# BRITISH PARLIAMENTARY ELECTION RESULTS 1918–1949

## (Revised Edition)

**Other Books in this Series Compiled and Edited by F.W.S. Craig**

# BRITISH PARLIAMENTARY ELECTION RESULTS

## 1918–1949

Compiled and Edited by
## F.W.S. CRAIG

REVISED EDITION

M

First published 1969 by Political Reference Publications
Revised edition published 1977 by
THE MACMILLAN PRESS LTD
London and Basingstoke
Associated companies in New York
Dublin Melbourne Johannesburg and Madras


ISBN 0 333 23048 5


Typeset by
Lithoset, Chichester
Printed in Great Britain by
The Scolar Press, Ilkley, West Yorkshire

# CONTENTS

FOREWORD to FIRST EDITION     vii

PREFACE     ix

ABBREVIATIONS and SYMBOLS     x

INTRODUCTORY NOTES     xii

ENGLAND:

    London Boroughs     1

    Provincial Boroughs     65

    Counties     287

WALES and MONMOUTHSHIRE:

    Boroughs     531

    Counties     545

SCOTLAND:

    Burghs     571

    Counties     609

NORTHERN IRELAND:

    Boroughs     649

    Counties     655

UNIVERSITIES:

    England     663

    Wales     672

    Scotland     673

    Northern Ireland     675

APPENDICES:

    1. Analysis of Voting in University Seats     676

    2. Analysis of Voting in Two-Member Seats     685

INDEX to CANDIDATES (Men)     721

INDEX to CANDIDATES (Women)     767

INDEX to CONSTITUENCIES     771

INDEX to FOOTNOTES     783

# FOREWORD TO FIRST EDITION

The substance of party controversy between the wars still echoes in the present, but the form of party competition was very different then from the tidy symmetry that has usually characterized electoral politics in England since 1950. In the inter-war period Britain had a multi-party system in which groupings and labels at times reflected a confusion that even a Frenchman might wonder at. The result is that anyone trying to find easily available and accurate information about election contests from Battersea to Inverness has been doomed to some disappointment.

The publication of F.W.S. Craig's voluminous researches into original electoral sources now makes available in one place general election and by-election results for each constituency in the United Kingdom from 1918 through 1949. In theory, the task is a straightforward one, for constituency boundaries remained virtually unaltered in the period. This fact also makes it meaningful to analyse electoral trends in each constituency during a 30-year period of many political changes.

In practice, the absence of party labels on ballots and the frequency of coalition government and Liberal party splits create major problems with such seemingly simple things as national totals of votes for each party. The editor has spent much time in patiently returning to local sources to verify the precise nuance of partisan attachment claimed by individual candidates. In addition, he has taken pains to correct typographical errors that occur even in official government publications.

In designing this volume for ready and frequent reference, the editor has applied the skills of a typographer as well as those of a psephologist. The result is a volume which has been promptly produced by technically advanced methods of automatic typesetting. It appears in a form that should maximize legibility and convenience.

The book is an innovation in another respect too. The materials contained on the following pages are also stored on magnetic tape convenient for computer analysis at the Survey Research Centre of the University of Strathclyde. Psephologists tired of testing their generalizations by slowly reading off figures from these pages may, upon application, have a computer read and tabulate constituency results for them.

RICHARD ROSE
*Professor of Politics*

*University of Strathclyde*
*Glasgow*
*September 1969*

**To Phyllis—**

*for her infinite patience*

# PREFACE

It is almost 8 years since this volume of parliamentary election results was first published and at that time it was intended that 1918 should be the starting date for a two volume work of reference. I certainly never envisaged researching elections prior to 1918 but pressure from readers persuaded me to carry the series back to 1832 in a further two volumes.

As I now write the Preface to a revised edition of the first volume published (now the third volume in date series) I must admit a feeling of relief that the series is now complete and the stage of revised editions has finally been reached. Eight years of research into the history of elections has been enjoyable but often tedious and I am now looking forward to being able to concentrate on the present and future rather than on the past.

This revised edition has been carefully updated against new sources of information and I have included analysis of the voting in the two-member constituencies and the detailed figures of the single transferable vote elections in the multi-member University constituencies. I am especially grateful to Mr. James Knight for providing a very useful and comprehensive Appendix which is particularly relevant at a time when electoral "reform" is once again attacting some attention.

The production of the first edition of this book, using (at that time) one of the most modern methods of type composition, could certainly never have been achieved without the infinite patience of my wife Phyllis who even after eight years still works tirelessly (if perhaps less good humouredly) to ensure that despite problems the production schedule of books is maintained. The dedication of this book to my wife is a most inadequate symbol of my gratitude to her. My eldest daughter Susan, who in 1969 was initiated into proof-reading, is now I'm afraid more interested in male politicians than in the statistics of politics. But at almost 19 years of age that is hardly surprising!

Even with the benefit of corrections sent to me by readers and a re-check of each page, it would be foolish to claim that this edition is entirely free from errors but they must surely be trivial. I will continue to be grateful to anyone who takes the trouble to write to me and point out any errors they may detect.

*Parliamantary Research Services*
*18 Lincoln Green*
*Chichester*
*West Sussex*

*April 1977*

F.W.S. CRAIG

*Compiler and Editor*

# ABBREVIATIONS and SYMBOLS

## PARTIES

Agric . . . . . . . . . . . . . . . . . Agriculturist/Farmers' candidate/Independent candidate
advocating agricultural policy

Agric P . . . . . . . . . . . . . . Agricultural Party

AWL . . . . . . . . . . . . . . . . . Anti-Waste League

BLP . . . . . . . . . . . . . . . . . Belfast Labour Party (subsequently became Northern
Ireland Labour Party)

BPP . . . . . . . . . . . . . . . . . British People's Party

BSP . . . . . . . . . . . . . . . . . British Socialist Party

BUF . . . . . . . . . . . . . . . . . British Union of Fascists (and National Socialists
from 1936)

C . . . . . . . . . . . . . . . . . . Conservative (or Unionist) Party

Co. . . . . . . . . . . . . . . . . . Coalition

Com . . . . . . . . . . . . . . . . . Communist Party of Great Britain

Const. . . . . . . . . . . . . . . . . Constitutionalist

Co-op . . . . . . . . . . . . . . . . Co-operative Party

CP. . . . . . . . . . . . . . . . . . Christian Pacifist

CS. . . . . . . . . . . . . . . . . . Christian Socialist

CW . . . . . . . . . . . . . . . . . Common Wealth Movement

CW Land P . . . . . . . . . . . . . Commonwealth Land Party

CWLP . . . . . . . . . . . . . . . . Commonwealth Labour Party (Northern Ireland)

Dem . . . . . . . . . . . . . . . . . Democrat

Dem P . . . . . . . . . . . . . . . . Democratic Party

EC . . . . . . . . . . . . . . . . . Empire Crusader (Empire Free Trade Crusade)

HLL . . . . . . . . . . . . . . . . . Highland Land League

ILP . . . . . . . . . . . . . . . . . Independent Labour Party

Ind . . . . . . . . . . . . . . . . . Independent (indicates an unofficial candidate when
placed before a party abbreviation)

Irish LP . . . . . . . . . . . . . . . Labour Party (Dublin)

L . . . . . . . . . . . . . . . . . . Liberal Party

Lab . . . . . . . . . . . . . . . . . Labour Party

Lab/Co-op . . . . . . . . . . . . . Labour Party/Co-operative Party joint candidate

LPP . . . . . . . . . . . . . . . . . Liverpool Protestant Party

N . . . . . . . . . . . . . . . . . . Irish Nationalist/Anti-Partitionist

NADSS . . . . . . . . . . . . . . . National Association of Discharged Sailors and Soldiers

Nat . . . . . . . . . . . . . . . . . National

Nat P . . . . . . . . . . . . . . . . National Party

NDP . . . . . . . . . . . . . . . . . National Democratic and Labour Party

NFDSS . . . . . . . . . . . . . . . National Federation of Discharged and Demobilized
Sailors and Soldiers

NFU . . . . . . . . . . . . . . . . . National Farmers' Union

NI Lab . . . . . . . . . . . . . . . Northern Ireland Labour Party

NL .................. National Liberal (candidate of Lloyd George's National Liberal Council, 1922-23 or of the National Liberal Organization (Liberal National Organization, 1931-48)).

NL & C .............. National Liberal and Conservative (joint candidate of the Conservative Party and the National Liberal Organization)

N Lab .............. National Labour Organization

NP ................. New Party

NPP ................ National Prohibition Party

NSP ................ National Socialist Party

PC ................. Plaid Cymru (pronounced *Plide Cumree*) - the Welsh (Nationalist) Party

Prog ............... Progressive

RCP ................ Revolutionary Communist Party

Rep ................ Irish Republican

SCPGB ............. Social Credit Party of Great Britain

SF ................. Sinn Fein (pronounced *Shin Fane)* - the Irish Republican Organization

SLP ................ Socialist Labour Party

SNP ................ Scottish National Party

Soc ................ Socialist

SP ................. Scottish Party

SPGB .............. Socialist Party of Great Britain

SPP ............... Scottish Prohibition Party

UEP ............... United Empire Party

WP ................ Women's Party

## MISCELLANEOUS

Bt. ................ Baronet

Dr. ................ Doctor

H.M. .............. His Majesty

Hon. .............. Honourable

Junr. ............. Junior

MP ................ Member of Parliament

Prof. ............. Professor

Rev. .............. Reverend

Rt. Hon. .......... Right Honourable (Member of the Privy Council)

Senr. ............. Senior

Unopp. ........... Unopposed

## SYMBOLS

†       before the name of a candidate in 1918 (Great Britain) or 1922 (Northern Ireland) indicates a member of the previous Parliament.

†       following a by-election electorate indicates that the total is approximate.

*       following the number of votes polled indicates a forfeited deposit.

*       following a 1945 electorate indicates that a minor boundary alteration had taken place

**      following a 1945 electorate indicates that a major boundary alteration had taken place.

# INTRODUCTORY NOTES

**General Note**    The name of the constituency at the top of each page is followed, within square brackets, by a consecutive reference number which is used in the indexes to candidates, constituencies and footnotes. The allocation of a distinctive reference number to each constituency was necessary in order to simplify and reduce the time taken for computer processing and indexing. This number should not be confused with the folio number which appears in small type at the foot of each page.

Under the name of each constituency are seven columns with the following headings:

**Election**    The year of each General Election and the date of any intervening by-election.

**Electors**    The number of electors on the Register in force at the time of the election.

**T'out**    Turnout — the number of electors voting (exclusive of spoilt ballot papers) expressed as a percentage of the total electorate. In the two-member constituencies the turnout percentage is calculated from the number of valid ballot papers counted and where this figure was not available an estimate has been made. See Appendix 2, p. 685.

**Candidate**    The initials and surname of the candidate.

**Party**    The party affiliation of the candidate.

**Votes**    The number of votes polled by the candidate.

**%**    The number of votes polled by the candidate expressed as a percentage of the total votes cast. If necessary the largest percentage has been adjusted to provide an exact total of 100.0%

At the foot of each set of voting figures appears the majority of the successful candidate and this is also expressed as a percentage.

**BY-ELECTIONS**    These are denoted by the year followed by the date (day/month) within round brackets. In the case of an unopposed return the date given is that of the close of nominations. The cause of the by-election is shown within square brackets above the year, and if the MP was elevated or succeeded to the Peerage, his new title is given.

Until the passing of the Re-Election of Ministers Act (1919) Amendment Act, 1926, MPs who were appointed to certain ministerial and other offices more than nine months after a proclamation summoning a new Parliament, were required to seek re-election to the House of Commons.

After the passing of the Amendment Act in July 1926, by-elections could only arise for one of the following reasons: (1) death; (2) elevation or succession to the Peerage; (3) acceptance of an office of profit under the Crown (including certain nominal offices to which MPs who wish to resign are appointed); (4) bankruptcy;

(5) lunacy; (6) election petition; (7) expulsion from the House of Commons; (8) sitting or voting in the House of Commons without taking the oath or affirmation of allegiance; (9) disqualification from having been elected to the House of Commons.

**CANDIDATES at the GENERAL ELECTION of 1918** There has always existed a great deal of confusion about party designations at the General Election of 1918 and extensive research has been carried out to ensure a high standard of accuracy.

The names and party designations of all official Coalition candidates were published in a pamphlet entitled *The Voter's Guide* issued by the Coalition Whips. An examination of this list has revealed a substantial number of errors and much of the confusion arose from the adoption of non-party men as Coalition candidates. The Whips appear to have assigned to these candidates the party 'label' considered most likely to win votes in a particular constituency.

A letter, signed by Lloyd George and Bonar Law, was sent to every approved Coalition candidate, but there was a great deal of confusion and the letter was sent in several instances to candidates who were hostile to the Coalition and who immediately repudiated Coalition support. This letter became known as the Coalition 'coupon'.

Apart from a number of errors in party designations, *The Voter's Guide* wrongly included the names of S. Chapman (Greenock), P.B. Malone (Tottenham, South) and W.T. Shaw (Forfarshire). The list omitted the names of three official candidates namely, H.H. Jones (Merionethshire), A. Neal (Sheffield, Hillsborough) and H.H. Whaite (Nottinghamshire, Broxtowe).

With regard to party designations, successful candidates have been given the 'label' appropriate to the whip which they accepted in the House of Commons and not necessarily the designation given them in the official list.

The substantial number of unofficial Labour candidates at this election was mainly due to the fact that a number of candidates sponsored by local Labour parties and trade unions were adopted too late to secure official endorsement by the National Executive.

**CANDIDATES at the GENERAL ELECTION of 1922** It was extremely difficult in many cases to distinguish Liberals and National Liberals at the General Election of 1922. The official lists of National Liberal candidates contained the names of all the former Coalition Labour and National Democratic Party MPs, many of whom never used the National Liberal 'label'. The list also included candidates who had not been adopted by any local Liberal organisation. To further complicate an already confused situation, agreement between Liberals and National Liberals was reached in a number of constituencies and this lead to the names of several candidates appearing in both official lists.

**CHANGE of PARTY ALLEGIANCE** When an MP seceded from a party after election and prior to the Dissolution, this is indicated by the new designation being shown within brackets. For example, C (Ind) indicates a change from Conservative to Independent.

During the period of National Government from 1931-40, a few Conservative MPs relinquished the National Government whip but claimed that this action did not affect their membership of the Conservative Parliamentary Party. The Conservative Whips however made it clear that MPs who resigned the National Government whip were no longer considered to be members of the Conservative Party in the House of Commons.

**CONSTITUENCY BOUNDARIES** Details of the area included within constituency boundaries in Great Britain from 1918-49 will be found in the Representation of the People Act, 1918 (Ninth Schedule). The boundaries of constituencies in Northern Ireland are given in the Government of Ireland Act, 1920 (Fifth Schedule, Part 2).

As a result of the House of Commons (Redistribution of Seats) Act, 1944, twenty abnormally large constituencies were to be divided and the number of seats in the House of Commons increased from 615 to 640. The Boundary Commission subsequently recommended the abolition of thirteen existing constituencies and the creation of thirty-eight new ones. In nine constituencies substantial boundary changes were proposed and in a further thirty-one, minor adjustments were recommended. Details of these changes will be found in the House of Commons (Redistribution of Seats) Order, 1945 (Statutory Instrument No. 701 of 1945).

Maps showing constituency boundaries in detail were included with the Boundary Commission reports published in 1917 and 1945.

**CO-OPERATIVE PARTY**  From after the General Election of 1918, all Co-operative Party candidates have been endorsed by the Labour Party and are designated Labour/Co-operative.

**DISSOLUTION VACANCIES**  Seats vacant at the Dissolution of a Parliament are indicated and the cause of the vacancy is given.

**ELECTION PETITIONS**  These are briefly recorded with a note of the outcome but detailed reports will be found in *The Times Law Reports,* Vol. 39, p. 423 (Derbyshire, North-Eastern) and *O'Malley and Hardcastle's Reports on Election Petitions,* Vol. 7 (Northumberland, Berwick-upon-Tweed; Oxford; Plymouth, Drake).

**ELECTORAL TRUCE, 1939-45**  From September 1939 until May 1945 a war-time electoral truce existed between the Conservative, Labour and Liberal parties. Each party undertook only to nominate a candidate for a seat held by them prior to a vacancy occurring.

**ELECTORATE STATISTICS**  The figures of electors at General Elections have been taken, except in 1918, from the *Returns of Election Expenses* compiled by the Home Office. For 1918 when no *Return of Election Expenses* was published, statistics of the electorate have been extracted from a *Return of Parliamentary and Local Government Electors* (House of Commons Papers (138) xix, 925).

Official figures of the electorate at by-elections were in a few cases not available and it has been necessary to give the number of electors on a previous Electoral Register. As this was usually the total on the Register for the preceding year, the error in turnout percentage is negligible.

**FORFEITED DEPOSITS**  A candidate forfeits his deposit of £150 if he is not elected and does not poll more than one-eighth of the total votes cast, exclusive of spoilt ballot papers. In a two-member constituency the total votes cast was deemed to be the total number of good ballot papers counted (first preference votes in the universities). In the Combined Scottish Universities which had three seats, a candidate had to poll more than one-eighth of the first preference votes divided by three.

**GENERAL ELECTION POLLING DATES**  Polling took place on the following dates:

| | |
|---|---|
| 1918 | Saturday, December 14 |
| 1922 | Wednesday, November 15 |
| 1923 | Thursday, December 6 |
| 1924 | Wednesday, October 29 |
| 1929 | Thursday, May 30 |
| 1931 | Tuesday, October 27 |
| 1935 | Thursday, November 14 |
| 1945 | Thursday, July 5 |

For a detailed time-table of each General Election see *British Electoral Facts 1885—1975* by F.W.S. Craig.

**GOVERNMENT PUBLICATIONS**  For a complete list of Bills, Acts and Parliamentary Papers relating to elections in the United Kingdom, see the *General Index to Parliamentary Papers, 1900—1949,* pp. 231-240 (London, H.M. Stationery Office, 1961).

**INDEPENDENT CANDIDATES** A detailed check has been made on the sponsorship and political background of all Independent candidates and where this revealed close party ties, they have been designated as Independent Conservative, Independent Labour, Independent Liberal, etc.

In all cases where an Independent stood as a representative of either a national or local organisation this is indicated in a footnote. If an Independent contested an election on a specific policy theme this is also noted.

Where an MP was refused re-adoption by his party and contested the seat as an Independent, details are given of the circumstances.

**INDEPENDENT LABOUR PARTY** Until August 1932, the Independent Labour Party (ILP) was affiliated to the Labour Party and prior to that date (with the undernoted exceptions) their candidates normally received Labour Party endorsement and are designated throughout this book as Labour candidates.

At the General Election of 1931, twenty-four members of the ILP declined to sign a form accepting the Standing Orders of the Parliamentary Labour Party and as a result they were refused endorsement. Of this number, nineteen sought election as ILP candidates. The remaining five, although ILP members, were the nominees of trade unions and local Labour parties and ran as unofficial Labour candidates. They have been designated as ILP or Independent Labour as was appropriate to the individual candidate.

At the by-elections in Renfrewshire, Eastern (November 1930) and Hampshire, New Forest and Christchurch (February 1932) ILP candidates were refused Labour Party endorsement and have been designated as ILP.

**IRELAND** The results of elections in Ireland between 1918 and 1922 (when the Irish Free State was created) are not included in this book.

**LIBERALS and the NATIONAL GOVERNMENT** At the General Election of 1931 and subsequent by-elections until November 21, 1933 (the day on which the Liberal Party severed its remaining links with the National Government and went into Opposition) the majority of Liberal candidates supported the National Government. The degree of support varied considerably and in most cases where a Liberal candidate was opposed by a Conservative, National Liberal or National Labour nominee, the Liberal was usually unwilling to promise full support to the National Government.

**MAJORITIES** In single-member constituencies, the majority (the lead of the first candidate over the second) is given below each result.

In the case of two-member constituencies the majority is calculated on the following basis:

Where the two candidates elected were of the *same* party, the majority is the lead of the lowest successful candidate over the highest unsuccessful candidate.

Where the two candidates elected were of *different* parties, the majorities shown are the lead of each successful candidate over the highest unsuccessful candidate of a different party.

In university constituencies returning more than one member, the elections were by Proportional Representation (single transferable vote) and figures of majority are inappropriate and have been omitted.

**MINISTERS CONTESTING BY-ELECTIONS** Candidates who were either Ministers or Junior Ministers at the time they contested by-elections are indicated in footnotes.

**NATIONAL CANDIDATES, 1931-45** At the General Elections of 1931, 1935, and 1945, it was found difficult in some cases to distinguish between Conservative and National candidates. The designation 'National' was used not only by non-party men, but also by a few Conservatives and former Labour MPs, who wished to indicate their support of the National Government without political ties. So far as information has been available, these candidates have been given the designation most appropriate to their political background.

Candidates standing under the National 'label' were presumed to be official National Government candidates unless they were opposed by a Conservative, National Liberal or National Labour nominee. Where this did happen, they have been designated Independent National although in fact they stood without the prefix but were presumably not acceptable to the National Government Whips.

Candidates who stood as Independents but indicated that they would support the National Government are designated National Independent.

It is important to appreciate the difference between the designations Independent National and National Independent.

**NATIONAL LIBERALS and LIBERAL NATIONALS** At the General Election of 1922, the Liberals who had been elected to the previous Parliament as supporters of the Coalition and were led by Lloyd George, fought as National Liberals to distinguish themselves from the official Liberal Party led by Asquith. During the early stages of the General Election of 1923 the two Liberal groups merged to fight that election as a united party.

The Liberal National Organization was formed on October 5, 1931 by Sir John (later Viscount) Simon. It was immediately joined by a number of Liberals and Independent Liberals who wished to give full support to the National Government. In June 1948 the name 'Liberal National' was changed to 'National Liberal' but to avoid confusion the designation of National Liberal has been used from 1931.

In May 1947, joint recommendations were issued by Lord Woolton, on behalf of the Conservative Party, and Lord Teviot, on behalf of the Liberal National Organization, which advocated that the two parties should come together in constituencies and form combined associations under a mutually agreed title.

Although candidates standing under this agreement did not appear at a General Election within the period covered by this book, there were two by-elections (in 1947 and 1949) at which joint National Liberal and Conservative candidates sought election. The actual designation used by candidates varied from one constituency to another but it was felt it would be less confusing if the designation 'National Liberal and Conservative' was applied and the numerous local variations disregarded.

**NORTHERN IRELAND PARTIES** Provided that they were endorsed by the Labour Party in London, no distinction is made between candidates of the Northern Ireland Labour Party and Labour candidates in Great Britain. The Northern Ireland Labour Party is an autonomous body but maintains co-operation with the British Labour Party on an informal and ad-hoc basis and there have only been three cases (at the General Election of 1924 in Belfast West and at two war-time by-elections) when a candidate did not receive Labour Party endorsement. The Irish Labour Party which has headquarters in Dublin should not be confused with the Northern Ireland Labour Party.

With the exception of Sinn Fein (banned in Northern Ireland since 1956) which is an organised political organisation, the nationalist movement in Northern Ireland comprised (until the formation of a Nationalist Party in May 1966) numerous small groups within each constituency. Candidates were selected by ballot at a convention held before each election and attended by representatives of local nationalist organisations.

For the sake of uniformity, candidates who described themselves as Anti-Partitionists rather than Nationalists have been given the Nationalist designation as the policy was always the same and the actual 'label' was a matter for local or personal choice.

Candidates who were supported and assisted by Sinn Fein but who were not official nominees of that organisation have been designated as Republicans.

**POSTPONED POLLS** Postponed polls at General Elections due to the death of a candidate (Lambeth, Kennington, 1918; Derbyshire, Western, 1923; Warwickshire, Rugby, 1929; Kingston-upon-Hull, Central, 1945) are indicated in footnotes. It should be noted that postponed polls are not considered by-elections but are part of the General Election, no new writ being issued.

At the General Election of 1945, voting was delayed in twenty-three constituencies because the national polling day fell during a local holiday week and the Postponement of Polling Day Act, 1945, altered the dates of polling as follows:

July 12   Barrow-in-Furness; Bolton; Carlisle; Morpeth; Warrington; Cheshire, Crewe; Lancashire, Darwen; Lancashire, Farnworth; Lancashire, Lonsdale; Edinburgh (all five constituencies); Greenock; Leith; Stirling and Falkirk Burghs; Berwickshire and Haddingtonshire; Midlothian and Peeblesshire, Northern; Midlothian and Peeblesshire, Peebles and Southern; Renfrewshire, Western; Stirlingshire and Clackmannanshire, Clackmannan and Eastern.

July 19   Nelson and Colne.

**SURNAMES and INITIALS** The surnames and initials of candidates at General Elections have been based, except in 1918, on the *Returns of Election Expenses* compiled by the Home Office. For 1918 when no *Return of Election Expenses* was published, the names have been extracted from *Debrett's House of Commons and Judicial Bench.* Every effort has been made to ensure that both the initials and spelling of surnames are correct and many doubtful spellings have been checked against local sources.

The names of candidates at by-elections have in most cases been taken from *The Times* and revised where necessary by extensive checking against other sources.

Degrees, decorations and service ranks have been omitted for reasons of space but members of the Privy Council and Baronets are indicated by a prefix or suffix.

It should be noted that married women frequently seek election under their maiden name, especially if they have been active in politics prior to marriage.

**UNIONISTS and ULSTER UNIONISTS** Conservative candidates in Scotland stand under the auspices of the Scottish Conservative and Unionist Association, and until the association added the word 'Conservative' to its title in April 1965, the majority of candidates ran as Unionists.

In Northern Ireland, Conservative candidates are sponsored by the Ulster Unionist Council and run as Unionists.

Throughout this book, Unionists in Scotland and Northern Ireland are designated as Conservatives.

**UNIVERSITY SEATS** In the four university constituencies returning more than one member, General Elections were conducted by Proportional Representation (single transferable vote). Figures are given, where applicable, for the first and final counts, with the first count figures shown within brackets. The successful candidates are placed in the order of their election irrespective of the number of votes credited to them in the final count.

The quota figure (the minimum number of votes required to secure election) is given below each result and an explanation of the system used plus a detailed analysis showing the transfer of votes is provided in Appendix 1, p. 676.

**VERIFICATION of OFFICIAL PARTY CANDIDATES** Despite many difficulties and with limited and not always accurate records and lists still available, a determined effort was made to try and ensure that all candidates who were not official nominees of a particular party have their party 'label' prefixed by the word Independent.

Especially during the complicated period of politics between 1918 and 1929 the fact that a candidate was the nominee of a party and had his name included in the official list, did not in several cases preclude him standing under some other 'label' which might appeal more to the electors. There are cases recorded in this volume of Communists standing under the designation Labour; Liberals who fought as Independents, and Conservatives who adopted the most unusual designation of all — 'Labour in the Conservative Interest'.

Although not always free from error, the principal sources used to verify official

Conservative, Labour and Liberal candidates were *The Constitutional Year Book, Labour Party Annual Conference Reports, The Liberal Year Book.*

**VOTING STATISTICS** The number of votes cast for candidates at General Elections have been taken, except in 1918, from the *Returns of Election Expenses* compiled by the Home Office. For 1918 when no *Return of Election Expenses* was published, figures of voting have been extracted from *Debrett's House of Commons and Judicial Bench.* The publishers of *Debrett* claimed that all figures were submitted to local Returning Officers for verification or revision and it was felt that this publication was an acceptable substitute for an official Return. In both *Debrett* and the *Returns of Election Expenses* some obvious errors were noticed and have been corrected.

By-election figures have in most cases been taken from *The Times* and revised where necessary by extensive checking against other sources.

# ENGLAND ——— LONDON BOROUGHS

| Election | Electors | T'out | Candidate | Party | Votes | % |
|----------|----------|-------|-----------|-------|-------|---|
| 1918 | 38,552 | 43.7 | R. Morris | Co L | 11,231 | 66.6 |
| | | | Mrs. C. Despard | Lab | 5,634 | 33.4 |
| | | | | | 5,597 | 33.2 |
| 1922 | 39,602 | 56.5 | S. Saklatvala | Lab | 11,311 | 50.5 |
| | | | H.C. Hogbin | NL | 9,290 | 41.6 |
| | | | V.C. Albu | L | 1,756* | 7.9 |
| | | | | | 2,021 | 8.9 |
| 1923 | 40,183 | 61.9 | H.C. Hogbin | L | 12,527 | 50.4 |
| | | | S. Saklatvala | Lab | 12,341 | 49.6 |
| | | | | | 186 | 0.8 |
| 1924 | 40,586 | 73.1 | S. Saklatvala | Com | 15,096 | 50.9 |
| | | | H.C. Hogbin | Const | 14,554 | 49.1 |
| | | | | | 542 | 1.8 |
| 1929 | 50,460 | 69.7 | W.S. Sanders | Lab | 13,265 | 37.8 |
| | | | A. Marsden | C | 10,833 | 30.8 |
| | | | S. Saklatvala | Com | 6,554 | 18.6 |
| | | | T.P. Brogan | L | 4,513 | 12.8 |
| | | | | | 2,432 | 7.0 |
| 1931 | 49,873 | 67.6 | A. Marsden | C | 18,688 | 55.4 |
| | | | W.S. Sanders | Lab | 11,985 | 35.6 |
| | | | S. Saklatvala | Com | 3,021* | 9.0 |
| | | | | | 6,703 | 19.8 |
| 1935 | 47,213 | 63.5 | W.S. Sanders | Lab | 17,596 | 58.7 |
| | | | A. Marsden | C | 12,393 | 41.3 |
| | | | | | 5,203 | 17.4 |

[Resignation]

| Election | Electors | T'out | Candidate | Party | Votes | % |
|----------|----------|-------|-----------|-------|-------|---|
| 1940 (17/4) | 42,725 | 25.1 | F.C.R. Douglas | Lab | 9,947 | 92.6 |
| | | | E.C. Joyce | Ind | 791* | 7.4 |
| | | | | | 9,156 | 85.2 |
| 1945 | 26,842 | 70.9 | F.C.R. Douglas | Lab | 14,070 | 73.9 |
| | | | J.W.F.G. Paget | C | 4,969 | 26.1 |
| | | | | | 9,101 | 47.8 |

[Resignation on appointment as Governor of Malta]

| Election | Electors | T'out | Candidate | Party | Votes | % |
|----------|----------|-------|-----------|-------|-------|---|
| 1946 (25/7) | 29,652 | 55.4 | D.P.T. Jay | Lab | 11,329 | 68.9 |
| | | | B.A. Shattock | C | 4,858 | 29.6 |
| | | | H. Dewar | ILP | 240* | 1.5 |
| | | | | | 6,471 | 39.3 |

Notes:—

1922-
1923:  Saklatvala was a member of the Communist Party but received Labour Party endorsement.

1940:  Joyce sought election as an 'Anti-War' candidate and received Communist Party support.

| Election | Electors | T'out | Candidate | Party | Votes | % |
|---|---|---|---|---|---|---|
| 1918 | 43,036 | 53.4 | Viscount Curzon | Co C | 15,670 | 68.2 |
| | | | †A.A. Lynch | Lab | 3,383 | 14.7 |
| | | | J.W. Molden | L | 2,273* | 9.9 |
| | | | J.E.P. Jenkin | Ind | 1,657* | 7.2 |
| | | | | | 12,287 | 53.5 |
| 1922 | 43,891 | 65.5 | Viscount Curzon | C | 17,685 | 61.5 |
| | | | A. Winfield | Lab | 11,050 | 38.5 |
| | | | | | 6,635 | 23.0 |
| 1923 | 44,062 | 63.5 | Viscount Curzon | C | 14,558 | 52.0 |
| | | | A. Winfield | Lab | 13,440 | 48.0 |
| | | | | | 1,118 | 4.0 |
| 1924 | 44,369 | 76.5 | Viscount Curzon | C | 19,588 | 57.7 |
| | | | A. Winfield | Lab | 14,371 | 42.3 |
| | | | | | 5,217 | 15.4 |

[Succession to the Peerage — Earl Howe]

| Election | Electors | T'out | Candidate | Party | Votes | % |
|---|---|---|---|---|---|---|
| 1929 | 44,786 | 57.7 | W. Bennett | Lab | 11,789 | 45.5 |
| (7/2) | | | H.R. Selley | C | 11,213 | 43.4 |
| | | | V.C. Albu | L | 2,858* | 11.1 |
| | | | | | 576 | 2.1 |
| 1929 | 57,018 | 72.5 | W. Bennett | Lab | 18,113 | 43.9 |
| | | | H.R. Selley | C | 17,695 | 42.8 |
| | | | W.J. West | L | 5,516 | 13.3 |
| | | | | | 418 | 1.1 |
| 1931 | 57,197 | 72.7 | H.R. Selley | C | 27,857 | 67.0 |
| | | | W. Bennett | Lab | 12,822 | 30.8 |
| | | | L.J. Cuming | NP | 909* | 2.2 |
| | | | | | 15,035 | 36.2 |
| 1935 | 55,546 | 66.8 | H.R. Selley | C | 21,268 | 57.3 |
| | | | H.G. Romeril | Lab | 15,821 | 42.7 |
| | | | | | 5,447 | 14.6 |
| 1945 | 42,987 | 72.9 | Mrs. C.S. Ganley | Lab/Co-op | 19,275 | 61.5 |
| | | | E. Partridge | C | 12,050 | 38.5 |
| | | | | | 7,225 | 23.0 |

Note:—

1918:  Jenkin was supported by and possibly the nominee of the local branch of the NFDSS.

| Election | Electors | T'out | Candidate | Party | Votes | % |
|---|---|---|---|---|---|---|
| 1918 | 25,008 | 45.1 | J.R. Lort-Williams | Co C | 5,639 | 50.0 |
| | | | †H.W.C. Carr-Gomm | L | 3,889 | 34.5 |
| | | | W. Godfrey | Lab | 1,750 | 15.5 |
| | | | | | 1,750 | 15.5 |
| 1922 | 29,166 | 63.4 | J.R. Lort-Williams | C | 6,749 | 36.5 |
| | | | C. Diamond | Lab | 6,703 | 36.3 |
| | | | H.W.C. Carr-Gomm | L | 5,034 | 27.2 |
| | | | | | 46 | 0.2 |
| 1923 | 29,457 | 63.8 | B. Smith | Lab | 9,019 | 48.0 |
| | | | J.R. Lort-Williams | C | 5,741 | 30.5 |
| | | | Dr. R. Hazleton | L | 4,035 | 21.5 |
| | | | | | 3,278 | 17.5 |
| 1924 | 29,906 | 70.5 | B. Smith | Lab | 12,703 | 60.3 |
| | | | C.G.L. du Cann | C | 8,375 | 39.7 |
| | | | | | 4,328 | 20.6 |
| 1929 | 36,133 | 65.9 | B. Smith | Lab | 14,664 | 61.6 |
| | | | J.G. Braithwaite | C | 4,594 | 19.3 |
| | | | Miss D. West | L | 4,556 | 19.1 |
| | | | | | 10,070 | 42.3 |
| 1931 | 36,111 | 64.3 | Mrs. N.C. Runge | C | 11,666 | 50.3 |
| | | | B. Smith | Lab | 11,536 | 49.7 |
| | | | | | 130 | 0.6 |
| 1935 | 33,899 | 71.3 | B. Smith | Lab | 14,416 | 59.7 |
| | | | Mrs. N.C. Runge | C | 9,751 | 40.3 |
| | | | | | 4,665 | 19.4 |
| 1945 | 18,098 | 68.1 | Rt. Hon. Sir B. Smith | Lab | 9,741 | 79.1 |
| | | | Mrs. N.C. Runge | C | 2,577 | 20.9 |
| | | | | | 7,164 | 58.2 |

[Resignation on appointment as Chairman of the West Midlands Divisional Coal Board]

| Election | Electors | T'out | Candidate | Party | Votes | % |
|---|---|---|---|---|---|---|
| 1946 (19/11) | 21,952 | 50.9 | R.J. Mellish | Lab | 7,265 | 65.0 |
| | | | E.D. Martell | L | 2,821 | 25.3 |
| | | | F.F.A. Burden | C | 1,084* | 9.7 |
| | | | | | 4,444 | 39.7 |

# BERMONDSEY, WEST [4]

| Election | Electors | T'out | Candidate | Party | Votes | % |
|---|---|---|---|---|---|---|
| 1918 | 23,100 | 45.5 | †H.J. Glanville | L | 4,260 | 40.6 |
| | | | C.R. Scriven | Co L | 2,998 | 28.5 |
| | | | Dr. A. Salter | Lab | 1,956 | 18.6 |
| | | | H.T.A. Becker | Ind | 1,294* | 12.3 |
| | | | | | 1,262 | 12.1 |
| 1922 | 26,168 | 64.6 | Dr. A. Salter | Lab | 7,550 | 44.6 |
| | | | Rev. R.M. Kedward | L | 5,225 | 30.9 |
| | | | C.R. Scriven | NL | 2,814 | 16.6 |
| | | | C.L. Nordon | Ind C | 1,328* | 7.9 |
| | | | | | 2,325 | 13.7 |
| 1923 | 26,456 | 66.1 | Rev. R.M. Kedward | L | 9,186 | 52.5 |
| | | | Dr. A. Salter | Lab | 8,298 | 47.5 |
| | | | | | 888 | 5.0 |
| 1924 | 26,989 | 75.0 | Dr. A. Salter | Lab | 11,578 | 57.2 |
| | | | Rev. R.M. Kedward | L | 8,676 | 42.8 |
| | | | | | 2,902 | 14.4 |
| 1929 | 32,963 | 66.6 | Dr. A. Salter | Lab | 13,231 | 60.2 |
| | | | L.J. Stein | L | 4,865 | 22.2 |
| | | | H.C. Butcher | C | 3,852 | 17.6 |
| | | | | | 8,366 | 38.0 |
| 1931 | 32,904 | 63.4 | Dr. A. Salter | Lab | 10,039 | 48.1 |
| | | | N.A.H. Bower | C | 9,948 | 47.7 |
| | | | W. Hannington | Com | 873* | 4.2 |
| | | | | | 91 | 0.4 |
| 1935 | 30,803 | 65.8 | Dr. A. Salter | Lab | 12,603 | 62.2 |
| | | | F.R.A. Glanville | NL | 7,674 | 37.8 |
| | | | | | 4,929 | 24.4 |
| 1945 | 17,004 | 66.3 | R. Sargood | Lab | 8,139 | 72.2 |
| | | | Dr. W.B.J. Pemberton | NL | 2,238 | 19.8 |
| | | | F.H. Collier | L | 903* | 8.0 |
| | | | | | 5,901 | 52.4 |

Note:—

1918: Becker was supported by and possibly the nominee of the local branch of the NFDSS.

| Election | Electors | T'out | Candidate | Party | Votes | % |
|---|---|---|---|---|---|---|
| 1918 | 25,253 | 31.2 | †Sir E.A. Cornwall, Bt. | Co L | 4,448 | 56.4 |
| | | | W.L. Steel | Nat P | 2,312 | 29.3 |
| | | | W. Shadforth | Ind | 1,127 | 14.3 |
| | | | | | 2,136 | 27.1 |
| 1922 | 27,262 | 58.8 | G. Edmonds | L | 5,774 | 36.1 |
| | | | W. Windsor | Com | 5,659 | 35.3 |
| | | | E.A. Hoffgaard | C | 2,806 | 17.5 |
| | | | G.M. Garro-Jones | NL | 1,780* | 11.1 |
| | | | | | 115 | 0.8 |
| 1923 | 27,468 | 59.1 | W. Windsor | Lab | 7,415 | 45.7 |
| | | | G. Edmonds | L | 6,790 | 41.8 |
| | | | R.I. Tasker | C | 2,035 | 12.5 |
| | | | | | 625 | 3.9 |
| 1924 | 27,827 | 68.4 | W. Windsor | Lab | 9,560 | 50.2 |
| | | | G. Edmonds | L | 9,465 | 49.8 |
| | | | | | 95 | 0.4 |
| 1929 | 34,453 | 71.7 | H.L. Nathan | L | 11,690 | 47.4 |
| | | | W. Windsor | Lab | 11,101 | 44.9 |
| | | | J.A. Bell | C | 1,908* | 7.7 |
| | | | | | 589 | 2.5 |
| 1931 | 34,377 | 68.4 | H.L. Nathan | L (Ind L) (Lab) | 13,135 | 55.9 |
| | | | W. Barratt | Lab | 10,368 | 44.1 |
| | | | | | 2,767 | 11.8 |
| 1935 | 32,809 | 55.5 | D. Chater | Lab/Co-op | 11,581 | 63.5 |
| | | | J.B. Hobman | L | 6,644 | 36.5 |
| | | | | | 4,937 | 27.0 |
| 1945 | 19,225 | 66.9 | D. Chater | Lab/Co-op | 7,696 | 59.9 |
| | | | P.H.G. Wright | L | 3,979 | 30.9 |
| | | | Lord Buckhurst | C | 1,185* | 9.2 |
| | | | | | 3,717 | 29.0 |

Notes:—

1918: Shadforth sought election as a 'Health' candidate.

1922: Windsor sought election as a 'Labour' candidate despite the fact that he was an official Communist Party candidate and did not receive Labour Party endorsement.

| Election | Electors | T'out | Candidate | Party | Votes | % |
|---|---|---|---|---|---|---|
| 1918 | 19,510 | 41.6 | †Sir M.R.H. Wilson, Bt. | Co C | 4,240 | 52.3 |
| | | | E. Thurtle | Ind | 1,941 | ·23.9 |
| | | | H.M. Meyler | L | 1,935 | 23.8 |
| | | | | | 2,299 | 28.4 |
| 1922 | 21,129 | 59.9 | P.A. Harris | L | 5,152 | 40.7 |
| | | | J.J. Vaughan | Com | 4,034 | 31.9 |
| | | | Sir M.R.H. Wilson, Bt. | C | 3,474 | 27.4 |
| | | | | | 1,118 | 8.8 |
| 1923 | 21,320 | 62.2 | P.A. Harris | L | 5,735 | 43.3 |
| | | | J.J. Vaughan | Lab | 5,251 | 39.6 |
| | | | J.C.G. Leigh | C | 2,267 | 17.1 |
| | | | | | 484 | 3.7 |
| 1924 | 21,522 | 68.4 | P.A. Harris | L | 6,236 | 42.3 |
| | | | J.J. Vaughan | Com | 6,024 | 40.9 |
| | | | C.P. Norman | C | 2,467 | 16.8 |
| | | | | | 212 | 1.4 |
| 1929 | 27,583 | 64.1 | P.A. Harris | L | 8,109 | 45.9 |
| | | | C.J. Kelly | Lab | 6,849 | 38.7 |
| | | | Dr. R. Dunstan | Com | 1,368* | 7.7 |
| | | | H.J. Malone | C | 1,365* | 7.7 |
| | | | | | 1,260 | 7.2 |
| 1931 | 27,895 | 61.2 | P.A. Harris | L | 10,176 | 59.6 |
| | | | W.J. Humphreys | Lab | 3,923 | 23.0 |
| | | | J.J. Vaughan | Com | 2,970 | 17.4 |
| | | | | | 6,253 | 36.6 |
| 1935 | 27,484 | 61.7 | Sir P.A. Harris, Bt. | L | 9,011 | 53.1 |
| | | | G. Jeger | Lab | 7,945 | 46.9 |
| | | | | | 1,066 | 6.2 |
| 1945 | 17,032 | 68.3 | P. Holman | Lab/Co-op | 6,669 | 57.4 |
| | | | Rt. Hon. Sir P.A. Harris, Bt. | L | 4,213 | 36.2 |
| | | | O.H. Leicester | Nat | 750* | 6.4 |
| | | | | | 2,456 | 21.2 |

Notes:—

1918: Thurtle was the nominee of the local branch of the NFDSS.

1922: Vaughan sought election as a 'Labour' candidate despite the fact that he was an official Communist Party candidate and did not receive Labour Party endorsement.

1923: Vaughan was a member of the Communist Party but received Labour Party endorsement.

| Election | Electors | T'out | Candidate | Party | Votes | % |
|---|---|---|---|---|---|---|
| 1918 | 30,377 | 50.2 | †Sir F. Hall | Co C | 12,039 | 78.9 |
|  |  |  | C.R. Cooke-Taylor | L | 3,219 | 21.1 |
|  |  |  |  |  | 8,820 | 57.8 |
| 1922 | 32,486 | 64.0 | Sir F. Hall | C | 14,046 | 67.6 |
|  |  |  | C.R. Cooke-Taylor | L | 6,733 | 32.4 |
|  |  |  |  |  | 7,313 | 35.2 |
| 1923 | 33,185 | 61.3 | Sir F. Hall, Bt. | C | 10,855 | 53.4 |
|  |  |  | C.R. Cooke-Taylor | L | 9,488 | 46.6 |
|  |  |  |  |  | 1,367 | 6.8 |
| 1924 | 33,833 | 78.9 | Sir F. Hall, Bt. | C | 15,611 | 58.5 |
|  |  |  | Dr. C.A. Smith | Lab | 7,068 | 26.5 |
|  |  |  | C.R. Cooke-Taylor | L | 4,017 | 15.0 |
|  |  |  |  |  | 8,543 | 32.0 |
| 1929 | 42,638 | 72.1 | Sir F. Hall, Bt. | C | 15,009 | 48.8 |
|  |  |  | Dr. C.A. Smith | Lab | 9,309 | 30.3 |
|  |  |  | Dr. C.R. Cooke-Taylor | L | 6,442 | 20.9 |
|  |  |  |  |  | 5,700 | 18.5 |
| 1931 | 43,025 | 70.7 | Sir F. Hall, Bt. | C | 21,752 | 71.5 |
|  |  |  | F. Hughes | Lab | 4,747 | 15.6 |
|  |  |  | Dr. C.R. Cooke-Taylor | L | 3,924 | 12.9 |
|  |  |  |  |  | 17,005 | 55.9 |
| [Death] |  |  |  |  |  |  |
| 1932 (8/6) | 43,025 | 47.1 | B. Smith | C | 12,342 | 61.0 |
|  |  |  | Dr. C.R. Cooke-Taylor | L | 3,998 | 19.7 |
|  |  |  | Mrs. H.C. Bentwich | Lab | 3,905 | 19.3 |
|  |  |  |  |  | 8,344 | 41.3 |
| 1935 | 42,206 | 65.8 | B. Smith | C | 16,870 | 60.8 |
|  |  |  | J.V. Delahaye | Lab | 7,142 | 25.7 |
|  |  |  | Dr. C.R. Cooke-Taylor | L | 3,743 | 13.5 |
|  |  |  |  |  | 9,728 | 35.1 |
| 1945 | 33,062 | 71.4 | W.F. Vernon | Lab | 10,266 | 43.5 |
|  |  |  | Sir B. Smith | C | 10,055 | 42.6 |
|  |  |  | J.P.J. Ellis | L | 3,287 | 13.9 |
|  |  |  |  |  | 211 | 0.9 |

# CAMBERWELL, NORTH [8]

| Election | Electors | T'out | Candidate | Party | Votes | % |
|---|---|---|---|---|---|---|
| 1918 | 26,416 | 39.2 | H.N. Knights | Co C | 6,010 | 58.0 |
| | | | G. Hearn | L | 2,177 | 21.0 |
| | | | C.G. Ammon | Lab | 2,175 | 21.0 |
| | | | | | 3,833 | 37.0 |
| [Resignation] | | | | | | |
| 1922 | 28,709 | 50.8 | C.G. Ammon | Lab | 7,854 | 53.9 |
| (20/2) | | | R.J. Meller | C | 6,719 | 46.1 |
| | | | | | 1,135 | 7.8 |
| 1922 | 28,894 | 56.7 | C.G. Ammon | Lab | 8,320 | 50.8 |
| | | | Dame Helen Gwynne-Vaughan | C | 8,066 | 49.2 |
| | | | | | 254 | 1.6 |
| 1923 | 29,088 | 56.9 | C.G. Ammon | Lab | 10,620 | 64.2 |
| | | | Dame Helen Gwynne-Vaughan | C | 5,934 | 35.8 |
| | | | | | 4,686 | 28.4 |
| 1924 | 29,530 | 69.7 | C.G. Ammon | Lab | 11,300 | 54.9 |
| | | | Dame Helen Gwynne-Vaughan | C | 7,564 | 36.7 |
| | | | V.D. Duval | L | 1,729* | 8.4 |
| | | | | | 3,736 | 18.2 |
| 1929 | 35,711 | 63.1 | C.G. Ammon | Lab | 13,051 | 58.0 |
| | | | L.St.C. Grondona | C | 5,228 | 23.2 |
| | | | H.J. Edwards | L | 4,244 | 18.8 |
| | | | | | 7,823 | 34.8 |
| 1931 | 35,153 | 58.3 | A.L. Bateman | C | 10,634 | 51.9 |
| | | | C.G. Ammon | Lab | 9,869 | 48.1 |
| | | | | | 765 | 3.8 |
| 1935 | 32,517 | 55.6 | C.G. Ammon | Lab | 11,701 | 64.7 |
| | | | T.B. Martin | C | 5,924 | 32.8 |
| | | | T.F.R. Disher | Ind | 451* | 2.5 |
| | | | | | 5,777 | 31.9 |
| [Elevation to the Peerage — Lord Ammon] | | | | | | |
| 1944 | 29,661 | 11.2 | C.A.G. Manning | Lab | 2,655 | 79.8 |
| (30/3) | | | T.F.R. Disher | Ind | 674 | 20.2 |
| | | | | | 1,981 | 59.6 |
| 1945 | 15,506 | 60.5 | C.A.G. Manning | Lab | 7,186 | 76.6 |
| | | | E.R. Mayer | C | 1,394 | 14.9 |
| | | | T.F.R. Disher | Ind Nat | 794* | 8.5 |
| | | | | | 5,792 | 61.7 |

Note:—

1935: Disher sought election as a 'Radical Reform' candidate.

| Election | Electors | T'out | Candidate | Party | Votes | % |
|---|---|---|---|---|---|---|
| 1918 | 29,959 | 36.5 | †Rt. Hon. T.J. Macnamara | Co L | 6,986 | 63.9 |
| | | | W.G.W. Radford | C | 3,947 | 36.1 |
| | | | | | 3,039 | 27.8 |
| [Appointed Minister of Labour] | | | | | | |
| 1920 (31/3) | 30,751 | 47.9 | Rt. Hon. T.J. Macnamara | Co L | 6,618 | 44.9 |
| | | | Miss A.S. Lawrence | Lab | 4,733 | 32.1 |
| | | | J.C. Carroll | L | 3,386 | 23.0 |
| | | | | | 1,885 | 12.8 |
| 1922 | 31,353 | 53.6 | Rt. Hon. T.J. Macnamara | NL | 8,339 | 49.6 |
| | | | Dr. H.B.W. Morgan | Lab | 5,182 | 30.9 |
| | | | J.H. Harris | L | 3,270 | 19.5 |
| | | | | | 3,157 | 18.7 |
| 1923 | 31,753 | 61.9 | Rt. Hon. T.J. Macnamara | L | 6,843 | 34.8 |
| | | | Dr. H.B.W. Morgan | Lab | 6,763 | 34.4 |
| | | | E.T. Campbell | C | 6,045 | 30.8 |
| | | | | | 80 | 0.4 |
| 1924 | 32,347 | 74.8 | E.T. Campbell | C | 9,626 | 39.8 |
| | | | Dr. H.B.W. Morgan | Lab | 9,432 | 39.0 |
| | | | Rt. Hon. T.J. Macnamara | L | 5,138 | 21.2 |
| | | | | | 194 | 0.8 |
| 1929 | 41,282 | 66.8 | Dr. H.B.W. Morgan | Lab | 12,213 | 44.2 |
| | | | E.T. Campbell | C | 9,808 | 35.6 |
| | | | H. Harcourt | L | 5,559 | 20.2 |
| | | | | | 2,405 | 8.6 |
| 1931 | 41,184 | 63.8 | J.D. Cassels | C | 17,581 | 66.9 |
| | | | H.S.J. Hughes | Lab | 8,693 | 33.1 |
| | | | | | 8,888 | 33.8 |
| 1935 | 40,674 | 59.3 | Hon. O.M. Guest | C | 11,744 | 48.6 |
| | | | H.S.J. Hughes | Lab | 10,931 | 45.3 |
| | | | H.J. Edwards | L | 1,462* | 6.1 |
| | | | | | 813 | 3.3 |
| 1945 | 26,979 | 65.2 | Mrs. F.K. Corbet | Lab | 12,251 | 69.6 |
| | | | L.A. May | C | 5,346 | 30.4 |
| | | | | | 6,905 | 39.2 |

| Election | Electors | T'out | Candidate | Party | Votes | % |
|---|---|---|---|---|---|---|
| 1918 | 36,916 | 43.0 | †A.H.H. Richardson | Co L | 8,764 | 55.2 |
| | | | C.J. Hughes | Ind C | 4,550 | 28.7 |
| | | | C. Diamond | Lab | 2,559 | 16.1 |
| | | | | | 4,214 | 26.5 |
| 1922 | 38,189 | 66.1 | C.J. Hughes | C | 11,218 | 44.4 |
| | | | H. Lesser | NL | 6,739 | 26.7 |
| | | | W.A. Chambers | Lab | 5,964 | 23.6 |
| | | | G.S. Tetley | L | 1,329* | 5.3 |
| | | | | | 4,479 | 17.7 |
| 1923 | 38,611 | 61.4 | C.J. Hughes | C | 8,526 | 36.0 |
| | | | W.A. Chambers | Lab | 8,370 | 35.3 |
| | | | C.W. Tagg | L | 6,815 | 28.7 |
| | | | | | 156 | 0.7 |
| 1924 | 39,053 | 74.2 | E.H.J.N. Dalton | Lab | 13,361 | 46.1 |
| | | | Sir M. Archer-Shee | C | 12,414 | 42.9 |
| | | | J.N. Emery | L | 3,194* | 11.0 |
| | | | | | 947 | 3.2 |
| 1929 | 48,008 | 67.0 | J. Beckett | Lab | 15,751 | 49.0 |
| | | | J.D. Cooke | C | 10,246 | 31.8 |
| | | | G.I. Phillips | L | 6,187 | 19.2 |
| | | | | | 5,505 | 17.2 |
| 1931 | 47,933 | 69.8 | Viscount Borodale | C | 19,458 | 58.2 |
| | | | J. Beckett | ILP | 11,217 | 33.5 |
| | | | E.J. Titler | N Lab | 1,442* | 4.3 |
| | | | H. Beaumont | Lab | 1,350* | 4.0 |
| | | | | | 8,241 | 24.7 |
| 1935 | 45,826 | 64.8 | Viscount Borodale | C | 15,229 | 51.3 |
| | | | L. Silkin | Lab | 14,457 | 48.7 |
| | | | | | 772 | 2.6 |

[Succession to the Peerage — Earl Beatty]

| | | | | | | |
|---|---|---|---|---|---|---|
| 1936 (6/5) | 45,826 | 56.5 | L. Silkin | Lab | 13,007 | 50.2 |
| | | | P.G.A. Harvey | C | 12,907 | 49.8 |
| | | | | | 100 | 0.4 |
| 1945 | 28,822 | 65.3 | L. Silkin | Lab | 12,935 | 68.7 |
| | | | R.J.E.F. O'Connell | C | 5,896 | 31.3 |
| | | | | | 7,039 | 37.4 |

| Election | Electors | T'out | Candidate | Party | Votes | % |
|---|---|---|---|---|---|---|
| 1918 | 24,822 | 46.6 | †Sir S.J.G. Hoare, Bt. | Co C | 9,159 | 79.1 |
| | | | Miss E.F. Phipps | Ind Prog | 2,419 | 20.9 |
| | | | | | 6,740 | 58.2 |
| 1922 | 28,453 | 63.1 | Rt. Hon. Sir S.J.G. Hoare, Bt. | C | 13,437 | 74.9 |
| | | | Hon. B.A.W. Russell | Lab | 4,513 | 25.1 |
| | | | | | 8,924 | 49.8 |
| 1923 | 28,755 | 63.8 | Rt. Hon. Sir S.J.G. Hoare, Bt. | C | 10,461 | 57.0 |
| | | | Hon. B.A.W. Russell | Lab | 5,047 | 27.5 |
| | | | H.W. Preston | L | 2,846 | 15.5 |
| | | | | | 5,414 | 29.5 |
| 1924 | 29,582 | 71.1 | Rt. Hon. Sir S.J.G. Hoare, Bt. | C | 13,816 | 65.7 |
| | | | Hon. Mrs. D.W. Russell | Lab | 5,661 | 26.9 |
| | | | I.A. Williams | L | 1,557* | 7.4 |
| | | | | | 8,155 | 38.8 |
| 1929 | 41,945 | 63.1 | Rt. Hon. Sir S.J.G. Hoare, Bt. | C | 15,480 | 58.4 |
| | | | Rev. A.G. Prichard | Lab | 6,645 | 25.1 |
| | | | I.A. Williams | L | 4,360 | 16.5 |
| | | | | | 8,835 | 33.3 |
| 1931 | 42,531 | 65.2 | Rt. Hon. Sir S.J.G. Hoare, Bt. | C | 23,015 | 83.0 |
| | | | G.A. Foan | Lab | 4,726 | 17.0 |
| | | | | | 18,289 | 66.0 |
| 1935 | 41,061 | 61.7 | Rt. Hon. Sir S.J.G. Hoare, Bt. | C | 18,992 | 74.9 |
| | | | G.S. Sandilands | Lab | 6,348 | 25.1 |
| | | | | | 12,644 | 49.8 |

[Elevation to the Peerage — Viscount Templewood]

| Election | Electors | T'out | Candidate | Party | Votes | % |
|---|---|---|---|---|---|---|
| 1944 (11/10) | | | W.P. Sidney | C | Unopp. | |
| 1945 | 30,095 | 62.8 | A.H.P. Noble | C | 12,043 | 63.7 |
| | | | Miss M.D. Shufeldt | Lab | 5,874 | 31.1 |
| | | | Dr. Dorothy A. Sharpe | CW | 984* | 5.2 |
| | | | | | 6,169 | 32.6 |

Note:—

1918: Miss Phipps was the nominee of the National Federation of Women Teachers.

### (Two Seats)

| Election | Electors | T'out | Candidate | Party | Votes | % |
|---|---|---|---|---|---|---|
| 1918 | | | †Rt. Hon. A.J. Balfour | Co C | Unopp. | |
| | | | †Rt. Hon. Sir F.G. Banbury, Bt. | Co C | Unopp. | |

[Elevation to the Peerage — Earl of Balfour]

| Election | Electors | T'out | Candidate | Party | Votes | % |
|---|---|---|---|---|---|---|
| 1922 | 44,083[†] | 37.0 | E.C. Grenfell | C | 10,114 | 62.1 |
| (19/5) | | | Sir T.V. Bowater, Bt. | Ind C | 6,178 | 37.9 |
| | | | | | 3,936 | 24.2 |
| | | | | | | |
| 1922 | | | Rt. Hon. Sir F.G. Banbury, Bt. | C | Unopp. | |
| | | | E.C. Grenfell | C | Unopp. | |
| | | | | | | |
| 1923 | | | Rt. Hon. Sir F.G. Banbury, Bt. | C | Unopp. | |
| | | | E.C. Grenfell | C | Unopp. | |

[Elevation to the Peerage — Lord Banbury of Southam]

| Election | Electors | T'out | Candidate | Party | Votes | % |
|---|---|---|---|---|---|---|
| 1924 | 44,130 | 41.9 | Sir T.V. Bowater, Bt. | C | 12,962 | 70.1 |
| (1/2) | | | H. Bell | L | 5,525 | 29.9 |
| | | | | | 7,437 | 40.2 |
| | | | | | | |
| 1924 | | | Sir T.V. Bowater, Bt. | C | Unopp. | |
| | | | E.C. Grenfell | C | Unopp | |
| | | | | | | |
| 1929 | 46,469 | 45.2 | Sir T.V. Bowater, Bt. | C | 16,149 | 43.9 |
| | | | E.C. Grenfell | C | 16,092 | 43.7 |
| | | | T.O. Jacobsen | L | 4,579 | 12.4 |
| | | | | | 11,513 | 31.3 |
| | | | | | | |
| 1931 | | | Sir T.V. Bowater, Bt. | C | Unopp. | |
| | | | E.C. Grenfell | C | Unopp. | |

[Elevation of Grenfell to the Peerage — Lord St. Just]

| Election | Electors | T'out | Candidate | Party | Votes | % |
|---|---|---|---|---|---|---|
| 1935 (26/6) | | | Sir A.G. Anderson | C | Unopp. | |
| | | | | | | |
| 1935 | | | Sir A.G. Anderson | C | Unopp. | |
| | | | Sir T.V. Bowater, Bt. | C | Unopp. | |

[Death of Bowater]

| Election | Electors | T'out | Candidate | Party | Votes | % |
|---|---|---|---|---|---|---|
| 1938 (6/4) | | | Sir G.T. Broadbridge, Bt. | C | Unopp. | |

[Resignation of Anderson]

| Election | Electors | T'out | Candidate | Party | Votes | % |
|---|---|---|---|---|---|---|
| 1940 (5/2) | | | Rt. Hon. Sir A.R. Duncan | Nat | Unopp. | |
| | | | | | | |
| 1945 | 10,851 | 63.9 | Rt. Hon. Sir A.R. Duncan | Nat | 5,332 | 39.5 |
| | | | Sir G.T. Broadbridge, Bt. | C | 5,309 | 39.3 |
| | | | Sir A. McFadyean | L | 1,487 | 11.0 |
| | | | S.W. Alexander | Ind | 1,379 | 10.2 |
| | | | | | 3,845 | 28.5 |
| | | | | | 3,822 | 28.3 |

[Elevation to the Peerage — Lord Broadbridge]

| Election | Electors | T'out | Candidate | Party | Votes | % |
|---|---|---|---|---|---|---|
| 1945 | 11,650 | 51.6 | Rt. Hon. R. Assheton | C | 4,506 | 75.0 |
| (31/10) | | | A.S. Comyns Carr | L | 1,503 | 25.0 |
| | | | | | 3,003 | 50.0 |

Notes:—
1940: Duncan was President of the Board of Trade.
1945: Alexander sought election as a 'Free Trade' candidate.

# DEPTFORD [13]

| Election | Electors | T'out | Candidate | Party | Votes | % |
|---|---|---|---|---|---|---|
| 1918 | 51,611 | 50.2 | †Rt. Hon. C.W. Bowerman | Lab | 14,073 | 54.4 |
| | | | J.T. Prestige | C | 9,711 | 37.5 |
| | | | F.A. Rumsey | Ind | 2,106* | 8.1 |
| | | | | | 4,362 | 16.9 |
| 1922 | 53,195 | 66.2 | Rt. Hon. C.W. Bowerman | Lab | 18,512 | 52.6 |
| | | | M.J. Pike | C | 16,687 | 47.4 |
| | | | | | 1,825 | 5.2 |
| 1923 | 54,135 | 63.3 | Rt. Hon. C.W. Bowerman | Lab | 21,576 | 63.0 |
| | | | M.J. Pike | C | 12,666 | 37.0 |
| | | | | | 8,910 | 26.0 |
| 1924 | 55,797 | 72.0 | Rt. Hon. C.W. Bowerman | Lab | 21,903 | 54.5 |
| | | | J. Hargreaves | C | 18,279 | 45.5 |
| | | | | | 3,624 | 9.0 |
| 1929 | 71,242 | 68.2 | Rt. Hon. C.W. Bowerman | Lab | 26,848 | 55.2 |
| | | | E.E. Gates | C | 14,832 | 30.5 |
| | | | H.C. Bevan | L | 6,935 | 14.3 |
| | | | | | 12,016 | 24.7 |
| 1931 | 71,406 | 68.3 | D.A. Hanley | C | 26,558 | 54.4 |
| | | | Rt. Hon. C.W. Bowerman | Lab | 22,244 | 45.6 |
| | | | | | 4,314 | 8.8 |
| 1935 | 68,026 | 69.3 | W.H. Green | Lab/Co-op | 27,021 | 57.3 |
| | | | Sir M. Campbell | C | 20,129 | 42.7 |
| | | | | | 6,892 | 14.6 |
| 1945 | 44,182 | 68.7 | J.C. Wilmot | Lab | 22,313 | 73.5 |
| | | | B.E.D. Cuddon | C | 8,059 | 26.5 |
| | | | | | 14,254 | 47.0 |

[Seat Vacant at Dissolution (Elevation to the Peerage — Lord Wilmot of Selmeston)]

Note:—

   1918:   Rumsey was the nominee of the local branch of the NFDSS.

| Election | Electors | T'out | Candidate | Party | Votes | % |
|----------|----------|-------|-----------|-------|-------|---|
| 1918 | 34,873 | 39.5 | †M. Archer-Shee | Co C (C) | 8,782 | 63.8 |
| | | | †H.E.A. Cotton | L | 4,981 | 36.2 |
| | | | | | 3,801 | 27.6 |
| 1922 | 38,705 | 54.3 | M. Archer-Shee | C | 9,382 | 44.6 |
| | | | E.H. Gilpin | L | 6,384 | 30.4 |
| | | | G.M. Gillett | Lab | 4,903 | 23.3 |
| | | | C.R. Morden | Ind Lab | 349* | 1.7 |
| | | | | | 2,998 | 14.2 |
| 1923 | 39,109 | 53.8 | G.M. Gillett | Lab | 8,907 | 42.4 |
| | | | Sir M. Archer-Shee | C | 7,063 | 33.6 |
| | | | A.H. Scott | L | 5,054 | 24.0 |
| | | | | | 1,844 | 8.8 |
| 1924 | 39,701 | 66.3 | G.M. Gillett | Lab | 12,363 | 47.0 |
| | | | E.A. Taylor | C | 11,643 | 44.2 |
| | | | R. Shaw | L | 2,324* | 8.8 |
| | | | | | 720 | 2.8 |
| 1929 | 48,225 | 66.0 | G.M. Gillett | Lab (N Lab) | 17,970 | 56.5 |
| | | | W. Ray | C | 9,026 | 28.3 |
| | | | W.J. Pinard | L | 4,855 | 15.2 |
| | | | | | 8,944 | 28.2 |
| 1931 | 47,222 | 58.1 | Sir G.M. Gillett | N Lab | 17,292 | 63.1 |
| | | | T.E. Williams | Lab/Co-op | 10,133 | 36.9 |
| | | | | | 7,159 | 26.2 |
| 1935 | 42,736 | 56.2 | Rev. G.S. Woods | Lab/Co-op | 13,408 | 55.8 |
| | | | Sir G.M. Gillett | N Lab | 10,600 | 44.2 |
| | | | | | 2,808 | 11.6 |
| 1945 | 21,615 | 63.9 | J.F.F. Platts-Mills | Lab (Ind Lab) | 9,786 | 70.8 |
| | | | F.F.A. Burden | C | 4,029 | 29.2 |
| | | | | | 5,757 | 41.6 |

Note:—

1945: Platts-Mills joined the Labour Independent Group when it was formed in June 1949.

| Election | Electors | T'out | Candidate | Party | Votes | % |
|---|---|---|---|---|---|---|
| 1918 | 36,228 | 40.8 | Sir H.G. Norris | Co C | 10,242 | 69.4 |
| | | | D. Cook | Ind Lab | 2,883 | 19.5 |
| | | | F. Coysh | L | 1,644* | 11.1 |
| | | | | | 7,359 | 49.9 |
| 1922 | 37,180 | 58.0 | K.P. Vaughan-Morgan | C | 13,282 | 61.5 |
| | | | J. Palmer | Lab | 5,393 | 25.0 |
| | | | M.G. Liverman | L | 2,907 | 13.5 |
| | | | | | 7,889 | 36.5 |
| 1923 | 38,403 | 58.0 | K.P. Vaughan-Morgan | C | 9,757 | 43.9 |
| | | | J. Palmer | Lab | 7,683 | 34.5 |
| | | | R.C. Hawkin | L | 4,817 | 21.6 |
| | | | | | 2,074 | 9.4 |
| 1924 | 39,151 | 69.1 | K.P. Vaughan-Morgan | C | 16,657 | 61.6 |
| | | | J. Palmer | Lab | 10,403 | 38.4 |
| | | | | | 6,254 | 23.2 |
| 1929 | 51,066 | 66.8 | Sir K.P. Vaughan-Morgan | C | 15,130 | 44.3 |
| | | | J. Palmer | Lab | 13,425 | 39.4 |
| | | | J.H. Greenwood | L | 5,551 | 16.3 |
| | | | | | 1,705 | 4.9 |
| 1931 | 51,688 | 66.1 | Sir K.P. Vaughan-Morgan | C | 23,438 | 68.7 |
| | | | Sir H.J. Maynard | Lab | 8,917 | 26.1 |
| | | | J.H. Greenwood | L | 1,788* | 5.2 |
| | | | | | 14,521 | 42.6 |
| [Death] | | | | | | |
| 1933 (25/10) | 51,642 | 59.5 | J.C. Wilmot | Lab | 17,790 | 57.9 |
| | | | W.J. Waldron | C | 12,950 | 42.1 |
| | | | | | 4,840 | 15.8 |
| 1935 | 50,682 | 71.9 | Hon. W.W. Astor | C | 18,743 | 51.4 |
| | | | J.C. Wilmot | Lab | 17,689 | 48.6 |
| | | | | | 1,054 | 2.8 |
| 1945 | 38,311 | 73.8 | R.M.M. Stewart | Lab | 15,662 | 55.4 |
| | | | Hon. W.W. Astor | C | 10,309 | 36.4 |
| | | | P.M. Syrett | L | 2,315* | 8.2 |
| | | | | | 5,353 | 19.0 |

# FULHAM, WEST [16]

| Election | Electors | T'out | Candidate | Party | Votes | % |
|---|---|---|---|---|---|---|
| 1918 | 39,953 | 46.9 | Sir C.S. Cobb | Co C | 12,182 | 64.9 |
| | | | R.M. Gentry | Lab | 4,435 | 23.7 |
| | | | Sir H.G. Fordham | L | 1,139* | 6.1 |
| | | | W.J. Allen | Ind | 995* | 5.3 |
| | | | | | 7,747 | 41.2 |
| 1922 | 39,562 | 58.4 | Sir C.S. Cobb | C | 14,875 | 64.4 |
| | | | R.M. Gentry | Lab | 8,210 | 35.6 |
| | | | | | 6,665 | 28.8 |
| 1923 | 40,134 | 62.9 | Sir C.S. Cobb | C | 9,965 | 39.5 |
| | | | R.M. Gentry | Lab | 8,687 | 34.4 |
| | | | C.W. Courtenay | L | 6,604 | 26.1 |
| | | | | | 1,278 | 5.1 |
| 1924 | 40,386 | 71.3 | Sir C.S. Cobb | C | 17,109 | 59.4 |
| | | | R.M. Gentry | Lab | 11,706 | 40.6 |
| | | | | | 5,403 | 18.8 |
| 1929 | 50,610 | 71.3 | Dr. G.E. Spero | Lab | 16,190 | 44.9 |
| | | | Sir C.S. Cobb | C | 13,979 | 38.7 |
| | | | G.A. Gale | L | 5,920 | 16.4 |
| | | | | | 2,211 | 6.2 |

[Resignation]

| Election | Electors | T'out | Candidate | Party | Votes | % |
|---|---|---|---|---|---|---|
| 1930 (6/5) | 50,610 | 63.6 | Sir C.S. Cobb | C | 16,223 | 50.4 |
| | | | J.W. Banfield | Lab | 15,983 | 49.6 |
| | | | | | 240 | 0.8 |
| 1931 | 50,991 | 71.4 | Sir C.S. Cobb | C | 24,257 | 66.6 |
| | | | J.W. Banfield | Lab | 12,164 | 33.4 |
| | | | | | 12,093 | 33.2 |
| 1935 | 49,480 | 69.9 | Sir C.S. Cobb | C | 18,461 | 53.4 |
| | | | Dr. M. Follick | Lab | 14,978 | 43.3 |
| | | | E.J. Johnson | L | 1,132* | 3.3 |
| | | | | | 3,483 | 10.1 |

[Death]

| Election | Electors | T'out | Candidate | Party | Votes | % |
|---|---|---|---|---|---|---|
| 1938 (6/4) | 48,469 | 65.5 | Dr. Edith Summerskill | Lab | 16,583 | 52.2 |
| | | | C.J. Busby | C | 15,162 | 47.8 |
| | | | | | 1,421 | 4.4 |
| 1945 | 41,329 | 76.3 | Dr. Edith Summerskill | Lab | 19,537 | 61.9 |
| | | | P.B. Lucas | C | 12,016 | 38.1 |
| | | | | | 7,521 | 23.8 |

Note:—

1918: Allen was supported by and possibly the nominee of the local branch of the NFDSS.

# GREENWICH [17]

| Election | Electors | T'out | Candidate | Party | Votes | % |
|---|---|---|---|---|---|---|
| 1918 | 43,756 | 48.1 | †I.H. Benn | Co C | 14,576 | 69.3 |
| | | | J. Bermingham | Lab | 6,471 | 30.7 |
| | | | | | 8,105 | 38.6 |
| 1922 | 46,005 | 60.4 | G.H. Hume | C | 16,934 | 60.9 |
| | | | E.T. Palmer | Lab | 10,860 | 39.1 |
| | | | | | 6,074 | 21.8 |
| 1923 | 46,741 | 61.8 | E.T. Palmer | Lab | 12,314 | 42.7 |
| | | | G.H. Hume | C | 10,746 | 37.2 |
| | | | C.G.L. du Cann | L | 5,806 | 20.1 |
| | | | | | 1,568 | 5.5 |
| 1924 | 47,716 | 75.2 | Sir G.H. Hume | C | 18,473 | 51.5 |
| | | | E.T. Palmer | Lab | 17,409 | 48.5 |
| | | | | | 1,064 | 3.0 |
| 1929 | 62,342 | 70.4 | E.T. Palmer | Lab | 20,328 | 46.3 |
| | | | Sir G.H. Hume | C | 16,710 | 38.1 |
| | | | W.P. Campbell | L | 6,870 | 15.6 |
| | | | | | 3,618 | 8.2 |
| 1931 | 63,385 | 71.0 | Sir G.H. Hume | C | 29,278 | 65.0 |
| | | | E.T. Palmer | Lab | 13,722 | 30.5 |
| | | | Mrs. K.S. Duncan | Com | 2,024* | 4.5 |
| | | | | | 15,556 | 34.5 |
| 1935 | 63,292 | 67.9 | Sir G.H. Hume | C | 22,526 | 52.4 |
| | | | J. Reeves | Lab/Co-op | 20,436 | 47.6 |
| | | | | | 2,090 | 4.8 |
| 1945 | 48,163 | 69.9 | J. Reeves | Lab | 22,078 | 65.6 |
| | | | A.W.S. Agar | C | 11,580 | 34.4 |
| | | | | | 10,498 | 31.2 |

| Election | Electors | T'out | Candidate | Party | Votes | % |
|----------|----------|-------|-----------|-------|-------|---|
| 1918 | | | W.J.U. Woolcock | Co L | Unopp. | |
| 1922 | 35,033 | 60.3 | Sir A.L. Lever, Bt. | NL | 9,795 | 46.4 |
| | | | Rt. Hon. T.M. Wood | L | 6,825 | 32.3 |
| | | | A.A. Lynch | Lab | 4,507 | 21.3 |
| | | | | | 2,970 | 14.1 |
| 1923 | 35,334 | 62.8 | L.B. Franklin | L | 8,569 | 38.6 |
| | | | Sir D.T. Keymer | C | 7,252 | 32.7 |
| | | | E.E. Hunter | Lab | 6,354 | 28.7 |
| | | | | | 1,317 | 5.9 |
| 1924 | 35,969 | 74.2 | Sir R.V. Gower | C | 11,414 | 42.7 |
| | | | E.E. Hunter | Lab | 9,684 | 36.3 |
| | | | L.B. Franklin | L | 5,594 | 21.0 |
| | | | | | 1,730 | 6.4 |
| 1929 | 47,774 | 70.0 | F.C. Watkins | Lab | 12,462 | 37.3 |
| | | | A.C. Bossom | C | 10,814 | 32.3 |
| | | | L.B. Franklin | L | 10,186 | 30.4 |
| | | | | | 1,648 | 5.0 |
| 1931 | 48,025 | 67.8 | J.C. Lockwood | C | 16,963 | 52.1 |
| | | | F.C. Watkins | Lab | 9,295 | 28.5 |
| | | | L.B. Franklin | L | 6,316 | 19.4 |
| | | | | | 7,668 | 23.6 |
| 1935 | 48,990 | 60.6 | F.C. Watkins | Lab | 15,332 | 51.6 |
| | | | J.C. Lockwood | C | 14,375 | 48.4 |
| | | | | | 957 | 3.2 |
| 1945 | 33,638 | 65.5 | H. Hynd | Lab | 14,810 | 67.2 |
| | | | R.R. Harris | C | 4,889 | 22.2 |
| | | | S.W. Magnus | L | 2,348* | 10.6 |
| | | | | | 9,921 | 45.0 |

# HACKNEY, NORTH [19]

| Election | Electors | T'out | Candidate | Party | Votes | % |
|---|---|---|---|---|---|---|
| 1918 | 27,871 | 50.2 | †W.R. Greene | Co C | 9,873 | 70.6 |
| | | | W. Burrows | L | 4,119 | 29.4 |
| | | | | | 5,754 | 41.2 |
| | | | | | | |
| 1922 | 33,706 | 63.5 | Sir W.R. Greene, Bt. | C | 13,002 | 60.8 |
| | | | P. Guedalla | L | 8,387 | 39.2 |
| | | | | | 4,615 | 21.6 |
| | | | | | | |
| 1923 | 33,825 | 61.2 | J.H. Harris | L | 11,177 | 54.0 |
| | | | Sir W.R. Greene, Bt. | C | 9,523 | 46.0 |
| | | | | | 1,654 | 8.0 |
| | | | | | | |
| 1924 | 34,012 | 74.2 | A.U.M. Hudson | C | 11,975 | 47.5 |
| | | | J.H. Harris | L | 7,181 | 28.4 |
| | | | Dr. Stella Churchill | Lab | 6,097 | 24.1 |
| | | | | | 4,794 | 19.1 |
| | | | | | | |
| 1929 | 45,722 | 68.6 | A.U.M. Hudson | C | 11,199 | 35.7 |
| | | | F.G. Bowles | Lab | 10,333 | 32.9 |
| | | | J.H. Harris | L | 9,844 | 31.4 |
| | | | | | 866 | 2.8 |
| | | | | | | |
| 1931 | 46,017 | 64.3 | A.U.M. Hudson | C | 20,545 | 69.5 |
| | | | F.G. Bowles | Lab | 9,022 | 30.5 |
| | | | | | 11,523 | 39.0 |
| | | | | | | |
| 1935 | 47,294 | 61.1 | A.U.M. Hudson | C | 15,000 | 51.9 |
| | | | F.G. Bowles | Lab | 13,920 | 48.1 |
| | | | | | 1,080 | 3.8 |
| | | | | | | |
| 1945 | 38,512 | 69.2 | H.E. Goodrich | Lab | 17,337 | 65.0 |
| | | | Sir A.U.M. Hudson, Bt. | C | 5,771 | 21.7 |
| | | | Mrs. D.M. Gorsky | L | 3,546 | 13.3 |
| | | | | | 11,566 | 43.3 |

| Election | Electors | T'out | Candidate | Party | Votes | % |
|---|---|---|---|---|---|---|
| 1918 | 25,212 | 55.4 | H.W. Bottomley | Ind | 11,145 | 79 7 |
| | | | A. Henri | Co L | 2,830 | 20.3 |
| | | | | | 8,315 | 59.4 |

[Expulsion from the House of Commons]

| | | | | | | |
|---|---|---|---|---|---|---|
| 1922 | 32,262[†] | 56.3 | C.C.A.L. Erskine-Bolst | Co C | 9,118 | 50.2 |
| (18/8) | | | G.W.H. Knight | Lab | 9,046 | 49.8 |
| | | | | | 72 | 0.4 |
| | | | | | | |
| 1922 | 33,284 | 70.0 | C.C.A.L. Erskine-Bolst | C | 14,017 | 60.2 |
| | | | G.W.H. Knight | Lab | 9,276 | 39.8 |
| | | | | | 4,741 | 20.4 |
| | | | | | | |
| 1923 | 34,037 | 65.8 | H.S. Morrison | Lab | 9,578 | 42.8 |
| | | | G.M. Garro-Jones | L | 6,757 | 30.2 |
| | | | C.C.A.L. Erskine-Bolst | C | 6,047 | 27.0 |
| | | | | | 2,821 | 12.6 |
| | | | | | | |
| 1924 | 34,565 | 72.5 | G.M. Garro-Jones | L | 13,415 | 53.5 |
| | | | H.S. Morrison | Lab | 11,651 | 46.5 |
| | | | | | 1,764 | 7.0 |
| | | | | | | |
| 1929 | 43,997 | 69.2 | H.S. Morrison | Lab | 15,590 | 51.2 |
| | | | Sir T.J.P. Lever, Bt. | C | 8,222 | 27.0 |
| | | | Miss M.M. Gibbon | L | 6,302 | 20.7 |
| | | | J.T. Murphy | Com | 331* | 1.1 |
| | | | | | 7,368 | 24.2 |
| | | | | | | |
| 1931 | 44,373 | 64.8 | Miss F.M. Graves | C | 15,920 | 55.4 |
| | | | Rt. Hon. H.S. Morrison | Lab | 12,827 | 44.6 |
| | | | | | 3,093 | 10.8 |
| | | | | | | |
| 1935 | 43,051 | 62.0 | Rt. Hon. H.S. Morrison | Lab | 15,830 | 59.3 |
| | | | Miss F.M. Graves | C | 10,876 | 40.7 |
| | | | | | 4,954 | 18.6 |
| | | | | | | |
| 1945 | 30,006 | 67.4 | H.W. Butler | Lab | 10,432 | 51.6 |
| | | | S.L. Price | NL | 4,901 | 24.2 |
| | | | W. Rust | Com | 4,891 | 24.2 |
| | | | | | 5,531 | 27.4 |

Note:—

1918: Bottomley was expelled from the House of Commons on August 1, 1922, as a result of being convicted at the Central Criminal Court on May 29, 1922. He was sentenced to seven years penal servitude for fraudulent conversion. See House of Commons Papers, 1922 (138) XVII, 473.

| Election | Electors | T'out | Candidate | Party | Votes | % |
|----------|----------|-------|-----------|-------|-------|---|
| 1918 | 26,656 | 46.7 | H. Foreman | Co C | 5,785 | 46.5 |
| | | | E. Young | L | 2,542 | 20.4 |
| | | | J.C. Walker | Nat P | 2,075 | 16.7 |
| | | | C.R. Morden | Lab | 2,048 | 16.4 |
| | | | | | 3,243 | 26.1 |
| 1922 | 29,904 | 60.0 | Sir H. Foreman | C | 8,303 | 46.3 |
| | | | J.P. Gardner | Lab | 5,350 | 29.8 |
| | | | F. Coysh | L | 4,278 | 23.9 |
| | | | | | 2,953 | 16.5 |
| 1923 | 31,331 | 63.0 | J.P. Gardner | Lab | 8,101 | 41.0 |
| | | | E. Ashmead-Bartlett | C | 7,256 | 36.8 |
| | | | F. Coysh | L | 4,374 | 22.2 |
| | | | | | 845 | 4.2 |
| 1924 | 32,194 | 74.2 | E. Ashmead-Bartlett | C | 12,925 | 54.1 |
| | | | J.P. Gardner | Lab | 10,970 | 45.9 |
| | | | | | 1,955 | 8.2 |

[Resignation]

| Election | Electors | T'out | Candidate | Party | Votes | % |
|----------|----------|-------|-----------|-------|-------|---|
| 1926 (28/5) | 34,017[†] | 72.2 | J.P. Gardner | Lab | 13,095 | 53.4 |
| | | | S. Gluckstein | C | 9,484 | 38.6 |
| | | | G.P. Murfitt | L | 1,974* | 8.0 |
| | | | | | 3,611 | 14.8 |
| 1929 | 44,789 | 70.0 | J.P. Gardner | Lab | 17,601 | 56.2 |
| | | | Sir M. Hays | C | 13,744 | 43.8 |
| | | | | | 3,857 | 12.4 |
| 1931 | 45,693 | 69.6 | Hon. Mary A. Pickford | C | 18,815 | 59.2 |
| | | | J.P. Gardner | Lab | 11,838 | 37.2 |
| | | | E.F. Bramley | Com | 697* | 2.2 |
| | | | R.E.N. Braden | NP | 431* | 1.4 |
| | | | | | 6,977 | 22.0 |

[Death]

| Election | Electors | T'out | Candidate | Party | Votes | % |
|----------|----------|-------|-----------|-------|-------|---|
| 1934 (24/4) | 45,216 | 56.7 | F.R. West | Lab | 14,263 | 55.7 |
| | | | C.P. Davis | C | 10,747 | 41.9 |
| | | | E.F. Bramley | Com | 614* | 2.4 |
| | | | | | 3,516 | 13.8 |

[Seat Vacant at Dissolution (Death)]

| Election | Electors | T'out | Candidate | Party | Votes | % |
|----------|----------|-------|-----------|-------|-------|---|
| 1935 | 44,570 | 65.7 | D.N. Pritt | Lab (Ind Lab) | 15,464 | 52.8 |
| | | | N.A.H. Bower | C | 13,830 | 47.2 |
| | | | | | 1,634 | 5.6 |
| 1945 | 40,444 | 73.0 | D.N. Pritt | Ind Lab | 18,845 | 63.8 |
| | | | L. Caplan | C | 7,516 | 25.5 |
| | | | W.H. Church | Lab | 3,165* | 10.7 |
| | | | | | 11,329 | 38.3 |

Note:—

1945: Pritt became chairman of the Labour Independent Group when it was formed in June 1949.

# HAMMERSMITH, SOUTH  [22]

| Election | Electors | T'out | Candidate | Party | Votes | % |
|---|---|---|---|---|---|---|
| 1918 | 27,996 | 46.8 | †Rt. Hon. Sir W.J. Bull | Co C | 8,592 | 65.6 |
| | | | T.A. Robertson | L | 2,555 | 19.5 |
| | | | J.T. Westcott | Lab | 1,958 | 14.9 |
| | | | | | 6,037 | 46.1 |
| 1922 | 30,618 | 56.4 | Rt. Hon. Sir W.J. Bull, Bt. | C | 10,877 | 63.0 |
| | | | W. Albery | Lab | 6,397 | 37.0 |
| | | | | | 4,480 | 26.0 |
| 1923 | 30,879 | 61.1 | Rt. Hon. Sir W.J. Bull, Bt. | C | 8,184 | 43.4 |
| | | | W. Albery | Lab | 6,974 | 36.9 |
| | | | E.D. Wetton | L | 3,723 | 19.7 |
| | | | | | 1,210 | 6.5 |
| 1924 | 31,633 | 72.3 | Rt. Hon. Sir W.J. Bull, Bt. | C | 12,679 | 55.4 |
| | | | Rt. Hon. C. Addison | Lab | 8,804 | 38.5 |
| | | | E.D. Wetton | L | 1,393* | 6.1 |
| | | | | | 3,875 | 16.9 |
| 1929 | 42,841 | 67.3 | D. Chater | Lab/Co-op | 12,630 | 43.8 |
| | | | Sir J. Ferguson | C | 12,218 | 42.4 |
| | | | J.J. Davies | L | 3,976 | 13.8 |
| | | | | | 412 | 1.4 |
| 1931 | 43,250 | 68.0 | J.D. Cooke | C | 21,018 | 71.5 |
| | | | D. Chater | Lab/Co-op | 8,390 | 28.5 |
| | | | | | 12,628 | 43.0 |
| 1935 | 41,104 | 60.1 | J.D. Cooke | C | 15,377 | 62.3 |
| | | | W.T. Adams | Lab | 9,309 | 37.7 |
| | | | | | 6,068 | 24.6 |
| 1945 | 32,779 | 65.7 | W.T. Adams | Lab/Co-op | 12,502 | 58.0 |
| | | | Sir J.D. Cooke | C | 9,044 | 42.0 |
| | | | | | 3,458 | 16.0 |
| [Death] | | | | | | |
| 1949 (24/2) | 47,545 | 60.6 | W.T. Williams | Lab/Co-op | 15,223 | 52.8 |
| | | | A. Fell | C | 13,610 | 47.2 |
| | | | | | 1,613 | 5.6 |

# HAMPSTEAD  [23]

| Election | Electors | T'out | Candidate | Party | Votes | % |
|---|---|---|---|---|---|---|
| 1918 | 32,544 | 58.1 | G. Balfour | Co C | 13,393 | 70.8 |
|  |  |  | B.S. MacKay | Lab | 3,646 | 19.3 |
|  |  |  | J.H. Wrentmore | Nat P | 1,881* | 9.9 |
|  |  |  |  |  | 9,747 | 51.5 |
| 1922 | 38,781 | 63.1 | G. Balfour | C | 14,596 | 59.7 |
|  |  |  | A. Clavering | NL | 5,582 | 22.8 |
|  |  |  | L.S. Fletcher | L | 4,282 | 17.5 |
|  |  |  |  |  | 9,014 | 36.9 |
| 1923 | 39,711 | 58.0 | G. Balfour | C | 13,513 | 58.6 |
|  |  |  | L.S. Fletcher | L | 9,538 | 41.4 |
|  |  |  |  |  | 3,975 | 17.2 |
| 1924 | 40,309 | 67.2 | G. Balfour | C | 21,432 | 79.1 |
|  |  |  | C.T. Hendin | Lab | 5,662 | 20.9 |
|  |  |  |  |  | 15,770 | 58.2 |
| 1929 | 63,861 | 62.8 | G. Balfour | C | 23,370 | 58.3 |
|  |  |  | F.E. Dawkins | Lab | 8,473 | 21.1 |
|  |  |  | M.L. Freedman | L | 8,273 | 20.6 |
|  |  |  |  |  | 14,897 | 37.2 |
| 1931 | 64,527 | 65.7 | G. Balfour | C | 36,928 | 87.1 |
|  |  |  | H. Smith | Lab | 5,475 | 12.9 |
|  |  |  |  |  | 31,453 | 74.2 |
| 1935 | 65,576 | 59.0 | G. Balfour | C | 28,334 | 73.2 |
|  |  |  | H. Smith | Lab | 6,987 | 18.0 |
|  |  |  | J.L. Young | L | 3,396* | 8.8 |
|  |  |  |  |  | 21,347 | 55.2 |
| [Death] |  |  |  |  |  |  |
| 1941 | 65,511 | 17.3 | C. Challen | C | 7,630 | 67.4 |
| (27/11) |  |  | N.P. Billing | Nat Ind | 2,734 | 24.1 |
|  |  |  | W.R. Hipwell | Ind Prog | 636* | 5.6 |
|  |  |  | A.L. Dolland | Ind | 326* | 2.9 |
|  |  |  |  |  | 4,896 | 43.3 |
| 1945 | 55,446 | 68.4 | C. Challen | C | 19,652 | 51.8 |
|  |  |  | W.J. Field | Lab | 18,294 | 48.2 |
|  |  |  |  |  | 1,358 | 3.6 |

Notes:—

1941:  Billing advocated a policy of aerial reprisals against Germany.

Dolland advocated a policy of all-out-aid to Russia.

| Election | Electors | T'out | Candidate | Party | Votes | % |
|---|---|---|---|---|---|---|
| 1918 | 20,371 | 39.1 | †Sir J.F. Remnant, Bt. | Co C | 6,874 | 86.3 |
| | | | J.H. Worrall | Ind Lab | 1,091 | 13.7 |
| | | | | | 5,783 | 72.6 |
| 1922 | 26,991 | 47.2 | Sir J.F. Remnant, Bt. | C | 8,996 | 70.5 |
| | | | J.S. Stooke-Vaughan | L | 3,757 | 29.5 |
| | | | | | 5,239 | 41.0 |
| 1923 | 27,218 | 48.8 | Sir J.F. Remnant, Bt. | C | 7,892 | 59.4 |
| | | | J.S. Stooke-Vaughan | L | 3,349 | 25.2 |
| | | | A. West | Lab | 2,044 | 15.4 |
| | | | | | 4,543 | 34.2 |
| 1924 | 27,490 | 55.1 | Sir J.F. Remnant, Bt. | C | 11,428 | 75.5 |
| | | | W.W. Messer | Lab | 3,718 | 24.5 |
| | | | | | 7,710 | 51.0 |

[Elevation to the Peerage – Lord Remnant]

| Election | Electors | T'out | Candidate | Party | Votes | % |
|---|---|---|---|---|---|---|
| 1928 | 27,357 | 39.0 | S.J. Bevan | C | 6,365 | 59.7 |
| (28/6) | | | P. Allott | Lab | 2,238 | 21.0 |
| | | | T.E. Morton | L | 2,062 | 19.3 |
| | | | | | 4,127 | 38.7 |
| 1929 | 32,862 | 54.1 | S.J. Bevan | C | 10,093 | 56.8 |
| | | | F.W. Hickinbottom | Lab | 4,530 | 25.5 |
| | | | T.E. Morton | L | 3,150 | 17.7 |
| | | | | | 5,563 | 31.3 |
| 1931 | 33,543 | 56.7 | S.J. Bevan | C | 16,094 | 84.7 |
| | | | F.W. Hickinbottom | Lab | 2,916 | 15.3 |
| | | | | | 13,178 | 69.4 |

[Seat Vacant at Dissolution (Death)]

| Election | Electors | T'out | Candidate | Party | Votes | % |
|---|---|---|---|---|---|---|
| 1935 | 32,641 | 49.0 | Sir R.I. Tasker | C | 11,654 | 72.9 |
| | | | R.S. Jefferies | Lab | 4,325 | 27.1 |
| | | | | | 7,329 | 45.8 |
| 1945 | 16,394 | 68.3 | Hon. J.W.M. Aitken | C | 6,061 | 54.1 |
| | | | Miss I. Marcousé | Lab | 5,136 | 45.9 |
| | | | | | 925 | 8.2 |

| Election | Electors | T'out | Candidate | Party | Votes | % |
|---|---|---|---|---|---|---|
| 1918 | 37,078 | 51.7 | A.B. Raper | Co C | 9,352 | 48.8 |
| | | | †E. Smallwood | L | 5,968 | 31.1 |
| | | | A.J. Lewer | Lab | 3,122 | 16.3 |
| | | | C.E. Copplestone | Nat P | 575* | 3.0 |
| | | | F.A. Wickhart | Ind | 147* | 0.8 |
| | | | | | 3,384 | 17.7 |
| 1922 | 43,676 | 59.4 | A.U.M. Hudson | C | 11,954 | 46.1 |
| | | | Sir G. Baring, Bt. | L | 8,107 | 31.2 |
| | | | Dr. Ethel Bentham | Lab | 5,900 | 22.7 |
| | | | | | 3,847 | 14.9 |
| 1923 | 44,402 | 60.0 | A.S. Comyns Carr | L | 10,670 | 40.1 |
| | | | A.U.M. Hudson | C | 9,038 | 33.9 |
| | | | Dr. Ethel Bentham | Lab | 6,941 | 26.0 |
| | | | | | 1,632 | 6.2 |
| 1924 | 44,978 | 70.8 | R.I. Tasker | C | 14,174 | 44.5 |
| | | | Dr. Ethel Bentham | Lab | 10,280 | 32.3 |
| | | | A.S. Comyns Carr | L | 7,406 | 23.2 |
| | | | | | 3,894 | 12.2 |
| 1929 | 60,202 | 66.4 | Dr. Ethel Bentham | Lab | 15,199 | 38.0 |
| | | | R.I. Tasker | C | 13,641 | 34.1 |
| | | | E. Middleton | L | 11,136 | 27.9 |
| | | | | | 1,558 | 3.9 |
| [Death] | | | | | | |
| 1931 (19/2) | 61,126 | 50.0 | Mrs. E.L. Manning | Lab | 10,591 | 34.7 |
| | | | A.C. Critchley | EC & UEP | 8,314 | 27.2 |
| | | | Miss T. Cazalet | C | 7,182 | 23.5 |
| | | | H.E. Crawfurd | L | 4,450 | 14.6 |
| | | | | | 2,277 | 7.5 |
| 1931 | 61,635 | 65.4 | Miss T. Cazalet | C | 27,221 | 67.5 |
| | | | Mrs. E.L. Manning | Lab | 13,111 | 32.5 |
| | | | | | 14,110 | 35.0 |
| 1935 | 60,135 | 57.8 | Miss T. Cazalet | C | 18,248 | 52.5 |
| | | | G.D. Jones | Lab | 13,810 | 39.8 |
| | | | C.H. Blackburn | L | 2,670* | 7.7 |
| | | | | | 4,438 | 12.7 |
| 1945 | 43,660 | 66.2 | E.G.M. Fletcher | Lab | 18,936 | 65.5 |
| | | | Mrs. T. Cazalet-Keir | C | 9,960 | 34.5 |
| | | | | | 8,976 | 31.0 |

Notes:—

1931: Critchley was the nominee of a joint EC and UEP selection committee.
(19/2)

1935: Miss Cazalet became Mrs. Cazalet-Keir upon her marriage in 1939.

| Election | Electors | T'out | Candidate | Party | Votes | % |
|---|---|---|---|---|---|---|
| 1918 | 41,769 | 49.6 | †Hon. Sir N.J. Moore | Co C | 14,183 | 68.5 |
| | | | J. Arnall | BSP | 4,000 | 19.3 |
| | | | N.T.C. Sargant | L | 2,529* | 12.2 |
| | | | | | 10,183 | 49.2 |
| 1922 | 47,059 | 61.1 | Hon. Sir N.J. Moore | C | 13,520 | 47.0 |
| | | | Miss E. Picton-Turbervill | Lab | 7,993 | 27.8 |
| | | | N.T.C. Sargant | L | 7,256 | 25.2 |
| | | | | | 5,527 | 19.2 |
| 1923 | 48,002 | 61.6 | Sir W.H. Cowan | C | 10,802 | 36.5 |
| | | | N.T.C. Sargant | L | 10,219 | 34.6 |
| | | | G. Bennett | Lab | 8,556 | 28.9 |
| | | | | | 583 | 1.9 |
| 1924 | 48,573 | 72.2 | Sir W.H. Cowan | C | 15,562 | 44.4 |
| | | | E.G. Culpin | Lab | 12,376 | 35.3 |
| | | | N.T.C. Sargant | L | 7,136 | 20.3 |
| | | | | | 3,186 | 9.1 |
| 1929 | 64,241 | 68.0 | R.S. Young | Lab | 18,272 | 41.8 |
| | | | G.C. Touche | C | 15,207 | 34.8 |
| | | | Lady Crosfield | L | 10,210 | 23.4 |
| | | | | | 3,065 | 7.0 |
| 1931 | 65,486 | 66.5 | A.W. Goodman | C | 28,790 | 66.1 |
| | | | R.S. Young | Lab | 14,783 | 33.9 |
| | | | | | 14,007 | 32.2 |
| 1935 | 63,835 | 59.7 | A.W. Goodman | C | 20,744 | 54.4 |
| | | | R.S. Young | Lab | 17,359 | 45.6 |
| | | | | | 3,385 | 8.8 |
| [Death] | | | | | | |
| 1937 | 63,747 | 40.4 | Dr. L. Haden-Guest | Lab | 13,523 | 52.5 |
| (13/10) | | | Sir W.H. Sugden | C | 12,227 | 47.5 |
| | | | | | 1,296 | 5.0 |
| 1945 | 51,322 | 67.2 | Dr. L. Haden-Guest | Lab | 23,234 | 67.4 |
| | | | Hon. C.A.U. Rhys | C | 11,240 | 32.6 |
| | | | | | 11,994 | 34.8 |

[Seat Vacant at Dissolution (Elevation to the Peerage — Lord Haden-Guest)]

| Election | Electors | T'out | Candidate | Party | Votes | % |
|---|---|---|---|---|---|---|
| 1918 | 28,976 | 44.1 | C.F. Higham | Co C | 6,885 | 53.9 |
|  |  |  | †Rt. Hon. T. Wiles | L | 5,883 | 46.1 |
|  |  |  |  |  | 1,002 | 7.8 |
| 1922 | 34,029 | 64.2 | C.S. Garland | C | 7,877 | 36.1 |
|  |  |  | Rt. Hon. T. Wiles | L | 7,352 | 33.6 |
|  |  |  | F.W. Pethick-Lawrence | Lab | 6,634 | 30.3 |
|  |  |  |  |  | 525 | 2.5 |
| 1923 | 34,462 | 60.9 | W.S. Cluse | Lab | 7,764 | 37.0 |
|  |  |  | E. Brotherton-Ratcliffe | L | 7,531 | 35.9 |
|  |  |  | C.S. Garland | C | 5,691 | 27.1 |
|  |  |  |  |  | 233 | 1.1 |
| 1924 | 34,818 | 69.4 | W.S. Cluse | Lab | 10,347 | 42.8 |
|  |  |  | T.F. Howard | C | 8,668 | 35.9 |
|  |  |  | E. Brotherton-Ratcliffe | L | 5,158 | 21.3 |
|  |  |  |  |  | 1,679 | 6.9 |
| 1929 | 44,490 | 66.2 | W.S. Cluse | Lab | 13,737 | 46.6 |
|  |  |  | T.F. Howard | C | 9,418 | 32.0 |
|  |  |  | F. Milton | L | 6,316 | 21.4 |
|  |  |  |  |  | 4,319 | 14.6 |
| 1931 | 44,716 | 64.8 | T.F. Howard | C | 18,071 | 62.4 |
|  |  |  | W.S. Cluse | Lab | 10,910 | 37.6 |
|  |  |  |  |  | 7,161 | 24.8 |
| 1935 | 42,188 | 56.7 | W.S. Cluse | Lab | 12,526 | 52.4 |
|  |  |  | T.F. Howard | C | 11,398 | 47.6 |
|  |  |  |  |  | 1,128 | 4.8 |
| 1945 | 27,759 | 64.0 | W.S. Cluse | Lab | 12,893 | 72.6 |
|  |  |  | T.F. Howard | C | 4,877 | 27.4 |
|  |  |  |  |  | 8,016 | 45.2 |

| Election | Electors | T'out | Candidate | Party | Votes | % |
|---|---|---|---|---|---|---|
| 1918 | 26,197 | 42.1 | Sir G.S. Elliott | Co C | 4,996 | 45.4 |
| | | | †Rt. Hon. T. Lough | L | 2,616 | 23.7 |
| | | | J.T. Sheppard | Lab | 2,300 | 20.9 |
| | | | E.M. Taylor | Ind | 1,105* | 10.0 |
| | | | | | 2,380 | 21.7 |
| 1922 | 32,775 | 57.5 | J.A.St.G.F. Despencer-Robertson | C | 7,335 | 38.9 |
| | | | H. Mills | L | 6,643 | 35.3 |
| | | | W.J. Lewington | Lab | 4,856 | 25.8 |
| | | | | | 692 | 3.6 |
| 1923 | 33,351 | 57.7 | F. Montague | Lab | 7,955 | 41.4 |
| | | | J.A.St.G.F. Despencer-Robertson | C | 5,829 | 30.3 |
| | | | J.W. Molden | L | 5,443 | 28.3 |
| | | | | | 2,126 | 11.1 |
| 1924 | 33,427 | 67.2 | F. Montague | Lab | 10,174 | 45.3 |
| | | | J.A.St.G.F. Despencer-Robertson | C | 9,499 | 42.3 |
| | | | J.W. Molden | L | 2,780* | 12.4 |
| | | | | | 675 | 3.0 |
| 1929 | 41,466 | 60.2 | F. Montague | Lab | 13,768 | 55.2 |
| | | | J.A.St.G.F. Despencer-Robertson | C | 6,921 | 27.7 |
| | | | D.E. Evans | L | 4,267 | 17.1 |
| | | | | | 6,847 | 27.5 |
| 1931 | 42,180 | 58.0 | P.W. Donner | C | 14,487 | 59.2 |
| | | | F. Montague | Lab | 9,977 | 40.8 |
| | | | | | 4,510 | 18.4 |
| 1935 | 39,177 | 52.6 | F. Montague | Lab | 11,340 | 55.0 |
| | | | Viscount Duncannon | C | 9,280 | 45.0 |
| | | | | | 2,060 | 10.0 |
| 1945 | 25,926 | 60.1 | F. Montague | Lab | 11,496 | 73.8 |
| | | | E.T. Hope | C | 4,090 | 26.2 |
| | | | | | 7,406 | 47.6 |

[Elevation to the Peerage — Lord Amwell]

| Election | Electors | T'out | Candidate | Party | Votes | % |
|---|---|---|---|---|---|---|
| 1947 (25/9) | 29,859 | 51.4 | A. Evans | Lab | 8,760 | 57.2 |
| | | | T.F. Howard | C | 4,084 | 26.6 |
| | | | E.T. Malindine | L | 2,459 | 16.0 |
| | | | L.J. Wildman | Ind | 33* | 0.2 |
| | | | | | 4,676 | 30.6 |

Notes:—

1918: Taylor was supported by and possibly the nominee of the local branch of the NFDSS.

1947: Wildman announced shortly after nominations closed that he was retiring from the contest owing to pressure of business. However, he did make an eve of poll appearance in the constituency and issued a leaflet complaining about the quality of beer.

| Election | Electors | T'out | Candidate | Party | Votes | % |
|---|---|---|---|---|---|---|
| 1918 | 38,045 | 44.2 | †A.H. Burgoyne | Co C | 13,176 | 78.3 |
| | | | W.J. Jarrett | Lab | 3,653 | 21.7 |
| | | | | | 9,523 | 56.6 |
| 1922 | 42,328 | 54.9 | P.G. Gates | C | 12,328 | 53.1 |
| | | | W.J. Jarrett | Lab | 6,225 | 26.8 |
| | | | Dr. C.W. Hayward | L | 4,666 | 20.1 |
| | | | | | 6,103 | 26.3 |
| 1923 | 43,050 | 55.8 | P.G. Gates | C | 9,458 | 39.4 |
| | | | W.J. Jarrett | Lab | 8,888 | 37.0 |
| | | | L.J. Stein | L | 5,672 | 23.6 |
| | | | | | 570 | 2.4 |
| 1924 | 44,015 | 69.6 | P.G. Gates | C | 16,255 | 53.0 |
| | | | F.R. West | Lab | 14,401 | 47.0 |
| | | | | | 1,854 | 6.0 |
| 1929 | 59,500 | 68.5 | F.R. West | Lab | 19,701 | 48.4 |
| | | | P.G. Gates | C | 15,511 | 38.1 |
| | | | Lady Stewart | L | 5,516 | 13.5 |
| | | | | | 4,190 | 10.3 |
| 1931 | 60,821 | 71.9 | J.A.L. Duncan | C | 27,860 | 63.7 |
| | | | F.R. West | Lab | 15,843 | 36.3 |
| | | | | | 12,017 | 27.4 |
| 1935 | 58,691 | 60.6 | J.A.L. Duncan | C | 18,907 | 53.2 |
| | | | F. Carter | Lab | 15,309 | 43.1 |
| | | | J.S. Spon | L | 1,323* | 3.7 |
| | | | | | 3,598 | 10.1 |
| 1945 | 42,365 | 70.2 | G.H.R. Rogers | Lab | 16,838 | 56.6 |
| | | | J.A.L. Duncan | C | 10,699 | 36.0 |
| | | | J.R. Colclough | L | 2,212* | 7.4 |
| | | | | | 6,139 | 20.6 |

| Election | Electors | T'out | Candidate | Party | Votes | % |
|----------|----------|-------|-----------|-------|-------|---|
| 1918 | 30,888 | 51.8 | Sir W.H. Davison | Co C | 10,693 | 66.8 |
|  |  |  | E. Makins | Nat P | 5,306 | 33.2 |
|  |  |  |  |  | 5,387 | 33.6 |
| 1922 | 35,684 | 58.1 | Sir W.H. Davison | C | 15,760 | 76.0 |
|  |  |  | F.W. Cavendish-Bentinck | Ind | 4,964 | 24.0 |
|  |  |  |  |  | 10,796 | 52.0 |
| 1923 |  |  | Sir W.H. Davison | C | Unopp. |  |
| 1924 |  |  | Sir W.H. Davison | C | Unopp. |  |
| 1929 | 70,593 | 59.5 | Sir W.H. Davison | C | 28,049 | 66.9 |
|  |  |  | Sir H.M. Seely, Bt. | L | 7,570 | 18.0 |
|  |  |  | R. Goddard | Ind C | 6,354 | 15.1 |
|  |  |  |  |  | 20,479 | 48.9 |
| 1931 |  |  | Sir W.H. Davison | C | Unopp. |  |
| 1935 | 69,520 | 62.0 | Sir W.H. Davison | C | 38,297 | 88.9 |
|  |  |  | C.H. Hartwell | Lab | 4,779* | 11.1 |
|  |  |  |  |  | 33,518 | 77.8 |
| 1945 | 46,797 | 67.9 | Sir W.H. Davison | C | 22,166 | 69.8 |
|  |  |  | Mrs. P. Strauss | Lab | 6,014 | 18.9 |
|  |  |  | F.N. Beaufort-Palmer | L | 3,586* | 11.3 |
|  |  |  |  |  | 16,152 | 50.9 |

[Elevation to the Peerage — Lord Broughshane]

| Election | Electors | T'out | Candidate | Party | Votes | % |
|----------|----------|-------|-----------|-------|-------|---|
| 1945 (20/11) | 52,750 | 36.8 | Rt. Hon. R.K. Law | C | 15,846 | 81.7 |
|  |  |  | L.D. Spicer | L | 3,559 | 18.3 |
|  |  |  |  |  | 12,287 | 63.4 |

Notes:—

   1922: Cavendish-Bentinck was incorrectly designated by the press as a National Liberal. He stated in his election address that he was free of all party ties but anti-Conservative.

   1929: Goddard was the nominee of the South Kensington Conservative Emergency Association which was formed by a number of former members of the official Conservative Association who had resigned in protest over the re-adoption of Sir W.H. Davison as the Conservative candidate.

| Election | Electors | T'out | Candidate | Party | Votes | % |
|---|---|---|---|---|---|---|
| 1918 | 37,745 | 42.8 | †D. Dalziel | Co C | 9,902 | 61.3 |
| | | | S. Kelley | Ind | 3,641 | 22.6 |
| | | | H. Norton | L | 2,594 | 16.1 |
| | | | | | 6,261 | 38.7 |
| 1922 | 39,004 | 52.8 | Sir D. Dalziel, Bt. | C | 11,284 | 54.8 |
| | | | F.J. Laverack | L | 9,316 | 45.2 |
| | | | | | 1,968 | 9.6 |
| 1923 | 39,189 | 51.9 | F.J. Laverack | L | 10,881 | 53.5 |
| | | | Sir D. Dalziel, Bt. | C | 9,476 | 46.5 |
| | | | | | 1,405 | 7.0 |
| 1924 | 40,134 | 69.4 | Sir D. Dalziel, Bt. | C | 15,755 | 56.6 |
| | | | J. Adams | Lab | 7,210 | 25.9 |
| | | | F.J. Laverack | L | 4,871 | 17.5 |
| | | | | | 8,545 | 30.7 |

[Elevation to the Peerage — Lord Dalziel]

| Election | Electors | T'out | Candidate | Party | Votes | % |
|---|---|---|---|---|---|---|
| 1927 (27/6) | 39,953 | 53.9 | N.C.D. Colman | C | 10,358 | 48.1 |
| | | | J. Adams | Lab | 6,032 | 28.0 |
| | | | F.J. Laverack | L | 5,134 | 23.9 |
| | | | | | 4,326 | 20.1 |
| 1929 | 50,956 | 62.4 | N.C.D. Colman | C | 14,252 | 44.9 |
| | | | A.B. Bishop | Lab | 10,089 | 31.7 |
| | | | A.S. Quick | L | 7,438 | 23.4 |
| | | | | | 4,163 | 13.2 |
| 1931 | 52,569 | 60.9 | N.C.D. Colman | C | 24,673 | 77.0 |
| | | | E.A. Radice | Lab | 7,358 | 23.0 |
| | | | | | 17,315 | 54.0 |
| 1935 | 51,713 | 58.5 | N.C.D. Colman | C | 17,414 | 57.6 |
| | | | M. Lipton | Lab | 10,908 | 36.1 |
| | | | A.S. Quick | L | 1,911* | 6.3 |
| | | | | | 6,506 | 21.5 |
| 1945 | 37,493 | 65.4 | M. Lipton | Lab | 15,583 | 63.6 |
| | | | N.C.D. Colman | C | 8,928 | 36.4 |
| | | | | | 6,655 | 27.2 |

Notes:—

1918: Kelley was supported by and possibly the nominee of the local branch of the NFDSS.

1922: Laverack was supported by the Anti-Waste League.

## LAMBETH, KENNINGTON  [32]

| Election | Electors | T'out | Candidate | Party | Votes | % |
|---|---|---|---|---|---|---|
| 1918 | 37,322 | 29.7 | H.G. Purchase | Co L | 4,705 | 42.4 |
| | | | Mrs. A. Lucas | C | 3,573 | 32.2 |
| | | | W. Glennie | Lab | 2,817 | 25.4 |
| | | | | | 1,132 | 10.2 |
| 1922 | 36,451 | 58.4 | F.C. Harrison | C | 10,081 | 47.3 |
| | | | H. Gosling | Lab | 7,670 | 36.1 |
| | | | H.G. Purchase | NL | 3,522 | 16.6 |
| | | | | | 2,411 | 11.2 |
| 1923 | 36,729 | 57.6 | T.S.B. Williams | Lab | 8,292 | 39.2 |
| | | | Sir R. Blair | C | 7,782 | 36.8 |
| | | | T.O. Jacobsen | L | 5,075 | 24.0 |
| | | | | | 510 | 2.4 |
| 1924 | 37,629 | 70.3 | G. Harvey | C | 14,898 | 56.3 |
| | | | T.S.B. Williams | Lab | 11,572 | 43.7 |
| | | | | | 3,326 | 12.6 |
| 1929 | 46,290 | 60.1 | L.W. Matters | Lab | 15,477 | 55.7 |
| | | | G. Harvey | C | 12,328 | 44.3 |
| | | | | | 3,149 | 11.4 |
| 1931 | 46,600 | 61.3 | G. Harvey | C | 18,371 | 64.3 |
| | | | L.W. Matters | Lab | 10,188 | 35.7 |
| | | | | | 8,183 | 28.6 |
| 1935 | 43,583 | 55.7 | G. Harvey | C | 12,401 | 51.1 |
| | | | L.W. Matters | Lab | 11,856 | 48.9 |
| | | | | | 545 | 2.2 |
| [Death] | | | | | | |
| 1939 | 43,907 | 40.6 | J.C. Wilmot | Lab | 10,715 | 60.1 |
| (24/5) | | | A. Kennedy | C | 7,119 | 39.9 |
| | | | | | 3,596 | 20.2 |
| 1945 | 29,529 | 62.2 | C.W. Gibson | Lab | 12,910 | 70.2 |
| | | | S.H. Stanley | C | 5,471 | 29.8 |
| | | | | | 7,439 | 40.4 |

Notes:—

1918: Polling was delayed until December 24 owing to the death, after nomination, of the Conservative candidate, F.A. Lucas.

1922: Harrison was supported by the Anti-Waste League.

# LAMBETH, NORTH [33]

| Election | Electors | T'out | Candidate | Party | Votes | % |
|---|---|---|---|---|---|---|
| 1918 | 28,777 | 40.9 | F. Briant | L | 7,326 | 62.3 |
| | | | †Sir W. Houghton-Gastrell | Co C | 4,441 | 37.7 |
| | | | | | 2,885 | 24.6 |
| 1922 | 30,320 | 62.2 | F. Briant | L | 8,132 | 43.1 |
| | | | E.R. Bird | C | 7,362 | 39.1 |
| | | | Mrs. B.A. Gould | Lab | 3,353 | 17.8 |
| | | | | | 770 | 4.0 |
| 1923 | 31,146 | 59.8 | F. Briant | L | 9,036 | 48.5 |
| | | | E.R. Bird | C | 5,509 | 29.6 |
| | | | F. Hughes | Lab | 4,089 | 21.9 |
| | | | | | 3,527 | 18.9 |
| 1924 | 31,866 | 67.0 | F. Briant | L | 7,943 | 37.2 |
| | | | G.R. Strauss | Lab | 7,914 | 37.1 |
| | | | J. Lazarus | C | 5,488 | 25.7 |
| | | | | | 29 | 0.1 |
| 1929 | 38,815 | 66.2 | G.R. Strauss | Lab | 11,264 | 43.8 |
| | | | F. Briant | L | 10,722 | 41.8 |
| | | | C.T. Wilson | C | 3,691 | 14.4 |
| | | | | | 542 | 2.0 |
| 1931 | 38,923 | 64.6 | F. Briant | L | 16,368 | 65.1 |
| | | | G.R. Strauss | Lab | 8,766 | 34.9 |
| | | | | | 7,602 | 30.2 |
| [Death] | | | | | | |
| 1934 (23/10) | 37,064 | 52.6 | G.R. Strauss | Lab | 11,281 | 57.9 |
| | | | J.W. Simpson | L | 4,968 | 25.5 |
| | | | S.F. Markham | N Lab | 2,927 | 15.0 |
| | | | Mrs. A.S.G. Brown | Ind | 305* | 1.6 |
| | | | | | 6,313 | 32.4 |
| 1935 | 35,211 | 54.2 | G.R. Strauss | Lab (Ind Lab) (Lab) | 10,577 | 55.4 |
| | | | E. Terrell | L | 8,521 | 44.6 |
| | | | | | 2,056 | 10.8 |
| 1945 | 20,233 | 64.4 | G.R. Strauss | Lab | 8,677 | 66.6 |
| | | | E.W. Bales | NL | 2,624 | 20.1 |
| | | | R.H. Walton | L | 1,730 | 13.3 |
| | | | | | 6,053 | 46.5 |

| Election | Electors | T'out | Candidate | Party | Votes | % |
|---|---|---|---|---|---|---|
| 1918 | 40,253 | 48.5 | †Rt. Hon. Sir H.S. Samuel | Co C | 12,848 | 65.8 |
| | | | H. Bignold | Ind | 6,665 | 34.2 |
| | | | | | 6,183 | 31.6 |
| 1922 | 43,029 | 61.7 | W. Greaves-Lord | C | 16,121 | 60.8 |
| | | | R.E.W. Kirby | L | 6,253 | 23.5 |
| | | | W.A. Hodgson | Lab | 4,180 | 15.7 |
| | | | | | 9,868 | 37.3 |
| 1923 | 43,495 | 59.4 | W. Greaves-Lord | C | 12,725 | 49.3 |
| | | | F.D. Lapthorn | L | 8,127 | 31.4 |
| | | | W.A. Hodgson | Lab | 5,002 | 19.3 |
| | | | | | 4,598 | 17.9 |
| 1924 | 44,315 | 70.2 | W. Greaves-Lord | C | 22,178 | 71.3 |
| | | | G.J. Anstey | Lab | 8,927 | 28.7 |
| | | | | | 13,251 | 42.6 |
| 1929 | 58,163 | 65.6 | Sir W. Greaves-Lord | C | 19,281 | 50.6 |
| | | | W.O. Reeves | Lab | 11,042 | 28.9 |
| | | | E.S. Layton | L | 7,823 | 20.5 |
| | | | | | 8,239 | 21.7 |
| 1931 | 59,555 | 63.9 | Sir W. Greaves-Lord | C | 30,851 | 81.0 |
| | | | Mrs. A.J. Anstey | Lab | 7,217 | 19.0 |
| | | | | | 23,634 | 62.0 |

[Resignation on appointment as a High Court Judge]

| Election | Electors | T'out | Candidate | Party | Votes | % |
|---|---|---|---|---|---|---|
| 1935 | 59,305 | 53.4 | E.D. Sandys | C | 16,147 | 51.1 |
| (14/3) | | | Mrs. B.A. Gould | Lab | 12,799 | 40.4 |
| | | | R. Findlay | Ind C | 2,698* | 8.5 |
| | | | | | 3,348 | 10.7 |
| 1935 | 59,219 | 62.2 | E.D. Sandys | C | 24,651 | 66.9 |
| | | | C.W. Gibson | Lab | 12,195 | 33.1 |
| | | | | | 12,456 | 33.8 |
| 1945 | 49,445 | 71.3 | R.A. Chamberlain | Lab | 16,667 | 47.3 |
| | | | Rt. Hon. E.D. Sandys | C | 14,644 | 41.5 |
| | | | A.D. Wintle | L | 3,944* | 11.2 |
| | | | | | 2,023 | 5.8 |

Notes:—

1918: Bignold was supported by and possibly the nominee of the local branch of the NFDSS.

1935: Findlay was opposed to the Government's policy on India. He was supported by
(14/3) Randolph Churchill.

# LEWISHAM, EAST [35]

| Election | Electors | T'out | Candidate | Party | Votes | % |
|---|---|---|---|---|---|---|
| 1918 | | | A. Pownall | Co C | Unopp. | |
| 1922 | 45,377 | 64.0 | A. Pownall | C | 16,726 | 57.6 |
| | | | E.W. Wilton | Lab | 8,402 | 28.9 |
| | | | J.C.L. Zorn | L | 3,906 | 13.5 |
| | | | | | 8,324 | 28.7 |
| 1923 | 48,812 | 62.6 | A. Pownall | C | 13,560 | 44.4 |
| | | | E.W. Wilton | Lab | 9,604 | 31.4 |
| | | | Sir E. Penton | L | 7,397 | 24.2 |
| | | | | | 3,956 | 13.0 |
| 1924 | 50,019 | 74.9 | A. Pownall | C | 23,842 | 63.6 |
| | | | J.C. Wilmot | Lab | 13,621 | 36.4 |
| | | | | | 10,221 | 27.2 |
| 1929 | 76,562 | 71.5 | Sir A. Pownall | C | 23,208 | 42.4 |
| | | | J.C. Wilmot | Lab | 22,806 | 41.7 |
| | | | Sir E. Penton | L | 8,729 | 15.9 |
| | | | | | 402 | 0.7 |
| 1931 | 82,606 | 74.9 | Sir A. Pownall | C | 41,354 | 66.9 |
| | | | J.C. Wilmot | Lab | 20,485 | 33.1 |
| | | | | | 20,869 | 33.8 |
| 1935 | 87,178 | 68.0 | Sir A. Pownall | C | 32,874 | 55.4 |
| | | | Mrs. F.K. Corbet | Lab | 26,425 | 44.6 |
| | | | | | 6,449 | 10.8 |
| 1945 | 79,318 | 76.2 | Rt. Hon. H.S. Morrison | Lab | 37,361 | 61.9 |
| | | | Sir A. Pownall | C | 22,142 | 36.6 |
| | | | F. Russell | Ind | 931* | 1.5 |
| | | | | | 15,219 | 25.3 |

# LEWISHAM, WEST  [36]

| Election | Electors | T'out | Candidate | Party | Votes | % |
|---|---|---|---|---|---|---|
| 1918 [Death] | | | †Sir E.F. Coates, Bt. | Co C | Unopp. | |
| 1921 (13/9) | 40,919 | 59.2 | Sir P. Dawson | C | 9,427 | 39.0 |
| | | | W.G. Windham | AWL | 8,580 | 35.4 |
| | | | F.W. Raffety | L | 6,211 | 25.6 |
| | | | | | 847 | 3.6 |
| 1922 | 42,455 | 58.1 | Sir P. Dawson | C | 16,216 | 65.7 |
| | | | B.L.A. O'Malley | L | 8,469 | 34.3 |
| | | | | | 7,747 | 31.4 |
| 1923 | 42,940 | 57.0 | Sir P. Dawson | C | 12,448 | 50.9 |
| | | | B.L.A. O'Malley | L | 12,009 | 49.1 |
| | | | | | 439 | 1.8 |
| 1924 | 44,078 | 75.5 | Sir P. Dawson | C | 19,723 | 59.3 |
| | | | Mrs. B. Drake | Lab | 6,781 | 20.4 |
| | | | B.L.A. O'Malley | L | 6,756 | 20.3 |
| | | | | | 12,942 | 38.9 |
| 1929 | 61,191 | 69.3 | Sir P. Dawson | C | 20,830 | 49.1 |
| | | | Mrs. C.M. Wadham | Lab | 10,958 | 25.9 |
| | | | A.R.N. Roberts | L | 10,590 | 25.0 |
| | | | | | 9,872 | 23.2 |
| 1931 | 63,946 | 69.2 | Sir P. Dawson | C | 34,289 | 77.5 |
| | | | R.M.M. Stewart | Lab | 9,956 | 22.5 |
| | | | | | 24,333 | 55.0 |
| 1935 | 65,679 | 63.9 | Sir P. Dawson | C | 27,173 | 64.7 |
| | | | R.M.M. Stewart | Lab | 14,803 | 35.3 |
| | | | | | 12,370 | 29.4 |
| [Death] | | | | | | |
| 1938 (24/11) | 67,641 | 58.4 | H. Brooke | C | 22,587 | 57.1 |
| | | | A.M. Skeffington | Lab | 16,939 | 42.9 |
| | | | | | 5,648 | 14.2 |
| 1945 | 50,918 | 73.6 | A.M. Skeffington | Lab | 20,008 | 53.4 |
| | | | H. Brooke | C | 17,492 | 46.6 |
| | | | | | 2,516 | 6.8 |

Note:—

1922:  Dawson was supported by the Anti-Waste League.

| Election | Electors | T'out | Candidate | Party | Votes | % |
|---|---|---|---|---|---|---|
| 1918 | 37,067 | 46.5 | W.G. Perring | Co C | 5,759 | 33.4 |
| | | | W.S.G. Aston | Nat P | 4,029 | 23.4 |
| | | | E.P.J. Barry | Ind | 3,571 | 20.7 |
| | | | L.B. Franklin | L | 1,831* | 10.6 |
| | | | H. Bundy | Ind Lab | 1,275* | 7.4 |
| | | | †A. Strauss | Ind Lab | 774* | 4.5 |
| | | | | | 1,730 | 10.0 |
| | | | | | | |
| 1922 | 37,761 | 45.6 | W.G. Perring | C | 10,792 | 62.6 |
| | | | J.W.A. Jennings | Ind L | 6,444 | 37.4 |
| | | | | | 4,348 | 25.2 |
| | | | | | | |
| 1923 | 37,751 | 59.7 | W.G. Perring | C | 8,721 | 38.7 |
| | | | J.W. Gordon | Lab | 6,954 | 30.8 |
| | | | H.A. Baker | L | 6,873 | 30.5 |
| | | | | | 1,767 | 7.9 |
| | | | | | | |
| 1924 | 38,225 | 72.0 | W.G. Perring | C | 14,044 | 51.0 |
| | | | J.W. Gordon | Lab | 10,481 | 38.1 |
| | | | A.C. Crane | L | 3,013* | 10.9 |
| | | | | | 3,563 | 12.9 |
| | | | | | | |
| 1929 | 49,185 | 69.0 | B. Bracken | C | 13,876 | 40.9 |
| | | | J.W. Gordon | Lab | 13,348 | 39.3 |
| | | | R. Myer | L | 6,723 | 19.8 |
| | | | | | 528 | 1.6 |
| | | | | | | |
| 1931 | 49,601 | 67.5 | B. Bracken | C | 23,901 | 71.4 |
| | | | Dr. Esther Rickards | Lab | 9,597 | 28.6 |
| | | | | | 14,304 | 42.8 |
| | | | | | | |
| 1935 | 47,864 | 60.3 | B. Bracken | C | 17,153 | 59.4 |
| | | | Mrs. C.S. Ganley | Lab/Co-op | 9,925 | 34.4 |
| | | | Dr. G. de P. Swietochowski | L | 1,795* | 6.2 |
| | | | | | 7,228 | 25.0 |
| | | | | | | |
| 1945 | 38,339 | 71.0 | Sir F.N. Mason-MacFarlane | Lab | 16,638 | 61.2 |
| | | | Rt. Hon. B. Bracken | C | 10,093 | 37.1 |
| | | | C. Groves | SPGB | 472* | 1.7 |
| | | | | | 6,545 | 24.1 |
| [Resignation] | | | | | | |
| 1946 | 43,678 | 53.9 | W.J. Field | Lab | 13,082 | 55.6 |
| (20/11) | | | H.F.L. Turner | C | 10,165 | 43.2 |
| | | | C. Groves | SPGB | 286* | 1.2 |
| | | | | | 2,917 | 12.4 |

Notes:—

1918: Barry was supported by and possibly the nominee of the local branch of the NFDSS.

1922: Jennings had official Liberal Party support withdrawn during the campaign. In February 1923, he was convicted at the Central Criminal Court and sentenced to four years imprisonment for cheque frauds.

## PADDINGTON, SOUTH  [38]

| Election | Electors | T'out | Candidate | Party | Votes | % |
|---|---|---|---|---|---|---|
| 1918 | | | †Sir H.P. Harris | Co C | Unopp. | |
| 1922 | 28,637 | 50.5 | H.D. King | C | 9,699 | 67.1 |
| | | | E.E. Sawyer | Ind C | 4,764 | 32.9 |
| | | | | | 4,935 | 34.2 |
| 1923 | 30,032 | 46.3 | H.D. King | C | 9,971 | 71.7 |
| | | | H.W.C. Carr-Gomm | L | 3,939 | 28.3 |
| | | | | | 6,032 | 43.4 |
| 1924 | | | H.D. King | C | Unopp. | |
| 1929 | | | H.D. King | C | Unopp. | |
| [Death] | | | | | | |
| 1930 (30/10) | 52,207 | 57.3 | E.A. Taylor | EC (C) | 11,209 | 37.4 |
| | | | Sir H. Lidiard | C | 10,268 | 34.3 |
| | | | Miss D. Evans | Lab | 7,944 | 26.6 |
| | | | Mrs. A.N. Stewart-Richardson | Ind UEP | 494* | 1.7 |
| | | | | | 941 | 3.1 |
| 1931 | 51,651 | 61.4 | E.A. Taylor | C | 27,206 | 85.7 |
| | | | Miss L.A. Cox | Lab | 4,532 | 14.3 |
| | | | | | 22,674 | 71.4 |
| 1935 | 48,570 | 55.7 | E.A. Taylor | C | 21,344 | 78.9 |
| | | | R.W. Thomson | Lab | 5,722 | 21.1 |
| | | | | | 15,622 | 57.8 |
| 1945 | 35,431 | 64.2 | E.A. Taylor | C | 13,131 | 57.8 |
| | | | C.F.H. Wegg-Prosser | Lab | 9,601 | 42.2 |
| | | | | | 3,530 | 15.6 |

Notes:—

1922: Sawyer was supported by the Anti-Waste League.

1930: Mrs. Stewart-Richardson was the nominee of the local branch of the UEP but her candidature was not endorsed by the UEP headquarters. Official UEP support was given to Taylor.

| Election | Electors | T'out | Candidate | Party | Votes | % |
|---|---|---|---|---|---|---|
| 1918 | 33,436 | 48.9 | †R. Blair | Co C | 8,109 | 49.7 |
| | | | G. Lansbury | Lab | 7,248 | 44.3 |
| | | | M. Dalton | L | 988* | 6.0 |
| | | | | | 861 | 5.4 |
| 1922 | 34,383 | 69.9 | G. Lansbury | Lab | 15,402 | 64.1 |
| | | | G.E. Duveen | C | 8,626 | 35.9 |
| | | | | | 6,776 | 28.2 |
| 1923 | 34,975 | 63.7 | G. Lansbury | Lab | 15,336 | 68.8 |
| | | | I.J. Albery | C | 6,941 | 31.2 |
| | | | | | 8,395 | 37.6 |
| 1924 | 35,446 | 72.1 | G. Lansbury | Lab | 15,740 | 61.6 |
| | | | H.A. Hill | C | 9,806 | 38.4 |
| | | | | | 5,934 | 23.2 |
| 1929 | 43,834 | 66.1 | G. Lansbury | Lab | 20,119 | 69.4 |
| | | | A.W. Goodman | C | 8,852 | 30.6 |
| | | | | | 11,267 | 38.8 |
| 1931 | 43,779 | 63.8 | Rt. Hon. G. Lansbury | Lab | 16,306 | 58.3 |
| | | | D.L.R. Guthrie | C | 11,642 | 41.7 |
| | | | | | 4,664 | 16.6 |
| 1935 | 41,653 | 59.5 | Rt. Hon. G. Lansbury | Lab | 19,064 | 77.0 |
| | | | H.E. Weber | C | 5,707 | 23.0 |
| | | | | | 13,357 | 54.0 |
| [Death] | | | | | | |
| 1940 (12/6) | 37,324 | 32.4 | C.W. Key | Lab | 11,594 | 95.8 |
| | | | Mrs. I. Brown | Com | 506* | 4.2 |
| | | | | | 11,088 | 91.6 |
| 1945 | 20,817 | 62.7 | C.W. Key | Lab | 10,982 | 84.1 |
| | | | C.K. Duthie | C | 2,075 | 15.9 |
| | | | | | 8,907 | 68.2 |

| Election | Electors | T'out | Candidate | Party | Votes | % |
|---|---|---|---|---|---|---|
| 1918 | 36,077 | 48.1 | †Sir A.W. Yeo | Co L | 8,571 | 49.4 |
|  |  |  | S. March | Lab | 4,446 | 25:6 |
|  |  |  | W.T. Allen | C | 4,339 | 25.0 |
|  |  |  |  |  | 4,125 | 23.8 |
| 1922 | 37,026 | 66.5 | S. March | Lab | 14,484 | 58.8 |
|  |  |  | Sir A.W. Yeo | NL | 10,146 | 41.2 |
|  |  |  |  |  | 4,338 | 17.6 |
| 1923 | 37,681 | 59.5 | S. March | Lab | 14,537 | 64.8 |
|  |  |  | H. Heathcote-Williams | L | 7,899 | 35.2 |
|  |  |  |  |  | 6,638 | 29.6 |
| 1924 | 38,336 | 67.6 | S. March | Lab | 16,224 | 62.6 |
|  |  |  | H. Heathcote-Williams | L | 9,709 | 37.4 |
|  |  |  |  |  | 6,515 | 25.2 |
| 1929 | 47,845 | 63.6 | S. March | Lab | 19,696 | 64.8 |
|  |  |  | H. Heathcote-Williams | L | 7,185 | 23.6 |
|  |  |  | E.M. Gorst | C | 3,532* | 11.6 |
|  |  |  |  |  | 12,511 | 41.2 |
| 1931 | 48,166 | 58.6 | D.M. Adams | Lab | 16,253 | 57.6 |
|  |  |  | H.L.M. Jones | L | 11,965 | 42.4 |
|  |  |  |  |  | 4,288 | 15.2 |
| 1935 | 46,231 | 55.3 | D.M. Adams | Lab | 18,715 | 73.2 |
|  |  |  | Mrs. D.V.C.E. Spearman | C | 6,862 | 26.8 |
|  |  |  |  |  | 11,853 | 46.4 |
| [Death] |  |  |  |  |  |  |
| 1942 (12/8) | 42,034 | 9.3 | W.H. Guy | Lab | 3,375 | 86.2 |
|  |  |  | Rev. P.H. Figgis | CS | 541 | 13.8 |
|  |  |  |  |  | 2,834 | 72.4 |
| 1945 | 19,667 | 66.2 | W.H. Guy | Lab | 11,620 | 89.2 |
|  |  |  | Miss J.H. Vickers | C | 1,403* | 10.8 |
|  |  |  |  |  | 10,217 | 78.4 |

# ST. MARYLEBONE  [41]

| Election | Electors | T'out | Candidate | Party | Votes | % |
|---|---|---|---|---|---|---|
| 1918 | | | †Sir S.E. Scott, Bt. | Co C | Unopp. | |
| 1922 | | | Rt. Hon. Sir D.M. Hogg | C | Unopp. | |
| 1923 | 47,998 | 52.5 | Rt. Hon. Sir D.M. Hogg | C | 16,763 | 66.6 |
| | | | J.J. Dodd | Lab | 8,424 | 33.4 |
| | | | | | 8,339 | 33.2 |
| 1924 | 50,611 | 65.5 | Rt. Hon. Sir D.M. Hogg | C | 24,359 | 73.5 |
| | | | G.E. Elmer | Lab | 8,782 | 26.5 |
| | | | | | 15,577 | 47.0 |

[Resignation on appointment as Lord Chancellor and elevation to the Peerage — Lord Hailsham]

| Election | Electors | T'out | Candidate | Party | Votes | % |
|---|---|---|---|---|---|---|
| 1928 (30/4) | 53,107 | 43.1 | Rt. Hon. Sir J.R. Rodd | C | 12,859 | 56.1 |
| | | | D.A. Ross | Lab | 6,721 | 29.4 |
| | | | B.A. Murray | L | 3,318 | 14.5 |
| | | | | | 6,138 | 26.7 |
| 1929 | 74,517 | 57.3 | Rt. Hon. Sir J.R. Rodd | C | 26,247 | 61.4 |
| | | | D.A. Ross | Lab | 10,960 | 25.7 |
| | | | C.M. Picciotto | L | 5,520 | 12.9 |
| | | | | | 15,287 | 35.7 |
| 1931 | 72,601 | 63.5 | Rt. Hon. Sir J.R. Rodd | C | 39,976 | 86.7 |
| | | | Dr. E.A. Whitfield | Lab | 6,147 | 13.3 |
| | | | | | 33,829 | 73.4 |

[Resignation]

| Election | Electors | T'out | Candidate | Party | Votes | % |
|---|---|---|---|---|---|---|
| 1932 (28/4) | 72,601 | 30.8 | A.S. Cunningham-Reid | C | 11,677 | 52.3 |
| | | | Sir B.P. Blackett | Ind C | 10,664 | 47.7 |
| | | | | | 1,013 | 4.6 |
| 1935 | 67,728 | 57.9 | A.S. Cunningham-Reid | C (Ind C) | 31,183 | 79.6 |
| | | | Dr. Elizabeth Jacobs | Lab | 8,008 | 20.4 |
| | | | | | 23,175 | 59.2 |
| 1945 | 48,570 | 68.3 | Sir W.W. Wakefield | C | 15,891 | 47.9 |
| | | | Dr. Elizabeth Jacobs | Lab | 10,740 | 32.4 |
| | | | A.S. Cunningham-Reid | Ind C | 3,824* | 11.5 |
| | | | T. Lodge | L | 2,711* | 8.2 |
| | | | | | 5,151 | 15.5 |

Notes:—

1932: Blackett was the nominee of the St. Marylebone Conservative Association which was formed by a number of former members of the St. Marylebone Conservative and Constitutional Union (the official Conservative organisation in the constituency) who had resigned in protest over the selection of a Conservative candidate. Both candidates claimed to be the official Conservative nominee and in the circumstances Baldwin decided not to send the customary letter of support to either candidate.

1945: Cunningham-Reid was the nominee of the St. Marylebone Conservative and Constitutional Union which had been disaffiliated in February 1943 by the National Union of Conservative and Unionist Associations. The St. Marylebone Conservative Association (which had remained active since the 1932 by-election) was recognised as the official Conservative constituency association.

| Election | Electors | T'out | Candidate | Party | Votes | % |
|---|---|---|---|---|---|---|
| 1918 | 33,747 | 51.9 | J.W. Lorden | Co C | 7,260 | 41.4 |
| | | | †Rt. Hon. Sir W.H. Dickinson | L | 5,596 | 32.0 |
| | | | J.G. Dale | Lab | 4,651 | 26.6 |
| | | | | | 1,664 | 9.4 |
| 1922 | 36,827 | 66.0 | J.W. Lorden | C | 9,156 | 37.7 |
| | | | J.G. Dale | Lab | 8,165 | 33.6 |
| | | | Rt. Hon. Sir W.H. Dickinson | L | 6,979 | 28.7 |
| | | | | | 991 | 4.1 |
| 1923 | 37,221 | 68.2 | J. Marley | Lab | 10,931 | 43.0 |
| | | | J.W. Lorden | C | 8,085 | 31.9 |
| | | | H.D. Roome | L | 6,363 | 25.1 |
| | | | | | 2,846 | 11.1 |
| 1924 | 37,721 | 79.2 | W.J.I. Fraser | C | 13,964 | 46.7 |
| | | | J. Marley | Lab | 13,171 | 44.1 |
| | | | H.D. Roome | L | 2,748* | 9.2 |
| | | | | | 793 | 2.6 |
| 1929 | 47,366 | 76.0 | J. Marley | Lab | 17,458 | 48.5 |
| | | | W.J.I. Fraser | C | 14,343 | 39.9 |
| | | | F. Coysh | L | 4,177* | 11.6 |
| | | | | | 3,115 | 8.6 |
| 1931 | 47,940 | 73.4 | W.J.I. Fraser | C | 22,490 | 63.9 |
| | | | J. Marley | Lab | 12,257 | 34.8 |
| | | | W.G. Shepherd | Com | 456* | 1.3 |
| | | | | | 10,233 | 29.1 |
| 1935 | 46,030 | 68.3 | Sir W.J.I. Fraser | C | 16,888 | 53.7 |
| | | | H.M. Tibbles | Lab | 13,287 | 42.3 |
| | | | W.O. Hall | L | 1,259* | 4.0 |
| | | | | | 3,601 | 11.4 |

[Resignation on appointment as a Governor of the British Broadcasting Corporation]

| Election | Electors | T'out | Candidate | Party | Votes | % |
|---|---|---|---|---|---|---|
| 1937 (4/2) | 45,632 | 50.9 | R.G. Grant-Ferris | C | 11,744 | 50.6 |
| | | | H.M. Tibbles | Lab | 11,476 | 49.4 |
| | | | | | 268 | 1.2 |
| 1945 | 36,979 | 71.0 | G. House | Lab | 16,738 | 63.8 |
| | | | R.G. Grant-Ferris | C | 9,108 | 34.7 |
| | | | J.B. Gilmore | Ind | 403* | 1.5 |
| | | | | | 7,630 | 29.1 |

[Death]

| Election | Electors | T'out | Candidate | Party | Votes | % |
|---|---|---|---|---|---|---|
| 1949 (10/3) | 43,229 | 65.1 | K. Robinson | Lab | 16,185 | 57.5 |
| | | | N.S. Shields | C | 11,118 | 39.5 |
| | | | J. Mahon | Com | 854* | 3.0 |
| | | | | | 5,067 | 18.0 |

Note:—

1945:  Gilmore sought election as a 'Sportsmen's' candidate.

# ST. PANCRAS, SOUTH-EAST [43]

| Election | Electors | T'out | Candidate | Party | Votes | % |
|---|---|---|---|---|---|---|
| 1918 | 27,411 | 47.2 | J.W.W. Hopkins | C | 4,884 | 37.8 |
| | | | R.L. Reiss | L | 3,594 | 27.8 |
| | | | P. Adams | Ind | 2,263 | 17.5 |
| | | | H.G. Romeril | Lab | 2,189 | 16.9 |
| | | | | | 1,290 | 10.0 |
| 1922 | 30,644 | 60.1 | J.W.W. Hopkins | C | 8,753 | 47.5 |
| | | | H.G. Romeril | Lab | 5,609 | 30.5 |
| | | | L.B. Franklin | L | 4,053 | 22.0 |
| | | | | | 3,144 | 17.0 |
| 1923 | 31,016 | 61.0 | H.G. Romeril | Lab | 7,866 | 41.6 |
| | | | J.W.W. Hopkins | C | 7,174 | 37.9 |
| | | | G. Swaffield | L | 3,890 | 20.5 |
| | | | | | 692 | 3.7 |
| 1924 | 31,679 | 72.6 | J.W.W. Hopkins | C | 12,538 | 54.5 |
| | | | H.G. Romeril | Lab | 10,463 | 45.5 |
| | | | | | 2,075 | 9.0 |
| 1929 | 41,186 | 66.8 | H.G. Romeril | Lab | 13,173 | 47.9 |
| | | | A.L. Beit | C | 10,543 | 38.3 |
| | | | Miss E. Edwardes | L | 3,798 | 13.8 |
| | | | | | 2,630 | 9.6 |
| 1931 | 41,367 | 65.5 | Sir A.L. Beit, Bt. | C | 18,064 | 66.7 |
| | | | H.G. Romeril | Lab | 8,684 | 32.1 |
| | | | S. Usmani | Com | 332* | 1.2 |
| | | | | | 9,380 | 34.6 |
| 1935 | 38,914 | 60.4 | Sir A.L. Beit, Bt. | C | 11,976 | 51.0 |
| | | | Dr. S.W. Jeger | Lab | 10,340 | 44.0 |
| | | | L.G. Bowman | L | 1,181* | 5.0 |
| | | | | | 1,636 | 7.0 |
| 1945 | 26,201 | 64.2 | Dr. S.W. Jeger | Lab | 10,030 | 59.6 |
| | | | Sir A.L. Beit, Bt. | C | 5,320 | 31.6 |
| | | | Mrs. A.B. Blackman | L | 1,474* | 8.8 |
| | | | | | 4,710 | 28.0 |

Note:—

1918: Adams at first received the Coalition Liberal 'coupon' but it was later withdrawn. He claimed to be free of any party allegiance and prior to the election had strongly criticised the Coalition.

## ST. PANCRAS, SOUTH-WEST  [44]

| Election | Electors | T'out | Candidate | Party | Votes | % |
|---|---|---|---|---|---|---|
| 1918 | 26,882 | 45.2 | †R.W. Barnett | Co C | 7,119 | 58.6 |
| | | | A.S. Comyns Carr | L | 4,679 | 38.5 |
| | | | J.C. Sherrott | Ind | 352* | 2.9 |
| | | | | | 2,440 | 20.1 |
| 1922 | 28,952 | 57.9 | R.W. Barnett | C | 8,289 | 49.4 |
| | | | A.S. Comyns Carr | L | 5,533 | 33.0 |
| | | | G. Horne | Lab | 2,947 | 17.6 |
| | | | | | 2,756 | 16.4 |
| 1923 | 29,733 | 56.9 | R.W. Barnett | C | 7,097 | 42.0 |
| | | | G. Horne | Lab | 5,321 | 31.4 |
| | | | W.C. Pilley | L | 4,505 | 26.6 |
| | | | | | 1,776 | 10.6 |
| 1924 | 30,666 | 66.9 | R.W. Barnett | C | 11,877 | 57.9 |
| | | | E.N. Bennett | Lab | 8,630 | 42.1 |
| | | | | | 3,247 | 15.8 |
| 1929 | 42,500 | 62.0 | W. Carter | Lab | 12,010 | 45.6 |
| | | | W.P. Spens | C | 10,231 | 38.8 |
| | | | H. Davies | L | 4,103 | 15.6 |
| | | | | | 1,779 | 6.8 |
| 1931 | 42,016 | 62.5 | G.G. Mitcheson | C | 18,737 | 71.4 |
| | | | W. Carter | Lab | 7,514 | 28.6 |
| | | | | | 11,223 | 42.8 |
| 1935 | 39,904 | 59.4 | G.G. Mitcheson | C | 13,035 | 55.0 |
| | | | J.E. Sears | Lab | 10,670 | 45.0 |
| | | | | | 2,365 | 10.0 |
| 1945 | 25,207 | 61.1 | H. Davies | Lab | 9,533 | 61.9 |
| | | | L.F. Heald | C | 5,862 | 38.1 |
| | | | | | 3,671 | 23.8 |

Note:—

1918: Sherrott sought election as an 'Independent Business' candidate.

# SHOREDITCH [45]

| Election | Electors | T'out | Candidate | Party | Votes | % |
|---|---|---|---|---|---|---|
| 1918 | 45,686 | 37.3 | †Rt. Hon. C. Addison | Co L (L) | 9,532 | 55.9 |
| | | | R.S. Sievier | C | 3,414 | 20.0 |
| | | | A. Walton | Ind Lab | 2,072* | 12.2 |
| | | | †H.G. Chancellor | L | 1,524* | 8.9 |
| | | | T. Warwick | Nat P | 504* | 3.0 |
| | | | | | 6,118 | 35.9 |
| 1922 | 51,040 | 47.4 | E.G. Price | NL | 9,084 | 37.6 |
| | | | E. Thurtle | Lab | 8,834 | 36.5 |
| | | | Rt. Hon. C. Addison | L | 6,273 | 25.9 |
| | | | | | 250 | 1.1 |
| 1923 | 51,726 | 47.4 | E. Thurtle | Lab | 13,874 | 56.6 |
| | | | E.G. Price | L | 10,658 | 43.4 |
| | | | | | 3,216 | 13.2 |
| 1924 | 52,698 | 59.5 | E. Thurtle | Lab | 16,608 | 53.0 |
| | | | Sir H.J. Reckitt, Bt. | L | 14,748 | 47.0 |
| | | | | | 1,860 | 6.0 |
| 1929 | 62,025 | 64.3 | E. Thurtle | Lab | 20,552 | 51.5 |
| | | | Sir H.J. Reckitt, Bt. | L | 12,981 | 32.6 |
| | | | Viscount Knebworth | C | 6,334 | 15.9 |
| | | | | | 7,571 | 18.9 |
| 1931 | 61,874 | 55.9 | C.H. Summersby | NL | 19,596 | 56.7 |
| | | | E. Thurtle | Lab | 14,988 | 43.3 |
| | | | | | 4,608 | 13.4 |
| 1935 | 58,333 | 51.9 | E. Thurtle | Lab | 18,602 | 61.4 |
| | | | S.S. Brooke | NL | 11,673 | 38.6 |
| | | | | | 6,929 | 22.8 |
| 1945 | 27,223 | 57.6 | E. Thurtle | Lab | 11,592 | 74.0 |
| | | | F. Boult | NL | 4,081 | 26.0 |
| | | | | | 7,511 | 48.0 |

Note:—

1918:  Walton was the nominee of the National Amalgamated Coal Porters' Union.

# SOUTHWARK, CENTRAL [46]

| Election | Electors | T'out | Candidate | Party | Votes | % |
|---|---|---|---|---|---|---|
| 1918 | 27,699 | 40.4 | †J.D. Gilbert | Co L | 8,060 | 72.1 |
| | | | Dr. L. Haden-Guest | Lab | 3,126 | 27.9 |
| | | | | | 4,934 | 44.2 |
| 1922 | 30,427 | 52.7 | J.D. Gilbert | NL | 10,522 | 65.6 |
| | | | G.D. Bell | Lab | 5,522 | 34.4 |
| | | | | | 5,000 | 31.2 |
| 1923 | 31,757 | 60.4 | J.D. Gilbert | L | 8,676 | 45.3 |
| | | | H. Day | Lab | 6,690 | 34.9 |
| | | | C.L. Nordon | C | 3,801 | 19.8 |
| | | | | | 1,986 | 10.4 |
| 1924 | 32,601 | 70.4 | H. Day | Lab | 9,199 | 40.0 |
| | | | J.D. Gilbert | L | 7,817 | 34.1 |
| | | | C.L. Nordon | C | 5,937 | 25.9 |
| | | | | | 1,382 | 5.9 |
| 1929 | 39,571 | 64.3 | H. Day | Lab | 13,318 | 52.3 |
| | | | E.H. Keeling | C | 6,256 | 24.6 |
| | | | J.R. Want | L | 5,878 | 23.1 |
| | | | | | 7,062 | 27.7 |
| 1931 | 39,252 | 62.1 | I.M. Horobin | Nat | 15,913 | 65.3 |
| | | | H. Day | Lab | 8,466 | 34.7 |
| | | | | | 7,447 | 30.6 |
| 1935 | 36,426 | 57.2 | H. Day | Lab | 11,098 | 53.3 |
| | | | E. Stanford | N Lab | 9,735 | 46.7 |
| | | | | | 1,363 | 6.6 |
| [Death] | | | | | | |
| 1940 (10/2) | 33,265 | 24.7 | J.H. Martin | Lab | 5,285 | 64.3 |
| | | | C.W. Searson | Ind | 1,550 | 18.9 |
| | | | Mrs. V. Van Der Elst | Nat Ind | 1,382 | 16.8 |
| | | | | | 3,735 | 45.4 |
| 1945 | 20,765 | 62.6 | J.H. Martin | Lab | 9,336 | 71.9 |
| | | | W.A. Steward | C | 3,654 | 28.1 |
| | | | | | 5,682 | 43.8 |
| [Resignation] | | | | | | |
| 1948 (29/4) | 27,440 | 48.7 | R.H. Jenkins | Lab | 8,744 | 65.4 |
| | | | J.M. Greenwood | C | 4,623 | 34.6 |
| | | | | | 4,121 | 30.8 |

Notes:—

1940: Searson sought election as an 'Anti-War' candidate. He had resigned from the Labour Party to fight the election and received Communist Party support.

Mrs. Van Der Elst advocated a policy of abolition of capital punishment.

| Election | Electors | T'out | Candidate | Party | Votes | % |
|---|---|---|---|---|---|---|
| 1918 | 22,366 | 40.4 | †E.A. Strauss | Co L | 4,254 | 47.1 |
| | | | Sir J.L. Harrington | Ind C | 2,183 | 24.2 |
| | | | G.A. Isaacs | Lab | 2,027 | 22.4 |
| | | | J.J. Gebbett | NFDSS | 573* | 6.3 |
| | | | | | 2,071 | 22.9 |
| 1922 | 24,541 | 56.1 | E.A. Strauss | NL | 7,435 | 54.0 |
| | | | Dr. L. Haden-Guest | Lab | 6,323 | 46.0 |
| | | | | | 1,112 | 8.0 |
| 1923 | 25,055 | 59.7 | Dr. L. Haden-Guest | Lab | 7,665 | 51.2 |
| | | | E.A. Strauss | L | 7,303 | 48.8 |
| | | | | | 362 | 2.4 |
| 1924 | 25,897 | 71.5 | Dr. L. Haden-Guest | Lab | 8,115 | 43.8 |
| | | | E.A. Strauss | L | 7,085 | 38.3 |
| | | | J.J. Llewellin | C | 3,305 | 17.9 |
| | | | | | 1,030 | 5.5 |

[Seeks re-election on leaving the Labour Party]

| Election | Electors | T'out | Candidate | Party | Votes | % |
|---|---|---|---|---|---|---|
| 1927 (28/3) | 26,601 | 62.8 | E.A. Strauss | L | 7,334 | 43.9 |
| | | | G.A. Isaacs | Lab | 6,167 | 36.9 |
| | | | Dr. L. Haden-Guest | Const | 3,215 | 19.2 |
| | | | | | 1,167 | 7.0 |
| 1929 | 32,340 | 65.2 | G.A. Isaacs | Lab | 9,660 | 45.8 |
| | | | E.A. Strauss | L | 9,228 | 43.8 |
| | | | M.R.A. Samuel | C | 2,198* | 10.4 |
| | | | | | 432 | 2.0 |
| 1931 | 31,784 | 63.2 | E.A. Strauss | NL | 13,045 | 64.9 |
| | | | G.A. Isaacs | Lab | 7,053 | 35.1 |
| | | | | | 5,992 | 29.8 |
| 1935 | 28,695 | 56.1 | E.A. Strauss | NL | 8,086 | 50.2 |
| | | | G.A. Isaacs | Lab | 8,007 | 49.8 |
| | | | | | 79 | 0.4 |

[Death]

| Election | Electors | T'out | Candidate | Party | Votes | % |
|---|---|---|---|---|---|---|
| 1939 (17/5) | 26,091 | 38.9 | G.A. Isaacs | Lab | 5,815 | 57.4 |
| | | | A.H. Henderson-Livesèy | NL | 4,322 | 42.6 |
| | | | | | 1,493 | 14.8 |
| 1945 | 14,108 | 61.1 | G.A. Isaacs | Lab | 5,943 | 69.0 |
| | | | E. Terrell | NL | 2,673 | 31.0 |
| | | | | | 3,270 | 38.0 |

Note:—

1927: Dr. Haden-Guest resigned from the Labour Party as a protest against the party's opposition to the Government's policy in China. He received local Conservative Party support.

| Election | Electors | T'out | Candidate | Party | Votes | % |
|---|---|---|---|---|---|---|
| 1918 | 27,512 | 36.1 | †J.A. Dawes | Co L | 7,208 | 72.6 |
| | | | T.E. Naylor | Lab | 2,718 | 27.4 |
| | | | | | 4,490 | 45.2 |
| [Death] | | | | | | |
| 1921 | 29,884 | 38.5 | T.E. Naylor | Lab | 6,561 | 57.0 |
| (14/12) | | | T.O. Jacobsen | Co L | 2,636 | 22.9 |
| | | | H.L.P. Boot | Ind C | 2,307 | 20.1 |
| | | | | | 3,925 | 34.1 |
| 1922 | 30,472 | 58.2 | M. Alexander | NL | 10,014 | 56.4 |
| | | | T.E. Naylor | Lab | 7,734 | 43.6 |
| | | | | | 2,280 | 12.8 |
| 1923 | 30,970 | 55.7 | T.E. Naylor | Lab | 9,374 | 54.3 |
| | | | M. Alexander | L | 7,884 | 45.7 |
| | | | | | 1,490 | 8.6 |
| 1924 | 31,436 | 68.1 | T.E. Naylor | Lab | 11,635 | 54.3 |
| | | | G.W. Lloyd | C | 7,387 | 34.5 |
| | | | Mrs. E.C. Elias | L | 2,388* | 11.2 |
| | | | | | 4,248 | 19.8 |
| 1929 | 37,999 | 58.9 | T.E. Naylor | Lab | 13,527 | 60.4 |
| | | | W.J. Squire | L | 4,766 | 21.3 |
| | | | E.G.H. Powell | C | 4,086 | 18.3 |
| | | | | | 8,761 | 39.1 |
| 1931 | 38,363 | 54.1 | E.G.H. Powell | C | 11,063 | 53.3 |
| | | | T.E. Naylor | Lab | 9,678 | 46.7 |
| | | | | | 1,385 | 6.6 |
| 1935 | 35,452 | 53.3 | T.E. Naylor | Lab | 11,942 | 63.2 |
| | | | E.G.H. Powell | C | 6,945 | 36.8 |
| | | | | | 4,997 | 26.4 |
| 1945 | 20,596 | 60.6 | T.E Naylor | Lab | 9,599 | 76.9 |
| | | | J.M Greenwood | C | 2,881 | 23.1 |
| | | | | | 6,718 | 53.8 |

| Election | Electors | T'out | Candidate | Party | Votes | % |
|---|---|---|---|---|---|---|
| 1918 | 29,275 | 33.4 | †Sir W. Pearce | Co L | 5,860 | 59.9 |
|  |  |  | †D.D. Sheehan | Lab | 2,470 | 25.2 |
|  |  |  | C.H. Rodwell | Nat P | 1,455 | 14.9 |
|  |  |  |  |  | 3,390 | 34.7 |
| 1922 | 30,261 | 57.8 | C.R. Attlee | Lab | 9,688 | 55.4 |
|  |  |  | Sir W. Pearce | NL | 7,789 | 44.6 |
|  |  |  |  |  | 1,899 | 10.8 |
| 1923 | 30,452 | 55.0 | C.R. Attlee | Lab | 11,473 | 68.5 |
|  |  |  | T. Miller-Jones | C | 5,288 | 31.5 |
|  |  |  |  |  | 6,185 | 37.0 |
| 1924 | 30,927 | 65.6 | C.R. Attlee | Lab | 11,713 | 57.7 |
|  |  |  | T. Miller-Jones | C | 5,692 | 28.1 |
|  |  |  | H. Marks | L | 2,869 | 14.2 |
|  |  |  |  |  | 6,021 | 29.6 |
| 1929 | 38,440 | 64.6 | C.R. Attlee | Lab | 13,872 | 55.9 |
|  |  |  | Hon. E.F. Morgan | C | 6,584 | 26.5 |
|  |  |  | J.J.J. Addis | L | 4,116 | 16.6 |
|  |  |  | W.T.L. Tapsell | Com | 245* | 1.0 |
|  |  |  |  |  | 7,288 | 29.4 |
| 1931 | 38,682 | 58.1 | C.R. Attlee | Lab | 11,354 | 50.5 |
|  |  |  | R. Girouard | C | 10,803 | 48.1 |
|  |  |  | H.L. Hodge | NP | 307* | 1.4 |
|  |  |  |  |  | 551 | 2.4 |
| 1935 | 37,020 | 59.3 | Rt. Hon. C.R. Attlee | Lab | 14,600 | 66.5 |
|  |  |  | C.J. Busby | C | 7,355 | 33.5 |
|  |  |  |  |  | 7,245 | 33.0 |
| 1945 | 16,367 | 61.2 | Rt. Hon. C.R. Attlee | Lab | 8,398 | 83.8 |
|  |  |  | A.N.P. Woodard | C | 1,618 | 16.2 |
|  |  |  |  |  | 6,780 | 67.6 |

# STEPNEY, MILE END [50]

| Election | Electors | T'out | Candidate | Party | Votes | % |
|---|---|---|---|---|---|---|
| 1918 | 22,131 | 43.1 | W.R. Preston | Co C | 6,025 | 63.2 |
| | | | W. Devenay | Lab | 2,392 | 25.1 |
| | | | C.J.O. Sanders | L | 1,119* | 11.7 |
| | | | | | 3,633 | 38.1 |
| 1922 | 22,885 | 64.2 | Sir W.R. Preston | C | 6,014 | 41.0 |
| | | | J. Scurr | Lab | 5,219 | 35.5 |
| | | | R.B. Solomon | L | 3,457 | 23.5 |
| | | | | | 795 | 5.5 |
| 1923 | 23,787 | 63.8 | J. Scurr | Lab | 6,219 | 41.0 |
| | | | Sir W.R. Preston | C | 4,741 | 31.2 |
| | | | R.B. Solomon | L | 4,215 | 27.8 |
| | | | | | 1,478 | 9.8 |
| 1924 | 24,245 | 70.7 | J. Scurr | Lab | 8,306 | 48.5 |
| | | | J.B. Dodge | C | 4,960 | 28.9 |
| | | | R.B. Solomon | L | 3,872 | 22.6 |
| | | | | | 3,346 | 19.6 |
| 1929 | 34,662 | 70.4 | J. Scurr | Lab | 11,489 | 47.1 |
| | | | J.B. Dodge | C | 7,401 | 30.3 |
| | | | S. Teff | L | 5,525 | 22.6 |
| | | | | | 4,088 | 16.8 |
| 1931 | 36,896 | 60.0 | Dr. W.J. O'Donovan | C | 12,399 | 56.0 |
| | | | J. Scurr | Lab | 9,738 | 44.0 |
| | | | | | 2,661 | 12.0 |
| 1935 | 36,294 | 63.5 | D. Frankel | Lab | 13,177 | 57.2 |
| | | | Dr. W.J. O'Donovan | C | 9,859 | 42.8 |
| | | | | | 3,318 | 14.4 |
| 1945 | 16,177 | 65.9 | P. Piratin | Com | 5,075 | 47.6 |
| | | | D. Frankel | Lab | 3,861 | 36.2 |
| | | | V. Motion | C | 1,722 | 16.2 |
| | | | | | 1,214 | 11.4 |

# STEPNEY, WHITECHAPEL and ST. GEORGE'S [51]

| Election | Electors | T'out | Candidate | Party | Votes | % |
|---|---|---|---|---|---|---|
| 1918 | 23,366 | 37.0 | †J.D. Kiley | L | 3,025 | 34.9 |
| | | | Dr. R. Ambrose | Lab | 2,522 | 29.2 |
| | | | G.A. Cohen | Co C | 2,489 | 28.8 |
| | | | J.R. Raphael | Ind | 614* | 7.1 |
| | | | | | 503 | 5.7 |
| 1922 | 24,333 | 64.1 | C.J. Mathew | Lab | 6,267 | 40.2 |
| | | | J.D. Kiley | L | 5,839 | 37.4 |
| | | | A. Instone | C | 3,502 | 22.4 |
| | | | | | 428 | 2.8 |
| [Death] | | | | | | |
| 1923 (8/2) | 24,333 | 60.5 | H. Gosling | Lab | 8,398 | 57.0 |
| | | | J.D. Kiley | L | 6,198 | 42.1 |
| | | | S.M. Holden | NPP | 130* | 0.9 |
| | | | | | 2,200 | 14.9 |
| 1923 | 24,800 | 58.3 | H. Gosling | Lab | 7,812 | 54.0 |
| | | | J.D. Kiley | L | 6,656 | 46.0 |
| | | | | | 1,156 | 8.0 |
| 1924 | 25,496 | 68.0 | H. Gosling | Lab | 10,147 | 58.5 |
| | | | H.L. Nathan | L | 7,193 | 41.5 |
| | | | | | 2,954 | 17.0 |
| 1929 | 35,996 | 60.3 | H. Gosling | Lab | 13,701 | 63.2 |
| | | | F.H. Sedgwick | L | 4,521 | 20.8 |
| | | | T.L.E.B. Guinness | C | 3,478 | 16.0 |
| | | | | | 9,180 | 42.4 |
| [Death] | | | | | | |
| 1930 (3/12) | 37,013 | 59.0 | J.H. Hall | Lab | 8,544 | 39.2 |
| | | | B. Janner | L | 7,445 | 34.1 |
| | | | T.L.E.B. Guinness | C | 3,735 | 17.1 |
| | | | H. Pollitt | Com | 2,106* | 9.6 |
| | | | | | 1,099 | 5.1 |
| 1931 | 38,214 | 62.0 | B. Janner | L | 11,013 | 46.5 |
| | | | J.H. Hall | Lab | 9,864 | 41.6 |
| | | | H. Pollitt | Com | 2,658* | 11.2 |
| | | | E. Lewis | NP | 154* | 0.7 |
| | | | | | 1,149 | 4.9 |
| 1935 | 38,626 | 63.3 | J.H. Hall | Lab | 13,374 | 54.7 |
| | | | B. Janner | L | 11,093 | 45.3 |
| | | | | | 2,281 | 9.4 |
| [Death] | | | | | | |
| 1942 (8/8) | | | W.J. Edwards | Lab | Unopp. | |
| 1945 | 18,887 | 66.4 | W.J. Edwards | Lab | 10,460 | 83.4 |
| | | | E.J.B. Nelson | C | 1,113* | 8.9 |
| | | | M.K. Staub | L | 965* | 7.7 |
| | | | | | 9,347 | 74.5 |

Note:—

1918:  Raphael was the nominee of the Whitechapel Street-Sellers' and Costers' Union.

| Election | Electors | T'out | Candidate | Party | Votes | % |
|---|---|---|---|---|---|---|
| 1918 | 20,090 | 54.4 | G.W.H. Jones | Co C | 5,918 | 54.1 |
| | | | H.J. Ormond | Ind | 2,829 | 25.9 |
| | | | P.H. Heffer | L | 2,181 | 20.0 |
| | | | | | 3,089 | 28.2 |
| 1922 | 23,821 | 65.0 | G.W.H. Jones | C | 9,753 | 63.0 |
| | | | P.H. Heffer | L | 5,737 | 37.0 |
| | | | | | 4,016 | 26.0 |
| 1923 | 24,605 | 63.5 | Dr. G.E. Spero | L | 8,365 | 53.5 |
| | | | G.W.H. Jones | C | 7,264 | 46.5 |
| | | | | | 1,101 | 7.0 |
| 1924 | 24,838 | 76.0 | G.W.H. Jones | C | 10,688 | 56.7 |
| | | | Dr. G.E. Spero | L | 4,758 | 25.2 |
| | | | L. Silkin | Lab | 3,420 | 18.1 |
| | | | | | 5,930 | 31.5 |
| 1929 | 33,855 | 70.0 | Sir G.W.H. Jones | C | 9,030 | 38.0 |
| | | | Rev. F.W. Norwood | L | 7,958 | 33.6 |
| | | | F.L. Kerran | Lab | 6,723 | 28.4 |
| | | | | | 1,072 | 4.4 |
| 1931 | 34,591 | 63.2 | Sir G.W.H. Jones | C | 16,035 | 73.3 |
| | | | F.L. Kerran | Lab | 5,837 | 26.7 |
| | | | | | 10,198 | 46.6 |
| 1935 | 34,208 | 61.5 | Sir G.W.H. Jones | C | 11,213 | 53.4 |
| | | | D. Weitzman | Lab | 7,448 | 35.4 |
| | | | J.H. Whitehouse | L | 2,364* | 11.2 |
| | | | | | 3,765 | 18.0 |
| 1945 | 26,987 | 67.3 | D. Weitzman | Lab | 9,356 | 51.5 |
| | | | Sir G.W.H. Jones | C | 5,155 | 28.4 |
| | | | H.H.C. Blake | L | 3,651 | 20.1 |
| | | | | | 4,201 | 23.1 |

## WANDSWORTH, BALHAM and TOOTING [53]

| Election | Electors | T'out | Candidate | Party | Votes | % |
|---|---|---|---|---|---|---|
| 1918 | 40,212 | 51.7 | †J.C.D. Denison-Pender | Co C | 12,405 | 59.7 |
| | | | F. Smith | Lab | 3,586 | 17.2 |
| | | | A.J. Hurley | Ind Dem | 1,805* | 8.7 |
| | | | M.H. Anderson | L | 1,542* | 7.4 |
| | | | W. Hunt | Ind C | 1,457* | 7.0 |
| | | | | | 8,819 | 42.5 |
| 1922 | 41,370 | 61.1 | Sir A. Butt | C | 17,239 | 68.2 |
| | | | J.W. Molden | L | 8,044 | 31.8 |
| | | | | | 9,195 | 36.4 |
| 1923 | 42,092 | 61.1 | Sir A. Butt | C | 12,695 | 49.4 |
| | | | G. Little | L | 7,477 | 29.1 |
| | | | E. Archbold | Lab | 5,536 | 21.5 |
| | | | | | 5,218 | 20.3 |
| 1924 | 42,765 | 70.3 | Sir A. Butt | C | 20,378 | 67.8 |
| | | | E. Archbold | Lab | 9,672 | 32.2 |
| | | | | | 10,706 | 35.6 |
| 1929 | 56,968 | 70.6 | Sir A. Butt, Bt. | C | 18,181 | 45.2 |
| | | | Dr. C.W. Brook | Lab | 13,499 | 33.6 |
| | | | Dr. W.H. Summerskill | L | 8,533 | 21.2 |
| | | | | | 4,682 | 11.6 |
| 1931 | 57,199 | 67.1 | Sir A. Butt, Bt. | C | 28,592 | 74.5 |
| | | | P.F. Pollard | Lab | 9,780 | 25.5 |
| | | | | | 18,812 | 49.0 |
| 1935 | 56,556 | 61.8 | Sir A. Butt, Bt. | C | 22,013 | 62.9 |
| | | | W.D. Lloyd | Lab | 12,960 | 37.1 |
| | | | | | 9,053 | 25.8 |
| [Resignation] | | | | | | |
| 1936 (23/7) | 56,556 | 49.2 | G.F. Doland | C | 14,959 | 53.7 |
| | | | W.J. Miller | Lab | 12,889 | 46.3 |
| | | | | | 2,070 | 7.4 |
| 1945 | 48,445 | 70.9 | H.R. Adams | Lab | 19,782 | 57.6 |
| | | | W.S. Edgson | C | 14,552 | 42.4 |
| | | | | | 5,230 | 15.2 |

| Election | Electors | T'out | Candidate | Party | Votes | % |
|---|---|---|---|---|---|---|
| 1918 | 27,825 | 50.8 | †Sir J. Norton-Griffiths | C | 7,771 | 55.0 |
| | | | G.P. Blizard | Lab | 3,382 | 23.9 |
| | | | †Hon. C.H.C. Guest | Co L | 2,988 | 21.1 |
| | | | | | 4,389 | 31.1 |
| 1922 | 29,154 | 61.4 | Sir J. Norton-Griffiths, Bt. | C | 12,470 | 69.7 |
| | | | L. Silkin | Lab | 5,420 | 30.3 |
| | | | | | 7,050 | 39.4 |
| 1923 | 29,733 | 62.0 | Sir J. Norton-Griffiths, Bt. | C | 8,774 | 47.7 |
| | | | G.P. Blizard | Lab | 5,294 | 28.7 |
| | | | E.M.C. Denny | L | 4,357 | 23.6 |
| | | | | | 3,480 | 19.0 |
| 1924 | 30,342 | 70.8 | Sir H. Jackson | C | 13,234 | 61.6 |
| | | | C. Latham | Lab | 8,235 | 38.4 |
| | | | | | 4,999 | 23.2 |
| 1929 | 39,258 | 69.5 | A.G. Church | Lab (N Lab) | 11,404 | 41.8 |
| | | | Sir H. Jackson | C | 11,104 | 40.7 |
| | | | A.W. Duthie | L | 4,784 | 17.5 |
| | | | | | 300 | 1.1 |
| 1931 | 39,463 | 68.7 | Sir H. Jackson | C | 19,159 | 70.7 |
| | | | J.L. Cohen | Lab | 7,512 | 27.7 |
| | | | A.M. Diston | NP | 424* | 1.6 |
| | | | | | 11,647 | 43.0 |
| 1935 | 38,664 | 65.0 | Sir H. Jackson, Bt. | C | 14,728 | 58.6 |
| | | | F.W. Davies | Lab | 10,405 | 41.4 |
| | | | | | 4,323 | 17.2 |
| [Death] | | | | | | |
| 1937 (29/4) | 38,478 | 63.2 | H.L. Nathan | Lab | 12,406 | 51.0 |
| | | | R. Jennings | C | 11,921 | 49.0 |
| | | | | | 485 | 2.0 |
| [Elevation to the Peerage — Lord Nathan] | | | | | | |
| 1940 (22/6) | | | Rt. Hon. E. Bevin | Lab | Unopp. | |
| 1945 | 31,349 | 73.6 | Rt. Hon. E. Bevin | Lab | 14,126 | 61.2 |
| | | | J.G. Smyth | C | 8,952 | 38.8 |
| | | | | | 5,174 | 22.4 |

Note:—

    1940:  Bevin was Minister of Labour and National Service.

# WANDSWORTH, CLAPHAM [55]

| Election | Electors | T'out | Candidate | Party | Votes | % |
|----------|----------|-------|-----------|-------|-------|---|
| 1918 | 34,640 | 46.9 | †Sir A.P. Du Cros, Bt. | Co C | 9,776 | 60.2 |
|  |  |  | H.H. Beamish | Ind | 3,070 | 18.9 |
|  |  |  | P.H. Thomas | L | 2,790 | 17.2 |
|  |  |  | W.J. Harvey | Ind | 594* | 3.7 |
|  |  |  |  |  | 6,706 | 41.3 |
| [Resignation] |  |  |  |  |  |  |
| 1922 (9/5) |  |  | Sir J. Leigh, Bt. | C | Unopp. |  |
| 1922 | 35,962 | 63.0 | Sir J. Leigh, Bt. | C | 13,285 | 58.7 |
|  |  |  | L. Spero | Lab | 4,919 | 21.7 |
|  |  |  | E.A. Villiers | L | 4,444 | 19.6 |
|  |  |  |  |  | 8,366 | 37.0 |
| 1923 | 36,498 | 60.7 | Sir J. Leigh, Bt. | C | 10,287 | 46.4 |
|  |  |  | L. Spero | Lab | 6,404 | 28.9 |
|  |  |  | T.G. Graham | L | 5,479 | 24.7 |
|  |  |  |  |  | 3,883 | 17.5 |
| 1924 | 36,872 | 69.5 | Sir J. Leigh, Bt. | C | 16,404 | 64.1 |
|  |  |  | C. Diamond | Lab | 9,204 | 35.9 |
|  |  |  |  |  | 7,200 | 28.2 |
| 1929 | 48,061 | 67.3 | Sir J. Leigh, Bt. | C | 13,507 | 41.7 |
|  |  |  | J.A. Skinner | Lab | 9,871 | 30.5 |
|  |  |  | O.P. Davies | L | 8,991 | 27.8 |
|  |  |  |  |  | 3,636 | 11.2 |
| 1931 | 48,136 | 66.1 | Sir J. Leigh, Bt. | C | 21,648 | 68.0 |
|  |  |  | Miss H.A. Browning | ILP | 7,317 | 23.0 |
|  |  |  | J.H. Clarke | L | 2,869* | 9.0 |
|  |  |  |  |  | 14,331 | 45.0 |
| 1935 | 47,612 | 60.5 | Sir J. Leigh, Bt. | C | 17,458 | 60.6 |
|  |  |  | Miss M.M. Whately | Lab | 11,368 | 39.4 |
|  |  |  |  |  | 6,090 | 21.2 |
| 1945 | 39,657 | 70.8 | J.R. Battley | Lab | 15,205 | 54.1 |
|  |  |  | R.L. Lowndes | C | 10,014 | 35.7 |
|  |  |  | C.E. Paterson | L | 2,850* | 10.2 |
|  |  |  |  |  | 5,191 | 18.4 |

Note:—

1918: Beamish was supported by and possibly the nominee of the local branch of the NFDSS.

# WANDSWORTH, PUTNEY [56]

| Election | Electors | T'out | Candidate | Party | Votes | % |
|---|---|---|---|---|---|---|
| 1918 | 31,437 | 43.4 | †S. Samuel | Co C | 8,677 | 63.6 |
| | | | Hon. J.G. Jenkins | Nat P | 4,968 | 36.4 |
| | | | | | 3,709 | 27.2 |
| 1922 | 33,346 | 61.8 | S. Samuel | C | 9,739 | 47.2 |
| | | | C. Prescott-Decie | Ind C | 5,556 | 27.0 |
| | | | H. Higgs | L | 5,317 | 25.8 |
| | | | | | 4,183 | 20.2 |
| 1923 | | | S. Samuel | C | Unopp. | |
| 1924 | 35,030 | 68.4 | S. Samuel | C | 17,341 | 72.4 |
| | | | J.M. Allen | Lab | 6,609 | 27.6 |
| | | | | | 10,732 | 44.8 |
| 1929 | 49,594 | 62.1 | S. Samuel | C | 19,657 | 63.8 |
| | | | J.C. Lawder | Lab | 11,136 | 36.2 |
| | | | | | 8,521 | 27.6 |
| 1931 | 50,538 | 66.3 | S. Samuel | C | 27,318 | 81.6 |
| | | | J.C. Lawder | Lab | 6,172 | 18.4 |
| | | | | | 21,146 | 63.2 |
| [Death] | | | | | | |
| 1934 (28/11) | 49,642 | 57.5 | M.R.A. Samuel | C | 15,599 | 54.7 |
| | | | Dr. Edith Summerskill | Lab | 12,936 | 45.3 |
| | | | | | 2,663 | 9.4 |
| 1935 | 49,901 | 68.5 | M.R.A. Samuel | C | 22,288 | 65.1 |
| | | | A.A. Watson | Lab | 10,895 | 31.9 |
| | | | Mrs. V. Van Der Elst | Ind | 1,021* | 3.0 |
| | | | | | 11,393 | 33.2 |
| [Death] | | | | | | |
| 1942 (8/5) | 51,066 | 23.0 | H.N. Linstead | C | 8,788 | 74.9 |
| | | | B. Acworth | Ind | 2,939 | 25.1 |
| | | | | | 5,849 | 49.8 |
| 1945 | 45,796 | 73.6 | H.N. Linstead | C | 16,356 | 48.5 |
| | | | P.D. Stewart | Lab | 12,469 | 37.0 |
| | | | Sir R.T.D. Acland, Bt. | CW | 2,686* | 8.0 |
| | | | I.J. Hyam | L | 2,041* | 6.1 |
| | | | Mrs. E.E.F. Tennant | Ind C | 144* | 0.4 |
| | | | | | 3,887 | 11.5 |

Notes:—

1922: Higgs was supported by the Anti-Waste League.

1935: Mrs. Van Der Elst advocated a policy of abolition of capital punishment.

# WANDSWORTH, STREATHAM [57]

| Election | Electors | T'out | Candidate | Party | Votes | % |
|---|---|---|---|---|---|---|
| 1918 | 26,842 | 58.6 | W.L. Mitchell | Co C | 11,457 | 72.9 |
| | | | J.A. Compston | L | 2,417 | 15.4 |
| | | | F.H. Bellamy | Nat P | 1,844* | 11.7 |
| | | | | | 9,040 | 57.5 |
| 1922 | 28,186 | 63.0 | Sir W.L. Mitchell | C | 12,282 | 69.1 |
| | | | O.A. Minns | L | 5,483 | 30.9 |
| | | | | | 6,799 | 38.2 |
| 1923 | 28,837 | 61.3 | Sir W.L. Mitchell | C | 10,598 | 60.0 |
| | | | C.G. Parsloe | L | 7,075 | 40.0 |
| | | | | | 3,523 | 20.0 |
| 1924 | 29,906 | 77.7 | Sir W.L. Mitchell | C | 15,936 | 68.5 |
| | | | C.G. Parsloe | L | 4,111 | 17.7 |
| | | | A.M. Wall | Com | 3,204 | 13.8 |
| | | | | | 11,825 | 50.8 |
| 1929 | 48,387 | 68.9 | Sir W.L. Mitchell | C | 19,024 | 57.0 |
| | | | P.L.E. Rawlins | L | 8,191 | 24.6 |
| | | | F. Hughes | Lab | 6,134 | 18.4 |
| | | | | | 10,833 | 32.4 |
| 1931 | 50,070 | 71.3 | Sir W.L. Mitchell | C | 30,358 | 85.0 |
| | | | Mrs. B. Fraser | Lab | 5,343 | 15.0 |
| | | | | | 25,015 | 70.0 |
| 1935 | 52,067 | 64.1 | Sir W.L. Mitchell | C | 25,429 | 76.2 |
| | | | A.M. Skeffington | Lab | 7,951 | 23.8 |
| | | | | | 17,478 | 52.4 |
| [Resignation] | | | | | | |
| 1939 (7/12) | | | D. Robertson | C | Unopp. | |
| 1945 | 45,970 | 72.7 | D. Robertson | C | 17,462 | 52.2 |
| | | | J. Gross | Lab | 11,296 | 33.8 |
| | | | C.W.E. Remnant | L | 4,677 | 14.0 |
| | | | | | 6,166 | 18.4 |

# WESTMINSTER, ABBEY [58]

| Election | Electors | T'out | Candidate | Party | Votes | % |
|---|---|---|---|---|---|---|
| 1918 | | | †W.L.A.B. Burdett-Coutts | Co C | Unopp. | |
| [Death] | | | | | | |
| 1921 | 36,952 | 38.5 | J.S. Nicholson | C | 6,204 | 43.6 |
| (25/8) | | | R.V.K. Applin | AWL | 4,970 | 34.9 |
| | | | A. Lupton | L | 3,053 | 21.5 |
| | | | | | 1,234 | 8.7 |
| 1922 | 36,763 | 49.0 | J.S. Nicholson | C | 13,620 | 75.6 |
| | | | J.G. Butler | Lab | 2,454 | 13.6 |
| | | | S.R. Drury-Lowe | Ind | 1,950* | 10.8 |
| | | | | | 11,166 | 62.0 |
| 1923 | | | J.S. Nicholson | C | Unopp. | |
| [Death] | | | | | | |
| 1924 | 36,999 | 61.6 | O.W. Nicholson | C | 8,187 | 35.9 |
| (19/3) | | | Rt. Hon. W.L.S. Churchill | Const | 8,144 | 35.8 |
| | | | A.F. Brockway | Lab | 6,156 | 27.0 |
| | | | J.S. Duckers | L | 291* | 1.3 |
| | | | | | 43 | 0.1 |
| 1924 | 38,069 | 58.4 | O.W. Nicholson | C | 17,915 | 80.6 |
| | | | A.H. Woolf | Lab | 4,308 | 19.4 |
| | | | | | 13,607 | 61.2 |
| 1929 | 48,524 | 50.7 | O.W. Nicholson | C | 18,195 | 74.0 |
| | | | J.H. MacDonnell | Lab | 6,406 | 26.0 |
| | | | | | 11,789 | 48.0 |
| 1931 | | | O.W. Nicholson | C | Unopp. | |
| [Resignation] | | | | | | |
| 1932 | | | S. Herbert | C | Unopp. | |
| (12/7) | | | | | | |
| 1935 | 47,538 | 49.2 | S. Herbert | C | 18,117 | 77.5 |
| | | | W.S. Kennedy | Lab | 5,255 | 22.5 |
| | | | | | 12,862 | 55.0 |
| [Death] | | | | | | |
| 1939 | 47,396 | 30.3 | Sir H. Webbe | C | 9,678 | 67.4 |
| (17/5) | | | G. Carritt | Ind Prog | 4,674 | 32.6 |
| | | | | | 5,004 | 34.8 |
| 1945 | 28,823 | 58.5 | Sir H. Webbe | C | 9,160 | 54.4 |
| | | | J.N. Hutchinson | Lab | 4,408 | 26.1 |
| | | | G. Carritt | Com | 2,964 | 17.6 |
| | | | N. Leith-Hay-Clark | Dem P | 326* | 1.9 |
| | | | | | 4,752 | 28.3 |

Notes:—

1921: Nicholson was supported by Horatio Bottomley's Independent Parliamentary Group.

1939: Carritt was supported by the local Labour and Liberal parties and advocated a 'Popular Front' policy.

| Election | Electors | T'out | Candidate | Party | Votes | % |
|---|---|---|---|---|---|---|
| 1918 | 29,080 | 39.9 | †Rt. Hon. W.H. Long | Co C | 10,453 | 90.2 |
| | | | H.T.M. Bell | L | 1,140* | 9.8 |
| | | | | | 9,313 | 80.4 |
| [Elevation to the Peerage — Viscount Long] | | | | | | |
| 1921 | 31,690 | 39.8 | J.M.M. Erskine | AWL | 7,244 | 57.5 |
| (7/6) | | | Sir H.M. Jessel, Bt. | Co C | 5,356 | 42.5 |
| | | | | | 1,888 | 15.0 |
| 1922 | 32,316 | 62.2 | J.M.M. Erskine | Ind C (C) | 11,252 | 55.9 |
| | | | Rt. Hon. L.O. Wilson | C | 7,559 | 37.6 |
| | | | Miss M.S. Ailen | L | 1,303* | 6.5 |
| | | | | | 3,693 | 18.3 |
| 1923 | | | J.M.M. Erskine | C | Unopp. | |
| 1924 | | | J.M.M. Erskine | C | Unopp. | |
| 1929 | 53,914 | 53.3 | Rt. Hon. Sir L. Worthington-Evans, Bt. | C | 22,448 | 78.1 |
| | | | J.G. Butler | Lab | 6,294 | 21.9 |
| | | | | | 16,154 | 56.2 |
| [Death] | | | | | | |
| 1931 | 54,156 | 53.1 | A.D. Cooper | C | 17,242 | 59.9 |
| (19/3) | | | Sir E.W. Petter | Ind C | 11,532 | 40.1 |
| | | | | | 5,710 | 19.8 |
| 1931 | | | A.D. Cooper | C | Unopp. | |
| 1935 | 54,442 | 55.2 | Rt. Hon. A.D. Cooper | C | 25,424 | 84.6 |
| | | | Hon. Mrs. A. Fremantle | Lab | 4,643 | 15.4 |
| | | | | | 20,781 | 69.2 |
| 1945 | 34,010 | 57.2 | Hon. A. Howard | C | 13,086 | 67.2 |
| | | | W.B.D. Brown | CW | 5,314 | 27.3 |
| | | | Miss D. Crisp | Ind | 1,069* | 5.5 |
| | | | | | 7,772 | 39.9 |

Notes:—

1922:  Erskine was the nominee of the St. George's, Hanover Square, Independent Conservative Association which was formed shortly after his election in 1921. He was also supported by the Anti-Waste League.

1931:  Petter was supported by Lord Beaverbrook and the 'Daily Express'.
(19/3)

| Election | Electors | T'out | Candidate | Party | Votes | % |
|---|---|---|---|---|---|---|
| 1918 | | | †Rt. Hon. W. Crooks | Lab | Unopp. | |
| [Resignation] | | | | | | |
| 1921 (2/3) | 34,099† | 78.5 | R. Gee | Co C | 13,724 | 51.3 |
| | | | J.R. MacDonald | Lab | 13,041 | 48.7 |
| | | | | | 683 | 2.6 |
| 1922 | 33,993 | 80.4 | H. Snell | Lab | 15,620 | 57.1 |
| | | | R. Gee | C | 11,714 | 42.9 |
| | | | | | 3,906 | 14.2 |
| 1923 | 34,429 | 74.4 | H. Snell | Lab | 15,766 | 61.6 |
| | | | E.A. Taylor | C | 9,839 | 38.4 |
| | | | | | 5,927 | 23.2 |
| 1924 | 34,935 | 81.6 | H. Snell | Lab | 16,660 | 58.4 |
| | | | D.A. Gooch | C | 11,862 | 41.6 |
| | | | | | 4,798 | 16.8 |
| 1929 | 42,808 | 75.6 | H. Snell | Lab | 20,447 | 63.2 |
| | | | E.S. Shrapnell-Smith | C | 11,906 | 36.8 |
| | | | | | 8,541 | 26.4 |
| [Elevation to the Peerage - Lord Snell] | | | | | | |
| 1931 (15/4) | 42,886 | 66.6 | E.G. Hicks | Lab | 16,200 | 56.7 |
| | | | E.S. Shrapnell-Smith | C | 12,357 | 43.3 |
| | | | | | 3,843 | 13.4 |
| 1931 | 42,857 | 76.3 | E.G. Hicks | Lab | 16,658 | 50.9 |
| | | | J.F. Finn | C | 16,050 | 49.1 |
| | | | | | 608 | 1.8 |
| 1935 | 42,450 | 71.3 | E.G. Hicks | Lab | 17,563 | 58.0 |
| | | | J.F. Finn | C | 12,721 | 42.0 |
| | | | | | 4,842 | 16.0 |
| 1945 | 36,851 | 72.7 | E.G. Hicks | Lab | 18,983 | 70.9 |
| | | | Dr. R.F.B. Bennett | C | 7,237 | 27.0 |
| | | | H.H. Wright | Ind | 571* | 2.1 |
| | | | | | 11,746 | 43.9 |

# WOOLWICH, WEST  [61]

| Election | Electors | T'out | Candidate | Party | Votes | % |
|---|---|---|---|---|---|---|
| 1918 | 34,248 | 60.0 | Sir H.K. Wood | Co C | 12,348 | 60.1 |
|  |  |  | A.G. Cameron | Lab | 7,088 | 34.5 |
|  |  |  | W.A. Adam | Ind C | 1,109* | 5.4 |
|  |  |  |  |  | 5,260 | 25.6 |
| 1922 | 34,242 | 70.1 | Sir H.K. Wood | C | 14,453 | 60.2 |
|  |  |  | J.T. Sheppard | Lab | 9,550 | 39.8 |
|  |  |  |  |  | 4,903 | 20.4 |
| 1923 | 35,032 | 67.8 | Sir H.K. Wood | C | 12,380 | 52.2 |
|  |  |  | W. Barefoot | Lab | 11,357 | 47.8 |
|  |  |  |  |  | 1,023 | 4.4 |
| 1924 | 36,153 | 79.7 | Sir H.K. Wood | C | 16,504 | 57.3 |
|  |  |  | W. Barefoot | Lab | 12,304 | 42.7 |
|  |  |  |  |  | 4,200 | 14.6 |
| 1929 | 50,014 | 76.8 | Rt. Hon. Sir H.K. Wood | C | 17,296 | 45.0 |
|  |  |  | W. Barefoot | Lab | 16,964 | 44.2 |
|  |  |  | A.S. Phillips | L | 4,140* | 10.8 |
|  |  |  |  |  | 332 | 0.8 |
| 1931 | 52,917 | 77.4 | Rt. Hon. Sir H.K. Wood | C | 26,441 | 64.6 |
|  |  |  | J. Reeves | Lab/Co-op | 14,520 | 35.4 |
|  |  |  |  |  | 11,921 | 29.2 |
| 1935 | 55,452 | 75.8 | Rt. Hon. Sir H.K. Wood | C | 24,649 | 58.7 |
|  |  |  | A.G. Wansbrough | Lab | 17,373 | 41.3 |
|  |  |  |  |  | 7,276 | 17.4 |
| [Death] |  |  |  |  |  |  |
| 1943 (10/11) | 60,400 | 20.8 | F.W. Beech | C | 8,204 | 65.2 |
|  |  |  | W.T. Colyer | ILP | 3,419 | 27.2 |
|  |  |  | L.J. Ellis | Ind | 958* | 7.6 |
|  |  |  |  |  | 4,785 | 38.0 |
| 1945 | 53,288 | 72.1 | H. Berry | Lab | 23,655 | 61.6 |
|  |  |  | F.W. Beech | C | 14,771 | 38.4 |
|  |  |  |  |  | 8,884 | 23.2 |

Note:—

1943: Ellis was the founder of an organisation called the British Citizens' League.

# ENGLAND —— PROVINCIAL BOROUGHS

# ACCRINGTON [62]

| Election | Electors | T'out | Candidate | Party | Votes | % |
|---|---|---|---|---|---|---|
| 1918 | 42,160 | 69.5 | E. Gray | Co C | 13,808 | 47.2 |
| | | | †Rt. Hon. H.T. Baker | L | 8,378 | 28.6 |
| | | | C.R. Buxton | Lab | 6,369 | 21.7 |
| | | | W. Hammond | NDP | 738* | 2.5 |
| | | | | | 5,430 | 18.6 |
| 1922 | 41,960 | 88.7 | C.R. Buxton | Lab | 16,462 | 44.3 |
| | | | E. Gray | C | 11,408 | 30.6 |
| | | | Rt. Hon. H.T. Baker | L | 9,359 | 25.1 |
| | | | | | 5,054 | 13.7 |
| 1923 | 42,507 | 86.5 | J.H. Edwards | L | 19,981 | 54.3 |
| | | | C.R. Buxton | Lab | 16,793 | 45.7 |
| | | | | | 3,188 | 8.6 |
| 1924 | 42,786 | 90.1 | J.H. Edwards | Const (L) | 20,391 | 52.9 |
| | | | C.R. Buxton | Lab | 18,148 | 47.1 |
| | | | | | 2,243 | 5.8 |
| 1929 | 54,591 | 88.7 | T. Snowden | Lab | 25,336 | 52.3 |
| | | | J.H. Edwards | L | 23,110 | 47.7 |
| | | | | | 2,226 | 4.6 |
| 1931 | 54,688 | 89.6 | H.A. Procter | C | 30,799 | 62.9 |
| | | | T. Snowden | Lab | 18,177 | 37.1 |
| | | | | | 12,622 | 25.8 |
| 1935 | 53,358 | 87.1 | H.A. Procter | C | 25,273 | 54.4 |
| | | | F.G. Burgess | Lab | 21,203 | 45.6 |
| | | | | | 4,070 | 8.8 |
| 1945 | 52,175 | 83.1 | W.T. Scott-Elliot | Lab | 21,102 | 48.7 |
| | | | H.A. Procter | C | 16,025 | 36.9 |
| | | | G.V. Mortimer | L | 6,247 | 14.4 |
| | | | | | 5,077 | 11.8 |

## ALTRINCHAM and SALE  [63]

| Election | Electors | T'out | Candidate | | Party | Votes | % |
|----------|----------|-------|-----------|--|-------|-------|---|
| 1945 | 59,768 | 80.2 | F.J. Erroll | | C | 26,656 | 55.6 |
| | | | M.C. Joseph | | Lab | 21,275 | 44.4 |
| | | | | | | 5,381 | 11.2 |

| Election | Electors | T'out | Candidate | Party | Votes | % |
|---|---|---|---|---|---|---|
| 1918 | 25,715 | 68.4 | †Rt. Hon. Sir A.H. Stanley | Co C | 10,261 | 58.3 |
| | | | T.F. Lister | NFDSS | 7,334 | 41.7 |
| | | | | | 2,927 | 16.6 |
| [Elevation to the Peerage — Lord Ashfield] | | | | | | |
| 1920 | 24,912 | 82.3 | Sir W. de Frece | Co C | 8,864 | 43.3 |
| (31/1) | | | W.C. Robinson | Lab | 8,127 | 39.6 |
| | | | Sir A.H. Marshall | L | 3,511 | 17.1 |
| | | | | | 737 | 3.7 |
| 1922 | 25,014 | 83.3 | Sir W. de Frece | C | 12,006 | 57.6 |
| | | | T.W. Gillinder | Lab | 8,834 | 42.4 |
| | | | | | 3,172 | 15.2 |
| 1923 | 25,327 | 85.3 | Sir W. de Frece | C | 7,813 | 36.2 |
| | | | H.T. Greenwood | L | 7,574 | 35.1 |
| | | | Miss E.C. Wilkinson | Lab | 6,208 | 28.7 |
| | | | | | 239 | 1.1 |
| 1924 | 25,736 | 88.3 | C.W.J. Homan | C | 8,971 | 39.5 |
| | | | C.J.L. Malone | Lab | 7,451 | 32.8 |
| | | | H.T. Greenwood | L | 6,292 | 27.7 |
| | | | | | 1,520 | 6.7 |
| [Adjudicated a bankrupt] | | | | | | |
| 1928 | 26,497 | 89.1 | A. Bellamy | Lab | 9,567 | 40.6 |
| (29/10) | | | G.C. Touche | C | 7,161 | 30.3 |
| | | | W.G. Greenwood | L | 6,874 | 29.1 |
| | | | | | 2,406 | 10.3 |
| 1929 | 34,471 | 85.9 | A. Bellamy | Lab | 13,170 | 44.4 |
| | | | J. Broadbent | C | 9,763 | 33.0 |
| | | | W.G. Greenwood | L | 6,693 | 22.6 |
| | | | | | 3,407 | 11.4 |
| [Death] | | | | | | |
| 1931 | 34,784 | 80.2 | J. Broadbent | C | 12,420 | 44.6 |
| (30/4) | | | J.W. Gordon | Lab | 11,005 | 39.4 |
| | | | A. Young | NP | 4,472 | 16.0 |
| | | | | | 1,415 | 5.2 |
| 1931 | 34,974 | 85.3 | J. Broadbent | C | 15,652 | 52.5 |
| | | | J.W. Gordon | Lab | 11,074 | 37.1 |
| | | | J.T. Middleton | L | 2,696* | 9.0 |
| | | | C.B. Hobhouse | NP | 424* | 1.4 |
| | | | | | 4,578 | 15.4 |
| 1935 | 34,785 | 81.0 | F.B. Simpson | Lab | 14,140 | 50.2 |
| | | | J. Broadbent | C | 14,026 | 49.8 |
| | | | | | 114 | 0.4 |
| [Death] | | | | | | |
| 1939 | | | Rt. Hon. Sir W.A. Jowitt | Lab | Unopp. | |
| (28/10) | | | | | | |

| Election | Electors | T'out | Candidate | Party | Votes | % |
|----------|----------|-------|-----------|-------|-------|---|
| 1945 | 33,834 | 78.6 | Rt. Hon. Sir W.A. Jowitt | Lab | 14,998 | 56.4 |
|  |  |  | F.H.G.H. Goodhart | C | 11,604 | 43.6 |
|  |  |  |  |  | 3,394 | 12.8 |

[Resignation on appointment as Lord Chancellor and elevation to the Peerage — Lord Jowitt]

| Election | Electors | T'out | Candidate | Party | Votes | % |
|----------|----------|-------|-----------|-------|-------|---|
| 1945 | 33,834 | 70.5 | H. Rhodes | Lab | 12,889 | 54.1 |
| (2/10) |  |  | Sir R.A. Cary | C | 8,360 | 35.0 |
|  |  |  | A. Beale | L | 2,604* | 10.9 |
|  |  |  |  |  | 4,529 | 19.1 |

Note:—

1923: Miss Wilkinson was a member of the Communist Party but received Labour Party endorsement.

## BARKING [65]

| Election | Electors | T'out | Candidate | Party | Votes | % |
|---|---|---|---|---|---|---|
| 1945 | 47,373 | 73.4 | Dr. S. Hastings | Lab | 24,504 | 70.5 |
| | | | K.E.B. Glenny | C | 5,593 | 16.1 |
| | | | C.H. Willcock | L | 4,674 | 13.4 |
| | | | | | 18,911 | 54.4 |

## BARNSLEY [66]

| Election | Electors | T'out | Candidate | Party | Votes | % |
|---|---|---|---|---|---|---|
| 1918 | | | †Sir J. Walton, Bt. | Co L | Unopp. | |
| 1922 | 35,307 | 75.7 | J. Potts | Lab | 14,728 | 55.1 |
| | | | M. Moore | NL | 12,011 | 44.9 |
| | | | | | 2,717 | 10.2 |
| 1923 | 35,684 | 74.1 | J. Potts | Lab | 12,674 | 48.0 |
| | | | W. Craven-Ellis | C | 6,884 | 26.0 |
| | | | J. Neal | L | 6,881 | 26.0 |
| | | | | | 5,790 | 22.0 |
| 1924 | 36,469 | 78.2 | J. Potts | Lab | 14,738 | 51.7 |
| | | | J. Neal | L | 13,785 | 48.3 |
| | | | | | 953 | 3.4 |
| 1929 | 49,361 | 82.3 | J. Potts | Lab | 21,855 | 53.8 |
| | | | Rt. Hon. Sir W. Sutherland | L | 12,517 | 30.8 |
| | | | W. Craven-Ellis | C | 6,265 | 15.4 |
| | | | | | 9,338 | 23.0 |
| 1931 | 49,902 | 84.2 | R.J. Soper | NL | 21,392 | 50.9 |
| | | | J. Potts | Lab | 20,622 | 49.1 |
| | | | | | 770 | 1.8 |
| 1935 | 52,077 | 82.6 | J. Potts | Lab | 25,318 | 58.9 |
| | | | R.J. Soper | NL | 17,683 | 41.1 |
| | | | | | 7,635 | 17.8 |
| [Death] | | | | | | |
| 1938 (16/6) | 50,376 | 72.7 | F. Collindridge | Lab | 23,566 | 64.4 |
| | | | H.W.S. Howard | NL | 13,052 | 35.6 |
| | | | | | 10,514 | 28.8 |
| 1945 | 52,211 | 80.4 | F. Collindridge | Lab | 30,614 | 72.9 |
| | | | R.J. Soper | NL | 11,382 | 27.1 |
| | | | | | 19,232 | 45.8 |

# BARROW-IN-FURNESS [67]

| Election | Electors | T'out | Candidate | Party | Votes | % |
|---|---|---|---|---|---|---|
| 1918 | 37,697 | 66.1 | R.B. Chadwick | C | 12,608 | 50.6 |
| | | | †C. Duncan | Lab | 12,309 | 49.4 |
| | | | | | 299 | 1.2 |
| 1922 | 35,609 | 87.1 | D.G. Somerville | C | 16,478 | 53.1 |
| | | | J. Bromley | Lab | 14,551 | 46.9 |
| | | | | | 1,927 | 6.2 |
| 1923 | 34,187 | 86.3 | D.G. Somerville | C | 13,996 | 47.5 |
| | | | J. Bromley | Lab | 13,576 | 46.0 |
| | | | W.H. Wandless | L | 1,931* | 6.5 |
| | | | | | 420 | 1.5 |
| 1924 | 33,714 | 89.9 | J. Bromley | Lab | 15,512 | 51.2 |
| | | | D.G. Somerville | C | 14,802 | 48.8 |
| | | | | | 710 | 2.4 |
| 1929 | 40,708 | 86.8 | J. Bromley | Lab | 19,798 | 56.0 |
| | | | K.M. Cameron | C | 15,551 | 44.0 |
| | | | | | 4,247 | 12.0 |
| 1931 | 41,195 | 88.9 | Sir J. Walker-Smith | C | 20,794 | 56.8 |
| | | | D. Adams | Lab | 15,835 | 43.2 |
| | | | | | 4,959 | 13.6 |
| 1935 | 42,213 | 85.4 | Sir J. Walker-Smith | C | 18,136 | 50.3 |
| | | | P.G. Barstow | Lab | 17,919 | 49.7 |
| | | | | | 217 | 0.6 |
| 1945 | 49,669 | 79.7 | W. Monslow | Lab | 25,939 | 65.5 |
| | | | Sir J. Walker-Smith | C | 13,648 | 34.5 |
| | | | | | 12,291 | 31.0 |

## BATH  [68]

| Election | Electors | T'out | Candidate | Party | Votes | % |
|---|---|---|---|---|---|---|
| 1918 | 31,512 | 66.2 | †C.T. Foxcroft | Co C | 15,605 | 74.8 |
|  |  |  | A.J. Bethell | Lab | 5,244 | 25.2 |
|  |  |  |  |  | 10,361 | 49.6 |
| 1922 | 33,023 | 82.4 | C.T. Foxcroft | C | 13,666 | 50.2 |
|  |  |  | E.H. Spender | L | 8,699 | 32.0 |
|  |  |  | H.H. Elvin | Lab | 4,849 | 17.8 |
|  |  |  |  |  | 4,967 | 18.2 |
| 1923 | 33,520 | 79.1 | F.W. Raffety | L | 13,694 | 51.6 |
|  |  |  | C.T. Foxcroft | C | 12,830 | 48.4 |
|  |  |  |  |  | 864 | 3.2 |
| 1924 | 34,042 | 84.5 | C.T. Foxcroft | C | 16,067 | 55.8 |
|  |  |  | F.W. Raffety | L | 8,800 | 30.6 |
|  |  |  | W.B. Scobell | Lab | 3,914 | 13.6 |
|  |  |  |  |  | 7,267 | 25.2 |
| [Death] |  |  |  |  |  |  |
| 1929 (21/3) | 35,373 | 70.1 | Hon. C.W. Baillie-Hamilton | C | 11,171 | 45.0 |
|  |  |  | S.R. Daniels | L | 7,255 | 29.3 |
|  |  |  | G.G. Desmond | Lab | 6,359 | 25.7 |
|  |  |  |  |  | 3,916 | 15.7 |
| 1929 | 46,877 | 81.3 | Hon. C.W. Baillie-Hamilton | C | 17,845 | 46.9 |
|  |  |  | S.R. Daniels | L | 11,485 | 30.1 |
|  |  |  | G.G. Desmond | Lab | 8,769 | 23.0 |
|  |  |  |  |  | 6,360 | 16.8 |
| 1931 | 47,932 | 80.6 | T.L.E.B. Guinness | C | 24,696 | 64.0 |
|  |  |  | S.R. Daniels | L | 8,241 | 21.3 |
|  |  |  | G.G. Desmond | Lab | 5,680 | 14.7 |
|  |  |  |  |  | 16,455 | 42.7 |
| 1935 | 49,022 | 74.5 | T.L.E.B. Guinness | C | 20,670 | 56.6 |
|  |  |  | S.R. Daniels | L | 8,650 | 23.7 |
|  |  |  | G.G. Desmond | Lab | 7,185 | 19.7 |
|  |  |  |  |  | 12,020 | 32.9 |
| 1945 | 59,681 | 77.5 | I.J. Pitman | C | 20,196 | 43.6 |
|  |  |  | Mrs. D.H. Archibald | Lab | 18,120 | 39.2 |
|  |  |  | P.W. Hopkins | L | 7,952 | 17.2 |
|  |  |  |  |  | 2,076 | 4.4 |

# BATLEY and MORLEY [69]

| Election | Electors | T'out | Candidate | Party | Votes | % |
|---|---|---|---|---|---|---|
| 1918 | 38,211 | 66.9 | †G.A. France | Co L | 13,519 | 52.9 |
| | | | B. Turner | Lab | 12,051 | 47.1 |
| | | | | | 1,468 | 5.8 |
| 1922 | 38,148 | 85.2 | B. Turner | Lab | 15,005 | 46.1 |
| | | | J.A. Compston | L | 9,443 | 29.1 |
| | | | J. Potter | C | 8,054 | 24.8 |
| | | | | | 5,562 | 17.0 |
| 1923 | 38,548 | 73.8 | B. Turner | Lab | 14,964 | 52.6 |
| | | | W. Forrest | L | 13,480 | 47.4 |
| | | | | | 1,484 | 5.2 |
| 1924 | 38,839 | 83.3 | W. Forrest | L | 16,369 | 50.6 |
| | | | B. Turner | Lab | 15,966 | 49.4 |
| | | | | | 403 | 1.2 |
| 1929 | 50,272 | 84.1 | B. Turner | Lab | 24,621 | 58.3 |
| | | | W. Forrest | L | 17,641 | 41.7 |
| | | | | | 6,980 | 16.6 |
| 1931 | 50,142 | 85.9 | W.D. Wills | C | 26,378 | 61.2 |
| | | | Sir B. Turner | Lab | 16,700 | 38.8 |
| | | | | | 9,678 | 22.4 |
| 1935 | 49,868 | 79.3 | W. Brooke | Lab | 21,182 | 53.6 |
| | | | W.D. Wills | C | 18,354 | 46.4 |
| | | | | | 2,828 | 7.2 |
| [Death] | | | | | | |
| 1939 (9/3) | 49,757 | 72.6 | H. Beaumont | Lab | 20,020 | 55.4 |
| | | | W.D. Wills | C | 16,124 | 44.6 |
| | | | | | 3,896 | 10.8 |
| 1945 | 48,334 | 80.7 | H. Beaumont | Lab | 22,682 | 58.1 |
| | | | G.W. Hirst | C | 11,090 | 28.4 |
| | | | A. Mitchell | L | 5,256 | 13.5 |
| | | | | | 11,592 | 29.7 |
| [Death] | | | | | | |
| 1949 (17/2) | 50,830 | 81.3 | Dr. A.D.D. Broughton | Lab | 24,514 | 59.3 |
| | | | A.M. Ramsden | C | 16,828 | 40.7 |
| | | | | | 7,686 | 18.6 |

Note:—

1945: Mitchell sought election as an 'Independent Liberal' but his name was included in the official list of Liberal Party candidates.

| Election | Electors | T'out | Candidate | Party | Votes | % |
|----------|----------|-------|-----------|-------|-------|---|
| 1945 | 56,557 | 76.7 | Mrs. J.L. Adamson | Lab | 24,686 | 56.9 |
| | | | J.C. Lockwood | C | 12,923 | 29.8 |
| | | | W. Smith | L | 5,750 | 13.3 |
| | | | | | 11,763 | 27.1 |

[Resignation on appointment as Deputy-Chairman of the National Assistance Board]

| Election | Electors | T'out | Candidate | Party | Votes | % |
|----------|----------|-------|-----------|-------|-------|---|
| 1946 | 61,583 | 61.2 | E.A. Bramall | Lab | 19,759 | 52.5 |
| (22/7) | | | J.C. Lockwood | C | 17,908 | 47.5 |
| | | | | | 1,851 | 5.0 |

## BIRKENHEAD, EAST [71]

| Election | Electors | T'out | Candidate | Party | Votes | % |
|---|---|---|---|---|---|---|
| 1918 | 33,297 | 60.7 | †A. Bigland | Co C | 13,012 | 64.5 |
| | | | J. Finigan | Lab | 5,399 | 26.7 |
| | | | H.G. White | L | 1,787* | 8.8 |
| | | | | | 7,613 | 37.8 |
| 1922 | 32,809 | 77.5 | H.G. White | L | 14,690 | 57.8 |
| | | | A. Bigland | C | 10,745 | 42.2 |
| | | | | | 3,945 | 15.6 |
| 1923 | 33,658 | 74.1 | H.G. White | L | 15,845 | 63.5 |
| | | | L. Lees | C | 9,091 | 36.5 |
| | | | | | 6,754 | 27.0 |
| 1924 | 34,696 | 81.0 | W.H. Stott | C | 11,328 | 40.3 |
| | | | H.G. White | L | 9,275 | 33.0 |
| | | | J. Coulthard | Lab | 7,496 | 26.7 |
| | | | | | 2,053 | 7.3 |
| 1929 | 46,563 | 78.8 | H.G. White | L | 13,157 | 35.9 |
| | | | C.E.R. Brocklebank | C | 11,860 | 32.3 |
| | | | J. Coulthard | Lab | 11,654 | 31.8 |
| | | | | | 1,297 | 3.6 |
| 1931 | 46,556 | 79.1 | H.G. White | L | 26,938 | 73.2 |
| | | | C. McVey | Lab | 9,868 | 26.8 |
| | | | | | 17,070 | 46.4 |
| 1935 | 46,385 | 74.2 | H.G. White | L | 16,548 | 48.1 |
| | | | S.J. Hill | C | 9,854 | 28.6 |
| | | | Mrs. M.A. Mercer | Lab | 8,028 | 23.3 |
| | | | | | 6,694 | 19.5 |
| 1945 | 44,247 | 73.6 | F. Soskice | Lab | 14,790 | 45.5 |
| | | | Rt. Hon. H.G. White | L | 10,140 | 31.1 |
| | | | F.N. Bucher | C | 7,624 | 23.4 |
| | | | | | 4,650 | 14.4 |

# BIRKENHEAD, WEST [72]

| Election | Electors | T'out | Candidate | Party | Votes | % |
|---|---|---|---|---|---|---|
| 1918 | 30,068 | 60.9 | H.M. Grayson | Co C | 10,881 | 59.4 |
| | | | W.H. Egan | Lab | 5,673 | 31.0 |
| | | | H. Bickersteth | L | 1,755* | 9.6 |
| | | | | | 5,208 | 28.4 |
| 1922 | 29,843 | 75.6 | W.H. Stott | C | 12,176 | 54.0 |
| | | | W.H. Egan | Lab | 10,371 | 46.0 |
| | | | | | 1,805 | 8.0 |
| 1923 | 30,841 | 72.4 | W.H. Egan | Lab | 12,473 | 55.8 |
| | | | W.H. Stott | C | 9,862 | 44.2 |
| | | | | | 2,611 | 11.6 |
| 1924 | 31,774 | 81.1 | E. Nuttall | C | 13,059 | 50.7 |
| | | | W.H. Egan | Lab | 12,723 | 49.3 |
| | | | | | 336 | 1.4 |
| 1929 | 42,773 | 79.5 | W.H. Egan | Lab | 15,634 | 45.9 |
| | | | E. Nuttall | C | 13,410 | 39.5 |
| | | | R.P. Fletcher | L | 4,946 | 14.6 |
| | | | | | 2,224 | 6.4 |
| 1931 | 42,600 | 82.2 | J.S. Allen | C | 22,336 | 63.8 |
| | | | W.H. Egan | Lab | 12,682 | 36.2 |
| | | | | | 9,654 | 27.6 |
| 1935 | 42,316 | 74.7 | J.S. Allen | C | 17,684 | 55.9 |
| | | | C. McVey | Lab | 13,931 | 44.1 |
| | | | | | 3,753 | 11.8 |
| 1945 | 36,156 | 75.1 | P.H. Collick | Lab | 15,568 | 57.3 |
| | | | A.R. Moody | C | 11,591 | 42.7 |
| | | | | | 3,977 | 14.6 |

# BIRMINGHAM, ACOCK'S GREEN [73]

| Election | Electors | T'out | Candidate | Party | Votes | % |
|---|---|---|---|---|---|---|
| 1945 | 55,880 | 72.1 | H.C. Usborne | Lab | 19,951 | 49.5 |
| | | | A.T. Maxwell | C | 15,797 | 39.2 |
| | | | W.P. Hamsher | L | 4,546* | 11.3 |
| | | | | | 4,154 | 10.3 |

# BIRMINGHAM, ASTON [74]

| Election | Electors | T'out | Candidate | Party | Votes | % |
|---|---|---|---|---|---|---|
| 1918 | 35,443 | 45.2 | †Rt. Hon. E. Cecil | Co C | 9,997 | 62.4 |
| | | | J.W. Banfield | Lab | 4,451 | 27.8 |
| | | | J.H. Dooley | NFDSS | 1,561* | 9.8 |
| | | | | | 5,546 | 34.6 |
| 1922 | 36,113 | 72.5 | Rt. Hon. Sir E. Cecil | C | 15,913 | 60.8 |
| | | | J.P. Cotter | Lab | 10,279 | 39.2 |
| | | | | | 5,634 | 21.6 |
| 1923 | 36,416 | 65.0 | Rt. Hon. Sir E. Cecil | C | 13,291 | 56.2 |
| | | | P. Bower | Lab | 7,541 | 31.8 |
| | | | J.C. Tillotson | L | 2,846* | 12.0 |
| | | | | | 5,750 | 24.4 |
| 1924 | 36,391 | 71.7 | Rt. Hon. Sir E. Cecil | C | 14,244 | 54.6 |
| | | | E.J.St.L. Strachey | Lab | 11,859 | 45.4 |
| | | | | | 2,385 | 9.2 |
| 1929 | 45,687 | 78.3 | E.J.St.L. Strachey | Lab (NP) (Ind) | 18,672 | 52.2 |
| | | | J.P. Whiteley | C | 17,114 | 47.8 |
| | | | | | 1,558 | 4.4 |
| 1931 | 44,123 | 73.4 | A.O.J. Hope | C | 22,959 | 70.8 |
| | | | T.J. May | Lab | 6,212 | 19.2 |
| | | | E.J.St.L. Strachey | Ind | 3,236* | 10.0 |
| | | | | | 16,747 | 51.6 |
| 1935 | 42,527 | 64.7 | Hon. A.O.J. Hope | C | 18,933 | 68.8 |
| | | | R.P. Messel | Lab | 8,578 | 31.2 |
| | | | | | 10,355 | 37.6 |

[Resignation on appointment as Governor of Madras]

| Election | Electors | T'out | Candidate | Party | Votes | % |
|---|---|---|---|---|---|---|
| 1939 (17/5) | 40,308 | 45.0 | E.O. Kellett | C | 12,023 | 66.3 |
| | | | Dr. S. Segal | Lab | 6,122 | 33.7 |
| | | | | | 5,901 | 32.6 |

[Death]

| Election | Electors | T'out | Candidate | Party | Votes | % |
|---|---|---|---|---|---|---|
| 1943 (9/6) | 39,262 | 22.2 | R.M. Prior | C | 6,316 | 72.5 |
| | | | G. Hall | CW | 1,886 | 21.6 |
| | | | S.H. Davis | Ind | 515* | 5.9 |
| | | | | | 4,430 | 50.9 |
| 1945 | 35,948 | 67.6 | W.L. Wyatt | Lab | 15,031 | 61.9 |
| | | | F.B. Normansell | C | 9,264 | 38.1 |
| | | | | | 5,767 | 23.8 |

# BIRMINGHAM, DERITEND [75]

| Election | Electors | T'out | Candidate | Party | Votes | % |
|---|---|---|---|---|---|---|
| 1918 | 37,442 | 30.7 | J.W. Dennis | Co C | 9,495 | 82.7 |
| | | | A. Brampton | L | 1,990 | 17.3 |
| | | | | | 7,505 | 65.4 |
| 1922 | 36,985 | 64.7 | J.S. Crooke | C | 11,700 | 48.9 |
| | | | F. Longden | Lab | 6,892 | 28.8 |
| | | | H. Willison | L | 5,331 | 22.3 |
| | | | | | 4,808 | 20.1 |
| 1923 | 37,671 | 56.8 | J.S. Crooke | C | 12,015 | 56.1 |
| | | | F. Longden | Lab | 9,396 | 43.9 |
| | | | | | 2,619 | 12.2 |
| 1924 | 37,980 | 69.3 | J.S. Crooke | C | 13,552 | 51.5 |
| | | | F. Longden | Lab/Co-op | 12,760 | 48.5 |
| | | | | | 792 | 3.0 |
| 1929 | 47,262 | 70.6 | F. Longden | Lab/Co-op | 16,932 | 50.7 |
| | | | J.S. Crooke | C | 14,165 | 42.5 |
| | | | Mrs. B. Hornabrook | L | 2,268* | 6.8 |
| | | | | | 2,767 | 8.2 |
| 1931 | 45,671 | 71.9 | J.S. Crooke | C | 21,684 | 66.0 |
| | | | F. Longden | Lab/Co-op | 11,163 | 34.0 |
| | | | | | 10,521 | 32.0 |
| 1935 | 42,078 | 59.6 | J.S. Crooke | C | 14,925 | 59.5 |
| | | | F. Longden | Lab/Co-op | 10,144 | 40.5 |
| | | | | | 4,781 | 19.0 |
| 1945 | 23,693 | 63.0 | F. Longden | Lab/Co-op | 9,749 | 65.3 |
| | | | G.R. Matthews | C | 5,172 | 34.7 |
| | | | | | 4,577 | 30.6 |

# BIRMINGHAM, DUDDESTON [76]

| Election | Electors | T'out | Candidate | Party | Votes | % |
|---|---|---|---|---|---|---|
| 1918 | 34,167 | 32.4 | E. Hallas | Co NDP (Lab) | 8,796 | 79.4 |
| | | | Dr. J.F. Crowley | L | 2,280 | 20.6 |
| | | | | | 6,516 | 58.8 |
| 1922 | 34,388 | 62.3 | Sir E.V. Hiley | C | 13,091 | 61.1 |
| | | | M. Brothers | Lab | 8,331 | 38.9 |
| | | | | | 4,760 | 22.2 |
| 1923 | 34,553 | 56.9 | J.B. Burman | C | 11,712 | 59.6 |
| | | | G.F. Sawyer | Lab | 7,309 | 37.2 |
| | | | A. Ford | Ind | 634* | 3.2 |
| | | | | | 4,403 | 22.4 |
| 1924 | 34,673 | 64.3 | J.B. Burman | C | 11,407 | 51.2 |
| | | | G.F. Sawyer | Lab | 10,892 | 48.8 |
| | | | | | 515 | 2.4 |
| 1929 | 43,507 | 68.6 | G.F. Sawyer | Lab | 18,204 | 61.0 |
| | | | J.B. Burman | C | 11,639 | 39.0 |
| | | | | | 6,565 | 22.0 |
| 1931 | 41,492 | 64.4 | O.E. Simmonds | C | 16,332 | 61.1 |
| | | | G.F. Sawyer | Lab | 9,789 | 36.6 |
| | | | B. Moore | Com | 327* | 1.2 |
| | | | J. Williams | NP | 284* | 1.1 |
| | | | | | 6,543 | 24.5 |
| 1935 | 39,144 | 53.7 | O.E. Simmonds | C | 12,146 | 57.8 |
| | | | G.F. Sawyer | Lab | 8,884 | 42.2 |
| | | | | | 3,262 | 15.6 |
| 1945 | 26,047 | 63.5 | Mrs. E.A. Wills | Lab/Co-op | 10,745 | 65.0 |
| | | | Sir O.E. Simmonds | C | 5,791 | 35.0 |
| | | | | | 4,954 | 30.0 |

Note:—

1923:   Ford sought election as a 'Free Trade' candidate.

| Election | Electors | T'out | Candidate | Party | Votes | % |
|---|---|---|---|---|---|---|
| 1918 | 37,013 | 48.0 | †Sir F.W. Lowe, Bt. | Co C | 13,565 | 76.4 |
| | | | Sir J. Barnsley | L | 4,184 | 23.6 |
| | | | | | 9,381 | 52.8 |
| 1922 | | | Sir F.W. Lowe, Bt. | C | Unopp. | |
| 1923 | 37,779 | 56.7 | Sir F.W. Lowe, Bt. | C | 15,459 | 72.2 |
| | | | A.W. Bowkett | L | 5,962 | 27.8 |
| | | | | | 9,497 | 44.4 |
| 1924 | 37,874 | 64.9 | Sir F.W. Lowe, Bt. | C | 18,822 | 76.6 |
| | | | F.R. Sharkey | Lab | 5,744 | 23.4 |
| | | | | | 13,078 | 53.2 |
| 1929 | 52,366 | 70.0 | Rt. Hon. A.N. Chamberlain | C | 23,350 | 63.7 |
| | | | W.H.D. Caple | Lab | 8,590 | 23.4 |
| | | | P.R.C. Young | L | 4,720 | 12.9 |
| | | | | | 14,760 | 40.3 |
| 1931 | 53,955 | 70.9 | Rt. Hon. A.N. Chamberlain | C | 33,085 | 86.5 |
| | | | W.W. Blaylock | Lab | 5,157 | 13.5 |
| | | | | | 27,928 | 73.0 |
| 1935 | 55,474 | 62.4 | Rt. Hon. A.N. Chamberlain | C | 28,243 | 81.6 |
| | | | J. Adshead | Lab | 6,381 | 18.4 |
| | | | | | 21,862 | 63.2 |
| [Death] | | | | | | |
| 1940 (18/12) | | | P.F.B. Bennett | C | Unopp. | |
| 1945 | 58,199 | 69.1 | Sir P.F.B. Bennett | C | 21,497 | 53.5 |
| | | | G.C. Barrow | Lab | 12,879 | 32.0 |
| | | | A.A. Shenfield | L | 5,832 | 14.5 |
| | | | | | 8,618 | 21.5 |

| Election | Electors | T'out | Candidate | Party | Votes | % |
|----------|----------|-------|-----------|-------|-------|---|
| 1918 | 34,239 | 56.1 | †Sir A.H.D.R. Steel-Maitland, Bt. | Co C | 12,678 | 66.0 |
| | | | A.E. Eyton | Ind Lab | 5,211 | 27.1 |
| | | | R.H.E.H. Somerset | L | 1,329* | 6.9 |
| | | | | | 7,467 | 38.9 |
| 1922 | | | Sir A.H.D.R. Steel-Maitland, Bt. | C | Unopp. | |
| 1923 | 37,450 | 59.4 | Sir A.H.D.R. Steel-Maitland, Bt. | C | 14,683 | 66.0 |
| | | | A.E. Eyton | Lab | 7,574 | 34.0 |
| | | | | | 7,109 | 32.0 |
| 1924 | 38,864 | 72.5 | Sir A.H.D.R. Steel-Maitland, Bt. | C | 16,754 | 59.5 |
| | | | C.J. Simmons | Lab | 11,412 | 40.5 |
| | | | | | 5,342 | 19.0 |
| 1929 | 60,472 | 78.7 | C.J. Simmons | Lab | 20,665 | 43.5 |
| | | | Rt. Hon. Sir A.H.D.R. Steel-Maitland, Bt. | C | 20,532 | 43.1 |
| | | | H.J.H. Dyer | L | 6,395 | 13.4 |
| | | | | | 133 | 0.4 |
| 1931 | 67,448 | 77.6 | J.F. Eales | C | 35,672 | 68.1 |
| | | | C.J. Simmons | Lab | 16,676 | 31.9 |
| | | | | | 18,996 | 36.2 |
| 1935 | 72,524 | 65.5 | J.F. Eales | C | 27,716 | 58.3 |
| | | | C.J. Simmons | Lab | 17,757 | 37.4 |
| | | | H.C. Bell | Ind | 2,050* | 4.3 |
| | | | | | 9,959 | 20.9 |
| [Death] | | | | | | |
| 1936 (20/10) | 74,038 | 64.7 | J.A.C. Wright | C | 27,068 | 56.5 |
| | | | C.J. Simmons | Lab | 20,834 | 43.5 |
| | | | | | 6,234 | 13.0 |
| 1945 | 83,152 | 68.8 | J. Silverman | Lab | 34,786 | 60.8 |
| | | | J.A.C. Wright | C | 22,457 | 39.2 |
| | | | | | 12,329 | 21.6 |

Note:-

1935: Bell sought election as a 'National Dividend' candidate. He was supported by the Social Credit Secretariat.

## BIRMINGHAM, HANDSWORTH [79]

| Election | Electors | T'out | Candidate | Party | Votes | % |
|---|---|---|---|---|---|---|
| 1918 | 37,254 | 57.2 | †E.C. Meysey-Thompson | Co C | 12,019 | 56.4 |
| | | | N. Tiptaft | Ind | 4,697 | 22.1 |
| | | | H.J. Odell | Ind Lab | 4,576 | 21.5 |
| | | | | | 7,322 | 34.3 |
| 1922 | 38,164 | 82.9 | O.S. Locker-Lampson | C | 18,859 | 59.6 |
| | | | N. Tiptaft | Ind | 12,790 | 40.4 |
| | | | | | 6,069 | 19.2 |
| 1923 | | | O.S. Locker-Lampson | C | Unopp. | |
| 1924 | 38,872 | 78.6 | O.S. Locker-Lampson | C | 20,056 | 65.6 |
| | | | P.J. Noel-Baker | Lab | 10,516 | 34.4 |
| | | | | | 9,540 | 31.2 |
| 1929 | 52,025 | 78.5 | O.S. Locker-Lampson | C | 22,035 | 53.9 |
| | | | L.A. Fenn | Lab | 11,959 | 29.3 |
| | | | A.G. Bagnall | L | 6,857 | 16.8 |
| | | | | | 10,076 | 24.6 |
| 1931 | 52,660 | 75.1 | O.S. Locker-Lampson | C | 30,989 | 78.4 |
| | | | L.A. Fenn | Lab | 8,548 | 21.6 |
| | | | | | 22,441 | 56.8 |
| 1935 | 53,567 | 61.7 | O.S. Locker-Lampson | C | 24,135 | 73.0 |
| | | | A.G. Chattaway | Lab | 8,910 | 27.0 |
| | | | | | 15,225 | 46.0 |
| 1945 | 56,890 | 72.4 | H. Roberts | C | 15,607 | 37.9 |
| | | | C.R. Bence | Lab | 14,142 | 34.3 |
| | | | N. Tiptaft | Nat Ind | 5,112* | 12.4 |
| | | | Mrs. B.E. Lewis | L | 4,945* | 12.0 |
| | | | Mrs. J. Eden | Com | 1,390* | 3.4 |
| | | | | | 1,465 | 3.6 |

Notes:—

1918: Tiptaft was supported by the local branch of the NFDSS.

1922: Tiptaft was leader of the Progressive Group in Birmingham City Council at the time of the election.

| Election | Electors | T'out | Candidate | Party | Votes | % |
|---|---|---|---|---|---|---|
| 1918 | 27,117 | 59.6 | Sir H. Austin | Co C | 8,809 | 54.5 |
| | | | T. Hackett | Co-op | 4,917 | 30.4 |
| | | | W.N. Birkett | L | 2,435 | 15.1 |
| | | | | | 3,892 | 24.1 |
| 1922 | 28,857 | 74.0 | Sir H. Austin | C | 8,870 | 41.6 |
| | | | Mrs. E. Barton | Lab/Co-op | 7,017 | 32.8 |
| | | | W. Meakin | L | 5,474 | 25.6 |
| | | | | | 1,853 | 8.8 |
| 1923 | 29,652 | 74.1 | Sir H. Austin | C | 9,545 | 43.4 |
| | | | Mrs. E. Barton | Lab/Co-op | 6,743 | 30.7 |
| | | | Mrs. E.M. Cadbury | L | 5,686 | 25.9 |
| | | | | | 2,802 | 12.7 |
| 1924 | 30,034 | 80.7 | R. Dennison | Lab | 10,497 | 43.3 |
| | | | Sir H. Austin | C | 10,364 | 42.8 |
| | | | J. Fryer | L | 3,370 | 13.9 |
| | | | | | 133 | 0.5 |
| 1929 | 41,602 | 82.8 | L. Beaumont-Thomas | C | 14,464 | 42.0 |
| | | | R. Dennison | Lab | 13,973 | 40.6 |
| | | | A.P. Marshall | L | 5,998 | 17.4 |
| | | | | | 491 | 1.4 |
| 1931 | 47,399 | 81.0 | L. Beaumont-Thomas | C | 22,063 | 57.5 |
| | | | G.R. Mitchison | Lab | 11,016 | 28.7 |
| | | | A.P. Marshall | L | 5,294 | 13.8 |
| | | | | | 11,047 | 28.8 |
| 1935 | 57,944 | 74.6 | J.R.H. Cartland | C | 24,559 | 56.8 |
| | | | G.R. Mitchison | Lab | 18,684 | 43.2 |
| | | | | | 5,875 | 13.6 |
| [Death] | | | | | | |
| 1941 (8/5) | 70,890 | 35.0 | B.A.J. Peto | C | 21,573 | 86.9 |
| | | | Dr. A.W.L. Smith | Ind | 1,696* | 6.8 |
| | | | S. Morris | Ind | 1,552* | 6.3 |
| | | | | | 19,877 | 80.1 |
| 1945 | 78,647 | 73.9 | A.R. Blackburn | Lab | 32,062 | 55.2 |
| | | | B.A.J. Peto | C | 19,764 | 34.0 |
| | | | B.S. White | L | 6,289* | 10.8 |
| | | | | | 12,298 | 21.2 |

Notes:—

1941:  Smith advocated a policy of aerial reprisals against Germany.

Morris sought election as a 'Pacifist' candidate. He was the nominee of the Peace Pledge Union.

# BIRMINGHAM, LADYWOOD [81]

| Election | Electors | T'out | Candidate | Party | Votes | % |
|---|---|---|---|---|---|---|
| 1918 | 33,330 | 40.6 | A.N. Chamberlain | Co C | 9,405 | 69.5 |
| | | | J.W. Kneeshaw | Lab | 2,572 | 19.0 |
| | | | Mrs. M.I.C. Ashby | L | 1,552* | 11.5 |
| | | | | | 6,833 | 50.5 |
| 1922 | 33,508 | 70.5 | Rt. Hon. A.N. Chamberlain | C | 13,032 | 55.2 |
| | | | Dr. R. Dunstan | Lab | 10,589 | 44.8 |
| | | | | | 2,443 | 10.4 |
| 1923 | 33,652 | 72.0 | Rt. Hon. A.N. Chamberlain | C | 12,884 | 53.2 |
| | | | Dr. R. Dunstan | Lab | 11,330 | 46.8 |
| | | | | | 1,554 | 6.4 |
| 1924 | 33,787 | 80.5 | Rt. Hon. A.N. Chamberlain | C | 13,374 | 49.1 |
| | | | O.E. Mosley | Lab | 13,297 | 48.9 |
| | | | A.W. Bowkett | L | 539* | 2.0 |
| | | | | | 77 | 0.2 |
| 1929 | 42,590 | 77.2 | W. Whiteley | Lab | 16,447 | 50.0 |
| | | | G.W. Lloyd | C | 16,436 | 50.0 |
| | | | | | 11 | 0.0 |
| 1931 | 41,129 | 78.1 | G.W. Lloyd | C | 23,057 | 71.8 |
| | | | W. Whiteley | Lab | 9,057 | 28.2 |
| | | | | | 14,000 | 43.6 |
| 1935 | 39,180 | 66.0 | G.W. Lloyd | C | 18,565 | 71.7 |
| | | | G.H. Humphreys | Lab | 7,311 | 28.3 |
| | | | | | 11,254 | 43.4 |
| 1945 | 34,541 | 69.9 | V.F. Yates | Lab | 13,503 | 55.9 |
| | | | Rt. Hon. G.W. Lloyd | C | 10,657 | 44.1 |
| | | | | | 2,846 | 11.8 |

## BIRMINGHAM, MOSELEY [82]

| Election | Electors | T'out | Candidate | Party | Votes | % |
|---|---|---|---|---|---|---|
| 1918 | 41,546 | 56.3 | Sir H. Rogers | Co C | 16,161 | 69.2 |
| | | | Dr. R. Dunstan | Lab | 3,789 | 16.2 |
| | | | W. Hill | L | 3,422 | 14.6 |
| | | | | | 12,372 | 53.0 |
| [Resignation] | | | | | | |
| 1921 (4/3) | | | P.J.H. Hannon | Co C | Unopp. | |
| 1922 | | | P.J.H. Hannon | C | Unopp. | |
| 1923 | 43,642 | 63.1 | P.J.H. Hannon | C | 19,628 | 71.3 |
| | | | Mrs. J. Clarkson | L | 7,904 | 28.7 |
| | | | | | 11,724 | 42.6 |
| 1924 | 44,876 | 70.2 | P.J.H. Hannon | C | 24,333 | 77.2 |
| | | | G.P. Blizard | Lab | 7,183 | 22.8 |
| | | | | | 17,150 | 54.4 |
| 1929 | 81,508 | 73.1 | P.J.H. Hannon | C | 33,820 | 56.8 |
| | | | Dr. F.G. Bushnell | Lab | 15,733 | 26.4 |
| | | | A.M. Meek | L | 9,388 | 15.7 |
| | | | G. Brigden | Ind Lab | 675* | 1.1 |
| | | | | | 18,087 | 30.4 |
| 1931 | 92,183 | 72.1 | P.J.H. Hannon | C | 53,041 | 79.8 |
| | | | F.G. Lloyd | Lab | 13,399 | 20.2 |
| | | | | | 39,642 | 59.6 |
| 1935 | 101,169 | 60.7 | P.J.H. Hannon | C | 43,885 | 71.4 |
| | | | J. Silverman | Lab | 17,543 | 28.6 |
| | | | | | 26,342 | 42.8 |
| 1945 | 61,850** | 69.7 | Sir P.J.H. Hannon | C | 22,063 | 51.2 |
| | | | A.L.N. Stephens | Lab | 21,070 | 48.8 |
| | | | | | 993 | 2.4 |

# BIRMINGHAM, SPARKBROOK [83]

| Election | Electors | T'out | Candidate | Party | Votes | % |
|---|---|---|---|---|---|---|
| 1918 | 37,123 | 52.5 | †L.C.M.S. Amery | Co C | 15,225 | 78.1 |
| | | | F. Spires | Co-op | 3,014 | 15.5 |
| | | | J.G. Hurst | L | 1,251* | 6.4 |
| | | | | | 12,211 | 62.6 |
| 1922 | 37,918 | 71.0 | Rt. Hon. L.C.M.S. Amery | C | 13,326 | 49.5 |
| | | | T.F. Duggan | L | 7,283 | 27.1 |
| | | | E.W. Hampton | Lab/Co-op | 6,310 | 23.4 |
| | | | | | 6,043 | 22.4 |
| 1923 | 37,890 | 63.7 | Rt. Hon. L.C.M.S. Amery | C | 13,523 | 56.0 |
| | | | E.W. Hampton | Lab | 5,948 | 24.6 |
| | | | D.L. Finnemore. | L | 4,676 | 19.4 |
| | | | | | 7,575 | 31.4 |
| 1924 | 38,058 | 71.1 | Rt. Hon. L.C.M.S. Amery | C | 15,718 | 58.1 |
| | | | S.B.M. Potter | Lab | 9,759 | 36.1 |
| | | | E.P. Ray | L | 1,580* | 5.8 |
| | | | | | 5,959 | 22.0 |
| 1929 | 47,041 | 73.1 | Rt. Hon. L.C.M.S. Amery | C | 15,867 | 46.2 |
| | | | A. Young | Lab | 12,875 | 37.4 |
| | | | T.F. Duggan | L | 5,645 | 16.4 |
| | | | | | 2,992 | 8.8 |
| 1931 | 46,073 | 69.6 | Rt. Hon. L.C.M.S. Amery | C | 23,517 | 73.4 |
| | | | G. Archibald | Lab | 8,538 | 26.6 |
| | | | | | 14,979 | 46.8 |
| 1935 | 44,647 | 57.3 | Rt. Hon. L.C.M.S. Amery | C | 17,509 | 68.5 |
| | | | H. Whittaker | Lab | 8,063 | 31.5 |
| | | | | | 9,446 | 37.0 |
| 1945 | 36,592 | 66.5 | P.L.E. Shurmer | Lab | 14,065 | 57.8 |
| | | | Rt. Hon. L.C.M.S. Amery | C | 8,431 | 34.6 |
| | | | R.P. Dutt | Com | 1,853* | 7.6 |
| | | | | | 5,634 | 23.2 |

# BIRMINGHAM, WEST [84]

| Election | Electors | T'out | Candidate | Party | Votes | % |
|---|---|---|---|---|---|---|
| 1918 | | | †Rt. Hon. J.A. Chamberlain | Co C | Unopp. | |
| [Appointed Lord Privy Seal] | | | | | | |
| 1921 (31/3) | | | Rt. Hon. J.A. Chamberlain | Co C | Unopp. | |
| 1922 | 37,263 | 67.1 | Rt. Hon. J.A. Chamberlain | C | 15,405 | 61.6 |
| | | | F. Smith | Lab | 9,599 | 38.4 |
| | | | | | 5,806 | 23.2 |
| 1923 | 37,433 | 63.9 | Rt. Hon. J.A. Chamberlain | C | 13,940 | 58.3 |
| | | | F. Smith | Lab | 9,983 | 41.7 |
| | | | | | 3,957 | 16.6 |
| 1924 | 37,754 | 58.2 | Rt. Hon. J.A. Chamberlain | C | 14,801 | 67.4 |
| | | | Dr. R. Dunstan | Com | 7,158 | 32.6 |
| | | | | | 7,643 | 34.8 |
| 1929 | 45,593 | 73.9 | Rt. Hon. Sir J.A. Chamberlain | C | 16,862 | 50.1 |
| | | | O.G. Willey | Lab | 16,819 | 49.9 |
| | | | | | 43 | 0.2 |
| 1931 | 43,442 | 75.9 | Rt. Hon. Sir J.A. Chamberlain | C | 22,448 | 68.1 |
| | | | O.G. Willey | Lab | 10,507 | 31.9 |
| | | | | | 11,941 | 36.2 |
| 1935 | 40,401 | 63.6 | Rt. Hon. Sir J.A. Chamberlain | C | 16,530 | 64.3 |
| | | | O.G. Willey | Lab | 9,159 | 35.7 |
| | | | | | 7,371 | 28.6 |
| [Death] | | | | | | |
| 1937 (29/4) | 39,600 | 56.0 | W.F. Higgs | C | 12,552 | 56.6 |
| | | | R.H.S. Crossman | Lab | 9,632 | 43.4 |
| | | | | | 2,920 | 13.2 |
| 1945 | 29,808 | 66.7 | C.J. Simmons | Lab | 12,639 | 63.5 |
| | | | W.F. Higgs | C | 7,253 | 36.5 |
| | | | | | 5,386 | 27.0 |

## BIRMINGHAM, YARDLEY [85]

| Election | Electors | T'out | Candidate | Party | Votes | % |
|---|---|---|---|---|---|---|
| 1918 | 36,575 | 53.2 | A.R. Jephcott | Co C | 10,960 | 56.3 |
|  |  |  | G. Shann | Lab | 7,466 | 38.3 |
|  |  |  | G. Jackson | L | 1,049* | 5.4 |
|  |  |  |  |  | 3,494 | 18.0 |
| 1922 | 38,045 | 70.5 | A.R. Jephcott | C | 15,586 | 58.1 |
|  |  |  | A.G. Gossling | Lab | 11,234 | 41.9 |
|  |  |  |  |  | 4,352 | 16.2 |
| 1923 | 38,591 | 64.4 | A.R. Jephcott | C | 13,300 | 53.5 |
|  |  |  | A.G. Gossling | Lab | 11,562 | 46.5 |
|  |  |  |  |  | 1,738 | 7.0 |
| 1924 | 39,235 | 77.3 | A.R. Jephcott | C | 16,149 | 53.2 |
|  |  |  | A.G. Gossling | Lab | 14,184 | 46.8 |
|  |  |  |  |  | 1,965 | 6.4 |
| 1929 | 63,068 | 77.8 | A.G. Gossling | Lab | 23,956 | 48.9 |
|  |  |  | E.W. Salt | C | 19,590 | 39.9 |
|  |  |  | C.A. Beaumont | L | 5,500* | 11.2 |
|  |  |  |  |  | 4,366 | 9.0 |
| 1931 | 64,117 | 76.7 | E.W. Salt | C | 32,061 | 65.2 |
|  |  |  | A.G. Gossling | Lab | 16,640 | 33.8 |
|  |  |  | E.J. Bartleet | NP | 479* | 1.0 |
|  |  |  |  |  | 15,421 | 31.4 |
| 1935 | 68,377 | 65.2 | E.W. Salt | C | 25,717 | 57.7 |
|  |  |  | C. Jarman | Lab | 18,879 | 42.3 |
|  |  |  |  |  | 6,838 | 15.4 |
| 1945 | 80,964 | 69.1 | W. Perrins | Lab | 33,835 | 60.5 |
|  |  |  | Sir E.W. Salt | C | 16,514 | 29.5 |
|  |  |  | C.F. Middleton | L | 5,583* | 10.0 |
|  |  |  |  |  | 17,321 | 31.0 |

# BLACKBURN [86]
## (Two Seats)

| Election | Electors | T'out | Candidate | Party | Votes | % |
|---|---|---|---|---|---|---|
| 1918 | 61,972 | 74.8 | †Rt. Hon. Sir H. Norman, Bt. | Co L | 32,076 | 41.4 |
| | | | P.T. Dean | Co C | 30,158 | 38.9 |
| | | | †P. Snowden | Lab | 15,274 | 19.7 |
| | | | | | 16,802 | 21.7 |
| | | | | | 14,884 | 19.2 |
| 1922 | 64,849 | 88.4 | Sir S.H.H. Henn | C | 28,280 | 25.5 |
| | | | Rt. Hon. Sir H. Norman, Bt. | NL | 27,071 | 24.4 |
| | | | J.P. Davies | Lab | 24,049 | 21.7 |
| | | | E. Porter | Lab | 23,402 | 21.1 |
| | | | T.C. Meech | L | 8,141 | 7.3 |
| | | | | | 4,231 | 3.8 |
| | | | | | 3,022 | 2.7 |
| 1923 | 65,389 | 85.0 | J. Duckworth | L | 31,117 | 29.1 |
| | | | Sir S.H.H. Henn | C | 28,505 | 26.6 |
| | | | J.P. Davies | Lab | 25,428 | 23.8 |
| | | | E. Porter | Lab | 21,903 | 20.5 |
| | | | | | 5,689 | 5.3 |
| | | | | | 3,077 | 2.8 |
| 1924 | 65,522 | 88.2 | J. Duckworth | L | 31,612 | 28.3 |
| | | | Sir S.H.H. Henn | C | 31,347 | 28.1 |
| | | | Mrs. M.A. Hamilton | Lab | 24,330 | 21.8 |
| | | | T.H. Gill | Lab | 24,317 | 21.8 |
| | | | | | 7,282 | 6.5 |
| | | | | | 7,017 | 6.3 |
| 1929 | 86,354 | 87.8 | Mrs. M.A. Hamilton | Lab | 37,256 | 26.1 |
| | | | T.H. Gill | Lab | 35,723 | 25.0 |
| | | | Sir S.H.H. Henn | C | 35,249 | 24.7 |
| | | | Viscount Erleigh | L | 34,504 | 24.2 |
| | | | | | 474 | 0.3 |
| 1931 | 86,824 | 87.4 | Sir W.D. Smiles | C | 50,105 | 33.3 |
| | | | G.S. Elliston | C | 49,953 | 33.1 |
| | | | Mrs. M.A. Hamilton | Lab | 25,643 | 17.0 |
| | | | T.H. Gill | Lab | 25,030 | 16.6 |
| | | | | | 24,310 | 16.1 |
| 1935 | 85,818 | 84.9 | G.S. Elliston | C | 37,932 | 26.2 |
| | | | Sir W.D. Smiles | C | 37,769 | 26.1 |
| | | | J. Bell | Lab | 34,571 | 23.9 |
| | | | G.H. Walker | Lab | 34,423 | 23.8 |
| | | | | | 3,198 | 2.2 |
| 1945 | 82,569 | 82.6 | L.J. Edwards | Lab | 35,182 | 26.0 |
| | | | Mrs. B.A. Castle | Lab | 35,145 | 26.0 |
| | | | D. Glover | C | 26,325 | 19.5 |
| | | | R.G. Parker | C | 25,807 | 19.1 |
| | | | R. Shackleton | L | 6,587* | 4.9 |
| | | | Mrs. M.A. MacInerney | L | 6,096* | 4.5 |
| | | | | | 8,820 | 6.5 |

# BLACKPOOL [87]

| Election | Electors | T'out | Candidate | Party | Votes | % |
|---|---|---|---|---|---|---|
| 1918 | 41,627 | 68.0 | A.L. Parkinson | Co C | 15,818 | 55.9 |
| | | | C.F. Critchley | Ind | 9,862 | 34.9 |
| | | | A. Gee | Lab | 2,608* | 9.2 |
| | | | | | 5,956 | 21.0 |
| 1922 | 46,292 | 78.3 | L.G.S. Molloy | C | 18,206 | 50.2 |
| | | | H.M. Meyler | L | 18,040 | 49.8 |
| | | | | | 166 | 0.4 |
| 1923 | 48,865 | 84.8 | H.M. Meyler | L | 22,264 | 53.7 |
| | | | Hon. V.A. Stanley | C | 19,192 | 46.3 |
| | | | | | 3,072 | 7.4 |
| 1924 | 51,914 | 85.8 | Sir W. de Frece | C | 25,839 | 58.0 |
| | | | H.M. Meyler | L | 18,712 | 42.0 |
| | | | | | 7,127 | 16.0 |
| 1929 | 86,744 | 81.1 | Sir W. de Frece | C | 32,912 | 46.8 |
| | | | M.E. Mitchell | L | 25,374 | 36.1 |
| | | | E.A. Machin | Lab | 12,049 | 17.1 |
| | | | | | 7,538 | 10.7 |
| 1931 | 91,099 | 79.6 | C.C.A.L. Erskine-Bolst | C | 53,010 | 73.1 |
| | | | R.E.H. Wallace | L | 19,524 | 26.9 |
| | | | | | 33,486 | 46.2 |
| 1935 | 100,529 | 74.0 | J.R. Robinson | C | 48,514 | 65.2 |
| | | | H. Thorneycroft | Lab | 13,598 | 18.3 |
| | | | H.G. Purchase | L | 12,245 | 16.5 |
| | | | | | 34,916 | 46.9 |

This constituency was divided in 1945.

Notes:—

1918: Critchley sought election as an 'Independent Progressive Coalition' candidate and received local Liberal Party support.

1931: Wallace was opposed to the National Government.

# BLACKPOOL, NORTH [88]

| Election | Electors | T'out | Candidate | Party | Votes | % |
|----------|----------|-------|-----------|-------|-------|---|
| 1945 | 76,168 | 68.0 | T.A.R.W. Low | C | 25,564 | 49.3 |
| | | | C.E.T. Thomas | Lab | 13,170 | 25.4 |
| | | | K.I. Hamilton | L | 11,452 | 22.1 |
| | | | A. Talbot | Nat Ind | 1,635* | 3.2 |
| | | | | | 12,394 | 23.9 |

## BLACKPOOL, SOUTH  [89]

| Election | Electors | T'out | Candidate | Party | Votes | % |
|---|---|---|---|---|---|---|
| 1945 | 68,136 | 72.3 | J.R. Robinson | C | 27,957 | 56.8 |
| | | | C.S. Hilditch | Lab | 11,914 | 24.2 |
| | | | A.J. Liddell Hart | L | 9,359 | 19.0 |
| | | | | | 16,043 | 32.6 |

# BOLTON [90]
## (Two Seats)

| Election | Electors | T'out | Candidate | Party | Votes | % |
|---|---|---|---|---|---|---|
| 1918 | | | †W. Edge | Co L | Unopp. | |
| | | | †R. Tootill | Lab | Unopp. | |
| 1922 | 84,342 | 87.2 | W. Russell | C | 37,491 | 29.3 |
| | | | Sir W. Edge | NL | 31,015 | 24.3 |
| | | | S. Lomax | Lab | 20,559 | 16.1 |
| | | | W.J. Abraham | Lab | 20,156 | 15.8 |
| | | | I. Edwards | L | 18,534 | 14.5 |
| | | | | | 16,932 | 13.2 |
| | | | | | 10,456 | 8.2 |
| 1923 | 85,613 | 80.0 | A. Law | Lab | 25,133 | 18.6 |
| | | | J.H. Cunliffe | C | 22,833 | 16.9 |
| | | | C. Hilton | C | 22,640 | 16.8 |
| | | | Sir W. Edge | L | 22,173 | 16.5 |
| | | | F. Eccles | Lab | 21,045 | 15.6 |
| | | | J.F. Steele | L | 21,040 | 15.6 |
| | | | | | 2,493 | 1.8 |
| | | | | | 660 | 0.4 |
| 1924 | 86,366 | 85.6 | J.H. Cunliffe | C | 34,690 | 23.7 |
| | | | C. Hilton | C | 33,405 | 22.8 |
| | | | A. Law | Lab | 30,632 | 20.9 |
| | | | W.H. Hutchinson | Lab | 28,918 | 19.8 |
| | | | J.P. Taylor | L | 10,036 | 6.9 |
| | | | A.E. Holt | L | 8,558* | 5.9 |
| | | | | | 2,773 | 1.9 |
| 1929 | 120,463 | 84.3 | A. Law | Lab | 43,520 | 24.0 |
| | | | M. Brothers | Lab | 37,888 | 20.9 |
| | | | C.F. Entwistle | C | 36,667 | 20.3 |
| | | | C. Hilton | C | 35,850 | 19.8 |
| | | | P.R. Barry | L | 27,074 | 15.0 |
| | | | | | 1,221 | 0.6 |
| 1931 | 122,912 | 81.3 | C.F. Entwistle | C | 66,385 | 33.9 |
| | | | Sir J. Haslam | C | 63,402 | 32.4 |
| | | | A. Law | Lab | 33,737 | 17.3 |
| | | | M. Brothers | Lab | 32,049 | 16.4 |
| | | | | | 29,665 | 15.1 |
| 1935 | 124,119 | 76.8 | C.F. Entwistle | C | 54,129 | 29.0 |
| | | | Sir J. Haslam | C | 52,465 | 28.2 |
| | | | A. Law | Lab | 39,890 | 21.4 |
| | | | J. Lynch | Lab | 39,871 | 21.4 |
| | | | | | 12,575 | 6.8 |
| [Death of Haslam] | | | | | | |
| 1940 (13/9) | | | Hon. Sir E.C.G. Cadogan | C | Unopp. | |
| 1945 | 120,551 | 78.1 | J.H. Jones | Lab | 44,595 | 24.0 |
| | | | J. Lewis | Lab | 43,266 | 23.3 |
| | | | Sir J.F.R. Reynolds, Bt. | C | 31,217 | 16.8 |
| | | | Sir C.F. Entwistle | C | 30,911 | 16.6 |
| | | | Rev. R.K. Spedding | L | 18,180 | 9.8 |
| | | | B.R. Connell | L | 17,710 | 9.5 |
| | | | | | 12,049 | 6.5 |

# BOOTLE [91]

| Election | Electors | T'out | Candidate | Party | Votes | % |
|---|---|---|---|---|---|---|
| 1918 | 33,419 | 58.5 | Sir T. Royden, Bt. | Co C | 12,312 | 63.0 |
| | | | E. Cathery | Ind | 7,235 | 37.0 |
| | | | | | 5,077 | 26.0 |
| 1922 | 33,148 | 71.1 | J. Burnie | L | 13,276 | 56.3 |
| | | | Sir A. Bicket | C | 9,867 | 41.9 |
| | | | J.E. Burke | Ind | 425* | 1.8 |
| | | | | | 3,409 | 14.4 |
| 1923 | 34,837 | 68.1 | J. Burnie | L | 10,444 | 44.1 |
| | | | V.L. Henderson | C | 9,991 | 42.1 |
| | | | J. Kinley | Lab | 3,272 | 13.8 |
| | | | | | 453 | 2.0 |
| 1924 | 35,305 | 77.0 | V.L. Henderson | C | 12,361 | 45.5 |
| | | | J. Kinley | Lab | 9,427 | 34.7 |
| | | | J. Burnie | L | 5,386 | 19.8 |
| | | | | | 2,934 | 10.8 |
| 1929 | 45,008 | 77.9 | J. Kinley | Lab | 15,294 | 43.6 |
| | | | Sir V.L. Henderson | C | 14,263 | 40.7 |
| | | | E.E. Edwards | L | 5,523 | 15.7 |
| | | | | | 1,031 | 2.9 |
| 1931 | 47,040 | 78.9 | C. de W. Crookshank | C | 22,966 | 61.9 |
| | | | J. Kinley | Lab | 14,160 | 38.1 |
| | | | | | 8,806 | 23.8 |
| 1935 | 48,031 | 71.3 | E. Errington | C | 16,653 | 48.6 |
| | | | J. Kinley | Lab | 13,285 | 38.8 |
| | | | J. Burnie | L | 4,319 | 12.6 |
| | | | | | 3,368 | 9.8 |
| 1945 | 38,720 | 69.7 | J. Kinley | Lab | 15,823 | 58.6 |
| | | | E. Errington | C | 11,180 | 41.4 |
| | | | | | 4,643 | 17.2 |

Note:—

1918: Cathery sought election as a 'Seamen's' candidate. He was supported by the National Sailors' and Firemen's Union.

| Election | Electors | T'out | Candidate | Party | Votes | % |
|---|---|---|---|---|---|---|
| 1918 | 33,079 | 64.1 | †H.P. Croft | Nat P (C) | 14,048 | 66.3 |
| | | | Rev. F.J. Hopkins | Lab | 5,302 | 25.0 |
| | | | T.D. Keighley | L | 1,854* | 8.7 |
| | | | | | 8,746 | 41.3 |
| 1922 | 37,598 | 79.8 | H.P. Croft | C | 15,690 | 52.3 |
| | | | C.B. Dallow | L | 10,181 | 33.9 |
| | | | H.K. Hargreaves | Ind C | 4,134 | 13.8 |
| | | | | | 5,509 | 18.4 |
| 1923 | 38,913 | 79.0 | H.P. Croft | C | 15,506 | 50.4 |
| | | | C.B. Dallow | L | 9,256 | 30.1 |
| | | | Miss M. Pallister | Lab | 5,986 | 19.5 |
| | | | | | 6,250 | 20.3 |
| 1924 | 41,038 | 69.1 | Sir H.P. Croft, Bt. | C | 20,620 | 72.7 |
| | | | Miss M. Pallister | Lab | 7,735 | 27.3 |
| | | | | | 12,885 | 45.4 |
| 1929 | 66,812 | 74.4 | Sir H.P. Croft, Bt. | C | 25,945 | 52.2 |
| | | | A. Mortimer | L | 15,890 | 31.9 |
| | | | M. Spencer | Lab | 7,900 | 15.9 |
| | | | | | 10,055 | 20.3 |
| 1931 | 70,858 | 70.3 | Sir H.P. Croft, Bt. | C | 39,859 | 80.0 |
| | | | J.H. Collingbourne | Lab | 9,943 | 20.0 |
| | | | | | 29,916 | 60.0 |
| 1935 | 73,335 | 62.6 | Sir H.P. Croft, Bt. | C | 32,645 | 71.1 |
| | | | M.S. Davidson | Lab | 13,279 | 28.9 |
| | | | | | 19,366 | 42.2 |

[Elevation to the Peerage — Lord Croft]

| Election | Electors | T'out | Candidate | Party | Votes | % |
|---|---|---|---|---|---|---|
| 1940 (27/6) | | | Sir C.E.L. Lyle, Bt. | C | Unopp. | |
| 1945 | 87,504 | 71.2 | Sir C.E.L. Lyle, Bt. | C | 34,544 | 55.5 |
| | | | B.T. Wigoder | L | 14,232 | 22.8 |
| | | | R.S.W. Pollard | Lab | 13,522 | 21.7 |
| | | | | | 20,312 | 32.7 |

[Elevation to the Peerage — Lord Lyle of Westbourne]

| Election | Electors | T'out | Candidate | Party | Votes | % |
|---|---|---|---|---|---|---|
| 1945 (15/11) | 86,796 | 56.5 | Rt. Hon. B. Bracken | C | 22,980 | 46.8 |
| | | | E.A.A. Shackleton | Lab | 16,526 | 33.7 |
| | | | B.T. Wigoder | L | 9,548 | 19.5 |
| | | | | | 6,454 | 13.1 |

Note:—

1922:  Hargreaves sought election as a 'Lloyd George Conservative'. He stated that although he was a Conservative he supported Lloyd George, hence the adoption of this unusual 'label'.

## BRADFORD, CENTRAL   [93]

| Election | Electors | T'out | Candidate | Party | Votes | % |
|---|---|---|---|---|---|---|
| 1918 | 44,549 | 54.7 | H.B. Ratcliffe | Co C | 12,434 | 51.0 |
|  |  |  | W. Leach | Lab | 7,636 | 31.3 |
|  |  |  | †Sir J. Hill, Bt. | L | 4,304 | 17.7 |
|  |  |  |  |  | 4,798 | 19.7 |
| 1922 | 44,689 | 75.4 | W. Leach | Lab | 14,296 | 42.4 |
|  |  |  | F.D. Moore | C | 12,171 | 36.1 |
|  |  |  | Rev. W. Paxton | L | 7,250 | 21.5 |
|  |  |  |  |  | 2,125 | 6.3 |
| 1923 | 44,991 | 71.0 | W. Leach | Lab | 14,241 | 44.6 |
|  |  |  | J. Pearson | C | 9,725 | 30.4 |
|  |  |  | Rev. W. Paxton | L | 7,973 | 25.0 |
|  |  |  |  |  | 4,516 | 14.2 |
| 1924 | 45,127 | 76.5 | A. Gadie | C | 17,854 | 51.7 |
|  |  |  | W. Leach | Lab | 16,652 | 48.3 |
|  |  |  |  |  | 1,202 | 3.4 |
| 1929 | 52,674 | 80.0 | W. Leach | Lab | 24,876 | 59.0 |
|  |  |  | A. Gadie | C | 17,265 | 41.0 |
|  |  |  |  |  | 7,611 | 18.0 |
| 1931 | 51,996 | 78.2 | G.H. Eady | C | 24,986 | 61.4 |
|  |  |  | W. Leach | Lab | 15,697 | 38.6 |
|  |  |  |  |  | 9,289 | 22.8 |
| 1935 | 47,906 | 66.0 | W. Leach | Lab | 16,397 | 51.8 |
|  |  |  | G.H. Eady | C | 15,241 | 48.2 |
|  |  |  |  |  | 1,156 | 3.6 |
| 1945 | 38,331 | 76.2 | M. Webb | Lab | 16,764 | 57.5 |
|  |  |  | T.L. Dallas | C | 7,776 | 26.6 |
|  |  |  | P.E. Trench | L | 4,655 | 15.9 |
|  |  |  |  |  | 8,988 | 30.9 |

# BRADFORD, EAST [94]

| Election | Electors | T'out | Candidate | Party | Votes | % |
|---|---|---|---|---|---|---|
| 1918 | 36,580 | 62.4 | C.E. Loseby | Co NDP | 9,390 | 41.1 |
| | | | †F.W. Jowett | Lab | 8,637 | 37.9 |
| | | | †Sir W.E.B. Priestley | L | 4,782 | 21.0 |
| | | | | | 753 | 3.2 |
| 1922 | 36,758 | 81.4 | F.W. Jowett | Lab | 13,573 | 45.4 |
| | | | C.E. Loseby | NL | 9,926 | 33.2 |
| | | | H.M. Dawson | L | 6,411 | 21.4 |
| | | | | | 3,647 | 12.2 |
| 1923 | 37,323 | 75.6 | F.W. Jowett | Lab | 13,579 | 48.1 |
| | | | E. Mitchell | L | 8,017 | 28.4 |
| | | | J. Clare | C | 6,622 | 23.5 |
| | | | | | 5,562 | 19.7 |
| 1924 | 37,658 | 80.8 | T.D. Fenby | L | 15,240 | 50.1 |
| | | | Rt. Hon. F.W. Jowett | Lab | 15,174 | 49.9 |
| | | | | | 66 | 0.2 |
| 1929 | 46,856 | 83.4 | Rt. Hon. F.W. Jowett | Lab | 21,398 | 54.7 |
| | | | T.D. Fenby | L | 17,701 | 45.3 |
| | | | | | 3,697 | 9.4 |
| 1931 | 46,494 | 82.4 | J. Hepworth | C | 22,532 | 58.8 |
| | | | Rt. Hon. F.W. Jowett | ILP | 15,779 | 41.2 |
| | | | | | 6,753 | 17.6 |
| 1935 | 46,176 | 73.1 | J. Hepworth | C | 11,131 | 33.0 |
| | | | Rt. Hon. F.W. Jowett | ILP | 8,983 | 26.6 |
| | | | W.L. Heywood | Lab | 7,329 | 21.7 |
| | | | T.D. Fenby | L | 6,312 | 18.7 |
| | | | | | 2,148 | 6.4 |

[Seat Vacant at Dissolution (Death)]

| Election | Electors | T'out | Candidate | Party | Votes | % |
|---|---|---|---|---|---|---|
| 1945 | 44,388 | 79.0 | F. McLeavy | Lab | 15,743 | 44.9 |
| | | | W.J. Taylor | C | 9,109 | 26.0 |
| | | | W. Ballantine | ILP | 5,195 | 14.8 |
| | | | J.S. Snowden | L | 5,010 | 14.3 |
| | | | | | 6,634 | 18.9 |

# BRADFORD, NORTH [95]

| Election | Electors | T'out | Candidate | Party | Votes | % |
|---|---|---|---|---|---|---|
| 1918 | 33,038 | 67.3 | A.B. Boyd-Carpenter | Co C | 11,042 | 49.7 |
| | | | J.H. Palin | Lab | 6,499 | 29.2 |
| | | | E. Binns | L | 4,688 | 21.1 |
| | | | | | 4,543 | 20.5 |
| 1922 | 33,508 | 84.0 | A.B. Boyd-Carpenter | C | 10,260 | 36.5 |
| | | | W.R. Rea | L | 9,008 | 32.0 |
| | | | J.H. Palin | Lab | 8,869 | 31.5 |
| | | | | | 1,252 | 4.5 |
| 1923 | 33,772 | 81.7 | W.R. Rea | L | 9,365 | 34.0 |
| | | | A.B. Boyd-Carpenter | C | 9,192 | 33.3 |
| | | | T. Blythe | Lab | 9,036 | 32.7 |
| | | | | | 173 | 0.7 |
| 1924 | 34,114 | 84.7 | E.J.S.H. Ramsden | C | 11,459 | 39.6 |
| | | | E.F. Wise | Lab | 9,442 | 32.7 |
| | | | W.R. Rea | L | 8,007 | 27.7 |
| | | | | | 2,017 | 6.9 |
| 1929 | 51,573 | 84.5 | R.N. Angell | Lab | 17,873 | 41.0 |
| | | | E.J.S.H. Ramsden | C | 15,413 | 35.4 |
| | | | J.B. Hobman | L | 10,290 | 23.6 |
| | | | | | 2,460 | 5.6 |
| 1931 | 52,864 | 83.1 | E.J.S.H. Ramsden | C | 31,537 | 71.8 |
| | | | P. Butler | Lab | 12,401 | 28.2 |
| | | | | | 19,136 | 43.6 |
| 1935 | 55,100 | 72.4 | Sir E.J.S.H. Ramsden | C | 21,150 | 53.1 |
| | | | Mrs. M.E. Nichol | Lab | 14,047 | 35.2 |
| | | | R. Kenney | Ind | 4,684* | 11.7 |
| | | | | | 7,103 | 17.9 |
| 1945 | 58,409 | 79.5 | Mrs. M.E. Nichol | Lab | 20,268 | 43.7 |
| | | | J.A. Benn | C | 16,824 | 36.2 |
| | | | B.R.W. Town | L | 9,337 | 20.1 |
| | | | | | 3,444 | 7.5 |

Note:—

1935: Kenney sought election as a 'National Dividend' candidate. He was supported by the Social Credit Secretariat.

# BRADFORD, SOUTH [96]

| Election | Electors | T'out | Candidate | Party | Votes | % |
|---|---|---|---|---|---|---|
| 1918 | 41,449 | 64.8 | F.V. Willey | Co C | 11,949 | 44.5 |
| | | | W. Hirst | Co-op | 8,291 | 30.9 |
| | | | G. Muff | L | 6,613 | 24.6 |
| | | | | | 3,658 | 13.6 |
| 1922 | 42,511 | 82.2 | H.H. Spencer | L | 13,259 | 38.0 |
| | | | W. Hirst | Lab/Co-op | 12,353 | 35.3 |
| | | | Hon. F.V. Willey | C | 9,334 | 26.7 |
| | | | | | 906 | 2.7 |
| 1923 | 42,967 | 76.9 | H.H. Spencer | L | 12,218 | 37.0 |
| | | | W. Hirst | Lab/Co-op | 11,543 | 34.9 |
| | | | G.G. Mitcheson | C | 9,270 | 28.1 |
| | | | | | 675 | 2.1 |
| 1924 | 43,495 | 82.2 | W. Hirst | Lab/Co-op | 13,919 | 39.0 |
| | | | G.G. Mitcheson | C | 11,586 | 32.4 |
| | | | H.H. Spencer | L | 10,237 | 28.6 |
| | | | | | 2,333 | 6.6 |
| 1929 | 57,301 | 83.0 | W. Hirst | Lab/Co-op | 23,251 | 48.9 |
| | | | F. Ogden | L | 12,279 | 25.8 |
| | | | G.W. Ferrand | C | 12,050 | 25.3 |
| | | | | | 10,972 | 23.1 |
| 1931 | 57,526 | 82.6 | H. Holdsworth | L | 31,531 | 66.3 |
| | | | W. Hirst | Lab/Co-op | 15,994 | 33.7 |
| | | | | | 15,537 | 32.6 |
| 1935 | 58,518 | 70.4 | H. Holdsworth | L (NL) | 24,081 | 58.4 |
| | | | W. Hirst | Lab/Co-op | 17,121 | 41.6 |
| | | | | | 6,960 | 16.8 |
| 1945 | 60,584 | 76.7 | M.F. Titterington | Lab/Co-op | 24,394 | 52.5 |
| | | | H.W. Peel | NL | 15,392 | 33.1 |
| | | | C.E. Hindley | L | 6,707 | 14.4 |
| | | | | | 9,002 | 19.4 |
| [Death] | | | | | | |
| 1949 (8/12) | 61,176 | 74.4 | G. Craddock | Lab | 23,335 | 51.3 |
| | | | J.L. Windle | NL & C | 19,313 | 42.4 |
| | | | C.J. Canning | Ind L | 2,882* | 6.3 |
| | | | | | 4,022 | 8.9 |

## BRIGHTON [97]
### (Two Seats)

| Election | Electors | T'out | Candidate | Party | Votes | % |
|---|---|---|---|---|---|---|
| 1918 | 82,449 | 51.4 | †G.C. Tryon | Co C | 32,958 | 39.7 |
| | | | †C. Thomas-Stanford | Co C | 32,561 | 39.2 |
| | | | T. Lewis | Lab | 8,971 | 10.8 |
| | | | G.W.A. Canter | Lab | 8,514 | 10.3 |
| | | | | | 23,590 | 28.4 |
| 1922 | 80,674 | 70.1 | Rt. Hon. G.C. Tryon | C | 28,549 | 32.0 |
| | | | A.C. Rawson | C | 26,844 | 30.0 |
| | | | C.B. Fry | L | 22,059 | 24.7 |
| | | | H. Wheater | Ind C | 11,913 | 13.3 |
| | | | | | 4,785 | 5.3 |
| 1923 | 82,475 | 69.3 | Rt. Hon. G.C. Tryon | C | 30,137 | 26.8 |
| | | | A.C. Rawson | C | 29,759 | 26.5 |
| | | | Rt. Hon. W. Runciman | L | 17,462 | 15.5 |
| | | | Sir H.S. Lunn | L | 16,567 | 14.7 |
| | | | A.G. Gordon | Lab | 9,545 | 8.5 |
| | | | H. Carden | Lab | 9,040 | 8.0 |
| | | | | | 12,297 | 11.0 |
| 1924 | 83,980 | 64.2 | Rt. Hon. G.C. Tryon | C | 39,387 | 42.5 |
| | | | A.C. Rawson | C | 39,253 | 42.3 |
| | | | A.G. Gordon | Lab | 14,072 | 15.2 |
| | | | | | 25,181 | 27.1 |
| 1929 | 122,641 | 66.4 | Sir A.C. Rawson | C | 46,515 | 29.1 |
| | | | Rt. Hon. G.C. Tryon | C | 46,287 | 29.0 |
| | | | Rev. L.S. Cheshire | Lab | 19,494 | 12.2 |
| | | | W. McLaine | Lab | 18,770 | 11.7 |
| | | | C.B. Dallow | L | 14,770 | 9.3 |
| | | | J.C. Brudenell-Bruce | L | 13,816 | 8.7 |
| | | | | | 26,793 | 16.8 |
| 1931 | 128,779 | 69.4 | Sir A.C. Rawson | C | 75,205 | 42.7 |
| | | | Rt. Hon. G.C. Tryon | C | 74,993 | 42.6 |
| | | | L.C. Cohen | Lab | 12,952 | 7.4 |
| | | | Mrs. R. Moore | Lab/Co-op | 12,878 | 7.3 |
| | | | | | 62,041 | 35.2 |
| 1935 | 129,356 | 62.6 | Rt. Hon. G.C. Tryon | C | 60,913 | 38.2 |
| | | | Sir A.C. Rawson | C | 60,724 | 38.0 |
| | | | A.G. Gordon | Lab | 19,287 | 12.1 |
| | | | L.C. Cohen | Lab | 18,743 | 11.7 |
| | | | | | 41,437 | 25.9 |

[Elevation to the Peerage — Lord Tryon]

| 1940 (9/5) | | | Lord Erskine | C | Unopp. | |
|---|---|---|---|---|---|---|

[Resignation of Erskine]

| 1941 (15/11) | | | A.A.H. Marlowe | C | Unopp. | |
|---|---|---|---|---|---|---|

[Resignation of Rawson]

| 1944 (3/2) | 123,310 | 22.1 | L.W.B. Teeling | C | 14,594 | 53.6 |
|---|---|---|---|---|---|---|
| | | | B.D. Briant | Nat Ind | 12,635 | 46.4 |
| | | | | | 1,959 | 7.2 |

➤

| Election | Electors | T'out | Candidate | Party | Votes | % |
|----------|----------|-------|-----------|-------|-------|---|
| 1945 | 124,714 | 65.9 | L.W.B. Teeling | C | 49,339 | 30.8 |
|  |  |  | A.A.H. Marlowe | C | 49,026 | 30.6 |
|  |  |  | J.T. Huddart | Lab | 31,074 | 19.4 |
|  |  |  | G.H. Barnard | Lab | 30,844 | 19.2 |
|  |  |  |  |  | 17,952 | 11.2 |

Notes:—

1922: Wheater sought election as a 'Free Conservative and Anti-Waste' candidate. He claimed to have been adopted by the Brighton and Hove Conservative Association and the Anti-Waste League but the official Conservative organisation in the constituency was the Brighton and Hove National Unionist Association who repudlated him. The Anti-Waste League did not include his name in their official list of supported candidates.

1944: Briant claimed to be a supporter of the National Government but he was repudiated by Winston Churchill.

# BRISTOL, CENTRAL [98]

| Election | Electors | T'out | Candidate | Party | Votes | % |
|---|---|---|---|---|---|---|
| 1918 | 36,038 | 53.7 | T.W.H. Inskip | Co C | 12,232 | 63.2 |
| | | | E. Bevin | Lab | 7,137 | 36.8 |
| | | | | | 5,095 | 26.4 |
| 1922 | 38,709 | 72.0 | Sir T.W.H. Inskip | C | 15,568 | 55.9 |
| | | | C.B. Thomson | Lab | 12,303 | 44.1 |
| | | | | | 3,265 | 11.8 |
| 1923 | 40,000 | 65.8 | Sir T.W.H. Inskip | C | 14,386 | 54.7 |
| | | | S.E. Walters | Lab | 11,932 | 45.3 |
| | | | | | 2,454 | 9.4 |
| 1924 | 40,252 | 77.5 | Sir T.W.H. Inskip | C | 17,177 | 55.1 |
| | | | J.A. Lovat-Fraser | Lab | 14,018 | 44.9 |
| | | | | | 3,159 | 10.2 |
| 1929 | 48,081 | 77.5 | J.H. Alpass | Lab | 20,749 | 55.7 |
| | | | Sir T.W.H. Inskip | C | 16,524 | 44.3 |
| | | | | | 4,225 | 11.4 |
| 1931 | 46,560 | 80.4 | Lord Apsley | C | 22,311 | 59.6 |
| | | | J.H. Alpass | Lab | 15,143 | 40.4 |
| | | | | | 7,168 | 19.2 |
| 1935 | 41,228 | 72.8 | Lord Apsley | C | 15,774 | 52.5 |
| | | | J.J. Taylor | Lab | 14,258 | 47.5 |
| | | | | | 1,516 | 5.0 |
| [Death] | | | | | | |
| 1943 (18/2) | 34,234 | 32.9 | Lady Apsley | C | 5,867 | 52.1 |
| | | | Miss J. Lee | Ind Lab | 4,308 | 38.2 |
| | | | J. McNair | ILP | 830* | 7.4 |
| | | | F.H. Dunn | Ind | 258* | 2.3 |
| | | | | | 1,559 | 13.9 |
| 1945 | 28,750 | 71.0 | S.S. Awbery | Lab | 13,045 | 63.9 |
| | | | Lady Apsley | C | 7,369 | 36.1 |
| | | | | | 5,676 | 27.8 |

Note:—

1943: Miss Lee was supported by the Common Wealth Movement.

| Election | Electors | T'out | Candidate | Party | Votes | % |
|---|---|---|---|---|---|---|
| 1918 | 33,679 | 56.5 | G.B. Britton | Co L | 9,434 | 49.6 |
| | | | L.H. Bateman | Lab | 8,135 | 42.8 |
| | | | †Rt. Hon. Sir C.E.H. Hobhouse, Bt. | L | 1,447* | 7.6 |
| | | | | | 1,299 | 6.8 |
| 1922 | 35,704 | 77.5 | H.S. Morris | NL | 13,910 | 50.3 |
| | | | L.H. Bateman | Lab | 13,759 | 49.7 |
| | | | | | 151 | 0.6 |
| 1923 | 36,105 | 76.5 | W.J. Baker | Lab | 14,828 | 53.7 |
| | | | H.S. Morris | L | 12,788 | 46.3 |
| | | | | | 2,040 | 7.4 |
| 1924 | 36,441 | 79.8 | W.J. Baker | Lab | 16,920 | 58.2 |
| | | | H.J. Maggs | L | 12,143 | 41.8 |
| | | | | | 4,777 | 16.4 |
| 1929 | 47,039 | 78.2 | W.J. Baker | Lab | 24,197 | 65.8 |
| | | | C. Gordon-Spencer | L | 12,576 | 34.2 |
| | | | | | 11,621 | 31.6 |
| [Death] | | | | | | |
| 1931 (16/1) | 46,881 | 66.6 | Hon. Sir R.S. Cripps | Lab | 19,261 | 61.8 |
| | | | P.J.F. Chapman-Walker | C | 7,937 | 25.4 |
| | | | E. Baker | L | 4,010 | 12.8 |
| | | | | | 11,324 | 36.4 |
| 1931 | 47,924 | 80.2 | Hon. Sir R.S. Cripps | Lab | 19,435 | 50.6 |
| | | | J.M. Spreull | C | 19,006 | 49.4 |
| | | | | | 429 | 1.2 |
| 1935 | 48,975 | 75.8 | Hon. Sir R.S. Cripps | Lab (Ind Lab) (Lab) | 22,009 | 59.3 |
| | | | A.G. Church | N Lab | 15,126 | 40.7 |
| | | | | | 6,883 | 18.6 |
| 1945 | 49,945 | 76.2 | Rt. Hon. Sir R.S. Cripps | Lab | 27,975 | 73.5 |
| | | | T.D. Corpe | C | 10,073 | 26.5 |
| | | | | | 17,902 | 47.0 |

Note:—

1931: Cripps was Solicitor-General.
(16/1)

# BRISTOL, NORTH [100]

| Election | Electors | T'out | Candidate | Party | Votes | % |
|---|---|---|---|---|---|---|
| 1918 | 34,657 | 54.6 | E.S. Gange | Co L | 11,400 | 60.2 |
| | | | J. Kaylor | Lab | 5,007 | 26.5 |
| | | | E.W. Petter | Nat P | 2,520 | 13.3 |
| | | | | | 6,393 | 33.7 |
| 1922 | 36,985 | 73.2 | Hon. C.H.C. Guest | NL | 17,495 | 64.6 |
| | | | W.H. Ayles | Lab | 9,567 | 35.4 |
| | | | | | 7,928 | 29.2 |
| 1923 | 37,424 | 74.4 | W.H. Ayles | Lab | 10,432 | 37.5 |
| | | | Hon. C.H.C. Guest | L | 8,770 | 31.5 |
| | | | E.W. Petter | C | 8,643 | 31.0 |
| | | | | | 1,662 | 6.0 |
| 1924 | 37,821 | 79.6 | Rt. Hon. F.E. Guest | L | 17,799 | 59.1 |
| | | | W.H. Ayles | Lab | 12,319 | 40.9 |
| | | | | | 5,480 | 18.2 |
| 1929 | 49,014 | 78.1 | W.H. Ayles | Lab | 18,619 | 48.7 |
| | | | Rt. Hon. F.E. Guest | Ind L | 12,932 | 33.8 |
| | | | J.O.M. Skelton | L | 6,713 | 17.5 |
| | | | | | 5,687 | 14.9 |
| 1931 | 50,504 | 80.9 | R.H. Bernays | L | 27,040 | 66.2 |
| | | | W.H. Ayles | Lab | 13,826 | 33.8 |
| | | | | | 13,214 | 32.4 |
| 1935 | 50,695 | 73.2 | R.H. Bernays | L (NL) | 20,977 | 56.5 |
| | | | W.H. Ayles | Lab | 16,149 | 43.5 |
| | | | | | 4,828 | 13.0 |

[Seat Vacant at Dissolution (Death)]

| Election | Electors | T'out | Candidate | Party | Votes | % |
|---|---|---|---|---|---|---|
| 1945 | 53,377 | 73.9 | W. Coldrick | Lab/Co-op | 22,819 | 57.8 |
| | | | J.H. Britton | NL | 16,648 | 42.2 |
| | | | | | 6,171 | 15.6 |

Notes:—

1924-
1929: Guest was the official candidate of the local Liberal Association at the General Election of 1924 but he also received support from the local Conservative Association. His campaign was conducted by a joint committee and he stated that he was prepared to support a Conservative Government under Baldwin's leadership. His position between the elections of 1924 and 1929 is difficult to define but although the 'Liberal Year Book' listed him as an Independent he appears to have been in receipt of the Liberal Party whip.

In January 1929 the Western Counties Liberal Association disaffiliated the North Bristol Liberal Association and set up a new organisation which adopted Skelton as their candidate. Shortly before the General Election, the Liberal Parliamentary Party endorsed Guest's receipt of the whip and he received a letter of support from the Chief Liberal Whip. However, on the eve of the election, Lloyd George who was Leader of the Liberal Party and chairman of the Parliamentary Party, sent a letter to Skelton recognising him as the only official Liberal candidate in the constituency.

1931-
1935: Bernays remained on the Government benches in the House of Commons when the Liberal Party went into Opposition in November 1933. He did not however take the National Liberal whip until September 1936.

# BRISTOL, SOUTH [101]

| Election | Electors | T'out | Candidate | Party | Votes | % |
|---|---|---|---|---|---|---|
| 1918 | 35,663 | 56.6 | †Sir W.H. Davies | Co L | 13,761 | 68.2 |
|  |  |  | T.C. Lewis | Lab | 6,409 | 31.8 |
|  |  |  |  |  | 7,352 | 36.4 |
| 1922 | 38,030 | 75.9 | Sir W.B. Rees | NL | 16,199 | 56.2 |
|  |  |  | D.J. Vaughan | Lab | 12,650 | 43.8 |
|  |  |  |  |  | 3,549 | 12.4 |
| 1923 | 38,675 | 74.8 | Sir W.B. Rees | L | 15,235 | 52.7 |
|  |  |  | D.J. Vaughan | Lab | 13,701 | 47.3 |
|  |  |  |  |  | 1,534 | 5.4 |
| 1924 | 39,056 | 83.0 | Sir W.B. Rees | L | 16,722 | 51.6 |
|  |  |  | D.J. Vaughan | Lab | 15,702 | 48.4 |
|  |  |  |  |  | 1,020 | 3.2 |
| 1929 | 51,628 | 80.9 | A.G. Walkden | Lab | 23,591 | 56.5 |
|  |  |  | Sir W.B. Rees | L | 18,194 | 43.5 |
|  |  |  |  |  | 5,397 | 13.0 |
| 1931 | 53,291 | 82.3 | N.K. Lindsay | C | 26,694 | 60.9 |
|  |  |  | A.G. Walkden | Lab | 17,174 | 39.1 |
|  |  |  |  |  | 9,520 | 21.8 |
| 1935 | 58,325 | 76.9 | A.G. Walkden | Lab | 22,586 | 50.3 |
|  |  |  | N.K. Lindsay | C | 20,153 | 45.0 |
|  |  |  | J.O.M. Skelton | L | 2,090* | 4.7 |
|  |  |  |  |  | 2,433 | 5.3 |
| 1945 | 56,434 | 75.1 | W.A. Wilkins | Lab | 24,929 | 58.8 |
|  |  |  | E.H.C. Leather | C | 12,379 | 29.2 |
|  |  |  | D.A. Jones | L | 5,083* | 12.0 |
|  |  |  |  |  | 12,550 | 29.6 |

# BRISTOL, WEST [102]

| Election | Electors | T'out | Candidate | Party | Votes | % |
|---|---|---|---|---|---|---|
| 1918 | | | †G.A. Gibbs | Co C | Unopp. | |
| [Appointed Treasurer of H.M. Household] | | | | | | |
| 1921 (9/4) | | | G.A. Gibbs | Co C | Unopp. | |
| 1922 | 38,013 | 76.9 | G.A. Gibbs | C | 18,124 | 62.0 |
| | | | F.W. Raffety | L | 11,100 | 38.0 |
| | | | | | 7,024 | 24.0 |
| 1923 | | | Rt. Hon. G.A. Gibbs | C | Unopp. | |
| 1924 | 39,752 | 75.1 | Rt. Hon. G.A. Gibbs | C | 23,574 | 79.0 |
| | | | M. Giles | Lab | 6,276 | 21.0 |
| | | | | | 17,298 | 58.0 |
| [Elevation to the Peerage — Lord Wraxall] | | | | | | |
| 1928 (2/2) | 43,900 | 67.6 | C.T. Culverwell | C | 16,970 | 57.2 |
| | | | Lady Clare Annesley | Lab | 7,702 | 26.0 |
| | | | W.N. Marcy | L | 4,996 | 16.8 |
| | | | | | 9,268 | 31.2 |
| 1929 | 60,844 | 77.7 | C.T. Culverwell | C | 25,416 | 53.7 |
| | | | Lady Clare Annesley | Lab | 11,961 | 25.3 |
| | | | W.N. Marcy | L | 9,909 | 21.0 |
| | | | | | 13,455 | 28.4 |
| 1931 | 65,740 | 79.3 | C.T. Culverwell | C | 43,264 | 83.0 |
| | | | F.E. White | Lab | 8,875 | 17.0 |
| | | | | | 34,389 | 66.0 |
| 1935 | 73,253 | 70.8 | C.T. Culverwell | C | 36,820 | 71.0 |
| | | | P.F. Williams | Lab | 15,058 | 29.0 |
| | | | | | 21,762 | 42.0 |
| 1945 | 88,599 | 74.7 | Rt. Hon. O.F.G. Stanley | C | 32,149 | 48.6 |
| | | | W.E. Balmer | Lab | 25,163 | 38.0 |
| | | | D. Allhusen | L | 8,849 | 13.4 |
| | | | | | 6,986 | 10.6 |

# BROMLEY [103]

| Election | Electors | T'out | Candidate | Party | Votes | % |
|---|---|---|---|---|---|---|
| 1918 | 40,709 | 52.0 | †Rt. Hon. H.W. Forster | Co C | 16,840 | 79.5 |
| | | | G.W.H. Knight | L | 4,339 | 20.5 |
| | | | | | 12,501 | 59.0 |

[Elevation to the Peerage — Lord Forster]

| Election | Electors | T'out | Candidate | Party | Votes | % |
|---|---|---|---|---|---|---|
| 1919 | 43,417 | 48.9 | Hon. C. James | Co C | 11,148 | 52.5 |
| (17/12) | | | F.P. Hodes | Lab | 10,077 | 47.5 |
| | | | | | 1,071 | 5.0 |
| | | | | | | |
| 1922 | 46,256 | 66.3 | Hon. C. James | C | 16,803 | 54.8 |
| | | | F.K. Griffith | L | 9,128 | 29.8 |
| | | | F.P. Hodes | Lab | 4,735 | 15.4 |
| | | | | | 7,675 | 25.0 |
| | | | | | | |
| 1923 | 46,976 | 64.1 | Hon. C. James | C | 13,495 | 44.8 |
| | | | F.K. Griffith | L | 12,612 | 41.9 |
| | | | W.G. Hall | Lab | 3,992 | 13.3 |
| | | | | | 883 | 2.9 |
| | | | | | | |
| 1924 | 48,028 | 78.6 | Hon. C. James | C | 20,272 | 53.7 |
| | | | F.K. Griffith | L | 11,580 | 30.7 |
| | | | H.J. Wallington | Lab | 5,876 | 15.6 |
| | | | | | 8,692 | 23.0 |
| | | | | | | |
| 1929 | 73,785 | 73.1 | Hon. C. James | C | 25,449 | 47.2 |
| | | | W.G. Fordham | L | 18,372 | 34.1 |
| | | | A.E. Ashworth | Lab | 10,105 | 18.7 |
| | | | | | 7,077 | 13.1 |

[Death]

| Election | Electors | T'out | Candidate | Party | Votes | % |
|---|---|---|---|---|---|---|
| 1930 | 73,785 | 53.4 | E.T. Campbell | C | 12,782 | 32.4 |
| (2/9) | | | W.G. Fordham | L | 11,176 | 28.4 |
| | | | V.C. Redwood | UEP | 9,483 | 24.1 |
| | | | A.E. Ashworth | Lab | 5,942 | 15.1 |
| | | | | | 1,606 | 4.0 |
| | | | | | | |
| 1931 | 80,499 | 70.0 | E.T. Campbell | C | 47,077 | 83.6 |
| | | | B.B. Gillis | Lab | 9,265 | 16.4 |
| | | | | | 37,812 | 67.2 |
| | | | | | | |
| 1935 | 90,532 | 65.1 | Sir E.T. Campbell | C | 39,741 | 67.5 |
| | | | C.W. Kendall | Lab | 11,800 | 20.0 |
| | | | H.C. Banting | L | 7,370 | 12.5 |
| | | | | | 27,941 | 47.5 |
| | | | | | | |
| 1945 | 81,938* | 70.9 | Sir E.T. Campbell, Bt. | C | 26,108 | 45.0 |
| | | | A. Bain | Lab | 19,849 | 34.1 |
| | | | J.C. Sayer | L | 12,177 | 20.9 |
| | | | | | 6,259 | 10.9 |

[Death]

| Election | Electors | T'out | Candidate | Party | Votes | % |
|---|---|---|---|---|---|---|
| 1945 | 87,797 | 60.6 | Rt. Hon. M.H. Macmillan | C | 26,367 | 49.6 |
| (14/11) | | | A. Bain | Lab | 20,810 | 39.1 |
| | | | J.C. Sayer | L | 5,990* | 11.3 |
| | | | | | 5,557 | 10.5 |

# BURNLEY [104]

| Election | Electors | T'out | Candidate | Party | Votes | % |
|---|---|---|---|---|---|---|
| 1918 | 50,870 | 71.4 | D.D. Irving | Lab | 15,217 | 41.9 |
| | | | Hon. H.G.H. Mulholland | Co C | 12,289 | 33.8 |
| | | | J.H. Grey | L | 8,825 | 24.3 |
| | | | | | 2,928 | 8.1 |
| 1922 | 50,111 | 88.7 | D.D. Irving | Lab | 17,385 | 39.1 |
| | | | H.E.J. Camps | C | 14,731 | 33.1 |
| | | | W.T. Layton | L | 12,339 | 27.8 |
| | | | | | 2,654 | 6.0 |
| 1923 | 51,086 | 87.3 | D.D. Irving | Lab | 16,848 | 37.8 |
| | | | H.E.J. Camps | C | 14,197 | 31.8 |
| | | | J. Whitehead | L | 13,543 | 30.4 |
| | | | | | 2,651 | 6.0 |
| [Death] | | | | | | |
| 1924 (28/2) | 51,086 | 82.4 | Rt. Hon. A. Henderson | Lab | 24,571 | 58.4 |
| | | | H.E.J. Camps | C | 17,534 | 41.6 |
| | | | | | 7,037 | 16.8 |
| 1924 | 51,162 | 88.4 | Rt. Hon. A. Henderson | Lab | 20,549 | 45.4 |
| | | | S.I. Fairbairn | C | 16,084 | 35.6 |
| | | | J. Whitehead | L | 8,601 | 19.0 |
| | | | | | 4,465 | 9.8 |
| 1929 | 67,781 | 89.6 | Rt. Hon. A. Henderson | Lab | 28,091 | 46.2 |
| | | | S.I. Fairbairn | C | 20,137 | 33.2 |
| | | | A.J.G. Edwards | L | 12,502 | 20.6 |
| | | | | | 7,954 | 13.0 |
| 1931 | 68,106 | 91.8 | G. Campbell | Nat (NL) | 35,126 | 56.2 |
| | | | Rt. Hon. A. Henderson | Lab | 26,917 | 43.0 |
| | | | J. Rushton | Com | 512* | 0.8 |
| | | | | | 8,209 | 13.2 |
| 1935 | 66,330 | 87.6 | W.A. Burke | Lab | 31,160 | 53.6 |
| | | | G. Campbell | NL | 26,965 | 46.4 |
| | | | | | 4,195 | 7.2 |
| 1945 | 62,849 | 80.4 | W.A. Burke | Lab | 32,122 | 63.5 |
| | | | H.H.M. Milnes | NL | 18,431 | 36.5 |
| | | | | | 13,691 | 27.0 |

Note:—

1918: Irving was also the nominee of the NSP.

# BURY [105]

| Election | Electors | T'out | Candidate | Party | Votes | % |
|----------|----------|-------|-----------|-------|-------|---|
| 1918 | 32,666 | 67.0 | C. Ainsworth | C | 10,043 | 45.9 |
| | | | †Sir G. Toulmin | Co L | 6,862 | 31.4 |
| | | | H.W. Wallace | Lab | 4,973 | 22.7 |
| | | | | | 3,181 | 14.5 |
| 1922 | 32,304 | 81.3 | C. Ainsworth | C | 10,830 | 41.2 |
| | | | H.W. Wallace | Lab | 9,643 | 36.7 |
| | | | W.A. Lewins | L | 5,795 | 22.1 |
| | | | | | 1,187 | 4.5 |
| 1923 | 32,803 | 80.8 | C. Ainsworth | C | 10,680 | 40.3 |
| | | | H.W. Wallace | Lab | 9,568 | 36.1 |
| | | | J. Duckworth | L | 6,251 | 23.6 |
| | | | | | 1,112 | 4.2 |
| 1924 | 32,982 | 86.5 | C. Ainsworth | C | 13,382 | 46.9 |
| | | | H.W. Wallace | Lab | 10,286 | 36.1 |
| | | | J. Duckworth | L | 4,847 | 17.0 |
| | | | | | 3,096 | 10.8 |
| 1929 | 43,216 | 81.4 | C. Ainsworth | C | 14,845 | 42.1 |
| | | | J. Bell | Lab | 13,175 | 37.5 |
| | | | C.S. Ickringill | L | 7,160 | 20.4 |
| | | | | | 1,670 | 4.6 |
| 1931 | 43,502 | 81.6 | C. Ainsworth | C | 24,975 | 70.3 |
| | | | J. Bell | Lab | 10,532 | 29.7 |
| | | | | | 14,443 | 40.6 |
| 1935 | 44,817 | 83.3 | A.E.L. Chorlton | C | 18,425 | 49.4 |
| | | | Dr. Edith Summerskill | Lab | 12,845 | 34.4 |
| | | | Dr. D.M. Johnson | L | 6,065 | 16.2 |
| | | | | | 5,580 | 15.0 |
| 1945 | 44,888 | 78.3 | W. Fletcher | C | 14,012 | 39.9 |
| | | | S. Hand | Lab | 13,902 | 39.6 |
| | | | A.W. James | L | 7,211 | 20.5 |
| | | | | | 110 | 0.3 |

# CAMBRIDGE [106]

| Election | Electors | T'out | Candidate | Party | Votes | % |
|----------|----------|-------|-----------|-------|-------|---|
| 1918 | 25,170 | 61.0 | †Rt. Hon. Sir E.C. Geddes | Co C | 11,553 | 75.3 |
|  |  |  | Rev. T.R. Williams | Lab | 3,789 | 24.7 |
|  |  |  |  |  | 7,764 | 50.6 |
| [Resignation] |  |  |  |  |  |  |
| 1922 | 27,833 | 80.4 | Sir D.G.C. Newton | C | 10,897 | 48.7 |
| (16/3) |  |  | E.H.J.N. Dalton | Lab | 6,954 | 31.1 |
|  |  |  | S.C. Morgan | L | 4,529 | 20.2 |
|  |  |  |  |  | 3,943 | 17.6 |
| 1922 | 28,402 | 81.2 | Sir D.G.C. Newton | C | 11,238 | 48.7 |
|  |  |  | S.C. Morgan | L | 7,005 | 30.4 |
|  |  |  | A.S. Firth | Lab | 4,810 | 20.9 |
|  |  |  |  |  | 4,233 | 18.3 |
| 1923 | 28,920 | 80.9 | Sir D.G.C. Newton | C | 9,814 | 42.0 |
|  |  |  | S.C. Morgan | L | 7,852 | 33.5 |
|  |  |  | A.S. Firth | Lab | 5,741 | 24.5 |
|  |  |  |  |  | 1,962 | 8.5 |
| 1924 | 29,372 | 81.9 | Sir D.G.C. Newton | C | 12,628 | 52.5 |
|  |  |  | A.S. Firth | Lab | 6,744 | 28.1 |
|  |  |  | F.R. Salter | L | 4,670 | 19.4 |
|  |  |  |  |  | 5,884 | 24.4 |
| 1929 | 40,227 | 79.8 | Sir D.G.C. Newton | C | 13,867 | 43.2 |
|  |  |  | D.R. Hardman | Lab | 10,116 | 31.5 |
|  |  |  | Sir M.S. Amos | L | 8,124 | 25.3 |
|  |  |  |  |  | 3,751 | 11.7 |
| 1931 | 42,186 | 75.6 | Sir D.G.C. Newton | C | 23,347 | 73.2 |
|  |  |  | Dr. A. Wood | Lab | 8,552 | 26.8 |
|  |  |  |  |  | 14,795 | 46.4 |
| [Elevation to the Peerage — Lord Eltisley] |  |  |  |  |  |  |
| 1934 | 42,939 | 67.8 | R.L. Tufnell | C | 14,896 | 51.2 |
| (8/2) |  |  | Dr. A. Wood | Lab | 12,176 | 41.8 |
|  |  |  | Rev. D. Macfadyen | L | 2,023* | 7.0 |
|  |  |  |  |  | 2,720 | 9.4 |
| 1935 | 44,197 | 73.2 | R.L. Tufnell | C | 18,927 | 58.5 |
|  |  |  | Dr. A. Wood | Lab | 13,436 | 41.5 |
|  |  |  |  |  | 5,491 | 17.0 |
| 1945 | 55,898 | 69.2 | A.L. Symonds | Lab | 19,671 | 50.9 |
|  |  |  | R.L. Tufnell | C | 18,989 | 49.1 |
|  |  |  |  |  | 682 | 1.8 |

## CARLISLE [107]

| Election | Electors | T'out | Candidate | Party | Votes | % |
|---|---|---|---|---|---|---|
| 1918 | 23,066 | 61.8 | W.T. Carr | Co L | 9,511 | 66.8 |
| | | | E. Lowthian | Lab | 4,736 | 33.2 |
| | | | | | 4,775 | 33.6 |
| 1922 | 24,969 | 84.0 | G. Middleton | Lab | 7,870 | 37.6 |
| | | | C.W.H. Lowther | C | 6,569 | 31.3 |
| | | | W.T. Carr | NL | 6,526 | 31.1 |
| | | | | | 1,301 | 6.3 |
| 1923 | 25,634 | 87.8 | G. Middleton | Lab | 9,120 | 40.5 |
| | | | Rt. Hon. W. Watson | C | 8,844 | 39.3 |
| | | | Hon. R.D. Denman | L | 4,541 | 20.2 |
| | | | | | 276 | 1.2 |
| 1924 | 26,326 | 89.1 | Rt. Hon. W. Watson | C | 12,787 | 54.5 |
| | | | G. Middleton | Lab | 10,676 | 45.5 |
| | | | | | 2,111 | 9.0 |

[Seat Vacant at Dissolution (Resignation on appointment as a Lord of Appeal in Ordinary and elevation to a Life Peerage — Lord Thankerton)]

| Election | Electors | T'out | Candidate | Party | Votes | % |
|---|---|---|---|---|---|---|
| 1929 | 34,984 | 90.4 | G. Middleton | Lab | 12,779 | 40.4 |
| | | | E.L. Spears | C | 10,362 | 32.8 |
| | | | A. Creighton | L | 8,484 | 26.8 |
| | | | | | 2,417 | 7.6 |
| 1931 | 36,376 | 86.7 | E.L. Spears | C | 18,079 | 57.3 |
| | | | G. Middleton | Lab | 13,445 | 42.7 |
| | | | | | 4,634 | 14.6 |
| 1935 | 38,608 | 88.3 | E.L. Spears | C | 16,591 | 48.7 |
| | | | A.E. Townend | Lab | 13,956 | 41.0 |
| | | | Miss B.E.M.S. Bliss | L | 3,525* | 10.3 |
| | | | | | 2,635 | 7.7 |
| 1945 | 46,427 | 79.1 | E. Grierson | Lab | 18,505 | 50.4 |
| | | | Sir E.L. Spears | C | 13,356 | 36.4 |
| | | | G.W. Iredell | L | 4,845 | 13.2 |
| | | | | | 5,149 | 14.0 |

# CHELTENHAM [108]

| Election | Electors | T'out | Candidate | Party | Vote | % |
|---|---|---|---|---|---|---|
| 1918 | 23,217 | 68.6 | †Sir J.T. Agg-Gardner | Co C | 9,602 | 60.3 |
| | | | Dr. R. Davies | Ind L | 6,317 | 39.7 |
| | | | | | 3,285 | 20.6 |
| 1922 | 23,997 | 81.8 | Sir J.T. Agg-Gardner | C | 11,383 | 58.0 |
| | | | C. Plaistowe | L | 8,237 | 42.0 |
| | | | | | 3,146 | 16.0 |
| 1923 | 24,768 | 79.5 | Sir J.T. Agg-Gardner | C | 10,514 | 53.4 |
| | | | C. Plaistowe | L | 9,170 | 46.6 |
| | | | | | 1,344 | 6.8 |
| 1924 | 25,454 | 82.7 | Rt. Hon. Sir J.T. Agg-Gardner | C | 11,909 | 56.6 |
| | | | J.S. Holmes | L | 9,146 | 43.4 |
| | | | | | 2,763 | 13.2 |
| [Death] | | | | | | |
| 1928 (26/9) | 26,265 | 80.3 | Sir W.R. Preston | C | 10,438 | 49.5 |
| | | | Sir J.F. Brunner, Bt. | L | 6,678 | 31.7 |
| | | | Miss F.B. Widdowson | Lab | 3,962 | 18.8 |
| | | | | | 3,760 | 17.8 |
| 1929 | 35,993 | 79.8 | Sir W.R. Preston | C | 15,279 | 53.2 |
| | | | F.W. Raffety | L | 8,533 | 29.7 |
| | | | W. Piggott | Lab | 4,920 | 17.1 |
| | | | | | 6,746 | 23.5 |
| 1931 | 36,974 | 75.2 | Sir W.R. Preston | C | 22,524 | 81.1 |
| | | | J. Ramage | Lab | 5,263 | 18.9 |
| | | | | | 17,261 | 62.2 |
| 1935 | 37,428 | 70.4 | Sir W.R. Preston | C | 18,574 | 70.5 |
| | | | Hon. Mrs. E. Pakenham | Lab | 7,784 | 29.5 |
| | | | | | 10,790 | 41.0 |
| [Resignation] | | | | | | |
| 1937 (22/6) | 37,947 | 69.3 | D.L. Lipson | Ind C | 10,533 | 40.0 |
| | | | R.T. Harper | C | 10,194 | 38.8 |
| | | | C.C. Poole | Lab | 5,570 | 21.2 |
| | | | | | 339 | 1.2 |
| 1945 | 49,282 | 75.4 | D.L. Lipson | Nat Ind | 16,081 | 43.3 |
| | | | Miss P.M. Warner | Lab | 11,095 | 29.9 |
| | | | W.W. Hicks Beach | C | 9,972 | 26.8 |
| | | | | | 4,986 | 13.4 |

| Election | Electors | T'out | Candidate | Party | Votes | % |
|---|---|---|---|---|---|---|
| 1918 | 62,066 | 62.4 | E. Manville | Co C | 17,380 | 44.8 |
| | | | R.C. Wallhead | Lab | 10,298 | 26.6 |
| | | | Sir C.C. Mansel, Bt. | L | 4,128* | 10.7 |
| | | | A.C. Bannington | Ind | 3,806* | 9.8 |
| | | | †D.M. Mason | Ind L | 3,145* | 8.1 |
| | | | | | 7,082 | 18.2 |
| 1922 | 60,952 | 80.8 | E. Manville | C | 20,986 | 42.6 |
| | | | R. Williams | Lab | 16,289 | 33.1 |
| | | | J.E. Darnton | L | 11,985 | 24.3 |
| | | | | | 4,697 | 9.5 |
| 1923 | 61,972 | 77.1 | A.A. Purcell | Lab | 16,346 | 34.2 |
| | | | Sir E. Manville | C | 15,726 | 32.9 |
| | | | H.P. Gisborne | L | 15,716 | 32.9 |
| | | | | | 620 | 1.3 |
| 1924 | 63,100 | 84.9 | A.B. Boyd-Carpenter | C | 22,712 | 42.4 |
| | | | A.A. Purcell | Lab | 17,888 | 33.4 |
| | | | H.P. Gisborne | L | 12,953 | 24.2 |
| | | | | | 4,824 | 9.0 |
| 1929 | 84,352 | 82.2 | P.J. Noel-Baker | Lab | 34,255 | 49.4 |
| | | | Sir A.B. Boyd-Carpenter | C | 22,536 | 32.5 |
| | | | J.W. McKay | L | 12,516 | 18.1 |
| | | | | | 11,719 | 16.9 |
| 1931 | 87,839 | 82.7 | W.F. Strickland | C | 44,305 | 61.0 |
| | | | P.J. Noel-Baker | Lab | 28,311 | 39.0 |
| | | | | | 15,994 | 22.0 |
| 1935 | 89,001 | 81.1 | W.F. Strickland | C | 37,313 | 51.7 |
| | | | P.J. Noel-Baker | Lab | 34,841 | 48.3 |
| | | | | | 2,472 | 3.4 |

This constituency was divided in 1945.

Note:—

1918: Bannington was supported by and possibly the nominee of the local branch of the NFDSS. He was also a member of the NSP.

# COVENTRY, EAST   [110]

| Election | Electors | T'out | Candidate | Party | Votes | % |
|----------|----------|-------|-----------|-------|-------|---|
| 1945 | 79,853 | 71.1 | R.H.S. Crossman | Lab | 34,379 | 60.5 |
| | | | H. Weston | C | 15,630 | 27.5 |
| | | | W. Alexander | Com | 3,986* | 7.0 |
| | | | C. Payne | L | 2,820* | 5.0 |
| | | | | | 18,749 | 33.0 |

| Election | Electors | T'out | Candidate | Party | Votes | % |
|---|---|---|---|---|---|---|
| 1945 | 92,991 | 66.1 | M. Edelman | Lab | 38,249 | 62.2 |
| | | | W.F. Strickland | C | 23,236 | 37.8 |
| | | | | | 15,013 | 24.4 |

| Election | Electors | T'out | Candidate | Party | Votes | % |
|---|---|---|---|---|---|---|
| 1918 | 43,669 | 54.1 | G.O. Borwick | Co C | 16,520 | 70.0 |
| | | | J. Trumble | L | 7,094 | 30.0 |
| | | | | | 9,426 | 40.0 |
| 1922 | | | G.K.M. Mason | C | Unopp. | |
| 1923 | 48,760 | 55.7 | G.K.M. Mason | C | 17,085 | 63.0 |
| | | | G.A. Foan | Lab | 10,054 | 37.0 |
| | | | | | 7,031 | 26.0 |
| 1924 | 50,697 | 72.8 | G.K.M. Mason | C | 25,972 | 70.3 |
| | | | G.A. Foan | Lab | 10,954 | 29.7 |
| | | | | | 15,018 | 40.6 |
| 1929 | 74,835 | 69.8 | G.K.M. Mason | C | 26,336 | 50.4 |
| | | | G.A. Foan | Lab | 13,852 | 26.5 |
| | | | C.W. Nunneley | L | 12,053 | 23.1 |
| | | | | | 12,484 | 23.9 |
| 1931 | 81,305 | 69.4 | G.K.M. Mason | C | 45,595 | 80.9 |
| | | | H.W. Ray | Lab | 10,795 | 19.1 |
| | | | | | 34,800 | 61.8 |
| 1935 | 83,986 | 64.6 | Hon. G.K.M. Mason | C | 36,383 | 67.1 |
| | | | F. Mitchell | Lab | 17,872 | 32.9 |
| | | | | | 18,511 | 34.2 |
| [Resignation] | | | | | | |
| 1940 (19/6) | 85,396 | 18.3 | H.U. Willink | C | 14,163 | 90.7 |
| | | | A.L. Lucas | Ind | 1,445* | 9.3 |
| | | | | | 12,718 | 81.4 |
| 1945 | 77,779* | 73.2 | Rt. Hon. H.U. Willink | C | 23,417 | 41.1 |
| | | | Miss M.G. Billson | Lab | 22,810 | 40.1 |
| | | | J.M. Howard | L | 10,714 | 18.8 |
| | | | | | 607 | 1.0 |
| [Resignation] | | | | | | |
| 1948 (11/3) | 89,606 | 74.8 | F.W. Harris | C | 36,200 | 54.0 |
| | | | Hon. H.G. Nicolson | Lab | 24,536 | 36.6 |
| | | | D.C.T. Bennett | L | 6,321* | 9.4 |
| | | | | | 11,664 | 17.4 |

| Election | Electors | T'out | Candidate | Party | Votes | % |
|---|---|---|---|---|---|---|
| 1918 | 45,115 | 55.0 | †I.Z. Malcolm | Co C | 17,813 | 71.8 |
| | | | H.T. Muggeridge | Lab | 7,006 | 28.2 |
| | | | | | 10,807 | 43.6 |
| [Resignation] | | | | | | |
| 1919 | 46,900 | 45.5 | Sir A.M. Smith | Co C | 11,777 | 55.2 |
| (14/11) | | | H. Houlder | L | 9,573 | 44.8 |
| | | | | | 2,204 | 10.4 |
| 1922 | 48,904 | 66.4 | Sir A.M. Smith | C | 15,356 | 47.3 |
| | | | H.T. Muggeridge | Lab | 8,942 | 27.5 |
| | | | T.W. Dobson | L | 8,183 | 25.2 |
| | | | | | 6,414 | 19.8 |
| 1923 | 49,634 | 63.4 | Sir W. Mitchell-Thomson, Bt. | C | 14,310 | 45.5 |
| | | | H.T. Muggeridge | Lab | 9,926 | 31.6 |
| | | | E.W. Cemlyn-Jones | L | 7,208 | 22.9 |
| | | | | | 4,384 | 13.9 |
| 1924 | 50,964 | 72.0 | Sir W. Mitchell-Thomson, Bt. | C | 23,734 | 64.6 |
| | | | H.T. Muggeridge | Lab | 12,979 | 35.4 |
| | | | | | 10,755 | 29.2 |
| 1929 | 70,107 | 67.4 | Rt. Hon. Sir W. Mitchell-Thomson, Bt. | C | 23,258 | 49.2 |
| | | | E.W. Wilton | Lab | 13,793 | 29.2 |
| | | | A.S. Elwell-Sutton | L | 10,218 | 21.6 |
| | | | | | 9,465 | 20.0 |
| 1931 | 74,081 | 68.3 | Rt. Hon. Sir W. Mitchell-Thomson, Bt. | C | 40,672 | 80.3 |
| | | | T. Crawford | Lab | 9,950 | 19.7 |
| | | | | | 30,722 | 60.6 |
| [Elevation to the Peerage — Lord Selsdon] | | | | | | |
| 1932 | 74,081 | 38.2 | H.G. Williams | C | 19,126 | 67.5 |
| (9/2) | | | R.P. Messel | Lab | 9,189 | 32.5 |
| | | | | | 9,937 | 35.0 |
| 1935 | 78,703 | 65.2 | H.G. Williams | C | 31,971 | 62.3 |
| | | | T. Crawford | Lab | 14,900 | 29.0 |
| | | | D.W.A. Llewellyn | L | 4,440* | 8.7 |
| | | | | | 17,071 | 33.3 |
| 1945 | 73,146* | 70.8 | D.R. Rees-Williams | Lab | 27,650 | 53.4 |
| | | | Sir H.G. Williams | C | 24,147 | 46.6 |
| | | | | | 3,503 | 6.8 |

## DAGENHAM  [114]

| Election | Electors | T'out | Candidate | Party | Votes | % |
|---|---|---|---|---|---|---|
| 1945 | 63,593 | 68.9 | J. Parker | Lab | 36,686 | 83.7 |
|  |  |  | A.E. Cooper | C | 7,147 | 16.3 |
|  |  |  |  |  | 29,539 | 67.4 |

| Election | Electors | T'out | Candidate | Party | Votes | % |
|---|---|---|---|---|---|---|
| 1918 | 28,660 | 67.8 | †Rt. Hon. H.P. Pease | Co C | 11,951 | 61.5 |
| | | | A.H. Scott | L | 7,494 | 38.5 |
| | | | | | 4,457 | 23.0 |
| 1922 | 30,411 | 88.0 | Rt. Hon. H.P. Pease | C | 13,286 | 49.7 |
| | | | W.J. Sherwood | Lab | 9,048 | 33.8 |
| | | | T. Crooks | L | 4,419 | 16.5 |
| | | | | | 4,238 | 15.9 |

[Elevation to the Peerage — Lord Daryngton of Witley]

| Election | Electors | T'out | Candidate | Party | Votes | % |
|---|---|---|---|---|---|---|
| 1923 | 30,411 | 85.3 | W.E. Pease | C | 14,684 | 56.6 |
| (28/2) | | | W.J. Sherwood | Lab | 11,271 | 43.4 |
| | | | | | 3,413 | 13.2 |
| 1923 | 31,801 | 86.8 | W.E. Pease | C | 11,638 | 42.2 |
| | | | W.J. Sherwood | Lab | 9,284 | 33.6 |
| | | | R.A. Wright | L | 6,697 | 24.2 |
| | | | | | 2,354 | 8.6 |
| 1924 | 32,735 | 86.1 | W.E. Pease | C | 15,174 | 53.8 |
| | | | A.L. Shepherd | Lab | 13,008 | 46.2 |
| | | | | | 2,166 | 7.6 |

[Death]

| Election | Electors | T'out | Candidate | Party | Votes | % |
|---|---|---|---|---|---|---|
| 1926 | 33,290 | 87.6 | A.L. Shepherd | Lab | 12,965 | 44.5 |
| (17/2) | | | E.H. Pease | C | 12,636 | 43.3 |
| | | | J.P. Dickie | L | 3,573* | 12.2 |
| | | | | | 329 | 1.2 |
| 1929 | 43,327 | 89.6 | A.L. Shepherd | Lab | 17,061 | 44.0 |
| | | | Viscount Castlereagh | C | 15,596 | 40.2 |
| | | | J.J. Richardson | L | 6,149 | 15.8 |
| | | | | | 1,465 | 3.8 |
| 1931 | 44,947 | 89.5 | C.U. Peat | C | 24,416 | 60.7 |
| | | | A.L. Shepherd | Lab | 15,798 | 39.3 |
| | | | | | 8,618 | 21.4 |
| 1935 | 47,676 | 84.8 | C.U. Peat | C | 22,320 | 55.2 |
| | | | A.L. Shepherd | Lab | 18,105 | 44.8 |
| | | | | | 4,215 | 10.4 |
| 1945 | 54,838 | 79.9 | D.R. Hardman | Lab | 21,442 | 49.0 |
| | | | C.U. Peat | C | 13,153 | 30.0 |
| | | | G.V. Rogers | L | 9,215 | 21.0 |
| | | | | | 8,289 | 19.0 |

| Election | Electors | T'out | Candidate | Party | Votes | % |
|---|---|---|---|---|---|---|
| 1945 | 71,591 | 74.9 | N.N. Dodds | Lab/Co-op | 36,666 | 68.4 |
| | | | R.E.W. Grubb | C | 16,951 | 31.6 |
| | | | | | 19,715 | 36.8 |

## DERBY [117]
### (Two Seats)

| Election | Electors | T'out | Candidate | Party | Votes | % |
|---|---|---|---|---|---|---|
| 1918 | 61,538 | 65.5 | †Rt. Hon. J.H. Thomas | Lab | 25,145 | 37.8 |
| | | | A. Green | C | 14,920 | 22.4 |
| | | | W.B. Rowbotham | L | 13,408 | 20.2 |
| | | | H.M. Smith | NDP | 13,012 | 19.6 |
| | | | | | 11,737 | 17.6 |
| | | | | | 1,512 | 2.2 |
| 1922 | 62,194 | 84.0 | Rt. Hon. J.H. Thomas | Lab | 25,215 | 27.0 |
| | | | C.H. Roberts | L | 24,068 | 25.8 |
| | | | A. Green | C | 22,240 | 23.9 |
| | | | W.R. Raynes | Lab | 21,677 | 23.3 |
| | | | | | 2,975 | 3.1 |
| | | | | | 1,828 | 1.9 |
| 1923 | 63,569 | 81.1 | Rt. Hon. J.H. Thomas | Lab | 24,887 | 29.0 |
| | | | W.R. Raynes | Lab | 20,318 | 23.7 |
| | | | H.F. Wright | C | 20,070 | 23.4 |
| | | | C.H. Roberts | L | 10,669 | 12.5 |
| | | | T.C. Newbold | Ind | 9,772 | 11.4 |
| | | | | | 248 | 0.3 |
| 1924 | 65,531 | 85.2 | Rt. Hon. J.H. Thomas | Lab | 27,423 | 25.7 |
| | | | Sir R.H. Luce | C | 25,425 | 23.8 |
| | | | W.R. Raynes | Lab | 25,172 | 23.6 |
| | | | Mrs. H. Hulse | C | 21,700 | 20.3 |
| | | | J. Henderson-Stewart | L | 7,083 | 6.6 |
| | | | | | 5,723 | 5.4 |
| | | | | | 253 | 0.2 |
| 1929 | 85,250 | 82.6 | Rt. Hon. J.H. Thomas | Lab (N Lab) | 39,688 | 30.0 |
| | | | W.R. Raynes | Lab | 36,237 | 27.4 |
| | | | Sir R.H. Luce | C | 24,553 | 18.6 |
| | | | J.A. Aiton | C | 20,443 | 15.4 |
| | | | L. du G. Peach | L | 11,317 | 8.6 |
| | | | | | 11,684 | 8.8 |
| 1931 | 85,542 | 84.5 | Rt. Hon. J.H. Thomas | N Lab | 49,257 | 35.4 |
| | | | W.A. Reid | C | 47,729 | 34.3 |
| | | | W.R. Raynes | Lab | 21,841 | 15.7 |
| | | | W. Halls | Lab | 20,241 | 14.6 |
| | | | | | 27,416 | 19.7 |
| | | | | | 25,888 | 18.6 |
| 1935 | 82,571 | 77.0 | W.A. Reid | C | 37,707 | 30.2 |
| | | | Rt. Hon. J.H. Thomas | N Lab | 37,566 | 30.1 |
| | | | H.A. Hind | Lab | 25,037 | 20.0 |
| | | | L.J. Barnes | Lab | 24,594 | 19.7 |
| | | | | | 12,670 | 10.2 |
| | | | | | 12,529 | 10.1 |
| [Resignation of Thomas] | | | | | | |
| 1936 (9/7) | 82,571 | 65.5 | P.J. Noel-Baker | Lab | 28,419 | 52.5 |
| | | | A.G. Church | N Lab | 25,666 | 47.5 |
| | | | | | 2,753 | 5.0 |

# DERBY (Cont.)

| Election | Electors | T'out | Candidate | Party | Votes | % |
|----------|----------|-------|-----------|-------|-------|---|
| 1945 | 82,326 | 77.5 | P.J. Noel-Baker | Lab | 42,196 | 33.6 |
| | | | C.A.B. Wilcock | Lab | 40,800 | 32.5 |
| | | | F.H.A.J. Lochrane | C | 21,460 | 17.1 |
| | | | J.M. Bemrose | C | 21,125 | 16.8 |
| | | | | | 19,340 | 15.4 |

Note:—

1923: Newbold stated that he was standing as an Independent and if elected his main endeavour would be devoted to the welfare of ex-servicemen.

The day following his nomination a meeting of the Full Street Branch of the British Legion in Derby adopted Newbold as their candidate by 25 votes to 7 with four abstentions. It was stated that due to the lack of time before polling day it would not be possible for other British Legion Branches in Derby to consider the question of supporting Newbold. Following this meeting several members resigned and complained that the adoption of Newbold was unconstitutional and undemocratic.

The circumstances surrounding his candidature are obscure but he did admit that there were several Conservatives among his sponsors and it appears probable that he had the backing of a number of Conservative supporters in Derby who felt that their party should have contested both seats.

# DEWSBURY [118]

| Election | Electors | T'out | Candidate | Party | Votes | % |
|---|---|---|---|---|---|---|
| 1918 | 27,592 | 67.3 | E.W. Pickering | Co C | 7,853 | 42.3 |
| | | | B. Riley | Lab | 5,596 | 30.1 |
| | | | †Rt. Hon. W. Runciman | L | 5,130 | 27.6 |
| | | | | | 2,257 | 12.2 |
| 1922 | 28,145 | 84.0 | B. Riley | Lab | 8,821 | 37.4 |
| | | | T.E. Harvey | L | 8,065 | 34.1 |
| | | | O. Peake | C | 6,744 | 28.5 |
| | | | | | 756 | 3.3 |
| 1923 | 28,431 | 70.7 | T.E. Harvey | L | 11,179 | 55.6 |
| | | | B. Riley | Lab | 8,923 | 44.4 |
| | | | | | 2,256 | 11.2 |
| 1924 | 28,677 | 84.3 | B. Riley | Lab | 9,941 | 41.1 |
| | | | F.W. Skelsey | C | 7,516 | 31.1 |
| | | | T.E. Harvey | L | 6,723 | 27.8 |
| | | | | | 2,425 | 10.0 |
| 1929 | 36,250 | 86.1 | B. Riley | Lab | 14,420 | 46.2 |
| | | | R.F. Walker | L | 10,607 | 34.0 |
| | | | J.W.W. Shuttleworth | C | 6,175 | 19.8 |
| | | | | | 3,813 | 12.2 |
| 1931 | 36,286 | 84.2 | W.R. Rea | L | 19,463 | 63.7 |
| | | | B. Riley | Lab | 11,101 | 36.3 |
| | | | | | 8,362 | 27.4 |
| 1935 | 36,875 | 80.8 | B. Riley | Lab | 14,066 | 47.2 |
| | | | J. Fennell | N Lab | 8,798 | 29.5 |
| | | | Sir W.R. Rea, Bt. | L | 6,933 | 23.3 |
| | | | | | 5,268 | 17.7 |
| 1945 | 36,217 | 80.1 | W.T. Paling | Lab | 16,330 | 56.2 |
| | | | E.E.R. Kilner | NL | 8,674 | 29.9 |
| | | | T.M. Banks | L | 4,023 | 13.9 |
| | | | | | 7,656 | 26.3 |

# DUDLEY [119]

| Election | Electors | T'out | Candidate | Party | Votes | % |
|---|---|---|---|---|---|---|
| 1918 | 25,103 | 60.4 | †Sir A.S.T. Griffith-Boscawen | Co C | 9,126 | 60.2 |
| | | | W.B. Steer | Lab | 6,046 | 39.8 |
| | | | | | 3,080 | 20.4 |
| [Appointed Minister of Agriculture and Fisheries] | | | | | | |
| 1921 | 25,305† | 79.9 | J. Wilson | Lab | 10,244 | 50.7 |
| (3/3) | | | Rt. Hon. Sir A.S.T. Griffith-Boscawen | Co C | 9,968 | 49.3 |
| | | | | | 276 | 1.4 |
| 1922 | 25,923 | 82.5 | C.E. Lloyd | C | 12,876 | 60.2 |
| | | | J. Wilson | Lab | 8,522 | 39.8 |
| | | | | | 4,354 | 20.4 |
| 1923 | 26,257 | 78.8 | C.E. Lloyd | C | 10,227 | 49.4 |
| | | | F.J. Ballard | L | 8,510 | 41.1 |
| | | | R.F. Smith | Lab | 1,958* | 9.5 |
| | | | | | 1,717 | 8.3 |
| 1924 | 26,826 | 80.2 | C.E. Lloyd | C | 11,199 | 52.1 |
| | | | O.R. Baldwin | Lab | 10,314 | 47.9 |
| | | | | | 885 | 4.2 |
| 1929 | 34,883 | 81.6 | O.R. Baldwin | Lab (Ind) (Lab) | 13,551 | 47.6 |
| | | | C.E. Lloyd | C | 10,508 | 36.9 |
| | | | T.I. Clough | L | 4,399 | 15.5 |
| | | | | | 3,043 | 10.7 |
| 1931 | 34,818 | 80.7 | D.J.B. Joel | C | 16,009 | 56.9 |
| | | | W. Hadgkiss | Lab | 12,105 | 43.1 |
| | | | | | 3,904 | 13.8 |
| 1935 | 33,823 | 75.3 | D.J.B. Joel | C | 13,958 | 54.8 |
| | | | Rt. Hon. W.W. Benn | Lab | 11,509 | 45.2 |
| | | | | | 2,449 | 9.6 |
| [Death] | | | | | | |
| 1941 | 31,966 | 34.7 | C.E. Lloyd | C | 6,234 | 56.1 |
| (23/7) | | | N.P. Billing | Nat Ind | 4,869 | 43.9 |
| | | | | | 1,365 | 12.2 |
| 1945 | 33,363 | 73.7 | G.E.C. Wigg | Lab | 15,439 | 62.8 |
| | | | E.T.C. Brinton | C | 9,156 | 37.2 |
| | | | | | 6,283 | 25.6 |

Notes:—

1921: Griffith-Boscawen retained office following his defeat and was elected for Somerest, Taunton at a by-election on April 8, 1921.

1941: Billing advocated a policy of aerial reprisals against Germany.

# EALING [120]

| Election | Electors | T'out | Candidate | Party | Votes | % |
|---|---|---|---|---|---|---|
| 1918 | 28,687 | 60.4 | †Sir H. Nield | Co C | 13,710 | 79.2 |
| | | | A.H. Chilton | Lab | 3,610 | 20.8 |
| | | | | | 10,100 | 58.4 |
| 1922 | 32,457 | 65.8 | Sir H. Nield | C | 14,507 | 67.9 |
| | | | A.H. Chilton | Lab | 6,128 | 28.7 |
| | | | L.M.M. Hall | Ind C | 719* | 3.4 |
| | | | | | 8,379 | 39.2 |
| 1923 | 33,699 | 69.0 | Sir H. Nield | C | 12,349 | 53.1 |
| | | | A.W. Bradford | L | 6,410 | 27.6 |
| | | | A.H. Chilton | Lab | 4,495 | 19.3 |
| | | | | | 5,939 | 25.5 |
| 1924 | 34,623 | 73.2 | Rt. Hon. Sir H. Nield | C | 18,572 | 73.3 |
| | | | A.H. Chilton | Lab | 6,765 | 26.7 |
| | | | | | 11,807 | 46.6 |
| 1929 | 51,253 | 73.4 | Rt. Hon. Sir H. Nield | C | 20,503 | 54.4 |
| | | | J.W. Maycock | Lab | 9,093 | 24.2 |
| | | | A.P. Grundy | L | 8,042 | 21.4 |
| | | | | | 11,410 | 30.2 |
| 1931 | 53,153 | 74.6 | Sir F.B. Sanderson, Bt. | C | 32,792 | 82.7 |
| | | | J.W. Maycock | Lab | 6,857 | 17.3 |
| | | | | | 25,935 | 65.4 |
| 1935 | 55,657 | 69.1 | Sir F.B. Sanderson, Bt. | C | 28,472 | 74.1 |
| | | | M. Auliff | Lab | 9,972 | 25.9 |
| | | | | | 18,500 | 48.2 |

This constituency was divided in 1945.

## EALING, EAST [121]

| Election | Electors | T'out | Candidate | Party | Votes | % |
|---|---|---|---|---|---|---|
| 1945 | 65,485 | 73.2 | Sir F.B. Sanderson, Bt. | C | 22,916 | 47.8 |
|  |  |  | D.J. Johnstone | Lab | 18,619 | 38.9 |
|  |  |  | H.W. Foster | L | 6,377 | 13.3 |
|  |  |  |  |  | 4,297 | 8.9 |

## EALING, WEST [122]

| Election | Electors | T'out | Candidate | Party | Votes | % |
|---|---|---|---|---|---|---|
| 1945 | 64,866 | 74.4 | J.H. Hudson | Lab/Co-op | 29,115 | 60.3 |
| | | | B. Sunley | C | 12,880 | 26.7 |
| | | | H.M. Lewis | L | 6,258 | 13.0 |
| | | | | | 16,235 | 33.6 |

## EAST HAM, NORTH  [123]

| Election | Electors | T'out | Candidate | Party | Votes | % |
|---|---|---|---|---|---|---|
| 1918 | 34,219 | 47.3 | †Sir J.H. Bethell, Bt. | Co L | 9,436 | 58.3 |
| | | | W. Mann | Nat P | 6,748 | 41.7 |
| | | | | | 2,688 | 16.6 |
| 1922 | 34,759 | 69.8 | C.W. Crook | C | 7,215 | 29.7 |
| | | | Miss A.S. Lawrence | Lab | 6,747 | 27.8 |
| | | | E. Edwards | NL | 4,775 | 19.7 |
| | | | H. Osborn | Ind | 4,021 | 16.6 |
| | | | J.N. Emery | L | 1,504* | 6.2 |
| | | | | | 468 | 1.9 |
| 1923 | 35,410 | 69.0 | Miss A.S. Lawrence | Lab | 8,727 | 35.7 |
| | | | E. Edwards | L | 8,311 | 34.0 |
| | | | C.W. Crook | C | 7,393 | 30.3 |
| | | | | | 416 | 1.7 |
| 1924 | 36,496 | 77.5 | C.W. Crook | C | 11,194 | 39.6 |
| | | | Miss A.S. Lawrence | Lab | 10,137 | 35.8 |
| | | | E. Edwards | L | 6,970 | 24.6 |
| | | | | | 1,057 | 3.8 |
| [Death] | | | | | | |
| 1926 | 37,057† | 71.7 | Miss A.S. Lawrence | Lab | 10,798 | 40.7 |
| (29/4) | | | G.W.S. Jarrett | C | 9,171 | 34.5 |
| | | | E.L. Burgin | L | 6,603 | 24.8 |
| | | | | | 1,627 | 6.2 |
| 1929 | 46,165 | 72.0 | Miss A.S. Lawrence | Lab | 13,969 | 42.1 |
| | | | J. Lees-Jones | C | 11,805 | 35.5 |
| | | | T.A. Evans | L | 7,459 | 22.4 |
| | | | | | 2,164 | 6.6 |
| 1931 | 47,002 | 73.4 | J. Mayhew | C | 22,730 | 65.9 |
| | | | Miss A.S. Lawrence | Lab | 11,769 | 34.1 |
| | | | | | 10,961 | 31.8 |
| 1935 | 46,252 | 65.0 | J. Mayhew | C | 15,295 | 50.9 |
| | | | T.W. Burden | Lab | 14,762 | 49.1 |
| | | | | | 533 | 1.8 |
| 1945 | 36,794 | 71.2 | P. Daines | Lab/Co-op | 18,373 | 70.2 |
| | | | Sir J. Mayhew | C | 7,814 | 29.8 |
| | | | | | 10,559 | 40.4 |

Note:—

1922:  Osborn sought election as a 'People's' candidate.

# EAST HAM, SOUTH  [124]

| Election | Electors | T'out | Candidate | Party | Votes | % |
|---|---|---|---|---|---|---|
| 1918 | 32,472 | 57.5 | †A.C. Edwards | Co NDP | 7,972 | 42.8 |
|  |  |  | R.F.F. Hamlett | C | 5,661 | 30.3 |
|  |  |  | †Rt. Hon. A. Henderson | Lab | 5,024 | 26.9 |
|  |  |  |  |  | 2,311 | 12.5 |
| 1922 | 33,070 | 66.3 | A.J. Barnes | Lab/Co-op | 10,566 | 48.1 |
|  |  |  | E. Smallwood | L | 6,567 | 30.0 |
|  |  |  | A.C. Edwards | NL | 4,793 | 21.9 |
|  |  |  |  |  | 3,999 | 18.1 |
| 1923 | 33,837 | 68.5 | A.J. Barnes | Lab/Co-op | 11,402 | 49.2 |
|  |  |  | E. Smallwood | L | 8,772 | 37.8 |
|  |  |  | H.J. Ward | C | 3,011 | 13.0 |
|  |  |  |  |  | 2,630 | 11.4 |
| 1924 | 34,651 | 75.9 | A.J. Barnes | Lab/Co-op | 13,644 | 51.9 |
|  |  |  | E.M.C. Denny | L | 12,656 | 48.1 |
|  |  |  |  |  | 988 | 3.8 |
| 1929 | 47,261 | 73.8 | A.J. Barnes | Lab/Co-op | 18,956 | 54.3 |
|  |  |  | H.J. Duggan | C | 8,854 | 25.4 |
|  |  |  | E.M.C. Denny | L | 7,085 | 20.3 |
|  |  |  |  |  | 10,102 | 28.9 |
| 1931 | 48,431 | 70.3 | M. Campbell-Johnston | C | 18,300 | 53.8 |
|  |  |  | A.J. Barnes | Lab/Co-op | 15,737 | 46.2 |
|  |  |  |  |  | 2,563 | 7.6 |
| 1935 | 47,950 | 66.6 | A.J. Barnes | Lab/Co-op | 18,949 | 59.3 |
|  |  |  | M. Campbell-Johnston | C | 12,993 | 40.7 |
|  |  |  |  |  | 5,956 | 18.6 |
| 1945 | 37,037 | 69.9 | A.J. Barnes | Lab/Co-op | 19,168 | 74.0 |
|  |  |  | M.G. Munthe | C | 6,734 | 26.0 |
|  |  |  |  |  | 12,434 | 48.0 |

# ECCLES [125]

| Election | Electors | T'out | Candidate | Party | Votes | % |
|---|---|---|---|---|---|---|
| 1918 | 34,702 | 55.4 | M. Stevens | Co C | 15,821 | 82.3 |
| | | | †R.D. Holt | L | 3,408 | 17.7 |
| | | | | | 12,413 | 64.6 |
| | | | | | | |
| 1922 | 35,912 | 77.7 | J. Buckle | Lab | 14,354 | 51.4 |
| | | | M. Stevens | C | 13,551 | 48.6 |
| | | | | | 803 | 2.8 |
| | | | | | | |
| 1923 | 36,585 | 78.2 | J. Buckle | Lab | 12,227 | 42.8 |
| | | | M. Stevens | C | 10,364 | 36.2 |
| | | | W.S. Ashton | L | 6,011 | 21.0 |
| | | | | | 1,863 | 6.6 |
| | | | | | | |
| 1924 | 38,257 | 82.7 | A. Bethel | C | 16,833 | 53.2 |
| | | | J. Buckle | Lab | 14,798 | 46.8 |
| | | | | | 2,035 | 6.4 |
| | | | | | | |
| 1929 | 50,203 | 81.9 | D.L. Mort | Lab | 20,489 | 49.8 |
| | | | A. Bethel | C | 12,232 | 29.8 |
| | | | H. Wilde | L | 8,374 | 20.4 |
| | | | | | 8,257 | 20.0 |
| | | | | | | |
| 1931 | 51,643 | 81.6 | J. Potter | C | 26,049 | 61.8 |
| | | | D.L. Mort | Lab | 16,101 | 38.2 |
| | | | | | 9,948 | 23.6 |
| | | | | | | |
| 1935 | 52,980 | 80.0 | R.A. Cary | C | 22,310 | 52.7 |
| | | | J. Grierson | Lab | 20,055 | 47.3 |
| | | | | | 2,255 | 5.4 |
| | | | | | | |
| 1945 | 57,059 | 78.9 | W.T. Proctor | Lab | 23,008 | 51.1 |
| | | | R.A. Cary | C | 15,562 | 34.6 |
| | | | A.G. Pollitt | L | 6,215 | 13.8 |
| | | | A.B. Brocklehurst | Ind Prog | 211* | 0.5 |
| | | | | | 7,446 | 16.5 |

Note:—

1945: Brocklehurst was supported by the Society of Friends (Quakers).

# EDMONTON [126]

| Election | Electors | T'out | Candidate | Party | Votes | % |
|----------|----------|-------|-----------|-------|-------|---|
| 1918 | 28,930 | 48.2 | Sir A.H. Warren | Co C | 6,891 | 49.4 |
| | | | F.A. Broad | Lab | 3,575 | 25.7 |
| | | | H.H. Vivian | L | 2,245 | 16.1 |
| | | | H. Barrass | Ind | 1,223* | 8.8 |
| | | | | | 3,316 | 23.7 |
| 1922 | 29,662 | 62.8 | F.A. Broad | Lab | 8,407 | 45.1 |
| | | | Sir A.H. Warren | C | 6,698 | 36.0 |
| | | | E.T. Rhymer | L | 3,522 | 18.9 |
| | | | | | 1,709 | 9.1 |
| 1923 | 30,423 | 54.8 | F.A. Broad | Lab | 10,735 | 64.4 |
| | | | R.S. Brown | C | 5,943 | 35.6 |
| | | | | | 4,792 | 28.8 |
| 1924 | 31,020 | 70.6 | F.A. Broad | Lab | 11,614 | 53.1 |
| | | | G.W.S. Jarrett | C | 10,278 | 46.9 |
| | | | | | 1,336 | 6.2 |
| 1929 | 42,586 | 69.5 | F.A. Broad | Lab | 17,555 | 59.3 |
| | | | G.W.S. Jarrett | C | 12,044 | 40.7 |
| | | | | | 5,511 | 18.6 |
| 1931 | 47,044 | 70.2 | J.R. Chalmers | C | 18,774 | 56.8 |
| | | | F.A. Broad | Lab/Co-op | 14,250 | 43.2 |
| | | | | | 4,524 | 13.6 |
| 1935 | 61,640 | 64.5 | F.A. Broad | Lab/Co-op | 21,940 | 55.2 |
| | | | J.R. Rutherford | C | 17,813 | 44.8 |
| | | | | | 4,127 | 10.4 |
| 1945 | 70,470 | 69.0 | E.F.M. Durbin | Lab | 33,163 | 68.2 |
| | | | G.M. Sparrow | C | 14,094 | 29.0 |
| | | | J.A. Ward | Ind Prog | 1,382* | 2.8 |
| | | | | | 19,069 | 39.2 |
| [Death] | | | | | | |
| 1948 (13/11) | 78,204 | 62.7 | A.H. Albu | Lab | 26,164 | 53.4 |
| | | | E.P. Hubbard | C | 22,837 | 46.6 |
| | | | | | 3,327 | 6.8 |

Notes:—

1918: Barrass was the nominee of a local organisation called the Edmonton Pro-Ally and Labour Party which was formed in August 1916 following a split in the Edmonton branch of the British Socialist Party.

1931: Chalmers changed his surname by Royal Licence in 1933 to Rutherford.

| Election | Electors | T'out | Candidate | Party | Votes | % |
|---|---|---|---|---|---|---|
| 1918 | 31,267 | 68.2 | †Sir R.H.S.D.L. Newman, Bt. | Co C | 12,524 | 58.7 |
| | | | L.W.J. Costello | L | 8,806 | 41.3 |
| | | | | | 3,718 | 17.4 |
| 1922 | 29,480 | 85.6 | Sir R.H.S.D.L. Newman, Bt. | C | 14,326 | 56.7 |
| | | | L.W.J. Costello | L | 10,920 | 43.3 |
| | | | | | 3,406 | 13.4 |
| 1923 | 30,354 | 72.6 | Sir R.H.S.D.L. Newman, Bt. | C | 14,908 | 67.7 |
| | | | G.L.R. Small | Lab | 7,123 | 32.3 |
| | | | | | 7,785 | 35.4 |
| 1924 | 30,729 | 82.1 | Sir R.H.S.D.L. Newman, Bt. | C (Ind) | 14,522 | 57.5 |
| | | | A.J. Penny | Lab | 6,359 | 25.2 |
| | | | T.F. Day | L | 4,359 | 17.3 |
| | | | | | 8,163 | 32.3 |
| 1929 | 41,056 | 81.9 | Sir R.H.S.D.L. Newman, Bt. | Ind | 16,642 | 49.5 |
| | | | J.L. Jones | Lab | 9,361 | 27.8 |
| | | | G.D. Roberts | C | 7,622 | 22.7 |
| | | | | | 7,281 | 21.7 |
| 1931 | 43,517 | 84.8 | A.C. Reed | C | 20,360 | 55.2 |
| | | | Lady Acland | L | 8,571 | 23.2 |
| | | | J.V. Delahaye | Lab | 7,958 | 21.6 |
| | | | | | 11,789 | 32.0 |
| 1935 | 45,964 | 75.9 | A.C. Reed | C | 21,192 | 60.8 |
| | | | J.S. Cripps | Lab | 13,674 | 39.2 |
| | | | | | 7,518 | 21.6 |
| 1945 | 50,971 | 74.3 | J.C. Maude | C | 16,420 | 43.4 |
| | | | R.J. Travess | Lab | 15,245 | 40.2 |
| | | | Mrs. F.E.G. Morgan | L | 6,220 | 16.4 |
| | | | | | 1,175 | 3.2 |

Note:—

1924: Newman's attitude and voting record on various political issues failed to satisfy the local Conservative Association who decided in 1927 to adopt another candidate at the next election. Newman then announced that he would seek re-election as an Independent and the Conservative whip was withdrawn from him.

| Election | Electors | T'out | Candidate | Party | Votes | % |
|---|---|---|---|---|---|---|
| 1918 | 55,443 | 54.6 | H.C. Surtees | Co C | 17,215 | 56.9 |
| | | | J. Brotherton | Lab | 7,212 | 23.8 |
| | | | †Sir H. Elverston | L | 5,833 | 19.3 |
| | | | | | 10,003 | 33.1 |
| 1922 | 54,741 | 78.4 | J. Brotherton | Lab | 18,795 | 43.8 |
| | | | H.C. Surtees | C | 13,424 | 31.3 |
| | | | J.P. Dickie | L | 10,679 | 24.9 |
| | | | | | 5,371 | 12.5 |
| 1923 | 55,525 | 73.2 | J.P. Dickie | L | 17,344 | 42.7 |
| | | | J. Brotherton | Lab | 16,689 | 41.1 |
| | | | G.F.S. Christie | C | 6,592 | 16.2 |
| | | | | | 655 | 1.6 |
| 1924 | 56,658 | 82.7 | J. Beckett | Lab | 23,514 | 50.2 |
| | | | H. Philipson | C | 14,178 | 30.2 |
| | | | J.P. Dickie | L | 9,185 | 19.6 |
| | | | | | 9,336 | 20.0 |
| 1929 | 73,099 | 73.9 | Sir J.B. Melville | Lab | 28,393 | 52.6 |
| | | | I.L. Orr-Ewing | C | 11,644 | 21.5 |
| | | | J. Fennell | L | 10,314 | 19.1 |
| | | | J.L. Watson | Ind | 3,688* | 6.8 |
| | | | | | 16,749 | 31.1 |
| [Death] | | | | | | |
| 1931 | 72,964 | 60.8 | H. Evans | Lab | 22,893 | 51.6 |
| (8/6) | | | C.M. Headlam | C | 21,501 | 48.4 |
| | | | | | 1,392 | 3.2 |
| [Seat Vacant at Dissolution (Death)] | | | | | | |
| 1931 | 73,872 | 78.3 | T. Magnay | NL | 34,764 | 60.1 |
| | | | E. Bevin | Lab | 21,826 | 37.7 |
| | | | J.S. Barr | NP | 1,077* | 1.9 |
| | | | J. Fennell | N Lab | 187* | 0.3 |
| | | | | | 12,938 | 22.4 |
| 1935 | 73,083 | 74.7 | T. Magnay | NL | 28,772 | 52.7 |
| | | | J.M. Wilson | Lab | 25,804 | 47.3 |
| | | | | | 2,968 | 5.4 |
| 1945 | 71,692 | 76.0 | K. Zilliacus | Lab (Ind Lab) | 36,736 | 67.5 |
| | | | T. Magnay | NL | 17,719 | 32.5 |
| | | | | | 19,017 | 35.0 |

Notes:—

1931:   Fennell retired after nomination in favour of Magnay.

1945:   Zilliacus joined the Labour Independent Group when it was formed in June 1949.

# GLOUCESTER [129]

| Election | Electors | T'out | Candidate | Party | Votes | % |
|---|---|---|---|---|---|---|
| 1918 | 25,006 | 66.3 | Sir J. Bruton | Co C | 8,470 | 51.1 |
| | | | T.H. Mordey | L | 5,246 | 31.6 |
| | | | W.L. Edwards | Lab | 2,860 | 17.3 |
| | | | | | 3,224 | 19.5 |
| 1922 | 25,784 | 84.7 | Sir J. Bruton | C | 7,922 | 36.3 |
| | | | M.P. Price | Lab | 7,871 | 36.0 |
| | | | A.W. Stanton | L | 6,050 | 27.7 |
| | | | | | 51 | 0.3 |
| 1923 | 26,324 | 86.5 | J.N. Horlick | C | 8,630 | 37.9 |
| | | | M.P. Price | Lab | 8,127 | 35.7 |
| | | | A.W. Stanton | L | 6,011 | 26.4 |
| | | | | | 503 | 2.2 |
| 1924 | 26,600 | 83.1 | J.N. Horlick | C | 10,525 | 47.7 |
| | | | M.P. Price | Lab | 8,005 | 36.2 |
| | | | T. Mathew | L | 3,566 | 16.1 |
| | | | | | 2,520 | 11.5 |
| 1929 | 33,716 | 83.6 | H.L. Boyce | C | 11,041 | 39.2 |
| | | | H. Nixon | Lab | 10,548 | 37.4 |
| | | | T.W. Casey | L | 6,589 | 23.4 |
| | | | | | 493 | 1.8 |
| 1931 | 34,473 | 82.5 | H.L. Boyce | C | 19,201 | 67.6 |
| | | | C.H. Fox | Lab | 9,223 | 32.4 |
| | | | | | 9,978 | 35.2 |
| 1935 | 34,786 | 79.0 | H.L. Boyce | C | 15,682 | 57.1 |
| | | | M. Turner-Samuels | Lab | 11,803 | 42.9 |
| | | | | | 3,879 | 14.2 |
| 1945 | 39,884 | 74.8 | M. Turner-Samuels | Lab | 14,010 | 47.0 |
| | | | Sir H.L. Boyce | C | 10,466 | 35.1 |
| | | | H.A. Guy | L | 5,338 | 17.9 |
| | | | | | 3,544 | 11.9 |

Note:—

1922-   Price had his name included in the first list of official Communist candidates at
1923:   the 1922 election but in a revised list he was described as "sympathetic" although
        not an actual member of the Communist Party.

At the 1923 election he was a member of the Communist Party but received
Labour Party endorsement.

# GREAT YARMOUTH  [130]

| Election | Electors | T'out | Candidate | Party | Votes | % |
|---|---|---|---|---|---|---|
| 1918 | 24,585 | 58.8 | †Sir A. Fell | Co C | 6,741 | 46.6 |
| | | | J.H. Wilson | L | 5,734 | 39.7 |
| | | | W. McConnell | Lab | 1,845 | 12.8 |
| | | | W.H. Dawson | Ind | 125* | 0.9 |
| | | | | | 1,007 | 6.9 |
| 1922 | 26,985 | 79.0 | A. Harbord | L | 9,836 | 46.1 |
| | | | C. de W. Crookshank | C | 8,917 | 41.8 |
| | | | A. Whiting | Lab | 2,574* | 12.1 |
| | | | | | 919 | 4.3 |
| 1923 | 27,844 | 79.2 | A. Harbord | L | 11,416 | 51.8 |
| | | | Sir J.A. Horne | C | 8,492 | 38.5 |
| | | | A. Wrigley | Lab | 2,138* | 9.7 |
| | | | | | 2,924 | 13.3 |
| 1924 | 28,447 | 79.9 | Sir F.C. Meyer, Bt. | C | 10,273 | 45.1 |
| | | | A. Harbord | L | 9,202 | 40.5 |
| | | | T.G. Tyler | Lab | 3,264 | 14.4 |
| | | | | | 1,071 | 4.6 |
| 1929 | 36,170 | 83.1 | A. Harbord | L (NL) | 13,147 | 43.7 |
| | | | Sir F.C. Meyer, Bt. | C | 11,570 | 38.5 |
| | | | G.F. Johnson | Lab | 5,347 | 17.8 |
| | | | | | 1,577 | 5.2 |
| 1931 | 37,109 | 72.1 | A. Harbord | NL | 21,008 | 78.6 |
| | | | J.H. Martin | Lab | 5,735 | 21.4 |
| | | | | | 15,273 | 57.2 |
| 1935 | 37,523 | 76.4 | A. Harbord | NL | 16,998 | 59.3 |
| | | | Dr. J. Lewis | Lab | 11,658 | 40.7 |
| | | | | | 5,340 | 18.6 |
| [Death] | | | | | | |
| 1941 (8/4) | | | P.W. Jewson | NL | Unopp. | |
| 1945 | 25,926 | 69.6 | E. Kinghorn | Lab | 10,079 | 55.8 |
| | | | P.W. Jewson | NL | 7,974 | 44.2 |
| | | | | | 2,105 | 11.6 |

Notes:—

1918:  Wilson sought election as a 'Patriotic Trade Unionist's and Seamen's' candidate. He claimed to have been adopted by both the local Liberal and National Democratic parties but as his name did not appear on the official list of the latter's candidates, he is therefore classed as a Liberal. His candidature was supported by the National Sailors' and Firemen's Union.

Dawson's candidature had been approved by the Executive of the NFDSS, but during the early stages of the campaign the NFDSS repudiated him.

# GRIMSBY [131]

| Election | Electors | T'out | Candidate | Party | Votes | % |
|---|---|---|---|---|---|---|
| 1918 | 47,189 | 56.7 | †T.G. Tickler | Co C | 13,688 | 51.2 |
| | | | C.E. Franklin | Lab | 9,015 | 33.7 |
| | | | J.W. Eason | Ind | 2,791* | 10.4 |
| | | | H.J.F. Crosby | Ind | 1,260* | 4.7 |
| | | | | | 4,673 | 17.5 |
| 1922 | 52,496 | 72.3 | T. Sutcliffe | C | 23,726 | 62.5 |
| | | | C.E. Franklin | Lab | 14,227 | 37.5 |
| | | | | | 9,499 | 25.0 |
| 1923 | 53,880 | 62.2 | T. Sutcliffe | C | 17,577 | 52.4 |
| | | | C.E. Franklin | Lab | 15,959 | 47.6 |
| | | | | | 1,618 | 4.8 |
| 1924 | 54,724 | 76.4 | W.J. Womersley | C | 21,487 | 51.4 |
| | | | C.E. Franklin | Lab | 14,874 | 35.6 |
| | | | T.E. Wing | L | 5,442 | 13.0 |
| | | | | | 6,613 | 15.8 |
| 1929 | 68,465 | 71.9 | W.J. Womersley | C | 27,001 | 54.8 |
| | | | E. Marklew | Lab | 22,254 | 45.2 |
| | | | | | 4,747 | 9.6 |
| 1931 | 71,897 | 69.3 | W.J. Womersley | C | 33,725 | 67.7 |
| | | | G.E. Farmery | Lab | 16,124 | 32.3 |
| | | | | | 17,601 | 35.4 |
| 1935 | 72,599 | 67.8 | Sir W.J. Womersley | C | 25,470 | 51.8 |
| | | | H. Brinton | Lab | 23,743 | 48.2 |
| | | | | | 1,727 | 3.6 |
| 1945 | 69,378 | 68.2 | Hon. K.G. Younger | Lab | 28,484 | 60.2 |
| | | | Rt. Hon. Sir W.J. Womersley | C | 18,841 | 39.8 |
| | | | | | 9,643 | 20.4 |

Note:—

1918: Crosby was supported by and possibly the nominee of the local branch of the NFDSS.

# HALIFAX [132]

| Election | Electors | T'out | Candidate | Party | Votes | % |
|---|---|---|---|---|---|---|
| 1918 | 49,017 | 53.4 | †Rt. Hon. J.H. Whitley | Co L | 22,136 | 84.6 |
| | | | A. McManus | SLP | 4,036 | 15.4 |
| | | | | | 18,100 | 69.2 |
| 1922 | | | Rt. Hon. J.H. Whitley | L | Unopp. | |
| 1923 | | | Rt. Hon. J.H. Whitley | L | Unopp. | |
| 1924 | | | Rt. Hon. J.H. Whitley | L | Unopp. | |
| [Resignation] | | | | | | |
| 1928 | 52,013 | 78.7 | A.W. Longbottom | Lab | 17,536 | 42.8 |
| (13/7) | | | H. Barnes | L | 12,585 | 30.8 |
| | | | Hon. F.S. Crossley | C | 10,804 | 26.4 |
| | | | | | 4,951 | 12.0 |
| 1929 | 69,301 | 81.3 | A.W. Longbottom | Lab | 23,776 | 42.2 |
| | | | G. Gledhill | C | 16,713 | 29.7 |
| | | | G.E. Dodds | L | 15,823 | 28.1 |
| | | | | | 7,063 | 12.5 |
| 1931 | 69,455 | 80.5 | G. Gledhill | C | 36,731 | 65.7 |
| | | | A.W. Longbottom | Lab | 16,601 | 29.7 |
| | | | F. Sykes | Ind L | 2,578* | 4.6 |
| | | | | | 20,130 | 36.0 |
| 1935 | 70,646 | 76.9 | G. Gledhill | C | 24,103 | 44.4 |
| | | | A.W. Longbottom | Lab | 21,471 | 39.5 |
| | | | A. Mitchell | L | 8,736 | 16.1 |
| | | | | | 2,632 | 4.9 |
| 1945 | 71,145 | 77.4 | D. Brook | Lab | 25,605 | 46.5 |
| | | | G. Gledhill | C | 14,824 | 26.9 |
| | | | A. Gelder | L | 14,631 | 26.6 |
| | | | | | 10,781 | 19.6 |

Notes:—

1918-
1924:  Whitley was the Speaker of the House of Commons from 1921.

1931:  Sykes sought election as an Anti-National Government candidate after the local
Liberal Association had decided not to put forward a candidate.

## HARROW, EAST [133]

| Election | Electors | T'out | Candidate | Party | Votes | % |
|---|---|---|---|---|---|---|
| 1945 | 77,017 | 77.2 | F.W. Skinnard | Lab | 27,613 | 46.4 |
| | | | F.A. Lincoln | C | 20,843 | 35.1 |
| | | | A.F.X.T. Gibbs | L | 7,513 | 12.6 |
| | | | Miss G.M. Driver | Com | 3,493* | 5.9 |
| | | | | | 6,770 | 11.3 |

## HARROW, WEST [134]

| Election | Electors | T'out | Candidate | Party | Votes | % |
|---|---|---|---|---|---|---|
| 1945 | 73,174 | 78.4 | N.A.H. Bower | C | 28,617 | 49.9 |
| | | | Mrs. B.J.K. Thompson | Lab | 18,961 | 33.0 |
| | | | Sir H.W. Young | L | 7,364 | 12.8 |
| | | | H.M. Lawson | CW · | 2,462* | 4.3 |
| | | | | | 9,656 | 16.9 |

# THE HARTLEPOOLS  [135]

| Election | Electors | T'out | Candidate | Party | Votes | % |
|---|---|---|---|---|---|---|
| 1918 | 39,578 | 64.1 | W.G.H. Gritten | C | 13,003 | 51.3 |
| | | | C. Macfarlane | Co L | 7,647 | 30.1 |
| | | | W.J. Sherwood | Lab | 4,733 | 18.6 |
| | | | | | 5,356 | 21.2 |
| 1922 | 41,206 | 87.2 | W.A. Jowitt | L | 18,252 | 50.8 |
| | | | W.G.H. Gritten | C | 17,685 | 49.2 |
| | | | | | 567 | 1.6 |
| 1923 | 42,071 | 87.5 | W.A. Jowitt | L | 17,101 | 46.4 |
| | | | W.G.H. Gritten | C | 16,956 | 46.1 |
| | | | G. Belt | Lab | 2,755* | 7.5 |
| | | | | | 145 | 0.3 |
| 1924 | 42,676 | 90.3 | Sir W.H. Sugden | C | 19,077 | 49.5 |
| | | | W.A. Jowitt | L | 15,724 | 40.8 |
| | | | C.M. Aitchison | Lab | 3,717* | 9.7 |
| | | | | | 3,353 | 8.7 |
| 1929 | 52,944 | 85.9 | W.G.H. Gritten | C | 17,271 | 38.0 |
| | | | S.N. Furness | L | 17,133 | 37.7 |
| | | | G. Oliver | Lab | 11,052 | 24.3 |
| | | | | | 138 | 0.3 |
| 1931 | 53,652 | 84.4 | W.G.H. Gritten | C | 30,842 | 68.1 |
| | | | A.A. MacGregor | Lab | 14,462 | 31.9 |
| | | | | | 16,380 | 36.2 |
| 1935 | 55,050 | 83.0 | W.G.H. Gritten | C | 21,828 | 47.8 |
| | | | C.A. Goatcher | Lab | 16,931 | 37.0 |
| | | | J. Scott-Cowell | L | 6,939 | 15.2 |
| | | | | | 4,897 | 10.8 |
| [Death] | | | | | | |
| 1943 (1/6) | 52,794 | 39.5 | T.G. Greenwell | C | 13,333 | 64.1 |
| | | | Miss E.F. Burton | CW | 3,634 | 17.4 |
| | | | O. Lupton | Ind | 2,351* | 11.3 |
| | | | W.R. Hipwell | Ind Prog | 1,510* | 7.2 |
| | | | | | 9,699 | 46.7 |
| 1945 | 52,612 | 76.1 | D.T. Jones | Lab | 16,502 | 41.3 |
| | | | T.G. Greenwell | C | 16,227 | 40.5 |
| | | | G.R. Vick | L | 6,903 | 17.2 |
| | | | H. Lane | Nat Ind | 390* | 1.0 |
| | | | | | 275 | 0.8 |

Note:—

1943: Lupton sought election as a 'People's' candidate. He was a prominent member of the local Labour Party.

# HASTINGS [136]

| Election | Electors | T'out | Candidate | Party | Votes | % |
|---|---|---|---|---|---|---|
| 1918 | 24,958 | 59.2 | L. Lyon | Co C | 11,210 | 75.9 |
| | | | J.G. Butler | Lab | 3,556 | 24.1 |
| | | | | | 7,654 | 51.8 |
| [Resignation] | | | | | | |
| 1921 | 27,386 | 78.0 | Lord Eustace Percy | Co C | 11,685 | 54.7 |
| (4/5) | | | R. Davies | Lab | 5,437 | 25.5 |
| | | | A. Blackman | L | 4,240 | 19.8 |
| | | | | | 6,248 | 29.2 |
| 1922 | 28,785 | 71.2 | Lord Eustace Percy | C | 13,991 | 68.3 |
| | | | R. Davies | Lab | 6,492 | 31.7 |
| | | | | | 7,499 | 36.6 |
| 1923 | 29,662 | 76.4 | Lord Eustace Percy | C | 11,914 | 52.6 |
| | | | Mrs. M.M.O. Gordon | L | 5,876 | 25.9 |
| | | | R. Davies | Lab | 4,859 | 21.5 |
| | | | | | 6,038 | 26.7 |
| 1924 | 30,195 | 70.5 | Lord Eustace Percy | C | 15,217 | 71.4 |
| | | | Mrs. M.M. Porter | Lab | 6,082 | 28.6 |
| | | | | | 9,135 | 42.8 |
| 1929 | 41,503 | 73.4 | Rt. Hon. Lord Eustace Percy | C | 15,928 | 52.3 |
| | | | T.A.E. Spearing | L | 8,004 | 26.3 |
| | | | B. Noble | Lab | 6,516 | 21.4 |
| | | | | | 7,924 | 26.0 |
| 1931 | 43,582 | 73.8 | Rt. Hon. Lord Eustace Percy | C | 22,640 | 70.3 |
| | | | Miss I.G. Goddard | Lab | 4,983 | 15.5 |
| | | | T.A.E. Spearing | L | 4,561 | 14.2 |
| | | | | | 17,657 | 54.8 |
| 1935 | 45,586 | 66.5 | Rt. Hon. Lord Eustace Percy | C | 20,905 | 69.0 |
| | | | W.W. Wood | Lab | 9,404 | 31.0 |
| | | | | | 11,501 | 38.0 |
| [Resignation] | | | | | | |
| 1937 | 45,470 | 65.3 | M.R. Hely-Hutchinson | C | 18,428 | 62.1 |
| (24/11) | | | W.W. Wood | Lab | 11,244 | 37.9 |
| | | | | | 7,184 | 24.2 |
| 1945 | 36,181 | 75.3 | E.M. Cooper-Key | C | 14,105 | 51.8 |
| | | | L. Gassman | Lab | 10,580 | 38.8 |
| | | | S.M. Parkman | Ind Prog | 2,564* | 9.4 |
| | | | | | 3,525 | 13.0 |

Note:—

1945: Parkman was the nominee of an organisation called the Hastings Independent Progressive Movement.

# HENDON, NORTH   [137]

| Election | Electors | T'out | Candidate | Party | Votes | % |
|---|---|---|---|---|---|---|
| 1945 | 51,196 | 74.9 | Mrs. B.A. Gould | Lab | 18,251 | 47.6 |
|  |  |  | E.W.C. Flavell | C | 13,607 | 35.5 |
|  |  |  | F.A. Sellers | L | 6,478 | 16.9 |
|  |  |  |  |  | 4,644 | 12.1 |

## HENDON, SOUTH   [138]

| Election | Electors | T'out | Candidate | Party | Votes | % |
|---|---|---|---|---|---|---|
| 1945 | 52,114 | 75.1 | Sir H.V.H.D. Lucas-Tooth, Bt. | C | 16,974 | 43.4 |
|  |  |  | Miss E.F. Burton | Lab | 14,917 | 38.1 |
|  |  |  | A.C. Forbes | L | 7,232 | 18.5 |
|  |  |  |  |  | 2,057 | 5.3 |

| Election | Electors | T'out | Candidate | Party | Votes | % |
|----------|----------|-------|-----------|-------|-------|---|
| 1945 | 72,344 | 74.3 | W.R. Williams | Lab | 29,192 | 54.3 |
| | | | R. Maudling | C | 22,623 | 42.1 |
| | | | W.H.G. Drake-Brockman | Ind Nat | 1,919* | 3.6 |
| | | | | | 6,569 | 12.2 |

| Election | Electors | T'out | Candidate | Party | Votes | % |
|---|---|---|---|---|---|---|
| 1918 [Death] | | | †W.K. Jones | Co C | Unopp. | |
| 1921 (10/11) | 45,510 | 65.7 | Viscount Ednam | C | 15,959 | 53.4 |
| | | | E.L. Burgin | L | 13,943 | 46.6 |
| | | | | | 2,016 | 6.8 |
| 1922 | 44,964 | 77.2 | Viscount Ednam | C | 18,462 | 53.2 |
| | | | E.L. Burgin | L | 16,239 | 46.8 |
| | | | | | 2,223 | 6.4 |
| 1923 | 46,312 | 76.6 | Viscount Ednam | C | 16,812 | 47.4 |
| | | | E.L. Burgin | L | 15,197 | 42.8 |
| | | | C.F. Healy | Lab | 3,487* | 9.8 |
| | | | | | 1,615 | 4.6 |
| 1924 | 47,174 | 81.6 | D.E. Wallace | C | 21,017 | 54.6 |
| | | | E.L. Burgin | L | 13,217 | 34.3 |
| | | | C.F. Healy | Lab | 4,277* | 11.1 |
| | | | | | 7,800 | 20.3 |
| 1929 | 66,620 | 75.2 | D.E. Wallace | C | 25,540 | 51.0 |
| | | | W. Thomson | L | 16,029 | 32.0 |
| | | | F.H. Wiltshire | Lab | 8,529 | 17.0 |
| | | | | | 9,511 | 19.0 |
| 1931 | 69,362 | 70.3 | D.E. Wallace | C | 41,194 | 84.5 |
| | | | H.A. Franklin | Lab | 7,585 | 15.5 |
| | | | | | 33,609 | 69.0 |
| 1935 | 70,167 | 67.0 | D.E. Wallace | C | 30,494 | 64.9 |
| | | | Mrs. M.M. Power | Lab | 10,320 | 21.9 |
| | | | H.J. Baxter | L | 6,206 | 13.2 |
| | | | | | 20,174 | 43.0 |
| [Death] | | | | | | |
| 1941 (28/5) | 72,298 | 21.1 | L.D. Gammans | C | 11,077 | 72.8 |
| | | | N.P. Billing | Nat Ind | 4,146 | 27.2 |
| | | | | | 6,931 | 45.6 |
| 1945 | 64,104 | 72.9 | L.D. Gammans | C | 24,684 | 52.8 |
| | | | W.G. Fiske | Lab | 12,015 | 25.7 |
| | | | G.J. Jones | Com | 10,058 | 21.5 |
| | | | | | 12,669 | 27.1 |

Note:—

1941: Billing advocated a policy of aerial reprisals against Germany.

# HUDDERSFIELD [141]

| Election | Electors | T'out | Candidate | Party | Votes | % |
|---|---|---|---|---|---|---|
| 1918 | 56,200 | 69.8 | Sir C. Sykes | Co L | 15,234 | 38.8 |
| | | | H. Snell | Lab | 12,737 | 32.5 |
| | | | E. Woodhead | L | 11,256 | 28.7 |
| | | | | | 2,497 | 6.3 |
| 1922 | 56,243 | 83.1 | Sir A.H. Marshall | L | 15,879 | 34.0 |
| | | | J.H. Hudson | Lab | 15,673 | 33.5 |
| | | | Sir C. Sykes, Bt. | NL | 15,212 | 32.5 |
| | | | | | 206 | 0.5 |
| 1923 | 58,029 | 81.9 | J.H. Hudson | Lab | 17,430 | 36.7 |
| | | | Sir A.H. Marshall | L | 17,404 | 36.6 |
| | | | C. Tinker | C | 12,694 | 26.7 |
| | | | | | 26 | 0.1 |
| 1924 | 59,176 | 88.5 | J.H. Hudson | Lab | 19,010 | 36.3 |
| | | | E. Hill | C | 16,745 | 32.0 |
| | | | Sir A.H. Marshall | L | 16,626 | 31.7 |
| | | | | | 2,265 | 4.3 |
| 1929 | 78,635 | 86.1 | J.H. Hudson | Lab | 25,966 | 38.3 |
| | | | W. Mabane | L | 21,398 | 31.6 |
| | | | Sir E. Hill | C | 20,361 | 30.1 |
| | | | | | 4,568 | 6.7 |
| 1931 | 80,492 | 83.3 | W. Mabane | NL | 47,056 | 70.1 |
| | | | J.H. Hudson | Lab | 20,034 | 29.9 |
| | | | | | 27,022 | 40.2 |
| 1935 | 83,103 | 73.2 | W. Mabane | NL | 37,009 | 60.8 |
| | | | W. Pickles | Lab | 23,844 | 39.2 |
| | | | | | 13,165 | 21.6 |
| 1945 | 88,064 | 78.4 | J.P.W. Mallalieu | Lab | 33,362 | 48.3 |
| | | | Rt. Hon. W. Mabane | NL | 24,496 | 35.5 |
| | | | R.F. Harrod | L | 11,199 | 16.2 |
| | | | | | 8,866 | 12.8 |

# HYTHE  [142]

| Election | Electors | T'out | Candidate | Party | Votes | % |
|---|---|---|---|---|---|---|
| 1918 | 19,896 | 61.6 | †Sir P.A.G.D. Sassoon, Bt. | Co C | 8,819 | 72.0 |
| | | | R.W. Forsyth | Lab | 3,427 | 28.0 |
| | | | | | 5,392 | 44.0 |
| 1922 | | | Sir P.A.G.D. Sassoon, Bt. | C | Unopp. | |
| 1923 | | | Sir P.A.G.D. Sassoon, Bt. | C | Unopp. | |
| 1924 | 21,058 | 79.7 | Sir P.A.G.D. Sassoon, Bt. | C | 12,843 | 76.5 |
| | | | C. Gallop | Lab | 3,936 | 23.5 |
| | | | | | 8,907 | 53.0 |
| 1929 | 31,745 | 70.8 | Sir P.A.G.D. Sassoon, Bt. | C | 12,982 | 57.8 |
| | | | Miss H.L. Holland | L | 6,912 | 30.7 |
| | | | Miss G.M. Colman | Lab | 2,597* | 11.5 |
| | | | | | 6,070 | 27.1 |
| 1931 | 33,256 | 71.8 | Rt. Hon. Sir P.A.G.D. Sassoon, Bt. | C | 20,277 | 84.9 |
| | | | Miss G.M. Colman | Lab | 3,608 | 15.1 |
| | | | | | 16,669 | 69.8 |
| 1935 | 35,205 | 68.3 | Rt. Hon. Sir P.A.G.D. Sassoon, Bt. | C | 15,359 | 63.9 |
| | | | R.H. Ellis | L | 8,688 | 36.1 |
| | | | | | 6,671 | 27.8 |
| [Death] | | | | | | |
| 1939 (20/7) | 35,535 | 62.4 | R.A. Brabner | C | 12,016 | 54.2 |
| | | | F.O. Darvall | L | 9,577 | 43.2 |
| | | | H.St.J.B. Philby | BPP | 576* | 2.6 |
| | | | | | 2,439 | 11.0 |
| [Seat Vacant at Dissolution (Death)] | | | | | | |
| 1945 | 23,575 | 73.3 | H.R. Mackeson | C | 8,048 | 46.6 |
| | | | D.G. Widdicombe | Lab | 6,091 | 35.2 |
| | | | A.D.B. James | L | 3,152 | 18.2 |
| | | | | | 1,957 | 11.4 |

# ILFORD [143]

| Election | Electors | T'out | Candidate | Party | Votes | % |
|---|---|---|---|---|---|---|
| 1918 | 40,749 | 58.3 | Sir W.P. Griggs | Co C | 15,870 | 66.8 |
| | | | Rev. H. Dunnico | Lab | 4,621 | 19.5 |
| | | | T.H. Garside | L | 3,261 | 13.7 |
| | | | | | 11,249 | 47.3 |
| [Death] | | | | | | |
| 1920 | 43,337[†] | 66.2 | F. Wise | Co C | 15,612 | 54.4 |
| (25/9) | | | J. King | Lab | 6,577 | 22.9 |
| | | | J.W.H. Thompson | L | 6,515 | 22.7 |
| | | | | | 9,035 | 31.5 |
| 1922 | 45,013 | 70.5 | F. Wise | C | 14,071 | 44.4 |
| | | | J.W.H. Thompson | L | 7,625 | 24.0 |
| | | | A. West | Lab | 5,414 | 17.1 |
| | | | F.C. Bramston | Ind C | 4,610 | 14.5 |
| | | | | | 6,446 | 20.4 |
| 1923 | 49,184 | 64.8 | Sir F. Wise | C | 14,136 | 44.4 |
| | | | J.W. Morris | L | 11,965 | 37.5 |
| | | | D. Chater | Lab | 5,775 | 18.1 |
| | | | | | 2,171 | 6.9 |
| 1924 | 52,243 | 74.8 | Sir F. Wise | C | 22,825 | 58.4 |
| | | | D. Chater | Lab | 8,460 | 21.7 |
| | | | J.W. Morris | L | 7,780 | 19.9 |
| | | | | | 14,365 | 36.7 |
| [Death] | | | | | | |
| 1928 | 60,487 | 67.5 | Sir G.C. Hamilton | C | 18,269 | 44.7 |
| (23/2) | | | A.S. Comyns Carr | L | 13,621 | 33.4 |
| | | | C.R. de Gruchy | Lab | 8,922 | 21.9 |
| | | | | | 4,648 | 11.3 |
| 1929 | 78,330 | 73.6 | Sir G.C. Hamilton | C | 24,414 | 42.4 |
| | | | A.S. Comyns Carr | L | 21,267 | 36.9 |
| | | | C.R. de Gruchy | Lab | 11,952 | 20.7 |
| | | | | | 3,147 | 5.5 |
| 1931 | 90,564 | 71.9 | Sir G.C. Hamilton | C | 43,737 | 67.2 |
| | | | P. Astins | Lab | 12,173 | 18.7 |
| | | | Dr. W.S.R. Thomas | L | 9,179 | 14.1 |
| | | | | | 31,564 | 48.5 |
| 1935 | 106,936 | 64.0 | Sir G.C. Hamilton | C | 43,208 | 63.1 |
| | | | P. Astins | Lab | 25,241 | 36.9 |
| | | | | | 17,967 | 26.2 |
| [Resignation] | | | | | | |
| 1937 | 111,817 | 37.3 | G.C. Hutchinson | C | 25,533 | 61.2 |
| (29/6) | | | P. Astins | Lab | 16,214 | 38.8 |
| | | | | | 9,319 | 22.4 |

This constituency was divided in 1945.

Note:—

1922: Bramston was the nominee of the Ilford Conservative Forward Association which was formed in 1922 by a number of members of the Ilford Conservative Association who had resigned in protest over the re-adoption of Wise as the Conservative candidate.

## ILFORD, NORTH  [144]

| Election | Electors | T'out | Candidate | Party | Votes | % |
|----------|----------|-------|-----------|-------|-------|---|
| 1945 | 61,619 | 71.4 | Mrs. M. Ridealgh | Lab/Co-op | 18,833 | 42.8 |
| | | | G.C. Hutchinson | C | 16,013 | 36.4 |
| | | | Lady Rhys Williams | L | 9,128 | 20.8 |
| | | | | | 2,820 | 6.4 |

## ILFORD, SOUTH [145]

| Election | Electors | T'out | Candidate | Party | Votes | % |
|---|---|---|---|---|---|---|
| 1945 | 56,784 | 71.0 | J. Ranger | Lab | 19,339 | 48.0 |
| | | | E.J. Boulton | C | 14,633 | 36.3 |
| | | | E.A.G. Holloway | L | 6,322 | 15.7 |
| | | | | | 4,706 | 11.7 |

# IPSWICH [146]

| Election | Electors | T'out | Candidate | Party | Votes | % |
|---|---|---|---|---|---|---|
| 1918 | 37,348 | 67.9 | †F.J.C. Ganzoni | Co C | 13,553 | 53.5 |
| | | | R.F. Jackson | Lab | 8,143 | 32.1 |
| | | | †G.H. Morgan | L | 3,663 | 14.4 |
| | | | | | 5,410 | 21.4 |
| 1922 | 38,924 | 82.4 | Sir F.J.C. Ganzoni | C | 17,134 | 53.4 |
| | | | R.F. Jackson | Lab | 14,924 | 46.6 |
| | | | | | 2,210 | 6.8 |
| 1923 | 39,606 | 78.7 | R.F. Jackson | Lab | 15,824 | 50.7 |
| | | | Sir F.J.C. Ganzoni | C | 15,364 | 49.3 |
| | | | | | 460 | 1.4 |
| 1924 | 40,379 | 87.7 | Sir F.J.C. Ganzoni | C | 19,621 | 55.4 |
| | | | R.F. Jackson | Lab | 15,791 | 44.6 |
| | | | | | 3,830 | 10.8 |
| 1929 | 54,474 | 85.7 | Sir F.J.C. Ganzoni, Bt. | C | 18,527 | 39.7 |
| | | | R.F. Jackson | Lab | 17,592 | 37.7 |
| | | | F.O. Darvall | L | 10,559 | 22.6 |
| | | | | | 935 | 2.0 |
| 1931 | 57,019 | 82.9 | Sir F.J.C. Ganzoni, Bt. | C | 29,782 | 63.0 |
| | | | R.F. Jackson | Lab | 17,490 | 37.0 |
| | | | | | 12,292 | 26.0 |
| 1935 | 60,643 | 82.1 | Sir F.J.C. Ganzoni, Bt. | C | 28,528 | 57.3 |
| | | | R.F. Jackson | Lab | 21,278 | 42.7 |
| | | | | | 7,250 | 14.6 |

[Elevation to the Peerage — Lord Belstead]

| Election | Electors | T'out | Candidate | Party | Votes | % |
|---|---|---|---|---|---|---|
| 1938 (16/2) | 62,840 | 82.8 | R.R. Stokes | Lab | 27,604 | 53.0 |
| | | | H.U. Willink | C | 24,443 | 47.0 |
| | | | | | 3,161 | 6.0 |
| 1945 | 66,740 | 79.9 | R.R. Stokes | Lab | 26,296 | 49.4 |
| | | | F.G.C. Fison | C | 18,177 | 34.1 |
| | | | D.M.S. Mowat | L | 8,819 | 16.5 |
| | | | | | 8,119 | 15.3 |

# KINGSTON UPON HULL, CENTRAL [147]

| Election | Electors | T'out | Candidate | Party | Votes | % |
|---|---|---|---|---|---|---|
| 1918 | 31,421 | 54.9 | †Sir M. Sykes, Bt. | Co C | 13,805 | 80.1 |
| | | | Rev. R.M. Kedward | L | 3,434 | 19.9 |
| | | | | | 10,371 | 60.2 |
| [Death] | | | | | | |
| 1919 | 31,421 | 51.9 | Hon. J.M. Kenworthy | L | 8,616 | 52.8 |
| (29/3) | | | Lord Eustace Percy | Co C | 7,699 | 47.2 |
| | | | | | 917 | 5.6 |
| 1922 | 35,037 | 79.1 | Hon. J.M. Kenworthy | L | 15,374 | 55.5 |
| | | | H.W. Looker | C | 12,347 | 44.5 |
| | | | | | 3,027 | 11.0 |
| 1923 | 36,085 | 73.0 | Hon. J.M. Kenworthy | L | 15,847 | 60.1 |
| | | | E. Wooll | C | 10,507 | 39.9 |
| | | | | | 5,340 | 20.2 |
| 1924 | 36,514 | 77.1 | Hon. J.M. Kenworthy | L | 15,234 | 54.1 |
| | | | L.E. Gaunt | C | 12,904 | 45.9 |
| | | | | | 2,330 | 8.2 |
| [Seeks re-election on joining the Labour Party] | | | | | | |
| 1926 | 36,820 | 82.8 | Hon. J.M. Kenworthy | Lab | 16,145 | 52.9 |
| (29/11) | | | L.E. Gaunt | C | 11,466 | 37.6 |
| | | | C.I. Kerr | L | 2,885* | 9.5 |
| | | | | | 4,679 | 15.3 |
| 1929 | 44,439 | 78.3 | Hon. J.M. Kenworthy | Lab | 18,815 | 54.1 |
| | | | L. Kimball | C | 11,181 | 32.1 |
| | | | A.S. Doran | L | 4,802 | 13.8 |
| | | | | | 7,634 | 22.0 |
| 1931 | 43,153 | 83.2 | B.K. Barton | C | 19,773 | 55.1 |
| | | | Hon. J.M. Kenworthy | Lab | 16,113 | 44.9 |
| | | | | | 3,660 | 10.2 |
| 1935 | 38,912 | 72.2 | W. Windsor | Lab | 14,851 | 52.9 |
| | | | B.K. Barton | C | 13,232 | 47.1 |
| | | | | | 1,619 | 5.8 |
| 1945 | 20,482 | 73.0 | M. Hewitson | Lab | 8,786 | 58.7 |
| | | | Mrs. D.V.C.E. Spearman | C | 4,106 | 27.5 |
| | | | C.S. Bell | L | 2,062 | 13.8 |
| | | | | | 4,680 | 31.2 |

Note:—

1945: Polling was delayed until July 19 owing to the death, after nomination, of the Labour candidate, W. Windsor.

# KINGSTON UPON HULL, EAST  [148]

| Election | Electors | T'out | Candidate | Party | Votes | % |
|---|---|---|---|---|---|---|
| 1918 | 31,316 | 58.2 | C.K. Murchison | Co C | 9,566 | 52.5 |
| | | | †Rt. Hon. T.R. Ferens | L | 4,947 | 27.1 |
| | | | R.H. Farrah | Lab | 3,725 | 20.4 |
| | | | | | 4,619 | 25.4 |
| 1922 | 33,795 | 82.5 | L.R. Lumley | C | 12,248 | 43.9 |
| | | | C.J. Vasey | L | 8,711 | 31.2 |
| | | | A. Stark | Lab | 6,934 | 24.9 |
| | | | | | 3,537 | 12.7 |
| 1923 | 34,908 | 79.4 | L.R. Lumley | C | 10,657 | 38.5 |
| | | | C.J. Vasey | L | 9,600 | 34.6 |
| | | | A. Stark | Lab | 7,468 | 26.9 |
| | | | | | 1,057 | 3.9 |
| 1924 | 35,467 | 81.8 | L.R. Lumley | C | 12,296 | 42.4 |
| | | | G. Muff | Lab | 11,130 | 38.4 |
| | | | F.C. Thornborough | L | 5,140 | 17.7 |
| | | | W.E. Mashford | Ind | 444* | 1.5 |
| | | | | | 1,166 | 4.0 |
| 1929 | 49,212 | 83.4 | G. Muff | Lab | 20,023 | 48.8 |
| | | | L.R. Lumley | C | 13,810 | 33.6 |
| | | | R. Stephens | L | 7,217 | 17.6 |
| | | | | | 6,213 | 15.2 |
| 1931 | 50,494 | 83.2 | J.J.H. Nation | C | 24,003 | 57.1 |
| | | | G. Muff | Lab | 18,026 | 42.9 |
| | | | | | 5,977 | 14.2 |
| 1935 | 51,087 | 75.6 | G. Muff | Lab | 19,054 | 49.3 |
| | | | J.J.H. Nation | C | 15,448 | 40.0 |
| | | | R. Stephens | L | 4,133* | 10.7 |
| | | | | | 3,606 | 9.3 |
| 1945 | 40,024 | 75.6 | H. Pursey | Lab | 19,443 | 64.2 |
| | | | R.A. Alec-Smith | C | 7,439 | 24.6 |
| | | | A.E. Marshall | L | 3,379* | 11.2 |
| | | | | | 12,004 | 39.6 |

Note:—

1924: Mashford advocated a policy urging a fairer deal for industrial insurance policy holders.

| Election | Electors | T'out | Candidate | Party | Votes | % |
|----------|----------|-------|-----------|-------|-------|---|
| 1918 | 31,417 | 58.1 | A.L. Ward | C | 10,898 | 59.7 |
| | | | †Hon. G.G. Wilson | L | 3,827 | 21.0 |
| | | | A. Gould | Lab | 3,528 | 19.3 |
| | | | | | 7,071 | 38.7 |
| 1922 | 33,885 | 77.0 | A.L. Ward | C | 14,904 | 57.1 |
| | | | Sir J.N. Barran, Bt. | L | 11,204 | 42.9 |
| | | | | | 3,700 | 14.2 |
| 1923 | 34,251 | 73.7 | A.L. Ward | C | 12,674 | 50.2 |
| | | | Sir J.N. Barran, Bt. | L | 12,559 | 49.8 |
| | | | | | 115 | 0.4 |
| 1924 | 34,835 | 81.2 | A.L. Ward | C | 15,072 | 53.3 |
| | | | Sir J.N. Barran, Bt. | L | 8,080 | 28.5 |
| | | | F.L. Kerran | Lab | 5,151 | 18.2 |
| | | | | | 6,992 | 24.8 |
| 1929 | 44,913 | 79.1 | A.L. Ward | C | 14,764 | 41.6 |
| | | | W. Pickles | Lab | 10,700 | 30.1 |
| | | | Mrs. C.B. Alderton | L | 10,059 | 28.3 |
| | | | | | 4,064 | 11.5 |
| 1931 | 45,759 | 79.8 | Sir A.L. Ward, Bt. | C | 26,549 | 72.7 |
| | | | J.H. Baum | Lab | 9,946 | 27.3 |
| | | | | | 16,603 | 45.4 |
| 1935 | 46,281 | 72.0 | Sir A.L. Ward, Bt. | C | 19,278 | 57.9 |
| | | | E.P. Young | Lab | 14,044 | 42.1 |
| | | | | | 5,234 | 15.8 |
| 1945 | 37,247 | 76.9 | R.W.G. Mackay | Lab | 13,944 | 48.7 |
| | | | Sir A.L. Ward, Bt. | C | 10,450 | 36.5 |
| | | | H.S. Freemantle | L | 4,235 | 14.8 |
| | | | | | 3,494 | 12.2 |

Note:—

1918: Wilson was issued with the Coalition 'coupon' but repudiated it.

| Election | Electors | T'out | Candidate | Party | Votes | % |
|---|---|---|---|---|---|---|
| 1918 | 32,601 | 49.7 | C.F. Entwistle | L | 6,724 | 41.5 |
| | | | J.R. Bell | Co Lab | 5,005 | 30.9 |
| | | | R. Mell | Lab | 3,121 | 19.3 |
| | | | A.E. Shakesby | NFDSS | 695* | 4.3 |
| | | | P.S. Newbound | Ind | 650* | 4.0 |
| | | | | | 1,719 | 10.6 |
| 1922 | 35,182 | 72.5 | C.F. Entwistle | L | 10,360 | 40.7 |
| | | | H.B. Grotrian | C | 9,597 | 37.6 |
| | | | J. Arnott | Lab | 4,859 | 19.0 |
| | | | Rev. D. Pughe | NL | 692* | 2.7 |
| | | | | | 763 | 3.1 |
| 1923 | 35,832 | 70.3 | C.F. Entwistle | L | 10,316 | 41.0 |
| | | | H.B. Grotrian | C | 8,883 | 35.3 |
| | | | J. Arnott | Lab | 5,973 | 23.7 |
| | | | | | 1,433 | 5.7 |
| 1924 | 36,240 | 75.4 | H.B. Grotrian | C | 11,190 | 40.9 |
| | | | C.F. Entwistle | L | 8,155 | 29.9 |
| | | | J. Arnott | Lab | 7,965 | 29.2 |
| | | | | | 3,035 | 11.0 |
| 1929 | 47,219 | 76.6 | J. Arnott | Lab | 14,903 | 41.2 |
| | | | H.B. Grotrian | C | 12,464 | 34.4 |
| | | | H.A. Crowe | L | 8,826 | 24.4 |
| | | | | | 2,439 | 6.8 |
| 1931 | 49,322 | 78.6 | R.K. Law | C | 25,909 | 66.8 |
| | | | J. Arnott | Lab | 12,857 | 33.2 |
| | | | | | 13,052 | 33.6 |
| 1935 | 49,632 | 68.8 | R.K. Law | C | 17,406 | 51.0 |
| | | | J. Arnott | Lab | 13,975 | 40.9 |
| | | | F.V. Baxter | L | 2,749* | 8.1 |
| | | | | | 3,431 | 10.1 |
| 1945 | 42,320 | 74.5 | S.H. Smith | Lab | 18,606 | 59.0 |
| | | | Rt. Hon. R.K. Law | C | 10,294 | 32.6 |
| | | | E.E. Dalton | L | 2,645* | 8.4 |
| | | | | | 8,312 | 26.4 |

Notes:—

1918: Bell was incorrectly described in the official list of Coalition candidates as a nominee of the National Democratic Party. He may have been given local support by the NDP but was not officially supported or sponsored by that party. His candidature was supported by the National Sailors' and Firemen's Union and he sought election as a 'Coalition Labour and Seamen's' candidate.

Newbound sought election as an 'Independent Business' candidate. He was a supporter of Horatio Bottomley.

## KINGSTON UPON THAMES [151]

| Election | Electors | T'out | Candidate | Party | Votes | % |
|---|---|---|---|---|---|---|
| 1918 | 35,656 | 51.7 | J.G.D. Campbell | Co C | 13,596 | 73.8 |
| | | | T.H. Dumper | Lab | 2,502 | 13.6 |
| | | | A.E. Ely | L | 2,325 | 12.6 |
| | | | | | 11,094 | 60.2 |
| 1922 | 38,265 | 59.3 | F.G. Penny | C | 15,136 | 66.7 |
| | | | H. Day | Ind | 7,563 | 33.3 |
| | | | | | 7,573 | 33.4 |
| 1923 | 39,044 | 53.9 | F.G. Penny | C | 12,968 | 61.6 |
| | | | W. Freeman | L | 8,095 | 38.4 |
| | | | | | 4,873 | 23.2 |
| 1924 | 39,868 | 71.3 | F.G. Penny | C | 19,933 | 70.2 |
| | | | A.B. Bishop | Lab | 5,640 | 19.8 |
| | | | W. Freeman | L | 2,850* | 10.0 |
| | | | | | 14,293 | 50.4 |
| 1929 | 56,004 | 68.9 | F.G. Penny | C | 20,911 | 54.1 |
| | | | J.W. Fawcett | Lab | 8,903 | 23.1 |
| | | | F.J. Powell | L | 8,796 | 22.8 |
| | | | | | 12,008 | 31.0 |
| 1931 | 62,867 | 69.3 | Sir F.G. Penny | C | 35,925 | 82.5 |
| | | | J.W. Fawcett | Lab | 7,613 | 17.5 |
| | | | | | 28,312 | 65.0 |
| 1935 | 74,476 | 65.5 | Sir F.G. Penny, Bt. | C | 32,953 | 67.5 |
| | | | G.H. Loman | Lab | 10,014 | 20.5 |
| | | | F.J. Powell | L | 5,832* | 12.0 |
| | | | | | 22,939 | 47.0 |

[Elevation to the Peerage — Lord Marchwood]

| Election | Electors | T'out | Candidate | Party | Votes | % |
|---|---|---|---|---|---|---|
| 1937 (1/7) | 78,387 | 38.1 | P.M.R. Royds | C | 19,887 | 66.6 |
| | | | G.H. Loman | Lab | 9,972 | 33.4 |
| | | | | | 9,915 | 33.2 |
| 1945 | 88,692* | 74.0 | J.A. Boyd-Carpenter | C | 37,085 | 56.5 |
| | | | G.H. Elvin | Lab | 28,516 | 43.5 |
| | | | | | 8,569 | 13.0 |

Note:—

1922: Day received local support from the Labour and Liberal parties.

| Election | Electors | T'out | Candidate | Party | Votes | % |
|---|---|---|---|---|---|---|
| 1918 | 43,496 | 37.4 | †R. Armitage | Co L | 11,474 | 70.6 |
| | | | E. Terry | Ind | 2,634 | 16.2 |
| | | | J. Smith | Co-op | 2,146 | 13.2 |
| | | | | | 8,840 | 54.4 |
| 1922 | 42,738 | 66.1 | A.W. Willey | C | 14,137 | 50.0 |
| | | | H.H. Slesser | Lab | 7,844 | 27.8 |
| | | | R. Armitage | L | 6,260 | 22.2 |
| | | | | | 6,293 | 22.2 |
| [Death] | | | | | | |
| 1923 | 42,738† | 64.3 | Sir C.H. Wilson | C | 13,085 | 47.6 |
| (26/7) | | | H.H. Slesser | Lab | 11,359 | 41.4 |
| | | | G. Stone | L | 3,026* | 11.0 |
| | | | | | 1,726 | 6.2 |
| 1923 | 43,972 | 60.1 | Sir C.H. Wilson | C | 14,853 | 56.2 |
| | | | H.H. Slesser | Lab | 11,574 | 43.8 |
| | | | | | 3,279 | 12.4 |
| 1924 | 44,532 | 61.0 | Sir C.H. Wilson | C | 16,182 | 59.6 |
| | | | E.J.C. Neep | Lab | 10,975 | 40.4 |
| | | | | | 5,207 | 19.2 |
| 1929 | 56,417 | 68.9 | Hon. R.D. Denman | Lab (N Lab) | 17,322 | 44.6 |
| | | | Sir C.H. Wilson | C | 15,958 | 41.0 |
| | | | M.J. Landa | L | 5,607 | 14.4 |
| | | | | | 1,364 | 3.6 |
| 1931 | 56,082 | 66.2 | Hon. R.D. Denman | N Lab | 26,496 | 71.4 |
| | | | M. Turner-Samuels | Lab | 10,633 | 28.6 |
| | | | | | 15,863 | 42.8 |
| 1935 | 51,182 | 61.4 | Hon. R.D. Denman | N Lab (Nat) | 17,747 | 56.4 |
| | | | F.W. Lindley | Lab | 13,701 | 43.6 |
| | | | | | 4,046 | 12.8 |
| 1945 | 36,830 | 63.5 | G. Porter | Lab | 13,370 | 57.2 |
| | | | C.S. Denman | C | 8,011 | 34.2 |
| | | | B.M. Sandelson | L | 2,017* | 8.6 |
| | | | | | 5,359 | 23.0 |

Note:—

1918: Terry was supported by the local branches of the three ex-servicemen organisations (NADSS, NFDSS, Comrades of the Great War).

| Election | Electors | T'out | Candidate | Party | Votes | % |
|---|---|---|---|---|---|---|
| 1918 | 37,904 | 49.0 | A.C. Farquharson | Co L | 13,863 | 74.7 |
| | | | G.H. Thompson | Lab | 3,423 | 18.4 |
| | | | H.F. Wyatt | Nat P | 1,282* | 6.9 |
| | | | | | 10,440 | 56.3 |
| 1922 | 37,383 | 71.8 | H.M. Butler | C | 13,771 | 51.4 |
| | | | E.O. Dodgson | L | 7,230 | 26.9 |
| | | | D. Stewart | Lab | 5,836 | 21.7 |
| | | | | | 6,541 | 24.5 |
| 1923 | 38,873 | 67.1 | Hon. Sir W.G. Beckett, Bt. | C | 14,066 | 54.0 |
| | | | E.O. Dodgson | L | 6,624 | 25.4 |
| | | | D. Stewart | Lab | 5,384 | 20.6 |
| | | | | | 7,442 | 28.6 |
| 1924 | 39,373 | 67.1 | Hon. Sir W.G. Beckett, Bt. | C | 18,502 | 70.0 |
| | | | S.C. Moore | Lab | 7,920 | 30.0 |
| | | | | | 10,582 | 40.0 |
| 1929 | 55,429 | 73.6 | O. Peake | C | 19,661 | 48.2 |
| | | | T. McCall | Lab | 11,180 | 27.4 |
| | | | T.E. Harvey | L | 9,944 | 24.4 |
| | | | | | 8,481 | 20.8 |
| 1931 | 59,948 | 74.0 | O. Peake | C | 34,964 | 78.8 |
| | | | L.J. Edwards | Lab | 9,427 | 21.2 |
| | | | | | 25,537 | 57.6 |
| 1935 | 66,551 | 66.8 | O. Peake | C | 30,636 | 69.0 |
| | | | L.J. Edwards | Lab | 13,792 | 31.0 |
| | | | | | 16,844 | 38.0 |
| 1945 | 75,625 | 71.9 | Rt. Hon. O. Peake | C | 22,848 | 42.0 |
| | | | R. Hodgson | Lab | 22,720 | 41.8 |
| | | | J.H.M. Scott | L | 8,824 | 16.2 |
| | | | | | 128 | 0.2 |

| Election | Electors | T'out | Candidate | Party | Votes | % |
|----------|----------|-------|-----------|-------|-------|---|
| 1918 | 36,829 | 51.9 | J.D. Birchall | Co C | 14,450 | 75.5 |
|  |  |  | J. Bromley | Lab | 4,680 | 24.5 |
|  |  |  |  |  | 9,770 | 51.0 |
| 1922 | 36,069 | 74.2 | J.D. Birchall | C | 12,343 | 46.1 |
|  |  |  | R.F. Walker | L | 7,891 | 29.5 |
|  |  |  | J. Badlay | Lab | 6,525 | 24.4 |
|  |  |  |  |  | 4,452 | 16.6 |
| 1923 | 37,045 | 73.9 | J.D. Birchall | C | 12,767 | 46.7 |
|  |  |  | F. Fountain | Lab/Co-op | 8,574 | 31.3 |
|  |  |  | R.F. Walker | L | 6,030 | 22.0 |
|  |  |  |  |  | 4,193 | 15.4 |
| 1924 | 38,039 | 74.6 | J.D. Birchall | C | 16,396 | 57.8 |
|  |  |  | Mrs. E.M. Penny | Lab/Co-op | 8,984 | 31.6 |
|  |  |  | G.R. Woodcock | L | 3,007* | 10.6 |
|  |  |  |  |  | 7,412 | 26.2 |
| 1929 | 54,076 | 74.3 | J.D. Birchall | C | 18,877 | 47.0 |
|  |  |  | D. Freeman | Lab | 13,050 | 32.5 |
|  |  |  | C.H. Boyle | L | 8,253 | 20.5 |
|  |  |  |  |  | 5,827 | 14.5 |
| 1931 | 56,984 | 73.6 | Sir J.D. Birchall | C | 31,671 | 75.5 |
|  |  |  | A.J. Dobbs | Lab | 10,294 | 24.5 |
|  |  |  |  |  | 21,377 | 51.0 |
| 1935 | 60,509 | 66.1 | Sir J.D. Birchall | C | 25,915 | 64.8 |
|  |  |  | A.J. Dobbs | Lab | 14,080 | 35.2 |
|  |  |  |  |  | 11,835 | 29.6 |
| [Resignation] |  |  |  |  |  |  |
| 1940 | 70,404 | 34.9 | J.J.C. Henderson | C | 23,882 | 97.1 |
| (13/3) |  |  | S. Allen | BUF | 722* | 2.9 |
|  |  |  |  |  | 23,160 | 94.2 |
| 1945 | 75,886 | 71.7 | Miss A.M. Bacon | Lab | 28,870 | 53.1 |
|  |  |  | J.J.C. Henderson | C | 20,406 | 37.5 |
|  |  |  | F.C. Wilson | L | 5,097* | 9.4 |
|  |  |  |  |  | 8,464 | 15.6 |

# LEEDS, SOUTH [155]

| Election | Electors | T'out | Candidate | Party | Votes | % |
|---|---|---|---|---|---|---|
| 1918 | 35,843 | 48.8 | †Sir W. Middlebrook | Co L | 10,609 | 60.6 |
| | | | F. Fountain | Lab | 5,510 | 31.5 |
| | | | J.A. Brook | Ind | 1,377* | 7.9 |
| | | | | | 5,099 | 29.1 |
| 1922 | 35,252 | 69.8 | H.C. Charleton | Lab | 13,210 | 53.7 |
| | | | Sir W. Middlebrook | L | 11,380 | 46.3 |
| | | | | | 1,830 | 7.4 |
| 1923 | 35,719 | 74.1 | H.C. Charleton | Lab | 11,705 | 44.2 |
| | | | R.J.N. Neville | C | 7,679 | 29.0 |
| | | | C.G. Gibson | L | 7,083 | 26.8 |
| | | | | | 4,026 | 15.2 |
| 1924 | 36,085 | 76.5 | H.C. Charleton | Lab | 12,799 | 46.3 |
| | | | B.T.G. Ford | C | 11,008 | 39.9 |
| | | | F. Geary | L | 3,801 | 13.8 |
| | | | | | 1,791 | 6.4 |
| 1929 | 45,084 | 76.2 | H.C. Charleton | Lab | 18,043 | 52.5 |
| | | | B.T.G. Ford | C | 9,433 | 27.5 |
| | | | E.K. Scott | L | 6,884 | 20.0 |
| | | | | | 8,610 | 25.0 |
| 1931 | 45,548 | 77.6 | B.N.H. Whiteside | C | 14,881 | 42.1 |
| | | | H.C. Charleton | Lab | 14,156 | 40.1 |
| | | | F. Boult | L | 6,291 | 17.8 |
| | | | | | 725 | 2.0 |
| 1935 | 44,886 | 73.7 | H.C. Charleton | Lab | 15,223 | 46.0 |
| | | | B.N.H. Whiteside | C | 14,207 | 43.0 |
| | | | W. Townend | SCPGB | 3,642* | 11.0 |
| | | | | | 1,016 | 3.0 |
| 1945 | 38,970 | 75.3 | H.T.N. Gaitskell | Lab | 17,899 | 61.0 |
| | | | A.M. Ramsden | C | 7,497 | 25.6 |
| | | | W. Barford | L | 3,933 | 13.4 |
| | | | | | 10,402 | 35.4 |

Note:—

1918: Brook was supported by the local branches of the three ex-servicemen organisations (NADSS, NFDSS, Comrades of the Great War).

## LEEDS, SOUTH-EAST [156]

| Election | Electors | T'out | Candidate | Party | Votes | % |
|---|---|---|---|---|---|---|
| 1918 | | | †J. O'Grady | Lab | Unopp. | |
| 1922 | 35,074 | 66.2 | J. O'Grady | Lab | 13,676 | 58.9 |
| | | | Miss M.P. Grant | L | 9,554 | 41.1 |
| | | | | | 4,122 | 17.8 |
| 1923 | 35,701 | 54.1 | J. O'Grady | Lab | 12,210 | 63.2 |
| | | | Hon. W.T. Whiteley | L | 7,110 | 36.8 |
| | | | | | 5,100 | 26.4 |
| 1924 | 35,994 | 71.8 | Sir H.H. Slesser | Lab | 15,133 | 58.6 |
| | | | Hon. W.T. Whiteley | L | 10,704 | 41.4 |
| | | | | | 4,429 | 17.2 |
| 1929 | 47,573 | 62.6 | Sir H.H. Slesser | Lab | 22,403 | 75.2 |
| | | | J.C. Spurr | C | 7,385 | 24.8 |
| | | | | | 15,018 | 50.4 |

[Resignation on appointment as a Lord Justice of Appeal]

| Election | Electors | T'out | Candidate | Party | Votes | % |
|---|---|---|---|---|---|---|
| 1929 (1/8) | 47,573 | 25.9 | J. Milner | Lab | 11,804 | 95.8 |
| | | | W.T.E. Brain | Com | 512* | 4.2 |
| | | | | | 11,292 | 91.6 |
| 1931 | 48,715 | 69.7 | J. Milner | Lab | 17,845 | 52.6 |
| | | | P.R. Le Mesurier | C | 16,109 | 47.4 |
| | | | | | 1,736 | 5.2 |
| 1935 | 47,555 | 62.5 | J. Milner | Lab | 19,552 | 65.7 |
| | | | P.R. Le Mesurier | C | 10,192 | 34.3 |
| | | | | | 9,360 | 31.4 |
| 1945 | 39,668 | 71.5 | Rt. Hon. J. Milner | Lab | 20,363 | 71.9 |
| | | | S. Beevers | C | 4,518 | 15.9 |
| | | | C.H. Tyers | L | 3,466* | 12.2 |
| | | | | | 15,845 | 56.0 |

# LEEDS, WEST  [157]

| Election | Electors | T'out | Candidate | Party | Votes | % |
|---|---|---|---|---|---|---|
| 1918 | 38,766 | 52.7 | J. Murray | Co L | 12,642 | 61.9 |
| | | | J. Arnott | Lab | 6,020 | 29.5 |
| | | | J.H. Chapman | Ind | 1,138* | 5.6 |
| | | | D.T. Barnes | Ind L | 619* | 3.0 |
| | | | | | 6,622 | 32.4 |
| 1922 | 38,259 | 67.6 | J. Murray | L | 13,391 | 51.7 |
| | | | T.W. Stamford | Lab | 12,487 | 48.3 |
| | | | | | 904 | 3.4 |
| 1923 | 39,175 | 71.6 | T.W. Stamford | Lab | 11,434 | 40.7 |
| | | | A.F.G. Renton | C | 9,432 | 33.6 |
| | | | J. Murray | L | 7,200 | 25.7 |
| | | | | | 2,002 | 7.1 |
| 1924 | 39,644 | 77.5 | T.W. Stamford | Lab | 13,057 | 42.5 |
| | | | A.F.G. Renton | C | 13,054 | 42.5 |
| | | | H. Brown | L | 4,597 | 15.0 |
| | | | | | 3 | 0.0 |
| 1929 | 50,107 | 79.4 | T.W. Stamford | Lab | 18,765 | 47.2 |
| | | | G.W. Martin | C | 13,129 | 33.0 |
| | | | R. Cleworth | L | 7,894 | 19.8 |
| | | | | | 5,636 | 14.2 |
| 1931 | 50,907 | 76.7 | S.V.T. Adams | C | 24,701 | 63.2 |
| | | | T.W. Stamford | Lab | 14,354 | 36.8 |
| | | | | | 10,347 | 26.4 |
| 1935 | 53,727 | 70.5 | S.V.T. Adams | C | 20,545 | 54.3 |
| | | | T.W. Stamford | Lab | 17,311 | 45.7 |
| | | | | | 3,234 | 8.6 |
| 1945 | 59,940 | 75.2 | T.W. Stamford | Lab | 26,593 | 59.1 |
| | | | S.V.T. Adams | C | 12,457 | 27.6 |
| | | | J. Booth | L | 6,008 | 13.3 |
| | | | | | 14,136 | 31.5 |
| [Death] | | | | | | |
| 1949 (21/7) | 61,112 | 65.1 | T.C. Pannell | Lab | 21,935 | 55.2 |
| | | | B. Mather | C | 17,826 | 44.8 |
| | | | | | 4,109 | 10.4 |

Note:—

1918: Chapman was supported by the local branches of the three ex-servicemen organisations (NADSS, NFDSS, Comrades of the Great War).

# LEICESTER, EAST [158]

| Election | Electors | T'out | Candidate | Party | Votes | % |
|---|---|---|---|---|---|---|
| 1918 | 37,687 | 65.6 | †Rt. Hon. Sir G. Hewart | Co L | 18,024 | 72.9 |
| | | | G. Banton | Lab | 6,697 | 27.1 |
| | | | | | 11,327 | 45.8 |

[Resignation on appointment as Lord Chief Justice of England and elevation to the Peerage — Lord Hewart]

| Election | Electors | T'out | Candidate | Party | Votes | % |
|---|---|---|---|---|---|---|
| 1922 (30/3) | 37,319 | 71.3 | G. Banton | Lab | 14,062 | 52.9 |
| | | | A.E. Marlow | Co L | 8,710 | 32.7 |
| | | | R.W. Allen | L | 3,825 | 14.4 |
| | | | | | 5,352 | 20.2 |
| 1922 | 37,749 | 76.9 | H.A. Evans | NL (C) | 15,164 | 52.3 |
| | | | G. Banton | Lab | 13,850 | 47.7 |
| | | | | | 1,314 | 4.6 |
| 1923 | 38,658 | 76.1 | G. Banton | Lab | 13,162 | 44.8 |
| | | | H.A. Evans | C | 8,247 | 28.0 |
| | | | J. Henderson-Stewart | L | 7,998 | 27.2 |
| | | | | | 4,915 | 16.8 |
| 1924 | 39,906 | 79.6 | J. de V. Loder | C | 16,090 | 50.7 |
| | | | G. Banton | Lab | 15,669 | 49.3 |
| | | | | | 421 | 1.4 |
| 1929 | 54,364 | 81.6 | E.F. Wise | Lab | 22,533 | 50.8 |
| | | | J. de V. Loder | C | 13,801 | 31.1 |
| | | | F. Lawson | L | 8,054 | 18.1 |
| | | | | | 8,732 | 19.7 |
| 1931 | 55,719 | 79.1 | A.M. Lyons | C | 30,265 | 68.7 |
| | | | E.F. Wise | Lab | 13,811 | 31.3 |
| | | | | | 16,454 | 37.4 |
| 1935 | 59,109 | 70.2 | A.M. Lyons | C | 20,442 | 49.2 |
| | | | F. Gould | Lab | 17,532 | 42.3 |
| | | | F. Lawson | L | 3,509* | 8.5 |
| | | | | | 2,910 | 6.9 |
| 1945 | 65,746 | 75.9 | T.N. Donovan | Lab | 28,414 | 57.0 |
| | | | A.M. Lyons | C | 15,182 | 30.4 |
| | | | D.G. Galloway | L | 6,306 | 12.6 |
| | | | | | 13,232 | 26.6 |

## LEICESTER, SOUTH [159]

| Election | Electors | T'out | Candidate | Party | Votes | % |
|---|---|---|---|---|---|---|
| 1918 | 35,909 | 66.7 | T.A. Blane | Co C | 18,498 | 77.2 |
| | | | F.F. Riley | Lab | 5,463 | 22.8 |
| | | | | | 13,035 | 54.4 |
| 1922 | 34,789 | 71.7 | W.G.W. Reynolds | C | 12,534 | 50.2 |
| | | | R.W. Allen | L | 12,425 | 49.8 |
| | | | | | 109 | 0.4 |
| 1923 | 35,710 | 71.0 | R.W. Allen | L | 14,692 | 57.9 |
| | | | W.G.W. Reynolds | C | 10,674 | 42.1 |
| | | | | | 4,018 | 15.8 |
| 1924 | 36,805 | 81.5 | C. Waterhouse | C | 15,005 | 50.0 |
| | | | H.B. Usher | Lab | 8,912 | 29.7 |
| | | | R.W. Allen | L | 6,079 | 20.3 |
| | | | | | 6,093 | 20.3 |
| 1929 | 53,890 | 80.4 | C. Waterhouse | C | 18,343 | 42.3 |
| | | | H.B. Usher | Lab | 16,198 | 37.4 |
| | | | H.G. Purchase | L | 8,811 | 20.3 |
| | | | | | 2,145 | 4.9 |
| 1931 | 54,208 | 78.7 | C. Waterhouse | C | 32,767 | 76.8 |
| | | | J. Dugdale | Lab | 9,892 | 23.2 |
| | | | | | 22,875 | 53.6 |
| 1935 | 54,500 | 70.2 | C. Waterhouse | C | 24,868 | 65.0 |
| | | | H.L. Maddock | Lab | 13,395 | 35.0 |
| | | | | | 11,473 | 30.0 |
| 1945 | 57,608 | 75.4 | H.W. Bowden | Lab | 19,541 | 45.0 |
| | | | Rt. Hon. C. Waterhouse | C | 18,373 | 42.3 |
| | | | T.A. Pratt | L | 5,509 | 12.7 |
| | | | | | 1,168 | 2.7 |

# LEICESTER, WEST [160]

| Election | Electors | T'out | Candidate | Party | Votes | % |
|---|---|---|---|---|---|---|
| 1918 | 40,634 | 66.2 | J.F. Green | Co NDP | 20,570 | 76.4 |
| | | | †J.R. MacDonald | Lab | 6,347 | 23.6 |
| | | | | | 14,223 | 52.8 |
| 1922 | 39,604 | 72.5 | A. Hill | Lab | 12,929 | 45.0 |
| | | | J.F. Green | NL | 8,137 | 28.4 |
| | | | Dr. G.E. Spero | L | 7,631 | 26.6 |
| | | | | | 4,792 | 16.6 |
| 1923 | 40,244 | 76.0 | F.W. Pethick-Lawrence | Lab | 13,634 | 44.6 |
| | | | Rt. Hon. W.L.S. Churchill | L | 9,236 | 30.2 |
| | | | A. Instone | C | 7,696 | 25.2 |
| | | | | | 4,398 | 14.4 |
| 1924 | 41,207 | 76.1 | F.W. Pethick-Lawrence | Lab | 16,047 | 51.2 |
| | | | Prof. M.A. Gerothwohl | L | 15,310 | 48.8 |
| | | | | | 737 | 2.4 |
| 1929 | 52,318 | 78.3 | F.W. Pethick-Lawrence | Lab | 22,635 | 55.3 |
| | | | P.V. Emrys-Evans | C | 10,691 | 26.1 |
| | | | C.W. Hartshorn | L | 7,617 | 18.6 |
| | | | | | 11,944 | 29.2 |
| 1931 | 53,252 | 74.6 | E.H. Pickering | L | 26,826 | 67.5 |
| | | | F.W. Pethick-Lawrence | Lab | 12,923 | 32.5 |
| | | | | | 13,903 | 35.0 |
| 1935 | 54,134 | 66.8 | Hon. H.G. Nicolson | N Lab (Nat) | 15,821 | 43.7 |
| | | | J. Morgan | Lab | 15,734 | 43.5 |
| | | | H.E. Crawfurd | L | 4,621 | 12.8 |
| | | | | | 87 | 0.2 |
| 1945 | 50,312 | 76.6 | B. Janner | Lab | 20,563 | 53.4 |
| | | | Hon. H.G. Nicolson | Nat | 13,348 | 34.6 |
| | | | J.A. Kirby | L | 4,639* | 12.0 |
| | | | | | 7,215 | 18.8 |

| Election | Electors | T'out | Candidate | Party | Votes | % |
|---|---|---|---|---|---|---|
| 1918 | 35,912 | 66.9 | †P.W. Raffan | L | 12,892 | 53.6 |
| | | | R.O. Jones | Lab | 11,146 | 46.4 |
| | | | | | 1,746 | 7.2 |
| 1922 | 37,050 | 89.9 | H. Twist | Lab | 15,006 | 45.0 |
| | | | H. Metcalfe | C | 11,279 | 33.9 |
| | | | J. Ashworth | L | 7,012 | 21.1 |
| | | | | | 3,727 | 11.1 |
| 1923 | 37,597 | 86.5 | J.J. Tinker | Lab | 13,989 | 43.0 |
| | | | R.A. Burrows | L | 9,854 | 30.3 |
| | | | H. Metcalfe | C | 8,664 | 26.7 |
| | | | | | 4,135 | 12.7 |
| 1924 | 38,010 | 88.2 | J.J. Tinker | Lab | 17,262 | 51.5 |
| | | | E. Owen | C | 16,247 | 48.5 |
| | | | | | 1,015 | 3.0 |
| 1929 | 50,982 | 88.3 | J.J. Tinker | Lab | 25,635 | 57.0 |
| | | | C.H. Grundy | C | 10,942 | 24.3 |
| | | | T. Hardy | L | 8,435 | 18.7 |
| | | | | | 14,693 | 32.7 |
| 1931 | 52,415 | 87.4 | J.J. Tinker | Lab | 23,965 | 52.3 |
| | | | P.T. Eckersley | C | 21,837 | 47.7 |
| | | | | | 2,128 | 4.6 |
| 1935 | | | J.J. Tinker | Lab | Unopp. | |
| 1945 | 57,476 | 80.9 | H. Boardman | Lab | 32,447 | 69.8 |
| | | | E. Heriot-Hill | C | 14,029 | 30.2 |
| | | | | | 18,418 | 39.6 |

Note:—

1918: Raffan was issued with the Coalition 'coupon' but repudiated it.

## LEYTON, EAST [162]

| Election | Electors | T'out | Candidate | Party | Votes | % |
|---|---|---|---|---|---|---|
| 1918 | 26,735 | 45.3 | C.J.L. Malone | Co L (BSP) (Com) | 4,319 | 35.7 |
| | | | E.E. Alexander | C | 4,119 | 34.0 |
| | | | W. Carter | Lab | 3,668 | 30.3 |
| | | | | | 200 | 1.7 |
| 1922 | 28,232 | 72.2 | E.E. Alexander | C | 7,866 | 38.6 |
| | | | W. Carter | Lab | 6,300 | 30.9 |
| | | | Sir W. Gibbons | NL | 4,568 | 22.4 |
| | | | E. Brotherton-Ratcliffe | L | 1,650* | 8.1 |
| | | | | | 1,566 | 7.7 |
| 1923 | 29,166 | 69.1 | A.G. Church | Lab | 7,944 | 39.5 |
| | | | E.E. Alexander | C | 6,533 | 32.4 |
| | | | T.T. Broad | L | 5,669 | 28.1 |
| | | | | | 1,411 | 7.1 |
| 1924 | 29,506 | 77.6 | E.E. Alexander | C | 10,649 | 46.4 |
| | | | A.G. Church | Lab | 9,087 | 39.7 |
| | | | R.W. Puddicombe | L | 3,174 | 13.9 |
| | | | | | 1,562 | 6.7 |
| 1929 | 35,680 | 72.6 | A.F. Brockway | Lab | 11,111 | 42.9 |
| | | | E.E. Alexander | C | 8,691 | 33.6 |
| | | | F.W. Davies | L | 6,096 | 23.5 |
| | | | | | 2,420 | 9.3 |
| 1931 | 36,598 | 75.7 | Sir F. Mills, Bt. | C | 17,285 | 62.4 |
| | | | A.F. Brockway | ILP | 10,433 | 37.6 |
| | | | | | 6,852 | 24.8 |
| 1935 | 35,011 | 67.1 | Sir F. Mills, Bt. | C | 10,836 | 46.1 |
| | | | A.E. Bechervaise | Lab | 10,507 | 44.7 |
| | | | E.T. Malindine | L | 2,161* | 9.2 |
| | | | | | 329 | 1.4 |
| 1945 | 29,093 | 68.2 | A.E. Bechervaise | Lab | 13,048 | 65.7 |
| | | | B.R. Braine | C | 6,802 | 34.3 |
| | | | | | 6,246 | 31.4 |

Note:—

1918: Malone attended the 1920 Labour Party Annual Conference as a delegate of the BSP. He claimed in a speech that he had never belonged to the official Liberal Party despite the fact that he accepted the Coalition Liberal 'coupon'.

As a result of a speech made at the Albert Hall in London on November 7, 1920, Malone was subsequently arrested and charged with an offence against the Defence of the Realm Regulations. He was convicted at Bow Street Magistrates Court on November 19, 1920, and sentenced to six months imprisonment in the second division.

# LEYTON, WEST  [163]

| Election | Electors | T'out | Candidate | Party | Votes | % |
|---|---|---|---|---|---|---|
| 1918 | 32,567 | 49.9 | H. Wrightson | Co C | 10,956 | 67.4 |
| | | | A.E. Newbould | L | 5,288 | 32.6 |
| | | | | | 5,668 | 34.8 |
| [Death] | | | | | | |
| 1919 (1/3) | 32,567 | 42.5 | A.E. Newbould | L | 7,934 | 57.3 |
| | | | J.F. Mason | Co C | 5,915 | 42.7 |
| | | | | | 2,019 | 14.6 |
| 1922 | 34,549 | 69.0 | J.D. Cassels | C | 11,157 | 46.8 |
| | | | A.E. Newbould | L | 7,021 | 29.4 |
| | | | A. Smith | Lab | 5,673 | 23.8 |
| | | | | | 4,136 | 17.4 |
| 1923 | 35,540 | 68.0 | J.D. Cassels | C | 8,349 | 34.5 |
| | | | A.E. Newbould | L | 8,285 | 34.3 |
| | | | A. Smith | Lab | 7,536 | 31.2 |
| | | | | | 64 | 0.2 |
| 1924 | 35,958 | 78.6 | J.D. Cassels | C | 13,212 | 46.7 |
| | | | A. Smith | Lab | 9,809 | 34.7 |
| | | | A.E. Newbould | L | 5,252 | 18.6 |
| | | | | | 3,403 | 12.0 |
| 1929 | 45,507 | 74.8 | Rev. R.W. Sorensen | Lab | 14,339 | 42.1 |
| | | | J.D. Cassels | C | 12,186 | 35.8 |
| | | | J. Johnston | L | 7,526 | 22.1 |
| | | | | | 2,153 | 6.3 |
| 1931 | 48,225 | 75.0 | Sir W.H. Sugden | C | 23,048 | 63.7 |
| | | | Rev. R.W. Sorensen | Lab | 13,138 | 36.3 |
| | | | | | 9,910 | 27.4 |
| 1935 | 48,071 | 68.0 | Rev. R.W. Sorensen | Lab | 16,408 | 50.2 |
| | | | Sir W.H. Sugden | C | 16,280 | 49.8 |
| | | | | | 128 | 0.4 |
| 1945 | 40,503 | 72.7 | Rev. R.W. Sorensen | Lab | 17,236 | 58.5 |
| | | | T.F.D. Rose | C | 8,507 | 28.9 |
| | | | Dr. B. Guyster | L | 3,708 | 12.6 |
| | | | | | 8,729 | 29.6 |

## LINCOLN [164]

| Election | Electors | T'out | Candidate | Party | Votes | % |
|---|---|---|---|---|---|---|
| 1918 | 31,365 | 74.4 | A.T. Davies | Co C | 11,114 | 47.7 |
| | | | R.A. Taylor | Lab | 6,658 | 28.5 |
| | | | †C.H. Roberts | L | 5,550 | 23.8 |
| | | | | | 4,456 | 19.2 |
| 1922 | 31,124 | 85.9 | A.T. Davies | C | 15,780 | 59.0 |
| | | | R.A. Taylor | Lab | 10,951 | 41.0 |
| | | | | | 4,829 | 18.0 |
| 1923 | 31,610 | 85.5 | A.T. Davies | C | 11,338 | 42.0 |
| | | | R.A. Taylor | Lab | 9,251 | 34.2 |
| | | | A.G. Macdonell | L | 6,447 | 23.8 |
| | | | | | 2,087 | 7.8 |
| 1924 | 31,768 | 88.5 | R.A. Taylor | Lab | 11,596 | 41.3 |
| | | | Sir G.C. Hamilton | C | 11,557 | 41.1 |
| | | | A.G. Macdonell | L | 4,952 | 17.6 |
| | | | | | 39 | 0.2 |
| 1929 | 39,419 | 88.5 | R.A. Taylor | Lab | 15,176 | 43.6 |
| | | | B.G. Lampard-Vachell | C | 11,978 | 34.3 |
| | | | R. Pattinson | L | 7,719 | 22.1 |
| | | | | | 3,198 | 9.3 |
| 1931 | 39,531 | 88.9 | W.S. Liddall | C | 20,688 | 58.9 |
| | | | R.A. Taylor | Lab | 14,455 | 41.1 |
| | | | | | 6,233 | 17.8 |
| 1935 | 39,526 | 84.0 | W.S. Liddall | C | 17,948 | 54.0 |
| | | | G. Deer | Lab | 15,264 | 46.0 |
| | | | | | 2,684 | 8.0 |
| 1945 | 42,457 | 80.3 | G. Deer | Lab | 14,052 | 41.3 |
| | | | Sir W.S. Liddall | C | 10,414 | 30.5 |
| | | | F.C. Truman | L | 9,625 | 28.2 |
| | | | | | 3,638 | 10.8 |

# LIVERPOOL, EAST TOXTETH [165]

| Election | Electors | T'out | Candidate | Party | Votes | % |
|---|---|---|---|---|---|---|
| 1918 | | | †J.S. Rankin | Co C | Unopp. | |
| | | | | | | |
| 1922 | 33,877 | 74.2 | J.S. Rankin | C | 15,149 | 60.3 |
| | | | Miss E.F. Rathbone | Ind | 9,984 | 39.7 |
| | | | | | 5,165 | 20.6 |
| | | | | | | |
| 1923 | | | J.S. Rankin | C | Unopp. | |
| | | | | | | |
| 1924 | 35,238 | 76.4 | A.E. Jacob | C | 16,139 | 59.9 |
| | | | C. Burden | Lab | 6,620 | 24.6 |
| | | | F.C. Bowring | L | 4,163 | 15.5 |
| | | | | | 9,519 | 35.3 |
| [Death] | | | | | | |
| 1929 | 36,388 | 61.7 | Hon. H.L. Mond | C | 9,692 | 43.2 |
| (19/3) | | | J.J. Cleary | Lab | 6,563 | 29.2 |
| | | | A.O. Roberts | L | 6,206 | 27.6 |
| | | | | | 3,129 | 14.0 |
| | | | | | | |
| 1929 | 48,812 | 75.5 | Hon. H.L. Mond | C | 17,678 | 47.9 |
| | | | J.J. Cleary | Lab | 9,904 | 26.9 |
| | | | A.O. Roberts | L | 9,287 | 25.2 |
| | | | | | 7,774 | 21.0 |
| [Succession to the Peerage — Lord Melchett] | | | | | | |
| 1931 | 49,518 | 45.6 | P.G.T. Buchan-Hepburn | C | 17,040 | 75.4 |
| (5/2) | | | C. Burden | Lab | 5,550 | 24.6 |
| | | | | | 11,490 | 50.8 |
| | | | | | | |
| 1931 | 50,357 | 74.0 | * P.G.T. Buchan-Hepburn | C | 28,187 | 75.6 |
| | | | A.S. Doran | L | 9,093 | 24.4 |
| | | | | | 19,094 | 51.2 |
| | | | | | | |
| 1935 | 52,543 | 65.2 | P.G.T. Buchan-Hepburn | C | 20,638 | 60.2 |
| | | | A.D. Dennis | L | 13,622 | 39.8 |
| | | | | | 7,016 | 20.4 |
| | | | | | | |
| 1945 | 52,484 | 70.1 | P.G.T. Buchan-Hepburn | C | 18,145 | 49.3 |
| | | | V.H.E. Baker | Lab | 12,376 | 33.6 |
| | | | Prof. W.L. Blease | L | 6,286 | 17.1 |
| | | | | | 5,769 | 15.7 |

Note:—

1922: Miss Rathbone was a member of Liverpool City Council at the time of the election. She received support from the Women's Citizenship Association and the local Liberal Party.

# LIVERPOOL, EDGE HILL [166]

| Election | Electors | T'out | Candidate | Party | Votes | % |
|---|---|---|---|---|---|---|
| 1918 | 30,683 | 50.3 | †Sir W.W. Rutherford | Co C | 9,832 | 63.8 |
| | | | P.J. Tevenan | Lab | 5,587 | 36.2 |
| | | | | | 4,245 | 27.6 |
| 1922 | 33,634 | 70.5 | Sir W.W. Rutherford | C | 14,186 | 59.8 |
| | | | J.H. Hayes | Lab | 9,520 | 40.2 |
| | | | | | 4,666 | 19.6 |
| [Resignation] | | | | | | |
| 1923 | 33,634 | 58.1 | J.H. Hayes | Lab | 10,300 | 52.7 |
| (6/3) | | | J.W. Hills | C | 9,250 | 47.3 |
| | | | | | 1,050 | 5.4 |
| 1923 | 34,021 | 69.9 | J.H. Hayes | Lab | 13,538 | 56.9 |
| | | | Hon. O.F.G. Stanley | C | 10,249 | 43.1 |
| | | | | | 3,289 | 13.8 |
| 1924 | 34,254 | 78.1 | J.H. Hayes | Lab | 14,168 | 53.0 |
| | | | D.C. Williams | C | 12,587 | 47.0 |
| | | | | | 1,581 | 6.0 |
| 1929 | 42,516 | 74.9 | J.H. Hayes | Lab | 17,650 | 55.4 |
| | | | Sir J.H. Rutherford, Bt. | C | 11,622 | 36.5 |
| | | | A.D. Dennis | L | 2,581* | 8.1 |
| | | | | | 6,028 | 18.9 |
| 1931 | 42,394 | 74.7 | Sir J.H. Rutherford, Bt. | C | 19,901 | 62.8 |
| | | | J.H. Hayes | Lab | 11,772 | 37.2 |
| | | | | | 8,129 | 25.6 |
| 1935 | 40,328 | 68.1 | A. Critchley | C | 13,882 | 50.5 |
| | | | J.H. Hayes | Lab | 13,581 | 49.5 |
| | | | | | 301 | 1.0 |
| 1945 | 30,661 | 66.1 | R. Clitherow | Lab | 13,150 | 64.9 |
| | | | W. Clothier | C | 7,111 | 35.1 |
| | | | | | 6,039 | 29.8 |
| [Death] | | | | | | |
| 1947 | 33,210 | 62.7 | A.J. Irvine | Lab | 10,827 | 52.1 |
| (11/9) | | | J.R. Bevins | C | 8,874 | 42.6 |
| | | | Sir H.W. Young | L | 910* | 4.4 |
| | | | D.W. Gibson | ILP | 154* | 0.7 |
| | | | C. Foster | Ind | 48* | 0.2 |
| | | | | | 1,953 | 9.5 |

Note:—

1923: Hills was Financial Secretary to the Treasury. He subsequently resigned.
(6/3)

| Election | Electors | T'out | Candidate | Party | Votes | % |
|---|---|---|---|---|---|---|
| 1918 | 25,606 | 47.4 | †Sir J.S. Harmood-Banner | Co C | 6,370 | 52.4 |
| | | | A.W. Brooksbank | Ind | 5,779 | 47.6 |
| | | | | | 591 | 4.8 |
| 1922 | 27,423 | 70.3 | Sir J.S. Harmood-Banner | C | 11,667 | 60.6 |
| | | | J. Toole | Lab | 7,600 | 39.4 |
| | | | | | 4,067 | 21.2 |
| 1923 | 28,193 | 59.8 | Sir J.S. Harmood-Banner | C | 9,183 | 54.5 |
| | | | H. Walker | Lab | 7,673 | 45.5 |
| | | | | | 1,510 | 9.0 |
| 1924 | 28,725 | 72.3 | H.C. Woodcock | C | 10,705 | 51.5 |
| | | | H. Walker | Lab | 10,075 | 48.5 |
| | | | | | 630 | 3.0 |
| 1929 | 35,430 | 75.9 | D. Hall Caine | Lab (N Lab) | 14,234 | 52.9 |
| | | | Miss M. Beavan | C | 12,667 | 47.1 |
| | | | | | 1,567 | 5.8 |
| 1931 | 34,969 | 71.3 | F. Hornby | C | 12,186 | 48.9 |
| | | | S.L. Treleaven | Lab | 7,786 | 31.2 |
| | | | D. Hall Caine | N Lab | 4,950 | 19.9 |
| | | | | | 4,400 | 17.7 |
| 1935 | 32,275 | 67.4 | B.V. Kirby | Lab | 10,962 | 50.4 |
| | | | R.H. Etherton | C | 10,785 | 49.6 |
| | | | | | 177 | 0.8 |
| 1945 | 22,084 | 62.9 | B.V. Kirby | Lab | 9,088 | 65.4 |
| | | | W. Hill | C | 4,806 | 34.6 |
| | | | | | 4,282 | 30.8 |

Note:—

1918: Brooksbank was the nominee of the local branch of the NFDSS.

# LIVERPOOL, EXCHANGE [168]

| Election | Electors | T'out | Candidate | Party | Votes | % |
|---|---|---|---|---|---|---|
| 1918 | 35,625 | 52.0 | †L.F. Scott | Co C | 10,286 | 55.6 |
| | | | A. Harford | N | 8,225 | 44.4 |
| | | | | | 2,061 | 11.2 |
| [Appointed Solicitor-General] | | | | | | |
| 1922 (13/3) | | | L.F. Scott | Co C | Unopp. | |
| 1922 | 37,797 | 74.8 | Sir L.F. Scott | C | 15,650 | 55.4 |
| | | | J. Devlin | N | 12,614 | 44.6 |
| | | | | | 3,036 | 10.8 |
| 1923 | 40,221 | 51.9 | Sir L.F. Scott | C | 10,551 | 50.5 |
| | | | W. Grogan | N | 10,322 | 49.5 |
| | | | | | 229 | 1.0 |
| 1924 | | | Sir L.F. Scott | C | Unopp. | |
| 1929 | 51,820 | 65.9 | Sir J.P. Reynolds, Bt. | C | 17,179 | 50.3 |
| | | | W.A. Robinson | Lab | 16,970 | 49.7 |
| | | | | | 209 | 0.6 |
| 1931 | 50,638 | 69.0 | Sir J.P. Reynolds, Bt. | C | 24,038 | 68.8 |
| | | | T. McLean | Lab | 10,894 | 31.2 |
| | | | | | 13,144 | 37.6 |
| [Death] | | | | | | |
| 1933 (19/1) | 50,060 | 55.2 | J.J. Shute | C | 15,198 | 55.0 |
| | | | S.S. Silverman | Lab | 12,412 | 45.0 |
| | | | | | 2,786 | 10.0 |
| 1935 | 46,404 | 65.7 | Sir J.J. Shute | C | 17,439 | 57.2 |
| | | | S. Mahon | Lab | 13,027 | 42.8 |
| | | | | | 4,412 | 14.4 |
| 1945 | 26,794 | 60.9 | Mrs. E.M. Braddock | Lab | 8,494 | 52.0 |
| | | | Sir J.J. Shute | C | 7,829 | 48.0 |
| | | | | | 665 | 4.0 |

# LIVERPOOL, FAIRFIELD [169]

| Election | Electors | T'out | Candidate | Party | Votes | % |
|---|---|---|---|---|---|---|
| 1918 | 27,727 | 54.9 | J.B.B. Cohen | C | 7,698 | 50.6 |
| | | | F.L. Joseph | Co L | 4,188 | 27.5 |
| | | | G. Porter | Lab | 3,337 | 21.9 |
| | | | | | 3,510 | 23.1 |
| 1922 | 30,938 | 64.0 | J.B.B. Cohen | C | 14,316 | 72.3 |
| | | | G. Porter | Lab | 5,478 | 27.7 |
| | | | | | 8,838 | 44.6 |
| 1923 | | | J.B.B. Cohen | C | Unopp. | |
| 1924 | 31,430 | 72.2 | J.B.B. Cohen | C | 14,277 | 62.9 |
| | | | Mrs. M.A. Mercer | Lab | 8,412 | 37.1 |
| | | | | | 5,865 | 25.8 |
| 1929 | 43,183 | 71.9 | J.B.B. Cohen | C | 16,436 | 52.9 |
| | | | J.H. Sutcliffe | Lab | 14,614 | 47.1 |
| | | | | | 1,822 | 5.8 |
| 1931 | 44,979 | 72.5 | C.E.R. Brocklebank | C | 24,636 | 75.6 |
| | | | A. Dodd | Lab | 7,960 | 24.4 |
| | | | | | 16,676 | 51.2 |
| 1935 | 48,241 | 61.7 | C.E.R. Brocklebank | C | 18,596 | 62.5 |
| | | | A.S. Moody | Lab | 11,155 | 37.5 |
| | | | | | 7,441 | 25.0 |
| 1945 | 48,033 | 65.8 | A.S. Moody | Lab | 14,475 | 45.7 |
| | | | Sir C.E.R. Brocklebank | C | 13,328 | 42.2 |
| | | | W.H. Ledsom | L | 3,816* | 12.1 |
| | | | | | 1,147 | 3.5 |

| Election | Electors | T'out | Candidate | Party | Votes | % |
|----------|----------|-------|-----------|-------|-------|---|
| 1918 | 30,760 | 50.0 | †J. de F. Pennefather | Co C | 10,380 | 67.4 |
|      |        |      | S. Mason | Lab | 5,012 | 32.6 |
|      |        |      |          |     | 5,368 | 34.8 |
| 1922 |        |      | J. de F. Pennefather | C | Unopp. | |
| 1923 |        |      | Sir J. de F. Pennefather, Bt. | C | Unopp. | |
| 1924 | 32,262 | 73.7 | Sir J. de F. Pennefather, Bt. | C | 14,392 | 60.6 |
|      |        |      | E. Sandham | Lab | 9,369 | 39.4 |
|      |        |      |          |     | 5,023 | 21.2 |
| 1929 | 40,646 | 72.9 | E. Sandham | Lab | 15,222 | 51.3 |
|      |        |      | R. Rankin | C | 14,429 | 48.7 |
|      |        |      |          |     | 793 | 2.6 |
| 1931 | 40,862 | 77.5 | R. Rankin | C | 14,303 | 45.2 |
|      |        |      | E. Sandham | ILP | 9,531 | 30.1 |
|      |        |      | Rev. H.D. Longbottom | LPP | 7,834 | 24.7 |
|      |        |      |          |     | 4,772 | 15.1 |
| 1935 | 39,150 | 69.5 | R. Rankin | C | 10,540 | 38.8 |
|      |        |      | J. Hamilton | Lab | 9,984 | 36.7 |
|      |        |      | Rev. H.D. Longbottom | LPP | 6,677 | 24.5 |
|      |        |      |          |     | 556 | 2.1 |
| 1945 | 30,630 | 64.2 | W. Keenan | Lab | 10,640 | 54.2 |
|      |        |      | A.O. Roberts | C | 6,414 | 32.6 |
|      |        |      | Rev. H.D. Longbottom | LPP | 2,601 | 13.2 |
|      |        |      |          |     | 4,226 | 21.6 |

| Election | Electors | T'out | Candidate | Party | Votes | % |
|---|---|---|---|---|---|---|
| 1918 | | | †T.P. O'Connor | N | Unopp. | |
| 1922 | | | T.P. O'Connor | N | Unopp. | |
| 1923 | | | T.P. O'Connor | N | Unopp. | |
| 1924 | | | Rt. Hon. T.P. O'Connor | N | Unopp. | |
| 1929 [Death] | | | Rt. Hon. T.P. O'Connor | N | Unopp. | |
| 1929 (14/12) | | | D.G. Logan | Lab | Unopp. | |
| 1931 | 39,975 | 68.7 | D.G. Logan | Lab | 15,521 | 56.5 |
| | | | E. Errington | C | 10,280 | 37.5 |
| | | | L.J. McGree | Com | 1,544* | 5.6 |
| | | | F. Abraham | Ind | 99* | 0.4 |
| | | | | | 5,241 | 19.0 |
| 1935 | 38,052 | 64.1 | D.G. Logan | Lab | 16,036 | 65.7 |
| | | | L.H. Wright | C | 8,372 | 34.3 |
| | | | | | 7,664 | 31.4 |
| 1945 | | | D.G. Logan | Lab | Unopp. | |

Note:—

1929: Logan had been associated with the Nationalist movement in Ireland for a number
(14/12) of years prior to joining the Labour Party.

# LIVERPOOL, WALTON [172]

| Election | Electors | T'out | Candidate | Party | Votes | % |
|---|---|---|---|---|---|---|
| 1918 | 29,128 | 55.1 | H.W.S. Chilcott | Co C | 11,457 | 71.4 |
| | | | R.D. Smith | Lab | 4,580 | 28.6 |
| | | | | | 6,877 | 42.8 |
| 1922 | | | Sir H.W.S. Chilcott | C | Unopp. | |
| 1923 | | | Sir H.W.S. Chilcott | C | Unopp. | |
| 1924 | 31,482 | 76.9 | Sir H.W.S. Chilcott | C | 13,387 | 55.3 |
| | | | T.W. Gillinder | Lab | 8,924 | 36.8 |
| | | | S. Skelton | L | 1,910* | 7.9 |
| | | | | | 4,463 | 18.5 |
| 1929 | 51,175 | 76.0 | R. Purbrick | C | 16,623 | 42.7 |
| | | | F.A.P. Rowe | Lab | 16,395 | 42.2 |
| | | | G.H. Howard-Jones | L | 5,857 | 15.1 |
| | | | | | 228 | 0.5 |
| 1931 | 54,605 | 77.5 | R. Purbrick | C | 31,135 | 73.6 |
| | | | F.A.P. Rowe | Lab | 11,183 | 26.4 |
| | | | | | 19,952 | 47.2 |
| 1935 | 57,136 | 64.2 | R. Purbrick | C | 22,623 | 61.6 |
| | | | F.L. McGhee | Lab | 14,079 | 38.4 |
| | | | | | 8,544 | 23.2 |
| 1945 | 60,776 | 69.4 | J. Haworth | Lab | 18,385 | 43.6 |
| | | | R. Purbrick | C | 15,749 | 37.4 |
| | | | E.R. Webster | L | 8,028 | 19.0 |
| | | | | | 2,636 | 6.2 |

# LIVERPOOL, WAVERTREE [173]

| Election | Electors | T'out | Candidate | Party | Votes | % |
|---|---|---|---|---|---|---|
| 1918 | 31,262 | 60.5 | Dr. N. Raw | Co C | 11,326 | 59.9 |
| | | | C. Wilson | Lab | 5,103 | 27.0 |
| | | | Sir A.A. Booth, Bt. | L | 2,484 | 13.1 |
| | | | | | 6,223 | 32.9 |
| 1922 | 33,558 | 69.5 | Sir H. Smith | C | 14,372 | 61.6 |
| | | | Rev. J.V. Laughland | Lab | 8,941 | 38.4 |
| | | | | | 5,431 | 23.2 |
| 1923 | 34,869 | 71.9 | H.R. Rathbone | L | 9,349 | 37.3 |
| | | | Sir H. Smith | C | 8,700 | 34.7 |
| | | | Rev. J.V. Laughland | Lab | 7,025 | 28.0 |
| | | | | | 649 | 2.6 |
| 1924 | 36,936 | 80.3 | J.A. Tinne | C | 14,063 | 47.4 |
| | | | W.A. Robinson | Lab | 10,383 | 35.0 |
| | | | H.R. Rathbone | L | 5,206 | 17.6 |
| | | | | | 3,680 | 12.4 |
| 1929 | 53,989 | 78.1 | J.A. Tinne | C | 16,880 | 40.0 |
| | | | S.L. Treleaven | Lab | 13,585 | 32.2 |
| | | | H.R. Rathbone | L | 11,723 | 27.8 |
| | | | | | 3,295 | 7.8 |

[Resignation]

| Election | Electors | T'out | Candidate | Party | Votes | % |
|---|---|---|---|---|---|---|
| 1931 (23/6) | 55,622 | 51.7 | A.R.N. Nall-Cain | C | 18,687 | 65.0 |
| | | | S.L. Treleaven | Lab | 10,042 | 35.0 |
| | | | | | 8,645 | 30.0 |
| 1931 | 57,171 | 75.2 | A.R.N. Nall-Cain | C | 33,476 | 77.9 |
| | | | C.G. Clark | Lab | 9,504 | 22.1 |
| | | | | | 23,972 | 55.8 |

[Succession to the Peerage — Lord Brocket]

| Election | Electors | T'out | Candidate | Party | Votes | % |
|---|---|---|---|---|---|---|
| 1935 (6/2) | 61,053 | 72.3 | J.J. Cleary | Lab | 15,611 | 35.4 |
| | | | J. Platt | C | 13,771 | 31.2 |
| | | | R.F.E.S. Churchill | Ind C | 10,575 | 23.9 |
| | | | T.A. Morris | L | 4,208* | 9.5 |
| | | | | | 1,840 | 4.2 |
| 1935 | 62,840 | 73.2 | P.S. Shaw | C | 26,915 | 58.5 |
| | | | J.J. Cleary | Lab | 19,068 | 41.5 |
| | | | | | 7,847 | 17.0 |
| 1945 | 72,250 | 73.1 | H.V.A.M. Raikes | C | 25,470 | 48.2 |
| | | | D.M. Van Abbé | Lab | 20,249 | 38.4 |
| | | | L.H. Storey | L | 7,063 | 13.4 |
| | | | | | 5,221 | 9.8 |

Note:—

1935: Churchill was opposed to the Government's policy on India.
(6/2)

# LIVERPOOL, WEST DERBY  [174]

| Election | Electors | T'out | Candidate | Party | Votes | % |
|---|---|---|---|---|---|---|
| 1918 | 31,276 | 55.1 | †Rt. Hon. Sir F.E. Smith, Bt. | Co C | 11,622 | 67.4 |
|  |  |  | G. Nelson | Lab | 5,618 | 32.6 |
|  |  |  |  |  | 6,004 | 34.8 |

[Resignation on appointment as Lord Chancellor and elevation to the Peerage — Earl of Birkenhead]

| | | | | | | |
|---|---|---|---|---|---|---|
| 1919 | 31,276 | 34.3 | Sir W.R. Hall | Co C | 6,062 | 56.5 |
| (26/2) |  |  | G. Nelson | Lab | 4,670 | 43.5 |
|  |  |  |  |  | 1,392 | 13.0 |
| 1922 | 35,330 | 65.0 | Sir W.R. Hall | C | 16,179 | 70.5 |
|  |  |  | D.R. Williams | Lab | 6,785 | 29.5 |
|  |  |  |  |  | 9,394 | 41.0 |
| 1923 | 37,618 | 63.5 | C.S. Jones | L | 12,942 | 54.2 |
|  |  |  | Sir W.R. Hall | C | 10,952 | 45.8 |
|  |  |  |  |  | 1,990 | 8.4 |
| 1924 | 38,579 | 77.2 | J.S. Allen | C | 15,667 | 52.5 |
|  |  |  | T.G. Adams | Lab | 8,807 | 29.6 |
|  |  |  | C.S. Jones | L | 5,321 | 17.9 |
|  |  |  |  |  | 6,860 | 22.9 |
| 1929 | 53,745 | 73.1 | Sir J.S. Allen | C | 16,794 | 42.7 |
|  |  |  | W.H. Moore | Lab | 14,124 | 36.0 |
|  |  |  | A.P. Jones | L | 8,368 | 21.3 |
|  |  |  |  |  | 2,670 | 6.7 |
| 1931 | 55,752 | 74.0 | Sir J.S. Allen | C | 32,202 | 78.0 |
|  |  |  | J.J. Cleary | Lab | 9,077 | 22.0 |
|  |  |  |  |  | 23,125 | 56.0 |

[Death]

| | | | | | | |
|---|---|---|---|---|---|---|
| 1935 |  |  | D.P.M. Fyfe | C | Unopp. |  |
| (6/7) |  |  |  |  |  |  |
| 1935 | 58,031 | 62.6 | D.P.M. Fyfe | C | 21,196 | 58.4 |
|  |  |  | J. Haworth | Lab | 10,218 | 28.1 |
|  |  |  | D.K. Mitchell | L | 4,911 | 13.5 |
|  |  |  |  |  | 10,978 | 30.3 |
| 1945 | 59,460 | 67.6 | Rt. Hon. Sir D.P.M. Fyfe | C | 21,798 | 54.3 |
|  |  |  | R.J. Lewis | Lab/Co-op | 18,370 | 45.7 |
|  |  |  |  |  | 3,428 | 8.6 |

# LIVERPOOL, WEST TOXTETH [175]

| Election | Electors | T'out | Candidate | Party | Votes | % |
|---|---|---|---|---|---|---|
| 1918 | 35,806 | 55.7 | †R.P. Houston | Co C | 13,083 | 65.6 |
| | | | W.A. Robinson | Lab | 6,850 | 34.4 |
| | | | | | 6,233 | 31.2 |
| 1922 | 36,500 | 69.1 | Sir R.P. Houston, Bt. | C | 15,030 | 59.6 |
| | | | J. Gibbins | Lab | 10,209 | 40.4 |
| | | | | | 4,821 | 19.2 |
| 1923 | 37,462 | 66.1 | Sir R.P. Houston, Bt. | C | 12,457 | 50.3 |
| | | | J. Gibbins | Lab | 12,318 | 49.7 |
| | | | | | 139 | 0.6 |
| [Resignation] | | | | | | |
| 1924 | 37,462† | 76.2 | J. Gibbins | Lab | 15,505 | 54.3 |
| (22/5) | | | T. White | C | 13,034 | 45.7 |
| | | | | | 2,471 | 8.6 |
| 1924 | 38,546 | 79.7 | J. Gibbins | Lab | 15,542 | 50.6 |
| | | | T. White | C | 15,163 | 49.4 |
| | | | | | 379 | 1.2 |
| 1929 | 47,608 | 76.2 | J. Gibbins | Lab | 19,988 | 55.1 |
| | | | G. Watson | C | 16,309 | 44.9 |
| | | | | | 3,679 | 10.2 |
| 1931 | 46,766 | 76.1 | C.T. Wilson | C | 20,633 | 57.9 |
| | | | J. Gibbins | Lab | 14,978 | 42.1 |
| | | | | | 5,655 | 15.8 |
| [Resignation on appointment as a Metropolitan Police Magistrate] | | | | | | |
| 1935 | 45,373 | 53.9 | J. Gibbins | Lab | 14,908 | 60.9 |
| (16/7) | | | J.W.J. Cremlyn | C | 9,565 | 39.1 |
| | | | | | 5,343 | 21.8 |
| 1935 | 44,634 | 78.6 | J. Gibbins | Lab | 18,543 | 52.9 |
| | | | R.F.E.S. Churchill | C | 16,539 | 47.1 |
| | | | | | 2,004 | 5.8 |
| 1945 | 36,104 | 68.5 | J. Gibbins | Lab | 14,780 | 59.7 |
| | | | J.R. Bevins | C | 9,966 | 40.3 |
| | | | | | 4,814 | 19.4 |

| Election | Electors | T'out | Candidate | Party | Votes | % |
|---|---|---|---|---|---|---|
| 1918 | 37,214 | 47.9 | A. Hailwood | Co C | 8,641 | 48.5 |
| | | | T. Lowth | Lab | 5,670 | 31.8 |
| | | | H.M. Stephenson | Nat P | 3,510 | 19.7 |
| | | | | | 2,971 | 16.7 |
| 1922 | 37,572 | 71.4 | T. Lowth | Lab | 14,031 | 52.3 |
| | | | A. Hailwood | C | 12,777 | 47.7 |
| | | | | | 1,254 | 4.6 |
| 1923 | 37,404 | 69.3 | T. Lowth | Lab | 15,673 | 60.4 |
| | | | A. Hailwood | C | 10,266 | 39.6 |
| | | | | | 5,407 | 20.8 |
| 1924 | 38,188 | 76.1 | T. Lowth | Lab | 15,941 | 54.9 |
| | | | Miss M.L.K. Jones | C | 13,115 | 45.1 |
| | | | | | 2,826 | 9.8 |
| 1929 | 46,158 | 72.0 | T. Lowth | Lab | 20,041 | 60.3 |
| | | | Miss M.L.K. Jones | C | 13,177 | 39.7 |
| | | | | | 6,864 | 20.6 |
| [Death] | | | | | | |
| 1931 (22/6) | 47,252 | 64.1 | J. Henderson | Lab | 15,294 | 50.5 |
| | | | S.L. Elborne | C | 14,980 | 49.5 |
| | | | | | 314 | 1.0 |
| 1931 | 47,658 | 78.3 | A.G. Fuller | C | 21,630 | 58.0 |
| | | | J. Henderson | Lab | 15,664 | 42.0 |
| | | | | | 5,966 | 16.0 |
| 1935 | 43,314 | 71.4 | J. Henderson | Lab | 16,364 | 52.9 |
| | | | A.G. Fuller | C | 14,556 | 47.1 |
| | | | | | 1,808 | 5.8 |
| 1945 | 32,899 | 68.2 | J. Henderson | Lab | 14,360 | 64.0 |
| | | | Mrs. N. Beer | C | 8,093 | 36.0 |
| | | | | | 6,267 | 28.0 |

[Seat Vacant at Dissolution (Elevation to the Peerage — Lord Henderson of Ardwick)].

## MANCHESTER, BLACKLEY [177]

| Election | Electors | T'out | Candidate | Party | Votes | % |
|---|---|---|---|---|---|---|
| 1918 | 24,857 | 58.9 | W.J.H. Briggs | C | 7,997 | 54.6 |
| | | | A.E. Townend | Lab | 3,659 | 25.0 |
| | | | P.M. Oliver | L | 2,986 | 20.4 |
| | | | | | 4,338 | 29.6 |
| 1922 | 25,585 | 81.4 | W.J.H. Briggs | C | 9,023 | 43.3 |
| | | | P.M. Oliver | L | 6,219 | 29.9 |
| | | | A.E. Townend | Lab | 5,580 | 26.8 |
| | | | | | 2,804 | 13.4 |
| 1923 | 25,927 | 75.4 | P.M. Oliver | L | 12,235 | 62.6 |
| | | | W.J.H. Briggs | C | 7,313 | 37.4 |
| | | | | | 4,922 | 25.2 |
| 1924 | 26,374 | 85.5 | W.J.H. Briggs | C | 9,737 | 43.2 |
| | | | P.M. Oliver | L | 6,609 | 29.3 |
| | | | W.A. Burke | Lab | 6,195 | 27.5 |
| | | | | | 3,128 | 13.9 |
| 1929 | 36,590 | 82.6 | P.M. Oliver | L | 11,006 | 36.4 |
| | | | W.J.H. Briggs | C | 10,118 | 33.5 |
| | | | W.A. Burke | Lab | 9,091 | 30.1 |
| | | | | | 888 | 2.9 |
| 1931 | 40,258 | 84.1 | J. Lees-Jones | C | 15,717 | 46.5 |
| | | | P.M. Oliver | L | 11,382 | 33.6 |
| | | | W.A. Burke | Lab | 6,752 | 19.9 |
| | | | | | 4,335 | 12.9 |
| 1935 | 44,314 | 78.1 | J. Lees-Jones | C | 15,355 | 44.3 |
| | | | P.M. Oliver | L | 9,893 | 28.6 |
| | | | W.E. Davies | Lab | 9,370 | 27.1 |
| | | | | | 5,462 | 15.7 |
| 1945 | 58,437 | 74.9 | J. Diamond | Lab | 19,561 | 44.7 |
| | | | J. Lees-Jones | C | 14,747 | 33.7 |
| | | | P.M. Oliver | L | 9,480 | 21.6 |
| | | | | | 4,814 | 11.0 |

# MANCHESTER, CLAYTON [178]

| Election | Electors | T'out | Candidate | Party | Votes | % |
|---|---|---|---|---|---|---|
| 1918 | 34,659 | 57.5 | E. Hopkinson | C | 12,285 | 61.6 |
| | | | †J.E. Sutton | Lab | 7,654 | 38.4 |
| | | | | | 4,631 | 23.2 |
| [Death] | | | | | | |
| 1922 | 34,851 | 73.7 | J.E. Sutton | Lab | 14,662 | 57.1 |
| (18/2) | | | W.H. Flanagan | C | 11,038 | 42.9 |
| | | | | | 3,624 | 14.2 |
| 1922 | 35,681 | 82.9 | W.H. Flanagan | C | 14,800 | 50.0 |
| | | | J.E. Sutton | Lab | 14,789 | 50.0 |
| | | | | | 11 | 0.0 |
| 1923 | 36,430 | 83.5 | J.E. Sutton | Lab | 17,255 | 56.7 |
| | | | W.H. Flanagan | C | 13,164 | 43.3 |
| | | | | | 4,091 | 13.4 |
| 1924 | 37,729 | 84.7 | J.E. Sutton | Lab | 17,338 | 54.2 |
| | | | T.E. Thorpe | C | 14,634 | 45.8 |
| | | | | | 2,704 | 8.4 |
| 1929 | 46,177 | 83.1 | J.E. Sutton | Lab | 21,103 | 55.0 |
| | | | W.H. Flanagan | C | 14,062 | 36.6 |
| | | | C.H. Travis | L | 3,207* | 8.4 |
| | | | | | 7,041 | 18.4 |
| 1931 | 47,038 | 83.4 | W.H. Flanagan | C | 22,072 | 56.2 |
| | | | J.E. Sutton | Lab | 17,169 | 43.8 |
| | | | | | 4,903 | 12.4 |
| 1935 | 46,475 | 77.0 | J. Jagger | Lab | 19,225 | 53.7 |
| | | | T.H. Hewlett | C | 16,557 | 46.3 |
| | | | | | 2,668 | 7.4 |
| [Death] | | | | | | |
| 1942 | 45,720 | 20.8 | H. Thorneycroft | Lab | 8,892 | 93.3 |
| (17/10) | | | E.H. Foot | Ind | 636* | 6.7 |
| | | | | | 8,256 | 86.6 |
| 1945 | 46,394 | 69.6 | H. Thorneycroft | Lab | 22,401 | 69.4 |
| | | | P. Smith | NL | 9,883 | 30.6 |
| | | | | | 12,518 | 38.8 |

| Election | Electors | T'out | Candidate | Party | Votes | % |
|---|---|---|---|---|---|---|
| 1918 | 34,569 | 51.0 | †Sir J.S. Randles | Co C | 12,290 | 69.8 |
| | | | Sir A.A. Haworth, Bt. | L | 5,326 | 30.2 |
| | | | | | 6,964 | 39.6 |
| 1922 | 39,343 | 61.2 | Sir E.F. Stockton | C | 13,919 | 57.8 |
| | | | Sir A.W. Barton | L | 10,148 | 42.2 |
| | | | | | 3,771 | 15.6 |
| 1923 | 38,218 | 59.4 | R.N. Barclay | L | 12,248 | 54.0 |
| | | | Sir E.F. Stockton | C | 10,449 | 46.0 |
| | | | | | 1,799 | 8.0 |
| 1924 | 40,487 | 59.0 | E.B. Fielden | C | 13,200 | 55.2 |
| | | | R.N. Barclay | L | 10,693 | 44.8 |
| | | | | | 2,507 | 10.4 |
| 1929 | 48,836 | 70.2 | E.B. Fielden | C | 13,691 | 39.9 |
| | | | R.N. Barclay | L | 11,112 | 32.4 |
| | | | A. Moss | Lab | 9,500 | 27.7 |
| | | | | | 2,579 | 7.5 |
| 1931 | 49,868 | 66.2 | E.B. Fielden | C | 24,261 | 73.5 |
| | | | E.A. Gower | Lab | 8,727 | 26.5 |
| | | | | | 15,534 | 47.0 |
| 1935 | 46,606 | 63.3 | P.T. Eckersley | C | 15,956 | 54.1 |
| | | | E.I. Mendel | Lab | 8,313 | 28.2 |
| | | | Sir G. Paish | L | 5,228 | 17.7 |
| | | | | | 7,643 | 25.9 |
| [Death] | | | | | | |
| 1940 (21/9) | | | T.H. Hewlett | C | Unopp. | |
| 1945 | 28,697 | 70.2 | N.H. Lever | Lab | 11,067 | 55.0 |
| | | | T.H. Hewlett | C | 7,050 | 35.0 |
| | | | H. Kenyon | L | 2,018* | 10.0 |
| | | | | | 4,017 | 20.0 |

| Election | Electors | T'out | Candidate | Party | Votes | % |
|---|---|---|---|---|---|---|
| 1918 | 33,382 | 58.0 | †Rt. Hon. J. Hodge | Lab | 13,047 | 67.4 |
| | | | H. White | Ind C | 5,005 | 25.9 |
| | | | J.T. Murphy | SLP | 1,300* | 6.7 |
| | | | | | 8,042 | 41.5 |
| 1922 | 35,567 | 79.0 | Rt. Hon. J. Hodge | Lab | 15,058 | 53.6 |
| | | | W. Heap | C | 13,057 | 46.4 |
| | | | | | 2,001 | 7.2 |
| 1923 | 35,963 | 74.5 | J. Compton | Lab | 16,080 | 60.0 |
| | | | W. Heap | C | 10,702 | 40.0 |
| | | | | | 5,378 | 20.0 |
| 1924 | 36,378 | 80.5 | J. Compton | Lab | 16,383 | 56.0 |
| | | | B.C. Sellars | C | 12,898 | 44.0 |
| | | | | | 3,485 | 12.0 |
| 1929 | 44,300 | 81.5 | J. Compton | Lab | 22,056 | 61.1 |
| | | | A.C. Critchley | C | 10,664 | 29.5 |
| | | | Mrs. B.A. Bayfield | L | 3,385* | 9.4 |
| | | | | | 11,392 | 31.6 |
| 1931 | 47,062 | 81.9 | E.A.G.S. Bailey | C | 21,228 | 55.1 |
| | | | J. Compton | Lab | 16,316 | 42.3 |
| | | | C. Flanagan | Com | 1,000* | 2.6 |
| | | | | | 4,912 | 12.8 |
| 1935 | 46,157 | 77.7 | J. Compton | Lab | 20,039 | 55.9 |
| | | | E.A.G.S. Bailey | C | 15,833 | 44.1 |
| | | | | | 4,206 | 11.8 |

[Death]

| Election | Electors | T'out | Candidate | Party | Votes | % |
|---|---|---|---|---|---|---|
| 1937 (18/2) | 46,337 | 66.8 | Rt. Hon. W.W. Benn | Lab | 17,849 | 57.7 |
| | | | A.C.M. Spearman | C | 13,091 | 42.3 |
| | | | | | 4,758 | 15.4 |

[Elevation to the Peerage — Viscount Stansgate]

| Election | Electors | T'out | Candidate | Party | Votes | % |
|---|---|---|---|---|---|---|
| 1942 (11/3) | | | W.H. Oldfield | Lab | Unopp. | |
| 1945 | 46,220 | 75.5 | W.H. Oldfield | Lab | 24,095 | 69.1 |
| | | | H. Sharp | C | 10,799 | 30.9 |
| | | | | | 13,296 | 38.2 |

# MANCHESTER, HULME  [181]

| Election | Electors | T'out | Candidate | Party | Votes | % |
|---|---|---|---|---|---|---|
| 1918 | 38,148 | 52.9 | J. Nall | C | 10,895 | 54.0 |
| | | | †C.T. Needham | L | 5,969 | 29.6 |
| | | | A. Hilton | Ind Lab | 2,572 | 12.8 |
| | | | G. Milner | Ind | 729* | 3.6 |
| | | | | | 4,926 | 24.4 |
| 1922 | 38,982 | 70.1 | J. Nall | C | 15,692 | 57.4 |
| | | | W. Davies | L | 11,639 | 42.6 |
| | | | | | 4,053 | 14.8 |
| 1923 | 39,234 | 71.5 | J. Nall | C | 10,035 | 35.8 |
| | | | W. Davies | L | 9,603 | 34.2 |
| | | | A. McElwee | Lab | 8,433 | 30.0 |
| | | | | | 432 | 1.6 |
| 1924 | 40,931 | 77.5 | Sir J. Nall | C | 15,374 | 48.5 |
| | | | A. McElwee | Lab | 13,080 | 41.2 |
| | | | F.J.M. Brunner | L | 3,277* | 10.3 |
| | | | | | 2,294 | 7.3 |
| 1929 | 47,362 | 72.6 | A. McElwee | Lab | 15,053 | 43.8 |
| | | | Sir J. Nall | C | 12,588 | 36.6 |
| | | | H. Allan | L | 6,728 | 19.6 |
| | | | | | 2,465 | 7.2 |
| 1931 | 49,256 | 73.0 | Sir J. Nall | C (Ind C) (C) | 25,185 | 70.0 |
| | | | A. McElwee | Lab | 9,219 | 25.6 |
| | | | Sir J.W. Pratt | NP | 1,565* | 4.4 |
| | | | | | 15,966 | 44.4 |
| 1935 | 42,448 | 66.7 | Sir J. Nall | C | 17,072 | 60.3 |
| | | | Mrs. B.A. Gould | Lab | 11,221 | 39.7 |
| | | | | | 5,851 | 20.6 |
| 1945 | 33,438 | 64.7 | F. Lee | Lab | 12,034 | 55.6 |
| | | | J.C. Currie | C | 9,600 | 44.4 |
| | | | | | 2,434 | 11.2 |

Notes:—

1918: Needham was issued with the Coalition 'coupon' but repudiated it.

Hilton was the nominee of the United Carters' and Motormen's Association.

Milner was supported by and possibly the nominee of the local branch of the NFDSS.

## MANCHESTER, MOSS SIDE   [182]

| Election | Electors | T'out | Candidate | Party | Votes | % |
|---|---|---|---|---|---|---|
| 1918 | 32,648 | 50.0 | G.B. Hurst | C | 10,621 | 65.0 |
| | | | T. Stott | L | 5,708 | 35.0 |
| | | | | | 4,913 | 30.0 |
| 1922 | 33,099 | 70.4 | G.B. Hurst | C | 11,932 | 51.2 |
| | | | T.R. Ackroyd | L | 6,743 | 28.9 |
| | | | T.W. Mercer | Lab/Co-op | 4,641 | 19.9 |
| | | | | | 5,189 | 22.3 |
| 1923 | 33,528 | 66.4 | T.R. Ackroyd | L | 12,210 | 54.8 |
| | | | G.B. Hurst | C | 9,097 | 40.9 |
| | | | J.C.D. Bustard | Ind | 949* | 4.3 |
| | | | | | 3,113 | 13.9 |
| 1924 | 34,716 | 69.3 | G.B. Hurst | C | 14,035 | 58.3 |
| | | | T.R. Ackroyd | L | 10,026 | 41.7 |
| | | | | | 4,009 | 16.6 |
| 1929 | 42,973 | 68.3 | Sir G.B. Hurst | C | 11,625 | 39.6 |
| | | | A.A. Purcell | Lab | 9,522 | 32.5 |
| | | | T.R. Ackroyd | L | 8,191 | 27.9 |
| | | | | | 2,103 | 7.1 |
| 1931 | 45,890 | 68.2 | Sir G.B. Hurst | C | 23,274 | 74.4 |
| | | | A.E. Davies | Lab | 8,012 | 25.6 |
| | | | | | 15,262 | 48.8 |
| 1935 | 40,973 | 63.2 | W.R. Duckworth | C | 15,199 | 58.7 |
| | | | L.M. Lever | Lab | 10,694 | 41.3 |
| | | | | | 4,505 | 17.4 |
| 1945 | 34,768 | 59.2 | W. Griffiths | Lab | 10,201 | 49.5 |
| | | | W.R. Duckworth | C | 7,423 | 36.0 |
| | | | H.D. Moore | L | 2,525* | 12.3 |
| | | | A.R. Edwards | Ind | 446* | 2.2 |
| | | | | | 2,778 | 13.5 |

Note:—

1945:   Edwards was the founder and nominee of the Moss Side Tenants' Protection Society.

## MANCHESTER, PLATTING   [183]

| Election | Electors | T'out | Candidate | Party | Votes | % |
|---|---|---|---|---|---|---|
| 1918 | | | †Rt. Hon. J.R. Clynes | Lab | Unopp. | |
| 1922 | 39,559 | 81.8 | Rt. Hon. J.R. Clynes | Lab | 15,683 | 48.5 |
| | | | F.H. Holmes | C | 14,814 | 45.8 |
| | | | W. Ramage | L | 1,847* | 5.7 |
| | | | | | 869 | 2.7 |
| 1923 | 39,898 | 78.1 | Rt. Hon. J.R. Clynes | Lab | 17,078 | 54.8 |
| | | | F.H. Holmes | C | 14,099 | 45.2 |
| | | | | | 2,979 | 9.6 |
| 1924 | 40,629 | 86.1 | Rt. Hon. J.R. Clynes | Lab | 17,233 | 49.2 |
| | | | F.H. Holmes | C | 16,228 | 46.4 |
| | | | E. Baker | L | 1,538* | 4.4 |
| | | | | | 1,005 | 2.8 |
| 1929 | 49,153 | 80.8 | Rt. Hon. J.R. Clynes | Lab | 22,969 | 57.9 |
| | | | A.E.L. Chorlton | C | 16,323 | 41.1 |
| | | | J.J. Vaughan | Com | 401* | 1.0 |
| | | | | | 6,646 | 16.8 |
| 1931 | 50,081 | 82.6 | A.E.L. Chorlton | C | 23,588 | 57.0 |
| | | | Rt. Hon. J.R. Clynes | Lab | 17,798 | 43.0 |
| | | | | | 5,790 | 14.0 |
| 1935 | 46,234 | 76.5 | Rt. Hon. J.R. Clynes | Lab | 18,352 | 51.9 |
| | | | J.W. Stansfield | C | 17,015 | 48.1 |
| | | | | | 1,337 | 3.8 |
| 1945 | 35,403 | 72.6 | H.J. Delargy | Lab | 16,427 | 63.9 |
| | | | Sir W.H. Sugden | C | 9,262 | 36.1 |
| | | | | | 7,165 | 27.8 |

## MANCHESTER, RUSHOLME [184]

| Election | Electors | T'out | Candidate | Party | Votes | % |
|---|---|---|---|---|---|---|
| 1918 | 30,421 | 62.9 | †R.B. Stoker | Co C | 12,447 | 65.1 |
| | | | W. Butterworth | L | 3,699 | 19.3 |
| | | | Mrs. E.P. Pethick-Lawrence | Lab | 2,985 | 15.6 |
| | | | | | 8,748 | 45.8 |
| [Death] | | | | | | |
| 1919 (7/10) | 30,421† | 67.5 | J.H. Thorpe | Co C | 9,394 | 45.7 |
| | | | Dr. R. Dunstan | Lab | 6,412 | 31.2 |
| | | | W.M.R. Pringle | L | 3,923 | 19.1 |
| | | | R.B. Crewdson | Nat P | 815* | 4.0 |
| | | | | | 2,982 | 14.5 |
| 1922 | 31,582 | 77.8 | J.H. Thorpe | C | 11,765 | 47.9 |
| | | | E.F.M. Sutton | L | 6,421 | 26.1 |
| | | | R.A.E. Wood | Lab | 6,397 | 26.0 |
| | | | | | 5,344 | 21.8 |
| 1923 | 32,253 | 78.0 | Rt. Hon. C.F.G. Masterman | L | 10,901 | 43.4 |
| | | | J.H. Thorpe | C | 8,876 | 35.3 |
| | | | W. Paul | Lab | 5,366 | 21.3 |
| | | | | | 2,025 | 8.1 |
| 1924 | 33,147 | 79.8 | F.B. Merriman | C | 13,341 | 50.4 |
| | | | Rt. Hon. C.F.G. Masterman | L | 7,772 | 29.4 |
| | | | W. Paul | Com | 5,328 | 20.2 |
| | | | | | 5,569 | 21.0 |
| 1929 | 42,289 | 78.7 | Sir F.B. Merriman | C | 14,230 | 42.8 |
| | | | P. Guedalla | L | 10,958 | 32.9 |
| | | | J. Adshead | Lab | 8,080 | 24.3 |
| | | | | | 3,272 | 9.9 |
| 1931 | 44,743 | 80.0 | Sir F.B. Merriman | C | 24,817 | 69.3 |
| | | | J. Adshead | Lab | 6,319 | 17.7 |
| | | | F.C. Thornborough | L | 4,658 | 13.0 |
| | | | | | 18,498 | 51.6 |

[Resignation on appointment as President of the Probate, Divorce and Admiralty Division of the High Court]

| Election | Electors | T'out | Candidate | Party | Votes | % |
|---|---|---|---|---|---|---|
| 1933 (21/11) | 45,112 | 60.8 | E.A. Radford | C | 13,904 | 50.8 |
| | | | Rev. G.S. Woods | Lab/Co-op | 11,005 | 40.1 |
| | | | Dr. P. McDougall | Ind L | 2,503* | 9.1 |
| | | | | | 2,899 | 10.7 |
| 1935 | 45,068 | 69.8 | E.A. Radford | C | 19,678 | 62.6 |
| | | | A. Knight | Lab | 9,258 | 29.4 |
| | | | Dr. P. McDougall | Ind L | 2,525* | 8.0 |
| | | | | | 10,420 | 33.2 |
| [Death] | | | | | | |
| 1944 (8/7) | 45,675 | 34.7 | F.W. Cundiff | C | 8,430 | 53.3 |
| | | | H. Blomerley | CW | 6,670 | 42.1 |
| | | | C.J. Taylor | Ind Lab | 734* | 4.6 |
| | | | | | 1,760 | 11.2 |

| Election | Electors | T'out | Candidate | Party | Votes | % |
|---|---|---|---|---|---|---|
| 1945 | 47,562 | 74.6 | H.L. Hutchinson | Lab (Ind Lab) | 15,408 | 43.4 |
|  |  |  | F.W. Cundiff | C | 15,398 | 43.4 |
|  |  |  | C.G. Chappell | L | 4,673 | 13.2 |
|  |  |  |  |  | 10 | 0.0 |

Notes:—

1923:  Paul was a member of the Communist Party but received Labour Party endorsement.

1933-
1935:  McDougall was supported by the Manchester Land Values League.

1945:  Hutchinson joined the Labour Independent Group when it was formed in June 1949.

# MANCHESTER, WITHINGTON [185]

| Election | Electors | T'out | Candidate | Party | Votes | % |
|---|---|---|---|---|---|---|
| 1918 | 27,601 | 61.0 | R.A.D. Carter | C | 11,677 | 69.3 |
| | | | G.F. Burditt | L | 5,166 | 30.7 |
| | | | | | 6,511 | 38.6 |
| 1922 | 29,311 | 77.4 | Dr. T. Watts | C | 11,678 | 51.5 |
| | | | E.D. Simon | L | 11,008 | 48.5 |
| | | | | | 670 | 3.0 |
| 1923 | 30,731 | 78.0 | E.D. Simon | L | 13,944 | 58.2 |
| | | | Dr. T. Watts | C | 10,026 | 41.8 |
| | | | | | 3,918 | 16.4 |
| 1924 | 32,712 | 81.8 | Dr. T. Watts | C | 13,633 | 50.9 |
| | | | E.D. Simon | L | 10,435 | 39.0 |
| | | | E. Whiteley | Lab | 2,467* | 9.2 |
| | | | K. Burke | Ind | 236* | 0.9 |
| | | | | | 3,198 | 11.9 |
| 1929 | 61,494 | 77.8 | E.D. Simon | L | 20,948 | 43.8 |
| | | | Sir T. Watts | C | 19,063 | 39.8 |
| | | | Dr. J. Robinson | Lab | 7,853 | 16.4 |
| | | | | | 1,885 | 4.0 |
| 1931 | 75,782 | 75.8 | E.L. Fleming | C | 36,097 | 62.8 |
| | | | P. Guedalla | L | 21,379 | 37.2 |
| | | | | | 14,718 | 25.6 |
| 1935 | 80,561 | 70.9 | E.L. Fleming | C | 35,564 | 62.3 |
| | | | D.S. Morton | Lab | 12,248 | 21.4 |
| | | | W.C. Ross | L | 9,298 | 16.3 |
| | | | | | 23,316 | 40.9 |
| 1945 | 89,806 | 74.2 | E.L. Fleming | C | 30,881 | 46.3 |
| | | | R. Edwards | Lab | 22,634 | 34.0 |
| | | | L.F. Behrens | L | 13,107 | 19.7 |
| | | | | | 8,247 | 12.3 |

Note:—

1924:  Burke sought election as an 'Anti-Socialist' candidate.

## MIDDLESBROUGH, EAST [186]

| Election | Electors | T'out | Candidate | Party | Votes | % |
|---|---|---|---|---|---|---|
| 1918 | 25,286 | 48.4 | †P. Williams | L | 8,470 | 69.2 |
| | | | F.W. Carey | Lab | 3,776 | 30.8 |
| | | | | | 4,694 | 38.4 |
| 1922 | 28,905 | 78.8 | J.W. Brown | C | 8,885 | 39.0 |
| | | | M.H. Connolly | Lab | 7,607 | 33.4 |
| | | | P. Williams | L | 6,295 | 27.6 |
| | | | | | 1,278 | 5.6 |
| 1923 | 29,430 | 77.3 | P. Williams | L | 9,241 | 40.6 |
| | | | M.H. Connolly | Lab | 7,712 | 33.9 |
| | | | J. Reid | C | 5,790 | 25.5 |
| | | | | | 1,529 | 6.7 |
| 1924 | 29,747 | 83.7 | Miss E.C. Wilkinson | Lab | 9,574 | 38.5 |
| | | | J.R.P. Warde-Aldam | C | 8,647 | 34.7 |
| | | | P. Williams | L | 6,688 | 26.8 |
| | | | | | 927 | 3.8 |
| 1929 | 36,512 | 80.8 | Miss E.C. Wilkinson | Lab | 12,215 | 41.3 |
| | | | E.J. Young | L | 9,016 | 30.6 |
| | | | J.W. Brown | C | 8,278 | 28.1 |
| | | | | | 3,199 | 10.7 |
| 1931 | 36,078 | 84.5 | E.J. Young | L | 18,409 | 60.4 |
| | | | Miss E.C. Wilkinson | Lab | 12,080 | 39.6 |
| | | | | | 6,329 | 20.8 |
| 1935 | 35,611 | 81.1 | A. Edwards | Lab | 12,699 | 44.0 |
| | | | B.C. Talbot | C | 12,632 | 43.7 |
| | | | E.J. Young | L | 3,565* | 12.3 |
| | | | | | 67 | 0.3 |
| 1945 | 34,922 | 76.7 | A. Edwards | Lab (Ind) (C) | 17,427 | 65.1 |
| | | | B. Chetwynd-Talbot | C | 9,352 | 34.9 |
| | | | | | 8,075 | 30.2 |

Note:—

1918: Williams was issued with the Coalition 'coupon' but repudiated it.

# MIDDLESBROUGH, WEST [187]

| Election | Electors | T'out | Candidate | Party | Votes | % |
|----------|----------|-------|-----------|-------|-------|---|
| 1918 | 32,286 | 50.5 | W.T. Thomson | L | 10,958 | 67.2 |
|  |  |  | C.T. Cramp | Lab | 5,350 | 32.8 |
|  |  |  |  |  | 5,608 | 34.4 |
| 1922 | 35,448 | 68.4 | W.T. Thomson | L | 16,811 | 69.4 |
|  |  |  | H.D. Levick | NL | 7,422 | 30.6 |
|  |  |  |  |  | 9,389 | 38.8 |
| 1923 | 35,362 | 68.6 | W.T. Thomson | L | 16,837 | 69.4 |
|  |  |  | J.D. White | Lab | 7,413 | 30.6 |
|  |  |  |  |  | 9,424 | 38.8 |
| 1924 [Death] |  |  | W.T. Thomson | L | Unopp. |  |
| 1928 (7/3) | 35,513 | 83.2 | F.K. Griffith | L | 10,717 | 36.2 |
|  |  |  | A.R. Ellis | Lab | 10,628 | 36.0 |
|  |  |  | S.A. Sadler | C | 8,213 | 27.8 |
|  |  |  |  |  | 89 | 0.2 |
| 1929 | 43,915 | 82.3 | F.K. Griffith | L | 14,674 | 40.6 |
|  |  |  | A.R. Ellis | Lab | 13,328 | 36.9 |
|  |  |  | A.E. Baucher | C | 8,137 | 22.5 |
|  |  |  |  |  | 1,346 | 3.7 |
| 1931 | 45,929 | 85.0 | F.K. Griffith | L | 26,011 | 66.6 |
|  |  |  | H. Kegie | Lab | 13,040 | 33.4 |
|  |  |  |  |  | 12,971 | 33.2 |
| 1935 | 47,666 | 79.4 | F.K. Griffith | L | 13,689 | 36.2 |
|  |  |  | H. Kegie | Lab | 12,764 | 33.7 |
|  |  |  | W.A. Spofforth | N Lab | 11,387 | 30.1 |
|  |  |  |  |  | 925 | 2.5 |

[Resignation on appointment as a County Court Judge]

| Election | Electors | T'out | Candidate | Party | Votes | % |
|----------|----------|-------|-----------|-------|-------|---|
| 1940 (7/8) [Death] |  |  | H. Johnstone | L | Unopp. |  |
| 1945 (14/5) |  |  | D.C.T. Bennett | L | Unopp. |  |
| 1945 | 48,595 | 77.2 | G. Cooper | Lab | 20,071 | 53.5 |
|  |  |  | D.C.T. Bennett | L | 17,458 | 46.5 |
|  |  |  |  |  | 2,613 | 7.0 |

Note:—

1918: Thomson was issued with the Coalition 'coupon' but repudiated it.

196

## MITCHAM [188]

| Election | Electors | T'out | Candidate | Party | Votes | % |
|---|---|---|---|---|---|---|
| 1945 | 63,545 | 73.4 | T. Braddock | Lab | 26,910 | 57.7 |
| | | | Rt. Hon. Sir M.A. Robertson | C | 19,742 | 42.3 |
| | | | | | 7,168 | 15.4 |

# MORPETH [189]

| Election | Electors | T'out | Candidate | Party | Votes | % |
|---|---|---|---|---|---|---|
| 1918 | 39,773 | 56.3 | J. Cairns | Lab | 7,677 | 34.3 |
| | | | F.C. Thornborough | L | 7,140 | 31.9 |
| | | | C.H. Meares | C | 4,320 | 19.3 |
| | | | G.D. Newton | Ind | 2,729* | 12.2 |
| | | | T.M. Allison | NDP | 511* | 2.3 |
| | | | | | 537 | 2.4 |
| 1922 | 43,098 | 72.1 | J. Cairns | Lab | 15,026 | 48.3 |
| | | | F.C. Thornborough | L | 10,007 | 32.2 |
| | | | C.S. Shortt | C | 6,045 | 19.5 |
| | | | | | 5,019 | 16.1 |
| [Death] | | | | | | |
| 1923 (21/6) | 43,098[†] | 76.9 | R. Smillie | Lab | 20,053 | 60.5 |
| | | | F.C. Thornborough | L | 13,087 | 39.5 |
| | | | | | 6,966 | 21.0 |
| 1923 | 44,323 | 59.4 | R. Smillie | Lab | 16,902 | 64.2 |
| | | | J. Dodd | L | 9,411 | 35.8 |
| | | | | | 7,491 | 28.4 |
| 1924 | 45,150 | 75.0 | R. Smillie | Lab | 19,248 | 56.8 |
| | | | Miss I.M.B. Ward | C | 10,828 | 32.0 |
| | | | J. Dodd | L | 3,805* | 11.2 |
| | | | | | 8,420 | 24.8 |
| 1929 | 55,126 | 75.5 | E. Edwards | Lab | 25,508 | 61.3 |
| | | | Miss I.M.B. Ward | C | 9,206 | 22.1 |
| | | | J. Ritson | L | 6,888 | 16.6 |
| | | | | | 16,302 | 39.2 |
| 1931 | 57,652 | 70.3 | G. Nicholson | C | 20,806 | 51.3 |
| | | | E. Edwards | Lab | 19,714 | 48.7 |
| | | | | | 1,092 | 2.6 |
| 1935 | 62,079 | 78.7 | R.J. Taylor | Lab | 28,900 | 59.2 |
| | | | G. Nicholson | C | 19,944 | 40.8 |
| | | | | | 8,956 | 18.4 |
| 1945 | 66,264 | 79.4 | R.J. Taylor | Lab | 38,521 | 73.2 |
| | | | G.J.M. Longden | C | 14,079 | 26.8 |
| | | | | | 24,442 | 46.4 |

Notes:—

1918: Thornborough was issued with the Coalition 'coupon' but repudiated it.
Newton was supported by the local branch of the NFDSS.

## NELSON and COLNE [190]

| Election | Electors | T'out | Candidate | Party | Votes | % |
|---|---|---|---|---|---|---|
| 1918 | 43,381 | 52.3 | †A. Smith | Lab | 14,075 | 62.0 |
| | | | F. Greenwood | L | 8,623 | 38.0 |
| | | | | | 5,452 | 24.0 |
| [Resignation] | | | | | | |
| 1920 (17/6) | 43,757† | 65.2 | R. Graham | Lab | 14,134 | 49.5 |
| | | | F.N. Wainwright | Co C | 8,577 | 30.1 |
| | | | W.R. Rea | L | 5,805 | 20.4 |
| | | | | | 5,557 | 19.4 |
| 1922 | 43,914 | 83.2 | A. Greenwood | Lab | 17,714 | 48.5 |
| | | | J.H.S. Aitken | L | 11,542 | 31.6 |
| | | | F.N. Wainwright | C | 7,286 | 19.9 |
| | | | | | 6,172 | 16.9 |
| 1923 | 44,432 | 83.4 | A. Greenwood | Lab | 17,083 | 46.1 |
| | | | J.H.S. Aitken | L | 10,103 | 27.3 |
| | | | Sir A. Nelson | C | 9,861 | 26.6 |
| | | | | | 6,980 | 18.8 |
| 1924 | 44,871 | 85.6 | A. Greenwood | Lab | 19,922 | 51.9 |
| | | | J.H.S. Aitken | L | 18,479 | 48.1 |
| | | | | | 1,443 | 3.8 |
| 1929 | 56,465 | 82.8 | A. Greenwood | Lab | 28,533 | 61.0 |
| | | | L.T. Thorp | C | 18,236 | 39.0 |
| | | | | | 10,297 | 22.0 |
| 1931 | 56,733 | 87.8 | L.T. Thorp | C (Ind C) | 28,747 | 57.7 |
| | | | Rt. Hon. A. Greenwood | Lab | 21,063 | 42.3 |
| | | | | | 7,684 | 15.4 |
| 1935 | 56,307 | 84.7 | S.S. Silverman | Lab | 26,011 | 54.5 |
| | | | L.T. Thorp | Ind C | 21,696 | 45.5 |
| | | | | | 4,315 | 9.0 |
| 1945 | 52,830 | 81.6 | S.S. Silverman | Lab | 25,610 | 59.4 |
| | | | H. Nicholls | C | 17,484 | 40.6 |
| | | | | | 8,126 | 18.8 |

| Election | Electors | T'out | Candidate | Party | Votes | % |
|---|---|---|---|---|---|---|
| 1918 | | | †J.C. Wedgwood | Ind L (Lab) | Unopp. | |
| 1922 | 30,300 | 79.5 | J.C. Wedgwood<br>A. Shaw | Lab<br>NL | 14,503<br>9,573<br>4,930 | 60.2<br>39.8<br>20.4 |
| 1923 | 30,565 | 64.2 | J.C. Wedgwood<br>J. Ravenshaw | Lab<br>C | 12,881<br>6,746<br>6,135 | 65.6<br>34.4<br>31.2 |
| 1924 | 30,816 | 80.0 | Rt. Hon. J.C. Wedgwood<br>A. Hassam | Lab<br>C | 14,226<br>10,425<br>3,801 | 57.7<br>42.3<br>15.4 |
| 1929 | 39,482 | 75.8 | Rt. Hon. J.C. Wedgwood<br>C.K. Tatham | Lab<br>C | 20,931<br>9,011<br>11,920 | 69.9<br>30.1<br>39.8 |
| 1931 | | | Rt. Hon. J.C. Wedgwood | Ind Lab<br>(Lab) | Unopp. | |
| 1935 | | | Rt. Hon. J.C. Wedgwood | Lab | Unopp. | |
| [Elevation to the Peerage — Lord Wedgwood] | | | | | | |
| 1942<br>(11/3) | | | J.D. Mack | Lab | Unopp. | |
| 1945 | 50,741 | 77.1 | J.D. Mack<br>G.A. Wade<br>N.W. Elliott | Lab<br>C<br>L | 25,903<br>8,380<br>4,838*<br>17,523 | 66.2<br>21.4<br>12.4<br>44.8 |

Note:—

1918: Wedgwood was issued with the Coalition 'coupon' but repudiated it. Although adopted by the local Liberal Association, he considered himself to be an Independent Liberal.

| Election | Electors | T'out | Candidate | Party | Votes | % |
|---|---|---|---|---|---|---|
| 1918 | 32,796 | 43.9 | G. Renwick | Co C | 9,414 | 65.4 |
| | | | J. Smith | Lab | 4,976 | 34.6 |
| | | | | | 4,438 | 30.8 |
| 1922 | 34,844 | 72.5 | C.P. Trevelyan | Lab | 13,709 | 54.2 |
| | | | Sir G. Renwick, Bt. | C | 8,639 | 34.2 |
| | | | J. Dodd | L | 2,923* | 11.6 |
| | | | | | 5,070 | 20.0 |
| 1923 | 35,193 | 67.4 | C.P. Trevelyan | Lab | 12,447 | 52.5 |
| | | | Hon. F.M.B. Fisher | C | 11,260 | 47.5 |
| | | | | | 1,187 | 5.0 |
| 1924 | 35,307 | 79.8 | Rt. Hon. C.P. Trevelyan | Lab | 14,542 | 51.6 |
| | | | Hon. F.M.B. Fisher | C | 13,646 | 48.4 |
| | | | | | 896 | 3.2 |
| 1929 | 41,683 | 73.7 | Rt. Hon. Sir C.P. Trevelyan, Bt. | Lab | 17,580 | 57.2 |
| | | | Viscount Adare | C | 13,161 | 42.8 |
| | | | | | 4,419 | 14.4 |
| 1931 | 40,437 | 80.5 | A. Denville | C | 20,309 | 62.4 |
| | | | Rt. Hon. Sir C.P. Trevelyan, Bt. | Ind Lab | 12,136 | 37.3 |
| | | | W.H.D. Caple | N Lab | 94* | 0.3 |
| | | | | | 8,173 | 25.1 |
| 1935 | 35,374 | 75.5 | A. Denville | C | 15,826 | 59.3 |
| | | | W. Monslow | Lab | 10,871 | 40.7 |
| | | | | | 4,955 | 18.6 |
| 1945 | 24,031 | 71.4 | L. Wilkes | Lab | 10,627 | 61.9 |
| | | | A. Denville | C | 6,536 | 38.1 |
| | | | | | 4,091 | 23.8 |

Note:—

1931: Caple retired after nomination in favour of Denville.

# NEWCASTLE UPON TYNE, EAST [193]

| Election | Electors | T'out | Candidate | Party | Votes | % |
|----------|----------|-------|-----------|-------|-------|---|
| 1918 | 30,719 | 48.7 | H. Barnes | Co L (L) | 8,682 | 58.1 |
| | | | †W. Hudson | Lab | 5,195 | 34.7 |
| | | | J. Thompson | Ind | 1,079* | 7.2 |
| | | | | | 3,487 | 23.4 |
| 1922 | 31,703 | 73.7 | J.N. Bell | Lab | 10,084 | 43.1 |
| | | | H. Barnes | L | 6,999 | 30.0 |
| | | | G. Stone | NL | 6,273 | 26.9 |
| | | | | | 3,085 | 13.1 |
| [Death] | | | | | | |
| 1923 (17/1) | 31,703 | 76.4 | Rt. Hon. A. Henderson | Lab | 11,066 | 45.7 |
| | | | H. Barnes | L | 6,682 | 27.6 |
| | | | R. Gee | C | 6,480 | 26.7 |
| | | | | | 4,384 | 18.1 |
| 1923 | 33,066 | 73.2 | Sir R.W. Aske, Bt. | L | 12,656 | 52.3 |
| | | | Rt. Hon. A. Henderson | Lab | 11,532 | 47.7 |
| | | | | | 1,124 | 4.6 |
| 1924 | 33,737 | 83.9 | M.H. Connolly | Lab | 13,120 | 46.4 |
| | | | Sir R.W. Aske, Bt. | L | 12,776 | 45.1 |
| | | | W. Temple | C | 2,420* | 8.5 |
| | | | | | 344 | 1.3 |
| 1929 | 43,797 | 79.4 | Sir R.W. Aske, Bt. | L (NL) | 17,856 | 51.3 |
| | | | M.H. Connolly | Lab | 16,921 | 48.7 |
| | | | | | 935 | 2.6 |
| 1931 | 44,757 | 86.5 | Sir R.W. Aske, Bt. | NL | 24,522 | 63.4 |
| | | | M. Alexander | Lab | 14,176 | 36.6 |
| | | | | | 10,346 | 26.8 |
| 1935 | 48,576 | 81.3 | Sir R.W. Aske, Bt. | NL | 23,146 | 58.6 |
| | | | B.B. Gillis | Lab | 16,322 | 41.4 |
| | | | | | 6,824 | 17.2 |
| 1945 | 51,977 | 72.9 | A. Blenkinsop | Lab | 26,116 | 68.9 |
| | | | R. O'Sullivan | NL | 11,774 | 31.1 |
| | | | | | 14,342 | 37.8 |

Note:—

1918:  Thompson was supported at first but later repudiated by the local branch of the NFDSS.

# NEWCASTLE UPON TYNE, NORTH  [194]

| Election | Electors | T'out | Candidate | Party | Votes | % |
|---|---|---|---|---|---|---|
| 1918 | 32,272 | 58.2 | N. Grattan-Doyle | Co C | 11,347 | 60.5 |
| | | | Sir G. Lunn | L | 4,322 | 23.0 |
| | | | R.J. Wilson | Lab | 3,102 | 16.5 |
| | | | | | 7,025 | 37.5 |
| 1922 | 32,987 | 73.9 | N. Grattan-Doyle | C | 14,931 | 61.2 |
| | | | Dr. R. W. Simpson | L | 8,017 | 32.9 |
| | | | J. Wilson | Ind Lab | 1,435* | 5.9 |
| | | | | | 6,914 | 28.3 |
| 1923 | 33,182 | 73.6 | N. Grattan-Doyle | C | 12,715 | 52.1 |
| | | | Dr. R.W. Simpson | L | 6,321 | 25.9 |
| | | | J. Beckett | Lab | 5,374 | 22.0 |
| | | | | | 6,394 | 26.2 |
| 1924 | 34,209 | 74.2 | Sir N. Grattan-Doyle | C | 18,386 | 72.5 |
| | | | H. Maw | Lab | 6,991 | 27.5 |
| | | | | | 11,395 | 45.0 |
| 1929 | 45,720 | 70.9 | Sir N. Grattan-Doyle | C | 17,962 | 55.4 |
| | | | E. Scott | Lab | 7,573 | 23.4 |
| | | | Dr. J.R. Crichton | L | 6,860 | 21.2 |
| | | | | | 10,389 | 32.0 |
| 1931 | 46,902 | 76.8 | Sir N. Grattan-Doyle | C | 30,245 | 83.9 |
| | | | R.J. Thomson | Lab | 5,791 | 16.1 |
| | | | | | 24,454 | 67.8 |
| 1935 | 47,503 | 70.3 | Sir N. Grattan-Doyle | C | 25,683 | 77.0 |
| | | | E. Gilbert | Lab | 7,693 | 23.0 |
| | | | | | 17,990 | 54.0 |
| [Resignation] | | | | | | |
| 1940 (7/6) | 47,166 | 22.0 | Sir C.M. Headlam, Bt. | Ind C (C) | 7,380 | 71.2 |
| | | | H. Grattan-Doyle | C | 2,982 | 28.8 |
| | | | | | 4,398 | 42.4 |
| 1945 | 47,047 | 73.0 | Sir C.M. Headlam, Bt. | C | 17,381 | 50.7 |
| | | | W.H. Shackleton | Lab/Co-op | 10,228 | 29.8 |
| | | | W. McKeag | L | 5,812 | 16.9 |
| | | | H.A.C. Ridsdale | CW | 904* | 2.6 |
| | | | | | 7,153 | 20.9 |

Note:—

1940: Headlam was the nominee of the Newcastle North (1940) Conservative Associat
ion, which was formed by a number of members of the Newcastle North
Conservative Association who had resigned in protest over the adoption of
Grattan-Doyle as the official Conservative candidate.

| Election | Electors | T'out | Candidate | Party | Votes | % |
|---|---|---|---|---|---|---|
| 1918 | 33,527 | 57.3 | †Rt. Hon. E. Shortt | Co L | 12,812 | 66.6 |
| | | | D. Adams | Lab | 6,411 | 33.4 |
| | | | | | 6,401 | 33.2 |
| 1922 | 32,964 | 80.5 | D. Adams | Lab | 11,654 | 43.9 |
| | | | C.B. Ramage | NL | 11,499 | 43.4 |
| | | | Hon. R.D. Denman | L | 3,367 | 12.7 |
| | | | | | 155 | 0.5 |
| 1923 | 33,621 | 79.3 | C.B. Ramage | L | 15,141 | 56.8 |
| | | | D. Adams | Lab | 11,527 | 43.2 |
| | | | | | 3,614 | 13.6 |
| 1924 | 34,304 | 83.8 | J.H. Palin | Lab | 13,089 | 45.5 |
| | | | C. Vernon | C | 8,459 | 29.4 |
| | | | C.B. Ramage | L | 7,208 | 25.1 |
| | | | | | 4,630 | 16.1 |
| 1929 | 47,121 | 76.8 | J.H. Palin | Lab | 16,856 | 46.6 |
| | | | Dr. J.W. Leech | C | 14,088 | 38.9 |
| | | | J. Dodd | L | 5,267 | 14.5 |
| | | | | | 2,768 | 7.7 |
| 1931 | 50,521 | 83.3 | Dr. J.W. Leech | C | 28,560 | 67.9 |
| | | | J.H. Palin | Lab | 13,514 | 32.1 |
| | | | | | 15,046 | 35.8 |
| 1935 | 56,732 | 75.1 | Dr. J.W. Leech | C | 25,526 | 60.0 |
| | | | W. Taylor | Lab | 17,052 | 40.0 |
| | | | | | 8,474 | 20.0 |
| [Death] | | | | | | |
| 1940 (5/7) | | | W. Nunn | C | Unopp. | |
| 1945 | 66,224 | 72.7 | E. Popplewell | Lab | 28,149 | 58.5 |
| | | | W. Nunn | C | 19,966 | 41.5 |
| | | | | | 8,183 | 17.0 |

# NORTHAMPTON [196]

| Election | Electors | T'out | Candidate | Party | Votes | % |
|---|---|---|---|---|---|---|
| 1918 | 46,007 | 62.5 | †C.A. McCurdy | Co L | 18,010 | 62.7 |
| | | | W. Halls | Lab | 10,735 | 37.3 |
| | | | | | 7,275 | 25.4 |
| [Appointed Food Controller] | | | | | | |
| 1920 | 44,573 | 67.1 | Rt. Hon. C.A. McCurdy | Co L | 16,650 | 55.6 |
| (1/4) | | | Miss M.G. Bondfield | Lab | 13,279 | 44.4 |
| | | | | | 3,371 | 11.2 |
| 1922 | 44,722 | 85.5 | Rt. Hon. C.A. McCurdy | NL | 19,974 | 52.3 |
| | | | Miss M.G. Bondfield | Lab | 14,498 | 37.9 |
| | | | H.H. Vivian | L | 3,753* | 9.8 |
| | | | | | 5,476 | 14.4 |
| 1923 | 45,599 | 84.3 | Miss M.G. Bondfield | Lab | 15,556 | 40.5 |
| | | | J.V. Collier | C | 11,520 | 30.0 |
| | | | Rt. Hon. C.A. McCurdy | L | 11,342 | 29.5 |
| | | | | | 4,036 | 10.5 |
| 1924 | 46,543 | 87.0 | Sir A.E.A. Holland | C | 16,017 | 39.5 |
| | | | Miss M.G. Bondfield | Lab | 15,046 | 37.2 |
| | | | J. Manfield | L | 9,436 | 23.3 |
| | | | | | 971 | 2.3 |
| [Death] | | | | | | |
| 1928 | 48,048 | 84.2 | C.J.L. Malone | Lab | 15,173 | 37.5 |
| (9/1) | | | A.F.G. Renton | C | 14,616 | 36.1 |
| | | | S.C. Morgan | L | 9,584 | 23.7 |
| | | | E.A. Hallwood | Ind C | 1,093* | 2.7 |
| | | | | | 557 | 1.4 |
| 1929 | 61,222 | 87.5 | C.J.L. Malone | Lab | 22,356 | 41.7 |
| | | | A.F.G. Renton | C | 20,177 | 37.7 |
| | | | Miss A.H. Schilizzi | L | 11,054 | 20.6 |
| | | | | | 2,179 | 4.0 |
| 1931 | 62,577 | 87.4 | Sir M.E. Manningham-Buller, Bt. | C | 34,817 | 63.6 |
| | | | C.J.L. Malone | Lab | 19,898 | 36.4 |
| | | | | | 14,919 | 27.2 |
| 1935 | 62,079 | 79.6 | Sir M.E. Manningham-Buller, Bt. | C | 25,438 | 51.5 |
| | | | R.T. Paget | Lab | 23,983 | 48.5 |
| | | | | | 1,455 | 3.0 |
| [Resignation] | | | | | | |
| 1940 | 59,267 | 30.0 | G.S. Summers | C | 16,587 | 93.4 |
| (6/12) | | | W.S. Seamark | CP | 1,167* | 6.6 |
| | | | | | 15,420 | 86.8 |
| 1945 | 65,134 | 75.4 | R.T. Paget | Lab | 27,681 | 56.4 |
| | | | G.S. Summers | C | 20,684 | 42.1 |
| | | | J.E. Bugby | Ind Lab | 749* | 1.5 |
| | | | | | 6,997 | 14.3 |

## NORWICH [197]

### (Two Seats)

| Election | Electors | T'out | Candidate | Party | Votes | % |
|---|---|---|---|---|---|---|
| 1918 | 60,342 | 55.2 | †Rt. Hon. G.H. Roberts | Co Lab | 26,642 | 45.1 |
| | | | †E.H. Young | L (Co L) | 25,555 | 43.3 |
| | | | H.E. Witard | Ind Lab | 6,856 | 11.6 |
| | | | | | 19,786 | 33.5 |
| | | | | | 18,699 | 31.7 |
| 1922 | 60,159 | 78.5 | Rt. Hon. G.H. Roberts | Ind (C) | 31,167 | 33.7 |
| | | | Rt. Hon. E.H. Young | NL | 31,151 | 33.7 |
| | | | H.E. Witard | Lab | 15,609 | 16.9 |
| | | | G.F. Johnson | Lab | 14,490 | 15.7 |
| | | | | | 15,558 | 16.8 |
| | | | | | 15,542 | 16.8 |
| 1923 | 61,168 | 79.8 | W.R. Smith | Lab | 20,077 | 20.9 |
| | | | Miss D. Jewson | Lab | 19,304 | 20.0 |
| | | | Rt. Hon. E.H. Young | L | 16,222 | 16.9 |
| | | | Rt. Hon. G.H. Roberts | C | 14,749 | 15.3 |
| | | | H.J. Copeman | L | 13,180 | 13.7 |
| | | | H.D. Swan | C | 12,713 | 13.2 |
| | | | | | 3,082 | 3.1 |
| 1924 | 61,995 | 85.7 | Rt. Hon. E.H. Young | L (Ind) (C) | 28,842 | 27.7 |
| | | | J.G. Fairfax | C | 28,529 | 27.4 |
| | | | W.R. Smith | Lab | 23,808 | 22.9 |
| | | | Miss D. Jewson | Lab | 22,931 | 22.0 |
| | | | | | 5,034 | 4.8 |
| | | | | | 4,721 | 4.5 |
| 1929 | 82,143 | 82.7 | G.H. Shakespeare | L (NL) | 33,974 | 26.2 |
| | | | W.R. Smith | Lab | 33,690 | 26.0 |
| | | | Miss D. Jewson | Lab | 31,040 | 24.0 |
| | | | J.G. Fairfax | C | 30,793 | 23.8 |
| | | | | | 2,934 | 2.2 |
| | | | | | 2,897 | 2.2 |
| 1931 | 83,755 | 82.0 | G.H. Shakespeare | NL | 40,925 | 30.4 |
| | | | G.A. Hartland | C | 38,883 | 28.9 |
| | | | W.R. Smith | Lab | 28,295 | 21.0 |
| | | | Miss D. Jewson | ILP | 26,537 | 19.7 |
| | | | | | 12,630 | 9.4 |
| | | | | | 10,588 | 7.9 |
| 1935 | 84,275 | 75.7 | G.H. Shakespeare | NL | 36,039 | 29.1 |
| | | | H.G. Strauss | C | 34,182 | 27.6 |
| | | | W.G. Hall | Lab | 24,670 | 20.0 |
| | | | C.J. Kelly | Lab | 22,055 | 17.8 |
| | | | A.F. Brockway | ILP | 6,737* | 5.5 |
| | | | | | 11,369 | 9.1 |
| | | | | | 9,512 | 7.6 |
| 1945 | 79,880 | 73.2 | Lady Noel-Buxton | Lab | 31,553 | 27.9 |
| | | | J. Paton | Lab | 31,229 | 27.7 |
| | | | Rt. Hon. Sir G.H. Shakespeare, Bt. | NL | 25,945 | 23.0 |
| | | | H.G. Strauss | C | 24,225 | 21.4 |
| | | | | | 5,284 | 4.7 |

Note:—

1918: Roberts was not an official Coalition candidate and did not receive a 'coupon'. He did however fully support the Coalition and sought election as a Coalition candidate.

# NOTTINGHAM, CENTRAL [198]

| Election | Electors | T'out | Candidate | Party | Votes | % |
|---|---|---|---|---|---|---|
| 1918 | 32,460 | 51.0 | A.R. Atkey | Co C | 10,552 | 63.8 |
| | | | E. Huntsman | L | 3,988 | 24.1 |
| | | | A. Kitson | Nat P | 1,999* | 12.1 |
| | | | | | 6,564 | 39.7 |
| 1922 | 33,311 | 68.9 | R.C. Berkeley | L | 11,481 | 50.0 |
| | | | A.R. Atkey | C | 11,459 | 50.0 |
| | | | | | 22 | 0.0 |
| 1923 | 33,808 | 72.8 | R.C. Berkeley | L | 13,208 | 53.7 |
| | | | A.R. Atkey | C | 11,403 | 46.3 |
| | | | | | 1,805 | 7.4 |
| 1924 | 34,411 | 76.6 | A.J. Bennett | C | 15,107 | 57.3 |
| | | | W.H. Coultate | Lab | 6,852 | 26.0 |
| | | | C.H. Roberts | L | 4,409 | 16.7 |
| | | | | | 8,255 | 31.3 |
| 1929 | 45,045 | 77.4 | A.J. Bennett | C | 14,571 | 41.7 |
| | | | Mrs. E. Barton | Lab/Co-op | 11,573 | 33.2 |
| | | | A. Brampton | L | 8,738 | 25.1 |
| | | | | | 2,998 | 8.5 |

[Resignation]

| Election | Electors | T'out | Candidate | Party | Votes | % |
|---|---|---|---|---|---|---|
| 1930 (27/5) | 45,045 | 61.1 | T.J. O'Connor | C | 14,946 | 54.3 |
| | | | A.E. Waterson | Lab/Co-op | 7,923 | 28.8 |
| | | | R.C. Berkeley | L | 4,648 | 16.9 |
| | | | | | 7,023 | 25.5 |
| 1931 | 44,185 | 76.4 | T.J. O'Connor | C | 25,828 | 76.5 |
| | | | A.E. Waterson | Lab/Co-op | 7,932 | 23.5 |
| | | | | | 17,896 | 53.0 |
| 1935 | 41,947 | 68.9 | T.J. O'Connor | C | 18,706 | 64.7 |
| | | | J.W. Allitt | Lab/Co-op | 10,193 | 35.3 |
| | | | | | 8,513 | 29.4 |

[Death]

| Election | Electors | T'out | Candidate | Party | Votes | % |
|---|---|---|---|---|---|---|
| 1940 (19/7) | | | Rt. Hon. Sir F.H. Sykes | C | Unopp. | |
| 1945 | 38,270 | 73.9 | G.S. de Freitas | Lab | 13,681 | 48.4 |
| | | | Rt. Hon. Sir F.H. Sykes | C | 10,947 | 38.7 |
| | | | D. Craven-Griffiths | L | 3,644 | 12.9 |
| | | | | | 2,734 | 9.7 |

# NOTTINGHAM, EAST [199]

| Election | Electors | T'out | Candidate | Party | Votes | % |
|---|---|---|---|---|---|---|
| 1918 | 29,377 | 49.5 | †Sir J.D. Rees | Co C | 9,549 | 65.7 |
| | | | T. Proctor | Lab | 2,817 | 19.4 |
| | | | J.N.D. Brookes | NFDSS | 2,166 | 14.9 |
| | | | | | 6,732 | 46.3 |
| [Death] | | | | | | |
| 1922 | 30,034† | 66.3 | J.P. Houfton | Co C | 10,404 | 52.3 |
| (29/6) | | | A.H. Jones | Lab/Co-op | 5,431 | 27.3 |
| | | | T.G. Graham | L | 4,065 | 20.4 |
| | | | | | 4,973 | 25.0 |
| 1922 | 30,610 | 66.2 | J.P. Houfton | C | 12,082 | 59.7 |
| | | | E.E.H. Atkin | L | 8,170 | 40.3 |
| | | | | | 3,912 | 19.4 |
| 1923 | 31,365 | 67.8 | W.N. Birkett | L | 11,355 | 53.4 |
| | | | J.P. Houfton | C | 9,919 | 46.6 |
| | | | | | 1,436 | 6.8 |
| 1924 | 32,411 | 74.7 | C.E.R. Brocklebank | C | 11,524 | 47.6 |
| | | | W.N. Birkett | L | 10,078 | 41.6 |
| | | | T. Mann | Com | 2,606* | 10.8 |
| | | | | | 1,446 | 6.0 |
| 1929 | 44,319 | 78.9 | W.N. Birkett | L | 14,049 | 40.2 |
| | | | L.H. Gluckstein | C | 11,110 | 31.8 |
| | | | J.H. Baum | Lab | 9,787 | 28.0 |
| | | | | | 2,939 | 8.4 |
| 1931 | 44,049 | 78.8 | L.H. Gluckstein | C | 17,484 | 50.3 |
| | | | W.N. Birkett | L | 11,901 | 34.3 |
| | | | W. Windsor | Lab | 5,339 | 15.4 |
| | | | | | 5,583 | 16.0 |
| 1935 | 42,551 | 68.1 | L.H. Gluckstein | C | 16,726 | 57.7 |
| | | | M.L. Freedman | Lab | 7,435 | 25.7 |
| | | | A.S. Comyns Carr | L | 4,819 | 16.6 |
| | | | | | 9,291 | 32.0 |
| 1945 | 41,734 | 72.0 | J. Harrison | Lab | 12,075 | 40.2 |
| | | | L.H. Gluckstein | C | 11,227 | 37.4 |
| | | | Hon. A.P.W. Seely | L | 5,658 | 18.8 |
| | | | G. Twells | Ind | 1,072* | 3.6 |
| | | | | | 848 | 2.8 |

| Election | Electors | T'out | Candidate | Party | Votes | % |
|---|---|---|---|---|---|---|
| 1918 | 30,528 | 47.9 | †Lord Henry Cavendish-Bentinck | Co C | 10,881 | 74.4 |
|  |  |  | H. Mills | Ind Lab | 3,738 | 25.6 |
|  |  |  |  |  | 7,143 | 48.8 |
| 1922 | 29,951 | 66.3 | Lord Henry Cavendish-Bentinck | C | 15,158 | 76.3 |
|  |  |  | H. Mills | Ind Lab | 4,706 | 23.7 |
|  |  |  |  |  | 10,452 | 52.6 |
| 1923 | 30,847 | 67.6 | Lord Henry Cavendish-Bentinck | C | 10,724 | 51.4 |
|  |  |  | H. Mills | Ind Lab | 5,176 | 24.8 |
|  |  |  | V.D. Duval | L | 4,966 | 23.8 |
|  |  |  |  |  | 5,548 | 26.6 |
| 1924 | 31,271 | 72.3 | Lord Henry Cavendish-Bentinck | C | 13,725 | 60.7 |
|  |  |  | H. Mills | Lab | 8,897 | 39.3 |
|  |  |  |  |  | 4,828 | 21.4 |
| 1929 | 42,920 | 80.4 | G.W.H. Knight | Lab (N Lab) | 14,800 | 42.9 |
|  |  |  | Lord Henry Cavendish-Bentinck | C | 14,252 | 41.3 |
|  |  |  | C.L. Hale | L | 5,445 | 15.8 |
|  |  |  |  |  | 548 | 1.6 |
| 1931 | 43,104 | 77.6 | G.W.H. Knight | N Lab | 22,852 | 68.3 |
|  |  |  | A.R. Ellis | Lab | 10,583 | 31.7 |
|  |  |  |  |  | 12,269 | 36.6 |
| 1935 | 41,976 | 71.0 | S.F. Markham | N Lab (Nat) | 15,559 | 52.3 |
|  |  |  | T.J. May | Lab | 10,963 | 36.8 |
|  |  |  | J. Mawdesley | L | 3,260* | 10.9 |
|  |  |  |  |  | 4,596 | 15.5 |
| 1945 | 39,989 | 75.9 | H.N. Smith | Lab/Co-op | 15,316 | 50.4 |
|  |  |  | S.F. Markham | Nat | 10,766 | 35.5 |
|  |  |  | R.J.R. Blindell | L | 4,272 | 14.1 |
|  |  |  |  |  | 4,550 | 14.9 |

# NOTTINGHAM, WEST [201]

| Election | Electors | T'out | Candidate | Party | Votes | % |
|---|---|---|---|---|---|---|
| 1918 | 30,105 | 42.6 | A. Hayday | Lab | 7,286 | 56.8 |
| | | | †A. Richardson | L | 5,552 | 43.2 |
| | | | | | 1,734 | 13.6 |
| 1922 | 30,332 | 72.5 | A. Hayday | Lab | 10,787 | 49.0 |
| | | | G.H. Powell | C | 6,050 | 27.5 |
| | | | A.L. Rea | L | 5,163 | 23.5 |
| | | | | | 4,737 | 21.5 |
| 1923 | 31,093 | 63.5 | A. Hayday | Lab | 12,366 | 62.7 |
| | | | J.L. Litchfield | C | 7,370 | 37.3 |
| | | | | | 4,996 | 25.4 |
| 1924 | 31,574 | 71.5 | A. Hayday | Lab | 12,782 | 56.6 |
| | | | C.E. Loseby | Const | 9,790 | 43.4 |
| | | | | | 2,992 | 13.2 |
| 1929 | 42,314 | 79.8 | A. Hayday | Lab | 18,593 | 55.1 |
| | | | W.E. Barron | L | 8,276 | 24.5 |
| | | | C.E. Loseby | C | 6,893 | 20.4 |
| | | | | | 10,317 | 30.6 |
| 1931 | 46,542 | 76.4 | A.C. Caporn | C | 20,596 | 57.9 |
| | | | A. Hayday | Lab | 14,963 | 42.1 |
| | | | | | 5,633 | 15.8 |
| 1935 | 51,394 | 71.4 | A. Hayday | Lab | 19,697 | 53.7 |
| | | | A.C. Caporn | C | 16,987 | 46.3 |
| | | | | | 2,710 | 7.4 |
| 1945 | 54,755 | 76.3 | T. O'Brien | Lab | 24,887 | 59.6 |
| | | | B.S. Townroe | C | 9,711 | 23.2 |
| | | | S.A.J. Young | L | 7,184 | 17.2 |
| | | | | | 15,176 | 36.4 |

## OLDHAM [202]
### (Two Seats)

| Election | Electors | T'out | Candidate | Party | Votes | % |
|---|---|---|---|---|---|---|
| 1918 | 71,378 | 59.5 | †E.R. Bartley-Denniss | Co C | 26,568 | 34.3 |
| | | | †Sir A.W. Barton | Co L (L) | 26,254 | 34.0 |
| | | | W.C. Robinson | Lab | 15,178 | 19.6 |
| | | | †W.R. Rea | L | 9,323 | 12.1 |
| | | | | | 11,390 | 14.7 |
| | | | | | 11,076 | 14.4 |
| 1922 | 70,583 | 78.8 | Sir E.W.M. Grigg | NL | 24,762 | 28.0 |
| | | | W.J. Tout | Lab | 24,434 | 27.7 |
| | | | S. Smethurst | C | 23,200 | 26.2 |
| | | | W.T. Davies | L | 9,812 | 11.1 |
| | | | Lady Emmott | L | 6,186* | 7.0 |
| | | | | | 1,562 | 1.8 |
| | | | | | 1,234 | 1.5 |
| 1923 | 71,001 | 76.3 | W.J. Tout | Lab | 20,939 | 23.4 |
| | | | Sir E.W.M. Grigg | L | 20,681 | 23.2 |
| | | | W.M. Wiggins | L | 17,990 | 20.1 |
| | | | W.E. Freeman | C | 15,819 | 17.7 |
| | | | S. Smethurst | C | 13,894 | 15.6 |
| | | | | | 2,949 | 3.3 |
| | | | | | 4,862 | 5.5 |
| 1924 | 71,834 | 86.7 | A.D. Cooper | C | 37,419 | 31.2 |
| | | | Sir E.W.M. Grigg | L | 36,761 | 30.7 |
| | | | W.J. Tout | Lab | 23,623 | 19.7 |
| | | | J. Wilson | Lab | 22,081 | 18.4 |
| | | | | | 13,796 | 11.5 |
| | | | | | 13,138 | 11.0 |

[Resignation of Grigg on appointment as Governor of Kenya]

| Election | Electors | T'out | Candidate | Party | Votes | % |
|---|---|---|---|---|---|---|
| 1925 (24/6) | 71,834† | 66.9 | W.M. Wiggins | L | 26,325 | 54.8 |
| | | | W.J. Tout | Lab | 21,702 | 45.2 |
| | | | | | 4,623 | 9.6 |
| 1929 | 95,109 | 81.2 | Rev. G. Lang | Lab | 34,223 | 26.2 |
| | | | J. Wilson | Lab | 32,727 | 25.0 |
| | | | A.D. Cooper | C | 29,424 | 22.5 |
| | | | J.S. Dodd | L | 20,810 | 15.9 |
| | | | Rev. G.J. Jenkins | L | 13,528 | 10.4 |
| | | | | | 3,303 | 2.5 |
| 1931 | 96,518 | 82.3 | A.C. Crossley | C | 50,693 | 32.5 |
| | | | H.W. Kerr | C | 50,395 | 32.3 |
| | | | Rev. G. Lang | Lab | 28,629 | 18.3 |
| | | | J. Wilson | Lab | 26,361 | 16.9 |
| | | | | | 21,766 | 14.0 |
| 1935 | 94,418 | 79.2 | H.W. Kerr | C | 36,738 | 25.5 |
| | | | J.S. Dodd | NL | 34,755 | 24.2 |
| | | | Rev. G. Lang | Lab | 34,316 | 23.8 |
| | | | M.B. Farr | Lab | 29,647 | 20.6 |
| | | | W.G. Ward | L | 8,534* | 5.9 |
| | | | | | 2,422 | 1.7 |
| | | | | | 439 | 0.4 |

| Election | Electors | T'out | Candidate | Party | Votes | % |
|---|---|---|---|---|---|---|
| 1945 | 89,005 | 76.3 | F. Fairhurst | Lab | 31,704 | 23.9 |
| | | | C.L. Hale | Lab | 31,327 | 23.6 |
| | | | H.W. Kerr | C | 26,911 | 20.3 |
| | | | J.S. Dodd | NL | 24,199 | 18.2 |
| | | | J.T. Middleton | L | 10,365 | 7.8 |
| | | | T.D.F. Powell | L | 8,264* | 6.2 |
| | | | | | 4,416 | 3.3 |

| Election | Electors | T'out | Candidate | Party | Votes | % |
|---|---|---|---|---|---|---|
| 1918 | 25,134 | 55.2 | †J.A.R. Marriott | Co C | 9,805 | 70.7 |
| | | | G.H. Higgins | L | 4,057 | 29.3 |
| | | | | | 5,748 | 41.4 |
| 1922 | 25,254 | 83.8 | F. Gray | L | 12,489 | 59.0 |
| | | | J.A.R. Marriott | C | 8,683 | 41.0 |
| | | | | | 3,806 | 18.0 |
| 1923 | 26,270 | 83.5 | F. Gray | L | 12,311 | 56.1 |
| | | | R.C. Bourne | C | 9,618 | 43.9 |
| | | | | | 2,693 | 12.2 |

[Election declared void on petition]

| Election | Electors | T'out | Candidate | Party | Votes | % |
|---|---|---|---|---|---|---|
| 1924 | 26,270† | 80.3 | R.C. Bourne | C | 10,079 | 47.8 |
| (5/6) | | | C.B. Fry | L | 8,237 | 39.1 |
| | | | K.M. Lindsay | Lab | 2,769 | 13.1 |
| | | | | | 1,842 | 8.7 |
| 1924 | 27,139 | 78.5 | R.C. Bourne | C | 12,196 | 57.3 |
| | | | Dr. R.O. Moon | L | 6,836 | 32.1 |
| | | | F. Ludlow | Lab | 2,260* | 10.6 |
| | | | | | 5,360 | 25.2 |
| 1929 | 38,668 | 72.2 | R.C. Bourne | C | 14,638 | 52.5 |
| | | | Dr. R.O. Moon | L | 8,581 | 30.7 |
| | | | J.L. Etty | Lab | 4,694 | 16.8 |
| | | | | | 6,057 | 21.8 |
| 1931 | | | R.C. Bourne | C | Unopp. | |
| 1935 | 38,557 | 67.3 | Rt. Hon. R.C. Bourne | C | 16,306 | 62.8 |
| | | | P.C. Gordon Walker | Lab | 9,661 | 37.2 |
| | | | | | 6,645 | 25.6 |

[Death]

| Election | Electors | T'out | Candidate | Party | Votes | % |
|---|---|---|---|---|---|---|
| 1938 | 36,929 | 76.3 | Hon. Q.M. Hogg | C | 15,797 | 56.1 |
| (27/10) | | | A.D.L. Lindsay | Ind Prog | 12,363 | 43.9 |
| | | | | | 3,434 | 12.2 |
| 1945 | 45,775 | 69.1 | Hon. Q.M. Hogg | C | 14,314 | 45.3 |
| | | | Hon. F.A. Pakenham | Lab | 11,451 | 36.2 |
| | | | A.C.W. Norman | L | 5,860 | 18.5 |
| | | | | | 2,863 | 9.1 |

Note:—

1938: Lindsay was supported by the Oxford City Labour Party and the local Liberal Association, both of whom withdrew their candidates when he agreed to seek election on a 'Popular Front' programme.

# PLYMOUTH, DEVONPORT  [204]

| Election | Electors | T'out | Candidate | Party | Votes | % |
|---|---|---|---|---|---|---|
| 1918 | 31,687 | 67.2 | †Sir C. Kinloch-Cooke | Co C | 13,240 | 62.2 |
|  |  |  | F. Bramley | Lab | 4,115 | 19.3 |
|  |  |  | S. Lithgow | L | 3,930 | 18.5 |
|  |  |  |  |  | 9,125 | 42.9 |
| 1922 | 31,268 | 79.1 | Sir C. Kinloch-Cooke | C | 10,459 | 42.3 |
|  |  |  | L. Hore-Belisha | L | 8,538 | 34.5 |
|  |  |  | R.B. Bates | Lab | 5,742 | 23.2 |
|  |  |  |  |  | 1,921 | 7.8 |
| 1923 | 32,491 | 82.7 | L. Hore-Belisha | L | 12,269 | 45.7 |
|  |  |  | Sir C. Kinloch-Cooke | C | 10,428 | 38.8 |
|  |  |  | J. Harris | Lab | 4,158 | 15.5 |
|  |  |  |  |  | 1,841 | 6.9 |
| 1924 | 33,159 | 84.4 | L. Hore-Belisha | L | 11,115 | 39.7 |
|  |  |  | S. Gluckstein | C | 10,534 | 37.6 |
|  |  |  | G.W.H. Knight | Lab | 6,350 | 22.7 |
|  |  |  |  |  | 581 | 2.1 |
| 1929 | 40,499 | 82.3 | L. Hore-Belisha | L (NL) | 15,233 | 45.7 |
|  |  |  | S. Gluckstein | C | 10,688 | 32.0 |
|  |  |  | Rev. D.B. Fraser | Lab | 7,428 | 22.3 |
|  |  |  |  |  | 4,545 | 13.7 |
| 1931 | 41,568 | 78.2 | L. Hore-Belisha | NL | 23,459 | 72.2 |
|  |  |  | P. Reed | Lab | 9,039 | 27.8 |
|  |  |  |  |  | 14,420 | 44.4 |
| 1935 | 42,355 | 72.3 | Rt. Hon. L. Hore-Belisha | NL (Nat Ind) | 20,852 | 68.1 |
|  |  |  | J. Brown | Lab | 9,756 | 31.9 |
|  |  |  |  |  | 11,096 | 36.2 |
| 1945 | 34,845 | 71.1 | M.M. Foot | Lab | 13,395 | 54.1 |
|  |  |  | Rt. Hon. L. Hore-Belisha | Nat | 11,382 | 45.9 |
|  |  |  |  |  | 2,013 | 8.2 |

| Election | Electors | T'out | Candidate | Party | Votes | % |
|---|---|---|---|---|---|---|
| 1918 | 42,833 | 54.7 | †Sir A.S. Benn | Co C | 17,188 | 73.4 |
| | | | T.W. Dobson | L | 6,225 | 26.6 |
| | | | | | 10,963 | 46.8 |
| | | | | | | |
| 1922 | 35,845 | 74.4 | Sir A.S. Benn | C | 11,698 | 43.9 |
| | | | J. Gorman | Lab | 8,359 | 31.4 |
| | | | S.J. Robins | L | 6,594 | 24.7 |
| | | | | | 3,339 | 12.5 |
| | | | | | | |
| 1923 | 36,284 | 77.9 | Sir A.S. Benn | C | 12,345 | 43.7 |
| | | | J.J.H. Moses | Lab | 11,849 | 41.9 |
| | | | E.E.H. Atkin | L | 4,082 | 14.4 |
| | | | | | 496 | 1.8 |
| | | | | | | |
| 1924 | 36,626 | 83.2 | Sir A.S. Benn | C | 14,669 | 48.1 |
| | | | J.J.H. Moses | Lab | 12,161 | 39.9 |
| | | | S. Stephens | L | 3,645* | 12.0 |
| | | | | | 2,508 | 8.2 |
| | | | | | | |
| 1929 | 46,801 | 80.5 | J.J.H. Moses | Lab | 16,684 | 44.3 |
| | | | Sir A.S. Benn, Bt. | C | 14,673 | 39.0 |
| | | | H.M. Pratt | L | 6,309 | 16.7 |
| | | | | | 2,011 | 5.3 |
| | | | | | | |
| 1931 | 47,388 | 79.6 | Rt. Hon. F.E. Guest | C | 25,063 | 66.4 |
| | | | J.J.H. Moses | Lab | 12,669 | 33.6 |
| | | | | | 12,394 | 32.8 |
| | | | | | | |
| 1935 | 49,194 | 74.8 | Rt. Hon. F.E. Guest | C | 21,446 | 58.3 |
| | | | J.J.H. Moses | Lab | 15,368 | 41.7 |
| | | | | | 6,078 | 16.6 |
| [Death] | | | | | | |
| 1937 | 49,088 | 54.6 | Hon. C.H.C. Guest | C | 15,778 | 58.8 |
| (15/6) | | | G.T. Garratt | Lab | 11,044 | 41.2 |
| | | | | | 4,734 | 17.6 |
| | | | | | | |
| 1945 | 41,380 | 71.6 | H.M. Medland | Lab | 15,070 | 50.8 |
| | | | Hon. C.H.C. Guest | C | 12,871 | 43.5 |
| | | | E.J. Trout | CW | 1,681* | 5.7 |
| | | | | | 2,199 | 7.3 |

Note:—

1929:  A petition was lodged relating to this election but was dismissed.

# PLYMOUTH, SUTTON   [206]

| Election | Electors | T'out | Candidate | Party | Votes | % |
|---|---|---|---|---|---|---|
| 1918 | 43,444 | 59.6 | †Hon. W. Astor | Co C | 17,091 | 65.9 |
| | | | W.T. Gay | Lab | 5,334 | 20.6 |
| | | | S. Ransom | L | 3,488 | 13.5 |
| | | | | | 11,757 | 45.3 |

[Succession to the Peerage — Viscount Astor]

| Election | Electors | T'out | Candidate | Party | Votes | % |
|---|---|---|---|---|---|---|
| 1919 | 38,539 | 72.5 | Viscountess Astor | Co C | 14,495 | 51.9 |
| (15/11) | | | W.T. Gay | Lab | 9,292 | 33.3 |
| | | | I. Foot | L | 4,139 | 14.8 |
| | | | | | 5,203 | 18.6 |
| 1922 | 37,696 | 78.0 | Viscountess Astor | C | 13,924 | 47.4 |
| | | | F.G.J. Woulfe-Brenan | Lab | 10,831 | 36.8 |
| | | | Dr. H.W. Bayly | Ind C | 4,643 | 15.8 |
| | | | | | 3,093 | 10.6 |
| 1923 | 37,921 | 77.9 | Viscountess Astor | C | 16,114 | 54.5 |
| | | | F.G.J. Woulfe-Brenan | Lab | 13,438 | 45.5 |
| | | | | | 2,676 | 9.0 |
| 1924 | 38,300 | 81.6 | Viscountess Astor | C | 18,174 | 58.1 |
| | | | F.G.J. Woulfe-Brenan | Lab | 13,095 | 41.9 |
| | | | | | 5,079 | 16.2 |
| 1929 | 47,423 | 81.1 | Viscountess Astor | C | 16,625 | 43.2 |
| | | | W. Westwood | Lab | 16,414 | 42.7 |
| | | | T.H. Aggett | L | 5,430 | 14.1 |
| | | | | | 211 | 0.5 |
| 1931 | 47,862 | 80.1 | Viscountess Astor | C | 24,277 | 63.3 |
| | | | G. Ward | Lab | 14,073 | 36.7 |
| | | | | | 10,204 | 26.6 |
| 1935 | 47,540 | 77.6 | Viscountess Astor | C | 21,491 | 58.3 |
| | | | G. Ward | Lab | 15,394 | 41.7 |
| | | | | | 6,097 | 16.6 |
| 1945 | 41,493 | 71.9 | Mrs. L.A. Middleton | Lab | 15,417 | 51.6 |
| | | | L.D. Grand | C | 10,738 | 36.0 |
| | | | Miss J.A. Gaved | L | 3,695* | 12.4 |
| | | | | | 4,679 | 15.6 |

Notes:—

1919:  Viscountess Astor was the first woman to sit in the House of Commons.

1922:  Bayly was the nominee of the Plymouth Conservative Imperial Party which was formed in the summer of 1922 with the object of promoting his candidature. He opposed Lady Astor's views on temperance and condemned the policy of prohibition. It was alleged during the campaign that he was supported and financed by local brewers.

| Election | Electors | T'out | Candidate | Party | Votes | % |
|---|---|---|---|---|---|---|
| 1918 | 35,964 | 58.2 | Sir T.A. Bramsdon | L | 10,929 | 52.2 |
| | | | Sir W.T. Dupree | Co C | 6,008 | 28.7 |
| | | | H. Hinshelwood | Lab | 4,004 | 19.1 |
| | | | | | 4,921 | 23.5 |
| 1922 | 36,695 | 77.9 | F.J. Privett | C | 7,666 | 26.9 |
| | | | Sir T. Fisher | NL | 7,659 | 26.8 |
| | | | Sir T.A. Bramsdon | L | 7,129 | 24.9 |
| | | | A.G. Gourd | Lab | 6,126 | 21.4 |
| | | | | | 7 | 0.1 |
| 1923 | 37,991 | 78.2 | Sir T.A. Bramsdon | L | 11,493 | 38.7 |
| | | | F.J. Privett | C | 10,231 | 34.4 |
| | | | F.P. Crozier | Lab | 7,991 | 26.9 |
| | | | | | 1,262 | 4.3 |
| 1924 | 37,966 | 80.3 | Sir H.S. Foster | C | 14,028 | 46.1 |
| | | | W.G. Hall | Lab | 10,525 | 34.5 |
| | | | F. Gray | L | 5,926 | 19.4 |
| | | | | | 3,503 | 11.6 |
| 1929 | 48,146 | 74.3 | W.G. Hall | Lab | 15,153 | 42.4 |
| | | | Sir T.W. Comyn-Platt | C | 13,628 | 38.1 |
| | | | C.W. Cohen | L | 6,993 | 19.5 |
| | | | | | 1,525 | 4.3 |
| 1931 | 49,927 | 78.4 | Hon. R.E.B. Beaumont | C | 24,623 | 62.9 |
| | | | W.G. Hall | Lab | 14,512 | 37.1 |
| | | | | | 10,111 | 25.8 |
| 1935 | 50,558 | 71.1 | Hon. R.E.B. Beaumont | C | 21,578 | 60.0 |
| | | | D. Freeman | Lab | 10,733 | 29.9 |
| | | | E.J. Thornley | L | 3,612* | 10.1 |
| | | | | | 10,845 | 30.1 |
| 1945 | 36,255 | 73.5 | J.W. Snow | Lab | 14,745 | 55.3 |
| | | | Hon. R.E.B. Beaumont | C | 11,345 | 42.6 |
| | | | W.R.C. Foster | Dem P | 561* | 2.1 |
| | | | | | 3,400 | 12.7 |

| Election | Electors | T'out | Candidate | Party | Votes | % |
|---|---|---|---|---|---|---|
| 1918 | 35,367 | 52.3 | †Sir B.G. Falle, Bt. | Co C | 11,427 | 61.8 |
| | | | L.J.W. Yexley | Ind | 7,063 | 38.2 |
| | | | | | 4,364 | 23.6 |
| 1922 | 35,236 | 71.9 | Sir B.G. Falle, Bt. | C | 14,168 | 55.9 |
| | | | A. Henderson | Lab | 6,808 | 26.9 |
| | | | T.H.F. Lapthorn | L | 4,368 | 17.2 |
| | | | | | 7,360 | 29.0 |
| 1923 | 36,717 | 71.7 | Sir B.G. Falle, Bt. | C | 13,229 | 50.2 |
| | | | Dr. O. Gleeson | Lab | 9,523 | 36.2 |
| | | | W.L. Williams | L | 3,584 | 13.6 |
| | | | | | 3,706 | 14.0 |
| 1924 | 37,168 | 75.0 | Sir B.G. Falle, Bt. | C | 17,597 | 63.1 |
| | | | Dr. O. Gleeson | Lab | 10,279 | 36.9 |
| | | | | | 7,318 | 26.2 |
| 1929 | 48,688 | 70.8 | Sir B.G. Falle, Bt. | C | 15,352 | 44.5 |
| | | | E. Archbold | Lab | 12,475 | 36.2 |
| | | | A.W. Palmer | L | 6,643 | 19.3 |
| | | | | | 2,877 | 8.3 |
| 1931 | 51,704 | 74.5 | Sir B.G. Falle, Bt. | C | 26,331 | 68.4 |
| | | | K.G.B. Dewar | Lab | 12,182 | 31.6 |
| | | | | | 14,149 | 36.8 |

[Elevation to the Peerage — Lord Portsea]

| Election | Electors | T'out | Candidate | Party | Votes | % |
|---|---|---|---|---|---|---|
| 1934 (19/2) | 52,965 | 55.7 | Sir R.J.B. Keyes, Bt. | C | 17,582 | 59.6 |
| | | | E.T. Humby | Lab | 11,904 | 40.4 |
| | | | | | 5,678 | 19.2 |
| 1935 | 53,123 | 64.9 | Sir R.J.B. Keyes, Bt. | C | 22,956 | 66.6 |
| | | | E.T. Humby | Lab | 11,502 | 33.4 |
| | | | | | 11,454 | 33.2 |

[Elevation to the Peerage — Lord Keyes]

| Election | Electors | T'out | Candidate | Party | Votes | % |
|---|---|---|---|---|---|---|
| 1943 (16/2) | 51,434 | 21.9 | Sir W.M. James | C | 6,735 | 59.7 |
| | | | T. Sargant | CW | 4,545 | 40.3 |
| | | | | | 2,190 | 19.4 |
| 1945 | 39,873 | 75.4 | D.W.T. Bruce | Lab | 15,352 | 51.1 |
| | | | Hon. G.R. Howard | C | 14,310 | 47.6 |
| | | | J.E.V. Keast | Dem P | 388* | 1.3 |
| | | | | | 1,042 | 3.5 |

Note:—

1918: Yexley sought election as a 'Naval and Lower-Deck' candidate. He was supported by the Lower-Deck Parliamentary Committee and also received local Liberal Party support.

# PORTSMOUTH, SOUTH [209]

| Election | Electors | T'out | Candidate | Party | Votes | % |
|---|---|---|---|---|---|---|
| 1918 | 37,427 | 62.0 | H.R. Cayzer | Co C | 15,842 | 68.3 |
| | | | Miss A.V. Garland | L | 4,283 | 18.5 |
| | | | J. Lacey | Lab | 3,070 | 13.2 |
| | | | | | 11,559 | 49.8 |
| 1922 | 39,426 | 73.7 | H.R. Cayzer | C | 19,960 | 68.7 |
| | | | Sir H.M. Lawson | L | 9,080 | 31.3 |
| | | | | | 10,880 | 37.4 |

[Resignation]

| Election | Electors | T'out | Candidate | Party | Votes | % |
|---|---|---|---|---|---|---|
| 1922 (13/12) | 39,426 | 57.7 | Rt. Hon. L.O. Wilson | C | 14,301 | 62.9 |
| | | | G.C. Thomas | Ind C | 8,434 | 37.1 |
| | | | | | 5,867 | 25.8 |

[Resignation on appointment as Governor of Bombay]

| Election | Electors | T'out | Candidate | Party | Votes | % |
|---|---|---|---|---|---|---|
| 1923 (13/8) | 39,426[†] | 54.9 | H.R. Cayzer | C | 11,884 | 54.9 |
| | | | Sir H.M. Lawson | L | 9,763 | 45.1 |
| | | | | | 2,121 | 9.8 |
| 1923 | 40,854 | 72.7 | H.R. Cayzer | C | 16,625 | 55.9 |
| | | | Miss J. Stephen | Lab | 7,388 | 24.9 |
| | | | S.R. Drury-Lowe | L | 5,698 | 19.2 |
| | | | | | 9,237 | 31.0 |
| 1924 | 41,417 | 74.2 | Sir H.R. Cayzer, Bt. | C | 22,423 | 73.0 |
| | | | Miss J. Stephen | Lab | 8,310 | 27.0 |
| | | | | | 14,113 | 46.0 |
| 1929 | 54,449 | 75.1 | Sir H.R. Cayzer, Bt. | C | 15,068 | 36.8 |
| | | | Miss J. Stephen | Lab | 10,127 | 24.8 |
| | | | F.J. Privett | Ind C | 9,505 | 23.2 |
| | | | C.M.C. Rudkin | L | 6,214 | 15.2 |
| | | | | | 4,941 | 12.0 |
| 1931 | 55,488 | 72.7 | Sir H.R. Cayzer, Bt. | C | 32,634 | 80.9 |
| | | | W.J. Beck | Lab | 7,715 | 19.1 |
| | | | | | 24,919 | 61.8 |
| 1935 | 54,463 | 66.9 | Sir H.R. Cayzer, Bt. | C | 27,416 | 75.2 |
| | | | J.W. Fawcett | Lab | 9,043 | 24.8 |
| | | | | | 18,373 | 50.4 |

[Elevation to the Peerage — Lord Rotherwick]

| Election | Electors | T'out | Candidate | Party | Votes | % |
|---|---|---|---|---|---|---|
| 1939 (12/7) | | | Sir J.M. Lucas, Bt. | C | Unopp. | |
| 1945 | 38,150 | 74.9 | Sir J.M. Lucas, Bt. | C | 15,810 | 55.3 |
| | | | J.F. Blitz | Lab | 12,783 | 44.7 |
| | | | | | 3,027 | 10.6 |

Notes:—

1922: Wilson was Parliamentary Secretary to the Treasury.
(13/12)

1929: Privett was the nominee of the Portsmouth South Constitutional Association which was formed in April 1929 with the object of promoting his candidature.

# PRESTON [210]
## (Two Seats)

| Election | Electors | T'out | Candidate | Party | Votes | % |
|---|---|---|---|---|---|---|
| 1918 | 57,795 | 69.6 | T. Shaw | Lab | 19,213 | 25.8 |
| | | | †Hon. G.F. Stanley | Co C | 18,970 | 25.4 |
| | | | J.J. O'Neill | L | 18,485 | 24.8 |
| | | | †W. Brookes | Co C | 17,928 | 24.0 |
| | | | | | 728 | 1.0 |
| | | | | | 485 | 0.6 |
| | | | | | | |
| 1922 | 57,953 | 87.8 | T. Shaw | Lab | 26,259 | 27.9 |
| | | | J.P. Hodge | L | 24,798 | 26.4 |
| | | | Hon. G.F. Stanley | C | 22,574 | 24.0 |
| | | | A.R.M. Camm | C | 20,410 | 21.7 |
| | | | | | 3,685 | 3.9 |
| | | | | | 2,224 | 2.4 |
| | | | | | | |
| 1923 | 59,406 | 87.2 | T. Shaw | Lab | 25,816 | 34.4 |
| | | | J.P. Hodge | L | 25,155 | 33.6 |
| | | | W.M. Kirkpatrick | C | 23,962 | 32.0 |
| | | | | | 1,854 | 2.4 |
| | | | | | 1,193 | 1.6 |
| | | | | | | |
| 1924 | 60,840 | 88.8 | Rt. Hon. T. Shaw | Lab | 27,009 | 26.3 |
| | | | A.R. Kennedy | C | 25,887 | 25.2 |
| | | | J.P. Hodge | L | 25,327 | 24.6 |
| | | | G. Barnes | C | 24,557 | 23.9 |
| | | | | | 1,682 | 1.7 |
| | | | | | 560 | 0.6 |

[Seat Vacant at Dissolution (Resignation of Kennedy on appointment as a County Court Judge)]

| Election | Electors | T'out | Candidate | Party | Votes | % |
|---|---|---|---|---|---|---|
| 1929 | 81,866 | 87.9 | Rt. Hon. T. Shaw | Lab | 37,705 | 29.5 |
| | | | W.A. Jowitt | L | 31,277 | 24.4 |
| | | | Dr. A.B. Howitt | C | 29,116 | 22.8 |
| | | | C.E.G.C. Emmott | C | 27,754 | 21.7 |
| | | | S.M. Holden | Ind Lab | 2,111* | 1.6 |
| | | | | | 8,589 | 6.7 |
| | | | | | 2,161 | 1.6 |

[Jowitt seeks re-election on joining the Labour Party]

| Election | Electors | T'out | Candidate | Party | Votes | % |
|---|---|---|---|---|---|---|
| 1929 (31/7) | 81,866 | 79.6 | Sir W.A. Jowitt | Lab (N Lab) | 35,608 | 54.6 |
| | | | Dr. A.B. Howitt | C | 29,168 | 44.8 |
| | | | S.M. Holden | Ind Lab | 410* | 0.6 |
| | | | | | 6,440 | 9.8 |
| | | | | | | |
| 1931 | 84,243 | 85.7 | W.M. Kirkpatrick | C | 46,276 | 32.5 |
| | | | A.C. Moreing | C | 45,843 | 32.2 |
| | | | Rt. Hon. T. Shaw | Lab | 25,710 | 18.0 |
| | | | E. Porter | Lab | 24,660 | 17.3 |
| | | | | | 20,133 | 14.2 |
| | | | | | | |
| 1935 | 84,291 | 82.6 | A.C. Moreing | C | 37,219 | 26.9 |
| | | | W.M. Kirkpatrick | C | 36,797 | 26.7 |
| | | | Dr. R.A. Lyster | Lab | 32,225 | 23.3 |
| | | | R.L. Reiss | Lab | 31,827 | 23.1 |
| | | | | | 4,572 | 3.4 |

| Election | Electors | T'out | Candidate | Party | Votes | % |
|---|---|---|---|---|---|---|
| [Resignation of Kirkwood on appointment as Representative in China of the Exports Credits Guarantee Department] | | | | | | |
| 1936 (25/11) | 84,535 | 79.0 | E.C. Cobb | C | 32,575 | 48.8 |
| | | | F.G. Bowles | Lab | 30.970 | 46.4 |
| | | | Miss F. White | Ind | 3,221* | 4.8 |
| | | | | | 1,605 | 2.4 |
| [Death of Moreing] | | | | | | |
| 1940 (25/9) | | | R.F.E.S. Churchill | C | Unopp. | |
| 1945 | 88,535 | 80.2 | Dr. S. Segal | Lab | 33,053 | 24.2 |
| | | | J.W. Sunderland | Lab | 32,889 | 24.1 |
| | | | R.F.E.S. Churchill | C | 29,129 | 21.4 |
| | | | J. Amery | C | 27,885 | 20.4 |
| | | | J.M. Toulmin | L | 8,251* | 6.1 |
| | | | P.J. Devine | Com | 5,168* | 3.8 |
| | | | | | 3,760 | 2.7 |
| [Death of Sunderland] | | | | | | |
| 1946 (31/1) | 89,282 | 64.9 | E.A.A. Shackleton | Lab | 32,189 | 55.6 |
| | | | H. Nicholls | C | 25,718 | 44.4 |
| | | | | | 6,471 | 11.2 |

Notes:—

1929-
1929:
(31/7)    Holden stated at the General Election that he was the nominee of an organisation called the British Reform and Women's Party (with headquarters in Manchester), which supported local option. At the by-election he was the nominee of the Preston Progressive Labour Party which was formed shortly after the General Election.

1936:    Miss White was the founder and nominee of the Spinsters Pensions' Association.

| Election | Electors | T'out | Candidate | Party | Votes | % |
|---|---|---|---|---|---|---|
| 1918 | 45,379 | 62.2 | †L.O. Wilson | Co C | 15,204 | 53.9 |
| | | | T.C. Morris | Lab | 8,410 | 29.8 |
| | | | F. Thoresby | L | 3,143* | 11.1 |
| | | | L.E. Quelch | NSP | 1,462* | 5.2 |
| | | | | | 6,794 | 24.1 |
| 1922 | 45,003 | 83.6 | Hon. E.C.G. Cadogan | C | 16,082 | 42.7 |
| | | | D. Hall Caine | Lab | 14,322 | 38.1 |
| | | | H.D. Roome | L | 7,212 | 19.2 |
| | | | | | 1,760 | 4.6 |
| 1923 | 45,308 | 82.1 | Dr. S. Hastings | Lab | 16,657 | 44.8 |
| | | | Hon. E.C.G. Cadogan | C | 15,115 | 40.7 |
| | | | F. Maddison | L | 5,406 | 14.5 |
| | | | | | 1,542 | 4.1 |
| 1924 | 46,234 | 85.8 | H.G. Williams | C | 21,338 | 53.8 |
| | | | Dr. S. Hastings | Lab | 18,337 | 46.2 |
| | | | | | 3,001 | 7.6 |
| 1929 | 62,873 | 85.0 | Dr. S. Hastings | Lab | 23,281 | 43.5 |
| | | | H.G. Williams | C | 22,429 | 42.0 |
| | | | Rev. D. Macfadyen | L | 7,733 | 14.5 |
| | | | | | 852 | 1.5 |
| 1931 | 65,009 | 84.0 | Dr. A.B. Howitt | C | 34,439 | 63.1 |
| | | | Dr. S. Hastings | Lab | 19,277 | 35.3 |
| | | | E.R. Troward | NP | 861* | 1.6 |
| | | | | | 15,162 | 27.8 |
| 1935 | 67,181 | 79.2 | Dr. A.B. Howitt | C | 27,540 | 51.8 |
| | | | Dr. S. Hastings | Lab | 22,949 | 43.2 |
| | | | J.W. Todd | L | 2,685* | 5.0 |
| | | | | | 4,591 | 8.6 |
| 1945 | 85,039 | 73.3 | I. Mikardo | Lab | 30,465 | 48.8 |
| | | | W.E.C. McIlroy | Nat | 24,075 | 38.6 |
| | | | R.N. Tronchin-James | L | 7,834 | 12.6 |
| | | | | | 6,390 | 10.2 |

## RICHMOND [212]

| Election | Electors | T'out | Candidate | Party | Votes | % |
|---|---|---|---|---|---|---|
| 1918 | 32,900 | 53.8 | C.B. Edgar | Co C | 8,364 | 47.4 |
| | | | Mrs. N.D. Fox | Ind | 3,615 | 20.4 |
| | | | R.J. Morrison | L | 3,491 | 19.7 |
| | | | W.W. Crotch | Ind | 2,220 | 12.5 |
| | | | | | 4,749 | 27.0 |
| 1922 | 34,719 | 68.8 | H.T.A. Becker | Ind C (C) | 12,075 | 50.6 |
| | | | C.B. Edgar | C | 6,032 | 25.3 |
| | | | Mrs. M.I.C. Ashby | L | 5,765 | 24.1 |
| | | | | | 6,043 | 25.3 |
| 1923 | 35,042 | 59.4 | H.T.A. Becker | C | 13,112 | 63.0 |
| | | | Mrs. M.I.C. Ashby | L | 7,702 | 37.0 |
| | | | | | 5,410 | 26.0 |
| 1924 | 35,704 | 72.8 | Hon. Sir N.J. Moore | C | 19,948 | 76.8 |
| | | | H. Parker | Lab | 6,034 | 23.2 |
| | | | | | 13,914 | 53.6 |
| 1929 | 55,936 | 70.6 | Hon. Sir N.J. Moore | C | 23,148 | 58.7 |
| | | | P. Butler | Lab | 9,520 | 24.1 |
| | | | W.H. Williamson | L | 6,802 | 17.2 |
| | | | | | 13,628 | 34.6 |
| 1931 | 58,070 | 72.0 | Hon. Sir N.J. Moore | C | 35,333 | 84.5 |
| | | | J.L. Thomson | Lab | 6,460 | 15.5 |
| | | | | | 28,873 | 69.0 |
| [Resignation] | | | | | | |
| 1932 (13/4) | | | Sir W. Ray | C | Unopp. | |
| 1935 | 59,322 | 69.8 | Sir W. Ray | C | 30,433 | 73.5 |
| | | | L. Gassman | Lab | 10,953 | 26.5 |
| | | | | | 19,480 | 47.0 |
| [Resignation] | | | | | | |
| 1937 (25/2) | 59,718 | 47.3 | G.S. Harvie-Watt | C | 20,546 | 72.7 |
| | | | G.H.R. Rogers | Lab | 7,709 | 27.3 |
| | | | | | 12,837 | 45.4 |
| 1945 | 59,759 | 76.4 | G.S. Harvie-Watt | C | 24,085 | 52.8 |
| | | | Dr. D.S. Murray | Lab | 15,760 | 34.5 |
| | | | G.A.D. Gordon | L | 5,029* | 11.0 |
| | | | D.G.H. Frank | CW | 753* | 1.7 |
| | | | | | 8,325 | 18.3 |

Note:—

1922: Becker was supported by the Anti-Waste League.

# ROCHDALE  [213]

| Election | Electors | T'out | Candidate | Party | Votes | % |
|---|---|---|---|---|---|---|
| 1918 | 46,598 | 64.5 | A.J. Law | Co C | 14,299 | 47.6 |
| | | | H.V. Phillipps | L | 6,452 | 21.5 |
| | | | R.H. Tawney | Lab | 4,956 | 16.5 |
| | | | J.J. Terrett | NDP | 2,358* | 7.8 |
| | | | J.F. Jones | Nat P | 1,992* | 6.6 |
| | | | | | 7,847 | 26.1 |
| 1922 | 46,723 | 87.1 | S. Burgess | Lab | 15,774 | 38.8 |
| | | | A.J. Law | C | 13,006 | 32.0 |
| | | | J.R.B. Muir | L | 11,894 | 29.2 |
| | | | | | 2,768 | 6.8 |
| 1923 | 47,207 | 87.8 | J.R.B. Muir | L | 15,087 | 36.4 |
| | | | S. Burgess | Lab | 13,525 | 32.6 |
| | | | N. Cockshutt | C | 12,845 | 31.0 |
| | | | | | 1,562 | 3.8 |
| 1924 | 47,859 | 90.3 | W.T. Kelly | Lab | 14,609 | 33.8 |
| | | | J.R.B. Muir | L | 14,492 | 33.5 |
| | | | T.E. Jesson | C | 14,112 | 32.7 |
| | | | | | 117 | 0.3 |
| 1929 | 62,744 | 87.6 | W.T. Kelly | Lab | 22,060 | 40.2 |
| | | | J.R.B. Muir | L | 16,957 | 30.8 |
| | | | Sir J. Haslam | C | 15,962 | 29.0 |
| | | | | | 5,103 | 9.4 |
| 1931 | 63,351 | 88.8 | T.E. Jesson | C | 25,346 | 45.0 |
| | | | W.T. Kelly | Lab | 18,329 | 32.6 |
| | | | G.E. Dodds | L | 12,572 | 22.4 |
| | | | | | 7,017 | 12.4 |
| 1935 | 63,854 | 84.7 | W.T. Kelly | Lab | 22,281 | 41.2 |
| | | | W.G. Murray | C | 20,486 | 37.9 |
| | | | G.E. Dodds | L | 11,311 | 20.9 |
| | | | | | 1,795 | 3.3 |
| [Resignation] | | | | | | |
| 1940 (20/7) | | | Dr. H.B.W. Morgan | Lab | Unopp. | |
| 1945 | 60,873 | 80.7 | Dr. H.B.W. Morgan | Lab | 22,047 | 44.9 |
| | | | E.M. Nicol | C | 16,852 | 34.3 |
| | | | C.G.C. Harvey | L | 10,211 | 20.8 |
| | | | | | 5,195 | 10.6 |

# ROCHESTER, CHATHAM [214]

| Election | Electors | T'out | Candidate | Party | Votes | % |
|---|---|---|---|---|---|---|
| 1918 | 31,000 | 59.2 | J.T.C. Moore-Brabazon | C | 11,454 | 62.4 |
| | | | D. Hubbard | Lab | 4,134 | 22.5 |
| | | | H.B.D. Woodcock | L | 2,778 | 15.1 |
| | | | | | 7,320 | 39.9 |
| 1922 | 31,525 | 69.8 | J.T.C. Moore-Brabazon | C | 11,335 | 51.5 |
| | | | Sir A.J. Callaghan | L | 10,682 | 48.5 |
| | | | | | 653 | 3.0 |
| 1923 | 32,212 | 74.6 | J.T.C. Moore-Brabazon | C | 9,994 | 41.6 |
| | | | Sir A.J. Callaghan | L | 8,227 | 34.3 |
| | | | Mrs. M.A. Hamilton | Lab | 5,794 | 24.1 |
| | | | | | 1,767 | 7.3 |
| 1924 | 32,481 | 77.8 | J.T.C. Moore-Brabazon | C | 13,184 | 52.2 |
| | | | W.H. Moore | Lab | 9,276 | 36.7 |
| | | | C.B. Dallow | L | 2,806* | 11.1 |
| | | | | | 3,908 | 15.5 |
| 1929 | 40,980 | 74.5 | S.F. Markham | Lab (N Lab) | 13,007 | 42.6 |
| | | | J.T.C. Moore-Brabazon | C | 12,231 | 40.1 |
| | | | G.H. Bryans | L | 5,284 | 17.3 |
| | | | | | 776 | 2.5 |
| 1931 | 42,356 | 75.5 | Sir P. Goff | C | 19,991 | 62.5 |
| | | | O.R. Baldwin | Lab | 10,837 | 33.9 |
| | | | M.F. Woodroffe | NP | 1,135* | 3.6 |
| | | | | | 9,154 | 28.6 |
| 1935 | 43,573 | 74.6 | L.F. Plugge | C | 19,212 | 59.1 |
| | | | H.T.N. Gaitskell | Lab | 13,315 | 40.9 |
| | | | | | 5,897 | 18.2 |
| 1945 | 48,270 | 72.1 | A.G. Bottomley | Lab | 19,250 | 55.3 |
| | | | L.F. Plugge | C | 15,534 | 44.7 |
| | | | | | 3,716 | 10.6 |

| Election | Electors | T'out | Candidate | Party | Votes | % |
|---|---|---|---|---|---|---|
| 1918 | 27,899 | 65.1 | †G.F. Hohler | Co C | 12,455 | 68.6 |
| | | | A.W. Tapp | Lab | 4,705 | 25.9 |
| | | | J.B. Cronin | Ind | 1,001* | 5.5 |
| | | | | | 7,750 | 42.7 |
| 1922 | 29,560 | 72.3 | G.F. Hohler | C | 12,425 | 58.1 |
| | | | M. Spencer | Lab | 8,944 | 41.9 |
| | | | | | 3,481 | 16.2 |
| 1923 | 29,919 | 73.9 | G.F. Hohler | C | 10,426 | 47.1 |
| | | | M. Spencer | Lab | 7,674 | 34.7 |
| | | | G.H. Bryans | L | 4,015 | 18.2 |
| | | | | | 2,752 | 12.4 |
| 1924 | 30,212 | 78.0 | Sir G.F. Hohler | C | 12,418 | 52.7 |
| | | | M. Spencer | Lab | 8,309 | 35.3 |
| | | | G.H. Bryans | L | 2,839* | 12.0 |
| | | | | | 4,109 | 17.4 |
| 1929 | 38,336 | 74.0 | Sir R.V. Gower | C | 13,612 | 48.0 |
| | | | G.P. Blizard | Lab | 11,207 | 39.5 |
| | | | R. Tyrer | L | 3,556 | 12.5 |
| | | | | | 2,405 | 8.5 |
| 1931 | 39,664 | 74.1 | Sir R.V. Gower | C | 20,277 | 69.0 |
| | | | Mrs. C.M. Wadham | Lab | 9,103 | 31.0 |
| | | | | | 11,174 | 38.0 |
| 1935 | 40,271 | 71.4 | Sir R.V. Gower | C | 18,726 | 65.1 |
| | | | E.F.M. Durbin | Lab | 10,032 | 34.9 |
| | | | | | 8,694 | 30.2 |
| 1945 | 39,765 | 71.3 | J. Binns | Lab | 15,110 | 53.3 |
| | | | J.B. Dodge | C | 13,254 | 46.7 |
| | | | | | 1,856 | 6.6 |

Note:—

1918: Cronin was supported by the Lower-Deck Parliamentary Committee.

## ROMFORD  [216]

| 1945 | 43,129 | 74.5 | T. Macpherson | Lab | 16,979 | 52.8 |
|      |        |      | M.L. Berryman | C | 11,202 | 34.9 |
|      |        |      | H.J.G. Hare | L | 3,957* | 12.3 |
|      |        |      |           |   | 5,777 | 17.9 |

| Election | Electors | T'out | Candidate | Party | Votes | % |
|---|---|---|---|---|---|---|
| 1918 | 35,717 | 63.6 | R. Waddington | Co C | 8,907 | 39.2 |
|  |  |  | G.W. Jones | Lab | 7,984 | 35.1 |
|  |  |  | †Sir J.H. Maden | L | 5,837 | 25.7 |
|  |  |  |  |  | 923 | 4.1 |
| 1922 | 35,553 | 85.0 | D. Halstead | C | 12,881 | 42.6 |
|  |  |  | G.W. Jones | Lab | 11,029 | 36.5 |
|  |  |  | R.D. Holt | L | 6,327 | 20.9 |
|  |  |  |  |  | 1,852 | 6.1 |
| 1923 | 36,016 | 83.8 | R. Waddington | C | 11,362 | 37.6 |
|  |  |  | E.J. Young | L | 9,592 | 31.8 |
|  |  |  | R.N. Angell | Lab | 9,230 | 30.6 |
|  |  |  |  |  | 1,770 | 5.8 |
| 1924 | 36,394 | 84.5 | R. Waddington | C | 12,836 | 41.7 |
|  |  |  | J. Bell | Lab | 9,951 | 32.4 |
|  |  |  | E.J. Young | L | 7,958 | 25.9 |
|  |  |  |  |  | 2,885 | 9.3 |
| 1929 | 46,280 | 87.7 | A. Law | Lab | 14,624 | 36.0 |
|  |  |  | E. Bayliss | L | 13,747 | 33.9 |
|  |  |  | Sir W.H. Sugden | C | 12,225 | 30.1 |
|  |  |  |  |  | 877 | 2.1 |
| 1931 | 46,163 | 87.6 | R.H. Cross | C | 16,206 | 40.1 |
|  |  |  | W.F. Dean | L | 13,089 | 32.4 |
|  |  |  | A. Law | Lab | 11,135 | 27.5 |
|  |  |  |  |  | 3,117 | 7.7 |
| 1935 | 46,200 | 86.1 | R.H. Cross | C | 15,650 | 39.4 |
|  |  |  | E. Walkden | Lab | 14,769 | 37.1 |
|  |  |  | A. Holgate | L | 9,343 | 23.5 |
|  |  |  |  |  | 881 | 2.3 |
| 1945 | 43,297 | 83.4 | G.H. Walker | Lab | 15,741 | 43.6 |
|  |  |  | Rt. Hon. Sir R.H. Cross, Bt. | C | 10,153 | 28.1 |
|  |  |  | A.W. Jones | L | 8,542 | 23.7 |
|  |  |  | W. Whittaker | Com | 1,663* | 4.6 |
|  |  |  |  |  | 5,588 | 15.5 |

| Election | Electors | T'out | Candidate | Party | Votes | % |
|---|---|---|---|---|---|---|
| 1918 | 40,523 | 63.2 | F.A. Kelley | C | 11,473 | 44.8 |
| | | | J. Walker | Lab | 9,757 | 38.1 |
| | | | Hon. J.M. Kenworthy | L | 3,805 | 14.9 |
| | | | E.S. Bardsley | NDP | 564* | 2.2 |
| | | | | | 1,716 | 6.7 |
| 1922 | 41,103 | 81.6 | F.A. Kelley | C | 17,093 | 51.0 |
| | | | J. Walker | Lab | 16,449 | 49.0 |
| | | | | | 644 | 2.0 |
| 1923 | 41,873 | 75.3 | F.W. Lindley | Lab | 16,983 | 53.9 |
| | | | Sir F.A. Kelley | C | 14,535 | 46.1 |
| | | | | | 2,448 | 7.8 |
| 1924 | 42,251 | 81.8 | F.W. Lindley | Lab | 18,860 | 54.6 |
| | | | H.J. Temple | C | 15,712 | 45.4 |
| | | | | | 3,148 | 9.2 |
| 1929 | 54,752 | 81.4 | F.W. Lindley | Lab | 26,937 | 60.4 |
| | | | H.P. Latham | C | 10,101 | 22.7 |
| | | | R. Charlesworth | L | 7,534 | 16.9 |
| | | | | | 16,836 | 37.7 |
| 1931 | 56,216 | 82.6 | G. Herbert | C | 23,596 | 50.8 |
| | | | F.W. Lindley | Lab | 22,834 | 49.2 |
| | | | | | 762 | 1.6 |
| [Resignation] | | | | | | |
| 1933 (27/2) | 56,682 | 73.5 | W. Dobbie | Lab | 28,767 | 69.1 |
| | | | H.M.C. Drummond-Wolff | C | 12,893 | 30.9 |
| | | | | | 15,874 | 38.2 |
| 1935 | 57,382 | 76.7 | W. Dobbie | Lab | 29,725 | 67.5 |
| | | | T.W. Casey | NL | 14,298 | 32.5 |
| | | | | | 15,427 | 35.0 |
| 1945 | 62,949 | 76.4 | W. Dobbie | Lab | 35,654 | 74.2 |
| | | | E.H. Phillips | NL | 12,420 | 25.8 |
| | | | | | 23,234 | 48.4 |

[Seat Vacant at Dissolution (Death)]

Note:—

| | |
|---|---|
| 1918-1923: | Kelley sought election on each occasion as an Independent despite the fact that he was adopted by the local Conservative Association and his name was always included in the official list of Conservative candidates. |

| Election | Electors | T'out | Candidate | Party | Votes | % |
|---|---|---|---|---|---|---|
| 1918 | 44,379 | 61.5 | J. Sexton | Lab | 15,583 | 57.1 |
|  |  |  | †R.P.W. Swift | Co C | 11,689 | 42.9 |
|  |  |  |  |  | 3,894 | 14.2 |
| 1922 | 44,166 | 80.0 | J. Sexton | Lab | 20,731 | 58.7 |
|  |  |  | E. Wooll | C | 14,587 | 41.3 |
|  |  |  |  |  | 6,144 | 17.4 |
| 1923 | 44,937 | 80.5 | J. Sexton | Lab | 20,086 | 55.5 |
|  |  |  | Miss M.E. Pilkington | C | 16,109 | 44.5 |
|  |  |  |  |  | 3,977 | 11.0 |
| 1924 | 45,980 | 83.1 | J. Sexton | Lab | 21,313 | 55.8 |
|  |  |  | Miss M.E. Pilkington | C | 16,908 | 44.2 |
|  |  |  |  |  | 4,405 | 11.6 |
| 1929 | 60,331 | 78.3 | J. Sexton | Lab | 27,665 | 58.6 |
|  |  |  | R.A. Spencer | C | 19,560 | 41.4 |
|  |  |  |  |  | 8,105 | 17.2 |
| 1931 | 63,174 | 78.9 | R.A. Spencer | C | 26,131 | 52.4 |
|  |  |  | Sir J. Sexton | Lab | 23,701 | 47.6 |
|  |  |  |  |  | 2,430 | 4.8 |
| 1935 | 65,542 | 82.6 | W.A. Robinson | Lab | 29,044 | 53.7 |
|  |  |  | R.A. Spencer | C | 25,063 | 46.3 |
|  |  |  |  |  | 3,981 | 7.4 |
| 1945 | 68,249 | 76.7 | H.W. Shawcross | Lab | 34,675 | 66.2 |
|  |  |  | F. Whitworth | C | 17,686 | 33.8 |
|  |  |  |  |  | 16,989 | 32.4 |

## SALFORD, NORTH [220]

| Election | Electors | T'out | Candidate | Party | Votes | % |
|---|---|---|---|---|---|---|
| 1918 | 34,490 | 47.1 | †B. Tillett | Lab | 12,079 | 74.4 |
| | | | F.W.R. Rycroft | L | 4,155 | 25.6 |
| | | | | | 7,924 | 48.8 |
| 1922 | 34,780 | 78.7 | B. Tillett | Lab | 11,368 | 41.5 |
| | | | S. Finburgh | C | 11,349 | 41.5 |
| | | | J.C. Jolly | L | 4,660 | 17.0 |
| | | | | | 19 | 0.0 |
| 1923 | 35,441 | 73.9 | B. Tillett | Lab | 13,377 | 51.1 |
| | | | S. Finburgh | C | 12,810 | 48.9 |
| | | | | | 567 | 2.2 |
| 1924 | 36,332 | 85.8 | S. Finburgh | C | 14,250 | 45.7 |
| | | | B. Tillett | Lab | 13,114 | 42.1 |
| | | | J. Rothwell | L | 3,818* | 12.2 |
| | | | | | 1,136 | 3.6 |
| 1929 | 46,938 | 80.0 | B. Tillett | Lab | 17,333 | 46.2 |
| | | | Dr. L. Haden-Guest | C | 13,607 | 36.2 |
| | | | J. Rothwell | L | 6,609 | 17.6 |
| | | | | | 3,726 | 10.0 |
| 1931 | 48,675 | 78.9 | J.P. Morris | C | 25,151 | 65.5 |
| | | | B. Tillett | Lab | 13,271 | 34.5 |
| | | | | | 11,880 | 31.0 |
| 1935 | 47,557 | 74.0 | J.P. Morris | C | 19,904 | 56.6 |
| | | | W. McAdam | Lab | 15,272 | 43.4 |
| | | | | | 4,632 | 13.2 |
| 1945 | 41,811 | 72.5 | W. McAdam | Lab | 18,327 | 60.5 |
| | | | J.E. Fitzsimons | C | 11,977 | 39.5 |
| | | | | | 6,350 | 21.0 |

## SALFORD, SOUTH [221]

| Election | Electors | T'out | Candidate | Party | Votes | % |
|---|---|---|---|---|---|---|
| 1918 | 37,301 | 53.8 | †Sir C.A. Montague-Barlow | Co C | 14,265 | 71.1 |
| | | | J. Gorman | Lab | 3,807 | 19.0 |
| | | | F.B.V. Norris | L | 1,994* | 9.9 |
| | | | | | 10,458 | 52.1 |
| 1922 | | | Rt. Hon. Sir C.A. Montague-Barlow | C | Unopp. | |
| 1923 | 36,465 | 72.2 | J. Toole | Lab | 12,097 | 46.0 |
| | | | Rt. Hon. Sir C.A. Montague-Barlow | C | 9,366 | 35.6 |
| | | | Sir E.R. Jones | L | 4,851 | 18.4 |
| | | | | | 2,731 | 10.4 |
| 1924 | 37,214 | 79.6 | E.A. Radford | C | 15,163 | 51.2 |
| | | | J. Toole | Lab | 14,455 | 48.8 |
| | | | | | 708 | 2.4 |
| 1929 | 46,942 | 78.7 | J. Toole | Lab | 20,100 | 54.4 |
| | | | E.A. Radford | C | 16,846 | 45.6 |
| | | | | | 3,254 | 8.8 |
| 1931 | 47,784 | 78.4 | Hon. J.J. Stourton | C | 22,140 | 59.1 |
| | | | J. Toole | Lab | 15,302 | 40.9 |
| | | | | | 6,838 | 18.2 |
| 1935 | 43,835 | 73.4 | Hon. J.J. Stourton | C | 16,236 | 50.5 |
| | | | J. Toole | Lab | 15,932 | 49.5 |
| | | | | | 304 | 1.0 |
| 1945 | 31,815 | 72.6 | E.A. Hardy | Lab | 13,941 | 60.4 |
| | | | M.R. O'Brien | C | 9,150 | 39.6 |
| | | | | | 4,791 | 20.8 |

| Election | Electors | T'out | Candidate | Party | Votes | % |
|----------|----------|-------|-----------|-------|-------|---|
| 1918 | 33,035 | 59.1 | F.W. Astbury | C | 9,478 | 48.5 |
| | | | Sir W. Stephens | Co L | 5,554 | 28.4 |
| | | | R.J. Davies | Lab | 4,503 | 23.1 |
| | | | | | 3,924 | 20.1 |
| 1922 | 33,059 | 81.8 | F.W. Astbury | C | 12,130 | 44.9 |
| | | | A. Law | Lab | 8,724 | 32.3 |
| | | | Sir W. Milligan | L | 6,174 | 22.8 |
| | | | | | 3,406 | 12.6 |
| 1923 | 33,628 | 76.5 | A.W.F. Haycock | Lab | 9,868 | 38.4 |
| | | | F.W. Astbury | C | 9,752 | 37.9 |
| | | | G.H. Morgan | L | 6,097 | 23.7 |
| | | | | | 116 | 0.5 |
| 1924 | 34,326 | 84.7 | F.W. Astbury | C | 16,719 | 57.5 |
| | | | A.W.F. Haycock | Lab | 12,369 | 42.5 |
| | | | | | 4,350 | 15.0 |
| 1929 | 43,806 | 83.4 | A.W.F. Haycock | Lab | 15,647 | 42.8 |
| | | | F.W. Astbury | C | 15,289 | 41.8 |
| | | | Miss M.P. Grant | L | 5,614 | 15.4 |
| | | | | | 358 | 1.0 |
| 1931 | 44,677 | 81.5 | F.W. Astbury | C (Ind C) (C) | 24,083 | 66.2 |
| | | | A.W.F. Haycock | Lab | 12,320 | 33.8 |
| | | | | | 11,763 | 32.4 |
| 1935 | 45,787 | 79.6 | J.F. Emery | C | 19,245 | 52.8 |
| | | | A.W.F. Haycock | Lab | 14,732 | 40.4 |
| | | | F. Kenyon | L | 2,492* | 6.8 |
| | | | | | 4,513 | 12.4 |
| 1945 | 43,625 | 76.8 | C. Royle | Lab | 17,010 | 50.7 |
| | | | J.F. Emery | C | 13,321 | 39.8 |
| | | | R. Pugh | L | 3,180* | 9.5 |
| | | | | | 3,689 | 10.9 |

| Election | Electors | T'out | Candidate | Party | Votes | % |
|----------|----------|-------|-----------|-------|-------|---|
| 1918 | 35,923 | 52.5 | T.W. Casey | Co L | 12,308 | 65.3 |
| | | | †W.C. Anderson | Lab | 6,539 | 34.7 |
| | | | | | 5,769 | 30.6 |
| 1922 | 34,671 | 68.6 | C.H. Wilson | Lab | 16,206 | 68.2 |
| | | | T.W. Casey | NL | 7,562 | 31.8 |
| | | | | | 8,644 | 36.4 |
| 1923 | 34,618 | 66.8 | C.H. Wilson | Lab | 13,581 | 58.7 |
| | | | G. Terrell | C | 6,106 | 26.4 |
| | | | H.A. Briggs | L | 3,438 | 14.9 |
| | | | | | 7,475 | 32.3 |
| 1924 | 34,843 | 75.9 | C.H. Wilson | Lab | 16,802 | 63.6 |
| | | | W.B. Faraday | C | 9,629 | 36.4 |
| | | | | | 7,173 | 27.2 |
| 1929 | 42,070 | 75.4 | C.H. Wilson | Lab | 19,152 | 60.3 |
| | | | W.B. Faraday | C | 6,190 | 19.5 |
| | | | T. Neville | L | 4,652 | 14.7 |
| | | | G.H. Fletcher | Com | 1,731* | 5.5 |
| | | | | | 12,962 | 40.8 |
| 1931 | 42,234 | 78.1 | C.F. Pike | C | 15,185 | 46.0 |
| | | | C.H. Wilson | Lab | 15,020 | 45.5 |
| | | | G.H. Fletcher | Com | 2,790* | 8.5 |
| | | | | | 165 | 0.5 |
| 1935 | 40,664 | 73.0 | C.H. Wilson | Lab | 18,663 | 62.8 |
| | | | C.F. Pike | C | 11,034 | 37.2 |
| | | | | | 7,629 | 25.6 |
| [Resignation] | | | | | | |
| 1944 (21/2) | | | J.B. Hynd | Lab | Unopp. | |
| 1945 | 36,316 | 79.4 | J.B. Hynd | Lab | 23,468 | 81.4 |
| | | | B. Paddon | C | 5,376 | 18.6 |
| | | | | | 18,092 | 62.8 |

# SHEFFIELD, BRIGHTSIDE  [224]

| Election | Electors | T'out | Candidate | Party | Votes | % |
|----------|----------|-------|-----------|-------|-------|---|
| 1918 | 36,453 | 52.0 | †Sir J.T. Walters | Co L | 12,164 | 64.2 |
| | | | R.E. Jones | Lab | 6,781 | 35.8 |
| | | | | | 5,383 | 28.4 |
| 1922 | 36,874 | 75.0 | A.A.W.H. Ponsonby | Lab | 16,692 | 60.4 |
| | | | Rt. Hon. Sir J.T. Walters | NL | 10,949 | 39.6 |
| | | | | | 5,743 | 20.8 |
| 1923 | 38,140 | 73.0 | A.A.W.H. Ponsonby | Lab | 14,741 | 53.0 |
| | | | M. Sheppard | C | 9,408 | 33.8 |
| | | | T.I. Clough | L | 3,684 | 13.2 |
| | | | | | 5,333 | 19.2 |
| 1924 | 38,979 | 78.9 | A.A.W.H. Ponsonby | Lab | 17,053 | 55.4 |
| | | | M. Sheppard | C | 13,708 | 44.6 |
| | | | | | 3,345 | 10.8 |
| 1929 | 47,521 | 77.3 | A.A.W.H. Ponsonby | Lab | 20,277 | 55.2 |
| | | | R.I. Money | C | 9,828 | 26.8 |
| | | | W.A. Lambert | L | 6,612 | 18.0 |
| | | | | | 10,449 | 28.4 |

[Elevation to the Peerage — Lord Ponsonby of Shulbrede]

| Election | Electors | T'out | Candidate | Party | Votes | % |
|----------|----------|-------|-----------|-------|-------|---|
| 1930 (6/2) | 47,521 | 52.4 | F. Marshall | Lab | 11,543 | 46.3 |
| | | | H.F. Russell | C | 8,612 | 34.6 |
| | | | W.A. Lambert | L | 3,650 | 14.7 |
| | | | J.T. Murphy | Com | 1,084* | 4.4 |
| | | | | | 2,931 | 11.7 |
| 1931 | 48,027 | 79.6 | H.F. Russell | C | 20,270 | 53.1 |
| | | | F. Marshall | Lab | 15,528 | 40.6 |
| | | | J.T. Murphy | Com | 1,571* | 4.1 |
| | | | E.C. Snelgrove | NP | 847* | 2.2 |
| | | | | | 4,742 | 12.5 |
| 1935 | 47,251 | 68.7 | F. Marshall | Lab | 18,985 | 58.5 |
| | | | H.F. Russell | C | 13,467 | 41.5 |
| | | | | | 5,518 | 17.0 |
| 1945 | 41,913 | 75.5 | F. Marshall | Lab | 19,373 | 61.2 |
| | | | H.B. Taylor | C | 8,177 | 25.8 |
| | | | H. Hill | Com | 4,115 | 13.0 |
| | | | | | 11,196 | 35.4 |

# SHEFFIELD, CENTRAL [225]

| Election | Electors | T'out | Candidate | Party | Votes | % |
|---|---|---|---|---|---|---|
| 1918 | 37,076 | 43.1 | †J.F. Hope | Co C | 9,361 | 58.7 |
| | | | A.J. Bailey | Ind Lab | 5,959 | 37.3 |
| | | | R.G. Murray | BSP | 643* | 4.0 |
| | | | | | 3,402 | 21.4 |
| 1922 | | | Rt. Hon. J.F. Hope | C | Unopp. | |
| 1923 | 34,756 | 61.3 | Rt. Hon. J.F. Hope | C | 9,727 | 45.7 |
| | | | T. Snowden | Lab | 8,762 | 41.1 |
| | | | J.H. Freeborough | L | 2,810 | 13.2 |
| | | | | | 965 | 4.6 |
| 1924 | 35,298 | 74.5 | Rt. Hon. J.F. Hope | C | 13,302 | 50.6 |
| | | | T. Snowden | Lab | 12,995 | 49.4 |
| | | | | | 307 | 1.2 |
| 1929 | 43,798 | 74.1 | P.C. Hoffman | Lab | 19,183 | 59.1 |
| | | | J.R.P. Warde-Aldam | C | 13,284 | 40.9 |
| | | | | | 5,899 | 18.2 |
| 1931 | 43,371 | 80.2 | W.W. Boulton | C | 21,589 | 62.0 |
| | | | P.C. Hoffman | Lab | 13,212 | 38.0 |
| | | | | | 8,377 | 24.0 |
| 1935 | 36,709 | 74.2 | W.W. Boulton | C | 13,828 | 50.8 |
| | | | P.C. Hoffman | Lab | 13,408 | 49.2 |
| | | | | | 420 | 1.6 |
| 1945 | 18,666 | 72.0 | H. Morris | Lab | 7,954 | 59.2 |
| | | | G.V. Hunt | C | 5,481 | 40.8 |
| | | | | | 2,473 | 18.4 |

Note:—

1918: Bailey was the nominee of the National Amalgamated Union of Labour.

| Election | Electors | T'out | Candidate | Party | Votes | % |
|---|---|---|---|---|---|---|
| 1918 | | | †Sir S. Roberts | Co C | Unopp. | |
| 1922 | | | Rt. Hon. Sir S. Roberts, Bt. | C | Unopp. | |
| 1923 | 29,504 | 69.5 | A. Harland | C | 13,047 | 63.6 |
| | | | H.F. Russell | L | 7,456 | 36.4 |
| | | | | | 5,591 | 27.2 |
| 1924 | 29,862 | 62.8 | A. Harland | C | 16,131 | 86.0 |
| | | | A. Taylor | Ind | 2,624 | 14.0 |
| | | | | | 13,507 | 72.0 |
| 1929 | 41,317 | 75.1 | Sir S. Roberts, Bt. | C | 17,165 | 55.3 |
| | | | H. Samuels | Lab | 7,983 | 25.7 |
| | | | R.S. Wells | L | 5,898 | 19.0 |
| | | | | | 9,182 | 29.6 |
| 1931 | | | Sir S. Roberts, Bt. | C | Unopp. | |
| 1935 | 43,668 | 71.0 | Sir R.G. Ellis, Bt. | C | 22,819 | 73.6 |
| | | | K.G. Brooks | Lab | 8,173 | 26.4 |
| | | | | | 14,646 | 47.2 |
| 1945 | 44,462 | 75.5 | P.G. Roberts | C | 18,120 | 54.0 |
| | | | S. Checkland | CW | 12,045 | 35.9 |
| | | | P.R. Nightingale | L | 3,391* | 10.1 |
| | | | | | 6,075 | 18.1 |

Note:—

1924: Taylor was the nominee of the Ecclesall Tenants' Protection Association.

## SHEFFIELD, HALLAM [227]

| Election | Electors | T'out | Candidate | Party | Votes | % |
|---|---|---|---|---|---|---|
| 1918 | | | D. Vickers | Co C | Unopp. | |
| | | | | | | |
| 1922 | 30,628 | 73.7 | Sir F.H. Sykes | C | 13,405 | 59.4 |
| | | | C.S. Rewcastle | L | 9,173 | 40.6 |
| | | | | | 4,232 | 18.8 |
| | | | | | | |
| 1923 | 30,667 | 75.0 | Sir F.H. Sykes | C | 12,119 | 52.7 |
| | | | A.J. Freeman | Lab | 5,506 | 23.9 |
| | | | C.S. Rewcastle | L | 5,383 | 23.4 |
| | | | | | 6,613 | 28.8 |
| | | | | | | |
| 1924 | 31,163 | 77.8 | Sir F.H. Sykes | C | 15,446 | 63.7 |
| | | | E. Snelgrove | Lab | 8,807 | 36.3 |
| | | | | | 6,639 | 27.4 |

[Resignation on appointment as Governor of Bombay]

| Election | Electors | T'out | Candidate | Party | Votes | % |
|---|---|---|---|---|---|---|
| 1928<br>(16/7) | 32,037 | 54.7 | L.W. Smith | C | 9,417 | 53.7 |
| | | | C.R. Flynn | Lab | 5,393 | 30.8 |
| | | | J.B. Hobman | L | 2,715 | 15.5 |
| | | | | | 4,024 | 22.9 |
| | | | | | | |
| 1929 | 42,422 | 73.2 | L.W. Smith | C | 18,920 | 60.9 |
| | | | B. Rawson | Lab | 12,133 | 39.1 |
| | | | | | 6,787 | 21.8 |
| | | | | | | |
| 1931 | 43,191 | 80.3 | L.W. Smith | C | 26,857 | 77.5 |
| | | | H.G. McGhee | Lab | 7,807 | 22.5 |
| | | | | | 19,050 | 55.0 |
| | | | | | | |
| 1935 | 44,140 | 71.7 | L.W. Smith | C | 21,298 | 67.3 |
| | | | Miss G.M. Colman | Lab | 10,346 | 32.7 |
| | | | | | 10,952 | 34.6 |

[Death]

| Election | Electors | T'out | Candidate | Party | Votes | % |
|---|---|---|---|---|---|---|
| 1939<br>(10/5) | 44,897 | 57.8 | R. Jennings | C | 16,033 | 61.7 |
| | | | C.S. Darvill | Lab | 9,939 | 38.3 |
| | | | | | 6,094 | 23.4 |
| | | | | | | |
| 1945 | 44,579 | 75.7 | R. Jennings | C | 15,874 | 47.1 |
| | | | J.F. Drabble | Lab | 13,009 | 38.5 |
| | | | G. Abrahams | L | 2,614* | 7.7 |
| | | | G.H. Cree | Com | 2,253* | 6.7 |
| | | | | | 2,865 | 8.6 |

# SHEFFIELD, HILLSBOROUGH [228]

| Election | Electors | T'out | Candidate | Party | Votes | % |
|---|---|---|---|---|---|---|
| 1918 | 36,084 | 42.2 | A. Neal | Co L | 11,171 | 73.4 |
|  |  |  | A. Lockwood | Co-op | 4,050 | 26.6 |
|  |  |  |  |  | 7,121 | 46.8 |
| 1922 | 36,091 | 74.7 | A.V. Alexander | Lab/Co-op | 15,130 | 56.2 |
|  |  |  | A. Neal | NL | 11,812 | 43.8 |
|  |  |  |  |  | 3,318 | 12.4 |
| 1923 | 36,956 | 73.3 | A.V. Alexander | Lab/Co-op | 15,087 | 55.7 |
|  |  |  | C. Boot | C | 8,369 | 30.9 |
|  |  |  | E. Woodhead | L | 3,636 | 13.4 |
|  |  |  |  |  | 6,718 | 24.8 |
| 1924 | 37,380 | 77.9 | A.V. Alexander | Lab/Co-op | 16,573 | 56.9 |
|  |  |  | N.G. Thwaites | C | 12,554 | 43.1 |
|  |  |  |  |  | 4,019 | 13.8 |
| 1929 | 47,036 | 77.6 | A.V. Alexander | Lab/Co-op | 20,941 | 57.3 |
|  |  |  | A. Harland | C | 10,489 | 28.8 |
|  |  |  | E.H.F. Morris | L | 5,053 | 13.9 |
|  |  |  |  |  | 10,452 | 28.5 |
| 1931 | 50,433 | 81.6 | J.G. Braithwaite | C | 23,819 | 57.9 |
|  |  |  | Rt. Hon. A.V. Alexander | Lab/Co-op | 17,319 | 42.1 |
|  |  |  |  |  | 6,500 | 15.8 |
| 1935 | 50,474 | 76.8 | Rt. Hon. A.V. Alexander | Lab/Co-op | 21,025 | 54.3 |
|  |  |  | J.G. Braithwaite | C | 17,721 | 45.7 |
|  |  |  |  |  | 3,304 | 8.6 |
| 1945 | 51,821 | 76.0 | Rt. Hon. A.V. Alexander | Lab/Co-op | 24,959 | 63.4 |
|  |  |  | R.H. Hobart | NL | 14,403 | 36.6 |
|  |  |  |  |  | 10,556 | 26.8 |

[Seat Vacant at Dissolution (Elevation to the Peerage — Viscount Alexander of Hillsborough)]

Note:—

1918: Neal's name was not included in the final official list of Coalition candidates, but this appears to have been an ommission through error for there is no doubt that he both received and accepted the 'coupon'.

# SHEFFIELD, PARK  [229]

| Election | Electors | T'out | Candidate | Party | Votes | % |
|---|---|---|---|---|---|---|
| 1918 | 31,241 | 49.6 | H.K. Stephenson | Co L | 12,339 | 79.6 |
| | | | A. Barton | Lab | 3,167 | 20.4 |
| | | | | | 9,172 | 59.2 |
| 1922 | 30,321 | 73.0 | H.K. Stephenson | NL (L) | 11,542 | 52.2 |
| | | | R. Morley | Lab | 10,578 | 47.8 |
| | | | | | 964 | 4.4 |
| 1923 | 31,016 | 74.1 | R.S. Deans | C | 9,648 | 41.9 |
| | | | G. Lathan | Lab | 9,050 | 39.4 |
| | | | H.K. Stephenson | L | 4,296 | 18.7 |
| | | | | | 598 | 2.5 |
| 1924 | 31,618 | 81.1 | R.S. Deans | C | 14,053 | 54.8 |
| | | | G. Lathan | Lab | 11,576 | 45.2 |
| | | | | | 2,477 | 9.6 |
| 1929 | 49,843 | 79.2 | G. Lathan | Lab | 20,304 | 51.4 |
| | | | R.S. Deans | C | 13,597 | 34.5 |
| | | | E.E. Dalton | L | 5,560 | 14.1 |
| | | | | | 6,707 | 16.9 |
| 1931 | 51,981 | 81.1 | Sir A.S. Benn, Bt. | C | 26,392 | 62.6 |
| | | | G. Lathan | Lab | 15,783 | 37.4 |
| | | | | | 10,609 | 25.2 |
| 1935 | 56,121 | 73.2 | G. Lathan | Lab | 21,153 | 51.5 |
| | | | Sir A.S. Benn, Bt. | C | 19,947 | 48.5 |
| | | | | | 1,206 | 3.0 |
| [Death] | | | | | | |
| 1942 (27/8) | | | T.W. Burden | Lab | Unopp. | |
| 1945 | 61,325 | 73.9 | T.W. Burden | Lab | 29,424 | 64.9 |
| | | | G.P. Stevens | C | 15,882 | 35.1 |
| | | | | | 13,542 | 29.8 |

[Seat Vacant at Dissolution (Elevation to the Peerage — Lord Burden)]

# SMETHWICK [230]

| Election | Electors | T'out | Candidate | Party | Votes | % |
|---|---|---|---|---|---|---|
| 1918 | 32,908 | 54.7 | J.E. Davison | Lab | 9,389 | 52.2 |
|  |  |  | Miss C. Pankhurst | WP | 8,614 | 47.8 |
|  |  |  |  |  | 775 | 4.4 |
| 1922 | 34,132 | 75.9 | J.E. Davison | Lab | 13,141 | 50.7 |
|  |  |  | A.H.A. Simcox | C | 12,759 | 49.3 |
|  |  |  |  |  | 382 | 1.4 |
| 1923 | 34,556 | 71.7 | J.E. Davison | Lab | 13,550 | 54.7 |
|  |  |  | C.E.R. Brocklebank | C | 11,217 | 45.3 |
|  |  |  |  |  | 2,333 | 9.4 |
| 1924 | 35,443 | 78.2 | J.E. Davison | Lab | 14,491 | 52.3 |
|  |  |  | M.J. Pike | C | 13,238 | 47.7 |
|  |  |  |  |  | 1,253 | 4.6 |
| [Resignation] |  |  |  |  |  |  |
| 1926 | 35,862 | 78.6 | O.E. Mosley | Lab | 16,077 | 57.1 |
| (21/12) |  |  | M.J. Pike | C | 9,495 | 33.7 |
|  |  |  | E. Bayliss | L | 2,600* | 9.2 |
|  |  |  |  |  | 6,582 | 23.4 |
| 1929 | 45,222 | 78.9 | Sir O.E. Mosley, Bt. | Lab (NP) | 19,550 | 54.8 |
|  |  |  | A.R. Wise | C | 12,210 | 34.2 |
|  |  |  | Miss M.E. Marshall | L | 3,909* | 11.0 |
|  |  |  |  |  | 7,340 | 20.6 |
| 1931 | 46,671 | 74.7 | A.R. Wise | C | 20,945 | 60.1 |
|  |  |  | W.E. Lawrence | Lab | 13,927 | 39.9 |
|  |  |  |  |  | 7,018 | 20.2 |
| 1935 | 44,695 | 70.7 | A.R. Wise | C | 16,575 | 52.5 |
|  |  |  | Dr. C.W. Brook | Lab | 15,023 | 47.5 |
|  |  |  |  |  | 1,552 | 5.0 |
| 1945 | 43,020 | 72.4 | A.J. Dobbs | Lab | 20,522 | 65.9 |
|  |  |  | G.H. Edgar | C | 10,637 | 34.1 |
|  |  |  |  |  | 9,885 | 31.8 |
| [Death] |  |  |  |  |  |  |
| 1945 | 43,020 | 65.4 | P.C. Gordon Walker | Lab | 19,364 | 68.8 |
| (1/10) |  |  | G.H. Edgar | C | 8,762 | 31.2 |
|  |  |  |  |  | 10,602 | 37.6 |

Note:—

1918: Miss Pankhurst's candidature had the approval and support of the Coalition although she did not actually receive a 'coupon'. Bonar Law the Conservative Party Leader, personally intervened to secure the withdrawal of a Conservative candidate and Lloyd George wrote her a letter of support during the campaign.

## SOUTHALL [231]

| Election | Electors | T'out | Candidate | Party | Votes | % |
|----------|----------|-------|-----------|-------|-------|---|
| 1945 | 78,649 | 74.2 | W.H. Ayles | Lab | 37,404 | 64.1 |
| | | | G.G. Baker | C | 13,347 | 22.9 |
| | | | W.A. Wakefield | L | 7,598 | 13.0 |
| | | | | | 24,057 | 41.2 |

## SOUTHAMPTON  [232]
### (Two Seats)

| Election | Electors | T'out | Candidate | Party | Votes | % |
|---|---|---|---|---|---|---|
| 1918 | 75,334 | 53.7 | †Sir I. Philipps | Co L | 26,884 | 36.4 |
| | | | †W.D. Ward | Co L | 16,843 | 22.8 |
| | | | E.K. Perkins | C | 15,548 | 21.0 |
| | | | T. Lewis | Lab | 7,828 | 10.6 |
| | | | F. Perriman | Lab | 6,776 | 9.2 |
| | | | | | 1,295 | 1.8 |
| 1922 | 75,316 | 68.5 | E.K. Perkins | C | 22,054 | 23.9 |
| | | | Lord Apsley | C | 20,351 | 22.0 |
| | | | T. Lewis | Lab | 14,868 | 16.1 |
| | | | Dr. E.H.M. Stancomb | Ind | 14,193 | 15.4 |
| | | | Sir I. Philipps | NL | 11,576 | 12.5 |
| | | | Rt. Hon. W.D. Ward | NL | 9,318 | 10.1 |
| | | | | | 5,483 | 5.9 |
| 1923 | 76,833 | 67.3 | Lord Apsley | C | 20,453 | 20.0 |
| | | | E.K. Perkins | C | 20,249 | 19.8 |
| | | | T. Lewis | Lab | 17,208 | 16.9 |
| | | | Rev. R.W. Sorensen | Lab | 16,679 | 16.4 |
| | | | F.J.G. Spranger | L | 13,724 | 13.5 |
| | | | C.N.D. Dixey | L | 13,657 | 13.4 |
| | | | | | 3,041 | 2.9 |
| 1924 | 78,776 | 67.5 | Lord Apsley | C | 30,703 | 29.3 |
| | | | E.K. Perkins | C | 30,201 | 28.8 |
| | | | T. Lewis | Lab | 22,183 | 21.1 |
| | | | Rev. R.W. Sorensen | Lab | 21,768 | 20.8 |
| | | | | | 8,018 | 7.7 |
| 1929 | 103,653 | 70.9 | T. Lewis | Lab | 32,249 | 22.4 |
| | | | R. Morley | Lab | 31,252 | 21.7 |
| | | | Lord Thirlestane and Boltoun | C | 27,898 | 19.4 |
| | | | A.S. Cunningham-Reid | C | 26,801 | 18.6 |
| | | | J.H. Whitehouse | L | 12,966 | 9.0 |
| | | | A.T. Lamsley | L | 12,836 | 8.9 |
| | | | | | 3,354 | 2.3 |
| 1931 | 107,376 | 76.1 | W. Craven-Ellis | C | 54,699 | 33.9 |
| | | | Sir C.C. Barrie | NL | 54,269 | 33.6 |
| | | | T. Lewis | Lab | 26,425 | 16.4 |
| | | | R. Morley | Lab | 26,061 | 16.1 |
| | | | | | 28,274 | 17.5 |
| | | | | | 27,844 | 17.2 |
| 1935 | 110,047 | 68.8 | W. Craven-Ellis | C | 44,896 | 30.0 |
| | | | Sir C.C. Barrie | NL | 43,697 | 29.3 |
| | | | T. Lewis | Lab | 30,751 | 20.6 |
| | | | R. Morley | Lab | 30,028 | 20.1 |
| | | | | | 14,145 | 9.4 |
| | | | | | 12,946 | 8.7 |

[Resignation of Barrie]

| 1940 (1/2) | | | Rt. Hon. Sir J.C.W. Reith | Nat | Unopp. | |

[Elevation of Reith to the Peerage — Lord Reith]

| 1940 (27/11) | | | Dr. W.S.R. Thomas | NL | Unopp. | |

| Election | Electors | T'out | Candidate | Party | Votes | % |
|---|---|---|---|---|---|---|
| 1945 | 95,898 | 72.6 | R. Morley | Lab | 37,556 | 28.8 |
| | | | T. Lewis | Lab | 37,054 | 28.4 |
| | | | W. Craven-Ellis | C | 24,367 | 18.7 |
| | | | Dr. W.S.R. Thomas | NL | 22,650 | 17.3 |
| | | | R. Fulljames | L | 8,878 | 6.8 |
| | | | | | 12,687 | 9.7 |

Notes:—

1922:  Stancomb sought election as a 'Health' candidate. He had previously been associated with the Labour Party.

1940:  Reith was Minister of Information
(1/2)

| Election | Electors | T'out | Candidate | Party | Votes | % |
|----------|----------|-------|-----------|-------|-------|---|
| 1918 | 36,357 | 53.9 | †Hon. R.E.C.L. Guinness | Co C | 12,392 | 63.3 |
| | | | J. Francis | Ind C | 4,242 | 21.6 |
| | | | C. Hubbard | L | 2,965 | 15.1 |
| | | | | | 8,150 | 41.7 |
| 1922 | 42,599 | 68.0 | Viscount Elveden | C | 17,920 | 61.9 |
| | | | H.G. Walker | L | 11,039 | 38.1 |
| | | | | | 6,881 | 23.8 |
| 1923 | 44,738 | 69.3 | Viscount Elveden | C | 15,566 | 50.2 |
| | | | J.D. Young | L | 15,453 | 49.8 |
| | | | | | 113 | 0.4 |
| 1924 | 47,259 | 79.3 | Viscount Elveden | C | 23,417 | 62.5 |
| | | | J.D. Young | L | 10,924 | 29.1 |
| | | | S.A. Moseley | Lab | 3,144* | 8.4 |
| | | | | | 12,493 | 33.4 |

[Succession to the Peerage — Earl of Iveagh]

| Election | Electors | T'out | Candidate | Party | Votes | % |
|----------|----------|-------|-----------|-------|-------|---|
| 1927 (19/11) | 53,039 | 73.2 | Countess of Iveagh | C | 21,221 | 54.6 |
| | | | Hon. D. Meston | L | 11,912 | 30.7 |
| | | | J.E. Harper | Lab | 4,777* | 12.3 |
| | | | E.A. Hailwood | Ind C | 917* | 2.4 |
| | | | | | 9,309 | 23.9 |
| 1929 | 73,815 | 67.0 | Countess of Iveagh | C | 27,605 | 55.8 |
| | | | Hon. D. Meston | L | 21,884 | 44.2 |
| | | | | | 5,721 | 11.6 |
| 1931 | 79,220 | 68.5 | Countess of Iveagh | C | 46,564 | 85.7 |
| | | | A.E. Bechervaise | Lab | 7,741 | 14.3 |
| | | | | | 38,823 | 71.4 |
| 1935 | 85,814 | 66.0 | H. Channon | C | 36,865 | 65.1 |
| | | | M. Gladstone | L | 11,934 | 21.1 |
| | | | Miss H.M. Keynes | Lab | 7,796 | 13.8 |
| | | | | | 24,931 | 44.0 |
| 1945 | 72,373 | 73.3 | H. Channon | C | 23,712 | 44.6 |
| | | | G.R. Sandison | Lab | 20,635 | 38.9 |
| | | | H.D. Tanner | L | 8,735 | 16.5 |
| | | | | | 3,077 | 5.7 |

Note:—

1918: Guinness became Viscount Elveden in 1919 on his father receiving an Earldom.

# SOUTHPORT [234]

| Election | Electors | T'out | Candidate | Party | Votes | % |
|---|---|---|---|---|---|---|
| 1918 | 33,150 | 61.6 | †G.D. Dalrymple-White | Co C | 14,707 | 72.0 |
| | | | A. Greenwood | Lab | 5,727 | 28.0 |
| | | | | | 8,980 | 44.0 |
| 1922 | 33,836 | 76.3 | G.D. Dalrymple-White | C | 13,733 | 53.2 |
| | | | Sir J.F. Brunner, Bt. | L | 12,068 | 46.8 |
| | | | | | 1,665 | 6.4 |
| 1923 | 34,871 | 75.9 | Sir J.F. Brunner, Bt. | L | 13,704 | 51.8 |
| | | | Sir T.W. Comyn-Platt | C | 12,776 | 48.2 |
| | | | | | 928 | 3.6 |
| 1924 | 36,310 | 78.7 | G.D. Dalrymple-White | C | 17,430 | 61.0 |
| | | | Sir J.F. Brunner, Bt. | L | 11,158 | 39.0 |
| | | | | | 6,272 | 22.0 |
| 1929 | 54,962 | 79.6 | Sir G.D. Dalrymple-White, Bt. | C | 21,161 | 48.3 |
| | | | C.B. Ramage | L | 17,220 | 39.4 |
| | | | A.L. Williams | Lab | 5,380* | 12.3 |
| | | | | | 3,941 | 8.9 |
| 1931 | 55,592 | 79.7 | R.S. Hudson | C | 30,307 | 68.4 |
| | | | R.M. Hughes | L | 13,983 | 31.6 |
| | | | | | 16,324 | 36.8 |
| 1935 | 57,951 | 70.9 | R.S. Hudson | C | 29,652 | 72.2 |
| | | | R.C. Willis | Lab | 11,419 | 27.8 |
| | | | | | 18,233 | 44.4 |
| 1945 | 68,456 | 74.2 | Rt. Hon. R.S. Hudson | C | 26,792 | 52.7 |
| | | | W. Hamling | Lab | 13,596 | 26.8 |
| | | | R. Martin | L | 10,404 | 20.5 |
| | | | | | 13,196 | 25.9 |

| Election | Electors | T'out | Candidate | Party | Votes | % |
|---|---|---|---|---|---|---|
| 1918 | 50,584 | 51.3 | †J.H. Wilson | Co L | 19,514 | 75.2 |
| | | | G.J. Rowe | Lab | 6,425 | 24.8 |
| | | | | | 13,089 | 50.4 |
| 1922 | 52,005 | 76.2 | E.A.St.A. Harney | L | 15,760 | 39.8 |
| | | | W. Lawther | Lab | 15,735 | 39.7 |
| | | | J.H. Wilson | NL | 8,121 | 20.5 |
| | | | | | 25 | 0.1 |
| 1923 | 52,557 | 73.5 | E.A.St.A. Harney | L | 22,912 | 59.3 |
| | | | W. Lawther | Lab | 15,717 | 40.7 |
| | | | | | 7,195 | 18.6 |
| 1924 | 53,122 | 75.3 | E.A.St.A. Harney | L | 23,171 | 57.9 |
| | | | W. Lawther | Lab | 16,852 | 42.1 |
| | | | | | 6,319 | 15.8 |
| 1929 | 61,629 | 72.9 | J.C. Ede | Lab | 18,938 | 42.2 |
| | | | Hon. H.B. Robson | L | 18,898 | 42.0 |
| | | | W. Nunn | C | 7,110 | 15.8 |
| | | | | | 40 | 0.2 |
| 1931 | 63,697 | 80.1 | H. Johnstone | L | 30,528 | 59.8 |
| | | | J.C. Ede | Lab | 20,512 | 40.2 |
| | | | | | 10,016 | 19.6 |
| 1935 | 62,847 | 72.8 | J.C. Ede | Lab | 22,031 | 48.1 |
| | | | H. Johnstone | L | 12,932 | 28.3 |
| | | | F.F.A. Burden | N Lab | 10,784 | 23.6 |
| | | | | | 9,099 | 19.8 |
| 1945 | 51,599 | 73.1 | Rt. Hon. J.C. Ede | Lab | 22,410 | 59.4 |
| | | | D.M. Parry | NL | 15,296 | 40.6 |
| | | | | | 7,114 | 18.8 |

Note:—

1918: Wilson sought election as a 'Coalition Trade Unionist's and Seamen's' candidate. He was supported by the National Sailors' and Firemen's Union.

# STOCKPORT [236]
## (Two Seats)

| Election | Electors | T'out | Candidate | Party | Votes | % |
|---|---|---|---|---|---|---|
| 1918 | | | †S.L. Hughes | Co L | Unopp. | |
| | | | †G.J. Wardle | Co Lab | Unopp. | |
| [Death of Hughes and resignation of Wardle] | | | | | | |
| 1920 | 60,508 | 75.7 | W. Greenwood | Co C | 22,847 | 25.7 |
| (27/3) | | | H. Fildes | Co L | 22,386 | 25.1 |
| | | | Sir L.G.C. Money | Lab | 16,042 | 18.0 |
| | | | S.F. Perry | Lab/Co-op | 14,434 | 16.2 |
| | | | A.A.G. Kindell | Ind | 5,644* | 6.3 |
| | | | J.J. Terrett | Ind | 5,443* | 6.1 |
| | | | W. O'Brien | Ind | 2,336* | 2.6 |
| | | | | | 6,805 | 7.7 |
| | | | | | 6,344 | 7.1 |
| 1922 | 63,010 | 83.4 | H. Fildes | NL | 35,241 | 34.4 |
| | | | W. Greenwood | C | 33,852 | 33.1 |
| | | | S.F. Perry | Lab/Co-op | 17,059 | 16.7 |
| | | | J.C.H. Robinson | Lab | 16,126 | 15.8 |
| | | | | | 18,182 | 17.7 |
| | | | | | 16,793 | 16.4 |
| 1923 | 63,781 | 81.7 | W. Greenwood | C | 20,308 | 22.4 |
| | | | C. Royle | L | 19,223 | 21.2 |
| | | | S.S. Hammersley | C | 18,129 | 20.0 |
| | | | H. Fildes | L | 16,756 | 18.4 |
| | | | A.E. Townend | Lab | 16,340 | 18.0 |
| | | | | | 3,552 | 4.0 |
| | | | | | 1,094 | 1.2 |
| 1924 | 64,689 | 85.9 | W. Greenwood | C | 28,057 | 31.6 |
| | | | S.S. Hammersley | C | 26,417 | 29.7 |
| | | | A.E. Townend | Lab | 21,986 | 24.8 |
| | | | C. Royle | L | 12,386 | 13.9 |
| | | | | | 4,431 | 4.9 |
| [Death of Greenwood] | | | | | | |
| 1925 | 64,689[†] | 85.7 | A.E. Townend | Lab | 20,219 | 36.5 |
| (17/9) | | | T. Eastham | C | 17,892 | 32.3 |
| | | | H. Fildes | L | 17,296 | 31.2 |
| | | | | | 2,327 | 4.2 |
| 1929 | 84,433 | 84.6 | A.E. Townend | Lab | 30,955 | 27.4 |
| | | | S.S. Hammersley | C | 29,043 | 25.7 |
| | | | H. Fildes | L | 22,595 | 20.0 |
| | | | E.N. Lingen-Barker | C | 22,047 | 19.5 |
| | | | C. Royle | Ind L | 8,355* | 7.4 |
| | | | | | 8,360 | 7.4 |
| | | | | | 6,448 | 5.7 |
| 1931 | 86,284 | 84.1 | S.S. Hammersley | C | 50,936 | 37.0 |
| | | | A.V.G. Dower | C | 47,757 | 34.7 |
| | | | A.E. Townend | Lab | 23,350 | 17.0 |
| | | | J.T. Abbott | ILP | 15,591 | 11.3 |
| | | | | | 24,407 | 17.7 |

# STOCKPORT (Cont.)

| Election | Electors | T'out | Candidate | Party | Votes | % |
|---|---|---|---|---|---|---|
| 1935 | 90,969 | 79.5 | Sir A.B. Gridley | C | 43,882 | 30.7 |
| | | | N.J. Hulbert | C | 43,001 | 30.0 |
| | | | J.H. Hudson | Lab | 28,798 | 20.1 |
| | | | C.T. Douthwaite | Lab | 27,528 | 19.2 |
| | | | | | 14,203 | 9.9 |
| 1945 | 99,836 | 77.2 | Sir A.B. Gridley | C | 31,039 | 20.6 |
| | | | N.J. Hulbert | C | 30,792 | 20.4 |
| | | | A.R. Stamp | Lab | 29,674 | 19.6 |
| | | | R.W. Casasola | Lab | 29,630 | 19.6 |
| | | | H. Sutherland | L | 14,994 | 9.9 |
| | | | F.W. Malbon | L | 14,942 | 9.9 |
| | | | | | 1,118 | 0.8 |

Notes:—

1918: Wardle was not an official Coalition candidate and did not receive a 'coupon'. He did however fully support the Coalition and sought election as a Coalition candidate.

1920: Kindell and Terrett were supported by Horatio Bottomley.

O'Brien sought election as a 'Irish Workers' Republican' candidate. He was the nominee of the Stockport Irish Election Committee and a prominent member of the Irish Labour Party. At the time of the election he was serving a prison sentence.

| Election | Electors | T'out | Candidate | Party | Votes | % |
|---|---|---|---|---|---|---|
| 1918 | | | †J.B. Watson | Co L | Unopp. | |
| 1922 | 37,991 | 85.9 | J.B. Watson | NL | 12,396 | 38.0 |
| | | | F.F. Riley | Lab | 11,183 | 34.3 |
| | | | R.S. Stewart | L | 9,041 | 27.7 |
| | | | | | 1,213 | 3.7 |
| 1923 | 38,872 | 87.5 | R.S. Stewart | L | 11,734 | 34.5 |
| | | | M.H. Macmillan | C | 11,661 | 34.3 |
| | | | F.F. Riley | Lab | 10,619 | 31.2 |
| | | | | | 73 | 0.2 |
| 1924 | 39,981 | 90.2 | M.H. Macmillan | C | 15,163 | 42.0 |
| | | | F.F. Riley | Lab | 11,948 | 33.1 |
| | | | R.S. Stewart | L | 8,971 | 24.9 |
| | | | | | 3,215 | 8.9 |
| 1929 | 52,739 | 87.1 | F.F. Riley | Lab | 18,961 | 41.2 |
| | | | M.H. Macmillan | C | 16,572 | 36.1 |
| | | | J.C. Hayes | L | 10,407 | 22.7 |
| | | | | | 2,389 | 5.1 |
| 1931 | 53,587 | 88.4 | M.H. Macmillan | C | 29,199 | 61.6 |
| | | | F.F. Riley | Lab | 18,168 | 38.4 |
| | | | | | 11,031 | 23.2 |
| 1935 | 55,216 | 86.3 | M.H. Macmillan | C (Ind C) (C) | 23,285 | 48.9 |
| | | | Miss A.S. Lawrence | Lab | 19,217 | 40.3 |
| | | | G.L. Tossell | L | 5,158* | 10.8 |
| | | | | | 4,068 | 8.6 |
| 1945 | 60,693 | 81.2 | G.R. Chetwynd | Lab | 27,128 | 55.1 |
| | | | Rt. Hon. M.H. Macmillan | C | 18,464 | 37.4 |
| | | | G.P. Evans | L | 3,718* | 7.5 |
| | | | | | 8,664 | 17.7 |

| Election | Electors | T'out | Candidate | Party | Votes | % |
|---|---|---|---|---|---|---|
| 1918 | 29,866 | 56.5 | †S. Finney | Lab | 7,474 | 44.3 |
| | | | S. Walker | Co C | 6,301 | 37.3 |
| | | | †Sir R.W. Essex | L | 3,108 | 18.4 |
| | | | | | 1,173 | 7.0 |
| 1922 | 30,119 | 78.2 | A. MacLaren | Lab | 11,872 | 50.4 |
| | | | S. Malkin | NL | 11,667 | 49.6 |
| | | | | | 205 | 0.8 |
| 1923 | 30,372 | 82.4 | W.E. Robinson | L | 12,543 | 50.1 |
| | | | A. MacLaren | Lab | 12,480 | 49.9 |
| | | | | | 63 | 0.2 |
| 1924 | 31,903 | 88.1 | A. MacLaren | Lab | 14,361 | 51.1 |
| | | | W. Allen | Const | 13,755 | 48.9 |
| | | | | | 606 | 2.2 |
| 1929 | 41,782 | 82.5 | A. MacLaren | Lab | 20,228 | 58.6 |
| | | | A.P. Harrison | C | 7,440 | 21.6 |
| | | | J. Joy | L | 6,815 | 19.8 |
| | | | | | 12,788 | 37.0 |
| 1931 | 42,782 | 82.5 | W. Allen | Nat (NL) | 18,647 | 52.9 |
| | | | A. MacLaren | Lab | 16,248 | 46.0 |
| | | | A. Rowland-Entwistle | CW Land P | 401* | 1.1 |
| | | | | | 2,399 | 6.9 |
| 1935 | 42,706 | 77.9 | A. MacLaren | Lab (Ind Lab) | 18,030 | 54.2 |
| | | | W. Allen | NL | 15,227 | 45.8 |
| | | | | | 2,803 | 8.4 |
| 1945 | 42,121 | 78.7 | A.E. Davies | Lab | 20,044 | 60.5 |
| | | | F.M. Bennett | NL | 9,877 | 29.8 |
| | | | A. MacLaren | Ind Lab | 3,223* | 9.7 |
| | | | | | 10,167 | 30.7 |

| Election | Electors | T'out | Candidate | Party | Votes | % |
|---|---|---|---|---|---|---|
| 1918 | 33,789 | 58.9 | J.A. Seddon | Co NDP | 8,032 | 40.4 |
| | | | H. Parker | Lab | 7,697 | 38.7 |
| | | | †R.L. Outhwaite | Ind L | 2,703 | 13.6 |
| | | | L.L. Grimwade | L | 1,459* | 7.3 |
| | | | | | 335 | 1.7 |
| | | | | | | |
| 1922 | 32,641 | 67.4 | H. Parker | Lab | 10,742 | 48.8 |
| | | | J.A. Seddon | NL | 6,312 | 28.7 |
| | | | J.H. Whitehouse | L | 4,942 | 22.5 |
| | | | | | 4,430 | 20.1 |
| | | | | | | |
| 1923 | 33,895 | 63.7 | H. Parker | Lab | 11,508 | 53.3 |
| | | | J.A. Seddon | C | 5,817 | 26.9 |
| | | | Mrs. A. Moody | L | 4,268 | 19.8 |
| | | | | | 5,691 | 26.4 |
| | | | | | | |
| 1924 | 34,682 | 73.5 | S. Clowes | Lab | 13,527 | 53.0 |
| | | | F. Collis | C | 11,973 | 47.0 |
| | | | | | 1,554 | 6.0 |
| [Death] | | | | | | |
| 1928 (23/4) | 35,976 | 69.9 | A. Hollins | Lab | 15,136 | 60.2 |
| | | | A. Denville | C | 6,604 | 26.3 |
| | | | W. Meakin | L | 3,390 | 13.5 |
| | | | | | 8,532 | 33.9 |
| | | | | | | |
| 1929 | 46,224 | 72.5 | A. Hollins | Lab | 20,785 | 62.1 |
| | | | E. Errington | C | 9,022 | 26.9 |
| | | | C.F. White | L | 3,696* | 11.0 |
| | | | | | 11,763 | 35.2 |
| | | | | | | |
| 1931 | 47,432 | 72.6 | H.K. Hales | C | 18,262 | 53.1 |
| | | | A. Hollins | Lab | 15,245 | 44.2 |
| | | | J.W.G. Peace | CW Land P | 946* | 2.7 |
| | | | | | 3,017 | 8.9 |
| | | | | | | |
| 1935 | 47,414 | 69.8 | A. Hollins | Lab | 17,211 | 52.0 |
| | | | H.K. Hales | C | 15,880 | 48.0 |
| | | | | | 1,331 | 4.0 |
| | | | | | | |
| 1945 | 43,764 | 73.6 | Dr. B. Stross | Lab | 21,915 | 68.0 |
| | | | J.P.A.L. Doran | C | 10,313 | 32.0 |
| | | | | | 11,602 | 36.0 |

| Election | Electors | T'out | Candidate | Party | Votes | % |
|---|---|---|---|---|---|---|
| 1918 | | | †J. Ward | Co L | Unopp. | |
| | | | | | | |
| 1922 | 40,023 | 68.0 | J. Ward | NL | 16,685 | 61.3 |
| | | | J. Watts | Lab | 10,522 | 38.7 |
| | | | | | 6,163 | 22.6 |
| | | | | | | |
| 1923 | 40,566 | 63.2 | J. Ward | L | 13,119 | 51.2 |
| | | | J. Watts | Lab | 12,502 | 48.8 |
| | | | | | 617 | 2.4 |
| | | | | | | |
| 1924 | 41,365 | 75.4 | J. Ward | Const (L) | 17,864 | 57.3 |
| | | | J. Watts | Lab | 13,318 | 42.7 |
| | | | | | 4,546 | 14.6 |
| | | | | | | |
| 1929 | 55,691 | 81.2 | Lady Cynthia Mosley | Lab (NP) | 26,548 | 58.7 |
| | | | J. Ward | L | 18,698 | 41.3 |
| | | | | | 7,850 | 17.4 |
| | | | | | | |
| 1931 | 57,612 | 75.9 | Mrs. I. Copeland | C | 19,918 | 45.6 |
| | | | E. Smith | Lab | 13,264 | 30.3 |
| | | | Sir O.E. Mosley, Bt. | NP | 10,534 | 24.1 |
| | | | | | 6,654 | 15.3 |
| | | | | | | |
| 1935 | 56,958 | 70.0 | E. Smith | Lab | 20,992 | 52.7 |
| | | | Mrs. I. Copeland | C | 18,867 | 47.3 |
| | | | | | 2,125 | 5.4 |
| | | | | | | |
| 1945 | 56,496 | 75.7 | E. Smith | Lab | 29,551 | 69.1 |
| | | | W.F. Wentworth-Sheilds | C | 13,203 | 30.9 |
| | | | | | 16,348 | 38.2 |

Note:—

1918-
1929:   Ward had been elected in 1906 as a Liberal-Labour member and between 1918 and 1929 stood under the title 'Independent Labour'. He was the product of a local Liberal-Conservative pact and also had the support of some local trade unions. The Liberal Party always claimed him as one of their members and it appears that he accepted their whip. In view of this he is designated as a Liberal, except in 1924 when the 'label' Constitutionalist was used by 'pact' candidates.

## SUNDERLAND [241]
### (Two Seats)

| Election | Electors | T'out | Candidate | Party | Votes | % |
|---|---|---|---|---|---|---|
| 1918 | 73,121 | 56.4 | †Sir H. Greenwood, Bt. | Co L | 27,646 | 43.9 |
| | | | R.M. Hudson | C | 25,698 | 40.8 |
| | | | †F.W. Goldstone | Lab | 9,603 | 15.3 |
| | | | | | 18,043 | 28.6 |
| | | | | | 16,095 | 25.5 |

[Appointed Chief Secretary to the Lord Lieutenant of Ireland]

| Election | Electors | T'out | Candidate | Party | Votes | % |
|---|---|---|---|---|---|---|
| 1920 | 76,216 | 55.4 | Sir H. Greenwood, Bt. | Co L | 22,813 | 54.0 |
| (24/4) | | | Dr. V.H. Rutherford | Lab | 14,379 | 34.0 |
| | | | E.M. Howe | L | 5,065* | 12.0 |
| | | | | | 8,434 | 20.0 |
| 1922 | 74,970 | 81.6 | W. Raine | C | 28,001 | 25.0 |
| | | | L. Thompson | C | 24,591 | 22.0 |
| | | | Rt. Hon. Sir H. Greenwood, Bt. | NL | 19,058 | 17.0 |
| | | | D.B. Lawley | Lab | 13,683 | 12.2 |
| | | | Dr. V.H. Rutherford | Lab | 13,490 | 12.1 |
| | | | L.A. Common | L | 13,036 | 11.7 |
| | | | | | 5,533 | 5.0 |
| 1923 | 76,916 | 77.9 | W. Raine | C | 23,497 | 19.9 |
| | | | L. Thompson | C | 23,379 | 19.8 |
| | | | L.A. Common | L | 22,438 | 19.0 |
| | | | Rt. Hon. Sir H. Greenwood, Bt. | L | 22,034 | 18.6 |
| | | | D.B. Lawley | Lab | 13,707 | 11.6 |
| | | | T.W. Gillinder | Lab | 13,184 | 11.1 |
| | | | | | 941 | 0.8 |
| 1924 | 78,361 | 84.6 | L. Thompson | C | 28,612 | 25.4 |
| | | | W. Raine | C | 28,608 | 25.3 |
| | | | J. MacVeagh | Lab | 21,823 | 19.3 |
| | | | L.A. Common | L | 20,139 | 17.8 |
| | | | I.C. Hannah | L | 13,731 | 12.2 |
| | | | | | 6,785 | 6.0 |
| 1929 | 101,875 | 81.1 | Dr. Marion Phillips | Lab | 31,794 | 19.5 |
| | | | A. Smith | Lab | 31,085 | 19.0 |
| | | | Sir W. Raine | C | 29,180 | 17.9 |
| | | | L. Thompson | C | 28,937 | 17.7 |
| | | | Dr. Elizabeth T. Morgan | L | 21,300 | 13.0 |
| | | | Sir J.W. Pratt | L | 21,142 | 12.9 |
| | | | | | 1,905 | 1.1 |

[Death of Smith]

| Election | Electors | T'out | Candidate | Party | Votes | % |
|---|---|---|---|---|---|---|
| 1931 | 103,363 | 73.1 | L. Thompson | C | 30,497 | 40.3 |
| (26/3) | | | J.T. Brownlie | Lab | 30,075 | 39.8 |
| | | | Dr. Elizabeth T. Morgan | L | 15,020 | 19.9 |
| | | | | | 422 | 0.5 |
| 1931 | 103,559 | 81.1 | L. Thompson | C | 53,386 | 32.3 |
| | | | S. Storey | C | 52,589 | 31.8 |
| | | | Dr. Marion Phillips | Lab | 29,707 | 18.0 |
| | | | D.N. Pritt | Lab | 29,680 | 17.9 |
| | | | | | 22,882 | 13.8 |

| Election | Electors | T'out | Candidate | Party | Votes | % |
|---|---|---|---|---|---|---|
| 1935 | 103,928 | 79.0 | S.N. Furness | NL | 49,001 | 30.2 |
| | | | S. Storey | C | 48,760 | 30.0 |
| | | | G.E.G. Catlin | Lab | 32,483 | 20.0 |
| | | | Mrs. E.L. Manning | Lab | 32,059 | 19.8 |
| | | | | | 16,518 | 10.2 |
| | | | | | 16,277 | 10.0 |
| 1945 | 90,729 | 77.2 | F.T. Willey | Lab | 38,769 | 28.1 |
| | | | R. Ewart | Lab | 36,711 | 26.6 |
| | | | S.N. Furness | NL | 29,366 | 21.3 |
| | | | S. Storey | C | 28,579 | 20.7 |
| | | | T.A. Richardson | Com | 4,501* | 3.3 |
| | | | | | 7,345 | 5.3 |

| Election | Electors | T'out | Candidate | Party | Votes | % |
|----------|----------|-------|-----------|-------|-------|---|
| 1945 | 55,742 | 75.7 | S.H. Marshall | C | 19,431 | 46.0 |
|  |  |  | Mrs. H.O. Judd | Lab | 17,293 | 41.0 |
|  |  |  | J.P. Hughes | L | 5,483 | 13.0 |
|  |  |  |  |  | 2,138 | 5.0 |

# TOTTENHAM, NORTH  [243]

| Election | Electors | T'out | Candidate | Party | Votes | % |
|---|---|---|---|---|---|---|
| 1918 | 34,463 | 55.7 | W.H. Prescott | Co C | 11,891 | 62.0 |
| | | | †P. Alden | L | 7,293 | 38.0 |
| | | | | | 4,598 | 24.0 |
| 1922 | 35,484 | 65.4 | R.C. Morrison | Lab/Co-op | 10,250 | 44.2 |
| | | | C.D. Roberts | C | 8,392 | 36.1 |
| | | | C. Baker | NL | 4,181 | 18.0 |
| | | | F. Bartle | Ind C | 395* | 1.7 |
| | | | | | 1,858 | 8.1 |
| 1923 | 36,846 | 69.3 | R.C. Morrison | Lab/Co-op | 12,696 | 49.7 |
| | | | Sir W.H. Prescott | C | 8,323 | 32.6 |
| | | | O.F. Broadway | L | 4,525 | 17.7 |
| | | | | | 4,373 | 17.1 |
| 1924 | 37,903 | 71.3 | R.C. Morrison | Lab/Co-op | 13,800 | 51.0 |
| | | | J.L. Sturrock | Const | 13,243 | 49.0 |
| | | | | | 557 | 2.0 |
| 1929 | 52,399 | 73.8 | R.C. Morrison | Lab/Co-op | 20,884 | 54.0 |
| | | | H.J. Solomon | C | 11,231 | 29.1 |
| | | | Hon. A.W.E. Holden | L | 6,535 | 16.9 |
| | | | | | 9,653 | 24.9 |
| 1931 | 55,922 | 71.2 | E. Doran | C | 22,172 | 55.7 |
| | | | R.C. Morrison | Lab/Co-op | 17,651 | 44.3 |
| | | | | | 4,521 | 11.4 |
| 1935 | 55,926 | 65.9 | R.C. Morrison | Lab/Co-op | 21,075 | 57.2 |
| | | | E. Doran | C | 13,066 | 35.5 |
| | | | L.C.A. Dubery | L | 2,697* | 7.3 |
| | | | | | 8,009 | 21.7 |
| 1945 | 50,234 | 70.3 | R.C. Morrison | Lab/Co-op | 25,360 | 71.8 |
| | | | B.H. Berry | C | 9,955 | 28.2 |
| | | | | | 15,405 | 43.6 |

[Elevation to the Peerage — Lord Morrison]

| Election | Electors | T'out | Candidate | Party | Votes | % |
|---|---|---|---|---|---|---|
| 1945 (13/12) | 51,576 | 39.5 | W.J. Irving | Lab/Co-op | 12,937 | 63.6 |
| | | | F.P. Crowder | C | 7,415 | 36.4 |
| | | | | | 5,522 | 27.2 |

# TOTTENHAM, SOUTH  [244]

| Election | Electors | T'out | Candidate | Party | Votes | % |
|---|---|---|---|---|---|---|
| 1918 | 34,474 | 45.3 | P.B. Malone | C | 6,632 | 42.4 |
| | | | †Sir L.G.C. Money | Lab | 5,779 | 37.0 |
| | | | A.E. Harvey | NDP | 1,916* | 12.3 |
| | | | A.E. Jay | Ind | 1,295* | 8.3 |
| | | | | | 853 | 5.4 |
| 1922 | 34,828 | 63.8 | P.B. Malone | C | 9,903 | 44.5 |
| | | | R.H. Tawney | Lab | 8,241 | 37.1 |
| | | | A.M. Mathews | L | 4,081 | 18.4 |
| | | | | | 1,662 | 7.4 |
| 1923 | 35,182 | 62.5 | P. Alden | Lab | 10,312 | 46.9 |
| | | | P.B. Malone | C | 7,687 | 35.0 |
| | | | Dr. A.G. Newell | L | 3,974 | 18.1 |
| | | | | | 2,625 | 11.9 |
| 1924 | 35,760 | 71.9 | P.B. Malone | C | 13,600 | 52.9 |
| | | | P. Alden | Lab | 12,099 | 47.1 |
| | | | | | 1,501 | 5.8 |
| 1929 | 45,970 | 67.5 | F. Messer | Lab | 14,423 | 46.4 |
| | | | P.B. Malone | C | 9,701 | 31.3 |
| | | | W. Stonestreet | L | 6,407 | 20.7 |
| | | | H.T.W. Sara | Com | 490* | 1.6 |
| | | | | | 4,722 | 15.1 |
| 1931 | 46,532 | 65.4 | F.N. Palmer | N Lab | 17,824 | 58.6 |
| | | | F. Messer | Lab | 12,602 | 41.4 |
| | | | | | 5,222 | 17.2 |
| 1935 | 44,687 | 60.5 | F. Messer | Lab | 15,834 | 58.5 |
| | | | F.N. Palmer | N Lab | 11,221 | 41.5 |
| | | | | | 4,613 | 17.0 |
| 1945 | 36,261 | 69.0 | F. Messer | Lab | 18,335 | 73.3 |
| | | | A.L. Bateman | C | 4,480 | 17.9 |
| | | | A.G. Church | Ind Nat | 2,193* | 8.8 |
| | | | | | 13,855 | 55.4 |

Notes:—

1918: Malone was incorrectly included in the final official list of Coalition candidates. He did not receive a 'coupon'.

Jay was the nominee of the local branch of the NFDSS.

## TWICKENHAM [245]

| Election | Electors | T'out | Candidate | Party | Votes | % |
|---|---|---|---|---|---|---|
| 1945 | 73,291 | 74.6 | E.H. Keeling | C | 26,045 | 47.6 |
| | | | A.J. Irvine | Lab | 22,736 | 41.6 |
| | | | G.G. Slack | L | 5,909* | 10.8 |
| | | | | | 3,309 | 6.0 |

| Election | Electors | T'out | Candidate | Party | Votes | % |
|---|---|---|---|---|---|---|
| 1918 | 26,467 | 63.8 | C. Percy | Co C | 5,883 | 34.7 |
| | | | †H.J. Craig | L | 5,434 | 32.2 |
| | | | G.H. Humphrey | Ind Lab | 2,566 | 15.2 |
| | | | H. Gregg | Ind | 2,495 | 14.8 |
| | | | D. Scott | Nat P | 517* | 3.1 |
| | | | | | 449 | 2.5 |
| 1922 | 28,029 | 83.5 | A.W. Russell | C | 11,244 | 48.1 |
| | | | H.J. Craig | L | 6,787 | 29.0 |
| | | | G.H. Humphrey | Lab | 5,362 | 22.9 |
| | | | | | 4,457 | 19.1 |
| 1923 | 28,963 | 81.1 | A.W. Russell | C | 9,612 | 41.0 |
| | | | H. Barnes | L | 9,008 | 38.3 |
| | | | W. Pitt | Lab | 4,875 | 20.7 |
| | | | | | 604 | 2.7 |
| 1924 | 29,363 | 84.6 | A.W. Russell | C | 11,210 | 45.2 |
| | | | H. Barnes | L | 6,820 | 27.4 |
| | | | J.S. Barr | Lab | 6,818 | 27.4 |
| | | | | | 4,390 | 17.8 |
| 1929 | 38,221 | 83.3 | A.W. Russell | C | 11,785 | 37.0 |
| | | | R. Irvin | L | 10,545 | 33.1 |
| | | | J.S. Barr | Lab | 9,503 | 29.9 |
| | | | | | 1,240 | 3.9 |
| 1931 | 40,419 | 84.1 | A.W. Russell | C | 17,607 | 51.8 |
| | | | S. Holmes | L | 8,295 | 24.4 |
| | | | T.H. Knight | Lab | 8,110 | 23.8 |
| | | | | | 9,312 | 27.4 |
| 1935 | 42,938 | 79.2 | A.W. Russell | C | 16,003 | 47.1 |
| | | | Dr. S. Segal | Lab | 10,145 | 29.8 |
| | | | S. Holmes | L | 7,868 | 23.1 |
| | | | | | 5,858 | 17.3 |
| 1945 | 39,528 | 76.7 | Miss G.M. Colman | Lab | 13,963 | 46.1 |
| | | | Sir A.W. Russell | C | 10,884 | 35.9 |
| | | | K.P. Chitty | L | 5,460 | 18.0 |
| | | | | | 3,079 | 10.2 |

| Election | Electors | T'out | Candidate | Party | Votes | % |
|----------|----------|-------|-----------|-------|-------|---|
| 1918 | 24,203 | 72.1 | Sir E.A. Brotherton, Bt. | Co C | 9,128 | 52.3 |
| | | | A. Bellamy | Lab | 5,882 | 33.7 |
| | | | †Sir A.H. Marshall | L | 2,448 | 14.0 |
| | | | | | 3,246 | 18.6 |
| 1922 | 23,960 | 84.4 | R.G. Ellis | C | 10,416 | 51.5 |
| | | | A. Bellamy | Lab | 9,798 | 48.5 |
| | | | | | 618 | 3.0 |
| 1923 | 24,649 | 80.9 | G.H. Sherwood | Lab | 7,966 | 39.9 |
| | | | R.G. Ellis | C | 7,345 | 36.8 |
| | | | E.J. Lassen | L | 4,640 | 23.3 |
| | | | | | 621 | 3.1 |
| 1924 | 25,080 | 84.8 | R.G. Ellis | C | 11,086 | 52.1 |
| | | | G.H. Sherwood | Lab | 10,192 | 47.9 |
| | | | | | 894 | 4.2 |
| 1929 | 32,053 | 85.6 | G.H. Sherwood | Lab | 13,393 | 48.8 |
| | | | R.G. Ellis | C | 10,180 | 37.1 |
| | | | L. Parish | L | 3,875 | 14.1 |
| | | | | | 3,213 | 11.7 |
| 1931 | 32,334 | 85.5 | Dr. G.B. Hillman | C | 15,881 | 57.4 |
| | | | G.H. Sherwood | Lab | 11,774 | 42.6 |
| | | | | | 4,107 | 14.8 |
| [Death] | | | | | | |
| 1932 (21/4) | 32,334 | 83.0 | Rt. Hon. A. Greenwood | Lab | 13,586 | 50.6 |
| | | | A.E. Greaves | C | 13,242 | 49.4 |
| | | | | | 344 | 1.2 |
| 1935 | 33,215 | 84.9 | Rt. Hon. A. Greenwood | Lab | 15,804 | 56.0 |
| | | | A.E. Greaves | C | 12,400 | 44.0 |
| | | | | | 3,404 | 12.0 |
| 1945 | 32,721 | 80.3 | Rt. Hon. A. Greenwood | Lab | 14,378 | 54.7 |
| | | | H. Watson | C | 8,268 | 31.5 |
| | | | G.L.J. Oliver | L | 3,613 | 13.8 |
| | | | | | 6,110 | 23.2 |

# WALLASEY [248]

| Election | Electors | T'out | Candidate | Party | Votes | % |
|---|---|---|---|---|---|---|
| 1918 | 42,174 | 62.8 | Dr. B.F.P. McDonald | Co C | 14,633 | 55.2 |
| | | | W.M. Citrine | Lab | 4,384 | 16.6 |
| | | | J.M. Hay | L | 4,055 | 15.3 |
| | | | T.D. Owen | Ind | 3,407 | 12.9 |
| | | | | | 10,249 | 38.6 |
| 1922 | 39,737 | 69.2 | Sir R.B. Chadwick | C | 17,508 | 63.7 |
| | | | T.A. Morris | L | 9,984 | 36.3 |
| | | | | | 7,524 | 27.4 |
| 1923 | 40,367 | 67.2 | Sir R.B. Chadwick | C | 13,995 | 51.6 |
| | | | T.A. Morris | L | 13,146 | 48.4 |
| | | | | | 849 | 3.2 |
| 1924 | 41,816 | 74.7 | Sir R.B. Chadwick | C | 22,599 | 72.4 |
| | | | J.H. Warren | Lab | 8,634 | 27.6 |
| | | | | | 13,965 | 44.8 |
| 1929 | 60,075 | 77.6 | Sir R.B. Chadwick | C | 21,457 | 46.0 |
| | | | H. Phillips | L | 13,628 | 29.2 |
| | | | J.D. Mack | Lab | 11,545 | 24.8 |
| | | | | | 7,829 | 16.8 |
| 1931 | 62,092 | 77.1 | J.T.C. Moore-Brabazon | C | 40,161 | 83.9 |
| | | | J.D. Mack | Lab | 7,712 | 16.1 |
| | | | | | 32,449 | 67.8 |
| 1935 | 62,654 | 66.1 | J.T.C. Moore-Brabazon | C | 27,949 | 67.4 |
| | | | J. Airey | Lab | 13,491 | 32.6 |
| | | | | | 14,458 | 34.8 |

[Elevation to the Peerage — Lord Brabazon of Tara]

| Election | Electors | T'out | Candidate | Party | Votes | % |
|---|---|---|---|---|---|---|
| 1942 (29/4) | 60,684 | 34.2 | G.L. Reakes | Ind | 12,596 | 60.6 |
| | | | J. Pennington | C | 6,584 | 31.7 |
| | | | Hon. L.H. Cripps | Ind | 1,597* | 7.7 |
| | | | | | 6,012 | 28.9 |
| 1945 | 57,113 | 75.2 | A.E. Marples | C | 18,448 | 42.9 |
| | | | G.L. Reakes | Ind | 14,638 | 34.1 |
| | | | T. Findley | Lab/Co-op | 9,879 | 23.0 |
| | | | | | 3,810 | 8.8 |

Notes:—

1918: Owen was the nominee of the local branch of the NFDSS.

1942: Reakes was a former member of the Labour Party who had resigned in 1938 at the time of the Munich crisis. He was assisted by Sir Richard Acland, who was still nominally a Liberal, but a few months later became a co-founder of the Common Wealth Movement.

# WALLSEND [249]

| Election | Electors | T'out | Candidate | Party | Votes | % |
|---|---|---|---|---|---|---|
| 1918 | 36,739 | 54.8 | M.T. Simm | Co NDP | 10,246 | 50.9 |
| | | | J. Chapman | Lab | 6,835 | 34.0 |
| | | | †Rt. Hon. J.M. Robertson | L | 3,047 | 15.1 |
| | | | | | 3,411 | 16.9 |
| 1922 | 37,001 | 82.2 | P.G. Hastings | Lab | 14,248 | 46.8 |
| | | | Hon. C.W. Lowther | C | 11,425 | 37.6 |
| | | | T.G. Graham | L | 2,908* | 9.6 |
| | | | M.T. Simm | NL | 1,840* | 6.0 |
| | | | | | 2,823 | 9.2 |
| 1923 | 38,435 | 75.6 | P.G. Hastings | Lab | 16,126 | 55.5 |
| | | | Hon. C.W. Lowther | C | 12,950 | 44.5 |
| | | | | | 3,176 | 11.0 |
| 1924 | 38,598 | 85.4 | Sir P.G. Hastings | Lab | 17,274 | 52.4 |
| | | | S. Howard | C | 15,672 | 47.6 |
| | | | | | 1,602 | 4.8 |

[Resignation]

| Election | Electors | T'out | Candidate | Party | Votes | % |
|---|---|---|---|---|---|---|
| 1926 (21/7) | 39,460† | 82.9 | Miss M.G. Bondfield | Lab | 18,866 | 57.7 |
| | | | S. Howard | C | 9,839 | 30.1 |
| | | | A.C. Curry | L | 4,000* | 12.2 |
| | | | | | 9,027 | 27.6 |
| 1929 | 50,578 | 80.2 | Miss M.G. Bondfield | Lab | 20,057 | 49.6 |
| | | | W. Waring | C | 12,952 | 31.9 |
| | | | S. Phillips | L | 6,790 | 16.7 |
| | | | W. Hannington | Com | 744* | 1.8 |
| | | | | | 7,105 | 17.7 |
| 1931 | 52,277 | 84.9 | Miss I.M.B. Ward | C | 25,999 | 58.6 |
| | | | Rt. Hon. Margaret G. Bondfield | Lab | 18,393 | 41.4 |
| | | | | | 7,606 | 17.2 |
| 1935 | 55,755 | 81.3 | Miss I.M.B. Ward | C | 23,842 | 52.6 |
| | | | Rt. Hon. Margaret G. Bondfield | Lab | 21,463 | 47.4 |
| | | | | | 2,379 | 5.2 |
| 1945 | 67,698 | 78.9 | J. McKay | Lab | 32,065 | 60.1 |
| | | | Miss I.M.B. Ward | C | 21,319 | 39.9 |
| | | | | | 10,746 | 20.2 |

# WALSALL [250]

| Election | Electors | T'out | Candidate | Party | Votes | % |
|---|---|---|---|---|---|---|
| 1918 | 42,900 | 64.7 | †Sir R.A. Cooper, Bt. | Nat P (C) | 14,491 | 52.3 |
| | | | J. Thickett | Lab | 8,336 | 30.0 |
| | | | W.H. Brown | L | 4,914 | 17.7 |
| | | | | | 6,155 | 22.3 |
| 1922 | 45,009 | 84.4 | P. Collins | L | 14,674 | 38.6 |
| | | | Lady Cooper | C | 14,349 | 37.8 |
| | | | R. Dennison | Lab | 8,946 | 23.6 |
| | | | | | 325 | 0.8 |
| 1923 | 45,339 | 82.6 | P. Collins | L | 16,304 | 43.5 |
| | | | S.K. Lewis | C | 14,141 | 37.8 |
| | | | A.C. Osburn | Lab | 7,007 | 18.7 |
| | | | | | 2,163 | 5.7 |
| 1924 | 46,407 | 86.2 | W. Preston | C | 15,168 | 37.9 |
| | | | P. Collins | L | 12,734 | 31.8 |
| | | | G.L.R. Small | Lab | 11,474 | 28.7 |
| | | | Dr. J.J. Lynch | Ind | 622* | 1.6 |
| | | | | | 2,434 | 6.1 |

[Disqualification of Preston who at the time of his election held contracts with the General Post Office]

| Election | Electors | T'out | Candidate | Party | Votes | % |
|---|---|---|---|---|---|---|
| 1925 (27/2) | 46,407 | 83.4 | W. Preston | C | 14,793 | 38.2 |
| | | | Rt. Hon. T.J. Macnamara | L | 12,300 | 31.8 |
| | | | G.L.R. Small | Lab | 11,610 | 30.0 |
| | | | | | 2,493 | 6.4 |
| 1929 | 60,233 | 85.9 | J.J. McShane | Lab | 20,524 | 39.6 |
| | | | W. Preston | C | 15,818 | 30.6 |
| | | | Rt. Hon. T.J. Macnamara | L | 15,425 | 29.8 |
| | | | | | 4,706 | 9.0 |
| 1931 | 63,110 | 86.3 | J.A. Leckie | Nat (NL) | 30,507 | 56.0 |
| | | | J.J. McShane | Lab | 23,952 | 44.0 |
| | | | | | 6,555 | 12.0 |
| 1935 | 65,957 | 75.3 | J.A. Leckie | NL | 28,563 | 57.5 |
| | | | W. Graham | Lab | 19,594 | 39.5 |
| | | | J.W. Harper | CS | 1,480* | 3.0 |
| | | | | | 8,969 | 18.0 |

[Death]

| Election | Electors | T'out | Candidate | Party | Votes | % |
|---|---|---|---|---|---|---|
| 1938 (16/11) | 66,226 | 75.9 | Sir G.E. Schuster | NL | 28,720 | 57.1 |
| | | | G. Jeger | Lab | 21,562 | 42.9 |
| | | | | | 7,158 | 14.2 |
| 1945 | 68,924 | 76.2 | W.T. Wells | Lab | 28,324 | 53.9 |
| | | | Sir G.E. Schuster | NL | 24,197 | 46.1 |
| | | | | | 4,127 | 7.8 |

| Election | Electors | T'out | Candidate | Party | Votes | % |
|---|---|---|---|---|---|---|
| 1918 | 28,363 | 55.6 | L.S. Johnson | Co C | 9,992 | 63.3 |
|  |  |  | †Rt. Hon. Sir J.A. Simon | L | 5,781 | 36.7 |
|  |  |  |  |  | 4,211 | 26.6 |
| 1922 | 29,013 | 67.6 | Sir L.S. Johnson | C | 9,178 | 46.8 |
|  |  |  | W.B. Steer | Lab | 6,382 | 32.6 |
|  |  |  | Dr. H.B. Brackenbury | L | 4,043 | 20.6 |
|  |  |  |  |  | 2,796 | 14.2 |
| 1923 | 29,151 | 67.8 | Sir L.S. Johnson | C | 7,081 | 35.9 |
|  |  |  | J.G. Dale | Lab | 6,837 | 34.6 |
|  |  |  | A.M. Mathews | L | 5,837 | 29.5 |
|  |  |  |  |  | 244 | 1.3 |
| 1924 | 29,861 | 78.0 | Rt. Hon. Sir H. Greenwood, Bt. | Const (C) | 11,312 | 48.5 |
|  |  |  | J.G. Dale | Lab | 8,246 | 35.4 |
|  |  |  | P.H. Heffer | L | 3,745 | 16.1 |
|  |  |  |  |  | 3,066 | 13.1 |
| 1929 | 38,102 | 73.1 | H.W. Wallace | Lab | 11,039 | 39.6 |
|  |  |  | Rt. Hon. J.F. Hope | C | 9,665 | 34.7 |
|  |  |  | Dr. J.G. Dridges | L | 7,145 | 25.7 |
|  |  |  |  |  | 1,374 | 4.9 |
| 1931 | 41,890 | 76.4 | Sir B.C. Beauchamp, Bt. | C | 18,815 | 58.8 |
|  |  |  | H.W. Wallace | Lab | 9,983 | 31.2 |
|  |  |  | A.C. Crane | L | 3,198* | 10.0 |
|  |  |  |  |  | 8,832 | 27.6 |
| 1935 | 45,258 | 69.0 | Sir B.C. Beauchamp, Bt. | C | 16,866 | 54.0 |
|  |  |  | H.W. Wallace | Lab | 14,378 | 46.0 |
|  |  |  |  |  | 2,488 | 8.0 |
| 1945 | 41,676 | 73.5 | H.W. Wallace | Lab | 15,650 | 51.1 |
|  |  |  | H.E. Harrison | C | 9,118 | 29.8 |
|  |  |  | N.P. Dew | L | 5,854 | 19.1 |
|  |  |  |  |  | 6,532 | 21.3 |

## WALTHAMSTOW, WEST  [252]

| Election | Electors | T'out | Candidate | Party | Votes | % |
|---|---|---|---|---|---|---|
| 1918 | 30,225 | 47.0 | C. Jesson | Co NDP | 7,330 | 51.6 |
| | | | V.L.T. McEntee | Lab | 4,167 | 29.3 |
| | | | E.J. Horniman | L | 2,707 | 19.1 |
| | | | | | 3,163 | 22.3 |
| 1922 | 31,710 | 63.8 | V.L.T. McEntee | Lab | 8,758 | 43.3 |
| | | | C. Jesson | NL | 6,253 | 30.9 |
| | | | H.E. Crawfurd | L | 5,228 | 25.8 |
| | | | | | 2,505 | 12.4 |
| 1923 | 32,188 | 65.5 | V.L.T. McEntee | Lab | 10,026 | 47.6 |
| | | | H.E. Crawfurd | L | 8,234 | 39.0 |
| | | | J. Lyne | C | 2,832 | 13.4 |
| | | | | | 1,792 | 8.6 |
| 1924 | 33,780 | 75.5 | H.E. Crawfurd | L | 12,991 | 50.9 |
| | | | V.L.T. McEntee | Lab | 12,521 | 49.1 |
| | | | | | 470 | 1.8 |
| 1929 | 40,510 | 73.3 | V.L.T. McEntee | Lab | 16,050 | 54.0 |
| | | | H.E. Crawfurd | L | 9,470 | 31.9 |
| | | | F.C. Bramston | C | 4,184 | 14.1 |
| | | | | | 6,580 | 22.1 |
| 1931 | 43,027 | 72.8 | V.L.T. McEntee | Lab | 14,144 | 45.2 |
| | | | C.H. Grundy | C | 13,137 | 41.9 |
| | | | S.W. Robinson | L | 4,053 | 12.9 |
| | | | | | 1,007 | 3.3 |
| 1935 | 43,847 | 65.0 | V.L.T. McEntee | Lab | 17,613 | 61.8 |
| | | | T.C. Catty | C | 10,874 | 38.2 |
| | | | | | 6,739 | 23.6 |
| 1945 | 38,169 | 70.1 | V.L.T. McEntee | Lab | 17,460 | 65.2 |
| | | | L.D. Spicer | L | 4,760 | 17.8 |
| | | | L.C. Curran | C | 4,550 | 17.0 |
| | | | | | 12,700 | 47.4 |

# WARRINGTON  [253]

| Election | Electors | T'out | Candidate | Party | Votes | % |
|---|---|---|---|---|---|---|
| 1918 | 33,912 | 70.2 | †H. Smith | Co C | 10,403 | 43.7 |
| | | | Sir P. Peacock | L | 8,011 | 33.7 |
| | | | I. Brassington | Lab | 5,377 | 22.6 |
| | | | | | 2,392 | 10.0 |
| 1922 | 34,207 | 84.7 | A.S. Cunningham-Reid | C | 15,394 | 53.1 |
| | | | J. Gregory | Lab | 13,570 | 46.9 |
| | | | | | 1,824 | 6.2 |
| 1923 | 34,604 | 86.1 | C. Dukes | Lab | 12,984 | 43.6 |
| | | | A.S. Cunningham-Reid | C | 12,314 | 41.3 |
| | | | Dr. J.F. Crowley | L | 4,511 | 15.1 |
| | | | | | 670 | 2.3 |
| 1924 | 35,203 | 91.0 | A.S. Cunningham-Reid | C | 16,788 | 52.4 |
| | | | C. Dukes | Lab | 15,251 | 47.6 |
| | | | | | 1,537 | 4.8 |
| 1929 | 47,798 | 89.3 | C. Dukes | Lab | 21,610 | 50.6 |
| | | | N.B. Goldie | C | 18,025 | 42.2 |
| | | | Miss A.V. Garland | L | 3,070* | 7.2 |
| | | | | | 3,585 | 8.4 |
| 1931 | 49,114 | 88.5 | N.B. Goldie | C | 24,400 | 56.2 |
| | | | C. Dukes | Lab | 19,055 | 43.8 |
| | | | | | 5,345 | 12.4 |
| 1935 | 49,601 | 84.8 | N.B. Goldie | C | 21,324 | 50.7 |
| | | | E. Porter | Lab | 20,720 | 49.3 |
| | | | | | 604 | 1.4 |
| 1945 | 48,016 | 73.7 | E. Porter | Lab | 22,265 | 62.9 |
| | | | Sir N.B. Goldie | C | 13,110 | 37.1 |
| | | | | | 9,155 | 25.8 |

# WEDNESBURY [254]

| Election | Electors | T'out | Candidate | Party | Votes | % |
|----------|----------|-------|-----------|-------|-------|---|
| 1918 | 34,415 | 66.2 | A. Short | Lab | 11,341 | 49.8 |
| | | | A.W. Maconochie | Co C | 10,464 | 45.9 |
| | | | R.L.G. Simpson | L | 988* | 4.3 |
| | | | | | 877 | 3.9 |
| 1922 | 37,501 | 85.5 | A. Short | Lab | 16,087 | 50.2 |
| | | | H.G. Williams | C | 15,982 | 49.8 |
| | | | | | 105 | 0.4 |
| 1923 | 39,024 | 88.7 | A. Short | Lab | 17,810 | 51.5 |
| | | | H.G. Williams | C | 16,791 | 48.5 |
| | | | | | 1,019 | 3.0 |
| 1924 | 40,035 | 89.9 | A. Short | Lab | 18,170 | 50.5 |
| | | | B.G. Lampard-Vachell | C | 17,832 | 49.5 |
| | | | | | 338 | 1.0 |
| 1929 | 49,971 | 89.7 | A. Short | Lab | 22,420 | 50.1 |
| | | | H. Rubin | C | 17,089 | 38.1 |
| | | | J.H. Stockdale | L | 5,249* | 11.7 |
| | | | T. Gee | Ind | 61* | 0.1 |
| | | | | | 5,331 | 12.0 |
| 1931 | 51,498 | 89.0 | Viscount Ednam | C | 25,000 | 54.5 |
| | | | A. Short | Lab | 20,842 | 45.5 |
| | | | | | 4,158 | 9.0 |

[Succession to the Peerage — Earl of Dudley]

| Election | Electors | T'out | Candidate | Party | Votes | % |
|----------|----------|-------|-----------|-------|-------|---|
| 1932 (26/7) | 51,498 | 78.0 | J.W. Banfield | Lab | 21,977 | 54.7 |
| | | | R.G. Davis | C | 18,198 | 45.3 |
| | | | | | 3,779 | 9.4 |
| 1935 | 54,500 | 78.1 | J.W. Banfield | Lab | 22,683 | 53.3 |
| | | | Rev. H. Dunnico | N Lab | 19,883 | 46.7 |
| | | | | | 2,800 | 6.6 |

[Seat Vacant at Dissolution (Death)]

| Election | Electors | T'out | Candidate | Party | Votes | % |
|----------|----------|-------|-----------|-------|-------|---|
| 1945 | 57,881 | 75.8 | S.N. Evans | Lab | 29,909 | 68.2 |
| | | | S. Earl | Nat | 13,974 | 31.8 |
| | | | | | 15,935 | 36.4 |

Note:—

    1929:  Gee sought election as a 'Workers' candidate.

## WEMBLEY, NORTH  [255]

| Election | Electors | T'out | Candidate | Party | Votes | % |
|---|---|---|---|---|---|---|
| 1945 | 46,784 | 76.8 | C.R. Hobson | Lab | 15,677 | 43.6 |
| | | | P.M. Scott | C | 15,245 | 42.4 |
| | | | I.C. Baillieu | L | 5,019 | 14.0 |
| | | | | | 432 | 1.2 |

| Election | Electors | T'out | Candidate | Party | Votes | % |
|----------|----------|-------|-----------|-------|-------|---|
| 1945 | 47,213 | 74.9 | C. Barton | Lab | 16,928 | 47.9 |
| | | | B.N.H. Whiteside | C | 13,497 | 38.1 |
| | | | J.J. Over | L | 4,958 | 14.0 |
| | | | | | 3,431 | 9.8 |

# WEST BROMWICH [257]

| Election | Electors | T'out | Candidate | Party | Votes | % |
|---|---|---|---|---|---|---|
| 1918 | 32,777 | 65.4 | F.O. Roberts | Lab | 11,572 | 54.0 |
|  |  |  | †Viscount Lewisham | Co C | 9,863 | 46.0 |
|  |  |  |  |  | 1,709 | 8.0 |
| 1922 | 32,768 | 85.7 | F.O. Roberts | Lab | 14,210 | 50.6 |
|  |  |  | H.E. Parkes | C | 11,263 | 40.1 |
|  |  |  | A.J.G. Edwards | L | 2,622* | 9.3 |
|  |  |  |  |  | 2,947 | 10.5 |
| 1923 | 33,898 | 85.0 | F.O. Roberts | Lab | 12,910 | 44.8 |
|  |  |  | H.E. Parkes | C | 11,146 | 38.7 |
|  |  |  | A.J.G. Edwards | L | 4,749 | 16.5 |
|  |  |  |  |  | 1,764 | 6.1 |
| 1924 | 34,503 | 86.4 | Rt. Hon. F.O. Roberts | Lab | 15,384 | 51.6 |
|  |  |  | H.A.R. Graham | C | 14,413 | 48.4 |
|  |  |  |  |  | 971 | 3.2 |
| 1929 | 45,371 | 83.1 | Rt. Hon. F.O. Roberts | Lab | 19,621 | 52.1 |
|  |  |  | J.I. Chesshire | C | 10,943 | 29.0 |
|  |  |  | W. Ramage | L | 7,119 | 18.9 |
|  |  |  |  |  | 8,678 | 23.1 |
| 1931 | 47,492 | 81.7 | A. Ramsay | C | 17,729 | 45.7 |
|  |  |  | Rt. Hon. F.O. Roberts | Lab | 17,204 | 44.4 |
|  |  |  | W. Ramage | L | 3,851* | 9.9 |
|  |  |  |  |  | 525 | 1.3 |
| 1935 | 49,848 | 74.8 | Rt. Hon. F.O. Roberts | Lab | 19,113 | 51.3 |
|  |  |  | R. Ashton | C | 18,175 | 48.7 |
|  |  |  |  |  | 938 | 2.6 |
| [Resignation] |  |  |  |  |  |  |
| 1941 (16/4) |  |  | J. Dugdale | Lab | Unopp. |  |
| 1945 | 55,145 | 72.5 | J. Dugdale | Lab | 27,979 | 69.9 |
|  |  |  | G.D.N. Nabarro | C | 12,028 | 30.1 |
|  |  |  |  |  | 15,951 | 39.8 |

# WEST HAM, PLAISTOW  [258]

| Election | Electors | T'out | Candidate | Party | Votes | % |
|---|---|---|---|---|---|---|
| 1918 | 33,890 | 37.8 | †W.J. Thorne | Lab | 12,156 | 94.9 |
| | | | A. Lupton | Ind L | 657* | 5.1 |
| | | | | | 11,499 | 89.8 |
| 1922 | 35,602 | 54.7 | W.J. Thorne | Lab | 12,321 | 63.3 |
| | | | F.G. Penny | C | 7,140 | 36.7 |
| | | | | | 5,181 | 26.6 |
| 1923 | 36,628 | 49.9 | W.J. Thorne | Lab | 13,638 | 74.6 |
| | | | F.G. Penny | C | 4,643 | 25.4 |
| | | | | | 8,995 | 49.2 |
| 1924 | 37,441 | 62.1 | W.J. Thorne | Lab | 15,609 | 67.1 |
| | | | F.G. Penny | C | 7,638 | 32.9 |
| | | | | | 7,971 | 34.2 |
| 1929 | 48,232 | 63.2 | W.J. Thorne | Lab | 23,635 | 77.5 |
| | | | S.M. Lancaster | C | 6,851 | 22.5 |
| | | | | | 16,784 | 55.0 |
| 1931 | | | W.J. Thorne | Lab | Unopp. | |
| 1935 | 47,495 | 53.1 | W.J. Thorne | Lab | 18,493 | 73.3 |
| | | | Miss M.D. Roddick | C | 6,730 | 26.7 |
| | | | | | 11,763 | 46.6 |
| 1945 | 28,974 | 68.4 | F.E. Jones | Lab | 17,351 | 87.6 |
| | | | J.B. Raper | C | 2,463* | 12.4 |
| | | | | | 14,888 | 75.2 |

| Election | Electors | T'out | Candidate | Party | Votes | % |
|----------|----------|-------|-----------|-------|-------|---|
| 1918 | 31,943 | 42.3 | J.J. Jones | NSP (Lab) | 6,971 | 51.6 |
| | | | T.W.C. Carthew | Co C | 4,259 | 31.5 |
| | | | D.J. Davis | Lab | 2,278 | 16.9 |
| | | | | | 2,712 | 20.1 |
| 1922 | 33,111 | 49.0 | J.J. Jones | Lab | 11,874 | 73.1 |
| | | | C.G. Lewis | C | 4,361 | 26.9 |
| | | | | | 7,513 | 46.2 |
| 1923 | 34,261 | 45.9 | J.J. Jones | Lab | 12,777 | 81.3 |
| | | | C.G. Lewis | C | 2,948 | 18.7 |
| | | | | | 9,829 | 62.6 |
| 1924 | 35,087 | 56.1 | J.J. Jones | Lab | 15,962 | 81.1 |
| | | | E. Doran | C | 3,732 | 18.9 |
| | | | | | 12,230 | 62.2 |
| 1929 | 45,080 | 60.7 | J.J. Jones | Lab | 23,451 | 85.7 |
| | | | L.W.B. Teeling | C | 3,903 | 14.3 |
| | | | | | 19,548 | 71.4 |
| 1931 | 44,632 | 67.1 | J.J. Jones | Lab | 19,851 | 77.8 |
| | | | Mrs. E.E.F. Tennant | C | 5,654 | 22.2 |
| | | | | | 14,197 | 55.6 |
| 1935 | 42,078 | 53.4 | J.J. Jones | Lab | 18,177 | 81.0 |
| | | | Mrs. E.E.F. Tennant | C | 4,276 | 19.0 |
| | | | | | 13,901 | 62.0 |
| [Resignation] | | | | | | |
| 1940 (22/2) | 38,575 | 40.1 | J.H. Hollins | Lab | 14,343 | 92.8 |
| | | | H. Pollitt | Com | 966* | 6.2 |
| | | | T.P. Moran | BUF | 151* | 1.0 |
| | | | | | 13,377 | 86.6 |
| 1945 | 15,591 | 65.8 | Dr. L. Comyns | Lab | 9,358 | 91.3 |
| | | | E. Elverston | C | 494* | 4.8 |
| | | | A.W. Davies | Ind | 401* | 3.9 |
| | | | | | 8,864 | 86.5 |

Note:—

1922: Lewis sought election as 'Labour in the Conservative interest'. He was however an official Conservative candidate and has been designated as such despite the rather curious 'label' he used at the time. He was the nominee of local Conservative working men's clubs.

| Election | Electors | T'out | Candidate | Party | Votes | % |
|---|---|---|---|---|---|---|
| 1918 | 31,458 | 42.3 | C.E.L. Lyle | Co C | 8,498 | 63.8 |
| | | | Rt. Hon. C.F.G. Masterman | L | 4,821 | 36.2 |
| | | | | | 3,677 | 27.6 |
| 1922 | 32,930 | 64.9 | T.E. Groves | Lab | 10,017 | 46.8 |
| | | | C.E.L. Lyle | C | 8,641 | 40.5 |
| | | | A.H. Scott | L | 2,704 | 12.7 |
| | | | | | 1,376 | 6.3 |
| 1923 | 33,664 | 61.8 | T.E. Groves | Lab | 11,466 | 55.1 |
| | | | F.V. Fisher | C | 5,443 | 26.2 |
| | | | W. Crow | L | 3,888 | 18.7 |
| | | | | | 6,023 | 28.9 |
| 1924 | 34,293 | 69.0 | T.E. Groves | Lab | 13,264 | 56.0 |
| | | | H.H. Balfour | C | 10,414 | 44.0 |
| | | | | | 2,850 | 12.0 |
| 1929 | 43,134 | 66.0 | T.E. Groves | Lab | 16,665 | 58.5 |
| | | | H.A. Procter | C | 8,018 | 28.2 |
| | | | A.C. Crane | L | 3,779 | 13.3 |
| | | | | | 8,647 | 30.3 |
| 1931 | 42,815 | 64.6 | T.E. Groves | Lab | 13,925 | 50.4 |
| | | | C.G. Wodehouse-Temple | C | 13,722 | 49.6 |
| | | | | | 203 | 0.8 |
| 1935 | 40,042 | 57.1 | T.E. Groves | Lab | 14,427 | 63.1 |
| | | | F.H.G.H. Goodhart | C | 8,452 | 36.9 |
| | | | | | 5,975 | 26.2 |
| 1945 | 25,295 | 60.9 | H.R. Nicholls | Lab | 11,484 | 74.6 |
| | | | R.M. Prior | C | 3,162 | 20.5 |
| | | | T.E. Groves | Ind | 749* | 4.9 |
| | | | | | 8,322 | 54.1 |

Note:—

1945: Groves had indicated his willingness to contest the General Election of 1945 but his name was not submitted to the Labour Party selection conference which, in December 1944, chose Nicholls as their prospective candidate.

Subsequently Groves announced that his son would contest the seat as an Independent but shortly before nomination day his son withdrew and Groves decided to seek re-election. The local Labour Party immediately expelled him.

| Election | Electors | T'out | Candidate | Party | Votes | % |
|---|---|---|---|---|---|---|
| 1918 | 30,752 | 46.8 | Sir E.E. Wild | Co C | 8,813 | 61.2 |
| | | | B.W. Gardner | Lab | 3,186 | 22.2 |
| | | | J.C. Nicholson | L | 2,380 | 16.6 |
| | | | | | 5,627 | 39.0 |
| 1922 | 31,913 | 69.4 | H.D.R. Margesson | C | 10,196 | 46.0 |
| | | | B.W. Gardner | Lab | 7,268 | 32.8 |
| | | | J.C. Nicholson | L | 4,692 | 21.2 |
| | | | | | 2,928 | 13.2 |
| 1923 | 32,756 | 67.2 | B.W. Gardner | Lab | 8,656 | 39.3 |
| | | | H.D.R. Margesson | C | 7,630 | 34.7 |
| | | | J.C. Carroll | L | 5,710 | 26.0 |
| | | | | | 1,026 | 4.6 |
| 1924 | 33,244 | 74.8 | H.P. Holt | C | 13,410 | 54.0 |
| | | | B.W. Gardner | Lab | 11,443 | 46.0 |
| | | | | | 1,967 | 8.0 |
| 1929 | 42,346 | 70.8 | B.W. Gardner | Lab | 14,703 | 49.0 |
| | | | M. Morgan | C | 9,681 | 32.3 |
| | | | W.J. Austin | L | 5,607 | 18.7 |
| | | | | | 5,022 | 16.7 |
| 1931 | 42,624 | 70.4 | A.J. Chotzner | C | 17,561 | 58.5 |
| | | | B.W. Gardner | Lab | 12,453 | 41.5 |
| | | | | | 5,108 | 17.0 |
| [Resignation] | | | | | | |
| 1934 (14/5) | 42,129 | 50.5 | B.W. Gardner | Lab | 11,998 | 56.4 |
| | | | J.R.J. Macnamara | C | 8,534 | 40.1 |
| | | | A.F. Brockway | ILP | 748* | 3.5 |
| | | | | | 3,464 | 16.3 |
| 1935 | 40,979 | 62.7 | B.W. Gardner | Lab | 13,685 | 53.2 |
| | | | S.R. Benson | C | 12,020 | 46.8 |
| | | | | | 1,665 | 6.4 |
| 1945 | 28,438 | 67.4 | A.W.J. Lewis | Lab | 14,281 | 74.5 |
| | | | C.K. Collins | C | 4,885 | 25.5 |
| | | | | | 9,396 | 49.0 |

# WIGAN [262]

| Election | Electors | T'out | Candidate | Party | Votes | % |
|---|---|---|---|---|---|---|
| 1918 | 38,811 | 69.4 | J.A. Parkinson | Lab | 12,914 | 48.0 |
| | | | †R.J.N. Neville | Co C | 11,584 | 43.0 |
| | | | R. Alstead | L | 2,434* | 9.0 |
| | | | | | 1,330 | 5.0 |
| 1922 | 39,929 | 88.9 | J.A. Parkinson | Lab | 20,079 | 56.5 |
| | | | A.E. Baucher | C | 15,436 | 43.5 |
| | | | | | 4,643 | 13.0 |
| 1923 | 40,105 | 85.0 | J.A. Parkinson | Lab | 19,637 | 57.6 |
| | | | Lord Balniel | C | 14,451 | 42.4 |
| | | | | | 5,186 | 15.2 |
| 1924 | 40,217 | 87.9 | J.A. Parkinson | Lab | 20,350 | 57.6 |
| | | | D.P.M. Fyfe | C | 15,006 | 42.4 |
| | | | | | 5,344 | 15.2 |
| 1929 | 54,008 | 86.9 | J.A. Parkinson | Lab | 27,462 | 58.5 |
| | | | E. Barlow | C | 18,144 | 38.7 |
| | | | F. Bright | Com | 1,307* | 2.8 |
| | | | | | 9,318 | 19.8 |
| 1931 | 54,689 | 84.2 | J.A. Parkinson | Lab | 23,544 | 51.1 |
| | | | G.D. Roberts | C | 22,526 | 48.9 |
| | | | | | 1,018 | 2.2 |
| 1935 | 55,784 | 81.7 | J.A. Parkinson | Lab | 27,950 | 61.3 |
| | | | R.G. Grant-Ferris | C | 17,646 | 38.7 |
| | | | | | 10,304 | 22.6 |
| [Death] | | | | | | |
| 1942 (11/3) | | | W. Foster | Lab | Unopp. | |
| 1945 | 57,281 | 80.4 | W. Foster | Lab | 31,392 | 68.2 |
| | | | E.C.L. Hulbert-Powell | C | 14,666 | 31.8 |
| | | | | | 16,726 | 36.4 |
| [Death] | | | | | | |
| 1948 (4/3) | 60,184 | 81.4 | R.W. Williams | Lab | 28,941 | 59.0 |
| | | | H. Dowling | C | 17,466 | 35.7 |
| | | | T. Rowlandson | Com | 1,647* | 3.4 |
| | | | O.L. Roberts | Ind | 932* | 1.9 |
| | | | | | 11,475 | 23.3 |

Note:—

1948: Roberts sought election as a 'King's Cavalier' candidate.

| Election | Electors | T'out | Candidate | Party | Votes | % |
|---|---|---|---|---|---|---|
| 1918 | 38,801 | 50.9 | †H.M. Mallaby-Deeley | Co C | 12,044 | 61.0 |
| | | | H.J. Lincoln | Lab | 4,941 | 25.0 |
| | | | H.J. Doree | L | 2,757 | 14.0 |
| | | | | | 7,103 | 36.0 |
| 1922 | 40,661 | 58.4 | Sir H.M. Mallaby-Deeley, Bt. | C | 12,525 | 52.8 |
| | | | H. Johnstone | L | 11,211 | 47.2 |
| | | | | | 1,314 | 5.6 |
| [Resignation] | | | | | | |
| 1923 (3/3) | 40,661 | 60.2 | H. Johnstone | L | 14,824 | 60.6 |
| | | | Hon. G.F. Stanley | C | 9,648 | 39.4 |
| | | | | | 5,176 | 21.2 |
| 1923 | 40,797 | 68.1 | H. Johnstone | L | 11,260 | 40.5 |
| | | | Hon. G.F. Stanley | C | 11,146 | 40.1 |
| | | | J.G. Butler | Lab | 5,392 | 19.4 |
| | | | | | 114 | 0.4 |
| 1924 | 41,870 | 76.0 | Hon. G.F. Stanley | C | 15,965 | 50.2 |
| | | | H. Johnstone | L | 7,992 | 25.1 |
| | | | W.D. Lloyd | Lab | 7,860 | 24.7 |
| | | | | | 7,973 | 25.1 |
| [Seat Vacant at Dissolution (Resignation on appointment as Governor of Madras)] | | | | | | |
| 1929 | 60,942 | 69.3 | D.G. Somerville | C | 17,090 | 40.4 |
| | | | W.D. Lloyd | Lab | 13,977 | 33.1 |
| | | | M.G. Liverman | L | 11,190 | 26.5 |
| | | | | | 3,113 | 7.3 |
| 1931 | 68,352 | 68.3 | D.G. Somerville | C | 28,993 | 62.1 |
| | | | W.D. Lloyd | Lab | 10,010 | 21.4 |
| | | | Dr. J.S. Bridges | L | 7,684 | 16.5 |
| | | | | | 18,983 | 40.7 |
| 1935 | 71,562 | 62.0 | D.G. Somerville | C | 25,613 | 57.7 |
| | | | M. Orbach | Lab | 15,523 | 35.0 |
| | | | Miss N.S. Parnell | L | 3,217* | 7.3 |
| | | | | | 10,090 | 22.7 |
| [Death] | | | | | | |
| 1938 (28/7) | 72,008 | 39.3 | S.S. Hammersley | C | 16,009 | 56.6 |
| | | | M. Orbach | Lab | 12,278 | 43.4 |
| | | | | | 3,731 | 13.2 |
| 1945 | 61,001* | 72.5 | M. Orbach | Lab | 23,457 | 53.0 |
| | | | S.S. Hammersley | C | 14,027 | 31.7 |
| | | | R.L.R. Morgan | L | 6,771 | 15.3 |
| | | | | | 9,430 | 21.3 |

Note:—

1923: Stanley was Under-Secretary of State for the Home Department. He subsequently
(3/3)   resigned.

| Election | Electors | T'out | Candidate | Party | Votes | % |
|---|---|---|---|---|---|---|
| 1918 | 36,449 | 53.3 | C. Pinkham | Co C | 10,503 | 54.1 |
| | | | S.P. Viant | Lab | 7,217 | 37.2 |
| | | | Dr. J.S. Crone | L | 1,697* | 8.7 |
| | | | | | 3,286 | 16.9 |
| 1922 | 38,787 | 66.7 | G.J. Furness | C | 13,328 | 51.5 |
| | | | S.P. Viant | Lab | 12,529 | 48.5 |
| | | | | | 799 | 3.0 |
| 1923 | 39,493 | 69.1 | S.P. Viant | Lab | 14,004 | 51.3 |
| | | | G.J. Furness | C | 8,256 | 30.3 |
| | | | D.C. Thomson | L | 5,030 | 18.4 |
| | | | | | 5,748 | 21.0 |
| 1924 | 40,562 | 77.6 | S.P. Viant | Lab | 14,884 | 47.3 |
| | | | M. Brice | C | 13,539 | 43.0 |
| | | | J. McCulloch | L | 3,061* | 9.7 |
| | | | | | 1,345 | 4.3 |
| 1929 | 53,702 | 73.4 | S.P. Viant | Lab | 20,583 | 52.3 |
| | | | M.S. McCorquodale | C | 12,779 | 32.4 |
| | | | A.L. Leighton | L | 6,038 | 15.3 |
| | | | | | 7,804 | 19.9 |
| 1931 | 55,058 | 71.7 | Mrs. M.C. Tate | C | 23,910 | 60.6 |
| | | | S.P. Viant | Lab | 15,550 | 39.4 |
| | | | | | 8,360 | 21.2 |
| 1935 | 55,811 | 64.3 | S.P. Viant | Lab | 19,402 | 54.1 |
| | | | S. Samuel | C | 16,472 | 45.9 |
| | | | | | 2,930 | 8.2 |
| 1945 | 52,213* | 70.5 | S.P. Viant | Lab | 26,566 | 72.2 |
| | | | J.B. Cartland | C | 10,236 | 27.8 |
| | | | | | 16,330 | 44.4 |

| Election | Electors | T'out | Candidate | Party | Votes | % |
|----------|----------|-------|-----------|-------|-------|---|
| 1918 | 36,258 | 46.1 | J. Hood | Co C | 13,652 | 81.6 |
|  |  |  | G.M. Edwardes Jones | Ind | 3,079 | 18.4 |
|  |  |  |  |  | 10,573 | 63.2 |
| 1922 | 37,677 | 62.0 | Sir J. Hood, Bt. | C | 16,751 | 71.7 |
|  |  |  | Dr. R.O. Moon | L | 6,627 | 28.3 |
|  |  |  |  |  | 10,124 | 43.4 |
| 1923 | 38,793 | 57.3 | Sir J. Hood, Bt. | C | 15,495 | 69.8 |
|  |  |  | M. Starr | Lab | 6,717 | 30.2 |
|  |  |  |  |  | 8,778 | 39.6 |
| 1924 | 39,604 | 72.2 | Sir J.C. Power, Bt. | C | 21,209 | 74.2 |
|  |  |  | M. Starr | Lab | 7,386 | 25.8 |
|  |  |  |  |  | 13,823 | 48.4 |
| 1929 | 59,654 | 68.8 | Sir J.C. Power, Bt. | C | 21,902 | 53.4 |
|  |  |  | T. Braddock | Lab | 9,924 | 24.2 |
|  |  |  | A. Peters | L | 9,202 | 22.4 |
|  |  |  |  |  | 11,978 | 29.2 |
| 1931 | 69,508 | 71.0 | Sir J.C. Power, Bt. | C | 39,643 | 80.4 |
|  |  |  | T. Braddock | Lab | 9,674 | 19.6 |
|  |  |  |  |  | 29,969 | 60.8 |
| 1935 | 80,283 | 67.6 | Sir J.C. Power, Bt. | C | 36,816 | 67.8 |
|  |  |  | T. Braddock | Lab | 17,452 | 32.2 |
|  |  |  |  |  | 19,364 | 35.6 |
| 1945 | 89,469* | 76.0 | A.M.F. Palmer | Lab | 30,188 | 44.4 |
|  |  |  | G.P. Hardy-Roberts | C | 28,820 | 42.4 |
|  |  |  | A.D. Kay | L | 6,501* | 9.6 |
|  |  |  | K.E. Horne | CW | 2,472* | 3.6 |
|  |  |  |  |  | 1,368 | 2.0 |

| Election | Electors | T'out | Candidate | Party | Votes | % |
|----------|----------|-------|-----------|-------|-------|---|
| 1918 | 28,504 | 59.9 | †T.E. Hickman | Co C | 10,343 | 60.5 |
| | | | J.W. Kynaston | Lab | 6,744 | 39.5 |
| | | | | | 3,599 | 21.0 |
| 1922 | 30,752 | 73.8 | C.K. Howard-Bury | C | 12,297 | 54.2 |
| | | | J. Baker | Lab | 10,392 | 45.8 |
| | | | | | 1,905 | 8.4 |
| 1923 | 32,670 | 74.9 | C.K. Howard-Bury | C | 10,186 | 41.6 |
| | | | J. Baker | Lab | 9,085 | 37.1 |
| | | | J. Prentice | L | 5,205 | 21.3 |
| | | | | | 1,101 | 4.5 |
| 1924 | 33,444 | 82.0 | J. Baker | Lab | 14,583 | 53.2 |
| | | | C.K. Howard-Bury | C | 12,840 | 46.8 |
| | | | | | 1,743 | 6.4 |
| 1929 | 43,093 | 85.4 | J. Baker | Lab | 18,679 | 50.7 |
| | | | S.J. Thompson | C | 13,635 | 37.1 |
| | | | G. Salter | L | 4,475* | 12.2 |
| | | | | | 5,044 | 13.6 |
| 1931 | 46,045 | 81.4 | G.K. Peto | C | 20,620 | 55.0 |
| | | | J. Baker | Lab | 16,847 | 45.0 |
| | | | | | 3,773 | 10.0 |
| 1935 | 51,528 | 70.9 | I.C. Hannah | C | 18,689 | 51.2 |
| | | | D.L. Mort | Lab | 17,820 | 48.8 |
| | | | | | 869 | 2.4 |
| [Death] | | | | | | |
| 1944 | 58,423 | 32.6 | W.E. Gibbons | C | 9,693 | 50.9 |
| (20/9) | | | A. Eaton | ILP | 9,344 | 49.1 |
| | | | | | 349 | 1.8 |
| 1945 | 64,436 | 73.0 | W. Nally | Lab/Co-op | 31,493 | 67.0 |
| | | | W.E. Gibbons | C | 14,691 | 31.2 |
| | | | A. Eaton | ILP | 849* | 1.8 |
| | | | | | 16,802 | 35.8 |

# WOLVERHAMPTON, EAST [267]

| Election | Electors | T'out | Candidate | Party | Votes | % |
|----------|----------|-------|-----------|-------|-------|---|
| 1918 | 30,437 | 48.6 | †G.R. Thorne | L | 7,660 | 51.8 |
| | | | Rev. J.A. Shaw | Co NDP | 7,138 | 48.2 |
| | | | | | 522 | 3.6 |
| 1922 | 31,381 | 80.4 | G.R. Thorne | L | 11,577 | 45.9 |
| | | | C.H. Pinson | C | 9,410 | 37.3 |
| | | | W.T.A. Foot | Lab | 3,076* | 12.2 |
| | | | Rev. J.A. Shaw | NL | 1,169* | 4.6 |
| | | | | | 2,167 | 8.6 |
| 1923 | | | G.R. Thorne | L | Unopp. | |
| 1924 | 32,602 | 80.6 | G.R. Thorne | L | 11,066 | 42.1 |
| | | | Sir T.J. Strangman | C | 10,013 | 38.1 |
| | | | D.R. Williams | Lab | 5,188 | 19.8 |
| | | | | | 1,053 | 4.0 |
| 1929 | 42,222 | 81.5 | G. Le M. Mander | L | 15,391 | 44.8 |
| | | | P.G.T. Buchan-Hepburn | C | 10,163 | 29.5 |
| | | | D.R. Williams | Lab | 8,840 | 25.7 |
| | | | | | 5,228 | 15.3 |
| 1931 | 43,162 | 78.6 | G. Le M. Mander | L | 14,945 | 44.1 |
| | | | A.T. Waters-Taylor | C | 12,628 | 37.2 |
| | | | J. Smith | Lab | 6,340 | 18.7 |
| | | | | | 2,317 | 6.9 |
| 1935 | 44,817 | 73.3 | G. Le M. Mander | L | 15,935 | 48.5 |
| | | | J.L. Brockhouse | C | 11,935 | 36.3 |
| | | | H.E. Lane | Lab | 4,985 | 15.2 |
| | | | | | 4,000 | 12.2 |
| 1945 | 50,825 | 73.3 | J. Baird | Lab | 17,763 | 47.7 |
| | | | Sir G. Le M. Mander | L | 11,206 | 30.1 |
| | | | W.F.C. Garthwaite | C | 8,266 | 22.2 |
| | | | | | 6,557 | 17.6 |

# WOLVERHAMPTON, WEST [268]

| Election | Electors | T'out | Candidate | Party | Votes | % |
|---|---|---|---|---|---|---|
| 1918 | 37,097 | 63.3 | †A.F. Bird | Co C | 13,329 | 56.8 |
| | | | A.G. Walkden | Lab | 10,158 | 43.2 |
| | | | | | 3,171 | 13.6 |
| [Death] | | | | | | |
| 1922 | 38,216 | 80.0 | Sir R.B. Bird, Bt. | Co C | 16,790 | 54.9 |
| (7/3) | | | A.G. Walkden | Lab | 13,799 | 45.1 |
| | | | | | 2,991 | 9.8 |
| 1922 | 39,449 | 83.5 | Sir R.B. Bird, Bt. | C | 17,738 | 53.9 |
| | | | A.G. Walkden | Lab | 15,190 | 46.1 |
| | | | | | 2,548 | 7.8 |
| 1923 | 39,941 | 79.5 | Sir R.B. Bird, Bt. | C | 15,990 | 50.4 |
| | | | W.J. Brown | Lab | 15,749 | 49.6 |
| | | | | | 241 | 0.8 |
| 1924 | 40,677 | 85.9 | Sir R.B. Bird, Bt. | C | 17,886 | 51.2 |
| | | | W.J. Brown | Lab | 17,046 | 48.8 |
| | | | | | 840 | 2.4 |
| 1929 | 51,061 | 84.1 | W.J. Brown | Lab (Ind Lab) | 21,103 | 49.1 |
| | | | Sir R.B. Bird, Bt. | C | 17,237 | 40.2 |
| | | | G.H. Roberts | L | 4,580* | 10.7 |
| | | | | | 3,866 | 8.9 |
| 1931 | 51,355 | 84.3 | Sir R.B. Bird, Bt. | C | 26,181 | 60.5 |
| | | | W.J. Brown | Ind Lab | 17,090 | 39.5 |
| | | | | | 9,091 | 21.0 |
| 1935 | 49,537 | 72.4 | Sir R.B. Bird, Bt. | C | 19,697 | 54.9 |
| | | | W.J. Brown | Ind Lab | 14,867 | 41.4 |
| | | | Rev. R. Lee | Lab | 1,325* | 3.7 |
| | | | | | 4,830 | 13.5 |
| 1945 | 47,297 | 74.8 | H.D. Hughes | Lab | 21,186 | 59.9 |
| | | | J. Beattie | C | 14,176 | 40.1 |
| | | | | | 7,010 | 19.8 |

# WOODFORD   [269]

| Election | Electors | T'out | Candidate | Party | Votes | % |
|---|---|---|---|---|---|---|
| 1945 | 58,256 | 65.5 | Rt. Hon. W.L.S. Churchill | C | 27,688 | 72.5 |
| | | | A. Hancock | Ind | 10,488 | 27.5 |
| | | | | | 17,200 | 45.0 |

# WORCESTER [270]

| Election | Electors | T'out | Candidate | Party | Votes | % |
|---|---|---|---|---|---|---|
| 1918 | 22,667 | 62.3 | †Rt. Hon. Sir E.A. Goulding, Bt. | Co C | 9,243 | 65.4 |
| | | | R.R. Fairbairn | L | 4,889 | 34.6 |
| | | | | | 4,354 | 30.8 |
| | | | | | | |
| 1922 | 23,694 | 82.4 | R.R. Fairbairn | L | 10,143 | 52.0 |
| | | | Hon. H. Lygon | C | 9,370 | 48.0 |
| | | | | | 773 | 4.0 |
| | | | | | | |
| 1923 | 25,094 | 85.8 | W.P.C. Greene | C | 10,971 | 50.9 |
| | | | R.R. Fairbairn | L | 9,743 | 45.3 |
| | | | P. Williams | Lab | 815* | 3.8 |
| | | | | | 1,228 | 5.6 |
| | | | | | | |
| 1924 | 25,617 | 83.4 | W.P.C. Greene | C | 11,956 | 56.0 |
| | | | R.R. Fairbairn | L | 6,139 | 28.7 |
| | | | P. Williams | Lab | 3,272 | 15.3 |
| | | | | | 5,817 | 27.3 |
| | | | | | | |
| 1929 | 32,764 | 85.4 | W.P.C. Greene | C | 13,182 | 47.2 |
| | | | K.M. Lindsay | Lab | 8,208 | 29.3 |
| | | | R.R. Fairbairn | L | 6,588 | 23.5 |
| | | | | | 4,974 | 17.9 |
| | | | | | | |
| 1931 | 33,674 | 79.7 | W.P.C. Greene | C | 16,357 | 61.0 |
| | | | R.R. Fairbairn | L | 6,611 | 24.6 |
| | | | H. Bolton | Lab | 3,874 | 14.4 |
| | | | | | 9,746 | 36.4 |
| | | | | | | |
| 1935 | 34,441 | 76.8 | W.P.C. Greene | C | 13,398 | 50.7 |
| | | | R.R. Fairbairn | L | 6,885 | 26.0 |
| | | | J. Ferguson | Lab | 6,152 | 23.3 |
| | | | | | 6,513 | 24.7 |
| | | | | | | |
| 1945 | 41,523 | 75.9 | Hon. G.R. Ward | C | 13,523 | 42.9 |
| | | | J. Evans | Lab/Co-op | 13,519 | 42.9 |
| | | | R.J. Bowker | L | 4,459 | 14.2 |
| | | | | | 4 | 0.0 |

| Election | Electors | T'out | Candidate | Party | Votes | % |
|---|---|---|---|---|---|---|
| 1918 | 38,340 | 69.0 | †Sir J.G. Butcher, Bt. | Co C | 16,269 | 61.5 |
| | | | †A.S. Rowntree | L | 5,363 | 20.3 |
| | | | T.H. Gill | Lab | 4,822 | 18.2 |
| | | | | | 10,906 | 41.2 |
| 1922 | 39,732 | 85.8 | Sir J.G. Butcher, Bt. | C | 15,163 | 44.5 |
| | | | T.H. Gill | Lab | 10,106 | 29.6 |
| | | | G.E. Dodds | L | 8,838 | 25.9 |
| | | | | | 5,057 | 14.9 |
| 1923 | 41,082 | 82.8 | J.A.R. Marriott | C | 14,772 | 43.4 |
| | | | J. King | Lab | 11,626 | 34.2 |
| | | | G.E. Dodds | L | 7,638 | 22.4 |
| | | | | | 3,146 | 9.2 |
| 1924 | 41,775 | 84.8 | Sir J.A.R. Marriott | C | 19,914 | 56.2 |
| | | | D. Adams | Lab | 15,500 | 43.8 |
| | | | | | 4,414 | 12.4 |
| 1929 | 53,989 | 85.1 | F.G. Burgess | Lab | 20,663 | 45.0 |
| | | | Sir J.A.R. Marriott | C | 17,363 | 37.8 |
| | | | D. Crockatt | L | 7,907 | 17.2 |
| | | | | | 3,300 | 7.2 |
| 1931 | 54,112 | 86.0 | L.R. Lumley | C | 30,216 | 64.9 |
| | | | F.G. Burgess | Lab | 16,310 | 35.1 |
| | | | | | 13,906 | 29.8 |
| 1935 | 54,074 | 82.5 | L.R. Lumley | C | 25,442 | 57.0 |
| | | | R.B. Fraser | Lab | 19,168 | 43.0 |
| | | | | | 6,274 | 14.0 |

[Resignation on appointment as Governor of Bombay]

| Election | Electors | T'out | Candidate | Party | Votes | % |
|---|---|---|---|---|---|---|
| 1937 (6/5) | 53,935 | 74.2 | Hon. C.I.C. Wood | C | 22,045 | 55.1 |
| | | | J. Dugdale | Lab | 17,986 | 44.9 |
| | | | | | 4,059 | 10.2 |
| 1945 | 57,956 | 76.2 | Dr. J. Corlett | Lab | 22,021 | 49.9 |
| | | | Lord Irwin | C | 17,949 | 40.6 |
| | | | G.H. Keighley-Bell | L | 4,208* | 9.5 |
| | | | | | 4,072 | 9.3 |

Note:—

1937:  Wood became Lord Irwin in 1944 on his father receiving an Earldom.

# ENGLAND —— COUNTIES

| Election | Electors | T'out | Candidate | Party | Votes | % |
|---|---|---|---|---|---|---|
| 1918 | 33,257 | 45.2 | †F.G. Kellaway | Co L | 10,933 | 72.7 |
| | | | H. Burridge | Ind | 4,096 | 27.3 |
| | | | | | 6,837 | 45.4 |

[Appointed Postmaster-General]

| Election | Electors | T'out | Candidate | Party | Votes | % |
|---|---|---|---|---|---|---|
| 1921 | 32,912 | 73.3 | Rt. Hon. F.G. Kellaway | Co L | 14,397 | 59.7 |
| (23/4) | | | F.F. Riley | Lab | 9,731 | 40.3 |
| | | | | | 4,666 | 19.4 |
| 1922 | 33,792 | 79.1 | S.R. Wells | C | 13,460 | 50.3 |
| | | | Rt. Hon. F.G. Kellaway | NL | 5,714 | 21.4 |
| | | | A. Sells | Lab | 5,477 | 20.5 |
| | | | Lady Lawson | L | 2,075* | 7.8 |
| | | | | | 7,746 | 28.9 |
| 1923 | 34,492 | 73.5 | S.R. Wells | C | 12,906 | 50.9 |
| | | | M. Gray | L | 12,449 | 49.1 |
| | | | | | 457 | 1.8 |
| 1924 | 35,227 | 81.7 | S.R. Wells | C | 15,000 | 52.1 |
| | | | M. Gray | L | 8,451 | 29.4 |
| | | | G. Dixon | Lab | 5,330 | 18.5 |
| | | | | | 6,549 | 22.7 |
| 1929 | 45,990 | 79.1 | S.R. Wells | C | 16,724 | 46.0 |
| | | | A.G.F. Machin | L | 10,520 | 28.9 |
| | | | G. Dixon | Lab | 9,147 | 25.1 |
| | | | | | 6,204 | 17.1 |
| 1931 | 47,352 | 73.2 | S.R. Wells | C | 25,030 | 72.2 |
| | | | Lady Clare Annesley | Lab | 9,654 | 27.8 |
| | | | | | 15,376 | 44.4 |
| 1935 | 49,370 | 73.1 | S.R. Wells | C | 22,476 | 62.3 |
| | | | N. Mickle | Lab | 13,604 | 37.7 |
| | | | | | 8,872 | 24.6 |
| 1945 | 65,262 | 72.9 | T.C. Skeffington-Lodge | Lab | 19,849 | 41.7 |
| | | | Sir S.R. Wells, Bt. | C | 19,561 | 41.1 |
| | | | L.J. Humphrey | L | 8,183 | 17.2 |
| | | | | | 288 | 0.6 |

# BEDFORDSHIRE, LUTON  [273]

| Election | Electors | T'out | Candidate | Party | Votes | % |
|---|---|---|---|---|---|---|
| 1918 | 37,051 | 52.5 | †C.B. Harmsworth | Co L | 13,501 | 69.4 |
|  |  |  | W. Ball | Lab | 5,964 | 30.6 |
|  |  |  |  |  | 7,537 | 38.8 |
| 1922 | 37,730 | 81.0 | Sir J.P. Hewett | C | 13,301 | 43.5 |
|  |  |  | H. Arnold | L | 10,137 | 33.2 |
|  |  |  | P. Alden | Lab | 7,107 | 23.3 |
|  |  |  |  |  | 3,164 | 10.3 |
| 1923 | 38,799 | 78.1 | Hon. G.W.A. Howard | L | 15,569 | 51.4 |
|  |  |  | Sir J.P. Hewett | C | 11,738 | 38.7 |
|  |  |  | W. Ball | Lab | 2,998* | 9.9 |
|  |  |  |  |  | 3,831 | 12.7 |
| 1924 | 39,701 | 82.6 | T.J. O'Connor | C | 15,443 | 47.1 |
|  |  |  | Hon. G.W.A. Howard | L | 11,495 | 35.1 |
|  |  |  | P.L. Millwood | Lab | 5,850 | 17.8 |
|  |  |  |  |  | 3,948 | 12.0 |
| 1929 | 54,661 | 81.5 | E.L. Burgin | L (NL) | 20,248 | 45.5 |
|  |  |  | T.J. O'Connor | C | 16,930 | 38.0 |
|  |  |  | Mrs. F.N.H. Bell | Lab | 7,351 | 16.5 |
|  |  |  |  |  | 3,318 | 7.5 |
| 1931 | 58,880 | 67.8 | E.L. Burgin | NL | 32,015 | 80.2 |
|  |  |  | J.H. MacDonnell | Lab | 7,897 | 19.8 |
|  |  |  |  |  | 24,118 | 60.4 |
| 1935 | 69,548 | 63.3 | E.L. Burgin | NL | 28,809 | 65.5 |
|  |  |  | F.L. Kerran | Lab | 15,181 | 34.5 |
|  |  |  |  |  | 13,628 | 31.0 |
| 1945 | 95,227 | 74.8 | W.N. Warbey | Lab | 39,335 | 55.2 |
|  |  |  | Dr. L.G. Brown | NL | 31,914 | 44.8 |
|  |  |  |  |  | 7,421 | 10.4 |

## BEDFORDSHIRE, MID [274]

| Election | Electors | T'out | Candidate | Party | Votes | % |
|---|---|---|---|---|---|---|
| 1918 | 29,961 | 54.8 | M.G. Townley | Co C | 9,073 | 55.2 |
| | | | †Sir A.W. Black | L | 7,352 | 44.8 |
| | | | | | 1,721 | 10.4 |
| | | | | | | |
| 1922 | 29,968 | 70.1 | F.C. Linfield | L | 11,874 | 56.5 |
| | | | M.G. Townley | C | 9,137 | 43.5 |
| | | | | | 2,737 | 13.0 |
| | | | | | | |
| 1923 | 30,511 | 72.6 | F.C. Linfield | L | 11,310 | 51.0 |
| | | | W.W. Warner | C | 9,287 | 41.9 |
| | | | R.L. Wigzell | Lab | 1,567* | 7.1 |
| | | | | | 2,023 | 9.1 |
| | | | | | | |
| 1924 | 30,964 | 76.5 | W.W. Warner | C | 12,317 | 52.0 |
| | | | F.C. Linfield | L | 11,356 | 48.0 |
| | | | | | 961 | 4.0 |
| | | | | | | |
| 1929 | 39,149 | 79.5 | M. Gray | L | 14,595 | 46.9 |
| | | | W.W. Warner | C | 12,682 | 40.7 |
| | | | H.W. Fenner | Lab | 3,853* | 12.4 |
| | | | | | 1,913 | 6.2 |
| | | | | | | |
| 1931 | 40,555 | 79.1 | A.T. Lennox-Boyd | C | 15,213 | 47.4 |
| | | | M. Gray | L | 13,726 | 42.8 |
| | | | H.W. Fenner | Lab | 3,156* | 9.8 |
| | | | | | 1,487 | 4.6 |
| | | | | | | |
| 1935 | 41,813 | 76.3 | A.T. Lennox-Boyd | C | 16,054 | 50.4 |
| | | | M. Gray | L | 11,623 | 36.4 |
| | | | T.H. Knight | Lab | 4,224 | 13.2 |
| | | | | | 4,431 | 14.0 |
| | | | | | | |
| 1945 | 51,545 | 73.1 | A.T. Lennox-Boyd | C | 13,954 | 37.0 |
| | | | W. Howell | Lab | 12,073 | 32.1 |
| | | | E.K. Martell | L | 11,641 | 30.9 |
| | | | | | 1,881 | 4.9 |

| Election | Electors | T'out | Candidate | Party | Votes | % |
|---|---|---|---|---|---|---|
| 1918 | | | J.T. Wigan | Co C | Unopp. | |
| [Resignation] | | | | | | |
| 1921 (14/5) | | | A.T. Loyd | Co C | Unopp. | |
| 1922 | 26,541 | 77.1 | A.T. Loyd | C | 10,507 | 51.3 |
| | | | E.A. Lessing | L | 9,967 | 48.7 |
| | | | | | 540 | 2.6 |
| 1923 | 27,183 | 79.5 | E.A. Lessing | L | 10,932 | 50.6 |
| | | | R.G.C. Glyn | C | 10,678 | 49.4 |
| | | | | | 254 | 1.2 |
| 1924 | 28,082 | 82.9 | R.G.C. Glyn | C | 13,117 | 56.4 |
| | | | E.A. Lessing | L | 8,805 | 37.8 |
| | | | D.F. Brundrit | Lab | 1,355* | 5.8 |
| | | | | | 4,312 | 18.6 |
| 1929 | 36,758 | 80.8 | R.G.C. Glyn | C | 14,094 | 47.4 |
| | | | E.A. Lessing | L | 11,896 | 40.1 |
| | | | A.E.E. Reade | Lab | 3,712* | 12.5 |
| | | | | | 2,198 | 7.3 |
| 1931 | | | R.G.C. Glyn | C | Unopp. | |
| 1935 | | | Sir R.G.C. Glyn, Bt. | C | Unopp. | |
| 1945 | 56,491 | 67.4 | Sir R.G.C. Glyn, Bt. | C | 16,968 | 44.5 |
| | | | D.H. Parkinson | Lab | 11,980 | 31.5 |
| | | | J.H.C. Miller | L | 7,031 | 18.5 |
| | | | J.C.D. Dunman | Com | 1,668* | 4.4 |
| | | | C.A.M. Freake | Ind | 419* | 1.1 |
| | | | | | 4,988 | 13.0 |

| Election | Electors | T'out | Candidate | Party | Votes | % |
|---|---|---|---|---|---|---|
| 1918 [Resignation] | | | †W.A. Mount | Co C | Unopp. | |
| 1922 (10/6) | | | H.C. Brown | Co C | Unopp. | |
| 1922 | 30,804 | 69.7 | H.C. Brown | C | 12,322 | 57.4 |
| | | | I.H. Stranger | L | 9,144 | 42.6 |
| | | | | | 3,178 | 14.8 |
| 1923 | 31,443 | 71.3 | I.H. Stranger | L | 11,226 | 50.1 |
| | | | H.C. Brown | C | 11,185 | 49.9 |
| | | | | | 41 | 0.2 |
| 1924 | 32,650 | 80.9 | H.C. Brown | C | 14,759 | 55.9 |
| | | | I.H. Stranger | L | 10,444 | 39.5 |
| | | | F.M. Jacques | Lab | 1,219* | 4.6 |
| | | | | | 4,315 | 16.4 |
| 1929 | 44,538 | 78.3 | H.C. Brown | C | 17,800 | 51.0 |
| | | | E.H. Brooks | L | 13,604 | 39.0 |
| | | | F.M. Jacques | Lab | 3,471* | 10.0 |
| | | | | | 4,196 | 12.0 |
| 1931 | | | H.C. Brown | C | Unopp. | |
| 1935 | 51,568 | 65.5 | H.C. Brown | C | 24,642 | 73.0 |
| | | | R. Russell | Lab | 9,125 | 27.0 |
| | | | | | 15,517 | 46.0 |
| 1945 | 71,443 | 65.4 | A.R. Hurd | C | 24,463 | 52.4 |
| | | | Mrs. I. Brook | Lab | 15,754 | 33.7 |
| | | | E.D.T. Vane | L | 6,052 | 13.0 |
| | | | G.B. Suggett | CW | 424* | 0.9 |
| | | | | | 8,709 | 18.7 |

| Election | Electors | T'out | Candidate | Party | Votes | % |
|----------|----------|-------|-----------|-------|-------|---|
| 1918 | 33,377 | 43.5 | †E. Gardner | Co C | 10,073 | 69.4 |
|  |  |  | C.S. Edgerley | Ind Lab | 4,448 | 30.6 |
|  |  |  |  |  | 5,625 | 38.8 |
| 1922 | 37,445 | 65.7 | A.A. Somerville | C | 17,504 | 71.2 |
|  |  |  | C.B. Crisp | L | 7,087 | 28.8 |
|  |  |  |  |  | 10,417 | 42.4 |
| 1923 | 37,945 | 57.1 | A.A. Somerville | C | 12,648 | 58.4 |
|  |  |  | C.B. Crisp | L | 9,023 | 41.6 |
|  |  |  |  |  | 3,625 | 16.8 |
| 1924 | 38,852 | 66.6 | A.A. Somerville | C | 20,370 | 78.7 |
|  |  |  | C.N.B. Crisp | Lab | 5,514 | 21.3 |
|  |  |  |  |  | 14,856 | 57.4 |
| 1929 | 53,156 | 67.6 | A.A. Somerville | C | 20,564 | 57.2 |
|  |  |  | E.R. Haylor | L | 11,314 | 31.5 |
|  |  |  | A.H. Chilton | Lab | 4,049* | 11.3 |
|  |  |  |  |  | 9,250 | 25.7 |
| 1931 |  |  | A.A. Somerville | C | Unopp. |  |
| 1935 |  |  | A.A. Somerville | C | Unopp. |  |
| [Death] |  |  |  |  |  |  |
| 1942 | 58,726 | 27.9 | C.E. Mott-Radclyffe | C | 9,557 | 58.4 |
| (30/6) |  |  | Hon. W. Douglas-Home | Ind Prog | 6,817 | 41.6 |
|  |  |  |  |  | 2,740 | 16.8 |
| 1945 | 73,159 | 67.9 | C.E. Mott-Radclyffe | C | 26,901 | 54.1 |
|  |  |  | Miss M. Nicholson | Lab | 16,420 | 33.1 |
|  |  |  | N.C. Tufnell | L | 6,331 | 12.8 |
|  |  |  |  |  | 10,481 | 21.0 |

Note:—

1918:  Edgerley sought election as an 'Unofficial Labour Coalition' candidate.

# BUCKINGHAMSHIRE, AYLESBURY [278]

| Election | Electors | T'out | Candidate | Party | Votes | % |
|----------|----------|-------|-----------|-------|-------|---|
| 1918 | | | †L.N. de Rothschild | Co C | Unopp. | |
| 1922 | 36,747 | 71.4 | L.N. de Rothschild | C | 13,406 | 51.1 |
| | | | T. Keens | L | 12,835 | 48.9 |
| | | | | | 571 | 2.2 |
| 1923 | 37,970 | 74.7 | T. Keens | L | 13,575 | 47.9 |
| | | | Sir A.H. Burgoyne | C | 13,504 | 47.6 |
| | | | F.C. Watkins | Lab | 1,275* | 4.5 |
| | | | | | 71 | 0.3 |
| 1924 | 39,448 | 82.0 | Sir A.H. Burgoyne | C | 18,132 | 56.0 |
| | | | T. Keens | L | 11,574 | 35.8 |
| | | | F.C. Watkins | Lab | 2,655* | 8.2 |
| | | | | | 6,558 | 20.2 |

[Seat Vacant at Dissolution (Death)]

| Election | Electors | T'out | Candidate | Party | Votes | % |
|----------|----------|-------|-----------|-------|-------|---|
| 1929 | 54,074 | 78.7 | M.W. Beaumont | C | 20,478 | 48.1 |
| | | | T. Keens | L | 17,594 | 41.3 |
| | | | F.G. Temple | Lab | 4,509* | 10.6 |
| | | | | | 2,884 | 6.8 |
| 1931 | 56,830 | 75.6 | M.W. Beaumont | C | 29,368 | 68.3 |
| | | | C.B. Dallow | L | 8,927 | 20.8 |
| | | | Miss D.V.A. Woodman | Lab | 4,677* | 10.9 |
| | | | | | 20,441 | 47.5 |
| 1935 | 61,315 | 70.2 | M.W. Beaumont | C | 24,728 | 57.4 |
| | | | Mrs. M. Wintringham | L | 13,622 | 31.6 |
| | | | E.W. Shearer | Lab | 4,716* | 11.0 |
| | | | | | 11,106 | 25.8 |

[Resignation]

| Election | Electors | T'out | Candidate | Party | Votes | % |
|----------|----------|-------|-----------|-------|-------|---|
| 1938 (19/5) | 63,624 | 63.0 | Sir H.S. Reed | C | 21,695 | 54.1 |
| | | | T.A. Robertson | L | 10,751 | 26.8 |
| | | | R. Groves | Lab | 7,666 | 19.1 |
| | | | | | 10,944 | 27.3 |
| 1945 | 73,737* | 69.5 | Sir H.S. Reed | C | 24,537 | 47.8 |
| | | | R. Groves | Lab | 16,445 | 32.1 |
| | | | G.D. Naylor | L | 10,302 | 20.1 |
| | | | | | 8,092 | 15.7 |

| Election | Electors | T'out | Candidate | Party | Votes | % |
|---|---|---|---|---|---|---|
| 1918 | 36,434 | 63.6 | G.E.W. Bowyer | Co C | 12,441 | 53.7 |
| | | | J. Scurr | Lab | 7,481 | 32.3 |
| | | | †Sir H.C.W. Verney, Bt. | L | 3,250 | 14.0 |
| | | | | | 4,960 | 21.4 |
| 1922 | 36,262 | 76.9 | G.E.W. Bowyer | C | 13,751 | 49.4 |
| | | | O. Connellan | Lab | 7,343 | 26.3 |
| | | | Rt. Hon. Sir C.E.H. Hobhouse, Bt. | L | 6,789 | 24.3 |
| | | | | | 6,408 | 23.1 |
| 1923 | 36,785 | 68.4 | G.E.W. Bowyer | C | 13,351 | 53.0 |
| | | | E.J. Pay | Lab | 11,824 | 47.0 |
| | | | | | 1,527 | 6.0 |
| 1924 | 37,394 | 78.1 | G.E.W. Bowyer | C | 15,129 | 51.8 |
| | | | E.J. Pay | Lab | 8,939 | 30.6 |
| | | | R. Kingesley-Johnson | L | 5,144 | 17.6 |
| | | | | | 6,190 | 21.2 |
| 1929 | 44,974 | 79.6 | G.E.W. Bowyer | C | 16,375 | 45.8 |
| | | | J.L. George | Lab | 11,718 | 32.7 |
| | | | N.E. Crump | L | 7,713 | 21.5 |
| | | | | | 4,657 | 13.1 |
| 1931 | 45,693 | 77.7 | Sir G.E.W. Bowyer | C | 23,783 | 67.0 |
| | | | J.L. George | Lab | 11,736 | 33.0 |
| | | | | | 12,047 | 34.0 |
| 1935 | 47,312 | 75.1 | Sir G.E.W. Bowyer, Bt. | C | 20,616 | 58.0 |
| | | | J.A. Sparks | Lab | 14,928 | 42.0 |
| | | | | | 5,688 | 16.0 |

[Elevation to the Peerage — Lord Denham]

| Election | Electors | T'out | Candidate | Party | Votes | % |
|---|---|---|---|---|---|---|
| 1937 (11/6) | 47,738 | 71.4 | J.P. Whiteley | C | 17,919 | 52.0 |
| | | | J.V. Delahaye | Lab | 12,820 | 37.0 |
| | | | E.J. Boyce | L | 3,348* | 9.8 |
| | | | | | 5,099 | 15.0 |

[Death]

| Election | Electors | T'out | Candidate | Party | Votes | % |
|---|---|---|---|---|---|---|
| 1943 (4/8) | | | Hon. G.L. Berry | C | Unopp. | |
| 1945 | 56,908 | 71.6 | A.M. Crawley | Lab | 22,302 | 54. |
| | | | Hon. G.L. Berry | C | 18,457 | 45. |
| | | | | | 3,845 | 9. |

| Election | Electors | T'out | Candidate | Party | Votes | % |
|----------|----------|-------|-----------|-------|-------|---|
| 1945 | 78,512 | 71.9 | B. Levy | Lab | 25,711 | 45.5 |
|  |  |  | E.C. Cobb | C | 23,287 | 41.2 |
|  |  |  | A.E. Ward | L | 7,487 | 13.3 |
|  |  |  |  |  | 2,424 | 4.3 |

| Election | Electors | T'out | Candidate | Party | Votes | % |
|---|---|---|---|---|---|---|
| 1918 | | | †W.B. Du Pre | Co C | Unopp. | |
| 1922 | 45,049 | 69.2 | W.B. Du Pre | C | 15,627 | 50.1 |
| | | | Lady Terrington | L | 11,154 | 35.8 |
| | | | S. Stennett | Lab | 4,403 | 14.1 |
| | | | | | 4,473 | 14.3 |
| 1923 | 46,521 | 68.2 | Lady Terrington | L | 14,910 | 46.9 |
| | | | W.B. Du Pre | C | 13,228 | 41.7 |
| | | | G. Young | Lab | 3,611* | 11.4 |
| | | | | | 1,682 | 5.2 |
| 1924 | 48,652 | 78.0 | Sir A.W.F. Knox | C | 20,820 | 54.8 |
| | | | Lady Terrington | L | 12,526 | 33.0 |
| | | | G. Young | Lab | 4,626* | 12.2 |
| | | | | | 8,294 | 21.8 |
| 1929 | 68,992 | 71.1 | Sir A.W.F. Knox | C | 23,231 | 47.4 |
| | | | L.J. Humphrey | L | 16,929 | 34.5 |
| | | | Mrs. R. Townsend | Lab | 8,899 | 18.1 |
| | | | | | 6,302 | 12.9 |
| 1931 | 77,109 | 67.5 | Sir A.W.F. Knox | C | 41,208 | 79.2 |
| | | | Dr. L. Haden-Guest | Lab | 10,821 | 20.8 |
| | | | | | 30,387 | 58.4 |
| 1935 | 87,230 | 61.4 | Sir A.W.F. Knox | C | 34,747 | 64.9 |
| | | | Dr. E.A. Whitfield | Lab | 18,817 | 35.1 |
| | | | | | 15,930 | 29.8 |
| 1945 | 63,049** | 71.9 | J.E. Haire | Lab | 20,482 | 45.1 |
| | | | R. Peake | C | 17,946 | 39.6 |
| | | | C.A.H. Chadwick | L | 6,916 | 15.3 |
| | | | | | 2,536 | 5.5 |

# CAMBRIDGESHIRE [282]

| Election | Electors | T'out | Candidate | Party | Votes | % |
|---|---|---|---|---|---|---|
| 1918 | 37,410 | 51.3 | †Rt. Hon. E.S. Montagu | Co L | 12,497 | 65.1 |
| | | | A.E. Stubbs | Ind Lab | 6,686 | 34.9 |
| | | | | | 5,811 | 30.2 |
| 1922 | 36,636 | 70.8 | H.S. Gray | C | 9,846 | 38.0 |
| | | | A.E. Stubbs | Lab | 9,167 | 35.3 |
| | | | Rt. Hon. E.S. Montagu | NL | 6,942 | 26.7 |
| | | | | | 679 | 2.7 |
| 1923 | 37,078 | 72.5 | R.G. Briscoe | C | 11,710 | 43.6 |
| | | | A.E. Stubbs | Lab | 8,554 | 31.8 |
| | | | Mrs. E. Dimsdale | L | 6,619 | 24.6 |
| | | | | | 3,156 | 11.8 |
| 1924 | 37,626 | 69.9 | R.G. Briscoe | C | 15,530 | 59.0 |
| | | | G.T. Garratt | Lab | 10,781 | 41.0 |
| | | | | | 4,749 | 18.0 |
| 1929 | 47,475 | 74.7 | R.G. Briscoe | C | 13,306 | 37.6 |
| | | | G.T. Garratt | Lab | 11,256 | 31.7 |
| | | | J.W. Payne | L | 10,904 | 30.7 |
| | | | | | 2,050 | 5.9 |
| 1931 | 49,300 | 70.5 | R.G. Briscoe | C | 23,742 | 68.3 |
| | | | G.T. Garratt | Lab | 11,013 | 31.7 |
| | | | | | 12,729 | 36.6 |
| 1935 | 52,736 | 67.8 | R.G. Briscoe | C | 19,087 | 53.4 |
| | | | J.R. Bellerby | Lab | 11,437 | 32.0 |
| | | | J.W. Payne | L | 5,223 | 14.6 |
| | | | | | 7,650 | 21.4 |
| 1945 | 63,302 | 69.9 | A.E. Stubbs | Lab | 18,714 | 42.3 |
| | | | S.G. Howard | C | 18,670 | 42.2 |
| | | | L.E. Goodman | L | 6,867 | 15.5 |
| | | | | | 44 | 0.1 |

| Election | Electors | T'out | Candidate | Party | Votes | % |
|----------|----------|-------|-----------|-------|-------|---|
| 1918 | 42,912 | 65.5 | †G.C. Hamilton | Co C | 20,421 | 72.7 |
| | | | G. Middleton | Lab | 7,685 | 27.3 |
| | | | | | 12,736 | 45.4 |
| 1922 | 45,085 | 79.8 | Sir G.C. Hamilton | C | 19,361 | 53.8 |
| | | | R. Alstead | L | 11,692 | 32.5 |
| | | | G. Benson | Lab | 4,930 | 13.7 |
| | | | | | 7,669 | 21.3 |
| 1923 | 45,871 | 76.6 | R. Alstead | L | 19,046 | 54.2 |
| | | | Sir G.C. Hamilton | C | 16,081 | 45.8 |
| | | | | | 2,965 | 8.4 |
| 1924 | 47,253 | 84.8 | C. Atkinson | C | 24,439 | 61.0 |
| | | | R. Alstead | L | 15,654 | 39.0 |
| | | | | | 8,785 | 22.0 |
| 1929 | 69,607 | 80.8 | C. Atkinson | C | 28,512 | 50.7 |
| | | | R. Alstead | L | 18,475 | 32.9 |
| | | | A.J. Dobbs | Lab | 9,242 | 16.4 |
| | | | | | 10,037 | 17.8 |
| 1931 | | | C. Atkinson | C | Unopp. | |

[Resignation on appointment as a High Court Judge]

| Election | Electors | T'out | Candidate | Party | Votes | % |
|----------|----------|-------|-----------|-------|-------|---|
| 1933 (14/6) | 78,244 | 63.4 | Sir E.W.M. Grigg | C | 25,392 | 51.2 |
| | | | P.M. Oliver | L | 15,892 | 32.0 |
| | | | J.H. Hudson | Lab | 8,333 | 16.8 |
| | | | | | 9,500 | 19.2 |
| 1935 | 100,341 | 72.0 | Sir E.W.M. Grigg | C | 50,719 | 70.2 |
| | | | A. Moss | Lab | 21,493 | 29.8 |
| | | | | | 29,226 | 40.4 |

This constituency was divided in 1945.

| Election | Electors | T'out | Candidate | Party | Votes | % |
|---|---|---|---|---|---|---|
| 1945 | 69,044 | 76.3 | W.S. Shepherd | C | 30,165 | 57.3 |
| | | | A.W.F. Haycock | Lab | 22,497 | 42.7 |
| | | | | | 7,668 | 14.6 |

| Election | Electors | T'out | Candidate | Party | Votes | % |
|---|---|---|---|---|---|---|
| 1918 | 27,369 | 65.2 | †Sir O.C. Philipps | Co C | 10,043 | 56.3 |
| | | | E. Paul | L | 4,993 | 28.0 |
| | | | A. Mason | Lab | 2,799 | 15.7 |
| | | | | | 5,050 | 28.3 |
| 1922 | 27,159 | 81.2 | Sir C.W. Cayzer, Bt. | C | 11,938 | 54.1 |
| | | | G. Muff | Lab | 5,414 | 24.6 |
| | | | J. Banks | L | 4,688 | 21.3 |
| | | | | | 6,524 | 29.5 |
| 1923 | 27,947 | 78.6 | Sir C.W. Cayzer, Bt. | C | 9,985 | 45.4 |
| | | | W.C. Llewelyn | L | 6,212 | 28.3 |
| | | | G. Muff | Lab | 5,773 | 26.3 |
| | | | | | 3,773 | 17.1 |
| 1924 | 28,657 | 81.9 | Sir C.W. Cayzer, Bt. | C | 12,491 | 53.2 |
| | | | W.C. Llewelyn | L | 5,538 | 23.6 |
| | | | G. Beardsworth | Lab | 5,451 | 23.2 |
| | | | | | 6,953 | 29.6 |
| 1929 | 39,590 | 82.3 | Sir C.W. Cayzer, Bt. | C | 13,454 | 41.3 |
| | | | A. Herbert | L | 13,292 | 40.8 |
| | | | W. Herron | Lab | 5,846 | 17.9 |
| | | | | | 162 | 0.5 |
| 1931 | 40,959 | 85.8 | Sir C.W. Cayzer, Bt. | C | 18,174 | 51.7 |
| | | | A. Herbert | L | 11,770 | 33.5 |
| | | | J. Lewis | Lab | 5,186 | 14.8 |
| | | | | | 6,404 | 18.2 |
| 1935 | 43,044 | 77.9 | Sir C.W. Cayzer, Bt. | C | 16,882 | 50.4 |
| | | | E.H.G. Evans | L | 10,183 | 30.4 |
| | | | Miss A.L. Bulley | Lab | 6,450 | 19.2 |
| | | | | | 6,699 | 20.0 |
| [Death] | | | | | | |
| 1940 (7/3) | | | B.E. Nield | C | Unopp. | |
| 1945 | 52,590 | 72.0 | B.E. Nield | C | 19,064 | 50.3 |
| | | | D.M. Hopkinson | Lab | 13,585 | 35.9 |
| | | | A.E.E. Jones | L | 5,229 | 13.8 |
| | | | | | 5,479 | 14.4 |

# CHESHIRE, CREWE  [286]

| Election | Electors | T'out | Candidate | Party | Votes | % |
|---|---|---|---|---|---|---|
| 1918 | 34,818 | 68.4 | Sir J. Davies | Co L | 13,392 | 56.2 |
|  |  |  | J.T. Brownlie | Lab | 10,439 | 43.8 |
|  |  |  |  |  | 2,953 | 12.4 |
| 1922 | 37,159 | 80.9 | E.G. Hemmerde | Lab | 15,311 | 50.9 |
|  |  |  | Sir J. Davies | NL | 14,756 | 49.1 |
|  |  |  |  |  | 555 | 1.8 |
| 1923 | 37,959 | 82.8 | E.G. Hemmerde | Lab | 14,628 | 46.5 |
|  |  |  | Sir T.J. Strangman | C | 8,734 | 27.8 |
|  |  |  | R.M. Montgomery | L | 8,068 | 25.7 |
|  |  |  |  |  | 5,894 | 18.7 |
| 1924 | 38,583 | 85.6 | E. Craig | C | 18,333 | 55.5 |
|  |  |  | E.G. Hemmerde | Lab | 14,705 | 44.5 |
|  |  |  |  |  | 3,628 | 11.0 |
| 1929 | 49,863 | 83.7 | J.W. Bowen | Lab | 20,948 | 50.2 |
|  |  |  | D.B. Somervell | C | 11,732 | 28.1 |
|  |  |  | W.C. Llewelyn | L | 9,076 | 21.7 |
|  |  |  |  |  | 9,216 | 22.1 |
| 1931 | 51,448 | 84.5 | D.B. Somervell | C | 25,141 | 57.8 |
|  |  |  | J.W. Bowen | Lab | 18,351 | 42.2 |
|  |  |  |  |  | 6,790 | 15.6 |
| 1935 | 52,744 | 80.3 | Sir D.B. Somervell | C | 21,729 | 51.3 |
|  |  |  | J.W. Bowen | Lab | 20,620 | 48.7 |
|  |  |  |  |  | 1,109 | 2.6 |
| 1945 | 62,853 | 74.6 | S.S. Allen | Lab | 28,416 | 60.6 |
|  |  |  | Rt. Hon. Sir D.B. Somervell | C | 18,468 | 39.4 |
|  |  |  |  |  | 9,948 | 21.2 |

| Election | Electors | T'out | Candidate | Party | Votes | % |
|---|---|---|---|---|---|---|
| 1918 | | | †H. Barnston | Co C | Unopp. | |
| [Appointed Comptroller of H.M. Household] | | | | | | |
| 1921 (19/4) | | | H. Barnston | Co C | Unopp. | |
| 1922 | | | H. Barnston | C | Unopp. | |
| 1923 | 22,547 | 76.4 | H. Barnston | C | 8,716 | 50. |
| | | | R.J. Russell | L | 8,520 | 49. |
| | | | | | 196 | 1. |
| 1924 | 23,409 | 86.9 | Sir H. Barnston, Bt. | C | 11,006 | 54. |
| | | | R.J. Russell | L | 9,337 | 45. |
| | | | | | 1,669 | 8. |
| [Death] | | | | | | |
| 1929 (20/3) | 23,760 | 80.6 | R.J. Russell | L | 10,223 | 53. |
| | | | R.G. Fenwick-Palmer | C | 8,931 | 46. |
| | | | | | 1,292 | 6. |
| 1929 | 30,593 | 86.8 | R.J. Russell | L (NL) | 13,688 | 51. |
| | | | R.G. Fenwick-Palmer | C | 12,862 | 48. |
| | | | | | 826 | 3. |
| 1931 | | | R.J. Russell | NL | Unopp. | |
| 1935 | | | R.J. Russell | NL | Unopp. | |
| [Death] | | | | | | |
| 1943 (7/4) | 32,715 | 56.1 | J.E. Loverseed | CW (Ind Lab) (Lab) | 8,023 | 43. |
| | | | T. Peacock | NL | 7,537 | 41 |
| | | | H. Heathcote-Williams | Ind L | 2,803 | 15. |
| | | | | | 486 | 2. |
| 1945 | 35,224 | 75.2 | Sir J.D. Barlow, Bt. | NL | 15,294 | 57. |
| | | | J.E. Loverseed | Lab | 7,392 | 27. |
| | | | D.M.C. Curtis | L | 3,808 | 14. |
| | | | | | 7,902 | 29. |

| Election | Electors | T'out | Candidate | Party | Votes | % |
|---|---|---|---|---|---|---|
| 1918 | | | †Sir A.J. Sykes, Bt. | Co C | Unopp. | |
| | | | | | | |
| 1922 | 35,002 | 77.2 | E. Makins | C | 15,650 | 57.9 |
| | | | P. Butlin | L | 11,388 | 42.1 |
| | | | | | 4,262 | 15.8 |
| | | | | | | |
| 1923 | 35,916 | 76.8 | E. Makins | C | 13,838 | 50.1 |
| | | | Hon. Sir A.L. Stanley | L | 13,758 | 49.9 |
| | | | | | 80 | 0.2 |
| | | | | | | |
| 1924 | 37,191 | 80.9 | E. Makins | C | 18,199 | 60.5 |
| | | | J.P. McDougall | L | 11,885 | 39.5 |
| | | | | | 6,314 | 21.0 |
| | | | | | | |
| 1929 | 52,479 | 80.5 | E. Makins | C | 22,605 | 53.5 |
| | | | A.E. Jalland | L | 19,629 | 46.5 |
| | | | | | 2,976 | 7.0 |
| | | | | | | |
| 1931 | | | E. Makins | C | Unopp. | |
| | | | | | | |
| 1935 | 62,230 | 76.3 | E. Makins | C | 30,252 | 63.7 |
| | | | H. Heathcote-Williams | L | 17,253 | 36.3 |
| | | | | | 12,999 | 27.4 |
| | | | | | | |
| 1945 | 76,223* | 77.1 | W.H. Bromley-Davenport | C | 33,056 | 56.2 |
| | | | F.L. Tyler | Lab | 14,416 | 24.5 |
| | | | L.L. Maitland | L | 10,703 | 18.2 |
| | | | F.W. Young | CW | 628* | 1.1 |
| | | | | | 18,640 | 31.7 |

| Election | Electors | T'out | Candidate | Party | Votes | % |
|---|---|---|---|---|---|---|
| 1918 | 36,577 | 67.1 | J.R. Remer | Co C | 14,277 | 58.2 |
| | | | W. Pimblott | Lab | 10,253 | 41.8 |
| | | | | | 4,024 | 16.4 |
| 1922 | 38,245 | 86.0 | J.R. Remer | C | 15,825 | 48.1 |
| | | | T.A. Jones | L | 10,477 | 31.9 |
| | | | A.J. Penston | Lab | 6,584 | 20.0 |
| | | | | | 5,348 | 16.2 |
| 1923 | 38,982 | 83.9 | J.R. Remer | C | 14,744 | 45.1 |
| | | | W.T. Davies | L | 11,259 | 34.4 |
| | | | A.J. Penston | Lab | 6,713 | 20.5 |
| | | | | | 3,485 | 10.7 |
| 1924 | 39,962 | 84.6 | J.R. Remer | C | 17,171 | 50.9 |
| | | | J. Williams | Lab | 10,187 | 30.1 |
| | | | H.K. Nield | L | 6,434 | 19.0 |
| | | | | | 6,984 | 20.8 |
| 1929 | 53,053 | 87.0 | J.R. Remer | C | 19,329 | 41.9 |
| | | | J. Williams | Lab | 13,911 | 30.2 |
| | | | J.S.B. Lloyd | L | 12,891 | 27.9 |
| | | | | | 5,418 | 11.7 |
| 1931 | 54,954 | 81.2 | J.R. Remer | C | 30,796 | 69.0 |
| | | | D.S. Morton | Lab | 13,854 | 31.0 |
| | | | | | 16,942 | 38.0 |
| 1935 | 58,529 | 78.9 | J.R. Remer | C | 24,249 | 52.5 |
| | | | G. Darling | Lab | 14,761 | 32.0 |
| | | | J.L. Poole | L | 7,151 | 15.5 |
| | | | | | 9,488 | 20.5 |
| [Resignation] | | | | | | |
| 1939 (22/11) | | | W.G. Weston | C | Unopp. | |
| 1945 | 64,448 | 80.1 | A.V. Harvey | C | 23,495 | 45.5 |
| | | | H.F. Urquhart | Lab | 20,442 | 39.6 |
| | | | E.A.B. Fletcher | L | 7,702 | 14.9 |
| | | | | | 3,053 | 5.9 |

| Election | Electors | T'out | Candidate | Party | Votes | % |
|---|---|---|---|---|---|---|
| 1918 | 39,269 | 64.1 | H. Dewhurst | Co C | 15,444 | 61.4 |
| | | | †J.F. Brunner | L | 9,723 | 38.6 |
| | | | | | 5,721 | 22.8 |
| 1922 | 39,856 | 71.6 | Lord Colum Crichton-Stuart | C | 15,454 | 54.2 |
| | | | J. Williams | Lab | 13,066 | 45.8 |
| | | | | | 2,388 | 8.4 |
| 1923 | 40,440 | 76.1 | Lord Colum Crichton-Stuart | C | 11,835 | 38.5 |
| | | | A. Mort | L | 9,765 | 31.7 |
| | | | J. Williams | Lab | 9,183 | 29.8 |
| | | | | | 2,070 | 6.8 |
| 1924 | 41,670 | 80.7 | Lord Colum Crichton-Stuart | C | 14,545 | 43.2 |
| | | | Mrs. B.A. Gould | Lab | 11,630 | 34.6 |
| | | | A. Mort | L | 7,465 | 22.2 |
| | | | | | 2,915 | 8.6 |
| 1929 | 53,988 | 83.6 | Lord Colum Crichton-Stuart | C | 15,477 | 34.3 |
| | | | Mrs. B.A. Gould | Lab | 15,473 | 34.3 |
| | | | J.D. Barlow | L | 14,163 | 31.4 |
| | | | | | 4 | 0.0 |
| 1931 | 55,290 | 82.8 | Lord Colum Crichton-Stuart | C | 30,061 | 65.6 |
| | | | Mrs. B.A. Gould | Lab | 15,746 | 34.4 |
| | | | | | 14,315 | 31.2 |
| 1935 | 57,231 | 77.9 | Lord Colum Crichton-Stuart | C | 24,316 | 54.5 |
| | | | T. Reid | Lab | 20,289 | 45.5 |
| | | | | | 4,027 | 9.0 |
| 1945 | 62,541 | 78.1 | J.G. Foster | C | 20,198 | 41.4 |
| | | | Prof. R.S.T. Chorley | Lab | 20,183 | 41.3 |
| | | | Sir F.J.M. Brunner, Bt. | L | 8,460 | 17.3 |
| | | | | | 15 | 0.1 |

| Election | Electors | T'out | Candidate | Party | Votes | % |
|---|---|---|---|---|---|---|
| 1918 | 43,711 | 60.0 | †Sir J. Wood, Bt. | C | 13,462 | 51.4 |
|  |  |  | W. Fowden | Lab | 6,508 | 24.8 |
|  |  |  | †T.O. Jacobsen | L | 6,241 | 23.8 |
|  |  |  |  |  | 6,954 | 26.6 |
| 1922 | 43,208 | 81.1 | J.P. Rhodes | C | 17,216 | 49.1 |
|  |  |  | J.L. Tattersall | L | 10,265 | 29.3 |
|  |  |  | P.H. Ward | Lab | 7,578 | 21.6 |
|  |  |  |  |  | 6,951 | 19.8 |
| 1923 | 44,045 | 72.2 | J.L. Tattersall | L | 17,082 | 53.7 |
|  |  |  | J.P. Rhodes | C | 14,708 | 46.3 |
|  |  |  |  |  | 2,374 | 7.4 |
| 1924 | 44,175 | 84.0 | E.W.H. Wood | C | 16,412 | 44.2 |
|  |  |  | W. Fowden | Lab | 12,509 | 33.7 |
|  |  |  | J.L. Tattersall | L | 8,201 | 22.1 |
|  |  |  |  |  | 3,903 | 10.5 |
| 1929 | 57,286 | 86.4 | H.H. Lawrie | Lab | 20,343 | 41.1 |
|  |  |  | E.W.H. Wood | C | 17,983 | 36.3 |
|  |  |  | P.H. Jones | L | 11,186 | 22.6 |
|  |  |  |  |  | 2,360 | 4.8 |
| 1931 | 58,315 | 86.9 | S. Hope | C | 27,557 | 54.4 |
|  |  |  | W. Dobbie | Lab | 14,251 | 28.1 |
|  |  |  | P.H. Jones | L | 8,849 | 17.5 |
|  |  |  |  |  | 13,306 | 26.3 |
| 1935 | 58,380 | 78.7 | P.R.R. Dunne | C | 25,502 | 55.5 |
|  |  |  | R.W. Casasola | Lab | 20,429 | 44.5 |
|  |  |  |  |  | 5,073 | 11.0 |
| [Resignation] |  |  |  |  |  |  |
| 1937 | 58,259 | 74.6 | H.B.T. Cox | C | 21,901 | 50.4 |
| (28/4) |  |  | Rev. G. Lang | Lab | 21,567 | 49.6 |
|  |  |  |  |  | 334 | 0.8 |
| 1945 | 57,189 | 80.5 | Rev. G. Lang | Lab | 20,597 | 44.7 |
|  |  |  | H.B.T. Cox | C | 16,227 | 35.2 |
|  |  |  | D.F. Burden | L | 9,240 | 20.1 |
|  |  |  |  |  | 4,370 | 9.5 |

| Election | Electors | T'out | Candidate | Party | Votes | % |
|---|---|---|---|---|---|---|
| 1918 | | | †G. Stewart | Co C | Unopp. | |
| 1922 | 34,150 | 74.0 | G. Stewart | C | 12,888 | 51.0 |
| | | | S.R. Dodds | L | 8,014 | 31.7 |
| | | | J.E.C. Grant | Lab | 4,363 | 17.3 |
| | | | | | 4,874 | 19.3 |
| 1923 | 35,518 | 71.6 | S.R. Dodds | L | 13,631 | 53.6 |
| | | | G. Stewart | C | 11,791 | 46.4 |
| | | | | | 1,840 | 7.2 |
| 1924 | 37,232 | 79.0 | J. Grace | C | 17,705 | 60.2 |
| | | | S.R. Dodds | L | 11,697 | 39.8 |
| | | | | | 6,008 | 20.4 |
| 1929 | 63,004 | 78.7 | J. Grace | C | 23,522 | 47.5 |
| | | | S.R. Dodds | L | 15,158 | 30.6 |
| | | | G. Beardsworth | Lab | 10,876 | 21.9 |
| | | | | | 8,364 | 16.9 |
| 1931 | 71,556 | 77.0 | G.C. Clayton | C | 44,935 | 81.5 |
| | | | S. Wormald | Lab | 10,177 | 18.5 |
| | | | | | 34,758 | 63.0 |
| 1935 | 82,413 | 69.7 | A.C. Graham | C | 41,617 | 72.5 |
| | | | S. Wormald | Lab | 15,801 | 27.5 |
| | | | | | 25,816 | 45.0 |
| 1945 | 110,570 | 74.9 | J.S.B. Lloyd | C | 42,544 | 51.4 |
| | | | Miss A.L. Bulley | Lab | 25,919 | 31.3 |
| | | | E.E. Dorman-Smith | L | 14,302 | 17.3 |
| | | | | | 16,625 | 20.1 |

| Election | Electors | T'out | Candidate | Party | Votes | % |
|---|---|---|---|---|---|---|
| 1918 | 30,279 | 69.1 | †Sir C.A. Hanson, Bt. | Co C | 12,228 | 58.4 |
| | | | I. Foot | L | 8,705 | 41.6 |
| | | | | | 3,523 | 16.8 |
| [Death] | | | | | | |
| 1922 (24/2) | 32,578 | 74.8 | I. Foot | L | 13,751 | 56.4 |
| | | | Sir F.C. Poole | Co C | 10,610 | 43.6 |
| | | | | | 3,141 | 12.8 |
| 1922 | 33,265 | 80.4 | I. Foot | L | 14,292 | 53.4 |
| | | | Sir F.C. Poole | C | 12,467 | 46.6 |
| | | | | | 1,825 | 6.8 |
| 1923 | 33,054 | 82.0 | I. Foot | L | 14,536 | 53.6 |
| | | | Sir F.C. Poole | C | 12,574 | 46.4 |
| | | | | | 1,962 | 7.2 |
| 1924 | 33,635 | 82.4 | G.J.C. Harrison | C | 14,163 | 51.1 |
| | | | I. Foot | L | 13,548 | 48.9 |
| | | | | | 615 | 2.2 |
| 1929 | 40,666 | 84.9 | I. Foot | L | 16,002 | 46.3 |
| | | | G.J.C. Harrison | C | 15,088 | 43.7 |
| | | | P. Reed | Lab | 3,437* | 10.0 |
| | | | | | 914 | 2.6 |
| 1931 | | | I. Foot | L | Unopp. | |
| 1935 | 42,190 | 82.3 | J.R. Rathbone | C | 17,485 | 50.4 |
| | | | I. Foot | L | 14,732 | 42.4 |
| | | | H.E.J. Falconer | Lab | 2,496* | 7.2 |
| | | | | | 2,753 | 8.0 |
| [Death] | | | | | | |
| 1941 (11/3) | | | Mrs. B.F. Rathbone | C | Unopp. | |
| 1945 | 46,188 | 76.1 | D. Marshall | C | 15,396 | 43.8 |
| | | | J.M. Foot | L | 13,348 | 38.0 |
| | | | J.H. Pitts | Lab | 6,401 | 18.2 |
| | | | | | 2,048 | 5.8 |

Note:—

1941:  Mrs. Rathbone became Mrs. Wright upon her marriage in 1942.

# CORNWALL, CAMBORNE [294]

| Election | Electors | T'out | Candidate | Party | Votes | % |
|---|---|---|---|---|---|---|
| 1918 | 32,575 | 41.8 | †Rt. Hon. F.D. Acland | L | 7,078 | 52.0 |
| | | | G. Nicholls | Lab | 6,546 | 48.0 |
| | | | | | 532 | 4.0 |
| 1922 | 34,097 | 60.5 | A.H. Moreing | NL | 8,191 | 39.7 |
| | | | Rt. Hon. L.S. Jones | L | 7,923 | 38.4 |
| | | | T. Proctor | Lab | 4,512 | 21.9 |
| | | | | | 268 | 1.3 |
| 1923 | 34,303 | 58.0 | Rt. Hon. L.S. Jones | L | 11,794 | 59.3 |
| | | | A.H. Moreing | L | 8,096 | 40.7 |
| | | | | | 3,698 | 18.6 |
| 1924 | 34,399 | 64.6 | A.H. Moreing | Const (C) | 9,530 | 42.9 |
| | | | Rt. Hon. L.S. Jones | L | 7,220 | 32.5 |
| | | | F.A.P. Rowe | Lab | 5,477 | 24.6 |
| | | | | | 2,310 | 10.4 |
| 1929 | 44,026 | 70.8 | Rt. Hon. L.S. Jones | L | 11,176 | 35.8 |
| | | | A.H. Moreing | C | 10,145 | 32.6 |
| | | | H.J. Sharman | Lab | 7,870 | 25.3 |
| | | | J.C. Roberts | Ind | 1,976* | 6.3 |
| | | | | | 1,031 | 3.2 |
| 1931 | 44,542 | 75.8 | P.G. Agnew | C | 14,664 | 43.4 |
| | | | Rt. Hon. L.S. Jones | L | 10,840 | 32.1 |
| | | | Miss K.F. Spurrell | ILP | 8,280 | 24.5 |
| | | | | | 3,824 | 11.3 |
| 1935 | 45,935 | 66.9 | P.G. Agnew | C | 14,826 | 48.3 |
| | | | Sir W. Peacock | L | 7,921 | 25.8 |
| | | | H.R.G. Greaves | Lab | 7,375 | 24.0 |
| | | | Miss K.F. Spurrell | ILP | 592* | 1.9 |
| | | | | | 6,905 | 22.5 |
| 1945 | 51,407 | 64.3 | P.G. Agnew | C | 12,257 | 37.1 |
| | | | F.H. Hayman | Lab | 11,673 | 35.3 |
| | | | Dr. T.R. Hill | L | 9,141 | 27.6 |
| | | | | | 584 | 1.8 |

Note:—

1923: Moreing's name also appeared on the official list of Conservative candidates. Local differences between the followers of Lloyd George and Asquith led to the nomination of two Liberal candidates, Moreing being the nominee of the Lloyd George Liberals and the local Conservative Association. Jones was backed by supporters of Asquith who had formed a committee known as the 'Liberal 600'.

The United Liberal Committee in London which had been formed to assist in selecting candidates and bring the two wings of the Liberal Party together, declared its neutrality during the campaign after it had failed to obtain local agreement.

| Election | Electors | T'out | Candidate | Party | Votes | % |
|---|---|---|---|---|---|---|
| 1918 | | | †Sir G.C. Marks | Co L | Unopp. | |
| 1922 | | | Sir G.C. Marks | NL | Unopp. | |
| 1923 | 29,120 | 75.6 | Sir G.C. Marks | L | 12,434 | 56.5 |
| | | | C.A. Petrie | C | 9,581 | 43.5 |
| | | | | | 2,853 | 13.0 |
| 1924 | 30,202 | 78.0 | A.M. Williams | C | 12,639 | 53.6 |
| | | | Sir G.C. Marks | L | 10,927 | 46.4 |
| | | | | | 1,712 | 7.2 |
| 1929 | 38,711 | 86.1 | Rt. Hon. Sir D. Maclean | L | 16,586 | 49.7 |
| | | | A.M. Williams | C | 14,095 | 42.3 |
| | | | F.E. Church | Lab | 2,654* | 8.0 |
| | | | | | 2,491 | 7.4 |
| 1931 | 40,020 | 85.7 | Rt. Hon. Sir D. Maclean | L | 16,867 | 49.1 |
| | | | A.M. Williams | C | 15,526 | 45.3 |
| | | | A. Bennett | Lab | 1,907* | 5.6 |
| | | | | | 1,341 | 3.8 |
| [Death] | | | | | | |
| 1932 (22/7) | 40,020 | 80.8 | Rt. Hon. Sir F.D. Acland, Bt. | L | 16,933 | 52.4 |
| | | | A.M. Williams | C | 15,387 | 47.6 |
| | | | | | 1,546 | 4.8 |
| 1935 | 41,164 | 79.9 | Rt. Hon. Sir F.D. Acland, Bt. | L | 16,872 | 51.3 |
| | | | E.R. Whitehouse | C | 16,036 | 48.7 |
| | | | | | 836 | 2.6 |
| [Death] | | | | | | |
| 1939 (13/7) | 41,191 | 79.3 | T.L. Horabin | L | 17,072 | 52.2 |
| | | | E.R. Whitehouse | C | 15,608 | 47.8 |
| | | | | | 1,464 | 4.4 |
| 1945 | 49,033 | 72.7 | T.L. Horabin | L (Ind) (Lab) | 18,836 | 52.8 |
| | | | T.P. Fulford | C | 16,171 | 45.4 |
| | | | J.H. Worrall | Ind Lab | 626* | 1.8 |
| | | | | | 2,665 | 7.4 |

| Election | Electors | T'out | Candidate | Party | Votes | % |
|---|---|---|---|---|---|---|
| 1918 | 35,074 | 56.6 | Sir E. Nicholl | Co C | 10,050 | 50.6 |
| | | | Sir A. Carkeek | L | 9,815 | 49.4 |
| | | | | | 235 | 1.2 |
| 1922 | 37,297 | 72.5 | D.E.B.K. Shipwright | C | 11,566 | 42.7 |
| | | | Sir C.C. Mansel, Bt. | L | 8,879 | 32.8 |
| | | | J. Harris | Lab | 4,482 | 16.6 |
| | | | G.H. Morgan | NL | 2,129* | 7.9 |
| | | | | | 2,687 | 9.9 |
| 1923 | 37,586 | 73.0 | Sir C.C. Mansel, Bt. | L | 17,015 | 62.0 |
| | | | D.E.B.K. Shipwright | C | 10,429 | 38.0 |
| | | | | | 6,586 | 24.0 |
| 1924 | 38,640 | 74.7 | G. Pilcher | C | 12,485 | 43.3 |
| | | | Sir C.C. Mansel, Bt. | L | 9,913 | 34.3 |
| | | | Rev. F.J. Hopkins | Lab | 6,462 | 22.4 |
| | | | | | 2,572 | 9.0 |
| 1929 | 49,186 | 78.4 | Rt. Hon. Sir J.T. Walters | L | 14,274 | 37.0 |
| | | | M. Petherick | C | 13,136 | 34.1 |
| | | | Rev. F.J. Hopkins | Lab | 11,166 | 28.9 |
| | | | | | 1,138 | 2.9 |
| 1931 | 50,767 | 79.8 | M. Petherick | C | 16,388 | 40.5 |
| | | | E.D. Simon | L | 14,006 | 34.6 |
| | | | A.L. Rowse | Lab | 10,098 | 24.9 |
| | | | | | 2,382 | 5.9 |
| 1935 | 52,559 | 77.6 | M. Petherick | C | 16,136 | 39.6 |
| | | | A.L. Rowse | Lab | 13,105 | 32.1 |
| | | | Sir R.W. Allen | L | 11,527 | 28.3 |
| | | | | | 3,031 | 7.5 |
| 1945 | 56,214 | 73.0 | E.M. King | Lab | 17,962 | 43.7 |
| | | | M. Petherick | C | 15,169 | 37.0 |
| | | | P. Harris | L | 7,917 | 19.3 |
| | | | | | 2,793 | 6.7 |

| Election | Electors | T'out | Candidate | Party | Votes | % |
|----------|----------|-------|-----------|-------|-------|---|
| 1918 | 28,537 | 51.7 | †Sir C.J. Cory, Bt. | Co L | 8,659 | 58.6 |
| | | | A.E. Dunn | Lab | 5,659 | 38.4 |
| | | | T.F.T. Michell | Ind C | 436* | 3.0 |
| | | | | | 3,000 | 20.2 |
| 1922 | 29,561 | 65.6 | J.A. Hawke | C | 10,388 | 53.5 |
| | | | Sir C.J. Cory, Bt. | NL | 9,016 | 46.5 |
| | | | | | 1,372 | 7.0 |
| 1923 | 29,877 | 71.4 | Sir C.J. Cory, Bt. | L | 9,922 | 46.5 |
| | | | J.A. Hawke | C | 8,652 | 40.6 |
| | | | A.E. Dunn | Lab | 2,749 | 12.9 |
| | | | | | 1,270 | 5.9 |
| 1924 | 30,512 | 69.1 | J.A. Hawke | C | 11,159 | 53.0 |
| | | | Sir C.J. Cory, Bt. | L | 9,912 | 47.0 |
| | | | | | 1,247 | 6.0 |

[Resignation on appointment as a High Court Judge]

| Election | Electors | T'out | Candidate | Party | Votes | % |
|----------|----------|-------|-----------|-------|-------|---|
| 1928 (6/3) | 31,096 | 77.4 | Mrs. H. Runciman | L | 10,241 | 42.6 |
| | | | Sir A. Caird | C | 9,478 | 39.4 |
| | | | Rev. F.J. Hopkins | Lab | 4,343 | 18.0 |
| | | | | | 763 | 3.2 |
| 1929 | 37,593 | 76.5 | Rt. Hon. W. Runciman | L (NL) | 12,443 | 43.2 |
| | | | Sir A. Caird | C | 11,411 | 39.7 |
| | | | W.E. Arnold-Forster | Lab | 4,920 | 17.1 |
| | | | | | 1,032 | 3.5 |
| 1931 | | | Rt. Hon. W. Runciman | NL | Unopp. | |
| 1935 | | | Rt. Hon. W. Runciman | NL | Unopp. | |

[Elevation to the Peerage — Viscount Runciman of Doxford]

| Election | Electors | T'out | Candidate | Party | Votes | % |
|----------|----------|-------|-----------|-------|-------|---|
| 1937 (30/6) | 39,149 | 66.1 | N.A. Beechman | NL | 13,044 | 50.4 |
| | | | Rt. Hon. I. Foot | L | 12,834 | 49.6 |
| | | | | | 210 | 0.8 |
| 1945 | 42,706 | 70.6 | N.A. Beechman | NL | 14,256 | 47.3 |
| | | | H. Brinton | Lab | 8,190 | 27.2 |
| | | | E.F. Allison | L | 7,692 | 25.5 |
| | | | | | 6,066 | 20.1 |

| Election | Electors | T'out | Candidate | Party | Votes | % |
|---|---|---|---|---|---|---|
| 1918 | | | C.W. Lowther | Co C (Ind) | Unopp. | |
| 1922 | 21,714 | 79.9 | Hon. D.S.P. Howard | C | 8,815 | 50.8 |
| | | | Hon. G.W.A. Howard | L | 8,544 | 49.2 |
| | | | | | 271 | 1.6 |
| 1923 | 22,075 | 83.2 | Hon. D.S.P. Howard | C | 9,288 | 50.6 |
| | | | R.D. Holt | L | 9,070 | 49.4 |
| | | | | | 218 | 1.2 |
| 1924 | 22,717 | 86.0 | Hon. D.S.P. Howard | C | 10,586 | 54.2 |
| | | | R.D. Holt | L | 6,821 | 34.9 |
| | | | B. Brooke | Lab | 2,125* | 10.9 |
| | | | | | 3,765 | 19.3 |

[Succession to the Peerage — Lord Strathcona and Mount Royal]

| Election | Electors | T'out | Candidate | Party | Votes | % |
|---|---|---|---|---|---|---|
| 1926 (17/9) | 22,607[†] | 82.0 | F.F. Graham | C | 8,867 | 47.8 |
| | | | R.D. Holt | L | 6,871 | 37.1 |
| | | | H.W. McIntyre | Lab | 2,793 | 15.1 |
| | | | | | 1,996 | 10.7 |
| 1929 | 27,653 | 83.7 | F.F. Graham | C | 10,392 | 44.9 |
| | | | R.D. Holt | L | 9,661 | 41.7 |
| | | | C.A. O'Donnell | Lab | 3,092 | 13.4 |
| | | | | | 731 | 3.2 |
| 1931 | 28,055 | 84.6 | F.F. Graham | C | 12,504 | 52.7 |
| | | | W.H.W. Roberts | L | 11,227 | 47.3 |
| | | | | | 1,277 | 5.4 |
| 1935 | 28,769 | 83.9 | W.H.W. Roberts | L | 12,521 | 51.9 |
| | | | Sir F.F. Graham, Bt. | C | 11,627 | 48.1 |
| | | | | | 894 | 3.8 |
| 1945 | 31,631 | 75.6 | W.H.W. Roberts | L | 12,053 | 50.4 |
| | | | R.N. Carr | C | 11,855 | 49.6 |
| | | | | | 198 | 0.8 |

Note:—

1918: Lowther joined Horatio Bottomley's Independent Parliamentary Group.

| Election | Electors | T'out | Candidate | Party | Votes | % |
|---|---|---|---|---|---|---|
| 1918 | | | †Rt. Hon. J.W. Lowther | Co C | Unopp. | |
| [Resignation] | | | | | | |
| 1921 | 20,719 | 74.0 | Sir H.C. Lowther | Co C | 7,678 | 50.1 |
| (13/5) | | | L. Collison | L | 7,647 | 49.9 |
| | | | | | 31 | 0.2 |
| 1922 | 21,498 | 83.0 | L. Collison | L | 9,114 | 51.1 |
| | | | Sir H.C. Lowther | C | 8,736 | 48.9 |
| | | | | | 378 | 2.2 |
| 1923 | 21,735 | 83.2 | A.C.N. Dixey | C | 9,205 | 50.9 |
| | | | L. Collison | L | 8,878 | 49.1 |
| | | | | | 327 | 1.8 |
| 1924 | 22,166 | 75.9 | A.C.N. Dixey | C | 11,431 | 67.9 |
| | | | F. Tait | Lab | 5,404 | 32.1 |
| | | | | | 6,027 | 35.8 |
| 1929 | 27,465 | 85.3 | A.C.N. Dixey | C | 10,595 | 45.2 |
| | | | A. Holgate | L | 8,750 | 37.4 |
| | | | A. Dodd | Lab | 4,073 | 17.4 |
| | | | | | 1,845 | 7.8 |
| 1931 | 28,070 | 86.6 | A.C.N. Dixey | C | 12,904 | 53.1 |
| | | | A. Holgate | L | 11,412 | 46.9 |
| | | | | | 1,492 | 6.2 |
| 1935 | 28,737 | 78.4 | A.V.G. Dower | C | 14,496 | 64.3 |
| | | | H. Smith | Lab | 8,036 | 35.7 |
| | | | | | 6,460 | 28.6 |
| 1945 | 30,676 | 79.3 | A.V.G. Dower | C | 9,198 | 37.8 |
| | | | N.F. Newsome | L | 6,579 | 27.0 |
| | | | L.F. Browne | Lab | 6,350 | 26.1 |
| | | | T. Mitchell | Nat Ind | 2,204* | 9.1 |
| | | | | | 2,619 | 10.8 |

Note:—

1918:   Lowther was the Speaker of the House of Commons.

## CUMBERLAND, WHITEHAVEN [300]

| Election | Electors | T'out | Candidate | Party | Votes | % |
|---|---|---|---|---|---|---|
| 1918 | 27,440 | 72.0 | †J.A. Grant | Co C | 10,736 | 54.4 |
| | | | T. Gavan-Duffy | Lab | 9,016 | 45.6 |
| | | | | | 1,720 | 8.8 |
| 1922 | 27,699 | 87.0 | T. Gavan-Duffy | Lab | 10,935 | 45.3 |
| | | | J.A. Grant | C | 8,956 | 37.2 |
| | | | H.K. Campbell | L | 4,209 | 17.5 |
| | | | | | 1,979 | 8.1 |
| 1923 | 28,203 | 83.1 | T. Gavan-Duffy | Lab | 12,419 | 53.0 |
| | | | R.S. Hudson | C | 11,029 | 47.0 |
| | | | | | 1,390 | 6.0 |
| 1924 | 28,234 | 88.2 | R.S. Hudson | C | 13,149 | 52.8 |
| | | | T. Gavan-Duffy | Lab | 11,741 | 47.2 |
| | | | | | 1,408 | 5.6 |
| 1929 | 34,006 | 88.1 | M.P. Price | Lab | 14,034 | 46.8 |
| | | | R.S. Hudson | C | 12,382 | 41.3 |
| | | | H.D. Naylor | L | 3,558* | 11.9 |
| | | | | | 1,652 | 5.5 |
| 1931 | 34,079 | 89.6 | W. Nunn | C | 16,286 | 53.3 |
| | | | M.P. Price | Lab | 14,255 | 46.7 |
| | | | | | 2,031 | 6.6 |
| 1935 | 34,646 | 87.3 | F. Anderson | Lab | 14,794 | 48.9 |
| | | | W. Nunn | C | 14,442 | 47.8 |
| | | | T. Stephenson | ILP | 1,004* | 3.3 |
| | | | | | 352 | 1.1 |
| 1945 | 36,696 | 82.8 | F. Anderson | Lab | 18,568 | 61.1 |
| | | | W.O. Hill | C | 11,821 | 38.9 |
| | | | | | 6,747 | 22.2 |

| Election | Electors | T'out | Candidate | Party | Votes | % |
|---|---|---|---|---|---|---|
| 1918 | 28,691 | 70.7 | T. Cape | Lab | 10,441 | 51.5 |
| | | | D.J. Mason | C | 5,946 | 29.3 |
| | | | R.S. Stewart | L | 2,968 | 14.6 |
| | | | R. Millican | Ind | 943* | 4.6 |
| | | | | | 4,495 | 22.2 |
| 1922 | 31,789 | 83.7 | T. Cape | Lab | 14,546 | 54.7 |
| | | | L.E. Gaunt | C | 12,064 | 45.3 |
| | | | | | 2,482 | 9.4 |
| 1923 | 32,425 | 83.5 | T. Cape | Lab | 15,296 | 56.5 |
| | | | L.E. Gaunt | C | 11,781 | 43.5 |
| | | | | | 3,515 | 13.0 |
| 1924 | 32,690 | 84.4 | T. Cape | Lab | 15,353 | 55.6 |
| | | | E. Davies | C | 12,243 | 44.4 |
| | | | | | 3,110 | 11.2 |
| 1929 | 38,915 | 81.2 | T. Cape | Lab | 20,591 | 65.2 |
| | | | Sir J.S.P. Mellor, Bt. | C | 10,995 | 34.8 |
| | | | | | 9,596 | 30.4 |
| 1931 | 39,152 | 85.9 | T. Cape | Lab | 18,469 | 54.9 |
| | | | Hon. C.W. Lowther | C | 15,165 | 45.1 |
| | | | | | 3,304 | 9.8 |
| 1935 | | | T. Cape | Lab | Unopp. | |
| 1945 | 42,617 | 80.5 | T.F. Peart | Lab | 24,876 | 72.5 |
| | | | G.C. White | C | 9,438 | 27.5 |
| | | | | | 15,438 | 45.0 |

Note:—

1918: Stewart was issued with the Coalition 'coupon' but repudiated it.

## DERBYSHIRE, BELPER   [302]

| Election | Electors | T'out | Candidate | Party | Votes | % |
|---|---|---|---|---|---|---|
| 1918 | | | †J.G. Hancock | L | Unopp. | |
| 1922 | 32,113 | 63.6 | J.G. Hancock | L | 12,494 | 61.1 |
| | | | O.W. Wright | Lab | 7,942 | 38.9 |
| | | | | | 4,552 | 22.2 |
| 1923 | 33,024 | 70.0 | H. Wragg | C | 9,662 | 41.8 |
| | | | O.W. Wright | Lab | 7,284 | 31.5 |
| | | | J.G. Hancock | L | 6,178 | 26.7 |
| | | | | | 2,378 | 10.3 |
| 1924 | 34,093 | 74.5 | H. Wragg | C | 14,766 | 58.2 |
| | | | J. Lees | Lab | 10,618 | 41.8 |
| | | | | | 4,148 | 16.4 |
| 1929 | 44,892 | 82.7 | J. Lees | Lab | 15,958 | 43.0 |
| | | | H. Wragg | C | 13,003 | 35.0 |
| | | | T.S. Anderson | L | 8,149 | 22.0 |
| | | | | | 2,955 | 8.0 |
| 1931 | 47,335 | 82.0 | H. Wragg | C | 23,361 | 60.2 |
| | | | J. Lees | Lab | 15,450 | 39.8 |
| | | | | | 7,911 | 20.4 |
| 1935 | 51,202 | 76.8 | H. Wragg | C | 20,078 | 51.1 |
| | | | J. Lees | Lab | 19,250 | 48.9 |
| | | | | | 828 | 2.2 |
| 1945 | 57,405 | 80.2 | G.A. Brown | Lab | 24,319 | 52.9 |
| | | | G. Hampson | C | 15,438 | 33.5 |
| | | | R.A. Burrows | L | 6,276 | 13.6 |
| | | | | | 8,881 | 19.4 |

Note:

1918: Hancock was issued with the Coalition 'coupon' but repudiated it.

| Election | Electors | T'out | Candidate | Party | Votes | % |
|---|---|---|---|---|---|---|
| 1918 | | | †B. Kenyon | L | Unopp. | |
| 1922 | | | B. Kenyon | L | Unopp. | |
| 1923 | 34,648 | 69.0 | B. Kenyon | L | 12,164 | 50.9 |
| | | | G. Benson | Lab | 6,198 | 25.9 |
| | | | R.F.H. Broomhead-Colton-Fox | C | 5,541 | 23.2 |
| | | | | | 5,966 | 25.0 |
| 1924 | 35,989 | 64.4 | B. Kenyon | L | 13,971 | 60.3 |
| | | | G. Benson | Lab | 9,206 | 39.7 |
| | | | | | 4,765 | 20.6 |
| 1929 | 48,278 | 77.8 | G. Benson | Lab | 20,296 | 54.1 |
| | | | R.J.E. Conant | C | 9,915 | 26.4 |
| | | | H. Cropper | L | 7,329 | 19.5 |
| | | | | | 10,381 | 27.7 |
| 1931 | 50,076 | 80.0 | R.J.E. Conant | C | 23,026 | 57.5 |
| | | | G. Benson | Lab | 17,046 | 42.5 |
| | | | | | 5,980 | 15.0 |
| 1935 | 52,758 | 79.8 | G. Benson | Lab | 21,439 | 51.0 |
| | | | R.J.E. Conant | C | 16,555 | 39.3 |
| | | | R.G. Hill | L | 4,096* | 9.7 |
| | | | | | 4,884 | 11.7 |
| 1945 | 60,686 | 77.3 | G. Benson | Lab | 29,459 | 62.8 |
| | | | Lord Andrew Cavendish | C | 17,424 | 37.2 |
| | | | | | 12,035 | 25.6 |

Note:—

1918: Kenyon was issued with the Coalition 'coupon' but repudiated it.

# DERBYSHIRE, CLAY CROSS [304]

| Election | Electors | T'out | Candidate | Party | Votes | % |
|---|---|---|---|---|---|---|
| 1918 | 29,181 | 50.6 | T.T. Broad | Co L | 7,987 | 54.1 |
| | | | F. Hall | Lab | 6,766 | 45.9 |
| | | | | | 1,221 | 8.2 |
| 1922 | 31,611 | 72.1 | C. Duncan | Lab | 13,206 | 57.9 |
| | | | Rt. Hon. C.F.G. Masterman | L | 6,294 | 27.6 |
| | | | T.T. Broad | NL | 3,294 | 14.5 |
| | | | | | 6,912 | 30.3 |
| 1923 | 34,729 | 61.4 | C. Duncan | Lab | 11,939 | 56.0 |
| | | | J. Sherwood-Kelly | C | 4,881 | 22.9 |
| | | | F.C. Thornborough | L | 4,488 | 21.1 |
| | | | | | 7,058 | 33.1 |
| 1924 | 33,737 | 67.2 | C. Duncan | Lab | 14,618 | 64.4 |
| | | | J. Sherwood-Kelly | C | 8,069 | 35.6 |
| | | | | | 6,549 | 28.8 |
| 1929 | 42,557 | 71.8 | C. Duncan | Lab | 24,480 | 80.2 |
| | | | A.M. Lyons | C | 6,055 | 19.8 |
| | | | | | 18,425 | 60.4 |
| 1931 | 43,931 | 74.6 | C. Duncan | Lab | 21,163 | 64.6 |
| | | | J. Weinberg | NL | 11,611 | 35.4 |
| | | | | | 9,552 | 29.2 |
| [Death] | | | | | | |
| 1933 (1/9) | 44,466 | 71.2 | Rt. Hon. A. Henderson | Lab | 21,931 | 69.3 |
| | | | J. Moores | C | 6,293 | 19.9 |
| | | | H. Pollitt | Com | 3,434* | 10.8 |
| | | | | | 15,638 | 49.4 |
| [Seat Vacant at Dissolution (Death)] | | | | | | |
| 1935 | 44,785 | 73.6 | A. Holland | Lab | 24,590 | 74.6 |
| | | | Miss E.B.H. Jackson | C | 8,391 | 25.4 |
| | | | | | 16,199 | 49.2 |
| [Death] | | | | | | |
| 1936 (5/11) | 44,651 | 72.4 | G. Ridley | Lab | 24,290 | 75.1 |
| | | | Miss E.B.H. Jackson | C | 8,042 | 24.9 |
| | | | | | 16,248 | 50.2 |
| [Death] | | | | | | |
| 1944 (14/4) | 44,535 | 40.3 | H. Neal | Lab | 13,693 | 76.3 |
| | | | P. Hicken | Ind | 2,336 | 13.0 |
| | | | Hon. W. Douglas-Home | Ind Prog | 1,911* | 10.7 |
| | | | | | 11,357 | 63.3 |
| 1945 | 47,456 | 70.7 | H. Neal | Lab | 27,538 | 82.1 |
| | | | W.P. Bull | C | 6,021 | 17.9 |
| | | | | | 21,517 | 64.2 |

Notes:—

1944: Hicken sought election as a 'Workers' Anti-Fascist' candidate.

Douglas-Home sought election as an 'Atlantic Charter' candidate.

| Election | Electors | T'out | Candidate | Party | Votes | % |
|---|---|---|---|---|---|---|
| 1918 | 33,075 | 62.3 | †S.H. Hill-Wood | Co C | 12,118 | 58.8 |
|  |  |  | C. Brookes | L | 8,504 | 41.2 |
|  |  |  |  |  | 3,614 | 17.6 |
| 1922 | 34,242 | 82.9 | Sir S.H. Hill-Wood, Bt. | C | 14,892 | 52.5 |
|  |  |  | F. Anderson | Lab | 7,698 | 27.1 |
|  |  |  | Hon. Lady Barlow | L | 5,802 | 20.4 |
|  |  |  |  |  | 7,194 | 25.4 |
| 1923 | 34,896 | 78.2 | Sir S.H. Hill-Wood, Bt. | C | 12,162 | 44.6 |
|  |  |  | R. McDougall | L | 9,432 | 34.6 |
|  |  |  | F. Anderson | Lab | 5,684 | 20.8 |
|  |  |  |  |  | 2,730 | 10.0 |
| 1924 | 35,588 | 76.8 | Sir S.H. Hill-Wood, Bt. | C | 14,560 | 53.3 |
|  |  |  | R. McDougall | L | 12,772 | 46.7 |
|  |  |  |  |  | 1,788 | 6.6 |
| 1929 | 47,066 | 80.9 | Sir A.J. Law | C | 16,406 | 43.1 |
|  |  |  | R. McDougall | L | 11,083 | 29.1 |
|  |  |  | G.H. Bagnall | Lab | 10,567 | 27.8 |
|  |  |  |  |  | 5,323 | 14.0 |
| 1931 | 48,489 | 76.8 | Sir A.J. Law | C | 27,577 | 74.1 |
|  |  |  | G.H. Bagnall | Lab | 9,640 | 25.9 |
|  |  |  |  |  | 17,937 | 48.2 |
| 1935 | 49,190 | 72.2 | Sir A.J. Law | C | 19,145 | 53.9 |
|  |  |  | R.W. Wright | Lab | 9,559 | 26.9 |
|  |  |  | L. Radcliffe | L | 6,831 | 19.2 |
|  |  |  |  |  | 9,586 | 27.0 |
| [Death] |  |  |  |  |  |  |
| 1939 (7/10) |  |  | A.H.E. Molson | C | Unopp. |  |
| 1945 | 51,136 | 77.8 | A.H.E. Molson | C | 18,113 | 45.5 |
|  |  |  | W.M. Halsall | Lab | 15,454 | 38.8 |
|  |  |  | T.S. Rothwell | L | 6,230 | 15.7 |
|  |  |  |  |  | 2,659 | 6.7 |

# DERBYSHIRE, ILKESTON [306]

| Election | Electors | T'out | Candidate | Party | Votes | % |
|---|---|---|---|---|---|---|
| 1918 | 28,896 | 61.0 | †Rt. Hon. J.E.B. Seely | Co L | 9,660 | 54.8 |
| | | | G.H. Oliver | Lab | 7,962 | 45.2 |
| | | | | | 1,698 | 9.6 |
| 1922 | 30,738 | 76.8 | G.H. Oliver | Lab | 9,432 | 40.0 |
| | | | Rt. Hon. J.E.B. Seely | NL | 8,348 | 35.3 |
| | | | W.M. Freeman | C | 5,841 | 24.7 |
| | | | | | 1,084 | 4.7 |
| 1923 | 31,503 | 69.4 | G.H. Oliver | Lab | 9,191 | 42.1 |
| | | | W.M. Freeman | C | 6,566 | 30.0 |
| | | | T.W. Casey | L | 6,112 | 27.9 |
| | | | | | 2,625 | 12.1 |
| 1924 | 32,243 | 76.1 | G.H. Oliver | Lab | 11,011 | 44.9 |
| | | | H.V.A.M. Raikes | C | 9,203 | 37.5 |
| | | | Hon. Lady Barlow | L | 4,320 | 17.6 |
| | | | | | 1,808 | 7.4 |
| 1929 | 42,430 | 80.7 | G.H. Oliver | Lab | 20,202 | 59.0 |
| | | | Dr. J.V. Shaw | L | 7,766 | 22.7 |
| | | | H.V.A.M. Raikes | C | 6,258 | 18.3 |
| | | | | | 12,436 | 36.3 |
| 1931 | 44,116 | 79.7 | A.J. Flint | N Lab | 17,587 | 50.0 |
| | | | G.H. Oliver | Lab | 17,585 | 50.0 |
| | | | | | 2 | 0.0 |
| 1935 | 45,427 | 81.7 | G.H. Oliver | Lab | 23,851 | 64.3 |
| | | | Sir C. Markham, Bt. | Nat | 13,250 | 35.7 |
| | | | | | 10,601 | 28.6 |
| 1945 | 49,007 | 81.0 | G.H. Oliver | Lab | 26,536 | 66.8 |
| | | | P.G. Hartley | C | 8,439 | 21.3 |
| | | | C.O. Foster | L | 4,720* | 11.9 |
| | | | | | 18,097 | 45.5 |

| Election | Electors | T'out | Candidate | Party | Votes | % |
|---|---|---|---|---|---|---|
| 1918 | 33,567 | 58.0 | J.S. Holmes | L | 6,117 | 31.4 |
| | | | F. Lee | Lab | 5,560 | 28.6 |
| | | | †G.R.H. Bowden | Ind C | 5,049 | 25.9 |
| | | | Marquess of Hartington | Co C | 2,738 | 14.1 |
| | | | | | 557 | 2.8 |
| 1922 | 35,683 | 77.3 | F. Lee | Lab | 9,359 | 33.9 |
| | | | J.S. Holmes | L | 9,344 | 33.9 |
| | | | C. Waterhouse | C | 8,878 | 32.2 |
| | | | | | 15 | 0.0 |
| 1923 | 36,712 | 75.8 | F. Lee | Lab | 10,971 | 39.5 |
| | | | C. Waterhouse | C | 8,768 | 31.5 |
| | | | P. Guedalla | L | 8,080 | 29.0 |
| | | | | | 2,203 | 8.0 |
| 1924 | 38,025 | 78.5 | F. Lee | Lab | 13,420 | 44.9 |
| | | | G.R.H. Bowden | C | 9,914 | 33.2 |
| | | | P. Guedalla | L | 6,529 | 21.9 |
| | | | | | 3,506 | 11.7 |
| 1929 | 49,718 | 79.8 | F. Lee | Lab | 21,633 | 54.6 |
| | | | R.E.H. Samuelson | C | 9,167 | 23.1 |
| | | | H.A. Briggs | L | 8,861 | 22.3 |
| | | | | | 12,466 | 31.5 |
| 1931 | 51,407 | 79.4 | J.B. Whyte | C | 20,719 | 50.8 |
| | | | F. Lee | Lab | 19,385 | 47.5 |
| | | | A.V. Williams | NP | 689* | 1.7 |
| | | | | | 1,334 | 3.3 |
| 1935 | 56,954 | 77.9 | F. Lee | Lab | 25,382 | 57.2 |
| | | | H.B.T. Cox | C | 15,802 | 35.6 |
| | | | A.T. Marwood | L | 3,186* | 7.2 |
| | | | | | 9,580 | 21.6 |
| [Death] | | | | | | |
| 1942 (2/3) | | | H. White | Lab | Unopp. | |
| 1945 | 69,091 | 79.0 | H. White | Lab | 35,795 | 65.6 |
| | | | R.E. Warlow | C | 18,789 | 34.4 |
| | | | | | 17,006 | 31.2 |

Note:—

1922: A petition was lodged relating to the election but was dismissed after a recount and scrutiny led to an increased majority for the Labour candidate. The original figures had been Lee 9,357; Holmes 9,352; Waterhouse 8,879; Labour majority, 5.

| Election | Electors | T'out | Candidate | Party | Votes | % |
|---|---|---|---|---|---|---|
| 1918 | 40,112 | 58.4 | H.H. Gregory | Co L | 15,504 | 66.2 |
| | | | S. Truman | Lab | 7,923 | 33.8 |
| | | | | | 7,581 | 32.4 |
| | | | | | | |
| 1922 | 43,172 | 79.8 | H.D. Lorimer | C | 14,664 | 42.6 |
| | | | S. Truman | Lab | 10,201 | 29.6 |
| | | | G. Owen | NL | 9,585 | 27.8 |
| | | | | | 4,463 | 13.0 |
| | | | | | | |
| 1923 | 44,171 | 75.7 | H.D. Lorimer | C | 12,902 | 38.5 |
| | | | A. Goodere | Lab | 10,919 | 32.7 |
| | | | G. Stone | L | 9,620 | 28.8 |
| | | | | | 1,983 | 5.8 |
| | | | | | | |
| 1924 | 45,359 | 81.9 | J.A. Grant | C | 16,448 | 44.3 |
| | | | A. Goodere | Lab | 15,033 | 40.5 |
| | | | A.J. Suenson-Taylor | L | 5,647 | 15.2 |
| | | | | | 1,415 | 3.8 |
| | | | | | | |
| 1929 | 63,413 | 83.4 | D.G. Pole | Lab | 25,101 | 47.4 |
| | | | Sir J.A. Grant, Bt. | C | 17,803 | 33.7 |
| | | | E.J. Johnson | L | 9,998 | 18.9 |
| | | | | | 7,298 | 13.7 |
| | | | | | | |
| 1931 | 70,345 | 82.3 | P.V. Emrys-Evans | C | 33,965 | 58.6 |
| | | | D.G. Pole | Lab | 23,958 | 41.4 |
| | | | | | 10,007 | 17.2 |
| | | | | | | |
| 1935 | 82,645 | 73.5 | P.V. Emrys-Evans | C | 31,321 | 51.5 |
| | | | F.A.P. Rowe | Lab | 29,462 | 48.5 |
| | | | | | 1,859 | 3.0 |
| | | | | | | |
| 1945 | 104,570 | 78.9 | A.J. Champion | Lab | 47,586 | 57.7 |
| | | | P.V. Emrys-Evans | C | 24,636 | 29.9 |
| | | | N. Heathcote | L | 10,255* | 12.4 |
| | | | | | 22,950 | 27.8 |

| Election | Electors | T'out | Candidate | Party | Votes | % |
|---|---|---|---|---|---|---|
| 1918 | 29,323 | 66.0 | C.F. White (Senr.) | L | 10,752 | 55.6 |
|  |  |  | †Earl of Kerry | Co C | 8,592 | 44.4 |
|  |  |  |  |  | 2,160 | 11.2 |
| 1922 | 30,231 | 86.1 | C.F. White (Senr.) | L | 13,060 | 50.2 |
|  |  |  | Marquess of Hartington | C | 12,973 | 49.8 |
|  |  |  |  |  | 87 | 0.4 |
| 1923 | 31,067 | 84.9 | Marquess of Hartington | C | 13,419 | 50.9 |
|  |  |  | W.C. Mallison | L | 12,966 | 49.1 |
|  |  |  |  |  | 453 | 1.8 |
| 1924 | 31,757 | 84.8 | Marquess of Hartington | C | 15,324 | 56.9 |
|  |  |  | W.C. Mallison | L | 11,612 | 43.1 |
|  |  |  |  |  | 3,712 | 13.8 |
| 1929 | 40,487 | 83.2 | Marquess of Hartington | C | 16,760 | 49.7 |
|  |  |  | W.C. Mallison | L | 13,277 | 39.4 |
|  |  |  | W. Wilkinson | Lab | 3,660* | 10.9 |
|  |  |  |  |  | 3,483 | 10.3 |
| 1931 |  |  | Marquess of Hartington | C | Unopp. |  |
| 1935 |  |  | Marquess of Hartington | C | Unopp. |  |

[Succession to the Peerage — Duke of Devonshire]

| Election | Electors | T'out | Candidate | Party | Votes | % |
|---|---|---|---|---|---|---|
| 1938 (2/6) | 43,410 | 79.4 | H.P. Hunloke | C | 16,740 | 48.6 |
|  |  |  | C.F. White (Junr.) | Lab | 11,216 | 32.5 |
|  |  |  | M. Gray | L | 6,515 | 18.9 |
|  |  |  |  |  | 5,524 | 16.1 |

[Resignation]

| Election | Electors | T'out | Candidate | Party | Votes | % |
|---|---|---|---|---|---|---|
| 1944 (17/2) | 43,371 | 65.4 | C.F. White (Junr.) | Ind Lab (Lab) | 16,336 | 57.7 |
|  |  |  | Marquess of Hartington | C | 11,775 | 41.5 |
|  |  |  | R. Goodall | Agric | 233* | 0.8 |
|  |  |  |  |  | 4,561 | 16.2 |
| 1945 | 45,981 | 81.7 | C.F. White (Junr.) | Lab | 18,331 | 48.8 |
|  |  |  | W.T. Aitken | C | 18,175 | 48.4 |
|  |  |  | R. Goodall | Agric | 1,068* | 2.8 |
|  |  |  |  |  | 156 | 0.4 |

Notes:—

1923: Polling was delayed until December 20 owing to the death, after nomination, of the Liberal candidate, C.F. White.

1944: White was the prospective Labour candidate for the constituency but resigned from the Labour Party (who were committed to the electoral truce) in order to fight the election. He received unofficial support from the local Labour Party and was also supported by the Common Wealth Movement.

| Election | Electors | T'out | Candidate | Party | Votes | % |
|---|---|---|---|---|---|---|
| 1918 | 31,790 | 69.1 | J.T.T. Rees | L (Co L) | 11,281 | 51.4 |
| | | | C.S. Parker | C | 10,679 | 48.6 |
| | | | | | 602 | 2.8 |
| 1922 | 33,004 | 83.1 | B.E. Peto | C | 13,793 | 50.3 |
| | | | J.T.T. Rees | L | 13,619 | 49.7 |
| | | | | | 174 | 0.6 |
| 1923 | 33,939 | 87.6 | J.T.T. Rees | L | 14,880 | 50.1 |
| | | | B.E. Peto | C | 13,614 | 45.8 |
| | | | R.W. Gifford | Lab | 1,225* | 4.1 |
| | | | | | 1,266 | 4.3 |
| 1924 | 34,632 | 85.9 | B.E. Peto | C (Ind C) (C) | 15,479 | 52.0 |
| | | | J.T.T. Rees | L | 14,284 | 48.0 |
| | | | | | 1,195 | 4.0 |
| 1929 | 43,596 | 86.8 | Sir B.E. Peto, Bt. | C | 17,382 | 45.9 |
| | | | D.M. Mason | L | 16,593 | 43.9 |
| | | | D.E. Mullins | Lab | 3,864* | 10.2 |
| | | | | | 789 | 2.0 |
| 1931 | 44,452 | 86.3 | Sir B.E. Peto, Bt. | C | 20,028 | 52.2 |
| | | | R.T.D. Acland | L | 18,318 | 47.8 |
| | | | | | 1,710 | 4.4 |
| 1935 | 45,830 | 83.8 | R.T.D. Acland | L (CW) | 19,432 | 50.6 |
| | | | B.G. Lampard-Vachell | C | 18,978 | 49.4 |
| | | | | | 454 | 1.2 |
| 1945 | 55,170 | 75.8 | C.H.M. Peto | C | 17,822 | 42.6 |
| | | | M.R. Bonham Carter | L | 13,752 | 32.9 |
| | | | I.A.J. Williams | Lab | 10,237 | 24.5 |
| | | | | | 4,070 | 9.7 |

| Election | Electors | T'out | Candidate | Party | Votes | % |
|----------|----------|-------|-----------|-------|-------|---|
| 1918 | | | †A.C. Morrison-Bell | Co C | Unopp. | |
| 1922 | 29,546 | 79.1 | A.C. Morrison-Bell | C | 12,972 | 55.5 |
| | | | J.G.H. Halse | L | 10,404 | 44.5 |
| | | | | | 2,568 | 11.0 |
| 1923 | 30,443 | 81.0 | Sir A.C. Morrison-Bell, Bt. | C | 12,470 | 50.6 |
| | | | J.G.H. Halse | L | 12,177 | 49.4 |
| | | | | | 293 | 1.2 |
| 1924 | 31,388 | 85.5 | Sir A.C. Morrison-Bell, Bt. | C | 14,804 | 55.2 |
| | | | J.G.H. Halse | L | 12,025 | 44.8 |
| | | | | | 2,779 | 10.4 |
| 1929 | 41,723 | 84.3 | Sir A.C. Morrison-Bell, Bt. | C | 17,911 | 50.9 |
| | | | J.G.H. Halse | L | 16,353 | 46.5 |
| | | | Mrs. F.R. Davies | Lab | 915* | 2.6 |
| | | | | | 1,558 | 4.4 |
| 1931 | 43,625 | 83.5 | C. Drewe | C | 21,854 | 60.0 |
| | | | J.G.H. Halse | L | 14,563 | 40.0 |
| | | | | | 7,291 | 20.0 |
| 1935 | 45,577 | 69.6 | C. Drewe | C | 22,805 | 71.9 |
| | | | J.R. Morris | Lab | 8,916 | 28.1 |
| | | | | | 13,889 | 43.8 |
| 1945 | 52,949 | 70.3 | C. Drewe | C | 24,499 | 65.8 |
| | | | H.T. Langdon | Lab | 12,739 | 34.2 |
| | | | | | 11,760 | 31.6 |

| Election | Electors | T'out | Candidate | Party | Votes | % |
|---|---|---|---|---|---|---|
| 1918 | 28,139 | 65.8 | †Rt. Hon. G. Lambert | L (Co L) | 10,424 | 56.3 |
|  |  |  | H.W.S. Sparkes | Co C | 8,093 | 43.7 |
|  |  |  |  |  | 2,331 | 12.6 |
| 1922 |  |  | Rt. Hon. G. Lambert | L | Unopp. |  |
| 1923 |  |  | Rt. Hon. G. Lambert | L | Unopp. |  |
| 1924 | 29,257 | 85.3 | C. Drewe | C | 12,811 | 51.3 |
|  |  |  | Rt. Hon. G. Lambert | L | 12,157 | 48.7 |
|  |  |  |  |  | 654 | 2.6 |
| 1929 | 35,884 | 87.4 | Rt. Hon. G. Lambert | L (NL) | 15,072 | 48.1 |
|  |  |  | C. Drewe | C | 13,567 | 43.2 |
|  |  |  | R.P. Messel | Lab | 2,731* | 8.7 |
|  |  |  |  |  | 1,505 | 4.9 |
| 1931 | 36,033 | 81.0 | Rt. Hon. G. Lambert | NL | 25,700 | 88.0 |
|  |  |  | R.P. Messel | Lab | 3,499* | 12.0 |
|  |  |  |  |  | 22,201 | 76.0 |
| 1935 | 36,176 | 72.9 | Rt. Hon. G. Lambert | NL | 20,767 | 78.7 |
|  |  |  | H.F. Chilcott | Lab | 5,610 | 21.3 |
|  |  |  |  |  | 15,157 | 57.4 |
| 1945 | 39,221 | 71.9 | Hon. G. Lambert | NL | 19,065 | 67.6 |
|  |  |  | C.D.C. Lang | Lab | 9,140 | 32.4 |
|  |  |  |  |  | 9,925 | 35.2 |

| Election | Electors | T'out | Candidate | Party | Votes | % |
|---|---|---|---|---|---|---|
| 1918 | 25,979 | 62.2 | C. Williams | Co C | 9,157 | 56.7 |
| | | | H. Geen | L | 7,005 | 43.3 |
| | | | | | 2,152 | 13.4 |
| 1922 | 27,651 | 77.6 | M.R. Thornton | L | 11,708 | 54.5 |
| | | | C. Williams | C | 9,757 | 45.5 |
| | | | | | 1,951 | 9.0 |
| 1923 | 28,242 | 77.7 | M.R. Thornton | L | 11,883 | 54.1 |
| | | | P.P. Kenyon-Slaney | C | 10,072 | 45.9 |
| | | | | | 1,811 | 8.2 |
| 1924 | 29,419 | 77.7 | P.P. Kenyon-Slaney | C | 12,058 | 52.8 |
| | | | M.R. Thornton | L | 10,786 | 47.2 |
| | | | | | 1,272 | 5.6 |
| [Death] | | | | | | |
| 1928 (11/10) | 30,755 | 77.3 | W.D. Wright | C | 10,745 | 45.2 |
| | | | R.T.H. Fletcher | L | 10,572 | 44.5 |
| | | | R. Davies | Lab | 2,449* | 10.3 |
| | | | | | 173 | 0.7 |
| 1929 | 38,786 | 82.0 | W.D. Wright | C | 14,192 | 44.7 |
| | | | Mrs. H. Runciman | L | 14,040 | 44.1 |
| | | | R. Davies | Lab | 3,574* | 11.2 |
| | | | | | 152 | 0.6 |
| 1931 | 39,637 | 83.3 | C.M. Patrick | C | 17,310 | 52.4 |
| | | | J.A. Day | L | 13,592 | 41.2 |
| | | | R. Davies | Lab | 2,124* | 6.4 |
| | | | | | 3,718 | 11.2 |
| 1935 | 42,560 | 77.9 | C.M. Patrick | C | 17,475 | 52.8 |
| | | | J.A. Day | L | 13,422 | 40.5 |
| | | | C.H. Townsend | Lab | 2,236* | 6.7 |
| | | | | | 4,053 | 12.3 |
| [Death] | | | | | | |
| 1942 (2/4) | | | H.G. Studholme | C | Unopp. | |
| 1945 | 55,589 | 75.6 | H.G. Studholme | C | 19,730 | 47.0 |
| | | | Rt. Hon. I. Foot | L | 13,764 | 32.7 |
| | | | J. Finnigan | Lab | 8,539 | 20.3 |
| | | | | | 5,966 | 14.3 |

| Election | Electors | T'out | Candidate | Party | Votes | % |
|---|---|---|---|---|---|---|
| 1918 | 25,925 | 64.8 | †C.R.S. Carew | Co C | 9,598 | 57.2 |
| | | | Sir E. Penton | L | 4,827 | 28.7 |
| | | | Rev. D.B. Fraser | Lab | 2,377 | 14.1 |
| | | | | | 4,771 | 28.5 |
| 1922 | 27,452 | 80.1 | H.W.S. Sparkes | C | 10,304 | 46.9 |
| | | | Rt. Hon. F.D. Acland | L | 10,230 | 46.5 |
| | | | F. Brown | Lab | 1,457* | 6.6 |
| | | | | | 74 | 0.4 |
| [Death] | | | | | | |
| 1923 (21/6) | 27,452† | 88.1 | Rt. Hon. F.D. Acland | L | 12,041 | 49.9 |
| | | | G.J. Acland-Troyte | C | 11,638 | 48.1 |
| | | | F. Brown | Ind Lab | 495* | 2.0 |
| | | | | | 403 | 1.8 |
| 1923 | 28,151 | 87.4 | Rt. Hon. F.D. Acland | L | 12,303 | 50.0 |
| | | | G.J. Acland-Troyte | C | 12,300 | 50.0 |
| | | | | | 3 | 0.0 |
| 1924 | 28,331 | 90.2 | G.J. Acland-Troyte | C | 13,601 | 53.2 |
| | | | Rt. Hon. F.D. Acland | L | 11,942 | 46.8 |
| | | | | | 1,659 | 6.4 |
| 1929 | 35,436 | 86.2 | G.J. Acland-Troyte | C | 15,423 | 50.5 |
| | | | D.M. Foot | L | 12,908 | 42.3 |
| | | | H.W. Wreford-Glanvill | Lab | 2,199* | 7.2 |
| | | | | | 2,515 | 8.2 |
| 1931 | | | G.J. Acland-Troyte | C | Unopp. | |
| 1935 | | | G.J. Acland-Troyte | C | Unopp. | |
| 1945 | 44,557 | 74.0 | D. Heathcoat-Amory | C | 16,919 | 51.3 |
| | | | G.C. Tompson | Lab | 8,634 | 26.2 |
| | | | C.H. Blackburn | L | 7,418 | 22.5 |
| | | | | | 8,285 | 25.1 |

# DEVON, TORQUAY [315]

| Election | Electors | T'out | Candidate | Party | Votes | % |
|---|---|---|---|---|---|---|
| 1918 | 32,584 | 65.3 | †C.R. Burn | Co C | 14,068 | 66.2 |
| | | | A.E.Y. Trestrail | Lab | 4,029 | 18.9 |
| | | | R. Cooke | L | 3,173 | 14.9 |
| | | | | | 10,039 | 47.3 |
| 1922 | 35,817 | 78.5 | C.R. Burn | C | 14,676 | 52.2 |
| | | | P.G. Thompson | L | 13,425 | 47.8 |
| | | | | | 1,251 | 4.4 |
| 1923 | 37,770 | 80.0 | P.G. Thompson | L | 15,294 | 50.6 |
| | | | C. Williams | C | 14,922 | 49.4 |
| | | | | | 372 | 1.2 |
| 1924 | 38,915 | 84.4 | C. Williams | C | 18,119 | 55.2 |
| | | | P.G. Thompson | L | 11,958 | 36.4 |
| | | | A. Moyle | Lab | 2,752* | 8.4 |
| | | | | | 6,161 | 18.8 |
| 1929 | 53,340 | 81.7 | C. Williams | C | 21,690 | 49.7 |
| | | | R.T.D. Acland | L | 16,337 | 37.5 |
| | | | H.M. Medland | Lab | 5,576 | 12.8 |
| | | | | | 5,353 | 12.2 |
| 1931 | 56,380 | 74.6 | C. Williams | C | 34,690 | 82.5 |
| | | | H.M. Medland | Lab | 7,351 | 17.5 |
| | | | | | 27,339 | 65.0 |
| 1935 | 59,835 | 71.0 | C. Williams | C | 27,008 | 63.6 |
| | | | H. Samways | L | 9,073 | 21.4 |
| | | | F. Scardifield | Lab | 6,387 | 15.0 |
| | | | | | 17,935 | 42.2 |
| 1945 | 72,973 | 71.4 | C. Williams | C | 25,479 | 48.9 |
| | | | G. Cornes | Lab | 13,590 | 26.1 |
| | | | S.G. Putt | L | 13,003 | 25.0 |
| | | | | | 11,889 | 22.8 |

## DEVON, TOTNES [316]

| Election | Electors | T'out | Candidate | Party | Votes | % |
|---|---|---|---|---|---|---|
| 1918 | 39,042 | 63.9 | †Rt. Hon. F.B. Mildmay | Co C | 14,680 | 58.8 |
| | | | J.A.R. Cairns | L | 10,266 | 41.2 |
| | | | | | 4,414 | 17.6 |
| 1922 | 40,417 | 78.1 | S.E. Harvey | C | 16,532 | 52.4 |
| | | | T.H.J. Underdown | L | 15,032 | 47.6 |
| | | | | | 1,500 | 4.8 |
| 1923 | 41,115 | 80.7 | H.H. Vivian | L | 16,845 | 50.8 |
| | | | S.E. Harvey | C | 16,343 | 49.2 |
| | | | | | 502 | 1.6 |
| 1924 | 42,757 | 86.1 | S.E. Harvey | C | 19,771 | 53.7 |
| | | | H.H. Vivian | L | 14,786 | 40.2 |
| | | | Miss K.F. Spurrell | Lab | 2,240* | 6.1 |
| | | | | | 4,985 | 13.5 |
| 1929 | 54,471 | 83.1 | S.E. Harvey | C | 21,673 | 47.8 |
| | | | P.F. Rowsell | L | 17,790 | 39.3 |
| | | | Miss K.F. Spurrell | Lab | 5,828 | 12.9 |
| | | | | | 3,883 | 8.5 |
| 1931 | 56,308 | 83.4 | S.E. Harvey | C | 26,765 | 57.0 |
| | | | E.R. Haylor | L | 20,203 | 43.0 |
| | | | | | 6,562 | 14.0 |
| 1935 | 58,434 | 79.2 | R.H. Rayner | C | 24,815 | 53.6 |
| | | | E.R. Haylor | L | 17,639 | 38.1 |
| | | | W.R.J. Henwood | Lab | 3,848* | 8.3 |
| | | | | | 7,176 | 15.5 |
| 1945 | 64,801 | 74.5 | R.H. Rayner | C | 24,638 | 51.1 |
| | | | J.R. Warde | Lab | 16,098 | 33.3 |
| | | | T.H. Aggett | L | 7,536 | 15.6 |
| | | | | | 8,540 | 17.8 |

## DORSET, EASTERN [317]

| Election | Electors | T'out | Candidate | Party | Votes | % |
|---|---|---|---|---|---|---|
| 1918 | 29,988 | 54.2 | †F.E. Guest | Co L | 11,944 | 73.4 |
| | | | A. Smith | Lab | 4,321 | 26.6 |
| | | | | | 7,623 | 46.8 |

[Appointed Secretary of State for Air]

| Election | Electors | T'out | Candidate | Party | Votes | % |
|---|---|---|---|---|---|---|
| 1921 (16/4) | | | Rt. Hon. F.E. Guest | Co L | Unopp. | |
| 1922 | 31,797 | 80.2 | G.R. Hall Caine | Ind C (C) | 12,513 | 49.1 |
| | | | Rev. F.J. Hopkins | Lab | 6,914 | 27.1 |
| | | | Rt. Hon. F.E. Guest | NL | 6,062 | 23.8 |
| | | | | | 5,599 | 22.0 |
| 1923 | 32,828 | 78.5 | G.R. Hall Caine | C | 12,480 | 48.5 |
| | | | R.E.W. Kirby | L | 7,535 | 29.2 |
| | | | Rev. F.J. Hopkins | Lab | 5,760 | 22.3 |
| | | | | | 4,945 | 19.3 |
| 1924 | 34,249 | 80.3 | G.R. Hall Caine | C | 14,479 | 52.6 |
| | | | A.E. Glassey | L | 8,828 | 32.1 |
| | | | E.J. Stocker | Lab | 4,205 | 15.3 |
| | | | | | 5,651 | 20.5 |
| 1929 | 51,756 | 81.5 | A.E. Glassey | L | 17,810 | 42.2 |
| | | | G.R. Hall Caine | C | 17,533 | 41.6 |
| | | | E.J. Stocker | Lab | 6,819 | 16.2 |
| | | | | | 277 | 0.6 |
| 1931 | 56,304 | 82.6 | G.R. Hall Caine | C | 20,711 | 44.5 |
| | | | A.E. Glassey | NL | 18,801 | 40.4 |
| | | | E.J. Stocker | Lab | 7,009 | 15.1 |
| | | | | | 1,910 | 4.1 |
| 1935 | 64,068 | 74.4 | G.R. Hall Caine | C | 25,520 | 53.5 |
| | | | F.W. Raffety | L | 11,349 | 23.8 |
| | | | E.J. Stocker | Lab | 10,822 | 22.7 |
| | | | | | 14,171 | 29.7 |
| 1945 | 80,816 | 75.0 | M.J. Wheatley | C | 26,561 | 43.8 |
| | | | C.F. Fletcher-Cooke | Lab | 25,093 | 41.4 |
| | | | J.A.H. Mander | L | 8,975 | 14.8 |
| | | | | | 1,468 | 2.4 |

## DORSET, NORTHERN [318]

| Election | Electors | T'out | Candidate | Party | Votes | % |
|---|---|---|---|---|---|---|
| 1918 | 24,334 | 61.0 | W.P. Colfox | Co C | 7,532 | 50.7 |
| | | | J.E. Emlyn-Jones | L | 7,320 | 49.3 |
| | | | | | 212 | 1.4 |
| 1922 | 24,539 | 84.2 | J.E. Emlyn-Jones | L | 10,805 | 52.3 |
| | | | C. Hanbury | C | 9,869 | 47.7 |
| | | | | | 936 | 4.6 |
| 1923 | 25,160 | 84.3 | J.E. Emlyn-Jones | L | 10,992 | 51.8 |
| | | | C. Hanbury | C | 10,211 | 48.2 |
| | | | | | 781 | 3.6 |
| 1924 | 25,616 | 86.5 | C. Hanbury | C | 11,819 | 53.3 |
| | | | J.E. Emlyn-Jones | L | 10,341 | 46.7 |
| | | | | | 1,478 | 6.6 |
| 1929 | 31,684 | 81.4 | C. Hanbury | C | 12,203 | 47.3 |
| | | | Hon. W. Borthwick | L | 11,281 | 43.8 |
| | | | C.G. Clark | Lab | 2,298* | 8.9 |
| | | | | | 922 | 3.5 |
| 1931 | 31,898 | 82.1 | C. Hanbury | C | 15,499 | 59.2 |
| | | | Hon. W. Borthwick | L | 10,682 | 40.8 |
| | | | | | 4,817 | 18.4 |
| 1935 | 32,714 | 79.7 | Sir C. Hanbury | C | 13,055 | 50.1 |
| | | | Hon. W. Borthwick | L | 9,871 | 37.9 |
| | | | G.H.L.F. Pitt-Rivers | Agric | 1,771* | 6.8 |
| | | | Miss M.M. Whitehead | Lab | 1,360* | 5.2 |
| | | | | | 3,184 | 12.2 |
| [Death] | | | | | | |
| 1937 (13/7) | 32,654 | 73.3 | A.V. Hambro | C | 12,247 | 51.1 |
| | | | Hon. W. Borthwick | L | 11,704 | 48.9 |
| | | | | | 543 | 2.2 |
| 1945 | 35,879 | 75.0 | C.F. Byers | L | 14,444 | 53.6 |
| | | | R.H. Glyn | C | 12,479 | 46.4 |
| | | | | | 1,965 | 7.2 |

Note:—

1935: Pitt-Rivers was the nominee of the North Dorset Agricultural Defence League.

| Election | Electors | T'out | Candidate | Party | Votes | % |
|---|---|---|---|---|---|---|
| 1918 | 28,224 | 57.9 | †A.V. Hambro | Co C | 11,175 | 68.4 |
| | | | B. Morgan | Lab | 5,159 | 31.6 |
| | | | | | 6,016 | 36.8 |
| 1922 | 28,149 | 75.2 | R.D.T. Yerburgh | C | 12,121 | 57.2 |
| | | | F. Maddison | L | 4,657 | 22.0 |
| | | | H. Pavely | Lab | 4,394 | 20.8 |
| | | | | | 7,464 | 35.2 |
| 1923 | 28,810 | 71.6 | R.D.T. Yerburgh | C | 11,057 | 53.5 |
| | | | R.S. Comben | L | 5,973 | 29.0 |
| | | | D.W. Thomas | Lab | 3,602 | 17.5 |
| | | | | | 5,084 | 24.5 |
| 1924 | 29,845 | 66.1 | R.D.T. Yerburgh | C | 13,900 | 70.5 |
| | | | W. Risdon | Lab | 5,821 | 29.5 |
| | | | | | 8,079 | 41.0 |
| 1929 | 39,396 | 75.5 | Viscount Cranborne | C | 14,632 | 49.2 |
| | | | C. Plaistowe | L | 8,168 | 27.4 |
| | | | A.W. Wiltshire | Lab | 6,959 | 23.4 |
| | | | | | 6,464 | 21.8 |
| 1931 | 41,062 | 73.3 | Viscount Cranborne | C | 21,284 | 70.7 |
| | | | A.W. Wiltshire | Lab | 8,809 | 29.3 |
| | | | | | 12,475 | 41.4 |
| 1935 | 43,499 | 70.1 | Viscount Cranborne | C | 17,637 | 57.8 |
| | | | A.W. Wiltshire | Lab | 8,580 | 28.2 |
| | | | F.W. King | L | 4,255 | 14.0 |
| | | | | | 9,057 | 29.6 |

[Called to the House of Lords as Lord Cecil of Essondon]

| Election | Electors | T'out | Candidate | Party | Votes | % |
|---|---|---|---|---|---|---|
| 1941 (22/2) | | | Viscount Hinchingbrooke | C | Unopp. | |
| 1945 | 46,513 | 73.6 | Viscount Hinchingbrooke | C | 14,626 | 42.7 |
| | | | P.S. Eastman | Lab | 12,460 | 36.4 |
| | | | W.E. Ward | L | 7,149 | 20.9 |
| | | | | | 2,166 | 6.3 |

| Election | Electors | T'out | Candidate | Party | Votes | % |
|---|---|---|---|---|---|---|
| 1918 | | | †Sir R. Williams, Bt. | Co C | Unopp. | |
| 1922 | 23,885 | 78.5 | W.P. Colfox | C | 11,649 | 62.1 |
| | | | T.C. Duke | Lab | 7,101 | 37.9 |
| | | | | | 4,548 | 24.2 |
| 1923 | 24,242 | 70.9 | W.P. Colfox | C | 10,100 | 58.8 |
| | | | Mrs. L. Simpson | Lab | 7,087 | 41.2 |
| | | | | | 3,013 | 17.6 |
| 1924 | 24,852 | 73.2 | W.P. Colfox | C | 12,426 | 68.3 |
| | | | Mrs. L. Simpson | Lab | 5,764 | 31.7 |
| | | | | | 6,662 | 36.6 |
| 1929 | 30,946 | 80.6 | W.P. Colfox | C | 12,247 | 49.1 |
| | | | G.E. Chappell | L | 7,921 | 31.8 |
| | | | T. Robins | Lab | 4,770 | 19.1 |
| | | | | | 4,326 | 17.3 |
| 1931 | 31,590 | 81.6 | W.P. Colfox | C | 15,510 | 60.2 |
| | | | G.E. Chappell | L | 10,271 | 39.8 |
| | | | | | 5,239 | 20.4 |
| 1935 | 32,817 | 77.9 | W.P. Colfox | C | 13,825 | 54.1 |
| | | | G.E. Chappell | L | 11,735 | 45.9 |
| | | | | | 2,090 | 8.2 |
| [Resignation] | | | | | | |
| 1941 (21/6) | | | K.S.D.W. Digby | C | Unopp. | |
| 1945 | 35,780 | 74.7 | K.S.D.W. Digby | C | 13,399 | 50.1 |
| | | | C.J. Kane | Lab | 8,215 | 30.8 |
| | | | G.H. Newsom | L | 5,098 | 19.1 |
| | | | | | 5,184 | 19.3 |

# DURHAM, BARNARD CASTLE  [321]

| Election | Electors | T'out | Candidate | Party | Votes | % |
|---|---|---|---|---|---|---|
| 1918 | 19,949 | 64.0 | J.E. Swan | Lab | 5,468 | 42.8 |
| | | | J.E. Rogerson | Co C | 3,837 | 30.1 |
| | | | A.E. Hillary | L | 2,180 | 17.1 |
| | | | O. Monkhouse | Agric | 1,274* | 10.0 |
| | | | | | 1,631 | 12.7 |
| 1922 | 20,791 | 78.5 | J.E. Rogerson | C | 8,271 | 50.7 |
| | | | J.E. Swan | Lab | 8,052 | 49.3 |
| | | | | | 219 | 1.4 |
| 1923 | 21,135 | 78.8 | M. Turner-Samuels | Lab | 9,171 | 55.1 |
| | | | J.E. Rogerson | C | 7,482 | 44.9 |
| | | | | | 1,689 | 10.2 |
| 1924 | 21,931 | 84.9 | C.M. Headlam | C | 9,465 | 50.8 |
| | | | M. Turner-Samuels | Lab | 9,152 | 49.2 |
| | | | | | 313 | 1.6 |
| 1929 | 26,488 | 83.4 | W. Lawther | Lab | 9,281 | 42.0 |
| | | | C.M. Headlam | C | 8,406 | 38.1 |
| | | | E. Spence | L | 4,402 | 19.9 |
| | | | | | 875 | 3.9 |
| 1931 | 27,006 | 85.2 | C.M. Headlam | C | 12,721 | 55.3 |
| | | | W. Lawther | Lab | 10,287 | 44.7 |
| | | | | | 2,434 | 10.6 |
| 1935 | 27,309 | 84.2 | T.M. Sexton | Lab | 11,458 | 49.8 |
| | | | Sir C.M. Headlam, Bt. | C | 10,138 | 44.1 |
| | | | A. Graham | L | 1,393* | 6.1 |
| | | | | | 1,320 | 5.7 |
| 1945 | 27,387 | 75.3 | S.R.C. Lavers | Lab | 12,024 | 58.3 |
| | | | Sir G. Le Q. Martel | C | 8,600 | 41.7 |
| | | | | | 3,424 | 16.6 |

Note:—

1918:  Monkhouse was the nominee of the NFU.

| Election | Electors | T'out | Candidate | Party | Votes | % |
|----------|----------|-------|-----------|-------|-------|---|
| 1918 | 32,685 | 60.8 | B.C. Spoor | Lab | 10,060 | 50.6 |
| | | | G.R. Vick | Co L | 7,417 | 37.3 |
| | | | Dr. V.H. Rutherford | L | 2,411* | 12.1 |
| | | | | | 2,643 | 13.3 |
| 1922 | 34,730 | 74.8 | B.C. Spoor | Lab | 13,946 | 53.7 |
| | | | E. Atherley-Jones | NL | 12,019 | 46.3 |
| | | | | | 1,927 | 7.4 |
| 1923 | 34,487 | 75.5 | B.C. Spoor | Lab | 13,328 | 51.2 |
| | | | J. Bainbridge | L | 6,686 | 25.7 |
| | | | R. Gee | C | 6,024 | 23.1 |
| | | | | | 6,642 | 25.5 |
| 1924 | 35,438 | 80.9 | B.C. Spoor | Lab | 15,786 | 55.1 |
| | | | J. Bainbridge | L | 12,868 | 44.9 |
| | | | | | 2,918 | 10.2 |
| [Death] | | | | | | |
| 1929 (7/2) | 34,787 | 74.4 | Mrs. F.R. Dalton | Lab | 14,797 | 57.1 |
| | | | A.C. Curry | L | 7,725 | 29.9 |
| | | | H. Thompson | C | 3,357 | 13.0 |
| | | | | | 7,072 | 27.2 |
| 1929 | 41,772 | 76.5 | E.H.J.N. Dalton | Lab | 17,838 | 55.8 |
| | | | A.C. Curry | L | 9,635 | 30.1 |
| | | | H. Thompson | C | 4,503 | 14.1 |
| | | | | | 8,203 | 25.7 |
| 1931 | 41,851 | 82.5 | A.C. Curry | NL (L) | 17,751 | 51.4 |
| | | | E.H.J.N. Dalton | Lab | 16,796 | 48.6 |
| | | | | | 955 | 2.8 |
| 1935 | 41,530 | 79.2 | E.H.J.N. Dalton | Lab | 20,481 | 62.3 |
| | | | A.C. Curry | L | 12,395 | 37.7 |
| | | | | | 8,086 | 24.6 |
| 1945 | 42,630 | 73.5 | Rt. Hon. E.H.J.N. Dalton | Lab | 20,100 | 64.1 |
| | | | W.J.W. Tily | NL | 11,240 | 35.9 |
| | | | | | 8,860 | 28.2 |

# DURHAM, BLAYDON  [323]

| Election | Electors | T'out | Candidate | Party | Votes | % |
|---|---|---|---|---|---|---|
| 1918 | 32,831 | 57.4 | †W. Waring | Co L | 9,937 | 52.8 |
| | | | W. Whiteley | Lab | 7,844 | 41.6 |
| | | | T.G. Graham | L | 1,064* | 5.6 |
| | | | | | 2,093 | 11.2 |
| 1922 | 35,434 | 77.0 | W. Whiteley | Lab | 14,722 | 53.9 |
| | | | F.R. Simpson | C | 7,963 | 29.2 |
| | | | F.W. Cook | NL | 4,606 | 16.9 |
| | | | | | 6,759 | 24.7 |
| 1923 | 35,764 | 62.1 | W. Whiteley | Lab | 15,073 | 67.9 |
| | | | G. Denson | C | 7,124 | 32.1 |
| | | | | | 7,949 | 35.8 |
| 1924 | 36,646 | 77.0 | W. Whiteley | Lab | 17,670 | 62.6 |
| | | | G. Denson | C | 10,549 | 37.4 |
| | | | | | 7,121 | 25.2 |
| 1929 | 45,204 | 79.5 | W. Whiteley | Lab | 21,221 | 59.1 |
| | | | R.C. White | C | 7,847 | 21.8 |
| | | | T. Magnay | L | 6,878 | 19.1 |
| | | | | | 13,374 | 37.3 |
| 1931 | 46,151 | 80.9 | T.B. Martin | C | 18,927 | 50.7 |
| | | | W. Whiteley | Lab | 18,431 | 49.3 |
| | | | | | 496 | 1.4 |
| 1935 | 48,006 | 80.8 | W. Whiteley | Lab | 24,148 | 62.3 |
| | | | C.E. Vickery | C | 14,622 | 37.7 |
| | | | | | 9,526 | 24.6 |
| 1945 | 52,619 | 79.4 | Rt. Hon. W. Whiteley | Lab | 29,931 | 71.7 |
| | | | E.C. Peake | C | 11,842 | 28.3 |
| | | | | | 18,089 | 43.4 |

## DURHAM, CHESTER-LE-STREET [324]

| Election | Electors | T'out | Candidate | Party | Votes | % |
|---|---|---|---|---|---|---|
| 1918 | | | †J.W. Taylor | Lab | Unopp. | |
| [Resignation] | | | | | | |
| 1919 | 36,321 | 63.7 | J.J. Lawson | Lab | 17,838 | 77.1 |
| (13/11) | | | D. Gilmour | NDP | 5,313 | 22.9 |
| | | | | | 12,525 | 54.2 |
| 1922 | 38,672 | 76.6 | J.J. Lawson | Lab | 20,296 | 68.5 |
| | | | D.F. Todd | C | 9,335 | 31.5 |
| | | | | | 10,961 | 37.0 |
| 1923 | 39,532 | 70.1 | J.J. Lawson | Lab | 20,712 | 74.7 |
| | | | C.R.S. Harris | C | 7,015 | 25.3 |
| | | | | | 13,697 | 49.4 |
| 1924 | 40,578 | 78.7 | J.J. Lawson | Lab | 22,700 | 71.0 |
| | | | M.D. McCarthy | C | 9,250 | 29.0 |
| | | | | | 13,450 | 42.0 |
| 1929 | 49,243 | 78.5 | J.J. Lawson | Lab | 26,975 | 69.8 |
| | | | E.G. Payne | C | 6,334 | 16.4 |
| | | | J.W. Wright | L | 5,340 | 13.8 |
| | | | | | 20,641 | 53.4 |
| 1931 | 50,668 | 79.4 | J.J. Lawson | Lab | 24,373 | 60.6 |
| | | | R.G. Kellett | C | 15,834 | 39.4 |
| | | | | | 8,539 | 21.2 |
| 1935 | 52,419 | 78.2 | J.J. Lawson | Lab | 29,111 | 71.0 |
| | | | C.R.I. Besley | C | 11,901 | 29.0 |
| | | | | | 17,210 | 42.0 |
| 1945 | 55,375 | 79.5 | Rt. Hon. J.J. Lawson | Lab | 33,788 | 76.8 |
| | | | Viscount Lambton | C | 10,228 | 23.2 |
| | | | | | 23,560 | 53.6 |

[Seat Vacant at Dissolution (Resignation on appointment as Vice-Chairman of the National Parks Commission)]

| Election | Electors | T'out | Candidate | Party | Votes | % |
|---|---|---|---|---|---|---|
| 1918 | 34,393 | 64.3 | †A. Williams | L | 7,576 | 34.3 |
| | | | R. Gee | Co NDP | 7,283 | 32.9 |
| | | | G.H. Stuart-Bunning | Lab | 7,268 | 32.8 |
| | | | | | 293 | 1.4 |
| 1922 | 37,886 | 82.0 | Rev. H. Dunnico | Lab | 14,469 | 46.5 |
| | | | A. Williams | L | 9,870 | 31.8 |
| | | | S.E.D. Wilson | C | 6,745 | 21.7 |
| | | | | | 4,599 | 14.7 |
| 1923 | 38,989 | 78.2 | Rev. H. Dunnico | Lab | 15,862 | 52.0 |
| | | | Miss H.U. Williams | L | 14,619 | 48.0 |
| | | | | | 1,243 | 4.0 |
| 1924 | 40,363 | 83.4 | Rev. H. Dunnico | Lab | 18,842 | 55.9 |
| | | | J.E. Davis | Const | 14,836 | 44.1 |
| | | | | | 4,006 | 11.8 |
| 1929 | 49,233 | 80.1 | Rev. H. Dunnico | Lab | 22,256 | 56.5 |
| | | | J.P. Dickie | L | 10,772 | 27.3 |
| | | | J.W. Watts | C | 6,400 | 16.2 |
| | | | | | 11,484 | 29.2 |
| 1931 | 50,940 | 83.2 | J.P. Dickie | NL | 22,474 | 53.0 |
| | | | Rev. H. Dunnico | Lab | 19,927 | 47.0 |
| | | | | | 2,547 | 6.0 |
| 1935 | 51,667 | 83.8 | D. Adams | Lab | 25,419 | 58.7 |
| | | | J.P. Dickie | NL | 17,897 | 41.3 |
| | | | | | 7,522 | 17.4 |
| [Death] | | | | | | |
| 1943 (15/11) | | | J.E. Glanville | Lab | Unopp. | |
| 1945 | 52,915 | 77.1 | J.E. Glanville | Lab | 28,617 | 70.1 |
| | | | J.A. McGilley | NL | 12,198 | 29.9 |
| | | | | | 16,419 | 40.2 |

# DURHAM, DURHAM [326]

| Election | Electors | T'out | Candidate | Party | Votes | % |
|---|---|---|---|---|---|---|
| 1918 | 29,037 | 61.4 | †J.W. Hills | Co C | 9,027 | 50.6 |
| | | | J. Ritson | Lab | 8,809 | 49.4 |
| | | | | | 218 | 1.2 |
| 1922 | 31,104 | 81.9 | J. Ritson | Lab | 14,068 | 55.2 |
| | | | J.W. Hills | C | 11,396 | 44.8 |
| | | | | | 2,672 | 10.4 |
| 1923 | 31,523 | 77.2 | J. Ritson | Lab | 13,819 | 56.8 |
| | | | T.A. Bradford | C | 10,530 | 43.2 |
| | | | | | 3,289 | 13.6 |
| 1924 | 32,163 | 85.2 | J. Ritson | Lab | 15,032 | 54.9 |
| | | | S.R. Streatfeild | C | 9,614 | 35.1 |
| | | | W. McKeag | L | 2,747* | 10.0 |
| | | | | | 5,418 | 19.8 |
| 1929 | 40,676 | 80.1 | J. Ritson | Lab | 18,514 | 56.8 |
| | | | W. McKeag | L | 7,266 | 22.3 |
| | | | G.M.A. Hamilton-Fletcher | C | 6,820 | 20.9 |
| | | | | | 11,248 | 34.5 |
| 1931 | 41,282 | 83.7 | W. McKeag | L (NL) | 17,406 | 50.4 |
| | | | J. Ritson | Lab | 17,136 | 49.6 |
| | | | | | 270 | 0.8 |
| 1935 | 42,753 | 85.2 | J. Ritson | Lab | 21,517 | 59.1 |
| | | | W. McKeag | NL | 14,910 | 40.9 |
| | | | | | 6,607 | 18.2 |
| 1945 | 45,684 | 79.8 | C.F. Grey | Lab | 24,135 | 66.2 |
| | | | J. Bunyan | NL | 12,331 | 33.8 |
| | | | | | 11,804 | 32.4 |

| Election | Electors | T'out | Candidate | Party | Votes | % |
|----------|----------|-------|-----------|-------|-------|---|
| 1918 | 32,552 | 61.8 | R. Richardson | Lab | 7,315 | 36.4 |
| | | | †T.E. Wing | L | 6,626 | 32.9 |
| | | | J. Lindsley | Co NDP | 6,185 | 30.7 |
| | | | | | 689 | 3.5 |
| 1922 | 35,871 | 78.4 | R. Richardson | Lab | 14,611 | 51.9 |
| | | | W.W. Shaw | C | 7,555 | 26.9 |
| | | | J.E. Johnston | L | 5,958 | 21.2 |
| | | | | | 7,056 | 25.0 |
| 1923 | 37,224 | 69.0 | R. Richardson | Lab | 15,225 | 59.3 |
| | | | A.C. Curry | L | 10,445 | 40.7 |
| | | | | | 4,780 | 18.6 |
| 1924 | 38,779 | 79.6 | R. Richardson | Lab | 17,857 | 57.8 |
| | | | A.C. Curry | L | 13,023 | 42.2 |
| | | | | | 4,834 | 15.6 |
| 1929 | 54,615 | 80.3 | R. Richardson | Lab | 25,056 | 57.1 |
| | | | T.E. Wing | L | 10,267 | 23.4 |
| | | | W.G. Pearson | C | 8,545 | 19.5 |
| | | | | | 14,789 | 33.7 |
| 1931 | 58,285 | 82.8 | R. Chapman | C | 25,549 | 53.0 |
| | | | R. Richardson | Lab | 22,700 | 47.0 |
| | | | | | 2,849 | 6.0 |
| 1935 | 65,403 | 82.0 | W.J. Stewart | Lab | 30,665 | 57.2 |
| | | | R. Chapman | C | 22,990 | 42.8 |
| | | | | | 7,675 | 14.4 |
| 1945 | 85,584 | 76.6 | W.R. Blyton | Lab | 43,730 | 66.7 |
| | | | T.B. Martin | C | 21,864 | 33.3 |
| | | | | | 21,866 | 33.4 |

| Election | Electors | T'out | Candidate | Party | Votes | % |
|---|---|---|---|---|---|---|
| 1918 | 37,389 | 55.0 | †G.M. Palmer | Co L | 12,544 | 61.0 |
| | | | J. Hill | Lab | 8,034 | 39.0 |
| | | | | | 4,510 | 22.0 |
| 1922 | 38,808 | 82.2 | R.J. Wilson | Lab | 17,208 | 53.9 |
| | | | C.H. Innes-Hopkins | C | 10,166 | 31.9 |
| | | | E.J. Young | L | 4,522 | 14.2 |
| | | | | | 7,042 | 22.0 |
| 1923 | 38,548 | 67.2 | R.J. Wilson | Lab | 16,570 | 63.9 |
| | | | J. Lindsley | C | 9,348 | 36.1 |
| | | | | | 7,222 | 27.8 |
| 1924 | 39,237 | 80.9 | R.J. Wilson | Lab | 18,203 | 57.4 |
| | | | A.E. Baucher | C | 13,527 | 42.6 |
| | | | | | 4,676 | 14.8 |
| 1929 | 48,313 | 75.3 | R.J. Wilson | Lab | 22,751 | 62.5 |
| | | | L.V. Rogers | C | 13,638 | 37.5 |
| | | | | | 9,113 | 25.0 |
| 1931 | 48,875 | 80.5 | W.G. Pearson | C | 21,263 | 54.1 |
| | | | R.J. Wilson | Lab | 18,071 | 45.9 |
| | | | | | 3,192 | 8.2 |
| 1935 | 47,408 | 80.8 | Miss E.C. Wilkinson | Lab | 20,324 | 53.1 |
| | | | W.G. Pearson | C | 17,974 | 46.9 |
| | | | | | 2,350 | 6.2 |
| 1945 | 45,135 | 76.0 | Rt. Hon. Ellen C. Wilkinson | Lab | 22,656 | 66.0 |
| | | | S. Holmes | NL | 11,649 | 34.0 |
| | | | | | 11,007 | 32.0 |
| [Death] | | | | | | |
| 1947 | 47,538 | 73.4 | E. Fernyhough | Lab | 20,694 | 59.3 |
| (7/5) | | | W. Scott | C | 13,078 | 37.5 |
| | | | W. Moody | Ind Lab | 1,114* | 3.2 |
| | | | | | 7,616 | 21.8 |

# DURHAM, SEAHAM  [329]

| Election | Electors | T'out | Candidate | Party | Votes | % |
|---|---|---|---|---|---|---|
| 1918 | 36,701 | 59.2 | †E. Hayward | L | 12,754 | 58.7 |
|  |  |  | J.J. Lawson | Lab | 8,988 | 41.3 |
|  |  |  |  |  | 3,766 | 17.4 |
| 1922 | 41,229 | 81.9 | S.J. Webb | Lab | 20,203 | 59.9 |
|  |  |  | T.A. Bradford | C | 8,315 | 24.6 |
|  |  |  | E. Hayward | L | 5,247 | 15.5 |
|  |  |  |  |  | 11,888 | 35.3 |
| 1923 | 41,854 | 71.3 | S.J. Webb | Lab | 21,281 | 71.3 |
|  |  |  | R.D. Ross | C | 8,546 | 28.7 |
|  |  |  |  |  | 12,735 | 42.6 |
| 1924 | 43,356 | 78.8 | Rt. Hon. S.J. Webb | Lab | 22,399 | 65.5 |
|  |  |  | R.D. Ross | C | 11,775 | 34.5 |
|  |  |  |  |  | 10,624 | 31.0 |
| 1929 | 58,353 | 84.2 | Rt. Hon. J.R. MacDonald | Lab (N Lab) | 35,615 | 72.5 |
|  |  |  | W.A. Fearnley-Whittingstall | C | 6,821 | 13.9 |
|  |  |  | H.A. Haslam | L | 5,266* | 10.7 |
|  |  |  | H. Pollitt | Com | 1,431* | 2.9 |
|  |  |  |  |  | 28,794 | 58.6 |
| 1931 | 60,795 | 86.7 | Rt. Hon. J.R. MacDonald | N Lab | 28,978 | 55.0 |
|  |  |  | W. Coxon | Lab | 23,027 | 43.7 |
|  |  |  | G. Lumley | Com | 677* | 1.3 |
|  |  |  |  |  | 5,951 | 11.3 |
| 1935 | 65,178 | 86.3 | E. Shinwell | Lab | 38,380 | 68.2 |
|  |  |  | Rt. Hon. J.R. MacDonald | N Lab | 17,882 | 31.8 |
|  |  |  |  |  | 20,498 | 36.4 |
| 1945 | 67,485 | 79.5 | E. Shinwell | Lab | 42,942 | 80.1 |
|  |  |  | M.V. Macmillan | C | 10,685 | 19.9 |
|  |  |  |  |  | 32,257 | 60.2 |

Note:—

    1918:   Hayward was issued with the Coalition 'coupon' but repudiated it.

# DURHAM, SEDGEFIELD  [330]

| Election | Electors | T'out | Candidate | Party | Votes | % |
|---|---|---|---|---|---|---|
| 1918 | 24,847 | 63.4 | R. Burdon | Co C | 6,627 | 42.1 |
| | | | J. Herriotts | Lab | 5,801 | 36.8 |
| | | | Sir C.W. Starmer | L | 3,333 | 21.1 |
| | | | | | 826 | 5.3 |
| 1922 | 29,407 | 76.1 | J. Herriotts | Lab | 9,756 | 43.6 |
| | | | E. Waddington | C | 9,067 | 40.5 |
| | | | C.H. Brown | L | 3,561 | 15.9 |
| | | | | | 689 | 3.1 |
| 1923 | 29,765 | 74.5 | L. Ropner | C | 11,093 | 50.0 |
| | | | J. Herriotts | Lab | 11,087 | 50.0 |
| | | | | | 6 | 0.0 |
| 1924 | 31,065 | 85.4 | L. Ropner | C | 13,968 | 52.7 |
| | | | J. Herriotts | Lab | 12,552 | 47.3 |
| | | | | | 1,416 | 5.4 |
| 1929 | 39,774 | 83.0 | J. Herriotts | Lab | 15,749 | 47.7 |
| | | | L. Ropner | C | 13,043 | 39.5 |
| | | | W. Leeson | L | 4,236 | 12.8 |
| | | | | | 2,706 | 8.2 |
| 1931 | 44,276 | 84.4 | R. Jennings | C | 21,956 | 58.8 |
| | | | J. Herriotts | Lab | 15,404 | 41.2 |
| | | | | | 6,552 | 17.6 |
| 1935 | 47,910 | 81.4 | J.R. Leslie | Lab | 20,375 | 52.3 |
| | | | R. Jennings | C | 18,604 | 47.7 |
| | | | | | 1,771 | 4.6 |
| 1945 | 54,860 | 77.3 | J.R. Leslie | Lab | 27,051 | 63.8 |
| | | | J.E.S. Walford | C | 15,360 | 36.2 |
| | | | | | 11,691 | 27.6 |

# DURHAM, SPENNYMOOR  [331]

| Election | Electors | T'out | Candidate | Party | Votes | % |
|---|---|---|---|---|---|---|
| 1918 | 31,617 | 55.8 | †S. Galbraith | L | 9,443 | 53.5 |
| | | | J. Batey | Lab | 8,196 | 46.5 |
| | | | | | 1,247 | 7.0 |
| 1922 | 33,710 | 81.2 | J. Batey | Lab | 13,766 | 50.3 |
| | | | R.A. Eden | C | 7,567 | 27.6 |
| | | | T.E. Wing | L | 6,046 | 22.1 |
| | | | | | 6,199 | 22.7 |
| 1923 | 33,962 | 69.7 | J. Batey | Lab | 15,567 | 65.7 |
| | | | W. Appleby | C | 8,116 | 34.3 |
| | | | | | 7,451 | 31.4 |
| 1924 | 34,865 | 78.3 | J. Batey | Lab | 17,211 | 63.0 |
| | | | H.C. Surtees | C | 10,101 | 37.0 |
| | | | | | 7,110 | 26.0 |
| 1929 | 39,961 | 72.7 | J. Batey | Lab | 20,858 | 71.8 |
| | | | F.P. Gourlay | C | 8,202 | 28.2 |
| | | | | | 12,656 | 43.6 |
| 1931 | 40,473 | 79.4 | J. Batey | Lab | 18,072 | 56.2 |
| | | | M.D. McCarthy | C | 14,072 | 43.8 |
| | | | | | 4,000 | 12.4 |
| 1935 | 40,566 | 74.4 | J. Batey | Lab | 21,473 | 71.2 |
| | | | M.D. McCarthy | C | 8,706 | 28.8 |
| | | | | | 12,767 | 42.4 |

[Resignation]

| 1942 (21/7) | | | J.D. Murray | Lab | Unopp. | |
|---|---|---|---|---|---|---|
| 1945 | 40,662 | 79.5 | J.D. Murray | Lab | 22,587 | 69.9 |
| | | | F.D. Nicholson | C | 7,510 | 23.2 |
| | | | C.J.F. Savill | Ind | 2,222* | 6.9 |
| | | | | | 15,077 | 46.7 |

| Election | Electors | T'out | Candidate | Party | Votes | % |
|---|---|---|---|---|---|---|
| 1918 | 33,429 | 50.2 | †Rt. Hon. E.G. Pretyman | Co C | 11,217 | 66.9 |
| | | | W.F. Toynbee | Lab | 5,551 | 33.1 |
| | | | | | 5,666 | 33.8 |
| 1922 | 35,128 | 61.0 | Rt. Hon. E.G. Pretyman | C | 11,267 | 52.6 |
| | | | S.W. Robinson | L | 6,380 | 29.8 |
| | | | Mrs. C.D. Rackham | Lab | 3,767 | 17.6 |
| | | | | | 4,887 | 22.8 |
| 1923 | 36,343 | 63.5 | S.W. Robinson | L | 12,877 | 55.8 |
| | | | Rt. Hon. E.G. Pretyman | C | 10,185 | 44.2 |
| | | | | | 2,692 | 11.6 |
| 1924 | 37,656 | 77.1 | Sir H.H. Curtis-Bennett | C | 15,875 | 54.7 |
| | | | S.W. Robinson | L | 10,244 | 35.3 |
| | | | N.H. Moller | Lab | 2,904* | 10.0 |
| | | | | | 5,631 | 19.4 |
| [Resignation] | | | | | | |
| 1926 | 39,652 | 70.5 | C.K. Howard-Bury | C | 13,395 | 47.8 |
| (30/11) | | | S.W. Robinson | L | 8,435 | 30.2 |
| | | | N.H. Moller | Lab | 6,140 | 22.0 |
| | | | | | 4,960 | 17.6 |
| 1929 | 51,966 | 75.1 | C.K. Howard-Bury | C | 17,094 | 43.8 |
| | | | S.W. Robinson | L | 13,034 | 33.4 |
| | | | N.H. Moller | Lab | 8,910 | 22.8 |
| | | | | | 4,060 | 10.4 |
| 1931 | 56,001 | 70.9 | Sir V.L. Henderson | C | 31,961 | 80.5 |
| | | | J.A. Sparks | Lab | 7,755 | 19.5 |
| | | | | | 24,206 | 61.0 |
| 1935 | 61,164 | 65.4 | J.R.J. Macnamara | C | 28,314 | 70.8 |
| | | | F. Hughes | Lab | 11,690 | 29.2 |
| | | | | | 16,624 | 41.6 |
| [Death] | | | | | | |
| 1945 | 78,806 | 54.1 | E.R. Millington | CW | 24,548 | 57.5 |
| (26/4) | | | B.C. Cook | C | 18,117 | 42.5 |
| | | | | | 6,431 | 15.0 |
| 1945 | 79,638* | 73.4 | E.R. Millington | CW (Lab) | 27,309 | 46.7 |
| | | | H. Ashton | C | 25,229 | 43.2 |
| | | | Miss H.M.A. Buckmaster | L | 5,909* | 10.1 |
| | | | | | 2,080 | 3.5 |

| Election | Electors | T'out | Candidate | Party | Votes | % |
|---|---|---|---|---|---|---|
| 1918 | 30,372 | 60.2 | †Rt. Hon. Sir L. Worthington-Evans, Bt. | Co C | 11,186 | 61.1 |
| | | | A. Conley | Lab | 7,112 | 38.9 |
| | | | | | 4,074 | 22.2 |
| 1922 | 29,779 | 77.9 | Rt. Hon. Sir L. Worthington-Evans, Bt. | C | 13,142 | 56.7 |
| | | | R.L. Reiss | Lab | 10,045 | 43.3 |
| | | | | | 3,097 | 13.4 |
| 1923 | 31,058 | 78.2 | Rt. Hon. Sir L. Worthington-Evans, Bt. | C | 10,535 | 43.4 |
| | | | R.L. Reiss | Lab | 8,316 | 34.2 |
| | | | Sir A.H. Goldfinch | L | 5,430 | 22.4 |
| | | | | | 2,219 | 9.2 |
| 1924 | 32,009 | 78.8 | Rt. Hon. Sir L. Worthington-Evans, Bt. | C | 14,283 | 56.6 |
| | | | R.L. Reiss | Lab | 10,953 | 43.4 |
| | | | | | 3,330 | 13.2 |
| 1929 | 41,947 | 79.4 | O. Lewis | C | 13,411 | 40.3 |
| | | | R.L. Reiss | Lab | 12,809 | 38.5 |
| | | | W.R. Elliston | L | 6,896 | 20.7 |
| | | | C.C. Gray | Ind C | 172* | 0.5 |
| | | | | | 602 | 1.8 |
| 1931 | 43,216 | 76.4 | O. Lewis | C | 22,285 | 67.5 |
| | | | E.A. Digby | Lab | 10,725 | 32.5 |
| | | | | | 11,560 | 35.0 |
| 1935 | 45,496 | 74.6 | O. Lewis | C | 19,915 | 58.7 |
| | | | H. Beaumont | Lab | 14,039 | 41.3 |
| | | | | | 5,876 | 17.4 |
| 1945 | 49,557 | 73.9 | C.G.P. Smith | Lab | 16,587 | 45.3 |
| | | | O. Lewis | C | 14,123 | 38.6 |
| | | | G.A. Routledge | L | 5,899 | 16.1 |
| | | | | | 2,464 | 6.7 |

# ESSEX, EPPING [334]

| Election | Electors | T'out | Candidate | Party | Votes | % |
|---|---|---|---|---|---|---|
| 1918 | 38,519 | 52.4 | †R.B. Colvin | Co C | 14,668 | 72.6 |
| | | | A.L. Horner | L | 4,164 | 20.6 |
| | | | J. Conoley | Ind | 1,367* | 6.8 |
| | | | | | 10,504 | 52.0 |
| 1922 | 40,209 | 63.5 | R.B. Colvin | C | 15,300 | 59.9 |
| | | | G.G. Sharp | L | 10,228 | 40.1 |
| | | | | | 5,072 | 19.8 |
| 1923 | 41,404 | 66.4 | Sir C.E.L. Lyle | C | 14,528 | 52.9 |
| | | | G.G. Sharp | L | 12,954 | 47.1 |
| | | | | | 1,574 | 5.8 |
| 1924 | 43,055 | 78.3 | Rt. Hon. W.L.S. Churchill | Const (C) | 19,843 | 58.9 |
| | | | G.G. Sharp | L | 10,080 | 29.9 |
| | | | J.R. McPhie | Lab | 3,768* | 11.2 |
| | | | | | 9,763 | 29.0 |
| 1929 | 65,758 | 75.2 | Rt. Hon. W.L.S. Churchill | C | 23,972 | 48.5 |
| | | | G.G. Sharp | L | 19,005 | 38.4 |
| | | | J.T.W. Newbold | Lab | 6,472 | 13.1 |
| | | | | | 4,967 | 10.1 |
| 1931 | 72,889 | 77.3 | Rt. Hon. W.L.S. Churchill | C | 35,956 | 63.8 |
| | | | A.S. Comyns Carr | L | 15,670 | 27.8 |
| | | | J. Ranger | Lab | 4,713* | 8.4 |
| | | | | | 20,286 | 36.0 |
| 1935 | 87,177 | 67.7 | Rt. Hon. W.L.S. Churchill | C | 34,849 | 59.1 |
| | | | G.G. Sharp | L | 14,430 | 24.4 |
| | | | J. Ranger | Lab | 9,758 | 16.5 |
| | | | | | 20,419 | 34.7 |
| 1945 | 50,861** | 71.4 | Mrs. E.L. Manning | Lab | 15,993 | 44.1 |
| | | | A.R. Wise | C | 15,006 | 41.3 |
| | | | Sir S.W. Robinson | L | 5,314 | 14.6 |
| | | | | | 987 | 2.8 |

Note:—

1918: Conoley sought election as a 'People's Progressive Coalition' candidate and pledged his support to the Labour Party on certain issues.

| Election | Electors | T'out | Candidate | Party | Votes | % |
|----------|----------|-------|-----------|-------|-------|---|
| 1918 | 27,421 | 55.9 | †H.K. Newton | Co C | 8,261 | 53.9 |
| | | | E.A. Digby | L | 7,064 | 46.1 |
| | | | | | 1,197 | 7.8 |
| 1922 | 28,432 | 71.6 | A.E. Hillary | L | 10,556 | 51.9 |
| | | | G. St. J. Strutt | C | 9,792 | 48.1 |
| | | | | | 764 | 3.8 |
| 1923 | 29,126 | 76.2 | A.E. Hillary | L | 12,059 | 54.3 |
| | | | Sir F.G. Rice | C | 10,142 | 45.7 |
| | | | | | 1,917 | 8.6 |
| 1924 | 30,047 | 79.0 | Sir F.G. Rice | C | 12,219 | 51.5 |
| | | | A.E. Hillary | L | 9,904 | 41.7 |
| | | | A. Barton | Lab | 1,604* | 6.8 |
| | | | | | 2,315 | 9.8 |
| 1929 | 40,478 | 76.3 | P.J. Pybus | L (NL) | 16,309 | 52.8 |
| | | | J. Mayhew | C | 13,609 | 44.1 |
| | | | J. Elliott | Ind C | 948* | 3.1 |
| | | | | | 2,700 | 8.7 |
| 1931 | 42,759 | 72.6 | P.J. Pybus | NL | 26,818 | 86.4 |
| | | | E.L. McKeag | Lab | 4,229 | 13.6 |
| | | | | | 22,589 | 72.8 |
| [Seat Vacant at Dissolution (Death)] | | | | | | |
| 1935 | 48,299 | 63.9 | J.S. Holmes | NL | 21,716 | 70.3 |
| | | | A.E. Appelbe | Lab | 9,170 | 29.7 |
| | | | | | 12,546 | 40.6 |
| 1945 | 42,986 | 68.7 | Sir J.S. Holmes | NL | 16,452 | 55.7 |
| | | | J. Hewett | Lab | 13,067 | 44.3 |
| | | | | | 3,385 | 11.4 |

## ESSEX, HORNCHURCH  [336]

| Election | Electors | T'out | Candidate | Party | Votes | % |
|---|---|---|---|---|---|---|
| 1945 | 66,529 | 72.1 | G.H.C. Bing | Lab | 26,856 | 55.9 |
| | | | J.T.D.H. Vaizey | C | 15,100 | 31.5 |
| | | | N.C. Jones | L | 5,807* | 12.1 |
| | | | Mrs. V. Van Der Elst | Ind | 232* | 0.5 |
| | | | | | 11,756 | 24.4 |

Note:—

1945:  Mrs. Van Der Elst advocated a policy of abolition of capital punishment.

| Election | Electors | T'out | Candidate | Party | Votes | % |
|---|---|---|---|---|---|---|
| 1918 | 28,127 | 56.7 | †Sir J.F. Flannery, Bt. | Co C | 8,138 | 51.1 |
| | | | G. Dallas | Lab | 6,315 | 39.6 |
| | | | E.W. Tanner | L | 1,490* | 9.3 |
| | | | | | 1,823 | 11.5 |
| 1922 | 29,252 | 74.8 | E.A. Ruggles-Brise | C | 10,337 | 47.2 |
| | | | G. Dallas | Lab | 6,085 | 27.8 |
| | | | J. Parish | L | 5,470 | 25.0 |
| | | | | | 4,252 | 19.4 |
| 1923 | 29,619 | 69.6 | V.G. Crittall | Lab | 10,329 | 50.1 |
| | | | E.A. Ruggles-Brise | C | 10,280 | 49.9 |
| | | | | | 49 | 0.2 |
| 1924 | 30,573 | 82.6 | E.A. Ruggles-Brise | C | 13,209 | 52.3 |
| | | | V.G. Crittall | Lab | 9,323 | 36.9 |
| | | | H.R.G. Brooks | L | 2,724* | 10.8 |
| | | | | | 3,886 | 15.4 |
| 1929 | 40,238 | 79.5 | E.A. Ruggles-Brise | C | 14,020 | 43.8 |
| | | | H. Evans | Lab | 11,224 | 35.1 |
| | | | H.A. May | L | 6,748 | 21.1 |
| | | | | | 2,796 | 8.7 |
| 1931 | 41,689 | 74.7 | E.A. Ruggles-Brise | C | 22,055 | 70.8 |
| | | | W.F. Toynbee | Lab | 9,078 | 29.2 |
| | | | | | 12,977 | 41.6 |
| 1935 | 43,395 | 73.8 | Sir E.A. Ruggles-Brise, Bt. | C | 17,072 | 53.4 |
| | | | W.F. Toynbee | Lab | 9,264 | 28.9 |
| | | | Miss H.M.A. Buckmaster | L | 5,680 | 17.7 |
| | | | | | 7,808 | 24.5 |
| [Death] | | | | | | |
| 1942 (25/6) | 44,887 | 44.4 | T.E.N. Driberg | Ind Lab (Lab) | 12,219 | 61.3 |
| | | | R.J. Hunt | C | 6,226 | 31.3 |
| | | | R.B. Matthews | Nat Ind & Agric | 1,476* | 7.4 |
| | | | | | 5,993 | 30.0 |
| 1945 | 49,978* | 74.5 | T.E.N. Driberg | Lab | 22,480 | 60.4 |
| | | | A.M.S. Stevenson | C | 14,753 | 39.6 |
| | | | | | 7,727 | 20.8 |

# ESSEX, ROMFORD [338]

| Election | Electors | T'out | Candidate | Party | Votes | % |
|---|---|---|---|---|---|---|
| 1918 | 37,055 | 48.4 | A.E. Martin | Co L | 10,300 | 57.5 |
| | | | W.H. Letts | Lab | 5,044 | 28.1 |
| | | | A. Whiting | NSP | 2,580 | 14.4 |
| | | | | | 5,256 | 29.4 |
| 1922 | 40,597 | 59.2 | A.E. Martin | NL | 14,070 | 58.5 |
| | | | A.E. Davies | Lab | 9,967 | 41.5 |
| | | | | | 4,103 | 17.0 |
| 1923 | 43,715 | 61.4 | Hon. C.A.U. Rhys | C | 9,585 | 35.8 |
| | | | A.E. Davies | Lab | 9,109 | 33.9 |
| | | | D.M. Mason | L | 8,144 | 30.3 |
| | | | | | 476 | 1.9 |
| 1924 | 46,708 | 74.5 | Hon. C.A.U. Rhys | C | 15,520 | 44.6 |
| | | | A.E. Davies | Lab | 13,312 | 38.3 |
| | | | D.M. Mason | L | 5,957 | 17.1 |
| | | | | | 2,208 | 6.3 |
| 1929 | 98,577 | 70.1 | H.T. Muggeridge | Lab | 31,045 | 44.9 |
| | | | Hon. C.A.U. Rhys | C | 22,525 | 32.6 |
| | | | A.F. Wood | L | 15,527 | 22.5 |
| | | | | | 8,520 | 12.3 |
| 1931 | 124,795 | 65.3 | W.G.D. Hutchison | C | 50,097 | 61.5 |
| | | | H.T. Muggeridge | Lab | 31,410 | 38.5 |
| | | | | | 18,687 | 23.0 |
| 1935 | 167,939 | 61.4 | J. Parker | Lab | 55,723 | 54.0 |
| | | | W.G.D. Hutchison | C | 47,416 | 46.0 |
| | | | | | 8,307 | 8.0 |

This constituency was divided in 1945.

| Election | Electors | T'out | Candidate | Party | Votes | % |
|----------|----------|-------|-----------|-------|-------|---|
| 1918 | 31,682 | 47.8 | †A.C.T. Beck | Co L (Ind) | 10,628 | 70.1 |
|  |  |  | J.J. Mallon | Lab | 4,531 | 29.9 |
|  |  |  |  |  | 6,097 | 40.2 |
| 1922 | 31,774 | 71.1 | W.F. Mitchell | C | 9,844 | 43.6 |
|  |  |  | W. Cash | Lab | 6,797 | 30.1 |
|  |  |  | W.D. Harbinson | NL | 3,097 | 13.7 |
|  |  |  | Dr. R.M. Wilson | L | 2,853 | 12.6 |
|  |  |  |  |  | 3,047 | 13.5 |
| 1923 | 32,212 | 67.7 | W.F. Mitchell | C | 9,652 | 44.3 |
|  |  |  | W. Cash | Lab | 6,398 | 29.3 |
|  |  |  | Dr. R.M. Wilson | L | 5,752 | 26.4 |
|  |  |  |  |  | 3,254 | 15.0 |
| 1924 | 32,590 | 73.1 | W.F. Mitchell | C | 12,289 | 51.6 |
|  |  |  | W. Cash | Lab | 6,340 | 26.6 |
|  |  |  | A.M. Mathews | L | 5,195 | 21.8 |
|  |  |  |  |  | 5,949 | 25.0 |
| 1929 | 40,253 | 75.8 | R.A. Butler | C | 13,561 | 44.5 |
|  |  |  | W. Cash | Lab | 8,642 | 28.3 |
|  |  |  | A.M. Mathews | L | 8,307 | 27.2 |
|  |  |  |  |  | 4,919 | 16.2 |
| 1931 | 41,159 | 70.4 | R.A. Butler | C | 22,501 | 77.7 |
|  |  |  | S.S. Wilson | Lab | 6,468 | 22.3 |
|  |  |  |  |  | 16,033 | 55.4 |
| 1935 | 42,371 | 69.2 | R.A. Butler | C | 19,669 | 67.1 |
|  |  |  | Mrs. C.D. Rackham | Lab | 9,633 | 32.9 |
|  |  |  |  |  | 10,036 | 34.2 |
| 1945 | 48,497 | 74.5 | Rt.Hon. R.A. Butler | C | 16,950 | 46.9 |
|  |  |  | S.S. Wilson | Lab | 15,792 | 43.7 |
|  |  |  | G.A. Edinger | L | 3,395* | 9.4 |
|  |  |  |  |  | 1,158 | 3.2 |

Notes:—

1918: Beck joined Horatio Bottomley's Independent Parliamentary Group.

1922: Harbinson sought election as a 'Constitutional and Democratic' candidate but his name was included in the official list of National Liberal candidates.

1945: Edinger sought election as an 'Independent Liberal' but his name was included in the official list of Liberal Party candidates.

| Election | Electors | T'out | Candidate | Party | Votes | % |
|---|---|---|---|---|---|---|
| 1918 | 36,213 | 50.9 | F. Hilder | Co C | 11,703 | 63.6 |
| | | | J.P. Cotter | Lab | 5,343 | 29.0 |
| | | | S.W. Robinson | L | 1,372* | 7.4 |
| | | | | | 6,360 | 34.6 |
| 1922 | 42,406 | 58.9 | F. Hilder | C | 13,522 | 54.1 |
| | | | P.C. Hoffman | Lab | 11,459 | 45.9 |
| | | | | | 2,063 | 8.2 |
| 1923 | 45,363 | 58.1 | P.C. Hoffman | Lab | 13,979 | 53.0 |
| | | | F. Hilder | C | 12,379 | 47.0 |
| | | | | | 1,600 | 6.0 |
| 1924 | 48,412 | 69.3 | H.W. Looker | C | 19,731 | 58.8 |
| | | | P.C. Hoffman | Lab | 13,820 | 41.2 |
| | | | | | 5,911 | 17.6 |
| 1929 | 76,466 | 65.3 | J.R.A. Oldfield | Lab | 18,756 | 37.6 |
| | | | H.W. Looker | C | 18,130 | 36.3 |
| | | | G.T. Veness | L | 13,030 | 26.1 |
| | | | | | 626 | 1.3 |
| 1931 | 85,420 | 66.8 | H.V.A.M. Raikes | C | 30,436 | 53.3 |
| | | | J.R.A. Oldfield | Lab | 20,066 | 35.2 |
| | | | F. Greene | N Lab | 6,539* | 11.5 |
| | | | | | 10,370 | 18.1 |
| 1935 | 98,558 | 59.5 | H.V.A.M. Raikes | C | 25,912 | 44.2 |
| | | | J.R.A. Oldfield | Lab | 24,942 | 42.5 |
| | | | A.M. Mathews | L | 7,797 | 13.3 |
| | | | | | 970 | 1.7 |
| 1945 | 72,412** | 65.7 | R.J. Gunter | Lab | 25,581 | 53.8 |
| | | | A. Jones | C | 21,990 | 46.2 |
| | | | | | 3,591 | 7.6 |

| Election | Electors | T'out | Candidate | Party | Votes | % |
|----------|----------|-------|-----------|-------|-------|---|
| 1945 | 43,024 | 76.9 | L.J. Solley | Lab (Ind Lab) | 23,171 | 70.0 |
| | | | T. Adam | C | 9,909 | 30.0 |
| | | | | | 13,262 | 40.0 |

Note:—

1945: Solley joined the Labour Independent Group when it was formed in June 1949.

| Election | Electors | T'out | Candidate | Party | Votes | % |
|---|---|---|---|---|---|---|
| 1918 | 35,049 | 56.3 | T. Davies | Co C | 11,171 | 56.7 |
| | | | J.H. Alpass | Ind Lab | 8,546 | 43.3 |
| | | | | | 2,625 | 13.4 |
| 1922 | 36,008 | 71.3 | T. Davies | C | 16,463 | 64.2 |
| | | | W.R. Robins | Lab | 9,195 | 35.8 |
| | | | | | 7,268 | 28.4 |
| 1923 | 36,573 | 63.6 | T. Davies | C | 15,406 | 66.2 |
| | | | W.R. Robins | Lab | 7,849 | 33.8 |
| | | | | | 7,557 | 32.4 |
| 1924 | 36,934 | 68.4 | Sir T. Davies | C | 18,201 | 72.0 |
| | | | J.H. Alpass | Lab | 7,078 | 28.0 |
| | | | | | 11,123 | 44.0 |
| 1929 | 46,109 | 76.3 | W.S. Morrison | C | 19,584 | 55.7 |
| | | | C. a'B. Williams | L | 8,629 | 24.5 |
| | | | E.W. Fredman | Lab | 6,987 | 19.8 |
| | | | | | 10,955 | 31.2 |
| 1931 | 47,467 | 71.7 | W.S. Morrison | C | 28,170 | 82.8 |
| | | | J. Griffin | Lab | 5,868 | 17.2 |
| | | | | | 22,302 | 65.6 |
| 1935 | | | W.S. Morrison | C | Unopp. | |
| 1945 | 59,890 | 67.7 | Rt. Hon. W.S. Morrison | C | 19,490 | 48.1 |
| | | | A.E.G. Hawkins | Lab | 12,380 | 30.5 |
| | | | C.M. Harris | L | 8,681 | 21.4 |
| | | | | | 7,110 | 17.6 |

| Election | Electors | T'out | Candidate | Party | Votes | % |
|---|---|---|---|---|---|---|
| 1918 | 27,624 | 56.1 | J. Wignall | Lab | 9,731 | 62.8 |
| | | | †Sir H. Webb, Bt. | Co L | 5,765 | 37.2 |
| | | | | | 3,966 | 25.6 |
| 1922 | 28,686 | 72.0 | J. Wignall | Lab | 10,820 | 52.4 |
| | | | A.G.C. Dinnick | Ind C | 5,976 | 28.9 |
| | | | Mrs. W.M. Tennant | NL | 3,861 | 18.7 |
| | | | | | 4,844 | 23.5 |
| 1923 | 29,174 | 64.7 | J. Wignall | Lab | 11,486 | 60.9 |
| | | | A.G.C. Dinnick | C | 7,383 | 39.1 |
| | | | | | 4,103 | 21.8 |
| 1924 | 29,696 | 70.0 | J. Wignall | Lab | 11,048 | 53.1 |
| | | | M.W. Beaumont | C | 9,739 | 46.9 |
| | | | | | 1,309 | 6.2 |
| [Death] | | | | | | |
| 1925 (14/7) | 29,696† | 80.9 | A.A. Purcell | Lab | 11,629 | 48.5 |
| | | | M.W. Beaumont | C | 8,607 | 35.8 |
| | | | H. West | L | 3,774 | 15.7 |
| | | | | | 3,022 | 12.7 |
| 1929 | 36,563 | 73.3 | D.J. Vaughan | Lab | 13,976 | 52.1 |
| | | | W.C.M. Cotts | C | 7,092 | 26.5 |
| | | | J.W. Westwood | L | 5,738 | 21.4 |
| | | | | | 6,884 | 25.6 |
| 1931 | 36,547 | 76.9 | Dr. J.V. Worthington | N Lab | 14,815 | 52.7 |
| | | | D.J. Vaughan | Lab | 13,291 | 47.3 |
| | | | | | 1,524 | 5.4 |
| 1935 | 37,643 | 77.3 | M.P. Price | Lab | 16,768 | 57.6 |
| | | | Sir J.V. Worthington | N Lab | 12,337 | 42.4 |
| | | | | | 4,431 | 15.2 |
| 1945 | 42,667 | 70.9 | M.P. Price | Lab | 19,721 | 65.2 |
| | | | J. Brown | Nat Ind | 10,529 | 34.8 |
| | | | | | 9,192 | 30.4 |

| Election | Flectors | T'out | Candidate | Party | Votes | % |
|---|---|---|---|---|---|---|
| 1918 | 34,685 | 61.3 | Sir R.A. Lister | Co L | 12,734 | 59.9 |
| | | | C.W. Kendall | Lab | 8,522 | 40.1 |
| | | | | | 4,212 | 19.8 |
| 1922 | 36,094 | 79.9 | S.W. Tubbs | C | 14,723 | 51.1 |
| | | | Rt. Hon. C.P. Allen | L | 9,041 | 31.3 |
| | | | S.E. Walters | Lab | 5,081 | 17.6 |
| | | | | | 5,682 | 19.8 |
| 1923 | 36,504 | 78.2 | Rt. Hon. F.E. Guest | L | 15,179 | 53.2 |
| | | | S.W. Tubbs | C | 13,355 | 46.8 |
| | | | | | 1,824 | 6.4 |
| 1924 | 37,336 | 78.9 | Sir F. Nelson | C | 15,973 | 54.2 |
| | | | Miss E. Picton-Turbervill | Lab | 7,418 | 25.2 |
| | | | A.W. Stanton | L | 6,057 | 20.6 |
| | | | | | 8,555 | 29.0 |
| 1929 | 48,776 | 81.6 | Sir F. Nelson | C | 17,700 | 44.4 |
| | | | A.W. Stanton | L | 11,728 | 29.5 |
| | | | F.E. White | Lab | 10,384 | 26.1 |
| | | | | | 5,972 | 14.9 |
| [Resignation] | | | | | | |
| 1931 (21/5) | 49,874 | 71.4 | W.R.D. Perkins | C | 17,641 | 49.6 |
| | | | Sir H.J. Maynard | Lab | 10,688 | 30.0 |
| | | | A.W. Stanton | L | 7,267 | 20.4 |
| | | | | | 6,953 | 19.6 |
| 1931 | 50,534 | 76.5 | W.R.D. Perkins | C | 27,612 | 71.4 |
| | | | F.W. Davies | Lab | 11,039 | 28.6 |
| | | | | | 16,573 | 42.8 |
| 1935 | 54,140 | 71.0 | W.R.D. Perkins | C | 24,282 | 63.2 |
| | | | Mrs. C.E.M. Borrett | Lab | 14,133 | 36.8 |
| | | | | | 10,149 | 26.4 |
| 1945 | 75,987 | 72.6 | B.T. Parkin | Lab | 22,495 | 40.8 |
| | | | W.R.D. Perkins | C | 21,546 | 39.0 |
| | | | P.E. Cadbury | L | 11,141 | 20.2 |
| | | | | | 949 | 1.8 |

# GLOUCESTERSHIRE, THORNBURY [345]

| Election | Electors | T'out | Candidate | Party | Votes | % |
|---|---|---|---|---|---|---|
| 1918 | 33,862 | 47.6 | †A. Rendall | Co L (L) | 9,999 | 62.0 |
| | | | T.D. Pilcher | Nat P | 6,132 | 38.0 |
| | | | | | 3,867 | 24.0 |
| 1922 | 34,655 | 77.9 | H.C. Woodcock | C | 10,682 | 39.5 |
| | | | A. Rendall | L | 10,578 | 39.2 |
| | | | J.H. Alpass | Lab | 5,749 | 21.3 |
| | | | | | 104 | 0.3 |
| 1923 | 35,695 | 75.6 | A. Rendall | L | 16,722 | 62.0 |
| | | | H.C. Woodcock | C | 10,252 | 38.0 |
| | | | | | 6,470 | 24.0 |
| 1924 | 36,672 | 79.5 | D.W. Gunston | C | 12,500 | 42.8 |
| | | | A. Rendall | L | 10,283 | 35.3 |
| | | | G. Elton | Lab | 6,376 | 21.9 |
| | | | | | 2,217 | 7.5 |
| 1929 | 49,645 | 82.5 | D.W. Gunston | C | 13,914 | 34.0 |
| | | | J.A. Day | L | 13,614 | 33.2 |
| | | | G. Elton | Lab | 13,445 | 32.8 |
| | | | | | 300 | 0.8 |
| 1931 | 52,547 | 79.7 | D.W. Gunston | C | 23,072 | 55.0 |
| | | | G.P. Blizard | Lab | 11,008 | 26.3 |
| | | | J.H. Whitehouse | L | 7,826 | 18.7 |
| | | | | | 12,064 | 28.7 |
| 1935 | 56,582 | 71.5 | D.W. Gunston | C | 19,180 | 47.4 |
| | | | F.A. Heron | Lab | 15,164 | 37.5 |
| | | | Rev. W.J. Jenkins | L | 6,104 | 15.1 |
| | | | | | 4,016 | 9.9 |
| 1945 | 75,286 | 76.4 | J.H. Alpass | Lab | 28,364 | 49.3 |
| | | | Sir D.W. Gunston, Bt. | C | 18,927 | 32.9 |
| | | | R.W. Brighton | L | 10,262 | 17.8 |
| | | | | | 9,437 | 16.4 |

| Election | Electors | T'out | Candidate | Party | Votes | % |
|---|---|---|---|---|---|---|
| 1918 | 25,228 | 48.0 | †Viscount Wolmer | Co C | 8,755 | 72.4 |
|  |  |  | H. Ainger | L | 3,342 | 27.6 |
|  |  |  |  |  | 5,413 | 44.8 |
| 1922 | 25,072 | 64.8 | Viscount Wolmer | C | 10,952 | 67.4 |
|  |  |  | H. Ainger | L | 5,296 | 32.6 |
|  |  |  |  |  | 5,656 | 34.8 |
| 1923 | 25,932 | 59.6 | Viscount Wolmer | C | 9,131 | 59.1 |
|  |  |  | A.J. Suenson-Taylor | L | 6,315 | 40.9 |
|  |  |  |  |  | 2,816 | 18.2 |
| 1924 | 26,956 | 68.2 | Viscount Wolmer | C | 14,081 | 76.6 |
|  |  |  | H. Beaumont | Lab | 4,313 | 23.4 |
|  |  |  |  |  | 9,768 | 53.2 |
| 1929 | 37,208 | 68.5 | Viscount Wolmer | C | 15,123 | 59.3 |
|  |  |  | H.F. Orpen | L | 5,984 | 23.5 |
|  |  |  | J.R. McPhie | Lab | 4,389 | 17.2 |
|  |  |  |  |  | 9,139 | 35.8 |
| 1931 | 39,952 | 65.6 | Rt. Hon. Viscount Wolmer | C | 22,134 | 84.4 |
|  |  |  | Miss M.R. Richardson | Lab | 4,091 | 15.6 |
|  |  |  |  |  | 18,043 | 68.8 |
| 1935 | 41,376 | 58.4 | Rt. Hon. Viscount Wolmer | C | 17,730 | 73.4 |
|  |  |  | V.G. Bailey | Ind Prog | 6,421 | 26.6 |
|  |  |  |  |  | 11,309 | 46.8 |

[Called to the House of Lords as Lord Selborne]

| Election | Electors | T'out | Candidate | Party | Votes | % |
|---|---|---|---|---|---|---|
| 1940 (26/11) |  |  | Rt. Hon. O. Lyttelton | C | Unopp. |  |
| 1945 | 49,172 | 68.9 | Rt. Hon. O. Lyttelton | C | 19,456 | 57.4 |
|  |  |  | T.H. Wintringham | CW | 14,435 | 42.6 |
|  |  |  |  |  | 5,021 | 14.8 |

Notes:—

1935:  Bailey was Directing-Secretary of the National Peace Council, a pacifist organisation.

1940:  Lyttelton was President of the Board of Trade.

# HAMPSHIRE, BASINGSTOKE  [347]

| Election | Electors | T'out | Candidate | Party | Votes | % |
|---|---|---|---|---|---|---|
| 1918 | 31,687 | 55.2 | †Rt. Hon. Sir A.C. Geddes | Co C | 11,218 | 64.1 |
| | | | A. Close | Ind Lab | 6,277 | 35.9 |
| | | | | | 4,941 | 28.2 |

[Resignation on appointment as United Kingdom Ambassador to the United States]

| | | | | | | |
|---|---|---|---|---|---|---|
| 1920 | 32,081 | 60.0 | Sir A.R. Holbrook | Co C | 8,515 | 44.2 |
| (31/3) | | | Sir H.C.W. Verney, Bt. | L | 5,393 | 28.0 |
| | | | J.H. Round | Lab | 5,352 | 27.8 |
| | | | | | 3,122 | 16.2 |
| 1922 | 33,364 | 66.9 | Sir A.R. Holbrook | C | 12,514 | 56.0 |
| | | | R.T.H. Fletcher | L | 6,780 | 30.4 |
| | | | S. Ledbury | Lab | 3,035 | 13.6 |
| | | | | | 5,734 | 25.6 |
| 1923 | 34,033 | 68.8 | R.T.H. Fletcher | L | 11,879 | 50.7 |
| | | | Sir A.R. Holbrook | C | 11,531 | 49.3 |
| | | | | | 348 | 1.4 |
| 1924 | 34,666 | 78.3 | Sir A.R. Holbrook | C | 15,558 | 57.3 |
| | | | R.T.H. Fletcher | L | 9,429 | 34.7 |
| | | | B. Greene | Lab | 2,172* | 8.0 |
| | | | | | 6,129 | 22.6 |
| 1929 | 44,197 | 74.2 | Viscount Lymington | C | 16,547 | 50.4 |
| | | | L.H.D. Jones | L | 11,595 | 35.4 |
| | | | W.J. Beck | Lab | 4,650 | 14.2 |
| | | | | | 4,952 | 15.0 |
| 1931 | 45,481 | 74.2 | Viscount Lymington | C | 23,523 | 69.7 |
| | | | Miss F.L. Josephy | L | 6,106 | 18.1 |
| | | | C.A. Goatcher | Lab | 4,124* | 12.2 |
| | | | | | 17,417 | 51.6 |

[Resignation]

| | | | | | | |
|---|---|---|---|---|---|---|
| 1934 | 46,686 | 64.4 | H.M.C. Drummond-Wolff | C | 16,147 | 53.7 |
| (19/4) | | | J.M. Foot | L | 9,262 | 30.8 |
| | | | J.W. Barker | Lab | 4,663 | 15.5 |
| | | | | | 6,885 | 22.9 |
| 1935 | 47,561 | 67.4 | P.W. Donner | C | 18,549 | 57.8 |
| | | | J.M. Foot | L | 10,317 | 32.2 |
| | | | J.S.W. Whybrew | Lab | 3,207* | 10.0 |
| | | | | | 8,232 | 25.6 |
| 1945 | 61,268 | 66.4 | P.W. Donner | C | 18,700 | 46.0 |
| | | | Mrs. E.A. Weston | Lab | 13,763 | 33.8 |
| | | | Hon. D.R. Rhys | L | 8,206 | 20.2 |
| | | | | | 4,937 | 12.2 |

| Election | Electors | T'out | Candidate | Party | Votes | % |
|---|---|---|---|---|---|---|
| 1918 | | | †J.H. Davidson | Co C | Unopp. | |
| 1922 | 34,480 | 67.4 | Sir J.H. Davidson | C | 17,008 | 73.1 |
| | | | C.H. Hoare | Lab | 6,245 | 26.9 |
| | | | | | 10,763 | 46.2 |
| 1923 | 35,685 | 59.7 | Sir J.H. Davidson | C | 14,787 | 69.4 |
| | | | J.B. Baker | Lab | 6,526 | 30.6 |
| | | | | | 8,261 | 38.8 |
| 1924 | 36,953 | 68.8 | Sir J.H. Davidson | C | 19,108 | 75.2 |
| | | | J.B. Baker | Lab | 6,304 | 24.8 |
| | | | | | 12,804 | 50.4 |
| 1929 | 53,538 | 68.0 | Sir J.H. Davidson | C | 19,756 | 54.2 |
| | | | C.P. Cross | L | 8,630 | 23.7 |
| | | | A.J. Pearson | Lab | 8,034 | 22.1 |
| | | | | | 11,126 | 30.5 |
| [Resignation] | | | | | | |
| 1931 (20/2) | 56,876 | 50.2 | Sir T.W.H. Inskip | C | 18,749 | 65.6 |
| | | | A.J. Pearson | Lab | 6,312 | 22.1 |
| | | | C.P. Cross | L | 3,517* | 12.3 |
| | | | | | 12,437 | 43.5 |
| 1931 | | | Sir T.W.H. Inskip | C | Unopp. | |
| 1935 | 68,402 | 61.9 | Rt. Hon. Sir T.W.H. Inskip | C | 31,794 | 75.1 |
| | | | R. Mack | Lab | 10,561 | 24.9 |
| | | | | | 21,233 | 50.2 |
| [Resignation on appointment as Lord Chancellor and elevation to the Peerage — Viscount Caldecote] | | | | | | |
| 1939 (6/10) | | | Sir R.D. White, Bt. | C | Unopp. | |
| 1945 | 96,374 | 71.0 | Sir R.D. White, Bt. | C | 35,882 | 52.5 |
| | | | E.A. Bramall | Lab | 32,501 | 47.5 |
| | | | | | 3,381 | 5.0 |

| Election | Electors | T'out | Candidate | Party | Votes | % |
|---|---|---|---|---|---|---|
| 1918 | | | †W.F. Perkins | Co C | Unopp. | |
| 1922 | | | W.W. Ashley | C | Unopp. | |
| 1923 | 37,475 | 68.8 | W.W. Ashley | C | 13,900 | 53.9 |
| | | | A.C.F. Boulton | L | 11,889 | 46.1 |
| | | | | | 2,011 | 7.8 |
| 1924 | 38,905 | 71.4 | Rt. Hon. W.W. Ashley | C | 17,945 | 64.6 |
| | | | A.C.F. Boulton | L | 6,681 | 24.1 |
| | | | C.L. Brighton | Lab | 3,137* | 11.3 |
| | | | | | 11,264 | 40.5 |
| 1929 | 54,884 | 72.6 | Rt. Hon. W.W. Ashley | C | 22,122 | 55.5 |
| | | | M.J. Cheke | L | 11,520 | 28.9 |
| | | | G.W. Austin | Lab | 6,206 | 15.6 |
| | | | | | 10,602 | 26.6 |
| 1931 | 59,357 | 71.9 | Rt. Hon. W.W. Ashley | C | 35,544 | 83.3 |
| | | | F. Stainer | Lab | 7,130 | 16.7 |
| | | | | | 28,414 | 66.6 |

[Elevation to the Peerage — Lord Mount Temple]

| Election | Electors | T'out | Candidate | Party | Votes | % |
|---|---|---|---|---|---|---|
| 1932 | 59,357 | 48.0 | J.D. Mills | C | 23,327 | 82.0 |
| (9/2) | | | Dr. C.A. Smith | ILP | 5,135 | 18.0 |
| | | | | | 18,192 | 64.0 |
| 1935 | 66,831 | 64.5 | J.D. Mills | C | 32,209 | 74.8 |
| | | | Mrs. C.D. Wadham | Lab | 10,876 | 25.2 |
| | | | | | 21,333 | 49.6 |
| 1945 | 87,904 | 71.3 | O.E. Crosthwaite-Eyre | C | 31,888 | 50.9 |
| | | | Dr. H.M. King | Lab | 22,478 | 35.9 |
| | | | J.W. Howlett | Ind L | 8,299 | 13.2 |
| | | | | | 9,410 | 15.0 |

Note:—

1932: Smith was put forward by the ILP after a decision by the local Labour Party not to contest the seat. Although the ILP was still affiliated to the Labour Party at the time of the by-election the Labour Party declined to endorse his candidature.

# HAMPSHIRE, PETERSFIELD [350]

| Election | Electors | T'out | Candidate | Party | Votes | % |
|---|---|---|---|---|---|---|
| 1918 | 28,473 | 52.7 | †W.G. Nicholson | Co C | 10,730 | 71.5 |
| | | | J. Pile | Lab | 4,267 | 28.5 |
| | | | | | 6,463 | 43.0 |
| 1922 | 29,873 | 65.7 | W.G. Nicholson | C | 12,600 | 64.2 |
| | | | D.L. Aman | Lab | 7,036 | 35.8 |
| | | | | | 5,564 | 28.4 |
| 1923 | 30,692 | 60.6 | W.G. Nicholson | C | 12,195 | 65.6 |
| | | | D.L. Aman | Lab | 6,403 | 34.4 |
| | | | | | 5,792 | 31.2 |
| 1924 | 31,627 | 66.3 | W.G. Nicholson | C | 14,646 | 69.8 |
| | | | G. Spencer | L | 3,755 | 17.9 |
| | | | G.G. Desmond | Lab | 2,582* | 12.3 |
| | | | | | 10,891 | 51.9 |
| 1929 | 41,587 | 68.2 | Rt. Hon. W.G. Nicholson | C | 15,605 | 55.0 |
| | | | V.G. Bailey | L | 9,334 | 32.9 |
| | | | Mrs. G.S. Massingham | Lab | 3,418* | 12.1 |
| | | | | | 6,271 | 22.1 |
| 1931 | 43,697 | 67.8 | Rt. Hon. W.G. Nicholson | C | 26,081 | 88.0 |
| | | | A.E. Albery | Lab | 3,559* | 12.0 |
| | | | | | 22,522 | 76.0 |
| 1935 | 45,655 | 63.4 | R.H. Dorman-Smith | C | 22,877 | 79.1 |
| | | | J.E.L. Birch | Lab | 6,061 | 20.9 |
| | | | | | 16,816 | 58.2 |

[Resignation on appointment as Governor of Burma]

| Election | Electors | T'out | Candidate | Party | Votes | % |
|---|---|---|---|---|---|---|
| 1941 (22/2) | | | Sir G.D. Jeffreys | C | Unopp. | |
| 1945 | 55,423 | 64.4 | Sir G.D. Jeffreys | C | 20,838 | 58.3 |
| | | | B.E. Goldstone | L | 8,269 | 23.2 |
| | | | T. Sargant | CW | 6,600 | 18.5 |
| | | | | | 12,569 | 35.1 |

| Election | Electors | T'out | Candidate | Party | Votes | % |
|---|---|---|---|---|---|---|
| 1918 | 32,747 | 48.1 | G.R.J. Hennessy | Co C | 10,166 | 64.6 |
| | | | W.J. West | L | 5,569 | 35.4 |
| | | | | | 4,597 | 29.2 |
| 1922 | 34,045 | 63.8 | G.R.J. Hennessy | C | 14,173 | 65.3 |
| | | | A.W.F. Haycock | Lab | 7,535 | 34.7 |
| | | | | | 6,638 | 30.6 |
| 1923 | 35,324 | 67.9 | G.R.J. Hennessy | C | 11,240 | 46.8 |
| | | | A.R. Stamp | Lab | 6,495 | 27.1 |
| | | | W.J. West | L | 6,252 | 26.1 |
| | | | | | 4,745 | 19.7 |
| 1924 | 36,583 | 71.8 | G.R.J. Hennessy | C | 15,026 | 57.2 |
| | | | A.R. Stamp | Lab | 8,216 | 31.3 |
| | | | W.J. West | L | 3,012* | 11.5 |
| | | | | | 6,810 | 25.9 |
| 1929 | 52,522 | 74.6 | Sir G.R.J. Hennessy, Bt. | C | 17,560 | 44.8 |
| | | | Dr. R.A. Lyster | Lab | 14,326 | 36.6 |
| | | | Miss F.L. Josephy | L | 7,278 | 18.6 |
| | | | | | 3,234 | 8.2 |
| 1931 | 57,895 | 77.1 | R.G. Ellis | C | 31,131 | 69.7 |
| | | | Dr. R.A. Lyster | Lab | 13,529 | 30.3 |
| | | | | | 17,602 | 39.4 |
| 1935 | 62,188 | 71.1 | G.E.H. Palmer | C | 28,506 | 64.4 |
| | | | A.L. Williams | Lab | 15,739 | 35.6 |
| | | | | | 12,767 | 28.8 |
| 1945 | 80,265 | 71.7 | G. Jeger | Lab | 30,290 | 52.6 |
| | | | G.E.H. Palmer | C | 27,259 | 47.4 |
| | | | | | 3,031 | 5.2 |

| Election | Electors | T'out | Candidate | Party | Votes | % |
|---|---|---|---|---|---|---|
| 1918 | 28,246 | 54.6 | †C.T. Pulley | Co C | 11,680 | 75.8 |
|  |  |  | S. Box | Lab | 3,730 | 24.2 |
|  |  |  |  |  | 7,950 | 51.6 |
| [Resignation] |  |  |  |  |  |  |
| 1921 | 27,316† | 62.5 | S. Roberts | Co C | 9,670 | 56.6 |
| (11/1) |  |  | E.W. Langford | L | 7,411 | 43.4 |
|  |  |  |  |  | 2,259 | 13.2 |
| 1922 | 27,774 | 62.0 | S. Roberts | C | 13,138 | 76.2 |
|  |  |  | J.J. Dodd | Lab | 4,094 | 23.8 |
|  |  |  |  |  | 9,044 | 52.4 |
| 1923 | 28,538 | 72.6 | S. Roberts | C | 11,448 | 55.3 |
|  |  |  | J.H. Whitehouse | L | 8,280 | 40.0 |
|  |  |  | S. Box | Lab | 981* | 4.7 |
|  |  |  |  |  | 3,168 | 15.3 |
| 1924 | 29,083 | 75.0 | S. Roberts | C | 13,210 | 60.6 |
|  |  |  | J.H. Whitehouse | L | 8,604 | 39.4 |
|  |  |  |  |  | 4,606 | 21.2 |
| 1929 | 36,984 | 78.9 | H.F. Owen | L | 14,208 | 48.7 |
|  |  |  | E.C. Romilly | C | 13,087 | 44.8 |
|  |  |  | H. Cooper | Lab | 1,901* | 6.5 |
|  |  |  |  |  | 1,121 | 3.9 |
| 1931 | 38,023 | 83.9 | J.P.L. Thomas | C | 19,418 | 60.9 |
|  |  |  | H.F. Owen | L | 12,465 | 39.1 |
|  |  |  |  |  | 6,953 | 21.8 |
| 1935 | 39,484 | 74.7 | J.P.L. Thomas | C | 18,234 | 61.9 |
|  |  |  | W.L. Dingley | L | 8,853 | 30.0 |
|  |  |  | G. Clarke | Lab | 2,397* | 8.1 |
|  |  |  |  |  | 9,381 | 31.9 |
| 1945 | 48,674 | 69.2 | J.P.L. Thomas | C | 17,439 | 51.8 |
|  |  |  | W. Pigott | Lab | 8,359 | 24.8 |
|  |  |  | A.P. Marshall | L | 7,871 | 23.4 |
|  |  |  |  |  | 9,080 | 27.0 |

Note:—

1931:  Owen was opposed to the National Government.

| Election | Electors | T'out | Candidate | Party | Votes | % |
|---|---|---|---|---|---|---|
| 1918 | 26,184 | 62.9 | C.L.A. Ward-Jackson | Co C | 8,308 | 50.5 |
| | | | E.G. Lamb | L | 5,291 | 32.1 |
| | | | E.W. Langford | Agric | 2,870 | 17.4 |
| | | | | | 3,017 | 18.4 |
| 1922 | 26,182 | 79.0 | E.W. Shepperson | C | 10,978 | 53.1 |
| | | | G. Le M. Mander | L | 9,698 | 46.9 |
| | | | | | 1,280 | 6.2 |
| 1923 | 26,658 | 75.8 | E.W. Shepperson | C | 11,582 | 57.3 |
| | | | J. Dockett | L | 8,614 | 42.7 |
| | | | | | 2,968 | 14.6 |
| 1924 | 27,033 | 71.6 | E.W. Shepperson | C | 12,470 | 64.4 |
| | | | G.A. Edinger | L | 6,897 | 35.6 |
| | | | | | 5,573 | 28.8 |
| 1929 | 33,046 | 76.3 | E.W. Shepperson | C | 13,237 | 52.5 |
| | | | G.A. Edinger | L | 11,990 | 47.5 |
| | | | | | 1,247 | 5.0 |
| 1931 | 33,432 | 79.9 | Sir E.W. Shepperson | C | 16,916 | 63.3 |
| | | | G.A. Edinger | L | 9,803 | 36.7 |
| | | | | | 7,113 | 26.6 |
| 1935 | 34,079 | 78.2 | Sir E.W. Shepperson | C | 14,180 | 53.2 |
| | | | A.E. Farr | L | 12,465 | 46.8 |
| | | | | | 1,715 | 6.4 |
| 1945 | 37,389 | 74.4 | A.E. Baldwin | C | 14,224 | 51.1 |
| | | | A.E. Farr | L | 13,586 | 48.9 |
| | | | | | 638 | 2.2 |

Note:—

1918: Langford was the nominee of the NFU.

| Election | Electors | T'out | Candidate | Party | Votes | % |
|---|---|---|---|---|---|---|
| 1945 | 53,338 | 73.8 | Dr. S.J.L. Taylor | Lab | 17,764 | 45.2 |
| | | | A.E.J. Clark | C | 17,082 | 43.4 |
| | | | Miss J.M. Henderson | L | 4,495* | 11.4 |
| | | | | | 682 | 1.8 |

| Election | Electors | T'out | Candidate | Party | Votes | % |
|---|---|---|---|---|---|---|
| 1918 | 25,752 | 50.4 | G.A. Talbot | Co C | 10,070 | 77.6 |
| | | | J. Hawkes | Lab | 2,913 | 22.4 |
| | | | | | 7,157 | 55.2 |
| [Death] | | | | | | |
| 1920 (9/11) | | | J.C.C. Davidson | Co C | Unopp. | |
| 1922 | 26,627 | 66.0 | J.C.C. Davidson | C | 11,847 | 67.4 |
| | | | J.H. Clynes | Lab | 5,726 | 32.6 |
| | | | | | 6,121 | 34.8 |
| 1923 | 26,990 | 65.8 | J.F. Dunn | L | 8,892 | 50.0 |
| | | | J.C.C. Davidson | C | 8,875 | 50.0 |
| | | | | | 17 | 0.0 |
| 1924 | 28,106 | 80.2 | J.C.C. Davidson | C | 12,985 | 57.6 |
| | | | J.F. Dunn | L | 7,994 | 35.5 |
| | | | Miss A. Sayle | Lab | 1,553* | 6.9 |
| | | | | | 4,991 | 22.1 |
| 1929 | 38,957 | 78.0 | Rt. Hon. J.C.C. Davidson | C | 15,145 | 49.8 |
| | | | C.T. Le Quesne | L | 11,631 | 38.3 |
| | | | A.E.R. Millar | Lab | 3,624* | 11.9 |
| | | | | | 3,514 | 11.5 |
| 1931 | 42,267 | 77.2 | Rt. Hon. J.C.C. Davidson | C | 21,946 | 67.2 |
| | | | C.T. Le Quesne | L | 8,021 | 24.6 |
| | | | A.E.R. Millar | Lab | 2,677* | 8.2 |
| | | | | | 13,925 | 42.6 |
| 1935 | 46,290 | 69.4 | Rt. Hon. Sir J.C.C. Davidson | C | 20,074 | 62.6 |
| | | | Mrs. M.I.C. Ashby | L | 7,078 | 22.0 |
| | | | C.W. James | Lab | 4,951 | 15.4 |
| | | | | | 12,996 | 40.6 |
| [Elevation to the Peerage — Viscount Davidson] | | | | | | |
| 1937 (22/6) | 47,281 | 55.0 | Viscountess Davidson | C | 14,992 | 57.7 |
| | | | Mrs. M.I.C. Ashby | L | 7,347 | 28.3 |
| | | | C.W. James | Lab | 3,651 | 14.0 |
| | | | | | 7,645 | 29.4 |
| 1945 | 62,091* | 71.2 | Viscountess Davidson | C | 19,536 | 44.2 |
| | | | Miss D.W. Mobbs | Lab | 14,426 | 32.7 |
| | | | T.A. Trotter | L | 10,219 | 23.1 |
| | | | | | 5,110 | 11.5 |

| Election | Electors | T'out | Candidate | Party | Votes | % |
|---|---|---|---|---|---|---|
| 1918 | 32,158 | 57.4 | †N.P. Billing | Ind | 9,628 | 52.1 |
| | | | E.B. Barnard | Nat P & Agric | 7,158 | 38.8 |
| | | | C. Harding | Lab | 1,679* | 9.1 |
| | | | | | 2,470 | 13.3 |
| [Resignation] | | | | | | |
| 1921 (16/6) | 32,426 | 55.1 | M.F. Sueter | AWL & Ind | 12,329 | 68.9 |
| | | | Sir E.H. Carlile, Bt. | Co C | 5,553 | 31.1 |
| | | | | | 6,776 | 37.8 |
| 1922 | 33,184 | 54.1 | M.F. Sueter | C | 11,406 | 63.6 |
| | | | T. Greenwood | L | 6,534 | 36.4 |
| | | | | | 4,872 | 27.2 |
| 1923 | 33,704 | 60.6 | M.F. Sueter | C | 10,660 | 52.2 |
| | | | T. Greenwood | L | 9,763 | 47.8 |
| | | | | | 897 | 4.4 |
| 1924 | 34,315 | 70.8 | M.F. Sueter | C | 14,582 | 60.0 |
| | | | T.M. Davies | L | 5,828 | 24.0 |
| | | | E. Selley | Lab | 3,885 | 16.0 |
| | | | | | 8,754 | 36.0 |
| 1929 | 45,893 | 74.7 | M.F. Sueter | C | 13,525 | 39.5 |
| | | | N.P. Billing | Ind | 10,149 | 29.6 |
| | | | T.E. Evans | L | 6,419 | 18.7 |
| | | | Dr. R.S. Edwards | Lab | 4,193* | 12.2 |
| | | | | | 3,376 | 9.9 |
| 1931 | 47,562 | 69.1 | M.F. Sueter | C | 25,751 | 78.4 |
| | | | Dr. R.S. Edwards | Lab | 7,092 | 21.6 |
| | | | | | 18,659 | 56.8 |
| 1935 | 52,270 | 62.5 | Sir M.F. Sueter | C | 21,193 | 64.8 |
| | | | Dr. R.S. Edwards | Lab | 11,492 | 35.2 |
| | | | | | 9,701 | 29.6 |
| 1945 | 65,070* | 70.4 | D.C. Walker-Smith | C | 19,877 | 43.3 |
| | | | L. Scutts | Lab | 17,349 | 37.9 |
| | | | T.P. Hughes | L | 7,587 | 16.6 |
| | | | A.B. Swain | Ind | 1,005* | 2.2 |
| | | | | | 2,528 | 5.4 |

Notes:—

1918:  Barnard was the nominee of both the Nat P and the NFU.

1921:  Sueter was the nominee of both the Anti-Waste League and Horatio Bottomley's Independent Parliamentary Group.

| Election | Electors | T'out | Candidate | Party | Votes | % |
|---|---|---|---|---|---|---|
| 1918 | 29,820 | 54.4 | †Rt. Hon. Lord Robert Cecil | Co C (C) | 9,828 | 60.6 |
| | | | R. Green | Lab | 5,661 | 34.9 |
| | | | G. Humm | Ind | 722* | 4.5 |
| | | | | | 4,167 | 25.7 |
| 1922 | 32,005 | 66.2 | Rt. Hon. Lord Robert Cecil | C | 13,124 | 62.0 |
| | | | B.S. MacKay | Lab | 8,049 | 38.0 |
| | | | | | 5,075 | 24.0 |
| 1923 | 33,197 | 67.7 | G.M. Kindersley | C | 11,157 | 49.7 |
| | | | B.S. MacKay | Lab | 5,913 | 26.3 |
| | | | Rev. D. Macfadyen | L | 5,390 | 24.0 |
| | | | | | 5,244 | 23.4 |
| 1924 | 34,060 | 69.5 | G.M. Kindersley | C | 14,019 | 59.2 |
| | | | J.A. Tayler | Lab | 5,773 | 24.4 |
| | | | Rev. D. Macfadyen | L | 3,881 | 16.4 |
| | | | | | 8,246 | 34.8 |
| 1929 | 44,967 | 73.4 | G.M. Kindersley | C | 14,786 | 44.8 |
| | | | Miss E. Lapthorn | L | 9,325 | 28.3 |
| | | | R.W. Gifford | Lab | 8,880 | 26.9 |
| | | | | | 5,461 | 16.5 |
| 1931 | 48,003 | 71.1 | Viscount Knebworth | C | 25,841 | 75.7 |
| | | | D.J. Freyer | Lab | 8,312 | 24.3 |
| | | | | | 17,529 | 51.4 |
| [Death] | | | | | | |
| 1933 (8/6) | 48,580 | 51.3 | Sir A.T. Wilson | C | 14,569 | 58.4 |
| | | | W. Bennett | Lab | 10,362 | 41.6 |
| | | | | | 4,207 | 16.8 |
| 1935 | 50,975 | 66.4 | Sir A.T. Wilson | C | 21,452 | 63.3 |
| | | | G.S. Lindgren | Lab | 12,417 | 36.7 |
| | | | | | 9,035 | 26.6 |
| [Death] | | | | | | |
| 1941 (10/3) | | | Hon. J.S. Berry | C | Unopp. | |
| 1945 | 67,331* | 72.4 | P.A. Jones | Lab | 20,779 | 42.7 |
| | | | Hon. J.S. Berry | C | 20,433 | 41.9 |
| | | | T. Darling | L | 7,515 | 15.4 |
| | | | | | 346 | 0.8 |

Note:—

1918: Humm was the nominee of the local branch of the NFDSS.

| Election | Electors | T'out | Candidate | Party | Votes | % |
|---|---|---|---|---|---|---|
| 1918 | | | †Sir E.H. Carlile, Bt. | Co C | Unopp. | |
| [Resignation] | | | | | | |
| 1919 (10/12) | 33,437 | 62.8 | F.E. Fremantle | Co C | 9,621 | 45.8 |
| | | | J.W. Brown | Lab | 8,908 | 42.4 |
| | | | M. Gray | L | 2,474* | 11.8 |
| | | | | | 713 | 3.4 |
| 1922 | 35,520 | 71.1 | F.E. Fremantle | C | 14,594 | 57.8 |
| | | | J.W. Brown | Lab | 10,662 | 42.2 |
| | | | | | 3,932 | 15.6 |
| 1923 | 36,474 | 68.8 | F.E. Fremantle | C | 11,968 | 47.7 |
| | | | C.B. Thomson | Lab | 6,640 | 26.5 |
| | | | H.K. Nield | L | 6,469 | 25.8 |
| | | | | | 5,328 | 21.2 |
| 1924 | 37,983 | 70.3 | F.E. Fremantle | C | 18,004 | 67.5 |
| | | | F. Herbert | Lab | 8,682 | 32.5 |
| | | | | | 9,322 | 35.0 |
| 1929 | 58,418 | 72.6 | F.E. Fremantle | C | 20,436 | 48.1 |
| | | | Miss M.M. Whately | Lab | 11,699 | 27.6 |
| | | | G.G. Honeyman | L | 10,299 | 24.3 |
| | | | | | 8,737 | 20.5 |
| 1931 | 65,365 | 71.9 | F.E. Fremantle | C | 36,690 | 78.1 |
| | | | Miss M.M. Whately | Lab | 10,289 | 21.9 |
| | | | | | 26,401 | 56.2 |
| 1935 | 79,885 | 62.6 | Sir F.E. Fremantle | C | 33,743 | 67.5 |
| | | | H.A. Franklin | Lab | 16,233 | 32.5 |
| | | | | | 17,510 | 35.0 |
| [Death] | | | | | | |
| 1943 (5/10) | | | Hon. J. Grimston | C | Unopp. | |
| 1945 | 71,893** | 72.6 | C.W. Dumpleton | Lab | 24,241 | 46.5 |
| | | | Hon. J. Grimston | C | 22,362 | 42.8 |
| | | | Miss E. Lakeman | L | 5,601* | 10.7 |
| | | | | | 1,879 | 3.7 |

| Election | Electors | T'out | Candidate | Party | Votes | % |
|----------|----------|-------|-----------|-------|-------|---|
| 1918 | 32,789 | 59.5 | D.H. Herbert | Co C | 11,155 | 57.2 |
| | | | G. Lathan | Lab | 4,952 | 25.4 |
| | | | F. Gray | L | 3,395 | 17.4 |
| | | | | | 6,203 | 31.8 |
| 1922 | 35,519 | 69.0 | D.H. Herbert | C | 12,040 | 49.2 |
| | | | J.J. Mallon | Lab | 8,561 | 34.9 |
| | | | R.A. Bateman | L | 3,896 | 15.9 |
| | | | | | 3,479 | 14.3 |
| 1923 | 35,773 | 68.5 | D.H. Herbert | C | 10,533 | 43.0 |
| | | | J.J. Mallon | Lab | 7,532 | 30.8 |
| | | | R.A. Bateman | L | 6,423 | 26.2 |
| | | | | | 3,001 | 12.2 |
| 1924 | 38,169 | 73.1 | D.H. Herbert | C | 15,271 | 54.7 |
| | | | H.H. Elvin | Lab | 7,417 | 26.6 |
| | | | Mrs. M.I.C. Ashby | L | 5,205 | 18.7 |
| | | | | | 7,854 | 28.1 |
| 1929 | 56,022 | 72.4 | Sir D.H. Herbert | C | 18,583 | 45.9 |
| | | | E. Terrell | L | 12,288 | 30.3 |
| | | | H. MacDonald | Lab | 9,665 | 23.8 |
| | | | | | 6,295 | 15.6 |
| 1931 | 61,261 | 71.0 | Sir D.H. Herbert | C | 34,076 | 78.3 |
| | | | F.M. Jacques | Lab | 9,423 | 21.7 |
| | | | | | 24,653 | 56.6 |
| 1935 | 67,826 | 63.5 | Rt. Hon. Sir D.H. Herbert | C | 28,196 | 65.4 |
| | | | S.W. Morgan | Lab | 14,906 | 34.6 |
| | | | | | 13,290 | 30.8 |

[Elevation to the Peerage — Lord Hemingford]

| Election | Electors | T'out | Candidate | Party | Votes | % |
|----------|----------|-------|-----------|-------|-------|---|
| 1943 (23/2) | 79,228 | 32.4 | W. Helmore | C | 13,839 | 53.9 |
| | | | A.R. Blackburn | CW | 11,838 | 46.1 |
| | | | | | 2,001 | 7.8 |
| 1945 | 95,276* | 73.3 | J. Freeman | Lab | 32,138 | 46.0 |
| | | | W. Helmore | C | 29,944 | 42.9 |
| | | | H.E.S. Harben | L | 7,743* | 11.1 |
| | | | | | 2,194 | 3.1 |

# HUNTINGDONSHIRE [360]

| Election | Electors | T'out | Candidate | Party | Votes | % |
|---|---|---|---|---|---|---|
| 1918 | 27,347 | 62.8 | †O.S. Locker-Lampson | Co C | 10,760 | 62.6 |
| | | | R.C. Grey | L | 6,416 | 37.4 |
| | | | | | 4,344 | 25.2 |
| 1922 | 28,143 | 70.7 | C.K. Murchison | C | 10,079 | 50.7 |
| | | | Mrs. L.M. Scott-Gatty | L | 5,123 | 25.7 |
| | | | D.J. Freyer | Lab | 4,697 | 23.6 |
| | | | | | 4,956 | 25.0 |
| 1923 | 28,554 | 69.6 | L.W.J. Costello | L | 10,465 | 52.7 |
| | | | C.K. Murchison | C | 9,404 | 47.3 |
| | | | | | 1,061 | 5.4 |
| 1924 | 28,957 | 77.8 | C.K. Murchison | C | 12,827 | 56.9 |
| | | | L.W.J. Costello | L | 9,703 | 43.1 |
| | | | | | 3,124 | 13.8 |
| 1929 | 36,691 | 77.2 | S.J. Peters | L (NL) | 12,889 | 45.6 |
| | | | Sir C.K. Murchison | C | 11,935 | 42.1 |
| | | | C.S. Giddins | Lab | 3,493* | 12.3 |
| | | | | | 954 | 3.5 |
| 1931 | 37,384 | 74.2 | S.J. Peters | NL | 23,102 | 83.3 |
| | | | M. Orbach | Lab | 4,624 | 16.7 |
| | | | | | 18,478 | 66.6 |
| 1935 | 38,005 | 66.2 | S.J. Peters | NL | 17,287 | 68.7 |
| | | | J.L. George | Lab | 7,861 | 31.3 |
| | | | | | 9,426 | 37.4 |
| 1945 | 46,754 | 65.7 | D.L-M. Renton | NL | 15,389 | 50.1 |
| | | | W.A. Waters | Lab | 9,458 | 30.8 |
| | | | H.D.L.G. Walston | L | 5,869 | 19.1 |
| | | | | | 5,931 | 19.3 |

# ISLE of ELY  [361]

| Election | Electors | T'out | Candidate | Party | Votes | % |
|---|---|---|---|---|---|---|
| 1918 | | | †C.R. Coote | Co L | Unopp. | |
| | | | | | | |
| 1922 | 36,966 | 72.0 | N. Coates | C | 13,552 | 50.9 |
| | | | C.R. Coote | NL | 7,359 | 27.7 |
| | | | W.G. Hall | Lab | 5,688 | 21.4 |
| | | | | | 6,193 | 23.2 |
| | | | | | | |
| 1923 | 37,656 | 68.1 | H.L. Mond | L | 11,476 | 44.7 |
| | | | M.G. Townley | C | 11,009 | 42.9 |
| | | | R.H.K. Hope | Lab | 3,172* | 12.4 |
| | | | | | 467 | 1.8 |
| | | | | | | |
| 1924 | 38,281 | 75.7 | Sir H.V.H.D. Lucas-Tooth, Bt. | C | 13,344 | 46.1 |
| | | | H.L. Mond | L | 11,381 | 39.3 |
| | | | D.J. Freyer | Lab | 4,235 | 14.6 |
| | | | | | 1,963 | 6.8 |
| | | | | | | |
| 1929 | 48,924 | 75.0 | J.A.E. de Rothschild | L | 16,111 | 43.9 |
| | | | Sir H.V.H.D. Lucas-Tooth, Bt. | C | 13,628 | 37.1 |
| | | | D.J. Freyer | Lab | 6,967 | 19.0 |
| | | | | | 2,483 | 6.8 |
| | | | | | | |
| 1931 | 50,849 | 63.2 | J.A.E. de Rothschild | L | 20,842 | 64.8 |
| | | | J.A. Whitehead | Agric | 6,993 | 21.8 |
| | | | F.J. Knowles | Lab | 4,302 | 13.4 |
| | | | | | 13,849 | 43.0 |
| | | | | | | |
| 1935 | 52,515 | 66.0 | J.A.E. de Rothschild | L | 17,671 | 51.0 |
| | | | W.F.C. Garthwaite | C | 16,972 | 49.0 |
| | | | | | 699 | 2.0 |
| | | | | | | |
| 1945 | 56,661 | 67.8 | E.A.H. Legge-Bourke | C | 15,592 | 40.6 |
| | | | A.F. Gray | Lab | 13,271 | 34.5 |
| | | | J.A.E. de Rothschild | L | 9,564 | 24.9 |
| | | | | | 2,321 | 6.1 |

Note:—

1931:  Whitehead sought election as an 'Independent Agricultural Protectionist' candidate.

| Election | Electors | T'out | Candidate | Party | Votes | % |
|----------|----------|-------|-----------|-------|-------|---|
| 1918 | 42,013 | 65.5 | †D.B. Hall | Co C | 16,274 | 59.2 |
|  |  |  | †Sir G. Baring, Bt. | L | 11,235 | 40.8 |
|  |  |  |  |  | 5,039 | 18.4 |
| 1922 | 44,637 | 75.4 | Sir E. Chatfeild-Clarke | L | 12,202 | 36.2 |
|  |  |  | J.T.W. Perowne | C | 10,620 | 31.6 |
|  |  |  | A.C.T. Veasey | Ind C | 7,061 | 21.0 |
|  |  |  | H.C. Shearman | Lab | 3,756* | 11.2 |
|  |  |  |  |  | 1,582 | 4.6 |
| 1923 | 45,530 | 76.6 | Rt. Hon. J.E.B. Seely | L | 16,249 | 46.6 |
|  |  |  | P.D. Macdonald | C | 16,159 | 46.3 |
|  |  |  | Mrs. E. Palmer | Lab | 2,475* | 7.1 |
|  |  |  |  |  | 90 | 0.3 |
| 1924 | 46,052 | 80.1 | P.D. Macdonald | C | 19,346 | 52.4 |
|  |  |  | Rt. Hon. J.E.B. Seely | L | 13,944 | 37.8 |
|  |  |  | H.E. Weaver | Lab | 3,620* | 9.8 |
|  |  |  |  |  | 5,402 | 14.6 |
| 1929 | 57,693 | 79.0 | P.D. Macdonald | C | 21,949 | 48.2 |
|  |  |  | St.J. Hutchinson | L | 17,383 | 38.1 |
|  |  |  | H.E. Weaver | Lab | 6,256 | 13.7 |
|  |  |  |  |  | 4,566 | 10.1 |
| 1931 | 59,574 | 71.1 | P.D. Macdonald | C | 32,728 | 77.2 |
|  |  |  | J.E. Drummond | Lab | 9,639 | 22.8 |
|  |  |  |  |  | 23,089 | 54.4 |
| 1935 | 60,965 | 69.4 | P.D. Macdonald | C | 26,748 | 63.2 |
|  |  |  | W.J. Miller | Lab | 15,586 | 36.8 |
|  |  |  |  |  | 11,162 | 26.4 |
| 1945 | 62,364 | 75.8 | Sir P.D. Macdonald | C | 22,036 | 46.7 |
|  |  |  | W.J. Miller | Lab | 19,252 | 40.7 |
|  |  |  | Miss M. O'Conor | L | 5,967 | 12.6 |
|  |  |  |  |  | 2,784 | 6.0 |

| Election | Electors | T'out | Candidate | Party | Votes | % |
|---|---|---|---|---|---|---|
| 1918 | 32,349 | 39.2 | S.S. Steel | Co C | 10,258 | 81.0 |
|  |  |  | W.H. Deedes | Ind Dem | 2,408 | 19.0 |
|  |  |  |  |  | 7,850 | 62.0 |
| 1922 | 35,240 | 64.2 | S.S. Steel | C | 15,638 | 69.1 |
|  |  |  | B. Noble | Lab | 6,977 | 30.9 |
|  |  |  |  |  | 8,661 | 38.2 |
| 1923 | 35,223 | 57.8 | S.S. Steel | C | 12,644 | 62.1 |
|  |  |  | B. Noble | Lab | 7,709 | 37.9 |
|  |  |  |  |  | 4,935 | 24.2 |
| 1924 | 35,659 | 70.4 | S.S. Steel | C | 15,159 | 60.4 |
|  |  |  | L.J. Humphrey | L | 5,487 | 21.8 |
|  |  |  | B. Noble | Lab | 4,473 | 17.8 |
|  |  |  |  |  | 9,672 | 38.6 |
| 1929 | 45,445 | 75.3 | Rev. R.M. Kedward | L | 15,753 | 46.0 |
|  |  |  | S.S. Steel | C | 14,579 | 42.6 |
|  |  |  | Dr. M. Follick | Lab | 3,885* | 11.4 |
|  |  |  |  |  | 1,174 | 3.4 |
| 1931 | 46,879 | 75.9 | Hon. M.H.R. Knatchbull | C | 20,891 | 58.7 |
|  |  |  | Rev. R.M. Kedward | NL | 14,681 | 41.3 |
|  |  |  |  |  | 6,210 | 17.4 |

[Succession to the Peerage — Lord Brabourne]

| Election | Electors | T'out | Candidate | Party | Votes | % |
|---|---|---|---|---|---|---|
| 1933 (17/3) | 47,434 | 70.9 | W.P. Spens | C | 16,051 | 47.7 |
|  |  |  | Rev. R.M. Kedward | L | 11,423 | 33.9 |
|  |  |  | W.J. Beck | Lab | 6,178 | 18.4 |
|  |  |  |  |  | 4,628 | 13.8 |
| 1935 | 48,910 | 73.6 | W.P. Spens | C | 21,323 | 59.2 |
|  |  |  | R.B. Matthews | L | 8,338 | 23.2 |
|  |  |  | W.J. Beck | Lab | 6,333 | 17.6 |
|  |  |  |  |  | 12,985 | 36.0 |

[Resignation on appointment as Chief Justice of India]

| Election | Electors | T'out | Candidate | Party | Votes | % |
|---|---|---|---|---|---|---|
| 1943 (10/2) | 49,899 | 27.7 | E.P. Smith | C | 9,648 | 69.7 |
|  |  |  | Mrs. C.E. Williamson | CW | 4,192 | 30.3 |
|  |  |  |  |  | 5,456 | 39.4 |
| 1945 | 50,933 | 71.0 | E.P. Smith | C | 18,800 | 51.9 |
|  |  |  | H.W. Lee | Lab | 12,575 | 34.8 |
|  |  |  | H.V. Strong | L | 4,804 | 13.3 |
|  |  |  |  |  | 6,225 | 17.1 |

Note:—

    1933:   Kedward was opposed to the National Government.

| Election | Electors | T'out | Candidate | Party | Votes | % |
|---|---|---|---|---|---|---|
| 1918 | 31,453 | 44.9 | †R.J. McNeill | Co C | 11,408 | 80.8 |
|  |  |  | E.T. Palmer | Lab | 2,719 | 19.2 |
|  |  |  |  |  | 8,689 | 61.6 |
| 1922 | 34,488 | 56.8 | R.J. McNeill | C | 13,954 | 71.2 |
|  |  |  | J.H.L. Sims | Lab | 5,639 | 28.8 |
|  |  |  |  |  | 8,315 | 42.4 |
| 1923 | 34,715 | 59.3 | R.J. McNeill | C | 12,017 | 58.4 |
|  |  |  | W.R. Heatley | L | 8,561 | 41.6 |
|  |  |  |  |  | 3,456 | 16.8 |
| 1924 | 36,045 | 65.9 | Rt. Hon. R.J. McNeill | C | 16,693 | 70.3 |
|  |  |  | D. Carnegie | L | 7,061 | 29.7 |
|  |  |  |  |  | 9,632 | 40.6 |

[Elevation to the Peerage — Lord Cushendun]

| Election | Electors | T'out | Candidate | Party | Votes | % |
|---|---|---|---|---|---|---|
| 1927 (24/11) | 39,229 | 60.8 | Sir W.A. Wayland | C | 13,657 | 57.3 |
|  |  |  | D. Carnegie | L | 10,175 | 42.7 |
|  |  |  |  |  | 3,482 | 14.6 |
| 1929 | 49,499 | 68.3 | Sir W.A. Wayland | C (Ind C) (C) | 19,181 | 56.7 |
|  |  |  | D. Carnegie | L | 9,937 | 29.4 |
|  |  |  | P.S. Eastman | Lab | 4,706 | 13.9 |
|  |  |  |  |  | 9,244 | 27.3 |
| 1931 | 54,740 | 66.2 | Sir W.A. Wayland | C | 30,328 | 83.7 |
|  |  |  | P. Winterton | Lab | 5,921 | 16.3 |
|  |  |  |  |  | 24,407 | 67.4 |
| 1935 | 55,417 | 64.4 | Sir W.A. Wayland | C | 26,552 | 74.3 |
|  |  |  | H.R. Adams | Lab | 9,164 | 25.7 |
|  |  |  |  |  | 17,388 | 48.6 |
| 1945 | 57,388 | 68.7 | J.B. White | C | 24,282 | 61.6 |
|  |  |  | J.D.M. Bell | Lab | 14,115 | 35.8 |
|  |  |  | Mrs. C.E. Williamson | CW | 1,017* | 2.6 |
|  |  |  |  |  | 10,167 | 25.8 |

## KENT, CHISLEHURST [365]

| Election | Electors | T'out | Candidate | Party | Votes | % |
|---|---|---|---|---|---|---|
| 1918 | 26,801 | 40.4 | A.W. Smithers | Co C | 8,314 | 76.8 |
| | | | A. Edmunds | Nat P | 2,507 | 23.2 |
| | | | | | 5,807 | 53.6 |
| | | | | | | |
| 1922 | 28,336 | 63.7 | R.C. Nesbitt | C | 11,801 | 65.4 |
| | | | D.M. Mason | L | 6,256 | 34.6 |
| | | | | | 5,545 | 30.8 |
| | | | | | | |
| 1923 | 28,961 | 60.5 | R.C. Nesbitt | C | 9,725 | 55.5 |
| | | | R.C.R. Nevill | L | 7,806 | 44.5 |
| | | | | | 1,919 | 11.0 |
| | | | | | | |
| 1924 | 30,029 | 72.7 | W. Smithers | C | 14,440 | 66.1 |
| | | | J.L. Thomson | Lab | 3,757 | 17.2 |
| | | | R.C.R. Nevill | L | 3,647 | 16.7 |
| | | | | | 10,683 | 48.9 |
| | | | | | | |
| 1929 | 45,116 | 69.6 | W. Smithers | C | 16,909 | 53.8 |
| | | | J.D. Bateman | L | 9,025 | 28.8 |
| | | | J.L. Thomson | Lab | 5,445 | 17.4 |
| | | | | | 7,884 | 25.0 |
| | | | | | | |
| 1931 | 54,589 | 69.8 | W. Smithers | C | 32,371 | 85.0 |
| | | | W.T. Colyer | Lab | 5,731 | 15.0 |
| | | | | | 26,640 | 70.0 |
| | | | | | | |
| 1935 | 85,028 | 66.1 | Sir W. Smithers | C | 38,705 | 68.9 |
| | | | W.T. Colyer | Lab | 12,227 | 21.8 |
| | | | J.A. Williams | L | 5,238* | 9.3 |
| | | | | | 26,478 | 47.1 |
| | | | | | | |
| 1945 | 71,246** | 72.4 | G.D. Wallace | Lab | 25,522 | 49.5 |
| | | | N.T.L. Fisher | C | 19,243 | 37.3 |
| | | | E.C.G. Hawkins | L | 6,824 | 13.2 |
| | | | | | 6,279 | 12.2 |

# KENT, DARTFORD  [366]

| Election | Electors | T'out | Candidate | Party | Votes | % |
|---|---|---|---|---|---|---|
| 1918 | 45,666 | 47.9 | †J. Rowlands | Co L | 15,626 | 71.4 |
| | | | W. Ling | Lab | 6,256 | 28.6 |
| | | | | | 9,370 | 42.8 |
| [Death] | | | | | | |
| 1920 | 44,281 | 61.3 | J.E. Mills | Lab | 13,610 | 50.2 |
| (27/3) | | | T.E. Wing | L | 4,562 | 16.8 |
| | | | R.J. Meller | Co C | 4,221 | 15.5 |
| | | | R.V.K. Applin | Nat P | 2,952* | 10.9 |
| | | | F.E. Fehr | Ind C | 1,802* | 6.6 |
| | | | | | 9,048 | 33.4 |
| 1922 | 47,132 | 71.2 | G.W.S. Jarrett | Const | 16,662 | 49.6 |
| | | | J.E. Mills | Lab | 14,744 | 43.9 |
| | | | Miss A.V. Garland | L | 2,175* | 6.5 |
| | | | | | 1,918 | 5.7 |
| 1923 | 48,320 | 70.0 | J.E. Mills | Lab | 18,329 | 54.2 |
| | | | G.W.S. Jarrett | Const | 15,500 | 45.8 |
| | | | | | 2,829 | 8.4 |
| 1924 | 49,804 | 79.2 | Hon. A. McDonnell | C | 20,108 | 51.0 |
| | | | J.E. Mills | Lab | 19,352 | 49.0 |
| | | | | | 756 | 2.0 |
| 1929 | 69,070 | 76.9 | J.E. Mills | Lab | 26,871 | 50.6 |
| | | | A. Edwards | C | 16,568 | 31.2 |
| | | | J.W. Williamson | L | 9,689 | 18.2 |
| | | | | | 10,303 | 19.4 |
| 1931 | 77,767 | 79.0 | F.E. Clarke | C | 34,095 | 55.5 |
| | | | J.E. Mills | Lab | 27,349 | 44.5 |
| | | | | | 6,746 | 11.0 |
| 1935 | 106,043 | 69.6 | F.E. Clarke | C | 38,242 | 51.8 |
| | | | Mrs. J.L. Adamson | Lab | 35,596 | 48.2 |
| | | | | | 2,646 | 3.6 |
| [Death] | | | | | | |
| 1938 | 129,543 | 68.5 | Mrs. J.L. Adamson | Lab | 46,514 | 52.4 |
| (7/11) | | | G.W. Mitchell | C | 42,276 | 47.6 |
| | | | | | 4,238 | 4.8 |

This constituency was divided in 1945.

Notes:—

1920:  Applin was supported by Horatio Bottomley.

1922:  Jarrett was the nominee of both the local National Liberal and Conservative associations. In a letter to 'The Times', he described himself as a 'constitutionalist' and that designation has been used.

1923:  Jarrett's name appeared on both the Liberal Party and the Conservative Party official lists of candidates.

| Election | Electors | T'out | Candidate | Party | Votes | % |
|---|---|---|---|---|---|---|
| 1918 | 35,170 | 46.5 | †Viscount Duncannon | Co C | 11,249 | 68.7 |
|  |  |  | A.M. Livingstone | L | 5,121 | 31:3 |
|  |  |  |  |  | 6,128 | 37.4 |

[Succession to the Peerage — Earl of Bessborough]

| 1921 | 34,890† | 71.0 | Sir T.A. Polson | Ind (AWL) | 13,947 | 56.3 |
| (12/1) |  |  | Hon. J.J. Astor | Co C | 10,817 | 43.7 |
|  |  |  |  |  | 3,130 | 12.6 |

| 1922 | 37,610 | 77.6 | Hon. J.J. Astor | C | 18,151 | 62.2 |
|  |  |  | Sir T.A. Polson | Ind C | 8,054 | 27.6 |
|  |  |  | L.J. Stein | L | 2,985* | 10.2 |
|  |  |  |  |  | 10,097 | 34.6 |

| 1923 |  |  | Hon. J.J. Astor | C | Unopp. |  |

[Unseated for voting in the House of Commons before taking the Oath]

| 1924 |  |  | Hon. J.J. Astor | C | Unopp. |  |
| (12/3) |  |  |  |  |  |  |

| 1924 | 38,580 | 74.7 | Hon. J.J. Astor | C | 21,186 | 73.5 |
|  |  |  | A.F. George | Lab | 7,627 | 26.5 |
|  |  |  |  |  | 13,559 | 47.0 |

| 1929 | 50,586 | 74.4 | Hon. J.J. Astor | C | 20,572 | 54.7 |
|  |  |  | E.L. McKeag | Lab | 8,864 | 23.6 |
|  |  |  | H.J. Baxter | L | 8,180 | 21.7 |
|  |  |  |  |  | 11,708 | 31.1 |

| 1931 | 54,106 | 73.0 | Hon. J.J. Astor | C | 29,743 | 75.3 |
|  |  |  | W. Moore | Lab | 9,781 | 24.7 |
|  |  |  |  |  | 19,962 | 50.6 |

| 1935 | 58,183 | 69.6 | Hon. J.J. Astor | C | 25,884 | 64.0 |
|  |  |  | W.H. Bennett | Lab | 14,588 | 36.0 |
|  |  |  |  |  | 11,296 | 28.0 |

| 1945 | 45,279 | 73.0 | J.R. Thomas | Lab | 17,373 | 52.5 |
|  |  |  | J.S-W. Arbuthnot | C | 15,691 | 47.5 |
|  |  |  |  |  | 1,682 | 5.0 |

Note:—

1921: Polson was supported by Horatio Bottomley but he joined the Anti-Waste League when it was founded shortly after the election. Bottomley did however continue to claim him as a member of the Independent Parliamentary Group.

# KENT, FAVERSHAM [368]

| Election | Electors | T'out | Candidate | Party | Votes | % |
|---|---|---|---|---|---|---|
| 1918 | 37,478 | 50.2 | †G.C.H. Wheler | Co C | 12,826 | 68.2 |
| | | | Rev. S.J.W. Morgan | Lab | 5,981 | 31.8 |
| | | | | | 6,845 | 36.4 |
| 1922 | 40,156 | 61.7 | G.C.H. Wheler | C | 13,675 | 55.2 |
| | | | Rev. S.J.W. Morgan | Lab | 11,096 | 44.8 |
| | | | | | 2,579 | 10.4 |
| 1923 | 40,676 | 63.4 | G.C.H. Wheler | C | 13,422 | 52.1 |
| | | | Rev. S.J.W. Morgan | Lab | 12,361 | 47.9 |
| | | | | | 1,061 | 4.2 |
| 1924 | 41,589 | 73.9 | G.C.H. Wheler | C | 14,432 | 46.9 |
| | | | Rev. S.J.W. Morgan | Lab | 9,180 | 29.9 |
| | | | A.J. Solomon | L | 7,132 | 23.2 |
| | | | | | 5,252 | 17.0 |
| [Death] | | | | | | |
| 1928 (25/1) | 43,122 | 72.4 | A. Maitland | C | 12,997 | 41.7 |
| | | | D.L. Aman | Lab | 11,313 | 36.2 |
| | | | J.F. Dunn | L | 5,813 | 18.6 |
| | | | E.A. Hailwood | Ind C | 1,090* | 3.5 |
| | | | | | 1,684 | 5.5 |
| 1929 | 52,047 | 75.5 | A. Maitland | C | 16,219 | 41.3 |
| | | | D.L. Aman | Lab | 15,275 | 38.9 |
| | | | Prof. M.A. Gerothwohl | L | 7,782 | 19.8 |
| | | | | | 944 | 2.4 |
| 1931 | 53,733 | 72.2 | A. Maitland | C | 25,568 | 65.9 |
| | | | H.N. Smith | Lab | 13,226 | 34.1 |
| | | | | | 12,342 | 31.8 |
| 1935 | 56,664 | 74.0 | A. Maitland | C | 22,881 | 54.6 |
| | | | H.N. Smith | Lab | 19,060 | 45.4 |
| | | | | | 3,821 | 9.2 |
| 1945 | 60,933 | 73.1 | P.L. Wells | Lab | 23,502 | 52.8 |
| | | | Sir A. Maitland | C | 21,037 | 47.2 |
| | | | | | 2,465 | 5.6 |

| Election | Electors | T'out | Candidate | Party | Votes | % |
|---|---|---|---|---|---|---|
| 1918 | 31,070 | 48.8 | †A. Richardson | Co C | 7,841 | 51.6 |
| | | | J. Butts | Lab | 3,254 | 21.5 |
| | | | H.E. Davis | Ind C | 1,817* | 12.0 |
| | | | C.E. Best | L | 1,271* | 8.4 |
| | | | H. Hinkley | Nat P | 985* | 6.5 |
| | | | | | 4,587 | 30.1 |
| 1922 | 31,972 | 63.0 | Sir A. Richardson | C | 8,166 | 40.6 |
| | | | G.A. Isaacs | Lab | 7,180 | 35.6 |
| | | | H.E. Davis | Ind C | 4,796 | 23.8 |
| | | | | | 986 | 5.0 |
| 1923 | 32,781 | 68.8 | G.A. Isaacs | Lab | 9,776 | 43.4 |
| | | | Sir A. Richardson | C | 9,657 | 42.8 |
| | | | L.H.D. Jones | L | 3,123 | 13.8 |
| | | | | | 119 | 0.6 |
| 1924 | 33,840 | 78.0 | I.J. Albery | C | 15,410 | 58.4 |
| | | | G.A. Isaacs | Lab | 10,969 | 41.6 |
| | | | | | 4,441 | 16.8 |
| 1929 | 44,226 | 71.8 | I.J. Albery | C | 14,644 | 46.1 |
| | | | W.J. Humphreys | Lab | 12,871 | 40.6 |
| | | | F.W. Kershaw | L | 4,220 | 13.3 |
| | | | | | 1,773 | 5.5 |
| 1931 | 46,124 | 75.7 | I.J. Albery | C | 22,410 | 64.2 |
| | | | B. Greene | Lab | 12,488 | 35.8 |
| | | | | | 9,922 | 28.4 |
| 1935 | 50,300 | 72.4 | I.J. Albery | C | 20,438 | 56.1 |
| | | | B. Greene | Lab | 15,994 | 43.9 |
| | | | | | 4,444 | 12.2 |
| 1945 | 55,293 | 74.5 | G. Allighan | Lab | 21,609 | 52.5 |
| | | | Sir I.J. Albery | C | 14,553 | 35.3 |
| | | | R.E. Goodfellow | L | 5,033* | 12.2 |
| | | | | | 7,056 | 17.2 |

[Expulsion from the House of Commons]

| 1947 | 61,684 | 77.3 | Sir R.T.D. Acland, Bt. | Lab | 24,692 | 51.8 |
|---|---|---|---|---|---|---|
| (26/11) | | | F.K. Taylor | C | 23,017 | 48.2 |
| | | | | | 1,675 | 3.6 |

Notes:—

1922: Davis sought election as an 'Anti-Waste' candidate but he was not officially supported by the Anti-Waste League.

1945: Allighan was expelled from the House of Commons on October 30, 1947, following a report of the Committee of Privileges which found him guilty of contempt of the House and a gross breach of privilege. See House of Commons Papers, 1946-47 (138) IX, 561.

| Election | Electors | T'out | Candidate | Party | Votes | % |
|---|---|---|---|---|---|---|
| 1918 [Death] | | | †N.C. Craig | Co C | Unopp. | |
| 1919 (15/11) | 31,767 | 52.8 | Hon. E.C. Harmsworth | C | 9,711 | 57.9 |
| | | | W.J. West | L | 7,058 | 42.1 |
| | | | | | 2,653 | 15.8 |
| 1922 | 38,500 | 68.4 | Hon. E.C. Harmsworth | C | 16,116 | 61.2 |
| | | | A.J. Suenson-Taylor | L | 10,226 | 38.8 |
| | | | | | 5,890 | 22.4 |
| 1923 | 39,679 | 69.5 | Hon. E.C. Harmsworth | C | 13,821 | 50.1 |
| | | | R.L. Rait | L | 13,773 | 49.9 |
| | | | | | 48 | 0.2 |
| 1924 | 41,395 | 77.6 | Hon. E.C. Harmsworth | C | 21,130 | 65.8 |
| | | | A.F.C.C. Luxmoore | L | 6,779 | 21.1 |
| | | | D.L. Aman | Lab | 4,202 | 13.1 |
| | | | | | 14,351 | 44.7 |
| 1929 | 58,330 | 73.3 | H.H. Balfour | C | 22,595 | 52.9 |
| | | | A.J. Suenson-Taylor | L | 15,648 | 36.6 |
| | | | E.J. Plaisted | Lab | 4,490* | 10.5 |
| | | | | | 6,947 | 16.3 |
| 1931 | 60,716 | 73.6 | H.H. Balfour | C | 33,173 | 74.2 |
| | | | G.I. Phillips | L | 11,517 | 25.8 |
| | | | | | 21,656 | 48.4 |
| 1935 | | | H.H. Balfour | C | Unopp. | |
| 1945 | 44,745 | 68.9 | E. Carson | C | 15,023 | 48.7 |
| | | | T.C. Boyd | Lab | 12,075 | 39.2 |
| | | | P.J. Willmett | L | 3,732* | 12.1 |
| | | | | | 2,948 | 9.5 |

Note:—

1919: Harmsworth joined the Anti-Waste League when it was formed in January 1921 and became leader of their parliamentary group. His actions were however approved by the local Conservative Association and he remained, at least nominally, a Conservative member.

| Election | Electors | T'out | Candidate | Party | Votes | % |
|----------|----------|-------|-----------|-------|-------|---|
| 1918 | 30,747 | 59.2 | †C. Bellairs | Co C | 11,931 | 65.5 |
|  |  |  | F.G. Burgess | Lab | 6,277 | 34.5 |
|  |  |  |  |  | 5,654 | 31.0 |
|  |  |  |  |  |  |  |
| 1922 | 32,916 | 78.5 | C. Bellairs | C | 8,928 | 34.6 |
|  |  |  | G.F. Clark | L | 8,895 | 34.4 |
|  |  |  | E.H.J.N. Dalton | Lab | 8,004 | 31.0 |
|  |  |  |  |  | 33 | 0.2 |
|  |  |  |  |  |  |  |
| 1923 | 34,037 | 78.9 | C. Bellairs | C | 11,244 | 41.9 |
|  |  |  | G.F. Clark | L | 9,047 | 33.7 |
|  |  |  | F.S. Cocks | Lab | 6,558 | 24.4 |
|  |  |  |  |  | 2,197 | 8.2 |
|  |  |  |  |  |  |  |
| 1924 | 34,811 | 69.8 | C. Bellairs | C | 16,121 | 66.3 |
|  |  |  | F.S. Cocks | Lab | 8,192 | 33.7 |
|  |  |  |  |  | 7,929 | 32.6 |
|  |  |  |  |  |  |  |
| 1929 | 45,317 | 77.0 | C. Bellairs | C | 14,254 | 40.8 |
|  |  |  | J. Morgan | Lab | 10,419 | 29.9 |
|  |  |  | T.F. Day | L | 10,222 | 29.3 |
|  |  |  |  |  | 3,835 | 10.9 |
|  |  |  |  |  |  |  |
| 1931 | 47,258 | 72.3 | A.C. Bossom | C | 27,394 | 80.2 |
|  |  |  | Mrs. G.S. Massingham | Lab | 6,770 | 19.8 |
|  |  |  |  |  | 20,624 | 60.4 |
|  |  |  |  |  |  |  |
| 1935 | 50,334 | 67.5 | A.C. Bossom | C | 24,644 | 72.5 |
|  |  |  | J.W. MacAlpine | Lab | 9,340 | 27.5 |
|  |  |  |  |  | 15,304 | 45.0 |
|  |  |  |  |  |  |  |
| 1945 | 56,347 | 71.0 | A.C. Bossom | C | 21,320 | 53.3 |
|  |  |  | O.L. Shaw | Lab | 18,295 | 45.7 |
|  |  |  | G. Murray | Dem P | 416* | 1.0 |
|  |  |  |  |  | 3,025 | 7.6 |

Note:—

1922: Clark sought election as an Independent candidate but he was the nominee of the local Liberal Association and is designated as such.

| Election | Electors | T'out | Candidate | Party | Votes | % |
|----------|----------|-------|-----------|-------|-------|---|
| 1945 | 57,625 | 72.7 | Sir W. Smithers | C | 20,388 | 48.6 |
| | | | A.R. Mais | Lab | 15,846 | 37.8 |
| | | | E.R. Goodfellow | L | 5,140* | 12.3 |
| | | | G.C. Milner | Ind | 528* | 1.3 |
| | | | | | 4,542 | 10.8 |

| Election | Electors | T'out | Candidate | Party | Votes | % |
|---|---|---|---|---|---|---|
| 1918 | 30,189 | 46.3 | T.J. Bennett | Co C | 10,650 | 76.2 |
| | | | J.E. Skinner | Ind Lab | 3,323 | 23.8 |
| | | | | | 7,327 | 52.4 |
| 1922 | 31,000 | 60.9 | Sir T.J. Bennett | C | 12,045 | 63.8 |
| | | | L.A. Goldie | Lab | 6,849 | 36.2 |
| | | | | | 5,196 | 27.6 |
| 1923 | 32,078 | 64.4 | R.S.A. Williams | L | 10,656 | 51.6 |
| | | | Sir T.J. Bennett | C | 9,987 | 48.4 |
| | | | | | 669 | 3.2 |
| 1924 | 32,660 | 74.8 | H.W. Styles | C | 15,125 | 61.9 |
| | | | R.S.A. Williams | L | 9,311 | 38.1 |
| | | | | | 5,814 | 23.8 |
| 1929 | 43,627 | 71.6 | Rt. Hon. Sir E.H. Young | C | 16,767 | 53.7 |
| | | | E.S. Liddiard | L | 7,844 | 25.1 |
| | | | H.H. Fyfe | Lab | 6,634 | 21.2 |
| | | | | | 8,923 | 28.6 |
| 1931 | | | Rt. Hon. Sir E.H. Young | C | Unopp. | |
| [Elevation to the Peerage — Lord Kennet] | | | | | | |
| 1935 (20/7) | | | C.E. Ponsonby | C | Unopp. | |
| 1935 | 48,559 | 65.3 | C.E. Ponsonby | C | 21,405 | 67.5 |
| | | | J. Horridge | L | 10,297 | 32.5 |
| | | | | | 11,108 | 35.0 |
| 1945 | 56,345* | 73.5 | C.E. Ponsonby | C | 18,893 | 45.6 |
| | | | J.S. Pudney | Lab | 14,947 | 36.1 |
| | | | Miss N. Muspratt | L | 6,906 | 16.7 |
| | | | K.F. Thompson | Com | 676* | 1.6 |
| | | | | | 3,946 | 9.5 |

| Election | Electors | T'out | Candidate | Party | Votes | % |
|---|---|---|---|---|---|---|
| 1918 | 37,448 | 57.4 | †H.H. Spender-Clay | Co C | 14,622 | 68.1 |
| | | | J. Palmer | Lab | 5,006 | 23.3 |
| | | | T.F. Buxton | L | 1,851* | 8.6 |
| | | | | | 9,616 | 44.8 |
| 1922 | 38,543 | 72.5 | H.H. Spender-Clay | C | 14,797 | 53.0 |
| | | | J.T. Davis | Lab | 7,665 | 27.4 |
| | | | A.C. Crane | L | 5,472 | 19.6 |
| | | | | | 7,132 | 25.6 |
| 1923 | 39,594 | 70.6 | H.H. Spender-Clay | C | 13,910 | 49.8 |
| | | | A.C. Crane | L | 7,433 | 26.6 |
| | | | J.T. Davis | Lab | 6,610 | 23.6 |
| | | | | | 6,477 | 23.2 |
| 1924 | 40,198 | 74.3 | H.H. Spender-Clay | C | 17,392 | 58.2 |
| | | | W.F. Toynbee | Lab | 6,564 | 22.0 |
| | | | J.M. Tucker | L | 5,898 | 19.8 |
| | | | | | 10,828 | 36.2 |
| 1929 | 52,855 | 72.3 | H.H. Spender-Clay | C | 19,018 | 49.8 |
| | | | G. Alchin | L | 10,025 | 26.2 |
| | | | W.F. Toynbee | Lab | 9,149 | 24.0 |
| | | | | | 8,993 | 23.6 |
| 1931 | 56,095 | 69.2 | Rt. Hon. H.H. Spender-Clay | C | 30,602 | 78.9 |
| | | | Mrs. C.E.M. Borrett | Lab | 8,208 | 21.1 |
| | | | | | 22,394 | 57.8 |
| 1935 | 56,106 | 68.2 | Rt. Hon. H.H. Spender-Clay | C | 23,460 | 61.3 |
| | | | F.M. Landau | Lab | 9,405 | 24.6 |
| | | | L.H.R. Pope-Hennessy | L | 5,403 | 14.1 |
| | | | | | 14,055 | 36.7 |
| [Death] | | | | | | |
| 1937 (23/3) | 56,717 | 58.2 | Sir A.W.M. Baillie, Bt. | C | 18,802 | 56.9 |
| | | | H. Smith | Lab | 8,147 | 24.7 |
| | | | R.B. Matthews | L | 6,073 | 18.4 |
| | | | | | 10,655 | 32.2 |
| 1945 | 63,441 | 72.9 | G.W. Williams | C | 23,081 | 49.8 |
| | | | Miss V. Dart | Lab | 16,590 | 35.9 |
| | | | J. Metcalfe | L | 5,351* | 11.6 |
| | | | Dr. E.F.St.J. Lyburn | Ind | 1,249* | 2.7 |
| | | | | | 6,491 | 13.9 |

Note:—

1945: Lyburn sought election as a 'Medical' candidate. He advocated the setting up of diagnostic clinics.

# LANCASHIRE, CHORLEY [375]

| Election | Electors | T'out | Candidate | Party | Votes | % |
|---|---|---|---|---|---|---|
| 1918 | 35,370 | 54.5 | D.H. Hacking | Co C | 13,059 | 67.7 |
| | | | E. Sandham | Lab | 6,222 | 32.3 |
| | | | | | 6,837 | 35.4 |
| 1922 | | | D.H. Hacking | C | Unopp. | |
| 1923 | 36,147 | 74.4 | D.H. Hacking | C | 14,715 | 54.7 |
| | | | Z. Hutchinson | Lab | 12,179 | 45.3 |
| | | | | | 2,536 | 9.4 |
| 1924 | 37,369 | 82.7 | D.H. Hacking | C | 17,844 | 57.7 |
| | | | Z. Hutchinson | Lab | 13,074 | 42.3 |
| | | | | | 4,770 | 15.4 |
| 1929 | 50,557 | 85.7 | D.H. Hacking | C | 19,728 | 45.6 |
| | | | W. Taylor | Lab | 18,369 | 42.4 |
| | | | H.E. Jones | L | 5,207* | 12.0 |
| | | | | | 1,359 | 3.2 |
| 1931 | 51,796 | 80.1 | Rt. Hon. D.H. Hacking | C | 28,749 | 69.3 |
| | | | J. Barrow | Lab | 12,734 | 30.7 |
| | | | | | 16,015 | 38.6 |
| 1935 | 53,222 | 78.4 | Rt. Hon. D.H. Hacking | C | 23,061 | 55.3 |
| | | | A. Whiting | Lab | 17,286 | 41.4 |
| | | | R. Edwards | ILP | 1,365* | 3.3 |
| | | | | | 5,775 | 13.9 |
| 1945 | 60,598 | 76.1 | C. Kenyon | Lab | 24,550 | 53.2 |
| | | | R.H. Brown | C | 21,595 | 46.8 |
| | | | | | 2,955 | 6.4 |

| Election | Electors | T'out | Candidate | Party | Votes | % |
|---|---|---|---|---|---|---|
| 1918 | 32,222 | 66.5 | A. Davies | Lab | 9,578 | 44.6 |
| | | | E.L. Hartley | C | 8,419 | 39.3 |
| | | | J.H. Batty | Co L | 3,443 | 16.1 |
| | | | | | 1,159 | 5.3 |
| 1922 | 33,393 | 85.3 | W. Brass | C | 15,586 | 54.7 |
| | | | A. Davies | Lab | 12,911 | 45.3 |
| | | | | | 2,675 | 9.4 |
| 1923 | 34,329 | 88.2 | W. Brass | C | 12,998 | 42.9 |
| | | | A. Davies | Lab | 11,469 | 37.9 |
| | | | H. Derbyshire | L | 5,810 | 19.2 |
| | | | | | 1,529 | 5.0 |
| 1924 | 34,617 | 88.6 | W. Brass | C | 16,637 | 54.2 |
| | | | D. Hall Caine | Lab | 14,041 | 45.8 |
| | | | | | 2,596 | 8.4 |
| 1929 | 43,113 | 91.5 | W. Brass | C | 16,035 | 40.7 |
| | | | W. Dobbie | Lab | 15,592 | 39.5 |
| | | | C.N. Glidewell | L | 7,826 | 19.8 |
| | | | | | 443 | 1.2 |
| 1931 | 44,002 | 89.3 | Sir W. Brass | C | 24,361 | 62.0 |
| | | | S.S. Awbery | Lab | 14,920 | 38.0 |
| | | | | | 9,441 | 24.0 |
| 1935 | 43,993 | 87.7 | Sir W. Brass | C | 21,163 | 54.9 |
| | | | S.S. Awbery | Lab | 17,411 | 45.1 |
| | | | | | 3,752 | 9.8 |
| 1945 | 43,534 | 83.2 | H.E. Randall | Lab | 19,443 | 53.7 |
| | | | R. Fort | C | 16,796 | 46.3 |
| | | | | | 2,647 | 7.4 |

| Election | Electors | T'out | Candidate | Party | Votes | % |
|---|---|---|---|---|---|---|
| 1918 | 31,203 | 71.3 | †Sir J. Rutherford, Bt. | Co C | 9,014 | 40.5 |
| | | | F. Hindle | L | 8,031 | 36.1 |
| | | | J. McGurk | Lab | 5,211 | 23.4 |
| | | | | | 983 | 4.4 |
| 1922 | 31,379 | 91.4 | Sir F.B. Sanderson, Bt. | C | 12,218 | 42.6 |
| | | | F. Hindle | L | 11,944 | 41.6 |
| | | | J. McGurk | Lab | 4,528 | 15.8 |
| | | | | | 274 | 1.0 |
| 1923 | 32,220 | 90.6 | F. Hindle | L | 14,242 | 48.8 |
| | | | Sir F.B. Sanderson, Bt. | C | 11,432 | 39.1 |
| | | | G. Thompson | Lab | 3,527* | 12.1 |
| | | | | | 2,810 | 9.7 |
| 1924 | 32,671 | 92.7 | Sir F.B. Sanderson, Bt. | C | 13,017 | 43.0 |
| | | | F. Hindle | L | 12,082 | 39.9 |
| | | | T. Ramsden | Lab | 5,188 | 17.1 |
| | | | | | 935 | 3.1 |
| 1929 | 41,664 | 92.3 | Rt. Hon. Sir H.L. Samuel | L | 15,714 | 40.9 |
| | | | Sir F.B. Sanderson, Bt. | C | 15,252 | 39.6 |
| | | | T. Ramsden | Lab | 7,504 | 19.5 |
| | | | | | 462 | 1.3 |
| 1931 | 42,031 | 92.2 | Rt. Hon. Sir H.L. Samuel | L | 18,923 | 48.8 |
| | | | A.C. Graham | C | 14,636 | 37.8 |
| | | | C. Rothwell | Lab | 5,184 | 13.4 |
| | | | | | 4,287 | 11.0 |
| 1935 | 41,390 | 89.9 | S.H.M. Russell | C | 15,292 | 41.1 |
| | | | Rt. Hon. Sir H.L. Samuel | L | 14,135 | 38.0 |
| | | | Mrs. F. Kerby | Lab | 7,778 | 20.9 |
| | | | | | 1,157 | 3.1 |
| [Death] | | | | | | |
| 1943 (15/12) | 39,229 | 45.0 | W.R.S. Prescott | C | 8,869 | 50.2 |
| | | | Miss H.C.M. Balfour | Ind L | 8,799 | 49.8 |
| | | | | | 70 | 0.4 |
| 1945 | 39,773 | 82.7 | W.R.S. Prescott | C | 13,623 | 41.4 |
| | | | R. Haines | Lab | 11,282 | 34.3 |
| | | | Miss H.C.M. Balfour | L | 7,979 | 24.3 |
| | | | | | 2,341 | 7.1 |

Note:—

1943: Miss Balfour was supported by the Common Wealth Movement.

# LANCASHIRE, FARNWORTH [378]

| Election | Electors | T'out | Candidate | Party | Votes | % |
|---|---|---|---|---|---|---|
| 1918 | 34,132 | 69.9 | E.A.A. Bagley | C | 10,237 | 42.9 |
|  |  |  | T. Greenall | Lab | 9,740 | 40.8 |
|  |  |  | Sir T.E. Flitcroft | L | 3,893 | 16.3 |
|  |  |  |  |  | 497 | 2.1 |
| 1922 | 34,606 | 84.8 | T. Greenall | Lab | 13,391 | 45.6 |
|  |  |  | E.A.A. Bagley | C | 10,037 | 34.2 |
|  |  |  | E. Rudd | L | 5,927 | 20.2 |
|  |  |  |  |  | 3,354 | 11.4 |
| 1923 | 35,351 | 73.5 | T. Greenall | Lab | 14,858 | 57.2 |
|  |  |  | A.L.W.K. Worsthorne | C | 11,134 | 42.8 |
|  |  |  |  |  | 3,724 | 14.4 |
| 1924 | 36,058 | 89.6 | T. Greenall | Lab | 15,327 | 47.5 |
|  |  |  | A.L.W.K. Worsthorne | C | 12,521 | 38.7 |
|  |  |  | J.C. Martin | L | 4,467 | 13.8 |
|  |  |  |  |  | 2,806 | 8.8 |
| 1929 | 47,841 | 87.5 | G. Rowson | Lab | 21,857 | 52.2 |
|  |  |  | Hon. Mary A. Pickford | C | 10,643 | 25.4 |
|  |  |  | E.F. Dyer | L | 9,381 | 22.4 |
|  |  |  |  |  | 11,214 | 26.8 |
| 1931 | 49,550 | 84.8 | J. Stones | C | 22,460 | 53.5 |
|  |  |  | G. Rowson | Lab | 19,553 | 46.5 |
|  |  |  |  |  | 2,907 | 7.0 |

[Seat Vacant at Dissolution (Death)]

| Election | Electors | T'out | Candidate | Party | Votes | % |
|---|---|---|---|---|---|---|
| 1935 | 51,739 | 82.4 | G. Rowson | Lab | 22,040 | 51.7 |
|  |  |  | E.I.G. Unsworth | C | 16,839 | 39.5 |
|  |  |  | J.M. Erskine | Ind | 3,763* | 8.8 |
|  |  |  |  |  | 5,201 | 12.2 |

[Death]

| Election | Electors | T'out | Candidate | Party | Votes | % |
|---|---|---|---|---|---|---|
| 1938 (27/1) | 52,784 | 77.9 | G. Tomlinson | Lab | 24,298 | 59.1 |
|  |  |  | H.F. Ryan | C | 16,835 | 40.9 |
|  |  |  |  |  | 7,463 | 18.2 |
| 1945 | 55,549 | 77.5 | G. Tomlinson | Lab | 28,462 | 66.1 |
|  |  |  | F. Howard | C | 14,570 | 33.9 |
|  |  |  |  |  | 13,892 | 32.2 |

Note:—

1935: Erskine sought election as a 'People's Peace' candidate. He received local Liberal Party support.

| Election | Electors | T'out | Candidate | Party | Votes | % |
|---|---|---|---|---|---|---|
| 1918 | 35,714 | 59.0 | †W.W. Ashley | Co C | 13,670 | 64.9 |
| | | | W.J. Tout | Lab | 7,400 | 35.1 |
| | | | | | 6,270 | 29.8 |
| 1922 | | | Lord Stanley | C | Unopp. | |
| 1923 | 39,090 | 76.1 | Lord Stanley | C | 16,510 | 55.5 |
| | | | R.P. Tomlinson | L | 13,230 | 44.5 |
| | | | | | 3,280 | 11.0 |
| 1924 | | | Lord Stanley | C | Unopp. | |
| 1929 | 61,702 | 74.9 | Lord Stanley | C | 29,894 | 64.7 |
| | | | J. Williamson | Lab | 16,318 | 35.3 |
| | | | | | 13,576 | 29.4 |
| 1931 | | | Lord Stanley | C | Unopp. | |
| 1935 | 77,942 | 72.0 | Rt. Hon. Lord Stanley | C | 39,731 | 70.8 |
| | | | T. McNamee | Lab | 16,379 | 29.2 |
| | | | | | 23,352 | 41.6 |
| [Death] | | | | | | |
| 1938 | 86,236 | 64.8 | C.G. Lancaster | C | 38,263 | 68.4 |
| (30/11) | | | Dr. Mabel P. Tylecote | Lab | 17,648 | 31.6 |
| | | | | | 20,615 | 36.8 |
| 1945 | 87,560* | 70.6 | C.G. Lancaster | C | 37,930 | 61.3 |
| | | | E. Hewitt | Lab | 22,102 | 35.8 |
| | | | K.E. Heath | CW | 1,784* | 2.9 |
| | | | | | 15,828 | 25.5 |

| Election | Electors | T'out | Candidate | Party | Votes | % |
|---|---|---|---|---|---|---|
| 1918 | 40,383 | 52.2 | †Rt. Hon. A.H. Illingworth | Co L | 14,250 | 67.6 |
| | | | H. Nobbs | Lab | 6,827 | 32.4 |
| | | | | | 7,423 | 35.2 |

[Elevation to the Peerage — Lord Illingworth]

| Election | Electors | T'out | Candidate | Party | Votes | % |
|---|---|---|---|---|---|---|
| 1921 | 39,856 | 80.9 | W. Halls | Lab | 13,430 | 41.7 |
| (8/6) | | | A. England | Co L | 13,125 | 40.7 |
| | | | C. Pickstone | L | 5,671 | 17.6 |
| | | | | | 305 | 1.0 |
| 1922 | 40,968 | 83.8 | A. England | NL | 19,016 | 55.4 |
| | | | W. Halls | Lab | 15,334 | 44.6 |
| | | | | | 3,682 | 10.8 |
| 1923 | 41,430 | 78.3 | A. England | L | 17,163 | 52.9 |
| | | | W. Halls | Lab | 15,273 | 47.1 |
| | | | | | 1,890 | 5.8 |
| 1924 | 42,529 | 81.0 | A. England | Const (L) | 19,131 | 55.6 |
| | | | A.G. Walkden | Lab | 15,307 | 44.4 |
| | | | | | 3,824 | 11.2 |
| 1929 | 54,757 | 79.3 | A. England | L (NL) | 22,692 | 52.2 |
| | | | A.C. Jones | Lab | 20,745 | 47.8 |
| | | | | | 1,947 | 4.4 |
| 1931 | 56,159 | 80.7 | J.C. Jackson | C | 32,429 | 71.5 |
| | | | J. Stott | Lab | 12,915 | 28.5 |
| | | | | | 19,514 | 43.0 |
| 1935 | 57,583 | 78.2 | R.W. Porritt | C | 27,226 | 60.5 |
| | | | T. McLean | Lab | 17,799 | 39.5 |
| | | | | | 9,427 | 21.0 |

[Death]

| Election | Electors | T'out | Candidate | Party | Votes | % |
|---|---|---|---|---|---|---|
| 1940 (28/8) | | | J.H. Wootton-Davies | C | Unopp. | |
| 1945 | 57,997 | 76.4 | J.E. Whittaker | Lab | 22,601 | 51.0 |
| | | | J.H. Wootton-Davies | C | 21,709 | 49.0 |
| | | | | | 892 | 2.0 |

[Death]

| Election | Electors | T'out | Candidate | Party | Votes | % |
|---|---|---|---|---|---|---|
| 1946 (21/2) | 58,204 | 75.6 | A.W.J. Greenwood | Lab | 22,238 | 50.5 |
| | | | A. Jones | C | 21,786 | 49.5 |
| | | | | | 452 | 1.0 |

| Election | Electors | T'out | Candidate | Party | Votes | % |
|----------|----------|-------|-----------|-------|-------|---|
| 1918 | 30,736 | 55.7 | †S. Walsh | Lab | 14,882 | 87.0 |
| | | | W. Paul | SLP | 2,231 | 13.0 |
| | | | | | 12,651 | 74.0 |
| 1922 | 31,974 | 80.0 | S. Walsh | Lab | 17,332 | 67.7 |
| | | | E.L. Fleming | C | 8,257 | 32.3 |
| | | | | | 9,075 | 35.4 |
| 1923 | 32,710 | 72.2 | S. Walsh | Lab | 17,365 | 73.5 |
| | | | Miss R.M. Parsons | C | 6,262 | 26.5 |
| | | | | | 11,103 | 47.0 |
| 1924 | 33,235 | 78.5 | Rt. Hon. S. Walsh | Lab | 18,272 | 70.0 |
| | | | E.V. Gabriel | C | 7,820 | 30.0 |
| | | | | | 10,452 | 40.0 |

[Seat Vacant at Dissolution (Death)]

| Election | Electors | T'out | Candidate | Party | Votes | % |
|----------|----------|-------|-----------|-------|-------|---|
| 1929 | 43,026 | 82.2 | G. Macdonald | Lab | 26,091 | 73.8 |
| | | | J.B. Walmsley | C | 9,260 | 26.2 |
| | | | | | 16,831 | 47.6 |
| 1931 | 44,454 | 82.5 | G. Macdonald | Lab | 23,237 | 63.4 |
| | | | R. Catterall | C | 13,440 | 36.6 |
| | | | | | 9,797 | 26.8 |
| 1935 | 46,899 | 77.3 | G. Macdonald | Lab | 26,334 | 72.6 |
| | | | H.F. Ryan | C | 9,928 | 27.4 |
| | | | | | 16,406 | 45.2 |

[Resignation on appointment as a Regional Controller of the Ministry of Fuel and Power]

| Election | Electors | T'out | Candidate | Party | Votes | % |
|----------|----------|-------|-----------|-------|-------|---|
| 1942 (20/10) | | | T.J. Brown | Lab | Unopp. | |
| 1945 | 48,883 | 78.9 | T.J. Brown | Lab | 28,702 | 74.4 |
| | | | Hon. R.E.P. Cecil | C | 9,875 | 25.6 |
| | | | | | 18,827 | 48.8 |

| Election | Electors | T'out | Candidate | Party | Votes | % |
|---|---|---|---|---|---|---|
| 1918 | 36,960 | 65.4 | Sir A. Hunter | Co C | 14,403 | 59.6 |
| | | | †Sir N.W. Helme | L | 9,778 | 40.4 |
| | | | | | 4,625 | 19.2 |
| 1922 | 36,121 | 79.2 | J.E. Singleton | C | 19,571 | 68.4 |
| | | | A.F. Brockway | Lab | 9,043 | 31.6 |
| | | | | | 10,528 | 36.8 |
| 1923 | 37,522 | 80.0 | J.J. O'Neill | L | 17,763 | 59.2 |
| | | | J.E. Singleton | C | 12,263 | 40.8 |
| | | | | | 5,500 | 18.4 |
| 1924 | 38,466 | 82.9 | Sir G. Strickland | C | 15,243 | 47.8 |
| | | | J.J. O'Neill | L | 11,085 | 34.7 |
| | | | H.M. Watkins | Lab | 5,572 | 17.5 |
| | | | | | 4,158 | 13.1 |

[Elevation to the Peerage — Lord Strickland]

| Election | Electors | T'out | Candidate | Party | Votes | % |
|---|---|---|---|---|---|---|
| 1928 (9/2) | 40,705 | 82.7 | R.P. Tomlinson | L | 14,689 | 43.7 |
| | | | H. Ramsbotham | C | 12,860 | 38.2 |
| | | | Rev. D.R. Davies | Lab | 6,101 | 18.1 |
| | | | | | 1,829 | 5.5 |
| 1929 | 52,774 | 83.9 | H. Ramsbotham | C | 17,414 | 39.3 |
| | | | R.P. Tomlinson | L | 16,977 | 38.3 |
| | | | R.P. Burnett | Lab | 9,903 | 22.4 |
| | | | | | 437 | 1.0 |
| 1931 | 55,708 | 76.3 | H. Ramsbotham | C | 32,185 | 75.7 |
| | | | R.C. Willis | Lab | 10,309 | 24.3 |
| | | | | | 21,876 | 51.4 |
| 1935 | 62,792 | 79.0 | H. Ramsbotham | C | 26,632 | 53.7 |
| | | | R.P. Tomlinson | L | 13,054 | 26.3 |
| | | | C. Royle | Lab | 9,938 | 20.0 |
| | | | | | 13,578 | 27.4 |

[Elevation to the Peerage — Lord Soulbury]

| Election | Electors | T'out | Candidate | Party | Votes | % |
|---|---|---|---|---|---|---|
| 1941 (15/10) | 66,290 | 41.9 | F.H.R. Maclean | C | 15,783 | 56.9 |
| | | | W.C. Ross | Ind L | 6,551 | 23.6 |
| | | | A.F. Brockway | ILP | 5,418 | 19.5 |
| | | | | | 9,232 | 33.3 |
| 1945 | 74,111 | 74.0 | F.H.R. Maclean | C | 27,090 | 49.5 |
| | | | A.E.V.A. Farrer | Lab | 19,367 | 35.3 |
| | | | E.S.T. Johnson | L | 8,357 | 15.2 |
| | | | | | 7,723 | 14.2 |

| Election | Electors | T'out | Candidate | Party | Votes | % |
|---|---|---|---|---|---|---|
| 1918 | 27,687 | 66.5 | †C.W.H. Lowther | Co C (Ind) | 9,662 | 52.5 |
| | | | D. Hunter | Lab | 4,472 | 24.3 |
| | | | †J. Bliss | L | 4,276 | 23.2 |
| | | | | | 5,190 | 28.2 |
| 1922 | 28,261 | 77.3 | M.S.N. Kennedy | C | 12,030 | 55.1 |
| | | | H. Maden | L | 5,790 | 26.5 |
| | | | T.M. Scott | Lab | 4,024 | 18.4 |
| | | | | | 6,240 | 28.6 |
| 1923 | 28,315 | 75.4 | H. Maden | L | 11,186 | 52.4 |
| | | | M.S.N. Kennedy | C | 10,176 | 47.6 |
| | | | | | 1,010 | 4.8 |
| 1924 | 28,171 | 83.3 | Lord Balniel | C | 13,460 | 57.4 |
| | | | H. Maden | L | 10,002 | 42.6 |
| | | | | | 3,458 | 14.8 |
| 1929 | 34,748 | 82.7 | Lord Balniel | C | 13,612 | 47.4 |
| | | | H. Maden | L | 7,805 | 27.2 |
| | | | J. Henderson | Lab | 7,303 | 25.4 |
| | | | | | 5,807 | 20.2 |
| 1931 | 35,232 | 83.0 | Lord Balniel | C | 17,423 | 59.6 |
| | | | H. Maden | L | 11,821 | 40.4 |
| | | | | | 5,602 | 19.2 |
| 1935 | 36,169 | 79.3 | Lord Balniel | C | 16,338 | 57.0 |
| | | | R.S. Armstrong | Lab | 6,946 | 24.2 |
| | | | H. Maden | L | 5,391 | 18.8 |
| | | | | | 9,392 | 32.8 |

[Succession to the Peerage — Earl of Crawford and Balcarres]

| Election | Electors | T'out | Candidate | Party | Votes | % |
|---|---|---|---|---|---|---|
| 1940 (12/4) | | | Sir W.J.I. Fraser | C | Unopp. | |
| 1945 | 41,466 | 77.2 | Sir W.J.I. Fraser | C | 18,571 | 58.0 |
| | | | S.W. Grundy | Lab | 13,436 | 42.0 |
| | | | | | 5,135 | 16.0 |

Note:—

1918: Lowther joined Horatio Bottomley's Independent Parliamentary Group.

| Election | Electors | T'out | Candidate | Party | Votes | % |
|---|---|---|---|---|---|---|
| 1918 | 36,563 | 58.3 | †Sir W.R.D. Adkins | Co L | 14,831 | 69.5 |
| | | | J. Battle | Lab | 6,501 | 30.5 |
| | | | | | 8,330 | 39.0 |
| [Appointed Recorder of Birmingham] | | | | | | |
| 1920 (22/11) | | | Sir W.R.D. Adkins | Co L | Unopp. | |
| 1922 | 37,034 | 68.4 | Sir W.R.D. Adkins | NL | 14,832 | 58.5 |
| | | | M.B. Farr | Lab | 10,505 | 41.5 |
| | | | | | 4,327 | 17.0 |
| 1923 | 37,585 | 72.8 | A.N. Stewart-Sandeman | C | 10,029 | 36.6 |
| | | | Sir W.R.D. Adkins | L | 9,500 | 34.7 |
| | | | M.B. Farr | Lab | 7,849 | 28.7 |
| | | | | | 529 | 1.9 |
| 1924 | 38,222 | 81.7 | A.N. Stewart-Sandeman | C | 16,005 | 51.3 |
| | | | M.B. Farr | Lab | 8,442 | 27.0 |
| | | | Sir W.R.D. Adkins | L | 6,763 | 21.7 |
| | | | | | 7,563 | 24.3 |
| 1929 | 52,005 | 79.8 | A.N. Stewart-Sandeman | C | 16,629 | 40.1 |
| | | | M.B. Farr | Lab | 14,368 | 34.6 |
| | | | D. Halliwell | L | 10,526 | 25.3 |
| | | | | | 2,261 | 5.5 |
| 1931 | 54,538 | 77.9 | Sir A.N. Stewart-Sandeman, Bt. | C | 31,702 | 74.6 |
| | | | T. McCall | Lab | 10,796 | 25.4 |
| | | | | | 20,906 | 49.2 |
| 1935 | 60,053 | 74.5 | Sir A.N. Stewart-Sandeman, Bt. | C | 27,369 | 61.1 |
| | | | J. Nuttall | Lab | 17,398 | 38.9 |
| | | | | | 9,971 | 22.2 |
| [Death] | | | | | | |
| 1940 (22/5) | 66,288 | 49.0 | E.E. Gates | C | 32,036 | 98.7 |
| | | | F. Haslam | BUF | 418* | 1.3 |
| | | | | | 31,618 | 97.4 |
| 1945 | 69,786 | 75.4 | E.E. Gates | C | 26,699 | 50.8 |
| | | | Dr. Mabel P. Tylecote | Lab | 25,908 | 49.2 |
| | | | | | 791 | 1.6 |

| Election | Electors | T'out | Candidate | Party | Votes | % |
|----------|----------|-------|-----------|-------|-------|---|
| 1918 | 40,469 | 52.8 | †A. Hopkinson | Co L (Ind) | 16,158 | 75.6 |
|  |  |  | W.H. Brown | Co-op | 5,227 | 24.4 |
|  |  |  |  |  | 10,931 | 51.2 |
| 1922 | 40,478 | 67.5 | A. Hopkinson | Ind | 15,953 | 58.4 |
|  |  |  | M.E. Mitchell | L | 11,376 | 41.6 |
|  |  |  |  |  | 4,577 | 16.8 |
| 1923 | 41,218 | 54.5 | A. Hopkinson | Ind | 11,426 | 50.8 |
|  |  |  | G. Jennison | L | 11,051 | 49.2 |
|  |  |  |  |  | 375 | 1.6 |
| 1924 | 41,682 | 75.3 | A. Hopkinson | Ind | 15,435 | 49.2 |
|  |  |  | T.W. Mercer | Lab/Co-op | 10,769 | 34.3 |
|  |  |  | G. Jennison | L | 5,162 | 16.5 |
|  |  |  |  |  | 4,666 | 14.9 |
| 1929 | 54,698 | 76.8 | H.M. Gibson | Lab/Co-op | 19,296 | 46.0 |
|  |  |  | A. Hopkinson | Ind | 14,267 | 33.9 |
|  |  |  | H. Housley | L | 8,467 | 20.1 |
|  |  |  |  |  | 5,029 | 12.1 |
| 1931 | 55,177 | 84.2 | A. Hopkinson | Nat Ind | 17,017 | 36.7 |
|  |  |  | H.M. Gibson | Lab/Co-op | 15,587 | 33.5 |
|  |  |  | E. Barlow | C | 13,873 | 29.8 |
|  |  |  |  |  | 1,430 | 3.2 |
| 1935 | 62,363 | 75.3 | A. Hopkinson | Nat Ind (Ind) (Nat Ind) | 24,569 | 52.3 |
|  |  |  | H.M. Gibson | Lab/Co-op | 22,399 | 47.7 |
|  |  |  |  |  | 2,170 | 4.6 |
| 1945 | 75,697 | 76.2 | Rev. G.S. Woods | Lab/Co-op | 27,435 | 47.5 |
|  |  |  | G.E. Rush | C | 18,452 | 32.0 |
|  |  |  | Miss M.W. Jalland | L | 7,128* | 12.4 |
|  |  |  | A. Hopkinson | Nat Ind | 4,671* | 8.1 |
|  |  |  |  |  | 8,983 | 15.5 |

Note:—

1918: Hopkinson was quoted, during the election, as saying that although he allowed himself to be called the Coalition candidate this did not bind him to support the Coalition Government. He went on to declare that he might vote against anything the Government did and he had simply taken their 'badge' (the 'coupon') because he felt it would be for the good of the country to do so. He was not a member of any party and had been adopted by both the local Conservative and Liberal associations.

| Election | Electors | T'out | Candidate | Party | Votes | % |
|---|---|---|---|---|---|---|
| 1918 | 24,397 | 73.0 | R. Young | Lab | 9,808 | 55.0 |
| | | | Hon. H. Lygon | Co C | 8,014 | 45.0 |
| | | | | | 1,794 | 10.0 |
| 1922 | 25,707 | 86.1 | R. Young | Lab | 12,312 | 55.6 |
| | | | Dr. H.B. Bates | C | 8,214 | 37.1 |
| | | | G.F. Clarke | Ind | 1,618* | 7.3 |
| | | | | | 4,098 | 18.5 |
| 1923 | 26,572 | 78.5 | R. Young | Lab | 12,492 | 59.9 |
| | | | Dr. H.B. Bates | C | 8,375 | 40.1 |
| | | | | | 4,117 | 19.8 |
| 1924 | 27,105 | 84.6 | R. Young | Lab | 12,875 | 56.1 |
| | | | J.A.W. Watts | C | 10,066 | 43.9 |
| | | | | | 2,809 | 12.2 |
| 1929 | 35,533 | 84.6 | R. Young | Lab | 18,176 | 60.5 |
| | | | R.C. Essenhigh | C | 11,887 | 39.5 |
| | | | | | 6,289 | 21.0 |
| 1931 | 36,965 | 85.9 | R.C. Essenhigh | C | 16,064 | 50.6 |
| | | | Sir R. Young | Lab | 15,683 | 49.4 |
| | | | | | 381 | 1.2 |
| 1935 | 40,321 | 84.8 | Sir R. Young | Lab | 19,992 | 58.5 |
| | | | R.C. Essenhigh | C | 14,201 | 41.5 |
| | | | | | 5,791 | 17.0 |
| 1945 | 53,393* | 76.2 | Sir R. Young | Lab | 25,197 | 62.0 |
| | | | K. Lewis | C | 15,465 | 38.0 |
| | | | | | 9,732 | 24.0 |

| Election | Electors | T'out | Candidate | Party | Votes | % |
|---|---|---|---|---|---|---|
| 1918 | 28,882 | 61.0 | J. Bell | Lab | 6,545 | 37.2 |
| | | | T. Fermor-Hesketh | Co C | 6,080 | 34.5 |
| | | | S. Hurst | Agric | 4,989 | 28.3 |
| | | | | | 465 | 2.7 |
| 1922 | 29,951 | 67.8 | F.N. Blundell | C | 11,921 | 58.7 |
| | | | J. Bell | Lab | 8,374 | 41.3 |
| | | | | | 3,547 | 17.4 |
| 1923 | 30,426 | 65.7 | F.N. Blundell | C | 10,598 | 53.0 |
| | | | R.B. Walker | Lab | 9,388 | 47.0 |
| | | | | | 1,210 | 6.0 |
| 1924 | 31,358 | 75.9 | F.N. Blundell | C | 13,392 | 56.3 |
| | | | R.B. Walker | Lab | 10,402 | 43.7 |
| | | | | | 2,990 | 12.6 |
| 1929 | 50,963 | 74.8 | S.T. Rosbotham | Lab (N Lab) | 20,350 | 53.4 |
| | | | F.N. Blundell | C | 17,761 | 46.6 |
| | | | | | 2,589 | 6.8 |
| 1931 | 56,472 | 71.7 | S.T. Rosbotham | N Lab | 30,368 | 75.0 |
| | | | F.V. King | Lab | 10,115 | 25.0 |
| | | | | | 20,253 | 50.0 |
| 1935 | 71,747 | 65.8 | Sir S.T. Rosbotham | N Lab | 27,624 | 58.5 |
| | | | F.V. King | Lab | 19,579 | 41.5 |
| | | | | | 8,045 | 17.0 |
| [Resignation] | | | | | | |
| 1939 (27/10) | | | W.S.R. King-Hall | N Lab (Nat Ind) | Unopp. | |
| 1945 | 93,874 | 69.3 | J.H. Wilson | Lab | 30,126 | 46.3 |
| | | | A.C. Greg | C | 23,104 | 35.5 |
| | | | W.S.R. King-Hall | Nat Ind | 11,848 | 18.2 |
| | | | | | 7,022 | 10.8 |

Note:—

1918:  Hurst was the nominee of the NFU.

| Election | Electors | T'out | Candidate | Party | Votes | % |
|---|---|---|---|---|---|---|
| 1918 | 35,239 | 61.7 | W.H. Sugden | Co C | 12,434 | 57.1 |
| | | | J. Crinion | Lab | 4,875 | 22.4 |
| | | | H. Fullerton | L | 4,451 | 20.5 |
| | | | | | 7,559 | 34.7 |
| 1922 | 35,318 | 83.4 | Sir W.H. Sugden | C | 12,388 | 42.1 |
| | | | W. Gorman | L | 11,295 | 38.3 |
| | | | J. Battle | Lab | 5,776 | 19.6 |
| | | | | | 1,093 | 3.8 |
| 1923 | 36,041 | 82.9 | W. Gorman | L | 14,836 | 49.6 |
| | | | Sir W.H. Sugden | C | 12,320 | 41.2 |
| | | | Rev. J.B. Turner | Lab | 2,740* | 9.2 |
| | | | | | 2,516 | 8.4 |
| 1924 | 36,449 | 86.3 | Dr. A.V. Davies | C | 13,859 | 44.0 |
| | | | W. Gorman | L | 11,433 | 36.4 |
| | | | A.E. Wood | Lab | 6,156 | 19.6 |
| | | | | | 2,426 | 7.6 |
| 1929 | 47,266 | 82.9 | Dr. A.V. Davies | C | 15,051 | 38.4 |
| | | | H. Derbyshire | L | 13,347 | 34.1 |
| | | | A.E. Wood | Lab | 10,763 | 27.5 |
| | | | | | 1,704 | 4.3 |
| 1931 | 47,838 | 85.9 | H. Sutcliffe | C | 21,044 | 51.2 |
| | | | R.F. Walker | L | 14,142 | 34.4 |
| | | | G. Illingworth | Lab | 5,913 | 14.4 |
| | | | | | 6,902 | 16.8 |
| 1935 | 48,063 | 81.7 | H. Sutcliffe | C | 20,510 | 52.3 |
| | | | R.F. Walker | L | 9,910 | 25.2 |
| | | | L. Oakes | Lab | 8,845 | 22.5 |
| | | | | | 10,600 | 27.1 |
| 1945 | 45,361 | 81.0 | H. Sutcliffe | C | 15,388 | 41.9 |
| | | | H. Rhodes | Lab | 13,753 | 37.4 |
| | | | A.M. Knight | L | 7,618 | 20.7 |
| | | | | | 1,635 | 4.5 |

| Election | Electors | T'out | Candidate | Party | Votes | % |
|----------|----------|-------|-----------|-------|-------|---|
| 1918 | 36,459 | 61.4 | T. Robinson | Co L | 17,161 | 76.7 |
| | | | J. Hallsworth | Lab | 5,216 | 23.3 |
| | | | | | 11,945 | 53.4 |
| | | | | | | |
| 1922 | 38,837 | 71.9 | Sir T. Robinson | NL | 19,185 | 68.7 |
| | | | A.H. Turner | Lab | 8,733 | 31.3 |
| | | | | | 10,452 | 37.4 |
| | | | | | | |
| 1923 | 40,415 | 67.9 | Sir T. Robinson | L | 15,971 | 58.2 |
| | | | J. Corlett | Lab | 11,451 | 41.8 |
| | | | | | 4,520 | 16.4 |
| | | | | | | |
| 1924 | 41,553 | 77.8 | Sir T. Robinson | Const (L) (Ind) | 20,826 | 64.4 |
| | | | Dr. J. Robinson | Lab | 11,520 | 35.6 |
| | | | | | 9,306 | 28.8 |
| | | | | | | |
| 1929 | 58,471 | 75.2 | Sir T. Robinson | Ind | 25,799 | 58.6 |
| | | | F. Anderson | Lab | 18,199 | 41.4 |
| | | | | | 7,600 | 17.2 |
| | | | | | | |
| 1931 | 66,063 | 78.4 | G.A. Renwick | C | 39,002 | 75.3 |
| | | | F. Anderson | Lab | 12,796 | 24.7 |
| | | | | | 26,206 | 50.6 |
| | | | | | | |
| 1935 | 74,697 | 72.5 | A.C. Crossley | C | 34,874 | 64.4 |
| | | | T. Myers | Lab | 19,278 | 35.6 |
| | | | | | 15,596 | 28.8 |
| [Death] | | | | | | |
| 1939 (8/12) | 80,112 | 36.6 | R.H. Etherton | C | 23,408 | 79.7 |
| | | | R. Edwards | ILP | 4,424 | 15.1 |
| | | | E.A. Gower | Com | 1,519* | 5.2 |
| | | | | | 18,984 | 64.6 |
| | | | | | | |
| 1945 | 83,003* | 78.5 | H.L. Austin | Lab | 35,715 | 54.8 |
| | | | R.H. Etherton | C | 29,421 | 45.2 |
| | | | | | 6,294 | 9.6 |

Note:—

| 1918-1929: | Robinson was the product of a Liberal-Conservative pact and stood under the title 'Independent Free Trade and Anti-Socialist' although he was always claimed by the Liberal Party as one of their candidates. In view of this he is designated as a Liberal, except in 1924 when the designation 'Constitutionalist' was used by 'pact' candidates. |
|---|---|

In a letter to 'The Daily News' (July 8, 1929) he stated that he had been an Independent MP since the Coalition was dissolved in 1922. "Notwithstanding this" he said, "my Liberal friends in the House of Commons generously continued to send me their Whip which I have regarded as an act of courtesy. To prevent however any possibility of misunderstanding in the future on this point, I arranged that the sending of the Whip to me should be discontinued in this Parliament."

| Election | Electors | T'out | Candidate | Party | Votes | % |
|---|---|---|---|---|---|---|
| 1918 | 26,806 | 59.2 | A. Buckley | Co C | 13,255 | 83.5 |
|  |  |  | S. Reeves | Lab | 2,619 | 16.5 |
|  |  |  |  |  | 10,636 | 67.0 |
| 1922 | 27,746 | 69.4 | A. Buckley | C | 12,967 | 67.3 |
|  |  |  | Mrs. N. Stewart-Brown | L | 6,300 | 32.7 |
|  |  |  |  |  | 6,667 | 34.6 |
| 1923 | 28,336 | 72.6 | M. Bullock | C | 10,615 | 51.6 |
|  |  |  | Sir R.L. Connell | L | 9,965 | 48.4 |
|  |  |  |  |  | 650 | 3.2 |
| 1924 | 29,083 | 75.0 | M. Bullock | C | 15,704 | 72.0 |
|  |  |  | G.F. Titt | Lab | 6,116 | 28.0 |
|  |  |  |  |  | 9,588 | 44.0 |
| 1929 | 42,423 | 78.2 | M. Bullock | C | 17,299 | 52.2 |
|  |  |  | J.C. Leigh | Lab | 8,142 | 24.5 |
|  |  |  | F.A. Sellers | L | 7,728 | 23.3 |
|  |  |  |  |  | 9,157 | 27.7 |
| 1931 |  |  | M. Bullock | C | Unopp. |  |
| 1935 |  |  | M. Bullock | C | Unopp. |  |
| 1945 | 54,409 | 76.2 | M. Bullock | C | 19,650 | 47.3 |
|  |  |  | P. Vos | Lab | 13,795 | 33.3 |
|  |  |  | J.D. Weir | L | 7,823 | 18.9 |
|  |  |  | C. Foster | Ind | 195* | 0.5 |
|  |  |  |  |  | 5,855 | 14.0 |

| Election | Electors | T'out | Candidate | Party | Votes | % |
|---|---|---|---|---|---|---|
| 1918 | 30,108 | 61.6 | †W.T. Wilson | Lab | 11,849 | 63.9 |
|  |  |  | J. Tonge | Ind L | 6,697 | 36.1 |
|  |  |  |  |  | 5,152 | 27.8 |
| [Death] |  |  |  |  |  |  |
| 1921 | 30,409 | 84.7 | R.J. Davies | Lab | 14,876 | 57.8 |
| (5/10) |  |  | J. Tonge | Co L | 10,867 | 42.2 |
|  |  |  |  |  | 4,009 | 15.6 |
| 1922 | 31,351 | 85.4 | R.J. Davies | Lab | 14,846 | 55.4 |
|  |  |  | J. Tonge | NL | 11,937 | 44.6 |
|  |  |  |  |  | 2,909 | 10.8 |
| 1923 | 32,081 | 79.3 | R.J. Davies | Lab | 15,347 | 60.3 |
|  |  |  | J. Haslam | C | 10,103 | 39.7 |
|  |  |  |  |  | 5,244 | 20.6 |
| 1924 | 32,587 | 88.1 | R.J. Davies | Lab | 16,033 | 55.8 |
|  |  |  | J. Haslam | C | 12,684 | 44.2 |
|  |  |  |  |  | 3,349 | 11.6 |
| 1929 | 41,648 | 87.1 | R.J. Davies | Lab | 22,305 | 61.4 |
|  |  |  | J.W. Lomax | C | 9,855 | 27.2 |
|  |  |  | E.E. Canney | L | 4,132* | 11.4 |
|  |  |  |  |  | 12,450 | 34.2 |
| 1931 | 42,230 | 85.5 | R.J. Davies | Lab | 19,301 | 53.5 |
|  |  |  | P. Higson | C | 16,801 | 46.5 |
|  |  |  |  |  | 2,500 | 7.0 |
| 1935 | 41,980 | 83.2 | R.J. Davies | Lab | 21,093 | 60.4 |
|  |  |  | H.O. Dixon | C | 13,851 | 39.6 |
|  |  |  |  |  | 7,242 | 20.8 |
| 1945 | 41,851 | 77.3 | R.J. Davies | Lab | 20,990 | 64.9 |
|  |  |  | S. Bell | C | 11,346 | 35.1 |
|  |  |  |  |  | 9,644 | 29.8 |

| Election | Electors | T'out | Candidate | Party | Votes | % |
|---|---|---|---|---|---|---|
| 1918 | 30,674 | 63.0 | †W.H. Walker | Co C | 11,515 | 59.6 |
| | | | T. Williamson | Lab | 7,821 | 40.4 |
| | | | | | 3,694 | 19.2 |
| [Elevation to the Peerage — Lord Wavertree] | | | | | | |
| 1919 | 30,674† | 71.1 | Rt. Hon. A. Henderson | Lab | 11,404 | 52.3 |
| (30/8) | | | Hon. F.M.B. Fisher | Co C | 10,417 | 47.7 |
| | | | | | 987 | 4.6 |
| 1922 | 31,784 | 86.8 | G.C. Clayton | C | 14,679 | 53.2 |
| | | | Rt. Hon. A. Henderson | Lab | 12,897 | 46.8 |
| | | | | | 1,782 | 6.4 |
| 1923 | 32,735 | 83.0 | G.C. Clayton | C | 12,808 | 47.1 |
| | | | J.P. Cotter | Lab | 12,020 | 44.2 |
| | | | H.T. Ellis | L | 2,355* | 8.7 |
| | | | | | 788 | 2.9 |
| 1924 | 33,553 | 85.8 | G.C. Clayton | C | 15,476 | 53.7 |
| | | | J.P. Cotter | Lab | 13,326 | 46.3 |
| | | | | | 2,150 | 7.4 |
| 1929 | 44,205 | 84.8 | A.G. Cameron | Lab | 19,125 | 51.0 |
| | | | G.C. Clayton | C | 18,376 | 49.0 |
| | | | | | 749 | 2.0 |
| 1931 | 46,219 | 87.5 | J.R. Robinson | C | 25,123 | 62.1 |
| | | | A.G. Cameron | Lab | 15,309 | 37.9 |
| | | | | | 9,814 | 24.2 |
| 1935 | 54,507 | 80.1 | R.A. Pilkington | C | 24,457 | 56.0 |
| | | | A.G. Cameron | Lab | 19,187 | 44.0 |
| | | | | | 5,270 | 12.0 |
| 1945 | 93,945 | 76.0 | C.N. Shawcross | Lab | 41,980 | 58.8 |
| | | | R.A. Pilkington | C | 29,382 | 41.2 |
| | | | | | 12,598 | 17.6 |

| Election | Electors | T'out | Candidate | Party | Votes | % |
|----------|----------|-------|-----------|-------|-------|---|
| 1918 | 32,242 | 58.6 | †Hon. H.D. McLaren | Co L | 12,545 | 66.4 |
| | | | †T. Richardson | Lab | 6,344 | 33.6 |
| | | | | | 6,201 | 32.8 |
| | | | | | | |
| 1922 | 33,937 | 81.0 | T.G.F. Paget | C | 11,251 | 40.9 |
| | | | C.J. Bundock | Lab | 8,740 | 31.8 |
| | | | Hon. H.D. McLaren | NL | 7,513 | 27.3 |
| | | | | | 2,511 | 9.1 |
| | | | | | | |
| 1923 | 35,090 | 80.3 | G. Ward | L | 11,596 | 41.2 |
| | | | T.G.F. Paget | C | 8,430 | 29.9 |
| | | | E. Hughes | Lab | 8,152 | 28.9 |
| | | | | | 3,166 | 11.3 |
| | | | | | | |
| 1924 | 35,925 | 80.8 | R. Gee | C | 10,114 | 34.9 |
| | | | G. Ward | L | 9,756 | 33.6 |
| | | | J. Minto | Lab | 9,143 | 31.5 |
| | | | | | 358 | 1.3 |
| [Resignation] | | | | | | |
| 1927 | 37,092 | 84.6 | Sir W. Edge | L | 11,981 | 38.2 |
| (31/5) | | | J. Minto | Lab | 11,710 | 37.3 |
| | | | E.L. Spears | C | 7,685 | 24.5 |
| | | | | | 271 | 0.9 |
| | | | | | | |
| 1929 | 47,912 | 85.9 | Sir W. Edge | L (NL) | 17,044 | 41.5 |
| | | | J. Minto | Lab | 15,244 | 37.0 |
| | | | S.L. Elborne | C | 8,861 | 21.5 |
| | | | | | 1,800 | 4.5 |
| | | | | | | |
| 1931 | 49,666 | 79.7 | Sir W. Edge | NL | 26,926 | 68.0 |
| | | | J. Morgan | Lab | 12,670 | 32.0 |
| | | | | | 14,256 | 36.0 |
| | | | | | | |
| 1935 | 52,893 | 73.3 | Sir W. Edge | NL | 22,969 | 59.2 |
| | | | C. Rothwell | Lab | 15,816 | 40.8 |
| | | | | | 7,153 | 18.4 |
| | | | | | | |
| 1945 | 60,588* | 77.6 | A.C. Allen | Lab | 26,151 | 55.6 |
| | | | J.M. Tucker | NL | 20,854 | 44.4 |
| | | | | | 5,297 | 11.2 |

| Election | Electors | T'out | Candidate | Party | Votes | % |
|---|---|---|---|---|---|---|
| 1918 | 27,742 | 63.3 | Sir K.A. Fraser, Bt. | Co C | 8,465 | 48.2 |
| | | | †P.A. Harris | L | 4,608 | 26.2 |
| | | | W.J. Baker | Lab | 4,495 | 25.6 |
| | | | | | 3,857 | 22.0 |
| 1922 | 28,594 | 76.9 | Sir K.A. Fraser, Bt. | C | 9,356 | 42.6 |
| | | | J.W. Black | L | 6,427 | 29.2 |
| | | | W.J. Baker | Lab | 6,205 | 28.2 |
| | | | | | 2,929 | 13.4 |
| 1923 | 29,505 | 69.1 | J.W. Black | L | 10,841 | 53.2 |
| | | | Sir K.A. Fraser, Bt. | C | 9,537 | 46.8 |
| | | | | | 1,304 | 6.4 |
| 1924 | 30,602 | 81.0 | L.P. Winby | C | 13,024 | 52.6 |
| | | | J.S. Hyder | Lab | 6,032 | 24.3 |
| | | | J.W. Black | L | 5,726 | 23.1 |
| | | | | | 6,992 | 28.3 |
| 1929 | 47,196 | 81.9 | Earl Castle Stewart | C | 16,164 | 41.8 |
| | | | F.J. Wise | Lab | 12,620 | 32.7 |
| | | | G. Nicholls | L | 9,846 | 25.5 |
| | | | | | 3,544 | 9.1 |
| 1931 | 51,228 | 78.1 | Earl Castle Stewart | C | 29,790 | 74.5 |
| | | | F.J. Wise | Lab | 10,212 | 25.5 |
| | | | | | 19,578 | 49.0 |
| [Resignation] | | | | | | |
| 1933 (28/11) | 52,486 | 72.3 | A.R.L.F. Tree | C | 19,320 | 50.9 |
| | | | W. Bennett | Lab | 12,460 | 32.9 |
| | | | W.C. Wilson | L | 6,144 | 16.2 |
| | | | | | 6,860 | 18.0 |
| 1935 | 55,396 | 72.3 | A.R.L.F. Tree | C | 25,308 | 63.2 |
| | | | R.M. Wood | Lab | 14,718 | 36.8 |
| | | | | | 10,590 | 26.4 |
| 1945 | 72,454 | 75.8 | H.C. Attewell | Lab | 23,353 | 42.5 |
| | | | A.R.L.F. Tree | C | 23,149 | 42.1 |
| | | | W.H. Kirby | L | 8,451 | 15.4 |
| | | | | | 204 | 0.4 |

| Election | Electors | T'out | Candidate | Party | Votes | % |
|---|---|---|---|---|---|---|
| 1918 | 30,581 | 59.8 | Hon. O.M. Guest | Co L | 11,918 | 65.1 |
| | | | H.W. Hallam | Lab | 6,381 | 34.9 |
| | | | | | 5,537 | 30.2 |
| 1922 | | | E.L. Spears | NL | Unopp. | |
| 1923 | 32,243 | 76.9 | E.L. Spears | L | 8,937 | 36.0 |
| | | | G.E. Winterton | Lab | 8,064 | 32.5 |
| | | | F.G. Rye | C | 7,805 | 31.5 |
| | | | | | 873 | 3.5 |
| 1924 | 33,323 | 83.7 | F.G. Rye | C | 11,114 | 39.9 |
| | | | G.E. Winterton | Lab | 9,751 | 34.9 |
| | | | E.L. Spears | L | 7,040 | 25.2 |
| | | | | | 1,363 | 5.0 |
| 1929 | 43,553 | 85.2 | G.E. Winterton | Lab | 14,854 | 40.0 |
| | | | F.G. Rye | C | 12,210 | 32.9 |
| | | | F.G. Hines | L | 10,044 | 27.1 |
| | | | | | 2,644 | 7.1 |
| 1931 | 44,954 | 81.8 | L. Kimball | C | 22,310 | 60.7 |
| | | | G.E. Winterton | Lab | 14,458 | 39.3 |
| | | | | | 7,852 | 21.4 |
| 1935 | 46,593 | 77.4 | L. Kimball | C | 15,396 | 42.7 |
| | | | G.E. Winterton | Lab | 14,653 | 40.6 |
| | | | W. Meakin | L | 6,003 | 16.7 |
| | | | | | 743 | 2.1 |
| 1945 | 53,086 | 74.7 | Dr. M. Follick | Lab | 21,152 | 53.3 |
| | | | L. Kimball | C | 12,401 | 31.3 |
| | | | C.A. Lidbury | L | 6,121 | 15.4 |
| | | | | | 8,751 | 22.0 |

| Election | Electors | T'out | Candidate | Party | Votes | % |
|---|---|---|---|---|---|---|
| 1918 | | | †C.E. Yate | Co C | Unopp. | |
| 1922 | 31,143 | 79.9 | Sir C.E. Yate, Bt. | C | 13,341 | 53.6 |
| | | | A. Richardson | L | 11,550 | 46.4 |
| | | | | | 1,791 | 7.2 |
| 1923 | 32,655 | 80.9 | Sir C.E. Yate, Bt. | C | 13,239 | 50.1 |
| | | | A. Richardson | L | 13,195 | 49.9 |
| | | | | | 44 | 0.2 |
| 1924 | 34,412 | 84.3 | W.L. Everard | C | 17,090 | 58.9 |
| | | | A. Richardson | L | 11,934 | 41.1 |
| | | | | | 5,156 | 17.8 |
| 1929 | 47,396 | 83.2 | W.L. Everard | C | 18,707 | 47.4 |
| | | | G.H. Dixon | L | 14,144 | 35.9 |
| | | | A.E. Stubbs | Lab | 6,569 | 16.7 |
| | | | | | 4,563 | 11.5 |
| 1931 | 50,318 | 76.4 | W.L. Everard | C | 30,355 | 78.9 |
| | | | A.E. Stubbs | Lab | 8,100 | 21.1 |
| | | | | | 22,255 | 57.8 |
| 1935 | 54,312 | 71.9 | W.L. Everard | C | 26,325 | 67.4 |
| | | | A.E. Stubbs | Lab | 12,724 | 32.6 |
| | | | | | 13,601 | 34.8 |
| 1945 | 67,440 | 76.6 | H.A. Nutting | C | 23,772 | 46.0 |
| | | | A. Crawford | Lab | 18,379 | 35.6 |
| | | | B.M. Butcher | L | 9,510 | 18.4 |
| | | | | | 5,393 | 10.4 |

# LINCOLNSHIRE (Parts of Holland), HOLLAND with BOSTON [397]

| Election | Electors | T'out | Candidate | Party | Votes | % |
|---|---|---|---|---|---|---|
| 1918 | 40,004 | 55.2 | W.S. Royce | Lab | 8,788 | 39.8 |
| | | | E.A.C. Belcher | Co C | 7,718 | 35.0 |
| | | | †Hon. A.G.V. Peel | L | 5,557 | 25.2 |
| | | | | | 1,070 | 4.8 |
| 1922 | 41,516 | 76.9 | W.S. Royce | Lab | 12,489 | 39.1 |
| | | | Sir H.W.C-R. Fairfax-Lucy, Bt. | C | 11,898 | 37.3 |
| | | | E.S. Agnew | L | 7,535 | 23.6 |
| | | | | | 591 | 1.8 |
| 1923 | 42,220 | 68.8 | W.S. Royce | Lab | 15,697 | 54.1 |
| | | | A.W. Dean | C | 13,331 | 45.9 |
| | | | | | 2,366 | 8.2 |
| [Death] | | | | | | |
| 1924 (31/7) | 42,220† | 77.2 | A.W. Dean | C | 12,907 | 39.6 |
| | | | E.H.J.N. Dalton | Lab | 12,101 | 37.1 |
| | | | R.P. Winfrey | L | 7,596 | 23.3 |
| | | | | | 806 | 2.5 |
| 1924 | 42,929 | 75.8 | A.W. Dean | C | 15,459 | 47.5 |
| | | | G.R.B. White | Lab | 10,689 | 32.8 |
| | | | R.P. Winfrey | L | 6,413 | 19.7 |
| | | | | | 4,770 | 14.7 |
| [Death] | | | | | | |
| 1929 (21/3) | 45,079 | 75.6 | J. Blindell | L | 13,000 | 38.1 |
| | | | G.R.B. White | Lab | 9,294 | 27.3 |
| | | | F.J. Van den Berg | C | 8,257 | 24.2 |
| | | | F.W. Dennis | Agric | 3,541* | 10.4 |
| | | | | | 3,706 | 10.8 |
| 1929 | 55,522 | 81.5 | J. Blindell | L (NL) | 19,792 | 43.8 |
| | | | F.J. Van den Berg | C | 15,877 | 35.1 |
| | | | C.E. Snook | Lab | 9,556 | 21.1 |
| | | | | | 3,915 | 8.7 |
| 1931 | 57,246 | 68.5 | J. Blindell | NL | 30,375 | 77.5 |
| | | | J. Parker | Lab | 8,840 | 22.5 |
| | | | | | 21,535 | 55.0 |
| 1935 | 60,384 | 63.6 | J. Blindell | NL | 25,162 | 65.5 |
| | | | E.E. Reynolds | Lab | 13,264 | 34.5 |
| | | | | | 11,898 | 31.0 |
| [Death] | | | | | | |
| 1937 (24/6) | 61,333 | 59.4 | H.W. Butcher | NL | 21,846 | 60.0 |
| | | | E.E. Reynolds | Lab | 14,556 | 40.0 |
| | | | | | 7,290 | 20.0 |
| 1945 | 66,136 | 72.9 | H.W. Butcher | NL | 26,939 | 55.9 |
| | | | A.E. Monks | Lab | 21,263 | 44.1 |
| | | | | | 5,676 | 11.8 |

## LINCOLNSHIRE (Parts of Kesteven, and Rutlandshire), GRANTHAM [398]

| Election | Electors | T'out | Candidate | Party | Votes | % |
|---|---|---|---|---|---|---|
| 1918 | 35,462 | 58.1 | †E. Royds | Co C | 9,972 | 48.4 |
| | | | R. Pattinson | L | 8,701 | 42.2 |
| | | | W.B. Harris | Ind Lab & Agric | 1,927* | 9.4 |
| | | | | | 1,271 | 6.2 |
| 1922 | 35,655 | 79.5 | R. Pattinson | L | 11,723 | 41.4 |
| | | | E. Royds | C | 11,295 | 39.8 |
| | | | J.H. Tones | Lab | 5,332 | 18.8 |
| | | | | | 428 | 1.6 |
| 1923 | 36,444 | 79.1 | Sir V.A.G.A. Warrender, Bt. | C | 12,552 | 43.5 |
| | | | R. Pattinson | L | 10,819 | 37.6 |
| | | | M.W. Moore | Lab | 5,440 | 18.9 |
| | | | | | 1,733 | 5.9 |
| 1924 | 37,021 | 80.4 | Sir V.A.G.A. Warrender, Bt. | C | 14,746 | 49.5 |
| | | | A. Lyle-Samuel | L | 7,730 | 26.0 |
| | | | M.W. Moore | Lab | 7,279 | 24.5 |
| | | | | | 7,016 | 23.5 |
| 1929 | 48,216 | 81.9 | Sir V.A.G.A. Warrender, Bt. | C | 16,121 | 40.8 |
| | | | R.H. Brown | L | 12,023 | 30.5 |
| | | | M.W. Moore | Lab | 11,340 | 28.7 |
| | | | | | 4,098 | 10.3 |
| 1931 | 49,432 | 79.5 | Sir V.A.G.A. Warrender, Bt. | C | 27,164 | 69.2 |
| | | | M.W. Moore | Lab | 12,115 | 30.8 |
| | | | | | 15,049 | 38.4 |
| 1935 | 51,494 | 74.2 | Sir V.A.G.A. Warrender, Bt. | C | 22,194 | 58.1 |
| | | | M.W. Moore | Lab | 16,009 | 41.9 |
| | | | | | 6,185 | 16.2 |

[Elevation to the Peerage — Lord Bruntisfield]

| Election | Electors | T'out | Candidate | Party | Votes | % |
|---|---|---|---|---|---|---|
| 1942 (25/3) | 54,317 | 42.6 | W.D. Kendall | Ind | 11,758 | 50.8 |
| | | | Sir A.M. Longmore | C | 11,391 | 49.2 |
| | | | | | 367 | 1.6 |
| 1945 | 62,783 | 75.9 | W.D. Kendall | Ind | 27,719 | 58.2 |
| | | | G.A. Worth | C | 12,206 | 25.6 |
| | | | T.S. Bavin | Lab | 7,728 | 16.2 |
| | | | | | 15,513 | 32.6 |

Note:—

1942: Kendall claimed to be a member of the Labour Party and during the early part of the campaign he was assisted by the local Labour Party who defied the electoral truce. After the Labour Party headquarters had intervened, the local party announced that they would in future observe the electoral truce and take no further part in the campaign.

## LINCOLNSHIRE (Parts of Kesteven, and Rutlandshire), RUTLAND and STAMFORD [399]

| Election | Electors | T'out | Candidate | Party | Votes | % |
|---|---|---|---|---|---|---|
| 1918 | 26,647 | 61.8 | †Hon. C.H-D. Willoughby | Co C | 8,838 | 53.6 |
| | | | F. Eccles | Lab | 7,639 | 46.4 |
| | | | | | 1,199 | 7.2 |
| 1922 | 27,074 | 81.2 | C.H. Dixon | C | 10,278 | 46.8 |
| | | | F. Eccles | Lab | 7,236 | 32.9 |
| | | | E. Clark | Agric | 4,471 | 20.3 |
| | | | | | 3,042 | 13.9 |
| [Death] | | | | | | |
| 1923 (30/10) | 27,409 | 71.5 | N.W. Smith-Carington | C | 11,196 | 57.1 |
| | | | A. Sells | Lab | 8,406 | 42.9 |
| | | | | | 2,790 | 14.2 |
| 1923 | 27,409 | 76.7 | N.W. Smith-Carington | C | 10,803 | 51.4 |
| | | | F.S. Hiley | L | 5,203 | 24.8 |
| | | | A. Sells | Lab | 5,005 | 23.8 |
| | | | | | 5,600 | 26.6 |
| 1924 | 27,869 | 71.5 | N.W. Smith-Carington | C | 13,286 | 66.7 |
| | | | H.F. Wheeler | Lab | 6,633 | 33.3 |
| | | | | | 6,653 | 33.4 |
| 1929 | 34,647 | 76.7 | N.W. Smith-Carington | C | 12,607 | 47.4 |
| | | | H.J. Jones | Lab | 7,403 | 27.9 |
| | | | H. Payne | L | 6,561 | 24.7 |
| | | | | | 5,204 | 19.5 |
| 1931 | 35,249 | 75.3 | N.W. Smith-Carington | C | 19,086 | 71.9 |
| | | | F.E. Church | Lab | 7,446 | 28.1 |
| | | | | | 11,640 | 43.8 |
| [Death] | | | | | | |
| 1933 (21/11) | 35,534 | 77.2 | Lord Willoughby de Eresby | C | 14,605 | 53.3 |
| | | | A.W. Gray | Lab | 12,818 | 46.7 |
| | | | | | 1,787 | 6.6 |
| 1935 | 35,770 | 78.4 | Lord Willoughby de Eresby | C | 16,799 | 59.9 |
| | | | A.W. Gray | Lab | 11,238 | 40.1 |
| | | | | | 5,561 | 19.8 |
| 1945 | 39,229 | 72.9 | Lord Willoughby de Eresby | C | 15,359 | 53.7 |
| | | | A.W. Gray | Lab | 13,223 | 46.3 |
| | | | | | 2,136 | 7.4 |

Note:—

1922: Clark was the nominee of the NFU.

# LINCOLNSHIRE (Parts of Lindsey), BRIGG [400]

| Election | Electors | T'out | Candidate | Party | Votes | % |
|---|---|---|---|---|---|---|
| 1918 | 29,054 | 60.5 | C.W.W. McLean | Co C | 8,310 | 47.2 |
| | | | D.J.K. Quibell | Lab | 4,789 | 27.3 |
| | | | †Sir W.A. Gelder | L | 4,475 | 25.5 |
| | | | | | 3,521 | 19.9 |
| 1922 | 30,685 | 80.3 | Sir B.D.G. Sheffield, Bt. | C | 15,463 | 62.7 |
| | | | D.J.K. Quibell | Lab | 9,185 | 37.3 |
| | | | | | 6,278 | 25.4 |
| 1923 | 31,818 | 72.8 | Sir B.D.G. Sheffield, Bt. | C | 12,412 | 53.6 |
| | | | D.J.K. Quibell | Lab | 10,753 | 46.4 |
| | | | | | 1,659 | 7.2 |
| 1924 | 33,124 | 80.9 | Sir B.D.G. Sheffield, Bt. | C | 15,125 | 56.4 |
| | | | D.J.K. Quibell | Lab | 11,669 | 43.6 |
| | | | | | 3,456 | 12.8 |
| 1929 | 43,226 | 82.5 | D.J.K. Quibell | Lab | 16,117 | 45.2 |
| | | | Sir B.D.G. Sheffield, Bt. | C | 12,506 | 35.0 |
| | | | A. Cairns | L | 7,060 | 19.8 |
| | | | | | 3,611 | 10.2 |
| 1931 | 45,565 | 82.1 | M.J. Hunter | C | 21,809 | 58.3 |
| | | | D.J.K. Quibell | Lab | 15,614 | 41.7 |
| | | | | | 6,195 | 16.6 |
| 1935 | 49,597 | 74.2 | D.J.K. Quibell | Lab | 18,495 | 50.3 |
| | | | M.J. Hunter | C | 18,292 | 49.7 |
| | | | | | 203 | 0.6 |
| 1945 | 60,899 | 74.6 | T. Williamson | Lab | 26,771 | 58.9 |
| | | | A.N. Dixon | C | 18,667 | 41.1 |
| | | | | | 8,104 | 17.8 |
| [Resignation] | | | | | | |
| 1948 (24/3) | 64,968 | 77.1 | E.L. Mallalieu | Lab | 27,333 | 54.6 |
| | | | A. Fell | C | 22,746 | 45.4 |
| | | | | | 4,587 | 9.2 |

## LINCOLNSHIRE (Parts of Lindsey), GAINSBOROUGH [401]

| Election | Electors | T'out | Candidate | Party | Votes | % |
|---|---|---|---|---|---|---|
| 1918 | 27,503 | 55.2 | J.E. Molson | Co C | 8,634 | 56.8 |
|  |  |  | †G.J. Bentham | L | 6,556 | 43.2 |
|  |  |  |  |  | 2,078 | 13.6 |
| 1922 | 27,219 | 77.6 | J.E. Molson | C | 9,015 | 42.7 |
|  |  |  | J.H. Seaverns | L | 7,216 | 34.2 |
|  |  |  | J. Read | Lab | 4,884 | 23.1 |
|  |  |  |  |  | 1,799 | 8.5 |
| 1923 | 27,294 | 75.4 | Sir R. Winfrey | L | 9,694 | 47.1 |
|  |  |  | J.E. Molson | C | 7,841 | 38.1 |
|  |  |  | J. Read | Lab | 3,039 | 14.8 |
|  |  |  |  |  | 1,853 | 9.0 |
| 1924 | 27,619 | 79.0 | H.F.C. Crookshank | C | 10,281 | 47.1 |
|  |  |  | F.J. Knowles | Lab | 5,958 | 27.3 |
|  |  |  | Sir R. Winfrey | L | 5,590 | 25.6 |
|  |  |  |  |  | 4,323 | 19.8 |
| 1929 | 33,977 | 79.7 | H.F.C. Crookshank | C | 10,058 | 37.1 |
|  |  |  | A. Neal | L | 9,991 | 36.9 |
|  |  |  | G. Deer | Lab | 7,032 | 26.0 |
|  |  |  |  |  | 67 | 0.2 |
| 1931 | 34,496 | 83.2 | H.F.C. Crookshank | C | 14,839 | 51.7 |
|  |  |  | H.G. Purchase | L | 8,009 | 27.9 |
|  |  |  | G. Deer | Lab | 5,856 | 20.4 |
|  |  |  |  |  | 6,830 | 23.8 |
| 1935 | 35,004 | 80.4 | H.F.C. Crookshank | C | 12,597 | 44.8 |
|  |  |  | J.J.T. Ferens | L | 10,840 | 38.5 |
|  |  |  | E. Pittwood | Lab | 4,698 | 16.7 |
|  |  |  |  |  | 1,757 | 6.3 |
| 1945 | 38,290 | 75.2 | Rt. Hon. H.F.C. Crookshank | C | 11,081 | 38.4 |
|  |  |  | G.S. Saville | Lab | 9,436 | 32.8 |
|  |  |  | R.D. Robinson | L | 8,284 | 28.8 |
|  |  |  |  |  | 1,645 | 5.6 |

## LINCOLNSHIRE (Parts of Lindsey), HORNCASTLE  [402]

| Election | Electors | T'out | Candidate | Party | Votes | % |
|---|---|---|---|---|---|---|
| 1918 | 23,854 | 68.2 | †W.E.G.A. Weigall | Co C | 8,826 | 54.3 |
| | | | S. Pattinson | L | 7,433 | 45.7 |
| | | | | | 1,393 | 8.6 |

[Resignation on appointment as Governor of South Australia]

| Election | Electors | T'out | Candidate | Party | Votes | % |
|---|---|---|---|---|---|---|
| 1920 (25/2) | 23,764 | 77.0 | S.V. Hotchkin | Co C | 8,140 | 44.5 |
| | | | S. Pattinson | L | 6,727 | 36.7 |
| | | | W. Holmes | Lab | 3,443 | 18.8 |
| | | | | | 1,413 | 7.8 |
| 1922 | 24,485 | 81.5 | S. Pattinson | L | 10,797 | 54.1 |
| | | | Lord Fermoy | C | 9,158 | 45.9 |
| | | | | | 1,639 | 8.2 |
| 1923 | 24,821 | 80.9 | S. Pattinson | L | 10,954 | 54.5 |
| | | | Sir J.P. Du Cane | C | 9,135 | 45.5 |
| | | | | | 1,819 | 9.0 |
| 1924 | 25,286 | 81.7 | H.C. Haslam | C | 10,912 | 52.8 |
| | | | S. Pattinson | L | 9,743 | 47.2 |
| | | | | | 1,169 | 5.6 |
| 1929 | 33,042 | 80.8 | H.C. Haslam | C | 12,837 | 48.1 |
| | | | F.C. Linfield | L | 10,168 | 38.1 |
| | | | J.R. Sanderson | Lab | 3,683 | 13.8 |
| | | | | | 2,669 | 10.0 |
| 1931 | 34,448 | 78.1 | H.C. Haslam | C | 18,100 | 67.3 |
| | | | G.H.J. Dutton | L | 8,788 | 32.7 |
| | | | | | 9,312 | 34.6 |
| 1935 | 36,851 | 69.4 | H.C. Haslam | C | 17,594 | 68.8 |
| | | | F.J. Knowles | Lab | 7,982 | 31.2 |
| | | | | | 9,612 | 37.6 |
| 1945 | 37,479 | 70.4 | J.F.W. Maitland | C | 14,019 | 53.1 |
| | | | G.W. Holderness | Lab | 7,052 | 26.7 |
| | | | F. Emerson | L | 5,329 | 20.2 |
| | | | | | 6,967 | 26.4 |

# LINCOLNSHIRE (Parts of Lindsey), LOUTH [403]

| Election | Electors | T'out | Candidate | Party | Votes | % |
|---|---|---|---|---|---|---|
| 1918 | 27,572 | 60.3 | H.L. Brackenbury | Co C | 9,055 | 54.5 |
| | | | †T. Davies | L | 7,559 | 45.5 |
| | | | | | 1,496 | 9.0 |
| [Death] | | | | | | |
| 1920 | 27,279† | 63.1 | T. Wintringham | L | 9,859 | 57.3 |
| (3/6) | | | C.H. Turnor | Co C | 7,354 | 42.7 |
| | | | | | 2,505 | 14.6 |
| [Death] | | | | | | |
| 1921 | 27,538 | 72.1 | Mrs. M. Wintringham | L | 8,386 | 42.2 |
| (22/9) | | | Sir A. Hutchings | C | 7,595 | 38.3 |
| | | | J.L. George | Lab | 3,873 | 19.5 |
| | | | | | 791 | 3.9 |
| 1922 | 28,468 | 78.5 | Mrs. M. Wintringham | L | 11,609 | 52.0 |
| | | | Sir A. Hutchings | C | 10,726 | 48.0 |
| | | | | | 883 | 4.0 |
| 1923 | 29,019 | 79.6 | Mrs. M. Wintringham | L | 12,104 | 52.4 |
| | | | G.K. Peto | C | 11,003 | 47.6 |
| | | | | | 1,101 | 4.8 |
| 1924 | 29,659 | 80.9 | A.P. Heneage | C | 12,674 | 52.8 |
| | | | Mrs. M. Wintringham | L | 11,330 | 47.2 |
| | | | | | 1,344 | 5.6 |
| 1929 | 38,624 | 81.8 | A.P. Heneage | C | 13,999 | 44.4 |
| | | | Mrs. M. Wintringham | L | 13,560 | 42.9 |
| | | | T. Holmes | Lab | 4,027 | 12.7 |
| | | | | | 439 | 1.5 |
| 1931 | 40,307 | 81.6 | A.P. Heneage | C | 18,434 | 56.1 |
| | | | J.R.B. Muir | L | 14,439 | 43.9 |
| | | | | | 3,995 | 12.2 |
| 1935 | 44,488 | 71.9 | A.P. Heneage | C | 19,705 | 61.6 |
| | | | J.H. Franklin | Lab | 12,261 | 38.4 |
| | | | | | 7,444 | 23.2 |
| 1945 | 49,184 | 71.9 | C. Osborne | C | 16,336 | 46.1 |
| | | | J.H. Franklin | Lab | 11,628 | 32.9 |
| | | | W.K. Carter | L | 7,176 | 20.3 |
| | | | S.R. Charlesworth | Ind | 233* | 0.7 |
| | | | | | 4,708 | 13.2 |

Notes:—

1920: Turnor, a member of the NDP, was adopted by the local Conservative Association and appears to have run as a Conservative rather than an NDP candidate. However, in a letter from W. Dudley Ward (a Coalition Liberal Whip) to Lloyd George on May 14, 1920 (Lloyd George papers F/22/1/35) Ward clearly states that Turnor was in fact an NDP candidate.

# MIDDLESEX, ACTON [404]

| Election | Electors | T'out | Candidate | Party | Votes | % |
|---|---|---|---|---|---|---|
| 1918 | 29,539 | 53.9 | Sir H.E. Brittain | Co C | 11,671 | 73.3 |
| | | | R. Dunsmore | Lab | 4,241 | 26.7 |
| | | | | | 7,430 | 46.6 |
| 1922 | 30,425 | 67.1 | Sir H.E. Brittain | C | 10,208 | 49.9 |
| | | | Miss M.R. Richardson | Lab | 5,342 | 26.2 |
| | | | C.N.D. Dixey | L | 4,877 | 23.9 |
| | | | | | 4,866 | 23.7 |
| 1923 | 31,394 | 63.5 | Sir H.E. Brittain | C | 8,943 | 44.9 |
| | | | H.A. Baldwin | Lab | 6,069 | 30.5 |
| | | | B.A. Levinson | L | 4,909 | 24.6 |
| | | | | | 2,874 | 14.4 |
| 1924 | 31,999 | 72.6 | Sir H.E. Brittain | C | 12,799 | 55.2 |
| | | | H.A. Baldwin | Lab | 5,583 | 24.0 |
| | | | B.A. Levinson | L | 3,074 | 13.2 |
| | | | Miss M.R. Richardson | Ind Lab | 1,775* | 7.6 |
| | | | | | 7,216 | 31.2 |
| 1929 | 42,276 | 75.5 | J.F. Shillaker | Lab | 13,208 | 41.4 |
| | | | Sir H.E. Brittain | C | 12,739 | 39.9 |
| | | | F. Medlicott | L | 5,981 | 18.7 |
| | | | | | 469 | 1.5 |
| 1931 | 47,865 | 75.5 | H.J. Duggan | C | 24,196 | 67.0 |
| | | | J.F. Shillaker | Lab | 11,924 | 33.0 |
| | | | | | 12,272 | 34.0 |
| 1935 | 48,258 | 67.8 | H.J. Duggan | C | 19,137 | 58.5 |
| | | | W. McLaine | Lab | 13,559 | 41.5 |
| | | | | | 5,578 | 17.0 |
| [Death] | | | | | | |
| 1943 (14/12) | 48,663 | 17.1 | H.C. Longhurst | C | 5,014 | 60.3 |
| | | | W.E. Padley | ILP | 2,336 | 28.1 |
| | | | Miss D. Crisp | Ind | 707* | 8.5 |
| | | | E. Godfrey | Ind | 258* | 3.1 |
| | | | | | 2,678 | 32.2 |
| 1945 | 44,887* | 77.7 | J.A. Sparks | Lab | 19,590 | 56.1 |
| | | | H.C. Longhurst | C | 12,134 | 34.8 |
| | | | F.J. Halpin | L | 3,172* | 9.1 |
| | | | | | 7,456 | 21.3 |

Notes:—

1924: Miss Richardson was the nominee of the Acton Democratic Labour Party which was formed in May 1924 by a number of former Labour Party members who had resigned the previous year due to a split in the local Labour Party. The policy of the Democratic Labour Party was left-wing and she received Communist Party support.

1943: Godfrey was the founder and leader of the English National Association, an organisation with alleged Fascist leanings, which he had originally formed as the British National Party. He sought election as an 'English Nationalist' candidate.

| Election | Electors | T'out | Candidate | Party | Votes | % |
|---|---|---|---|---|---|---|
| 1918 | 26,409 | 49.1 | W.G. Morden | Co C | 9,077 | 70.1 |
|  |  |  | W. Haywood | Lab | 2,620 | 20.2 |
|  |  |  | Mrs. R. Strachey | Ind | 1,263* | 9.7 |
|  |  |  |  |  | 6,457 | 49.9 |
| 1922 | 27,960 | 64.2 | W.G. Morden | C | 10,150 | 56.5 |
|  |  |  | Mrs. R. Strachey | Ind | 7,804 | 43.5 |
|  |  |  |  |  | 2,346 | 13.0 |
| 1923 | 28,245 | 62.6 | W.G. Morden | C | 9,648 | 54.5 |
|  |  |  | Mrs. R. Strachey | Ind | 4,828 | 27.3 |
|  |  |  | W. Haywood | Lab | 3,216 | 18.2 |
|  |  |  |  |  | 4,820 | 27.2 |
| 1924 | 28,606 | 72.5 | W.G. Morden | C | 12,098 | 58.3 |
|  |  |  | W. Haywood | Lab | 6,114 | 29.5 |
|  |  |  | J.C. Squire | L | 2,540* | 12.2 |
|  |  |  |  |  | 5,984 | 28.8 |
| 1929 | 40,088 | 72.2 | W.G. Morden | C | 14,025 | 48.4 |
|  |  |  | Dr. Stella Churchill | Lab | 10,978 | 37.9 |
|  |  |  | J. Stevenson | L | 3,957 | 13.7 |
|  |  |  |  |  | 3,047 | 10.5 |
| 1931 | 42,105 | 71.8 | H.P. Mitchell | C | 22,667 | 75.0 |
|  |  |  | G.E.G. Catlin | Lab | 7,572 | 25.0 |
|  |  |  |  |  | 15,095 | 50.0 |
| 1935 | 41,849 | 64.2 | H.P. Mitchell | C | 17,568 | 65.4 |
|  |  |  | F.W. Temple | Lab | 9,296 | 34.6 |
|  |  |  |  |  | 8,272 | 30.8 |
| 1945 | 40,491* | 75.8 | F.E. Noel-Baker | Lab | 17,693 | 57.6 |
|  |  |  | H.P. Mitchell | C | 13,006 | 42.4 |
|  |  |  |  |  | 4,687 | 15.2 |

| Election | Electors | T'out | Candidate | Party | Votes | % |
|---|---|---|---|---|---|---|
| 1918 | 30,031 | 54.8 | H.F. Bowles | Co C | 8,290 | 50.4 |
| | | | W.E. Hill | Lab | 6,176 | 37.5 |
| | | | Mrs. J.L. McEwan | L | 1,987* | 12.1 |
| | | | | | 2,114 | 12.9 |
| 1922 | 29,992 | 71.8 | T. Fermor-Hesketh | C | 11,725 | 54.4 |
| | | | G. Lathan | Lab | 9,820 | 45.6 |
| | | | | | 1,905 | 8.8 |
| 1923 | 30,580 | 68.5 | W.W. Henderson | Lab | 11,050 | 52.8 |
| | | | T. Fermor-Hesketh | C | 9,888 | 47.2 |
| | | | | | 1,162 | 5.6 |
| 1924 | 31,396 | 81.8 | R.V.K. Applin | C | 13,886 | 54.0 |
| | | | W.W. Henderson | Lab | 11,807 | 46.0 |
| | | | | | 2,079 | 8.0 |
| 1929 | 42,481 | 78.5 | W.W. Henderson | Lab | 14,427 | 43.3 |
| | | | R.V.K. Applin | C | 14,169 | 42.5 |
| | | | C.H. Durrad-Lang | L | 4,736 | 14.2 |
| | | | | | 258 | 0.8 |
| 1931 | 48,229 | 79.2 | R.V.K. Applin | C | 24,532 | 64.3 |
| | | | W. Mellor | Lab | 13,646 | 35.7 |
| | | | | | 10,886 | 28.6 |
| 1935 | 58,139 | 73.3 | B.B. Bull | C | 24,046 | 56.5 |
| | | | W. Mellor | Lab | 18,543 | 43.5 |
| | | | | | 5,503 | 13.0 |
| 1945 | 84,195* | 74.4 | E.A.J. Davies | Lab | 32,625 | 52.1 |
| | | | B.B. Bull | C | 20,935 | 33.4 |
| | | | J.P.C. Danny | L | 9,104 | 14.5 |
| | | | | | 11,690 | 18.7 |

| Election | Electors | T'out | Candidate | Party | Votes | % |
|---|---|---|---|---|---|---|
| 1918 | 28,848 | 59.7 | †J.R.P. Newman | Co C | 11,849 | 68.9 |
| | | | J.R. Leslie | Lab | 3,140 | 18.2 |
| | | | W.E. Martin | L | 2,221 | 12.9 |
| | | | | | 8,709 | 50.7 |
| 1922 | 30,843 | 72.4 | J.R.P. Newman | C | 11,883 | 53.2 |
| | | | T.A. Robertson | L | 10,440 | 46.8 |
| | | | | | 1,443 | 6.4 |
| 1923 | 31,650 | 76.0 | T.A. Robertson | L | 13,159 | 54.7 |
| | | | J.R.P. Newman | C | 10,883 | 45.3 |
| | | | | | 2,276 | 9.4 |
| 1924 | 32,984 | 79.5 | Hon. E.C.G. Cadogan | C | 15,277 | 58.3 |
| | | | T.A. Robertson | L | 10,942 | 41.7 |
| | | | | | 4,335 | 16.6 |
| 1929 | 50,243 | 77.2 | Hon. E.C.G. Cadogan | C | 18,920 | 48.8 |
| | | | T.A. Robertson | L | 14,065 | 36.2 |
| | | | J.G. Stone | Lab | 5,824 | 15.0 |
| | | | | | 4,855 | 12.6 |
| 1931 | 54,842 | 74.3 | Hon. E.C.G. Cadogan | C | 34,286 | 84.2 |
| | | | J.G. Stone | Lab | 6,440 | 15.8 |
| | | | | | 27,846 | 68.4 |
| 1935 | 60,374 | 70.3 | J.F.E. Crowder | C | 26,960 | 63.6 |
| | | | T.A. Robertson | L | 8,920 | 21.0 |
| | | | C.G. Lacey | Lab | 6,533 | 15.4 |
| | | | | | 18,040 | 42.6 |
| 1945 | 67,729* | 73.9 | J.F.E. Crowder | C | 24,256 | 48.5 |
| | | | C.G. Lacey | Lab | 18,611 | 37.2 |
| | | | D. Goldblatt | L | 7,164 | 14.3 |
| | | | | | 5,645 | 11.3 |

| Election | Electors | T'out | Candidate | Party | Votes | % |
|---|---|---|---|---|---|---|
| 1918 | 33,651 | 50.4 | O.E. Mosley | Co C (Ind) | 13,959 | 82.3 |
| | | | A.R. Chamberlayne | Ind | 3,007 | 17.7 |
| | | | | | 10,952 | 64.6 |
| 1922 | 35,592 | 65.1 | O.E. Mosley | Ind | 15,290 | 66.0 |
| | | | C.L.A. Ward-Jackson | C | 7,868 | 34.0 |
| | | | | | 7,422 | 32.0 |
| 1923 | 36,475 | 64.5 | O.E. Mosley | Ind (Lab) | 14,079 | 59.9 |
| | | | E.H.F. Morris | C | 9,433 | 40.1 |
| | | | | | 4,646 | 19.8 |
| 1924 | 38,644 | 78.5 | I. Salmon | C | 16,526 | 54.5 |
| | | | K.M. Lindsay | Lab | 9,507 | 31.3 |
| | | | Sir R. Blair | L | 4,320 | 14.2 |
| | | | | | 7,019 | 23.2 |
| 1929 | 70,849 | 74.3 | I. Salmon | C | 22,466 | 42.7 |
| | | | H. Beaumont | Lab | 15,684 | 29.8 |
| | | | C.E.P. Taylor | L | 12,554 | 23.8 |
| | | | W.J. Sholl | Ind C | 1,965* | 3.7 |
| | | | | | 6,782 | 12.9 |
| 1931 | 94,002 | 72.1 | I. Salmon | C | 48,068 | 71.0 |
| | | | G.S. Sandilands | Lab | 14,241 | 21.0 |
| | | | H.C. Banting | L | 5,444* | 8.0 |
| | | | | | 33,827 | 50.0 |
| 1935 | 130,682 | 64.4 | Sir I. Salmon | C | 52,729 | 62.7 |
| | | | Mrs. H.C. Bentwich | Lab | 31,422 | 37.3 |
| | | | | | 21,307 | 25.4 |
| [Death] | | | | | | |
| 1941 (2/12) | 168,594 | 10.7 | N.A.H. Bower | C | 14,540 | 80.9 |
| | | | Miss W.C. Henney | Ind Dem | 3,433 | 19.1 |
| | | | | | 11,107 | 61.8 |

This constituency was divided in 1945.

Notes:—

1918: Chamberlayne was the nominee of the Harrow Electors' League, a non-party organisation.

| Election | Electors | T'out | Candidate | Party | Votes | % |
|---|---|---|---|---|---|---|
| 1918 | 33,117 | 59.4 | P. Lloyd-Greame | Co C | 14,431 | 73.4 |
| | | | F. Bailey | Lab | 3,159 | 16.1 |
| | | | Mrs. E.H. Martyn | Ind Prog | 2,067* | 10.5 |
| | | | | | 11,272 | 57.3 |
| 1922 | 36,558 | 75.8 | Rt. Hon. Sir P. Lloyd-Greame | C | 17,402 | 62.8 |
| | | | J.D. Young | L | 5,650 | 20.4 |
| | | | C. Latham | Lab | 4,669 | 16.8 |
| | | | | | 11,752 | 42.4 |
| 1923 | 38,065 | 67.3 | Rt. Hon. Sir P. Lloyd-Greame | C | 13,278 | 51.9 |
| | | | Rt. Hon. J.M. Robertson | L | 7,324 | 28.6 |
| | | | C. Latham | Lab | 5,005 | 19.5 |
| | | | | | 5,954 | 23.3 |
| 1924 | 40,163 | 74.9 | Rt. Hon. Sir P. Lloyd-Greame | C | 19,183 | 63.8 |
| | | | A.J. Blue | L | 5,618 | 18.7 |
| | | | J.A. Skinner | Lab | 5,267 | 17.5 |
| | | | | | 13,565 | 45.1 |
| 1929 | 84,212 | 72.0 | Rt. Hon. Sir P. Cunliffe-Lister | C | 31,758 | 52.3 |
| | | | Dr. R. Lyons | Lab | 15,434 | 25.5 |
| | | | Mrs. M.I.C. Ashby | L | 13,449 | 22.2 |
| | | | | | 16,324 | 26.8 |
| 1931 | 113,780 | 71.7 | Rt. Hon. Sir P. Cunliffe-Lister | C | 66,305 | 81.2 |
| | | | Mrs. A.B. White | Lab | 15,305 | 18.8 |
| | | | | | 51,000 | 62.4 |
| 1935 | 164,786 | 64.4 | Sir R. Blair | C | 69,762 | 65.7 |
| | | | Mrs. A.B. White | Lab | 28,375 | 26.8 |
| | | | B.E. Goldstone | L | 7,920* | 7.5 |
| | | | | | 41,387 | 38.9 |

This constituency was divided in 1945.

Notes:—

1918: Mrs. Martyn was the nominee of the Women's Parliamentary League.

1924: Lloyd-Greame assumed the surname of Cunliffe-Lister shortly after the election.

| Election | Electors | T'uut | Candidate | Party | Votes | % |
|---|---|---|---|---|---|---|
| 1918 | 35,018 | 45.6 | Sir P.E. Pilditch | Co C | 12,423 | 77.7 |
| | | | F.E. Horton | Lab | 2,418 | 15.1 |
| | | | A.W. Leonard | Ind | 1,143* | 7.2 |
| | | | | | 10,005 | 62.6 |
| 1922 | 36,853 | 53.9 | Sir P.E. Pilditch | C | 12,849 | 64.7 |
| | | | A.G. Church | Lab | 7,015 | 35.3 |
| | | | | | 5,834 | 29.4 |
| 1923 | 38,023 | 46.0 | Sir P.E. Pilditch | C | 11,604 | 66.4 |
| | | | G.S. Cockrill | Lab | 5,868 | 33.6 |
| | | | | | 5,736 | 32.8 |
| 1924 | 39,405 | 64.6 | Sir P.E. Pilditch | C | 17,650 | 69.4 |
| | | | F.W. Temple | Lab | 7,792 | 30.6 |
| | | | | | 9,858 | 38.8 |
| 1929 | 56,292 | 69.0 | Sir P.E. Pilditch | C | 19,177 | 49.4 |
| | | | F.W. Temple | Lab | 11,946 | 30.7 |
| | | | W.A.J. Hillier | L | 7,727 | 19.9 |
| | | | | | 7,231 | 18.7 |
| 1931 | 63,404 | 68.3 | Sir R. Blaker, Bt. | C | 34,115 | 78.7 |
| | | | F.W. Temple | Lab | 9,214 | 21.3 |
| | | | | | 24,901 | 57.4 |
| 1935 | 76,110 | 58.0 | Sir R. Blaker, Bt. | C | 30,153 | 68.4 |
| | | | Dr. B. Lytton-Bernard | Lab | 13,957 | 31.6 |
| | | | | | 16,196 | 36.8 |
| 1945 | 76,840* | 70.3 | G.A. Pargiter | Lab | 28,064 | 52.0 |
| | | | I.D. Harvey | C | 19,725 | 36.5 |
| | | | H.B. Kerby | L | 6,222* | 11.5 |
| | | | | | 8,339 | 15.5 |

Note:—

1918:  Leonard was the nominee of the local branch of the NFDSS.

# MIDDLESEX, TWICKENHAM [411]

| Election | Electors | T'out | Candidate | Party | Votes | % |
|---|---|---|---|---|---|---|
| 1918 | 34,924 | 48.2 | †W. Joynson-Hicks | Co C | 14,015 | 83.2 |
| | | | Rev. H. Chalmers | Lab | 2,823 | 16.8 |
| | | | | | 11,192 | 66.4 |
| 1922 | | | Sir W. Joynson-Hicks, Bt. | C | Unopp. | |
| 1923 | 37,558 | 62.0 | Rt. Hon. Sir W. Joynson-Hicks, Bt. | C | 12,903 | 55.4 |
| | | | S. Sherman | Lab | 5,509 | 23.7 |
| | | | C. Baker | L | 4,858 | 20.9 |
| | | | | | 7,394 | 31.7 |
| 1924 | 38,353 | 70.0 | Rt. Hon. Sir W. Joynson-Hicks Bt. | C | 18,889 | 70.4 |
| | | | S. Sherman | Lab | 7,945 | 29.6 |
| | | | | | 10,944 | 40.8 |
| 1929 | 62,264 | 69.8 | Rt. Hon. Sir W. Joynson-Hicks Bt. | C | 21,087 | 48.5 |
| | | | T.J. Mason | Lab | 15,121 | 34.8 |
| | | | F.G. Paterson | L | 7,246 | 16.7 |
| | | | | | 5,966 | 13.7 |

[Elevation to the Peerage — Viscount Brentford]

| Election | Electors | T'out | Candidate | Party | Votes | % |
|---|---|---|---|---|---|---|
| 1929 (8/8) | 62,264 | 49.5 | Sir J. Ferguson | C | 14,705 | 47.7 |
| | | | T.J. Mason | Lab | 14,202 | 46.1 |
| | | | F.G. Paterson | L | 1,920* | 6.2 |
| | | | | | 503 | 1.6 |
| 1931 | 74,272 | 71.3 | Sir J. Ferguson | C | 39,161 | 74.0 |
| | | | P. Holman | Lab/Co-op | 13,763 | 26.0 |
| | | | | | 25,398 | 48.0 |

[Death]

| Election | Electors | T'out | Candidate | Party | Votes | % |
|---|---|---|---|---|---|---|
| 1932 (16/9) | 74,272 | 51.9 | H.R. Murray-Philipson | C | 21,688 | 56.2 |
| | | | P. Holman | Lab/Co-op | 16,881 | 43.8 |
| | | | | | 4,807 | 12.4 |

[Death]

| Election | Electors | T'out | Candidate | Party | Votes | % |
|---|---|---|---|---|---|---|
| 1934 (22/6) | 81,529 | 55.5 | A.C. Critchley | C | 25,395 | 56.1 |
| | | | P. Holman | Lab/Co-op | 19,890 | 43.9 |
| | | | | | 5,505 | 12.2 |
| 1935 | 90,923 | 66.5 | E.H. Keeling | C | 37,635 | 62.2 |
| | | | P. Holman | Lab/Co-op | 22,823 | 37.8 |
| | | | | | 14,812 | 24.4 |

This constituency was divided in 1945.

Note:—

1929: Ferguson had the active support of the Conservative Central Office withdrawn during
(8/8) the campaign. He advocated a policy of Empire free trade.

# MIDDLESEX, UXBRIDGE  [412]

| Election | Electors | T'out | Candidate | Party | Votes | % |
|---|---|---|---|---|---|---|
| 1918 | 29,707 | 55.9 | Hon. S. Peel | Co C | 9,814 | 59.1 |
| | | | H. Gosling | Lab | 6,251 | 37.6 |
| | | | N.M. Snowball | L | 545* | 3.3 |
| | | | | | 3,563 | 21.5 |
| 1922 | 32,229 | 73.0 | C.D. Burney | C | 12,391 | 52.7 |
| | | | W.J. Brown | Lab | 7,292 | 31.0 |
| | | | F.S. Evans | NL | 3,844 | 16.3 |
| | | | | | 5,099 | 21.7 |
| 1923 | 34,250 | 66.6 | C.D. Burney | C | 9,254 | 40.6 |
| | | | G.S. Hutchison | L | 7,423 | 32.5 |
| | | | R. Small | Lab | 6,146 | 26.9 |
| | | | | | 1,831 | 8.1 |
| 1924 | 36,141 | 71.8 | C.D. Burney | C | 13,525 | 52.1 |
| | | | R. Small | Lab | 8,459 | 32.6 |
| | | | J.S. Griffith-Jones | L | 3,976 | 15.3 |
| | | | | | 5,066 | 19.5 |
| 1929 | 59,603 | 72.2 | J.J. Llewellin | C | 17,770 | 41.2 |
| | | | R.F.O. Bridgeman | Lab | 16,422 | 38.2 |
| | | | R.C.C.J. Binney | L | 8,847 | 20.6 |
| | | | | | 1,348 | 3.0 |
| 1931 | 72,852 | 68.4 | J.J. Llewellin | C | 35,836 | 72.0 |
| | | | L.M. Worsnop | Lab | 11,609 | 23.3 |
| | | | R.F.O. Bridgeman | Ind | 2,358* | 4.7 |
| | | | | | 24,227 | 48.7 |
| 1935 | 98,527 | 65.2 | J.J. Llewellin | C | 34,727 | 54.0 |
| | | | L.M, Worsnop | Lab | 24,000 | 37.4 |
| | | | W. Ridgway | L | 5,514* | 8.6 |
| | | | | | 10,727 | 16.6 |
| 1945 | 78,904** | 73.0 | F. Beswick | Lab/Co-op | 25,190 | 43.7 |
| | | | Rt. Hon. J.J. Llewellin | C | 24,106 | 41.9 |
| | | | J.E. Aylett | L | 8,300 | 14.4 |
| | | | | | 1,084 | 1.8 |

Note:—

1931:  Bridgeman was the nominee of the League Against Imperialism. He sought
election as a 'Workers' candidate.

| Election | Electors | T'out | Candidate | Party | Votes | % |
|---|---|---|---|---|---|---|
| 1918 | 45,945 | 58.1 | †G.L.T. Locker-Lampson | Co C | 19,217 | 71.9 |
| | | | H.T. Rhys | Lab | 4,539 | 17.0 |
| | | | H.B. Holding | L | 2,957* | 11.1 |
| | | | | | 14,678 | 54.9 |
| 1922 | 47,153 | 66.5 | G.L.T. Locker-Lampson | C | 21,937 | 70.0 |
| | | | H.T. Rhys | Lab | 9,411 | 30.0 |
| | | | | | 12,526 | 40.0 |
| 1923 | 47,723 | 69.1 | G.L.T. Locker-Lampson | C | 15,344 | 46.5 |
| | | | J.T. Stevenson | L | 11,975 | 36.3 |
| | | | J. Bacon | Lab | 5,665 | 17.2 |
| | | | | | 3,369 | 10.2 |
| 1924 | 49,196 | 76.3 | G.L.T. Locker-Lampson | C | 21,725 | 57.9 |
| | | | H.T. Rhys | Lab | 8,648 | 23.0 |
| | | | J.T. Stevenson | L | 7,158 | 19.1 |
| | | | | | 13,077 | 34.9 |
| 1929 | 71,445 | 73.0 | Rt. Hon. G.L.T. Locker-Lampson | C | 24,821 | 47.6 |
| | | | H.T. Fraser | L | 14,995 | 28.7 |
| | | | E.P. Bell | Lab | 12,360 | 23.7 |
| | | | | | 9,826 | 18.9 |
| 1931 | 77,878 | 72.3 | Rt. Hon. G.L.T. Locker-Lampson | C | 44,364 | 78.7 |
| | | | E.P. Bell | Lab | 11,980 | 21.3 |
| | | | | | 32,384 | 57.4 |
| 1935 | 84,836 | 69.1 | A.B. Baxter | C | 36,384 | 62.1 |
| | | | Miss D.V.A. Woodman | Lab | 14,561 | 24.8 |
| | | | H.T. Fraser | L | 7,711 | 13.1 |
| | | | | | 21,823 | 37.3 |
| 1945 | 90,479 | 74.9 | A.B. Baxter | C | 29,429 | 43.4 |
| | | | W.A. Vant | Lab/Co-op | 23,544 | 34.7 |
| | | | E.T. Malindine | L | 14,836 | 21.9 |
| | | | | | 5,885 | 8.7 |

| Election | Electors | T'out | Candidate | Party | Votes | % |
|---|---|---|---|---|---|---|
| 1918 | 31,578 | 49.6 | M. Falcon | Co C | 7,030 | 44.9 |
| | | | F. Henderson | L | 6,691 | 42.8 |
| | | | W.B. Taylor | Agric | 1,926* | 12.3 |
| | | | | | 339 | 2.1 |
| 1922 | 32,204 | 70.2 | M. Falcon | C | 9,270 | 41.0 |
| | | | H.M. Seely | L | 8,962 | 39.7 |
| | | | G.E. Hewitt | Lab | 4,361 | 19.3 |
| | | | | | 308 | 1.3 |
| 1923 | 32,845 | 72.5 | H.M. Seely | L | 11,807 | 49.6 |
| | | | M. Falcon | C | 8,472 | 35.6 |
| | | | G.E. Hewitt | Lab | 3,530 | 14.8 |
| | | | | | 3,335 | 14.0 |
| 1924 | 33,470 | 75.6 | R.J.N. Neville | C | 11,283 | 44.6 |
| | | | H.M. Seely | L | 9,114 | 36.0 |
| | | | R.B. Bates | Lab | 4,907 | 19.4 |
| | | | | | 2,169 | 8.6 |
| 1929 | 43,327 | 77.6 | Viscount Elmley | L (NL) | 13,349 | 39.6 |
| | | | Sir R.J.N. Neville, Bt. | C | 12,434 | 37.0 |
| | | | W. Holmes | Lab | 7,856 | 23.4 |
| | | | | | 915 | 2.6 |
| 1931 | 45,366 | 71.7 | Viscount Elmley | NL | 25,945 | 79.8 |
| | | | W. Holmes | Lab | 6,562 | 20.2 |
| | | | | | 19,383 | 59.6 |
| 1935 | 50,229 | 66.8 | Viscount Elmley | NL | 23,108 | 68.8 |
| | | | N.R. Tillett | Lab | 10,461 | 31.2 |
| | | | | | 12,647 | 37.6 |

[Succession to the Peerage — Earl Beauchamp]

| Election | Electors | T'out | Candidate | Party | Votes | % |
|---|---|---|---|---|---|---|
| 1939 (26/1) | 54,719 | 53.1 | F. Medlicott | NL | 18,257 | 62.9 |
| | | | N.R. Tillett | Lab | 10,785 | 37.1 |
| | | | | | 7,472 | 25.8 |
| 1945 | 60,657 | 68.9 | F. Medlicott | NL | 23,307 | 55.8 |
| | | | N.R. Tillett | Lab | 18,467 | 44.2 |
| | | | | | 4,840 | 11.6 |

Notes:—

1918: Henderson sought election as an Independent supporter of the Coalition although he had been adopted by the local Liberal Association as their candidate and is designated as such.

Taylor was the nominee of the NFU.

| Election | Electors | T'out | Candidate | Party | Votes | % |
|---|---|---|---|---|---|---|
| 1918 | 33,349 | 59.7 | †N.P. Jodrell | Co C | 10,146 | 50.9 |
| | | | R.B. Walker | Lab | 9,780 | 49.1 |
| | | | | | 366 | 1.8 |
| 1922 | 35,131 | 75.5 | Sir N.P. Jodrell | C | 9,862 | 37.2 |
| | | | R.B. Walker | Lab | 8,683 | 32.7 |
| | | | G.G. Woodwark | L | 7,970 | 30.1 |
| | | | | | 1,179 | 4.5 |
| 1923 | 35,754 | 71.9 | G.G. Woodwark | L | 9,943 | 38.7 |
| | | | Sir N.P. Jodrell | C | 9,266 | 36.1 |
| | | | J. Stevenson | Lab | 6,488 | 25.2 |
| | | | | | 677 | 2.6 |
| 1924 | 36,289 | 77.6 | Lord Fermoy | C | 11,710 | 41.6 |
| | | | G.G. Woodwark | L | 9,184 | 32.6 |
| | | | J. Stevenson | Lab | 7,280 | 25.8 |
| | | | | | 2,526 | 9.0 |
| 1929 | 45,103 | 79.1 | Lord Fermoy | C | 14,501 | 40.7 |
| | | | W.B. Mitford | L | 10,806 | 30.3 |
| | | | Sir H.J. Maynard | Lab | 10,356 | 29.0 |
| | | | | | 3,695 | 10.4 |
| 1931 | 46,442 | 72.7 | Lord Fermoy | C | 23,687 | 70.2 |
| | | | D. Freeman | Lab | 10,054 | 29.8 |
| | | | | | 13,633 | 40.4 |
| 1935 | 48,764 | 71.7 | Hon. S.A. Maxwell | C | 17,492 | 50.0 |
| | | | F. Emerson | Lab | 12,062 | 34.5 |
| | | | F.O. Darvall | L | 5,418 | 15.5 |
| | | | | | 5,430 | 15.5 |
| [Death] | | | | | | |
| 1943 (12/2) | 49,581 | 39.8 | Lord Fermoy | C | 10,696 | 54.2 |
| | | | F.J. Wise | Ind Lab | 9,027 | 45.8 |
| | | | | | 1,669 | 8.4 |
| 1945 | 52,468 | 71.2 | F.J. Wise | Lab | 18,202 | 48.7 |
| | | | W.D. McCullough | C | 14,928 | 39.9 |
| | | | A.P.D. Penrose | L | 3,796* | 10.2 |
| | | | G.T. Bowles | Ind | 444* | 1.2 |
| | | | | | 3,274 | 8.8 |

Note:—

1945: Bowles sought election as a 'Liberty' candidate.

| Election | Electors | T'out | Candidate | Party | Votes | % |
|---|---|---|---|---|---|---|
| 1918 | 30,179 | 60.8 | H.D. King | Co Ind (Co C) | 9,274 | 50.6 |
| | | | †N.E. Buxton | L | 9,061 | 49.4 |
| | | | | | 213 | 1.2 |
| 1922 | 30,556 | 75.2 | N.E. Buxton | Lab | 12,004 | 52.2 |
| | | | R.B. Crewdson | C | 10,975 | 47.8 |
| | | | | | 1,029 | 4.4 |
| 1923 | 31,205 | 68.3 | N.E. Buxton | Lab | 12,278 | 57.6 |
| | | | B. Smith | C | 9,022 | 42.4 |
| | | | | | 3,256 | 15.2 |
| 1924 | 31,913 | 77.1 | Rt. Hon. N.E. Buxton | Lab | 11,978 | 48.7 |
| | | | T.R.A.M. Cook | C | 9,974 | 40.6 |
| | | | M. Alexander | L | 2,637* | 10.7 |
| | | | | | 2,004 | 8.1 |
| 1929 | 39,272 | 77.9 | Rt. Hon. N.E. Buxton | Lab | 14,544 | 47.5 |
| | | | T.R.A.M. Cook | C | 12,661 | 41.4 |
| | | | Mrs. Z.K. Hoffman | L | 3,407* | 11.1 |
| | | | | | 1,883 | 6.1 |

[Elevation to the Peerage — Lord Noel-Buxton]

| Election | Electors | T'out | Candidate | Party | Votes | % |
|---|---|---|---|---|---|---|
| 1930 (9/7) | 39,272 | 75.0 | Lady Noel-Buxton | Lab | 14,821 | 50.3 |
| | | | T.R.A.M. Cook | C | 14,642 | 49.7 |
| | | | | | 179 | 0.6 |
| 1931 | 40,139 | 82.3 | T.R.A.M. Cook | C | 19,988 | 60.5 |
| | | | Lady Noel-Buxton | Lab | 13,035 | 39.5 |
| | | | | | 6,953 | 21.0 |
| 1935 | 41,370 | 78.1 | T.R.A.M. Cook | C | 17,863 | 55.3 |
| | | | Lady Noel-Buxton | Lab | 14,465 | 44.7 |
| | | | | | 3,398 | 10.6 |
| 1945 | 42,657 | 70.9 | E.G. Gooch | Lab | 17,753 | 58.7 |
| | | | Sir T.R.A.M. Cook | C | 12,507 | 41.3 |
| | | | | | 5,246 | 17.4 |

Note:—

1918: King was designated as a Conservative in the official list of Coalition candidates, but he subsequently wrote to 'The Times' stating that he had left the Conservative Party prior to the election and should be classed as an Independent. Shortly after this he re-joined the Conservative Party.

| Election | Electors | T'out | Candidate | Party | Votes | % |
|----------|----------|-------|-----------|-------|-------|---|
| 1918 | 32,796 | 55.8 | Hon. W.H. Cozens-Hardy | L (Co L) | 11,755 | 64.3 |
| | | | G. Edwards | Lab | 6,536 | 35.7 |
| | | | | | 5,219 | 28.6 |

[Succession to the Peerage — Lord Cozens-Hardy]

| Election | Electors | T'out | Candidate | Party | Votes | % |
|----------|----------|-------|-----------|-------|-------|---|
| 1920 (27/7) | 32,131[†] | 58.5 | G. Edwards | Lab | 8,594 | 45.7 |
| | | | J.H. Batty | Co L | 6,476 | 34.5 |
| | | | C.H. Roberts | L | 3,718 | 19.8 |
| | | | | | 2,118 | 11.2 |
| 1922 | 32,326 | 70.8 | T.W. Hay | C | 12,734 | 55.6 |
| | | | G. Edwards | Lab | 10,159 | 44.4 |
| | | | | | 2,575 | 11.2 |
| 1923 | 32,937 | 68.3 | G. Edwards | Lab | 11,682 | 51.9 |
| | | | T.W. Hay | C | 10,821 | 48.1 |
| | | | | | 861 | 3.8 |
| 1924 | 33,409 | 76.5 | J.A. Christie | C | 14,189 | 55.5 |
| | | | G. Edwards | Lab | 11,376 | 44.5 |
| | | | | | 2,813 | 11.0 |
| 1929 | 40,701 | 76.0 | J.A. Christie | C | 12,978 | 42.0 |
| | | | G. Young | Lab | 10,686 | 34.5 |
| | | | I. Watkins-Evans | L | 7,268 | 23.5 |
| | | | | | 2,292 | 7.5 |
| 1931 | 41,551 | 77.8 | J.A. Christie | C | 21,195 | 65.5 |
| | | | E.G. Gooch | Lab | 11,148 | 34.5 |
| | | | | | 10,047 | 31.0 |
| 1935 | 43,294 | 73.5 | J.A. Christie | C | 18,420 | 57.9 |
| | | | C.G. Clark | Lab | 13,409 | 42.1 |
| | | | | | 5,011 | 15.8 |
| 1945 | 48,451 | 69.0 | C.P. Mayhew | Lab | 16,825 | 50.3 |
| | | | J.S. Allen | C | 10,862 | 32.5 |
| | | | J.H. Wilson | Ind C | 5,761 | 17.2 |
| | | | | | 5,963 | 17.8 |

Note:—

1945: Wilson was the nominee of the South Norfolk Independent Conservative Association which broke away from the official Conservative Association in 1944 as the result of a disagreement over the selection of a Conservative candidate.

| Election | Electors | T'out | Candidate | Party | Votes | % |
|---|---|---|---|---|---|---|
| 1918 | | | †Sir R. Winfrey | Co L | Unopp. | |
| 1922 | 32,305 | 59.1 | Sir R. Winfrey | NL | 10,432 | 54.7 |
| | | | W.B. Taylor | Lab | 8,655 | 45.3 |
| | | | | | 1,777 | 9.4 |
| 1923 | 32,543 | 64.7 | A. McLean | C | 11,269 | 53.5 |
| | | | W.B. Taylor | Lab | 9,779 | 46.5 |
| | | | | | 1,490 | 7.0 |
| 1924 | 33,131 | 72.0 | A. McLean | C | 13,838 | 58.0 |
| | | | W.B. Taylor | Lab | 10,004 | 42.0 |
| | | | | | 3,834 | 16.0 |
| 1929 | 39,277 | 74.1 | W.B. Taylor | Lab | 12,152 | 41.8 |
| | | | A. McLean | C | 11,382 | 39.1 |
| | | | V.D. Duval | L | 5,556 | 19.1 |
| | | | | | 770 | 2.7 |
| 1931 | 39,665 | 74.5 | A. McLean | C | 19,614 | 66.3 |
| | | | W.B. Taylor | Lab | 9,952 | 33.7 |
| | | | | | 9,662 | 32.6 |
| 1935 | 40,293 | 69.5 | S.S. de Chair | C | 16,060 | 57.4 |
| | | | S. Dye | Lab | 11,943 | 42.6 |
| | | | | | 4,117 | 14.8 |
| 1945 | 45,704 | 65.9 | S. Dye | Lab | 15,091 | 50.1 |
| | | | S.S. de Chair | C | 15,038 | 49.9 |
| | | | | | 53 | 0.2 |

| Election | Electors | T'out | Candidate | Party | Votes | % |
|---|---|---|---|---|---|---|
| 1918 | 30,288 | 62.7 | †Hon. E.A. FitzRoy | Co C | 11,176 | 58.8 |
| | | | W.J. Rogers | Lab | 7,824 | 41.2 |
| | | | | | 3,352 | 17.6 |
| 1922 | 30,387 | 72.1 | Hon. E.A. FitzRoy | C | 13,055 | 59.6 |
| | | | W.J. Rogers | Lab | 8,850 | 40.4 |
| | | | | | 4,205 | 19.2 |
| 1923 | 30,935 | 76.1 | Hon. E.A. FitzRoy | C | 10,514 | 44.7 |
| | | | C.I. Kerr | L | 8,914 | 37.8 |
| | | | L. Smith | Lab | 4,127 | 17.5 |
| | | | | | 1,600 | 6.9 |
| 1924 | 31,571 | 79.7 | Rt. Hon. E.A. FitzRoy | C | 12,683 | 50.4 |
| | | | C.I. Kerr | L | 12,483 | 49.6 |
| | | | | | 200 | 0.8 |
| 1929 | | | Rt. Hon. E.A. FitzRoy | C | Unopp. | |
| 1931 | | | Rt. Hon. E.A. FitzRoy | C | Unopp. | |
| 1935 | 39,095 | 76.0 | Rt. Hon. E.A. FitzRoy | C | 18,934 | 63.7 |
| | | | T.E. Barnes | Lab | 10,767 | 36.3 |
| | | | | | 8,167 | 27.4 |
| [Death] | | | | | | |
| 1943 | 40,541 | 48.7 | R.E. Manningham-Buller | C | 9,043 | 45.9 |
| (20/4) | | | D.G. Webb | CW | 6,591 | 33.4 |
| | | | W.G.E. Dyer | Ind L | 4,093 | 20.7 |
| | | | | | 2,452 | 12.5 |
| 1945 | 46,230 | 75.0 | R.E. Manningham-Buller | C | 14,863 | 42.8 |
| | | | P.F. Williams | Lab | 13,693 | 39.5 |
| | | | W.G.E. Dyer | L | 6,130 | 17.7 |
| | | | | | 1,170 | 3.3 |

Note:—

1924-  FitzRoy was the Speaker of the House of Commons from 1928.
1935:

| Election | Electors | Poll | Candidate | Party | Votes | % |
|---|---|---|---|---|---|---|
| 1918 | 34,624 | 65.1 | A.E. Waterson | Co-op (Lab/Co-op) | 10,299 | 45.7 |
| | | | L.W.W. Buxton | Co L | 7,761 | 34.4 |
| | | | A.F.H. Ferguson | Nat P | 4,489 | 19.9 |
| | | | | | 2,538 | 11.3 |
| 1922 | 35,024 | 81.0 | O. Parker | C | 14,333 | 50.5 |
| | | | A.E. Waterson | Lab/Co-op | 14,024 | 49.5 |
| | | | | | 309 | 1.0 |
| 1923 | 35,899 | 81.3 | S.F. Perry | Lab/Co-op | 12,718 | 43.5 |
| | | | O. Parker | C | 10,212 | 35.0 |
| | | | Sir A.W. Yeo | L | 6,273 | 21.5 |
| | | | | | 2,506 | 8.5 |
| 1924 | 36,574 | 84.3 | Sir M.E. Manningham-Buller, Bt. | C | 16,042 | 52.0 |
| | | | S.F. Perry | Lab/Co-op | 14,801 | 48.0 |
| | | | | | 1,241 | 4.0 |
| 1929 | 48,588 | 85.8 | S.F. Perry | Lab/Co-op | 18,253 | 43.8 |
| | | | J. Brown | C | 15,469 | 37.1 |
| | | | C.S. Rewcastle | L | 7,972 | 19.1 |
| | | | | | 2,784 | 6.7 |
| 1931 | 50,064 | 85.7 | J.F. Eastwood | C | 25,811 | 60.2 |
| | | | S.F. Perry | Lab/Co-op | 17,095 | 39.8 |
| | | | | | 8,716 | 20.4 |
| 1935 | 56,850 | 77.3 | J.F. Eastwood | C | 22,885 | 52.1 |
| | | | J.R. Sadler | Lab/Co-op | 21,042 | 47.9 |
| | | | | | 1,843 | 4.2 |

[Resignation on appointment as a Metropolitan Police Magistrate]

| Election | Electors | Poll | Candidate | Party | Votes | % |
|---|---|---|---|---|---|---|
| 1940 (6/3) | 64,838 | 37.8 | J.D. Profumo | C | 17,914 | 73.0 |
| | | | W. Ross | Ind | 6,616 | 27.0 |
| | | | | | 11,298 | 46.0 |
| 1945 | 74,091 | 75.1 | G.R. Mitchison | Lab | 29,868 | 53.6 |
| | | | J.D. Profumo | C | 23,424 | 42.1 |
| | | | J.C. Dempsey | CP | 2,381* | 4.3 |
| | | | | | 6,444 | 11.5 |

Note:—

1940:  Ross was a steel-worker and Labour councillor but he was disowned by the local Labour Party and the Labour Party National Executive. He sought election as a 'Workers' and Pensioners' Anti-War' candidate.

| Election | Electors | T'out | Candidate | Party | Votes | % |
|---|---|---|---|---|---|---|
| 1918 | 34,676 | 62.2 | †H.L.C. Brassey | Co C | 9,516 | 44.1 |
| | | | J. Mansfield | Lab | 8,832 | 41.0 |
| | | | T.I. Slater | L | 3,214 | 14.9 |
| | | | | | 684 | 3.1 |
| 1922 | 35,393 | 80.6 | Sir H.L.C. Brassey, Bt. | C | 13,560 | 47.5 |
| | | | J. Mansfield | Lab | 8,668 | 30.4 |
| | | | G. Nicholls | L | 6,290 | 22.1 |
| | | | | | 4,892 | 17.1 |
| 1923 | 36,049 | 74.4 | Sir H.L.C. Brassey, Bt. | C | 11,634 | 43.4 |
| | | | J. Mansfield | Lab | 8,177 | 30.5 |
| | | | D. Boyle | L | 7,014 | 26.1 |
| | | | | | 3,457 | 12.9 |
| 1924 | 36,461 | 77.2 | Sir H.L.C. Brassey, Bt. | C | 14,195 | 50.4 |
| | | | J. Mansfield | Lab | 9,180 | 32.6 |
| | | | D. Boyle | L | 4,786 | 17.0 |
| | | | | | 5,015 | 17.8 |
| 1929 | 46,704 | 80.6 | J.F. Horrabin | Lab | 14,743 | 39.2 |
| | | | Sir H.L.C. Brassey, Bt. | C | 14,218 | 37.7 |
| | | | J.W.F. Hill | L | 8,704 | 23.1 |
| | | | | | 525 | 1.5 |
| 1931 | 47,947 | 85.2 | Lord Burghley | C | 26,640 | 65.2 |
| | | | J.F. Horrabin | Lab | 14,206 | 34.8 |
| | | | | | 12,434 | 30.4 |
| 1935 | 49,573 | 80.8 | Lord Burghley | C | 22,677 | 56.6 |
| | | | E.A.J. Davies | Lab | 17,373 | 43.4 |
| | | | | | 5,304 | 13.2 |

[Resignation on appointment as Governor of Bermuda]

| Election | Electors | T'out | Candidate | Party | Votes | % |
|---|---|---|---|---|---|---|
| 1943 | 51,755 | 44.2 | Viscount Suirdale | C | 11,976 | 52.4 |
| (15/10) | | | S. Bennett | Ind Lab | 10,890 | 47.6 |
| | | | | | 1,086 | 4.8 |
| 1945 | 59,763 | 72.9 | S. Tiffany | Lab/Co-op | 22,056 | 50.7 |
| | | | Viscount Suirdale | C | 21,485 | 49.3 |
| | | | | | 571 | 1.4 |

Note:—

1943:   Bennett was supported by the Common Wealth Movement and the ILP.

| Election | Electors | T'out | Candidate | Party | Votes | % |
|---|---|---|---|---|---|---|
| 1918 | 31,669 | 61.9 | W.R. Smith | Lab | 10,290 | 52.5 |
| | | | M. Gray | Co L | 9,313 | 47.5 |
| | | | | | 977 | 5.0 |
| 1922 | 32,820 | 79.4 | G.H. Shakespeare | NL | 14,995 | 57.6 |
| | | | W.R. Smith | Lab | 11,057 | 42.4 |
| | | | | | 3,938 | 15.2 |
| 1923 | 33,226 | 79.9 | W.G. Cove | Lab | 11,175 | 42.1 |
| | | | G.H. Shakespeare | L | 8,638 | 32.5 |
| | | | R.M-D. Sanders | C | 6,747 | 25.4 |
| | | | | | 2,537 | 9.6 |
| 1924 | 33,934 | 84.0 | W.G. Cove | Lab | 11,381 | 40.0 |
| | | | R.A. Raphael | C | 8,900 | 31.2 |
| | | | H.M. Paul | L | 8,223 | 28.8 |
| | | | | | 2,481 | 8.8 |
| 1929 | 43,548 | 83.3 | G. Dallas | Lab | 15,300 | 42.2 |
| | | | R.P. Winfrey | L | 11,255 | 31.0 |
| | | | A.W.H. James | C | 9,703 | 26.8 |
| | | | | | 4,045 | 11.2 |
| 1931 | 44,638 | 81.2 | A.W.H. James | C | 22,127 | 61.0 |
| | | | G. Dallas | Lab | 14,137 | 39.0 |
| | | | | | 7,990 | 22.0 |
| 1935 | 46,337 | 77.3 | A.W.H. James | C | 18,085 | 50.5 |
| | | | G. Dallas | Lab | 17,713 | 49.5 |
| | | | | | 372 | 1.0 |
| 1945 | 52,213 | 74.4 | G.S. Lindgren | Lab | 22,416 | 57.7 |
| | | | Sir A.W.H. James | C | 16,426 | 42.3 |
| | | | | | 5,990 | 15.4 |

| Election | Electors | T'out | Candidate | Party | Votes | % |
|---|---|---|---|---|---|---|
| 1918 | 28,173 | 39.5 | †Sir F.D. Blake, Bt. | L (Co L) | 6,721 | 60.5 |
| | | | Hon. W.J.M. Watson-Armstrong | Ind | 4,397 | 39.5 |
| | | | | | 2,324 | 21.0 |
| 1922 | 29,136 | 66.2 | H. Philipson | NL | 11,933 | 61.9 |
| | | | Rt. Hon. W. Runciman | L | 7,354 | 38.1 |
| | | | | | 4,579 | 23.8 |

[Election declared void on petition]

| Election | Electors | T'out | Candidate | Party | Votes | % |
|---|---|---|---|---|---|---|
| 1923 (31/5) | 29,136† | 74.9 | Mrs. M. Philipson | C | 12,000 | 55.0 |
| | | | Hon. H.B. Robson | L | 5,858 | 26.8 |
| | | | G. Oliver | Lab | 3,966 | 18.2 |
| | | | | | 6,142 | 28.2 |
| 1923 | 30,216 | 73.4 | Mrs. M. Philipson | C | 10,636 | 48.0 |
| | | | Hon. H.B. Robson | L | 8,767 | 39.5 |
| | | | Mrs. E.M. Penny | Lab | 2,784 | 12.5 |
| | | | | | 1,869 | 8.5 |
| 1924 | 30,661 | 77.7 | Mrs. M. Philipson | C | 12,130 | 50.9 |
| | | | Hon. H.B. Robson | L | 8,165 | 34.3 |
| | | | J. Adams | Lab | 3,521 | 14.8 |
| | | | | | 3,965 | 16.6 |
| 1929 | 38,527 | 76.1 | A.J.K. Todd | C | 12,526 | 42.8 |
| | | | P. Williams | L | 11,372 | 38.8 |
| | | | H. Kegie | Lab | 5,402 | 18.4 |
| | | | | | 1,154 | 4.0 |
| 1931 | | | A.J.K. Todd | C (Ind C) (C) | Unopp. | |
| 1935 | 40,678 | 76.0 | Sir H.M. Seely, Bt. | L | 15,779 | 51.0 |
| | | | A.J.K. Todd | C | 15,145 | 49.0 |
| | | | | | 634 | 2.0 |

[Elevation to the Peerage — Lord Sherwood]

| Election | Electors | T'out | Candidate | Party | Votes | % |
|---|---|---|---|---|---|---|
| 1941 (18/8) | | | G.C. Grey | L | Unopp. | |

[Death]

| Election | Electors | T'out | Candidate | Party | Votes | % |
|---|---|---|---|---|---|---|
| 1944 (17/10) | 41,068 | 24.5 | Sir W.H. Beveridge | L | 8,792 | 87.4 |
| | | | W.D. Clark | Ind | 1,269 | 12.6 |
| | | | | | 7,523 | 74.8 |
| 1945 | 42,153 | 67.5 | R.A.F. Thorp | C | 12,315 | 43.3 |
| | | | Sir W.H. Beveridge | L | 10,353 | 36.4 |
| | | | J. Davis | Lab | 5,782 | 20.3 |
| | | | | | 1,962 | 6.9 |

Note:—

1918:   Watson-Armstrong sought election as an 'Independent Northumbrian' candidate.

| Election | Electors | T'out | Candidate | Party | Votes | % |
|---|---|---|---|---|---|---|
| 1918 | 25,341 | 62.4 | D. Clifton Brown | Co C | 7,763 | 48.9 |
|  |  |  | W. Weir | Lab | 4,168 | 26.2 |
|  |  |  | Hon. W.H.C. Beaumont | L | 3,948 | 24.9 |
|  |  |  |  |  | 3,595 | 22.7 |
| 1922 | 26,372 | 79.3 | D. Clifton Brown | C | 9,369 | 44.8 |
|  |  |  | V.H. Finney | L | 6,486 | 31.0 |
|  |  |  | G.W. Shield | Lab | 5,050 | 24.2 |
|  |  |  |  |  | 2,883 | 13.8 |
| 1923 | 26,732 | 75.5 | V.H. Finney | L | 11,293 | 56.0 |
|  |  |  | D. Clifton Brown | C | 8,887 | 44.0 |
|  |  |  |  |  | 2,406 | 12.0 |
| 1924 | 27,237 | 82.2 | D. Clifton Brown | C | 10,741 | 48.0 |
|  |  |  | V.H. Finney | L | 6,551 | 29.3 |
|  |  |  | C.R. Flynn | Lab | 5,089 | 22.7 |
|  |  |  |  |  | 4,190 | 18.7 |
| 1929 | 35,304 | 80.2 | D. Clifton Brown | C | 11,069 | 39.1 |
|  |  |  | Rt. Hon. Sir F.D. Acland, Bt. | L | 9,103 | 32.2 |
|  |  |  | E.O. Dunnico | Lab | 8,135 | 28.7 |
|  |  |  |  |  | 1,966 | 6.9 |
| 1931 | 35,520 | 79.2 | D. Clifton Brown | C | 20,578 | 73.1 |
|  |  |  | E.O. Dunnico | Lab | 7,557 | 26.9 |
|  |  |  |  |  | 13,021 | 46.2 |
| 1935 | 36,310 | 75.9 | D. Clifton Brown | C | 17,241 | 62.5 |
|  |  |  | E. Kinghorn | Lab | 10,324 | 37.5 |
|  |  |  |  |  | 6,917 | 25.0 |
| 1945 | 38,368 | 73.5 | D. Clifton Brown | C | 16,431 | 58.2 |
|  |  |  | E. Kavanagh | Lab | 11,786 | 41.8 |
|  |  |  |  |  | 4,645 | 16.4 |

Note:—

1935-
1945:   Clifton Brown was the Speaker of the House of Commons from 1943.

| Election | Electors | T'out | Candidate | Party | Votes | % |
|---|---|---|---|---|---|---|
| 1918 | 42,750 | 57.9 | †R. Mason | Co L | 14,065 | 56.9 |
| | | | E. Edwards | Lab | 10,666 | 43.1 |
| | | | | | 3,399 | 13.8 |
| 1922 | 46,354 | 76.6 | G.H. Warne | Lab | 16,032 | 45.2 |
| | | | R. White | C | 11,149 | 31.4 |
| | | | J. Neal | NL | 5,192 | 14.6 |
| | | | M. Davey | L | 3,134* | 8.8 |
| | | | | | 4,883 | 13.8 |
| 1923 | 47,828 | 68.4 | G.H. Warne | Lab | 18,583 | 56.8 |
| | | | H. Philipson | C | 14,131 | 43.2 |
| | | | | | 4,452 | 13.6 |
| 1924 | 50,446 | 79.4 | G.H. Warne | Lab | 21,159 | 52.9 |
| | | | Mrs. M.K. Middleton | C | 18,875 | 47.1 |
| | | | | | 2,284 | 5.8 |
| [Death] | | | | | | |
| 1929 (13/2) | 53,886 | 65.3 | G.W. Shield | Lab | 20,398 | 58.0 |
| | | | I.M. Moffatt-Pender | C | 9,612 | 27.3 |
| | | | H.A. Briggs | L | 5,183 | 14.7 |
| | | | | | 10,786 | 30.7 |
| 1929 | 67,390 | 76.1 | G.W. Shield | Lab | 27,930 | 54.5 |
| | | | B. Cruddas | C | 17,056 | 33.2 |
| | | | Rev. F. Waudby | L | 6,330* | 12.3 |
| | | | | | 10,874 | 21.3 |
| 1931 | 70,589 | 81.9 | B. Cruddas | C | 33,659 | 58.2 |
| | | | G.W. Shield | Lab | 24,126 | 41.8 |
| | | | | | 9,533 | 16.4 |
| 1935 | 76,348 | 79.6 | B. Cruddas | C | 30,859 | 50.8 |
| | | | E. Dowling | Lab | 29,904 | 49.2 |
| | | | | | 955 | 1.6 |
| [Resignation] | | | | | | |
| 1940 (29/7) | | | R.D. Scott | C | Unopp. | |
| 1945 | 88,089 | 77.5 | A. Robens | Lab | 40,948 | 60.0 |
| | | | R.D. Scott | C | 27,295 | 40.0 |
| | | | | | 13,653 | 20.0 |

# NOTTINGHAMSHIRE, BASSETLAW [426]

| Election | Electors | T'out | Candidate | Party | Votes | % |
|---|---|---|---|---|---|---|
| 1918 | | | †Sir W.E. Hume-Williams | Co C | Unopp. | |
| 1922 | 31,505 | 74.4 | Sir W.E. Hume-Williams, Bt. | C | 12,944 | 55.2 |
| | | | H.J. Odell | Lab | 10,502 | 44.8 |
| | | | | | 2,442 | 10.4 |
| 1923 | 32,161 | 76.6 | Sir W.E. Hume-Williams, Bt. | C | 10,419 | 42.3 |
| | | | A. Neal | L | 7,247 | 29.4 |
| | | | M.J. MacDonald | Lab | 6,973 | 28.3 |
| | | | | | 3,172 | 12.9 |
| 1924 | 33,651 | 81.8 | Sir W.E. Hume-Williams, Bt. | C | 12,732 | 46.3 |
| | | | M.J. MacDonald | Lab | 11,283 | 41.0 |
| | | | A. Neal | L | 3,505 | 12.7 |
| | | | | | 1,449 | 5.3 |
| 1929 | 49,184 | 82.0 | M.J. MacDonald | Lab (N Lab) | 23,681 | 58.7 |
| | | | Sir W.E. Hume-Williams, Bt. | C | 16,670 | 41.3 |
| | | | | | 7,011 | 17.4 |
| 1931 | 51,185 | 79.6 | M.J. MacDonald | N Lab | 27,136 | 66.6 |
| | | | H.M. Watkins | Lab | 13,582 | 33.4 |
| | | | | | 13,554 | 33.2 |
| 1935 | 53,422 | 79.9 | F.J. Bellenger | Lab | 21,903 | 51.3 |
| | | | Rt. Hon. M.J. MacDonald | N Lab | 20,764 | 48.7 |
| | | | | | 1,139 | 2.6 |
| 1945 | 61,573 | 78.6 | F.J. Bellenger | Lab | 30,382 | 62.8 |
| | | | R.E. Laycock | C | 18,005 | 37.2 |
| | | | | | 12,377 | 25.6 |

| Election | Electors | T'out | Candidate | Party | Votes | % |
|---|---|---|---|---|---|---|
| 1918 | 35,826 | 56.4 | G.A. Spencer | Lab | 11,150 | 55.2 |
| | | | †Sir C.H. Seely, Bt. | L | 4,681 | 23.2 |
| | | | H.H. Whaite | Co NDP | 4,374 | 21.6 |
| | | | | | 6,469 | 32.0 |
| 1922 | 38,475 | 59.8 | G.A. Spencer | Lab | 11,699 | 50.8 |
| | | | C.E. Tee | NL | 11,328 | 49.2 |
| | | | | | 371 | 1.6 |
| 1923 | 39,169 | 62.0 | G.A. Spencer | Lab | 13,219 | 54.5 |
| | | | G.J.S. Scovell | L | 11,049 | 45.5 |
| | | | | | 2,170 | 9.0 |
| 1924 | 40,171 | 68.7 | G.A. Spencer | Lab (Ind) | 15,276 | 55.4 |
| | | | T.E. Jackson | L | 12,313 | 44.6 |
| | | | | | 2,963 | 10.8 |
| 1929 | 51,249 | 81.2 | F.S. Cocks | Lab | 24,603 | 59.1 |
| | | | E.G. Cove | L | 9,814 | 23.6 |
| | | | G.E. Pierrepont | C | 7,194 | 17.3 |
| | | | | | 14,789 | 35.5 |
| 1931 | 53,766 | 78.6 | F.S. Cocks | Lab | 21,917 | 51.9 |
| | | | P.E. Springman | C | 20,327 | 48.1 |
| | | | | | 1,590 | 3.8 |
| 1935 | 58,045 | 73.5 | F.S. Cocks | Lab | 26,854 | 63.0 |
| | | | P.E. Springman | C | 15,804 | 37.0 |
| | | | | | 11,050 | 26.0 |
| 1945 | 70,089 | 78.3 | F.S. Cocks | Lab | 39,545 | 72.0 |
| | | | G.S.M. Bowman | C | 15,344 | 28.0 |
| | | | | | 24,201 | 44.0 |

Note:–

1918: Whaite stated during the election campaign that he was an Independent pledged to no party but shortly before polling day (too late for his name to appear on the final list of Coalition candidates) he received a 'coupon' under the auspices of the National Democratic Party who also gave him some local support.

| Election | Electors | T'out | Candidate | Party | Votes | % |
|---|---|---|---|---|---|---|
| 1918 | 39,041 | 52.5 | W. Carter | Lab | 8,957 | 43.6 |
| | | | G.W.S. Jarrett | Co NDP | 6,678 | 32.6 |
| | | | Miss V. Markham | L | 4,000 | 19.5 |
| | | | Dr. N.M. Tarachand | Ind | 878* | 4.3 |
| | | | | | 2,279 | 11.0 |
| 1922 | 41,868 | 74.3 | A.J. Bennett | L | 16,192 | 52.0 |
| | | | W. Carter | Lab | 14,917 | 48.0 |
| | | | | | 1,275 | 4.0 |
| 1923 | 42,937 | 75.9 | F.B. Varley | Lab | 18,813 | 57.8 |
| | | | A.J. Bennett | L | 13,757 | 42.2 |
| | | | | | 5,056 | 15.6 |
| 1924 | 44,094 | 74.8 | F.B. Varley | Lab | 19,441 | 59.0 |
| | | | C.L. Hanington | C | 13,535 | 41.0 |
| | | | | | 5,906 | 18.0 |

[Seat Vacant at Dissolution (Death)]

| Election | Electors | T'out | Candidate | Party | Votes | % |
|---|---|---|---|---|---|---|
| 1929 | 59,735 | 81.2 | C. Brown | Lab | 28,416 | 58.6 |
| | | | W. Collins | L | 10,517 | 21.7 |
| | | | S.R. Sidebottom | C | 9,035 | 18.6 |
| | | | Miss R. Smith | Com | 533* | 1.1 |
| | | | | | 17,899 | 36.9 |
| 1931 | 62,546 | 77.0 | C. Brown | Lab | 26,865 | 55.8 |
| | | | E.S.B. Hopkin | C | 21,303 | 44.2 |
| | | | | | 5,562 | 11.6 |
| 1935 | 67,251 | 69.5 | C. Brown | Lab | 31,803 | 68.0 |
| | | | A.C.M. Spearman | C | 14,962 | 32.0 |
| | | | | | 16,841 | 36.0 |

[Death]

| Election | Electors | T'out | Candidate | Party | Votes | % |
|---|---|---|---|---|---|---|
| 1941 (9/4) | | | H.B. Taylor | Lab | Unopp. | |
| 1945 | 75,768 | 75.8 | H.B. Taylor | Lab | 43,113 | 75.1 |
| | | | T. Lynch | C | 14,302 | 24.9 |
| | | | | | 28,811 | 50.2 |

| Election | Electors | T'out | Candidate | Party | Votes | % |
|---|---|---|---|---|---|---|
| 1918 | | | †J.R. Starkey | Co C | Unopp. | |
| 1922 | 29,777 | 79.9 | Marquess of Titchfield | C | 15,423 | 64.8 |
| | | | H. Nixon | Lab | 8,378 | 35.2 |
| | | | | | 7,045 | 29.6 |
| 1923 | 30,529 | 72.4 | Marquess of Titchfield | C | 12,357 | 55.9 |
| | | | L. Priestley | L | 9,741 | 44.1 |
| | | | | | 2,616 | 11.8 |
| 1924 | 31,458 | 74.2 | Marquess of Titchfield | C | 14,129 | 60.5 |
| | | | H. Varley | Lab | 5,076 | 21.8 |
| | | | J. Haslam | L | 4,124 | 17.7 |
| | | | | | 9,053 | 38.7 |
| 1929 | 44,826 | 77.0 | Marquess of Titchfield | C | 15,707 | 45.5 |
| | | | J. Haslam | L | 10,768 | 31.2 |
| | | | W.R.G. Haywood | Lab | 8,060 | 23.3 |
| | | | | | 4,939 | 14.3 |
| 1931 | 47,788 | 75.9 | Marquess of Titchfield | C | 25,445 | 70.1 |
| | | | J.R. Bellerby | Lab | 10,840 | 29.9 |
| | | | | | 14,605 | 40.2 |
| 1935 | 49,945 | 69.9 | Marquess of Titchfield | C | 21,793 | 62.4 |
| | | | A.W. Sharman | Lab | 13,127 | 37.6 |
| | | | | | 8,666 | 24.8 |

[Succession to the Peerage — Duke of Portland]

| Election | Electors | T'out | Candidate | Party | Votes | % |
|---|---|---|---|---|---|---|
| 1943 (8/6) | 51,785 | 44.2 | S. Shephard | C | 10,120 | 44.2 |
| | | | A. Dawrant | Ind Prog | 7,110 | 31.1 |
| | | | E.W. Moeran | CW | 3,189 | 13.9 |
| | | | J.T. Pepper | Ind L | 2,473* | 10.8 |
| | | | | | 3,010 | 13.1 |
| 1945 | 56,447 | 73.0 | S. Shephard | C | 18,580 | 45.1 |
| | | | H.V. Champion de Crespigny | Lab | 17,448 | 42.3 |
| | | | H.F. Calladine | L | 5,175 | 12.6 |
| | | | | | 1,132 | 2.8 |

Note:—

1943: Dawrant was supported by W.D. Kendall, M.P. (his brother-in-law) and W.J. Brown, M.P.

| Election | Electors | T'out | Candidate | Party | Votes | % |
|---|---|---|---|---|---|---|
| 1918 | 34,974 | 59.2 | H.B. Betterton | Co C | 10,848 | 52.4 |
| | | | C. Harris | Lab | 6,180 | 29.9 |
| | | | †Rt. Hon. L.S. Jones | L | 3,673 | 17.7 |
| | | | | | 4,668 | 22.5 |
| 1922 | 37,293 | 69.9 | H.B. Betterton | C | 14,822 | 56.8 |
| | | | R.N. Angell | Lab | 11,261 | 43.2 |
| | | | | | 3,561 | 13.6 |
| 1923 | 38,068 | 73.3 | H.B. Betterton | C | 12,427 | 44.5 |
| | | | J. Lewin | L | 8,581 | 30.8 |
| | | | J. Wilson | Lab | 6,882 | 24.7 |
| | | | | | 3,846 | 13.7 |
| 1924 | 39,360 | 69.3 | H.B. Betterton | C | 17,733 | 65.0 |
| | | | J.O. Whitwham | Lab | 9,548 | 35.0 |
| | | | | | 8,185 | 30.0 |
| 1929 | 57,758 | 79.5 | H.B. Betterton | C | 19,145 | 41.7 |
| | | | Miss F.B. Widdowson | Lab | 16,069 | 35.0 |
| | | | A.T. Marwood | L | 10,724 | 23.3 |
| | | | | | 3,076 | 6.7 |
| 1931 | 65,362 | 77.8 | Sir H.B. Betterton, Bt. | C | 36,670 | 72.1 |
| | | | Mrs. F.B. Paton | Lab | 14,176 | 27.9 |
| | | | | | 22,494 | 44.2 |

[Resignation on appointment as Chairman of the Unemployment Assistance Board]

| Election | Electors | T'out | Candidate | Party | Votes | % |
|---|---|---|---|---|---|---|
| 1934 (26/7) | 70,258 | 56.5 | R. Assheton | C | 19,374 | 48.8 |
| | | | H.J. Cadogan | Lab | 15,081 | 38.0 |
| | | | A.T. Marwood | L | 5,251 | 13.2 |
| | | | | | 4,293 | 10.8 |
| 1935 | 76,077 | 67.9 | R. Assheton | C | 32,320 | 62.6 |
| | | | H.J. Cadogan | Lab | 19,349 | 37.4 |
| | | | | | 12,971 | 25.2 |
| 1945 | 103,897 | 76.9 | Mrs. F.B. Paton | Lab | 43,303 | 54.2 |
| | | | Rt. Hon. R. Assheton | C | 36,544 | 45.8 |
| | | | | | 6,759 | 8.4 |

Note:—

1931:  Mrs. Paton was formerly Miss Widdowson.

| Election | Electors | T'out | Candidate | Party | Votes | % |
|---|---|---|---|---|---|---|
| 1918 | | | †Sir R. Rhys Williams, Bt. | Co L | Unopp. | |
| [Appointed Recorder of Cardiff] | | | | | | |
| 1922 (22/6) | | | Sir R. Rhys Williams, Bt. | Co L | Unopp. | |
| 1922 | 35,147 | 76.4 | A.J. Edmondson | C | 12,491 | 46.5 |
| | | | J.H. Early | L | 7,885 | 29.4 |
| | | | E.N. Bennett | Lab | 6,463 | 24.1 |
| | | | | | 4,606 | 17.1 |
| 1923 | 35,855 | 76.0 | A.J. Edmondson | C | 12,490 | 45.8 |
| | | | C.B. Fry | L | 12,271 | 45.0 |
| | | | E.N. Bennett | Lab | 2,500* | 9.2 |
| | | | | | 219 | 0.8 |
| 1924 | 36,097 | 79.3 | A.J. Edmondson | C | 15,053 | 52.7 |
| | | | Sir H.C.W. Verney, Bt. | L | 8,825 | 30.8 |
| | | | A.E. Monks | Lab | 4,733 | 16.5 |
| | | | | | 6,228 | 21.9 |
| 1929 | 45,937 | 78.7 | A.J. Edmondson | C | 16,444 | 45.5 |
| | | | R.W. Allen | L | 13,800 | 38.2 |
| | | | L.A. Wingfield | Lab | 5,894 | 16.3 |
| | | | | | 2,644 | 7.3 |
| 1931 | | | A.J. Edmondson | C | Unopp. | |
| 1935 | 50,682 | 65.8 | Sir A.J. Edmondson | C | 21,904 | 65.7 |
| | | | W.E. Wade | Lab | 11,456 | 34.3 |
| | | | | | 10,448 | 31.4 |
| 1945 | 64,816 | 70.6 | A.D. Dodds-Parker | C | 23,777 | 52.0 |
| | | | R.B.K. Roach | Lab | 21,951 | 48.0 |
| | | | | | 1,826 | 4.0 |

| Election | Electors | T'out | Candidate | Party | Votes | % |
|---|---|---|---|---|---|---|
| 1918 | 30,457 | 52.2 | R. Terrell | Co C | 10,757 | 67.7 |
| | | | E.L. Macnaghten | L | 5,138 | 32.3 |
| | | | | | 5,619 | 35.4 |
| 1922 | 31,246 | 69.6 | R. Terrell | C | 11,545 | 53.1 |
| | | | Sir R.H. Rew | L | 10,204 | 46.9 |
| | | | | | 1,341 | 6.2 |
| 1923 | 31,873 | 73.3 | R. Terrell | C | 12,092 | 51.8 |
| | | | Sir R.H. Rew | L | 11,266 | 48.2 |
| | | | | | 826 | 3.6 |
| 1924 | 32,613 | 70.2 | R.R. Henderson | C | 14,830 | 64.8 |
| | | | C.A. Bennett | L | 8,060 | 35.2 |
| | | | | | 6,770 | 29.6 |
| 1929 | 44,624 | 73.3 | R.R. Henderson | C | 16,943 | 51.9 |
| | | | G.E. Tritton | L | 9,786 | 29.9 |
| | | | B.B. Gillis | Lab | 5,962 | 18.2 |
| | | | | | 7,157 | 22.0 |
| 1931 | 48,425 | 68.6 | R.R. Henderson | C | 24,015 | 72.2 |
| | | | R.B. Matthews | L | 5,411 | 16.3 |
| | | | F.J. Hembury | Lab | 3,809* | 11.5 |
| | | | | | 18,604 | 55.9 |
| [Death] | | | | | | |
| 1932 | 48,425 | 48.9 | Sir G.W.G. Fox, Bt. | C | 16,553 | 69.9 |
| (25/2) | | | R.B. Matthews | L | 7,129 | 30.1 |
| | | | | | 9,424 | 39.8 |
| 1935 | 55,002 | 56.9 | Sir G.W.G. Fox, Bt. | C | 22,024 | 70.4 |
| | | | J.H. May | L | 9,254 | 29.6 |
| | | | | | 12,770 | 40.8 |
| 1945 | 79,133 | 66.3 | Sir G.W.G. Fox, Bt. | C | 22,286 | 42.5 |
| | | | J.S. Cook | Lab | 19,457 | 37.1 |
| | | | Hon. L.G.B. Brett | L | 10,718 | 20.4 |
| | | | | | 2,829 | 5.4 |

| Election | Electors | T'out | Candidate | Party | Votes | % |
|---|---|---|---|---|---|---|
| 1918 | | | †Sir B. Stanier, Bt. | Co C | Unopp. | |
| [Death] | | | | | | |
| 1922 (4/1) | | | Viscount Windsor | Co C | Unopp. | |
| | | | | | | |
| 1922 | 24,805 | 71.6 | Viscount Windsor | C | 11,787 | 66.3 |
| | | | E.C. Pryce | NL | 5,979 | 33.7 |
| | | | | | 5,808 | 32.6 |
| [Succession to the Peerage — Earl of Plymouth] | | | | | | |
| 1923 (19/4) | 24,805<sup>†</sup> | 73.0 | G. Windsor-Clive | C | 9,956 | 55.0 |
| | | | E.C. Pryce | L | 6,740 | 37.2 |
| | | | P.F. Pollard | Lab | 1,420* | 7.8 |
| | | | | | 3,216 | 17.8 |
| | | | | | | |
| 1923 | | | G. Windsor-Clive | C | Unopp. | |
| | | | | | | |
| 1924 | | | G. Windsor-Clive | C | Unopp. | |
| | | | | | | |
| 1929 | 32,233 | 76.5 | G. Windsor-Clive | C | 14,066 | 57.1 |
| | | | T. Hardwick | Lab | 5,323 | 21.6 |
| | | | A. Hanbury-Sparrow | L | 5,259 | 21.3 |
| | | | | | 8,743 | 35.5 |
| | | | | | | |
| 1931 | 32,778 | 74.4 | G. Windsor-Clive | C | 19,700 | 80.8 |
| | | | T. Hardwick | Lab | 4,683 | 19.2 |
| | | | | | 15,017 | 61.6 |
| | | | | | | |
| 1935 | 33,128 | 67.9 | G. Windsor-Clive | C | 16,355 | 72.7 |
| | | | T. Hardwick | Lab | 6,151 | 27.3 |
| | | | | | 10,204 | 45.4 |
| | | | | | | |
| 1945 | 35,990 | 71.1 | U. Corbett | C | 13,928 | 54.4 |
| | | | A.G. Parry-Jones | Lab | 6,358 | 24.9 |
| | | | C.J.G. Cameron | L | 4,307 | 16.8 |
| | | | C.E. Edwards | Nat Ind | 989* | 3.9 |
| | | | | | 7,570 | 29.5 |

Note:—

1945: Edwards was supported by the Farmers' Rights Association.

| Election | Electors | T'out | Candidate | Party | Votes | % |
|---|---|---|---|---|---|---|
| 1918 | 31,977 | 64.9 | †W.C. Bridgeman | Co C | 12,276 | 59.2 |
| | | | T. Morris | Lab | 8,467 | 40.8 |
| | | | | | 3,809 | 18.4 |
| | | | | | | |
| 1922 | 31,923 | 80.2 | Rt. Hon. W.C. Bridgeman | C | 12,837 | 50.2 |
| | | | R. Sidebottom | L | 6,660 | 26.0 |
| | | | T. Morris | Lab | 6,105 | 23.8 |
| | | | | | 6,177 | 24.2 |
| | | | | | | |
| 1923 | 32,595 | 75.8 | Rt. Hon. W.C. Bridgeman | C | 11,528 | 46.6 |
| | | | R. Sidebottom | L | 9,713 | 39.3 |
| | | | S.R. Campion | Lab | 3,477 | 14.1 |
| | | | | | 1,815 | 7.3 |
| | | | | | | |
| 1924 | 32,913 | 78.9 | Rt. Hon. W.C. Bridgeman | C | 14,316 | 55.1 |
| | | | R. Sidebottom | L | 6,143 | 23.7 |
| | | | T. Morris | Lab | 5,503 | 21.2 |
| | | | | | 8,173 | 31.4 |
| | | | | | | |
| 1929 | 41,953 | 78.8 | B.E.P. Leighton | C | 15,554 | 47.0 |
| | | | Prof. J.S. Jones | L | 10,565 | 32.0 |
| | | | H.S. Evans | Lab | 6,944 | 21.0 |
| | | | | | 4,989 | 15.0 |
| | | | | | | |
| 1931 | 42,928 | 74.7 | B.E.P. Leighton | C | 23,740 | 74.0 |
| | | | W.E. Warder | Lab | 8,343 | 26.0 |
| | | | | | 15,397 | 48.0 |
| | | | | | | |
| 1935 | | | B.E.P. Leighton | C | Unopp. | |
| | | | | | | |
| 1945 | 48,719 | 71.7 | O.B.S. Poole | C | 19,082 | 54.6 |
| | | | G.D.E. Boyd-Carpenter | Lab | 10,777 | 30.9 |
| | | | L.C. Burcher | L | 5,049 | 14.5 |
| | | | | | 8,305 | 23.7 |

| Election | Electors | T'out | Candidate | Party | Votes | % |
|---|---|---|---|---|---|---|
| 1918 | 25,459 | 60.4 | †G.B. Lloyd | Co C | 9,826 | 63.9 |
| | | | A. Taylor | Lab | 5,542 | 36.1 |
| | | | | | 4,284 | 27.8 |
| 1922 | 25,878 | 78.8 | Viscount Sandon | C | 10,999 | 53.9 |
| | | | J. Sunlight | L | 9,401 | 46.1 |
| | | | | | 1,598 | 7.8 |
| 1923 | 26,464 | 81.8 | J. Sunlight | L | 11,097 | 51.3 |
| | | | Viscount Sandon | C | 10,548 | 48.7 |
| | | | | | 549 | 2.6 |
| 1924 | 27,490 | 86.5 | Viscount Sandon | C | 13,220 | 55.6 |
| | | | J. Sunlight | L | 8,945 | 37.6 |
| | | | D.B. Lawley | Lab | 1,614* | 6.8 |
| | | | | | 4,275 | 18.0 |
| 1929 | 36,312 | 82.7 | G.A.V. Duckworth | C | 14,586 | 48.5 |
| | | | J. Sunlight | L | 11,794 | 39.3 |
| | | | A.A. Beach | Lab | 3,662* | 12.2 |
| | | | | | 2,792 | 9.2 |
| 1931 | 36,804 | 82.7 | G.A.V. Duckworth | C | 18,505 | 60.8 |
| | | | Dr. Elizabeth T. Morgan | L | 9,358 | 30.8 |
| | | | E. Porter | Lab | 2,567* | 8.4 |
| | | | | | 9,147 | 30.0 |
| 1935 | 37,753 | 74.2 | G.A.V. Duckworth | C | 18,401 | 65.7 |
| | | | C.C. Poole | Lab | 9,606 | 34.3 |
| | | | | | 8,795 | 31.4 |
| 1945 | 46,854 | 72.9 | J.A. Langford-Holt | C | 15,174 | 44.4 |
| | | | S.N. Chapman | Lab | 10,580 | 31.0 |
| | | | A.S. Comyns Carr | L | 8,412 | 24.6 |
| | | | | | 4,594 | 13.4 |

| Election | Electors | T'out | Candidate | Party | Votes | % |
|---|---|---|---|---|---|---|
| 1918 | | | †Sir C.S. Henry, Bt. | Co L | Unopp. | |
| [Death] | | | | | | |
| 1920 (7/2) | 32,053 | 71.0 | C.F. Palmer | Ind | 9,267 | 40.7 |
| | | | C. Duncan | Lab | 8,729 | 38.4 |
| | | | J. Bayley | Co L | 4,750 | 20.9 |
| | | | | | 538 | 2.3 |
| [Death] | | | | | | |
| 1920 (20/11) | 32,053† | 78.5 | Sir C.V.F. Townshend | Ind (C) | 14,565 | 57.9 |
| | | | C. Duncan | Lab | 10,600 | 42.1 |
| | | | | | 3,965 | 15.8 |
| 1922 | 32,844 | 67.8 | H.S. Button | C | 11,652 | 52.4 |
| | | | R.E. Jones | Lab | 10,603 | 47.6 |
| | | | | | 1,049 | 4.8 |
| 1923 | 33,253 | 66.0 | H. Nixon | Lab | 11,657 | 53.2 |
| | | | A.N. Fielden | C | 10,274 | 46.8 |
| | | | | | 1,383 | 6.4 |
| 1924 | 33,866 | 74.2 | T. Oakley | C | 14,003 | 55.7 |
| | | | H. Nixon | Lab | 11,132 | 44.3 |
| | | | | | 2,871 | 11.4 |
| 1929 | 42,823 | 76.7 | Miss E. Picton-Turbervill | Lab | 14,569 | 44.4 |
| | | | T. Oakley | C | 11,707 | 35.6 |
| | | | W.E. Boyes | L | 6,575 | 20.0 |
| | | | | | 2,862 | 8.8 |
| 1931 | 43,772 | 83.2 | J. Baldwin-Webb | C | 22,258 | 61.1 |
| | | | Miss E. Picton-Turbervill | Lab | 14,162 | 38.9 |
| | | | | | 8,096 | 22.2 |
| 1935 | 45,153 | 79.1 | J. Baldwin-Webb | C | 20,665 | 57.9 |
| | | | G.T. Garratt | Lab | 15,040 | 42.1 |
| | | | | | 5,625 | 15.8 |
| [Death] | | | | | | |
| 1941 (26/9) | 46,156 | 40.5 | W.A. Colegate | C | 9,946 | 53.1 |
| | | | N.P. Billing | Nat Ind | 7,121 | 38.1 |
| | | | A.P. Kennedy | Ind | 1,638* | 8.8 |
| | | | | | 2,825 | 15.0 |
| 1945 | 55,158 | 72.3 | I.O. Thomas | Lab | 22,453 | 56.3 |
| | | | W.A. Colegate | C | 17,422 | 43.7 |
| | | | | | 5,031 | 12.6 |

Notes:—

1920: Palmer was supported by Horatio Bottomley and joined the
(7/2) Independent Parliamentary Group.

1920: Townshend was supported by Horatio Bottomley and joined the
(20/11) Independent Parliamentary Group.

1941: Billing advocated a policy of aerial reprisals against Germany.

# SOMERSET, BRIDGWATER [437]

| Election | Electors | T'out | Candidate | Party | Votes | % |
|----------|----------|-------|-----------|-------|-------|---|
| 1918 | 29,411 | 62.4 | †Rt. Hon. R.A. Sanders | Co C | 12,587 | 68.6 |
|  |  |  | S.J. Plummer | Lab | 5,771 | 31.4 |
|  |  |  |  |  | 6,816 | 37.2 |
| 1922 | 30,657 | 78.2 | Rt. Hon. Sir R.A. Sanders, Bt. | C | 11,240 | 46.9 |
|  |  |  | W.E. Morse | L | 11,121 | 46.4 |
|  |  |  | T.S.B. Williams | Lab | 1,598* | 6.7 |
|  |  |  |  |  | 119 | 0.5 |
| 1923 | 31,317 | 83.4 | W.E. Morse | L | 13,778 | 52.7 |
|  |  |  | Rt. Hon. Sir R.A. Sanders, Bt. | C | 12,347 | 47.3 |
|  |  |  |  |  | 1,431 | 5.4 |
| 1924 | 32,111 | 84.4 | B.C. Wood | C | 14,283 | 52.7 |
|  |  |  | W.E. Morse | L | 10,842 | 40.0 |
|  |  |  | J.M. Boltz | Lab | 1,966* | 7.3 |
|  |  |  |  |  | 3,441 | 12.7 |
| 1929 | 41,068 | 80.4 | R.P. Croom-Johnson | C | 15,440 | 46.8 |
|  |  |  | J.W. Molden | L | 11,161 | 33.8 |
|  |  |  | J.M. Boltz | Lab | 6,423 | 19.4 |
|  |  |  |  |  | 4,279 | 13.0 |
| 1931 | 42,034 | 73.8 | R.P. Croom-Johnson | C | 24,041 | 77.5 |
|  |  |  | J.M. Boltz | Lab | 6,974 | 22.5 |
|  |  |  |  |  | 17,067 | 55.0 |
| 1935 | 43,367 | 72.7 | R.P. Croom-Johnson | C | 17,939 | 56.8 |
|  |  |  | N.D. Blake | L | 7,370 | 23.4 |
|  |  |  | A.W. Loveys | Lab | 6,240 | 19.8 |
|  |  |  |  |  | 10,569 | 33.4 |

[Resignation on appointment as a High Court Judge]

| | | | | | | |
|----------|----------|-------|-----------|-------|-------|---|
| 1938 (17/11) | 44,653 | 82.3 | C.V.O. Bartlett | Ind Prog | 19,540 | 53.2 |
|  |  |  | P.G. Heathcoat-Amory | C | 17,208 | 46.8 |
|  |  |  |  |  | 2,332 | 6.4 |
| 1945 | 53,896 | 72.7 | C.V.O. Bartlett | Ind Prog | 17,937 | 45.8 |
|  |  |  | G. Wills | C | 15,625 | 39.9 |
|  |  |  | N. Corkhill | Lab | 5,613 | 14.3 |
|  |  |  |  |  | 2,312 | 5.9 |

Note:—

1938: Bartlett was supported by the local Labour Party and stood on a 'Popular Front' programme. He also received support from the local Liberal Association and when the Common Wealth Movement was formed in 1942, he became a member of the National Committee but resigned two months later.

# SOMERSET, FROME  [438]

| Election | Electors | T'out | Candidate | Party | Votes | % |
|---|---|---|---|---|---|---|
| 1918 | 35,222 | 67.7 | P.A. Hurd | Co C | 11,118 | 46.6 |
|  |  |  | E. Gill | Lab | 10,454 | 43.9 |
|  |  |  | †Sir J.E. Barlow, Bt. | L | 2,004* | 8.4 |
|  |  |  | T.M.H. Kincaid-Smith | Nat P | 258* | 1.1 |
|  |  |  |  |  | 664 | 2.7 |
| 1922 | 35,698 | 82.2 | P.A. Hurd | C | 15,017 | 51.2 |
|  |  |  | E. Gill | Lab | 14,311 | 48.8 |
|  |  |  |  |  | 706 | 2.4 |
| 1923 | 36,628 | 79.7 | F. Gould | Lab | 15,902 | 54.4 |
|  |  |  | P.A. Hurd | C | 13,306 | 45.6 |
|  |  |  |  |  | 2,596 | 8.8 |
| 1924 | 37,438 | 82.9 | G.K. Peto | C | 16,397 | 52.8 |
|  |  |  | F. Gould | Lab | 14,652 | 47.2 |
|  |  |  |  |  | 1,745 | 5.6 |
| 1929 | 47,039 | 86.5 | F. Gould | Lab | 18,524 | 45.5 |
|  |  |  | G.K. Peto | C | 16,378 | 40.3 |
|  |  |  | C.S. Stratton-Hallett | L | 5,774 | 14.2 |
|  |  |  |  |  | 2,146 | 5.2 |
| 1931 | 48,778 | 87.3 | Viscount Weymouth | C | 24,858 | 58.3 |
|  |  |  | F. Gould | Lab | 17,748 | 41.7 |
|  |  |  |  |  | 7,110 | 16.6 |
| 1935 | 51,582 | 82.5 | Mrs. M.C. Tate | C | 19,684 | 46.3 |
|  |  |  | R.W.G. Mackay | Lab | 18,690 | 43.9 |
|  |  |  | P.W. Hopkins | L | 4,177* | 9.8 |
|  |  |  |  |  | 994 | 2.4 |
| 1945 | 68,954 | 78.3 | W.J. Farthing | Lab | 29,735 | 55.1 |
|  |  |  | Mrs. M.C. Tate | C | 24,228 | 44.9 |
|  |  |  |  |  | 5,507 | 10.2 |

| Election | Electors | T'out | Candidate | Party | Votes | % |
|----------|----------|-------|-----------|-------|-------|---|
| 1918 | 28,845 | 60.4 | †D.F. Boles | Co C | 12,619 | 72.4 |
|  |  |  | Rev. G.S. Woods | Lab | 4,816 | 27.6 |
|  |  |  |  |  | 7,803 | 44.8 |
| [Resignation] |  |  |  |  |  |  |
| 1921 (8/4) | 28,976† | 73.5 | Rt. Hon. Sir A.S.T. Griffith-Boscawen | Co C | 12,994 | 61.1 |
|  |  |  | J. Lunnon | Lab | 8,290 | 38.9 |
|  |  |  |  |  | 4,704 | 22.2 |
| 1922 | 29,567 | 79.1 | J.H. Simpson | L | 13,195 | 56.4 |
|  |  |  | Rt. Hon. Sir A.S.T. Griffith-Boscawen | C | 10,182 | 43.6 |
|  |  |  |  |  | 3,013 | 12.8 |
| 1923 | 30,088 | 82.6 | J.H. Simpson | L | 13,053 | 52.5 |
|  |  |  | A.H. Gault | C | 11,798 | 47.5 |
|  |  |  |  |  | 1,255 | 5.0 |
| 1924 | 31,235 | 85.6 | A.H. Gault | C | 13,930 | 52.1 |
|  |  |  | J.H. Simpson | L | 10,381 | 38.8 |
|  |  |  | Rev. G.S. Woods | Lab | 2,441* | 9.1 |
|  |  |  |  |  | 3,549 | 13.3 |
| 1929 | 39,926 | 82.2 | A.H. Gault | C | 15,083 | 45.9 |
|  |  |  | W.R. Rea | L | 11,121 | 33.9 |
|  |  |  | J.A. Sparks | Lab | 6,615 | 20.2 |
|  |  |  |  |  | 3,962 | 12.0 |
| 1931 | 41,006 | 75.4 | A.H. Gault | C | 22,564 | 72.9 |
|  |  |  | Dr. F.G. Bushnell | Lab | 8,367 | 27.1 |
|  |  |  |  |  | 14,197 | 45.8 |
| 1935 | 42,437 | 72.3 | E.T.R. Wickham | C | 19,443 | 63.4 |
|  |  |  | J. Lunnon | Lab | 11,219 | 36.6 |
|  |  |  |  |  | 8,224 | 26.8 |
| 1945 | 51,681 | 73.2 | V.J. Collins | Lab | 19,976 | 52.8 |
|  |  |  | E.T.R. Wickham | C | 17,858 | 47.2 |
|  |  |  |  |  | 2,118 | 5.6 |

Note:—

1921:  Griffith-Boscawen was Minister of Agriculture and Fisheries.

| Election | Electors | T'out | Candidate | Party | Votes | % |
|---|---|---|---|---|---|---|
| 1918 | 26,951 | 65.0 | †H. Greer | Co C | 9,786 | 55.8 |
| | | | J.C. Morland | L | 6,935 | 39.6 |
| | | | G.C.S. Hodgson | Nat P | 804* | 4.6 |
| | | | | | 2,851 | 16.2 |
| 1922 | 27,526 | 77.8 | R. Bruford | C | 10,210 | 47.7 |
| | | | A.L. Hobhouse | L | 7,156 | 33.4 |
| | | | L. Smith | Lab | 4,048 | 18.9 |
| | | | | | 3,054 | 14.3 |
| 1923 | 28,356 | 79.1 | A.L. Hobhouse | L | 10,818 | 48.2 |
| | | | R. Bruford | C | 9,909 | 44.2 |
| | | | C.H. Whitlow | Lab | 1,713* | 7.6 |
| | | | | | 909 | 4.0 |
| 1924 | 29,249 | 82.2 | Rt. Hon. Sir R.A. Sanders, Bt. | C | 12,642 | 52.6 |
| | | | A.L. Hobhouse | L | 8,668 | 36.1 |
| | | | W.T. Young | Lab | 2,726* | 11.3 |
| | | | | | 3,974 | 16.5 |
| 1929 | 36,219 | 82.5 | A.J. Muirhead | C | 13,026 | 43.6 |
| | | | A.L. Hobhouse | L | 12,382 | 41.4 |
| | | | Mrs. R.D.Q. Davies | Lab | 4,472 | 15.0 |
| | | | | | 644 | 2.2 |
| 1931 | 36,802 | 81.9 | A.J. Muirhead | C | 17,711 | 58.7 |
| | | | J.W.H. Thompson | L | 12,440 | 41.3 |
| | | | | | 5,271 | 17.4 |
| 1935 | 37,836 | 73.7 | A.J. Muirhead | C | 14,898 | 53.4 |
| | | | A.H. Jones | L | 7,277 | 26.1 |
| | | | W.J. Waring | Lab | 5,716 | 20.5 |
| | | | | | 7,621 | 27.3 |
| [Death] | | | | | | |
| 1939 (13/12) | | | D.C. Boles | C | Unopp. | |
| 1945 | 41,980 | 74.9 | D.C. Boles | C | 13,004 | 41.4 |
| | | | C. Morgan | Lab | 10,539 | 33.5 |
| | | | Lady Violet Bonham Carter | L | 7,910 | 25.1 |
| | | | | | 2,465 | 7.9 |

| Election | Electors | T'out | Candidate | Party | Votes | % |
|---|---|---|---|---|---|---|
| 1918 | 33,894 | 60.8 | †Sir G.A.H. Wills, Bt. | Co C | 13,494 | 65.5 |
|  |  |  | E.H. Thruston | L | 7,104 | 34.5 |
|  |  |  |  |  | 6,390 | 31.0 |
| 1922 | 36,234 | 77.9 | Lord Erskine | C | 15,552 | 55.1 |
|  |  |  | F.E.J. Murrell | L | 12,678 | 44.9 |
|  |  |  |  |  | 2,874 | 10.2 |
| 1923 | 37,588 | 78.6 | F.E.J. Murrell | L | 15,223 | 51.5 |
|  |  |  | Lord Erskine | C | 14,318 | 48.5 |
|  |  |  |  |  | 905 | 3.0 |
| 1924 | 39,457 | 81.7 | Lord Erskine | C | 17,987 | 55.8 |
|  |  |  | F.E.J. Murrell | L | 12,895 | 40.0 |
|  |  |  | R. Neft | Lab | 1,343* | 4.2 |
|  |  |  |  |  | 5,092 | 15.8 |
| 1929 | 55,135 | 77.8 | Lord Erskine | C | 21,898 | 51.1 |
|  |  |  | W.E. Morse | L | 16,219 | 37.8 |
|  |  |  | Mrs. C.E.M. Borrett | Lab | 4,766* | 11.1 |
|  |  |  |  |  | 5,679 | 13.3 |
| 1931 | 57,326 | 71.8 | Lord Erskine | C | 35,255 | 85.7 |
|  |  |  | W.B. Craig | Lab | 5,905 | 14.3 |
|  |  |  |  |  | 29,350 | 71.4 |

[Resignation on appointment as Governor of Madras]

| Election | Electors | T'out | Candidate | Party | Votes | % |
|---|---|---|---|---|---|---|
| 1934 | 60,213 | 57.2 | I.L. Orr-Ewing | C | 21,203 | 61.5 |
| (26/6) |  |  | H.F. Scott-Stokes | L | 7,551 | 21.9 |
|  |  |  | A.E. Millett | Lab | 5,715 | 16.6 |
|  |  |  |  |  | 13,652 | 39.6 |
| 1935 | 63,617 | 66.4 | I.L. Orr-Ewing | C | 27,735 | 65.6 |
|  |  |  | H.F. Scott-Stokes | L | 7,883 | 18.7 |
|  |  |  | G.H. Elvin | Lab | 6,625 | 15.7 |
|  |  |  |  |  | 19,852 | 46.9 |
| 1945 | 84,287 | 73.6 | I.L. Orr-Ewing | C | 30,730 | 49.5 |
|  |  |  | H.B.O. Cardew | Lab | 20,542 | 33.1 |
|  |  |  | S. Sanger | L | 10,804 | 17.4 |
|  |  |  |  |  | 10,188 | 16.4 |

| Election | Electors | T'out | Candidate | Party | Votes | % |
|---|---|---|---|---|---|---|
| 1918 | 33,747 | 61.8 | †Hon. A.N.H.M. Herbert | Co C | 10,522 | 50.4 |
| | | | W.T. Kelly | Lab | 7,589 | 36.4 |
| | | | J.R. Brough | L | 2,743 | 13.2 |
| | | | | | 2,933 | 14.0 |
| 1922 | 34,321 | 73.0 | Hon. A.N.H.M. Herbert | C | 15,468 | 61.8 |
| | | | W.T. Kelly | Lab | 9,581 | 38.2 |
| | | | | | 5,887 | 23.6 |
| [Death] | | | | | | |
| 1923 (30/10) | 35,103 | 80.8 | G.F. Davies | C | 13,205 | 46.5 |
| | | | W.T. Kelly | Lab | 8,140 | 28.7 |
| | | | C.W. Cohen | L | 7,024 | 24.8 |
| | | | | | 5,065 | 17.8 |
| 1923 | 35,103 | 81.1 | G.F. Davies | C | 12,690 | 44.6 |
| | | | C.W. Cohen | L | 10,715 | 37.6 |
| | | | W.T. Kelly | Lab | 5,080 | 17.8 |
| | | | | | 1,975 | 7.0 |
| 1924 | 35,872 | 83.6 | G.F. Davies | C | 14,477 | 48.3 |
| | | | C.W. Cohen | L | 9,320 | 31.1 |
| | | | J.L. George | Lab | 6,179 | 20.6 |
| | | | | | 5,157 | 17.2 |
| 1929 | 45,321 | 83.4 | G.F. Davies | C | 15,526 | 41.1 |
| | | | P.H. Heffer | L | 14,679 | 38.8 |
| | | | F.C.R. Douglas | Lab | 7,609 | 20.1 |
| | | | | | 847 | 2.3 |
| 1931 | 47,053 | 84.1 | G.F. Davies | C | 20,165 | 50.9 |
| | | | P.H. Heffer | L | 14,046 | 35.5 |
| | | | H.H. Fyfe | Lab | 5,377 | 13.6 |
| | | | | | 6,119 | 15.4 |
| 1935 | 48,425 | 77.8 | G.F. Davies | C | 17,640 | 46.8 |
| | | | J.D. Bateman | L | 12,482 | 33.1 |
| | | | A.E. Millett | Lab | 7,567 | 20.1 |
| | | | | | 5,158 | 13.7 |
| 1945 | 59,217 | 75.2 | W.H. Kingsmill | C | 16,815 | 37.8 |
| | | | M. MacPherson | Lab | 16,641 | 37.4 |
| | | | J.D. Bateman | L | 11,057 | 24.8 |
| | | | | | 174 | 0.4 |

# STAFFORDSHIRE, BURTON [443]

| Election | Electors | T'out | Candidate | Party | Votes | % |
|----------|----------|-------|-----------|-------|-------|---|
| 1918 | | | †J. Gretton | Co C (C) | Unopp. | |
| 1922 | | | J. Gretton | C | Unopp. | |
| 1923 | | | J. Gretton | C | Unopp. | |
| 1924 | 35,599 | 77.8 | J. Gretton | C | 20,550 | 74.2 |
| | | | F. Thoresby | Lab | 7,141 | 25.8 |
| | | | | | 13,409 | 48.4 |
| 1929 | 46,099 | 75.3 | Rt. Hon. J. Gretton | C | 18,243 | 52.6 |
| | | | W.T. Paling | Lab | 10,511 | 30.3 |
| | | | I.B. Lloyd | L | 5,943 | 17.1 |
| | | | | | 7,732 | 22.3 |
| 1931 | 46,819 | 74.6 | Rt. Hon. J. Gretton | C | 26,117 | 74.7 |
| | | | W.T. Paling | Lab | 8,832 | 25.3 |
| | | | | | 17,285 | 49.4 |
| 1935 | 48,110 | 65.6 | Rt. Hon. J. Gretton | C | 23,539 | 74.5 |
| | | | Mrs. G.N. Paling | Lab | 8,041 | 25.5 |
| | | | | | 15,498 | 49.0 |
| [Resignation] | | | | | | |
| 1943 (2/7) | | | J.F. Gretton | C | Unopp. | |
| 1945 | 53,587 | 66.8 | A.W. Lyne | Lab | 18,288 | 51.1 |
| | | | J.F. Gretton | C | 17,528 | 48.9 |
| | | | | | 760 | 2.2 |

| Election | Electors | T'out | Candidate | Party | Votes | % |
|---|---|---|---|---|---|---|
| 1918 | 37,284 | 41.7 | †J. Parker | Co Lab | 8,068 | 51.8 |
| | | | Sir W.B. Rees | L | 7,493 | 48.2 |
| | | | | | 575 | 3.6 |
| 1922 | 40,273 | 66.9 | W.M. Adamson | Lab | 9,889 | 36.8 |
| | | | J. Parker | Ind | 9,116 | 33.8 |
| | | | H.S. Abrahamson | L | 7,928 | 29.4 |
| | | | | | 773 | 3.0 |
| 1923 | 40,948 | 70.5 | W.M. Adamson | Lab | 11,956 | 41.4 |
| | | | W. Thorneycroft | C | 9,438 | 32.7 |
| | | | G. Le M. Mander | L | 7,465 | 25.9 |
| | | | | | 2,518 | 8.7 |
| 1924 | 42,473 | 74.2 | W.M. Adamson | Lab | 16,347 | 51.9 |
| | | | W. Thorneycroft | C | 15,166 | 48.1 |
| | | | | | 1,181 | 3.8 |
| 1929 | 62,871 | 77.5 | W.M. Adamson | Lab | 26,388 | 54.2 |
| | | | Hon. R.E.B. Beaumont | C | 15,055 | 30.9 |
| | | | Rev. A. Ray | L | 7,282 | 14.9 |
| | | | | | 11,333 | 23.3 |
| 1931 | 66,268 | 76.0 | Mrs. S.A. Ward | C | 27,498 | 54.6 |
| | | | W.M. Adamson | Lab | 22,833 | 45.4 |
| | | | | | 4,665 | 9.2 |
| 1935 | 76,735 | 71.4 | W.M. Adamson | Lab | 27,922 | 51.0 |
| | | | Mrs. S.A. Ward | C | 26,876 | 49.0 |
| | | | | | 1,046 | 2.0 |
| 1945 | 109,455 | 71.3 | Miss J. Lee | Lab | 48,859 | 62.6 |
| | | | C.W. Shelford | C | 29,225 | 37.4 |
| | | | | | 19,634 | 25.2 |

Note:—

1918: Parker was incorrectly designated as a Coalition Liberal in the official list of Coalition candidates.

## STAFFORDSHIRE, KINGSWINFORD  [445]

| Election | Electors | T'out | Candidate | Party | Votes | % |
|---|---|---|---|---|---|---|
| 1918 | 37,924 | 57.6 | C.H. Sitch | Lab | 10,397 | 47.6 |
| | | | A.E. Beck | C | 7,509 | 34.4 |
| | | | H.E. Brown | L | 3,943 | 18.0 |
| | | | | | 2,888 | 13.2 |
| 1922 | 39,306 | 75.2 | C.H. Sitch | Lab | 15,232 | 51.6 |
| | | | G.H. Beyfus | NL | 14,313 | 48.4 |
| | | | | | 919 | 3.2 |
| 1923 | 40,045 | 76.6 | C.H. Sitch | Lab | 15,174 | 49.5 |
| | | | W.H. Webb | C | 10,862 | 35.4 |
| | | | C.P. Blackwell | L | 4,633 | 15.1 |
| | | | | | 4,312 | 14.1 |
| 1924 | 40,470 | 82.6 | C.H. Sitch | Lab | 17,235 | 51.5 |
| | | | W.H. Webb | C | 16,208 | 48.5 |
| | | | | | 1,027 | 3.0 |
| 1929 | 53,530 | 79.0 | C.H. Sitch | Lab | 22,479 | 53.2 |
| | | | S.E. Garcke | C | 12,151 | 28.7 |
| | | | A.W. Bowkett | L | 7,639 | 18.1 |
| | | | | | 10,328 | 24.5 |
| 1931 | 55,138 | 75.1 | A.L.S. Todd | C | 21,934 | 52.9 |
| | | | C.H. Sitch | Lab | 19,495 | 47.1 |
| | | | | | 2,439 | 5.8 |
| 1935 | 58,490 | 71.5 | A. Henderson | Lab | 20,925 | 50.0 |
| | | | A.L.S. Todd | C | 20,909 | 50.0 |
| | | | | | 16 | 0.0 |
| 1945 | 67,293 | 73.7 | A. Henderson | Lab | 34,307 | 69.2 |
| | | | E.G. Taylor | C | 15,297 | 30.8 |
| | | | | | 19,010 | 38.4 |

| Election | Electors | T'out | Candidate | Party | Votes | % |
|---|---|---|---|---|---|---|
| 1918 | 30,055 | 67.7 | W. Bromfield | Lab | 10,510 | 51.7 |
|  |  |  | Sir G.R.A. Gaunt | Co L | 9,832 | 48.3 |
|  |  |  |  |  | 678 | 3.4 |
| 1922 | 32,175 | 78.7 | W. Bromfield | Lab | 12,857 | 50.8 |
|  |  |  | E. Hill | C | 12,473 | 49.2 |
|  |  |  |  |  | 384 | 1.6 |
| 1923 | 33,596 | 77.3 | W. Bromfield | Lab | 13,913 | 53.6 |
|  |  |  | E. Hill | C | 12,066 | 46.4 |
|  |  |  |  |  | 1,847 | 7.2 |
| 1924 | 34,686 | 79.5 | W. Bromfield | Lab | 14,256 | 51.7 |
|  |  |  | Hon. T.P.H. Cholmondeley | C | 13,305 | 48.3 |
|  |  |  |  |  | 951 | 3.4 |
| 1929 | 46,588 | 82.4 | W. Bromfield | Lab | 22,458 | 58.5 |
|  |  |  | E.G.W. Hulton | C | 15,953 | 41.5 |
|  |  |  |  |  | 6,505 | 17.0 |
| 1931 | 48,653 | 80.3 | A. Ratcliffe | C | 20,067 | 51.4 |
|  |  |  | W. Bromfield | Lab | 18,979 | 48.6 |
|  |  |  |  |  | 1,088 | 2.8 |
| 1935 | 54,412 | 75.1 | W. Bromfield | Lab | 23,432 | 57.4 |
|  |  |  | L.M. Thomas | N Lab | 17,419 | 42.6 |
|  |  |  |  |  | 6,013 | 14.8 |
| 1945 | 63,163 | 76.7 | H. Davies | Lab | 32,567 | 67.2 |
|  |  |  | T.W. Gimson | C | 15,904 | 32.8 |
|  |  |  |  |  | 16,663 | 34.4 |

| Election | Electors | T'out | Candidate | Party | Votes | % |
|---|---|---|---|---|---|---|
| 1918 | 29,535 | 51.5 | †Sir T.C.T. Warner, Bt. | Co L | 9,677 | 63.6 |
| | | | T. Riley | Lab | 5,548 | 36.4 |
| | | | | | 4,129 | 27.2 |
| 1922 | 32,100 | 62.0 | Sir T.C.T. Warner, Bt. | NL | 10,594 | 53.2 |
| | | | W.J. French | Lab | 9,316 | 46.8 |
| | | | | | 1,278 | 6.4 |
| 1923 | 32,580 | 69.7 | F. Hodges | Lab | 11,029 | 48.5 |
| | | | R.R. Wilson | C | 9,010 | 39.7 |
| | | | T.E. Morris | L | 2,683* | 11.8 |
| | | | | | 2,019 | 8.8 |
| 1924 | 33,751 | 80.3 | R.R. Wilson | C | 14,588 | 53.8 |
| | | | F. Hodges | Lab | 12,512 | 46.2 |
| | | | | | 2,076 | 7.6 |
| 1929 | 43,888 | 80.0 | J.A. Lovat-Fraser | Lab (N Lab) | 14,965 | 42.6 |
| | | | S. Samuel | C | 11,511 | 32.8 |
| | | | E.B. de Hamel | L | 8,643 | 24.6 |
| | | | | | 3,454 | 9.8 |
| 1931 | 57,589 | 73.7 | J.A. Lovat-Fraser | N Lab | 26,669 | 62.8 |
| | | | G.H. Jones | Lab | 15,790 | 37.2 |
| | | | | | 10,879 | 25.6 |
| 1935 | 68,064 | 64.2 | J.A. Lovat-Fraser | N Lab | 23,489 | 53.8 |
| | | | G.H. Jones | Lab | 20,191 | 46.2 |
| | | | | | 3,298 | 7.6 |
| [Death] | | | | | | |
| 1938 | 80,137 | 57.8 | C.C. Poole | Lab | 23,586 | 50.9 |
| (5/5) | | | G.B. Craddock | N Lab | 22,760 | 49.1 |
| | | | | | 826 | 1.8 |
| 1945 | 108,471* | 71.5 | C.C. Poole | Lab | 42,806 | 55.2 |
| | | | G.B. Craddock | Nat | 26,235 | 33.8 |
| | | | R.A. Lamb | L | 8,533* | 11.0 |
| | | | | | 16,571 | 21.4 |

| Election | Electors | T'out | Candidate | Party | Votes | % |
|---|---|---|---|---|---|---|
| 1918 | 23,140 | 54.0 | †Hon. W.G.A. Ormsby-Gore | Co C | 8,304 | 66.4 |
| | | | W. Meakin | L | 4,203 | 33.6 |
| | | | | | 4,101 | 32.8 |
| 1922 | 24,317 | 76.7 | Hon. W.G.A. Ormsby-Gore | C | 10,990 | 58.9 |
| | | | W. Holmes | Lab | 7,672 | 41.1 |
| | | | | | 3,318 | 17.8 |
| 1923 | 25,024 | 72.9 | Hon. W.G.A. Ormsby-Gore | C | 9,823 | 53.9 |
| | | | W.T. Scott | Lab | 8,412 | 46.1 |
| | | | | | 1,411 | 7.8 |
| 1924 | 25,260 | 79.1 | Hon. W.G.A. Ormsby-Gore | C | 12,404 | 62.1 |
| | | | W.T. Scott | Lab | 7,571 | 37.9 |
| | | | | | 4,833 | 24.2 |
| 1929 | 33,420 | 81.8 | Rt. Hon. W.G.A. Ormsby-Gore | C | 12,324 | 45.1 |
| | | | L. Smith | Lab | 10,011 | 36.6 |
| | | | Rev. A.S. Leyland | L | 5,000 | 18.3 |
| | | | | | 2,313 | 8.5 |
| 1931 | 34,535 | 78.5 | Rt. Hon. W.G.A. Ormsby-Gore | C | 18,467 | 68.1 |
| | | | L. Smith | Lab | 8,640 | 31.9 |
| | | | | | 9,827 | 36.2 |
| 1935 | 36,298 | 79.0 | Rt. Hon. W.G.A. Ormsby-Gore | C | 16,175 | 56.4 |
| | | | F.G. Lloyd | Lab | 12,514 | 43.6 |
| | | | | | 3,661 | 12.8 |

[Succession to the Peerage — Lord Harlech]

| Election | Electors | T'out | Candidate | Party | Votes | % |
|---|---|---|---|---|---|---|
| 1938 (9/6) | 37,719 | 77.1 | G.E.P. Thorneycroft | C | 16,754 | 57.6 |
| | | | F.G. Lloyd | Lab | 12,346 | 42.4 |
| | | | | | 4,408 | 15.2 |
| 1945 | 43,314 | 79.5 | S.T. Swingler | Lab | 17,923 | 52.1 |
| | | | G.E.P. Thorneycroft | C | 16,500 | 47.9 |
| | | | | | 1,423 | 4.2 |

## STAFFORDSHIRE, STONE [449]

| Election | Electors | T'out | Candidate | Party | Votes | % |
|----------|----------|-------|-----------|-------|-------|---|
| 1918 | 26,113 | 62.0 | Sir S.H. Child, Bt. | Co C | 7,568 | 46.7 |
|  |  |  | G. Townsend | L | 5,573 | 34.4 |
|  |  |  | J.Q. Lamb | Agric | 3,056 | 18.9 |
|  |  |  |  |  | 1,995 | 12.3 |
| 1922 | 28,273 | 71.4 | J.Q. Lamb | C | 7,742 | 38.3 |
|  |  |  | G. Townsend | L | 7,198 | 35.7 |
|  |  |  | W.L. Steel | Agric | 5,243 | 26.0 |
|  |  |  |  |  | 544 | 2.6 |
| 1923 | 29,151 | 67.5 | J.Q. Lamb | C | 10,001 | 50.8 |
|  |  |  | W. Meakin | L | 9,687 | 49.2 |
|  |  |  |  |  | 314 | 1.6 |
| 1924 | 29,994 | 74.9 | J.Q. Lamb | C | 12,856 | 57.3 |
|  |  |  | W. Meakin | L | 5,351 | 23.8 |
|  |  |  | C.A. Brook | Lab | 4,245 | 18.9 |
|  |  |  |  |  | 7,505 | 33.5 |
| 1929 | 41,268 | 76.9 | J.Q. Lamb | C | 13,965 | 44.0 |
|  |  |  | W. Meakin | L | 8,975 | 28.3 |
|  |  |  | G. Belt | Lab | 8,792 | 27.7 |
|  |  |  |  |  | 4,990 | 15.7 |
| 1931 | 43,847 | 74.6 | Sir J.Q. Lamb | C | 20,327 | 62.1 |
|  |  |  | W. Meakin | L | 6,407 | 19.6 |
|  |  |  | W.I. Simcock | Lab | 5,993 | 18.3 |
|  |  |  |  |  | 13,920 | 42.5 |
| 1935 | 50,708 | 66.3 | Sir J.Q. Lamb | C | 20,498 | 61.0 |
|  |  |  | W.I. Simcock | Lab | 13,099 | 39.0 |
|  |  |  |  |  | 7,399 | 22.0 |
| 1945 | 65,145 | 72.6 | Hon. H.C.P.J. Fraser | C | 20,279 | 42.9 |
|  |  |  | W.I. Simcock | Lab | 18,173 | 38.4 |
|  |  |  | J.H. Wedgwood | L | 8,853 | 18.7 |
|  |  |  |  |  | 2,106 | 4.5 |

# SUFFOLK (East), EYE  [450]

| Election | Electors | T'out | Candidate | Party | Votes | % |
|---|---|---|---|---|---|---|
| 1918 | 33,399 | 49.2 | A. Lyle-Samuel | Co L (L) | 10,072 | 61.3 |
| | | | F.W. French | C | 6,362 | 38.7 |
| | | | | | 3,710 | 22.6 |
| 1922 | 32,579 | 54.0 | A. Lyle-Samuel | L | 10,556 | 60.0 |
| | | | S.G. Howard | NL | 7,025 | 40.0 |
| | | | | | 3,531 | 20.0 |
| 1923 | 32,999 | 70.9 | Lord Huntingfield | C | 11,172 | 47.7 |
| | | | A. Lyle-Samuel | L | 9,244 | 39.5 |
| | | | C.W. Kendall | Lab | 2,984 | 12.8 |
| | | | | | 1,928 | 8.2 |
| 1924 | 33,841 | 74.5 | Lord Huntingfield | C | 13,450 | 53.3 |
| | | | Sir T.R. Bethell | L | 7,441 | 29.5 |
| | | | C.W. Kendall | Lab | 4,329 | 17.2 |
| | | | | | 6,009 | 23.8 |
| 1929 | 40,340 | 78.2 | E.L. Granville | L (NL) | 13,944 | 44.3 |
| | | | A.G. Soames | C | 12,880 | 40.8 |
| | | | O. Aves | Lab | 4,709 | 14.9 |
| | | | | | 1,064 | 3.5 |
| 1931 | | | E.L. Granville | NL | Unopp. | |
| 1935 | 41,334 | 70.7 | E.L. Granville | NL (Ind) (L) | 21,606 | 73.9 |
| | | | H.L. Self | Lab | 7,613 | 26.1 |
| | | | | | 13,993 | 47.8 |
| 1945 | 43,218 | 71.6 | E.L. Granville | L | 11,899 | 38.5 |
| | | | A.M. Borthwick | C | 10,950 | 35.4 |
| | | | R.B. Collingson | Lab | 8,089 | 26.1 |
| | | | | | 949 | 3.1 |

# SUFFOLK (East), LOWESTOFT [451]

| Election | Electors | T'out | Candidate | Party | Votes | % |
|---|---|---|---|---|---|---|
| 1918 | | | †Sir E. Beauchamp, Bt. | Co L | Unopp. | |
| 1922 | 35,012 | 71.0 | G. Rentoul | C | 14,154 | 57.0 |
| | | | B.C. Beauchamp | NL | 6,205 | 24.9 |
| | | | R.A. Mellanby | Lab | 4,511 | 18.1 |
| | | | | | 7,949 | 32.1 |
| 1923 | 35,881 | 67.6 | G. Rentoul | C | 11,103 | 45.8 |
| | | | F.G. Paterson | L | 8,362 | 34.5 |
| | | | R.A. Mellanby | Lab | 4,788 | 19.7 |
| | | | | | 2,741 | 11.3 |
| 1924 | 36,321 | 73.0 | G. Rentoul | C | 13,422 | 50.6 |
| | | | R.A. Mellanby | Lab | 6,570 | 24.8 |
| | | | F.G. Paterson | L | 6,532 | 24.6 |
| | | | | | 6,852 | 25.8 |
| 1929 | 46,359 | 73.8 | Sir G. Rentoul | C | 13,624 | 39.8 |
| | | | A.E. Owen-Jones | L | 10,707 | 31.3 |
| | | | B.W.R. Hall | Lab | 9,903 | 28.9 |
| | | | | | 2,917 | 8.5 |
| 1931 | 47,737 | 70.8 | Sir G. Rentoul | C | 22,886 | 67.8 |
| | | | E.J.C. Neep | Lab | 10,894 | 32.2 |
| | | | | | 11,992 | 35.6 |

[Resignation on appointment as a Metropolitan Police Magistrate]

| | | | | | | |
|---|---|---|---|---|---|---|
| 1934 | 48,900 | 67.9 | P.C. Loftus | C | 15,912 | 48.0 |
| (15/2) | | | Rev. R.W. Sorensen | Lab | 13,992 | 42.1 |
| | | | W. Smith | L | 3,304* | 9.9 |
| | | | | | 1,920 | 5.9 |
| 1935 | 49,871 | 69.0 | P.C. Loftus | C | 21,064 | 61.2 |
| | | | F.J. Wise | Lab | 13,348 | 38.8 |
| | | | | | 7,716 | 22.4 |
| 1945 | 44,764 | 67.7 | E. Evans | Lab | 12,759 | 42.1 |
| | | | P.C. Loftus | C | 10,996 | 36.3 |
| | | | M.P. Crosse | L | 6,545 | 21.6 |
| | | | | | 1,763 | 5.8 |

## SUFFOLK (East), WOODBRIDGE   [452]

| Election | Electors | T'out | Candidate | Party | Votes | % |
|---|---|---|---|---|---|---|
| 1918 | 30,413 | 51.0 | †R.F. Peel | Co C | 8,654 | 55.8 |
| | | | W.R. Elliston | L | 6,842 | 44.2 |
| | | | | | 1,812 | 11.6 |

[Resignation on appointment as Governor of St. Helena]

| | | | | | | |
|---|---|---|---|---|---|---|
| 1920 (28/7) | 30,300† | 61.4 | Sir A.C. Churchman, Bt. | Co C | 9,898 | 53.2 |
| | | | H.D. Harben | Lab | 8,707 | 46.8 |
| | | | | | 1,191 | 6.4 |
| 1922 | 31,646 | 69.1 | Sir A.C. Churchman, Bt. | C | 12,396 | 56.7 |
| | | | E.J.C. Neep | Lab | 9,476 | 43.3 |
| | | | | | 2,920 | 13.4 |
| 1923 | 32,067 | 70.9 | Sir A.C. Churchman, Bt. | C | 10,606 | 46.7 |
| | | | W.R. Elliston | L | 7,328 | 32.2 |
| | | | E.J.C. Neep | Lab | 4,810 | 21.1 |
| | | | | | 3,278 | 14.5 |
| 1924 | 32,869 | 74.3 | Sir A.C. Churchman, Bt. | C | 13,419 | 54.9 |
| | | | W.R. Elliston | L | 7,008 | 28.7 |
| | | | S. Mayer | Lab | 3,998 | 16.4 |
| | | | | | 6,411 | 26.2 |
| 1929 | 43,181 | 73.3 | F.G.C. Fison | C | 15,231 | 48.1 |
| | | | R.T.B. Fulford | L | 10,904 | 34.5 |
| | | | L. Spero | Lab | 5,507 | 17.4 |
| | | | | | 4,327 | 13.6 |
| 1931 | 44,686 | 70.6 | W. Ross Taylor | C | 25,654 | 81.3 |
| | | | Mrs. I.M.N. Keeble | Lab | 5,885 | 18.7 |
| | | | | | 19,769 | 62.6 |
| 1935 | 46,703 | 67.5 | W. Ross Taylor | C | 22,715 | 72.1 |
| | | | A.V. Smith | Lab | 8,808 | 27.9 |
| | | | | | 13,907 | 44.2 |
| 1945 | 47,891 | 71.4 | Hon. J.H. Hare | C | 16,073 | 47.0 |
| | | | J.M. Stewart | Lab | 11,380 | 33.3 |
| | | | D.B. Law | L | 6,740 | 19.7 |
| | | | | | 4,693 | 13.7 |

| Election | Electors | T'out | Candidate | Party | Votes | % |
|---|---|---|---|---|---|---|
| 1918 | | | †Hon. W.E. Guinness | Co C | Unopp. | |
| 1922 | | | Hon. W.E. Guinness | C | Unopp. | |
| 1923 | | | Hon. W.E. Guinness | C | Unopp. | |
| 1924 | 31,138 | 81.8 | Rt. Hon. W.E. Guinness | C | 16,073 | 63.1 |
| | | | J.A. Day | L | 9,392 | 36.9 |
| | | | | | 6,681 | 26.2 |

[Appointed Minister of Agriculture and Fisheries]

| | | | | | | |
|---|---|---|---|---|---|---|
| 1925 | 31,648 | 73.9 | Rt. Hon. W.E. Guinness | C | 14,700 | 62.8 |
| (1/12) | | | G. Nicholls | L | 8,703 | 37.2 |
| | | | | | 5,997 | 25.6 |
| 1929 | 38,938 | 77.8 | Rt. Hon. W.E. Guinness | C | 16,462 | 54.4 |
| | | | M.D. Lyon | L | 11,344 | 37.4 |
| | | | P. Astins | Lab | 2,490* | 8.2 |
| | | | | | 5,118 | 17.0 |
| 1931 | | | F.F.A. Heilgers | C | Unopp. | |
| 1935 | | | F.F.A. Heilgers | C | Unopp. | |

[Death]

| | | | | | | |
|---|---|---|---|---|---|---|
| 1944 | 40,971 | 50.8 | E.M. Keatinge | C | 11,705 | 56.2 |
| (29/2) | | | Mrs. M.I.C. Ashby | Ind L | 9,121 | 43.8 |
| | | | | | 2,584 | 12.4 |
| 1945 | 45,882 | 67.2 | G.B. Clifton-Brown | C | 15,013 | 48.8 |
| | | | Miss C.A.W. McCall | Lab | 9,195 | 29.8 |
| | | | H.C. Drayton | L | 5,863 | 19.0 |
| | | | E.C.G. England | CW | 750* | 2.4 |
| | | | | | 5,818 | 19.0 |

Note:—

1944: Mrs. Ashby was supported by the Common Wealth Movement.

## SUFFOLK (West), SUDBURY  [454]

| Election | Electors | T'out | Candidate | Party | Votes | % |
|---|---|---|---|---|---|---|
| 1918 | 26,437 | 48.4 | S.G. Howard | L (Co L) | 6,656 | 52.1 |
|  |  |  | R.G. Proby | Co C | 5,746 | 44.9 |
|  |  |  | J.R. Hicks | Agric | 390* | 3.0 |
|  |  |  |  |  | 910 | 7.2 |
| 1922 | 26,195 | 59.3 | H. Mercer | C | 7,298 | 47.0 |
|  |  |  | S.G. Howard | NL | 5,410 | 34.9 |
|  |  |  | E.W. Tanner | L | 2,813 | 18.1 |
|  |  |  |  |  | 1,888 | 12.1 |
| 1923 | 26,604 | 63.8 | J.F. Loverseed | L | 8,813 | 52.0 |
|  |  |  | H. Mercer | C | 8,148 | 48.0 |
|  |  |  |  |  | 665 | 4.0 |
| 1924 | 26,951 | 73.3 | H.W. Burton | C | 10,579 | 53.6 |
|  |  |  | J.F. Loverseed | L | 9,168 | 46.4 |
|  |  |  |  |  | 1,411 | 7.2 |
| 1929 | 31,850 | 75.9 | H.W. Burton | C | 9,715 | 40.2 |
|  |  |  | A.J. Sainsbury | L | 8,309 | 34.4 |
|  |  |  | W.J. Shingfield | Lab | 6,147 | 25.4 |
|  |  |  |  |  | 1,406 | 5.8 |
| 1931 | 31,869 | 76.7 | H.W. Burton | C | 13,500 | 55.3 |
|  |  |  | A.J. Sainsbury | L | 10,929 | 44.7 |
|  |  |  |  |  | 2,571 | 10.6 |
| 1935 | 32,594 | 72.8 | H.W. Burton | C | 11,700 | 49.3 |
|  |  |  | A.J. Sainsbury | L | 8,344 | 35.2 |
|  |  |  | H. Denton | Lab | 3,670 | 15.5 |
|  |  |  |  |  | 3,356 | 14.1 |
| 1945 | 35,408 | 69.5 | R. Hamilton | Lab | 9,906 | 40.3 |
|  |  |  | H.W. Burton | C | 9,659 | 39.2 |
|  |  |  | Mrs. M. Hitchcock | L | 5,045 | 20.5 |
|  |  |  |  |  | 247 | 1.1 |

## SURREY, CARSHALTON [455]

| Election | Electors | T'out | Candidate | Party | Votes | % |
|---|---|---|---|---|---|---|
| 1945 | 57,838 | 77.0 | A.H. Head | C | 20,181 | 45.3 |
| | | | W.F. Hawkins | Lab | 19,164 | 43.1 |
| | | | W.J.W.C. Barrow | L | 5,167* | 11.6 |
| | | | | | 1,017 | 2.2 |

# SURREY, CHERTSEY [456]

| Election | Electors | T'out | Candidate | Party | Votes | % |
|---|---|---|---|---|---|---|
| 1918 | 34,917 | 48.0 | †D. Macmaster | Co C | 13,531 | 80.7 |
| | | | T.T. Linsey | Lab | 3,232 | 19.3 |
| | | | | | 10,299 | 61.4 |
| [Death] | | | | | | |
| 1922 | 38,479 | 55.4 | Sir P.W. Richardson | C | 11,811 | 55.4 |
| (24/3) | | | Sir H. de la P. Gough | L | 9,490 | 44.6 |
| | | | | | 2,321 | 10.8 |
| 1922 | 40,020 | 58.2 | Sir P.W. Richardson | C | 14,081 | 60.4 |
| | | | H.S. Clark | L | 9,228 | 39.6 |
| | | | | | 4,853 | 20.8 |
| 1923 | 39,975 | 60.1 | Sir P.W. Richardson | C | 13,333 | 55.5 |
| | | | R.J. Marnham | L | 10,694 | 44.5 |
| | | | | | 2,639 | 11.0 |
| 1924 | 41,094 | 62.7 | Sir P.W. Richardson | C | 18,310 | 71.0 |
| | | | W.C. Smith | L | 7,471 | 29.0 |
| | | | | | 10,839 | 42.0 |
| 1929 | 60,711 | 63.5 | Sir P.W. Richardson | C | 21,433 | 55.6 |
| | | | M.B. Browne | L | 17,145 | 44.4 |
| | | | | | 4,288 | 11.2 |
| 1931 | 64,675 | 68.7 | Sir A.B. Boyd-Carpenter | C | 35,371 | 79.6 |
| | | | I.B. Lloyd | L | 9,063 | 20.4 |
| | | | | | 26,308 | 59.2 |
| 1935 | 73,261 | 60.2 | Sir A.B. Boyd-Carpenter | C | 31,484 | 71.4 |
| | | | M.B. Browne | L | 12,607 | 28.6 |
| | | | | | 18,877 | 42.8 |
| [Death] | | | | | | |
| 1937 | 77,824 | 39.2 | A. Marsden | C | 19,767 | 64.8 |
| (2/7) | | | E.R. Haylor | L-Prog | 10,722 | 35.2 |
| | | | | | 9,045 | 29.6 |
| 1945 | 100,843 | 71.0 | A. Marsden | C | 37,456 | 52.3 |
| | | | B. Barker | Lab | 25,194 | 35.2 |
| | | | W. Ridgway | L | 8,940* | 12.5 |
| | | | | | 12,262 | 17.1 |

Note:—

1937: Haylor stated that he had been invited to contest the election by a representative body of electors consisting of Liberals, members of the Labour Party, Cooperators, trade unionists, members of various progressive organisations and individuals attached to no party. He was a member of the Liberal Party and was supported by Viscount Samuel and Lloyd George.

## SURREY, EASTERN [457]

| Election | Electors | T'out | Candidate | Party | Votes | % |
|---|---|---|---|---|---|---|
| 1918 | 22,556 | 47.1 | †Sir S.A. Coats, Bt. | Co C | 8,795 | 82.8 |
| | | | G. Hayler | L | 1,830 | 17.2 |
| | | | | | 6,965 | 65.6 |
| 1922 | 25,069 | 64.5 | J.F.W. Galbraith | C | 12,498 | 77.3 |
| | | | Mrs. M. Pease | Lab | 3,667 | 22.7 |
| | | | | | 8,831 | 54.6 |
| 1923 | | | J.F.W. Galbraith | C | Unopp. | |
| 1924 | 27,228 | 70.7 | J.F.W. Galbraith | C | 15,999 | 83.1 |
| | | | R.O. Mennell | Lab | 3,249 | 16.9 |
| | | | | | 12,750 | 66.2 |
| 1929 | 45,998 | 69.9 | J.F.W. Galbraith | C | 19,578 | 60.9 |
| | | | Miss I. Swinburne | L | 7,435 | 23.1 |
| | | | R.O. Mennell | Lab | 5,152 | 16.0 |
| | | | | | 12,143 | 37.8 |
| 1931 | 53,230 | 71.4 | J.F.W. Galbraith | C | 33,771 | 88.9 |
| | | | Dr. M. Follick | Lab | 4,236* | 11.1 |
| | | | | | 29,535 | 77.8 |
| 1935 | 64,325 | 66.5 | C.E.G.C. Emmott | C | 33,776 | 78.9 |
| | | | H.E. Weaver | Lab | 9,025 | 21.1 |
| | | | | | 24,751 | 57.8 |
| 1945 | 78,283* | 74.5 | Hon. M.L. Astor | C | 31,117 | 53.3 |
| | | | H.E. Weaver | Lab | 17,708 | 30.4 |
| | | | D.P. Owen | L | 9,495 | 16.3 |
| | | | | | 13,409 | 22.9 |

# SURREY, EPSOM [458]

| Election | Electors | T'out | Candidate | Party | Votes | % |
|---|---|---|---|---|---|---|
| 1918 | 32,590 | 56.3 | Sir G.R. Blades | Co C | 13,556 | 73.9 |
| | | | J.C. Ede | Lab | 4,796 | 26.1 |
| | | | | | 8,760 | 47.8 |
| 1922 | 34,945 | 65.3 | Sir G.R. Blades, Bt. | C | 16,249 | 71.2 |
| | | | Dr. S. Hastings | Lab | 6,571 | 28.8 |
| | | | | | 9,678 | 42.4 |
| 1923 | 36,055 | 55.6 | Sir G.R. Blades, Bt. | C | 14,230 | 71.0 |
| | | | J. Langdon-Davies | Lab | 5,807 | 29.0 |
| | | | | | 8,423 | 42.0 |
| 1924 | 37,515 | 67.1 | Sir G.R. Blades, Bt. | C | 20,017 | 79.5 |
| | | | P. Butler | Lab | 5,149 | 20.5 |
| | | | | | 14,868 | 59.0 |

[Elevation to the Peerage — Lord Ebbisham]

| Election | Electors | T'out | Candidate | Party | Votes | % |
|---|---|---|---|---|---|---|
| 1928 (4/7) | 43,292 | 51.2 | A.R.J. Southby | C | 13,364 | 60.2 |
| | | | S.P. Kerr | L | 5,095 | 23.0 |
| | | | Miss H.M. Keynes | Lab | 3,719 | 16.8 |
| | | | | | 8,269 | 37.2 |
| 1929 | 63,268 | 67.7 | A.R.J. Southby | C | 24,720 | 57.8 |
| | | | S.P. Kerr | L | 10,422 | 24.3 |
| | | | Rev. S.J.W. Morgan | Lab | 7,662 | 17.9 |
| | | | | | 14,298 | 33.5 |
| 1931 | 74,905 | 69.0 | A.R.J. Southby | C | 44,076 | 85.3 |
| | | | Rev. S.J.W. Morgan | Lab | 7,571 | 14.7 |
| | | | | | 36,505 | 70.6 |
| 1935 | 105,844 | 65.4 | A.R.J. Southby | C | 49,948 | 72.1 |
| | | | Rev. S.J.W. Morgan | Lab | 19,286 | 27.9 |
| | | | | | 30,662 | 44.2 |
| 1945 | 72,732** | 74.6 | Sir A.R.J. Southby, Bt. | C | 27,081 | 50.0 |
| | | | E.A.A. Shackleton | Lab | 20,533 | 37.8 |
| | | | J.M. Fowler | L | 6,643* | 12.2 |
| | | | | | 6,548 | 12.2 |

[Resignation]

| Election | Electors | T'out | Candidate | Party | Votes | % |
|---|---|---|---|---|---|---|
| 1947 (4/12) | 78,156 | 70.5 | Rt. Hon. M.S. McCorquodale | C | 33,633 | 61.0 |
| | | | R. Bishop | Lab | 17,339 | 31.5 |
| | | | D.A.S. Cairns | L | 4,121* | 7.5 |
| | | | | | 16,294 | 29.5 |

| Election | Electors | T'out | Candidate | Party | Votes | % |
|---|---|---|---|---|---|---|
| 1918 | 32,720 | 44.0 | A.M. Samuel | Co C | 7,558 | 52.5 |
| | | | J. Hayes | Lab | 3,534 | 24.6 |
| | | | J.H. Harris | Ind C | 3,289 | 22.9 |
| | | | | | 4,024 | 27.9 |
| 1922 | 34,980 | 56.8 | A.M. Samuel | C | 14,557 | 73.3 |
| | | | T.H. Marshall | Lab | 5,312 | 26.7 |
| | | | | | 9,245 | 46.6 |
| 1923 | 35,314 | 59.6 | A.M. Samuel | C | 12,534 | 59.6 |
| | | | C. a'B. Williams | L | 4,979 | 23.7 |
| | | | Mrs. A.E. Corner | Lab | 3,520 | 16.7 |
| | | | | | 7,555 | 35.9 |
| 1924 | 36,255 | 63.1 | A.M. Samuel | C | 18,272 | 79.8 |
| | | | Mrs. A.E. Corner | Lab | 4,613 | 20.2 |
| | | | | | 13,659 | 59.6 |
| 1929 | 52,597 | 66.9 | A.M. Samuel | C | 21,050 | 59.9 |
| | | | J.W. Todd | L | 9,268 | 26.3 |
| | | | F.N. Palmer | Lab | 4,866 | 13.8 |
| | | | | | 11,782 | 33.6 |
| 1931 | | | A.M. Samuel | C | Unopp. | |
| 1935 | 60,121 | 59.8 | Sir A.M. Samuel, Bt. | C | 28,211 | 78.5 |
| | | | D.M. Fraser | Lab | 7,725 | 21.5 |
| | | | | | 20,486 | 57.0 |

[Elevation to the Peerage — Lord Mancroft]

| Election | Electors | T'out | Candidate | Party | Votes | % |
|---|---|---|---|---|---|---|
| 1937 | 61,680 | 50.0 | G. Nicholson | C | 20,580 | 66.7 |
| (23/3) | | | P. Pain | Lab | 7,792 | 25.3 |
| | | | L.T. Thorp | Ind C | 2,327* | 7.5 |
| | | | E. Miller | Ind | 154* | 0.5 |
| | | | | | 12,788 | 41.4 |
| 1945 | 75,134 | 68.6 | G. Nicholson | C | 31,557 | 61.2 |
| | | | T.W. Gittins | Lab | 20,013 | 38.8 |
| | | | | | 11,544 | 22.4 |

Notes:—

1937: Thorp was supported by the Liberty Restoration League.

Miller sought election as a 'King's and the People's Champion' candidate.

| Election | Electors | T'out | Candidate | Party | Votes | % |
|---|---|---|---|---|---|---|
| 1918 | 36,427 | 50.0 | †W.E. Horne | Co C | 13,149 | 72.1 |
| | | | W. Bennett | Lab | 5,078 | 27.9 |
| | | | | | 8,071 | 44.2 |
| 1922 | 39,087 | 65.4 | Sir H.C. Buckingham | C | 18,045 | 70.6 |
| | | | W. Bennett | Lab | 7,514 | 29.4 |
| | | | | | 10,531 | 41.2 |
| 1923 | 39,931 | 67.6 | Sir H.C. Buckingham | C | 14,117 | 52.3 |
| | | | S.P. Kerr | L | 7,601 | 28.2 |
| | | | W. Bennett | Lab | 5,260 | 19.5 |
| | | | | | 6,516 | 24.1 |
| 1924 | 41,164 | 71.3 | Sir H.C. Buckingham | C | 18,273 | 62.3 |
| | | | S.F. Markham | Lab | 6,227 | 21.2 |
| | | | S.P. Kerr | L | 4,842 | 16.5 |
| | | | | | 12,046 | 41.1 |
| 1929 | 58,958 | 72.1 | Sir H.C. Buckingham | C | 20,550 | 48.3 |
| | | | S.S. Brooke | L | 15,984 | 37.6 |
| | | | L.M. Worsnop | Lab | 5,996 | 14.1 |
| | | | | | 4,566 | 10.7 |
| [Death] | | | | | | |
| 1931 (25/8) | | | Hon. C.A.U. Rhys | C | Unopp. | |
| 1931 | 62,625 | 72.3 | Hon. C.A.U. Rhys | C | 39,008 | 86.2 |
| | | | S. Peck | Lab | 6,242 | 13.8 |
| | | | | | 32,766 | 72.4 |
| 1935 | 68,163 | 69.3 | Sir J.J. Jarvis, Bt. | C | 35,384 | 74.9 |
| | | | F.A. Campbell | Lab | 11,833 | 25.1 |
| | | | | | 23,551 | 49.8 |
| 1945 | 88,393 | 74.8 | Sir J.J. Jarvis, Bt. | C | 33,091 | 50.0 |
| | | | V.G. Wilkinson | Lab | 21,789 | 32.9 |
| | | | J.G.C. Ruston | L | 11,281 | 17.1 |
| | | | | | 11,302 | 17.1 |

## SURREY, MITCHAM [461]

| Election | Electors | T'out | Candidate | Party | Votes | % |
|---|---|---|---|---|---|---|
| 1918 | 28,952 | 43.6 | Dr. T.C. Worsfold | Co C | 7,651 | 60.6 |
| | | | S. Barrow | L | 4,968 | 39.4 |
| | | | | | 2,683 | 21.2 |
| 1922 | 31,927 | 52.7 | Dr. T.C. Worsfold | C | 10,934 | 65.0 |
| | | | A.E. Bennetts | L | 5,898 | 35.0 |
| | | | | | 5,036 | 30.0 |
| [Resignation] | | | | | | |
| 1923 | 31,927 | 66.2 | J.C. Ede | Lab | 8,029 | 38.0 |
| (3/3) | | | Rt. Hon. Sir A.S.T. Griffith- | | | |
| | | | Boscawen | C | 7,196 | 34.1 |
| | | | A.E. Brown | L | 3,214 | 15.2 |
| | | | J.T. Catterall | Ind C | 2,684 | 12.7 |
| | | | | | 833 | 3.9 |
| 1923 | 32,755 | 63.2 | R.J. Meller | C | 10,829 | 52.3 |
| | | | J.C. Ede | Lab | 9,877 | 47.7 |
| | | | | | 952 | 4.6 |
| 1924 | 34,435 | 74.8 | R.J. Meller | C | 15,984 | 62.0 |
| | | | J.C. Ede | Lab | 9,776 | 38.0 |
| | | | | | 6,208 | 24.0 |
| 1929 | 60,311 | 70.2 | R.J. Meller | C | 20,254 | 47.9 |
| | | | B.S. MacKay | Lab | 13,057 | 30.8 |
| | | | R.V. Jones | L | 9,016 | 21.3 |
| | | | | | 7,197 | 17.1 |
| 1931 | 72,991 | 70.0 | R.J. Meller | C | 38,948 | 76.3 |
| | | | W. Graham | Lab | 12,124 | 23.7 |
| | | | | | 26,824 | 52.6 |
| 1935 | 91,889 | 66.7 | Sir R.J. Meller | C | 35,239 | 57.5 |
| | | | P. Winterton | Lab | 26,087 | 42.5 |
| | | | | | 9,152 | 15.0 |
| [Death] | | | | | | |
| 1940 | | | Rt. Hon. Sir M.A. Robertson | C | Unopp. | |
| (19/8) | | | | | | |

This constituency was divided in 1945.

Note:—

1923: Griffith-Boscawen was Minister of Health. He subsequently resigned.
(3/3)

| Election | Electors | T'out | Candidate | Party | Votes | % |
|---|---|---|---|---|---|---|
| 1918 | | | G.K. Cockerill | Co C | Unopp. | |
| 1922 | | | G.K. Cockerill | C | Unopp. | |
| 1923 | | | G.K. Cockerill | C | Unopp. | |
| 1924 | 35,070 | 74.0 | G.K. Cockerill | C | 19,877 | 76.6 |
| | | | W. Graham | Lab | 6,061 | 23.4 |
| | | | | | 13,816 | 53.2 |
| 1929 | 51,314 | 74.8 | Sir G.K. Cockerill | C | 20,851 | 54.3 |
| | | | H.J. Hamblen | L | 9,532 | 24.8 |
| | | | P.H. Collick | Lab | 8,012 | 20.9 |
| | | | | | 11,319 | 29.5 |
| 1931 | 54,577 | 75.1 | G.C. Touche | C | 33,934 | 82.7 |
| | | | P.H. Collick | Lab | 7,076 | 17.3 |
| | | | | | 26,858 | 65.4 |
| 1935 | 58,783 | 69.9 | G.C. Touche | C | 30,340 | 73.8 |
| | | | I.L. Lewis | Lab | 10,748 | 26.2 |
| | | | | | 19,592 | 47.6 |
| 1945 | 65,884* | 72.9 | G.C. Touche | C | 27,419 | 57.1 |
| | | | C.J. Garnsworthy | Lab | 20,623 | 42.9 |
| | | | | | 6,796 | 14.2 |

| Election | Electors | T'out | Candidate | Party | Votes | % |
|---|---|---|---|---|---|---|
| 1918 | 29,863 | 59.8 | †R.S. Gwynne | Co C | 11,357 | 63.6 |
| | | | T.B. Hasdell | Lab | 4,641 | 26.0 |
| | | | Sir A.J. Callaghan | L | 1,852* | 10.4 |
| | | | | | 6,716 | 37.6 |
| 1922 | 31,281 | 77.2 | R.S. Gwynne | C | 14,601 | 60.5 |
| | | | E. Duke | L | 9,550 | 39.5 |
| | | | | | 5,051 | 21.0 |
| 1923 | 32,033 | 77.0 | R.S. Gwynne | C | 13,276 | 53.8 |
| | | | Rt. Hon. T. Wiles | L | 11,396 | 46.2 |
| | | | | | 1,880 | 7.6 |
| 1924 | 33,318 | 77.6 | Rt. Hon. Sir G.A. Lloyd | C | 17,533 | 67.9 |
| | | | J.J. Davies | L | 4,168 | 16.1 |
| | | | D.J. Davis | Lab | 4,138 | 16.0 |
| | | | | | 13,365 | 51.8 |

[Resignation on appointment as United Kingdom High Commissioner in Egypt and the Sudan]

| Election | Electors | T'out | Candidate | Party | Votes | % |
|---|---|---|---|---|---|---|
| 1925 (17/6) | 33,318† | 65.5 | Sir W.R. Hall | C | 12,741 | 58.4 |
| | | | H. Johnstone | L | 5,386 | 24.7 |
| | | | T.S.B. Williams | Lab | 3,696 | 16.9 |
| | | | | | 7,355 | 33.7 |
| 1929 | 48,951 | 74.5 | E. Marjoribanks | C | 18,157 | 49.9 |
| | | | R.S. Chatfield | Lab | 8,204 | 22.5 |
| | | | C.S.S. Burt | L | 7,812 | 21.4 |
| | | | P.E. Hurst | Ind C | 2,277* | 6.2 |
| | | | | | 9,953 | 27.4 |
| 1931 | 50,956 | 71.9 | E. Marjoribanks | C | 31,240 | 85.3 |
| | | | A.J. Marshall | Lab | 5,379 | 14.7 |
| | | | | | 25,861 | 70.6 |

[Death]

| Election | Electors | T'out | Candidate | Party | Votes | % |
|---|---|---|---|---|---|---|
| 1932 (28/4) | | | J. Slater | C | Unopp. | |

[Death]

| Election | Electors | T'out | Candidate | Party | Votes | % |
|---|---|---|---|---|---|---|
| 1935 (29/3) | | | C.S. Taylor | C | Unopp. | |
| 1935 | | | C.S. Taylor | C | Unopp. | |
| 1945 | 44,238 | 77.2 | C.S. Taylor | C | 18,173 | 53.3 |
| | | | D.N. Smith | Lab | 12,637 | 37.0 |
| | | | J.S. Gowland | L | 2,797* | 8.2 |
| | | | W.R. Hipwell | Ind Nat | 524* | 1.5 |
| | | | | | 5,536 | 16.3 |

| Election | Electors | T'out | Candidate | Party | Votes | % |
|---|---|---|---|---|---|---|
| 1918 | 35,955 | 52.3 | †H.S. Cautley | Co C | 12,584 | 67.0 |
| | | | D.G. Pole | Lab | 6,208 | 33.0 |
| | | | | | 6,376 | 34.0 |
| 1922 | 38,664 | 58.2 | H.S. Cautley | C | 15,981 | 71.0 |
| | | | T. Crawford | Lab | 6,527 | 29.0 |
| | | | | | 9,454 | 42.0 |
| 1923 | 39,405 | 52.4 | H.S. Cautley | C | 14,215 | 68.8 |
| | | | T. Crawford | Lab | 6,451 | 31.2 |
| | | | | | 7,764 | 37.6 |
| 1924 | 40,500 | 70.2 | Sir H.S. Cautley, Bt. | C | 18,365 | 64.6 |
| | | | G.F. Mowatt | L | 5,604 | 19.7 |
| | | | J. Morgan | Lab | 4,479 | 15.7 |
| | | | | | 12,761 | 44.9 |
| 1929 | 55,352 | 68.5 | Sir H.S. Cautley, Bt. | C | 21,940 | 57.9 |
| | | | Miss B.E.M.S. Bliss | L | 9,718 | 25.6 |
| | | | T. Crawford | Lab | 6,265 | 16.5 |
| | | | | | 12,222 | 32.3 |
| 1931 | 57,697 | 69.2 | Sir H.S. Cautley, Bt. | C | 34,826 | 87.2 |
| | | | E.F.M. Durbin | Lab | 5,121 | 12.8 |
| | | | | | 29,705 | 74.4 |
| 1935 | 61,302 | 61.2 | Sir H.S. Cautley, Bt. | C | 29,440 | 78.4 |
| | | | S. Seuffert | Lab | 8,097 | 21.6 |
| | | | | | 21,343 | 56.8 |

[Elevation to the Peerage — Lord Cautley]

| Election | Electors | T'out | Candidate | Party | Votes | % |
|---|---|---|---|---|---|---|
| 1936 (23/7) | 61,302 | 45.5 | R.S. Clarke | C | 22,207 | 79.6 |
| | | | A.E. Millett | Lab | 5,708 | 20.4 |
| | | | | | 16,499 | 59.2 |
| 1945 | 69,860 | 70.9 | R.S. Clarke | C | 28,273 | 57.1 |
| | | | D.G. Packham | Lab | 12,519 | 25.3 |
| | | | J.C. McLaughlin | L | 8,711 | 17.6 |
| | | | | | 15,754 | 31.8 |

481

# SUSSEX (East), LEWES  [465]

| Election | Electors | T'out | Candidate | Party | Votes | % |
|---|---|---|---|---|---|---|
| 1918 | 22,500 | 55.1 | †W.R. Campion | Co C | 7,792 | 62.8 |
|  |  |  | T. Pargeter | Lab | 4,164 | 33.6 |
|  |  |  | A.E. Gardiner | Ind | 452* | 3.6 |
|  |  |  |  |  | 3,628 | 29.2 |
| 1922 | 25,801 | 64.6 | W.R. Campion | C | 11,345 | 68.0 |
|  |  |  | H.M. Black | Lab | 5,328 | 32.0 |
|  |  |  |  |  | 6,017 | 36.0 |
| 1923 | 27,361 | 58.1 | W.R. Campion | C | 9,474 | 59.6 |
|  |  |  | B.W.R. Hall | Lab | 6,422 | 40.4 |
|  |  |  |  |  | 3,052 | 19.2 |

[Resignation on appointment as Governor of Western Australia]

| | | | | | | |
|---|---|---|---|---|---|---|
| 1924 (9/7) | 27,361† | 67.3 | T.P.H. Beamish | C | 9,584 | 52.0 |
|  |  |  | B.W.R. Hall | Lab | 6,112 | 33.2 |
|  |  |  | H. Williams | L | 2,718 | 14.8 |
|  |  |  |  |  | 3,472 | 18.8 |
| 1924 | 28,517 | 64.7 | T.P.H. Beamish | C | 13,399 | 72.7 |
|  |  |  | B.W.R. Hall | Lab | 5,043 | 27.3 |
|  |  |  |  |  | 8,356 | 45.4 |
| 1929 | 40,291 | 70.4 | T.P.H. Beamish | C | 15,230 | 53.7 |
|  |  |  | A.G. Gordon | Lab | 7,698 | 27.1 |
|  |  |  | H.P. Woodgate | L | 5,452 | 19.2 |
|  |  |  |  |  | 7,532 | 26.6 |
| 1931 | 43,711 | 70.9 | J. de V. Loder | C | 25,181 | 81.3 |
|  |  |  | F.R. Hancock | Lab | 5,795 | 18.7 |
|  |  |  |  |  | 19,386 | 62.6 |
| 1935 | 54,658 | 64.4 | Hon. J. de V. Loder | C | 24,644 | 70.0 |
|  |  |  | F.R. Hancock | Lab | 10,559 | 30.0 |
|  |  |  |  |  | 14,085 | 40.0 |

[Succession to the Peerage — Lord Wakehurst]

| | | | | | | |
|---|---|---|---|---|---|---|
| 1936 (18/6) | 54,658 | 40.6 | T.P.H. Beamish | C | 14,646 | 66.0 |
|  |  |  | A.G. Gordon | Lab | 7,557 | 34.0 |
|  |  |  |  |  | 7,089 | 32.0 |
| 1945 | 71,144 | 71.8 | T.V.H. Beamish | C | 26,170 | 51.2 |
|  |  |  | A.E. Oram | Lab/Co-op | 18,511 | 36.3 |
|  |  |  | P. Cadogan | L | 6,374* | 12.5 |
|  |  |  |  |  | 7,659 | 14.9 |

Note:—

1918: Gardiner sought election as an 'Independent and Silver Badge' candidate but there is no information available as to whether or not he was supported by any of the local ex-servicemen organisations.

# SUSSEX (East), RYE   [466]

| Election | Electors | T'out | Candidate | Party | Votes | % |
|---|---|---|---|---|---|---|
| 1918 | 27,153 | 53.1 | †G.L. Courthorpe | Co C | 10,378 | 72.0 |
|  |  |  | G. Ellis | L | 4,034 | 28.0 |
|  |  |  |  |  | 6,344 | 44.0 |
| 1922 | 29,490 | 62.4 | G.L. Courthorpe | C | 10,922 | 59.3 |
|  |  |  | G. Ellis | L | 7,488 | 40.7 |
|  |  |  |  |  | 3,434 | 18.6 |
| 1923 | 29,995 | 69.4 | G.L. Courthorpe | C | 11,167 | 53.6 |
|  |  |  | G. Ellis | L | 9,651 | 46.4 |
|  |  |  |  |  | 1,516 | 7.2 |
| 1924 | 31,103 | 71.2 | G.L. Courthorpe | C | 14,871 | 67.1 |
|  |  |  | G. Ellis | L | 7,289 | 32.9 |
|  |  |  |  |  | 7,582 | 34.2 |
| 1929 | 43,966 | 72.2 | Sir G.L. Courthorpe, Bt. | C | 18,061 | 56.9 |
|  |  |  | W.S. Osborn | L | 10,198 | 32.1 |
|  |  |  | G.A. Greenwood | Lab | 3,505* | 11.0 |
|  |  |  |  |  | 7,863 | 24.8 |
| 1931 |  |  | Sir G.L. Courthorpe, Bt. | C | Unopp. |  |
| 1935 | 49,498 | 64.2 | Sir G.L. Courthorpe, Bt. | C | 22,604 | 71.2 |
|  |  |  | Miss D.F. Osborn | L | 9,162 | 28.8 |
|  |  |  |  |  | 13,442 | 42.4 |
| 1945 | 47,547 | 70.8 | W.N. Cuthbert | C | 19,701 | 58.6 |
|  |  |  | E.B. Simmons | Lab | 7,414 | 22.0 |
|  |  |  | R. Ogden | L | 6,530 | 19.4 |
|  |  |  |  |  | 12,287 | 36.6 |

| Election | Electors | T'out | Candidate | Party | Votes | % |
|---|---|---|---|---|---|---|
| 1918 | 42,131 | 50.3 | †Rt. Hon. Lord Edmund Talbot | Co C | 14,491 | 68.4 |
| | | | F.E. Green | Lab | 6,705 | 31.6 |
| | | | | | 7,786 | 36.8 |

[Resignation on appointment as Lord-Lieutenant of Ireland]

| Election | Electors | T'out | Candidate | Party | Votes | % |
|---|---|---|---|---|---|---|
| 1921 (23/4) | | | Sir W.B.M. Bird | Co C | Unopp. | |
| 1922 | 45,364 | 57.9 | Sir W.B.M. Bird | C | 19,494 | 74.3 |
| | | | R.H.K. Hope | Lab | 6,752 | 25.7 |
| | | | | | 12,742 | 48.6 |
| 1923 | 46,257 | 60.2 | C.M.C. Rudkin | L | 14,513 | 52.1 |
| | | | Sir W.B.M. Bird | C | 13,348 | 47.9 |
| | | | | | 1,165 | 4.2 |
| 1924 | 48,170 | 72.4 | J.S. Courtauld | C | 20,710 | 59.3 |
| | | | C.M.C. Rudkin | L | 12,416 | 35.6 |
| | | | R.H.K. Hope | Lab | 1,765* | 5.1 |
| | | | | | 8,294 | 23.7 |
| 1929 | 67,276 | 64.9 | J.S. Courtauld | C | 26,278 | 60.2 |
| | | | J.F. Dunn | L | 17,398 | 39.8 |
| | | | | | 8,880 | 20.4 |
| 1931 | 72,751 | 68.5 | J.S. Courtauld | C | 43,756 | 87.8 |
| | | | C.W. Higgins | Lab | 6,085* | 12.2 |
| | | | | | 37,671 | 75.6 |
| 1935 | 81,239 | 59.5 | J.S. Courtauld | C | 37,882 | 78.3 |
| | | | C.W. Higgins | Lab | 10,484 | 21.7 |
| | | | | | 27,398 | 56.6 |

[Death]

| Election | Electors | T'out | Candidate | Party | Votes | % |
|---|---|---|---|---|---|---|
| 1942 (18/5) | 92,222 | 29.2 | Hon. L.W. Joynson-Hicks | C | 15,634 | 58.1 |
| | | | G. le B. Kidd | Ind | 10,564 | 39.3 |
| | | | A.A.W. Tribe | Ind C | 706* | 2.6 |
| | | | | | 5,070 | 18.8 |
| 1945 | 83,577* | 67.9 | Hon. L.W. Joynson-Hicks | C | 30,989 | 54.6 |
| | | | Mrs. R.F. Chamberlayne | Lab | 13,670 | 24.1 |
| | | | G. le B. Kidd | L | 11,345 | 20.0 |
| | | | M.H. Woodard | Nat Ind | 625* | 1.1 |
| | | | P.T. Carter | Dem P | 118* | 0.2 |
| | | | | | 17,319 | 30.5 |

Notes:—

1942: Kidd was supported by Sir Richard Acland, M.P., W.D. Kendall, M.P. and W.J. Brown, M.P.

1945: Woodard sought election as a 'National Independent Youth' candidate.

## SUSSEX (West), HORSHAM   [468]

| Election | Electors | T'out | Candidate | Party | Votes | % |
|----------|----------|-------|-----------|-------|-------|---|
| 1945 | 58,395 | 68.0 | Rt. Hon. Earl Winterton | C | 21,814 | 54.9 |
| | | | A.F.H. Lindner | Lab | 11,664 | 29.4 |
| | | | C.A.W. Williamson | L | 6,216 | 15.7 |
| | | | | | 10,150 | 25.5 |

| Election | Electors | T'out | Candidate | Party | Votes | % |
|----------|----------|-------|-----------|-------|-------|---|
| 1918 | 43,142 | 42.2 | †Earl Winterton | Co C | 15,644 | 86.0 |
|  |  |  | E.M. Rodocanachi | Ind | 2,544 | 14.0 |
|  |  |  |  |  | 13,100 | 72.0 |
| 1922 |  |  | Earl Winterton | C | Unopp. |  |
| 1923 | 45,438 | 59.0 | Earl Winterton | C | 17,925 | 66.8 |
|  |  |  | E. Stanford | Lab | 8,892 | 33.2 |
|  |  |  |  |  | 9,033 | 33.6 |
| 1924 | 47,557 | 65.7 | Rt. Hon. Earl Winterton | C | 23,715 | 75.9 |
|  |  |  | E. Stanford | Lab | 7,537 | 24.1 |
|  |  |  |  |  | 16,178 | 51.8 |
| 1929 | 70,220 | 66.1 | Rt. Hon. Earl Winterton | C | 27,872 | 60.1 |
|  |  |  | P. Boyden | L | 10,905 | 23.5 |
|  |  |  | Miss H.M. Keynes | Lab | 7,611 | 16.4 |
|  |  |  |  |  | 16,967 | 36.6 |
| 1931 | 75,485 | 67.3 | Rt. Hon. Earl Winterton | C | 44,886 | 88.3 |
|  |  |  | Miss H.M. Keynes | Lab | 5,932* | 11.7 |
|  |  |  |  |  | 38,954 | 76.6 |
| 1935 | 89,513 | 60.3 | Rt. Hon. Earl Winterton | C | 41,478 | 76.9 |
|  |  |  | H.W. Paton | Lab | 12,466 | 23.1 |
|  |  |  |  |  | 29,012 | 53.8 |

This constituency was divided in 1945.

## SUSSEX (West), WORTHING [470]

| Election | Electors | T'out | Candidate | Party | Votes | % |
|---|---|---|---|---|---|---|
| 1945 | 68,621 | 72.0 | O.L. Prior-Palmer | C | 31,337 | 63.5 |
| | | | A.W. Wright | Lab | 11,570 | 23.4 |
| | | | W. Parnell-Smith | L | 6,483 | 13.1 |
| | | | | | 19,767 | 40.1 |

| Election | Electors | T'out | Candidate | Party | Votes | % |
|----------|----------|-------|-----------|-------|-------|---|
| 1918 | 43,458 | 55.9 | H. Maddocks | Co C | 11,198 | 46.2 |
| | | | I. Gregory | Lab | 6,269 | 25.8 |
| | | | W.H. Grant | L | 5,707 | 23.5 |
| | | | W. Dyson | NDP | 1,101* | 4.5 |
| | | | | | 4,929 | 20.4 |
| 1922 | 47,777 | 69.8 | H. Maddocks | C | 12,765 | 38.3 |
| | | | J. Stevenson | Lab | 10,842 | 32.5 |
| | | | T. Slack | L | 9,730 | 29.2 |
| | | | | | 1,923 | 5.8 |
| 1923 | 49,460 | 72.6 | H. Willison | L | 14,518 | 40.4 |
| | | | Sir H. Maddocks | C | 10,940 | 30.5 |
| | | | T. Barron | Lab | 10,437 | 29.1 |
| | | | | | 3,578 | 9.9 |
| 1924 | 51,414 | 78.7 | A.O.J. Hope | C | 15,242 | 37.7 |
| | | | F. Smith | Lab | 12,679 | 31.3 |
| | | | H. Willison | L | 12,550 | 31.0 |
| | | | | | 2,563 | 6.4 |
| 1929 | 72,551 | 84.1 | F. Smith | Lab | 27,102 | 44.4 |
| | | | H. Willison | L | 19,104 | 31.3 |
| | | | A.O.J. Hope | C | 14,819 | 24.3 |
| | | | | | 7,998 | 13.1 |
| 1931 | 79,518 | 78.0 | E.T.T. North | C | 25,839 | 41.6 |
| | | | F. Smith | Lab | 23,375 | 37.7 |
| | | | H. Willison | NL | 12,811 | 20.7 |
| | | | | | 2,464 | 3.9 |
| 1935 | 90,422 | 75.9 | R.T.H. Fletcher | Lab | 33,237 | 48.4 |
| | | | J. Moores | C | 28,000 | 40.8 |
| | | | W.T. Stanton | L | 7,384* | 10.8 |
| | | | | | 5,237 | 7.6 |

[Elevation to the Peerage — Lord Winster]

| | | | | | | |
|----------|----------|-------|-----------|-------|-------|---|
| 1942 (9/3) | | | F.G. Bowles | Lab | Unopp. | |
| 1945 | 66,698** | 78.4 | F.G. Bowles | Lab | 30,587 | 58.4 |
| | | | Hon. J.M. Fitzroy-Newdegate | C | 12,267 | 23.5 |
| | | | P.J.A. Calvocoressi | L | 8,986 | 17.2 |
| | | | L. Melling | Ind Prog | 468* | 0.9 |
| | | | | | 18,320 | 34.9 |

| Election | Electors | T'out | Candidate | Party | Votes | % |
|---|---|---|---|---|---|---|
| 1918 | 31,726 | 59.0 | †J.L. Baird | Co C | 11,325 | 60.5 |
| | | | O.F. Maclagan | L | 7,399 | 39.5 |
| | | | | | 3,926 | 21.0 |
| 1922 | 32,599 | 76.9 | D.E. Wallace | C | 11,934 | 47.6 |
| | | | Hon. A.G.V. Peel | L | 8,196 | 32.7 |
| | | | T.H. Holt-Hughes | Lab | 4,940 | 19.7 |
| | | | | | 3,738 | 14.9 |
| 1923 | 33,363 | 75.2 | A.E. Brown | L | 13,798 | 55.0 |
| | | | D.E. Wallace | C | 11,286 | 45.0 |
| | | | | | 2,512 | 10.0 |
| 1924 | 33,903 | 84.7 | H.D.R. Margesson | C | 14,434 | 50.3 |
| | | | A.E. Brown | L | 10,524 | 36.6 |
| | | | H. Yates | Lab | 3,768 | 13.1 |
| | | | | | 3,910 | 13.7 |
| 1929 | 43,515 | 84.8 | H.D.R. Margesson | C | 15,147 | 41.1 |
| | | | J. Morgan | Lab | 11,588 | 31.4 |
| | | | R.H. Bernays | L | 10,158 | 27.5 |
| | | | | | 3,559 | 9.7 |
| 1931 | 44,363 | 78.9 | H.D.R. Margesson | C | 24,493 | 69.9 |
| | | | E.J. Pay | Lab | 10,523 | 30.1 |
| | | | | | 13,970 | 39.8 |
| 1935 | 45,996 | 73.8 | Rt. Hon. H.D.R. Margesson | C | 20,905 | 61.5 |
| | | | H.W. Fenner | Lab | 13,061 | 38.5 |
| | | | | | 7,844 | 23.0 |

[Elevation to the Peerage — Viscount Margesson]

| Election | Electors | T'out | Candidate | Party | Votes | % |
|---|---|---|---|---|---|---|
| 1942 (29/4) | 49,252 | 38.5 | W.J. Brown | Ind | 9,824 | 51.8 |
| | | | Sir C.V. Holbrook | C | 9,145 | 48.2 |
| | | | | | 679 | 3.6 |
| 1945 | 62,794* | 73.5 | W.J. Brown | Ind | 18,615 | 40.3 |
| | | | J. Lakin | C | 17,049 | 37.0 |
| | | | R.H. Lewis | Lab | 10,470 | 22.7 |
| | | | | | 1,566 | 3.3 |

Notes:—

    1929:  Polling was delayed until June 13 owing to the death, after nomination, of the Labour candidate, H. Yates.

    1942:  Brown received considerable unofficial support from the local Labour Party.

| Election | Electors | T'out | Candidate | Party | Votes | % |
|----------|----------|-------|-----------|-------|-------|---|
| 1945 | 67,249 | 71.9 | M.A. Lindsay | C | 26,696 | 55.2 |
| | | | R.H. Jenkins | Lab | 21,647 | 44.8 |
| | | | | | 5,049 | 10.4 |

| Election | Electors | T'out | Candidate | Party | Votes | % |
|---|---|---|---|---|---|---|
| 1945 | 65,160 | 74.5 | Sir J.S.P. Mellor, Bt. | C | 28,225 | 58.2 |
| | | | F.W. Mulley | Lab | 18,261 | 37.6 |
| | | | Mrs. J. Purser | CW | 2,043* | 4.2 |
| | | | | | 9,964 | 20.6 |

| Election | Electors | T'out | Candidate | Party | Votes | % |
|---|---|---|---|---|---|---|
| 1918 | | | †H. Wilson-Fox | Co C | Unopp. | |
| [Death] | | | | | | |
| 1922 (17/1) | 35,692 | 60.0 | Sir P.W. Newson, Bt. | Co C | 14,732 | 68.8 |
| | | | G.H. Jones | Lab | 6,671 | 31.2 |
| | | | | | 8,061 | 37.6 |
| 1922 | | | Sir P.W. Newson, Bt. | C | Unopp. | |
| 1923 | | | Sir E.M. Iliffe | C | Unopp. | |
| 1924 | | | Sir E.M. Iliffe | C | Unopp. | |
| 1929 | 60,087 | 73.6 | Sir E.M. Iliffe | C | 29,807 | 67.4 |
| | | | G. Horwill | Lab | 14,402 | 32.6 |
| | | | | | 15,405 | 34.8 |
| [Resignation] | | | | | | |
| 1929 (2/12) | 60,087 | 60.3 | Rt. Hon. Sir A.H.D.R. Steel-Maitland, Bt. | C | 23,495 | 64.8 |
| | | | G. Horwill | Lab | 12,759 | 35.2 |
| | | | | | 10,736 | 29.6 |
| 1931 | 66,421 | 73.9 | Rt. Hon. Sir A.H.D.R. Steel-Maitland, Bt. | C | 41,571 | 84.7 |
| | | | J. Willbery | Lab | 7,525 | 15.3 |
| | | | | | 34,046 | 69.4 |
| [Death] | | | | | | |
| 1935 (10/5) | | | Sir J.S.P. Mellor, Bt. | C | Unopp. | |
| 1935 | 83,139 | 64.6 | Sir J.S.P. Mellor, Bt. | C | 42,675 | 79.5 |
| | | | J.A. Yates | Lab | 11,026 | 20.5 |
| | | | | | 31,649 | 59.0 |

This constituency was divided in 1945.

| Election | Electors | T'out | Candidate | Party | Votes | % |
|---|---|---|---|---|---|---|
| 1918 | | | †Sir E.M. Pollock, Bt. | Co C | Unopp. | |
| | | | | | | |
| 1922 | | | Rt. Hon. Sir E.M. Pollock, Bt. | C | Unopp. | |
| [Seat Vacant at Dissolution (Resignation on appointment as Master of the Rolls)] | | | | | | |
| 1923 | 43,175 | 72.9 | R.A. Eden | C | 16,337 | 51.8 |
| | | | G. Nicholls | L | 11,134 | 35.4 |
| | | | Countess of Warwick | Lab | 4,015 | 12.8 |
| | | | | | 5,203 | 16.4 |
| | | | | | | |
| 1924 | 44,191 | 73.6 | R.A. Eden | C | 19,575 | 60.2 |
| | | | G. Nicholls | L | 12,966 | 39.8 |
| | | | | | 6,609 | 20.4 |
| | | | | | | |
| 1929 | 62,406 | 77.5 | R.A. Eden | C | 23,045 | 47.6 |
| | | | W.L. Dingley | L | 17,585 | 36.4 |
| | | | C.G. Garton | Lab | 7,741 | 16.0 |
| | | | | | 5,460 | 11.2 |
| | | | | | | |
| 1931 | 66,058 | 72.4 | R.A. Eden | C | 38,584 | 80.6 |
| | | | C.G. Garton | Ind Lab | 9,261 | 19.4 |
| | | | | | 29,323 | 61.2 |
| | | | | | | |
| 1935 | 71,091 | 65.7 | Rt. Hon. R.A. Eden | C | 35,746 | 76.6 |
| | | | J. Perry | Lab | 10,930 | 23.4 |
| | | | | | 24,816 | 53.2 |
| | | | | | | |
| 1945 | 87,620* | 69.0 | Rt. Hon. R.A. Eden | C | 37,110 | 61.3 |
| | | | D.P. Chesworth | Lab | 19,476 | 32.2 |
| | | | W.L. Dingley | L | 3,908* | 6.5 |
| | | | | | 17,634 | 29.1 |

| Election | Electors | T'out | Candidate | Party | Votes | % |
|----------|----------|-------|-----------|-------|-------|---|
| 1918 | | | †J.W. Weston | Co C | Unopp. | |
| 1922 | | | J.W. Weston | C | Unopp. | |
| 1923 | | | J.W. Weston | C | Unopp. | |
| 1924 | 31,376 | 80.2 | Hon. O.F.G. Stanley | C | 17,935 | 71.2 |
| | | | R.P. Burnett | Lab | 7,242 | 28.8 |
| | | | | | 10,693 | 42.4 |
| 1929 | 42,139 | 81.9 | Hon. O.F.G. Stanley | C | 17,101 | 49.6 |
| | | | W.G. Ward | L | 13,223 | 38.3 |
| | | | W. Bone | Lab | 4,184* | 12.1 |
| | | | | | 3,878 | 11.3 |
| 1931 | | | Hon. O.F.G. Stanley | C | Unopp. | |
| 1935 | 44,797 | 73.8 | Rt. Hon. O.F.G. Stanley | C | 22,634 | 68.5 |
| | | | Mrs. E.V. Short | Lab | 10,417 | 31.5 |
| | | | | | 12,217 | 37.0 |
| 1945 | 48,117 | 76.9 | W.M.F. Vane | C | 19,717 | 53.3 |
| | | | H.B. Richardson | Lab | 9,674 | 26.1 |
| | | | A.G.D. Acland | L | 7,313 | 19.8 |
| | | | F.B. Price-Heywood | Ind | 306* | 0.8 |
| | | | | | 10,043 | 27.2 |

| Election | Electors | T'out | Candidate | Party | Votes | % |
|---|---|---|---|---|---|---|
| 1918 | 27,013 | 61.3 | †G. Terrell | Co C | 8,786 | 53.1 |
| | | | A.J. Bennett | L | 4,839 | 29.2 |
| | | | R. George | Lab | 2,939 | 17.7 |
| | | | | | 3,947 | 23.9 |
| 1922 | 27,682 | 78.0 | A.J. Bonwick | L | 10,494 | 48.6 |
| | | | G. Terrell | C | 10,006 | 46.3 |
| | | | W.R. Roberts | Lab | 1,098* | 5.1 |
| | | | | | 488 | 2.3 |
| 1923 | 28,315 | 81.6 | A.J. Bonwick | L | 11,953 | 51.7 |
| | | | V.A. Cazalet | C | 11,156 | 48.3 |
| | | | | | 797 | 3.4 |
| 1924 | 29,135 | 83.2 | V.A. Cazalet | C | 13,227 | 54.6 |
| | | | A.J. Bonwick | L | 11,015 | 45.4 |
| | | | | | 2,212 | 9.2 |
| 1929 | 35,404 | 82.2 | V.A. Cazalet | C | 13,550 | 46.6 |
| | | | Sir F.J.M. Brunner, Bt. | L | 11,819 | 40.6 |
| | | | W.R. Robins | Lab | 3,717 | 12.8 |
| | | | | | 1,731 | 6.0 |
| 1931 | 36,282 | 83.7 | V.A. Cazalet | C | 17,232 | 56.8 |
| | | | H.W.S. Howard | L | 10,928 | 36.0 |
| | | | W.R. Robins | Lab | 2,194* | 7.2 |
| | | | | | 6,304 | 20.8 |
| 1935 | 37,210 | 77.5 | V.A. Cazalet | C | 15,370 | 53.3 |
| | | | A.W. Stanton | L | 9,949 | 34.5 |
| | | | W.R. Robins | Lab | 3,527* | 12.2 |
| | | | | | 5,421 | 18.8 |
| [Death] | | | | | | |
| 1943 (24/8) | 39,648 | 41.4 | D.M. Eccles | C | 8,310 | 50.6 |
| | | | Dr. D.M. Johnson | Ind L | 8,115 | 49.4 |
| | | | | | 195 | 1.2 |
| 1945 | 53,524 | 69.7 | D.M. Eccles | C | 15,889 | 42.6 |
| | | | A. Tomlinson | Lab | 11,866 | 31.8 |
| | | | Dr. D.M. Johnson | L | 9,547 | 25.6 |
| | | | | | 4,023 | 10.8 |

Note:—

1945: Johnson sought election as an 'Independent Liberal' but his name was included in the official list of Liberal Party candidates.

| Election | Electors | T'out | Candidate | Party | Votes | % |
|----------|----------|-------|-----------|-------|-------|---|
| 1918 | 25,091 | 53.1 | W.C.H. Bell | Co C | 8,512 | 63.8 |
|  |  |  | J. Currie | L | 4,823 | 36.2 |
|  |  |  |  |  | 3,689 | 27.6 |
| 1922 | 24,937 | 64.9 | W.C.H. Bell | C | 9,598 | 59.3 |
|  |  |  | Lady Currie | L | 6,578 | 40.7 |
|  |  |  |  |  | 3,020 | 18.6 |
| 1923 | 25,588 | 69.5 | E. Macfadyen | L | 9,202 | 51.8 |
|  |  |  | W.C.H. Bell | C | 8,574 | 48.2 |
|  |  |  |  |  | 628 | 3.6 |
| 1924 | 26,195 | 76.2 | P.A. Hurd | C | 12,157 | 60.9 |
|  |  |  | E. Macfadyen | L | 7,807 | 39.1 |
|  |  |  |  |  | 4,350 | 21.8 |
| 1929 | 32,371 | 77.5 | P.A. Hurd | C | 11,979 | 47.8 |
|  |  |  | E. Macfadyen | L | 10,728 | 42.7 |
|  |  |  | R.P. Sheppard | Lab | 2,391* | 9.5 |
|  |  |  |  |  | 1,251 | 5.1 |
| 1931 | 33,075 | 76.2 | P.A. Hurd | C | 16,702 | 66.3 |
|  |  |  | J.W. Molden | L | 8,501 | 33.7 |
|  |  |  |  |  | 8,201 | 32.6 |
| 1935 | 33,715 | 72.2 | Sir P.A. Hurd | C | 14,438 | 59.3 |
|  |  |  | Miss F.L. Josephy | L | 9,903 | 40.7 |
|  |  |  |  |  | 4,535 | 18.6 |
| 1945 | 38,911 | 69.9 | M.C. Hollis | C | 12,796 | 47.0 |
|  |  |  | W.E. Cave | Lab | 8,120 | 29.9 |
|  |  |  | Miss F.L. Josephy | L | 6,278 | 23.1 |
|  |  |  |  |  | 4,676 | 17.1 |

| Election | Electors | T'out | Candidate | Party | Votes | % |
|---|---|---|---|---|---|---|
| 1918 | 29,144 | 59.0 | †H. Morrison | Co C | 9,168 | 53.3 |
| | | | A.E. Brown | L | 8,018 | 46.7 |
| | | | | | 1,150 | 6.6 |
| 1922 | 28,911 | 81.1 | H. Morrison | C | 11,882 | 50.7 |
| | | | A.E. Brown | L | 11,559 | 49.3 |
| | | | | | 323 | 1.4 |
| 1923 | 30,026 | 80.2 | Hon. H.L.F. Moulton | L | 12,375 | 51.4 |
| | | | H. Morrison | C | 11,710 | 48.6 |
| | | | | | 665 | 2.8 |
| 1924 | 31,393 | 81.8 | H. Morrison | C | 14,475 | 56.3 |
| | | | Hon. H.L.F. Moulton | L | 9,138 | 35.6 |
| | | | D. Freeman | Lab | 2,071* | 8.1 |
| | | | | | 5,337 | 20.7 |
| 1929 | 40,453 | 81.9 | H. Morrison | C | 15,672 | 47.3 |
| | | | Mrs. L.B. Masterman | L | 13,022 | 39.3 |
| | | | F.R. Hancock | Lab | 4,435 | 13.4 |
| | | | | | 2,650 | 8.0 |
| [Resignation] | | | | | | |
| 1931 (11/3) | 41,243 | 71.1 | J.A.St.G.F. Despencer-Robertson | C | 15,800 | 53.9 |
| | | | Mrs. L.B. Masterman | L | 9,588 | 32.7 |
| | | | F.R. Hancock | Lab | 3,939 | 13.4 |
| | | | | | 6,212 | 21.2 |
| 1931 | 41,950 | 71.9 | J.A.St.G.F. Despencer-Robertson | C | 23,189 | 76.9 |
| | | | A.B. Lemon | Lab | 6,956 | 23.1 |
| | | | | | 16,233 | 53.8 |
| 1935 | 43,781 | 66.2 | J.A.St.G.F. Despencer-Robertson | C | 20,707 | 71.5 |
| | | | E.J. Plaisted | Lab | 8,259 | 28.5 |
| | | | | | 12,448 | 43.0 |
| [Death] | | | | | | |
| 1942 (8/7) | 44,893 | 39.7 | J.G. Morrison | C | 12,076 | 67.8 |
| | | | W.R. Hipwell | Ind Prog | 3,218 | 18.1 |
| | | | J.D. Monro | Ind Dem | 2,519 | 14.1 |
| | | | | | 8,858 | 49.7 |
| 1945 | 53,583 | 71.0 | J.G. Morrison | C | 16,742 | 44.0 |
| | | | J.A.L. Caunter | Lab | 12,344 | 32.5 |
| | | | A. Campbell-Johnson | L | 8,946 | 23.5 |
| | | | | | 4,398 | 11.5 |

Note:—

1942: Monro was at first supported but later repudiated by J.B. Priestley's '1941 Committee'.

| Election | Electors | T'out | Candidate | Party | Votes | % |
|---|---|---|---|---|---|---|
| 1918 | 31,406 | 67.0 | Sir F.W. Young | Co C | 10,180 | 48.4 |
| | | | J. Compton | Lab | 8,393 | 39.9 |
| | | | H. Walker | L | 2,460* | 11.7 |
| | | | | | 1,787 | 8.5 |
| 1922 | 33,000 | 80.0 | R.M. Banks | C | 14,886 | 56.4 |
| | | | J. Compton | Lab | 11,502 | 43.6 |
| | | | | | 3,384 | 12.8 |
| 1923 | 33,787 | 82.8 | R.M. Banks | C | 12,625 | 45.1 |
| | | | G.W.H. Knight | Lab | 9,121 | 32.6 |
| | | | W.L. Rocke | L | 6,231 | 22.3 |
| | | | | | 3,504 | 12.5 |
| 1924 | 34,938 | 81.0 | R.M. Banks | C | 15,602 | 55.1 |
| | | | R.H. Tawney | Lab | 12,698 | 44.9 |
| | | | | | 2,904 | 10.2 |
| 1929 | 45,250 | 85.5 | Rt. Hon. C. Addison | Lab | 16,885 | 43.6 |
| | | | Sir R.M. Banks | C | 14,724 | 38.1 |
| | | | F.C. Thornborough | L | 7,060 | 18.3 |
| | | | | | 2,161 | 5.5 |
| 1931 | 47,609 | 85.5 | Sir R.M. Banks | C | 22,756 | 55.9 |
| | | | Rt. Hon. C. Addison | Lab | 17,962 | 44.1 |
| | | | | | 4,794 | 11.8 |

[Resignation on appointment as a County Court Judge]

| Election | Electors | T'out | Candidate | Party | Votes | % |
|---|---|---|---|---|---|---|
| 1934 | 47,877 | 81.8 | Rt. Hon. C. Addison | Lab | 20,902 | 53.4 |
| (25/10) | | | W.W. Wakefield | C | 18,253 | 46.6 |
| | | | | | 2,649 | 6.8 |
| 1935 | 48,052 | 84.3 | W.W. Wakefield | C | 20,732 | 51.2 |
| | | | Rt. Hon. C. Addison | Lab | 19,757 | 48.8 |
| | | | | | 975 | 2.4 |
| 1945 | 59,878 | 73.8 | T. Reid | Lab | 27,545 | 62.3 |
| | | | A.M. Gibb | C | 16,641 | 37.7 |
| | | | | | 10,904 | 24.6 |

| Election | Electors | T'out | Candidate | Party | Votes | % |
|---|---|---|---|---|---|---|
| 1918 | 29,208 | 64.6 | G.L. Palmer | Co C | 9,261 | 49.1 |
| | | | †Hon. G.W.A. Howard | L | 6,064 | 32.1 |
| | | | E.N. Bennett | Lab | 3,537 | 18.8 |
| | | | | | 3,197 | 17.0 |
| 1922 | 29,310 | 81.0 | C.W. Darbishire | L | 9,903 | 41.7 |
| | | | G.L. Palmer | C | 9,262 | 39.0 |
| | | | G. Ward | Lab | 4,572 | 19.3 |
| | | | | | 641 | 2.7 |
| 1923 | 30,102 | 83.5 | C.W. Darbishire | L | 10,867 | 43.2 |
| | | | W.W. Shaw | C | 9,891 | 39.4 |
| | | | G. Ward | Lab | 4,372 | 17.4 |
| | | | | | 976 | 3.8 |
| 1924 | 30,784 | 84.9 | W.W. Shaw | C | 11,559 | 44.2 |
| | | | C.W. Darbishire | L | 9,848 | 37.7 |
| | | | G. Ward | Lab | 4,731 | 18.1 |
| | | | | | 1,711 | 6.5 |
| [Death] | | | | | | |
| 1927 (16/6) | 31,321 | 84.6 | Hon. R.E.O. Long | C | 10,623 | 40.1 |
| | | | H. Johnstone | L | 10,474 | 39.5 |
| | | | G. Ward | Lab | 5,396 | 20.4 |
| | | | | | 149 | 0.6 |
| 1929 | 38,119 | 87.1 | Hon. R.E.O. Long | C | 12,907 | 38.8 |
| | | | H. Johnstone | L | 12,840 | 38.7 |
| | | | G. Ward | Lab | 7,458 | 22.5 |
| | | | | | 67 | 0.1 |
| 1931 | 38,744 | 85.4 | R.V. Grimston | C | 16,949 | 51.2 |
| | | | J.H. Harris | L | 11,014 | 33.3 |
| | | | M.F. Hackett | Lab | 5,127 | 15.5 |
| | | | | | 5,935 | 17.9 |
| 1935 | 40,253 | 80.1 | R.V. Grimston | C | 15,804 | 49.0 |
| | | | C.C. Byers | L | 10,789 | 33.5 |
| | | | R.St.J. Reade | Lab | 5,641 | 17.5 |
| | | | | | 5,015 | 15.5 |
| 1945 | 48,716 | 75.4 | R.V. Grimston | C | 14,328 | 39.0 |
| | | | G. Ward | Lab | 13,397 | 36.5 |
| | | | W.G. Milne | L | 9,004 | 24.5 |
| | | | | | 931 | 2.5 |

| Election | Electors | T'out | Candidate | Party | Votes | % |
|---|---|---|---|---|---|---|
| 1918 | | | †S. Baldwin | Co C | Unopp. | |
| [Appointed President of the Board of Trade] | | | | | | |
| 1921 | 25,440 | 63.7 | Rt. Hon. S. Baldwin | Co C | 14,537 | 89.6 |
| (19/4) | | | H. Mills | Ind Lab | 1,680* | 10.4 |
| | | | | | 12,857 | 79.2 |
| 1922 | 26,177 | 64.7 | Rt. Hon. S. Baldwin | C | 11,192 | 66.1 |
| | | | S. Hancock | L | 5,748 | 33.9 |
| | | | | | 5,444 | 32.2 |
| 1923 | 26,765 | 68.8 | Rt. Hon. S. Baldwin | C | 12,395 | 67.3 |
| | | | S. Hancock | L | 6,026 | 32.7 |
| | | | | | 6,369 | 34.6 |
| 1924 | | | Rt. Hon. S. Baldwin | C | Unopp. | |
| 1929 | 36,979 | 71.3 | Rt. Hon. S. Baldwin | C | 16,593 | 62.9 |
| | | | S.B. Carter | L | 7,186 | 27.3 |
| | | | S. Hancock | Lab | 2,575* | 9.8 |
| | | | | | 9,407 | 35.6 |
| 1931 | | | Rt. Hon. S. Baldwin | C | Unopp. | |
| 1935 | | | Rt. Hon. S. Baldwin | C | Unopp. | |
| [Elevation to the Peerage — Earl Baldwin of Bewdley] | | | | | | |
| 1937 | 38,916 | 60.6 | R.J.E. Conant | C | 15,054 | 63.9 |
| (24/6) | | | Dr. D.M. Johnson | L | 8,511 | 36.1 |
| | | | | | 6,543 | 27.8 |
| 1945 | 46,828 | 67.5 | R.J.E. Conant | C | 17,393 | 55.0 |
| | | | G. Samson | L | 14,223 | 45.0 |
| | | | | | 3,170 | 10.0 |

| Election | Electors | T'out | Candidate | Party | Votes | % |
|---|---|---|---|---|---|---|
| 1918 | 28,931 | 58.5 | †B.M. Eyres-Monsell | Co C | 10,479 | 62.0 |
| | | | W.P. Ellis | L | 3,570 | 21.1 |
| | | | W.M. Fielding | Lab | 2,863 | 16.9 |
| | | | | | 6,909 | 40.9 |
| 1922 | 29,230 | 65.7 | B.M. Eyres-Monsell | C | 11,502 | 59.9 |
| | | | R. Aldington | Lab | 7,715 | 40.1 |
| | | | | | 3,787 | 19.8 |
| 1923 | 29,729 | 67.7 | Rt. Hon. B.M. Eyres-Monsell | C | 10,976 | 54.5 |
| | | | W.H. Collett | L | 5,453 | 27.1 |
| | | | R. Aldington | Lab | 3,705 | 18.4 |
| | | | | | 5,523 | 27.4 |
| 1924 | 30,270 | 66.4 | Rt. Hon. B.M. Eyres-Monsell | C | 13,176 | 65.5 |
| | | | R. Aldington | Lab | 3,473 | 17.3 |
| | | | B.R. Swift | L | 3,454 | 17.2 |
| | | | | | 9,703 | 48.2 |
| 1929 | 39,721 | 76.4 | Rt. Hon. B.M. Eyres-Monsell | C | 14,694 | 48.4 |
| | | | S. Davies | L | 11,519 | 38.0 |
| | | | R. Aldington | Lab | 4,138 | 13.6 |
| | | | | | 3,175 | 10.4 |
| 1931 | | | Rt. Hon. Sir B.M. Eyres-Monsell | C | Unopp. | |
| 1935 | 43,394 | 66.4 | R. De la Bère | C | 18,757 | 65.1 |
| | | | W.E. Warder | Lab | 6,264 | 21.8 |
| | | | C. a'B. Williams | L | 3,774 | 13.1 |
| | | | | | 12,493 | 43.3 |
| 1945 | 52,764 | 63.3 | R. De la Bère | C | 17,835 | 53.4 |
| | | | D.J. McGuffie | L | 7,849 | 23.5 |
| | | | D.L. Donnelly | CW | 7,727 | 23.1 |
| | | | | | 9,986 | 29.9 |

| Election | Electors | T'out | Candidate | Party | Votes | % |
|---|---|---|---|---|---|---|
| 1918 | 39,798 | 58.4 | †E.A. Knight | Co C | 13,497 | 58.0 |
| | | | J. Baker | Lab | 9,760 | 42.0 |
| | | | | | 3,737 | 16.0 |
| 1922 | 41,286 | 70.0 | J.S. Wardlaw-Milne | C | 19,711 | 68.2 |
| | | | J.H. Bruce | Lab | 9,203 | 31.8 |
| | | | | | 10,508 | 36.4 |
| 1923 | 41,939 | 69.4 | J.S. Wardlaw-Milne | C | 15,469 | 53.1 |
| | | | H.G. Purchase | L | 9,663 | 33.2 |
| | | | L. Tolley | Lab | 3,990 | 13.7 |
| | | | | | 5,806 | 19.9 |
| 1924 | 42,770 | 71.3 | J.S. Wardlaw-Milne | C | 18,040 | 59.1 |
| | | | J.C. Leigh | Lab | 6,792 | 22.3 |
| | | | H.G. Purchase | L | 5,667 | 18.6 |
| | | | | | 11,248 | 36.8 |
| 1929 | 59,421 | 75.6 | J.S. Wardlaw-Milne | C | 21,643 | 48.1 |
| | | | F.G. Lloyd | Lab | 12,246 | 27.3 |
| | | | J.W. Hughes | L | 11,050 | 24.6 |
| | | | | | 9,397 | 20.8 |
| 1931 | 62,530 | 69.0 | J.S. Wardlaw-Milne | C | 33,359 | 77.3 |
| | | | Miss J. Stephen | Lab | 9,814 | 22.7 |
| | | | | | 23,545 | 54.6 |
| 1935 | 68,098 | 60.2 | Sir J.S. Wardlaw-Milne | C | 28,494 | 69.5 |
| | | | C. Coombes | Lab | 12,485 | 30.5 |
| | | | | | 16,009 | 39.0 |
| 1945 | 87,253 | 70.7 | L. Tolley | Lab | 34,421 | 55.8 |
| | | | Sir J.S. Wardlaw-Milne | C | 27,247 | 44.2 |
| | | | | | 7,174 | 11.6 |

| Election | Electors | T'out | Candidate | Party | Votes | % |
|---|---|---|---|---|---|---|
| 1918 | 42,205 | 55.0 | †Rt. Hon. J.W. Wilson | L | 8,920 | 38.5 |
| | | | Miss M.R. Macarthur | Lab | 7,587 | 32.7 |
| | | | F.V. Fisher | Co NDP | 6,690 | 28.8 |
| | | | | | 1,333 | 5.8 |
| 1922 | 46,346 | 75.8 | D.P. Pielou | C | 18,200 | 51.8 |
| | | | Rt. Hon. J.W. Wilson | L | 16,949 | 48.2 |
| | | | | | 1,251 | 3.6 |
| 1923 | 47,241 | 78.5 | D.P. Pielou | C | 14,764 | 39.8 |
| | | | H.E. Palfrey | L | 13,269 | 35.8 |
| | | | W. Wellock | Lab | 9,050 | 24.4 |
| | | | | | 1,495 | 4.0 |
| 1924 | 48,466 | 83.7 | D.P. Pielou | C | 16,023 | 39.5 |
| | | | W. Wellock | Lab | 14,113 | 34.8 |
| | | | G. Le M. Mander | L | 10,418 | 25.7 |
| | | | | | 1,910 | 4.7 |
| [Death] | | | | | | |
| 1927 (23/2) | 49,587 | 79.8 | W. Wellock | Lab | 16,561 | 41.9 |
| | | | H.C. Hogbin | C | 13,462 | 34.0 |
| | | | A.J.G. Edwards | L | 9,535 | 24.1 |
| | | | | | 3,099 | 7.9 |
| 1929 | 66,145 | 84.0 | W. Wellock | Lab | 21,343 | 38.4 |
| | | | Sir H.S. Reed | C | 17,675 | 31.8 |
| | | | D.L. Finnemore | L | 16,537 | 29.8 |
| | | | | | 3,668 | 6.6 |
| 1931 | 70,324 | 82.0 | R.H. Morgan | C | 22,652 | 39.3 |
| | | | W. Wellock | Lab | 18,910 | 32.8 |
| | | | D.L. Finnemore | L | 16,121 | 27.9 |
| | | | | | 3,742 | 6.5 |
| 1935 | 80,598 | 70.9 | R.H. Morgan | C | 24,898 | 43.5 |
| | | | W. Wellock | Lab | 19,597 | 34.3 |
| | | | D.L. Finnemore | L | 12,684 | 22.2 |
| | | | | | 5,301 | 9.2 |
| 1945 | 97,095 | 74.2 | A. Moyle | Lab | 34,912 | 48.5 |
| | | | R.H. Morgan | C | 18,979 | 26.3 |
| | | | R.K. Brown | L | 18,159 | 25.2 |
| | | | | | 15,933 | 22.2 |

| Election | Electors | T'out | Candidate | Party | Votes | % |
|---|---|---|---|---|---|---|
| 1918 | 27,288 | 56.0 | A.H. Moreing | Co L | 9,310 | 60.9 |
| | | | G.H. Dawson | Ind Lab | 3,176 | 20.8 |
| | | | A. Taylor | L | 2,792 | 18.3 |
| | | | | | 6,134 | 40.1 |
| 1922 | 28,385 | 82.5 | Sir G.R.A. Gaunt | C | 12,012 | 51.3 |
| | | | T.D. Fenby | L | 11,411 | 48.7 |
| | | | | | 601 | 2.6 |
| 1923 | 29,076 | 84.1 | Sir G.R.A. Gaunt | C | 12,336 | 50.4 |
| | | | T.D. Fenby | L | 12,122 | 49.6 |
| | | | | | 214 | 0.8 |
| 1924 | 30,074 | 82.9 | Sir G.R.A. Gaunt | C | 13,966 | 56.0 |
| | | | H.A. Briggs | L | 10,962 | 44.0 |
| | | | | | 3,004 | 12.0 |

[Resignation]

| Election | Electors | T'out | Candidate | Party | Votes | % |
|---|---|---|---|---|---|---|
| 1926 (5/5) | 30,388[†] | 81.7 | A.N. Braithwaite | C | 12,089 | 48.7 |
| | | | Sir H.C.W. Verney, Bt. | L | 10,537 | 42.5 |
| | | | H.C. Laycock | Lab | 2,191* | 8.8 |
| | | | | | 1,552 | 6.2 |
| 1929 | 38,884 | 80.4 | A.N. Braithwaite | C | 15,625 | 50.0 |
| | | | S.S. Lamert | L | 13,885 | 44.4 |
| | | | H.H. Vickers | Lab | 1,766* | 5.6 |
| | | | | | 1,740 | 5.6 |
| 1931 | | | A.N. Braithwaite | C | Unopp. | |
| 1935 | 41,899 | 78.4 | A.N. Braithwaite | C | 18,090 | 55.1 |
| | | | T. Macleod | L | 14,763 | 44.9 |
| | | | | | 3,327 | 10.2 |
| 1945 | 43,145 | 71.7 | G. Wadsworth | L | 15,935 | 51.5 |
| | | | Sir A.N. Braithwaite | C | 14,985 | 48.5 |
| | | | | | 950 | 3.0 |

| Election | Electors | T'out | Candidate | Party | Votes | % |
|----------|----------|-------|-----------|-------|-------|---|
| 1918 | 25,741 | 57.9 | †A.S. Wilson | Co C | 9,387 | 63.0 |
| | | | F. Maddison | L | 5,521 | 37.0 |
| | | | | | 3,866 | 26.0 |
| 1922 | 27,421 | 79.1 | W.A. Bowdler | L | 11,479 | 52.9 |
| | | | A.S. Wilson | C | 10,200 | 47.1 |
| | | | | | 1,279 | 5.8 |
| 1923 | 28,085 | 78.1 | S.S. Savery | C | 11,099 | 50.6 |
| | | | W.A. Bowdler | L | 10,846 | 49.4 |
| | | | | | 253 | 1.2 |
| 1924 | 28,449 | 81.1 | S.S. Savery | C | 12,911 | 56.0 |
| | | | C.N.D. Dixey | L | 10,162 | 44.0 |
| | | | | | 2,749 | 12.0 |
| 1929 | 38,147 | 80.1 | S.S. Savery | C | 14,544 | 47.6 |
| | | | C.N.D. Dixey | L | 13,525 | 44.3 |
| | | | J.W. Hewitt | Lab | 2,481* | 8.1 |
| | | | | | 1,019 | 3.3 |
| 1931 | 42,734 | 81.8 | S.S. Savery | C | 21,560 | 61.6 |
| | | | Miss A. Mackinnon | L | 10,471 | 30.0 |
| | | | J.L. Schultz | Lab | 2,927* | 8.4 |
| | | | | | 11,089 | 31.6 |
| 1935 | 57,466 | 72.2 | S.S. Savery | C | 22,249 | 53.6 |
| | | | Miss A. Mackinnon | L | 10,348 | 24.9 |
| | | | J.L. Schultz | Lab | 8,906 | 21.5 |
| | | | | | 11,901 | 28.7 |
| [Death] | | | | | | |
| 1939 | 67,967 | 66.3 | J.G. Braithwaite | C | 17,742 | 39.4 |
| (15/2) | | | Miss A. Mackinnon | L | 11,590 | 25.7 |
| | | | J.L. Schultz | Lab | 9,629 | 21.4 |
| | | | R.C.J. Chichester-Constable | Ind C | 6,103 | 13.5 |
| | | | | | 6,152 | 13.7 |
| 1945 | 77,475 | 75.4 | J.G. Braithwaite | C | 25,181 | 43.1 |
| | | | C.F.C. Lawson | Lab | 23,036 | 39.5 |
| | | | R.T.B. Fulford | L | 10,165 | 17.4 |
| | | | | | 2,145 | 3.6 |

Note:—

1939: Chichester-Constable was supported by the East Yorkshire Executive Committee of the National Farmers' Union and two (out of four) of the NFU branches in the constituency. He opposed the Government's agricultural policy.

| Election | Electors | T'out | Candidate | Party | Votes | % |
|---|---|---|---|---|---|---|
| 1918 | 23,481 | 57.1 | †Hon. F.S. Jackson | Co C | 9,023 | 67.3 |
| | | | T.D. Fenby | L | 4,384 | 32.7 |
| | | | | | 4,639 | 34.6 |
| 1922 | 24,975 | 71.1 | Hon. F.S. Jackson | C | 10,748 | 60.5 |
| | | | H.J. Winn | Agric | 7,021 | 39.5 |
| | | | | | 3,727 | 21.0 |
| 1923 | | | Hon. F.S. Jackson | C | Unopp. | |
| 1924 | | | Hon. F.S. Jackson | C | Unopp. | |

[Resignation on appointment as Governor of Bengal]

| Election | Electors | T'out | Candidate | Party | Votes | % |
|---|---|---|---|---|---|---|
| 1926 | 26,682 | 73.6 | W.H. Carver | C | 10,653 | 54.2 |
| (25/11) | | | F.C. Linfield | L | 6,668 | 34.0 |
| | | | J.W. Kneeshaw | Lab | 2,318* | 11.8 |
| | | | | | 3,985 | 20.2 |
| 1929 | 35,164 | 76.8 | W.H. Carver | C | 13,823 | 51.2 |
| | | | E. Baker | L | 13,170 | 48.8 |
| | | | | | 653 | 2.4 |
| 1931 | | | W.H. Carver | C | Unopp. | |
| 1935 | 41,093 | 69.2 | W.H. Carver | C | 18,155 | 63.9 |
| | | | E. Baker | L | 7,837 | 27.5 |
| | | | J. Richardson | Lab | 2,459* | 8.6 |
| | | | | | 10,318 | 36.4 |
| 1945 | 53,679 | 71.1 | C.W.H. Glossop | C | 21,348 | 56.0 |
| | | | T. Neville | Lab/Co-op | 11,161 | 29.2 |
| | | | J.E. Wilson | L | 5,669 | 14.8 |
| | | | | | 10,187 | 26.8 |

[Resignation]

| Election | Electors | T'out | Candidate | Party | Votes | % |
|---|---|---|---|---|---|---|
| 1947 | 54,384 | 67.0 | G.W. Odey | C | 23,344 | 64.0 |
| (27/11) | | | T. Neville | Lab/Co-op | 9,298 | 25.5 |
| | | | J.E. Wilson | L | 3,819* | 10.5 |
| | | | | | 14,046 | 38.5 |

Note:—

1922: Winn was the nominee of the NFU.

## YORKSHIRE (North Riding), CLEVELAND  [490]

| Election | Electors | T'out | Candidate | Party | Votes | % |
|---|---|---|---|---|---|---|
| 1918 | 36,843 | 66.2 | Sir P. Goff | Co C | 8,701 | 35.6 |
| | | | H. Dack | Lab | 8,610 | 35.3 |
| | | | †Rt. Hon. H.L. Samuel | L | 7,089 | 29.1 |
| | | | | | 91 | 0.3 |
| 1922 | 43,105 | 82.4 | Sir P. Goff | C | 13,369 | 37.7 |
| | | | Sir C.W. Starmer | L | 11,668 | 32.8 |
| | | | H. Dack | Lab | 10,483 | 29.5 |
| | | | | | 1,701 | 4.9 |
| 1923 | 43,339 | 80.4 | Sir C.W. Starmer | L | 13,326 | 38.2 |
| | | | Sir P. Goff | C | 11,855 | 34.0 |
| | | | R. Dennison | Lab | 9,683 | 27.8 |
| | | | | | 1,471 | 4.2 |
| 1924 | 44,040 | 86.3 | Sir P. Goff | C | 16,578 | 43.6 |
| | | | W.T. Mansfield | Lab | 11,153 | 29.4 |
| | | | Sir C.W. Starmer | L | 10,260 | 27.0 |
| | | | | | 5,425 | 14.2 |
| 1929 | 55,463 | 84.3 | W.T. Mansfield | Lab | 16,938 | 36.3 |
| | | | Sir P. Goff | C | 15,255 | 32.6 |
| | | | Sir C.W. Starmer | L | 14,535 | 31.1 |
| | | | | | 1,683 | 3.7 |
| 1931 | 58,973 | 85.9 | R.T. Bower | C | 30,608 | 60.4 |
| | | | W.T. Mansfield | Lab | 20,060 | 39.6 |
| | | | | | 10,548 | 20.8 |
| 1935 | 61,961 | 81.2 | R.T. Bower | C | 26,508 | 52.7 |
| | | | W.T. Mansfield | Lab | 23,776 | 47.3 |
| | | | | | 2,732 | 5.4 |
| 1945 | 74,332 | 76.0 | O.G. Willey | Lab | 27,660 | 49.0 |
| | | | R.T. Bower | C | 19,739 | 34.9 |
| | | | M.R. Shawcross | L | 9,108 | 16.1 |
| | | | | | 7,921 | 14.1 |

| Election | Electors | T'out | Candidate | Party | Votes | % |
|---|---|---|---|---|---|---|
| 1918 | 30,710 | 48.1 | M.J. Wilson | Co C | 9,857 | 66.8 |
| | | | W. Parlour | Agric | 4,907 | 33.2 |
| | | | | | 4,950 | 33.6 |
| 1922 | | | M.J. Wilson | C | Unopp. | |
| 1923 | | | M.J. Wilson | C | Unopp. | |
| 1924 | | | M.J. Wilson | C | Unopp. | |
| 1929 | 43,314 | 79.4 | T.L. Dugdale | C | 19,763 | 57.5 |
| | | | J.D. Hinks | L | 14,634 | 42.5 |
| | | | | | 5,129 | 15.0 |
| 1931 | | | T.L. Dugdale | C | Unopp. | |
| 1935 | 47,658 | 68.1 | T.L. Dugdale | C | 25,088 | 77.3 |
| | | | A.J. Best | Lab | 7,369 | 22.7 |
| | | | | | 17,719 | 54.6 |
| 1945 | 50,836 | 68.2 | Sir T.L. Dugdale, Bt. | C | 18,332 | 52.9 |
| | | | M.W. Darwin | L | 9,427 | 27.2 |
| | | | G.H. Metcalfe | Lab | 6,104 | 17.6 |
| | | | R.N. Chesterton | CW | 813* | 2.3 |
| | | | | | 8,905 | 25.7 |

Note:—

1918: Parlour was the nominee of the NFU.

| Election | Electors | T'out | Candidate | Party | Votes | % |
|---|---|---|---|---|---|---|
| 1918 | 34,578 | 60.1 | †Hon. W.G. Beckett | Co C | 11,764 | 56.6 |
| | | | F.O.S. Sitwell | L | 7,994 | 38.5 |
| | | | J.W. Rowntree | Lab | 1,025* | 4.9 |
| | | | | | 3,770 | 18.1 |
| 1922 | 38,846 | 76.2 | S. Herbert | C | 16,358 | 55.2 |
| | | | S.P. Turnbull | L | 13,262 | 44.8 |
| | | | | | 3,096 | 10.4 |
| 1923 | 40,383 | 76.4 | S. Herbert | C | 15,927 | 51.6 |
| | | | A. Mitchell | L | 14,933 | 48.4 |
| | | | | | 994 | 3.2 |
| 1924 | 41,640 | 78.9 | S. Herbert | C | 18,911 | 57.5 |
| | | | A. Mitchell | L | 11,223 | 34.2 |
| | | | H.D. Rowntree | Lab | 2,713* | 8.3 |
| | | | | | 7,688 | 23.3 |
| 1929 | 53,846 | 79.7 | S. Herbert | C | 20,710 | 48.3 |
| | | | H.P. Gisborne | L | 17,549 | 40.9 |
| | | | H.D. Rowntree | Lab | 4,645* | 10.8 |
| | | | | | 3,161 | 7.4 |
| [Resignation] | | | | | | |
| 1931 (6/5) | 54,389 | 75.5 | H.P. Latham | C | 21,618 | 52.7 |
| | | | J.R.B. Muir | L | 19,429 | 47.3 |
| | | | | | 2,189 | 5.4 |
| 1931 | 55,546 | 69.5 | Sir H.P. Latham, Bt. | C | 32,025 | 83.0 |
| | | | P.S. Eastman | Lab | 6,575 | 17.0 |
| | | | | | 25,450 | 66.0 |
| 1935 | 57,631 | 74.7 | Sir H.P. Latham, Bt. | C | 23,210 | 53.9 |
| | | | J.R.B. Muir | L | 16,668 | 38.7 |
| | | | T.W. Coates | Lab | 3,195* | 7.4 |
| | | | | | 6,542 | 15.2 |
| [Resignation] | | | | | | |
| 1941 (24/9) | 57,381 | 35.9 | A.C.M. Spearman | C | 12,518 | 60.8 |
| | | | W.R. Hipwell | Ind Prog | 8,086 | 39.2 |
| | | | | | 4,432 | 21.6 |
| 1945 | 59,171 | 69.0 | A.C.M. Spearman | C | 20,786 | 50.9 |
| | | | L.H. Razzall | L | 10,739 | 26.3 |
| | | | D.H. Curry | Lab | 9,289 | 22.8 |
| | | | | | 10,047 | 24.6 |

| Election | Electors | T'out | Candidate | Party | Votes | % |
|----------|----------|-------|-----------|-------|-------|---|
| 1918 | 26,765 | 52.2 | †E.R. Turton | Co C | 9,656 | 69.1 |
|  |  |  | S.S. Lockwood | L | 4,317 | 30.9 |
|  |  |  |  |  | 5,339 | 38.2 |
| 1922 |  |  | E.R. Turton | C | Unopp. |  |
| 1923 | 27,636 | 66.9 | E.R. Turton | C | 11,545 | 62.5 |
|  |  |  | W.H. Sessions | L | 6,939 | 37.5 |
|  |  |  |  |  | 4,606 | 25.0 |
| 1924 | 28,855 | 71.5 | E.R. Turton | C | 13,564 | 65.7 |
|  |  |  | W.H. Sessions | L | 7,072 | 34.3 |
|  |  |  |  |  | 6,492 | 31.4 |

[Seat Vacant at Dissolution (Death)]

| Election | Electors | T'out | Candidate | Party | Votes | % |
|----------|----------|-------|-----------|-------|-------|---|
| 1929 | 36,820 | 73.7 | R.H. Turton | C | 16,084 | 59.2 |
|  |  |  | T. Sunley | L | 11,069 | 40.8 |
|  |  |  |  |  | 5,015 | 18.4 |
| 1931 |  |  | R.H. Turton | C | Unopp. |  |
| 1935 |  |  | R.H. Turton | C | Unopp. |  |
| 1945 | 52,051 | 65.4 | R.H. Turton | C | 20,483 | 60.1 |
|  |  |  | E.W. Moeran | CW | 13,572 | 39.9 |
|  |  |  |  |  | 6,911 | 20.2 |

# YORKSHIRE (West Riding), BARKSTON ASH [494]

| Election | Electors | T'out | Candidate | Party | Votes | % |
|---|---|---|---|---|---|---|
| 1918 | 32,919 | 61.4 | †G.R. Lane-Fox | Co C | 12,365 | 61.2 |
| | | | J.A. Rhodes | L | 6,809 | 33.7 |
| | | | D. Milner | Ind Lab | 1,035* | 5.1 |
| | | | | | 5,556 | 27.5 |
| 1922 | | | G.R. Lane-Fox | C | Unopp. | |
| 1923 | 34,604 | 76.1 | G.R. Lane-Fox | C | 12,932 | 49.1 |
| | | | G.L. Ward | Lab | 7,964 | 30.3 |
| | | | J. Lambert | L | 5,425 | 20.6 |
| | | | | | 4,968 | 18.8 |
| 1924 | 35,792 | 80.2 | G.R. Lane-Fox | C | 16,817 | 58.6 |
| | | | W. Dobbie | Lab | 11,894 | 41.4 |
| | | | | | 4,923 | 17.2 |
| 1929 | 47,940 | 80.2 | Rt. Hon. G.R. Lane-Fox | C | 20,116 | 52.3 |
| | | | Rev. G.S. Woods | Lab/Co-op | 18,321 | 47.7 |
| | | | | | 1,795 | 4.6 |
| 1931 | 50,387 | 84.4 | L. Ropner | C | 27,924 | 65.7 |
| | | | Rev. G.S. Woods | Lab/Co-op | 14,585 | 34.3 |
| | | | | | 13,339 | 31.4 |
| 1935 | 53,777 | 78.5 | L. Ropner | C | 25,714 | 60.9 |
| | | | F. Smithson | Lab/Co-op | 16,525 | 39.1 |
| | | | | | 9,189 | 21.8 |
| 1945 | 64,624 | 75.5 | L. Ropner | C | 24,438 | 50.1 |
| | | | B. Hazell | Lab | 24,322 | 49.9 |
| | | | | | 116 | 0.2 |

# YORKSHIRE (West Riding), COLNE VALLEY [495]

| Election | Electors | T'out | Candidate | Party | Votes | % |
|----------|----------|-------|-----------|-------|-------|---|
| 1918 | 39,085 | 58.9 | †F.W. Mallalieu | Co L | 13,541 | 58.8 |
| | | | W. Whiteley | Lab | 9,473 | 41.2 |
| | | | | | 4,068 | 17.6 |
| 1922 | 40,724 | 78.5 | P. Snowden | Lab | 12,614 | 39.5 |
| | | | T. Brooke | C | 11,332 | 35.4 |
| | | | F.W. Mallalieu | L | 8,042 | 25.1 |
| | | | | | 1,282 | 4.1 |
| 1923 | 41,212 | 79.0 | P. Snowden | Lab | 13,136 | 40.4 |
| | | | T. Brooke | C | 11,215 | 34.4 |
| | | | P.H. Heffer | L | 8,223 | 25.2 |
| | | | | | 1,921 | 6.0 |
| 1924 | 41,794 | 78.6 | Rt. Hon. P. Snowden | Lab | 14,215 | 43.3 |
| | | | F. Thorpe | C | 10,972 | 33.4 |
| | | | R.F. Walker | L | 7,651 | 23.3 |
| | | | | | 3,243 | 9.9 |
| 1929 | 54,351 | 82.5 | Rt. Hon. P. Snowden | Lab (N Lab) | 21,667 | 48.3 |
| | | | R.B. Carrow | C | 12,532 | 28.0 |
| | | | F. Brook | L | 10,630 | 23.7 |
| | | | | | 9,135 | 20.3 |
| 1931 | 55,197 | 79.1 | E.L. Mallalieu | L | 17,119 | 39.2 |
| | | | E. Marklew | Lab | 13,734 | 31.5 |
| | | | E.ff.W. Lascelles | C | 12,581 | 28.8 |
| | | | M.A.E. Franklin | N Lab | 202* | 0.5 |
| | | | | | 3,385 | 7.7 |
| 1935 | 55,739 | 76.0 | E. Marklew | Lab | 16,725 | 39.5 |
| | | | E.L. Mallalieu | L | 12,946 | 30.6 |
| | | | M.G. Crofton | C | 10,917 | 25.8 |
| | | | W.G. Bagnall | Ind | 1,754* | 4.1 |
| | | | | | 3,779 | 8.9 |
| [Death] | | | | | | |
| 1939 (27/7) | 55,776 | 63.7 | W.G. Hall | Lab | 17,277 | 48.6 |
| | | | E.L. Mallalieu | L | 9,228 | 26.0 |
| | | | C.F. Pike | C | 9,012 | 25.4 |
| | | | | | 8,049 | 22.6 |
| 1945 | 54,403 | 79.0 | W.G. Hall | Lab | 23,488 | 54.6 |
| | | | S.W. Smith | C | 11,593 | 27.0 |
| | | | G.K. Lawrence | L | 7,890 | 18.4 |
| | | | | | 11,895 | 27.6 |

Note:—

1931:   Franklin retired after nomination in favour of Mallalieu.

# YORKSHIRE (West Riding), DONCASTER [496]

| Election | Electors | T'out | Candidate | Party | Votes | % |
|----------|----------|-------|-----------|-------|-------|---|
| 1918 | 35,114 | 58.6 | R. Nicholson | Co L | 15,431 | 75.0 |
|  |  |  | R. Morley | Lab | 5,153 | 25.0 |
|  |  |  |  |  | 10,278 | 50.0 |
| 1922 | 37,310 | 77.4 | W. Paling | Lab | 13,437 | 46.5 |
|  |  |  | Sir R.C.A.B. Bewicke-Copley | C | 8,279 | 28.7 |
|  |  |  | R. Nicholson | NL | 7,161 | 24.8 |
|  |  |  |  |  | 5,158 | 17.8 |
| 1923 | 39,027 | 68.4 | W. Paling | Lab | 16,198 | 60.6 |
|  |  |  | W.St.A. Warde-Aldam | C | 10,514 | 39.4 |
|  |  |  |  |  | 5,684 | 21.2 |
| 1924 | 40,633 | 77.0 | W. Paling | Lab | 16,496 | 52.7 |
|  |  |  | A.S. Matthews | C | 14,800 | 47.3 |
|  |  |  |  |  | 1,696 | 5.4 |
| 1929 | 58,213 | 77.6 | W. Paling | Lab | 25,295 | 56.0 |
|  |  |  | E.A. Phillips | C | 11,016 | 24.4 |
|  |  |  | J.T. Clarke | L | 8,842 | 19.6 |
|  |  |  |  |  | 14,279 | 31.6 |
| 1931 | 61,444 | 80.7 | A.H.E. Molson | C | 27,205 | 54.9 |
|  |  |  | W. Paling | Lab | 22,363 | 45.1 |
|  |  |  |  |  | 4,842 | 9.8 |
| 1935 | 66,925 | 77.7 | A. Short | Lab | 29,963 | 57.6 |
|  |  |  | A.H.E. Molson | C | 22,011 | 42.4 |
|  |  |  |  |  | 7,952 | 15.2 |
| [Death] |  |  |  |  |  |  |
| 1938 (17/11) | 68,632 | 75.4 | J. Morgan | Lab | 31,735 | 61.3 |
|  |  |  | A. Monteith | NL | 20,027 | 38.7 |
|  |  |  |  |  | 11,708 | 22.6 |
| [Death] |  |  |  |  |  |  |
| 1941 (6/2) |  |  | E. Walkden | Lab | Unopp. |  |
| 1945 | 76,539 | 74.5 | E. Walkden | Lab (Ind Lab) | 40,050 | 70.2 |
|  |  |  | H.A. Taylor | C | 16,999 | 29.8 |
|  |  |  |  |  | 23,051 | 40.4 |

# YORKSHIRE (West Riding), DON VALLEY   [497]

| Election | Electors | T'out | Candidate | Party | Votes | % |
|----------|----------|-------|-----------|-------|-------|---|
| 1918 | 28,724 | 45.9 | J. Walton | Co NDP | 6,095 | 46.2 |
|  |  |  | †H.B. Lees-Smith | L | 3,868 | 29.3 |
|  |  |  | E. Hough | Lab | 3,226 | 24.5 |
|  |  |  |  |  | 2,227 | 16.9 |
| 1922 | 32,175 | 65.4 | T. Williams | Lab | 9,903 | 47.0 |
|  |  |  | J. Walton | NL | 5,797 | 27.6 |
|  |  |  | J.H. Freeborough | L | 5,332 | 25.4 |
|  |  |  |  |  | 4,106 | 19.4 |
| 1923 | 34,339 | 62.2 | T. Williams | Lab | 12,898 | 60.4 |
|  |  |  | J.W. Reynolds | C | 8,451 | 39.6 |
|  |  |  |  |  | 4,447 | 20.8 |
| 1924 | 37,184 | 72.8 | T. Williams | Lab | 14,598 | 53.9 |
|  |  |  | J.W. Reynolds | C | 12,463 | 46.1 |
|  |  |  |  |  | 2,135 | 7.8 |
| 1929 | 61,604 | 69.7 | T. Williams | Lab | 31,466 | 73.3 |
|  |  |  | W.S. Liddall | C | 11,467 | 26.7 |
|  |  |  |  |  | 19,999 | 46.6 |
| 1931 | 66,197 | 71.2 | T. Williams | Lab | 27,599 | 58.6 |
|  |  |  | S. Hardwick | C | 19,506 | 41.4 |
|  |  |  |  |  | 8,093 | 17.2 |
| 1935 | 68,816 | 70.0 | T. Williams | Lab | 33,220 | 68.9 |
|  |  |  | J.S-W. Arbuthnot | C | 14,961 | 31.1 |
|  |  |  |  |  | 18,259 | 37.8 |
| 1945 | 76,487 | 73.2 | Rt. Hon. T. Williams | Lab | 40,153 | 71.7 |
|  |  |  | J.J.A.N. Ross | C | 15,832 | 28.3 |
|  |  |  |  |  | 24,321 | 43.4 |

# YORKSHIRE (West Riding), ELLAND [498]

| Election | Electors | T'out | Candidate | Party | Votes | % |
|---|---|---|---|---|---|---|
| 1918 | 34,584 | 67.0 | G.T. Ramsden | Co C | 8,917 | 38.4 |
|  |  |  | H. Dawson | L | 7,028 | 30.4 |
|  |  |  | D. Hardaker | Lab | 5,923 | 25.6 |
|  |  |  | †C.P. Trevelyan | Ind Lab | 1,286* | 5.6 |
|  |  |  |  |  | 1,889 | 8.0 |
| 1922 | 35,145 | 81.9 | W.C. Robinson | Lab | 10,590 | 36.8 |
|  |  |  | Sir R.N. Kay | NL | 10,160 | 35.3 |
|  |  |  | G.T. Ramsden | C | 8,039 | 27.9 |
|  |  |  |  |  | 430 | 1.5 |
| 1923 | 35,008 | 70.0 | Sir R.N. Kay | L | 12,476 | 50.9 |
|  |  |  | W.C. Robinson | Lab | 12,031 | 49.1 |
|  |  |  |  |  | 445 | 1.8 |
| 1924 | 35,214 | 84.1 | W.C. Robinson | Lab | 11,690 | 39.5 |
|  |  |  | A.N. Braithwaite | C | 11,202 | 37.8 |
|  |  |  | Sir R.N. Kay | L | 6,713 | 22.7 |
|  |  |  |  |  | 488 | 1.7 |
| 1929 | 46,499 | 83.6 | C.R. Buxton | Lab | 17,012 | 43.7 |
|  |  |  | S. Howard | C | 11,150 | 28.7 |
|  |  |  | W.H. Sessions | L | 10,734 | 27.6 |
|  |  |  |  |  | 5,862 | 15.0 |
| 1931 | 47,210 | 82.5 | T. Levy | C | 25,378 | 65.2 |
|  |  |  | C.R. Buxton | Lab | 13,563 | 34.8 |
|  |  |  |  |  | 11,815 | 30.4 |
| 1935 | 48,396 | 77.2 | T. Levy | C | 19,498 | 52.2 |
|  |  |  | C.R. Buxton | Lab | 17,856 | 47.8 |
|  |  |  |  |  | 1,642 | 4.4 |
| 1945 | 48,833 | 79.9 | F.A. Cobb | Lab | 19,632 | 50.3 |
|  |  |  | T. Levy | C | 11,570 | 29.7 |
|  |  |  | J. Wilson | L | 7,805 | 20.0 |
|  |  |  |  |  | 8,062 | 20.6 |

# YORKSHIRE (West Riding), HEMSWORTH [499]

| Election | Electors | T'out | Candidate | Party | Votes | % |
|----------|----------|-------|-----------|-------|-------|---|
| 1918 | 25,137 | 58.0 | J. Guest | Lab | 8,102 | 55.5 |
| | | | J. Scholefield | Co C | 6,490 | 44.5 |
| | | | | | 1,612 | 11.0 |
| 1922 | 29,643 | 76.3 | J. Guest | Lab | 14,295 | 63.2 |
| | | | Dr. F.W. Crossley-Holland | NL | 8,317 | 36.8 |
| | | | | | 5,978 | 26.4 |
| 1923 | 30,644 | 61.3 | J. Guest | Lab | 13,159 | 70.1 |
| | | | H. Conway-Jones | L | 5,624 | 29.9 |
| | | | | | 7,535 | 40.2 |
| 1924 | 32,257 | 69.7 | J. Guest | Lab | 15,593 | 69.3 |
| | | | H.R. Brown | C | 6,902 | 30.7 |
| | | | | | 8,691 | 38.6 |
| 1929 | 43,100 | 75.8 | J. Guest | Lab | 26,075 | 79.9 |
| | | | R.A. Broughton | C | 6,578 | 20.1 |
| | | | | | 19,497 | 59.8 |

[Seat Vacant at Dissolution (Death)]

| | | | | | | |
|----------|----------|-------|-----------|-------|-------|---|
| 1931 | 45,914 | 72.9 | G. Price | Lab | 23,609 | 70.5 |
| | | | W.F.C. Garthwaite | C | 9,867 | 29.5 |
| | | | | | 13,742 | 41.0 |

[Death]

| | | | | | | |
|----------|----------|-------|-----------|-------|-------|---|
| 1934 (17/5) | | | G.A. Griffiths | Lab | Unopp. | |
| 1935 | 48,863 | 72.3 | G.A. Griffiths | Lab | 28,298 | 80.1 |
| | | | F.H. Collier | C | 7,032 | 19.9 |
| | | | | | 21,266 | 60.2 |
| 1945 | 51,684 | 80.8 | G.A. Griffiths | Lab | 33,984 | 81.4 |
| | | | R.W.P. Dawson | C | 7,778 | 18.6 |
| | | | | | 26,206 | 62.8 |

[Death]

| | | | | | | |
|----------|----------|-------|-----------|-------|-------|---|
| 1946 (21/2) | | | H.E. Holmes | Lab | Unopp. | |

## YORKSHIRE (West Riding), KEIGHLEY [500]

| Election | Electors | T'out | Candidate | Party | Votes | % |
|---|---|---|---|---|---|---|
| 1918 | 34,934 | 65.4 | R. Clough | Co C | 8,820 | 38.6 |
| | | | †W.H. Somervell | L | 7,709 | 33.7 |
| | | | W. Bland | Lab | 6,324 | 27.7 |
| | | | | | 1,111 | 4.9 |
| 1922 | 37,005 | 81.6 | H.B. Lees-Smith | Lab | 13,978 | 46.3 |
| | | | W.A. Brigg | L | 9,262 | 30.7 |
| | | | C.H. Foulds | C | 6,955 | 23.0 |
| | | | | | 4,716 | 15.6 |
| 1923 | 37,060 | 77.4 | R.R. Pilkington | L | 14,609 | 50.9 |
| | | | H.B. Lees-Smith | Lab | 14,083 | 49.1 |
| | | | | | 526 | 1.8 |
| 1924 | 37,887 | 82.8 | H.B. Lees-Smith | Lab | 14,105 | 45.0 |
| | | | T.P. Perks | C | 8,922 | 28.4 |
| | | | T.A. Jones | L | 8,339 | 26.6 |
| | | | | | 5,183 | 16.6 |
| 1929 | 48,518 | 84.9 | H.B. Lees-Smith | Lab | 18,412 | 44.7 |
| | | | D. Rhodes | L | 11,905 | 28.9 |
| | | | A. Smith | C | 10,858 | 26.4 |
| | | | | | 6,507 | 15.8 |
| 1931 | 49,242 | 83.9 | G.S. Harvie-Watt | C | 19,079 | 46.2 |
| | | | Rt. Hon. H.B. Lees-Smith | Lab | 13,192 | 31.9 |
| | | | W.J.C. Briggs | L | 9,044 | 21.9 |
| | | | | | 5,887 | 14.3 |
| 1935 | 50,530 | 78.9 | Rt. Hon. H.B. Lees-Smith | Lab | 20,124 | 50.5 |
| | | | G.S. Harvie-Watt | C | 19,756 | 49.5 |
| | | | | | 368 | 1.0 |
| [Death] | | | | | | |
| 1942 (13/2) | | | I. Thomas | Lab | Unopp. | |
| 1945 | 51,345 | 82.2 | I. Thomas | Lab (Ind) (C) | 22,222 | 52.7 |
| | | | H.A. Dalrymple-White | C | 10,865 | 25.7 |
| | | | N. Robson | L | 9,116 | 21.6 |
| | | | | | 11,357 | 27.0 |

| Election | Electors | T'out | Candidate | Party | Votes | % |
|---|---|---|---|---|---|---|
| 1918 | | | †F. Hall | Lab | Unopp. | |
| 1922 | 32,073 | 68.3 | F. Hall | Lab | 16,040 | 73.3 |
| | | | E.G. Bearcroft | NL | 5,855 | 26.7 |
| | | | | | 10,185 | 46.6 |
| 1923 | 32,223 | 61.5 | F. Hall | Lab | 15,455 | 78.0 |
| | | | Dr. G.B. Hillman | C | 4,365 | 22.0 |
| | | | | | 11,090 | 56.0 |
| 1924 | | | F. Hall | Lab | Unopp. | |
| 1929 | 41,279 | 75.8 | F. Hall | Lab | 26,008 | 83.1 |
| | | | A. Coates | C | 5,276 | 16.9 |
| | | | | | 20,732 | 66.2 |
| 1931 | 41,666 | 78.8 | F. Hall | Lab | 22,877 | 69.6 |
| | | | J.N. Cumberbirch | C | 9,974 | 30.4 |
| | | | | | 12,903 | 39.2 |

[Death]

| Election | Electors | T'out | Candidate | Party | Votes | % |
|---|---|---|---|---|---|---|
| 1933 (8/5) | | | T. Smith | Lab | Unopp. | |
| 1935 | 42,219 | 77.7 | T. Smith | Lab | 26,705 | 81.4 |
| | | | E.O. Moss | C | 6,106 | 18.6 |
| | | | | | 20,599 | 62.8 |
| 1945 | 41,945 | 79.9 | T. Smith | Lab | 28,238 | 84.3 |
| | | | J.H. Hulbert | C | 5,259 | 15.7 |
| | | | | | 22,979 | 68.6 |

[Resignation on appointment as Labour Director of the North-Eastern Divisional Coal Board]

| Election | Electors | T'out | Candidate | Party | Votes | % |
|---|---|---|---|---|---|---|
| 1947 (11/2) | 43,797 | 54.6 | G.O. Sylvester | Lab | 19,085 | 79.8 |
| | | | J.E. Powell | C | 4,258 | 17.8 |
| | | | Dr. W.D. Hartley | Ind | 579* | 2.4 |
| | | | | | 14,827 | 62.0 |

# YORKSHIRE (West Riding), PENISTONE   [502]

| Election | Electors | T'out | Candidate | Party | Votes | % |
|---|---|---|---|---|---|---|
| 1918 | 31,928 | 58.4 | †S. Arnold | L | 7,338 | 39.4 |
| | | | P.G. Smith | Co C | 6,744 | 36.2 |
| | | | F.W. Southern | Ind Lab | 4,556 | 24.4 |
| | | | | | 594 | 3.2 |
| [Resignation] | | | | | | |
| 1921 | 32,988† | 71.7 | W. Gillis | Lab | 8,560 | 36.2 |
| (5/3) | | | W.M.R. Pringle | L | 7,984 | 33.7 |
| | | | Sir J.P. Hinchliffe | Co L | 7,123 | 30.1 |
| | | | | | 576 | 2.5 |
| 1922 | 34,071 | 73.1 | W.M.R. Pringle | L | 8,924 | 35.8 |
| | | | W. Gillis | Lab | 8,382 | 33.7 |
| | | | C. Hodgkinson | C | 7,600 | 30.5 |
| | | | | | 542 | 2.1 |
| 1923 | 34,612 | 71.8 | W.M.R. Pringle | L | 9,164 | 36.9 |
| | | | R. Smith | Lab | 8,329 | 33.5 |
| | | | C. Hodgkinson | C | 7,369 | 29.6 |
| | | | | | 835 | 3.4 |
| 1924 | 35,358 | 80.6 | R. Smith | Lab | 10,997 | 38.5 |
| | | | C. Hodgkinson | C | 9,718 | 34.1 |
| | | | W.M.R. Pringle | L | 7,799 | 27.4 |
| | | | | | 1,279 | 4.4 |
| 1929 | 46,810 | 81.6 | R. Smith | Lab | 17,286 | 45.2 |
| | | | F.G. Bibbings | C | 10,640 | 27.9 |
| | | | A. Mitchell | L | 10,277 | 26.9 |
| | | | | | 6,646 | 17.3 |
| 1931 | 49,985 | 81.9 | C.W.H. Glossop | C | 19,556 | 47.7 |
| | | | R. Smith | Lab | 14,584 | 35.6 |
| | | | T. Neville | L | 6,821 | 16.7 |
| | | | | | 4,972 | 12.1 |
| 1935 | 60,904 | 73.3 | H.G. McGhee | Lab | 23,869 | 53.5 |
| | | | C.W.H. Glossop | C | 20,783 | 46.5 |
| | | | | | 3,086 | 7.0 |
| 1945 | 81,268 | 75.1 | H.G. McGhee | Lab | 40,180 | 65.8 |
| | | | R.G. Davis | C | 20,869 | 34.2 |
| | | | | | 19,311 | 31.6 |

| Election | Electors | T'out | Candidate | Party | Votes | % |
|---|---|---|---|---|---|---|
| 1918 | 29,841 | 45.6 | †Rt. Hon. Sir J. Compton-Rickett | Co L | 8,561 | 62.9 |
| | | | I. Burns | Lab | 5,047 | 37.1 |
| | | | | | 3,514 | 25.8 |
| [Death] | | | | | | |
| 1919 | 29,841† | 61.5 | W. Forrest | Co L | 9,920 | 54.0 |
| (6/9) | | | I. Burns | Lab | 8,445 | 46.0 |
| | | | | | 1,475 | 8.0 |
| 1922 | 31,747 | 73.9 | T. Smith | Lab | 9,111 | 38.9 |
| | | | J. Scholefield | C | 8,485 | 36.1 |
| | | | W. Forrest | NL | 5,879 | 25.0 |
| | | | | | 626 | 2.8 |
| 1923 | 33,425 | 73.5 | T. Smith | Lab | 11,134 | 45.3 |
| | | | A.N. Braithwaite | C | 8,872 | 36.1 |
| | | | Miss M.P. Grant | L | 4,567 | 18.6 |
| | | | | | 2,262 | 9.2 |
| 1924 | 35,148 | 76.2 | C.R.I. Brooke | C | 13,745 | 51.3 |
| | | | T. Smith | Lab | 13,044 | 48.7 |
| | | | | | 701 | 2.6 |
| 1929 | 45,254 | 80.1 | T. Smith | Lab | 17,335 | 47.8 |
| | | | C.R.I. Brooke | C | 10,040 | 27.7 |
| | | | H. Powis | L | 8,892 | 24.5 |
| | | | | | 7,295 | 20.1 |
| 1931 | 46,745 | 80.9 | T.E. Sotheron-Estcourt | C | 20,941 | 55.4 |
| | | | T. Smith | Lab | 16,870 | 44.6 |
| | | | | | 4,071 | 10.8 |
| 1935 | 48,900 | 75.7 | A. Hills | Lab | 19,783 | 53.4 |
| | | | V.B.J. Seely | NL | 17,257 | 46.6 |
| | | | | | 2,526 | 6.8 |
| [Death] | | | | | | |
| 1941 | | | P.G. Barstow | Lab | Unopp. | |
| (24/7) | | | | | | |
| 1945 | 54,537 | 74.7 | P.G. Barstow | Lab | 24,690 | 60.6 |
| | | | K. Hargreaves | C | 16,048 | 39.4 |
| | | | | | 8,642 | 21.2 |

| Election | Electors | T'out | Candidate | Party | Votes | % |
|---|---|---|---|---|---|---|
| 1918 | 31,487 | 58.6 | A.R. Barrand | Co L | 13,860 | 75.2 |
| | | | G.R. Carter | Lab | 4,583 | 24.8 |
| | | | | | 9,277 | 50.4 |
| 1922 | 32,506 | 82.0 | F.H. Fawkes | C | 12,396 | 46.5 |
| | | | A.R. Barrand | L | 8,439 | 31.7 |
| | | | P. Myers | Lab | 5,818 | 21.8 |
| | | | | | 3,957 | 14.8 |
| 1923 | 33,316 | 79.1 | Sir F. Watson | C | 11,537 | 43.7 |
| | | | Rt. Hon. Sir J.T. Walters | L | 9,330 | 35.4 |
| | | | P. Myers | Lab | 5,499 | 20.9 |
| | | | | | 2,207 | 8.3 |
| 1924 | 34,334 | 80.5 | Sir F. Watson | C | 14,090 | 51.0 |
| | | | P. Myers | Lab | 7,001 | 25.3 |
| | | | E. Woodhead | L | 6,545 | 23.7 |
| | | | | | 7,089 | 25.7 |
| 1929 | 49,796 | 81.8 | C.G. Gibson | C | 16,729 | 41.0 |
| | | | A.W. Brown | Lab | 12,336 | 30.3 |
| | | | H.S. Houldsworth | L | 11,685 | 28.7 |
| | | | | | 4,393 | 10.7 |
| 1931 | 52,195 | 79.9 | C.G. Gibson | C | 31,701 | 76.0 |
| | | | W. Pickles | Lab | 10,013 | 24.0 |
| | | | | | 21,688 | 52.0 |
| 1935 | 56,245 | 76.0 | C.G. Gibson | C | 22,107 | 51.7 |
| | | | J.C. Smuts | L | 10,682 | 25.0 |
| | | | Miss L.A. Cox | Lab | 9,977 | 23.3 |
| | | | | | 11,425 | 26.7 |
| 1945 | 66,632 | 78.7 | M. Stoddart-Scott | C | 22,755 | 43.4 |
| | | | D.W. Healey | Lab | 21,104 | 40.2 |
| | | | T.H. Clarke | L | 8,592 | 16.4 |
| | | | | | 1,651 | 3.2 |

| Election | Electors | T'out | Candidate | Party | Votes | % |
|---|---|---|---|---|---|---|
| 1918 | | | †Hon. E.F.L. Wood | Co C | Unopp. | |
| 1922 | | | Rt. Hon. E.F.L. Wood | C | Unopp. | |
| 1923 | | | Rt. Hon. E.F.L. Wood | C | Unopp. | |
| 1924 | | | Rt. Hon. E.F.L. Wood | C | Unopp. | |
| [Resignation on appointment as Viceroy of India] | | | | | | |
| 1925 (5/12) | 37,338 | 74.6 | J.W. Hills | C | 16,433 | 59.0 |
| | | | J. Murray | L | 11,422 | 41.0 |
| | | | | | 5,011 | 18.0 |
| 1929 | 55,191 | 76.2 | J.W. Hills | C | 23,173 | 55.1 |
| | | | F. Boult | L | 14,542 | 34.6 |
| | | | A. Godfrey | Lab | 4,339* | 10.3 |
| | | | | | 8,631 | 20.5 |
| 1931 | 58,381 | 73.7 | Rt. Hon. J.W. Hills | C | 37,898 | 88.1 |
| | | | R.J. Hall | Lab | 5,125* | 11.9 |
| | | | | | 32,773 | 76.2 |
| 1935 | 58,159 | 68.6 | Rt. Hon. J.W. Hills | C | 30,804 | 77.2 |
| | | | R.J. Hall | Lab | 9,116 | 22.8 |
| | | | | | 21,688 | 54.4 |
| [Death] | | | | | | |
| 1939 (23/2) | 58,603 | 57.1 | C. York | C | 23,257 | 69.5 |
| | | | R.J. Hall | Lab | 10,213 | 30.5 |
| | | | | | 13,044 | 39.0 |
| 1945 | 69,374 | 69.8 | C. York | C | 29,674 | 61.3 |
| | | | R. Hartley | Lab | 12,599 | 26.0 |
| | | | Mrs. M. Cowley | L | 6,122 | 12.7 |
| | | | | | 17,075 | 35.3 |

| Election | Electors | T'out | Candidate | Party | Votes | % |
|---|---|---|---|---|---|---|
| 1918 | 31,965 | 56.3 | T.W. Grundy | Lab | 9,917 | 55.1 |
| | | | E.G. Bearcroft | Co NDP | 4,894 | 27.2 |
| | | | A.E.M. Turner | L | 3,177 | 17.7 |
| | | | | | 5,023 | 27.9 |
| 1922 | | | T.W. Grundy | Lab | Unopp. | |
| 1923 | 36,397 | 64.0 | T.W. Grundy | Lab | 15,967 | 68.6 |
| | | | F.R. Wade | C | 7,323 | 31.4 |
| | | | | | 8,644 | 37.2 |
| 1924 | 37,860 | 75.9 | T.W. Grundy | Lab | 18,750 | 65.3 |
| | | | F.R. Wade | C | 9,985 | 34.7 |
| | | | | | 8,765 | 30.6 |
| 1929 | 51,261 | 77.8 | T.W. Grundy | Lab | 30,405 | 76.3 |
| | | | C.F. Pike | C | 9,460 | 23.7 |
| | | | | | 20,945 | 52.6 |
| 1931 | 54,184 | 77.5 | T.W. Grundy | Lab | 26,185 | 62.3 |
| | | | A.G. Olliver | C | 15,812 | 37.7 |
| | | | | | 10,373 | 24.6 |
| 1935 | 62,530 | 73.8 | E. Dunn | Lab | 33,271 | 72.0 |
| | | | A.G. Olliver | C | 12,907 | 28.0 |
| | | | | | 20,364 | 44.0 |

[Seat Vacant at Dissolution (Death)]

| Election | Electors | T'out | Candidate | Party | Votes | % |
|---|---|---|---|---|---|---|
| 1945 | 78,636 | 75.2 | D. Griffiths | Lab | 44,499 | 75.2 |
| | | | J.H. Bull | C | 14,669 | 24.8 |
| | | | | | 29,830 | 50.4 |

# YORKSHIRE (West Riding), ROTHWELL  [507]

| Election | Electors | T'out | Candidate | Party | Votes | % |
|----------|----------|-------|-----------|-------|-------|---|
| 1918 | 33,899 | 63.5 | W. Lunn | Lab | 9,998 | 46.4 |
|  |  |  | H.C.B. Wilson | Co C | 6,621 | 30.8 |
|  |  |  | J.A. Yonge | L | 4,909 | 22.8 |
|  |  |  |  |  | 3,377 | 15.6 |
| 1922 | 36,227 | 78.4 | W. Lunn | Lab | 17,831 | 62.8 |
|  |  |  | A.N. Braithwaite | C | 10,580 | 37.2 |
|  |  |  |  |  | 7,251 | 25.6 |
| 1923 | 37,611 | 60.9 | W. Lunn | Lab | 15,115 | 66.0 |
|  |  |  | B.P. Wilson | L | 7,788 | 34.0 |
|  |  |  |  |  | 7,327 | 32.0 |
| 1924 | 38,635 | 69.3 | W. Lunn | Lab | 16,540 | 61.8 |
|  |  |  | B.P. Wilson | L | 10,240 | 38.2 |
|  |  |  |  |  | 6,300 | 23.6 |
| 1929 | 55,869 | 79.2 | W. Lunn | Lab | 27,320 | 61.7 |
|  |  |  | J.W. Harrison | C | 8,799 | 19.9 |
|  |  |  | H. Holdsworth | L | 8,141 | 18.4 |
|  |  |  |  |  | 18,521 | 41.8 |
| 1931 | 58,974 | 79.9 | W. Lunn | Lab | 24,897 | 52.9 |
|  |  |  | C.H. Stringer | C | 22,198 | 47.1 |
|  |  |  |  |  | 2,699 | 5.8 |
| 1935 | 64,730 | 75.4 | W. Lunn | Lab | 31,472 | 64.5 |
|  |  |  | Mrs. G. Beaumont | C | 17,352 | 35.5 |
|  |  |  |  |  | 14,120 | 29.0 |
| [Death] |  |  |  |  |  |  |
| 1942 (7/8) |  |  | T.J. Brooks | Lab | Unopp. |  |
| 1945 | 78,588 | 75.3 | T.J. Brooks | Lab | 43,829 | 74.0 |
|  |  |  | Sir A. Pilkington, Bt. | C | 15,370 | 26.0 |
|  |  |  |  |  | 28,459 | 48.0 |

# YORKSHIRE (West Riding), SHIPLEY  [508]

| Election | Electors | T'out | Candidate | Party | Votes | % |
|---|---|---|---|---|---|---|
| 1918 | 35,566 | 63.0 | H.N. Rae | Co L | 16,700 | 74.6 |
| | | | T. Snowden | Lab | 5,690 | 25.4 |
| | | | | | 11,010 | 49.2 |
| | | | | | | |
| 1922 | 36,781 | 81.7 | Sir H.N. Rae | NL | 12,201 | 40.6 |
| | | | W. Mackinder | Lab | 11,160 | 37.2 |
| | | | A. Davy | L | 6,674 | 22.2 |
| | | | | | 1,041 | 3.4 |
| | | | | | | |
| 1923 | 37,552 | 82.7 | W. Mackinder | Lab | 11,918 | 38.4 |
| | | | P.J. Pybus | L | 10,262 | 33.0 |
| | | | R. Garnett | C | 8,872 | 28.6 |
| | | | | | 1,656 | 5.4 |
| | | | | | | |
| 1924 | 38,120 | 86.4 | W. Mackinder | Lab | 11,862 | 36.0 |
| | | | Hon. T.H.R. Plumer | C | 11,266 | 34.2 |
| | | | P.J. Pybus | L | 9,800 | 29.8 |
| | | | | | 596 | 1.8 |
| | | | | | | |
| 1929 | 51,838 | 85.0 | W. Mackinder | Lab | 18,654 | 42.3 |
| | | | Sir R. Clough | C | 13,693 | 31.1 |
| | | | F.W. Hirst | L | 11,712 | 26.6 |
| | | | | | 4,961 | 11.2 |
| [Death] | | | | | | |
| 1930 | 52,856 | 80.0 | J.H. Lockwood | C | 15,238 | 36.0 |
| (6/11) | | | W.A. Robinson | Lab | 13,573 | 32.1 |
| | | | A. Davy | L | 12,785 | 30.2 |
| | | | W. Gallacher | Com | 701* | 1.7 |
| | | | | | 1,665 | 3.9 |
| | | | | | | |
| 1931 | 53,464 | 79.7 | J.H. Lockwood | C | 27,304 | 64.1 |
| | | | W.A. Robinson | Lab | 14,725 | 34.5 |
| | | | W.J. Leaper | NP | 601* | 1.4 |
| | | | | | 12,579 | 29.6 |
| | | | | | | |
| 1935 | 57,670 | 77.5 | A.C. Jones | Lab | 16,102 | 36.0 |
| | | | P.G. Illingworth | L | 11,595 | 25.9 |
| | | | T. Howarth | C | 10,998 | 24.6 |
| | | | J.H. Lockwood | Ind C | 6,025 | 13.5 |
| | | | | | 4,507 | 10.1 |
| | | | | | | |
| 1945 | 62,240 | 80.2 | A.C. Jones | Lab | 25,027 | 50.1 |
| | | | H.B.H. Hylton-Foster | C | 17,097 | 34.2 |
| | | | E. Robinson | L | 7,820 | 15.7 |
| | | | | | 7,930 | 15.9 |

Note:—

1935: Lockwood was not re-adopted by the local Conservative Association but decided
to contest the constituency as an Independent.

# YORKSHIRE (West Riding), SKIPTON [509]

| Election | Electors | T'out | Candidate | Party | Votes | % |
|---|---|---|---|---|---|---|
| 1918 | 35,722 | 64.2 | R.F. Roundell | Co C | 12,599 | 55.0 |
|  |  |  | W.A. Brigg | L | 10,318 | 45.0 |
|  |  |  |  |  | 2,281 | 10.0 |
| 1922 | 37,220 | 85.2 | R.F. Roundell | C | 13,251 | 41.7 |
|  |  |  | Sir H.C.W. Verney, Bt. | L | 10,228 | 32.3 |
|  |  |  | T. Snowden | Lab | 8,229 | 26.0 |
|  |  |  |  |  | 3,023 | 9.4 |
| 1923 | 37,965 | 83.6 | R.F. Roundell | C | 12,676 | 39.9 |
|  |  |  | Sir H.C.W. Verney, Bt. | L | 11,285 | 35.6 |
|  |  |  | O.G. Willey | Lab | 7,767 | 24.5 |
|  |  |  |  |  | 1,391 | 4.3 |
| 1924 | 38,790 | 83.8 | E.R. Bird | C | 14,924 | 46.0 |
|  |  |  | T. Woffenden | L | 8,947 | 27.5 |
|  |  |  | O.G. Willey | Lab | 8,626 | 26.5 |
|  |  |  |  |  | 5,977 | 18.5 |
| 1929 | 50,369 | 83.4 | E.R. Bird | C | 16,588 | 39.5 |
|  |  |  | J.P. Davies | Lab | 13,088 | 31.2 |
|  |  |  | T. Woffenden | L | 12,320 | 29.3 |
|  |  |  |  |  | 3,500 | 8.3 |
| 1931 | 51,169 | 80.3 | E.R. Bird | C | 28,013 | 68.2 |
|  |  |  | J.P. Davies | Lab | 13,053 | 31.8 |
|  |  |  |  |  | 14,960 | 36.4 |
| [Death] |  |  |  |  |  |  |
| 1933 | 51,039 | 82.7 | G.W. Rickards | C | 18,136 | 43.0 |
| (7/11) |  |  | J.P. Davies | Lab | 14,157 | 33.5 |
|  |  |  | R.C. Denby | L | 9,219 | 21.8 |
|  |  |  | J. Rushton | Com | 704* | 1.7 |
|  |  |  |  |  | 3,979 | 9.5 |
| 1935 | 51,041 | 79.6 | G.W. Rickards | C | 22,847 | 56.2 |
|  |  |  | J.P. Davies | Lab | 17,788 | 43.8 |
|  |  |  |  |  | 5,059 | 12.4 |
| [Death] |  |  |  |  |  |  |
| 1944 | 49,608 | 54.9 | H.M. Lawson | CW | 12,222 | 44.9 |
| (7/1) |  |  | H. Riddiough | C | 12,001 | 44.0 |
|  |  |  | J. Toole | Ind Lab | 3,029* | 11.1 |
|  |  |  |  |  | 221 | 0.9 |
| 1945 | 52,937 | 81.5 | G.B. Drayson | C | 17,905 | 41.5 |
|  |  |  | J.P. Davies | Lab | 15,704 | 36.4 |
|  |  |  | E. Townsend | L | 9,546 | 22.1 |
|  |  |  |  |  | 2,201 | 5.1 |

Note:—

1944: Toole was a member of the Labour Party and was expelled for breaking the electoral truce.

# YORKSHIRE (West Riding), SOWERBY [510]

| Election | Electors | T'out | Candidate | Party | Votes | % |
|----------|----------|-------|-----------|-------|-------|---|
| 1918 | 34,286 | 65.2 | R.H. Barker | Ind | 8,287 | 37.0 |
| | | | J.W. Ogden | Lab | 7,306 | 32.7 |
| | | | †J.S. Higham | L | 6,778 | 30.3 |
| | | | | | 981 | 4.3 |
| 1922 | 35,022 | 83.9 | W.A. Simpson-Hinchliffe | C | 11,710 | 39.9 |
| | | | A. Williams | L | 8,144 | 27.7 |
| | | | J.W. Ogden | Lab | 7,496 | 25.5 |
| | | | F. Roebuck | NL | 2,023* | 6.9 |
| | | | | | 3,566 | 12.2 |
| 1923 | 35,378 | 81.0 | A. Williams | L | 11,350 | 39.6 |
| | | | W.A. Simpson-Hinchliffe | C | 9,932 | 34.6 |
| | | | A. Dawson | Lab | 7,389 | 25.8 |
| | | | | | 1,418 | 5.0 |
| 1924 | 35,500 | 83.2 | G.R.D. Shaw | C | 11,181 | 37.8 |
| | | | A. Williams | L | 9,480 | 32.1 |
| | | | A. Dawson | Lab | 8,881 | 30.1 |
| | | | | | 1,701 | 5.7 |
| 1929 | 45,780 | 83.4 | W.J. Tout | Lab | 14,223 | 37.2 |
| | | | W.A. Colegate | C | 12,057 | 31.6 |
| | | | T.G. Graham | L | 11,890 | 31.2 |
| | | | | | 2,166 | 5.6 |
| 1931 | 46,104 | 81.1 | M.S. McCorquodale | C | 25,511 | 68.3 |
| | | | W.J. Tout | Lab | 11,857 | 31.7 |
| | | | | | 13,654 | 36.6 |
| 1935 | 45,803 | 75.9 | M.S. McCorquodale | C | 18,707 | 53.8 |
| | | | W.J. Tout | Lab | 16,035 | 46.2 |
| | | | | | 2,672 | 7.6 |
| 1945 | 42,557 | 81.9 | J.W. Belcher | Lab | 17,710 | 50.8 |
| | | | M.S. McCorquodale | C | 10,777 | 30.9 |
| | | | D.E. Moore | L | 6,373 | 18.3 |
| | | | | | 6,933 | 19.9 |
| [Resignation] | | | | | | |
| 1949 (16/3) | 43,457 | 80.7 | A.L.N.D. Houghton | Lab | 18,606 | 53.1 |
| | | | P.E.O. Bryan | C | 16,454 | 46.9 |
| | | | | | 2,152 | 6.2 |

Note:—

1918: Barker's sponsorship is interesting and worth recording.

Some time prior to the announcement of a General Election, a Conservative candidate had been selected to contest the constituency but when an election became imminent, the Coalition Whips prevailed upon the local Conservative Association to withdraw their candidate in favour of Higham who was issued with the 'coupon' which he subsequently repudiated.

A group of local Conservatives, annoyed at Higham's attitude and the fact that they had no candidate of their own, persuaded the local branch of the NADSS to sponsor Barker who was known to be a Conservative. During the campaign Barker had considerable support from the Conservative organisation in the constituency and although there is no information as to which (if any) whip he accepted in the House of Commons, his voting record indicated fairly consistent support for the Coalition.

# YORKSHIRE (West Riding), SPEN VALLEY [511]

| Election | Electors | T'out | Candidate | Party | Votes | % |
|---|---|---|---|---|---|---|
| 1918 | 38,827 | 49.4 | †Rt. Hon. Sir T.P. Whittaker | Co L | 10,664 | 55.6 |
| | | | T. Myers | Lab | 8,508 | 44.4 |
| | | | | | 2,156 | 11.2 |
| [Death] | | | | | | |
| 1919 | 39,667 | 76.5 | T. Myers | Lab | 11,962 | 39.4 |
| (20/12) | | | Rt. Hon. Sir J.A. Simon | L | 10,244 | 33.8 |
| | | | B.C. Fairfax | Co L | 8,134 | 26.8 |
| | | | | | 1,718 | 5.6 |
| 1922 | 40,107 | 84.6 | Rt. Hon. Sir J.A. Simon | L | 13,306 | 39.2 |
| | | | T. Myers | Lab | 12,519 | 36.9 |
| | | | W.O.R. Holton | C | 8,104 | 23.9 |
| | | | | | 787 | 2.3 |
| 1923 | 40,678 | 82.7 | Rt. Hon. Sir J.A. Simon | L | 13,672 | 40.6 |
| | | | T. Myers | Lab | 12,597 | 37.4 |
| | | | E.J.S.H. Ramsden | C | 7,390 | 22.0 |
| | | | | | 1,075 | 3.2 |
| 1924 | 40,978 | 79.2 | Rt. Hon. Sir J.A. Simon | L | 18,474 | 56.9 |
| | | | T. Myers | Lab | 13,999 | 43.1 |
| | | | | | 4,475 | 13.8 |
| 1929 | 53,480 | 79.6 | Rt. Hon. Sir J.A. Simon | L (Ind L) (NL) | 22,039 | 51.7 |
| | | | H.H. Elvin | Lab | 20,300 | 47.7 |
| | | | S. Usmani | Com | 242* | 0.6 |
| | | | | | 1,739 | 4.0 |
| 1931 | 54,097 | 82.0 | Rt. Hon. Sir J.A. Simon | NL | 28,647 | 64.6 |
| | | | H.H. Elvin | Lab | 15,691 | 35.4 |
| | | | | | 12,956 | 29.2 |
| 1935 | 55,358 | 77.1 | Rt. Hon. Sir J.A. Simon | NL | 21,671 | 50.8 |
| | | | I. Thomas | Lab | 21,029 | 49.2 |
| | | | | | 642 | 1.6 |

[Resignation on appointment as Lord Chancellor and elevation to the Peerage — Viscount Simon]

| Election | Electors | T'out | Candidate | Party | Votes | % |
|---|---|---|---|---|---|---|
| 1940 (1/6) | | | W.E. Woolley | NL | Unopp. | |
| 1945 | 55,218 | 82.1 | G.M. Sharp | Lab | 25,698 | 56.7 |
| | | | W.E. Woolley | NL | 19,621 | 43.3 |
| | | | | | 6,077 | 13.4 |

| Election | Electors | T'out | Candidate | Party | Votes | % |
|----------|----------|-------|-----------|-------|-------|---|
| 1918 | 36,004 | 60.5 | G.H. Hirst | Lab | 13,029 | 59.8 |
| | | | T.W.H. Mitchell | Co C | 5,315 | 24.4 |
| | | | †F.H. Booth | L | 3,453 | 15.8 |
| | | | | | 7,714 | 35.4 |
| 1922 | | | G.H. Hirst | Lab | Unopp. | |
| 1923 | | | G.H. Hirst | Lab | Unopp. | |
| 1924 | | | G.H. Hirst | Lab | Unopp. | |
| 1929 | 58,398 | 80.3 | G.H. Hirst | Lab | 35,276 | 75.1 |
| | | | P.B. Nicholson | L | 7,955 | 17.0 |
| | | | B.H. Oates | C | 3,684* | 7.9 |
| | | | | | 27,321 | 58.1 |
| 1931 | 60,055 | 77.1 | G.H. Hirst | Lab | 31,861 | 68.8 |
| | | | Mrs. C.I. Hilyer | NL | 14,462 | 31.2 |
| | | | | | 17,399 | 37.6 |
| [Death] | | | | | | |
| 1933 (22/12) | | | W. Paling | Lab | Unopp. | |
| 1935 | 62,205 | 73.4 | W. Paling | Lab | 37,471 | 82.1 |
| | | | A.G. Hargreaves | C | 8,167 | 17.9 |
| | | | | | 29,304 | 64.2 |
| 1945 | 67,399 | 78.3 | Rt. Hon. W. Paling | Lab | 44,080 | 83.6 |
| | | | Mrs. A.L.G. Dower | C | 8,670 | 16.4 |
| | | | | | 35,410 | 67.2 |

# WALES and MONMOUTHSHIRE ——— BOROUGHS

## CAERNARVON DISTRICT of BOROUGHS [513]

### (Caernarvon, Bangor, Conway, Pwllheli)

| Election | Electors | T'out | Candidate | Party | Votes | % |
|---|---|---|---|---|---|---|
| 1918 | 23,787 | 63.4 | †Rt. Hon. D. Lloyd George | Co L | 13,993 | 92.7 |
|  |  |  | A. Harrison | Ind | 1,095* | 7.3 |
|  |  |  |  |  | 12,898 | 85.4 |
| 1922 |  |  | Rt. Hon. D. Lloyd George | NL | Unopp. |  |
| 1923 | 24,488 | 80.9 | Rt. Hon. D. Lloyd George | L | 12,499 | 63.1 |
|  |  |  | A.L. Jones | C | 7,323 | 36.9 |
|  |  |  |  |  | 5,176 | 26.2 |
| 1924 | 25,281 | 77.0 | Rt. Hon. D. Lloyd George | L | 16,058 | 82.5 |
|  |  |  | Prof. A.E. Zimmern | Lab | 3,401 | 17.5 |
|  |  |  |  |  | 12,657 | 65.0 |
| 1929 | 35,083 | 81.8 | Rt. Hon. D. Lloyd George | L | 16,647 | 58.0 |
|  |  |  | J.B. Davies | C | 7,514 | 26.2 |
|  |  |  | T.A. Rhys | Lab | 4,536 | 15.8 |
|  |  |  |  |  | 9,133 | 31.8 |
| 1931 | 35,879 | 80.3 | Rt. Hon. D. Lloyd George | L | 17,101 | 59.3 |
|  |  |  | F.P. Gourlay | C | 11,714 | 40.7 |
|  |  |  |  |  | 5,387 | 18.6 |
| 1935 | 37,313 | 77.4 | Rt. Hon. D. Lloyd George | L | 19,242 | 66.6 |
|  |  |  | A.R.P. Du Cros | C | 9,633 | 33.4 |
|  |  |  |  |  | 9,609 | 33.2 |

[Elevation to the Peerage — Earl Lloyd George of Dwyfor)

| Election | Electors | T'out | Candidate | Party | Votes | % |
|---|---|---|---|---|---|---|
| 1945 | 46,910 | 58.8 | D.R.S. Davies | L | 20,754 | 75.2 |
| (26/4) |  |  | Prof. J.E. Daniel | PC | 6,844 | 24.8 |
|  |  |  |  |  | 13,910 | 50.4 |
| 1945 | 47,041 | 73.8 | D.A. Price-White | C | 11,432 | 32.9 |
|  |  |  | D.R.S. Davies | L | 11,096 | 32.0 |
|  |  |  | W.E.E. Jones | Lab | 10,625 | 30.6 |
|  |  |  | Prof. J.E. Daniel | PC | 1,560* | 4.5 |
|  |  |  |  |  | 336 | 0.9 |

Note:—

1931: Lloyd George was opposed to the National Government.

| Election | Electors | T'out | Candidate | Party | Votes | % |
|---|---|---|---|---|---|---|
| 1918 | 36,557 | 56.9 | J.C. Gould | C | 8,542 | 41.1 |
| | | | J.E. Edmunds | Lab | 4,663 | 22.4 |
| | | | G.F. Forsdike | L | 4,172 | 20.1 |
| | | | R. Hughes | Ind C | 3,419 | 16.4 |
| | | | | | 3,879 | 18.7 |
| 1922 | 37,326 | 74.4 | J.C. Gould | C | 13,885 | 50.0 |
| | | | J.E. Edmunds | Lab | 8,169 | 29.4 |
| | | | C.F. Sanders | L | 5,732 | 20.6 |
| | | | | | 5,716 | 20.6 |
| 1923 | 37,444 | 71.4 | J.C. Gould | C | 10,261 | 38.4 |
| | | | J.E. Edmunds | Lab | 8,563 | 32.0 |
| | | | I. Watkins-Evans | L | 7,923 | 29.6 |
| | | | | | 1,698 | 6.4 |
| 1924 | 38,026 | 76.8 | L. Lougher | C | 14,537 | 49.7 |
| | | | D.G. Pole | Lab | 9,864 | 33.8 |
| | | | A.J.G. Edwards | L | 4,805 | 16.5 |
| | | | | | 4,673 | 15.9 |
| 1929 | 47,282 | 78.2 | E.N. Bennett | Lab (N Lab) | 14,469 | 39.1 |
| | | | Sir L. Lougher | C | 12,903 | 34.9 |
| | | | B. Janner | L | 9,623 | 26.0 |
| | | | | | 1,566 | 4.2 |
| 1931 | 48,065 | 72.6 | Sir E.N. Bennett | N Lab | 24,120 | 69.2 |
| | | | E. Archbold | Lab | 10,758 | 30.8 |
| | | | | | 13,362 | 38.4 |
| 1935 | 47,912 | 68.7 | Sir E.N. Bennett | N Lab (Nat) | 16,954 | 51.6 |
| | | | J. Dugdale | Lab | 12,094 | 36.7 |
| | | | W.G. Brown | L | 3,863* | 11.7 |
| | | | | | 4,860 | 14.9 |
| 1945 | 46,580 | 72.2 | T.G. Thomas | Lab | 16,506 | 49.1 |
| | | | C.S. Hallinan | C | 11,982 | 35.7 |
| | | | P.T.H. Morgan | L | 5,121 | 15.2 |
| | | | | | 4,524 | 13.4 |

| Election | Electors | T'out | Candidate | Party | Votes | % |
|---|---|---|---|---|---|---|
| 1918 | 30,164 | 64.6 | Sir W.H. Seager | L (Co L) | 7,963 | 40.8 |
| | | | Lord Colum Crichton-Stuart | C | 5,978 | 30.7 |
| | | | A.J. Williams | Lab | 5,554 | 28.5 |
| | | | | | 1,985 | 10.1 |
| 1922 | 29,532 | 81.0 | L. Lougher | C | 8,804 | 36.8 |
| | | | Sir H. Webb, Bt. | L | 7,622 | 31.8 |
| | | | A.J. Williams | Lab | 7,506 | 31.4 |
| | | | | | 1,182 | 5.0 |
| 1923 | 30,100 | 79.3 | Sir H. Webb, Bt. | L | 8,536 | 35.8 |
| | | | E.H.J.N. Dalton | Lab | 7,812 | 32.7 |
| | | | L. Lougher | C | 7,513 | 31.5 |
| | | | | | 724 | 3.1 |
| 1924 | 30,218 | 82.3 | Sir C. Kinloch-Cooke | C | 10,036 | 40.3 |
| | | | H.M. Lloyd | Lab | 8,156 | 32.8 |
| | | | Rt. Hon. Sir D. Maclean | L | 6,684 | 26.9 |
| | | | | | 1,880 | 7.5 |
| 1929 | 40,061 | 82.1 | J.E. Edmunds | Lab | 12,813 | 39.0 |
| | | | J.E. Emlyn-Jones | L | 10,500 | 31.9 |
| | | | Sir C. Kinloch-Cooke, Bt. | C | 9,563 | 29.1 |
| | | | | | 2,313 | 7.1 |
| 1931 | 40,316 | 80.2 | O.T. Morris | C | 12,465 | 38.6 |
| | | | J.E. Edmunds | Lab | 10,292 | 31.8 |
| | | | J.E. Emlyn-Jones | L | 9,559 | 29.6 |
| | | | | | 2,173 | 6.8 |
| 1935 | 41,076 | 73.1 | O.T. Morris | C | 16,048 | 53.5 |
| | | | W. Bennett | Lab | 11,362 | 37.8 |
| | | | A.W. Pile | L | 2,623* | 8.7 |
| | | | | | 4,686 | 15.7 |

[Resignation on appointment as a County Court Judge]

| Election | Electors | T'out | Candidate | Party | Votes | % |
|---|---|---|---|---|---|---|
| 1942 | 40,254 | 33.1 | Rt. Hon. Sir P.J. Grigg | Nat | 10,030 | 75.2 |
| (13/4) | | | A.F. Brockway | ILP | 3,311 | 24.8 |
| | | | | | 6,719 | 50.4 |
| 1945 | 42,950 | 74.8 | H.A. Marquand | Lab | 16,299 | 50.7 |
| | | | Rt. Hon. Sir P.J. Grigg | Nat | 11,306 | 35.2 |
| | | | J.E. Emlyn-Jones | L | 4,523 | 14.1 |
| | | | | | 4,993 | 15.5 |

Note:—

    1942: Grigg was Secretary of State for War.

# CARDIFF, SOUTH [516]

| Election | Electors | T'out | Candidate | Party | Votes | % |
|----------|----------|-------|-----------|-------|-------|---|
| 1918 | 28,307 | 57.8 | †J.H. Cory | C | 7,922 | 48.5 |
|  |  |  | J.T. Clatworthy | Lab | 4,303 | 26.3 |
|  |  |  | E. Curran | L | 4,126 | 25.2 |
|  |  |  |  |  | 3,619 | 22.2 |
| 1922 | 29,033 | 74.9 | Sir J.H. Cory, Bt. | C | 7,929 | 36.4 |
|  |  |  | B.C. Freyberg | L | 6,996 | 32.2 |
|  |  |  | D.G. Pole | Lab | 6,831 | 31.4 |
|  |  |  |  |  | 933 | 4.2 |
| 1923 | 29,511 | 70.6 | A. Henderson | Lab | 7,899 | 37.9 |
|  |  |  | Sir J.H. Cory, Bt. | C | 7,473 | 35.8 |
|  |  |  | W.T. Layton | L | 5,474 | 26.3 |
|  |  |  |  |  | 426 | 2.1 |
| 1924 | 29,388 | 78.8 | H.A. Evans | C | 11,542 | 49.8 |
|  |  |  | A. Henderson | Lab | 9,324 | 40.3 |
|  |  |  | E.G. Davies | L | 2,287* | 9.9 |
|  |  |  |  |  | 2,218 | 9.5 |
| 1929 | 38,097 | 79.4 | A. Henderson | Lab | 13,686 | 45.3 |
|  |  |  | E.T. Neathercoat | C | 10,030 | 33.1 |
|  |  |  | C.J. Cole | L | 6,550 | 21.6 |
|  |  |  |  |  | 3,656 | 12.2 |
| 1931 | 38,659 | 77.8 | H.A. Evans | C | 17,976 | 59.8 |
|  |  |  | A. Henderson | Lab | 12,092 | 40.2 |
|  |  |  |  |  | 5,884 | 19.6 |
| 1935 | 38,681 | 75.8 | H.A. Evans | C | 14,925 | 50.9 |
|  |  |  | H.L. Nathan | Lab | 14,384 | 49.1 |
|  |  |  |  |  | 541 | 1.8 |
| 1945 | 39,303 | 73.9 | L.J. Callaghan | Lab | 17,489 | 60.2 |
|  |  |  | Sir H.A. Evans | C | 11,545 | 39.8 |
|  |  |  |  |  | 5,944 | 20.4 |

Note:—

1922: Freyberg sought election as an Independent although he had been adopted by the local Liberal Association as their candidate. He did not commit himself to supporting either Lloyd George or Asquith.

| Election | Electors | T'out | Candidate | Party | Votes | % |
|----------|----------|-------|-----------|-------|-------|---|
| 1918 | 41,651 | 69.8 | †C.B. Stanton | Co NDP | 22,824 | 78.6 |
| | | | Rev. T.E. Nicholas | Lab | 6,229 | 21.4 |
| | | | | | 16,595 | 57.2 |
| 1922 | 45,285 | 79.9 | G.H. Hall | Lab | 20,704 | 57.2 |
| | | | C.B. Stanton | NL | 15,487 | 42.8 |
| | | | | | 5,217 | 14.4 |
| 1923 | 46,148 | 83.3 | G.H. Hall | Lab | 22,379 | 58.2 |
| | | | W.M. Llewellyn | L | 16,050 | 41.8 |
| | | | | | 6,329 | 16.4 |
| 1924 | 47,267 | 83.7 | G.H. Hall | Lab | 24,343 | 61.6 |
| | | | D. Bowen | L | 15,201 | 38.4 |
| | | | | | 9,142 | 23.2 |
| 1929 | 54,134 | 84.5 | G.H. Hall | Lab | 29,550 | 64.6 |
| | | | E.J. Roderick | L | 10,594 | 23.2 |
| | | | A.H.E. Molson | C | 5,573* | 12.2 |
| | | | | | 18,956 | 41.4 |
| 1931 | | | G.H. Hall | Lab | Unopp. | |
| 1935 | | | G.H. Hall | Lab | Unopp. | |
| 1945 | 53,630 | 76.1 | Rt. Hon. G.H. Hall | Lab | 34,398 | 84.3 |
| | | | C.G. Clover | C | 6,429 | 15.7 |
| | | | | | 27,969 | 68.6 |

[Elevation to the Peerage — Viscount Hall]

| Election | Electors | T'out | Candidate | Party | Votes | % |
|----------|----------|-------|-----------|-------|-------|---|
| 1946 | 53,911 | 65.7 | D.E. Thomas | Lab | 24,215 | 68.3 |
| (5/12) | | | W.I. Samuel | PC | 7,090 | 20.0 |
| | | | A.L. Hallinan | C | 4,140* | 11.7 |
| | | | | | 17,125 | 48.3 |

| Election | Electors | T'out | Candidate | Party | Votes | % |
|---|---|---|---|---|---|---|
| 1918 | 35,049 | 76.5 | †Sir E.R. Jones | Co L | 14,127 | 52.7 |
| | | | J. Winstone | Lab | 12,682 | 47.3 |
| | | | | | 1,445 | 5.4 |
| 1922 | 36,514 | 90.6 | R.C. Wallhead | Lab | 17,516 | 53.0 |
| | | | Sir R. Mathias, Bt. | Ind | 15,552 | 47.0 |
| | | | | | 1,964 | 6.0 |
| 1923 | 37,413 | 86.8 | R.C. Wallhead | Lab | 19,511 | 60.1 |
| | | | D.R. Thomas | L | 7,403 | 22.8 |
| | | | A.C. Fox-Davies | C | 5,548 | 17.1 |
| | | | | | 12,108 | 37.3 |
| 1924 | 38,276 | 86.9 | R.C. Wallhead | Lab | 19,882 | 59.8 |
| | | | A.C. Fox-Davies | C | 13,383 | 40.2 |
| | | | | | 6,499 | 19.6 |
| 1929 | 44,408 | 85.8 | R.C. Wallhead | Lab | 22,701 | 59.6 |
| | | | J. Jenkins | L | 8,696 | 22.8 |
| | | | F.B. Bradley-Birt | C | 6,712 | 17.6 |
| | | | | | 14,005 | 36.8 |
| 1931 | 43,908 | 80.8 | R.C. Wallhead | ILP (Lab) | 24,623 | 69.4 |
| | | | S. Davies | NP | 10,834 | 30.6 |
| | | | | | 13,789 | 38.8 |
| [Death] | | | | | | |
| 1934 (5/6) | 44,286 | 81.1 | S.O. Davies | Lab | 18,645 | 51.8 |
| | | | J.V. Evans | L | 10,376 | 28.9 |
| | | | Rev. C. Stephen | ILP | 3,508* | 9.8 |
| | | | W. Hannington | Com | 3,409* | 9.5 |
| | | | | | 8,269 | 22.9 |
| 1935 | 43,842 | 68.8 | S.O. Davies | Lab | 20,530 | 68.0 |
| | | | C. Stanfield | ILP | 9,640 | 32.0 |
| | | | | | 10,890 | 36.0 |
| 1945 | 44,540 | 68.6 | S.O. Davies | Lab | 24,879 | 81.4 |
| | | | S. Jennings | Ind Lab | 5,693 | 18.6 |
| | | | | | 19,186 | 62.8 |

Note:—

1922: Mathias sought election as an 'Independent and Anti-Socialist' candidate. He was the nominee of the local National Liberal Association and also received support from the Merthyr Conservative Association.

| Election | Electors | T'out | Candidate | Party | Votes | % |
|---|---|---|---|---|---|---|
| 1918 | 40,146 | 62.2 | †L. Haslam | Co L | 14,080 | 56.4 |
|  |  |  | J.W. Bowen | Lab | 10,234 | 41.0 |
|  |  |  | B.P. Thomas | Ind Dem | 647* | 2.6 |
|  |  |  |  |  | 3,846 | 15.4 |
| [Death] |  |  |  |  |  |  |
| 1922 | 42,645 | 79.2 | R.G. Clarry | C | 13,515 | 40.0 |
| (18/10) |  |  | J.W. Bowen | Lab | 11,425 | 33.8 |
|  |  |  | W.L. Moore | L | 8,841 | 26.2 |
|  |  |  |  |  | 2,090 | 6.2 |
| 1922 | 42,645 | 82.1 | R.G. Clarry | C | 19,019 | 54.3 |
|  |  |  | J.W. Bowen | Lab | 16,000 | 45.7 |
|  |  |  |  |  | 3,019 | 8.6 |
| 1923 | 42,899 | 85.2 | R.G. Clarry | C | 14,424 | 39.5 |
|  |  |  | J.W. Bowen | Lab | 14,100 | 38.6 |
|  |  |  | H. Davies | L | 8,015 | 21.9 |
|  |  |  |  |  | 324 | 0.9 |
| 1924 | 45,138 | 85.7 | R.G. Clarry | C | 20,426 | 52.8 |
|  |  |  | J.W. Bowen | Lab | 18,263 | 47.2 |
|  |  |  |  |  | 2,163 | 5.6 |
| 1929 | 56,392 | 83.8 | J. Walker | Lab | 18,653 | 39.5 |
|  |  |  | R.G. Clarry | C | 15,841 | 33.5 |
|  |  |  | S.I. Cohen | L | 12,735 | 27.0 |
|  |  |  |  |  | 2,812 | 6.0 |
| 1931 | 57,035 | 82.5 | R.G. Clarry | C | 27,829 | 59.1 |
|  |  |  | J. Walker | Lab | 19,238 | 40.9 |
|  |  |  |  |  | 8,591 | 18.2 |
| 1935 | 56,780 | 79.4 | R.G. Clarry | C | 23,300 | 51.7 |
|  |  |  | P. Freeman | Lab | 21,755 | 48.3 |
|  |  |  |  |  | 1,545 | 3.4 |
| [Death] |  |  |  |  |  |  |
| 1945 | 60,248 | 50.0 | R.M. Bell | C | 16,424 | 54.5 |
| (17/5) |  |  | R. Edwards | ILP | 13,722 | 45.5 |
|  |  |  |  |  | 2,702 | 9.0 |
| 1945 | 60,378 | 72.8 | P. Freeman | Lab | 23,845 | 54.2 |
|  |  |  | R.M. Bell | C | 14,754 | 33.6 |
|  |  |  | W.R. Crawshay | L | 5,362* | 12.2 |
|  |  |  |  |  | 9,091 | 20.6 |

## RHONDDA, EAST [520]

| Election | Electors | T'out | Candidate | Party | Votes | % |
|---|---|---|---|---|---|---|
| 1918 | | | D.W. Morgan | Lab | Unopp. | |
| 1922 | 38,516 | 80.9 | D.W. Morgan | Lab | 17,146 | 55.0 |
| | | | F.W. Heale | NL | 14,025 | 45.0 |
| | | | | | 3,121 | 10.0 |
| 1923 | 39,802 | 74.6 | D.W. Morgan | Lab | 21,338 | 71.9 |
| | | | A.J. Orchard | C | 8,346 | 28.1 |
| | | | | | 12,992 | 43.8 |
| 1924 | | | D.W. Morgan | Lab | Unopp. | |
| 1929 | 44,834 | 84.7 | D.W. Morgan | Lab | 19,010 | 50.2 |
| | | | R.D. Chalke | L | 10,269 | 27.0 |
| | | | A.L. Horner | Com | 5,789 | 15.2 |
| | | | J.F. Powell | C | 2,901* | 7.6 |
| | | | | | 8,741 | 23.2 |
| 1931 | 44,039 | 73.7 | D.W. Morgan | Lab | 22,086 | 68.1 |
| | | | A.L. Horner | Com | 10,359 | 31.9 |
| | | | | | 11,727 | 36.2 |
| [Death] | | | | | | |
| 1933 (28/3) | 44,311 | 74.9 | W.H. Mainwaring | Lab | 14,127 | 42.6 |
| | | | A.L. Horner | Com | 11,228 | 33.8 |
| | | | W.D. Thomas | L | 7,851 | 23.6 |
| | | | | | 2,899 | 8.8 |
| 1935 | 44,243 | 80.8 | W.H. Mainwaring | Lab | 22,088 | 61.8 |
| | | | H. Pollitt | Com | 13,655 | 38.2 |
| | | | | | 8,433 | 23.6 |
| 1945 | 41,832 | 82.8 | W.H. Mainwaring | Lab | 16,733 | 48.4 |
| | | | H. Pollitt | Com | 15,761 | 45.5 |
| | | | J.K. Davies | PC | 2,123* | 6.1 |
| | | | | | 972 | 2.9 |

# RHONDDA, WEST  [521]

| Election | Electors | T'out | Candidate | Party | Votes | % |
|---|---|---|---|---|---|---|
| 1918 | | | †Rt. Hon. W. Abraham | Lab | Unopp. | |
| [Resignation] | | | | | | |
| 1920 | 34,203† | 70.2 | W. John | Lab | 14,035 | 58.5 |
| (21/12) | | | G. Rowlands | Co C | 9,959 | 41.5 |
| | | | | | 4,076 | 17.0 |
| 1922 | 34,632 | 83.7 | W. John | Lab | 18,001 | 62.1 |
| | | | G. Rowlands | C | 10,990 | 37.9 |
| | | | | | 7,011 | 24.2 |
| 1923 | 35,462 | 78.5 | W. John | Lab | 18,206 | 65.4 |
| | | | J.R. Jones | L | 9,640 | 34.6 |
| | | | | | 8,566 | 30.8 |
| 1924 | | | W. John | Lab | Unopp. | |
| 1929 | 41,161 | 86.7 | W. John | Lab | 23,238 | 65.1 |
| | | | R.M. Hughes | L | 9,247 | 25.9 |
| | | | W.A. Prichard | C | 3,210* | 9.0 |
| | | | | | 13,991 | 39.2 |
| 1931 | 40,950 | 66.7 | W. John | Lab | 23,024 | 84.3 |
| | | | J.L. Davies | Com | 4,296 | 15.7 |
| | | | | | 18,728 | 68.6 |
| 1935 | | | W. John | Lab | Unopp. | |
| 1945 | | | W. John | Lab | Unopp. | |

Note:—

1922: Rowlands sought election as 'Labour in the Conservative interest'. He was however an official Conservative candidate and has been designated as such despite the rather unusual 'label' which he used. He was the nominee of Conservative working men's clubs.

## SWANSEA, EAST [522]

| Election | Electors | T'out | Candidate | Party | Votes | % |
|---|---|---|---|---|---|---|
| 1918 | 27,185 | 64.1 | †T.J. Williams | Co L | 11,071 | 63.6 |
| | | | D. Williams | Lab | 6,341 | 36.4 |
| | | | | | 4,730 | 27.2 |
| [Death] | | | | | | |
| 1919 (10/7) | 27,185† | 64.0 | D. Matthews | Co L | 9,250 | 53.1 |
| | | | D. Williams | Lab | 8,158 | 46.9 |
| | | | | | 1,092 | 6.2 |
| 1922 | 27,246 | 81.7 | D. Williams | Lab | 11,333 | 50.9 |
| | | | E. Harris | NL | 10,926 | 49.1 |
| | | | | | 407 | 1.8 |
| 1923 | 27,365 | 81.1 | D. Williams | Lab | 12,735 | 57.4 |
| | | | T.A. Jones | L | 9,463 | 42.6 |
| | | | | | 3,272 | 14.8 |
| 1924 | 27,836 | 80.7 | D. Williams | Lab | 12,274 | 54.6 |
| | | | W.D. Rees | L | 10,186 | 45.4 |
| | | | | | 2,088 | 9.2 |
| 1929 | 36,001 | 81.9 | D. Williams | Lab | 16,665 | 56.5 |
| | | | A. Hopkins | L | 9,825 | 33.3 |
| | | | P.P. Jones | C | 3,003* | 10.2 |
| | | | | | 6,840 | 23.2 |
| 1931 | 35,918 | 84.4 | D. Williams | Lab | 17,126 | 56.5 |
| | | | R.D. Chalke | L | 13,177 | 43.5 |
| | | | | | 3,949 | 13.0 |
| 1935 | | | D. Williams | Lab | Unopp. | |
| [Resignation] | | | | | | |
| 1940 (5/2) | | | D.L. Mort | Lab | Unopp. | |
| 1945 | 33,762 | 74.7 | D.L. Mort | Lab | 19,127 | 75.8 |
| | | | R. Harding | NL | 6,102 | 24.2 |
| | | | | | 13,025 | 51.6 |

## SWANSEA, WEST [523]

| Election | Electors | T'out | Candidate | Party | Votes | % |
|---|---|---|---|---|---|---|
| 1918 | 31,884 | 67.4 | †Rt. Hon. Sir A.M. Mond, Bt. | Co L | 8,579 | 40.0 |
|  |  |  | D. Davies | C | 7,398 | 34.4 |
|  |  |  | J.J. Powlesland | Lab | 5,510 | 25.6 |
|  |  |  |  |  | 1,181 | 5.6 |
| 1922 | 31,178 | 83.9 | Rt. Hon. Sir A.M. Mond, Bt. | NL | 9,278 | 35.5 |
|  |  |  | W.A.S. Hewins | C | 8,476 | 32.4 |
|  |  |  | H.W. Samuel | Lab | 8,401 | 32.1 |
|  |  |  |  |  | 802 | 3.1 |
| 1923 | 31,237 | 85.3 | H.W. Samuel | Lab | 9,260 | 34.8 |
|  |  |  | Rt. Hon. Sir A.M. Mond, Bt. | L | 9,145 | 34.3 |
|  |  |  | W.A.S. Hewins | C | 8,238 | 30.9 |
|  |  |  |  |  | 115 | 0.5 |
| 1924 | 31,674 | 87.0 | Rt. Hon. W. Runciman | L | 10,033 | 36.4 |
|  |  |  | H.W. Samuel | Lab | 9,188 | 33.4 |
|  |  |  | W.A.S. Hewins | C | 8,324 | 30.2 |
|  |  |  |  |  | 845 | 3.0 |
| 1929 | 40,021 | 81.7 | H.W. Samuel | Lab | 13,268 | 40.6 |
|  |  |  | C.I. Kerr | L | 12,625 | 38.6 |
|  |  |  | A.W.E. Wynne | C | 6,794 | 20.8 |
|  |  |  |  |  | 643 | 2.0 |
| 1931 | 41,680 | 84.4 | L. Jones | NL | 20,603 | 58.5 |
|  |  |  | H.W. Samuel | Lab | 14,587 | 41.5 |
|  |  |  |  |  | 6,016 | 17.0 |
| 1935 | 44,373 | 80.0 | L. Jones | NL | 18,784 | 52.9 |
|  |  |  | P. Morris | Lab | 16,703 | 47.1 |
|  |  |  |  |  | 2,081 | 5.8 |
| 1945 | 41,772 | 74.7 | P. Morris | Lab | 18,098 | 58.0 |
|  |  |  | Sir L. Jones | NL | 13,089 | 42.0 |
|  |  |  |  |  | 5,009 | 16.0 |

# WALES and MONMOUTHSHIRE ——— COUNTIES

| Election | Electors | T'out | Candidate | Party | Votes | % |
|---|---|---|---|---|---|---|
| 1918 | 25,836 | 69.4 | Sir O. Thomas | Ind Lab (Lab) (Ind Lab) | 9,038 | 50.4 |
| | | | †Rt. Hon. Sir E.J. Ellis-Griffith, Bt. | Co L | 8,898 | 49.6 |
| | | | | | 140 | 0.8 |
| 1922 | 27,320 | 80.5 | Sir O. Thomas | Ind Lab | 11,929 | 54.2 |
| | | | Sir R.J. Thomas, Bt. | NL | 10,067 | 45.8 |
| | | | | | 1,862 | 8.4 |
| [Death] | | | | | | |
| 1923 (7/4) | 27,320 | 76.4 | Sir R.J. Thomas, Bt. | L | 11,116 | 53.3 |
| | | | E.T. John | Lab | 6,368 | 30.5 |
| | | | R.O. Roberts | C | 3,385 | 16.2 |
| | | | | | 4,748 | 22.8 |
| 1923 | | | Sir R.J. Thomas, Bt. | L | Unopp. | |
| 1924 | 28,343 | 74.0 | Sir R.J. Thomas, Bt. | L | 13,407 | 63.9 |
| | | | C.O. Jones | Lab | 7,580 | 36.1 |
| | | | | | 5,827 | 27.8 |
| 1929 | 33,392 | 79.8 | Miss M. Lloyd George | L | 13,181 | 49.4 |
| | | | W. Edwards | Lab | 7,563 | 28.4 |
| | | | A. Hughes | C | 5,917 | 22.2 |
| | | | | | 5,618 | 21.0 |
| 1931 | 33,700 | 75.5 | Miss M. Lloyd George | L | 14,839 | 58.3 |
| | | | A. Hughes | C | 10,612 | 41.7 |
| | | | | | 4,227 | 16.6 |
| 1935 | 33,930 | 74.4 | Miss M. Lloyd George | L | 11,227 | 44.5 |
| | | | F.J.W. Williams | C | 7,045 | 27.9 |
| | | | H. Jones | Lab | 6,959 | 27.6 |
| | | | | | 4,182 | 16.6 |
| 1945 | 34,210 | 70.6 | Lady Megan Lloyd George | L | 12,610 | 52.2 |
| | | | C. Hughes | Lab | 11,529 | 47.8 |
| | | | | | 1,081 | 4.4 |

Note:—

1931: Miss Lloyd George was opposed to the National Government.

| Election | Electors | T'out | Candidate | Party | Votes | % |
|---|---|---|---|---|---|---|
| 1918 | | | †S. Robinson | Co L | Unopp. | |
| 1922 | 38,815 | 77.9 | W.A. Jenkins | NL | 20,405 | 67.4 |
| | | | E.T. John | Lab | 9,850 | 32.6 |
| | | | | | 10,555 | 34.8 |
| 1923 | | | W.A. Jenkins | L | Unopp. | |
| 1924 | 39,943 | 83.6 | W.D'A. Hall | C | 12,834 | 38.4 |
| | | | W.A. Jenkins | L | 10,374 | 31.1 |
| | | | E.T. John | Lab | 10,167 | 30.5 |
| | | | | | 2,460 | 7.3 |
| 1929 | 49,031 | 87.7 | P. Freeman | Lab | 14,511 | 33.7 |
| | | | W.D'A. Hall | C | 14,324 | 33.3 |
| | | | E.W. Cemlyn-Jones | L | 14,182 | 33.0 |
| | | | | | 187 | 0.4 |
| 1931 | 49,199 | 87.1 | W.D'A. Hall | C | 25,620 | 59.8 |
| | | | P. Freeman | Lab | 17,223 | 40.2 |
| | | | | | 8,397 | 19.6 |
| 1935 | 49,827 | 84.3 | Hon. I.G. Guest | Nat | 22,079 | 52.6 |
| | | | Dr. L. Haden-Guest | Lab | 19,910 | 47.4 |
| | | | | | 2,169 | 5.2 |

[Succession to the Peerage — Viscount Wimborne]

| Election | Electors | T'out | Candidate | Party | Votes | % |
|---|---|---|---|---|---|---|
| 1939 (1/8) | 48,486 | 79.9 | W.F. Jackson | Lab | 20,679 | 53.4 |
| | | | Hon. R.H. Philipps | C | 18,043 | 46.6 |
| | | | | | 2,636 | 6.8 |
| 1945 | 52,689 | 80.0 | T.E. Watkins | Lab | 19,725 | 46.8 |
| | | | Hon. O.M. Guest | C | 14,089 | 33.4 |
| | | | D. Lewis | L | 8,335 | 19.8 |
| | | | | | 5,636 | 13.4 |

# CAERNARVONSHIRE [526]

| Election | Electors | T'out | Candidate | Party | Votes | % |
|---|---|---|---|---|---|---|
| 1918 | 36,460 | 64.6 | C.E. Breese | Co L | 10,488 | 44.5 |
| | | | R.T. Jones | Ind Lab | 8,145 | 34.6 |
| | | | †E.W. Davies | L | 4,937 | 20.9 |
| | | | | | 2,343 | 9.9 |
| 1922 | 37,450 | 70.6 | R.T. Jones | Lab | 14,016 | 53.0 |
| | | | C.E. Breese | NL | 12,407 | 47.0 |
| | | | | | 1,609 | 6.0 |
| 1923 | 38,136 | 74.9 | G. Owen | L | 15,043 | 52.7 |
| | | | R.T. Jones | Lab | 13,521 | 47.3 |
| | | | | | 1,522 | 5.4 |
| 1924 | 38,647 | 76.6 | G. Owen | L | 15,033 | 50.8 |
| | | | R.T. Jones | Lab | 14,564 | 49.2 |
| | | | | | 469 | 1.6 |
| 1929 | 47,481 | 81.4 | G. Owen | L | 18,507 | 47.8 |
| | | | R.T. Jones | Lab | 14,867 | 38.5 |
| | | | D.F. Jones | C | 4,669* | 12.1 |
| | | | Rev. L.E. Valentine | PC | 609* | 1.6 |
| | | | | | 3,640 | 9.3 |
| 1931 | 48,003 | 80.0 | G. Owen | L | 14,993 | 39.0 |
| | | | W.E.E. Jones | Lab | 14,299 | 37.2 |
| | | | W.P.O. Evans | Nat Ind | 7,990 | 20.8 |
| | | | Prof. J.E. Daniel | PC | 1,136* | 3.0 |
| | | | | | 694 | 1.8 |
| 1935 | 49,284 | 74.9 | G. Owen | L | 17,947 | 48.6 |
| | | | W.E.E. Jones | Lab | 16,450 | 44.5 |
| | | | Prof. J.E. Daniel | PC | 2,534* | 6.9 |
| | | | | | 1,497 | 4.1 |
| 1945 | 51,295 | 77.7 | G.O. Roberts | Lab | 22,043 | 55.3 |
| | | | Sir G. Owen | L | 15,637 | 39.3 |
| | | | W.A. Bebb | PC | 2,152* | 5.4 |
| | | | | | 6,406 | 16.0 |

Note:—

1931: Owen was opposed to the National Government.

| Election | Electors | T'out | Candidate | Party | Votes | % |
|----------|----------|-------|-----------|-------|-------|---|
| 1918 | | | †M.L. Vaughan-Davies | Co L | Unopp. | |
| [Elevation to the Peerage — Lord Ystwyth] | | | | | | |
| 1921 | 30,751† | 80.1 | E. Evans | Co L | 14,111 | 57.3 |
| (18/2) | | | W.L. Williams | L | 10,521 | 42.7 |
| | | | | | 3,590 | 14.6 |
| 1922 | 32,695 | 76.9 | E. Evans | NL | 12,825 | 51.0 |
| | | | R.H. Morris | L | 12,310 | 49.0 |
| | | | | | 515 | 2.0 |
| 1923 | 32,881 | 81.0 | R.H. Morris | Ind L (L) | 12,469 | 46.9 |
| | | | E. Evans | L | 7,391 | 27.7 |
| | | | Earl of Lisburne | C | 6,776 | 25.4 |
| | | | | | 5,078 | 19.2 |
| 1924 | | | R.H. Morris | L | Unopp. | |
| 1929 | 38,704 | 73.2 | R.H. Morris | L | 17,127 | 60.5 |
| | | | E.C.L. Fitzwilliams | C | 11,198 | 39.5 |
| | | | | | 5,929 | 21.0 |
| 1931 | 39,206 | 67.5 | R.H. Morris | L | 20,113 | 76.0 |
| | | | J.L. Jones | Lab | 6,361 | 24.0 |
| | | | | | 13,752 | 52.0 |
| [Resignation on appointment as a Metropolitan Police Magistrate] | | | | | | |
| 1932 | 39,206 | 70.4 | D.O. Evans | L | 13,437 | 48.7 |
| (22/9) | | | E.C.L. Fitzwilliams | C | 8,866 | 32.1 |
| | | | Rev. D.M. Jones | Lab | 5,295 | 19.2 |
| | | | | | 4,571 | 16.6 |
| 1935 | 39,851 | 65.1 | D.O. Evans | L | 15,846 | 61.1 |
| | | | R.M. Hughes | Lab | 10,085 | 38.9 |
| | | | | | 5,761 | 22.2 |
| [Seat Vacant at Dissolution (Death)] | | | | | | |
| 1945 | 41,597 | 71.2 | E.R. Bowen | L | 18,912 | 63.8 |
| | | | I.J. Morgan | Lab | 10,718 | 36.2 |
| | | | | | 8,194 | 27.6 |

# CARMARTHENSHIRE, CARMARTHEN [528]

| Election | Electors | T'out | Candidate | Party | Votes | % |
|---|---|---|---|---|---|---|
| 1918 | | | †J. Hinds | Co L | Unopp. | |
| | | | | | | |
| 1922 | 36,213 | 82.7 | J. Hinds | NL (L) | 12,530 | 41.9 |
| | | | Hon. G.W.R.V. Coventry | C | 8,805 | 29.4 |
| | | | D. Johns | Agric | 4,775 | 15.9 |
| | | | H. Llewelyn-Williams | L | 3,847 | 12.8 |
| | | | | | 3,725 | 12.5 |
| | | | | | | |
| 1923 | 36,779 | 78.3 | Rt. Hon. Sir E.J. Ellis-Griffith, Bt. | L | 12,988 | 45.1 |
| | | | Sir A. Stephens | C | 8,677 | 30.1 |
| | | | R. Williams | Lab | 7,132 | 24.8 |
| | | | | | 4,311 | 15.0 |
| [Resignation] | | | | | | |
| 1924 (14/8) | 36,779† | 78.9 | Rt. Hon. Sir A.M. Mond, Bt. | L | 12,760 | 44.0 |
| | | | Rev. E.T. Owen | Lab | 8,351 | 28.8 |
| | | | Sir A. Stephens | C | 7,896 | 27.2 |
| | | | | | 4,409 | 15.2 |
| | | | | | | |
| 1924 | 37,155 | 67.9 | Rt. Hon. Sir A.M. Mond, Bt. | L (C) | 17,281 | 68.5 |
| | | | Rev. E.T. Owen | Lab | 7,953 | 31.5 |
| | | | | | 9,328 | 37.0 |
| [Elevation to the Peerage — Lord Melchett] | | | | | | |
| 1928 (28/6) | 37,482 | 76.6 | W.N. Jones | L | 10,201 | 35.5 |
| | | | D. Hopkin | Lab | 10,154 | 35.4 |
| | | | Sir C.C. Mansel, Bt. | C | 8,361 | 29.1 |
| | | | | | 47 | 0.1 |
| | | | | | | |
| 1929 | 46,110 | 85.8 | D. Hopkin | Lab | 15,130 | 38.2 |
| | | | W.N. Jones | L | 14,477 | 36.6 |
| | | | Hon. J.B. Coventry | C | 9,961 | 25.2 |
| | | | | | 653 | 1.6 |
| | | | | | | |
| 1931 | 46,507 | 84.5 | R.T. Evans | L | 15,532 | 39.6 |
| | | | D. Hopkin | Lab | 14,318 | 36.4 |
| | | | D.W.C. Davies-Evans | C | 9,434 | 24.0 |
| | | | | | 1,214 | 3.2 |
| | | | | | | |
| 1935 | 48,217 | 79.3 | D. Hopkin | Lab | 18,146 | 47.4 |
| | | | R.T. Evans | L | 12,911 | 33.8 |
| | | | E.O. Kellett | C | 7,177 | 18.8 |
| | | | | | 5,235 | 13.6 |
| [Resignation on appointment as a Metropolitan Police Magistrate] | | | | | | |
| 1941 (26/3) | | | R.M. Hughes | Lab | Unopp. | |
| | | | | | | |
| 1945 | 50,462 | 75.9 | R.H. Morris | L | 19,783 | 51.7 |
| | | | R.M. Hughes | Lab | 18,504 | 48.3 |
| | | | | | 1,279 | 3.4 |

Note:—

1922:   Johns was the nominee of the NFU.

| Election | Electors | T'out | Candidate | Party | Votes | % |
|---|---|---|---|---|---|---|
| 1918 | 44,657 | 68.9 | †J.T. Jones | Co L | 16,344 | 53.1 |
| | | | Dr. J.H. Williams | Lab | 14,409 | 46.9 |
| | | | | | 1,935 | 6.2 |
| 1922 | 48,795 | 80.3 | Dr. J.H. Williams | Lab | 23,213 | 59.3 |
| | | | G.C. Williams | NL | 15,947 | 40.7 |
| | | | | | 7,266 | 18.6 |
| 1923 | 49.825 | 76.8 | Dr. J.H. Williams | Lab | 21,063 | 55.1 |
| | | | R.T. Evans | L | 11,765 | 30.7 |
| | | | L. Beaumont-Thomas | C | 5,442 | 14.2 |
| | | | | | 9,298 | 24.4 |
| 1924 | 51,213 | 75.7 | Dr. J.H. Williams | Lab | 20,516 | 52.9 |
| | | | R.T. Evans | L | 18,257 | 47.1 |
| | | | | | 2,259 | 5.8 |
| 1929 | 65,255 | 79.1 | Dr. J.H. Williams | Lab | 28,595 | 55.4 |
| | | | R.T. Evans | L | 19,075 | 36.9 |
| | | | J.P.L. Thomas | C | 3,969* | 7.7 |
| | | | | | 9,520 | 18.5 |
| 1931 | 67,047 | 78.1 | Dr. J.H. Williams | Lab | 34,196 | 65.3 |
| | | | F.J. Rees | C | 18,163 | 34.7 |
| | | | | | 16,033 | 30.6 |
| 1935 | | | Dr. J.H. Williams | Lab | Unopp. | |
| [Death] | | | | | | |
| 1936 | 70,380 | 68.4 | J. Griffiths | Lab | 32,188 | 66.8 |
| (26/3) | | | W.A. Jenkins | NL | 15,967 | 33.2 |
| | | | | | 16,221 | 33.6 |
| 1945 | 73,385 | 74.8 | J. Griffiths | Lab | 44,514 | 81.1 |
| | | | G.O. George | C | 10,397 | 18.9 |
| | | | | | 34,117 | 62.2 |

# DENBIGHSHIRE, DENBIGH [530]

| Election | Electors | T'out | Candidate | Party | Votes | % |
|---|---|---|---|---|---|---|
| 1918 | 30,448 | 58.2 | Sir D.S. Davies | Co L | 14,773 | 83.3 |
| | | | †E.T. John | Lab | 2,958 | 16.7 |
| | | | | | 11,815 | 66.6 |
| | | | | | | |
| 1922 | 31,403 | 76.7 | J.C. Davies | NL | 12,975 | 53.9 |
| | | | Hon. Mrs. A.G. Brodrick | C | 9,138 | 37.9 |
| | | | L.G. Williams | L | 1,974* | 8.2 |
| | | | | | 3,837 | 16.0 |
| | | | | | | |
| 1923 | 31,997 | 63.6 | E.W. Davies | L | 12,164 | 59.8 |
| | | | D. Rhys | C | 8,186 | 40.2 |
| | | | | | 3,978 | 19.6 |
| | | | | | | |
| 1924 | 32,979 | 72.5 | E.W. Davies | L | 12,671 | 53.0 |
| | | | Hon. Mrs. A.G. Brodrick | C | 11,250 | 47.0 |
| | | | | | 1,421 | 6.0 |
| | | | | | | |
| 1929 | 43,173 | 79.7 | J.H. Morris-Jones | L (NL) | 21,305 | 61.9 |
| | | | A.C. Graham | C | 13,116 | 38.1 |
| | | | | | 8,189 | 23.8 |
| | | | | | | |
| 1931 | | | J.H. Morris-Jones | NL | Unopp. | |
| | | | | | | |
| 1935 | 46,158 | 75.1 | J.H. Morris Jones | NL (Ind) (NL) | 17,372 | 50.1 |
| | | | J.C. Davies | L | 12,329 | 35.6 |
| | | | J.R. Hughes | Lab | 4,963 | 14.3 |
| | | | | | 5,043 | 14.5 |
| | | | | | | |
| 1945 | 54,572 | 74.8 | Sir J.H. Morris-Jones | NL | 17,023 | 41.7 |
| | | | E.H.G. Evans | L | 12,101 | 29.6 |
| | | | W.L. Mars-Jones | Lab | 11,702 | 28.7 |
| | | | | | 4,922 | 12.1 |

| Election | Electors | T'out | Candidate | Party | Votes | % |
|----------|----------|-------|-----------|-------|-------|---|
| 1918 | 39,259 | 69.7 | Sir R.J. Thomas, Bt. | Co L | 20,874 | 76.3 |
| | | | H. Hughes | Lab | 6,500 | 23.7 |
| | | | | | 14,374 | 52.6 |
| 1922 | 39,446 | 84.4 | R. Richards | Lab | 11,940 | 35.8 |
| | | | E.R. Davies | NL | 10,842 | 32.6 |
| | | | R.C. Roberts | C | 10,508 | 31.6 |
| | | | | | 1,098 | 3.2 |
| 1923 | 40,789 | 81.1 | R. Richards | Lab | 12,918 | 39.0 |
| | | | H.A. Morgan | L | 11,037 | 33.4 |
| | | | E.F. Bushby | C | 9,131 | 27.6 |
| | | | | | 1,881 | 5.6 |
| 1924 | 41,686 | 82.6 | C.P. Williams | L | 19,154 | 55.6 |
| | | | R. Richards | Lab | 15,291 | 44.4 |
| | | | | | 3,863 | 11.2 |
| 1929 | 52,310 | 84.9 | R. Richards | Lab | 20,584 | 46.4 |
| | | | C.P. Williams | L | 13,997 | 31.5 |
| | | | Sir E.F. Bushby | C | 9,820 | 22.1 |
| | | | | | 6,587 | 14.9 |
| 1931 | 54,048 | 79.8 | A.O. Roberts | L | 22,474 | 52.1 |
| | | | R. Richards | Lab | 20,653 | 47.9 |
| | | | | | 1,821 | 4.2 |
| 1935 | 55,665 | 75.5 | R. Richards | Lab | 23,650 | 56.3 |
| | | | A.O. Roberts | L | 18,367 | 43.7 |
| | | | | | 5,283 | 12.6 |
| 1945 | 62,446 | 76.8 | R. Richards | Lab | 26,854 | 56.0 |
| | | | D.L. Milne | NL | 13,714 | 28.6 |
| | | | J.D. Williams | L | 6,960 | 14.5 |
| | | | J.R. Hayes-Jones | Ind | 430* | 0.9 |
| | | | | | 13,140 | 27.4 |

Note:—

1945: Hayes-Jones advocated a policy of Welsh nationalism.

| Election | Electors | T'out | Candidate | Party | Votes | % |
|---|---|---|---|---|---|---|
| 1918 | | | †T.H. Parry | Co L | Unopp. | |
| 1922 | 47,999 | 79.4 | T.H. Parry | NL | 16,854 | 44.2 |
| | | | A.L. Jones | C | 15,080 | 39.6 |
| | | | Rev. D.G. Jones | Lab | 6,163 | 16.2 |
| | | | | | 1,774 | 4.6 |
| 1923 | 49,728 | 69.4 | T.H. Parry | L | 19,609 | 56.8 |
| | | | E.H.G. Roberts | C | 14,926 | 43.2 |
| | | | | | 4,683 | 13.6 |
| 1924 | 51,205 | 80.2 | E.H.G. Roberts | C | 19,054 | 46.4 |
| | | | T.H. Parry | L | 14,169 | 34.5 |
| | | | Rev. D.G. Jones | Lab | 7,821 | 19.1 |
| | | | | | 4,885 | 11.9 |
| 1929 | 68,687 | 81.3 | F. Llewellyn-Jones | L (NL) | 24,012 | 43.0 |
| | | | E.H.G. Roberts | C | 19,536 | 35.0 |
| | | | C.O. Jones | Lab | 12,310 | 22.0 |
| | | | | | 4,476 | 8.0 |
| 1931 | 72,602 | 77.9 | F. Llewellyn-Jones | NL (L) | 40,405 | 71.4 |
| | | | Miss F. Edwards | Lab | 16,158 | 28.6 |
| | | | | | 24,247 | 42.8 |
| 1935 | 77,768 | 76.3 | G. Rowlands | C | 26,644 | 44.9 |
| | | | J.E. Emlyn-Jones | L | 16,536 | 27.9 |
| | | | C.O. Jones | Lab | 16,131 | 27.2 |
| | | | | | 10,108 | 17.0 |
| 1945 | 93,287 | 76.7 | E.N.C. Birch | C | 27,800 | 38.8 |
| | | | Miss E.L. Jones | Lab | 26,761 | 37.4 |
| | | | J.W. Hughes | L | 17,007 | 23.8 |
| | | | | | 1,039 | 1.4 |

| Election | Electors | T'out | Candidate | Party | Votes | % |
|---|---|---|---|---|---|---|
| 1918 | 30,415 | 71.4 | J. Edwards | Co L | 13,635 | 62.8 |
| | | | R. Williams | Lab | 7,758 | 35.7 |
| | | | T.G. Jones | Ind | 324* | 1.5 |
| | | | | | 5,877 | 27.1 |
| 1922 | 34,716 | 88.6 | J.R. MacDonald | Lab | 14,318 | 46.6 |
| | | | S.H. Byass | C | 11,111 | 36.1 |
| | | | J. Edwards | NL | 5,328 | 17.3 |
| | | | | | 3,207 | 10.5 |
| 1923 | 35,952 | 87.2 | J.R. MacDonald | Lab | 17,439 | 55.6 |
| | | | S.H. Byass | C | 13,927 | 44.4 |
| | | | | | 3,512 | 11.2 |
| 1924 | 37,200 | 89.6 | Rt. Hon. J.R. MacDonald | Lab | 17,724 | 53.1 |
| | | | W.H. Williams | L | 15,624 | 46.9 |
| | | | | | 2,100 | 6.2 |
| 1929 | 45,613 | 87.0 | W.G. Cove | Lab | 22,194 | 55.9 |
| | | | W.H. Williams | L | 13,155 | 33.2 |
| | | | F.B. Reece | C | 4,330* | 10.9 |
| | | | | | 9,039 | 22.7 |
| 1931 | 46,689 | 84.4 | W.G. Cove | Lab | 23,029 | 58.4 |
| | | | E. Curran | L | 16,378 | 41.6 |
| | | | | | 6,651 | 16.8 |
| 1935 | | | W.G. Cove | Lab | Unopp. | |
| 1945 | 54,381 | 79.3 | W.G. Cove | Lab | 31,286 | 72.5 |
| | | | D.T. Llewellyn | C | 11,860 | 27.5 |
| | | | | | 19,426 | 45.0 |

Note:—

1918: Jones was the nominee of the local branch of the NFDSS. He retired after nomination in favour of Edwards.

| Election | Electors | T'out | Candidate | Party | Votes | % |
|---|---|---|---|---|---|---|
| 1918 | 32,790 | 64.0 | A. Onions | Lab | 11,496 | 54.8 |
| | | | W.R. Edmunds | L | 9,482 | 45.2 |
| | | | | | 2,014 | 9.6 |
| [Death] | | | | | | |
| 1921 (24/8) | 34,511 | 73.2 | M. Jones | Lab | 13,699 | 54.2 |
| | | | W.R. Edmunds | Co L | 8,958 | 35.5 |
| | | | R. Stewart | Com | 2,592* | 10.3 |
| | | | | | 4,741 | 18.7 |
| 1922 | 35,795 | 78.6 | M. Jones | Lab | 16,082 | 57.2 |
| | | | A. McLean | C | 12,057 | 42.8 |
| | | | | | 4,025 | 14.4 |
| 1923 | 36,592 | 77.0 | M. Jones | Lab | 16,535 | 58.7 |
| | | | G. Rowlands | C | 6,493 | 23.0 |
| | | | S.R. Jenkins | L | 5,152 | 18.3 |
| | | | | | 10,042 | 35.7 |
| 1924 | 37,868 | 79.3 | M. Jones | Lab | 17,723 | 59.0 |
| | | | G. Rowlands | C | 12,293 | 41.0 |
| | | | | | 5,430 | 18.0 |
| 1929 | 45,173 | 81.1 | M. Jones | Lab | 21,248 | 57.9 |
| | | | Miss A.G. Roberts | L | 8,190 | 22.4 |
| | | | O.T. Morris | C | 6,357 | 17.4 |
| | | | J.R. Wilson | Com | 829* | 2.3 |
| | | | | | 13,058 | 35.5 |
| 1931 | 44,509 | 76.6 | M. Jones | Lab | 23,061 | 67.6 |
| | | | Mrs. C. Bowen-Davies | C | 11,044 | 32.4 |
| | | | | | 12,017 | 35.2 |
| 1935 | 45,057 | 72.3 | M. Jones | Lab | 24,846 | 76.3 |
| | | | Mrs. N.J. Stoneham | C | 7,738 | 23.7 |
| | | | | | 17,108 | 52.6 |
| [Death] | | | | | | |
| 1939 (4/7) | 42,678 | 68.4 | N. Edwards | Lab | 19,847 | 68.0 |
| | | | R.M. Bell | C | 9,349 | 32.0 |
| | | | | | 10,498 | 36.0 |
| 1945 | 47,170 | 77.1 | N. Edwards | Lab | 29,158 | 80.2 |
| | | | J.F.M. de Courcy | C | 7,189 | 19.8 |
| | | | | | 21,969 | 60.4 |

Note:—

1923: Rowlands sought election as 'Labour in the Conservative interest'. He was however an official Conservative candidate and has been designated as such despite the rather unusual 'label' he used. He was the nominee of Conservative working men's clubs.

| Election | Electors | T'out | Candidate | Party | Votes | % |
|----------|----------|-------|-----------|-------|-------|---|
| 1918 | 29,667 | 62.2 | †J. Williams | Lab | 10,109 | 54.8 |
| | | | D.H. Williams | L | 8,353 | 45.2 |
| | | | | | 1,756 | 9.6 |
| [Death] | | | | | | |
| 1922 (20/7) | 31,679† | 73.0 | D.R. Grenfell | Lab | 13,296 | 57.5 |
| | | | D.H. Williams | Co L | 9,841 | 42.5 |
| | | | | | 3,455 | 15.0 |
| 1922 | 33,084 | 74.6 | D.R. Grenfell | Lab | 13,388 | 54.2 |
| | | | F.W. Davies | L | 11,302 | 45.8 |
| | | | | | 2,086 | 8.4 |
| 1923 | 34,250 | 73.0 | D.R. Grenfell | Lab | 14,771 | 59.1 |
| | | | Mrs. L. Folland | L | 10,219 | 40.9 |
| | | | | | 4,552 | 18.2 |
| 1924 | 35,631 | 75.5 | D.R. Grenfell | Lab | 15,374 | 57.2 |
| | | | E.T. Neathercoat | C | 11,516 | 42.8 |
| | | | | | 3,858 | 14.4 |
| 1929 | 48,060 | 79.6 | D.R. Grenfell | Lab | 20,664 | 54.0 |
| | | | F.W. Davies | L | 11,055 | 28.9 |
| | | | A.T. Lennox-Boyd | C | 6,554 | 17.1 |
| | | | | | 9,609 | 25.1 |
| 1931 | 49,232 | 83.5 | D.R. Grenfell | Lab | 21,963 | 53.4 |
| | | | Sir E.R. Jones | L | 19,157 | 46.6 |
| | | | | | 2,806 | 6.8 |
| 1935 | 52,376 | 76.1 | D.R. Grenfell | Lab | 26,632 | 66.8 |
| | | | G.C. Hutchinson | Nat | 13,239 | 33.2 |
| | | | | | 13,393 | 33.6 |
| 1945 | 58,238 | 76.9 | D.R. Grenfell | Lab | 30,676 | 68.5 |
| | | | J. Aeron-Thomas | NL | 14,115 | 31.5 |
| | | | | | 16,561 | 37.0 |

| Election | Electors | T'out | Candidate | Party | Votes | % |
|---|---|---|---|---|---|---|
| 1918 | 34,041 | 63.0 | W. Cope | Co C | 13,307 | 62.0 |
|  |  |  | R.L. Jones | Lab | 6,607 | 30.8 |
|  |  |  | Dr. C.F.G. Sixsmith | Ind | 1,539* | 7.2 |
|  |  |  |  |  | 6,700 | 31.2 |
| 1922 | 38,698 | 76.8 | W. Cope | C | 13,129 | 44.1 |
|  |  |  | J.A. Lovat-Fraser | Lab | 9,031 | 30.4 |
|  |  |  | J.C. Meggitt | L | 7,577 | 25.5 |
|  |  |  |  |  | 4,098 | 13.7 |
| 1923 | 40,388 | 72.1 | W. Cope | C | 11,050 | 37.9 |
|  |  |  | E.W. David | L | 10,213 | 35.1 |
|  |  |  | T.F. Worrall | Lab | 7,871 | 27.0 |
|  |  |  |  |  | 837 | 2.8 |
| 1924 | 42,166 | 80.2 | W. Cope | C | 15,801 | 46.8 |
|  |  |  | C.E. Lloyd | Lab | 11,609 | 34.3 |
|  |  |  | E.W. David | L | 6,389 | 18.9 |
|  |  |  |  |  | 4,192 | 12.5 |
| 1929 | 63,802 | 82.5 | C.E. Lloyd | Lab | 21,468 | 40.8 |
|  |  |  | Sir W. Cope, Bt. | C | 18,799 | 35.7 |
|  |  |  | E.G. Davies | L | 12,352 | 23.5 |
|  |  |  |  |  | 2,669 | 5.1 |
| 1931 | 67,680 | 81.8 | P. Munro | C | 33,590 | 60.7 |
|  |  |  | C.E. Lloyd | Lab | 21,767 | 39.3 |
|  |  |  |  |  | 11,823 | 21.4 |
| 1935 | 73,693 | 77.0 | P. Munro | C | 29,099 | 51.3 |
|  |  |  | C.E. Lloyd | Lab | 27,677 | 48.7 |
|  |  |  |  |  | 1,422 | 2.6 |
| [Death] |  |  |  |  |  |  |
| 1942 (10/6) | 82,232 | 41.5 | C.H.A. Lakin | C | 19,408 | 56.8 |
|  |  |  | R.W.G. Mackay | Ind Lab | 13,753 | 40.3 |
|  |  |  | R.M.R. Paton | Ind | 975* | 2.9 |
|  |  |  |  |  | 5,655 | 16.5 |
| 1945 | 96,106 | 73.8 | A.L. Ungoed-Thomas | Lab | 33,706 | 47.5 |
|  |  |  | C.H.A. Lakin | C | 27,108 | 38.2 |
|  |  |  | M.E. Bransby-Williams | L | 10,132 | 14.3 |
|  |  |  |  |  | 6,598 | 9.3 |

Note:—

1942:  Paton advocated a policy of Welsh nationalism.

| Election | Electors | T'out | Candidate | Party | Votes | % |
|---|---|---|---|---|---|---|
| 1918 | 38,929 | 70.6 | †J.H. Edwards | Co L | 17,818 | 64.8 |
| | | | Rev. H. Morgan | Lab | 9,670 | 35.2 |
| | | | | | 8,148 | 29.6 |
| 1922 | 43,638 | 75.4 | W. Jenkins | Lab | 19,566 | 59.5 |
| | | | J.H. Edwards | NL | 13,331 | 40.5 |
| | | | | | 6,235 | 19.0 |
| 1923 | 45,084 | 73.9 | W. Jenkins | Lab | 20,764 | 62.3 |
| | | | T. Elias | L | 12,562 | 37.7 |
| | | | | | 8,202 | 24.6 |
| 1924 | | | W. Jenkins | Lab | Unopp. | |
| 1929 | 59,584 | 82.1 | W. Jenkins | Lab | 29,455 | 60.2 |
| | | | J. Jones | L | 14,554 | 29.8 |
| | | | D.J. Evans | C | 4,892* | 10.0 |
| | | | | | 14,901 | 30.4 |
| 1931 | 61,550 | 78.4 | Sir W. Jenkins | Lab | 30,873 | 64.0 |
| | | | D.G. Davies | L | 17,389 | 36.0 |
| | | | | | 13,484 | 28.0 |
| 1935 [Death] | | | Sir W. Jenkins | Lab | Unopp. | |
| 1945 (15/5) | 67,083 | 58.0 | D.J. Williams | Lab | 30,847 | 79.2 |
| | | | W.I. Samuel | PC | 6,290 | 16.2 |
| | | | J.R. Haston | RCP | 1,781* | 4.6 |
| | | | | | 24,557 | 63.0 |
| 1945 | 67,164 | 74.6 | D.J. Williams | Lab | 37,957 | 75.8 |
| | | | D. Bowen | C | 8,466 | 16.9 |
| | | | W.I. Samuel | PC | 3,659* | 7.3 |
| | | | | | 29,491 | 58.9 |

# GLAMORGANSHIRE, OGMORE [538]

| Election | Electors | T'out | Candidate | Party | Votes | % |
|---|---|---|---|---|---|---|
| 1918 | | | V. Hartshorn | Lab | Unopp. | |
| | | | | | | |
| 1922 | 39,673 | 78.3 | V. Hartshorn | Lab | 17,321 | 55.8 |
| | | | J.W. Jones | NL | 7,498 | 24.1 |
| | | | Mrs. D.C. Edmondes | C | 6,257 | 20.1 |
| | | | | | 9,823 | 31.7 |
| | | | | | | |
| 1923 | | | V. Hartshorn | Lab | Unopp. | |
| | | | | | | |
| 1924 | | | Rt.Hon. V. Hartshorn | Lab | Unopp. | |
| | | | | | | |
| 1929 | 48,786 | 82.8 | Rt.Hon. V. Hartshorn | Lab | 22,900 | 56.7 |
| | | | D.L. Powell | L | 11,804 | 29.2 |
| | | | H. Abbott | C | 4,164* | 10.3 |
| | | | J.R. Campbell | Com | 1,525* | 3.8 |
| | | | | | 11,096 | 27.5 |

[Death]

| Election | Electors | T'out | Candidate | Party | Votes | % |
|---|---|---|---|---|---|---|
| 1931 | 48,406 | 50.8 | E.J. Williams | Lab | 19,356 | 78.8 |
| (19/5) | | | J.R. Campbell | Com | 5,219 | 21.2 |
| | | | | | 14,137 | 57.6 |
| | | | | | | |
| 1931 | 49,203 | 76.9 | E.J. Williams | Lab | 23,064 | 61.0 |
| | | | Sir T.G. Jones | C | 11,653 | 30.8 |
| | | | J.R. Campbell | Com | 3,099* | 8.2 |
| | | | | | 11,411 | 30.2 |
| | | | | | | |
| 1935 | | | E.J. Williams | Lab | Unopp. | |
| | | | | | | |
| 1945 | 56,644 | 75.6 | E.J. Williams | Lab | 32,715 | 76.4 |
| | | | O.G. Davies | C | 7,712 | 18.0 |
| | | | T.R. Morgan | PC | 2,379* | 5.6 |
| | | | | | 25,003 | 58.4 |

[Resignation on appointment as United Kingdom High Commissioner in Australia]

| Election | Electors | T'out | Candidate | Party | Votes | % |
|---|---|---|---|---|---|---|
| 1946 | 58,361 | 33.1 | J. Evans | Lab | 13,632 | 70.6 |
| (4/6) | | | T.R. Morgan | PC | 5,685 | 29.4 |
| | | | | | 7,947 | 41.2 |

| Election | Electors | T'out | Candidate | Party | Votes | % |
|---|---|---|---|---|---|---|
| 1918 | 34,778 | 68.3 | T.A. Lewis | Co L | 13,327 | 56.1 |
| | | | D.L. Davies | Lab | 10,152 | 42.8 |
| | | | A. Seaton | C | 260* | 1.1 |
| | | | | | 3,175 | 13.3 |

[Appointed a Lord Commissioner of the Treasury]

| | | | | | | |
|---|---|---|---|---|---|---|
| 1922 | 40,017[†] | 72.9 | T.I. Mardy-Jones | Lab | 16,630 | 57.0 |
| (25/7) | | | T.A. Lewis | Co L | 12,550 | 43.0 |
| | | | | | 4,080 | 14.0 |
| | | | | | | |
| 1922 | 41,087 | 76.8 | T.I. Mardy-Jones | Lab | 14,884 | 47.2 |
| | | | Sir R. Rhys Williams, Bt. | NL | 8,667 | 27.5 |
| | | | J.G. Jones | C | 7,994 | 25.3 |
| | | | | | 6,217 | 19.7 |
| | | | | | | |
| 1923 | 40,379 | 76.0 | T.I. Mardy-Jones | Lab | 16,837 | 54.9 |
| | | | D. Rees | L | 13,839 | 45.1 |
| | | | | | 2,998 | 9.8 |
| | | | | | | |
| 1924 | 41,099 | 79.6 | T.I. Mardy-Jones | Lab | 18,301 | 55.9 |
| | | | D.J. Evans | C | 14,425 | 44.1 |
| | | | | | 3,876 | 11.8 |
| | | | | | | |
| 1929 | 47,860 | 82.0 | T.I. Mardy-Jones | Lab | 20,835 | 53.1 |
| | | | J.V. Evans | L | 14,421 | 36.8 |
| | | | Miss M.L.G. Williams | C | 3,967* | 10.1 |
| | | | | | 6,414 | 16.3 |

[Resignation]

| | | | | | | |
|---|---|---|---|---|---|---|
| 1931 | 46,936 | 73.6 | D.L. Davies | Lab | 20,687 | 59.9 |
| (19/3) | | | G.C.H. Crawshay | L | 8,368 | 24.2 |
| | | | D.J. Evans | C | 5,489 | 15.9 |
| | | | | | 12,319 | 35.7 |
| | | | | | | |
| 1931 | 47,346 | 78.7 | D.L. Davies | Lab | 21,751 | 58.3 |
| | | | B. Acworth | L | 13,937 | 37.4 |
| | | | T.I. Mardy-Jones | Ind Lab | 1,110* | 3.0 |
| | | | W. Lowell | NP | 466* | 1.3 |
| | | | | | 7,814 | 20.9 |
| | | | | | | |
| 1935 | | | D.L. Davies | Lab | Unopp. | |

[Death]

| | | | | | | |
|---|---|---|---|---|---|---|
| 1938 | 47,238 | 78.3 | A. Pearson | Lab | 22,159 | 59.9 |
| (11/2) | | | Lady Rhys Williams | NL | 14,810 | 40.1 |
| | | | | | 7,349 | 19.8 |
| | | | | | | |
| 1945 | 53,598 | 75.7 | A. Pearson | Lab | 27,823 | 68.6 |
| | | | C.G. Treherne | C | 7,260 | 17.9 |
| | | | J.E. Williams | L | 5,464 | 13.5 |
| | | | | | 20,563 | 50.7 |

Notes:—

1918: Seaton retired after nomination in favour of Lewis.

1922: Lewis resigned office following his defeat.
(25/7)

| Election | Electors | T'out | Candidate | Party | Votes | % |
|---|---|---|---|---|---|---|
| 1918 | | | †H.H. Jones | L | Unopp. | |
| 1922 | 22,017 | 77.1 | H.H. Jones | L | 9,903 | 58.3 |
| | | | J.J. Roberts | Lab | 7,071 | 41.7 |
| | | | | | 2,832 | 16.6 |
| 1923 | 22,666 | 80.2 | H.H. Jones | L | 11,005 | 60.5 |
| | | | J.J. Roberts | Lab | 7,181 | 39.5 |
| | | | | | 3,824 | 21.0 |
| 1924 | 23,013 | 83.9 | H.H. Jones | L | 9,228 | 47.8 |
| | | | J.J. Roberts | Lab | 6,393 | 33.1 |
| | | | R. Vaughan | C | 3,677 | 19.1 |
| | | | | | 2,835 | 14.7 |
| 1929 | 28,836 | 85.2 | H.H. Jones | L | 11,865 | 48.2 |
| | | | J.J. Roberts | Lab | 7,980 | 32.5 |
| | | | C. Phibbs | C | 4,731 | 19.3 |
| | | | | | 3,885 | 15.7 |
| 1931 | 28,973 | 82.6 | H.H. Jones | L | 9,756 | 40.8 |
| | | | J.H. Howard | Lab | 7,807 | 32.6 |
| | | | C. Phibbs | C | 6,372 | 26.6 |
| | | | | | 1,949 | 8.2 |
| 1935 | 28,985 | 81.6 | H.H. Jones | L | 9,466 | 40.0 |
| | | | T.W. Jones | Lab | 8,317 | 35.2 |
| | | | C. Phibbs | C | 5,868 | 24.8 |
| | | | | | 1,149 | 4.8 |
| 1945 | 28,845 | 82.2 | E.O. Roberts | L | 8,495 | 35.8 |
| | | | H.M. Jones | Lab | 8,383 | 35.4 |
| | | | C.P. Hughes | C | 4,374 | 18.5 |
| | | | G.R. Evans | PC | 2,448* | 10.3 |
| | | | | | 112 | 0.4 |

Note:—

    1918: Jones was issued with the Coalition 'coupon' but repudiated it.

| Election | Electors | T'out | Candidate | Party | Votes | % |
|---|---|---|---|---|---|---|
| 1918 | | | †Rt. Hon. W. Brace | Lab | Unopp. | |
| [Resignation on appointment as Chief Labour Adviser to the Department of Mines] | | | | | | |
| 1920 (21/12) | 32,960† | 70.8 | G. Barker<br>G.H. Morgan | Lab<br>Co L | 15,492<br>7,842<br>7,650 | 66.4<br>33.6<br>32.8 |
| 1922 | | | G. Barker | Lab | Unopp. | |
| 1923 | | | G. Barker | Lab | Unopp. | |
| 1924 | | | G. Barker | Lab | Unopp. | |
| 1929 | 37,972 | 82.4 | G. Daggar<br>W.R. Meredith<br>P.J.F. Chapman-Walker | Lab<br>L<br>C | 20,175<br>8,425<br>2,697*<br>11,750 | 64.5<br>26.9<br>8.6<br>37.6 |
| 1931 | | | G. Daggar | Lab | Unopp. | |
| 1935 | | | G. Daggar | Lab | Unopp. | |
| 1945 | 40,749 | 81.1 | G. Daggar<br>Dr. J.J. Hayward | Lab<br>C | 28,615<br>4,422<br>24,193 | 86.6<br>13.4<br>73.2 |

## MONMOUTHSHIRE, BEDWELLTY [542]

| Election | Electors | T'out | Candidate | Party | Votes | % |
|---|---|---|---|---|---|---|
| 1918 | 30,938 | 70.8 | C. Edwards | Lab | 11,730 | 53.6 |
| | | | W.H. Williams | Co L | 10,170 | 46.4 |
| | | | | | 1,560 | 7.2 |
| 1922 | 33,741 | 81.2 | C. Edwards | Lab | 17,270 | 63.0 |
| | | | C.E. Bagram | C | 10,132 | 37.0 |
| | | | | | 7,138 | 26.0 |
| 1923 | 35,051 | 74.2 | C. Edwards | Lab | 17,564 | 67.6 |
| | | | W.H. Williams | L | 8,436 | 32.4 |
| | | | | | 9,128 | 35.2 |
| 1924 | | | C. Edwards | Lab | Unopp. | |
| 1929 | 44,023 | 74.9 | C. Edwards | Lab | 26,021 | 79.0 |
| | | | H.G. Griffith | C | 6,936 | 21.0 |
| | | | | | 19,085 | 58.0 |
| 1931 | | | C. Edwards | Lab | Unopp. | |
| 1935 | | | Sir C. Edwards | Lab | Unopp. | |
| 1945 | 47,716 | 77.8 | Rt. Hon. Sir C. Edwards | Lab | 30,480 | 82.1 |
| | | | H.L. Tett | C | 6,641 | 17.9 |
| | | | | | 23,839 | 64.2 |

| Election | Electors | T'out | Candidate | Party | Votes | % |
|----------|----------|-------|-----------|-------|-------|---|
| 1918 [Resignation] | | | †Rt. Hon. T. Richards | Lab | Unopp. | |
| 1920 (26/7) | | | E. Davies | Lab | Unopp. | |
| 1922 | 33,119 | 78.2 | E. Davies | Lab | 16,947 | 65.4 |
| | | | M. Morgan | C | 8,951 | 34.6 |
| | | | | | 7,996 | 30.8 |
| 1923 | 33,171 | 75.8 | E. Davies | Lab | 16,492 | 65.6 |
| | | | C.G. Davies | L | 8,639 | 34.4 |
| | | | | | 7,853 | 31.2 |
| 1924 | | | E. Davies | Lab | Unopp. | |
| 1929 | 38,781 | 85.9 | A. Bevan | Lab | 20,088 | 60.3 |
| | | | W. Griffiths | L | 8,924 | 26.8 |
| | | | M. Brace | C | 4,287 | 12.9 |
| | | | | | 11,164 | 33.5 |
| 1931 | | | A. Bevan | Lab | Unopp. | |
| 1935 | 38,908 | 82.6 | A. Bevan | Lab (Ind Lab) (Lab) | 25,007 | 77.8 |
| | | | Miss F.E. Scarborough | C | 7,145 | 22.2 |
| | | | | | 17,862 | 55.6 |
| 1945 | 41,146 | 82.6 | A. Bevan | Lab | 27,209 | 80.1 |
| | | | C.S. Parker | C | 6,758 | 19.9 |
| | | | | | 20,451 | 60.2 |

| Election | Electors | T'out | Candidate | Party | Votes | % |
|---|---|---|---|---|---|---|
| 1918 | 27,575 | 55.7 | C.L. Forestier-Walker | C | 9,164 | 59.7 |
| | | | H.M. Martineau | L | 6,189 | 40.3 |
| | | | | | 2,975 | 19.4 |
| 1922 | | | C.L. Forestier-Walker | C | Unopp. | |
| 1923 | 29,889 | 70.9 | C.L. Forestier-Walker | C | 12,697 | 59.9 |
| | | | M. Griffith | L | 8,487 | 40.1 |
| | | | | | 4,210 | 19.8 |
| 1924 | 31,031 | 74.1 | C.L. Forestier-Walker | C | 16,510 | 71.8 |
| | | | L.H. Bateman | Lab | 6,469 | 28.2 |
| | | | | | 10,041 | 43.6 |
| 1929 | 42,070 | 78.9 | Sir C.L. Forestier-Walker. Bt. | C | 16,353 | 49.3 |
| | | | R.C. Williams | L | 8,582 | 25.8 |
| | | | L.H. Bateman | Lab | 8,268 | 24.9 |
| | | | | | 7,771 | 23.5 |
| 1931 | 44,929 | 78.0 | Sir C.L. Forestier-Walker, Bt. | C | 24,829 | 70.8 |
| | | | Rev. D. Hughes | Lab | 10,217 | 29.2 |
| | | | | | 14,612 | 41.6 |
| [Death] | | | | | | |
| 1934 (14/6) | 45,885 | 69.2 | J.A. Herbert | C | 20,640 | 65.0 |
| | | | Rev. D. Hughes | Lab | 11,094 | 35.0 |
| | | | | | 9,546 | 30.0 |
| 1935 | 47,792 | 76.8 | J.A. Herbert | C | 23,262 | 63.4 |
| | | | M.M. Foot | Lab | 13,454 | 36.6 |
| | | | | | 9,808 | 26.8 |
| [Resignation on appointment as Governor of Bengal] | | | | | | |
| 1939 (25/7) | 49,690 | 58.2 | L.R. Pym | C | 17,358 | 60.1 |
| | | | F.R. Hancock | Lab | 11,543 | 39.9 |
| | | | | | 5,815 | 20.2 |
| 1945 | 59,359 | 72.0 | L.R. Pym | C | 22,195 | 51.9 |
| | | | A.B.L. Oakley | Lab | 20,543 | 48.1 |
| | | | | | 1,652 | 3.8 |
| [Death] | | | | | | |
| 1945 (30/10) | 60,013 | 66.7 | G.E.P. Thorneycroft | C | 21,092 | 52.7 |
| | | | A.B.L. Oakley | Lab | 18,953 | 47.3 |
| | | | | | 2,139 | 5.4 |

| Election | Electors | T'out | Candidate | Party | Votes | % |
|---|---|---|---|---|---|---|
| 1918 | 30,002 | 72.1 | T. Griffiths | Lab | 8,438 | 39.0 |
| | | | Sir L.W. Llewelyn | Co C | 7,021 | 32.5 |
| | | | †Rt. Hon. R. McKenna | L | 6,160 | 28.5 |
| | | | | | 1,417 | 6.5 |
| 1922 | 32,439 | 85.0 | T. Griffiths | Lab | 11,198 | 40.6 |
| | | | Sir T.G. Jones | C | 8,654 | 31.4 |
| | | | Sir R.L. Connell | L | 7,733 | 28.0 |
| | | | | | 2,544 | 9.2 |
| 1923 | 33,369 | 81.6 | T. Griffiths | Lab | 13,770 | 50.6 |
| | | | S.J. Robins | L | 13,444 | 49.4 |
| | | | | | 326 | 1.2 |
| 1924 | 34,587 | 84.5 | T. Griffiths | Lab | 15,378 | 52.6 |
| | | | L. Beaumont-Thomas | C | 13,831 | 47.4 |
| | | | | | 1,547 | 5.2 |
| 1929 | 40,888 | 84.6 | T. Griffiths | Lab | 17,805 | 51.5 |
| | | | G.C.H. Crawshay | L | 12,581 | 36.4 |
| | | | G. Rowlands | C | 4,188* | 12.1 |
| | | | | | 5,224 | 15.1 |
| 1931 | 41,090 | 82.0 | T. Griffiths | Lab | 18,981 | 56.3 |
| | | | T. Keens | NL | 14,709 | 43.7 |
| | | | | | 4,272 | 12.6 |
| 1935 | 41,887 | 78.5 | A. Jenkins | Lab | 22,346 | 67.9 |
| | | | L. Caplan | C | 10,555 | 32.1 |
| | | | | | 11,791 | 35.8 |
| 1945 | 46,122 | 77.0 | A. Jenkins | Lab | 27,455 | **77.3** |
| | | | J.G. Weeple | C | 8,072 | **22.7** |
| | | | | | 19,383 | **54.6** |
| [Death] | | | | | | |
| 1946 (23/7) | 47,093 | 64.8 | D.G. West | Lab | 22,359 | 73.2 |
| | | | P. Welch | C | 8,170 | 26.8 |
| | | | | | 14,189 | 46.4 |

| Election | Electors | T'out | Candidate | Party | Votes | % |
|----------|----------|-------|-----------|-------|-------|---|
| 1918 | | | †D. Davies | L | Unopp. | |
| 1922 | | | D. Davies | L | Unopp. | |
| 1923 | | | D. Davies | L | Unopp. | |
| 1924 | 24,338 | 79.4 | D. Davies | L | 14,942 | 77.3 |
| | | | A. Davies | Lab | 4,384 | 22.7 |
| | | | | | 10,558 | 54.6 |
| 1929 | 31,142 | 88.3 | E.C. Davies | L (NL) | 12,779 | 46.5 |
| | | | J.M. Naylor | C | 10,651 | 38.7 |
| | | | J. Evans | Lab | 4,069 | 14.8 |
| | | | | | 2,128 | 7.8 |
| 1931 | | | E.C. Davies | NL | Unopp. | |
| 1935 | | | E.C. Davies | NL (Ind L) (L) | Unopp. | |
| 1945 | 32,190 | 77.4 | E.C. Davies | L | 14,018 | 56.3 |
| | | | P.L.W. Owen | C | 10,895 | 43.7 |
| | | | | | 3,123 | 12.6 |

Notes:—

1918: Davies was issued with the Coalition 'coupon' but repudiated it.

1924: Davies announced in 1926 that owing to the policy being pursued by the Liberal Party under the leadership of Lloyd George he would not be willing to seek re-election as a Liberal candidate. There is no evidence of him actually relinquishing the Liberal whip and apparently until the Dissolution he remained, at least nominally, a Liberal member.

# PEMBROKESHIRE [547]

| Election | Electors | T'out | Candidate | Party | Votes | % |
|----------|----------|-------|-----------|-------|-------|---|
| 1918 | 42,808 | 64.3 | Sir E.D. Jones, Bt. | Co L | 19,200 | 69.8 |
| | | | I. Gwynne | Lab | 7,712 | 28.0 |
| | | | G.B. Thomas | CS | 597* | 2.2 |
| | | | | | 11,488 | 41.8 |
| 1922 | 43,631 | 71.7 | G. Lloyd George | NL | 21,569 | 69.0 |
| | | | W.J. Jenkins | Lab | 9,703 | 31.0 |
| | | | | | 11,866 | 38.0 |
| 1923 | 44,134 | 77.9 | G. Lloyd George | L | 13,173 | 38.3 |
| | | | C.W.M. Price | C | 11,682 | 34.0 |
| | | | W.J. Jenkins | Lab | 9,511 | 27.7 |
| | | | | | 1,491 | 4.3 |
| 1924 | 44,980 | 80.2 | C.W.M. Price | C | 14,575 | 40.4 |
| | | | G. Lloyd George | L | 13,045 | 36.2 |
| | | | W.J. Jenkins | Lab | 8,455 | 23.4 |
| | | | | | 1,530 | 4.2 |
| 1929 | 54,302 | 83.8 | G. Lloyd George | L | 19,050 | 41.8 |
| | | | C.W.M. Price | C | 14,235 | 31.3 |
| | | | W.J. Jenkins | Lab | 12,235 | 26.9 |
| | | | | | 4,815 | 10.5 |
| 1931 | 55,291 | 79.9 | G. Lloyd George | L | 24,606 | 55.7 |
| | | | C.W.M. Price | C | 19,560 | 44.3 |
| | | | | | 5,046 | 11.4 |
| 1935 | 56,537 | 79.1 | G. Lloyd George | L | 16,734 | 37.4 |
| | | | G.E. Allison | C | 15,660 | 35.0 |
| | | | W.J. Jenkins | Lab | 12,341 | 27.6 |
| | | | | | 1,074 | 2.4 |
| 1945 | 63,388 | 72.3 | Rt. Hon. G. Lloyd George | L (NL & C) | 22,997 | 50.2 |
| | | | W. Fienburgh | Lab | 22,829 | 49.8 |
| | | | | | 168 | 0.4 |

Notes:—

1931: Lloyd George was opposed to the National Government.

1945: Lloyd George, although an official Liberal candidate, had accepted office in the National (Caretaker) Government and supported Churchill. He contested the election with the full support of the local Conservative Association and as a result of the Woolton-Teviot Agreement of 1947, a united Liberal-Conservative organisation was formed in the constituency.

# SCOTLAND ——— BURGHS

| Election | Electors | T'out | Candidate | Party | Votes | % |
|---|---|---|---|---|---|---|
| 1918 | 33,072 | 36.4 | F.H. Rose | Ind Lab (Lab) (Ind Lab) (Lab) | 6,128 | 50.9 |
| | | | †D.V. Pirie | Co L | 5,918 | 49.1 |
| | | | | | 210 | 1.8 |
| 1922 | 34,603 | 56.9 | F.H. Rose | Lab | 10,958 | 55.7 |
| | | | W.M. Cameron | NL | 6,615 | 33.6 |
| | | | J. Johnston | L | 2,113* | 10.7 |
| | | | | | 4,343 | 22.1 |
| 1923 | 34,098 | 53.0 | F.H. Rose | Lab | 9,138 | 50.6 |
| | | | W.F. Lumsden | C | 4,820 | 26.7 |
| | | | W.M. Cameron | L | 4,099 | 22.7 |
| | | | | | 4,318 | 23.9 |
| 1924 | 33,826 | 64.4 | F.H. Rose | Lab | 13,249 | 60.8 |
| | | | Dr. Laura S. Sandeman | C | 8,545 | 39.2 |
| | | | | | 4,704 | 21.6 |
| [Death] | | | | | | |
| 1928 (16/8) | 35,738 | 56.8 | W.W. Benn | Lab | 10,646 | 52.5 |
| | | | Dr. Laura S. Sandeman | C | 4,696 | 23.1 |
| | | | A. Ferguson | Com | 2,618 | 12.9 |
| | | | J.R. Rutherford | L | 2,337* | 11.5 |
| | | | | | 5,950 | 29.4 |
| 1929 | 46,934 | 62.5 | W.W. Benn | Lab | 17,826 | 60.8 |
| | | | R.C. Berkeley | L | 9,799 | 33.4 |
| | | | A. Ferguson | Com | 1,686* | 5.8 |
| | | | | | 8,027 | 27.4 |
| 1931 | 48,618 | 73.4 | J.G. Burnett | C | 22,931 | 64.3 |
| | | | Rt. Hon. W.W. Benn | Lab | 8,753 | 24.5 |
| | | | Mrs. H. Crawfurd | Com | 3,980* | 11.2 |
| | | | | | 14,178 | 39.8 |
| 1935 | 52,858 | 65.9 | G.M. Garro-Jones | Lab | 16,952 | 48.7 |
| | | | J.G. Burnett | C | 13,990 | 40.2 |
| | | | A.F. Macintosh | ILP | 3,871* | 11.1 |
| | | | | | 2,962 | 8.5 |
| 1945 | 57,109 | 67.2 | H.S.J. Hughes | Lab | 26,753 | 69.6 |
| | | | Lady Grant of Monymusk | C | 9,623 | 25.1 |
| | | | A.W. Walker | SNP | 2,021* | 5.3 |
| | | | | | 17,130 | 44.5 |

# ABERDEEN, SOUTH [549]

| Election | Electors | T'out | Candidate | Party | Votes | % |
|----------|----------|-------|-----------|-------|-------|---|
| 1918 | 38,800 | 43.9 | F.C. Thomson | Co C | 10,625 | 62.4 |
|  |  |  | †Sir J. Fleming | L | 3,535 | 20.8 |
|  |  |  | Prof. J.R. Watson | Ind | 2,868 | 16.8 |
|  |  |  |  |  | 7,090 | 41.6 |
| 1922 | 39,619 | 57.5 | F.C. Thomson | C | 13,208 | 58.0 |
|  |  |  | Sir C.E. Mallet | L | 9,573 | 42.0 |
|  |  |  |  |  | 3,635 | 16.0 |
| 1923 | 39,229 | 60.7 | F.C. Thomson | C | 11,258 | 47.3 |
|  |  |  | J. Paton | Lab | 6,911 | 29.0 |
|  |  |  | Sir C.E. Mallet | L | 5,641 | 23.7 |
|  |  |  |  |  | 4,347 | 18.3 |
| 1924 | 38,958 | 68.8 | F.C. Thomson | C | 16,092 | 60.1 |
|  |  |  | G. Archibald | Lab | 10,699 | 39.9 |
|  |  |  |  |  | 5,393 | 20.2 |
| 1929 | 52,692 | 67.2 | Sir F.C. Thomson, Bt. | C | 21,548 | 60.8 |
|  |  |  | W.H.P. Martin | Lab | 13,868 | 39.2 |
|  |  |  |  |  | 7,680 | 21.6 |
| 1931 | 53,560 | 75.8 | Sir F.C. Thomson, Bt. | C | 33,988 | 83.7 |
|  |  |  | G. Catto | Lab | 6,627 | 16.3 |
|  |  |  |  |  | 27,361 | 67.4 |
| [Death] |  |  |  |  |  |  |
| 1935 (21/5) | 55,958 | 56.6 | Sir J.D.W. Thomson, Bt. | C | 20,925 | 66.0 |
|  |  |  | J.F. Duncan | Lab | 10,760 | 34.0 |
|  |  |  |  |  | 10,165 | 32.0 |
| 1935 | 56,319 | 65.9 | Sir J.D.W. Thomson, Bt. | C | 25,270 | 68.1 |
|  |  |  | G.R. McIntosh | Lab | 11,817 | 31.9 |
|  |  |  |  |  | 13,453 | 36.2 |
| 1945 | 57,200 | 71.9 | Sir J.D.W. Thomson, Bt. | C | 19,214 | 46.8 |
|  |  |  | W. McLaine | Lab | 17,398 | 42.3 |
|  |  |  | J.L. Milne | L | 4,501* | 10.9 |
|  |  |  |  |  | 1,816 | 4.5 |
| [Resignation] |  |  |  |  |  |  |
| 1946 (26/11) | 60,500 | 65.6 | Lady Grant of Monymusk | C | 21,750 | 54.8 |
|  |  |  | A.J. Irvine | Lab | 17,911 | 45.2 |
|  |  |  |  |  | 3,839 | 9.6 |

Note:—

1946: Lady Grant of Monymusk became Lady Tweedsmuir upon her marriage in 1948.

## AYR DISTRICT of BURGHS [550]

### (Ayr, Ardrossan, Irvine, Prestwick, Saltcoats, Troon)

| Election | Electors | T'out | Candidate | Party | Votes | % |
|---|---|---|---|---|---|---|
| 1918 | 31,379 | 62.2 | †Sir G. Younger, Bt. | Co C | 9,565 | 49.1 |
| | | | M.M. Wood | L | 5,410 | 27.7 |
| | | | Rev. C. Stephen | Lab | 4,534 | 23.2 |
| | | | | | 4,155 | 21.4 |
| 1922 | 35,346 | 71.1 | Rt. Hon. Sir J.L. Baird, Bt. | C | 11,179 | 44.5 |
| | | | P.W. Raffan | L | 7,402 | 29.5 |
| | | | J.M. Airlie | Lab | 6,533 | 26.0 |
| | | | | | 3,777 | 15.0 |
| 1923 | 34,852 | 70.0 | Rt. Hon. Sir J.L. Baird, Bt. | C | 10,206 | 41.8 |
| | | | J.M. Airlie | Lab | 7,732 | 31.7 |
| | | | W.H. Pringle | L | 6,467 | 26.5 |
| | | | | | 2,474 | 10.1 |
| 1924 | 35,316 | 73.5 | Rt. Hon. Sir J.L. Baird, Bt. | C | 16,153 | 62.3 |
| | | | J.M. Airlie | Lab | 9,787 | 37.7 |
| | | | | | 6,366 | 24.6 |

[Resignation on appointment as Governor-General of Australia]

| Election | Electors | T'out | Candidate | Party | Votes | % |
|---|---|---|---|---|---|---|
| 1925 (12/6) | 35,316† | 71.0 | T.C.R. Moore | C | 11,601 | 46.2 |
| | | | P.J. Dollan | Lab | 8,813 | 35.2 |
| | | | W.M.R. Pringle | L | 4,656 | 18.6 |
| | | | | | 2,788 | 11.0 |
| 1929 | 49,142 | 74.8 | T.C.R. Moore | C | 16,874 | 45.9 |
| | | | Mrs. C.M. Shaw | Lab | 13,429 | 36.5 |
| | | | R. Lorimer | L | 6,479 | 17.6 |
| | | | | | 3,445 | 9.4 |
| 1931 | 49,732 | 76.9 | T.C.R. Moore | C | 28,256 | 73.9 |
| | | | Mrs. C.M. Shaw | Lab | 9,974 | 26.1 |
| | | | | | 18,282 | 47.8 |
| 1935 | 53,662 | 73.0 | T.C.R. Moore | C | 25,893 | 66.1 |
| | | | A.W. Brady | Lab | 13,274 | 33.9 |
| | | | | | 12,619 | 32.2 |
| 1945 | 62,182 | 71.5 | Sir T.C.R. Moore | C | 22,593 | 50.8 |
| | | | W. Ross | Lab | 21,865 | 49.2 |
| | | | | | 728 | 1.6 |

## DUMBARTON DISTRICT of BURGHS [551]
### (Dumbarton, Clydebank)

| Election | Electors | T'out | Candidate | Party | Votes | % |
|---|---|---|---|---|---|---|
| 1918 | 31,678 | 70.4 | J. Taylor | Co L | 11,734 | 52.6 |
| | | | D. Kirkwood | Lab | 10,566 | 47.4 |
| | | | | | 1,168 | 5.2 |
| 1922 | 33,463 | 76.2 | D. Kirkwood | Lab | 16,397 | 64.3 |
| | | | J. Taylor | NL | 9,107 | 35.7 |
| | | | | | 7,290 | 28.6 |
| 1923 | 32,349 | 68.0 | D. Kirkwood | Lab | 13,472 | 61.3 |
| | | | W.B. Munro | C | 8,520 | 38.7 |
| | | | | | 4,952 | 22.6 |
| 1924 | 32,293 | 76.1 | D. Kirkwood | Lab | 14,562 | 59.2 |
| | | | W.B. Munro | C | 10,027 | 40.8 |
| | | | | | 4,535 | 18.4 |
| 1929 | 39,474 | 77.1 | D. Kirkwood | Lab | 19,193 | 63.1 |
| | | | C. Milne | C | 11,225 | 36.9 |
| | | | | | 7,968 | 26.2 |
| 1931 | 39,253 | 80.7 | D. Kirkwood | Ind Lab (ILP) (Lab) | 16,335 | 51.6 |
| | | | M.J. McCracken | C | 15,338 | 48.4 |
| | | | | | 997 | 3.2 |
| 1935 | 39,744 | 78.8 | D. Kirkwood | Lab | 20,409 | 65.2 |
| | | | M.J. McCracken | C | 10,909 | 34.8 |
| | | | | | 9,500 | 30.4 |
| 1945 | 34,067 | 73.2 | D. Kirkwood | Lab | 16,262 | 65.2 |
| | | | J. Richardson | C | 8,676 | 34.8 |
| | | | | | 7,586 | 30.4 |

Note:—

1918: Taylor was supported by the NDP who claimed him as one of their MPs. He was however the nominee of the local Liberal Association and appears to have considered himself a Coalition Liberal with NDP support.

## DUNDEE [552]
### (Two Seats)

| Election | Electors | T'out | Candidate | Party | Votes | % |
|---|---|---|---|---|---|---|
| 1918 | 83,676 | 46.6 | †Rt. Hon. W.L.S. Churchill | Co L | 25,788 | 37.5 |
| | | | †A. Wilkie | Lab | 24,822 | 36.1 |
| | | | E. Scrymgeour | SPP | 10,423 | 15.1 |
| | | | J.S. Brown | Lab | 7,769 | 11.3 |
| | | | | | 15,365 | 22.4 |
| | | | | | 14,399 | 21.0 |
| 1922 | 78,007 | 80.5 | E. Scrymgeour | SPP | 32,578 | 27.6 |
| | | | E.D. Morel | Lab | 30,292 | 25.6 |
| | | | D.J. MacDonald | NL | 22,244 | 18.8 |
| | | | Rt. Hon. W.L.S. Churchill | NL | 20,466 | 17.3 |
| | | | R.R. Pilkington | L | 6,681* | 5.7 |
| | | | W. Gallacher | Com | 5,906* | 5.0 |
| | | | | | 10,334 | 8.8 |
| | | | | | 8,048 | 6.8 |
| 1923 | 78,561 | 72.7 | E. Scrymgeour | SPP | 25,753 | 25.1 |
| | | | E.D. Morel | Lab | 23,345 | 22.7 |
| | | | Sir J.W. Pratt | L | 23,031 | 22.4 |
| | | | F.W. Wallace | C | 20,253 | 19.7 |
| | | | W. Gallacher | Com | 10,380 | 10.1 |
| | | | | | 2,722 | 2.7 |
| | | | | | 314 | 0.3 |
| 1924 | 78,297 | 83.8 | E.D. Morel | Lab | 32,846 | 26.5 |
| | | | E. Scrymgeour | SPP | 29,193 | 23.5 |
| | | | F.W. Wallace | C | 28,118 | 22.7 |
| | | | Sir A.R. Duncan | L | 25,566 | 20.6 |
| | | | R. Stewart | Com | 8,340 | 6.7 |
| | | | | | 4,728 | 3.8 |
| | | | | | 1,075 | 0.8 |

[Death of Morel]

| Election | Electors | T'out | Candidate | Party | Votes | % |
|---|---|---|---|---|---|---|
| 1924 (22/12) | 78,297 | 42.4 | T. Johnston | Lab | 22,973 | 69.2 |
| | | | E.D. Simon | L | 10,234 | 30.8 |
| | | | | | 12,739 | 38.4 |
| 1929 | 109,126 | 82.5 | E. Scrymgeour | SPP | 50,073 | 29.2 |
| | | | M. Marcus | Lab | 47,602 | 27.7 |
| | | | J. Henderson-Stewart | L | 33,890 | 19.8 |
| | | | F.W. Wallace | C | 33,868 | 19.7 |
| | | | R. Stewart | Com | 6,160* | 3.6 |
| | | | | | 16,183 | 9.4 |
| | | | | | 13,712 | 7.9 |
| 1931 | 109,272 | 84.8 | D.M. Foot | L | 52,048 | 29.6 |
| | | | Miss F. Horsbrugh | C | 48,556 | 27.7 |
| | | | M. Marcus | Lab | 32,573 | 18.6 |
| | | | E. Scrymgeour | SPP | 32,229 | 18.3 |
| | | | R. Stewart | Com | 10,264* | 5.8 |
| | | | | | 19,475 | 11.0 |
| | | | | | 15,983 | 9.1 |

| Election | Electors | T'out | Candidate | Party | Votes | % |
|----------|----------|-------|-----------|-------|-------|---|
| 1935 | 112,398 | 84.7 | Miss F. Horsbrugh | C | 50,542 | 26.8 |
| | | | D.M. Foot | L | 49,632 | 26.4 |
| | | | M. Marcus | Lab | 44,457 | 23.6 |
| | | | R. Gibson | Lab | 43,747 | 23.2 |
| | | | | | 6,085 | 3.2 |
| | | | | | 5,175 | 2.8 |
| | | | | | | |
| 1945 | 110,563 | 79.2 | T.F. Cook | Lab | 48,804 | 28.6 |
| | | | E.J.St.L. Strachey | Lab | 48,393 | 28.4 |
| | | | D.M. Foot | L | 33,230 | 19.5 |
| | | | Rt. Hon. Florence Horsbrugh | C | 32,309 | 18.9 |
| | | | A. Donaldson | SNP | 7,776* | 4.6 |
| | | | | | 15,163 | 8.9 |

Note:—

1918—1931: Scrymgeour had been at one time a member of the Labour Party and he received considerable support from the local Labour Party.

## (Dunfermline, Cowdenbeath, Inverkeithing, Lochgelly)

| Election | Electors | T'out | Candidate | Party | Votes | % |
|---|---|---|---|---|---|---|
| 1918 | 27,993 | 55.2 | J. Wallace | Co L | 6,886 | 44.6 |
| | | | W.M. Watson | Ind Lab | 5,076 | 32.8 |
| | | | †A.A.W.H. Ponsonby | Ind Dem | 3,491 | 22.6 |
| | | | | | 1,810 | 11.8 |
| 1922 | 29,815 | 77.5 | W.M. Watson | Lab | 11,652 | 50.4 |
| | | | J. Wallace | NL | 11,451 | 49.6 |
| | | | | | 201 | 0.8 |
| 1923 | 30,296 | 77.7 | W.M. Watson | Lab | 12,606 | 53.6 |
| | | | J. Wallace | L | 10,931 | 46.4 |
| | | | | | 1,675 | 7.2 |
| 1924 | 30,518 | 78.7 | W.M. Watson | Lab | 13,887 | 57.9 |
| | | | F.J. Robertson | L | 10,118 | 42.1 |
| | | | | | 3,769 | 15.8 |
| 1929 | 35,305 | 74.1 | W.M. Watson | Lab | 15,288 | 58.5 |
| | | | A. Beaton | C | 9,146 | 35.0 |
| | | | J.V. Leckie | Com | 1,712* | 6.5 |
| | | | | | 6,142 | 23.5 |
| 1931 | 36,299 | 80.2 | J. Wallace | NL | 16,863 | 57.9 |
| | | | W.M. Watson | Lab | 12,247 | 42.1 |
| | | | | | 4,616 | 15.8 |
| 1935 | 38,134 | 81.6 | W.M. Watson | Lab | 16,271 | 52.3 |
| | | | Sir J. Wallace | NL | 14,848 | 47.7 |
| | | | | | 1,423 | 4.6 |
| 1945 | 46,672 | 73.0 | W.M. Watson | Lab | 22,021 | 64.7 |
| | | | J. Henderson | NL | 12,028 | 35.3 |
| | | | | | 9,993 | 29.4 |

Note:—

1918: Watson was the nominee of the Fife, Kinross and Clackmannan Miners' Association.

# EDINBURGH, CENTRAL  [554]

| Election | Electors | T'out | Candidate | Party | Votes | % |
|---|---|---|---|---|---|---|
| 1918 | 30,867 | 45.2 | W. Graham | Lab | 7,161 | 51.3 |
| | | | J. Dobbie | Co L | 6,797 | 48.7 |
| | | | | | 364 | 2.6 |
| 1922 | 30,970 | 71.8 | W. Graham | Lab | 12,876 | 57.9 |
| | | | Sir G. McCrae | NL | 9,371 | 42.1 |
| | | | | | 3,505 | 15.8 |
| 1923 | 32,492 | 59.7 | W. Graham | Lab | 13,186 | 67.9 |
| | | | T. Lamb | L | 6,225 | 32.1 |
| | | | | | 6,961 | 35.8 |
| 1924 | 32,744 | 68.8 | W. Graham | Lab | 13,628 | 60.5 |
| | | | A. Beaton | C | 8,897 | 39.5 |
| | | | | | 4,731 | 21.0 |
| 1929 | 40,975 | 69.3 | Rt. Hon. W. Graham | Lab | 16,762 | 59.0 |
| | | | H. Alexander | L | 6,745 | 23.8 |
| | | | J.H. Mackie | C | 4,889 | 17.2 |
| | | | | | 10,017 | 35.2 |
| 1931 | 39,306 | 74.2 | J.C.M. Guy | C | 17,293 | 59.3 |
| | | | Rt. Hon. W. Graham | Lab | 10,566 | 36.2 |
| | | | F. Douglas | Com | 1,319* | 4.5 |
| | | | | | 6,727 | 23.1 |
| 1935 | 36,201 | 64.5 | J.C.M. Guy | C | 12,612 | 54.0 |
| | | | A. Gilzean | Lab | 9,659 | 41.4 |
| | | | Dr. R.A. Barlow | L | 1,086* | 4.6 |
| | | | | | 2,953 | 12.6 |
| [Resignation] | | | | | | |
| 1941 (11/12) | 33,641 | 20.0 | F.C. Watt | C | 4,771 | 71.0 |
| | | | T. Taylor | ILP | 1,950 | 29.0 |
| | | | | | 2,821 | 42.0 |
| 1945 | 33,783 | 59.5 | A. Gilzean | Lab | 10,921 | 54.3 |
| | | | F.C. Watt | C | 6,701 | 33.3 |
| | | | N.A. Donald | L | 2,262* | 11.2 |
| | | | H. Sleigh | Ind | 232* | 1.2 |
| | | | | | 4,220 | 21.0 |

Note:—

1945: Sleigh advocated a policy of Scottish nationalism.

| Election | Electors | T'out | Candidate | Party | Votes | % |
|---|---|---|---|---|---|---|
| 1918 | 25,895 | 52.5 | †J.M. Hogge | L | 8,460 | 62.2 |
| | | | A.E. Balfour | Co NDP | 5,136 | 37.8 |
| | | | | | 3,324 | 24.4 |
| 1922 | 26,724 | 66.0 | J.M. Hogge | L | 10,551 | 59.8 |
| | | | S. McDonald | NL | 7,088 | 40.2 |
| | | | | | 3,463 | 19.6 |
| 1923 | 27,219 | 58.5 | J.M. Hogge | L | 10,876 | 68.3 |
| | | | C.J.M. Mancor | C | 5,045 | 31.7 |
| | | | | | 5,831 | 36.6 |
| 1924 | 27,474 | 76.7 | Dr. T.D. Shiels | Lab | 9,330 | 44.3 |
| | | | C. Milne | C | 6,105 | 29.0 |
| | | | J.M. Hogge | L | 5,625 | 26.7 |
| | | | | | 3,225 | 15.3 |
| 1929 | 38,553 | 76.5 | Dr. T.D. Shiels | Lab | 13,933 | 47.3 |
| | | | T.P. McDonald | L | 8,687 | 29.4 |
| | | | R.C. Thyne | C | 6,889 | 23.3 |
| | | | | | 5,246 | 17.9 |
| 1931 | 39,676 | 76.8 | D.M. Mason | L | 17,372 | 57.0 |
| | | | Dr. T.D. Shiels | Lab | 10,244 | 33.6 |
| | | | Rev. T.T. Alexander | SNP | 2,872* | 9.4 |
| | | | | | 7,128 | 23.4 |
| 1935 | 44,997 | 68.6 | F.W. Pethick-Lawrence | Lab | 13,341 | 43.2 |
| | | | Miss M.G. Cowan | C | 12,229 | 39.6 |
| | | | D.M. Mason | L | 5,313 | 17.2 |
| | | | | | 1,112 | 3.6 |
| 1945 | 49,292 | 69.4 | Rt. Hon. F.W. Pethick-Lawrence | Lab | 19,300 | 56.4 |
| | | | W.A. Sinclair | C | 12,771 | 37.3 |
| | | | F.C. Yeaman | SNP | 2,149* | 6.3 |
| | | | | | 6,529 | 19.1 |

[Elevation to the Peerage — Lord Pethick-Lawrence]

| | | | | | | |
|---|---|---|---|---|---|---|
| 1945 (3/10) | 49,292 | 51.0 | Rt. Hon. G.R. Thomson | Lab | 15,482 | 61.6 |
| | | | T.G.D. Galbraith | C | 9,665 | 38.4 |
| | | | | | 5,817 | 23.2 |

[Resignation on appointment as Lord Justice Clerk — Lord Thomson]

| | | | | | | |
|---|---|---|---|---|---|---|
| 1947 (27/11) | 53,073 | 63.0 | Rt. Hon. J.T. Wheatley | Lab | 16,906 | 50.6 |
| | | | D.M. Matthews | NL & C | 11,490 | 34.3 |
| | | | J.D.B. Junor | L | 3,379* | 10.1 |
| | | | Mrs. M. Dott | SNP | 1,682* | 5.0 |
| | | | | | 5,416 | 16.3 |

Notes:—

1945: Thomson was Lord Advoacte.
(3/10)

1947: Wheatley was Lord Advocate.

# EDINBURGH, NORTH [556]

| Election | Electors | T'out | Candidate | Party | Votes | % |
|---|---|---|---|---|---|---|
| 1918 | 35,611 | 53.0 | †Rt. Hon. J.A. Clyde | Co C | 11,879 | 63.0 |
| | | | J. Johnston | L | 6,986 | 37.0 |
| | | | | | 4,893 | 26.0 |

[Resignation on appointment as Lord Justice General and Lord President of the Court of Session — Lord Clyde]

| | | | | | | |
|---|---|---|---|---|---|---|
| 1920 | 35,663 | 62.3 | P.J. Ford | Co C | 9,944 | 44.8 |
| (9/4) | | | Rt. Hon. W. Runciman | L | 8,469 | 38.1 |
| | | | D.G. Pole | Lab | 3,808 | 17.1 |
| | | | | | 1,475 | 6.7 |
| 1922 | 36,038 | 66.5 | P.J. Ford | C | 14,805 | 61.8 |
| | | | P.H. Allan | L | 9,165 | 38.2 |
| | | | | | 5,640 | 23.6 |
| 1923 | 37,202 | 66.3 | P.W. Raffan | L | 13,744 | 55.7 |
| | | | P.J. Ford | C | 10,909 | 44.3 |
| | | | | | 2,835 | 11.4 |
| 1924 | 37,599 | 78.0 | P.J. Ford | C | 14,461 | 49.4 |
| | | | Miss E. Stewart | Lab | 8,192 | 27.9 |
| | | | P.W. Raffan | L | 6,669 | 22.7 |
| | | | | | 6,269 | 21.5 |
| 1929 | 47,728 | 73.8 | Sir P.J. Ford | C | 13,993 | 39.7 |
| | | | Miss E. Stewart | Lab | 11,340 | 32.2 |
| | | | W. Mitchell | L | 9,877 | 28.1 |
| | | | | | 2,653 | 7.5 |
| 1931 | 47,234 | 74.4 | Sir P.J. Ford, Bt. | C | 26,361 | 75.0 |
| | | | R. Gibson | Lab | 8,771 | 25.0 |
| | | | | | 17,590 | 50.0 |
| 1935 | 46,786 | 66.7 | A.G. Erskine-Hill | C | 20,776 | 66.5 |
| | | | G.W. Crawford | Lab | 8,654 | 27.7 |
| | | | Miss C. Macmillan | L | 1,798* | 5.8 |
| | | | | | 12,122 | 38.8 |
| 1945 | 44,039 | 64.6 | E.G. Willis | Lab | 12,825 | 45.1 |
| | | | Sir A.G. Erskine-Hill, Bt. | C | 12,270 | 43.1 |
| | | | C.H. Johnston | L | 3,344* | 11.8 |
| | | | | | 555 | 2.0 |

| Election | Electors | T'out | Candidate | Party | Votes | % |
|---|---|---|---|---|---|---|
| 1918 | 32,087 | 61.8 | C.D. Murray | Co C | 14,874 | 75.0 |
| | | | D. Caird | L | 4,966 | 25.0 |
| | | | | | 9,908 | 50.0 |

[Appointed Solicitor-General for Scotland]

| Election | Electors | T'out | Candidate | Party | Votes | % |
|---|---|---|---|---|---|---|
| 1920 (9/4) | 32,656 | 59.3 | C.D. Murray | Co C | 11,176 | 57.7 |
| | | | D.T. Holmes | L | 8,177 | 42.3 |
| | | | | | 2,999 | 15.4 |
| 1922 | 32,152 | 69.2 | Sir S. Chapman | C | 14,843 | 66.7 |
| | | | Mrs. C.B. Alderton | L | 7,408 | 33.3 |
| | | | | | 7,435 | 33.4 |
| 1923 | 32,745 | 70.2 | Sir S. Chapman | C | 12,804 | 55.7 |
| | | | W. Hope | L | 10,194 | 44.3 |
| | | | | | 2,610 | 11.4 |
| 1924 | 33,447 | 73.6 | Sir S. Chapman | C | 15,854 | 64.4 |
| | | | D.C. Thomson | L | 8,777 | 35.6 |
| | | | | | 7,077 | 28.8 |
| 1929 | 45,794 | 75.2 | Sir S. Chapman | C | 19,541 | 56.7 |
| | | | Dr. A.P. Laurie | L | 9,849 | 28.6 |
| | | | A. Woodburn | Lab | 5,050 | 14.7 |
| | | | | | 9,692 | 28.1 |
| 1931 | | | Sir S. Chapman | C | Unopp. | |
| 1935 | 48,284 | 67.6 | Sir S. Chapman | C | 27,254 | 83.6 |
| | | | Mrs. B. Woodburn | Lab | 5,365 | 16.4 |
| | | | | | 21,889 | 67.2 |
| 1945 | 50,348 | 66.4 | Sir W.Y. Darling | C | 23,652 | 70.8 |
| | | | W.P. Earsman | Lab | 9,767 | 29.2 |
| | | | | | 13,885 | 41.6 |

| Election | Electors | T'out | Candidate | Party | Votes | % |
|---|---|---|---|---|---|---|
| 1918 | 33,835 | 53.3 | J.G. Jameson | Co C | 9,172 | 50.8 |
| | | | †Sir J.E. Parrott | L | 6,220 | 34.5 |
| | | | J.A. Young | Lab | 2,642 | 14.7 |
| | | | | | 2,952 | 16.3 |
| 1922 | 34,899 | 68.9 | H.V. Phillipps | L | 12,355 | 51.4 |
| | | | J.G. Jameson | C | 11,689 | 48.6 |
| | | | | | 666 | 2.8 |
| 1923 | 35,809 | 74.4 | H.V. Phillipps | L | 11,010 | 41.3 |
| | | | I. MacIntyre | C | 8,778 | 33.0 |
| | | | G. Mathers | Lab | 6,836 | 25.7 |
| | | | | | 2,232 | 8.3 |
| 1924 | 36,618 | 79.3 | I. MacIntyre | C | 10,628 | 36.6 |
| | | | G. Mathers | Lab | 9,603 | 33.1 |
| | | | H.V. Phillipps | L | 8,790 | 30.3 |
| | | | | | 1,025 | 3.5 |
| 1929 | 54,695 | 74.8 | G. Mathers | Lab | 15,795 | 38.6 |
| | | | W.G. Normand | C | 12,966 | 31.7 |
| | | | H.V. Phillipps | L | 12,126 | 29.7 |
| | | | | | 2,829 | 6.9 |
| 1931 | 55,707 | 79.2 | W.G. Normand | C | 31,407 | 71.2 |
| | | | G. Mathers | Lab | 12,704 | 28.8 |
| | | | | | 18,703 | 42.4 |

[Resignation on appointment as Lord Justice General and Lord President of the Court of Session — Lord Normand]

| Election | Electors | T'out | Candidate | Party | Votes | % |
|---|---|---|---|---|---|---|
| 1935 (2/5) | 60,354 | 51.2 | T.M. Cooper | C | 16,373 | 53.0 |
| | | | W. McAdam | Lab | 10,462 | 33.9 |
| | | | Sir G. Paish | L | 4,059 | 13.1 |
| | | | | | 5,911 | 19.1 |
| 1935 | 61,403 | 68.1 | Rt. Hon. T.M. Cooper | C | 28,023 | 67.0 |
| | | | J. Welch | Lab | 13,794 | 33.0 |
| | | | | | 14,229 | 34.0 |

[Resignation on appointment as Lord Justice Clerk — Lord Cooper]

| Election | Electors | T'out | Candidate | Party | Votes | % |
|---|---|---|---|---|---|---|
| 1941 (12/7) | | | G.I.C. Hutchison | C | Unopp. | |
| 1945 | 62,196 | 67.5 | G.I.C. Hutchison | C | 19,894 | 47.3 |
| | | | G.G. Stott | Lab | 18,840 | 44.9 |
| | | | J.G. Thomson | L | 3,256* | 7.8 |
| | | | | | 1,054 | 2.4 |

| Election | Electors | T'out | Candidate | Party | Votes | % |
|---|---|---|---|---|---|---|
| 1918 | 37,980 | 52.0 | †A.M. Scott | Co L | 10,887 | 55.2 |
| | | | J. Maxton | Lab | 7,860 | 39.8 |
| | | | Miss E.G. Murray | Ind | 991* | 5.0 |
| | | | | | 3,027 | 15.4 |
| 1922 | 36,627 | 76.7 | J. Maxton | Lab | 17,890 | 63.7 |
| | | | A.M. Scott | NL | 10,198 | 36.3 |
| | | | | | 7,692 | 27.4 |
| 1923 | 36,522 | 66.5 | J. Maxton | Lab | 15,735 | 64.8 |
| | | | J.B. Black | C | 6,101 | 25.1 |
| | | | T.R. Anderson | L | 2,445* | 10.1 |
| | | | | | 9,634 | 39.7 |
| 1924 | 36,571 | 75.1 | J. Maxton | Lab | 16,850 | 61.3 |
| | | | M.J. McCracken | C | 10,633 | 38.7 |
| | | | | | 6,217 | 22.6 |
| 1929 | 43,421 | 71.6 | J. Maxton | Lab | 21,033 | 67.7 |
| | | | M.J. McCracken | C | 10,049 | 32.3 |
| | | | | | 10,984 | 35.4 |
| 1931 | 40,340 | 70.8 | J. Maxton | ILP | 16,630 | 58.2 |
| | | | Dr. Catherine I. Gavin | C | 11,941 | 41.8 |
| | | | | | 4,689 | 16.4 |
| 1935 | 37,537 | 72.6 | J. Maxton | ILP | 17,691 | 64.9 |
| | | | A.D.M. Shaw | C | 8,951 | 32.9 |
| | | | S.P. McLaren | Lab | 594* | 2.2 |
| | | | | | 8,740 | 32.0 |
| 1945 | 34,217 | 58.2 | J. Maxton | ILP | 13,220 | 66.4 |
| | | | R.C. Brooman-White | C | 6,695 | 33.6 |
| | | | | | 6,525 | 32.8 |
| [Death] | | | | | | |
| 1946 (29/8) | 34,716† | 53.3 | J. Carmichael | ILP (Lab) | 6,351 | 34.3 |
| | | | J.T. Wheatley | Lab | 5,180 | 28.0 |
| | | | V. Warren | C | 3,987 | 21.6 |
| | | | Miss W. Wood | Ind | 2,575 | 13.9 |
| | | | G.A. Aldred | Ind Soc | 405* | 2.2 |
| | | | | | 1,171 | 6.3 |

Notes:—

1946: Miss Wood advocated a policy of Scottish nationalism.

Aldred was founder and leader of the United Socialist Movement, a left-wing propaganda organisation.

# GLASGOW, CAMLACHIE [560]

| Election | Electors | T'out | Candidate | Party | Votes | % |
|---|---|---|---|---|---|---|
| 1918 | 37,319 | 58.1 | †H.J. Mackinder | Co C | 13,645 | 62.9 |
| | | | H.B. Guthrie | Lab | 7,192 | 33.1 |
| | | | D. Browning | L | 860* | 4.0 |
| | | | | | 6,453 | 29.8 |
| 1922 | 35,249 | 81.0 | Rev. C. Stephen | Lab | 15,181 | 53.2 |
| | | | Sir H.J. Mackinder | C | 11,459 | 40.2 |
| | | | W.C. Smith | L | 1,896* | 6.6 |
| | | | | | 3,722 | 13.0 |
| 1923 | 35,046 | 71.8 | Rev. C. Stephen | Lab | 14,143 | 56.2 |
| | | | Sir H.S. Keith | C | 11,027 | 43.8 |
| | | | | | 3,116 | 12.4 |
| 1924 | 35,918 | 80.6 | Rev. C. Stephen | Lab | 14,588 | 50.4 |
| | | | P.D. Ridge-Beedle | C | 14,373 | 49.6 |
| | | | | | 215 | 0.8 |
| 1929 | 42,960 | 78.6 | Rev. C. Stephen | Lab | 17,946 | 53.1 |
| | | | J. Stevenson | C | 14,161 | 42.0 |
| | | | J.M. MacCormick | SNP | 1,646* | 4.9 |
| | | | | | 3,785 | 11.1 |
| 1931 | 43,136 | 78.2 | J. Stevenson | C | 18,461 | 54.7 |
| | | | Rev. C. Stephen | ILP | 15,282 | 45.3 |
| | | | | | 3,179 | 9.4 |
| 1935 | 42,747 | 74.8 | Rev. C. Stephen | ILP | 15,070 | 47.2 |
| | | | J. Stevenson | C | 14,186 | 44.3 |
| | | | W. Reid | Lab | 2,732* | 8.5 |
| | | | | | 884 | 2.9 |
| 1945 | 41,480 | 65.0 | Rev. C. Stephen | ILP (Lab) | 15,558 | 57.7 |
| | | | C.S. McFarlane | C | 11,399 | 42.3 |
| | | | | | 4,159 | 15.4 |
| [Death] | | | | | | |
| 1948 (28/1) | 44,709 | 56.8 | C.S. McFarlane | C | 11,085 | 43.7 |
| | | | J.M. Inglis | Lab | 10,690 | 42.1 |
| | | | Miss A. Maxton | ILP | 1,622* | 6.4 |
| | | | R.B. Wilkie | Ind | 1,320* | 5.2 |
| | | | G.A. Aldred | Ind Soc | 345* | 1.4 |
| | | | E.R. Goodfellow | L | 312* | 1.2 |
| | | | | | 395 | 1.6 |

Notes:—

1948: Wilkie advocated a policy of Scottish nationalism.

Aldred was founder and leader of the United Socialist Movement, a left-wing propaganda organisation.

## GLASGOW, CATHCART [561]

| Election | Electors | T'out | Candidate | Party | Votes | % |
|---|---|---|---|---|---|---|
| 1918 | 34,293 | 61.8 | †J.W. Pratt | Co L | 16,310 | 76.9 |
| | | | Dr. G.B. Clark | Lab | 4,899 | 23.1 |
| | | | | | 11,411 | 53.8 |
| 1922 | 33,198 | 81.0 | J.P. Hay | Lab | 9,137 | 34.0 |
| | | | Sir A.R. Duncan | NL | 9,104 | 33.8 |
| | | | R. MacDonald | C | 8,661 | 32.2 |
| | | | | | 33 | 0.2 |
| 1923 | 33,040 | 77.5 | R. MacDonald | C | 10,817 | 42.3 |
| | | | J.P. Hay | Lab | 8,884 | 34.7 |
| | | | T.G. Robertson | L | 5,894 | 23.0 |
| | | | | | 1,933 | 7.6 |
| 1924 | 35,076 | 80.8 | R. MacDonald | C | 18,440 | 65.0 |
| | | | J.P. Hay | Lab | 9,915 | 35.0 |
| | | | | | 8,525 | 30.0 |
| 1929 | 45,545 | 78.6 | J. Train | C | 15,435 | 43.1 |
| | | | J.P. Hay | Lab | 12,983 | 36.3 |
| | | | J. Gray | L | 7,388 | 20.6 |
| | | | | | 2,452 | 6.8 |
| 1931 | 45,398 | 79.5 | J. Train | C | 26,642 | 73.8 |
| | | | A.L. Ritchie | Lab | 8,919 | 24.7 |
| | | | J. Mellick | NP | 529* | 1.5 |
| | | | | | 17,723 | 49.1 |
| 1935 | 46,172 | 74.3 | J. Train | C | 21,331 | 62.1 |
| | | | A.A. MacGregor | Lab | 12,995 | 37.9 |
| | | | | | 8,336 | 24.2 |
| [Death] | | | | | | |
| 1942 (28/4) | 46,239 | 39.1 | F. Beattie | C | 10,786 | 59.7 |
| | | | Hon. W. Douglas-Home | Ind Prog | 3,807 | 21.0 |
| | | | J. Carmichael | ILP | 2,493 | 13.8 |
| | | | W. Whyte | Ind | 1,000* | 5.5 |
| | | | | | 6,979 | 38.7 |
| 1945 | 46,442 | 67.6 | F. Beattie | C | 18,472 | 58.8 |
| | | | N. Jackson | Lab | 12,923 | 41.2 |
| | | | | | 5,549 | 17.6 |
| [Death] | | | | | | |
| 1946 (12/2) | 46,911 | 55.6 | J. Henderson | C | 13,696 | 52.5 |
| | | | A.B. Mackay | Lab | 9,689 | 37.1 |
| | | | Dr. W.O.G. Taylor | SNP | 2,700* | 10.4 |
| | | | | | 4,007 | 15.4 |

Note:—

1942: Whyte advocated a policy of Scottish nationalism.

| Election | Electors | T'out | Candidate | Party | Votes | % |
|----------|----------|-------|-----------|-------|-------|---|
| 1918 | 42,329 | 52.9 | †Rt. Hon. A.B. Law | Co C | 17,653 | 78.8 |
|  |  |  | D.J.M. Quin | Ind Lab | 4,736 | 21.2 |
|  |  |  |  |  | 12,917 | 57.6 |
| 1922 | 43,351 | 71.2 | Rt. Hon. A.B. Law | C | 15,437 | 49.9 |
|  |  |  | E.R. Mitchell | Lab | 12,923 | 41.9 |
|  |  |  | Sir G. Paish | L | 2,518* | 8.2 |
|  |  |  |  |  | 2,514 | 8.0 |

[Seat Vacant at Dissolution (Death)]

| Election | Electors | T'out | Candidate | Party | Votes | % |
|----------|----------|-------|-----------|-------|-------|---|
| 1923 | 43,292 | 67.5 | Sir W. Alexander | C | 13,392 | 45.8 |
|  |  |  | E.R. Mitchell | Lab | 12,976 | 44.4 |
|  |  |  | Rt. Hon. H.J. Tennant | L | 2,870* | 9.8 |
|  |  |  |  |  | 416 | 1.4 |
| 1924 | 44,010 | 70.2 | Sir W. Alexander | C | 18,258 | 59.1 |
|  |  |  | J.D. White | Lab | 12,617 | 40.9 |
|  |  |  |  |  | 5,641 | 18.2 |
| 1929 | 49,983 | 72.0 | Sir W. Alexander | C | 18,336 | 50.9 |
|  |  |  | C.M. Aitchison | Lab | 17,663 | 49.1 |
|  |  |  |  |  | 673 | 1.8 |
| 1931 | 46,160 | 71.5 | Sir W. Alexander | C | 21,547 | 65.3 |
|  |  |  | W.H.P. Martin | Lab | 11,456 | 34.7 |
|  |  |  |  |  | 10,091 | 30.6 |
| 1935 | 44,504 | 67.2 | Sir W. Alexander | C | 16,707 | 55.9 |
|  |  |  | R.R. Stokes | Lab | 13,186 | 44.1 |
|  |  |  |  |  | 3,521 | 11.8 |
| 1945 | 35,734 | 59.6 | J.R.H. Hutchison | C | 9,365 | 44.0 |
|  |  |  | J. McInnes | Lab | 7,849 | 36.9 |
|  |  |  | R.H. Cooney | Com | 2,709 | 12.7 |
|  |  |  | N.M. Glen | L | 1,072* | 5.0 |
|  |  |  | G.A. Aldred | Ind Soc | 300* | 1.4 |
|  |  |  |  |  | 1,516 | 7.1 |

Note:—

1945: Aldred was founder and leader of the United Socialist Movement, a left-wing propaganda organisation.

| Election | Electors | T'out | Candidate | Party | Votes | % |
|---|---|---|---|---|---|---|
| 1918 | 40,765 | 53.2 | †Rt. Hon. G.N. Barnes | Co Lab | 14,247 | 65.7 |
| | | | J. Maclean | Lab | 7,436 | 34.3 |
| | | | | | 6,811 | 31.4 |
| 1922 | 40,251 | 75.1 | G. Buchanan | Lab | 16,478 | 54.5 |
| | | | J.E. Harper | NL | 8,276 | 27.4 |
| | | | J. Maclean | Ind Com | 4,027 | 13.3 |
| | | | F.J. Robertson | L | 1,456* | 4.8 |
| | | | | | 8,202 | 27.1 |
| 1923 | 40,331 | 63.5 | G. Buchanan | Lab | 17,211 | 67.2 |
| | | | R. McLellan | C | 8,392 | 32.8 |
| | | | | | 8,819 | 34.4 |
| 1924 | 40,483 | 73.0 | G. Buchanan | Lab | 19,480 | 65.9 |
| | | | R. McLellan | C | 10,092 | 34.1 |
| | | | | | 9,388 | 31.8 |
| 1929 | 49,004 | 68.5 | G. Buchanan | Lab | 25,134 | 74.8 |
| | | | M. Bloch | C | 8,457 | 25.2 |
| | | | | | 16,677 | 49.6 |
| 1931 | 47,372 | 70.0 | G. Buchanan | Ind Lab (ILP) | 19,278 | 58.1 |
| | | | M. Bloch | C | 11,264 | 34.0 |
| | | | H. McShane | Com | 2,626* | 7.9 |
| | | | | | 8,014 | 24.1 |
| 1935 | 46,076 | 66.1 | G. Buchanan | ILP (Lab) | 22,860 | 75.0 |
| | | | M. Bloch | C | 5,824 | 19.1 |
| | | | A. Burnett | Lab | 1,786* | 5.9 |
| | | | | | 17,036 | 55.9 |
| 1945 | 46,394 | 56.8 | G. Buchanan | Lab | 21,073 | 80.0 |
| | | | I.A. Mactaggart | C | 5,269 | 20.0 |
| | | | | | 15,804 | 60.0 |

[Resignation on appointment as Chairman of the National Assistance Board]

| Election | Electors | T'out | Candidate | Party | Votes | % |
|---|---|---|---|---|---|---|
| 1948 (30/9) | 50,243 | 50.0 | Mrs. A. Cullen | Lab | 13,706 | 54.5 |
| | | | W. Roxburgh | C | 7,181 | 28.6 |
| | | | P. Kerrigan | Com | 4,233 | 16.9 |
| | | | | | 6,525 | 25.9 |

Notes:—

1918: Barnes was strictly speaking an unofficial Coalition candidate. He did not receive a 'coupon'.

1922: Maclean sought election as a Communist but his candidature was not endorsed by the Communist Party.

589

# GLASGOW, GOVAN [564]

| Election | Electors | T'out | Candidate | Party | Votes | % |
|----------|----------|-------|-----------|-------|-------|---|
| 1918 | 31,652 | 63.2 | N. Maclean | Lab | 9,577 | 47.8 |
| | | | A. McClure | Co C | 8,762 | 43.8 |
| | | | †D.T. Holmes | L | 1,678* | 8.4 |
| | | | | | 815 | 4.0 |
| 1922 | 30,539 | 81.1 | N. Maclean | Lab | 15,441 | 62.3 |
| | | | Miss H. Fraser | NL | 9,336 | 37.7 |
| | | | | | 6,105 | 24.6 |
| 1923 | 30,790 | 68.5 | N. Maclean | Lab | 13,987 | 66.3 |
| | | | H.A. Watt | L | 7,095 | 33.7 |
| | | | | | 6,892 | 32.6 |
| 1924 | 31,497 | 76.0 | N. Maclean | Lab | 15,132 | 63.2 |
| | | | H. Stanley | C | 8,815 | 36.8 |
| | | | | | 6,317 | 26.4 |
| 1929 | 40,103 | 75.1 | N. Maclean | Ind Lab (Lab) | 17,384 | 57.7 |
| | | | Marquess of Douglas and Clydesdale | C | 12,736 | 42.3 |
| | | | | | 4,648 | 15.4 |
| 1931 | 39,099 | 75.4 | N. Maclean | Lab | 15,047 | 51.0 |
| | | | A. McClure | C | 14,442 | 49.0 |
| | | | | | 605 | 2.0 |
| 1935 | 41,444 | 74.7 | N. Maclean | Lab | 15,791 | 51.0 |
| | | | A. McClure | C | 10,211 | 33.0 |
| | | | T. Taylor | ILP | 4,959 | 16.0 |
| | | | | | 5,580 | 18.0 |
| 1945 | 44,197 | 63.9 | N. Maclean | Lab | 18,668 | 66.1 |
| | | | J.N. Browne | C | 9,586 | 33.9 |
| | | | | | 9,082 | 32.2 |

Note:—

1929: Maclean had been until 1929, a nominee of the Govan Branch of the ILP but at a meeting held in April 1929 to select a candidate for the General Election, the ILP refused to re-nominate him. After a vote had been taken, T.A. Kerr (an ILP member) was selected as the Labour candidate. Maclean then announced that he would seek re-election as an Independent and prior to nomination day Kerr decided to withdraw.

Owing to the local circumstances, Maclean's candidature could not be endorsed by the Labour Party and he fought the election as an unofficial Labour candidate.

| Election | Electors | T'out | Candidate | Party | Votes | % |
|---|---|---|---|---|---|---|
| 1918 | 26,798 | 63.4 | Sir R.S. Horne | Co C | 12,803 | 75.4 |
| | | | J. Izett | Lab | 4,186 | 24.6 |
| | | | | | 8,617 | 50.8 |
| 1922 | 25,951 | 75.5 | Rt. Hon. Sir R.S. Horne | C | 12,272 | 62.7 |
| | | | E.J. Donaldson | L | 7,313 | 37.3 |
| | | | | | 4,959 | 25.4 |
| 1923 | 26,165 | 73.2 | Rt. Hon. Sir R.S. Horne | C | 9,757 | 51.0 |
| | | | J.L. Kinloch | Lab | 5,059 | 26.4 |
| | | | E.J. Donaldson | L | 4,331 | 22.6 |
| | | | | | 4,698 | 24.6 |
| 1924 | 27,522 | 78.2 | Rt. Hon. Sir R.S. Horne | C | 14,572 | 67.7 |
| | | | J.L. Kinloch | Lab | 6,957 | 32.3 |
| | | | | | 7,615 | 35.4 |
| 1929 | 36,660 | 74.9 | Rt. Hon. Sir R.S. Horne | C | 17,395 | 63.3 |
| | | | W.S. Cormack | Lab | 10,065 | 36.7 |
| | | | | | 7,330 | 26.6 |
| 1931 | 36,020 | 80.0 | Rt. Hon. Sir R.S. Horne | C | 21,279 | 73.8 |
| | | | C.A. O'Donnell | Ind Lab | 7,539 | 26.2 |
| | | | | | 13,740 | 47.6 |
| 1935 | 36,772 | 73.2 | Rt. Hon. Sir R.S. Horne | C | 18,367 | 68.2 |
| | | | J. McCulloch | Lab | 8,566 | 31.8 |
| | | | | | 9,801 | 36.4 |

[Elevation to the Peerage — Viscount Horne of Slamannan]

| Election | Electors | T'out | Candidate | Party | Votes | % |
|---|---|---|---|---|---|---|
| 1937 (10/6) | 37,177 | 56.1 | Rt. Hon. J.S.C. Reid | C | 12,539 | 60.2 |
| | | | G. McAllister | Lab | 6,202 | 29.7 |
| | | | J.M. MacCormick | SNP | 1,886* | 9.0 |
| | | | D.J. Black | Ind | 221* | 1.1 |
| | | | | | 6,337 | 30.5 |
| 1945 | 38,669 | 65.8 | Rt. Hon. J.S.C. Reid | C | 14,909 | 58.5 |
| | | | H.T. MacCalman | Lab | 8,545 | 33.6 |
| | | | J.G. Wilson | L | 2,003* | 7.9 |
| | | | | | 6,364 | 24.9 |

[Resignation on appointment as a Lord of Appeal — Lord Reid]

| Election | Electors | T'out | Candidate | Party | Votes | % |
|---|---|---|---|---|---|---|
| 1948 (25/11) | 41,405 | 56.7 | T.G.D. Galbraith | C | 16,060 | 68.4 |
| | | | T.A. MacNair | Lab | 7,419 | 31.6 |
| | | | | | 8,641 | 36.8 |

Notes:—

1931: O'Donnell was the nominee of the local Labour Party who contested the seat despite a decision of Glasgow Burgh Labour Party not to put forward a candidate due to lack of sufficient local organisation and finance.

1937: Reid was Solicitor-General for Scotland.

Black sought election as a 'Liberal-Unionist' candidate but he had no connection with either party.

# GLASGOW, KELVINGROVE [566]

| Election | Electors | T'out | Candidate | Party | Votes | % |
|---|---|---|---|---|---|---|
| 1918 | 39,702 | 53.5 | †J.M. MacLeod | Co C | 13,648 | 64.2 |
| | | | W.G. Leechman | Ind Lab | 5,012 | 23.6 |
| | | | G. MacPherson | L | 2,582* | 12.2 |
| | | | | | 8,636 | 40.6 |
| 1922 | 38,031 | 64.5 | W. Hutchison | C | 13,442 | 54.8 |
| | | | R. Roxburgh | L | 11,094 | 45.2 |
| | | | | | 2,348 | 9.6 |
| 1923 | 37,692 | 68.2 | W. Hutchison | C | 11,025 | 42.9 |
| | | | A. Ferguson | Com | 10,021 | 39.0 |
| | | | A.J. Grieve | L | 4,662 | 18.1 |
| | | | | | 1,004 | 3.9 |
| [Death] | | | | | | |
| 1924 | 39,779 | 70.5 | W.E. Elliot | C | 15,488 | 55.3 |
| (23/5) | | | A. Ferguson | Lab | 11,167 | 39.8 |
| | | | Sir J.W. Pratt | L | 1,372* | 4.9 |
| | | | | | 4,321 | 15.5 |
| 1924 | 39,841 | 77.5 | W.E. Elliot | C | 18,034 | 58.4 |
| | | | T.A. Kerr | Lab | 12,844 | 41.6 |
| | | | | | 5,190 | 16.8 |
| 1929 | 46,507 | 74.9 | W.E. Elliot | C | 17,031 | 48.9 |
| | | | J. Winning | Lab | 15,173 | 43.6 |
| | | | W. Reid | L | 2,623* | 7.5 |
| | | | | | 1,858 | 5.3 |
| 1931 | 44,197 | 76.7 | W.E. Elliot | C | 21,481 | 63.4 |
| | | | J. Winning | ILP | 12,415 | 36.6 |
| | | | | | 9,066 | 26.8 |
| 1935 | 42,837 | 72.5 | Rt. Hon. W.E. Elliot | C | 15,100 | 48.7 |
| | | | H. McNeil | Lab | 14,951 | 48.1 |
| | | | H.G. Rae | L | 1,004* | 3.2 |
| | | | | | 149 | 0.6 |
| 1945 | 43,225 | 61.7 | J.L. Williams | Lab | 12,273 | 46.0 |
| | | | Rt. Hon. W.E. Elliot | C | 12,185 | 45.7 |
| | | | C.M. Grieve | SNP | 1,314* | 4.9 |
| | | | C.J.E. Morgan | L | 919* | 3.4 |
| | | | | | 88 | 0.3 |

Notes:—

1923: Ferguson sought election as a 'Labour' candidate despite the fact that he was an official Communist Party candidate and did not receive Labour Party endorsement.

1924: Ferguson's candidature had been endorsed by the National Executive of the
(23/5) Labour Party, but the Labour Party Annual Conference Report for 1924 reported that due to developments during the campaign it had been found impossible to render further official support. He was a member of the Communist Party at the time of the election.

## GLASGOW, MARYHILL [567]

| Election | Electors | T'out | Candidate | Party | Votes | % |
|---|---|---|---|---|---|---|
| 1918 | 34,622 | 57.2 | †Sir W. Mitchell-Thomson, Bt. | Co C | 11,913 | 60.2 |
| | | | J.W. Muir | Lab | 5,531 | 27.9 |
| | | | †H.A. Watt | L | 2,363* | 11.9 |
| | | | | | 6,382 | 32.3 |
| 1922 | 33,991 | 81.3 | J.W. Muir | Lab | 13,058 | 47.3 |
| | | | Sir W. Mitchell-Thomson, Bt. | C | 10,951 | 39.6 |
| | | | Miss A.S. Swan | L | 3,617 | 13.1 |
| | | | | | 2,107 | 7.7 |
| 1923 | 33,781 | 77.1 | J.W. Muir | Lab | 12,508 | 48.1 |
| | | | J.B. Couper | C | 10,342 | 39.7 |
| | | | W.C. Smith | L | 3,179* | 12.2 |
| | | | | | 2,166 | 8.4 |
| 1924 | 34,930 | 84.2 | J.B. Couper | C | 15,460 | 52.6 |
| | | | J.W. Muir | Lab | 13,947 | 47.4 |
| | | | | | 1,513 | 5.2 |
| 1929 | 45,333 | 79.8 | J.S. Clarke | Lab | 18,311 | 50.6 |
| | | | J.B. Couper | C | 14,922 | 41.2 |
| | | | Rev. H.T. Cape | L | 2,955* | 8.2 |
| | | | | | 3,389 | 9.4 |
| 1931 | 47,880 | 78.0 | D. Jamieson | C | 20,710 | 55.5 |
| | | | J.S. Clarke | Lab | 16,613 | 44.5 |
| | | | | | 4,097 | 11.0 |
| 1935 | 53,817 | 73.3 | J.J. Davidson | Lab | 21,706 | 55.0 |
| | | | G.I.C. Hutchison | C | 17,735 | 45.0 |
| | | | | | 3,971 | 10.0 |
| 1945 | 58,857 | 66.8 | W. Hannan | Lab | 23,595 | 60.1 |
| | | | W.R. McLean | C | 15,693 | 39.9 |
| | | | | | 7,902 | 20.2 |

# GLASGOW, PARTICK [568]

| Election | Electors | T'out | Candidate | Party | Votes | % |
|---|---|---|---|---|---|---|
| 1918 | 28,376 | 61.1 | †Sir R. Balfour, Bt. | Co L | 12,156 | 70.1 |
| | | | W. Mackie | Lab | 5,173 | 29.9 |
| | | | | | 6,983 | 40.2 |
| 1922 | 27,048 | 66.7 | Sir R.J. Collie | NL | 11,754 | 65.2 |
| | | | Sir D.M. Stevenson, Bt. | L | 6,282 | 34.8 |
| | | | | | 5,472 | 30.4 |
| 1923 | 26,806 | 71.1 | A. Young | Lab/Co-op | 8,397 | 44.0 |
| | | | Sir A.M. Smith | C | 6,315 | 33.1 |
| | | | A.M. Scott | L | 4,358 | 22.9 |
| | | | | | 2,082 | 10.9 |
| 1924 | 27,660 | 82.4 | G.H.M. Broun-Lindsay | C | 13,167 | 57.8 |
| | | | A. Young | Lab/Co-op | 9,612 | 42.2 |
| | | | | | 3,555 | 15.6 |
| 1929 | 36,517 | 78.8 | A.S. McKinlay | Lab | 13,110 | 45.6 |
| | | | G.H.M. Broun-Lindsay | C | 12,701 | 44.1 |
| | | | J. Taylor | L | 2,975* | 10.3 |
| | | | | | 409 | 1.5 |
| 1931 | 36,134 | 83.5 | C.G. MacAndrew | C | 18,904 | 62.7 |
| | | | A.S. McKinlay | Lab | 11,252 | 37.3 |
| | | | | | 7,652 | 25.4 |
| 1935 | 36,999 | 78.2 | A.S.L. Young | C | 15,616 | 54.0 |
| | | | A.S. McKinlay | Lab | 13,316 | 46.0 |
| | | | | | 2,300 | 8.0 |
| 1945 | 38,899 | 69.0 | A.S.L. Young | C | 13,851 | 51.6 |
| | | | G.A. Younger | Lab/Co-op | 12,998 | 48.4 |
| | | | | | 853 | 3.2 |

| Election | Electors | T'out | Candidate | Party | Votes | % |
|---|---|---|---|---|---|---|
| 1918 | | | †J. Gilmour | Co C | Unopp. | |
| [Appointed a Lord Commissioner of the Treasury] | | | | | | |
| 1921 (14/4) | | | Sir J. Gilmour, Bt. | Co C | Unopp. | |
| 1922 | 29,670 | 78.7 | Rt. Hon. Sir J. Gilmour, Bt. | C | 14,920 | 63.9 |
| | | | A.B. Mackay | Lab | 5,759 | 24.7 |
| | | | T.R. Anderson | L | 2,658* | 11.4 |
| | | | | | 9,161 | 39.2 |
| 1923 | 31,612 | 66.0 | Rt. Hon. Sir J. Gilmour, Bt. | C | 14,013 | 67.2 |
| | | | J. Rankin | Lab | 6,836 | 32.8 |
| | | | | | 7,177 | 34.4 |
| 1924 | 35,788 | 76.5 | Rt. Hon. Sir J. Gilmour, Bt. | C | 20,622 | 75.3 |
| | | | J. Rankin | Lab | 6,749 | 24.7 |
| | | | | | 13,873 | 50.6 |
| 1929 | 44,945 | 71.8 | Rt. Hon. Sir J. Gilmour, Bt. | C | 22,328 | 69.2 |
| | | | W. Muter | Lab | 9,936 | 30.8 |
| | | | | | 12,392 | 38.4 |
| 1931 | 44,192 | 77.2 | Rt. Hon. Sir J. Gilmour, Bt. | C | 27,772 | 81.5 |
| | | | J. Rankin | Lab | 6,323 | 18.5 |
| | | | | | 21,449 | 63.0 |
| 1935 | 44,348 | 70.1 | Rt. Hon. Sir J. Gilmour, Bt. | C | 22,408 | 72.1 |
| | | | J. McInnes | Lab | 8,670 | 27.9 |
| | | | | | 13,738 | 44.2 |
| [Death] | | | | | | |
| 1940 (30/4) | 45,518 | 44.5 | T.D. Galbraith | C | 17,850 | 88.1 |
| | | | J. Nicholson | Ind Lab | 2,401* | 11.9 |
| | | | | | 15,449 | 76.2 |
| 1945 | 46,397 | 68.2 | T.D. Galbraith | C | 20,072 | 63.5 |
| | | | A.B. Mackay | Lab | 10,630 | 33.6 |
| | | | W.J. Voisey-Youldon | CW | 932* | 2.9 |
| | | | | | 9,442 | 29.9 |

Note:—

1940: Nicholson was the nominee of the local Labour Party which was disaffiliated by the National Executive Committee of the Labour Party for breaking the electoral truce.

| Election | Electors | T'out | Candidate | Party | Votes | % |
|---|---|---|---|---|---|---|
| 1918 | 38,439 | 48.2 | Hon. C.G. Murray | Co C (C) | 10,844 | 58.6 |
|  |  |  | J. Stewart | Lab | 6,147 | 33.2 |
|  |  |  | †Rt. Hon. T.M. Wood | L | 1,521* | 8.2 |
|  |  |  |  |  | 4,697 | 25.4 |
| 1922 | 37,145 | 76.7 | J. Stewart | Lab | 16,114 | 56.6 |
|  |  |  | J.B. Couper | C | 10,343 | 36.3 |
|  |  |  | J.A. Fleming | L | 2,025* | 7.1 |
|  |  |  |  |  | 5,771 | 20.3 |
| 1923 | 37,238 | 65.6 | J. Stewart | Lab | 15,240 | 62.3 |
|  |  |  | Miss V.M.C. Roberton | C | 9,204 | 37.7 |
|  |  |  |  |  | 6,036 | 24.6 |
| 1924 | 37,059 | 74.3 | J. Stewart | Lab | 16,299 | 59.2 |
|  |  |  | J. Johnston | L | 11,238 | 40.8 |
|  |  |  |  |  | 5,061 | 18.4 |
| 1929 | 43,742 | 72.0 | J. Stewart | Lab | 19,445 | 61.8 |
|  |  |  | A.N. Forman | C | 11,430 | 36.3 |
|  |  |  | G.W. Middleton | Com | 613* | 1.9 |
|  |  |  |  |  | 8,015 | 25.5 |
| [Death] |  |  |  |  |  |  |
| 1931 (7/5) | 41,112 | 54.1 | W. Leonard | Lab/Co-op | 10,044 | 45.2 |
|  |  |  | J.A. Kennedy | C | 8,662 | 39.0 |
|  |  |  | Miss E. Campbell | SNP | 3,521 | 15.8 |
|  |  |  |  |  | 1,382 | 6.2 |
| 1931 | 40,858 | 74.2 | W. Leonard | Lab/Co-op | 13,545 | 44.7 |
|  |  |  | F. Shoesmith | C | 12,734 | 42.0 |
|  |  |  | Miss E. Campbell | SNP | 4,021 | 13.3 |
|  |  |  |  |  | 811 | 2.7 |
| 1935 | 39,986 | 67.8 | W. Leonard | Lab/Co-op | 16,708 | 61.6 |
|  |  |  | H. Black | C | 10,411 | 38.4 |
|  |  |  |  |  | 6,297 | 23.2 |
| 1945 | 37,745 | 61.1 | W. Leonard | Lab/Co-op | 14,520 | 62.9 |
|  |  |  | W.R. Milligan | C | 8,553 | 37.1 |
|  |  |  |  |  | 5,967 | 25.8 |

| Election | Electors | T'out | Candidate | Party | Votes | % |
|----------|----------|-------|-----------|-------|-------|---|
| 1918 | 31,488 | 62.7 | T.B.S. Adair | Co C | 9,901 | 50.2 |
| | | | J. Wheatley | Lab | 9,827 | 49.8 |
| | | | | | 74 | 0.4 |
| 1922 | 29,639 | 83.9 | J. Wheatley | Lab | 14,695 | 59.1 |
| | | | T.B.W. Ramsay | NL | 9,704 | 39.0 |
| | | | G.A. Aldred | Ind Com | 470* | 1.9 |
| | | | | | 4,991 | 20.1 |
| 1923 | 29,708 | 71.0 | J. Wheatley | Lab | 12,624 | 59.8 |
| | | | F.J. Robertson | L | 8,471 | 40.2 |
| | | | | | 4,153 | 19.6 |
| 1924 | 30,324 | 81.8 | Rt. Hon. J. Wheatley | Lab | 12,714 | 51.3 |
| | | | J.M.R. Miller | C | 12,084 | 48.7 |
| | | | | | 630 | 2.6 |
| 1929 | 42,193 | 76.9 | Rt. Hon. J. Wheatley | Lab | 19,594 | 60.4 |
| | | | H.J. Moss | C | 12,870 | 39.6 |
| | | | | | 6,724 | 20.8 |
| [Death] | | | | | | |
| 1930 (26/6) | 42,193 | 59.2 | J. McGovern | Lab | 10,699 | 42.9 |
| | | | W.P. Templeton | C | 10,303 | 41.2 |
| | | | J.M. McNicol | SNP | 2,527* | 10.1 |
| | | | S. Saklatvala | Com | 1,459* | 5.8 |
| | | | | | 396 | 1.7 |
| 1931 | 43,819 | 77.8 | J. McGovern | ILP | 16,301 | 47.8 |
| | | | J. Lucas | C | 15,530 | 45.6 |
| | | | J.Y. Marshall | Lab | 1,856* | 5.4 |
| | | | W.E. Stevenson | NP | 402* | 1.2 |
| | | | | | 771 | 2.2 |
| 1935 | 46,696 | 74.5 | J. McGovern | ILP | 18,377 | 52.8 |
| | | | R.S. Russell | C | 13,802 | 39.7 |
| | | | G. Beggs | Lab | 2,610* | 7.5 |
| | | | | | 4,575 | 13.1 |
| 1945 | 50,498 | 66.6 | J. McGovern | ILP (Lab) | 11,947 | 35.4 |
| | | | W.G. Bennett | C | 10,453 | 31.1 |
| | | | J.S. Dallas | Lab | 6,910 | 20.6 |
| | | | P. Kerrigan | Com | 4,122* | 12.3 |
| | | | I. Queen | Ind | 186* | 0.6 |
| | | | | | 1,494 | 4.3 |

Notes:—

1922: Aldred was founder and leader of the Anti-Parliamentary Communist Federation which he formed in Glasgow during 1919.

1945: Queen was a member of the British Legion and fought the election on issues affecting ex-servicemen.

| Election | Electors | T'out | Candidate | Party | Votes | % |
|---|---|---|---|---|---|---|
| 1918 | 33,599 | 60.9 | F.A. Macquisten | Co C | 10,786 | 52.7 |
| | | | G.D.B. Hardie | Lab | 7,996 | 39.1 |
| | | | †W.M.R. Pringle | L | 1,669* | 8.2 |
| | | | | | 2,790 | 13.6 |
| 1922 | 33,230 | 78.5 | G.D.B. Hardie | Lab | 15,771 | 60.5 |
| | | | F.A. Macquisten | C | 10,311 | 39.5 |
| | | | | | 5,460 | 21.0 |
| 1923 | 34,277 | 68.1 | G.D.B. Hardie | Lab | 14,535 | 62.3 |
| | | | D.A. Guild | C | 8,814 | 37.7 |
| | | | | | 5,721 | 24.6 |
| 1924 | 34,907 | 79.3 | G.D.B. Hardie | Lab | 15,635 | 56.5 |
| | | | D.A. Guild | C | 12,043 | 43.5 |
| | | | | | 3,592 | 13.0 |
| 1929 | 43,757 | 73.6 | G.D.B. Hardie | Lab | 21,079 | 65.5 |
| | | | J. McSkimming | C | 11,110 | 34.5 |
| | | | | | 9,969 | 31.0 |
| 1931 | 45,268 | 75.4 | C.E.G.C. Emmott | C | 16,092 | 47.2 |
| | | | G.D.B. Hardie | Lab | 16,058 | 47.0 |
| | | | A. Haimes | Com | 1,997* | 5.8 |
| | | | | | 34 | 0.2 |
| 1935 | 45,190 | 71.1 | G.D.B. Hardie | Lab | 20,286 | 63.1 |
| | | | J. McNicol | C | 11,859 | 36.9 |
| | | | | | 8,427 | 26.2 |
| [Death] | | | | | | |
| 1937 (7/9) | 46,684 | 50.9 | Mrs. A. Hardie | Lab | 14,859 | 62.6 |
| | | | A.D.M. Shaw | C | 8,881 | 37.4 |
| | | | | | 5,978 | 25.2 |
| 1945 | 52,532 | 63.6 | J.C. Forman | Lab/Co-op | 21,698 | 65.0 |
| | | | R.H.S. Calver | C | 11,690 | 35.0 |
| | | | | | 10,008 | 30.0 |

| Election | Electors | T'out | Candidate | Party | Votes | % |
|---|---|---|---|---|---|---|
| 1918 | 35,960 | 53.9 | V.L. Henderson | Co C | 12,250 | 63.2 |
| | | | J.D. MacDougall | BSP | 3,751 | 19.4 |
| | | | †J.D. White | L | 3,369 | 17.4 |
| | | | | | 8,499 | 43.8 |
| 1922 | 33,792 | 75.4 | T. Henderson | Lab/Co-op | 14,190 | 55.7 |
| | | | V.L. Henderson | C | 9,977 | 39.2 |
| | | | C. de B. Murray | L | 1,310* | 5.1 |
| | | | | | 4,213 | 16.5 |
| 1923 | 33,713 | 63.1 | T. Henderson | Lab/Co-op | 12,787 | 60.1 |
| | | | D. Macdonald | L | 8,479 | 39.9 |
| | | | | | 4,308 | 20.2 |
| 1924 | 34,373 | 73.1 | T. Henderson | Lab/Co-op | 14,067 | 56.0 |
| | | | D. Macdonald | L | 11,074 | 44.0 |
| | | | | | 2,993 | 12.0 |
| 1929 | 40,743 | 75.7 | T. Henderson | Lab/Co-op | 17,864 | 57.9 |
| | | | I. Spencer | C | 12,992 | 42.1 |
| | | | | | 4,872 | 15.8 |
| 1931 | 39,026 | 73.4 | Dr. W.H. McLean | C | 15,067 | 52.6 |
| | | | T. Henderson | Lab/Co-op | 13,579 | 47.4 |
| | | | | | 1,488 | 5.2 |
| 1935 | 37,582 | 69.3 | T. Henderson | Lab/Co-op | 12,253 | 47.0 |
| | | | Dr. W.H. McLean | C | 10,354 | 39.8 |
| | | | J. Carmichael | ILP | 3,423 | 13.2 |
| | | | | | 1,899 | 7.2 |
| 1945 | 35,499 | 62.0 | J. Rankin | Lab/Co-op | 13,153 | 59.7 |
| | | | H.R. Black | C | 8,871 | 40.3 |
| | | | | | 4,282 | 19.4 |

| Election | Electors | T'out | Candidate | Party | Votes | % |
|---|---|---|---|---|---|---|
| 1918 | 34,182 | 66.6 | †G.P. Collins | L (Co L) (L) | 10,933 | 48.0 |
| | | | S. Chapman | C | 7,246 | 31.8 |
| | | | F. Shaw | Lab | 2,542* | 11.2 |
| | | | N. Haughey | Ind Lab | 2,050* | 9.0 |
| | | | | | 3,687 | 16.2 |
| 1922 | 33,835 | 84.8 | Sir G.P. Collins | L | 10,520 | 36.6 |
| | | | A. Geddes | Com | 9,776 | 34.1 |
| | | | J. Denholm | C | 8,404 | 29.3 |
| | | | | | 744 | 2.5 |
| 1923 | 34,006 | 78.4 | Sir G.P. Collins | L | 16,337 | 61.3 |
| | | | A. Geddes | Com | 10,335 | 38.7 |
| | | | | | 6,002 | 22.6 |
| 1924 | 33,693 | 77.8 | Sir G.P. Collins | L | 12,752 | 48.6 |
| | | | A. Geddes | Com | 7,590 | 29.0 |
| | | | S. Kelly | Lab | 5,874 | 22.4 |
| | | | | | 5,162 | 19.6 |
| 1929 | 43,720 | 78.7 | Sir G.P. Collins | L (NL) | 11,190 | 32.5 |
| | | | W. Leonard | Lab/Co-op | 9,697 | 28.2 |
| | | | A. Geddes | Com | 7,005 | 20.4 |
| | | | A.D. Gibb | C | 6,517 | 18.9 |
| | | | | | 1,493 | 4.3 |
| 1931 | 43,946 | 80.3 | Sir G.P. Collins | NL | 18,013 | 51.1 |
| | | | T. Irwin | Lab | 10,850 | 30.7 |
| | | | A. Ferguson | Com | 6,440 | 18.2 |
| | | | | | 7,163 | 20.4 |
| 1935 | 45,668 | 84.4 | Rt. Hon. Sir G.P. Collins | NL | 20,299 | 52.7 |
| | | | T. Irwin | Lab | 16,945 | 44.0 |
| | | | J.L. Kinloch | SNP | 1,286* | 3.3 |
| | | | | | 3,354 | 8.7 |
| [Death] | | | | | | |
| 1936 | 46,340 | 83.3 | R. Gibson | Lab | 20,594 | 53.4 |
| (26/11) | | | V.E. Cornelius | NL | 17,990 | 46.6 |
| | | | | | 2,604 | 6.8 |

[Resignation on appointment as Chairman of the Scottish Land Court — Lord Gibson]

| | | | | | | |
|---|---|---|---|---|---|---|
| 1941 | | | H. McNeil | Lab | Unopp. | |
| (10/7) | | | | | | |

| Election | Electors | T'out | Candidate | Party | Votes | % |
|----------|----------|-------|-----------|-------|-------|---|
| 1945 | 50,561 | 68.0 | H. McNeil | Lab | 16,186 | 47.0 |
| | | | Lord Malcolm Douglas-Hamilton | C | 8,097 | 23.6 |
| | | | J.R. Campbell | Com | 5,900 | 17.2 |
| | | | G.G. Honeyman | L | 4,180* | 12.2 |
| | | | | | 8,089 | 23.4 |

Notes:—

1918: Chapman's name appeared on the final official list of Coalition candidates despite the fact that the Coalition Whips had previously agreed not to issue a 'coupon' for this constituency. This was presumably an error and immediately after the list was published the Coalition Liberal Whip sent a telegram to Collins making it clear that there was no official Coalition candidate for the constituency.

Haughey was the nominee of the Greenock and District Dockers' Union.

1922-
1923: Geddes sought election as a 'Labour' candidate despite the fact that he was an official Communist Party candidate and did not receive Labour Party endorsement.

# KIRKCALDY DISTRICT of BURGHS [575]

## (Kirkcaldy, Buckhaven, Methil and Innerleven, Burntisland, Dysart, Kinghorn)

| Election | Electors | T'out | Candidate | Party | Votes | % |
|---|---|---|---|---|---|---|
| 1918 | | | †Rt. Hon. Sir J.H. Dalziel, Bt. | Co L | Unopp. | |
| [Resignation] | | | | | | |
| 1921 (4/3) | 33,326† | 65.6 | T. Kennedy | Lab | 11,674 | 53.4 |
| | | | Sir R.C. Lockhart | Co L | 10,199 | 46.6 |
| | | | | | 1,475 | 6.8 |
| 1922 | 31,342 | 79.3 | Sir R. Hutchison | NL | 12,762 | 51.4 |
| | | | T. Kennedy | Lab | 12,089 | 48.6 |
| | | | | | 673 | 2.8 |
| 1923 | 32,033 | 81.7 | T. Kennedy | Lab | 14,221 | 54.4 |
| | | | Sir R. Hutchison | L | 11,937 | 45.6 |
| | | | | | 2,284 | 8.8 |
| 1924 | 32,588 | 81.8 | T. Kennedy | Lab | 14,038 | 52.7 |
| | | | J. Murray | L | 12,607 | 47.3 |
| | | | | | 1,431 | 5.4 |
| 1929 | 40,437 | 72.2 | T. Kennedy | Lab | 17,410 | 59.6 |
| | | | H.J. Scrymgeour-Wedderburn | C | 11,805 | 40.4 |
| | | | | | 5,605 | 19.2 |
| 1931 | 41,483 | 81.1 | A. Russell | C | 19,132 | 56.9 |
| | | | Rt. Hon. T. Kennedy | Lab | 14,492 | 43.1 |
| | | | | | 4,640 | 13.8 |
| 1935 | 43,232 | 79.9 | Rt. Hon. T. Kennedy | Lab | 19,457 | 56.3 |
| | | | A. Russell | C | 15,086 | 43.7 |
| | | | | | 4,371 | 12.6 |
| [Resignation] | | | | | | |
| 1944 (17/2) | 43,030 | 37.2 | T.F. Hubbard | Lab | 8,268 | 51.6 |
| | | | D.C.C. Young | SNP | 6,621 | 41.3 |
| | | | H. Hilditch | CS | 1,136* | 7.1 |
| | | | | | 1,647 | 10.3 |
| 1945 | 44,883 | 76.2 | T.F. Hubbard | Lab | 15,401 | 45.0 |
| | | | C.W.G. Guest | C | 10,099 | 29.5 |
| | | | D.C.C. Young | SNP | 5,811 | 17.0 |
| | | | J. McArthur | Com | 2,898* | 8.5 |
| | | | | | 5,302 | 15.5 |

| Election | Electors | T'out | Candidate | Party | Votes | % |
|---|---|---|---|---|---|---|
| 1918 | 42,507 | 52.2 | †W.W. Benn | L | 10,338 | 46.6 |
| | | | †G.W. Currie | Co C | 7,613 | 34.3 |
| | | | S. Burgess | Lab | 4,251 | 19.1 |
| | | | | | 2,725 | 12.3 |
| 1922 | 39,048 | 71.5 | W.W. Benn | L | 13,971 | 50.1 |
| | | | A.M. MacRobert | C | 7,372 | 26.4 |
| | | | R.F. Wilson | Lab | 6,567 | 23.5 |
| | | | | | 6,599 | 23.7 |
| 1923 | 39,385 | 59.1 | W.W. Benn | L | 15,004 | 64.5 |
| | | | R.F. Wilson | Lab | 8,267 | 35.5 |
| | | | | | 6,737 | 29.0 |
| 1924 | 39,480 | 70.5 | W.W. Benn | L | 16,569 | 59.6 |
| | | | R.F. Wilson | Lab | 11,250 | 40.4 |
| | | | | | 5,319 | 19.2 |

[Resignation on joining the Labour Party]

| Election | Electors | T'out | Candidate | Party | Votes | % |
|---|---|---|---|---|---|---|
| 1927 (23/3) | 39,795 | 73.9 | A.E. Brown | L | 12,461 | 42.3 |
| | | | R.F. Wilson | Lab | 12,350 | 42.0 |
| | | | A. Beaton | C | 4,607 | 15.7 |
| | | | | | 111 | 0.3 |
| 1929 | 50,801 | 71.5 | A.E. Brown | L (Ind L) (NL) | 20,613 | 56.7 |
| | | | A.H. Paton | Lab | 15,715 | 43.3 |
| | | | | | 4,898 | 13.4 |
| 1931 | 50,979 | 75.0 | A.E. Brown | NL | 24,847 | 65.0 |
| | | | A. Woodburn | Lab | 13,400 | 35.0 |
| | | | | | 11,447 | 30.0 |
| 1935 | 49,933 | 65.5 | Rt. Hon. A.E. Brown | NL | 18,888 | 57.7 |
| | | | D.C. Thomson | Lab | 13,819 | 42.3 |
| | | | | | 5,069 | 15.4 |
| 1945 | 46,581 | 69.1 | J.H. Hoy | Lab | 19,571 | 60.9 |
| | | | Rt. Hon. A.E. Brown | NL | 10,116 | 31.4 |
| | | | J. Cormack | Ind | 2,493* | 7.7 |
| | | | | | 9,455 | 29.5 |

Note:—

1945: Cormack was the founder of the Protestant Action Society, an organisation he formed in Edinburgh during 1932.

# MONTROSE DISTRICT of BURGHS [577]

## (Montrose, Arbroath, Brechin, Forfar, Inverbervie)

| Election | Electors | T'out | Candidate | Party | Votes | % |
|---|---|---|---|---|---|---|
| 1918 | 24,956 | 49.1 | J.L. Sturrock | Co L | 9,309 | 76.0 |
| | | | H.N. Brailsford | Lab | 2,940 | 24.0 |
| | | | | | 6,369 | 52.0 |
| 1922 | 24,628 | 62.7 | J.L. Sturrock | NL | 8,407 | 54.4 |
| | | | J. Carnegie | Lab | 7,044 | 45.6 |
| | | | | | 1,363 | 8.8 |
| 1923 | 25,031 | 62.9 | J.L. Sturrock | L | 8,717 | 55.3 |
| | | | J. Carnegie | Lab | 7,032 | 44.7 |
| | | | | | 1,685 | 10.6 |
| 1924 | 23,568 | 68.5 | Sir R. Hutchison | L | 9,226 | 57.2 |
| | | | T. Barron | Lab | 6,914 | 42.8 |
| | | | | | 2,312 | 14.4 |
| 1929 | 29,573 | 71.3 | Sir R. Hutchison | L (Ind L) (NL) | 11,715 | 55.5 |
| | | | T. Irwin | Lab | 9,381 | 44.5 |
| | | | | | 2,334 | 11.0 |
| 1931 | 29,956 | 74.6 | Sir R. Hutchison | NL | 17,212 | 77.0 |
| | | | A.F. Macintosh | Lab | 5,137 | 23.0 |
| | | | | | 12,075 | 54.0 |

[Elevation to the Peerage — Lord Hutchison of Montrose]

| Election | Electors | T'out | Candidate | Party | Votes | % |
|---|---|---|---|---|---|---|
| 1932 (28/6) | 29,956 | 56.7 | C.I. Kerr | NL | 7,963 | 46.9 |
| | | | Rt. Hon. T. Kennedy | Lab | 7,030 | 41.4 |
| | | | D. Emslie | SNP | 1,996*· | 11.7 |
| | | | | | 933 | 5.5 |
| 1935 | 30,941 | 70.6 | C.I. Kerr | NL | 15,198 | 69.6 |
| | | | J.E. Harper | Lab | 6,632 | 30.4 |
| | | | | | 8,566 | 39.2 |

[Elevation to the Peerage — Lord Teviot]

| Election | Electors | T'out | Candidate | Party | Votes | % |
|---|---|---|---|---|---|---|
| 1940 (5/7) | | | Hon. J.S. Maclay | NL | Unopp. | |
| 1945 | 33,162 | 72.3 | Hon. J.S. Maclay | NL | 13,966 | 58.2 |
| | | | T.A. MacNair | Lab | 10,011 | 41.8 |
| | | | | | 3,955 | 16.4 |

| Election | Electors | T'out | Candidate | Party | Votes | % |
|---|---|---|---|---|---|---|
| 1918 | 38,508 | 57.6 | †Sir J.M. McCallum | L | 7,542 | 34.0 |
| | | | J.M. Biggar | Co-op | 7,436 | 33.5 |
| | | | J. Taylor | Co NDP | 7,201 | 32.5 |
| | | | | | 106 | 0.5 |
| [Death] | | | | | | |
| 1920 (12/2) | 39,235 | 77.6 | Rt. Hon. H.H. Asquith | L | 14,736 | 48.4 |
| | | | J.M. Biggar | Lab/Co-op | 11,902 | 39.1 |
| | | | J.A.D. McKean | Co C | 3,795* | 12.5 |
| | | | | | 2,834 | 9.3 |
| 1922 | 38,093 | 78.0 | Rt. Hon. H.H. Asquith | L | 15,005 | 50.5 |
| | | | J.M. Biggar | Lab/Co-op | 14,689 | 49.5 |
| | | | | | 316 | 1.0 |
| 1923 | 37,792 | 77.1 | Rt. Hon. H.H. Asquith | L | 9,723 | 33.4 |
| | | | J.M. Biggar | Lab/Co-op | 7,977 | 27.4 |
| | | | A.D.M. Shaw | C | 7,758 | 26.6 |
| | | | D.D. Cormack | Ind Lab | 3,685 | 12.6 |
| | | | | | 1,746 | 6.0 |
| 1924 | 37,901 | 84.1 | E.R. Mitchell | Lab | 17,057 | 53.5 |
| | | | Rt. Hon. H.H. Asquith | L | 14,829 | 46.5 |
| | | | | | 2,228 | 7.0 |
| 1929 | 51,385 | 78.2 | J. Welsh | Lab | 22,425 | 55.8 |
| | | | J. McCulloch | L | 10,640 | 26.5 |
| | | | Miss M.G. Cowan | C | 7,094 | 17.7 |
| | | | | | 11,785 | 29.3 |
| 1931 | 53,373 | 79.4 | Hon. J.P. Maclay | L | 26,187 | 61.8 |
| | | | J. Welsh | Lab | 16,183 | 38.2 |
| | | | | | 10,004 | 23.6 |
| 1935 | 55,473 | 80.3 | Hon. J.P. Maclay | L | 22,466 | 50.4 |
| | | | O.R. Baldwin | Lab | 22,077 | 49.6 |
| | | | | | 389 | 0.8 |
| 1945 | 61,286 | 73.9 | Viscount Corvedale | Lab | 25,156 | 55.6 |
| | | | T.G.D. Galbraith | C | 14,826 | 32.7 |
| | | | Lady Glen-Coats | L | 4,532* | 10.0 |
| | | | A.R. Eagles | Ind | 765* | 1.7 |
| | | | | | 10,330 | 22.9 |
| [Succession to the Peerage — Earl Baldwin of Bewdley] | | | | | | |
| 1948 (18/2) | 63,008 | 76.0 | D.H. Johnston | Lab | 27,213 | 56.8 |
| | | | J.M. MacCormick | Nat | 20,668 | 43.2 |
| | | | | | 6,545 | 13.6 |

Notes:—

1923: Cormack was the nominee of the local Labour Party who refused to accept Biggar as the official Labour candidate.

1931-
1935: Maclay remained on the Government benches in the House of Commons when the Liberal Party went into Opposition in November 1933. Although remaining an official Liberal member and not joining the National Liberal group, he gave general support to the National Government.

1945: Viscount Corvedale was formerly O.R. Baldwin.

1948: Johnston was Solicitor-General for Scotland.

MacCormick was at first adopted by the local Liberal Association but subsequently an agreement was reached with the Conservative Association and he sought election as a 'National' candidate.

# STIRLING and FALKIRK DISTRICT of BURGHS  [579]

## (Stirling, Falkirk, Grangemouth)

| Election | Electors | T'out | Candidate | Party | Votes | % |
|---|---|---|---|---|---|---|
| 1918 | 29,443 | 49.4 | †Rt. Hon. J.A.M. Macdonald | L | 9,350 | 64.3 |
| | | | A. Logan | Lab | 5,201 | 35.7 |
| | | | | | 4,149 | 28.6 |
| 1922 | 28,986 | 71.7 | H. Murnin | Lab | 11,073 | 53.3 |
| | | | Rt. Hon. J.A.M. Macdonald | NL | 9,717 | 46.7 |
| | | | | | 1,356 | 6.6 |
| 1923 | 29,668 | 71.7 | Sir G. McCrae | L | 10,721 | 50.4 |
| | | | H. Murnin | Lab | 10,565 | 49.6 |
| | | | | | 156 | 0.8 |
| 1924 | 30,592 | 81.6 | H. Murnin | Lab | 13,436 | 53.9 |
| | | | Sir G. McCrae | L | 11,512 | 46.1 |
| | | | | | 1,924 | 7.8 |
| 1929 | 41,036 | 79.1 | H. Murnin | Lab | 15,408 | 47.4 |
| | | | D. Jamieson | C | 10,164 | 31.3 |
| | | | A. Ratcliffe | Ind | 6,902 | 21.3 |
| | | | | | 5,244 | 16.1 |
| 1931 | 42,179 | 81.4 | J.S.C. Reid | C | 21,844 | 63.6 |
| | | | H. Murnin | Lab | 12,483 | 36.4 |
| | | | | | 9,361 | 27.2 |
| 1935 | 44,702 | 78.4 | J.C. Westwood | Lab | 17,958 | 51.2 |
| | | | J.S.C. Reid | C | 17,087 | 48.8 |
| | | | | | 871 | 2.4 |
| 1945 | 45,666 | 71.5 | Rt. Hon. J.C. Westwood | Lab | 18,326 | 56.1 |
| | | | J.F.G. Thomson | C | 14,323 | 43.9 |
| | | | | | 4,003 | 12.2 |
| [Death] | | | | | | |
| 1948 (7/10) | 47,544 | 72.9 | M. MacPherson | Lab | 17,001 | 49.0 |
| | | | W.D.H.C. Forbes | C | 14,826 | 42.8 |
| | | | R. Curran | SNP | 2,831* | 8.2 |
| | | | | | 2,175 | 6.2 |

Notes:—

1918-
1922: Macdonald's position in relation to the Coalition Government on one hand and the Liberal Party on the other is difficult to define. Although elected as a Liberal without prefix in 1918 he gave fairly consistent support to the Coalition Government.

At the General Election of 1922 his name appeared on the official list of National Liberal candidates but he maintained that he was a Liberal and Free Trader and not a National Liberal. He did however receive support from the local Conservative Association and as a result of an examination of the text of his election address and several of his speeches, the designation National Liberal is considered to be an accurate indication of his political views.

1929: Ratcliffe sought election as a 'Protestant and Progressive' candidate. He was supported by the Scottish Protestant League.

# SCOTLAND ——— COUNTIES

| Election | Electors | T'out | Candidate | Party | Votes | % |
|---|---|---|---|---|---|---|
| 1918 | 26,315 | 47.3 | A.T. Gordon | Co C | 6,546 | 52.6 |
| | | | †J.M. Henderson | L | 5,908 | 47.4 |
| | | | | | 638 | 5.2 |
| [Death] | | | | | | |
| 1919 | 26,315 | 50.1 | M.M. Wood | L | 4,950 | 37.5 |
| (16/4) | | | L.F.W. Davidson | Co C | 4,764 | 36.1 |
| | | | J.F. Duncan | Lab | 3,482 | 26.4 |
| | | | | | 186 | 1.4 |
| 1922 | 28,573 | 56.9 | M.M. Wood | L | 9,779 | 60.1 |
| | | | R.W. Smith | C | 6,481 | 39.9 |
| | | | | | 3,298 | 20.2 |
| 1923 | 28,329 | 64.7 | M.M. Wood | L | 9,818 | 53.6 |
| | | | R.W. Smith | C | 8,507 | 46.4 |
| | | | | | 1,311 | 7.2 |
| 1924 | 28,658 | 71.7 | R.W. Smith | C | 9,130 | 44.4 |
| | | | M.M. Wood | L | 7,639 | 37.2 |
| | | | J. Newman | Lab | 3,791 | 18.4 |
| | | | | | 1,491 | 7.2 |
| 1929 | 39,182 | 63.0 | R.W. Smith | C | 10,773 | 43.6 |
| | | | F. Martin | L | 9,540 | 38.7 |
| | | | A.F. Macintosh | Lab | 4,357 | 17.7 |
| | | | | | 1,233 | 4.9 |
| 1931 | 38,098 | 76.8 | R.W. Smith | C | 16,501 | 56.4 |
| | | | R.C. Berkeley | L | 12,758 | 43.6 |
| | | | | | 3,743 | 12.8 |
| 1935 | 39,984 | 66.8 | Sir R.W. Smith | C | 14,697 | 55.0 |
| | | | G.G. Stott | Lab | 6,128 | 23.0 |
| | | | Dr. W.S.R. Thomas | L | 5,873 | 22.0 |
| | | | | | 8,569 | 32.0 |
| 1945 | 43,984 | 68.3 | H.R. Spence | C | 15,702 | 52.3 |
| | | | D.S. Hay | Lab | 7,997 | 26.6 |
| | | | I.R.M. Davies | L | 6,348 | 21.1 |
| | | | | | 7,705 | 25.7 |

| Election | Electors | T'out | Candidate | Party | Votes | % |
|---|---|---|---|---|---|---|
| 1918 | 25,622 | 34.2 | †Sir W.H. Cowan | Co L | 4,430 | 50.5 |
| | | | F.L. Wallace | Ind L | 4,343 | 49.5 |
| | | | | | 87 | 1.0 |
| 1922 | 29,230 | 45.3 | F. Martin | L | 8,018 | 60.5 |
| | | | Sir W.H. Cowan | NL | 5,227 | 39.5 |
| | | | | | 2,791 | 21.0 |
| 1923 | 27,318 | 57.6 | F. Martin | L | 8,793 | 55.9 |
| | | | F.L. Wallace | C | 6,949 | 44.1 |
| | | | | | 1,844 | 11.8 |
| 1924 | 27,026 | 59.0 | R.J.G. Boothby | C | 7,363 | 46.1 |
| | | | F. Martin | L | 4,680 | 29.4 |
| | | | W.S. Cormack | Lab | 3,899 | 24.5 |
| | | | | | 2,683 | 16.7 |
| 1929 | 35,039 | 67.0 | R.J.G. Boothby | C | 13,354 | 56.9 |
| | | | Rev. J.E. Hamilton | Lab | 10,110 | 43.1 |
| | | | | | 3,244 | 13.8 |
| 1931 | 34,527 | 65.7 | R.J.G. Boothby | C | 16,396 | 72.2 |
| | | | F. Martin | Lab | 6,299 | 27.8 |
| | | | | | 10,097 | 44.4 |
| 1935 | 35,839 | 62.4 | R.J.G. Boothby | C | 12,748 | 57.0 |
| | | | F. Martin | Lab | 9,627 | 43.0 |
| | | | | | 3,121 | 14.0 |
| 1945 | 36,837 | 65.7 | R.J.G. Boothby | C | 13,290 | 54.9 |
| | | | J.R. Allan | Lab | 10,918 | 45.1 |
| | | | | | 2,372 | 9.8 |

| Election | Electors | T'out | Candidate | Party | Votes | % |
|---|---|---|---|---|---|---|
| 1918 | | | †Hon. A.C. Murray | Co L (L) | Unopp. | |
| 1922 | 22,405 | 44.6 | Hon. A.C. Murray | L | 6,224 | 62.3 |
| | | | W. Mitchell | NL | 3,767 | 37.7 |
| | | | | | 2,457 | 24.6 |
| 1923 | 22,502 | 57.8 | C.M. Barclay-Harvey | C | 6,639 | 51.0 |
| | | | Hon. A.C. Murray | L | 6,369 | 49.0 |
| | | | | | 270 | 2.0 |
| 1924 | 22,502 | 67.3 | C.M. Barclay-Harvey | C | 8,260 | 54.5 |
| | | | J. Scott | L | 6,889 | 45.5 |
| | | | | | 1,371 | 9.0 |
| 1929 | 28,690 | 66.3 | J. Scott | L | 9,839 | 51.8 |
| | | | C.M. Barclay-Harvey | C | 9,171 | 48.2 |
| | | | | | 668 | 3.6 |
| 1931 | 28,749 | 80.5 | C.M. Barclay-Harvey | C | 14,266 | 61.6 |
| | | | J. Scott | L | 8,890 | 38.4 |
| | | | | | 5,376 | 23.2 |
| 1935 | 29,528 | 75.6 | C.M. Barclay-Harvey | C | 12,477 | 55.9 |
| | | | A.J. Irvine | L | 9,841 | 44.1 |
| | | | | | 2,636 | 11.8 |

[Resignation on appointment as Governor of South Australia]

| Election | Electors | T'out | Candidate | Party | Votes | % |
|---|---|---|---|---|---|---|
| 1939 (30/3) | 29,558 | 71.4 | C.N. Thornton-Kemsley | C | 11,111 | 52.7 |
| | | | A.J. Irvine | L | 9,990 | 47.3 |
| | | | | | 1,121 | 5.4 |
| 1945 | 30,901 | 68.7 | C.N. Thornton-Kemsley | C | 10,932 | 51.5 |
| | | | J.D.B. Junor | L | 10,290 | 48.5 |
| | | | | | 642 | 3.0 |

| Election | Electors | T'out | Candidate | Party | Votes | % |
|---|---|---|---|---|---|---|
| 1918 | 28,293 | 52.0 | W. Sutherland | Co L | 11,970 | 81.4 |
| | | | L.M. Weir | HLL | 2,733 | 18.6 |
| | | | | | 9,237 | 62.8 |

[Appointed a Lord Commissioner of the Treasury]

| | | | | | | |
|---|---|---|---|---|---|---|
| 1920 | 31,262 | 50.2 | Sir W. Sutherland | Co L | 10,187 | 64.9 |
| (10/3) | | | Rev. M. MacCallum | Lab | 5,498 | 35.1 |
| | | | | | 4,689 | 29.8 |
| 1922 | 32,333 | 51.8 | Rt. Hon. Sir W. Sutherland | NL | 9,848 | 58.8 |
| | | | H.A. Watt | L | 6,897 | 41.2 |
| | | | | | 2,951 | 17.6 |
| 1923 | 32,134 | 53.3 | Rt. Hon. Sir W. Sutherland | L | 9,020 | 52.7 |
| | | | F.A. Macquisten | C | 8,100 | 47.3 |
| | | | | | 920 | 5.4 |
| 1924 | 31,878 | 62.7 | F.A. Macquisten | C | 9,240 | 46.2 |
| | | | Rt. Hon. Sir W. Sutherland | L | 6,211 | 31.1 |
| | | | Dr. I.H. MacIver | Lab | 4,532 | 22.7 |
| | | | | | 3,029 | 15.1 |
| 1929 | 40,198 | 62.7 | F.A. Macquisten | C | 11,108 | 44.1 |
| | | | B.A. Murray | L | 8,089 | 32.1 |
| | | | J.L. Kinloch | Lab | 6,001 | 23.8 |
| | | | | | 3,019 | 12.0 |
| 1931 | | | F.A. Macquisten | C | Unopp. | |
| 1935 | 43,716 | 56.6 | F.A. Macquisten | C | 13,260 | 53.6 |
| | | | B.A. Murray | L | 11,486 | 46.4 |
| | | | | | 1,774 | 7.2 |

[Death]

| | | | | | | |
|---|---|---|---|---|---|---|
| 1940 | 41,005 | 47.9 | D. McCallum | C | 12,317 | 62.8 |
| (10/4) | | | W. Power | SNP | 7,308 | 37.2 |
| | | | | | 5,009 | 25.6 |
| 1945 | 43,822 | 63.7 | D. McCallum | C | 15,791 | 56.5 |
| | | | A.M. Weir | Lab | 8,889 | 31.9 |
| | | | J.M. Bannerman | L | 3,228* | 11.6 |
| | | | | | 6,902 | 24.6 |

| Election | Electors | T'out | Candidate | Party | Votes | % |
|---|---|---|---|---|---|---|
| 1918 | 37,158 | 55.3 | †Sir A.G. Hunter-Weston | Co C | 12,638 | 61.5 |
|  |  |  | R. Smith | Lab | 5,848 | 28.5 |
|  |  |  | H.F. Campbell | L | 2,059* | 10.0 |
|  |  |  |  |  | 6,790 | 33.0 |
| 1922 | 39,817 | 59.5 | Sir A.G. Hunter-Weston | C | 14,368 | 60.6 |
|  |  |  | J. Paton | Lab | 9,323 | 39.4 |
|  |  |  |  |  | 5,045 | 21.2 |
| 1923 | 39,685 | 55.9 | Sir A.G. Hunter-Weston | C | 12,320 | 55.6 |
|  |  |  | P.C. Stephen | Lab | 9,855 | 44.4 |
|  |  |  |  |  | 2,465 | 11.2 |
| 1924 | 40,076 | 65.6 | Sir A.G. Hunter-Weston | C | 16,203 | 61.7 |
|  |  |  | P.C. Stephen | Lab | 10,075 | 38.3 |
|  |  |  |  |  | 6,128 | 23.4 |
| 1929 | 50,032 | 65.2 | Sir A.G. Hunter-Weston | C | 18,331 | 56.2 |
|  |  |  | A. Sloan | Lab | 14,294 | 43.8 |
|  |  |  |  |  | 4,037 | 12.4 |
| 1931 | 51,095 | 67.9 | Sir A.G. Hunter-Weston | C | 24,467 | 70.5 |
|  |  |  | A. Sloan | ILP | 10,227 | 29.5 |
|  |  |  |  |  | 14,240 | 41.0 |
| 1935 | 53,682 | 66.6 | Sir C.G. MacAndrew | C | 22,391 | 62.6 |
|  |  |  | M. Shinwell | Lab | 13,358 | 37.4 |
|  |  |  |  |  | 9,033 | 25.2 |
| 1945 | 59,657 | 68.5 | Sir C.G. MacAndrew | C | 21,652 | 53.0 |
|  |  |  | J.T. Wheatley | Lab | 19,209 | 47.0 |
|  |  |  |  |  | 2,443 | 6.0 |

| Election | Electors | T'out | Candidate | Party | Votes | % |
|---|---|---|---|---|---|---|
| 1918 | 32,298 | 62.6 | †Hon. A. Shaw | Co L | 13,568 | 67.1 |
| | | | P. Malcolm | Co-op | 6,652 | 32.9 |
| | | | | | 6,916 | 34.2 |
| 1922 | 33,210 | 71.5 | Hon. A. Shaw | L | 12,991 | 54.7 |
| | | | R. Climie | Lab | 10,752 | 45.3 |
| | | | | | 2,239 | 9.4 |

[Seat Vacant at Dissolution (Resignation)]

| | | | | | | |
|---|---|---|---|---|---|---|
| 1923 | 33,652 | 75.7 | R. Climie | Lab | 10,992 | 43.2 |
| | | | Rt. Hon. Sir D. Maclean | L | 8,185 | 32.1 |
| | | | A.M. Mackay | C | 6,298 | 24.7 |
| | | | | | 2,807 | 11.1 |
| 1924 | 34,315 | 79.5 | C.G. MacAndrew | C | 14,237 | 52.2 |
| | | | R. Climie | Lab | 13,054 | 47.8 |
| | | | | | 1,183 | 4.4 |
| 1929 | 46,310 | 77.8 | R. Climie | Lab | 17,368 | 48.2 |
| | | | C.G. MacAndrew | C | 10,939 | 30.4 |
| | | | J.R. Rutherford | L | 7,700 | 21.4 |
| | | | | | 6,429 | 17.8 |

[Death]

| | | | | | | |
|---|---|---|---|---|---|---|
| 1929 (27/11) | 46,310 | 71.7 | Rt. Hon. C.M. Aitchison | Lab (N Lab) | 18,465 | 55.6 |
| | | | C.G. MacAndrew | C | 13,270 | 40.0 |
| | | | Mrs. I. Brown | Com | 1,448* | 4.4 |
| | | | | | 5,195 | 15.6 |
| 1931 | 46,006 | 79.5 | Rt. Hon. C.M. Aitchison | N Lab | 21,803 | 59.6 |
| | | | J. Pollock | ILP | 14,767 | 40.4 |
| | | | | | 7,036 | 19.2 |

[Resignation on appointment as Lord Justice Clerk — Lord Aitchison]

| | | | | | | |
|---|---|---|---|---|---|---|
| 1933 (2/11) | 46,796 | 77.3 | K.M. Lindsay | N Lab | 12,577 | 34.8 |
| | | | Rev. J. Barr | Lab | 9,924 | 27.4 |
| | | | J. Pollock | ILP | 7,575 | 20.9 |
| | | | Sir A.M. MacEwen | SNP & SP | 6,098 | 16.9 |
| | | | | | 2,653 | 7.4 |
| 1935 | 47,734 | 78.8 | K.M. Lindsay | N Lab (Nat Ind) | 19,115 | 50.9 |
| | | | J. Crawford | Lab | 12,558 | 33.4 |
| | | | J. Pollock | ILP | 3,582* | 9.5 |
| | | | T.W. Campbell | SNP | 2,346* | 6.2 |
| | | | | | 6,557 | 17.5 |
| 1945 | 52,721 | 76.1 | Mrs. C.M. Shaw | Lab | 23,837 | 59.4 |
| | | | G.E.O. Walker | C | 16,300 | 40.6 |
| | | | | | 7,537 | 18.8 |

[Resignation]

| | | | | | | |
|---|---|---|---|---|---|---|
| 1946 (5/12) | 55,022 | 68.4 | W. Ross | Lab | 22,456 | 59.7 |
| | | | G.E.O. Walker | C | 12,239 | 32.5 |
| | | | G. Dott | SNP | 2,932* | 7.8 |
| | | | | | 10,217 | 27.2 |

Notes:—
1929 (27/11): Aitchison was Lord Advocate.

## AYRSHIRE and BUTE, SOUTH AYRSHIRE [586]

| Election | Electors | T'out | Candidate | Party | Votes | % |
|---|---|---|---|---|---|---|
| 1918 | 27,691 | 61.5 | J. Brown | Lab | 6,358 | 37.3 |
| | | | J.B. Pollok-McCall | Co C | 5,495 | 32.3 |
| | | | W. Robertson | L | 4,555 | 26.7 |
| | | | H.R. Wallace | Ind C | 627* | 3.7 |
| | | | | | 863 | 5.0 |
| 1922 | 30,488 | 67.9 | J. Brown | Lab | 11,511 | 55.6 |
| | | | Sir W. Reid | NL | 9,180 | 44.4 |
| | | | | | 2,331 | 11.2 |
| 1923 | 30,419 | 65.7 | J. Brown | Lab | 11,169 | 55.9 |
| | | | Sir C. Fergusson, Bt. | C | 8,807 | 44.1 |
| | | | | | 2,362 | 11.8 |
| 1924 | 30,228 | 74.3 | J. Brown | Lab | 11,313 | 50.4 |
| | | | C.I.A. Dubs | C | 11,136 | 49.6 |
| | | | | | 177 | 0.8 |
| 1929 | 39,551 | 73.9 | J. Brown | Lab | 16,981 | 58.1 |
| | | | C.I.A. Dubs | C | 12,240 | 41.9 |
| | | | | | 4,741 | 16.2 |
| 1931 | 38,359 | 79.3 | J.O. MacAndrew | C | 16,675 | 54.8 |
| | | | Rt. Hon. J. Brown | Lab | 13,733 | 45.2 |
| | | | | | 2,942 | 9.6 |
| 1935 | 40,465 | 78.0 | Rt. Hon. J. Brown | Lab | 18,190 | 57.6 |
| | | | J.O. MacAndrew | C | 13,386 | 42.4 |
| | | | | | 4,804 | 15.2 |
| [Death] | | | | | | |
| 1939 (20/4) | 41,460 | 74.5 | A. Sloan | Lab | 17,908 | 58.0 |
| | | | Dr. Catherine I. Gavin | C | 12,986 | 42.0 |
| | | | | | 4,922 | 16.0 |
| 1945 | 46,137 | 75.0 | A. Sloan | Lab | 21,235 | 61.3 |
| | | | R. Mathew | C | 13,382 | 38.7 |
| | | | | | 7,853 | 22.6 |
| [Death] | | | | | | |
| 1946 (7/2) | 46,555 | 69.0 | E. Hughes | Lab | 20,434 | 63.6 |
| | | | R. Mathew | C | 11,705 | 36.4 |
| | | | | | 8,729 | 27.2 |

| Election | Electors | T'out | Candidate | Party | Votes | % |
|----------|----------|-------|-----------|-------|-------|---|
| 1918 | | | †C.C. Barrie | Co L | Unopp. | |
| 1922 | | | Sir C.C. Barrie | L | Unopp. | |
| 1923 | | | Sir C.C. Barrie | L | Unopp. | |
| 1924 | 28,855 | 55.4 | W.P. Templeton | C | 6,829 | 42.7 |
| | | | Sir C.C. Barrie | L | 5,426 | 34.0 |
| | | | Rev. A.W. Groundwater | Lab | 3,722 | 23.3 |
| | | | | | 1,403 | 8.7 |
| 1929 | 32,868 | 63.8 | M.M. Wood | L | 9,278 | 44.3 |
| | | | W.P. Templeton | C | 6,720 | 32.0 |
| | | | A.A. MacGregor | Lab | 4,982 | 23.7 |
| | | | | | 2,558 | 12.3 |
| 1931 | | | M.M. Wood | L | Unopp. | |
| 1935 | 32,518 | 70.5 | Sir J.E.R. Findlay, Bt. | C | 11,771 | 51.3 |
| | | | Sir M.M. Wood | L | 11,168 | 48.7 |
| | | | | | 603 | 2.6 |
| 1945 | 32,483 | 66.5 | W.S. Duthie | C | 10,689 | 49.5 |
| | | | I.A.D. Millar | L | 6,401 | 29.6 |
| | | | D. Macpherson | Lab | 4,524 | 20.9 |
| | | | | | 4,288 | 19.9 |

| Election | Electors | T'out | Candidate | Party | Votes | % |
|---|---|---|---|---|---|---|
| 1918 | 32,763 | 48.6 | †J.D. Hope | Co L | 8,584 | 53.9 |
| | | | R.W. Foulis | Lab | 4,783 | 30.0 |
| | | | †Rt. Hon. H.J. Tennant | L | 2,557 | 16.1 |
| | | | | | 3,801 | 23.9 |
| 1922 | 33,119 | 60.1 | W. Waring | NL | 6,342 | 31.9 |
| | | | R. Spence | Lab | 5,842 | 29.3 |
| | | | W.H. Pringle | L | 4,422 | 22.2 |
| | | | J.D. Hope | Ind L | 3,300 | 16.6 |
| | | | | | 500 | 2.6 |
| 1923 | 33,381 | 69.4 | R. Spence | Lab | 8,576 | 37.0 |
| | | | C. de W. Crookshank | C | 8,508 | 36.7 |
| | | | W. Waring | L | 6,084 | 26.3 |
| | | | | | 68 | 0.3 |
| 1924 | 34,017 | 75.3 | C. de W. Crookshank | C | 11,745 | 45.8 |
| | | | R. Spence | Lab | 8,882 | 34.7 |
| | | | W.H. Pringle | L | 4,986 | 19.5 |
| | | | | | 2,863 | 11.1 |
| 1929 | 45,043 | 69.6 | G. Sinkinson | Lab | 11,761 | 37.5 |
| | | | J.H.F. McEwen | C | 11,435 | 36.5 |
| | | | Sir J.W. Greig | L | 8,132 | 26.0 |
| | | | | | 326 | 1.0 |
| 1931 | 45,797 | 74.8 | J.H.F. McEwen | C | 25,169 | 73.5 |
| | | | G. Sinkinson | Lab | 9,089 | 26.5 |
| | | | | | 16,080 | 47.0 |
| 1935 | 47,447 | 71.9 | J.H.F. McEwen | C | 19,839 | 58.1 |
| | | | J.J. Fraser | Lab | 14,299 | 41.9 |
| | | | | | 5,540 | 16.2 |
| 1945 | 49,641 | 70.3 | J.J. Robertson | Lab | 19,037 | 54.5 |
| | | | J.H.F. McEwen | C | 15,880 | 45.5 |
| | | | | | 3,157 | 9.0 |

Note:—

1922: Hope had been refused re-adoption by the local Liberal Association and the Conservative Association in the constituency also declined to support him. As a result he decided to contest the seat as an Independent Liberal.

| Election | Electors | T'out | Candidate | Party | Votes | % |
|----------|----------|-------|-----------|-------|-------|---|
| 1918 | 21,237 | 50.9 | †Sir R.L. Harmsworth, Bt. | Co L | 6,769 | 62.6 |
| | | | F.J. Robertson | L | 4,036 | 37.4 |
| | | | | | 2,733 | 25.2 |
| 1922 | 22,501 | 60.1 | Sir A.H.M. Sinclair, Bt. | NL | 7,715 | 57.1 |
| | | | Sir R.L. Harmsworth, Bt. | L | 5,803 | 42.9 |
| | | | | | 1,912 | 14.2 |
| 1923 | | | Sir A.H.M. Sinclair, Bt. | L | Unopp. | |
| 1924 | | | Sir A.H.M. Sinclair, Bt. | L | Unopp. | |
| 1929 | 27,399 | 66.5 | Sir A.H.M. Sinclair, Bt. | L | 13,462 | 73.9 |
| | | | J.A.L. Duncan | C | 3,041 | 16.7 |
| | | | C.G. Oman | Ind Lab | 1,711* | 9.4 |
| | | | | | 10,421 | 57.2 |
| 1931 | | | Rt. Hon. Sir A.H.M. Sinclair, Bt. | L | Unopp. | |
| 1935 | 27,811 | 60.0 | Rt. Hon. Sir A.H.M. Sinclair, Bt. | L | 12,071 | 72.3 |
| | | | W. Bruce | Nat | 4,621 | 27.7 |
| | | | | | 7,450 | 44.6 |
| 1945 | 25,989 | 64.0 | E.L. Gandar-Dower | C (Ind) | 5,564 | 33.5 |
| | | | R.I.A. MacInnes | Lab | 5,558 | 33.4 |
| | | | Rt. Hon. Sir A.H.M. Sinclair, Bt. | L | 5,503 | 33.1 |
| | | | | | 6 | 0.1 |

Note:—

1929: Oman was the nominee of the Wick branch of the ILP. His candidature was not however endorsed by the Labour Party.

# DUMFRIESSHIRE [590]

| Election | Electors | T'out | Candidate | Party | Votes | % |
|---|---|---|---|---|---|---|
| 1918 | 36,394 | 57.4 | W. Murray | Co C | 13,345 | 63.8 |
| | | | †Rt. Hon. J.W. Gulland | L | 7,562 | 36.2 |
| | | | | | 5,783 | 27.6 |
| 1922 | 33,113 | 73.5 | Dr. W.A. Chapple | L | 13,296 | 54.6 |
| | | | H. Keswick | C | 11,055 | 45.4 |
| | | | | | 2,241 | 9.2 |
| 1923 | 33,728 | 72.6 | Dr. W.A. Chapple | L | 13,107 | 53.5 |
| | | | J. Charteris | C | 11,380 | 46.5 |
| | | | | | 1,727 | 7.0 |
| 1924 | 34,079 | 80.8 | J. Charteris | C | 12,718 | 46.2 |
| | | | Dr. W.A. Chapple | L | 8,472 | 30.8 |
| | | | Mrs. A.J. Dollan | Lab | 6,342 | 23.0 |
| | | | | | 4,246 | 15.4 |
| 1929 | 44,050 | 81.4 | Dr. J. Hunter | L | 16,174 | 45.1 |
| | | | J. Charteris | C | 12,984 | 36.2 |
| | | | W.H. Marwick | Lab | 6,687 | 18.7 |
| | | | | | 3,190 | 8.9 |
| 1931 | 44,564 | 77.6 | Dr. J. Hunter | L (NL) | 26,873 | 77.7 |
| | | | J.S. Paterson | Lab | 7,693 | 22.3 |
| | | | | | 19,180 | 55.4 |
| [Death] | | | | | | |
| 1935 (12/9) | 45,904 | 58.7 | Sir H. Fildes | NL | 16,271 | 60.3 |
| | | | J. Downie | Lab/Co-op | 10,697 | 39.7 |
| | | | | | 5,574 | 20.6 |
| 1935 | 45,847 | 73.6 | Sir H. Fildes | NL | 22,053 | 65.4 |
| | | | J. Downie | Lab/Co-op | 11,685 | 34.6 |
| | | | | | 10,368 | 30.8 |
| 1945 | 48,092 | 72.2 | N.M.S. Macpherson | NL | 16,465 | 47.4 |
| | | | D. Dunwoodie | Lab/Co-op | 12,388 | 35.7 |
| | | | I. McColl | L | 5,850 | 16.9 |
| | | | | | 4,077 | 11.7 |

| Election | Electors | T'out | Candidate | Party | Votes | % |
|---|---|---|---|---|---|---|
| 1918 | 34,284 | 66.8 | Sir W.H. Raeburn | Co C | 12,765 | 55.8 |
| | | | W.H.P. Martin | Lab | 7,072 | 30.9 |
| | | | †A.A. Allen | L | 3,048 | 13.3 |
| | | | | | 5,693 | 24.9 |
| 1922 | 38,559 | 69.0 | Sir W.H. Raeburn | C | 13,407 | 50.4 |
| | | | W.H.P. Martin | Lab | 13,216 | 49.6 |
| | | | | | 191 | 0.8 |
| 1923 | 38,539 | 70.7 | W.H.P. Martin | Lab | 11,705 | 43.0 |
| | | | D.P. Fleming | C | 9,802 | 36.0 |
| | | | J.S. Holmes | L | 5,726 | 21.0 |
| | | | | | 1,903 | 7.0 |
| 1924 | 38,469 | 75.6 | D.P. Fleming | C | 16,223 | 55.8 |
| | | | W.H.P. Martin | Lab | 12,872 | 44.2 |
| | | | | | 3,351 | 11.6 |

[Resignation on appointment as a Senator of the College of Justice — Lord Fleming]

| Election | Electors | T'out | Candidate | Party | Votes | % |
|---|---|---|---|---|---|---|
| 1926 | 35,239 | 75.0 | J.G. Thom | C | 12,680 | 48.0 |
| (29/1) | | | W.H.P. Martin | Lab | 11,610 | 43.9 |
| | | | W. Reid | L | 2,146* | 8.1 |
| | | | | | 1,070 | 4.1 |
| 1929 | 49,113 | 81.0 | W. Brooke | Lab | 18,153 | 45.7 |
| | | | J.G. Thom | C | 16,576 | 41.6 |
| | | | H.W. Guthrie | L | 5,071 | 12.7 |
| | | | | | 1,577 | 4.1 |
| 1931 | 54,625 | 82.8 | J.G. Thom | C | 28,762 | 63.6 |
| | | | W. Brooke | Lab | 16,474 | 36.4 |
| | | | | | 12,288 | 27.2 |

[Resignation on appointment as a High Court Judge in India]

| Election | Electors | T'out | Candidate | Party | Votes | % |
|---|---|---|---|---|---|---|
| 1932 | 54,625 | 70.5 | Hon. A.D. Cochrane | C | 16,749 | 43.5 |
| (17/3) | | | Rt. Hon. T. Johnston | Lab | 13,704 | 35.6 |
| | | | R. Gray | SNP | 5,178 | 13.4 |
| | | | H. McIntyre | Com | 2,870* | 7.5 |
| | | | | | 3,045 | 7.9 |
| 1935 | 61,216 | 80.5 | Hon. A.D. Cochrane | C | 24,776 | 50.3 |
| | | | T. Cassells | Lab | 20,679 | 41.9 |
| | | | R. Gray | SNP | 3,841* | 7.8 |
| | | | | | 4,097 | 8.4 |

[Resignation on appointment as Governor of Burma]

| Election | Electors | T'out | Candidate | Party | Votes | % |
|---|---|---|---|---|---|---|
| 1936 | 61,216 | 68.6 | T. Cassells | Lab | 20,187 | 48.1 |
| (18/3) | | | A.P. Duffes | C | 19,203 | 45.7 |
| | | | R. Gray | SNP | 2,599* | 6.2 |
| | | | | | 984 | 2.4 |

[Resignation on appointment as Sheriff Substitute of Inverness-shire, Moray and Nairn]

| Election | Electors | T'out | Candidate | Party | Votes | % |
|---|---|---|---|---|---|---|
| 1941 | 66,510 | 38.7 | A.S. McKinlay | Lab | 21,900 | 85.0 |
| (27/2) | | | M. MacEwen | Com | 3,862 | 15.0 |
| | | | | | 18,038 | 70.0 |
| 1945 | 78,100 | 71.7 | A.S. McKinlay | Lab | 28,383 | 50.7 |
| | | | R.A. Allan | C | 27,636 | 49.3 |
| | | | | | 747 | 1.4 |

# FIFE, EASTERN  [592]

| Election | Electors | T'out | Candidate | Party | Votes | % |
|---|---|---|---|---|---|---|
| 1918 | 30,689 | 54.0 | Sir A. Sprot, Bt. | C | 8,996 | 54.2 |
| | | | †Rt. Hon. H.H. Asquith | L | 6,994 | 42.2 |
| | | | W.P. Morgan | Ind Prog | 591* | 3.6 |
| | | | | | 2,002 | 12.0 |
| 1922 | 33,772 | 67.2 | J.D. Millar | L | 12,697 | 56.0 |
| | | | Sir A. Sprot, Bt. | C | 9,987 | 44.0 |
| | | | | | 2,710 | 12.0 |
| 1923 | 34,068 | 67.8 | J.D. Millar | L | 12,825 | 55.5 |
| | | | Sir A. Sprot, Bt. | C | 10,275 | 44.5 |
| | | | | | 2,550 | 11.0 |
| 1924 | 34,555 | 69.2 | Hon. A.D. Cochrane | C | 12,664 | 53.0 |
| | | | J.D. Millar | L | 11,242 | 47.0 |
| | | | | | 1,422 | 6.0 |
| 1929 | 45,612 | 73.3 | J.D. Millar | L (NL) | 14,329 | 42.9 |
| | | | Hon. A.D. Cochrane | C | 13,748 | 41.1 |
| | | | W.R. Garson | Lab | 5,350 | 16.0 |
| | | | | | 581 | 1.8 |
| 1931 [Death] | | | J.D. Millar | NL | Unopp. | |
| 1933 (2/2) | 46,011 | 65.6 | J. Henderson-Stewart | NL | 15,770 | 52.2 |
| | | | J.C. Westwood | Lab | 6,635 | 22.0 |
| | | | J.L. Anderson | Agric P | 4,404 | 14.6 |
| | | | D.E. Keir | Ind L | 2,296* | 7.6 |
| | | | E. Linklater | SNP | 1,083* | 3.6 |
| | | | | | 9,135 | 30.2 |
| 1935 | 47,807 | 71.0 | J. Henderson-Stewart | NL | 27,915 | 82.3 |
| | | | A.K. Davidson | Lab | 6,016 | 17.7 |
| | | | | | 21,899 | 64.6 |
| 1945 | 50,387 | 70.8 | J. Henderson-Stewart | NL | 24,765 | 69.4 |
| | | | S.P. McLaren | Lab/Co-op | 10,920 | 30.6 |
| | | | | | 13,845 | 38.8 |

Note:—

1933:  Keir was opposed to the National Government.

| Election | Electors | T'out | Candidate | Party | Votes | % |
|---|---|---|---|---|---|---|
| 1918 | 30,452 | 48.2 | †Rt. Hon. W. Adamson | Lab | 10,664 | 72.6 |
| | | | J.H. Menzies | Co C | 4,020 | 27.4 |
| | | | | | 6,644 | 45.2 |
| 1922 | | | Rt. Hon. W. Adamson | Lab | Unopp. | |
| 1923 | 32,491 | 57.4 | Rt. Hon. W. Adamson | Lab | 12,204 | 65.4 |
| | | | P. Hodge | Ind Lab | 6,459 | 34.6 |
| | | | | | 5,745 | 30.8 |
| 1924 | 32,882 | 63.0 | Rt. Hon. W. Adamson | Lab | 14,685 | 70.9 |
| | | | J. MacRobert | C | 6,015 | 29.1 |
| | | | | | 8,670 | 41.8 |
| 1929 | 42,252 | 69.7 | Rt. Hon. W. Adamson | Lab | 17,668 | 60.0 |
| | | | W. Gallacher | Com | 6,040 | 20.5 |
| | | | A.B. Brown | C | 5,727 | 19.5 |
| | | | | | 11,628 | 39.5 |
| 1931 | 43,237 | 71.4 | C. Milne | C | 12,977 | 42.1 |
| | | | Rt. Hon. W. Adamson | Lab | 11,063 | 35.8 |
| | | | W. Gallacher | Com | 6,829 | 22.1 |
| | | | | | 1,914 | 6.3 |
| 1935 | 46,281 | 77.8 | W. Gallacher | Com | 13,462 | 37.4 |
| | | | Rt. Hon. W. Adamson | Lab | 12,869 | 35.7 |
| | | | C. Milne | C | 9,667 | 26.9 |
| | | | | | 593 | 1.7 |
| 1945 | 55,419 | 75.4 | W. Gallacher | Com | 17,636 | 42.1 |
| | | | W.W. Hamilton | Lab | 15,580 | 37.3 |
| | | | Dr. R.S. Stevenson | NL | 8,597 | 20.6 |
| | | | | | 2,056 | 4.8 |

Note:—

1923: Hodge was the nominee of the Fife, Kinross and Clackmannan Mineworkers' Reform Union, a breakaway movement from the Fife, Kinross and Clackmannan Miners' Association of which Adamson was General Secretary.

| Election | Electors | T'out | Candidate | Party | Votes | % |
|----------|----------|-------|-----------|-------|-------|---|
| 1918 | 24,611 | 44.2 | W.T. Shaw | C | 5,697 | 52.4 |
|  |  |  | †J. Falconer | L | 5,179 | 47.6 |
|  |  |  |  |  | 518 | 4.8 |
| 1922 | 24,040 | 65.0 | J. Falconer | L | 8,567 | 54.8 |
|  |  |  | W.T. Shaw | C | 7,071 | 45.2 |
|  |  |  |  |  | 1,496 | 9.6 |
| 1923 | 23,828 | 60.3 | J. Falconer | L | 7,605 | 52.9 |
|  |  |  | W.T. Shaw | C | 6,758 | 47.1 |
|  |  |  |  |  | 847 | 5.8 |
| 1924 | 23,916 | 68.3 | Sir H. Hope | C | 8,022 | 49.1 |
|  |  |  | J. Falconer | L | 4,581 | 28.0 |
|  |  |  | C.N. Gallie | Lab | 3,736 | 22.9 |
|  |  |  |  |  | 3,441 | 21.1 |
| 1929 | 29,737 | 70.7 | Sir H. Hope | C | 8,852 | 42.2 |
|  |  |  | W. Scott | L | 6,901 | 32.8 |
|  |  |  | C.N. Gallie | Lab | 5,257 | 25.0 |
|  |  |  |  |  | 1,951 | 9.4 |
| 1931 | 30,114 | 75.2 | W.T. Shaw | C | 13,912 | 61.4 |
|  |  |  | W. Scott | L | 8,731 | 38.6 |
|  |  |  |  |  | 5,181 | 22.8 |
| 1935 | 31,381 | 71.5 | W.T. Shaw | C | 13,505 | 60.2 |
|  |  |  | W. Scott | L | 8,922 | 39.8 |
|  |  |  |  |  | 4,583 | 20.4 |
| 1945 | 38,286 | 68.9 | Hon. S. Ramsay | C | 13,615 | 51.6 |
|  |  |  | E.S. Douglas | Lab | 8,199 | 31.1 |
|  |  |  | C.P. Fothergill | L | 4,575 | 17.3 |
|  |  |  |  |  | 5,416 | 20.5 |

Note:—

1918:   Shaw's name was incorrectly included in the final official list of Coalition candidates. He did not receive a 'coupon'.

# GALLOWAY [595]

## (Kirkcudbrightshire and Wigtownshire)

| Election | Electors | T'out | Candidate | Party | Votes | % |
|---|---|---|---|---|---|---|
| 1918 | | | †G. McMicking | Co L | Unopp. | |
| 1922 | 29,645 | 77.5 | C.R. Dudgeon | L | 12,406 | 54.0 |
| | | | Rt. Hon. W. Watson | C | 10,557 | 46.0 |
| | | | | | 1,849 | 8.0 |
| 1923 | | | C.R. Dudgeon | L | Unopp. | |
| 1924 | 30,107 | 76.8 | Sir A.J. Henniker-Hughan, Bt. | C | 12,268 | 53.1 |
| | | | C.R. Dudgeon | L | 10,852 | 46.9 |
| | | | | | 1,416 | 6.2 |
| [Death] | | | | | | |
| 1925 | 29,992 | 83.3 | S.R. Streatfeild | C | 10,846 | 43.5 |
| (17/11) | | | C.R. Dudgeon | L | 9,918 | 39.7 |
| | | | J. Mitchell | Lab | 4,207 | 16.8 |
| | | | | | 928 | 3.8 |
| 1929 | 39,621 | 80.1 | C.R. Dudgeon | L | 13,461 | 42.4 |
| | | | S.R. Streatfeild | C | 13,360 | 42.1 |
| | | | H. McNeill | Lab | 4,903 | 15.5 |
| | | | | | 101 | 0.3 |
| 1931 | 40,312 | 80.6 | J.H. Mackie | C | 18,903 | 58.3 |
| | | | E.M. Campbell | L | 9,176 | 28.2 |
| | | | H. McNeill | Lab | 3,418* | 10.5 |
| | | | C.R. Dudgeon | NP | 986* | 3.0 |
| | | | | | 9,727 | 30.1 |
| 1935 | | | J.H. Mackie | C | Unopp. | |
| 1945 | 47,922 | 69.9 | J.H. Mackie | Ind C (C) | 13,647 | 40.7 |
| | | | R.N. Hales | Lab | 11,822 | 35.3 |
| | | | B.E. Fergusson | C | 8,032 | 24.0 |
| | | | | | 1,825 | 5.4 |

Notes:—

1929: Dudgeon resigned from the Liberal Party and joined the New Party immediately following the announcement of a Dissolution.

1945: Mackie had been refused re-adoption by the local Conservative Association and he decided to contest the seat as an Independent Conservative. In March 1948 he was granted the Conservative whip.

| Election | Electors | T'out | Candidate | Party | Votes | % |
|---|---|---|---|---|---|---|
| 1918 | 29,263 | 37.3 | †T.B. Morison | Co L | 7,991 | 73.2 |
| | | | G.J. Bruce | HLL | 2,930 | 26.8 |
| | | | | | 5,061 | 46.4 |

[Resignation on appointment as a Senator of the College of Justice — Lord Morison]

| Election | Electors | T'out | Candidate | Party | Votes | % |
|---|---|---|---|---|---|---|
| 1922 (16/3) | 32,695[†] | 50.1 | Sir M. Macdonald | Co L | 8,340 | 51.0 |
| | | | A.H. Livingstone | L | 8,024 | 49.0 |
| | | | | | 316 | 2.0 |
| 1922 | 34,244 | 54.3 | Sir M. Macdonald | NL | 9,796 | 52.7 |
| | | | A.M. Livingstone | L | 8,785 | 47.3 |
| | | | | | 1,011 | 5.4 |
| 1923 | 33,230 | 46.9 | Sir M. Macdonald | L | 10,194 | 65.4 |
| | | | A.D. Kinloch | Lab | 5,385 | 34.6 |
| | | | | | 4,809 | 30.8 |
| 1924 | 33,875 | 54.1 | Sir M. Macdonald | L | 11,468 | 62.6 |
| | | | T. Henderson | Lab | 6,863 | 37.4 |
| | | | | | 4,605 | 25.2 |
| 1929 | 43,387 | 58.6 | Sir M. Macdonald | L (NL) | 14,042 | 55.3 |
| | | | D.N. Mackay | Lab | 11,369 | 44.7 |
| | | | | | 2,673 | 10.6 |
| 1931 | 46,289 | 61.9 | Sir M. Macdonald | NL | 18,702 | 65.3 |
| | | | D.N. Mackay | Lab | 5,941 | 20.7 |
| | | | J.M. MacCormick | SNP | 4,016 | 14.0 |
| | | | | | 12,761 | 44.6 |
| 1935 | 45,930 | 57.8 | Sir M. Macdonald | NL (Ind L) | 14,985 | 56.4 |
| | | | H. Fraser | Lab | 7,297 | 27.5 |
| | | | J.M. MacCormick | SNP | 4,273 | 16.1 |
| | | | | | 7,688 | 28.9 |
| 1945 | 47,335 | 59.0 | Sir M. Macdonald | Ind L | 12,090 | 43.2 |
| | | | N.G. Maclean | Lab | 9,655 | 34.6 |
| | | | J.M. MacCormick | L | 6,200 | 22.2 |
| | | | | | 2,435 | 8.6 |

Note:—

1935-
1945:   Macdonald announced his resignation from the National Liberal Parliamentary Party in March 1942 but emphasized that he would remain an adherent of the party in the country and preserve his National Liberal 'label'.

Prior to the General Election, the local Liberal Association decided to adopt MacCormick in preference to Macdonald. As a result of this decision a number of people who had supported him formed a new Liberal Association and he was adopted as an Independent Liberal pledged to support Churchill.

| Election | Electors | T'out | Candidate | Party | Votes | % |
|---|---|---|---|---|---|---|
| 1918 | 20,685 | 51.2 | †Rt. Hon. J.I. Macpherson | Co L | 8,358 | 78.9 |
| | | | H. Munro | HLL | 2,238 | 21.1 |
| | | | | | 6,120 | 57.8 |
| 1922 | 24,624 | 42.4 | Rt. Hon. J.I. Macpherson | NL | 5,923 | 56.7 |
| | | | J. Macdonald | L | 4,521 | 43.3 |
| | | | | | 1,402 | 13.4 |
| 1923 | | | Rt. Hon. J.I. Macpherson | L | Unopp. | |
| 1924 | | | Rt. Hon. J.I. Macpherson | L | Unopp. | |
| 1929 | 29,281 | 55.6 | Rt. Hon. J.I. Macpherson | L (NL) | 9,564 | 58.8 |
| | | | H.D. MacIntosh | Lab | 6,710 | 41.2 |
| | | | | | 2,854 | 17.6 |
| 1931 | | | Rt. Hon. J.I. Macpherson | NL | Unopp. | |
| 1935 | 27,754 | 50.8 | Rt. Hon. Sir J.I. Macpherson,Bt. | NL | 10,810 | 76.7 |
| | | | J.M. MacDiarmid | Lab | 3,284 | 23.3 |
| | | | | | 7,526 | 53.4 |

[Elevation to the Peerage — Lord Strathcarron]

| Election | Electors | T'out | Candidate | Party | Votes | % |
|---|---|---|---|---|---|---|
| 1936 (10/2) | 27,754 | 65.1 | Rt. Hon. M.J. MacDonald | N Lab (Nat) | 8,949 | 49.5 |
| | | | H. McNeil | Lab | 5,967 | 33.0 |
| | | | R.F.E.S. Churchill | C | 2,427 | 13.4 |
| | | | Dr. W.S.R. Thomas | L | 738* | 4.1 |
| | | | | | 2,982 | 16.5 |
| 1945 | 25,866 | 61.9 | J. MacLeod | Ind L | 10,061 | 62.8 |
| | | | A.M. Mackintosh | Lab | 5,959 | 37.2 |
| | | | | | 4,102 | 25.6 |

Notes:—

1936:  MacDonald was Secretary of State for the Dominions.

Churchill was the nominee of the local Conservative Association who refused to support MacDonald as the official candidate of the National Government.

1945:  MacLeod was the nominee of the local Liberal Association which was an independent organisation and not affilliated to either the Liberal or National Liberal parties. He declared himself a supporter of Churchill and in the House of Commons aligned himself with the National Liberal group.

| Election | Electors | T'out | Candidate | Party | Votes | % |
|---|---|---|---|---|---|---|
| 1918 | 18,236 | 43.6 | Dr. D. Murray | L | 3,765 | 47.3 |
| | | | W.D.M. Cotts | Co L | 3,375 | 42.5 |
| | | | H. McCowan | HLL | 809* | 10.2 |
| | | | | | 390 | 4.8 |
| 1922 | 21,089 | 54.1 | Sir W.D.M. Cotts, Bt. | NL | 6,177 | 54.1 |
| | | | Dr. D. Murray | L | 5,238 | 45.9 |
| | | | | | 939 | 8.2 |
| 1923 | 21,359 | 40.1 | A.M. Livingstone | L | 3,391 | 39.6 |
| | | | W.S. Morrison | C | 3,158 | 36.9 |
| | | | H. McCowan | Ind Lab | 2,011 | 23.5 |
| | | | | | 233 | 2.7 |
| 1924 | 21,604 | 39.1 | A.M. Livingstone | L | 4,579 | 54.2 |
| | | | W.S. Morrison | C | 2,418 | 28.6 |
| | | | A.G. Burns | Lab | 1,454 | 17.2 |
| | | | | | 2,161 | 25.6 |
| 1929 | 27,284 | 40.5 | T.B.W. Ramsay | L (NL) | 4,877 | 44.1 |
| | | | J.M. MacDiarmid | Lab | 3,589 | 32.5 |
| | | | I.M. Moffatt-Pender | C | 2,593 | 23.4 |
| | | | | | 1,288 | 11.6 |
| 1931 | 28,720 | 36.8 | T.B.W. Ramsay | NL | 5,793 | 54.8 |
| | | | I.M. Moffatt-Pender | C | 4,785 | 45.2 |
| | | | | | 1,008 | 9.6 |
| 1935 | 28,195 | 46.8 | M.K. Macmillan | Lab | 5,421 | 41.0 |
| | | | T.B.W. Ramsay | NL | 4,076 | 30.9 |
| | | | Sir A.M. MacEwen | SNP | 3,704 | 28.1 |
| | | | | | 1,345 | 10.1 |
| 1945 | 24,311 | 53.3 | M.K. Macmillan | Lab | 5,914 | 45.7 |
| | | | H.M. Sinclair | L | 4,277 | 33.0 |
| | | | I.N. Macleod | C | 2,756 | 21.3 |
| | | | | | 1,637 | 12.7 |

Note:—

1923: McCowan was the nominee of the Stornoway branch of the ILP. His candidature was not however endorsed by the Labour Party.

| Election | Electors | T'out | Candidate | Party | Votes | % |
|---|---|---|---|---|---|---|
| 1918 | 26,572 | 69.2 | D.H. Macdonald | Co C | 9,359 | 50.9 |
| | | | J. Robertson | Lab | 9,027 | 49.1 |
| | | | | | 332 | 1.8 |
| [Death] | | | | | | |
| 1919 (16/7) | 26,572[†] | 71.9 | J. Robertson | Lab | 13,135 | 68.8 |
| | | | J. Moffat | Co L | 5,967 | 31.2 |
| | | | | | 7,168 | 37.6 |
| 1922 | 31,149 | 78.2 | J. Robertson | Lab | 13,872 | 57.0 |
| | | | P.D. Ridge-Beedle | C | 10,484 | 43.0 |
| | | | | | 3,388 | 14.0 |
| 1923 | 32,342 | 73.1 | J. Robertson | Lab | 14,211 | 60.2 |
| | | | P.D. Ridge-Beedle | C | 7,569 | 32.0 |
| | | | J.D. Scott | L | 1,846* | 7.8 |
| | | | | | 6,642 | 28.2 |
| 1924 | 32,665 | 79.3 | J. Robertson | Lab | 14,591 | 56.3 |
| | | | Mrs. H.B. Shaw | C | 11,314 | 43.7 |
| | | | | | 3,277 | 12.6 |
| [Death] | | | | | | |
| 1926 (26/3) | 33,505 | 74.2 | J. Sullivan | Lab | 14,830 | 59.7 |
| | | | A.M. Mackay | C | 8,740 | 35.2 |
| | | | E.J. Young | L | 1,276* | 5.1 |
| | | | | | 6,090 | 24.5 |
| 1929 | 42,312 | 72.7 | J. Sullivan | Lab | 17,006 | 55.2 |
| | | | Mrs. H.B. Shaw | C | 12,077 | 39.3 |
| | | | Mrs. H. Crawfurd | Com | 1,677* | 5.5 |
| | | | | | 4,929 | 15.9 |
| 1931 | 42,668 | 77.7 | Mrs. H.B. Shaw | C | 16,571 | 50.0 |
| | | | J. Sullivan | Lab | 14,423 | 43.5 |
| | | | B. McCourt | Com | 2,163* | 6.5 |
| | | | | | 2,148 | 6.5 |
| 1935 | 44,080 | 78.6 | J.C. Welsh | Lab | 20,900 | 60.3 |
| | | | Mrs. H.B. Shaw | C | 13,761 | 39.7 |
| | | | | | 7,139 | 20.6 |
| 1945 | 52,854 | 73.0 | J. Timmons | Lab | 25,369 | 65.8 |
| | | | Mrs. H.B. Shaw | C | 13,207 | 34.2 |
| | | | | | 12,162 | 31.6 |

# LANARKSHIRE, COATBRIDGE [600]

| Election | Electors | T'out | Candidate | Party | Votes | % |
|---|---|---|---|---|---|---|
| 1918 | 31,557 | 64.8 | A.L.H. Buchanan | Co C | 13,188 | 64.5 |
|  |  |  | O. Coyle | Lab | 7,254 | 35.5 |
|  |  |  |  |  | 5,934 | 29.0 |
| 1922 | 30,650 | 80.1 | J.C. Welsh | Lab | 12,038 | 49.0 |
|  |  |  | A.L.H. Buchanan | C | 9,724 | 39.6 |
|  |  |  | D.P. Blades | L | 2,802* | 11.4 |
|  |  |  |  |  | 2,314 | 9.4 |
| 1923 | 30,892 | 71.7 | J.C. Welsh | Lab | 12,292 | 55.5 |
|  |  |  | J.B. Young | C | 9,865 | 44.5 |
|  |  |  |  |  | 2,427 | 11.0 |
| 1924 | 30,356 | 84.0 | J.C. Welsh | Lab | 12,782 | 50.1 |
|  |  |  | T.C.R. Moore | C | 12,725 | 49.9 |
|  |  |  |  |  | 57 | 0.2 |
| 1929 | 37,299 | 82.3 | J.C. Welsh | Lab | 16,879 | 55.0 |
|  |  |  | Lord Dunglass | C | 9,210 | 30.0 |
|  |  |  | R. Irvine | L | 4,610 | 15.0 |
|  |  |  |  |  | 7,669 | 25.0 |
| 1931 | 37,911 | 83.4 | W.P. Templeton | C | 16,223 | 51.3 |
|  |  |  | J.C. Welsh | Lab | 14,722 | 46.6 |
|  |  |  | W.W. Gilmour | NP | 674* | 2.1 |
|  |  |  |  |  | 1,501 | 4.7 |
| 1935 | 39,029 | 78.5 | Rev. J. Barr | Lab | 17,535 | 57.2 |
|  |  |  | T.D.K. Murray | C | 13,121 | 42.8 |
|  |  |  |  |  | 4,414 | 14.4 |
| 1945 | 40,104 | 76.0 | Mrs. J. Mann | Lab | 18,619 | 61.1 |
|  |  |  | R.S. Russell | C | 11,842 | 38.9 |
|  |  |  |  |  | 6,777 | 22.2 |

# LANARKSHIRE, HAMILTON [601]

| Election | Electors | T'out | Candidate | Party | Votes | % |
|---|---|---|---|---|---|---|
| 1918 | 25,013 | 66.4 | D.M. Graham | Lab | 6,988 | 42.1 |
| | | | H.S. Keith | Co C | 4,819 | 29.0 |
| | | | D. Gilmour | NDP | 4,297 | 25.9 |
| | | | †J.H. Whitehouse | Ind L | 504* | 3.0 |
| | | | | | 2,169 | 13.1 |
| 1922 | 27,385 | 78.3 | D.M. Graham | Lab | 12,365 | 57.6 |
| | | | Sir H.S. Keith | C | 9,089 | 42.4 |
| | | | | | 3,276 | 15.2 |
| 1923 | 27,617 | 73.5 | D.M. Graham | Lab | 11,858 | 58.4 |
| | | | Miss H. Fraser | L | 8,436 | 41.6 |
| | | | | | 3,422 | 16.8 |
| 1924 | 27,930 | 76.5 | D.M. Graham | Lab | 13,003 | 60.8 |
| | | | A.D. Gibb | C | 8,372 | 39.2 |
| | | | | | 4,631 | 21.6 |
| 1929 | 34,248 | 72.2 | D.M. Graham | Lab | 16,595 | 67.1 |
| | | | R. McLellan | C | 7,752 | 31.3 |
| | | | F. Moore | Com | 395* | 1.6 |
| | | | | | 8,843 | 35.8 |
| 1931 | 34,004 | 77.7 | D.M. Graham | Lab | 14,233 | 53.9 |
| | | | R.H.S. Calver | C | 12,180 | 46.1 |
| | | | | | 2,053 | 7.8 |
| 1935 | 35,041 | 74.0 | D.M. Graham | Lab | 17,049 | 65.7 |
| | | | R.H.S. Calver | C | 8,884 | 34.3 |
| | | | | | 8,165 | 31.4 |
| [Death] | | | | | | |
| 1943 (29/1) | 35,934 | 36.8 | T. Fraser | Lab | 10,725 | 81.1 |
| | | | J. Letham | Ind | 2,505 | 18.9 |
| | | | | | 8,220 | 62.2 |
| 1945 | 38,934 | 70.0 | T. Fraser | Lab | 20,015 | 73.5 |
| | | | J.U. Baillie | C | 7,226 | 26.5 |
| | | | | | 12,789 | 47.0 |

Note:—

1918: Keith and Gilmour both received the 'coupon' and each claimed to be the official Coalition candidate. This was presumably an error by the Coalition Whips and in the final official list of candidates only Keith's name appeared.

| Election | Electors | T'out | Candidate | Party | Votes | % |
|---|---|---|---|---|---|---|
| 1918 | 27,434 | 68.5 | W.E. Elliot | Co C | 12,976 | 69.0 |
| | | | J.C. Welsh | Lab | 5,821 | 31.0 |
| | | | | | 7,155 | 38.0 |
| 1922 | 29,074 | 75.0 | W.E. Elliot | C | 12,005 | 55.0 |
| | | | T.S. Dickson | Lab | 9,812 | 45.0 |
| | | | | | 2,193 | 10.0 |
| 1923 | 30,071 | 74.9 | T.S. Dickson | Lab | 11,384 | 50.5 |
| | | | W.E. Elliot | C | 11,154 | 49.5 |
| | | | | | 230 | 1.0 |
| 1924 | 31,164 | 84.3 | S. Mitchell | C | 12,714 | 48.4 |
| | | | T.S. Dickson | Lab | 11,426 | 43.5 |
| | | | Miss E.B. Mitchell | L | 2,126* | 8.1 |
| | | | | | 1,288 | 4.9 |
| 1929 | 39,201 | 78.8 | T.S. Dickson | Lab | 15,054 | 48.7 |
| | | | S. Mitchell | C | 12,652 | 41.0 |
| | | | J.M. Weir | L | 3,177* | 10.3 |
| | | | | | 2,402 | 7.7 |
| 1931 | 39,389 | 82.5 | Lord Dunglass | C | 20,675 | 63.6 |
| | | | J. Gibson | ILP | 11,815 | 36.4 |
| | | | | | 8,860 | 27.2 |
| 1935 | 41,197 | 76.0 | Lord Dunglass | C | 17,759 | 56.7 |
| | | | J. Gibson | Lab | 10,950 | 35.0 |
| | | | W. Carlin | ILP | 2,583* | 8.3 |
| | | | | | 6,809 | 21.7 |
| 1945 | 45,026 | 74.8 | T. Steele | Lab | 17,784 | 52.8 |
| | | | Lord Dunglass | C | 15,900 | 47.2 |
| | | | | | 1,884 | 5.6 |

| Election | Electors | T'out | Candidate | Party | Votes | % |
|---|---|---|---|---|---|---|
| 1918 | 27,816 | 64.2 | R.F.W.R. Nelson | Co C | 6,972 | 39.0 |
| | | | †J.D. Millar | L | 4,817 | 27.0 |
| | | | J.T.W. Newbold | Lab | 4,135 | 23.2 |
| | | | H. Ferguson | Ind C | 1,923* | 10.8 |
| | | | | | 2,155 | 12.0 |
| 1922 | 30,443 | 81.5 | J.T.W. Newbold | Com | 8,262 | 33.3 |
| | | | H. Ferguson | Ind C | 7,214 | 29.1 |
| | | | J. Maxwell | L | 5,359 | 21.6 |
| | | | D.J. Colville | NL | 3,966 | 16.0 |
| | | | | | 1,048 | 4.2 |
| 1923 | 30,109 | 77.4 | H. Ferguson | C | 9,793 | 42.0 |
| | | | J.T.W. Newbold | Com | 8,712 | 37.4 |
| | | | J. Maxwell | L | 4,799 | 20.6 |
| | | | | | 1,081 | 4.6 |
| 1924 | 29,871 | 82.3 | Rev. J. Barr | Lab | 12,816 | 52.1 |
| | | | H. Ferguson | C | 11,776 | 47.9 |
| | | | | | 1,040 | 4.2 |
| 1929 | 36,094 | 79.6 | Rev. J. Barr | Lab | 16,650 | 58.0 |
| | | | J. Ford | C | 7,502 | 26.1 |
| | | | H. Archibald | L | 3,597 | 12.5 |
| | | | Mrs. I. Brown | Com | 984* | 3.4 |
| | | | | | 9,148 | 31.9 |
| 1931 | 36,671 | 82.4 | T. Ormiston | C | 15,513 | 51.3 |
| | | | Rev. J. Barr | Lab | 14,714 | 48.7 |
| | | | | | 799 | 2.6 |
| 1935 | 38,320 | 75.9 | J. Walker | Lab | 14,755 | 50.7 |
| | | | T. Ormiston | C | 14,325 | 49.3 |
| | | | | | 430 | 1.4 |
| [Death] | | | | | | |
| 1945 (12/4) | 41,180 | 54.0 | Dr. R.D. McIntyre | SNP | 11,417 | 51.4 |
| | | | A. Anderson | Lab | 10,800 | 48.6 |
| | | | | | 617 | 2.8 |
| 1945 | 41,258 | 72.8 | A. Anderson | Lab | 15,831 | 52.7 |
| | | | Dr. R.D. McIntyre | SNP | 8,022 | 26.7 |
| | | | J.H. Hamilton | C | 6,197 | 20.6 |
| | | | | | 7,809 | 26.0 |

Note:—

1918- Ferguson was associated with the Orange (Protestant) movement in
1922: Lanarkshire.

# LANARKSHIRE, NORTHERN  [604]

| Election | Electors | T'out | Candidate | Party | Votes | % |
|---|---|---|---|---|---|---|
| 1918 | 40,014 | 41.6 | R. McLaren | Co C | 7,175 | 43.1 |
| | | | J. Sullivan | Lab | 5,673 | 34.1 |
| | | | A.G. Erskine-Hill | L | 3,068 | 18.5 |
| | | | J.R. Auld | Ind | 710* | 4.3 |
| | | | | | 1,502 | 9.0 |
| 1922 | 30,359 | 72.1 | J. Sullivan | Lab | 10,349 | 47.3 |
| | | | R. McLaren | C | 7,957 | 36.4 |
| | | | J.C. Carroll | L | 3,569 | 16.3 |
| | | | | | 2,392 | 10.9 |
| 1923 | 31,942 | 65.3 | J. Sullivan | Lab | 10,526 | 50.5 |
| | | | A. McClure | C | 7,165 | 34.3 |
| | | | E.R. McNab | L | 3,168 | 15.2 |
| | | | | | 3,361 | 16.2 |
| 1924 | 32,194 | 79.9 | Sir A. Sprot, Bt. | C | 13,880 | 53.9 |
| | | | J. Sullivan | Lab | 11,852 | 46.1 |
| | | | | | 2,028 | 7.8 |
| [Death] | | | | | | |
| 1929 (21/3) | 33,215 | 82.3 | Miss J. Lee | Lab | 15,711 | 57.5 |
| | | | Lord Scone | C | 9,133 | 33.4 |
| | | | Miss E.B. Mitchell | L | 2,488* | 9.1 |
| | | | | | 6,578 | 24.1 |
| 1929 | 45,247 | 78.6 | Miss J. Lee | Lab | 19,884 | 55.9 |
| | | | Lord Scone | C | 15,680 | 44.1 |
| | | | | | 4,204 | 11.8 |
| 1931 | 53,596 | 82.2 | W.J. Anstruther-Gray | C | 24,384 | 55.3 |
| | | | Miss J. Lee | ILP | 19,691 | 44.7 |
| | | | | | 4,693 | 10.6 |
| 1935 | 59,307 | 78.1 | W.J. Anstruther-Gray | C | 22,301 | 48.1 |
| | | | Miss J. Lee | ILP | 17,267 | 37.3 |
| | | | G. McAllister | Lab | 6,763 | 14.6 |
| | | | | | 5,034 | 10.8 |
| 1945 | 69,190 | 73.3 | Miss M.M. Herbison | Lab | 30,251 | 59.6 |
| | | | W.J. Anstruther-Gray | C | 20,489 | 40.4 |
| | | | | | 9,762 | 19.2 |

| Election | Electors | T'out | Candidate | Party | Votes | % |
|---|---|---|---|---|---|---|
| 1918 | 37,518 | 57.0 | A.K. Rodger | Co L | 12,641 | 59.1 |
| | | | W. Regan | Lab | 8,759 | 40.9 |
| | | | | | 3,882 | 18.2 |
| 1922 | 32,487 | 78.4 | W. Wright | Lab | 14,029 | 55.1 |
| | | | J. Train | NL | 11,440 | 44.9 |
| | | | | | 2,589 | 10.2 |
| 1923 | 33,007 | 72.3 | W. Wright | Lab | 13,021 | 54.5 |
| | | | R. McLaren | C | 7,652 | 32.1 |
| | | | J. Taylor | L | 3,201 | 13.4 |
| | | | | | 5,369 | 22.4 |
| 1924 | 33,081 | 80.1 | W. Wright | Lab | 13,796 | 52.1 |
| | | | R. McLaren | C | 12,707 | 47.9 |
| | | | | | 1,089 | 4.2 |
| 1929 | 44,378 | 75.7 | W. Wright | Lab | 17,538 | 52.2 |
| | | | A.P. Duffes | C | 12,249 | 36.5 |
| | | | J.D. MacDougall | L | 2,945* | 8.8 |
| | | | A.B. Moffat | Com | 842* | 2.5 |
| | | | | | 5,289 | 15.7 |
| [Death] | | | | | | |
| 1931 (21/5) | 46,804 | 69.6 | D. Hardie | Lab | 16,736 | 51.4 |
| | | | H.J. Moss | C | 15,853 | 48.6 |
| | | | | | 883 | 2.8 |
| 1931 | 47,848 | 81.6 | H.J. Moss | C | 22,185 | 56.8 |
| | | | D. Hardie | Lab | 16,866 | 43.2 |
| | | | | | 5,319 | 13.6 |
| 1935 | 51,063 | 80.0 | A. Chapman | C | 20,712 | 50.7 |
| | | | D. Hardie | Lab | 20,131 | 49.3 |
| | | | | | 581 | 1.4 |
| 1945 | 54,280 | 76.4 | G. McAllister | Lab | 24,738 | 59.6 |
| | | | A. Chapman | C | 16,736 | 40.4 |
| | | | | | 8,002 | 19.2 |

# LINLITHGOWSHIRE [606]

| Election | Electors | T'out | Candidate | Party | Votes | % |
|---|---|---|---|---|---|---|
| 1918 | 32,562 | 66.4 | J. Kidd | Co C | 12,898 | 59.7 |
| | | | E. Shinwell | Lab | 8,723 | 40.3 |
| | | | | | 4,175 | 19.4 |
| 1922 | 35,582 | 76.5 | E. Shinwell | Lab | 12,625 | 46.4 |
| | | | J. Kidd | C | 8,993 | 33.0 |
| | | | J. Orr | L | 5,605 | 20.6 |
| | | | | | 3,632 | 13.4 |
| 1923 | 36,459 | 71.7 | E. Shinwell | Lab | 13,304 | 50.9 |
| | | | J. Kidd | C | 8,149 | 31.2 |
| | | | J. Johnston | L | 4,691 | 17.9 |
| | | | | | 5,155 | 19.7 |
| 1924 | 36,122 | 80.0 | J. Kidd | C | 14,765 | 51.1 |
| | | | E. Shinwell | Lab | 14,123 | 48.9 |
| | | | | | 642 | 2.2 |
| [Death] | | | | | | |
| 1928 (4/4) | 36,082 | 81.5 | E. Shinwell | Lab | 14,446 | 49.1 |
| | | | Miss M.H. Kidd | C | 9,268 | 31.5 |
| | | | J.D. Young | L | 5,690 | 19.4 |
| | | | | | 5,178 | 17.6 |
| 1929 | 44,962 | 77.9 | E. Shinwell | Lab | 18,063 | 51.6 |
| | | | Sir A.W.M. Baillie, Bt. | C | 11,241 | 32.1 |
| | | | Dr. J.F. Orr | L | 5,722 | 16.3 |
| | | | | | 6,822 | 19.5 |
| 1931 | 45,612 | 82.1 | Sir A.W.M. Baillie, Bt. | C | 20,476 | 54.7 |
| | | | E. Shinwell | Lab | 16,956 | 45.3 |
| | | | | | 3,520 | 9.4 |
| 1935 | 47,813 | 80.8 | G. Mathers | Lab | 20,905 | 54.1 |
| | | | Sir A.W.M. Baillie, Bt. | C | 17,730 | 45.9 |
| | | | | | 3,175 | 8.2 |
| 1945 | 52,752 | 73.2 | G. Mathers | Lab | 24,762 | 64.1 |
| | | | R.M. Speir | C | 13,871 | 35.9 |
| | | | | | 10,891 | 28.2 |

| Election | Electors | T'out | Candidate | Party | Votes | % |
|---|---|---|---|---|---|---|
| 1918 | 25,291 | 49.4 | †Sir J.A. Hope, Bt. | Co C | 7,762 | 62.1 |
| | | | J.B. Cadzow | Ind | 4,737 | 37.9 |
| | | | | | 3,025 | 24.2 |
| 1922 | 24,939 | 72.7 | G.A.C. Hutchison | C | 7,416 | 40.9 |
| | | | A.B. Clarke | Lab | 6,942 | 38.3 |
| | | | E.R. McNab | L | 3,770 | 20.8 |
| | | | | | 474 | 2.6 |
| 1923 | 25,278 | 74.7 | A.B. Clarke | Lab | 8,570 | 45.3 |
| | | | G.A.C. Hutchison | C | 6,731 | 35.7 |
| | | | C. de B. Murray | L | 3,578 | 19.0 |
| | | | | | 1,839 | 9.6 |
| 1924 | 25,889 | 79.2 | G.A.C. Hutchison | C | 11,320 | 55.2 |
| | | | A.B. Clarke | Lab | 9,173 | 44.8 |
| | | | | | 2,147 | 10.4 |
| [Death] | | | | | | |
| 1929 (29/1) | 28,586 | 66.0 | A.B. Clarke | Lab | 7,917 | 42.0 |
| | | | D.J. Colville | C | 6,965 | 36.9 |
| | | | D.E. Keir | L | 3,130 | 16.6 |
| | | | J.L.T.C. Spence | SNP | 842* | 4.5 |
| | | | | | 952 | 5.1 |
| 1929 | 36,471 | 78.8 | D.J. Colville | C | 11,219 | 39.1 |
| | | | A.B. Clarke | Lab | 10,779 | 37.5 |
| | | | D.E. Keir | L | 6,726 | 23.4 |
| | | | | | 440 | 1.6 |
| 1931 | 39,296 | 78.2 | D.J. Colville | C | 22,211 | 72.3 |
| | | | A.B. Clarke | Lab | 8,501 | 27.7 |
| | | | | | 13,710 | 44.6 |
| 1935 | 50,687 | 74.3 | D.J. Colville | C | 23,711 | 62.9 |
| | | | J. Lean | Lab | 13,970 | 37.1 |
| | | | | | 9,741 | 25.8 |
| [Resignation on appointment as Governor of Bombay] | | | | | | |
| 1943 (11/2) | 64,626 | 34.6 | Sir T.D.K. Murray | C | 11,620 | 51.9 |
| | | | T.H. Wintringham | CW | 10,751 | 48.1 |
| | | | | | 869 | 3.8 |
| 1945 | 73,831 | 70.1 | Lord John Hope | C | 24,834 | 47.9 |
| | | | J. Lean | Lab | 23,657 | 45.7 |
| | | | Mrs. K. Wintringham | CW | 3,299* | 6.4 |
| | | | | | 1,177 | 2.2 |

Note:—

1943:   Murray was Solicitor-General for Scotland.

| Election | Electors | T'out | Candidate | Party | Votes | % |
|---|---|---|---|---|---|---|
| 1918 | 23,310 | 52.6 | †Rt. Hon. Sir D. Maclean | L | 7,429 | 60.6 |
|  |  |  | J. Gold | Lab | 4,830 | 39.4 |
|  |  |  |  |  | 2,599 | 21.2 |
| 1922 | 23,453 | 75.7 | J.C. Westwood | Lab | 6,394 | 36.0 |
|  |  |  | A. Crawford | C | 5,992 | 33.7 |
|  |  |  | Rt. Hon. Sir D. Maclean | L | 5,377 | 30.3 |
|  |  |  |  |  | 402 | 2.3 |
| 1923 | 23,831 | 76.9 | J.C. Westwood | Lab | 7,882 | 43.0 |
|  |  |  | A. Crawford | C | 6,203 | 33.8 |
|  |  |  | W. Mitchell | L | 4,245 | 23.2 |
|  |  |  |  |  | 1,679 | 9.2 |
| 1924 | 24,210 | 78.8 | J.C. Westwood | Lab | 7,797 | 40.8 |
|  |  |  | Hon. C.W. Baillie-Hamilton | C | 6,723 | 35.3 |
|  |  |  | W. Mitchell | L | 4,550 | 23.9 |
|  |  |  |  |  | 1,074 | 5.5 |
| 1929 | 32,420 | 75.7 | J.C. Westwood | Lab | 11,161 | 45.5 |
|  |  |  | H.R. Murray-Philipson | C | 7,736 | 31.5 |
|  |  |  | J. McGowan | L | 5,648 | 23.0 |
|  |  |  |  |  | 3,425 | 14.0 |
| 1931 | 33,394 | 79.7 | A.H.M. Ramsay | C | 17,435 | 65.5 |
|  |  |  | J.C. Westwood | Lab | 9,185 | 34.5 |
|  |  |  |  |  | 8,250 | 31.0 |
| 1935 | 34,536 | 74.9 | A.H.M. Ramsay | C (Ind) | 13,671 | 52.8 |
|  |  |  | D.J. Pryde | Lab | 12,209 | 47.2 |
|  |  |  |  |  | 1,462 | 5.6 |
| 1945 | 37,931 | 73.5 | D.J. Pryde | Lab | 15,546 | 55.8 |
|  |  |  | J.L. Clyde | C | 9,050 | 32.4 |
|  |  |  | L. Gellatly | L | 3,299* | 11.8 |
|  |  |  |  |  | 6,496 | 23.4 |

Note:—

1935: Ramsay was detained in Brixton Prison, London, from May 23, 1940 until September 26, 1944 under Defence Regulation 18b. He was immediately disowned by the local Conservative Association.

| Election | Electors | T'out | Candidate | Party | Votes | % |
|---|---|---|---|---|---|---|
| 1918 | | | †Rt. Hon. Sir A. Williamson, Bt. | Co L | Unopp. | |
| [Elevation to the Peerage — Lord Forres] | | | | | | |
| 1922 (21/6) | | | T.M. Guthrie | Co L | Unopp. | |
| 1922 | 24,691 | 49.0 | T.M. Guthrie | NL (L) | 6,263 | 51.8 |
| | | | J. Scott | L | 5,832 | 48.2 |
| | | | | | 431 | 3.6 |
| 1923 | 24,798 | 61.3 | Hon. J. Stuart | C | 8,116 | 53.4 |
| | | | T.M. Guthrie | L | 7,089 | 46.6 |
| | | | | | 1,027 | 6.8 |
| 1924 | 25,539 | 61.7 | Hon. J. Stuart | C | 9,762 | 61.9 |
| | | | B.S. MacKay | Lab | 6,005 | 38.1 |
| | | | | | 3,757 | 23.8 |
| 1929 | 29,669 | 68.6 | Hon. J. Stuart | C | 8,896 | 43.7 |
| | | | J.F. Duncan | Lab | 6,566 | 32.3 |
| | | | J.E. Tennant | L | 4,889 | 24.0 |
| | | | | | 2,330 | 11.4 |
| 1931 | | | Hon. J. Stuart | C | Unopp. | |
| 1935 | 30,488 | 65.9 | Hon. J. Stuart | C | 12,755 | 63.5 |
| | | | J.D. Vassie | Lab | 7,347 | 36.5 |
| | | | | | 5,408 | 27.0 |
| 1945 | 33,639 | 61.8 | Rt. Hon. J. Stuart | C | 12,809 | 61.6 |
| | | | S. Shaw | Lab | 7,993 | 38.4 |
| | | | | | 4,816 | 23.2 |

| Election | Electors | T'out | Candidate | Party | Votes | % |
|----------|----------|-------|-----------|-------|-------|---|
| 1918 [Death] | | | †J.C. Wason | Co L | Unopp. | |
| 1921 (17/5) | | | Sir M. Smith | Co L | Unopp. | |
| 1922 | 24,084 | 37.4 | Sir R.W. Hamilton | L | 4,814 | 53.5 |
| | | | Sir M. Smith | NL | 4,189 | 46.5 |
| | | | | | 625 | 7.0 |
| 1923 | 24,167 | 39.1 | Sir R.W. Hamilton | L | 5,129 | 54.3 |
| | | | R.J.G. Boothby | C | 4,318 | 45.7 |
| | | | | | 811 | 8.6 |
| 1924 | | | Sir R.W. Hamilton | L | Unopp. | |
| 1929 | 31,683 | 43.1 | Sir R.W. Hamilton | L | 8,256 | 60.4 |
| | | | B.H.H. Neven-Spence | C | 5,404 | 39.6 |
| | | | | | 2,852 | 20.8 |
| 1931 | | | Sir R.W. Hamilton | L | Unopp. | |
| 1935 | 31,480 | 46.3 | B.H.H. Neven-Spence | C | 8,406 | 57.6 |
| | | | Sir R.W. Hamilton | L | 6,180 | 42.4 |
| | | | | | 2,226 | 15.2 |
| 1945 | 31,493 | 55.5 | B.H.H. Neven-Spence | C | 6,304 | 36.0 |
| | | | J. Grimond | L | 5,975 | 34.2 |
| | | | P.J.L. Smith | Lab | 5,208 | 29.8 |
| | | | | | 329 | 1.8 |

Note:—

| 1918-1924: | The Representation of the People Act, 1918, made provision for the poll in this constituency to remain open for two consecutive days. This was repealed in 1926. |
|---|---|

| Election | Electors | T'out | Candidate | Party | Votes | % |
|---|---|---|---|---|---|---|
| 1918 | 23,888 | 60.9 | J. Gardiner | L (Co L) | 7,579 | 52.1 |
| | | | †A. Stirling | Co C | 6,975 | 47.9 |
| | | | | | 604 | 4.2 |
| 1922 | | | J. Gardiner | NL | Unopp. | |
| 1923 | 25,221 | 72.6 | Duchess of Atholl | C | 9,235 | 50.4 |
| | | | P.A. Molteno | L | 9,085 | 49.6 |
| | | | | | 150 | 0.8 |
| 1924 | 25,978 | 72.6 | Duchess of Atholl | C | 13,565 | 72.0 |
| | | | J.M. MacDiarmid | Lab | 5,286 | 28.0 |
| | | | | | 8,279 | 44.0 |
| 1929 | 33,408 | 75.5 | Duchess of Atholl | C | 12,245 | 48.6 |
| | | | Dr. G.F. Barbour | L | 9,128 | 36.2 |
| | | | Rev. W.D. Stewart | Lab | 3,834 | 15.2 |
| | | | | | 3,117 | 12.4 |
| 1931 | 33,862 | 79.0 | Duchess of Atholl | C (Ind C) (C) | 16,228 | 60.6 |
| | | | T.A. Robertson | L | 10,533 | 39.4 |
| | | | | | 5,695 | 21.2 |
| 1935 | 34,232 | 73.9 | Duchess of Atholl | C (Ind C) | 15,238 | 60.2 |
| | | | Mrs. M.I. MacDonald | L | 10,069 | 39.8 |
| | | | | | 5,169 | 20.4 |

[Seeks re-election]

| Election | Electors | T'out | Candidate | Party | Votes | % |
|---|---|---|---|---|---|---|
| 1938 (21/12) | 33,482 | 66.6 | W.M. Snadden | C | 11,808 | 52.9 |
| | | | Duchess of Atholl | Ind | 10,495 | 47.1 |
| | | | | | 1,313 | 5.8 |
| 1945 | 36,096 | 67.4 | W.M. Snadden | C | 16,536 | 68.0 |
| | | | Rev. C. McKinnon | Lab | 7,782 | 32.0 |
| | | | | | 8,754 | 36.0 |

Note:—

1938: The Duchess of Atholl resigned the National Government whip in April 1938 as a protest against the Government's policy on Spain. At a meeting of the local Conservative Association held in November 1938 it was decided by a majority of 273 to 167 votes to seek a new candidate for the next election. Five days after this meeting the Duchess announced that she would resign her seat and fight the resulting by-election as an Independent opposed to the Government's foreign policy.

| Election | Electors | T'out | Candidate | Party | Votes | % |
|---|---|---|---|---|---|---|
| 1918 | | | †W. Young | Co L | Unopp. | |
| | | | | | | |
| 1922 | 34,590 | 71.1 | A.N. Skelton | C | 11,387 | 46.3 |
| | | | W. Henderson | L | 5,874 | 23.9 |
| | | | W. Westwood | Lab | 4,651 | 18.9 |
| | | | W.R. Gourlay | NL | 2,689* | 10.9 |
| | | | | | 5,513 | 22.4 |
| | | | | | | |
| 1923 | 34,635 | 68.7 | R.M. Mitchell | L | 12,655 | 53.2 |
| | | | A.N. Skelton | C | 11,134 | 46.8 |
| | | | | | 1,521 | 6.4 |
| | | | | | | |
| 1924 | 34,992 | 75.3 | A.N. Skelton | C | 13,022 | 49.4 |
| | | | R.M. Mitchell | L | 7,998 | 30.4 |
| | | | C. Roberts | Lab | 5,316 | 20.2 |
| | | | | | 5,024 | 19.0 |
| | | | | | | |
| 1929 | 45,923 | 76.7 | A.N. Skelton | C | 14,229 | 40.4 |
| | | | F. Norie-Miller | L | 12,699 | 36.1 |
| | | | Mrs. H.E. Gault | Lab | 8,291 | 23.5 |
| | | | | | 1,530 | 4.3 |
| | | | | | | |
| 1931 | 47,145 | 81.4 | Lord Scone | C | 19,254 | 50.2 |
| | | | F. Norie-Miller | L | 15,396 | 40.1 |
| | | | Mrs. H.E. Gault | ILP | 3,705* | 9.7 |
| | | | | | 3,858 | 10.1 |

[Succession to the Peerage — Earl of Mansfield and Mansfield]

| Election | Electors | T'out | Candidate | Party | Votes | % |
|---|---|---|---|---|---|---|
| 1935 (16/4) | 48,160 | 52.9 | F. Norie-Miller | NL | 17,516 | 68.7 |
| | | | A.S. McKinlay | Lab | 7,984 | 31.3 |
| | | | | | 9,532 | 37.4 |
| | | | | | | |
| 1935 | 48,815 | 64.0 | T. Hunter | C | 23,011 | 73.7 |
| | | | R. Gunn | Lab | 8,209 | 26.3 |
| | | | | | 14,802 | 47.4 |
| | | | | | | |
| 1945 | 54,558 | 65.3 | A. Gomme-Duncan | C | 22,484 | 63.1 |
| | | | W. Hughes | Lab | 11,617 | 32.6 |
| | | | J.B. Brown | SNP | 1,547* | 4.3 |
| | | | | | 10,867 | 30.5 |

| Election | Electors | T'out | Candidate | Party | Votes | % |
|----------|----------|-------|-----------|-------|-------|---|
| 1918 | 28,066 | 64.7 | J. Johnstone | Co L | 13,107 | 72.2 |
|  |  |  | R. Spence | Lab | 5,048 | 27.8 |
|  |  |  |  |  | 8,059 | 44.4 |
| 1922 | 28,394 | 80.6 | R. Nichol | Lab | 9,708 | 42.5 |
|  |  |  | Sir F. Lobnitz | C | 9,158 | 40.0 |
|  |  |  | J. Johnstone | L | 4,013 | 17.5 |
|  |  |  |  |  | 550 | 2.5 |
| 1923 | 29,095 | 75.9 | R. Nichol | Lab | 9,857 | 44.6 |
|  |  |  | Sir F. Lobnitz | C | 9,349 | 42.3 |
|  |  |  | W. Crawford | L | 2,887 | 13.1 |
|  |  |  |  |  | 508 | 2.3 |
| 1924 | 29,493 | 83.5 | A.M. MacRobert | C | 13,716 | 55.7 |
|  |  |  | R. Nichol | Lab | 10,903 | 44.3 |
|  |  |  |  |  | 2,813 | 11.4 |

[Appointed Solicitor-General for Scotland]

| Election | Electors | T'out | Candidate | Party | Votes | % |
|----------|----------|-------|-----------|-------|-------|---|
| 1926 (29/1) | 30,211 | 75.2 | A.M. MacRobert | C | 11,817 | 52.0 |
|  |  |  | Rev. J.M. Munro | Lab | 10,889 | 48.0 |
|  |  |  |  |  | 928 | 4.0 |
| 1929 | 45,525 | 77.8 | Rt. Hon. A.M. MacRobert | C | 18,487 | 52.2 |
|  |  |  | Rev. J.M. Munro | Lab | 16,924 | 47.8 |
|  |  |  |  |  | 1,563 | 4.4 |

[Death]

| Election | Electors | T'out | Candidate | Party | Votes | % |
|----------|----------|-------|-----------|-------|-------|---|
| 1930 (28/11) | 53,417 | 69.0 | Marquess of Douglas and Clydesdale | C | 19,753 | 53.6 |
|  |  |  | T. Irwin | ILP | 12,293 | 33.3 |
|  |  |  | W.O. Brown | SNP | 4,818 | 13.1 |
|  |  |  |  |  | 7,460 | 20.3 |
| 1931 | 57,911 | 80.7 | Marquess of Douglas and Clydesdale | C | 27,740 | 59.4 |
|  |  |  | J. Strain | Lab/Co-op | 12,477 | 26.7 |
|  |  |  | W.O. Brown | SNP | 6,498 | 13.9 |
|  |  |  |  |  | 15,263 | 32.7 |
| 1935 | 83,201 | 75.9 | Marquess of Douglas and Clydesdale | C | 35,121 | 55.6 |
|  |  |  | J. Barr | Lab/Co-op | 21,475 | 34.0 |
|  |  |  | W.O. Brown | SNP | 6,593* | 10.4 |
|  |  |  |  |  | 13,646 | 21.6 |

[Succession to the Peerage — Duke of Hamilton and Brandon]

| Election | Electors | T'out | Candidate | Party | Votes | % |
|----------|----------|-------|-----------|-------|-------|---|
| 1940 (9/5) | 98,083 | 43.4 | E.G.R. Lloyd | C | 34,316 | 80.7 |
|  |  |  | Miss A. Maxton | ILP | 8,206 | 19.3 |
|  |  |  |  |  | 26,110 | 61.4 |
| 1945 | 117,431 | 67.2 | E.G.R. Lloyd | C | 42,310 | 53.6 |
|  |  |  | D. McArthur | Lab/Co-op | 36,634 | 46.4 |
|  |  |  |  |  | 5,676 | 7.2 |

Note:—

1930: Irwin had committed himself to conditions imposed by the ILP upon its candidates, and as a result, the National Executive Committee of the Labour Party decided that in the circumstances it could not endorse his candidature.

| Election | Electors | T'out | Candidate | Party | Votes | % |
|----------|----------|-------|-----------|-------|-------|---|
| 1918 | 28,542 | 65.3 | †J.W. Greig | Co L | 11,524 | 61.8 |
| | | | R. Murray | Lab | 7,126 | 38.2 |
| | | | | | 4,398 | 23.6 |
| 1922 | 28,868 | 75.6 | R. Murray | Lab | 11,787 | 54.0 |
| | | | Sir J.W. Greig | NL | 10,051 | 46.0 |
| | | | | | 1,736 | 8.0 |
| 1923 | 29,426 | 77.0 | R. Murray | Lab | 10,904 | 48.1 |
| | | | A.T. Taylor | C | 7,602 | 33.6 |
| | | | J. Scott | L | 4,149 | 18.3 |
| | | | | | 3,302 | 14.5 |
| 1924 | 29,029 | 84.5 | A.D.M. Shaw | C | 13,267 | 54.1 |
| | | | R. Murray | Lab | 11,252 | 45.9 |
| | | | | | 2,015 | 8.2 |
| 1929 | 37,947 | 81.6 | Dr. R. Forgan | Lab (NP) | 14,419 | 46.5 |
| | | | A.T. Taylor | C | 12,183 | 39.4 |
| | | | F.S. Anderson | L | 2,682* | 8.7 |
| | | | R.E. Muirhead | SNP | 1,667* | 5.4 |
| | | | | | 2,236 | 7.1 |
| 1931 | 38,894 | 83.2 | H.J. Scrymgeour-Wedderburn | C | 17,318 | 53.5 |
| | | | Mrs. J. Mann | ILP | 10,203 | 31.5 |
| | | | R.E. Muirhead | SNP | 3,547* | 11.0 |
| | | | Dr. R. Forgan | NP | 1,304* | 4.0 |
| | | | | | 7,115 | 22.0 |
| 1935 | 39,396 | 81.0 | H.J. Scrymgeour-Wedderburn | C | 15,906 | 49.8 |
| | | | Mrs. J. Mann | Lab | 12,407 | 38.9 |
| | | | R.E. Muirhead | SNP | 3,609* | 11.3 |
| | | | | | 3,499 | 10.9 |
| 1945 | 43,940 | 70.2 | T. Scollan | Lab | 15,050 | 48.8 |
| | | | H.J. Scrymgeour-Wedderburn | C | 13,836 | 44.9 |
| | | | R.B. Wilkie | SNP | 1,955* | 6.3 |
| | | | | | 1,214 | 3.9 |

| Election | Electors | T'out | Candidate | Party | Votes | % |
|----------|----------|-------|-----------|-------|-------|---|
| 1918 | 33,604 | 55.4 | †Rt. Hon. R. Munro | Co L | 13,043 | 70.1 |
|  |  |  | T. Hamilton | Lab | 5,574 | 29.9 |
|  |  |  |  |  | 7,469 | 40.2 |

[Seat Vacant at Dissolution (Resignation on appointment as Lord Justice Clerk — Lord Alness)]

| | | | | | | |
|----------|----------|-------|-----------|-------|-------|---|
| 1922 | 32,752 | 61.2 | Sir T. Henderson | NL | 10,356 | 51.6 |
|  |  |  | Sir A.H. Grant | L | 9,698 | 48.4 |
|  |  |  |  |  | 658 | 3.2 |
| 1923 | 33,185 | 78.7 | Earl of Dalkeith | C | 11,258 | 43.1 |
|  |  |  | Sir T. Henderson | L | 8,046 | 30.8 |
|  |  |  | G. Dallas | Lab | 6,811 | 26.1 |
|  |  |  |  |  | 3,212 | 12.3 |
| 1924 | 34,594 | 80.0 | Earl of Dalkeith | C | 12,684 | 45.9 |
|  |  |  | J.M. Wylie | L | 7,737 | 27.9 |
|  |  |  | G. Dallas | Lab | 7,266 | 26.2 |
|  |  |  |  |  | 4,947 | 18.0 |
| 1929 | 45,287 | 78.5 | Earl of Dalkeith | C | 13,510 | 38.0 |
|  |  |  | A.R. McDougal | L | 12,232 | 34.4 |
|  |  |  | R. Gibson | Lab | 9,803 | 27.6 |
|  |  |  |  |  | 1,278 | 3.6 |
| 1931 | 45,975 | 84.4 | Earl of Dalkeith | C | 21,394 | 55.1 |
|  |  |  | D.E. Keir | L | 17,420 | 44.9 |
|  |  |  |  |  | 3,974 | 10.2 |

[Seat Vacant at Dissolution (Succession to the Peerage — Duke of Buccleuch)]

| | | | | | | |
|----------|----------|-------|-----------|-------|-------|---|
| 1935 | 47,037 | 78.0 | Lord William Scott | C | 18,342 | 50.0 |
|  |  |  | A.R. McDougal | L | 12,264 | 33.4 |
|  |  |  | J.A.C. Thomson | Lab | 6,099 | 16.6 |
|  |  |  |  |  | 6,078 | 16.6 |
| 1945 | 47,492 | 73.6 | Lord William Scott | C | 13,232 | 37.9 |
|  |  |  | A.J.F. Macdonald | L | 11,604 | 33.2 |
|  |  |  | L.P. Thomas | Lab | 10,107 | 28.9 |
|  |  |  |  |  | 1,628 | 4.7 |

| Election | Electors | T'out | Candidate | Party | Votes | % |
|---|---|---|---|---|---|---|
| 1918 | 31,916 | 55.0 | R.G.C. Glyn | Co C | 6,771 | 38.5 |
| | | | H.J. May | Co-op | 5,753 | 32.8 |
| | | | †Dr. W.A. Chapple | L | 5,040 | 28.7 |
| | | | | | 1,018 | 5.7 |
| 1922 | 31,563 | 77.9 | L.M. Weir | Lab | 10,312 | 42.0 |
| | | | C.M. Aitchison | L | 7,379 | 30.0 |
| | | | R.G.C. Glyn | C | 6,888 | 28.0 |
| | | | | | 2,933 | 12.0 |
| 1923 | 31,976 | 64.2 | L.M. Weir | Lab | 10,492 | 51.1 |
| | | | C.M. Aitchison | L | 10,043 | 48.9 |
| | | | | | 449 | 2.2 |
| 1924 | 32,195 | 77.0 | L.M. Weir | Lab | 13,032 | 52.6 |
| | | | E.J. Donaldson | L | 11,752 | 47.4 |
| | | | | | 1,280 | 5.2 |
| 1929 | 42,567 | 78.0 | L.M. Weir | Lab | 17,677 | 53.2 |
| | | | H.P. Mitchell | C | 8,778 | 26.4 |
| | | | E.J. Donaldson | L | 6,760 | 20.4 |
| | | | | | 8,899 | 26.8 |
| 1931 | 43,854 | 77.7 | J.W. Johnston | C | 20,425 | 59.9 |
| | | | L.M. Weir | Lab | 13,669 | 40.1 |
| | | | | | 6,756 | 19.8 |
| 1935 | 46,203 | 76.3 | L.M. Weir | Lab | 14,881 | 42.1 |
| | | | J.W. Johnston | C | 13,738 | 39.0 |
| | | | G.G. Honeyman | L | 5,062 | 14.4 |
| | | | D.W. Gibson | ILP | 1,573* | 4.5 |
| | | | | | 1,143 | 3.1 |
| [Death] | | | | | | |
| 1939 | 47,237 | 35.4 | A. Woodburn | Lab | 15,645 | 93.7 |
| (13/10) | | | A. Stewart | Ind | 1,060* | 6.3 |
| | | | | | 14,585 | 87.4 |
| 1945 | 54,632 | 71.7 | A. Woodburn | Lab | 24,622 | 62.9 |
| | | | Sir J.E. Gilmour, Bt. | C | 14,522 | 37.1 |
| | | | | | 10,100 | 25.8 |

Note:—

1939: Stewart was the nominee of the Scottish Anti-War and No Conscription League Council. He was an organiser of the Peace Pledge Union and also received the support of the ILP, the Scottish Socialist Party and a number of other pacifist organisations.

| Election | Electors | T'out | Candidate | Party | Votes | % |
|---|---|---|---|---|---|---|
| 1918 | 22,463 | 59.1 | †H. Hope | Co C | 6,893 | 51.9 |
| | | | T. Johnston | Lab | 3,809 | 28.7 |
| | | | R.B. Cunninghame Graham | L | 2,582 | 19.4 |
| | | | | | 3,084 | 23.2 |
| 1922 | 22,974 | 74.1 | T. Johnston | Lab | 8,919 | 52.4 |
| | | | Sir H. Hope | C | 8,104 | 47.6 |
| | | | | | 815 | 4.8 |
| 1923 | 23,832 | 74.7 | T. Johnston | Lab | 9,242 | 51.9 |
| | | | Sir H. Hope | C | 6,182 | 34.7 |
| | | | R.I.A. MacInnes | L | 2,390 | 13.4 |
| | | | | | 3,060 | 17.2 |
| 1924 | 24,420 | 81.0 | G.D. Fanshawe | C | 10,043 | 50.7 |
| | | | T. Johnston | Lab | 9,749 | 49.3 |
| | | | | | 294 | 1.4 |
| 1929 | 32,383 | 82.7 | T. Johnston | Lab | 15,179 | 56.7 |
| | | | G.D. Fanshawe | C | 11,589 | 43.3 |
| | | | | | 3,590 | 13.4 |
| 1931 | 32,999 | 84.0 | J.C. Ker | C | 14,771 | 53.3 |
| | | | Rt. Hon. T. Johnston | Lab | 12,952 | 46.7 |
| | | | | | 1,819 | 6.6 |
| 1935 | 35,336 | 82.3 | Rt. Hon. T. Johnston | Lab | 16,015 | 55.1 |
| | | | A.P. Duffes | C | 13,053 | 44.9 |
| | | | | | 2,962 | 10.2 |
| 1945 | 39,414 | 75.0 | A. Balfour | Lab | 16,066 | 54.4 |
| | | | J.C.L. Anderson | C | 13,489 | 45.6 |
| | | | | | 2,577 | 8.8 |

Note:—

1922: W. Wright (L) was nominated for this election but died the following day. A new nomination day was arranged but no Liberal candidate was nominated.

# NORTHERN IRELAND —— BOROUGHS

| Election | Electors | T'out | Candidate | Party | Votes | % |
|---|---|---|---|---|---|---|
| 1922 | | | †H. Dixon | C | Unopp. | |
| 1923 | | | Rt. Hon. H. Dixon | C | Unopp. | |
| 1924 | | | Rt. Hon. H. Dixon | C | Unopp. | |
| 1929 | 56,426 | 65.7 | Rt. Hon. H. Dixon | C | 27,855 | 75.1 |
| | | | D. Ireland | L | 9,230 | 24.9 |
| | | | | | 18,625 | 50.2 |
| 1931 | 57,166 | 66.2 | Rt. Hon. H. Dixon | C | 28,431 | 75.1 |
| | | | J. Campbell | Lab | 9,410 | 24.9 |
| | | | | | 19,021 | 50.2 |
| 1935 | | | Rt. Hon. H. Dixon | C | Unopp. | |

[Elevation to the Peerage — Lord Glentoran]

| Election | Electors | T'out | Candidate | Party | Votes | % |
|---|---|---|---|---|---|---|
| 1940 (8/2) | | | H.P. Harland | C | Unopp. | |
| 1945 | 60,175 | 63.2 | T.L. Cole | C | 21,443 | 56.4 |
| | | | T.W. Boyd | Lab | 16,574 | 43.6 |
| | | | | | 4,869 | 12.8 |

# BELFAST, NORTH [619]

| Election | Electors | T'out | Candidate | Party | Votes | % |
|---|---|---|---|---|---|---|
| 1922 | | | †T.E. McConnell | C | Unopp. | |
| 1923 | 46,844 | 68.2 | T.E. McConnell | C | 16,771 | 52.5 |
| | | | T.G. Henderson | Ind C | 15,171 | 47.5 |
| | | | | | 1,600 | 5.0 |
| 1924 | 46,902 | 75.4 | T.E. McConnell | C | 34,182 | 96.6 |
| | | | H.C. Corvin | SF | 1,192* | 3.4 |
| | | | | | 32,990 | 93.2 |
| 1929 | 61,438 | 72.9 | T. Somerset | C | 27,812 | 62.1 |
| | | | T.G. Henderson | Ind C | 10,909 | 24.4 |
| | | | D. Wilson | Ind | 6,059 | 13.5 |
| | | | | | 16,903 | 37.7 |
| 1931 | | | T. Somerset | C | Unopp. | |
| 1935 | | | T. Somerset | C | Unopp. | |
| 1945 | 73,231 | 63.6 | W.F. Neill | C | 25,761 | 55.3 |
| | | | W.J. Leeburn | Lab | 20,845 | 44.7 |
| | | | | | 4,916 | 10.6 |

Note:—

1929: Wilson sought election as a 'Temperance Unionist and Local Optionist' candidate. He was the nominee of the North Belfast Temperance Council.

| Election | Electors | T'out | Candidate | Party | Votes | % |
|---|---|---|---|---|---|---|
| 1922 | | | †T. Moles | C | Unopp. | |
| 1923 | | | Rt. Hon. T. Moles | C | Unopp. | |
| 1924 | | | Rt. Hon. T. Moles | C | Unopp. | |
| 1929 | 59,025 | 64.7 | W.J. Stewart | C | 24,019 | 62.9 |
| | | | P.J. Woods | Ind C | 14,148 | 37.1 |
| | | | | | 9,871 | 25.8 |
| 1931 | | | W.J. Stewart | C | Unopp. | |
| 1935 | | | W.J. Stewart | C | Unopp. | |
| 1945 | 70,140 | 66.4 | C.H. Gage | C | 24,282 | 52.2 |
| | | | Rt. Hon. H.C. Midgley | CWLP | 14,096 | 30.3 |
| | | | J. Morrow | Lab | 8,166 | 17.5 |
| | | | | | 10,186 | 21.9 |

# BELFAST, WEST [621]

| Election | Electors | T'out | Candidate | Party | Votes | % |
|---|---|---|---|---|---|---|
| 1922 | | | †R.J. Lynn | C | Unopp. | |
| 1923 | 67,161 | 70.3 | R.J. Lynn | C | 24,975 | 52.9 |
| | | | H.C. Midgley | BLP | 22,255 | 47.1 |
| | | | | | 2,720 | 5.8 |
| 1924 | 66,010 | 79.1 | Sir R.J. Lynn | C | 28,435 | 54.5 |
| | | | H.C. Midgley | NI Lab | 21,122 | 40.4 |
| | | | P. Nash | SF | 2,688* | 5.1 |
| | | | | | 7,313 | 14.1 |
| 1929 | 77,721 | 73.9 | W.E.D. Allen | C (NP) | 33,274 | 57.9 |
| | | | F. MacDermot | N | 24,177 | 42.1 |
| | | | | | 9,097 | 15.8 |
| 1931 | 77,993 | 68.1 | A.C. Browne | C | 31,113 | 58.6 |
| | | | T.J. Campbell | N | 22,006 | 41.4 |
| | | | | | 9,107 | 17.2 |
| 1935 | 79,902 | 68.0 | A.C. Browne | C | 34,060 | 62.6 |
| | | | C.E. Leddy | Rep | 20,313 | 37.4 |
| | | | | | 13,747 | 25.2 |
| [Death] | | | | | | |
| 1943 (9/2) | 78,763 | 54.8 | J. Beattie | NI Lab (Lab) (Ind Lab) | 19,936 | 46.2 |
| | | | S.K. Cunningham | C | 14,426 | 33.4 |
| | | | W.M. Wilton | Ind C | 7,551 | 17.5 |
| | | | H.C. Corvin | Ind Rep | 1,250* | 2.9 |
| | | | | | 5,510 | 12.8 |
| 1945 | 78,674 | 73.1 | J. Beattie | Ind Lab (Irish LP) | 30,787 | 53.5 |
| | | | S.K. Cunningham | C | 26,729 | 46.5 |
| | | | | | 4,058 | 7.0 |

Notes:—

1935: Leddy was supported by Sinn Fein.

1943: Beattie's candidature was not endorsed by the British Labour Party owing to the electoral truce but he joined the Parliamentary Labour Party shortly after being elected.

Wilton was the nominee of the Ulster Independent Unionist Association which he had formed in November 1938. The Association's aim was to stimulate the Government to more vigorous action on economic affairs.

Corvin sought election as a Republican but he was disowned by both the Nationalist and Sinn Fein organisations in Belfast.

# NORTHERN IRELAND ——— COUNTIES

# ANTRIM [622]

## (Two Seats)

| Election | Electors | T'out | Candidate | Party | Votes | % |
|---|---|---|---|---|---|---|
| 1922 | | | †C.C. Craig | C | Unopp. | |
| | | | †Rt. Hon. R.W.H. O'Neill | C | Unopp. | |
| 1923 | | | Rt. Hon. C.C. Craig | C | Unopp. | |
| | | | Rt. Hon. R.W.H. O'Neill | C | Unopp. | |
| 1924 | 98,616 | 64.2 | Rt. Hon. C.C. Craig | C | 60,868 | 49.0 |
| | | | Rt. Hon. R.W.H. O'Neill | C | 60,764 | 49.0 |
| | | | P. McCormick | SF | 2,514* | 2.0 |
| | | | | | 58,250 | 47.0 |
| 1929 | 123,474 | 58.6 | Rt. Hon. R.W.H. O'Neill | C | 53,864 | 37.6 |
| | | | Sir J. McConnell, Bt. | C | 52,851 | 36.8 |
| | | | G. Henderson | L | 18,985 | 13.2 |
| | | | R.N. Boyd | L | 17,824 | 12.4 |
| | | | | | 33,866 | 23.6 |
| 1931 | | | Sir J. McConnell, Bt. | C | Unopp. | |
| | | | Rt. Hon. Sir R.W.H. O'Neill, Bt. | C | Unopp. | |
| 1935 | | | Sir J. McConnell, Bt. | C | Unopp. | |
| | | | Rt. Hon. Sir R.W.H. O'Neill, Bt. | C | Unopp. | |

[Death of McConnell]

| Election | Electors | T'out | Candidate | Party | Votes | % |
|---|---|---|---|---|---|---|
| 1943 (11/2) | 135,795 | 45.0 | J.D. Campbell | C | 42,371 | 69.4 |
| | | | R. Getgood | NI Lab | 17,253 | 28.3 |
| | | | R.H. Press | Ind C | 1,432* | 2.3 |
| | | | | | 25,118 | 41.1 |

[Seat Vacant at Dissolution (Death of Campbell)]

| Election | Electors | T'out | Candidate | Party | Votes | % |
|---|---|---|---|---|---|---|
| 1945 | 134,528 | 56.2 | Rt. Hon. Sir R.W.H. O'Neill, Bt. | C | 57,259 | 43.1 |
| | | | S.G. Haughton | C | 57,232 | 43.1 |
| | | | H. Holmes | Lab | 18,403 | 13.8 |
| | | | | | 38,829 | 29.3 |

Notes:—

1943:   Getgood's candidature was not endorsed by the British Labour Party owing to the electoral truce.

Press was the nominee of the Ulster Progressive Unionist Association, which was formed in 1938 by W.J. Stewart, Conservative MP for Belfast, South. The Association's aim was to stimulate the Government to more vigorous action on economic affairs.

| Election | Electors | T'out | Candidate | Party | Votes | % |
|----------|----------|-------|-----------|-------|-------|---|
| 1922 | | | †Sir W.J. Allen | C | Unopp. | |
| 1923 | | | Sir W.J. Allen | C | Unopp. | |
| 1924 | 54,376 | 75.0 | Sir W.J. Allen | C | 29,021 | 71.2 |
| | | | Dr. J.T. McKee | SF | 11,756 | 28.8 |
| | | | | | 17,265 | 42.4 |
| 1929 | 66,527 | 60.2 | Sir W.J. Allen | C | 26,966 | 67.4 |
| | | | W.R. Todd | L | 13,052 | 32.6 |
| | | | | | 13,914 | 34.8 |
| 1931 | | | Sir W.J. Allen | C | Unopp. | |
| 1935 | 68,582 | 73.3 | Sir W.J. Allen | C | 34,002 | 67.6 |
| | | | C.E. McGleenan | Rep | 16,284 | 32.4 |
| | | | | | 17,718 | 35.2 |
| 1945 | | | Sir W.J. Allen | C | Unopp. | |
| [Death] | | | | | | |
| 1948 | 70,337 | 86.9 | J.R.E. Harden | C | 36,736 | 60.1 |
| (5/3) | | | S. O'Reilly | N | 24,422 | 39.9 |
| | | | | | 12,314 | 20.2 |

Note:—

1935:   McGleenan was supported by Sinn Fein.

# DOWN [624]

## (Two Seats)

| Election | Electors | T'out | Candidate | Party | Votes | % |
|---|---|---|---|---|---|---|
| 1922 | | | †D.D. Reid | C | Unopp. | |
| | | | †Very Rev. J.M. Simms | C | Unopp. | |
| 1923 | | | D.D. Reid | C | Unopp. | |
| | | | Very Rev. J.M. Simms | C | Unopp. | |
| 1924 | 96,285 | 70.5 | D.D. Reid | C | 58,929 | 46.5 |
| | | | Very Rev. J.M. Simms | C | 58,777 | 46.4 |
| | | | M. Murney | SF | 8,941 | 7.1 |
| | | | | | 49,836 | 39.3 |
| 1929 | 127,346 | 58.9 | D.D. Reid | C | 54,073 | 36.3 |
| | | | Very Rev. J.M. Simms | C | 53,943 | 36.2 |
| | | | R.D. Pollock | L | 20,999 | 14.1 |
| | | | D. Johnston | L | 20,013 | 13.4 |
| | | | | | 32,944 | 22.1 |
| 1931 | | | Viscount Castlereagh | C | Unopp. | |
| | | | D.D. Reid | C | Unopp. | |
| 1935 | 134,467 | 64.6 | D.D. Reid | C | 66,324 | 43.5 |
| | | | Viscount Castlereagh | C | 65,829 | 43.2 |
| | | | P.F. O'Hagan | Rep | 20,236 | 13.3 |
| | | | | | 45,593 | 29.9 |
| [Death of Reid] | | | | | | |
| 1939 (10/5) | | | Rev. Dr. J. Little | C (Ind C) | Unopp. | |
| 1945 | 145,524 | 49.3 | Rev. Dr. J. Little | Ind C | 46,732 | 40.4 |
| | | | Sir W.D. Smiles | C | 24,148 | 20.9 |
| | | | J.M. Blakiston-Houston | C | 22,730 | 19.6 |
| | | | J. Brown | Ind C | 22,163 | 19.1 |
| | | | | | 24,002 | 20.8 |
| | | | | | 1,985 | 1.8 |
| [Death of Little] | | | | | | |
| 1946 (6/6) | 147,978 | 66.6 | C.H. Mullan | C | 50,699 | 51.4 |
| | | | D.L. Donnelly | Lab | 28,846 | 29.3 |
| | | | Rev. J.H. Little | Ind C | 16,895 | 17.1 |
| | | | J. Brown | Ind C | 2,125* | 2.2 |
| | | | | | 21,853 | 22.1 |

Notes:—

1935:  O'Hagan was supported by Sinn Fein.

1945:  Little's resignation from the Conservative Party in May 1945 arose as a result of a meeting held to adopt two Conservative candidates for the forthcoming General Election. Little objected to his name being added to a list of six other Conservatives who had been put forward for the vacancy caused by the retirement of Viscount Castlereagh. He considered that his re-adoption should not be subjected to a ballot and walked out of the meeting after announcing that he would seek re-election as an Independent Conservative.

1945-1946:  Brown sought election as a 'Democratic Unionist, Farmers' and Industries' candidate.

## (Two Seats)

| Election | Electors | T'out | Candidate | Party | Votes | % |
|---|---|---|---|---|---|---|
| 1922 | 97,904 | 85.7 | †T.J.S. Harbison | N | 45,236 | 27.0 |
| | | | C. Healy | N | 44,817 | 26.8 |
| | | | J.A. Pringle | C | 38,640 | 23.1 |
| | | | W.E.D. Allen | C | 38,589 | 23.1 |
| | | | | | 6,177 | 3.7 |
| 1923 | 96,497 | 84.8 | T.J.S. Harbison | N | 44,003 | 27.0 |
| | | | C. Healy | N | 43,668 | 26.8 |
| | | | J.A. Pringle | C | 37,733 | 23.1 |
| | | | Sir C.F. Falls | C | 37,682 | 23.1 |
| | | | | | 5,935 | 3.7 |
| 1924 | 97,044 | 53.3 | Sir C.F. Falls | C | 44,716 | 43.5 |
| | | | J.A. Pringle | C | 44,711 | 43.4 |
| | | | M. McCartan | SF | 6,812 | 6.6 |
| | | | T. Corrigan | SF | 6,685 | 6.5 |
| | | | | | 37,899 | 36.8 |
| 1929 | | | J. Devlin | N | Unopp. | |
| | | | T.J.S. Harbison | N | Unopp. | |
| [Death of Harbison] | | | | | | |
| 1931 (7/3) | | | C. Healy | N | Unopp. | |
| 1931 | 116,965 | 82.7 | J. Devlin | N | 50,650 | 26.5 |
| | | | C. Healy | N | 50,397 | 26.4 |
| | | | H.M. Irwin | C | 45,101 | 23.6 |
| | | | Y.A. Burges | C | 44,921 | 23.5 |
| | | | | | 5,296 | 2.8 |
| [Death of Devlin] | | | | | | |
| 1934 (27/6) | 118,884 | 39.4 | J.F. Stewart | N | 28,790 | 61.4 |
| | | | D. McCrossan | Ind N & Agric | 18,089 | 38.6 |
| | | | | | 10,701 | 22.8 |
| 1935 | 118,322 | 82.4 | P. Cunningham | N | 50,891 | 26.2 |
| | | | A. Mulvey | N | 50,603 | 26.1 |
| | | | R.E. Dean | C | 46,625 | 24.0 |
| | | | J.M. Blakiston-Houston | C | 46,000 | 23.7 |
| | | | | | 3,978 | 2.1 |
| 1945 | 114,977 | 88.7 | P. Cunningham | N | 55,373 | 27.3 |
| | | | A. Mulvey | N | 55,144 | 27.1 |
| | | | T. Lyons | C | 46,392 | 22.8 |
| | | | Miss N.A. Cooper | C | 46,260 | 22.8 |
| | | | | | 8,752 | 4.3 |

Note:—

1922-1923: Healy was interned by the Northern Ireland Government from May 22, 1922 until February 11, 1924.

| Election | Electors | T'out | Candidate | Party | Votes | % |
|---|---|---|---|---|---|---|
| 1922 | 63,505 | 63.9 | †Hon. Sir M.M. Macnaghten | C | 30,743 | 75.7 |
|  |  |  | E.L. Macnaghten | Ind N | 9,861 | 24.3 |
|  |  |  |  |  | 20,882 | 51.4 |
| 1923 |  |  | Hon. Sir M.M. Macnaghten | C | Unopp. |  |
| 1924 | 63,087 | 59.1 | Hon. Sir M.M. Macnaghten | C | 30,875 | 82.8 |
|  |  |  | C. MacWhinney | SF | 5,869 | 15.8 |
|  |  |  | W.H.C. Galt | Ind C | 517* | 1.4 |
|  |  |  |  |  | 25,006 | 67.0 |

[Resignation on appointment as a High Court Judge]

| Election | Electors | T'out | Candidate | Party | Votes | % |
|---|---|---|---|---|---|---|
| 1929 (29/1) |  |  | R.D. Ross | C | Unopp. |  |
| 1929 |  |  | R.D. Ross | C | Unopp. |  |
| 1931 |  |  | R.D. Ross | C | Unopp. |  |
| 1935 |  |  | Sir R.D. Ross, Bt. | C | Unopp. |  |
| 1945 | 89,979 | 88.1 | Sir R.D. Ross, Bt. | C | 40,214 | 50.7 |
|  |  |  | Dr. D.J. Cavanagh | N | 37,561 | 47.4 |
|  |  |  | M.W. Gordon | Lab | 1,471* | 1.9 |
|  |  |  |  |  | 2,653 | 3.3 |

Note:—

1922: E.L. Macnaghten sought election as a 'Protestant Home-Ruler and Anti-Partitionist' candidate. He was disowned by both the Nationalist and Sinn Fein organisations in the constituency.

# UNIVERSITIES ——— ENGLAND, WALES, SCOTLAND, N. IRELAND

# CAMBRIDGE UNIVERSITY  [627]

## (Two Seats)

| Election | Electors | T'out | Candidate | Party | Votes | % |
|---|---|---|---|---|---|---|
| 1918 | 9,282 | 62.3 | †J.F.P. Rawlinson | Co C | 1,929 | |
| | | | | | (2,034) | 35.1 |
| | | | †Sir J. Larmor | Co C | 1,986 | |
| | | | | | (1,891) | 32.7 |
| | | | W.C.D. Whetham | Ind | 1,229 | |
| | | | | | (1,220) | 21.1 |
| | | | J.C. Squire | Lab | 641 | |
| | | | | | (640*) | 11.1 |
| | | | | Quota: | 1,929 | |
| 1922 | 13,592 | 63.7 | J.F.P. Rawlinson | C | 4,192 | 48.4 |
| | | | J.R.M. Butler | Ind L | 3,453 | 39.8 |
| | | | Prof. W.R. Sorley | C | 1,018* | 11.8 |
| | | | | Quota: | 2,888 | |
| 1923 | 14,974 | 68.8 | Rt. Hon. J.F.P. Rawlinson | C | 3,434 | |
| | | | | | (4,207) | 40.9 |
| | | | Sir G.G.G. Butler | C | 3,560 | |
| | | | | | (2,844) | 27.6 |
| | | | J.R.M. Butler | Ind L | 3,283 | |
| | | | | | (3,248) | 31.5 |
| | | | | Quota: | 3,434 | |
| 1924 | 16,621 | 71.2 | Rt. Hon. J.F.P. Rawlinson | C | 4,569 | 38.6 |
| | | | Sir G.G.G. Butler | C | 4,026 | 34.0 |
| | | | J.R.M. Butler | Ind L | 3,241 | 27.4 |
| | | | | Quota: | 3,946 | |

[Death of Rawlinson]

| 1926 (13/2) | | | J.J. Withers | C | Unopp. | |

[Seat Vacant at Dissolution (Death of Butler)]

| 1929 | 23,978 | 66.7 | J.J. Withers | C | 5,330 | |
| | | | | | (6,356) | 39.7 |
| | | | G.H.A. Wilson | C | 6,046 | |
| | | | | | (5,069) | 31.7 |
| | | | H.D. Henderson | L | 3,131 | |
| | | | | | (3,099) | 19.4 |
| | | | Dr. A. Wood | Lab | 1,480 | |
| | | | | | (1,463*) | 9.2 |
| | | | | Quota: | 5,330 | |
| 1931 | | | G.H.A. Wilson | C | Unopp. | |
| | | | Sir J.J. Withers | C | Unopp. | |

[Resignation of Wilson]

| 1935 (23/2) | | | K.W.M. Pickthorn | C | Unopp. | |
| 1935 | 33,617 | 53.5 | Sir J.J. Withers | C | 7,602 | 42.3 |
| | | | K.W.M. Pickthorn | C | 6,917 | 38.5 |
| | | | H.L. Elvin | Lab | 3,453 | 19.2 |
| | | | | Quota: | 5,991 | |

[Death of Withers]

| 1940 (19–23/2) | 39,171 | 38.9 | Dr. A.V. Hill | Ind C | 9,840 | 64.6 |
| | | | Prof. J.A. Ryle | Ind Prog | 5,387 | 35.4 |
| | | | | | 4,453 | 29.2 |

| Election | Electors | T'out | Candidate | Party | Votes | % |
|----------|----------|-------|-----------|-------|-------|---|
| 1945 | 42,012 | 52.6 | K.W.M. Pickthorn | C | 7,364 | |
| | | | | | (10,202) | 46.2 |
| | | | H.W. Harris | Ind | 6,556 | |
| | | | | | (3,574) | 16.2 |
| | | | J.B. Priestley | Ind Prog | 5,745 | |
| | | | | | (5,041) | 22.8 |
| | | | Dr. C. Hill | Ind | — | |
| | | | | | (2,238*) | 10.1 |
| | | | E.L. Howard-Williams | Nat Ind | — | |
| | | | | | (1,036*) | 4.7 |
| | | | | Quota: | 7,364 | |

General Elections were conducted by Proportional Representation (single transferable vote). For an explanation of the arrangement of the figures given in the Votes column see the Introductory Notes (University Seats) at the front of this book.

## COMBINED ENGLISH UNIVERSITIES [628]

### (Birmingham, Bristol, Durham, Leeds, Liverpool, Manchester, Reading (from 1928), Sheffield)

### (Two Seats)

| Election | Electors | T'out | Candidate | Party | Votes | % |
|---|---|---|---|---|---|---|
| 1918 | 2,357 | 84.6 | †Rt. Hon. H.A.L. Fisher | Co L | 665 (959) | 48.0 |
| | | | Sir W.M. Conway | Co C | 777 (303) | 15.2 |
| | | | J.A. Hobson | Lab | 481 (366) | 18.4 |
| | | | H.G. Williams | C | — (366) | 18.4 |
| | | | | Quota: | 665 | |
| 1922 | 3,967 | 74.3 | Sir W.M. Conway | C | 983 (968) | 32.8 |
| | | | Rt. Hon. H.A.L. Fisher | NL | 1,009 (815) | 27.7 |
| | | | Prof. J. Strong | Ind | 813 (571) | 19.4 |
| | | | L.S. Woolf | Lab | — (361*) | 12.2 |
| | | | W.B. Faraday | Ind C | — (141*) | 4.8 |
| | | | S.C. Lawrence | Ind C | — (90*) | 3.1 |
| | | | | Quota: | 983 | |
| 1923 | 5,008 | 77.4 | Sir W.M. Conway | C | 1,711 | 44.1 |
| | | | Rt. Hon. H.A.L. Fisher | L | 1,316 | 34.0 |
| | | | Prof. J.J. Findlay | Lab | 850 | 21.9 |
| | | | | Quota: | 1,293 | |
| 1924 | 5,655 | 78.2 | Sir W.M. Conway | C | 1,476 (2,231) | 50.4 |
| | | | Rt. Hon. H.A.L. Fisher | L | 2,064 (1,333) | 30.1 |
| | | | Prof. J.J. Findlay | Lab | 885 (861) | 19.5 |
| | | | | Quota: | 1,476 | |
| [Resignation of Fisher] | | | | | | |
| 1926 (8-12/3) | 6,513 | 66.7 | Sir A. Hopkinson | C | 2,343 | 53.9 |
| | | | J.R.B. Muir | L | 2,000 | 46.1 |
| | | | | | 343 | 7.8 |
| 1929 | 13,775 | 72.6 | Sir W.M. Conway | C | 4,321 (2,679) | 26.8 |
| | | | Miss E.F. Rathbone | Ind | 3,394 (3,331) | 33.3 |
| | | | Prof. R.S. Conway | L | 2,281 (2,231) | 22.3 |
| | | | Sir L.A. Selby-Bigge, Bt. | C | — (1,762) | 17.6 |
| | | | | Quota: | 3,335 | |

| Election | Electors | T'out | Candidate | Party | Votes | % |
|---|---|---|---|---|---|---|
| 1931 | 19,109 | 71.7 | Miss E.F. Rathbone | Ind | 4,567 | |
| | | | | | (5,096) | 37.2 |
| | | | Sir R.H. Craddock | C | 4,858 | |
| | | | | | (3,633) | 26.5 |
| | | | Rt. Hon. Sir W.A. Jowitt | N Lab | 3,632 | |
| | | | | | (2,759) | 20.1 |
| | | | H.G. Williams | C | — | |
| | | | | | (1,748) | 12.8 |
| | | | Hon. H.G. Nicolson | NP | — | |
| | | | | | (461*) | 3.4 |
| | | | | Quota: | 4,567 | |
| | | | | | | |
| 1935 | | | Sir R.H. Craddock | C | Unopp. | |
| | | | Miss E.F. Rathbone | Ind | Unopp. | |
| [Death of Craddock] | | | | | | |
| 1937 | 28,808 | 48.3 | T.E. Harvey | Ind Prog | 6,596 | 47.4 |
| (15—19/3) | | | Rt. Hon. Sir F. Lindley | C | 4,952 | 35.6 |
| | | | Sir H.B. Brackenbury | Ind | 2,373 | 17.0 |
| | | | | | 1,644 | 11.8 |
| | | | | | | |
| 1945 | 41,976 | 50.0 | Miss E.F. Rathbone | Ind | 6,992 | |
| | | | | | (11,176) | 53.3 |
| | | | K.M. Lindsay | Ind | 5,826 | |
| | | | | | (1,923) | 9.2 |
| | | | S. Wormald | Ind Lab | 4,675 | |
| | | | | | (3,212) | 15.3 |
| | | | E.C. Arden | Nat Ind | — | |
| | | | | | (2,433*) | 11.6 |
| | | | Prof. J.H. Richardson | Ind | — | |
| | | | | | (1,124*) | 5.3 |
| | | | A.R. Foxall | Ind | — | |
| | | | | | (1,105*) | 5.3 |
| | | | | Quota: | 6,992 | |
| [Death of Rathbone] | | | | | | |
| 1946 | 43,438 | 42.1 | H.G. Strauss | C | 5,483 | 30.0 |
| (13—18/3) | | | Mrs. M.D. Stocks | Ind | 5,124 | 28.0 |
| | | | Sir E.D. Simon | Ind | 4,028 | 22.0 |
| | | | S. Wormald | Ind Lab | 3,414 | 18.7 |
| | | | G.S. Oddie | BPP | 239* | 1.3 |
| | | | | | 359 | 2.0 |

General Elections were conducted by Proportional Representation (single transferable vote). For an explanation of the arrangement of the figures given in the Votes column see the Introductory Notes (University Seats) at the front of this book.

| Election | Electors | T'out | Candidate | Party | Votes | % |
|---|---|---|---|---|---|---|
| 1918 | 9,797 | 69.0 | †Sir P. Magnus, Bt. | Co C | 2,810 | 41.5 |
| | | | S.J. Webb | Lab | 2,141 | 31.7 |
| | | | A.A. Somerville | Ind | 885 | 13.1 |
| | | | Sir W.P. Herringham | Ind | 715* | 10.6 |
| | | | C.L. Nordon | Ind | 210* | 3.1 |
| | | | | | 669 | 9.8 |
| 1922 | 11,000 | 67.6 | Sir S. Russell-Wells | C | 3,833 | 51.5 |
| | | | Prof. A.F. Pollard | L | 2,180 | 29.3 |
| | | | H.G. Wells | Lab | 1,427 | 19.2 |
| | | | | | 1,653 | 22.2 |
| 1923 | 11,293 | 71.3 | Sir S. Russell-Wells | C | 4,037 | 50.2 |
| | | | Prof. A.F. Pollard | L | 2,593 | 32.2 |
| | | | H.G. Wells | Lab | 1,420 | 17.6 |
| | | | | | 1,444 | 18.0 |
| [Seat Vacant at Dissolution (Death)] | | | | | | |
| 1924 | 11,997 | 72.0 | Dr. E.G.G. Graham-Little | Ind | 3,202 | 37.0 |
| | | | Sir J.R. Bradford | C | 2,813 | 32.6 |
| | | | Prof. A.F. Pollard | L | 1,539 | 17.8 |
| | | | Dr. F.G. Bushnell | Lab | 1,087 | 12.6 |
| | | | | | 389 | 4.4 |
| 1929 | 15,558 | 70.5 | Dr. E.G.G. Graham-Little | Ind | 5,869 | 53.5 |
| | | | W.T. Layton | L | 2,923 | 26.6 |
| | | | Sir J.W. Gilbert | C | 2,179 | 19.9 |
| | | | | | 2,946 | 26.9 |
| 1931 | 16,501 | 70.3 | Sir E.G.G. Graham-Little | Nat Ind | 8,461 | 73.0 |
| | | | A.G. Church | Ind Nat | 3,134 | 27.0 |
| | | | | | 5,327 | 46.0 |
| 1935 | 17,949 | 71.7 | Sir E.G.G. Graham-Little | Nat Ind | 8,958 | 69.6 |
| | | | Sir R.N. Angell | Lab | 3,918 | 30.4 |
| | | | | | 5,040 | 39.2 |
| 1945 | 23,948 | 63.0 | Sir E.G.G. Graham-Little | Nat Ind | 7,618 | 50.5 |
| | | | Mrs. M.D. Stocks | Ind Prog | 7,469 | 49.5 |
| | | | | | 149 | 1.0 |

Note:—

1918: Somerville sought election as a 'Teachers' candidate.

## OXFORD UNIVERSITY [630]

### (Two Seats)

| Election | Electors | T'out | Candidate | Party | Votes | % |
|----------|----------|-------|-----------|-------|-------|---|
| 1918 | 7,907 | 70.4 | †Rt. Hon. Lord Hugh Cecil | Co C (C) | 1,855 | |
| | | | | | (2,771) | 49.8 |
| | | | †Rt. Hon. R.E. Prothero | Co C | 2,546 | |
| | | | | | (1,716) | 30.9 |
| | | | Prof. G.G.A. Murray | L | 812 | |
| | | | | | (742) | 13.3 |
| | | | H.S. Furniss | Lab | 351 | |
| | | | | | (335*) | 6.0 |
| | | | | Quota: | 1,855 | |

[Elevation of Prothero to the Peerage — Lord Ernle]

| Election | Electors | T'out | Candidate | Party | Votes | % |
|----------|----------|-------|-----------|-------|-------|---|
| 1919 | 7,907 | 62.9 | Prof. C.W.C. Oman | Co C | 2,613 | 52.5 |
| (19–24/3) | | | Prof. G.G.A. Murray | L | 1,330 | 26.7 |
| | | | J.A.L. Riley | Ind | 1,032 | 20.8 |
| | | | | | 1,283 | 25.8 |
| 1922 | 9,374 | 60.2 | Rt. Hon. Lord Hugh Cecil | C | 1,883 | |
| | | | | | (3,185) | 56.4 |
| | | | Sir C.W.C. Oman | C | 2,170 | |
| | | | | | (1,018) | 18.0 |
| | | | Prof. G.G.A. Murray | L | 1,594 | |
| | | | | | (1,444) | 25.6 |
| | | | | Quota: | 1,883 | |
| 1923 | 10,814 | 75.2 | Rt. Hon. Lord Hugh Cecil | C | 2,712 | |
| | | | | | (3,560) | 43.8 |
| | | | Sir C.W.C. Oman | C | 2,950 | |
| | | | | | (2,206) | 27.1 |
| | | | Prof. G.G.A. Murray | L | 2,472 | |
| | | | | | (2,368) | 29.1 |
| | | | | Quota: | 2,712 | |
| 1924 | 10,773 | 80.8 | Rt. Hon. Lord Hugh Cecil | C | 2,901 | |
| | | | | | (4,320) | 49.6 |
| | | | Sir C.W.C. Oman | C | 2,968 | |
| | | | | | (1,738) | 20.0 |
| | | | Prof. G.G.A. Murray | Ind | 2,832 | |
| | | | | | (2,643) | 30.4 |
| | | | | Quota: | 2,901 | |
| 1929 | 15,770 | 72.7 | Rt. Hon. Lord Hugh Cecil | C | 3,822 | |
| | | | | | (6,012) | 52.4 |
| | | | Sir C.W.C. Oman | C | 4,112 | |
| | | | | | (2,174) | 19.0 |
| | | | Prof. G.G.A. Murray | L | 3,529 | |
| | | | | | (3,277) | 28.6 |
| | | | | Quota: | 3,822 | |
| 1931 | | | Rt. Hon. Lord Hugh Cecil | C | Unopp. | |
| | | | Sir C.W.C. Oman | C | Unopp. | |
| 1935 | 22,413 | 68.0 | Rt. Hon. Lord Hugh Cecil | C | 5,081 | |
| | | | | | (7,365) | 48.3 |
| | | | A.P. Herbert | Ind | 5,206 | |
| | | | | | (3,390) | 22.3 |
| | | | C.R.M.F. Cruttwell | C | 3,697 | |
| | | | | | (1,803*) | 11.8 |
| | | | Prof. J.L. Stocks | Lab | — | |
| | | | | | (2,683) | 17.6 |
| | | | | Quota: | 5,081 | |

| Election | Electors | T'out | Candidate | Party | Votes | % |
|----------|----------|-------|-----------|-------|-------|---|
| [Resignation of Cecil on appointment as Provost of Eton College] | | | | | | |
| 1937 | 24,021 | 62.9 | Sir J.A. Salter | Ind | 7,580 | 50.2 |
| (23–27/2) | | | Sir E.F. Buzzard, Bt. | C | 3,917 | 25.9 |
| | | | Prof. F.A. Lindemann | Ind C | 3,608 | 23.9 |
| | | | | | 3,663 | 24.3 |
| 1945 | 28,865 | 53.1 | Rt. Hon. Sir J.A. Salter | Ind | 6,771 | 44.2 |
| | | | A.P. Herbert | Ind | 5,136 | 33.5 |
| | | | G.D.H. Cole | Lab | 3,414 | 22.3 |
| | | | | Quota: | 5,108 | |

General Elections were conducted by Proportional Representation (single transferable vote). For an explanation of the arrangement of the figures given in the Votes column see the Introductory Notes (University Seats) at the front of this book.

| Election | Electors | T'out | Candidate | Party | Votes | % |
|---|---|---|---|---|---|---|
| 1918 | 1,066 | 85.8 | †Rt. Hon. J.H. Lewis | Co L | 739 | 80.8 |
| | | | Mrs. H.M. Mackenzie | Lab | 176 | 19.2 |
| | | | | | 563 | 61.6 |
| 1922 | 1,441 | 87.2 | T.A. Lewis | NL | 497 | 39.5 |
| | | | Rt. Hon. Sir E.J. Ellis-Griffith, Bt. | L | 451 | 35.9 |
| | | | Dr. Olive A. Wheeler | Lab | 309 | 24.6 |
| | | | | | 46 | 3.6 |

[Seat Vacant at Dissolution (Death)]

| Election | Electors | T'out | Candidate | Party | Votes | % |
|---|---|---|---|---|---|---|
| 1923 | 1,922 | 83.1 | G.M.L. Davies | CP (Lab) | 570 | 35.7 |
| | | | Rev. J. Jones | L | 560 | 35.1 |
| | | | J. Edwards | Ind L | 467 | 29.2 |
| | | | | | 10 | 0.6 |
| 1924 | 2,252 | 79.0 | E. Evans | L | 1,057 | 59.4 |
| | | | G.M.L. Davies | Lab | 721 | 40.6 |
| | | | | | 336 | 18.8 |
| 1929 | 3,623 | 74.4 | E. Evans | L | 1,712 | 63.5 |
| | | | Rev. D. Richards | Lab | 671 | 24.9 |
| | | | Sir C.C. Mansel, Bt. | C | 314* | 11.6 |
| | | | | | 1,041 | 38.6 |
| 1931 | 5,121 | 61.4 | E. Evans | L | 2,229 | 70.9 |
| | | | J.S. Lewis | PC | 914 | 29.1 |
| | | | | | 1,315 | 41.8 |
| 1935 | 7,325 | 62.3 | E. Evans | L | 2,796 | 61.3 |
| | | | I. Davies | Lab | 1,768 | 38.7 |
| | | | | | 1,028 | 22.6 |

[Resignation on appointment as a County Court Judge]

| Election | Electors | T'out | Candidate | Party | Votes | % |
|---|---|---|---|---|---|---|
| 1943 (25–29/1) | 11,079 | 53.4 | Prof. W.J. Gruffydd | L | 3,098 | 52.3 |
| | | | J.S. Lewis | PC | 1,330 | 22.5 |
| | | | A.T. Davies | Ind | 755 | 12.8 |
| | | | E. Davies | Ind Lab | 634* | 10.7 |
| | | | N.L. Evans | Ind Lab | 101* | 1.7 |
| | | | | | 1,768 | 29.8 |
| 1945 | 11,847 | 58.5 | Prof. W.J. Gruffydd | L | 5,239 | 75.5 |
| | | | Dr. Gwenan Jones | PC | 1,696 | 24.5 |
| | | | | | 3,543 | 51.0 |

# COMBINED SCOTTISH UNIVERSITIES [632]
## (Aberdeen, Edinburgh, Glasgow, St. Andrews)
### (Three Seats)

| Election | Electors | T'out | Candidate | Party | Votes | % |
|---|---|---|---|---|---|---|
| 1918 | 27,283 | 47.4 | †Sir W.W. Cheyne, Bt. | Co C | 3,719 | 28.7 |
| | | | D.M. Cowan | Co L | 3,499 | 27.1 |
| | | | †Rt. Hon. Sir H. Craik | Co C | 3,286 | 25.4 |
| | | | Dr. P. Macdonald | Lab | 1,581 | 12.2 |
| | | | Prof. W.R. Smith | Ind | 850 | 6.6 |
| | | | | **Quota:** | **3,234** | |
| | | | | | | |
| 1922 | | | Sir G.A. Berry | C | Unopp. | |
| | | | D.M. Cowan | L | Unopp. | |
| | | | Rt. Hon. Sir H. Craik | C | Unopp. | |
| | | | | | | |
| 1923 | | | Sir G.A. Berry | C | Unopp. | |
| | | | D.M. Cowan | L | Unopp. | |
| | | | Rt. Hon. Sir H. Craik | C | Unopp. | |
| | | | | | | |
| 1924 | 31,977 | 55.1 | Rt. Hon. Sir H. Craik | C | 4,405 | |
| | | | | | (7,188) | 40.8 |
| | | | D.M. Cowan | L | 5,011 | |
| | | | | | (5,011) | 28.4 |
| | | | Sir G.A. Berry | C | 6,529 | |
| | | | | | (3,781) | 21.5 |
| | | | Rev. J.M. Munro | Lab | 1,674 | |
| | | | | | (1,639) | 9.3 |
| | | | | **Quota:** | **4,405** | |

**[Death of Craik]**

| Election | Electors | T'out | Candidate | Party | Votes | % |
|---|---|---|---|---|---|---|
| 1927<br>(26–29/4) | 35,120 | 55.1 | J. Buchan | C | 16,963 | 87.7 |
| | | | H.B. Guthrie | Lab | 2,378* | 12.3 |
| | | | | | 14,585 | 75.4 |
| | | | | | | |
| 1929 | 43,192 | 58.1 | J. Buchan | C | 6,276 | |
| | | | | | (9,959) | 39.7 |
| | | | D.M. Cowan | L | 6,698 | |
| | | | | | (6,698) | 26.7 |
| | | | Sir G.A. Berry | C | 9,262 | |
| | | | | | (5,755) | 22.9 |
| | | | Dr. J. Kerr | Lab | 2,867 | |
| | | | | | (2,691) | 10.7 |
| | | | | **Quota:** | **6,276** | |
| | | | | | | |
| 1931 | | | J. Buchan | C | Unopp. | |
| | | | D.M. Cowan | L | Unopp. | |
| | | | A.N. Skelton | C | Unopp. | |

**[Death of Cowan]**

| Election | Electors | T'out | Candidate | Party | Votes | % |
|---|---|---|---|---|---|---|
| 1934<br>(7–12/3) | 51,522 | 44.3 | Dr. G.A. Morrison | L (NL) | 18,070 | 79.2 |
| | | | R. Gibson | Lab | 4,750 | 20.8 |
| | | | | | 13,320 | 58.4 |

**[Resignation of Buchan on appointment as Governor-General of Canada]**

| Election | Electors | T'out | Candidate | Party | Votes | % |
|---|---|---|---|---|---|---|
| 1935<br>(17–22/6) | 51,522† | 48.1 | Prof. J.G. Kerr | C | 20,507 | 82.7 |
| | | | Mrs. N. Mitchison | Lab | 4,293 | 17.3 |
| | | | | | 16,214 | 65.4 |

| Election | Electors | T'out | Candidate | Party | Votes | % |
|---|---|---|---|---|---|---|
| 1935 | 52,981 | 51.2 | Prof. J.G. Kerr | C | 8,252 | 30.4 |
| | | | Dr. G.A. Morrison | NL | 7,529 | 27.8 |
| | | | A.N. Skelton | C | 7,479 | 27.6 |
| | | | Prof. A.D. Gibb | SNP | 3,865 | 14.2 |
| | | | | Quota: | 6,782 | |

[Death of Skelton]

| 1936 | 52,981 | 54.8 | Rt. Hon. J.R. MacDonald | N Lab | 16,393 | 56.5 |
| (27—31/1) | | | Prof. A.D. Gibb | SNP | 9,034 | 31.1 |
| | | | D.C. Thomson | Lab | 3,597* | 12.4 |
| | | | | | 7,359 | 25.4 |

[Death of MacDonald]

| 1938 | 55,272 | 52.1 | Rt. Hon. Sir J. Anderson | Nat | 14,042 | 48.8 |
| (21—25/2) | | | Dr. Frances H. Melville | Ind | 5,618 | 19.5 |
| | | | Prof. A.D. Gibb | SNP | 5,246 | 18.2 |
| | | | Sir P.C. Mitchell | Ind Prog | 3,868 | 13.5 |
| | | | | | 8,424 | 29.3 |

[Resignation of Morrison]

| 1945 | 63,581 | 44.6 | Sir J. Boyd Orr | Ind | 20,197 | 71.2 |
| (9—13/4) | | | R.M. Munro | NL | 8,177 | 28.8 |
| | | | | | 12,020 | 42.4 |

| 1945 | 63,581 | 51.6 | Rt. Hon. Sir J. Anderson | Nat | 8,198 | |
| | | | | | (16,011) | 48.8 |
| | | | Sir J. Boyd Orr | Ind | 8,198 | |
| | | | | | (10,685) | 32.6 |
| | | | Sir J.G. Kerr | C | 8,999 | |
| | | | | | (1,361) | 4.2 |
| | | | Dr. H.G. Sutherland | Lab | 4,075 | |
| | | | | | (2,860) | 8.7 |
| | | | R.S. Weir | L | 3,319 | |
| | | | | | (1,872) | 5.7 |
| | | | | Quota: | 8,198 | |

[Resignation of Boyd Orr on appointment as Director-General of the United Nations Food and Agricultural Organisation]

| 1946 | 64,062 | 50.7 | Rt. Hon. W.E. Elliot | C | 22,152 | 68.2 |
| (22—27/11) | | | Dr. C.E.M. Joad | Lab | 3,731* | 11.5 |
| | | | J.M. Bannerman | L | 2,593* | 8.0 |
| | | | J.G. Jameson | Ind | 2,080* | 6.4 |
| | | | Dr. R.S. Stevenson | NL | 1,938* | 5.9 |
| | | | | | 18,421 | 56.7 |

General Elections were conducted by Proportional Representation (single transferable vote). For an explanation of the arrangement of the figures given in the Votes column see the Introductory Notes (University Seats) at the front of this book.

Notes:—

1931: Cowan remained on the Government benches in the House of Commons when the Liberal Party went into Opposition in November 1933. Although remaining an official Liberal member and not joining the National Liberal group, he gave general support to the National Government.

1934: Morrison was a supporter of the National Government and subsequently joined the National Liberal group.

1936: MacDonald was Lord President of the Council.

1946: Jameson, a member of the Federal Union, fought the election as an advocate of the Union's policy although his candidature was not officially sponsored by that organisation.

| Election | Electors | T'out | Candidate | Party | Votes | % |
|---|---|---|---|---|---|---|
| 1922 | | | †Sir W. Whitla | C | Unopp. | |
| 1923 | | | T. Sinclair | C | Unopp. | |
| 1924 | | | T. Sinclair | C | Unopp. | |
| 1929 | | | T. Sinclair | C | Unopp. | |
| 1931 | | | T. Sinclair | C | Unopp. | |
| 1935 [Resignation] | | | T. Sinclair | C | Unopp. | |
| 1940 (2/11) | | | Prof. D.L. Savory | C | Unopp. | |
| 1945 | 5,134 | 51.6 | Prof. D.L. Savory | C | 1,923 | 72.5 |
| | | | T. Cusack | Ind | 728 | 27.5 |
| | | | | | 1,195 | 45.0 |

# Appendix 1

## ANALYSIS OF VOTING IN UNIVERSITY SEATS

Though the Speaker's Conference of 1916-17 recommended the use of proportional representation in boroughs of three members the Representation of the People Act 1918 made two separate provisions only one of which was implemented. Section 20(1) provided that where a university constituency had two or more members "any election. . .shall be according to the principle of proportional representation each elector having one transferable vote. . ." Under Section 20(2) Commissioners to prepare a scheme for one hundred members to be elected by proportional representation were never appointed.

From December 1918 to July 1945 three British university constituencies[1] returned two members each and one three members so that in eight general elections nine members for four university constituencies were returnable by the single transferable vote. Three single member constituencies returned one member each making a total of twelve. University representation was abolished by the Representation of the People Act, 1948 which therefore also brought proportional representation to an end in British parliamentary elections.

For over thirty years members sat in the House of Commons who had been elected by two different methods, the vast majority by the X-vote and a tiny minority by the single transferable vote.

Section 41(6) said "The expression 'transferable vote' means a vote:—
(a) capable of being given so as to indicate the voter's preference for the candidates in order; and
(b) capable of being transferred to the next choice when the vote is not required to give a prior choice the necessary quota of votes, or when, owing to the deficiency in the number of the votes given for a prior choice that choice is eliminated from the list of candidates"
This definition appears in a number of subsequent Acts, Orders and Bills and, with a very slight change in wording, in the Northern Ireland Assembly Act 1973 Section 2(3).

Detailed regulations were made, Statutory Instrument No. 1348 of 1918, which prescribed in legal language the method of voting and the counting and transfer of votes. They have remained the basis of the legal rules for the conduct of single transferable vote elections in the whole of the British Isles[2] ever since. Peripheral additions have refined and clarified various points without changing the fundamental logic of the system.

The application of the single transferable vote to four university constituencies demonstrated the mechanics of the system in real situations which are shown in the detailed results on the following pages.

Unfortunately because only one constituency had as many as three seats and the other three each had only two, the second object of the system, to provide for the representation of a reasonable spectrum of substantial groups of opinion, could not be attained. The constituencies were too small. For example, Professor Gilbert Murray stood five times for Oxford from 1918 to 1929 but never received enough votes from the regular transfer of Lord Hugh Cecil's surpluses to reach the quota of just over one-third of the votes. Three times at the end of the count he had over 30% of the votes, a substantial body of opinion indeed which could not be represented in a constituency of only two seats. Sir Alan Herbert gives a detailed account of the counting process in the 1935 election[3] when he eventually received just over one-third of the votes after the transfer to him of one-fifth of Lord Hugh's surplus and nearly half of Professor Stock's votes.

Combined English Universities 1945 illustrates two points. Though Kenneth Lindsay was fourth on first preference votes he was nevertheless elected with Miss

Eleanor Rathbone after the transfer of her surplus and the votes of eliminated candidates. Section 27 of the 1918 Act made an anomalous rule by which a deposit was only returnable in a one or two member constituency if a candidate received more than one-eighth of the first preference votes. While this might have been suitable when voting was by one or two X's it was inappropriate in a single transferable vote election. The Irish Free State corrected the anomaly by expressing the minimum vote required as a proportion of the quota calculated at the point of elimination. A candidate who had more first preferences than Lindsay lost his deposit even though he had half a quota on elimination.

The rule was different in a three-member constituency when the return of the deposit required only 1/24 of first preference votes (1/8 of 1/3). Sir John Graham Kerr would have suffered in Combined Scottish 1945 had he not been elected third after starting fifth and last.

The multi-member university elections are untypical in that there were several instances where the required number of candidates each received a quota of first preference votes. The voters formed themselves into constituencies of opinion without the assistance of the Returning Officer in Combined Scottish 1918 and 1935, Cambridge 1922, 1924 and 1935, Combined English 1923, and Oxford 1945. There were also six uncontested elections. Even if the comparative harshness of the deposit rule in two-member constituencies discouraged candidates, this did not apply to Combined Scottish. Tacit understanding between parties and candidates and a hangover from pre-first world war customs may be a possible explanation.

This is the only trial which has been made so far (April 1977) of proportional representation by the single transferable vote in British parliamentary history. It was of limited nature as a test.

*JAMES KNIGHT*

[1]   The University of Dublin elected two members in 1918.

[2]   i.e. including the Republic of Ireland (Irish Free State to 1948)

[3]   A.P. Herbert, *The Ayes Have It*, pp. 16-31 (London, 1937)

## CAMBRIDGE UNIVERSITY
### (Two Seats)

### 1918

Electors: 9,282
Turnout: 62.3
Quota: 1,929

| Candidate | Party | Stage I | Stage II Rawlinson's Surplus | | Result |
|---|---|---|---|---|---|
| Rawlinson | Co C | 2,034 | − 105 | 1,929 | First |
| Larmor | Co C | 1,891 | 95 | 1,986 | Second |
| Whetham | Ind | 1,220 | 9 | 1,229 | Runner Up |
| Squire | Lab | 640* | 1 | 641 | Unsuccessful |
| Non-transferable | | | | | |
| Total | | 5,785 | | 5,785 | |

### 1923

Electors: 14,974
Turnout: 68.8
Quota: 3,434

| Candidate | Party | Stage I | Stage II Rawlinson's Surplus | | Result |
|---|---|---|---|---|---|
| Rawlinson | C | 4,207 | − 773 | 3,434 | First |
| Butler | Ind L | 3,248 | 35 | 3,283 | Runner Up |
| Butler | C | 2,844 | 716 | 3,560 | Second |
| Non-transferable | | | 22 | 22 | |
| Total | | 10,299 | | 10,299 | |

### 1929

Electors: 23,978
Turnout: 66.7
Quota: 5,330

| Candidate | Party | Stage I | Stage II Withers' Surplus | | Result |
|---|---|---|---|---|---|
| Withers | C | 6,356 | − 1,026 | 5,330 | First |
| Wilson | C | 5,069 | 977 | 6,046 | Second |
| Henderson | L | 3,099 | 32 | 3,131 | Runner Up |
| Wood | Lab | 1,463* | 17 | 1,480 | Unsuccessful |
| Non-transferable | | | | | |
| Total | | 15,987 | | 15,987 | |

## CAMBRIDGE UNIVERSITY (Cont.)

### 1945

Electors: 42,012
Turnout: 52.6
Quota: 7,364

| Candidate | Party | Stage I | Stage II Pickthorn's Surplus | | Stage III Williams' Votes | | Stage IV Hill's Votes | | Result |
|-----------|-------|---------|---------|---------|---------|---------|---------|---------|--------|
| Pickthorn | C | 10,202 | − 2,838 | 7,364 | | 7,364 | | 7,364 | First |
| Priestley | Ind Prog | 5,041 | 87 | 5,128 | 110 | 5,238 | 507 | 5,745 | Runner Up |
| Harris | Ind | 3,574 | 1,135 | 4,709 | 476 | 5,185 | 1,371 | 6,556 | Second |
| Hill | Ind | 2,238* | 854 | 3,092 | 503 | 3,595 | − 3,595 | | Eliminated |
| Williams | Nat Ind | 1,036* | 762 | 1,798 | − 1,798 | | | | Eliminated |
| Non-transferable | | | | | 709 | 709 | 1,717 | 2,426 | |
| | | | | | | | | | |
| Total | | 22,091 | | 22,091 | | 22,091 | | 22,091 | |

## COMBINED ENGLISH UNIVERSITIES

### (Two Seats)

### 1918

Electors: 2,357
Turnout: 84.6
Quota: 665

| Candidate | Party | Stage I | Stage II Fisher's Surplus | | Stage III Williams' Votes | | Result |
|---|---|---|---|---|---|---|---|
| Fisher | Co L | 959 | −294 | 665 | | 665 | First |
| Hobson | Lab | 366 | 88 | 454 | 27 | 481 | Runner Up |
| Williams | C | 366 | 44 | 410 | −410 | | Eliminated |
| Conway | Co C | 303 | 162 | 465 | 312 | 777 | Second |
| Non-transferable | | | | | 71 | 71 | |
| Total | | 1,994 | | 1,994 | | 1,994 | |

### 1922

Electors: 3,967
Turnout: 74.3
Quota: 983

| Candidate | Party | Stage I | Stage II Lawrence's Votes | | Stage III Faraday's Votes | | Stage IV Conway's Surplus | | Stage V Woolf's Votes | | Result |
|---|---|---|---|---|---|---|---|---|---|---|---|
| Conway | C | 968 | 14 | 982 | 111 | 1,093 | −110 | 983 | | 983 | First |
| Fisher | NL | 815 | 6 | 821 | 28 | 849 | 34 | 883 | 126 | 1,009 | Second |
| Strong | Ind | 571 | 4 | 575 | 20 | 595 | 16 | 611 | 202 | 813 | Runner Up |
| Woolf | Lab | 361* | | 361 | 4 | 365 | 1 | 366 | −366 | | Eliminated |
| Faraday | Ind C | 141* | 65 | 206 | −206 | | | | | | Eliminated |
| Lawrence | Ind C | 90* | −90 | | | | | | | | Eliminated |
| Non-transferable | | | 1 | 1 | 43 | 44 | 59 | 103 | 38 | 141 | |
| Total | | 2,946 | | 2,946 | | 2,946 | | 2,946 | | 2,946 | |

### 1924

Electors: 5,655
Turnout: 78.2
Quota: 1,476

| Candidate | Party | Stage I | Stage II Conway's Surplus | | Result |
|---|---|---|---|---|---|
| Conway | C | 2,231 | −755 | 1,476 | First |
| Fisher | L | 1,333 | 731 | 2,064 | Second |
| Findlay | Lab | 861 | 24 | 885 | Runner Up |
| Non-transferable | | | | | |
| Total | | 4,425 | | 4,425 | |

## COMBINED ENGLISH UNIVERSITIES (Cont.)

### 1929

Electors: 13,775
Turnout: 72.6
Quota: 3,335

| Candidate | Party | Stage I | Stage II Selby-Bigge's Votes | | Result |
|---|---|---|---|---|---|
| Rathbone | Ind | 3,331 | 63 | 3,394 | First |
| Conway | C | 2,679 | 1,642 | 4,321 | Second |
| Conway | L | 2,231 | 50 | 2,281 | Runner Up |
| Selby-Bigge | C | 1,762 | −1,762 | | Eliminated |
| Non-transferable | | | 7 | 7 | |
| Total | | 10,003 | | 10,003 | |

### 1931

Electors: 19,109
Turnout: 71.7
Quota: 4,567

| Candidate | Party | Stage I | Stage II Rathbone's Surplus | | Stage III Nicholson's Votes | | Stage IV Williams' Votes | | Result |
|---|---|---|---|---|---|---|---|---|---|
| Rathbone | Ind | 5,096 | −529 | 4,567 | | 4,567 | | 4,567 | First |
| Craddock | C | 3,633 | 52 | 3,685 | 69 | 3,754 | 1,104 | 4,858 | Second |
| Jowitt | N Lab | 2,759 | 244 | 3,003 | 204 | 3,207 | 425 | 3,632 | Runner Up |
| Williams | C | 1,748 | 71 | 1,819 | 103 | 1,922 | −1,922 | | Eliminated |
| Nicolson | NP | 461* | 162 | 623 | −623 | | | | Eliminated |
| Non-transferable | | | | | 247 | 247 | 393 | 640 | |
| Total | | 13,697 | | 13,697 | | 13,697 | | 13,697 | |

### 1945

Electors: 41,976
Turnout: 50.0
Quota: 6,992

| Candidate | Party | Stage I | Stage II Rathbone's Surplus | | Stage III Foxall's Votes | | Stage IV Richardson's Votes | | Stage V Arden's Votes | | Result |
|---|---|---|---|---|---|---|---|---|---|---|---|
| Rathbone | Ind | 11,176 | −4,184 | 6,992 | | 6,992 | | 6,992 | | 6,992 | First |
| Wormald | Ind | 3,212 | 761 | 3,973 | 108 | 4,081 | 392 | 4,473 | 202 | 4,675 | Runner Up |
| Arden | Ind | 2,433* | 640 | 3,073 | 316 | 3,389 | 440 | 3,829 | −3,829 | | Eliminated |
| Lindsay | Ind | 1,923 | 1,580 | 3,503 | 353 | 3,856 | 672 | 4,528 | 1,298 | 5,826 | Second |
| Richardson | Ind | 1,124* | 871 | 1,995 | 346 | 2,341 | −2,341 | | | | Eliminated |
| Foxall | Ind | 1,105* | 332 | 1,437 | −1,437 | | | | | | Eliminated |
| Non-transferable | | | | | 314 | 314 | 837 | 1,151 | 2,329 | 3,480 | |
| Total | | 20,973 | | 20,973 | | 20,973 | | 20,973 | | 20,973 | |

## OXFORD UNIVERSITY

### (Two Seats)

### 1918

Electors: 7,907
Turnout: 70.4
Quota: 1,855

| Candidate | Party | Stage I | Stage II Cecil's Surplus | | Result |
|---|---|---|---|---|---|
| Cecil | Co C | 2,771 | − 916 | 1,855 | First |
| Prothero | Co C | 1,716 | 830 | 2,546 | Second |
| Murray | L | 742 | 70 | 812 | Runner Up |
| Furniss | Lab | 335* | 16 | 351 | Unsuccessful |
| Non-transferable | | | | | |
| Total | | 5,564 | | 5,564 | |

### 1922

Electors: 9,374
Turnout: 60.2
Quota: 1,883

| Candidate | Party | Stage I | Stage II Cecil's Surplus | | Result |
|---|---|---|---|---|---|
| Cecil | C | 3,185 | − 1,302 | 1,883 | First |
| Murray | L | 1,444 | 150 | 1,594 | Runner Up |
| Oman | C | 1,018 | 1,152 | 2,170 | Second |
| Non-transferable | | | | | |
| Total | | 5,647 | | 5,647 | |

### 1923

Electors: 10,814
Turnout: 75.2
Quota: 2,712

| Candidate | Party | Stage I | Stage II Cecil's Surplus | | Result |
|---|---|---|---|---|---|
| Cecil | C | 3,560 | − 848 | 2,712 | First |
| Murray | L | 2,368 | 104 | 2,472 | Runner Up |
| Oman | C | 2,206 | 744 | 2,950 | Second |
| Non-transferable | | | | | |
| Total | | 8,134 | | 8,134 | |

## OXFORD UNIVERSITY   (Cont.)

### 1924

Electors: 10,773
Turnout: 80.8
Quota: 2,901

| Candidate | Party | Stage I | Stage II Cecil's Surplus | | Result |
|---|---|---|---|---|---|
| Cecil | C | 4,320 | − 1,419 | 2,901 | First |
| Murray | Ind | 2,643 | 189 | 2,832 | Runner Up |
| Oman | C | 1,738 | 1,230 | 2,968 | Second |
| Non-transferable | | | | | |
| Total | | 8,701 | | 8,701 | |

### 1929

Electors: 15,770
Turnout: 72.7
Quota: 3,822

| Candidate | Party | Stage I | Stage II Cecil's Surplus | | Result |
|---|---|---|---|---|---|
| Cecil | C | 6,012 | − 2,190 | 3,822 | First |
| Murray | L | 3,277 | 252 | 3,529 | Runner Up |
| Oman | C | 2,174 | 1,938 | 4,112 | Second |
| Non-transferable | | | | | |
| Total | | 11,463 | | 11,463 | |

### 1935

Electors: 22,413
Turnout: 68.0
Quota: 5,081

| Candidate | Party | Stage I | Stage II Cecil's Surplus | | Stage III Stocks' Votes | | Result |
|---|---|---|---|---|---|---|---|
| Cecil | C | 7,365 | − 2,284 | 5,081 | | 5,081 | First |
| Herbert | Ind | 3,390 | 474 | 3,864 | 1,342 | 5,206 | Second |
| Stocks | Lab | 2,683 | 93 | 2,776 | − 2,776 | | Eliminated |
| Cruttwell | C | 1,803* | 1,717 | 3,520 | 177 | 3,697 | Runner Up |
| Non-transferable | | | | | 1,257 | 1,257 | |
| Total | | 15,241 | | 15,241 | | 15,241 | |

## COMBINED SCOTTISH UNIVERSITIES
### (Three Seats)

### 1924

Electors: 31,977
Turnout: 55.1
Quota: 4,405

| Candidate | Party | Stage I | Stage II Craik's Surplus | | Result |
|-----------|-------|---------|--------|--------|--------|
| Craik | C | 7,188 | −2,783 | 4,405 | First |
| Cowan | L | 5,011 | | 5,011 | Second |
| Berry | C | 3,781 | 2,748 | 6,529 | Third |
| Munro | Lab | 1,639 | 35 | 1,674 | Runner Up |
| Non-transferable | | | | | |
| Total | | 17,619 | | 17,619 | |

### 1929

Electors: 43,192
Turnout: 58.1
Quota: 6,276

| Candidate | Party | Stage I | Stage II Buchan's Surplus | | Result |
|-----------|-------|---------|--------|--------|--------|
| Buchan | C | 9,959 | −3,683 | 6,276 | First |
| Cowan | L | 6,698 | | 6,698 | Second |
| Berry | C | 5,755 | 3,507 | 9,262 | Third |
| Kerr | Lab | 2,691 | 176 | 2,867 | Runner Up |
| Non transferable | | | | | |
| Total | | 25,103 | | 25,103 | |

### 1945

Electors: 63,581
Turnout: 51.6
Quota: 8,198

| Candidate | Party | Stage I | Stage II Anderson's Surplus | | Stage III Orr's Surplus | | Result |
|-----------|-------|---------|--------|--------|--------|--------|--------|
| Anderson | Nat | 16,011 | −7,813 | 8,198 | | 8,198 | First |
| Boyd Orr | Ind | 10,685 | | 10,685 | −2,487 | 8,198 | Second |
| Sutherland | Lab | 2,860 | 321 | 3,181 | 894 | 4,075 | Runner Up |
| Weir | L | 1,872 | 744 | 2,616 | 703 | 3,319 | Unsuccessf |
| Kerr | C | 1,361 | 6,748 | 8,109 | 890 | 8,999 | Third |
| Non-transferable | | | | | | | |
| Total | | 32,789 | | 32,789 | | 32,789 | |

## Appendix 2

## ANALYSIS OF VOTING IN TWO-MEMBER SEATS

The following is a detailed analysis of the voting in the fifteen territorial constituencies in which each elector had two votes, and returned two Members of Parliament.

Figures have been extracted from local newspaper reports and where the analysis did not agree precisely with the official total of votes cast for each candidate, minor adjustments have been made to correct what were probably typographical or arithmetical errors.

Returning Officers were under no obligation to provide an analysis of the voting but in the vast majority of elections, figures were obtained by the local press either directly from the Returning Officers or through election agents. In the relatively few instances where figures have not been found it is likely that the method of counting used at the election made an analysis impossible. Where an analysis proved unobtainable the total number of valid ballot papers included in the count is given (this figure coming from either press reports or Home Office Returns) and the number of 'plumpers' can be calculated (ballot papers multiplied by 2 minus total votes cast equals 'plumpers') if required. Only in a very few cases has it been impossible to find an exact figure for the total number of ballot papers and an estimate has been made which should be fairly accurate.

The presentation of the figures requires little explanation. The number of 'plumpers' is followed by an analysis of the voting for pairs of candidates. Finally, a total is given of the number of votes (i.e. ballot papers) cast which is in effect the number of persons voting, and also a total of the individual votes which made up the result.

Occasionally the analysis figures included a total for doubtful ballot papers which had been rejected in the initial stages of the count but subsequently found to be valid either wholly or in part. In these cases the figures have been included, in *italic* type within brackets, following the number of 'plumpers', the total figure representing the number of ballot papers involved. In instances where only a partial analysis was published the total figures for 'plumpers' and voters have been included even though some of the figures making up the total may be missing.

### CITY of LONDON [12]

| | |
|---|---|
| **1918** | Unopposed |
| **1922** | Unopposed |
| **1923** | Unopposed |
| **1924** | Unopposed |
| **1929** | Analysis not available — Ballot papers 20,983 (including spoilt papers) |
| **1931** | Unopposed |
| **1935** | Unopposed |
| **1945** | Analysis not available — Ballot Papers 6,935 |

## BLACKBURN [86]

### 1918

| Candidate | Party | Votes | Result |
|---|---|---|---|
| Norman | Co L | 1,199 | 32,076 |
| Dean | Co C | 1,043 | 30,158 |
| Snowden | Lab | 12,994 | 15,274 |
| **Total Plumpers** | | **15,236** | |
| Norman/Dean | Co L/Co C | 28,856 | |
| Norman/Snowden | Co L/Lab | 2,021 | |
| Dean/Snowden | Co C/Lab | 259 | |
| **Total** | | **46,372** | **77,508** |

### 1922

| | | | |
|---|---|---|---|
| Henn | C | 1,510 | 28,280 |
| Norman | NL | 301 | 27,071 |
| Davies | Lab | 71 | 24,049 |
| Porter | Lab | 189 | 23,402 |
| Meech | L | 1,652 | 8,141 |
| **Total Plumpers** | | **3,723** | |
| Henn/Norman | C/NL | 24,253 | |
| Henn/Davies | C/Lab | 493 | |
| Henn/Porter | C/Lab | 639 | |
| Henn/Meech | C/L | 1,385 | |
| Norman/Davies | NL/Lab | 257 | |
| Norman/Porter | NL/Lab | 325 | |
| Norman/Meech | NL/L | 1,935 | |
| Davies/Porter | Lab/Lab | 21,154 | |
| Davies/Meech | Lab/L | 2,074 | |
| Porter/Meech | Lab/L | 1,095 | |
| **Total** | | **57,333** | **110,943** |

### 1923

| | | | |
|---|---|---|---|
| Duckworth | L | 1,730 | 31,117 |
| Henn | C | 2,148 | 28,505 |
| Davies | Lab | 240 | 25,428 |
| Porter | Lab | 125 | 21,903 |
| **Total Plumpers** | | **4,243** | |
| Duckworth/Henn | L/C | 25,518 | |
| Duckworth/Davies | L/Lab | 3,450 | |
| Duckworth/Porter | L/Lab | 419 | |
| Henn/Davies | C/Lab | 609 | |
| Henn/Porter | C/Lab | 230 | |
| Davies/Porter | Lab/Lab | 21,129 | |
| **Total** | | **55,598** | **106,953** |

### 1924

| | | | |
|---|---|---|---|
| Duckworth | L | 1,361 | 31,612 |
| Henn | C | 2,129 | 31,347 |
| Hamilton | Lab | 194 | 24,330 |
| Gill | Lab | 252 | 24,317 |
| **Total Plumpers** | | **3,936** | |
| Duckworth/Henn | L/C | 28,586 | |
| Duckworth/Hamilton | L/Lab | 835 | |
| Duckworth/Gill | L/Lab | 830 | |
| Henn/Hamilton | C/Lab | 349 | |
| Henn/Gill | C/Lab | 283 | |
| Hamilton/Gill | Lab/Lab | 22,952 | |
| **Total** | | **57,771** | **111,606** |

# ANALYSIS OF VOTING IN TWO-MEMBER SEATS

## 1929

| Candidate | Party | Votes | Result |
|---|---|---|---|
| Hamilton | Lab | 479 | 37,256 |
| Gill | Lab | 290 | 35,723 |
| Henn | C | 5,440 | 35,249 |
| Erleigh | L | 2,719 | 34,504 |
| **Total Plumpers** | | **8,928** | |
| Hamilton/Gill | Lab/Lab | 33,697 | |
| Hamilton/Henn | Lab/C | 977 | |
| Hamilton/Erleigh | Lab/L | 2,103 | |
| Gill/Henn | Lab/C | 443 | |
| Gill/Erleigh | Lab/L | 1,293 | |
| Henn/Erleigh | C/L | 28,389 | |
| **Total** | | **75,830** | **142,732** |

## 1931

| Candidate | Party | Votes | Result |
|---|---|---|---|
| Smiles | C | 285 | 50,105 |
| Elliston | C | 275 | 49,953 |
| Hamilton | Lab | 284 | 25,643 |
| Gill | Lab | 135 | 25,030 |
| **Total Plumpers** | | **979** | |
| Smiles/Elliston | C/C | 48,628 | |
| Smiles/Hamilton | C/Lab | 1,030 | |
| Smiles/Gill | C/Lab | 162 | |
| Elliston/Hamilton | C/Lab | 323 | |
| Elliston/Gill | C/Lab | 727 | |
| Hamilton/Gill | Lab/Lab | 24,006 | |
| **Total** | | **75,855** | **150,731** |

## 1935

| Candidate | Party | Votes | Result |
|---|---|---|---|
| Elliston | C | 267 | 37,932 |
| Smiles | C | 338 | 37,769 |
| Bell | Lab | 267 | 34,571 |
| Walker | Lab | 223 | 34,423 |
| **Total Plumpers** | | **1,095** | |
| Elliston/Smiles | C/C | 36,221 | |
| Elliston/Bell | C/Lab | 1,221 | |
| Elliston/Walker | C/Lab | 223 | |
| Smiles/Bell | C/Lab | 158 | |
| Smiles/Walker | C/Lab | 1,052 | |
| Bell/Walker | Lab/Lab | 32,925 | |
| **Total** | | **72,895** | **144,695** |

## 1945

| Candidate | Party | Votes | Result |
|---|---|---|---|
| Edwards | Lab | 266 | 35,182 |
| Castle | Lab | 428 | 35,145 |
| Glover | C | 326 | 26,325 |
| Parker | C | 146 | 25,807 |
| Shackleton | L | 97 | 6,587 |
| Macinerney | L | 69 | 6,096 |
| **Total Plumpers** | | **1,332** | |
| Edwards/Castle | Lab/Lab | 34,145 | |
| Edwards/Glover | Lab/C | 346 | |
| Edwards/Parker | Lab/C | 83 | |
| Edwards/Shackleton | Lab/L | 223 | |
| Edwards/Macinerney | Lab/L | 119 | |

## 1945 (Cont.)

| Candidate | Party | Votes | Result |
|---|---|---|---|
| Castle/Glover | Lab/C | 116 | |
| Castle/Parker | Lab/C | 68 | |
| Castle/Shackleton | Lab/L | 182 | |
| Castle/Macinerney | Lab/L | 206 | |
| Glover/Parker | C/C | 24,636 | |
| Glover/Shackleton | C/L | 370 | |
| Glover/Macinerney | C/L | 531 | |
| Parker/Shackleton | C/L | 709 | |
| Parker/Macinerney | C/L | 165 | |
| Shackleton/Macinerney | L/L | 5,006 | |
| **Total** | | **68,237** | **135,142** |

## BOLTON [90]

**1918**                          Unopposed

**1922**

| Candidate | Party | Votes | Result |
|-----------|-------|-------|--------|
| Russell | C | 8,460 | 37,491 |
| Edge | NL | 2,124 | 31,015 |
| Lomax | Lab | 240 | 20,559 |
| Abraham | Lab | 253 | 20,156 |
| Edwards | L | 8,312 | 18,534 |
| **Total Plumpers** | | **19,389** | |
| Russell/Edge | C/NL | 24,644 | |
| Russell/Lomax | C/Lab | 662 | |
| Russell/Abraham | C/Lab | 618 | |
| Russell/Edwards | C/L | 3,107 | |
| Edge/Lomax | NL/Lab | 441 | |
| Edge/Abraham | NL/Lab | 305 | |
| Edge/Edwards | NL/L | 3,501 | |
| Lomax/Abraham | Lab/Lab | 17,291 | |
| Lomax/Edwards | Lab/L | 1,925 | |
| Abraham/Edwards | Lab/L | 1,689 | |
| **Total** | | **73,572** | **127,755** |

**1923**

| | | | |
|-----------|-------|-------|--------|
| Law | Lab | 591 | 25,133 |
| Cunliffe | C | 216 | 22,833 |
| Hilton | C | 151 | 22,640 |
| Edge | L | 647 | 22,173 |
| Eccles | Lab | 87 | 21,045 |
| Steele | L | 478 | 21,040 |
| **Total Plumpers** | | **2,170** | |
| Law/Cunliffe | Lab/C | 278 | |
| Law/Hilton | Lab/C | 269 | |
| Law/Edge | Lab/L | 2,111 | |
| Law/Eccles | Lab/Lab | 20,251 | |
| Law/Steele | Lab/L | 1,633 | |
| Cunliffe/Hilton | C/C | 21,453 | |
| Cunliffe/Edge | C/L | 482 | |
| Cunliffe/Eccles | C/Lab | 185 | |
| Cunliffe/Steele | C/L | 219 | |
| Hilton/Edge | C/L | 363 | |
| Hilton/Eccles | C/Lab | 213 | |
| Hilton/Steele | C/L | 191 | |
| Edge/Eccles | L/Lab | 167 | |
| Edge/Steele | L/L | 18,405 | |
| Eccles/Steele | Lab/L | 142 | |
| **Total** | | **68,532** | **134,864** |

**1924**

| | | | |
|-----------|-------|-------|--------|
| Cunliffe | C | 422 | 34,690 |
| Hilton | C | 96 | 33,405 |
| Law | Lab | 476 | 30,632 |
| Hutchinson | Lab | 96 | 28,918 |
| Taylor | L | 376 | 10,036 |
| Holt | L | 71 | 8,558 |
| **Total Plumpers** | | **1,537** | |

## 1924 (Cont.)

| Candidate | Party | Votes | Result |
|---|---|---|---|
| Cunliffe/Hilton | C/C | 32,812 | |
| Cunliffe/Law | C/Lab | 452 | |
| Cunliffe/Hutchinson | C/Lab | 72 | |
| Cunliffe/Taylor | C/L | 762 | |
| Cunliffe/Holt | C/L | 170 | |
| Hilton/Law | C/Lab | 112 | |
| Hilton/Hutchinson | C/Lab | 50 | |
| Hilton/Taylor | C/L | 156 | |
| Hilton/Holt | C/L | 179 | |
| Law/Hutchinson | Lab/Lab | 28,484 | |
| Law/Taylor | Lab/L | 899 | |
| Law/Holt | Lab/L | 209 | |
| Hutchinson/Taylor | Lab/L | 65 | |
| Hutchinson/Holt | Lab/L | 151 | |
| Taylor/Holt | L/L | 7,778 | |
| **Total** | | **73,888** | **146,239** |

## 1929

| Candidate | Party | Votes | Result |
|---|---|---|---|
| Law | Lab | 2,308 | 43,520 |
| Brothers | Lab | 231 | 37,888 |
| Entwistle | C | 647 | 36,667 |
| Hilton | C | 393 | 35,850 |
| Barry | L | 18,522 | 27,074 |
| **Total Plumpers** | | **22,101** | |
| Law/Brothers | Lab/Lab | 35,749 | |
| Law/Entwistle | Lab/C | 497 | |
| Law/Hilton | Lab/C | 620 | |
| Law/Barry | Lab/L | 4,346 | |
| Brothers/Entwistle | Lab/C | 122 | |
| Brothers/Hilton | Lab/C | 95 | |
| Brothers/Barry | Lab/L | 1,691 | |
| Entwistle/Hilton | C/C | 33,814 | |
| Entwistle/Barry | C/L | 1,587 | |
| Hilton/Barry | C/L | 928 | |
| **Total** | | **101,550** | **180,999** |

## 1931

| Candidate | Party | Votes | Result |
|---|---|---|---|
| Entwistle | C | 1,827 | 66,385 |
| Haslam | C | 414 | 63,402 |
| Law | Lab | 1,350 | 33,737 |
| Brothers | Lab | 758 | 32,049 |
| **Total Plumpers** | | **4,349** | |
| Entwistle/Haslam | C/C | 62,242 | |
| Entwistle/Law | C/Lab | 1,590 | |
| Entwistle/Brothers | C/Lab | 726 | |
| Haslam/Law | C/Lab | 489 | |
| Haslam/Brothers | C/Lab | 257 | |
| Law/Brothers | Lab/Lab | 30,308 | |
| **Total** | | **99,961** | **195,573** |

## 1935

| Candidate | Party | Votes | Result |
|---|---|---|---|
| Entwistle | C | 906 | 54,129 |
| Haslam | C | 405 | 52,465 |
| Law | Lab | 1,388 | 39,890 |
| Lynch | Lab | 1,640 | 39,871 |
| **Total Plumpers** | | **4,339** | |

## 1935 (Cont.)

| Candidate | Party | Votes | Result |
|---|---|---|---|
| Entwistle/Haslam | C/C | 51,015 | |
| Entwistle/Law | C/Lab | 1,106 | |
| Entwistle/Lynch | C/Lab | 1,102 | |
| Haslam/Law | C/Lab | 656 | |
| Haslam/Lynch | C/Lab | 389 | |
| Law/Lynch | Lab/Lab | 36,740 | |
| **Total** | | **95,347** | **186,355** |

## 1945

| Candidate | Party | Votes | Result |
|---|---|---|---|
| Jones | Lab | 473 | 44,595 |
| Lewis | Lab | 130 | 43,266 |
| Reynolds | C | 775 | 31,217 |
| Entwistle | C | 671 | 30,911 |
| Spedding | L | 246 | 18,180 |
| Connell | L | 226 | 17,710 |
| **Total Plumpers** | | **2,521** | |
| Jones/Lewis | Lab/Lab | 42,674 | |
| Jones/Reynolds | Lab/C | 286 | |
| Jones/Entwistle | Lab/C | 244 | |
| Jones/Spedding | Lab/L | 515 | |
| Jones/Connell | Lab/L | 403 | |
| Lewis/Reynolds | Lab/C | 149 | |
| Lewis/Entwistle | Lab/C | 116 | |
| Lewis/Spedding | Lab/L | 109 | |
| Lewis/Connell | Lab/L | 88 | |
| Reynolds/Entwistle | C/C | 28,187 | |
| Reynolds/Spedding | C/L | 1,306 | |
| Reynolds/Connell | C/L | 514 | |
| Entwistle/Spedding | C/L | 609 | |
| Entwistle/Connell | C/L | 1,084 | |
| Spedding/Connell | L/L | 15,395 | |
| **Total** | | **94,200** | **185,879** |

## BRIGHTON [97]

### 1918

| Candidate | Party | Votes | Result |
|-----------|-------|------:|-------:|
| Tryon | Co C | 773 | 32,958 |
| Thomas-Stanford | Co C | 358 | 32,561 |
| Lewis | Lab | 430 | 8,971 |
| Canter | Lab | 139 | 8,514 |
| **Total Plumpers** | | **1,700** | |
| Tryon/Thomas-Stanford | Co C/Co C | 31,930 | |
| Tryon/Lewis | Co C/Lab | 159 | |
| Tryon/Canter | Co C/Lab | 96 | |
| Thomas-Stanford/Lewis | Co C/Lab | 188 | |
| Thomas-Stanford/Canter | Co C/Lab | 85 | |
| Lewis/Canter | Lab/Lab | 8,194 | |
| **Total** | | **42,352** | **83,004** |

### 1922

| Candidate | Party | Votes | Result |
|-----------|-------|------:|-------:|
| Tryon | C | 1,110 | 28,549 |
| Rawson | C | 328 | 26,844 |
| Fry | L | 16,981 | 22,059 |
| Wheater | Ind C | 5,290 | 11,913 |
| **Total Plumpers** | | **23,709** | |
| Tryon/Rawson | C/C | 24,942 | |
| Tryon/Fry | C/L | 840 | |
| Tryon/Wheater | C/Ind C | 1,657 | |
| Rawson/Fry | C/L | 423 | |
| Rawson/Wheater | C/Ind C | 1,151 | |
| Fry/Wheater | L/Ind C | 3,815 | |
| **Total** | | **56,537** | **89,365** |

### 1923

| Candidate | Party | Votes | Result |
|-----------|-------|------:|-------:|
| Tryon | C | 617 | 30,137 |
| Rawson | C | 325 | 29,759 |
| Runciman | L | 373 | 17,462 |
| Lunn | L | 123 | 16,567 |
| Gordon | Lab | 200 | 9,545 |
| Carden | Lab | 118 | 9,040 |
| **Total Plumpers** | | **1,756** | |
| Tryon/Rawson | C/C | 28,764 | |
| Tryon/Runciman | C/L | 610 | |
| Tryon/Lunn | C/L | 38 | |
| Tryon/Gordon | C/Lab | 87 | |
| Tryon/Carden | C/Lab | 21 | |
| Rawson/Runciman | C/L | 277 | |
| Rawson/Lunn | C/L | 282 | |
| Rawson/Gordon | C/Lab | 90 | |
| Rawson/Carden | C/Lab | 21 | |
| Runciman/Lunn | L/L | 15,937 | |
| Runciman/Gordon | L/Lab | 204 | |
| Runciman/Carden | L/Lab | 61 | |
| Lunn/Gordon | L/Lab | 166 | |
| Lunn/Carden | L/Lab | 21 | |
| Gordon/Carden | Lab/Lab | 8,798 | |
| **Total** | | **57,133** | **112,510** |

## 1924

| Candidate | Party | Votes | Result |
|---|---|---|---|
| Tryon | C | 951 | 39,387 |
| Rawson | C | 618 | 39,253 |
| Gordon | Lab | 13,481 | 14,072 |
| Total Plumpers | | **15,050** | |
| Tryon/Rawson | C/C | 38,240 | |
| Tryon/Gordon | C/Lab | 196 | |
| Rawson/Gordon | C/Lab | 395 | |
| Total | | **53,881** | **92,712** |

## 1929

| Candidate | Party | Votes | Result |
|---|---|---|---|
| Rawson | C | 671 | 46,515 |
| Tryon | C | 570 | 46,287 |
| Cheshire | Lab | 488 | 19,494 |
| McLaine | Lab | 459 | 18,770 |
| Dallow | L | 583 | 14,770 |
| Brudenell-Bruce | L | 433 | 13,816 |
| Total Plumpers | | **3,204** | |
| Rawson/Tryon | C/C | 45,567 | |
| Rawson/Cheshire | C/Lab | 45 | |
| Rawson/McLaine | C/Lab | 72 | |
| Rawson/Dallow | C/L | 96 | |
| Rawson/Brudenell-Bruce | C/L | 64 | |
| Tryon/Cheshire | C/Lab | 25 | |
| Tryon/McLaine | C/Lab | 22 | |
| Tryon/Dallow | C/L | 39 | |
| Tryon/Brudenell-Bruce | C/L | 64 | |
| Cheshire/McLaine | Lab/Lab | 16,771 | |
| Cheshire/Dallow | Lab/L | 840 | |
| Cheshire/Brudenell-Bruce | Lab/L | 1,325 | |
| McLaine/Dallow | Lab/L | 1,364 | |
| McLaine/Brudenell-Bruce | Lab/L | 82 | |
| Dallow/Brudenell-Bruce | L/L | 11,848 | |
| Total | | **81,428** | **159,652** |

## 1931

| Candidate | Party | Votes | Result |
|---|---|---|---|
| Rawson | C | 1,098 | 75,205 |
| Tryon | C | 882 | 74,993 |
| Cohen | Lab | 422 | 12,952 |
| Moore | Lab | 280 | 12,878 |
| Total Plumpers | | **2,682** | |
| Rawson/Tryon | C/C | 73,925 | |
| Rawson/Cohen | C/Lab | 68 | |
| Rawson/Moore | C/Lab | 114 | |
| Tryon/Cohen | C/Lab | 82 | |
| Tryon/Moore | C/Lab | 104 | |
| Cohen/Moore | Lab/Lab | 12,380 | |
| Total | | **89,355** | **176,028** |

## 1935

| Candidate | Party | Votes | Result |
|---|---|---|---|
| Tryon | C | 742 | 60,913 |
| Rawson | C | 654 | 60,724 |
| Gordon | Lab | 518 | 19,287 |
| Cohen | Lab | 433 | 18,743 |
| Total Plumpers | | **2,347** | |

## 1935 (Cont.)

| Candidate | Party | Votes | Result |
|---|---|---|---|
| Tryon/Rawson | C/C | 59,705 | |
| Tryon/Gordon | C/Lab | 352 | |
| Tryon/Cohen | C/Lab | 114 | |
| Rawson/Gordon | C/Lab | 293 | |
| Rawson/Cohen | C/Lab | 72 | |
| Gordon/Cohen | Lab/Lab | 18,124 | |
| **Total** | | | |
| | | **81,007** | **159,667** |

## 1945

| | | | |
|---|---|---|---|
| Teeling | C | 1,483 | 49,339 |
| Marlowe | C | 1,097 | 49,026 |
| Huddart | Lab | 831 | 31,074 |
| Barnard | Lab | 776 | 30,844 |
| **Total Plumpers** | | **4,187** | |
| Teeling/Marlowe | C/C | 47,639 | |
| Teeling/Huddart | C/Lab | 132 | |
| Teeling/Barnard | C/Lab | 85 | |
| Marlowe/Huddart | C/Lab | 209 | |
| Marlowe/Barnard | C/Lab | 81 | |
| Huddart/Barnard | Lab/Lab | 29,902 | |
| **Total** | | | |
| | | **82,235** | **160,283** |

## DERBY  [117]

### 1918

| Candidate | Party | Votes | Result |
|---|---|---|---|
| Thomas | Lab | 6,986 | 25,145 |
| Green | C | 4,815 | 14,920 |
| Rowbotham | L | 796 | 13,408 |
| Smith | NDP | 1,562 | 13,012 |
| **Total Plumpers** | | **14,159** | |
| Thomas/Green | Lab/C | 2,456 | |
| Thomas/Rowbotham | Lab/L | 11,780 | |
| Thomas/Smith | Lab/NDP | 3,923 | |
| Green/Rowbotham | C/L | 477 | |
| Green/Smith | C/NDP | 7,172 | |
| Rowbotham/Smith | L/NDP | 355 | |
| **Total** | | **40,322** | **66,485** |

### 1922

Analysis not available — Ballot Papers 52,246 (including spoilt papers).

### 1923

| | | | |
|---|---|---|---|
| Thomas | Lab | 594 | 24,887 |
| Raynes | Lab | 184 | 20,318 |
| Wright | C | 12,033 | 20,070 |
| Roberts | L | 3,844 | 10,669 |
| Newbold | Ind | 677 | 9,772 |
| **Total Plumpers** | | **17,332** | |
| Thomas/Raynes | Lab/Lab | 19,484 | |
| Thomas/Wright | Lab/C | 721 | |
| Thomas/Roberts | Lab/L | 3,463 | |
| Thomas/Newbold | Lab/Ind | 625 | |
| Raynes/Wright | Lab/C | 147 | |
| Raynes/Roberts | Lab/L | 378 | |
| Raynes/Newbold | Lab/Ind | 125 | |
| Wright/Roberts | C/L | 904 | |
| Wright/Newbold | C/Ind | 6,265 | |
| Roberts/Newbold | L/Ind | 2,080 | |
| **Total** | | **51,524** | **85,716** |

### 1924

| | | | |
|---|---|---|---|
| Thomas | Lab | 369 | 27,423 |
| Luce | C | 1,008 | 25,425 |
| Raynes | Lab | 125 | 25,172 |
| Hulse | C | 98 | 21,700 |
| Henderson-Stewart | L | 3,287 | 7,083 |
| **Total Plumpers** | | **4,887** | |
| Thomas/Luce | Lab/C | 767 | |
| Thomas/Raynes | Lab/Lab | 24,796 | |
| Thomas/Hulse | Lab/C | 64 | |
| Thomas/Henderson-Stewart | Lab/L | 1,427 | |
| Luce/Raynes | C/Lab | 114 | |
| Luce/Hulse | C/C | 21,404 | |
| Luce/Henderson-Stewart | C/L | 2,132 | |
| Raynes/Hulse | Lab/C | 17 | |
| Raynes/Henderson-Stewart | Lab/L | 120 | |
| Hulse/Henderson-Stewart | C/L | 117 | |
| **Total** | | **55,845** | **106,803** |

## 1929

| Candidate | Party | Votes | Result |
|---|---|---|---|
| Thomas | Lab | 584 | 39,688 |
| Raynes | Lab | 325 | 36,237 |
| Luce | C | 1,201 | 24,553 |
| Aiton | C | 72 | 20,443 |
| Peach | L | 6,464 | 11,317 |
| **Total Plumpers** | | **8,646** | |
| Thomas/Raynes | Lab/Lab | 35,426 | |
| Thomas/Luce | Lab/C | 1,188 | |
| Thomas/Aiton | Lab/C | 59 | |
| Thomas/Peach | Lab/L | 2,431 | |
| Raynes/Luce | Lab/C | 79 | |
| Raynes/Aiton | Lab/C | 7 | |
| Raynes/Peach | Lab/L | 400 | |
| Luce/Aiton | C/C | 20,184 | |
| Luce/Peach | C/L | 1,901 | |
| Aiton/Peach | C/L | 121 | |
| **Total** | | **70,442** | **132,238** |

## 1931

| Candidate | Party | Votes | Result |
|---|---|---|---|
| Thomas | N Lab | 2,761 | 49,257 |
| Reid | C | 2,274 | 47,729 |
| Raynes | Lab | 346 | 21,841 |
| Halls | Lab | 93 | 20,241 |
| **Total Plumpers** | | **5,474** | |
| Thomas/Reid | N Lab/C | 45,062 | |
| Thomas/Raynes | N Lab/Lab | 1,277 | |
| Thomas/Halls | N Lab/Lab | 157 | |
| Reid/Raynes | C/Lab | 310 | |
| Reid/Halls | C/Lab | 83 | |
| Raynes/Halls | Lab/Lab | 19,908 | |
| **Total** | | **72,271** | **139,068** |

## 1935

| Candidate | Party | Votes | Result |
|---|---|---|---|
| Reid | C | 876 | 37,707 |
| Thomas | N Lab | 727 | 37,566 |
| Hind | Lab | 364 | 25,037 |
| Barnes | Lab | 245 | 24,594 |
| **Total Plumpers** | | **2,212** | |
| Reid/Thomas | C/N Lab | 36,147 | |
| Reid/Hind | C/Lab | 485 | |
| Reid/Barnes | C/Lab | 199 | |
| Thomas/Hind | N Lab/Lab | 365 | |
| Thomas/Barnes | N Lab/Lab | 327 | |
| Hind/Barnes | Lab/Lab | 23,823 | |
| **Total** | | **63,558** | **124,904** |

## 1945

| Candidate | Party | Votes | Result |
|---|---|---|---|
| Noel-Baker | Lab | 1,007 | 42,196 |
| Wilcock | Lab | 250 | 40,800 |
| Lochrane | C | 432 | 21,460 |
| Bemrose | C | 276 | 21,125 |
| **Total Plumpers** | | **1,965** | |
| Noel-Baker/Wilcock | Lab/Lab | 40,309 | |
| Noel-Baker/Lochrane | Lab/C | 486 | |

## 1945 (Cont.)

| Candidate | Party | Votes | Result |
|---|---|---|---|
| Noel-Baker/Bemrose | Lab/C | 394 | |
| Wilcock/Lochrane | Lab/C | 164 | |
| Wilcock/Bemrose | Lab/C | 77 | |
| Lochrane/Bemrose | C/C | 20,378 | |
| Total | | 63,773 | 125,581 |

## NORWICH [197]

### 1918

| Candiate | Party | Votes | Result |
|---|---|---|---|
| Roberts | Co Lab | 1,382 | 26,642 |
| Young | L | 1,264 | 25,555 |
| Witard | Ind Lab | 4,927 | 6,856 |
| **Total Plumpers** | | **7,573** | |
| Roberts/Young | Co Lab/L | 23,811 | |
| Roberts/Witard | Co Lab/Ind Lab | 1,449 | |
| Young/Witard | L/Ind Lab | 480 | |
| **Total** | | **33,313** | **59,053** |

### 1922

| | | | |
|---|---|---|---|
| Roberts | Ind | 577 | 31,167 |
| Young | NL | 915 | 31,151 |
| Witard | Lab | 440 | 15,609 |
| Johnson | Lab | 111 | 14,490 |
| **Total Plumpers** | | **2,043** | |
| Roberts/Young | Ind/NL | 29,474 | |
| Roberts/Witard | Ind/Lab | 767 | |
| Roberts/Johnson | Ind/Lab | 349 | |
| Young/Witard | NL/Lab | 567 | |
| Young/Johnson | NL/Lab | 195 | |
| Witard/Johnson | Lab/Lab | 13,835 | |
| **Total** | | **47,230** | **92,417** |

### 1923

| | | | |
|---|---|---|---|
| Smith | Lab | 294 | 20,077 |
| Jewson | Lab | 179 | 19,304 |
| Young | L | 352 | 16,222 |
| Roberts | C | 321 | 14,749 |
| Copeman | L | 75 | 13,180 |
| Swan | C | 104 | 12,713 |
| **Total Plumpers** | | **1,325** | |
| Smith/Jewson | Lab/Lab | 18,588 | |
| Smith/Young | Lab/L | 726 | |
| Smith/Roberts | Lab/C | 285 | |
| Smith/Copeman | Lab/L | 102 | |
| Smith/Swan | Lab/C | 82 | |
| Jewson/Young | Lab/L | 208 | |
| Jewson/Roberts | Lab/C | 100 | |
| Jewson/Copeman | Lab/L | 146 | |
| Jewson/Swan | Lab/C | 83 | |
| Young/Roberts | L/C | 1,867 | |
| Young/Copeman | L/L | 12,765 | |
| Young/Swan | L/C | 304 | |
| Roberts/Copeman | C/L | 64 | |
| Roberts/Swan | C/C | 12,112 | |
| Copeman/Swan | L/C | 28 | |
| **Total** | | **48,785** | **96,245** |

### 1924

| | | | |
|---|---|---|---|
| Young | L | 822 | 28,842 |
| Fairfax | C | 946 | 28,529 |
| Smith | Lab | 249 | 23,808 |
| Jewson | Lab | 167 | 22,931 |
| **Total Plumpers** | | **2,184** | |

## 1924 (Cont.)

| Candidate | Party | Votes | Result |
|---|---|---|---|
| Young/Fairfax | L/C | 27,131 | |
| Young/Smith | L/Lab | 745 | |
| Young/Jewson | L/Lab | 144 | |
| Fairfax/Smith | C/Lab | 323 | |
| Fairfax/Jewson | C/Lab | 129 | |
| Smith/Jewson | Lab/Lab | 22,491 | |
| **Total** | | **53,147** | **104,110** |

## 1929

| | | | |
|---|---|---|---|
| Shakespeare | L | 3,123 | 33,974 |
| Smith | Lab | 366 | 33,690 |
| Jewson | Lab | 280 | 31,040 |
| Fairfax | C | 2,676 | 30,793 |
| **Total Plumpers** | | **6,445** | |
| Shakespeare/Smith | L/Lab | 2,846 | |
| Shakespeare/Jewson | L/Lab | 535 | |
| Shakespeare/Fairfax | L/C | 27,470 | |
| Smith/Jewson | Lab/Lab | 30,028 | |
| Smith/Fairfax | Lab/C | 450 | |
| Jewson/Fairfax | Lab/C | 197 | |
| **Total** | | **67,971** | **129,497** |

## 1931

| | | | |
|---|---|---|---|
| Shakespeare | NL | 1,013 | 40,925 |
| Hartland | C | 869 | 38,883 |
| Smith | Lab | 509 | 28,295 |
| Jewson | ILP | 351 | 26,537 |
| **Total Plumpers** | | **2,742** | |
| Shakespeare/Hartland | NL/C | 37,596 | |
| Shakespeare/Smith | NL/Lab | 1,919 | |
| Shakespeare/Jewson | NL/ILP | 397 | |
| Hartland/Smith | C/Lab | 248 | |
| Hartland/Jewson | C/ILP | 170 | |
| Smith/Jewson | Lab/ILP | 25,619 | |
| **Total** | | **68,691** | **134,640** |

## 1935

| | | | |
|---|---|---|---|
| Shakespeare | NL | 790 | 36,039 |
| Strauss | C | 530 | 34,182 |
| Hall | Lab | 207 | 24,670 |
| Kelly | Lab | 150 | 22,055 |
| Brockway | ILP | 2,266 | 6,737 |
| **Total Plumpers** | | **3,943** | |
| Shakespeare/Strauss | NL/C | 33,458 | |
| Shakespeare/Hall | NL/Lab | 829 | |
| Shakespeare/Kelly | NL/Lab | 274 | |
| Shakespeare/Brockway | NL/ILP | 688 | |
| Strauss/Hall | C/Lab | 50 | |
| Strauss/Kelly | C/Lab | 39 | |
| Strauss/Brockway | C/ILP | 105 | |
| Hall/Kelly | Lab/Lab | 20,749 | |
| Hall/Brockway | Lab/ILP | 2,835 | |
| Kelly/Brockway | Lab/ILP | 843 | |
| **Total** | | **63,813** | **123,683** |

## 1945

| Candidate | Party | Votes | Result |
|---|---|---|---|
| Noel-Buxton | Lab | 1,059 | 31,553 |
| Paton | Lab | 824 | 31,229 |
| Shakespeare | NL | 1,458 | 25,945 |
| Strauss | C | 639 | 24,225 |
| **Total Plumpers** | | **3,980** | |
| Noel-Buxton/Paton | Lab/Lab | 29,783 | |
| Noel-Buxton/Shakespeare | Lab/NL | 615 | |
| Noel-Buxton/Strauss | Lab/C | 96 | |
| Paton/Shakespeare | Lab/NL | 502 | |
| Paton/Strauss | Lab/C | 120 | |
| Shakespeare/Strauss | NL/C | 23,370 | |
| **Total** | | **58,466** | **112,952** |

## OLDHAM [202]

### 1918

| Candidate | Party | Votes | Result |
|---|---|---|---|
| Bartley-Denniss | Co C | 929 | 26,568 |
| Barton | Co L | 379 | 26,254 |
| Robinson | Lab | 5,486 | 15,178 |
| Rea | L | 889 | 9,323 |
| Total Plumpers | | 7,683 | |
| Bartley-Denniss/Barton | Co C/Co L | 23,947 | |
| Bartley-Denniss/Robinson | Co C/Lab | 1,399 | |
| Bartley-Denniss/Rea | Co C/L | 293 | |
| Barton/Robinson | Co L/Lab | 1,040 | |
| Barton/Rea | Co L/L | 888 | |
| Robinson/Rea | Lab/L | 7,253 | |
| Total | | 42,503 | 77,323 |

### 1922

| | | | |
|---|---|---|---|
| Grigg | NL | 629 | 24,762 |
| Tout | Lab | 20,771 | 24,434 |
| Smethurst | C | 1,009 | 23,200 |
| Davies | L | 363 | 9,812 |
| Emmott | L | 98 | 6,186 |
| Total Plumpers | | 22,870 | |
| Grigg/Tout | NL/Lab | 950 | |
| Grigg/Smethurst | NL/C | 20,753 | |
| Grigg/Davies | NL/L | 2,113 | |
| Grigg/Emmott | NL/L | 317 | |
| Tout/Smethurst | Lab/C | 978 | |
| Tout/Davies | Lab/L | 1,535 | |
| Tout/Emmott | Lab/L | 200 | |
| Smethurst/Davies | C/L | 345 | |
| Smethurst/Emmott | C/L | 115 | |
| Davies/Emmott | L/L | 5,456 | |
| Total | | 55,632 | 88,394 |

### 1923

| | | | |
|---|---|---|---|
| Tout | Lab | 17,435 | 20,939 |
| Grigg | L | 587 | 20,681 |
| Wiggins | L | 131 | 17,990 |
| Freeman | C | 633 | 15,819 |
| Smethurst | C | 207 | 13,894 |
| Total Plumpers | | 18,993 | |
| Tout/Grigg | Lab/L | 1,916 | |
| Tout/Wiggins | Lab/L | 786 | |
| Tout/Freeman | Lab/C | 648 | |
| Tout/Smethurst | Lab/C | 154 | |
| Grigg/Wiggins | L/L | 16,721 | |
| Grigg/Freeman | L/C | 1,177 | |
| Grigg/Smethurst | L/C | 280 | |
| Wiggins/Freeman | L/C | 230 | |
| Wiggins/Smethurst | L/C | 122 | |
| Freeman/Smethurst | C/C | 13,131 | |
| Total | | 54,158 | 89,323 |

## 1924

| Candidate | Party | Votes | Result |
|---|---|---|---|
| Cooper | C | 2,562 | 37,419 |
| Grigg | L | 1,510 | 36,761 |
| Tout | Lab | 611 | 23,623 |
| Wilson | Lab | 47 | 22,081 |
| Total Plumpers | | 4,730 | |
| Cooper/Grigg | C/L | 34,357 | |
| Cooper/Tout | C/Lab | 420 | |
| Cooper/Wilson | C/Lab | 80 | |
| Grigg/Tout | L/Lab | 766 | |
| Grigg/Wilson | L/Lab | 128 | |
| Tout/Wilson | Lab/Lab | 21,826 | |
| Total | | 62,307 | 119,884 |

## 1929

| Candidate | Party | Votes | Result |
|---|---|---|---|
| Lang | Lab | 793 | 34,223 |
| Wilson | Lab | 335 | 32,727 |
| Cooper | C | 21,726 | 29,424 |
| Dodd | L | 727 | 20,810 |
| Jenkins | L | 123 | 13,528 |
| Total Plumpers | | 23,704 | |
| Lang/Wilson | Lab/Lab | 32,025 | |
| Lang/Cooper | Lab/C | 449 | |
| Lang/Dodd | Lab/L | 595 | |
| Lang/Jenkins | Lab/L | 361 | |
| Wilson/Cooper | Lab/C | 168 | |
| Wilson/Dodd | Lab/L | 169 | |
| Wilson/Jenkins | Lab/L | 30 | |
| Cooper/Dodd | C/L | 6,693 | |
| Cooper/Jenkins | C/L | 388 | |
| Dodd/Jenkins | L/L | 12,626 | |
| Total | | 77,208 | 130.712 |

## 1931

| Candidate | Party | Votes | Result |
|---|---|---|---|
| Crossley | C | 832 | 50,693 |
| Kerr | C | 527 | 50,395 |
| Lang | Lab | 1,279 | 28,629 |
| Wilson | Lab | 162 | 26,361 |
| Total Plumpers | | 2,800 | |
| Crossley/Kerr | C/C | 49,155 | |
| Crossley/Lang | C/Lab | 650 | |
| Crossley/Wilson | C/Lab | 56 | |
| Kerr/Lang | C/Lab | 635 | |
| Kerr/Wilson | C/Lab | 78 | |
| Lang/Wilson | Lab/Lab | 26,065 | |
| Total | | 79,439 | 156,078 |

## 1935

| Candidate | Party | Votes | Result |
|---|---|---|---|
| Kerr | C | 1,273 | 36,738 |
| Dodd | NL | 368 | 34,755 |
| Lang | Lab | 1,107 | 34,316 |
| Farr | Lab | 134 | 29,647 |
| Ward | L | 2,724 | 8,534 |
| Total Plumpers | | 5,606 | |
| Kerr/Dodd | C/NL | 31,715 | |
| Kerr/Lang | C/Lab | 1,947 | |

## 1935 (Cont.)

| Candidate | Party | Votes | Result |
|---|---|---|---|
| Kerr/Farr | C/Lab | 504 | |
| Kerr/Ward | C/L | 1,299 | |
| Dodd/Lang | NL/Lab | 428 | |
| Dodd/Farr | NL/Lab | 1,106 | |
| Dodd/Ward | NL/L | 1,138 | |
| Lang/Farr | Lab/Lab | 27,682 | |
| Lang/Ward | Lab/L | 3,152 | |
| Farr/Ward | Lab/L | 221 | |
| **Total** | | **74,798** | **143,990** |

**1945**　　　　Analysis not available—Ballot Papers 67,885 (estimated)

## PRESTON [210]

### 1918

| Candidate | Party | Votes | Result |
|---|---|---|---|
| Shaw | Lab | 2,993 | 19,213 |
| Stanley | Co C | 518 | 18,970 |
| O'Neill | L | 2,292 | 18,485 |
| Brookes | Co C | 127 | 17,928 |
| **Total Plumpers** | | **5,930** | |
| Shaw/Stanley | Lab/Co C | 626 | |
| Shaw/O'Neill | Lab/L | 15,357 | |
| Shaw/Brookes | Lab/Co C | 237 | |
| Stanley/O'Neill | Co C/L | 549 | |
| Stanley/Brookes | Co C/Co C | 17,277 | |
| O'Neill/Brookes | L/Co C | 287 | |
| **Total** | | **40,263** | **74,596** |

### 1922

| | | | |
|---|---|---|---|
| Shaw | Lab | 3,388 | 26,259 |
| Hodge | L | 2,156 | 24,798 |
| Stanley | C | 1,708 | 22,574 |
| Camm | C | 445 | 20,410 |
| **Total Plumpers** | | **7,697** | |
| Shaw/Hodge | Lab/L | 21,369 | |
| Shaw/Stanley | Lab/C | 1,055 | |
| Shaw/Camm | Lab/C | 447 | |
| Hodge/Stanley | L/C | 783 | |
| Hodge/Camm | L/C | 490 | |
| Stanley/Camm | C/C | 19,028 | |
| **Total** | | **50,869** | **94,041** |

### 1923

| | | | |
|---|---|---|---|
| Shaw | Lab | 3,650 | 25,816 |
| Hodge | L | 2,858 | 25,155 |
| Kirkpatrick | C | 22,169 | 23,962 |
| **Total Plumpers** | | **28,677** | |
| Shaw/Hodge | Lab/L | 21,335 | |
| Shaw/Kirkpatrick | Lab/C | 831 | |
| Hodge/Kirkpatrick | L/C | 962 | |
| **Total** | | **51,805** | **74,933** |

### 1924

| | | | |
|---|---|---|---|
| Shaw | Lab | 3,113 | 27,009 |
| Kennedy | C | 664 | 25,887 |
| Hodge | L | 1,441 | 25,327 |
| Barnes | C | 102 | 24,557 |
| **Total Plumpers** | | **5,320** | |
| Shaw/Kennedy | Lab/C | 604 | |
| Shaw/Hodge | Lab/L | 23,112 | |
| Shaw/Barnes | Lab/C | 180 | |
| Kennedy/Hodge | C/L | 559 | |
| Kennedy/Barnes | C/C | 24,060 | |
| Hodge/Barnes | L/C | 215 | |
| **Total** | | **54,050** | **102,780** |

## 1929

| Candidate | Party | Votes | Result |
|---|---|---|---|
| Shaw | Lab | 10,718 | 37,705 |
| Jowitt | L | 4,498 | 31,277 |
| Howitt | C | 422 | 29,116 |
| Emmott | C | 250 | 27,754 |
| Holden | Ind Lab | 41 | 2,111 |
| **Total Plumpers** | | **15,929** | |
| Shaw/Jowitt | Lab/L | 24,675 | |
| Shaw/Howitt | Lab/C | 489 | |
| Shaw/Emmott | Lab/C | 153 | |
| Shaw/Holden | Lab/Ind Lab | 1,670 | |
| Jowitt/Howitt | L/C | 1,465 | |
| Jowitt/Emmott | L/C | 468 | |
| Jowitt/Holden | L/Ind Lab | 171 | |
| Howitt/Emmott | C/C | 26,697 | |
| Howitt/Holden | C/Ind Lab | 43 | |
| Emmott/Holden | C/Ind Lab | 186 | |
| **Total** | | **71,946** | **127,963** |

## 1931

| | | | |
|---|---|---|---|
| Kirkpatrick | C | 597 | 46,276 |
| Moreing | C | 202 | 45,843 |
| Shaw | Lab | 925 | 25,710 |
| Porter | Lab | 191 | 24,660 |
| **Total Plumpers** | | **1,915** | |
| Kirkpatrick/Moreing | C/C | 45,264 | |
| Kirkpatrick/Shaw | C/Lab | 325 | |
| Kirkpatrick/Porter | C/Lab | 90 | |
| Moreing/Shaw | C/Lab | 229 | |
| Moreing/Porter | C/Lab | 148 | |
| Shaw/Porter | Lab/Lab | 24,231 | |
| **Total** | | **72,202** | **142,489** |

## 1935

| | | | |
|---|---|---|---|
| Moreing | C | 391 | 37,219 |
| Kirkpatrick | C | 382 | 36,797 |
| Lyster | Lab | 329 | 32,225 |
| Reiss | Lab | 128 | 31,827 |
| **Total Plumpers** | | **1,230** | |
| Moreing/Kirkpatrick | C/C | 35,837 | |
| Moreing/Lyster | C/Lab | 477 | |
| Moreing/Reiss | C/Lab | 514 | |
| Kirkpatrick/Lyster | C/Lab | 406 | |
| Kirkpatrick/Reiss | C/Lab | 172 | |
| Lyster/Reiss | Lab/Lab | 31,013 | |
| **Total** | | **69,649** | **138,068** |

## 1945

| | | | |
|---|---|---|---|
| Segal | Lab | 444 | 33,053 |
| Sunderland | Lab | 605 | 32,889 |
| Churchill | C | 954 | 29,129 |
| Amery | C | 153 | 27,885 |
| Toulmin | L | 2,488 | 8,251 |
| Devine | Com | 909 | 5,168 |
| **Total Plumpers** | | **5,553** | |

## 1945 (Cont.)

| Candidate | Party | Votes | Result |
|---|---|---|---|
| Segal/Sunderland | Lab/Lab | 29,035 | |
| Segal/Churchill | Lab/C | 100 | |
| Segal/Amery | Lab/C | 61 | |
| Segal/Toulmin | Lab/L | 1,184 | |
| Segal/Devine | Lab/Com | 2,229 | |
| Sunderland/Churchill | Lab/C | 126 | |
| Sunderland/Amery | Lab/C | 49 | |
| Sunderland/Toulmin | Lab/L | 1,827 | |
| Sunderland/Devine | Lab/Com | 1,247 | |
| Churchill/Amery | C/C | 26,596 | |
| Churchill/Toulmin | C/L | 1,183 | |
| Churchill/Devine | C/Com | 170 | |
| Amery/Toulmin | C/L | 991 | |
| Amery/Devine | C/Com | 35 | |
| Toulmin/Devine | L/Com | 578 | |
| **Total** | | **70,964** | **136,375** |

## SOUTHAMPTON [232]

### 1918

| Candidate | Party | Votes | Result |
|---|---|---|---|
| Philipps | Co L | 942 | 26,884 |
| Ward | Co L | 365 | 16,843 |
| Perkins | C | 4,910 | 15,548 |
| Lewis | Lab | 654 | 7,828 |
| Perriman | Lab | 222 | 6,776 |
| **Total Plumpers** | | **7,093** | |
| Philipps/Ward | Co L/Co L | 15,935 | |
| Philipps/Perkins | Co L/C | 9,381 | |
| Philipps/Lewis | Co L/Lab | 348 | |
| Philipps/Perriman | Co L/Lab | 278 | |
| Ward/Perkins | Co L/C | 377 | |
| Ward/Lewis | Co L/Lab | 112 | |
| Ward/Perriman | Co L/Lab | 54 | |
| Perkins/Lewis | C/Lab | 686 | |
| Perkins/Perriman | C/Lab | 194 | |
| Lewis/Perriman | Lab/Lab | 6,028 | |
| **Total** | | **40,486** | **73,879** |

### 1922

| Candidate | Party | Votes | Result |
|---|---|---|---|
| Perkins | C | 495 | 22,054 |
| Apsley | C | 216 | 20,351 |
| Lewis | Lab | 7,097 | 14,868 |
| Stancomb | Ind | 2,838 | 14,193 |
| Philipps | NL | 167 | 11,576 |
| Ward | NL | 83 | 9,318 |
| **Total Plumpers** | | **10,896** | |
| Perkins/Apsley | C/C | 19,462 | |
| Perkins/Lewis | C/Lab | 235 | |
| Perkins/Stancomb | C/Ind | 1,494 | |
| Perkins/Philipps | C/NL | 292 | |
| Perkins/Ward | C/NL | 76 | |
| Apsley/Lewis | C/Lab | 124 | |
| Apsley/Stancomb | C/Ind | 365 | |
| Apsley/Philipps | C/NL | 148 | |
| Apsley/Ward | C/NL | 36 | |
| Lewis/Stancomb | Lab/Ind | 7,105 | |
| Lewis/Philipps | Lab/NL | 259 | |
| Lewis/Ward | Lab/NL | 48 | |
| Stancomb/Philipps | Ind/NL | 2,013 | |
| Stancomb/Ward | Ind/NL | 378 | |
| Philipps/Ward | NL/NL | 8,697 | |
| **Total** | | **51,628** | **92,360** |

### 1923

| Candidate | Party | Votes | Result |
|---|---|---|---|
| Apsley | C | 276 | 20,453 |
| Perkins | C | 172 | 20,249 |
| Lewis | Lab | 598 | 17,208 |
| Sorensen | Lab | 93 | 16,679 |
| Spranger | L | 132 | 13,724 |
| Dixey | L | 111 | 13,657 |
| **Total Plumpers** | | **1,382** | |
| Apsley/Perkins | C/C | 19,738 | |
| Apsley/Lewis | C/Lab | 71 | |
| Apsley/Sorensen | C/Lab | 46 | |
| Apsley/Spranger | C/L | 129 | |
| Apsley/Dixey | C/L | 193 | |

## 1923 (Cont.)

| Candidate | Party | Votes | Result |
|---|---|---|---|
| Perkins/Lewis | C/Lab | 145 | |
| Perkins/Sorensen | C/Lab | 79 | |
| Perkins/Spranger | C/L | 56 | |
| Perkins/Dixey | C/L | 59 | |
| Lewis/Sorensen | Lab/Lab | 16,042 | |
| Lewis/Spranger | Lab/L | 218 | |
| Lewis/Dixey | Lab/L | 134 | |
| Sorensen/Spranger | Lab/L | 224 | |
| Sorensen/Dixey | Lab/L | 195 | |
| Spranger/Dixey | L/L | 12,966 | |
| **Total** | | **51,676** | **101,970** |

## 1924

| Candidate | Party | Votes | Result |
|---|---|---|---|
| Apsley | C | 532 | 30,703 |
| Perkins | C | 173 | 30,201 |
| Lewis | Lab | 612 | 22,183 |
| Sorensen | Lab | 234 | 21,768 |
| **Total Plumpers** | | **1,551** | |
| Apsley/Perkins | C/C | 29,668 | |
| Apsley/Lewis | C/Lab | 309 | |
| Apsley/Sorensen | C/Lab | 194 | |
| Perkins/Lewis | C/Lab | 141 | |
| Perkins/Sorensen | C/Lab | 219 | |
| Lewis/Sorensen | Lab/Lab | 21,121 | |
| **Total** | | **53,203** | **104,855** |

## 1929

| Candidate | Party | Votes | Result |
|---|---|---|---|
| Lewis | Lab | 1,101 | 32,249 |
| Morley | Lab | 291 | 31,252 |
| Thirlestane & Boltoun | C | 714 | 27,898 |
| Cunningham-Reid | C | 485 | 26,801 |
| Whitehouse | L | 187 | 12,966 |
| Lamsley | L | 174 | 12,836 |
| **Total Plumpers** | | **2,952** | |
| Lewis/Morley | Lab/Lab | 30,668 | |
| Lewis/Thirlestane & Boltoun | Lab/C | 52 | |
| Lewis/Cunningham-Reid | Lab/C | 33 | |
| Lewis/Whitehouse | Lab/L | 103 | |
| Lewis/Lamsley | Lab/L | 292 | |
| Morley/Thirlestane & Boltoun | Lab/C | 85 | |
| Morley/Cunningham-Reid | Lab/C | 19 | |
| Morley/Whitehouse | Lab/L | 73 | |
| Morley/Lamsley | Lab/L | 116 | |
| Thirlestane & Boltoun/ Cunningham-Reid | C/C | 25,874 | |
| Thirlestane & Boltoun/ Whitehouse | C/L | 781 | |
| Thirlestane & Boltoun/Lamsley | C/L | 392 | |
| Cunningham-Reid/Whitehouse | C/L | 175 | |
| Cunningham-Reid/Lamsley | C/L | 215 | |
| Whitehouse/Lamsley | C/L | 11,647 | |
| **Total** | | **73,477** | **144,002** |

## 1931

| Candidate | Party | Votes | Result |
|---|---|---|---|
| Craven-Ellis | C | 873 | 54,699 |
| Barrie | NL | 481 | 54,269 |
| Lewis | Lab | 511 | 26,425 |
| Morley | Lab | 183 | 26,061 |
| **Total Plumpers** | | **2,048** | |
| Craven-Ellis/Barrie | C/NL | 53,603 | |
| Craven-Ellis/Lewis | C/Lab | 141 | |
| Craven-Ellis/Morley | C/Lab | 82 | |
| Barrie/Lewis | NL/Lab | 81 | |
| Barrie/Morley | NL/Lab | 104 | |
| Lewis/Morley | Lab/Lab | 25,692 | |
| **Total** | | **81,751** | **161,454** |

## 1935

Analysis not available—Ballot Papers 75,686 (estimated)

## 1945

| Candidate | Party | Votes | Result |
|---|---|---|---|
| Morley | Lab | 903 | 37,556 |
| Lewis | Lab | 1,318 | 37,054 |
| Craven-Ellis | C | 2,236 | 24,367 |
| Thomas | NL | 342 | 22,650 |
| Fulljames | L | 3,886 | 8,878 |
| **Total Plumpers** | | **8,685** | |
| Morley/Lewis | Lab/Lab | 34,903 | |
| Morley/Craven-Ellis | Lab/C | 253 | |
| Morley/Thomas | Lab/NL | 583 | |
| Morley/Fulljames | Lab/L | 914 | |
| Lewis/Craven-Ellis | Lab/C | 136 | |
| Lewis/Thomas | Lab/NL | 94 | |
| Lewis/Fulljames | Lab/L | 603 | |
| Craven-Ellis/Thomas | C/NL | 19,949 | |
| Craven-Ellis/Fulljames | C/L | 1,793 | |
| Thomas/Fulljames | NL/L | 1,682 | |
| **Total** | | **69,595** | **130,505** |

## STOCKPORT [236]

**1918**                    Unopposed

**1920** (23/7)

| Candidate | Party | Votes | Result |
|---|---|---|---|
| Greenwood | Co C | 258 | 22,847 |
| Fildes | Co L | 192 | 22,386 |
| Money | Lab | 396 | 16,042 |
| Perry | Lab | 84 | 14,434 |
| Kindell | Ind | 103 | 5,644 |
| Terrett | Ind | 55 | 5,443 |
| O'Brien | Ind | 1,285 | 2,336 |
| **Total Plumpers** | | **2,373** | |
| Greenwood/Fildes | Co C/Co L | 21,172 | |
| Money/Perry | Lab/Lab | 13,529 | |
| Kindell/Terrett | Ind/Ind | 4,186 | |
| **Total** | | **45,789** | **89,132** |
| Note: | | A complete analysis is not available | |

**1922**

| | | | |
|---|---|---|---|
| Fildes | NL | 1,377 | 35,241 |
| Greenwood | C | 1,217 | 33,852 |
| Perry | Lab | 262 | 17,059 |
| Robinson | Lab | 262 | 16,126 |
| **Total Plumpers** | | **3,118** | |
| Fildes/Greenwood | NL/C | 31,703 | |
| Perry/Robinson | Lab/Lab | 14,844 | |
| **Total** | | **52,539** | **102,278** |
| Note: | | A complete analysis is not available | |

**1923**

| | | | |
|---|---|---|---|
| Greenwood | C | 377 | 20,308 |
| Royle | L | 384 | 19,223 |
| Hammersley | C | 84 | 18,129 |
| Fildes | L | 269 | 16,756 |
| Townend | Lab | 12,285 | 16,340 |
| **Total Plumpers** | | **13,399** | |
| Greenwood/Hammersley | C/C | 17,631 | |
| Royle/Fildes | L/L | 14,687 | |
| **Total** | | **52,095** | **90,756** |
| Note: | | A complete analysis is not available | |

**1924**

| | | | |
|---|---|---|---|
| Greenwood | C | 369 (43) | 28,057 |
| Hammersley | C | 201 (35) | 26,417 |
| Townend | Lab | 16,606 (42) | 21,986 |
| Royle | L | 5,027 (23) | 12,386 |
| **Total Plumpers** | | **22,203 (83)** | |
| Greenwood/Hammersley | C/C | 25,342 | |
| Greenwood/Townend | C/Lab | 354 | |
| Greenwood/Royle | C/L | 1,949 | |
| Hammersley/Townend | C/Lab | 218 | |
| Hammersley/Royle | C/L | 621 | |
| Townend/Royle | Lab/L | 4,766 | |
| **Total** | | **55,536** | **88,846** |

## ANALYSIS OF VOTING IN TWO-MEMBER SEATS

### 1929

| Candidate | Party | Votes | Result |
|---|---|---|---|
| Townend | Lab | 22,459 | 30,955 |
| Hammersley | C | | 29,043 |
| Fildes | L | 6,200 | 22,595 |
| Lingen-Barker | C | | 22,047 |
| Royle | Ind L | 231 | 8,355 |
| **Total Plumpers** | | **29,825** | |
| Hammersley/Lingen-Barker | | 21,645 | |
| **Total** | | **71,410** | **112,995** |
| Note: | A complete analysis is not available | | |

### 1931

| Hammersley | C | | 50,936 |
|---|---|---|---|
| Dower | C | | 47,757 |
| Townend | Lab | 5,664 | 23,350 |
| Abbott | ILP | 136 | 15,591 |
| **Total Plumpers** | | **7,542** | |
| Hammersley/Dower | C/C | 47,013 | |
| Townend/Abbott | Lab/ILP | 15,058 | |
| **Total** | | **72,588** | **137,634** |
| Note: | A complete analysis is not available | | |

### 1935

| Gridley | C | | 43,882 |
|---|---|---|---|
| Hulbert | C | | 43,001 |
| Hudson | Lab | | 28,798 |
| Douthwaite | Lab | | 27,528 |
| **Total Plumpers** | | **1,435** | |
| Gridley/Hulbert | C/C | 39,571 | |
| Hudson/Douthwaite | Lab/Lab | 24,308 | |
| **Total** | | **72,322** | **143,209** |
| Note: | A complete analysis is not available | | |

### 1945

| Gridley | C | | 31,039 |
|---|---|---|---|
| Hulbert | C | | 30,792 |
| Stamp | Lab | | 29,674 |
| Casasola | Lab | | 29,630 |
| Sutherland | L | | 14,994 |
| Malbon | L | | 14,942 |
| **Total Plumpers** | | **3,000 (estimated)** | |
| Gridley/Hulbert | C/C | 29,183 | |
| Stamp/Casasola | Lab/Lab | 27,267 | |
| Sutherland/Malbon | L/L | 12,555 | |
| **Total** | | **77,035 (estimated)** | **151,071** |
| Note: | A complete analysis is not available | | |

## SUNDERLAND [241]

### 1918

| Candidate | Party | Votes | Result |
|---|---|---|---|
| Greenwood | Co L | 6,997 | 27,646 |
| Hudson | C | 8,754 | 25,698 |
| Goldstone | Lab | 3,726 | 9,603 |
| **Total Plumpers** | | **19,477** | |
| Greenwood/Hudson | Co L/C | 15,858 | |
| Greenwood/Goldstone | Co L/Lab | 1,086 | |
| Hudson/Goldstone | C/Lab | 4,791 | |
| Total | | **41,212** | **62,947** |

### 1922

| Candidate | Party | Votes | Result |
|---|---|---|---|
| Raine | C | 561 | 28,001 |
| Thompson | C | 289 | 24,591 |
| Greenwood | NL | 7,104 | 19,058 |
| Lawley | Lab | 227 | 13,683 |
| Rutherford | Lab | 138 | 13,490 |
| Common | L | 2,132 | 13,036 |
| **Total Plumpers** | | **10,451** | |
| Raine/Thompson | C/C | 23,192 | |
| Raine/Greenwood | C/NL | 2,408 | |
| Raine/Lawley | C/Lab | 332 | |
| Raine/Rutherford | C/Lab | 381 | |
| Raine/Common | C/L | 1,127 | |
| Thompson/Greenwood | C/NL | 349 | |
| Thompson/Lawley | C/Lab | 150 | |
| Thompson/Rutherford | C/Lab | 416 | |
| Thompson/Common | C/L | 195 | |
| Greenwood/Lawley | NL/Lab | 625 | |
| Greenwood/Rutherford | NL/Lab | 271 | |
| Greenwood/Common | NL/L | 8,301 | |
| Lawley/Rutherford | Lab/Lab | 11,676 | |
| Lawley/Common | Lab/L | 673 | |
| Rutherford/Common | Lab/L | 608 | |
| Total | | **61,155** | **111,859** |

### 1923

| Candidate | Party | Votes | Result |
|---|---|---|---|
| Raine | C | 145 | 23,497 |
| Thompson | C | 177 | 23,379 |
| Common | L | 545 | 22,438 |
| Greenwood | L | 435 | 22,034 |
| Lawley | Lab | 296 | 13,707 |
| Gillinder | Lab | 49 | 13,184 |
| **Total Plumpers** | | **1,647** | |
| Raine/Thompson | C/C | 22,865 | |
| Raine/Common | C/L | 143 | |
| Raine/Greenwood | C/L | 167 | |
| Raine/Lawley | C/Lab | 116 | |
| Raine/Gillinder | C/Lab | 61 | |
| Thompson/Common | C/L | 146 | |
| Thompson/Greenwood | C/L | 129 | |
| Thompson/Lawley | C/Lab | 50 | |
| Thompson/Gillinder | C/Lab | 12 | |
| Common/Greenwood | L/L | 20,750 | |
| Common/Lawley | L/Lab | 495 | |
| Common/Gillinder | L/Lab | 359 | |
| Greenwood/Lawley | L/Lab | 300 | |

## 1923 (Cont.)

| Candidate | Party | Votes | Result |
|---|---|---|---|
| Greenwood/Gillinder | L/Lab | 253 | |
| Lawley/Gillinder | Lab/Lab | 12,450 | |
| **Total** | | **59,943** | **118,239** |

## 1924

| Candidate | Party | Votes | Result |
|---|---|---|---|
| Thompson | C | 237 | 28,612 |
| Raine | C | 214 | 28,608 |
| MacVeagh | Lab | 17,475 | 21,823 |
| Common | L | 1,691 | 20,139 |
| Hannah | L | 102 | 13,731 |
| **Total Plumpers** | | **19,719** | |
| Thompson/Raine | C/C | 27,731 | |
| Thompson/MacVeagh | C/Lab | 72 | |
| Thompson/Common | C/L | 543 | |
| Thompson/Hannah | C/L | 29 | |
| Raine/MacVeagh | C/Lab | 61 | |
| Raine/Common | C/L | 582 | |
| Raine/Hannah | C/L | 20 | |
| MacVeagh/Common | Lab/L | 3,979 | |
| MacVeagh/Hannah | Lab/L | 236 | |
| Common/Hannah | L/L | 13,344 | |
| **Total** | | **66,316** | **112,913** |

## 1929

| Candidate | Party | Votes | Result |
|---|---|---|---|
| Phillips | Lab | 411 | 31,794 |
| Smith | Lab | 370 | 31,085 |
| Raine | C | 296 | 29,180 |
| Thompson | C | 167 | 28,937 |
| Morgan | L | 240 | 21,300 |
| Pratt | L | 358 | 21,142 |
| **Total Plumpers** | | **1,842** | |
| Phillips/Smith | Lab/Lab | 29,602 | |
| Phillips/Raine | Lab/C | 133 | |
| Phillips/Thompson | Lab/C | 59 | |
| Phillips/Morgan | Lab/L | 970 | |
| Phillips/Pratt | Lab/L | 619 | |
| Smith/Raine | Lab/C | 146 | |
| Smith/Thompson | Lab/C | 168 | |
| Smith/Morgan | Lab/L | 427 | |
| Smith/Pratt | Lab/L | 372 | |
| Raine/Thompson | C/C | 28,371 | |
| Raine/Morgan | C/L | 79 | |
| Raine/Pratt | C/L | 155 | |
| Thompson/Morgan | C/L | 59 | |
| Thompson/Pratt | C/L | 113 | |
| Morgan/Pratt | L/L | 19,525 | |
| **Total** | | **82,640** | **163,438** |

## 1931

| Candidate | Party | Votes | Result |
|---|---|---|---|
| Thompson | C | 979 | 53,386 |
| Storey | C | 297 | 52,589 |
| Phillips | Lab | 711 | 29,707 |
| Pritt | Lab | 521 | 29,680 |
| **Total Plumpers** | | **2,508** | |

## 1931 (Cont.)

| Candidate | Party | Votes | Result |
|---|---|---|---|
| Thompson/Storey | C/C | 52,050 | |
| Thompson/Phillips | C/Lab | 175 | |
| Thompson/Pritt | C/Lab | 182 | |
| Storey/Phillips | C/Lab | 43 | |
| Storey/Pritt | C/Lab | 199 | |
| Phillips/Pritt | Lab/Lab | 28,778 | |
| **Total** | | **83,935** | **165,362** |

## 1935

| | | | |
|---|---|---|---|
| Furness | NL | 415 | 49,001 |
| Storey | C | 591 | 48,760 |
| Catlin | Lab | 497 | 32,483 |
| Manning | Lab | 316 | 32,059 |
| **Total Plumpers** | | **1,819** | |
| Furness/Storey | NL/C | 47,339 | |
| Furness/Catlin | NL/Lab | 829 | |
| Furness/Manning | NL/Lab | 418 | |
| Storey/Catlin | C/Lab | 331 | |
| Storey/Manning | C/Lab | 499 | |
| Catlin/Manning | Lab/Lab | 30,826 | |
| **Total** | | **82,061** | **162,303** |

## 1945

| | | | |
|---|---|---|---|
| Willey | Lab | 550 | 38,769 |
| Ewart | Lab | 300 | 36,711 |
| Furness | NL | 503 | 29,366 |
| Storey | C | 324 | 28,579 |
| Richardson | Com | 517 | 4,501 |
| **Total Plumpers** | | **2,194** | |
| Willey/Ewart | Lab/Lab | 34,912 | |
| Willey/Furness | Lab/NL | 437 | |
| Willey/Storey | Lab/C | 321 | |
| Willey/Richardson | Lab/Com | 2,549 | |
| Ewart/Furness | Lab/NL | 420 | |
| Ewart/Storey | Lab/C | 88 | |
| Ewart/Richardson | Lab/Com | 991 | |
| Furness/Storey | NL/C | 27,704 | |
| Furness/Richardson | NL/Com | 302 | |
| Storey/Richardson | C/Com | 142 | |
| **Total** | | **70,060** | **137,926** |

## DUNDEE [552]

### 1918

| Candidate | Party | Votes | Result |
|---|---|---|---|
| Churchill | Co L | 3,480 | 25,788 |
| Wilkie | Lab | 1,226 | 24,822 |
| Scrymgeour | SPP | 3,884 | 10,423 |
| Brown | Lab | 658 | 7,769 |
| Total Plumpers | | 9,248 | |
| Churchill/Wilkie | Co L/Lab | 20,752 | |
| Churchill/Scrymgeour | Co L/SPP | 955 | |
| Churchill/Brown | Co L/Lab | 601 | |
| Wilkie/Scrymgeour | Lab/SPP | 959 | |
| Wilkie/Brown | Lab/Lab | 1,885 | |
| Scrymgeour/Brown | SPP/Lab | 4,625 | |
| Total | | 39,025 | 68,802 |

### 1922

| Candidate | Party | Votes | Result |
|---|---|---|---|
| Scrymgeour | SPP | 5,015 | 32,578 |
| Morel | Lab | 1,018 | 30,292 |
| Macdonald | NL | 252 | 22,244 |
| Churchill | NL | 587 | 20,466 |
| Pilkington | L | 381 | 6,681 |
| Gallacher | Com | 128 | 5,906 |
| Total Plumpers | | 7,381 | |
| Scrymgeour/Morel | SPP/Lab | 21,621 | |
| Scrymgeour/Macdonald | SPP/NL | 2,092 | |
| Scrymgeour/Churchill | SPP/NL | 1,661 | |
| Scrymgeour/Pilkington | SPP/L | 1,490 | |
| Scrymgeour/Gallacher | SPP/Com | 699 | |
| Morel/Macdonald | Lab/NL | 658 | |
| Morel/Churchill | Lab/NL | 552 | |
| Morel/Pilkington | Lab/L | 1,630 | |
| Morel/Gallacher | Lab/Com | 4,813 | |
| Macdonald/Churchill | NL/NL | 16,798 | |
| Macdonald/Pilkington | NL/L | 2,315 | |
| Macdonald/Gallacher | NL/Com | 129 | |
| Churchill/Pilkington | NL/L | 798 | |
| Churchill/Gallacher | NL/Com | 70 | |
| Pilkington/Gallacher | L/Com | 67 | |
| Total | | 62,774 | 118,167 |

### 1923

| Candidate | Party | Votes | Result |
|---|---|---|---|
| Scrymgeour | SPP | 5,130 | 25,753 |
| Morel | Lab | 1,762 | 23,345 |
| Pratt | L | 2,138 | 23,031 |
| Wallace | C | 2,151 | 20,253 |
| Gallacher | Com | 331 | 10,380 |
| Total Plumpers | | 11,512 | |
| Scrymgeour/Morel | SPP/Lab | 10,480 | |
| Scrymgeour/Pratt | SPP/L | 5,935 | |
| Scrymgeour/Wallace | SPP/C | 3,574 | |
| Scrymgeour/Gallacher | SPP/Com | 634 | |
| Morel/Pratt | Lab/L | 1,168 | |
| Morel/Wallace | Lab/C | 696 | |
| Morel/Gallacher | Lab/Com | 9,239 | |
| Pratt/Wallace | L/C | 13,723 | |
| Pratt/Gallacher | L/Com | 67 | |
| Wallace/Gallacher | C/Com | 109 | |
| Total | | 57,137 | 102,762 |

# ANALYSIS OF VOTING IN TWO-MEMBER SEATS

## 1924

| Candidate | Party | Votes | Result |
|---|---|---|---|
| Morel | Lab | 3,000 | 32,846 |
| Scrymgeour | SPP | 3,431 | 29,193 |
| Wallace | C | 408 | 28,118 |
| Duncan | L | 213 | 25,566 |
| Stewart | Com | 71 | 8,340 |
| **Total Plumpers** | | **7,123** | |
| Morel/Scrymgeour | Lab/SPP | 21,173 | |
| Morel/Wallace | Lab/C | 467 | |
| Morel/Duncan | Lab/L | 260 | |
| Morel/Stewart | Lab/Com | 7,946 | |
| Scrymgeour/Wallace | SPP/C | 3,243 | |
| Scrymgeour/Duncan | SPP/L | 1,117 | |
| Scrymgeour/Stewart | SPP/Com | 229 | |
| Wallace/Duncan | C/L | 23,941 | |
| Wallace/Stewart | C/Com | 59 | |
| Duncan/Stewart | L/Com | 35 | |
| **Total** | | **65,593** | **124,063** |

## 1929

| Candidate | Party | Votes | Result |
|---|---|---|---|
| Scrymgeour | SPP | 1,588 | 50,073 |
| Marcus | Lab | 1,098 | 47,602 |
| Henderson-Stewart | L | 1,521 | 33,890 |
| Wallace | C | 2,536 | 33,868 |
| Stewart | Com | 1,668 | 6,160 |
| **Total Plumpers** | | **8,411** | |
| Scrymgeour/Marcus | SPP/Lab | 42,711 | |
| Scrymgeour/Henderson-Stewart | SPP/L | 3,315 | |
| Scrymgeour/Wallace | SPP/C | 1,851 | |
| Scrymgeour/Stewart | SPP/Com | 608 | |
| Marcus/Henderson-Stewart | Lab/L | 954 | |
| Marcus/Wallace | Lab/C | 250 | |
| Marcus/Stewart | Lab/Com | 2,589 | |
| Henderson-Stewart/Wallace | L/C | 28,018 | |
| Henderson-Stewart/Stewart | L/Com | 82 | |
| Wallace/Stewart | C/Com | 1,213 | |
| **Total** | | **90,002** | **171,593** |

## 1931

| Candidate | Party | Votes | Result |
|---|---|---|---|
| Foot | L | 989 | 52,048 |
| Horsbrugh | C | 610 | 48,556 |
| Marcus | Lab | 1,466 | 32,573 |
| Scrymgeour | SPP | 1,722 | 32,229 |
| Stewart | Com | 4,811 | 10,264 |
| **Total Plumpers** | | **9,598** | |
| Foot/Horsbrugh | L/C | 47,078 | |
| Foot/Marcus | L/Lab | 848 | |
| Foot/Scrymgeour | L/SPP | 3,022 | |
| Foot/Stewart | L/Com | 111 | |
| Horsbrugh/Marcus | C/Lab | 244 | |
| Horsbrugh/Scrymgeour | C/SPP | 571 | |
| Horsbrugh/Stewart | C/Com | 53 | |
| Marcus/Scrymgeour | Lab/SPP | 25,820 | |
| Marcus/Stewart | Lab/Com | 4,195 | |
| Scrymgeour/Stewart | SPP/Com | 1,094 | |
| **Total** | | **92,634** | **175,670** |

## 1935

| Candidate | Party | Votes | Result |
|---|---|---|---|
| Horsbrugh | C | 1,413 | 50,542 |
| Foot | L | 433 | 49,632 |
| Marcus | Lab | 185 | 44,457 |
| Gibson | Lab | 73 | 43,747 |
| **Total Plumpers** | | **2,104** | |
| Horsbrugh/Foot | C/L | 47,875 | |
| Horsbrugh/Marcus | C/Lab | 879 | |
| Horsbrugh/Gibson | C/Lab | 375 | |
| Foot/Marcus | L/Lab | 709 | |
| Foot/Gibson | L/Lab | 615 | |
| Marcus/Gibson | Lab/Lab | 42,684 | |
| **Total** | | **95,241** | **188,378** |

## 1945

| Candidate | Party | Votes | Result |
|---|---|---|---|
| Cook | Lab | 532 | 48,804 |
| Strachey | Lab | 449 | 48,393 |
| Foot | L | 969 | 33,230 |
| Horsbrugh | C | 1,900 | 32,309 |
| Donaldson | SNP | 668 | 7,776 |
| **Total Plumpers** | | **4,518** | |
| Cook/Strachey | Lab/Lab | 46,538 | |
| Cook/Foot | Lab/L | 584 | |
| Cook/Horsbrugh | Lab/C | 157 | |
| Cook/Donaldson | Lab/SNP | 993 | |
| Strachey/Foot | Lab/L | 800 | |
| Strachey/Horsbrugh | Lab/C | 197 | |
| Strachey/Donaldson | Lab/SNP | 409 | |
| Foot/Horsbrugh | L/C | 27,613 | |
| Foot/Donaldson | L/SNP | 3,264 | |
| Horsbrugh/Donaldson | C/SNP | 2,442 | |
| **Total** | | **87,515** | **170,512** |

## ANTRIM [622]

| 1922 | Unopposed |
|------|-----------|
| 1923 | Unopposed |
| 1924 | Analysis not available — Ballot Papers 63,323 (estimated) |
| 1929 | Analysis not available — Ballot Papers 72,314 |
| 1931 | Unopposed |
| 1935 | Unopposed |
| 1945 | Analysis not available — Ballot Papers 75,662 |

## DOWN [624]

**1922**          Unopposed

**1923**          Unopposed

**1924**          Analysis not available — Ballot Papers 67,870

**1929**          Analysis not available — Ballot Papers 75,014 (estimated)

**1931**          Unopposed

**1935**          Analysis not available — Ballot Papers 86,845 (estimated)

**1945**          Analysis not available — Ballot Papers 71,752

## FERMANAGH and TYRONE [625]

**1922**                         Analysis not available — Ballot Papers 83,947


**1923**                         Analysis not available — Ballot Papers 81,823

Note: An unoffical analysis was published in the local press as follows: Harbinson (N) 272; Healy (N) 118; Pringle (C) 75; Falls (C) 95; Harbinson/Healy (N/N) 43,300; Harbinson/Pringle (N/C) 180; Harbinson/Falls (N/C) 167; Healy/Pringle (N/C) 112; Healy/Falls (N/C) 54; Pringle/Falls (C/C) 37,265. This analysis was not completely accurate as it gave a total of 82,638 ballot papers instead of 81,823 as announced by the Returning Officer.


**1924**                         Analysis not available — Ballot Papers 51,687


**1929**                         Unopposed


**1931**                         Analysis not available — Ballot Papers 96,760

Note: An unofficial figure for the number of 'straight' votes was published in the local press as follows: Devlin/Healy (N/N) 49,949; Irwin/Burges (C/C) 44,410.


**1935**                         Analysis not available — Ballot Papers 97,516


**1945**                         Analysis not available — Ballot Papers 102,031

# INDEX TO CANDIDATES

This index lists the names of all candidates at General Elections from 1918 to 1945 and at intervening by-elections up to the end of December 1949. The number or numbers following the name of each candidate indicate the constituency reference number which is given after the name of the constituency, at the top of each page. It does *not* refer to the folio number which appears in small type at the foot of each page.

Owing to the very limited biographical information which is available about many of the candidates during this period, there is no doubt that some errors must have occurred. Every entry has been verified as far as possible but compiling an index of this size is complicated by changes in surnames (by marriage or deed poll), the adoption of additional hyphenated surnames and by the acquirement of courtesy titles.

The problems which arise in checking that a John Smith who contested a constituency in 1918 was the same, or a different person, who fought an election many years later will be appreciated by those who have researched information on candidates, especially prior to 1950.

Men and women candidates are listed in separate sections of the index and double surnames (hyphenated and un-hyphenated) have been cross-indexed for ease of reference.

## SECTION ONE — — — MEN

### A

Abbé, D.M. Van, see Van Abbé
Abbott, H., 538
Abbott, J.T., 236
Abraham, F., 171
Abraham, Rt. Hon. W., 521
Abraham, W.J., 90
Abrahams, G., 227
Abrahamson, H.S., 444
Ackroyd, T.R., 182
Acland, A.G.D., 477
Acland, Rt. Hon. Sir F.D., Bt., 294, 295, 314, 424
Acland, Sir R.T.D., Bt., 56, 310, 315, 369

Acland-Troyte, G.J., 314
Acworth, B., 56, 539
Adair, T.B.S., 571
Adam, T., 341
Adam, W.A., 61
Adams, D., 67, 195, 271, 325
Adams, D.M., 40
Adams, H.R., 53, 364
Adams, James (1), 423
Adams, James (2), 31
Adams, P., 43
Adams, S.V.T., 157
Adams, T.G. 174

Adams, W.T., 22
Adamson, Rt.Hon. W., 593
Adamson, W.M., 444
Adare, Viscount 192
Addis, J.J.J., 49
Addison, Rt. Hon. C., 22, 45, 481
Adkins, Sir W.R.D., 384
Adshead, J., 77, 184
Aeron-Thomas, J., 535
Agar, A.W.S., 17
Aggett, T.H., 206, 316
Agg-Gardner, Rt. Hon. Sir J.T., 108
Agnew, E.S., 397
Agnew, P.G., 294
Ainger, H., 346
Ainsworth, C., 105
Airey, J., 248
Airlie, J.M., 550
Aitchison, Rt. Hon. C.M., 135, 562, 585, 616
Aitken, J.H.S., 190
Aitken, Hon. J.W.M., 24
Aitken, W.T., 309
Aiton, J.A., 117
Albery, A.E., 350
Albery, Sir I.J., 39, 369
Albery, W., 22
Albu, A.H., 126
Albu, V.C., 1, 2
Alchin, G., 374
Aldam, J.R.P.W., see Warde-Aldam
Aldam, W.St.A.W., see Warde-Aldam
Alden, P., 243, 244, 273
Aldington, R., 484
Aldred, G.A., 559, 560, 562, 571
Alec-Smith, R.A., 148
Alexander, Rt. Hon. A.V., 228
Alexander, E.E., 162
Alexander, H., 554
Alexander, M., 48, 193, 416
Alexander, S.W., 12
Alexander, Rev. T.T., 555
Alexander, William, 110
Alexander, Sir William, 562
Allan, H., 181
Allan, J.R., 581
Allan, P.H., 556
Allan, R.A., 591
Allen, A.A., 591
Allen, A.C., 393
Allen, Rt. Hon. C.P., 344
Allen, J.M., 56
Allen, John Sandeman, 72, 417
Allen, Sir John Sandeman, 174
Allen, Sir R.W., 158, 159, 296, 431
Allen, S., 154
Allen, S.S., 286
Allen, W., 238
Allen, W.E.D., 621, 625
Allen, Sir William James, 623
Allen, William Jones, 16
Allen, W.T., 40
Allhusen, D., 102
Allighan, G., 369
Allison, E.F., 297
Allison, G.E., 547
Allison, T.M., 189
Allitt, J.W., 198

Allott, P., 24
Alpass, J.H., 98, 342, 345
Alstead, R., 262, 283
Aman, D.L., 350, 368, 370
Ambrose, Dr. R., 51
Amery, J., 210
Amery, Rt. Hon. L.C.M.S., 83
Ammon, C.G., 8
Amory, D.H., see Heathcoat-Amory
Amory, P.G.H., see Heathcoat-Amory
Amos, Sir M.S., 106
Anderson, A., 603
Anderson, Sir A.G., 12
Anderson, F., 300, 305, 389
Anderson, F.S., 614
Anderson, Rt. Hon. Sir J., 632
Anderson, J.C.L., 617
Anderson, J.L., 592
Anderson, M.H., 53
Anderson, T.R., 559, 569
Anderson, T.S., 302
Anderson, W.C., 223
Angell, Sir R.N., 95, 217, 430, 629
Anstey, G.J., 34
Anstruther-Gray, W.J., 604
Appelbe, A.E., 335
Appleby, W., 331
Applin, R.V.K., 58, 366, 406
Apsley, Lord 98, 232
Arbuthnot, J.S-W., 367, 497
Archbold, E., 53, 208, 514
Archer-Shee, Sir M., 10, 14
Archibald, G., 83, 549
Archibald, H., 603
Arden, E.C., 628
Armitage, R., 152
Armstrong, R.S., 383
Armstrong, Hon. W.J.M.J., see Watson-
  Armstrong
Arnall, J., 26
Arnold, H., 273
Arnold, S., 502
Arnold-Foster, W.E., 297
Arnott, J., 150, 157
Ashley, Rt.Hon. W.W., 349, 379
Ashmead-Bartlett, E., 21
Ashton, H., 332
Ashton, R., 257
Ashton, W.S., 125
Ashworth, A.E., 103
Ashworth, J., 161
Aske, Sir R.W., Bt., 193
Asquith, Rt.Hon. H.H., 578, 592
Assheton, Rt.Hon. R., 12, 430
Astbury, F.W., 222
Astins, P., 143, 453
Aston, W.S.G., 37
Astor, Hon. J.J., 367
Astor, Hon. M.L., 457
Astor, Hon. W., 206
Astor, Hon. W.W., 15
Atherley-Jones, E., 322
Atkey, A.R., 198
Atkin, E.E.H., 199, 205
Atkinson, C., 283
Attewell, H.C., 394
Attlee, Rt.Hon. C.R., 49

Auld, J.R., 604
Auliff, M., 120
Austin, G.W., 349
Austin, Sir H., 80
Austin, H.L., 389
Austin, W.J., 261
Aves, O., 450
Awbery, S.S., 98, 376
Ayles, W.H., 100, 231
Aylett, J.E., 412

**B**

Bacon, J., 413
Badlay, J., 154
Bagley, E.A.A., 378
Bagnall, A.G., 79
Bagnall, G.H., 305
Bagnall, W.G., 495
Bagram, C.E., 542
Bailey, A.J., 225
Bailey, E.A.G.S., 180
Bailey, F., 409
Bailey, V.G., 346, 350
Baillie, Sir A.W.M., Bt., 374, 606
Baillie, J.U., 601
Baillie-Hamilton, Hon. C.W., 68, 608
Baillieu, I.C., 255
Bain, A., 103
Bainbridge, J., 322
Baird, J., 267
Baird, Rt. Hon. Sir J.L., Bt., 472, 550
Baker, C., 243, 411
Baker, E., 99, 183, 489
Baker, F.E.N., see Noel-Baker
Baker, G.G., 231
Baker, H.A., 37
Baker, Rt. Hon. H.T., 62
Baker, J., 266, 485
Baker, J.B., 348
Baker, P.J.N., see Noel-Baker
Baker, V.H.E., 165
Baker, W.J., 99, 394
Baldwin, A.E., 353
Baldwin, H.A., 404
Baldwin, O.R., see Corvedale, Viscount
Baldwin, Rt. Hon. S., 483
Baldwin-Webb, J., 436
Bales, E.W., 33
Balfour, A., 617
Balfour, A.E., 555
Balfour, Rt. Hon. A.J., 12
Balfour, G., 23
Balfour, H.H., 260, 370
Balfour, Sir R., Bt., 568
Ball, W., 273
Ballantine, W., 94
Ballard, F.J., 119
Balmer, W.E., 102
Balniel, Lord, 262, 383
Banbury, Rt. Hon. Sir F.G., Bt., 12
Banfield, J.W., 16, 74, 254
Banks, J., 285
Banks, Sir R.M., 481
Banks, T.M., 118
Banner, Sir J.S.H., see Harmood-Banner
Bannerman, J.M., 583, 632

Bannington, A.C., 109
Banting, H.C., 103, 408
Banton, G., 158
Barbour, Dr. G.F., 611
Barclay, R.N., 179
Barclay-Harvey, C.M., 582
Bardsley, E.S., 218
Barefoot, W., 61
Barford, W., 155
Baring, Sir G., Bt., 25, 362
Barker, B., 456
Barker, E.N.L., see Lingen-Barker
Barker, G., 541
Barker, J.W., 347
Barker, R.H., 510
Barlow, Rt. Hon. Sir C.A.M., see Montague-Barlow
Barlow, E., 262, 385
Barlow, Sir J.D., Bt., 287, 290
Barlow, Sir J.E., Bt., 438
Barlow, Dr. R.A., 554
Barnard, E.B., 356
Barnard, G.H., 97
Barnes, A.J., 124
Barnes, D.T., 157
Barnes, G., 210
Barnes, Rt. Hon. G.N., 563
Barnes, H., 132, 193, 246
Barnes, L.J., 117
Barnes, T.E., 419
Barnett, R.W., 44
Barnsley, Sir J., 77
Barnston, Sir H., Bt., 287
Barr, James, 613
Barr, Rev. James, 585, 600, 603
Barr, J.S., 128, 246
Barran, Sir J.N., Bt., 149
Barrand, A.R., 504
Barrass, H., 126
Barratt, W., 5
Barrie, Sir C.C., 232, 587
Barron, T., 471, 577
Barron, W.E., 201
Barrow, G.C., 77
Barrow, J., 375
Barrow, S., 461
Barrow, W.J.W.C., 455
Barry, E.P.J., 37
Barry, P.R., 90
Barstow, P.G., 67, 503
Bartle, F., 243
Bartleet, E.J., 85
Bartlett, E.A., see Ashmead-Bartlett
Bartlett, C.V.O., 437
Bartley-Denniss, E.R., 202
Barton, A., 229, 335
Barton, Sir A.W., 179, 202
Barton, B.K., 147
Barton, C., 256
Bateman, A.L., 8, 244
Bateman, J.D., 365, 442
Bateman, L.H., 99, 544
Bateman, R.A., 359
Bates, Dr. H.B., 386
Bates, R.B., 204, 414
Batey, J., 331
Battle, J., 384, 388

Battley, J.R., 55
Batty, J.H., 376, 417
Baucher, A.E., 187, 262, 328
Baum, J.H., 149, 199
Bavin, T.S., 398
Baxter, A.B., 413
Baxter, F.V., 150
Baxter, H.J., 140, 367
Bayley, J., 436
Bayliss, E., 217, 230
Bayly, Dr. H.W., 206
Beach, A.A., 435
Beach, W.W. Hicks, see Hicks Beach
Beale, A., 64
Beamish, H.H., 55
Beamish, T.P.H., 465
Beamish, T.V.H., 465
Bearcroft, E.G., 501, 506
Beardsworth, G., 285, 292
Beaton, A., 553, 554, 576
Beattie, F., 561
Beattie, James, 268
Beattie, John, 621
Beauchamp, Sir B.C., Bt., 251, 451
Beauchamp, Sir E., Bt., 451
Beaufort-Palmer, F.N., 30
Beaumont, C.A., 85
Beaumont, H., 10, 69, 333, 346, 408
Beaumont, M.W., 278, 343
Beaumont, Hon. R.E.B., 207, 444
Beaumont, Hon. W.H.C., 424
Beaumont-Thomas, L., 80, 529, 545
Bebb, W.A., 526
Bechervaise, A.E., 162, 233
Beck, A.C.T., 339
Beck, A.E., 445
Beck, W.J., 209, 347, 363
Becker, H.T.A., 4, 212
Beckett, J., 10, 128, 194
Beckett, Hon. Sir W.G., Bt., 153, 492
Beech, F.W., 61
Beechman, N.A., 297
Beedle, P.D.R., see Ridge-Beedle
Beevers, S., 156
Beggs, G., 571
Behrens, L.F., 185
Beit, Sir A.L., Bt., 43
Belcher, E.A.C., 397
Belcher, J.W., 510
Belisha, Rt. Hon. L.H., see Hore-Belisha
Bell, Sir A.C.M., Bt., see Morrison-Bell
Bell, C.S., 147
Bell, E.P., 413
Bell, G.D., 46
Bell, G.H.K., see Keighley-Bell
Bell, H., 12
Bell, H.C., 78
Bell, H.T.M., 59
Bell, J., 86, 105, 217, 387
Bell, J.A., 5
Bell, J.D.M., 364
Bell, J.N., 193
Bell, J.R., 150
Bell, R.M., 519, 534
Bell, S., 391
Bell, W.C.H., 479
Bellairs, C., 371

Bellamy, A., 64, 247
Bellamy, F.H., 57
Bellenger, F.J., 426
Bellerby, J.R., 282, 429
Belt, G., 135, 449
Bemrose, J.M., 117
Bence, C.R., 79
Benn, Sir A.S., Bt., 205, 229
Benn, I.H., 17
Benn, J.A., 95
Benn, Rt. Hon. W.W., 119, 180, 548, 576
Bennett, A., 295
Bennett, A.J., 198, 428, 478
Bennett, C.A., 432
Bennett, D.C.T., 112, 187
Bennett, Sir E.N., 44, 431, 482, 514
Bennett, F.M., 238
Bennett, G., 26
Bennett, Sir H.H.C., see Curtis-Bennett
Bennett, Sir P.F.B., 77
Bennett, Dr. R.F.B., 60
Bennett, S., 421
Bennett, Sir T.J., 373
Bennett, W., 2, 357, 394, 460, 515
Bennett, W.G., 571
Bennett, W.H., 367
Bennetts, A.E., 461
Benson, G., 283, 303
Benson, S.R., 261
Bentham, G.J., 401
Bentinck, F.W.C., see Cavendish-Bentinck
Bentinck, Lord Henry Cavendish, see
   Cavendish-Bentinck
Bère, R. De la, see De la Bère
Berg, F.J. Van den, see Van den Berg
Berkeley, R.C., 198, 548, 580
Bermingham, J., 17
Bernard, Dr. B.L., see Lytton-Bernard
Bernays, R.H., 100, 472
Berry, B.H., 243
Berry, Sir G.A., 632
Berry, Hon. G.L., 279
Berry, H., 61
Berry, Hon. J.S., 357
Berryman, M.L., 216
Besley, C.R.I., 324
Best, A.J., 491
Best, C.E., 369
Beswick, F., 412
Bethel, A., 125
Bethell, A.J., 68
Bethell, Sir J.H., Bt., 123
Bethell, Sir T.R., 450
Betterton, Sir H.B., Bt., 430
Bevan, A., 543
Bevan, H.C., 13
Bevan, S.J., 24
Beveridge, Sir W.H., 423
Bevin, Rt. Hon. E., 54, 98, 128
Bevins, J.R., 166, 175
Bewicke-Copley, Sir R.C.A.B., 496
Beyfus, G.H., 445
Bibbings, F.G., 502
Bickersteth, H., 72
Bicket, Sir A., 91
Biggar, J.M., 578
Bigge, Sir A.A.S., Bt., see Selby-Bigge

Bigland, A., 71
Bignold, H., 34
Billing, N.P., 23, 119, 140, 356, 436
Bing, G.H.C., 336
Binney, R.C.C.J., 412
Binns, E., 95
Binns, J., 215
Birch, E.N.C., 532
Birch, J.E.L., 350
Birchall, Sir J.D., 154
Bird, A.F., 268
Bird, E.R., 33, 509
Bird, Sir R.B., Bt., 268
Bird, Sir W.B.M., 467
Birkett, W.N., 80, 199
Birt, F.B.B., see Bradley-Birt
Bishop, A.B., 31, 151
Bishop, R., 458
Black, Sir A.W., 274
Black, D.J., 565
Black, H., 570
Black, H.M., 465
Black, H.R., 573
Black, J.B., 559
Black, J.W., 394
Blackburn, A.R., 80, 359
Blackburn, C.H., 25, 314
Blackett, Sir B.P., 41
Blackman, A., 136
Blackwell, C.P., 445
Blades, D.P., 600
Blades, Sir G.R., Bt., 458
Blair, Sir Reginald, 32, 39, 409
Blair, Sir Robert, 408
Blake, Sir F.D., Bt., 423
Blake, H.H.C., 52
Blake, N.D., 437
Blaker, Sir R., Bt., 410
Blakiston-Houston, J.M., 624, 625
Bland, W., 500
Blane, T.A., 159
Blaylock, W.W., 77
Blease, Prof. W.L., 165
Blenkinsop, A., 193
Blindell, J., 397
Blindell, R.J.R., 200
Bliss, J., 383
Blitz, J.F., 209
Blizard, G.P., 54, 82, 215, 345
Bloch, M., 563
Blomerley, H., 184
Blue, A.J., 409
Blundell, F.N., 387
Blythe, T., 95
Blyton, W.R., 327
Boardman, H., 161
Boles, D.C., 440
Boles, D.F., 439
Bolst, C.C.A.L.E., see Erskine-Bolst
Bolton, H., 270
Boltoun, Lord Thirlestane and, see Thirlestane
Boltz, J.M., 437
Bone, W., 477
Bonham Carter, M.R., 310
Bonwick, A.J., 478
Boot, C., 228
Boot, H.L.P., 48

Booth, Sir A A., Bt., 173
Booth, F.H., 512
Booth, J., 157
Boothby, R.J.G., 581, 610
Borodale, Viscount, 10
Borthwick, A.M., 450
Borthwick, Hon. W., 318
Borwick, G.O., 112
Boscawen, Rt. Hon. Sir A.S.T.G., see
    Griffith-Boscawen
Bossom, A.C., 18, 371
Bottomley, A.G., 214
Bottomley, H.W., 20
Boult, F., 45, 155, 505
Boulton, A.C.F., 349
Boulton, E.J., 145
Boulton, W.W., 225
Bourke, E.A.H.L., see Legge-Bourke
Bourne, Rt. Hon. R.C., 203
Bowater, Sir T.V., Bt., 12
Bowden, G.R.H., 307
Bowden, H.W., 159
Bowdler, W.A., 488
Bowen, D., 517, 537
Bowen, E.R., 527
Bowen, J.W., 286, 519
Bower, N.A.H., 4, 21, 134, 408
Bower, P., 74
Bower, R.T., 490
Bowerman, Rt. Hon. C.W., 13
Bowker, R.J., 270
Bowkett, A.W., 77, 81, 445
Bowles, F.G., 19, 210, 471
Bowles, G.T., 415
Bowles, H.F., 406
Bowman, G.S.M., 427
Bowman, L.G., 43
Bowring, F.C., 165
Bowyer, Sir G.E.W., Bt., 279
Box, S., 352
Boyce, E.J., 279
Boyce, Sir H.L., 129
Boyd, A.T.L., see Lennox-Boyd
Boyd, R.N., 622
Boyd, T.C., 370
Boyd, T.W., 618
Boyd-Carpenter, Sir A.B., 95, 109, 456
Boyd-Carpenter, G.D.E., 434
Boyd-Carpenter, J.A., 151
Boyd Orr, Sir J., 632
Boyden, P., 469
Boyes, W.E., 436
Boyle, C.H., 154
Boyle, D., 421
Brabazon, J.T.C.M., see Moore-Brabazon
Brabner, R.A., 142
Brace, M., 543
Brace, Rt. Hon. W., 541
Bracken, Rt. Hon. B., 37, 92
Brackenbury, Sir H.B., 251, 628
Brackenbury, H.L., 403
Braddock, T., 188, 265
Braden, R.E.N., 21
Bradford, A.W., 120
Bradford, Sir J.R., 629
Bradford, T.A., 326, 329
Bradley-Birt, F.B., 518

Brady, A.W., 550
Brailsford, H.N., 577
Brain, W.T.E., 156
Braine, B.R., 162
Braithwaite, Sir A.N., 487, 498, 503, 507
Braithwaite, J.G., 3, 228, 488
Bramall, E.A., 70, 348
Bramley, E.F., 21
Bramley, F., 204
Brampton, A., 75, 198
Bramsdon, Sir T.A., 207
Bramston, F.C., 143, 252
Bransby-Williams, M.E., 536
Brass, Sir W., 376
Brassey, Sir H.L.C., Bt., 421
Brassington, I., 253
Breese, C.E., 526
Brenan, F.G.J.W., see Woulfe-Brenan
Brett, Hon. L.G.B., 432
Briant, B.D., 97
Briant, F., 33
Brice, M., 264
Bridgeman, R.F.O., 412
Bridgeman, Rt. Hon. W.C., 434
Bridges, Dr. J.S., 251, 263
Brigden, G., 82
Brigg, W.A., 500, 509
Briggs, H.A., 223, 307, 425, 487
Briggs, W.J.C., 500
Briggs, W.J.H., 177
Bright, F., 262
Brighton, C.L., 349
Brighton, R.W., 345
Brinton, E.T.C., 119
Brinton, H., 131, 297
Briscoe, R.G., 282
Brise, Sir E.A.R., Bt., see Ruggles-Brise
Brittain, Sir H.E., 404
Britton, G.B., 99
Britton, J.H., 100
Broad, F.A., 126
Broad, T.T., 162, 304
Broadbent, J., 64
Broadbridge, Sir G.T., Bt., 12
Broadway, O.F., 243
Brockhouse, J.L., 267
Brocklebank, Sir C.E.R., 71, 169, 199, 230
Brocklehurst, A.B., 125
Brockman, W.H.G.D., see Drake-Brockman
Brockway, A.F., 58, 162, 197, 261, 382, 515
Brogan, T.P., 1
Bromfield, W., 446
Bromley, J., 67, 154
Bromley-Davenport, W.H., 288
Brook, C.A., 449
Brook, Dr. C.W., 53, 230
Brook, D., 132
Brook, F., 495
Brook, J.A., 155
Brooke, B., 298
Brooke, C.R.I., 503
Brooke, H., 36
Brooke, S.S., 45, 460
Brooke, T., 495
Brooke, W., 69, 591
Brookes, C., 305
Brookes, J.N.D., 199

Brookes, W., 210
Brooks, E.H., 276
Brooks, H.R.G., 337
Brooks, K.G., 226
Brooks, T.J., 507
Brooksbank, A.W., 167
Brooman-White, R.C., 559
Broomhead-Colton-Fox, R.F.H., 303
Brothers, M., 76, 90
Brotherton, Sir E.A., Bt., 247
Brotherton, J., 128
Brotherton-Ratcliffe, E., 27, 162
Brough, J.R., 442
Broughton, Dr. A.D.D., 69
Broughton, R.A., 499
Broun-Lindsay, G.H.M., 568
Brown, A.B., 593
Brown, Rt. Hon. A.E., 461, 472, 480, 576
Brown, A.W., 504
Brown, C., 428
Brown, C.H., 330
Brown, D. Clifton, see Clifton Brown
Brown, F., 314
Brown, G.A., 302
Brown, G.B.C., see Clifton-Brown
Brown, H., 157
Brown, H.C., 276
Brown, H.E., 445
Brown, H.R., 499
Brown, Rt.Hon. James, 586
Brown, James, 624
Brown, John (1), 420
Brown, John (2), 204, 343
Brown, J.B., 612
Brown, J.S., 552
Brown, John Wesley, 186
Brown, John William, 358
Brown, Dr. L.G., 273
Brown, R.H., 375, 398
Brown, R.K., 486
Brown, R.S., 126
Brown, T.J., 381
Brown, W.B.D., 59
Brown, W.G., 514
Brown, William Henry (1), 250
Brown, William Henry (2), 385
Brown, W.J., 268, 412, 472
Brown, W.O., 613
Browne, A.C., 621
Browne, J.N., 564
Browne, L.F., 299
Browne, M.B., 456
Browning, D., 560
Brownlie, J.T., 241, 286
Bruce, D.W.T., 208
Bruce, G.J., 596
Bruce, J.C.B., see Brudenell-Bruce
Bruce, J.H., 485
Bruce, W., 589
Brudenell-Bruce, J.C., 97
Bruford, R., 440
Brundrit, D.F., 275
Brunner, Sir F.J.M., Bt., 181, 290, 478
Brunner, Sir J.F., Bt., 108, 234, 290
Bruton, Sir J., 129
Bryan, P.E.O., 510
Bryans, G.H., 214, 215

Buchan, J., 632
Buchan-Hepburn, P.G.T., 165, 267
Buchanan, A.L.H., 600
Buchanan, G., 563
Bucher, F.N., 71
Buckhurst, Lord, 5
Buckingham, Sir H.C., 460
Buckle, J., 125
Buckley, A., 390
Bugby, J.E., 196
Bull, B.B., 406
Bull, J.H., 506
Bull, Rt. Hon. Sir W.J., Bt., 22
Bull, W.P., 304
Buller, Sir M.E.M., Bt., see Manningham-Buller
Buller, R.E.M., see Manningham-Buller
Bullock, M., 390
Bundock, C.J., 393
Bundy, H., 37
Bunning, G.H.S., see Stuart-Bunning
Bunyan, J., 326
Burcher, L.C., 434
Burden, C., 165
Burden, D.F., 291
Burden, F.F.A., 3, 14, 235
Burden, T.W., 123, 229
Burdett-Coutts, W.L.A.B., 58
Burditt, G.F., 185
Burdon, R., 330
Burges, Y.A., 625
Burgess, F.G., 62, 271, 371
Burgess, S., 213, 576
Burghley, Lord, 421
Burgin, E.L., 123, 140, 273
Burgoyne, Sir A.H., 29, 278
Burke, J.E., 91
Burke, K., 185
Burke, W.A., 104, 177
Burman, J.B., 76
Burn, C.R., 315
Burnett, A., 563
Burnett, J.G., 548
Burnett, R.P., 382, 477
Burney, C.D., 412
Burnie, J., 91
Burns, A.G., 598
Burns, I., 503
Burridge, H., 272
Burrows, Robert Abraham, 161
Burrows, Robert Allanson, 302
Burrows, W., 19
Burt, C.S.S., 463
Burton, H.W., 454
Bury, C.K.H., see Howard-Bury
Busby, C.J., 16, 49
Bushby, Sir E.F., 531
Bushnell, Dr. F.G., 82, 439, 629
Bustard, J.C.D., 182
Butcher, B.M., 396
Butcher, H.C., 4
Butcher, H.W., 397
Butcher, Sir J.G., Bt., 271
Butler, Sir G.G.G., 627
Butler, H.M., 153
Butler, H.W., 20
Butler, J.G., 58, 59, 136, 263
Butler, J.R.M., 627

Butler, P., 95, 212, 458
Butler, Rt. Hon. R.A., 339
Butlin, P., 288
Butt, Sir A., Bt., 53
Butterworth, W., 184
Button, H.S., 436
Butts, J., 369
Buxton, C.R., 62, 498
Buxton, L.W.W., 420
Buxton, Rt. Hon. N.E., 416
Buxton, T.F., 374
Buzzard, Sir E.F., Bt., 630
Byass, S.H., 533
Byers, C.C., 482
Byers, C.F., 318

C

Cadbury, P.E., 344
Cadogan, Hon. Sir E.C.G., 90, 211, 407
Cadogan, H.J., 430
Cadogan, P., 465
Cadzow, J.B., 607
Cain, A.R.N.N., see Nall-Cain
Caine, D. Hall, see Hall Caine
Caine, G.R. Hall, see Hall Caine
Caird, Sir A., 297
Caird, D., 557
Cairns, A., 400
Cairns, D.A.S., 458
Cairns, J., 189
Cairns, J.A.R., 316
Calladine, H.F., 429
Callaghan, Sir A.J., 214, 463
Callaghan, L.J., 516
Calver, R.H.S., 572, 601
Calvocoressi, P.J.A., 471
Cameron, A.G., 61, 392
Cameron, C.J.G., 433
Cameron, K.M., 67
Cameron, W.M., 548
Camm, A.R.M., 210
Campbell, E.M., 595
Campbell, Sir E.T., Bt., 9, 103
Campbell, F.A., 460
Campbell, G., 104
Campbell, H.F., 584
Campbell, H.K., 300
Campbell, J., 618
Campbell, J.D., 622
Campbell, J.G.D., 151
Campbell, J.R., 538, 574
Campbell, Sir M., 13
Campbell, T.J., 621
Campbell, T.W., 585
Campbell, W.P., 17
Campbell-Johnson, A., 480
Campbell-Johnston, M., 124
Campion, S.R., 434
Campion, W.R., 465
Camps, H.E.J., 104
Cane, Sir J.P. Du, see Du Cane
Cann, C.G.L. du, see du Cann
Canney, E.E., 391
Canning, C.J., 96
Canter, G.W.A., 97
Cape, Rev. H.T., 567

Cape, T., 301
Caplan, L., 21, 545
Caple, W.H.D., 77, 192
Caporn, A.C., 201
Carden, H., 97
Cardew, H.B.O., 441
Carew, C.R.S., 314
Carey, F.W., 186
Carington, N.W.S., see Smith-Carington
Carkeek, Sir A., 296
Carlile, Sir E.H., Bt., 356, 358
Carlin, W., 602
Carmichael, J., 559, 561, 573
Carnegie, D., 364
Carnegie, J., 577
Carpenter, Sir A.B.B., see Boyd-Carpenter
Carpenter, G.D.E.B., see Boyd-Carpenter
Carpenter, J.A.B., see Boyd-Carpenter
Carr, A.S. Comyns, see Comyns Carr
Carr, R.N., 298
Carr, W.T., 107
Carr-Gomm, H.W.C., 3, 38
Carritt, G., 58
Carroll, J.C., 9, 261, 604
Carrow, R.B., 495
Carson, Hon. E., 370
Carter, F., 29
Carter, G.R., 504
Carter, M.R. Bonham, see Bonham Carter
Carter, P.T., 467
Carter, R.A.D., 185
Carter, S.B., 483
Carter, William (1), 428
Carter, William (2), 44, 162
Carter, W.K., 403
Carthew, T.W.C., 259
Cartland, J.B., 264
Cartland, J.R.H., 80
Carver, W.H., 489
Cary, Sir R.A., 64, 125
Casasola, R.W., 236, 291
Casey, T.W., 129, 218, 223, 306
Cash, W., 339
Cassells, T., 591
Cassels, J.D., 9, 163
Castlereagh, Viscount, 115, 624
Castle Stewart, Earl, 394
Cathery, E., 91
Catlin, G.E.G., 241, 405
Catterall, J.T., 461
Catterall, R., 381
Catto, G., 549
Catty, T.C., 252
Caunter, J.A.L., 480
Cautley, Sir H.S., Bt., 464
Cavanagh, Dr. D.J., 626
Cave, W.E., 479
Cavendish, Lord Andrew, 303
Cavendish-Bentinck, F.W., 30
Cavendish-Bentinck, Lord Henry, 200
Cayzer, Sir C.W., Bt., 285
Cayzer, Sir H.R., Bt., 209
Cazalet, V.A., 478
Cecil, Rt. Hon. Sir E., 74
Cecil, Rt. Hon. Lord Hugh, 630
Cecil, Rt. Hon. Lord Robert, 357
Cecil, Hon. R.E.P., 381

Cemlyn-Jones, E.W., 113, 525
Chadwick, C.A.H., 281
Chadwick, Sir R.B., 67, 248
Chair, S.S. de, see de Chair
Chalke, R.D., 520, 522
Challen, C., 23
Chalmers, Rev. H., 411
Chalmers, J.R., see Rutherford, J.R.
Chamberlain, Rt. Hon. A.N., 77, 81
Chamberlain, Rt. Hon. Sir J.A., 84
Chamberlain, R.A., 34
Chamberlayne, A.R., 408
Chambers, W.A., 10
Champion, A.J., 308
Champion de Crespigny, H.V., 429
Chancellor, H.G., 45
Channon, H., 233
Chapman, A., 605
Chapman, J., 249
Chapman, J.H., 157
Chapman, R., 327
Chapman, Sir S., 557, 574
Chapman, S.N., 435
Chapman-Walker, P.J.F., 99, 541
Chappell, C.G., 184
Chappell, G.E., 320
Chapple, Dr. W.A., 590, 616
Charlesworth, R., 218
Charlesworth, S.R., 403
Charleton, H.C., 155
Charteris, J., 590
Chater, D., 5, 22, 143
Chatfeild-Clarke, Sir E., 362
Chatfield, R.S., 463
Chattaway, A.G., 79
Checkland, S., 226
Cheke, M.J., 349
Cheshire, Rev. L.S., 97
Chesshire, J.I., 257
Chesterton, R.N., 491
Chesworth, D.P., 476
Chetwynd, G.R., 237
Chetwynd-Talbot, B., 186
Cheyne, Sir W.W., Bt., 632
Chichester-Constable, R.C.J., 488
Chilcott, H.F., 312
Chilcott, Sir H.W.S., 172
Child, Sir S.H., Bt., 449
Chilton, A.H., 120, 277
Chitty, K.P., 246
Cholmondeley, Hon. T.P.H., 446
Chorley, Prof. R.S.T., 290
Chorlton, A.E.L., 105, 183
Chotzner, A.J., 261
Christie, G.F.S., 128
Christie, J.A., 417
Church, A.G., 54, 99, 117, 162, 244, 410, 629
Church, F.E., 295, 399
Church, W.H., 21
Churchill, R.F.E.S., 173, 175, 210, 597
Churchill, Rt. Hon. W.L.S., 58, 160, 269, 334, 552
Churchman, Sir A.C., Bt., 452
Citrine, W.M., 248
Clare, J., 94
Clark, A.E.J., 354
Clark, C.G., 173, 318, 417
Clark, E., 399

Clark, Dr. G.B., 561
Clark, G.F., 371
Clark, H.S., 456
Clark, N.L.H., see Leith-Hay-Clark
Clark, W.D., 423
Clarke, A.B., 607
Clarke, Sir E.C., see Chatfeild-Clarke
Clarke, F.E., 366
Clarke, G., 352
Clarke, G.F., 386
Clarke, J.H., 55
Clarke, J.S., 567
Clarke, J.T., 496
Clarke, R.S., 464
Clarke, T.H., 504
Clarry, R.G., 519
Clatworthy, J.T., 516
Clavering, A., 23
Clay, Rt. Hon. H.H.S., see Spender-Clay
Clayton, G.C., 292, 392
Cleary, J.J., 165, 173, 174
Cleworth, R., 157
Clifton Brown, D., 424
Clifton-Brown, G.B., 453
Climie, R., 585
Clitherow, R., 166
Clive, G.W., see Windsor-Clive
Close, A., 347
Clothier, W., 166
Clough, Sir R., 500, 508
Clough, T.I., 119, 224
Clover, C.G., 517
Clowes, S., 239
Cluse, W.S., 27
Clyde, Rt. Hon. J.A., 556
Clyde, J.L., 608
Clydesdale, Marquess of Douglas and, 564, 613
Clynes, J.H., 355
Clynes, Rt. Hon. J.R., 183
Coates, A., 501
Coates, Sir E.F., Bt., 36
Coates, N., 361
Coates, T.W., 492
Coats, Sir S.A., Bt., 457
Cobb, Sir C.S., 16
Cobb, E.C., 210, 280
Cobb, F.A., 498
Cochrane, Hon. A.D., 591, 592
Cockerill, Sir G.K., 462
Cockrill, G.S., 410
Cocks, F.S., 371, 427
Cockshutt, N., 213
Cohen, C.W., 207, 442
Cohen, G.A., 51
Cohen, J.B.B., 169
Cohen, J.L., 54
Cohen, L.C., 97
Cohen, S.I., 519
Colclough, J.R., 29
Coldrick, W., 100
Cole, C.J., 516
Cole, G.D.H., 630
Cole, T.L., 618
Colegate, W.A., 436, 510
Colfox, W.P., 318, 320
Collett, W.H., 484
Collick, P.H., 72, 462

Cullie, Sir D.J., 568
Collier, F.H., 4, 499
Collier, J.V., 196
Collindridge, F., 66
Collingbourne, J.H., 92
Collingson, R.B., 450
Collins, C.K., 261
Collins, Rt. Hon. Sir G.P., 574
Collins, P., 250
Collins, V.J., 439
Collins, W., 428
Collis, F., 239
Collison, L., 299
Colman, N.C.D., 31
Colton-Fox, R.F.H.B., see Broomhead-Colton-Fox
Colville, D.J., 603, 607
Colvin, R.B., 334
Colyer, W.T., 61, 365
Comben, R.S., 319
Common, L.A., 241
Compston, J.A., 57, 69
Compton, J., 180, 481
Compton-Rickett, Sir J., 503
Comyn-Platt, Sir T.W., 207, 234
Comyns, Dr. L., 259
Comyns Carr, A.S., 12, 25, 44, 143, 199, 334, 435
Conant, R.J.E., 303, 483
Conley, A., 333
Connell, B.R., 90
Connell, Sir R.L., 390, 545
Connellan, O., 279
Connolly, M.H., 186, 193
Conoley, J., 334
Constable, R.C.J.C., see Chichester-Constable
Conway, Prof. R.S., 628
Conway, Sir W.M., 628
Conway-Jones, H., 499
Cook, B.C., 332
Cook, D., 15
Cook, F.W., 323
Cook, J.S., 432
Cook, T.F., 552
Cook, Sir T.R.A.M., 416
Cooke, C.F., see Fletcher-Cooke
Cooke, Sir C.K., Bt., see Kinloch-Cooke
Cooke, Sir J.D., 10, 22
Cooke, R., 315
Cooke-Taylor, Dr. C.R., 7
Coombes, C., 485
Cooney, R.H., 562
Cooper, Rt. Hon. A.D., 59, 202
Cooper, A.E., 114
Cooper, G., 187
Cooper, H., 352
Cooper, Sir R.A., Bt., 250
Cooper, Rt. Hon. T.M., 558
Cooper-Key, E.M., 136
Coote, C.R., 361
Cope, Sir W., Bt., 536
Copeman, H.J., 197
Copley, Sir R.C.A.B.B., see Bewicke-Copley
Copplestone, C.E., 25
Corbett, U., 433
Corkhill, N., 437
Corlett, Dr. J., 271, 389
Cormack, D.D., 578

Cormack, J., 576
Cormack, W.S., 565, 581
Cornelius, V.E., 574
Cornes, G., 315
Cornwall, Sir E.A., Bt., 5
Corpe, T.D., 99
Corrigan, T., 625
Corvedale, Viscount (formerly O.R. Baldwin) 119, 214, 578
Corvin, H.C., 619, 621
Cory, Sir C.J., Bt., 297
Cory, Sir J.H., Bt., 516
Costello, L.W.J., 127, 360
Cotter, J.P., 74, 340, 392
Cotton, H.E.A., 14
Cotts, W.C.M., 343
Cotts, Sir W.D.M., Bt., 598
Coultate, W.H., 198
Coulthard, J., 71
Couper, J.B., 567, 570
Courcy, J.F.M. de, see de Courcy
Courtauld, J.S., 467
Courtenay, C.W., 16
Courthorpe, Sir G.L., Bt., 466
Coutts, W.L.A.B.B., see Burdett-Coutts
Cove, E.G., 427
Cove, W.G., 422, 533
Coventry, Hon. G.W.R.V., 528
Coventry, Hon. J.B., 528
Cowan, D.M., 632
Cowan, Sir W.H., 26, 581
Cowell, J.S., see Scott-Cowell
Cox, H.B.T., 291, 307
Coxon, W., 329
Coyle, O., 600
Coysh, F., 15, 21, 42
Cozens-Hardy, Hon. W.H., 417
Craddock, G., 96
Craddock, G.B., 447
Craddock, Sir R.H., 628
Craig, Rt. Hon. C.C., 622
Craig, E., 286
Craig, H.J., 246
Craig, N.C., 370
Craig, W.B., 441
Craik, Rt. Hon. Sir H., 632
Cramp, C.T., 187
Cranborne, Viscount, 319
Crane, A.C., 37, 251, 260, 374
Craven-Ellis, W., 66, 232
Craven-Griffiths, D., 198
Crawford, Archibald (1), 608
Crawford, Archibald (2), 396
Crawford, G.W., 556
Crawford, J., 585
Crawford, T., 113, 464
Crawford, W., 613
Crawfurd, H.E., 25, 160, 252
Crawley, A.M., 279
Crawshay, G.C.H., 539, 545
Crawshay, W.R., 519
Cree, G.H., 227
Creighton, A., 107
Cremlyn, J.W.J., 175
Crespigny, H.V. Champion de, see Champion de Crespigny
Crewdson, R.B., 184, 416

Crichton, Dr. J.R., 194
Crichton-Stuart, Lord Colum, 290, 515
Crinion, J., 388
Cripps, J.S., 127
Cripps, Hon. L.H., 248
Cripps, Rt. Hon. Sir R.S., 99
Crisp, C.B., 277
Crisp, C.N.B., 277
Critchley, A., 166
Critchley, A.C., 25, 180, 411
Critchley, C.F., 87
Crittall, V.G., 337
Crockatt, D., 271
Croft, Sir H.P., Bt., 92
Crofton, M.G., 495
Crone, Dr. J.S., 264
Cronin, J.B., 215
Crook, C.W., 123
Crooke, J.S., 75
Crooks, T., 115
Crooks, Rt. Hon. W., 60
Crookshank, C. de W., 91, 130, 588
Crookshank, Rt. Hon. H.F.C., 401
Croom-Johnson, R.P., 437
Cropper, H., 303
Cros, Sir A.P. Du, Bt., see Du Cros
Cros, A.R.P. Du, see Du Cros
Crosby, H.J.F., 131
Cross, C.P., 348
Cross, Rt. Hon. Sir R.H., Bt., 217
Crosse, M.P., 451
Crossley, A.C., 202, 389
Crossley, Hon. F.S., 132
Crossley-Holland, Dr. F.W., 499
Crossman, R.H.S., 84, 110
Crosthwaite-Eyre, O.E., 349
Crotch, W.W., 212
Crow, W., 260
Crowder, F.P., 243
Crowder, J.F.E., 407
Crowe, H.A., 150
Crowley, Dr. J.F., 76, 253
Crozier, F.P., 207
Cruddas, B., 425
Crump, N.E., 279
Cruttwell, C.R.M.F., 630
Cuddon, B.E.D., 13
Culpin, E.G., 26
Culverwell, C.T., 102
Cumberbirch, J.N., 501
Cuming, L.J., 2
Cundiff, F.W., 184
Cunliffe, J.H., 90
Cunliffe-Lister, Rt. Hon. Sir P. (formerly Lloyd-Greame), 409
Cunningham, P., 625
Cunningham, S.K., 621
Cunningham-Reid, A.S., 41, 232, 253
Cunninghame Graham, R.B., 617
Curran, E., 516, 533
Curran, L.C., 252
Curran, R., 579
Currie, G.W., 576
Currie, J., 479
Currie, J.C., 181
Curry, A.C., 249, 322, 327
Curry, D.H., 492

Curtis, D.M.C., 287
Curtis-Bennett, Sir H.H., 332
Curzon, Viscount, 2
Cusack, T., 633
Cuthbert, W.N., 466

**D**

Dack, H., 490
Daggar, G., 541
Daines, P., 123
Dale, J.G., 42, 251
Dalkeith, Earl of, 615
Dallas, G., 337, 422, 615
Dallas, J.S., 571
Dallas, T.L., 93
Dallow, C.B., 92, 97, 214, 278
Dalrymple-White, Sir G.D., Bt., 234
Dalrymple-White, H.A., 500
Dalton, E.E., 150, 229
Dalton, Rt. Hon. E.H.J.N., 10, 106, 322, 371, 397, 515
Dalton, M., 39
Dalziel, Sir D., Bt., 31
Dalziel, Rt. Hon. Sir J.H., Bt., 575
Daniel, Prof. J.E., 513, 526
Daniels, S.R., 68
Danny, J.P.C., 406
Darbishire, C.W., 482
Darling, G., 289
Darling, T., 357
Darling, Sir W.Y., 557
Darnton, J.E., 109
Darvall, F.O., 142, 146, 415
Darvill, C.S., 227
Darwin, M.W., 491
Davenport, W.H.B., see Bromley-Davenport
Davey, M., 425
David, E.W., 536
Davidson, A.K., 592
Davidson, Rt. Hon. Sir J.C.C., 355
Davidson, Sir J.H., 348
Davidson, J.J., 567
Davidson, L.F.W., 580
Davidson, M.S., 92
Davies, Alfred, 376
Davies, Arthur, 546
Davies, A.C.F., see Fox-Davies
Davies, Albert Edward, 238
Davies, Albert Emil, 182, 338
Davies, Alfred T., 164
Davies, Alun T., 631
Davies, Dr. A.V., 388
Davies, A.W., 259
Davies, C.G., 543
Davies, David (1), 523
Davies, David (2), 546
Davies, D.G., 537
Davies, D.L., 539
Davies, Rev. D.R., 382
Davies, D.R.S., 513
Davies, Sir D.S., 530
Davies, Edward, 301
Davies, Evan (1), 543
Davies, Evan (2), 631
Davies, E.A.J., 406, 421
Davies, E.C., 546

Davies, E.G., 516, 538
Davies, E.R., 531
Davies, E.W., 526, 530
Davies, Frank W., 54, 162, 344
Davies, Frederick W., 535
Davies, G.F., 442
Davies, G.M.L., 631
Davies, Harold, 446
Davies, Haydn, 44
Davies, Henry, 519
Davies, I., 631
Davies, I.R.M., 580
Davies, Sir J., 286
Davies, J.B., 513
Davies, J.C., 530
Davies, J.H.W., see Wootton-Davies
Davies, J.J., 22, 463
Davies, J.K., 520
Davies, John Langdon, see Langdon-Davies
Davies, John Leigh, 521
Davies, J.P., 86, 509
Davies, M.L.V., see Vaughan-Davies
Davies, O.G., 538
Davies, O.P., 55
Davies, Richard, 136, 313
Davies, Dr. Richard, 108
Davies, R.J., 222, 391
Davies, S., 484, 518
Davies, S.O., 518
Davies, Sir Thomas, 342
Davies, Timothy, 403
Davies, T.M., 356
Davies, W., 181
Davies, W.E., 177
Davies, Sir W.H., 101
Davies, W.T., 202, 289
Davies-Evans, D.W.C., 528
Davis, C.P., 21
Davis, D.J., 259, 463
Davis, H.E., 369
Davis, J., 423
Davis, J.E., 325
Davis, J.T., 374
Davis, R.G., 254, 502
Davis, S.H., 74
Davison, J.E., 230
Davison, Sir W.H., 30
Davy, A., 508
Dawes, J.A., 48
Dawkins, F.E., 23
Dawrant, A., 429
Dawson, A., 510
Dawson, G.H., 487
Dawson, H., 498
Dawson, H.M., 94
Dawson, Sir P., 36
Dawson, R.W.P., 499
Dawson, W.H., 130
Day, H., 46, 151
Day, J.A., 313, 345, 453
Day, T.F., 127, 371
Dean, A.W., 397
Dean, P.T., 86
Dean, R.E., 625
Dean, W.F., 217
Deans, R.S., 229
de Chair, S.S., 418

Decie, C.P., see Prescott-Decie
de Courcy, J.F.M., 534
de Crespigny, H.V. Champion, see
 Champion de Crespigny
Deedes, W.H., 363
Deeley, Sir H.M.M., Bt., see Mallaby-Deeley
Deer, G., 164, 401
de Eresby, Lord Willoughby, see Willoughby
 de Eresby
de Frece, Sir W., 64, 87
de Freitas, G.S., 198
de Gruchy, C.R., 143
de Hamel, E.B., 447
De la Bère, R., 484
Delahaye, J.V., 7, 127, 279
Delargy, H.J., 183
Dempsey, J.C., 420
Denby, R.C., 509
Denholm, J., 574
Denison-Pender, J.C.D., 53
Denman, C.S., 152
Denman, Hon. R.D., 107, 152, 195
Dennis, A.D., 165, 166
Dennis, F.W., 397
Dennis, J.W., 75
Dennison, R., 80, 250, 490
Denniss, E.R.B., see Bartley-Denniss
Denny, E.M.C., 54, 124
Denson, G., 323
Denton, H., 454
Denville, A., 192, 239
Derbyshire, H., 376, 388
de Rothschild, J.A.E., see Rothschild
de Rothschild, L.N., see Rothschild
Desmond, G.G., 68, 350
Despencer-Robertson, J.A.St.G.F., 28, 480
Devenay, W., 50
Devine, P.J., 210
Devlin, J., 168, 625
Dew, N.P., 251
Dewar, H., 1
Dewar, K.G.B., 208
Dewhurst, H., 290
Diamond, C., 3, 10, 55
Diamond, J., 177
Dickie, J.P., 115, 128, 325
Dickinson, Rt. Hon. Sir W.H., 42
Dickson, T.S., 602
Digby, E.A., 333, 335
Digby, K.S.D.W., 320
Dingley, W.L., 352, 476
Dinnick, A.G.C., 343
Disher, T.F.R., 8
Diston, A.M., 54
Dixey, A.C.N., 299
Dixey, C.N.D., 232, 404, 488
Dixon, A.N., 400
Dixon, C.H., 399
Dixon, G., 272
Dixon, G.H., 396
Dixon, Rt. Hon. H., 618
Dixon, H.O., 391
Dobbie, J., 554
Dobbie, W., 218, 291, 376, 494
Dobbs, A.J., 154, 230, 283
Dobson, T.W., 113, 205
Dockett, J., 353

Dodd, A., 169, 299
Dodd, J., 189, 192, 195
Dodd, J.J., 41, 352
Dodd, J.S., 202
Dodds, G.E., 132, 213, 271
Dodds, N.N., 116
Dodds, S.R., 292
Dodds-Parker, A.D., 431
Dodge, J.B., 50, 215
Dodgson, E.O., 153
Doland, G.F., 53
Dollan, P.J., 550
Dolland, A.L., 23
Donald, N.A., 554
Donaldson, A., 552
Donaldson, E.J., 565, 616
Donnelly, D.L., 484, 624
Donner, P.W., 28, 347
Donovan, T.N., 158
Dooley, J.H., 74
Doran, A.S., 147, 165
Doran, E., 243, 259
Doran, J.P.A.L., 239
Doree, H.J., 263
Dorman-Smith, E.E., 292
Dorman-Smith, R.H., 350
Dott, G., 585
Douglas, E.S., 594
Douglas, F., 554
Douglas, F.C.R., 1, 442
Douglas and Clydesdale, Marquess of, see
 Clydesdale
Douglas-Hamilton, Lord Malcolm, 574
Douglas-Home, Hon. W., 277, 304, 561
Douthwaite, C.T., 236
Dower, A.V.G., 236, 299
Dower, E.L.G., see Gandar-Dower
Dowling, E., 425
Dowling, H., 262
Downie, J., 590
Doyle, H.G., see Grattan-Doyle
Doyle, Sir N.G., see Grattan-Doyle
Drabble, J.F., 227
Drake-Brockman, W.H.G., 139
Drayson, G.B., 509
Drayton, H.C., 453
Drewe, C., 311, 312
Driberg, T.E.N., 337
Drummond, J.E., 362
Drummond-Wolff, H.M.C., 218, 347
Drury-Lowe, S.R., 58, 209
Dubery, L.C.A., 243
Dubs, C.I.A., 586
Du Cane, Sir J.P., 402
du Cann, C.G.L., 3, 17
Duckers, J.S., 58
Duckworth, G.A.V., 435
Duckworth, James, 105
Duckworth, John, 86
Duckworth, W.R., 182
Du Cros, Sir A.P., Bt., 55
Du Cros, A.R.P., 513
Dudgeon, C.R., 595
Duffes, A.P., 591, 605, 617
Duffy, T.G., see Gavan-Duffy
Dugdale, J., 159, 257, 271, 514
Dugdale, Sir T.L., Bt., 491

Duggan, H.J., 124, 404
Duggan, T.F., 83
Duke, E., 463
Duke, T.C., 320
Dukes, C., 253
Dumper, T.H., 151
Dumpleton, C.W., 358
Duncan, A.G., see Gomme-Duncan
Duncan, Rt. Hon. Sir A.R., 12, 552, 561
Duncan, C., 67, 304, 436
Duncan, J.A.L., 29, 589
Duncan, J.F., 549, 580, 609
Duncannon, Viscount (Vere Brabazon Ponsonby)
367
Duncannon, Viscount (Frederick Edward
Neuflize Ponsonby), 28
Dunglass, Lord, 600, 602
Dunman, J.C.D., 275
Dunn, A.E., 297
Dunn, E., 506
Dunn, F.H., 98
Dunn, J.F., 355, 368, 467
Dunne, P.R.R., 291
Dunnico, E.O., 424
Dunnico, Rev. H., 143, 254, 325
Dunsmore, R., 404
Dunstan, Dr. R., 6, 81, 82, 84, 184
Dunwoodie, D., 590
Du Pre, W.B., 281
Dupree, Sir W.T., 207
Durbin, E.F.M., 126, 215, 464
Durrad-Lang, C.H., 406
Duthie, A.W., 54
Duthie, C.K., 39
Duthie, W.S., 587
Dutt, R.P., 83
Dutton, G.H.J., 402
Duval, V.D., 8, 200, 418
Duveen, G.E., 39
Dye, S., 418
Dyer, E.F., 378
Dyer, H.J.H., 78
Dyer, W.G.E., 419
Dyson, W., 471

D

Eady, G.H., 93
Eagles, A.R., 578
Eales, J.F., 78
Earl, S., 254
Early, J.H., 431
Earsman, W.P., 557
Eason, J.W., 131
Eastham, T., 236
Eastman, P.S., 319, 364, 492
Eastwood, J.F., 420
Eaton, A., 266
Eccles, D.M., 478
Eccles, F., 90, 399
Eckersley, P.T., 161, 179
Ede, Rt. Hon. J.C., 235, 458, 461
Edelman, M., 111
Eden, Rt. Hon. R.A., 331, 476
Edgar, C.B., 212
Edgar, G.H., 230
Edge, Sir W., 90, 393

Edgerley, C.S., 277
Edgson, W.S., 53
Edinger, G.A., 339, 353
Edmonds, G., 5
Edmondson, Sir A.J., 431
Edmunds, A., 365
Edmunds, J.E., 514, 515
Edmunds, W.R., 534
Ednam, Viscount, 140, 254
Edwardes Jones, G.M., 265
Edwards, Alfred, 186
Edwards, Ashley, 366
Edwards, A.C., 124
Edwards, A.J.G., 104, 257, 486, 514
Edwards, A.R., 182
Edwards, Rt. Hon. Sir C., 542
Edwards, C.E., 433
Edwards, Ebenezer, 189, 425
Edwards, Ernest, 123
Edwards, E.E., 91
Edwards, G., 417
Edwards, H.J., 8, 9
Edwards, I., 90
Edwards, J., 533, 631
Edwards, J.H., 62, 537
Edwards, L.J., 86, 153
Edwards, N., 534
Edwards, Reginald, 185
Edwards, Robert, 375, 389, 519
Edwards, Dr. R.S., 356
Edwards, W., 524
Edwards, W.J., 51
Edwards, W.L., 129
Egan, W.H., 72
Elborne, S.L., 176, 393
Elias, T., 537
Elliot, Rt. Hon. W.E., 566, 602, 632
Elliot, W.T.S., see Scott-Elliot
Elliott, Sir G.S., 28
Elliott, J., 335
Elliott, N.W., 191
Ellis, A.R., 187, 200
Ellis, G., 466
Ellis, H.T., 392
Ellis, J.P.J., 7
Ellis, L.J., 61
Ellis, Sir R.G., Bt., 226, 247, 351
Ellis, R.H., 142
Ellis, W.C., see Craven-Ellis
Ellis, W.P., 484
Ellis-Griffith, Rt. Hon. Sir E.J., Bt., 524, 528,
631
Elliston, G.S., 86
Elliston, W.R., 333, 452
Elmer, G.E., 41
Elmley, Viscount, 414
Elton, G., 345
Elveden, Viscount (formerly Hon. R.E.C.L.
Guinness), 233
Elverston, E., 259
Elverston, Sir H., 128
Elvin, G.H., 151, 441
Elvin, H.H., 68, 359, 511
Elvin, H.L., 627
Elwell-Sutton, A.S., 113
Ely, A.E., 151
Emerson, F., 402, 415

Emery, J.F., 222
Emery, J.N., 10, 123
Emlyn-Jones, J.E., 318, 515, 532
Emmott, C.E.G.C., 210, 457, 572
Emrys-Evans, P.V., 160, 308
Emslie, D., 577
England, A., 380
England, E.C.G., 453
Entwistle, A.R., see Rowland-Entwistle
Entwistle, Sir C.F., 90, 150
Erleigh, Viscount, 86
Errington, E., 91, 171, 239
Erroll, F.J., 63
Erskine, Lord, 97, 441
Erskine, J.M., 378
Erskine, J.M.M., 59
Erskine-Bolst, C.C.A.L., 20, 87
Erskine-Hill, Sir A.G., Bt., 556, 604
Essenhigh, R.C., 386
Essex, Sir R.W., 238
Estcourt, T.E.S., see Sotheron-Estcourt
Etherton, R.H., 167, 389
Etty, J.L., 203
Evans, A., 28
Evans, D.E., 28
Evans, D.J., 537, 539
Evans, D.O., 527
Evans, D.W.C.D., see Davies-Evans
Evans, Edward, 451
Evans, Ernest, 527, 631
Evans, E.H.G., 285, 530
Evans, F.S., 412
Evans, G.P., 237
Evans, G.R., 540
Evans, H., 128, 337
Evans, Sir H.A., 158, 516
Evans, H.S., 434
Evans, I.W., see Watkins-Evans
Evans, John (1), 538, 546
Evans, John (2), 270
Evans, J.V., 518, 539
Evans, Rt. Hon. Sir L.W., Bt., see
    Worthington-Evans
Evans, N.L., 631
Evans, P.V.E., see Emrys-Evans
Evans, R.T., 528, 529
Evans, S.N., 254
Evans, T.A., 123
Evans, T.E., 356
Evans, W.P.O., 526
Everard, W.L., 396
Ewart, R., 241
Ewing, I.L.O., see Orr-Ewing
Eyre, O.E.C., see Crosthwaite-Eyre
Eyres-Monsell, Rt. Hon. Sir B.M., 484
Eyton, A.E., 78

F

Fairbairn, R.R., 270
Fairbairn, S.I., 104
Fairfax, B.C., 511
Fairfax, J.G., 197
Fairfax-Lucy, Sir H.W.C-R., Bt., 397
Fairhurst, F., 202
Falcon, M., 414
Falconer, H.E.J., 293

Falconer, J., 594
Falle, Sir B.G., Bt., 208
Falls, Sir C.F., 625
Fanshawe, G.D., 617
Faraday, W.B., 223, 628
Farmery, G.E., 131
Farquharson, A.C., 153
Farr, A.E., 353
Farr, M.B., 202, 384
Farrah, R.H., 148
Farrer, A.E.V.A., 382
Farthing, W.J., 438
Fawcett, J.W., 151, 209
Fawkes, F.H., 504
Fearnley-Whittingstall, W.A., 329
Fehr, F.E., 366
Fell, Anthony, 22, 400
Fell, Sir Arthur, 130
Fenby, T.D., 94, 487, 489
Fenn, L.A., 79
Fennell, J., 118, 128
Fenner, H.W., 274, 472
Fenwick-Palmer, R.G., 287
Ferens, J.J.T., 401
Ferens, Rt. Hon. T.R., 148
Ferguson, A., 548, 566, 574
Ferguson, A.F.H., 420
Ferguson, H., 603
Ferguson, James, 270
Ferguson, Sir John, 22, 411
Fergusson, B.E., 595
Fergusson, Sir C., Bt., 586
Fermor-Hesketh, T., 387, 406
Fermoy, Lord, 402, 415
Fernyhough, E., 328
Ferrand, G.W., 96
Ferris, R.G.G., see Grant-Ferris
Field, W.J., 23, 37
Fielden, A.N., 436
Fielden, E.B., 179
Fielding, W.M., 484
Fienburgh, W., 547
Figgis, Rev. P.H., 40
Fildes, Sir H., 236, 590
Finburgh, S., 220
Findlay, Sir J.E.R., Bt., 587
Findlay, Prof. J.J., 628
Findlay, R., 34
Findley, T., 248
Finigan, J., 71
Finn, J.F., 60
Finnemore, D.L., 83, 486
Finney, S., 238
Finney, V.H., 424
Finnigan, J., 313
Firth, A.S., 106
Fisher, Hon. F.M.B., 192, 392
Fisher, F.V., 260, 486
Fisher, Rt. Hon. H.A.L., 628
Fisher, N.T.L., 365
Fisher, Sir T., 207
Fiske, W.G., 140
Fison, F.G.C., 146, 452
FitzRoy, Rt. Hon. E.A., 419
Fitzroy-Newdegate, Hon. J.M., 471
Fitzsimons, J.E., 220
Fitzwilliams, E.C.L., 527

Flanagan, C., 180
Flanagan, W.H., 178
Flannery, Sir J.F., Bt., 337
Flavell, E.W.C., 137
Fleming, D.P., 591
Fleming, E.L., 185, 381
Fleming, Sir J., 549
Fleming, J.A., 570
Fletcher, E.A.B., 289
Fletcher, E.G.M., 25
Fletcher, G.H., 223
Fletcher, G.M.A.H., see Hamilton-Fletcher
Fletcher, L.S., 23
Fletcher, R.P., 72
Fletcher, R.T.H., 313, 347, 471
Fletcher, W., 105
Fletcher-Cooke, C.F., 317
Flint, A.J., 306
Flitcroft, Sir T.E., 378
Flynn, C.R., 227, 424
Foan, G.A., 11, 112
Follick, Dr. M., 16, 363, 395, 457
Foot, D.M., 314, 552
Foot, E.H., 178
Foot, I., 206, 293, 297, 313
Foot, J.M., 293, 347
Foot, M.M., 204, 544
Foot, W.T.A., 267
Forbes, A.C., 138
Forbes, W.D.H.C., 579
Ford, A., 76
Ford, B.T.G., 155
Ford, J., 603
Ford, Sir P.J., Bt., 556
Fordham, Sir H.G., 16
Fordham, W.G., 103
Foreman, Sir H., 21
Forestier-Walker, Sir C.L., Bt., 544
Forgan, Dr. R., 614
Forman, A.N., 570
Forman, J.C., 572
Forrest, W., 69, 503
Forsdike, G.F., 514
Forster, Rt. Hon. H.W., 103
Forsyth, R.W., 142
Fort, R., 376
Foster, C., 166, 390
Foster, C.O., 306
Foster, H.B.H.H., see Hylton-Foster
Foster, Sir H.S., 207
Foster, H.W., 121
Foster, J.G., 290
Foster, W., 262
Foster, W.E.A., see Arnold-Foster
Foster, W.R.C., 207
Fothergill, C.P., 594
Foulds, C.H., 500
Foulis, R.W., 588
Fountain, F., 154, 155
Fowden, W., 291
Fowler, J.M., 458
Fox, C.H., 129
Fox, Rt. Hon. G.R.L., see Lane-Fox
Fox, Sir G.W.G., Bt., 432
Fox, H.W., see Wilson-Fox
Fox, R.F.H.B.C., see Broomhead-Colton-Fox
Fox-Davies, A.C., 518

Foxall, A.R., 628
Foxcroft, C.T., 68
France, G.A., 69
Francis, J., 233
Frank, D.G.H., 212
Frankel, D., 50
Franklin, C.E., 131
Franklin, H.A., 140, 358
Franklin, J.H., 403
Franklin, L.B., 18, 37, 43
Franklin, M.A.E., 495
Fraser, Rev. D.B., 204, 314
Fraser, D.M., 459
Fraser, H., 596
Fraser, Hon. H.C.P.J., 449
Fraser, H.T., 413
Fraser, J.A.L., see Lovat-Fraser
Fraser, J.J., 588
Fraser, Sir K.A., Bt., 394
Fraser, R.B., 271
Fraser, T., 601
Fraser, Sir W.J.I., 42, 383
Freake, C.A.M., 275
Frece, Sir W. de, see de Frece
Fredman, E.W., 342
Freeborough, J.H., 225, 497
Freedman, M.L., 23, 199
Freeman, A.J., 227
Freeman, D., 154, 207, 415, 480
Freeman, J., 359
Freeman, P., 519, 525
Freeman, W., 151
Freeman, W.F., 202
Freeman, W.M., 306
Freemantle, H.S., 149
Freitas, G.S. de, see de Freitas
Fremantle, Sir F.E., 358
French, F.W., 450
French, W.J., 447
Freyberg, B.C., 516
Freyer, D.J., 357, 360, 361
Fry, C.B., 97, 203, 431
Fryer, J., 80
Fulford, R.T.B., 452, 488
Fulford, T.P., 295
Fuller, A.G., 176
Fullerton, H., 388
Fulljames, R., 232
Furness, G.J., 264
Furness, S.N., 135, 241
Furniss, H.S., 630
Fyfe, Rt. Hon. Sir D.P.M., 174, 262
Fyfe, H.H., 373, 442

G

Gabriel, E.V., 381
Gadie, A., 93
Gage, C.H., 620
Gaitskell, H.T.N., 155, 214
Galbraith, J.F.W., 457
Galbraith, S., 331
Galbraith, T.D., 569
Galbraith, T.G.D., 555, 565, 578
Gale, G.A., 16
Gallacher, W., 508, 552, 593
Gallie, C.N., 594

Gallop, C., 142
Galloway, D.G., 158
Galt, W.H.C., 626
Gammans, L.D., 140
Gandar-Dower, E.L., 589
Gange, E.S., 100
Ganzoni, Sir F.J.C., Bt., 146
Garcke, S.E., 445
Gardiner, A.E., 465
Gardiner, J., 611
Gardner, B.W., 261
Gardner, E., 277
Gardner, J.P., 21
Gardner, Rt. Hon. Sir J.T.A., see Agg-Gardner
Garland, C.S., 27
Garnett, R., 508
Garnsworthy, C.J., 462
Garratt, G.T., 205, 282, 436
Garro-Jones, G.M., 5, 20, 548
Garside, T.H., 143
Garson, W.R., 592
Garthwaite, W.F.C., 267, 361, 499
Garton, C.G., 476
Gassman, L., 136, 212
Gastrell, Sir W.H., see Houghton-Gastrell
Gates, E.E., 13, 384
Gates, P.G., 29
Gault, A.H., 439
Gaunt, Sir G.R.A., 446, 487
Gaunt, L.E., 147, 301
Gavan-Duffy, T., 300
Gay, W.T., 206
Geary, F., 155
Gebbett, J.J., 47
Geddes, A., 574
Geddes, Rt. Hon. Sir A.C., 347
Geddes, Rt. Hon. Sir E.C., 106
Gee, A., 87
Gee, R., 60, 193, 322, 325, 393
Gee, T., 254
Geen, H., 313
Gelder, A., 132
Gelder, Sir W.A., 400
Gellatly, L., 608
Gentry, R.M., 16
George, A.F., 367
George, Rt. Hon. D. Lloyd, see Lloyd George
George, Rt. Hon. G. Lloyd, see Lloyd George
George, G.O., 529
George, J.L., 279, 360, 403, 442
George, R., 478
Gerothwohl, Prof. M.A., 160, 368
Getgood, R., 622
Gibb, Prof. A.D., 574, 601, 632
Gibb, A.M., 481
Gibbins, J., 175
Gibbons, Sir W., 162
Gibbons, W.E., 266
Gibbs, A.F.X.T., 133
Gibbs, Rt. Hon. G.A., 102
Gibson, C.G., 155, 504
Gibson, C.W., 32, 34
Gibson, D.W., 166, 616
Gibson, H.M., 385
Gibson, J., 602
Gibson, R., 552, 556, 574, 615, 632
Giddins, C.S., 360

Gifford, R.W., 310, 357
Gilbert, E., 194
Gilbert, J.D., 46
Gilbert, Sir J.W., 629
Giles, M., 102
Gill, E., 438
Gill, T.H., 86, 271
Gillett, Sir G.M., 14
Gillinder, T.W., 64, 172, 241
Gillis, B.B., 103, 193, 432
Gillis, W., 502
Gilmore, J.B., 42
Gilmour, D., 324, 601
Gilmour, Rt. Hon. Sir J., Bt., 569
Gilmour, Sir J.E., Bt., 616
Gilmour, W.W., 600
Gilpin, E.H., 14
Gilzean, A., 554
Gimson, T.W., 446
Girouard, R., 49
Gisborne, H.P., 109, 492
Gittins, T.W., 459
Gladstone, M., 233
Glanvill, H.W.W., see Wreford-Glanvill
Glanville, F.R.A., 4
Glanville, H.J., 4
Glanville, J.E., 325
Glassey, A.E., 317
Gledhill, G., 132
Gleeson, Dr. O., 208
Glen, N.M., 562
Glennie, W., 32
Glenny, K.E.B., 65
Glidewell, C.N., 376
Glossop, C.W.H., 489, 502
Glover, D., 86
Gluckstein, L.H., 199
Gluckstein, S., 21, 204
Glyn, Sir R.G.C., Bt., 275, 616
Glyn, R.H., 318
Goatcher, C.A., 135, 347
Goddard, R., 30
Godfrey, A., 505
Godfrey, E., 404
Godfrey, W., 3
Goff, Sir P., 214, 490
Gold, J., 608
Goldblatt, G., 407
Goldfinch, Sir A.H., 333
Goldie, L.A., 373
Goldie, Sir N.B., 253
Goldstone, B.E., 350, 409
Goldstone, F.W., 241
Gomm, H.W.C.C., see Carr-Gomm
Gomme-Duncan, A., 612
Gooch, D.A., 60
Gooch, E.G., 416, 417
Goodall, R., 309
Goodere, A., 308
Goodfellow, E.R., 372, 560
Goodfellow, R.E., 369
Goodhart, F.H.G.H., 64, 260
Goodman, A.W., 26, 39
Goodman, L.E., 282
Goodrich, H.E., 19
Gordon, A.G., 97, 465
Gordon, A.T., 580

Gordon, G.A.D., 212
Gordon, J.W., 37, 64
Gordon, M.W., 626
Gordon-Spencer, C., 99
Gordon Walker, P.C., 203, 230
Gore, Rt. Hon. W.G.A.O., see Ormsby-Gore
Gorman, J., 205, 221
Gorman, W., 388
Gorst, E.M., 40
Gosling, H., 32, 51, 412
Gossling, A.G., 85
Gough, Sir H. de la P., 456
Gould, A., 149
Gould, F., 158, 438
Gould, J.C., 514
Goulding, Rt. Hon. Sir E.A., Bt., 270
Gourd, A.G., 207
Gourlay, F.P., 331, 513
Gourlay, W.R., 612
Gower, E.A., 179, 389
Gower, Sir R.V., 18, 215
Gowland, J.S., 463
Grace, J., 292
Graham, A., 321
Graham, A.C., 292, 377, 530
Graham, D.M., 601
Graham, Sir F.F., Bt., 298
Graham, H.A.R., 257
Graham, R., 190
Graham, R.B. Cunninghame, see Cunninghame
  Graham
Graham, T.G., 55, 199, 249, 323, 510
Graham, Rt. Hon. William, 554
Graham, William, 250, 461, 462
Graham-Little, Sir E.G.G., 629
Grand, L.D., 206
Grant, Sir A.H., 615
Grant, Sir J.A., Bt., 300, 308
Grant, J.E.C., 292
Grant, W.H., 471
Grant-Ferris, R.G., 42, 262
Granville, E.L., 450
Grattan-Doyle, H., 194
Grattan-Doyle, Sir N., 194
Gray, A.F., 361
Gray, A.W., 399
Gray, C.C., 333
Gray, E., 62
Gray, F., 203, 207, 359
Gray, H.S., 282
Gray, J., 561
Gray, M., 272, 274, 309, 358, 422
Gray, R., 591
Gray, W.J.A., see Anstruther-Gray
Grayson, H.M., 72
Greaves, A.E., 247
Greaves, H.R.G., 294
Greaves-Lord, Sir W., 34
Green, A., 117
Green, F.E., 467
Green, J.F., 160
Green, R., 357
Green, W.H., 13
Greenall, T., 378
Greene, B., 347, 369
Greene, F., 340
Greene, W.P.C., 270

Greene, Sir W.R., Bt., 19
Greenwell, T.G., 135
Greenwood, Rt. Hon. A., 190, 234, 247
Greenwood, A.W.J., 380
Greenwood, F., 190
Greenwood, G.A., 466
Greenwood, Rt. Hon. Sir H., Bt., 241, 251
Greenwood, H.T., 64
Greenwood, J.H., 15
Greenwood, J.M., 46, 48
Greenwood, T., 356
Greenwood, W., 236
Greenwood, W.G., 64
Greer, H., 440
Greg, A.C., 387
Gregg, H., 246
Gregory, H.H., 308
Gregory, I., 471
Gregory, J., 253
Greig, Sir J.W., 588, 614
Grenfell, D.R., 535
Grenfell, E.C., 12
Gretton, Rt. Hon. J., 443
Gretton, J.F., 443
Grey, C.F., 326
Grey, G.C., 423
Grey, J.H., 104
Grey, R.C., 360
Gridley, Sir A.B., 236
Grierson, E., 107
Grierson, J., 125
Grieve, A.J., 566
Grieve, C.M., 566
Griffin, J., 342
Griffith, Rt. Hon. Sir E.J.E., Bt., see Ellis-Griffith
Griffith, F.K., 103, 187
Griffith, H.G., 542
Griffith, M., 544
Griffith-Boscawen, Rt. Hon. Sir A.S.T., 119,
  439, 461
Griffith-Jones, J.S., 412
Griffiths, D., 506
Griffiths, D.C., see Craven-Griffiths
Griffiths, G.A., 499
Griffiths, J., 529
Griffiths, Sir J.N., Bt., see Norton-Griffiths
Griffiths, T., 545
Griffiths, William (1), 182
Griffiths, William (2), 543
Grigg, Sir E.W.M., 202, 283
Grigg, Rt. Hon. Sir P.J., 515
Griggs, Sir W.P., 143
Grimond, J., 610
Grimston, Hon. J., 358
Grimston, R.V., 482
Grimwade, L.L., 239
Gritten, W.G.H., 135
Grogan, W., 168
Grondona, L.St.C., 8
Gross, J., 57
Grotrian, H.B., 150
Groundwater, Rev. A.W., 587
Groves, C., 37
Groves, R., 278
Groves, T.E., 260
Grubb, R.E.W., 116
Gruchy, C.R. de, see de Gruchy

Gruffydd, Prof. W.J., 631
Grundy, A.P., 120
Grundy, C.H., 161, 252
Grundy, S.W., 383
Grundy, T.W., 506
Guedalla, P., 19, 184, 185, 307
Guest, Hon. C.H.C., 54, 100, 205
Guest, C.W.G., 575
Guest, Rt. Hon. F.E., 100, 205, 317, 344
Guest, Hon. I.G., 525
Guest, J., 499
Guest, Dr. L.H., see Haden-Guest
Guest, Hon. O.M., 9, 395, 525
Guild, D.A., 572
Guinness, Hon. R.E.C.L., see Elveden, Viscount
Guinness, T.L.E.B., 51, 68
Guinness, Rt. Hon. W.E., 453
Gulland, Rt. Hon. J.W., 590
Gunn, R., 612
Gunston, Sir D.W., Bt., 345
Gunter, R.J., 340
Guthrie, D.L.R., 39
Guthrie, H.B., 560, 632
Guthrie, H.W., 591
Guthrie, T.M., 609
Guy, H.A., 129
Guy, J.C.M., 554
Guy, W.H., 40
Guyster, Dr. B., 163
Gwynne, I., 547
Gwynne, R.S., 463

H

Hackett, M.F., 482
Hackett, T., 80
Hacking, Rt. Hon. D.H., 375
Haden-Guest, Dr. L., 26, 46, 47, 220, 281, 525
Hadgkiss, W., 119
Hailwood, A., 176
Hailwood, E.A., 196, 233, 368
Haimes, A., 572
Haines, R., 377
Haire, J.E., 281
Hale, C.L., 200, 202
Hales, H.K., 239
Hales, R.N., 595
Hall, B.W.R., 451, 465
Hall, D.B., 362
Hall, Frank, 304
Hall, Sir Frederick, Bt., 7
Hall, Frederick, 501
Hall, G., 74
Hall, Rt. Hon. G.H., 517
Hall, J.H., 51
Hall, L.M.M., 120
Hall, R.J., 505
Hall, W.D'A., 525
Hall, W.G., 103, 197, 207, 361, 495
Hall, W.O., 42
Hall, Sir W.R., 174, 463
Hall, W.S.R.K., see King-Hall
Hall Caine, D., 167, 211, 376
Hall Caine, G.R., 317
Hallam, H.W., 395
Hallas, E., 76
Hallett, C.S.S., see Stratton-Hallett

Hallinan, A.L., 517
Hallinan, C.S., 514
Halliwell, D., 384
Halls, W., 117, 196, 380
Hallsworth, J., 389
Halpin, F.J., 404
Halsall, W.M., 305
Halse, J.G.H., 311
Halstead, D., 217
Hamblen, H.J., 462
Hambro, A.V., 318, 319
Hamel, E.B. de, see de Hamel
Hamilton, Hon. C.W.B., see Baillie-Hamilton
Hamilton, Sir G.C., 143, 164, 283
Hamilton, J., 170
Hamilton, Rev. J.E., 581
Hamilton, J.H., 603
Hamilton, K.I., 88
Hamilton, Lord Malcolm Douglas, see
  Douglas-Hamilton
Hamilton, R., 454
Hamilton, Sir R.W., 610
Hamilton, T., 615
Hamilton, W.W., 593
Hamilton-Fletcher, G.M.A., 326
Hamlett, R.F.F., 124
Hamling, W., 234
Hammersley, S.S., 236, 263
Hammond, W., 62
Hampson, G., 302
Hampton, E.W., 83
Hamsher, W.P., 73
Hanbury, Sir C., 318
Hanbury-Sparrow, A., 433
Hancock, A., 269
Hancock, F.R., 465, 480, 544
Hancock, J.G., 302
Hancock, S., 483
Hand, S., 105
Hanington, C.L., 428
Hanley, D.A., 13
Hannah, I.C., 241, 266
Hannan, W., 567
Hannington, W., 4, 249, 518
Hannon, Sir P.J.H., 82
Hanson, Sir C.A., Bt., 293
Harben, H.D., 452
Harben, H.E.S., 359
Harbinson, W.D., 339
Harbison, T.J.S., 625
Harbord, A., 130
Harcourt, H., 9
Hardaker, D., 498
Harden, J.R.E., 623
Hardie, D., 605
Hardie, G.D.B., 572
Harding, C., 356
Harding, R., 522
Hardman, D.R., 106, 115
Hardwick, S., 497
Hardwick, T., 433
Hardy, E.A., 221
Hardy, T., 161
Hardy, Hon. W.H.C., see Cozens-Hardy
Hardy-Roberts, G.P., 265
Hare, H.J.G., 216
Hare, Hon. J.H., 452

Harford, A., 168
Hargreaves, A.G., 512
Hargreaves, H.K., 92
Hargreaves, J., 13
Hargreaves, K., 503
Harland, A., 226, 228
Harland, H.P., 618
Harmwood-Banner, Sir J.S., 167
Harmsworth, C.B., 273
Harmsworth, Hon. E.C., 370
Harmsworth, Sir R.L., Bt., 589
Harney, E.A.St.A., 235
Harper, J.E., 233, 563, 577
Harper, J.W., 250
Harper, R.T., 108
Harrington, Sir J.L., 47
Harris, C., 430
Harris, C.M., 342
Harris, C.R.S., 324
Harris, E., 522
Harris, F.W., 112
Harris, Sir H.P., 38
Harris, H.W., 627
Harris, J., 204, 296
Harris, John Henry, 459
Harris, John Hobbis, 9, 19, 482
Harris, P., 296
Harris, Rt. Hon. Sir P.A., Bt., 6, 394
Harris, R.R., 18
Harris, W.B., 398
Harrison, A., 513
Harrison, A.P., 238
Harrison, F.C., 32
Harrison, G.J.C., 293
Harrison, H.E., 251
Harrison, J., 199
Harrison, J.W., 507
Harrod, R.F., 141
Hart, A.J. Liddell, see Liddell Hart
Hartington, Marquess of (Edward William
    Spencer Cavendish), 307, 309
Hartington, Marquess of (William John
    Robert Cavendish), 309
Hartland, G.A., 197
Hartley, E.L., 376
Hartley, P.G., 306
Hartley, R., 505
Hartley, Dr. W.D., 501
Hartshorn, C.W., 160
Hartshorn, Rt. Hon. V., 538
Hartwell, C.H., 30
Harvey, A.E., 244
Harvey, A.V., 289
Harvey, C.G.C., 213
Harvey, C.M.B., see Barclay-Harvey
Harvey, G., 32
Harvey, I.D., 410
Harvey, P.G.A., 10
Harvey, S.E., 316
Harvey, T.E., 118, 153, 628
Harvey, W.J., 55
Harvie-Watt, G.S., 212, 500
Hasdell, T.B., 463
Haslam, F., 384
Haslam, H.A., 329
Haslam, H.C., 402
Haslam, James, 429

Haslam, Sir John, 90, 213, 391
Haslam, L., 519
Hassam, A., 191
Hastings, Sir P.G., 249
Hastings, Dr. S., 65, 211, 458
Haston, J.R., 537
Haughey; N., 574
Haughton, S.G., 622
Hawke, J.A., 297
Hawkes, J., 355
Hawkin, R.C., 15
Hawkins, A.E.G., 342
Hawkins, E.C.G., 365
Hawkins, W.F., 455
Haworth, Sir A.A., Bt., 179
Haworth, J., 172, 174
Hay, D.S., 580
Hay, J.M., 248
Hay, J.P., 561
Hay, T.W., 417
Hay-Clark, N.L., see Leith-Hay-Clark
Haycock, A.W.F., 222, 284, 351
Hayday, A., 201
Hayes, J., 459
Hayes, J.C., 237
Hayes, J.H., 166
Hayes-Jones, J.R., 531
Hayler, G., 457
Haylor, E.R., 277, 316, 456
Hayman, F.H., 294
Hays, Sir M., 21
Hayward, Dr. C.W., 29
Hayward, E., 329
Hayward, Dr. J.J., 541
Haywood, W., 405
Haywood, W.R.G., 429
Hazell, B., 494
Hazleton, Dr. R., 3
Head, A.H., 455
Headlam, Sir C.M., Bt., 128, 194, 321
Heald, L.F., 44
Heale, F.W., 520
Healey, D.W., 504
Healy, C., 625
Healy, C.F., 140
Heap, W., 180
Hearn, G., 8
Heath, K.E., 379
Heathcoat-Amory, D., 314
Heathcoat-Amory, P.G., 437
Heathcote, N., 308
Heathcote-Williams, H., 40, 287, 288
Heatley, W.R., 364
Heffer, P.H., 52, 251, 442, 495
Heilgers, F.F.A., 453
Helme, Sir N.W., 382
Helmore, W., 359
Hely-Hutchinson, M.R., 136
Hembury, F.J., 432
Hemmerde, E.G., 286
Henderson, Rt. Hon. Arthur, 104, 124, 193, 304
    392
Henderson, Arthur, 208, 445, 516
Henderson, F., 414
Henderson, G., 622
Henderson, H.D., 627
Henderson, James, 553

Henderson, John, 561
Henderson, Joseph, 176, 383
Henderson, J.J.C., 154
Henderson, J.M., 580
Henderson, R.R., 432
Henderson, Sir Thomas, 615
Henderson, Thomas (1), 573
Henderson, Thomas (2), 596
Henderson, T.G., 619
Henderson, Sir V.L., 91, 332, 573
Henderson, W., 612
Henderson, W.W., 406
Henderson-Livesey, A.H., 47
Henderson-Stewart, J., 117, 158, 552, 602
Hendin, C.T., 23
Heneage, A.P., 403
Henn, Sir S.H.H., 86
Hennessy, Sir G.R.J., Bt., 351
Hennessy, L.H.R.P., see Pope-Hennessy
Henniker-Hughan, Sir A.J., Bt., 595
Henri, A., 20
Henry, Sir C.S., Bt., 436
Henwood, W.R.J., 316
Hepburn, P.G.T.B., see Buchan-Hepburn
Hepworth, J., 94
Herbert, A., 285
Herbert, Hon. A.N.H.M., 442
Herbert, A.P., 630
Herbert, Rt. Hon. Sir D.H., 359
Herbert, F., 358
Herbert, G., 218
Herbert, J.A., 544
Herbert, S., 58, 492
Heriot-Hill, E., 161
Heron, F.A., 345
Herringham, Sir W.P., 629
Herriotts, J., 330
Herron, W., 285
Hesketh, T.F., see Fermor-Hesketh
Hewart, Rt. Hon. Sir G., 158
Hewett, J., 335
Hewett, Sir J.P., 273
Hewins, W.A.S., 523
Hewitson, M., 147
Hewitt, E., 379
Hewitt, G.E., 414
Hewitt, J.W., 488
Hewlett, T.H., 178, 179
Heywood, F.B.P., see Price-Heywood
Heywood, W.L., 94
Hicken, P., 304
Hickinbottom, F.W., 24
Hickman, T.E., 266
Hicks, E.G., 60
Hicks, J.R., 454
Hicks, Hon. L.W.J., see Joynson-Hicks
Hicks, Rt. Hon. Sir W.J., Bt., see Joynson-Hicks
Hicks Beach, W.W., 108
Higgins, C.W., 467
Higgins, G.H., 203
Higgs, H., 56
Higgs, W.F., 84
Higham, C.F., 27
Higham, J.S., 510
Higson, P., 391
Hilder, F., 340
Hilditch, C.S., 89

Hilditch, H., 575
Hiley, Sir E.V., 76
Hiley, F.S., 399
Hill, A., 160
Hill, Sir A.G.E., Bt., see Erskine-Hill
Hill, Dr. A.V., 627
Hill, Dr. C., 627
Hill, Sir E., 141, 446
Hill, E.H., see Heriot-Hill
Hill, H., 224
Hill, H.A., 39
Hill, Sir James, Bt., 93
Hill, John, 328
Hill, J.W.F., 421
Hill, R.G., 303
Hill, S.J., 71
Hill, Dr. T.R., 294
Hill, Wilfred, 82
Hill, William, 167
Hill, W.E., 406
Hill, W.O., 300
Hill-Wood, Sir S.H., Bt., 305
Hillary, A.E., 321, 335
Hillier, W.A.J., 410
Hillman, Dr. G.B., 247, 501
Hills, A., 503
Hills, Rt. Hon. J.W., 166, 326, 505
Hilton, A., 181
Hilton, C., 90
Hinchingbrooke, Viscount, 319
Hinchliffe, Sir J.P., 502
Hinchliffe, W.A.S., see Simpson-Hinchliffe
Hind, H.A., 117
Hindle, F., 377
Hindley, C.E., 96
Hinds, J., 528
Hines, F.G., 395
Hinkley, H., 369
Hinks, J.D., 491
Hinshelwood, H., 207
Hipwell, W.R., 23, 135, 463, 480, 492
Hirst, F.W., 508
Hirst, G.H., 512
Hirst, G.W., 69
Hirst, W., 96
Hoare, C.H., 348
Hoare, Rt. Hon. Sir S.J.G., Bt., 11
Hobart, R.H., 228
Hobhouse, A.L., 440
Hobhouse, C.B., 64
Hobhouse, Rt. Hon. Sir C.E.H., Bt., 99, 279
Hobman, J.B., 5, 95, 227
Hobson, C.R., 255
Hobson, J.A., 628
Hodes, F.P., 103
Hodge, H.L., 49
Hodge, Rt. Hon. J., 180
Hodge, J.P., 210
Hodge, P., 593
Hodges, F., 447
Hodgkinson, C., 502
Hodgson, G.C.S., 440
Hodgson, R., 153
Hodgson, W.A., 34
Hoffgaard, E.A., 5
Hoffman, P.C., 225, 340
Hogbin, H.C., 1, 486

Hogg, Rt. Hon. Sir D.M., 41
Hogg, Hon. Q.M., 203
Hogge, J.M., 555
Hohler, Sir G.F., 215
Holbrook, Sir A.R., 347
Holbrook, Sir C.V., 472
Holden, Hon. A.W.E., 243
Holden, S.M., 51, 210
Holderness, G.W., 402
Holding, H.B., 413
Holdsworth, H., 96, 507
Holgate, A., 217, 299
Holland, A., 304
Holland, Sir A.E.A., 196
Holland, Dr. F.W.C., see Crossley-Holland
Hollins, A., 239
Hollins, J.H., 259
Hollis, M.C., 479
Holloway, E.A.G., 145
Holman, P., 6, 411
Holmes, D.T., 557, 564
Holmes, F.H., 183
Holmes, H., 622
Holmes, H.E., 499
Holmes, Sir J.S., 108, 307, 335, 591
Holmes, S., 246, 328
Holmes, T., 403
Holmes, W., 402, 414, 448
Holt, A.E., 90
Holt, H.P., 261
Holt, J.A.L., see Langford-Holt
Holt, R.D., 125, 217, 298
Holt-Hughes, T.H., 472
Holton, W.O.R., 511
Homan, C.W.J., 64
Home, Hon. W.D., see Douglas-Home
Honeyman, G.G., 358, 574, 616
Hood, Sir J., Bt., 265
Hope, Hon. A.O.J., 74, 471
Hope, E.T., 28
Hope, Sir H., 594, 617
Hope, Lord John, 607
Hope, Sir J.A., Bt., 607
Hope, J.D., 588
Hope, Rt. Hon. J.F., 225, 251
Hope, R.H.K., 361, 467
Hope, S., 291
Hope, W., 557
Hopkin, D., 528
Hopkin, E.S.B., 428
Hopkins, A., 522
Hopkins, C.H.I., see Innes-Hopkins
Hopkins, Rev. F.J., 92, 296, 297, 317
Hopkins, J.W.W., 43
Hopkins, P.W., 68, 438
Hopkinson, Sir Alfred, 628
Hopkinson, Austin, 385
Hopkinson, D.M., 285
Hopkinson, E., 178
Horabin, T.L., 295
Hore-Belisha, Rt. Hon. L., 204
Horlick, J.N., 129
Hornby, F., 167
Horne, G., 44
Horne, Sir J.A., 130
Horne, K.E., 265
Horne, Rt. Hon. Sir R.S., 565

Horne, W.L., 460
Horner, Arthur Leonard, 334
Horner, Arthur Lewis, 520
Horniman, E.J., 252
Horobin, I.M., 46
Horrabin, J.F., 421
Horridge, J., 373
Horton, F.E., 410
Horwill, G., 475
Hotchkin, S.V., 402
Houfton, J.P., 199
Hough, E., 497
Houghton, A.L.N.D., 510
Houghton-Gastrell, Sir W., 33
Houlder, H., 113
Houldsworth, H.S., 504
House, G., 42
Housley, H., 385
Houston, J.M.B., see Blakiston-Houston
Houston, Sir R.P., Bt., 175
Howard, Hon. A., 59
Howard, Hon. D.S.P., 298
Howard, F., 378
Howard, Hon. G.R., 208
Howard, Hon. G.W.A., 273, 298, 482
Howard, H.W.S., 66, 478
Howard, J.H., 540
Howard, J.M., 112
Howard, S., 249, 498
Howard, Stephen Gerald, 282, 450
Howard, Stephen Goodwin, 454
Howard, T.F., 27, 28
Howard-Bury, C.K., 266, 332
Howard-Jones, G.H., 172
Howard-Williams, E.L., 627
Howarth, T., 508
Howe, E.M., 241
Howell, W., 274
Howitt, Dr. A.B., 210, 211
Howlett, J.W., 349
Hoy, J.H., 576
Hubbard, C., 233
Hubbard, D., 214
Hubbard, E.P., 126
Hubbard, T.F., 575
Huddart, J.T., 97
Hudson, Sir A.U.M., Bt., 19, 25
Hudson, J.H., 122, 141, 236, 283
Hudson, R.M., 241
Hudson, Rt. Hon. R.S., 234, 300
Hudson, W., 193
Hughan, Sir A.J.H., Bt., see Henniker-Hughan
Hughes, A., 524
Hughes, C., 524
Hughes, C.J., 10
Hughes, C.P., 540
Hughes, Rev. D., 544
Hughes, E., 393, 586
Hughes, F., 7, 33, 57, 332
Hughes, H., 531
Hughes, H.D., 268
Hughes, H.S.J., 9, 548
Hughes, J.P., 242
Hughes, J.R., 530
Hughes, John William, 485
Hughes, John Williams, 532
Hughes, R., 514

Hughes, R.M., 234, 521, 527, 528
Hughes, S.L., 236
Hughes, T.H.H., see Holt-Hughes
Hughes, T.P., 356
Hughes, W., 612
Hulbert, J.H., 501
Hulbert, N.J., 236
Hulbert-Powell, E.C.L., 262
Hulton, E.G.W., 446
Humby, E.T., 208
Hume, Sir G.H., 17
Hume-Williams, Sir W.E., Bt., 426
Humm, G., 357
Humphrey, G.H., 246
Humphrey, L.J., 272, 281, 363
Humphreys, G.H., 81
Humphreys, W.J., 6, 369
Hunloke, H.P., 309
Hunt, G.V., 225
Hunt, R.J., 337
Hunt, W., 53
Hunter, Sir A., 382
Hunter, D., 383
Hunter, E.E., 18
Hunter, Dr. J., 590
Hunter, M.J., 400
Hunter, T., 612
Hunter-Weston, Sir A.G., 584
Huntingfield, Lord, 450
Huntsman, E., 198
Hurd, A.R., 276
Hurd, Sir P.A., 438, 479
Hurley, A.J., 53
Hurst, Sir G.B., 182
Hurst, J.G., 83
Hurst, P.E., 463
Hurst, S., 387
Hutchings, Sir A., 403
Hutchinson, G.C., 143, 144, 535
Hutchinson, H.L., 184
Hutchinson, J.N., 58
Hutchinson, M.R.H., see Hely-Hutchinson
Hutchinson, St.J., 362
Hutchinson, W.H., 90
Hutchinson, Z., 375
Hutchison, G.A.C., 607
Hutchison, G.I.C., 558, 567
Hutchison, G.S., 412
Hutchison, J.R.H., 562
Hutchison, Sir R., 575, 577
Hutchison, W., 566
Hutchison, W.G.D., 338
Hyam, I.J., 56
Hyder, J.S., 394
Hylton-Foster, H.B.H., 508
Hynd, H., 18
Hynd, J.B., 223

I

Ickringill, C.S., 105
Iliffe, Sir E.M., 475
Illingworth, Rt. Hon. A.H., 380
Illingworth, G., 388
Illingworth, P.G., 508
Inglis, J.M., 560
Innes-Hopkins, C.H., 328

Inskip, Rt. Hon. Sir T.W.H., 98, 348
Instone, A., 51, 160
Iredell, G.W., 107
Ireland, D., 618
Irvin, R., 246
Irvine, A.J., 166, 245, 549, 582
Irvine, R., 600
Irving, D.D., 104
Irving, W.J., 243
Irwin, Lord (formerly Hon. C.I.C. Wood), 271
Irwin, H.M., 625
Irwin, T., 574, 577, 613
Isaacs, G.A., 47, 369
Izett, J., 565

J

Jackson, C.L.A.W., see Ward-Jackson
Jackson, Hon. F.S., 489
Jackson, G., 85
Jackson, Sir H., Bt., 54
Jackson, J.C., 380
Jackson, N., 561
Jackson, R.F., 146
Jackson, T.E., 427
Jackson, W.F., 525
Jacob, A.E., 165
Jacobsen, T.O., 12, 32, 48, 291
Jacques, F.M., 276, 359
Jagger, J., 178
Jalland, A.E., 288
James, A.D.B., 142
James, A.W., 105
James, Sir A.W.H., 422
James, Hon. C., 103
James, C.W., 355
James, R.N.T., see Tronchin-James
James, Sir W.M., 208
Jameson, J.G., 558, 632
Jamieson, D., 567, 579
Janner, B., 51, 160, 514
Jarman, C., 85
Jarrett, G.W.S., 123, 126, 366, 428
Jarrett, W.J., 29
Jarvis, Sir J.J., Bt., 460
Jay, A.E., 244
Jay, D.P.T., 1
Jefferies, R.S., 24
Jeffreys, Sir G.D., 350
Jeger, G., 6, 250, 351
Jeger, Dr. S.W., 43
Jenkin, J.E.P., 2
Jenkins, A., 545
Jenkins, Rev. G.J., 202
Jenkins, J., 518
Jenkins, Hon. J.G., 56
Jenkins, R.H., 46, 473
Jenkins, S.R., 534
Jenkins, Sir W., 537
Jenkins, W.A., 525, 529
Jenkins, Rev. Wilfred J., 345
Jenkins, William J., 547
Jennings, J.W.A., 37
Jennings, R., 54, 227, 330
Jennings, S., 518
Jennison, G., 385
Jephcott, A.R., 85

Jessel, Sir H.M., Bt., 59
Jesson, C., 252
Jesson, T.E., 213
Jewson, P.W., 130
Joad, Dr. C.E.M., 632
Jodrell, Sir N.P., 415
Joel, D.J.B., 119
John, E.T., 524, 525, 530
John, W., 521
Johns, D., 528
Johnson, A.C., see Campbell-Johnson
Johnson, Dr. D.M., 105, 478, 483
Johnson, E.J., 16, 308
Johnson, E.S.T., 382
Johnson, G.F., 130, 197
Johnson, Sir L.S., 251
Johnson, R.K., see Kingesley-Johnson
Johnson, R.P.C., see Croom-Johnson
Johnston, C.H., 556
Johnston, D., 624
Johnston, D.H., 578
Johnston, J., 163, 548, 556, 570, 606
Johnston, J.E., 327
Johnston, J.W., 616
Johnston, M.C., see Campbell-Johnston
Johnston, Rt. Hon. T., 552, 591, 617
Johnstone, D.J., 121
Johnstone, H., 187, 235, 263, 463, 482
Johnstone, J., 613
Jolly, J.C., 220
Jones, A., 340, 380
Jones, A.C., 380, 508
Jones, A.E.E., 285
Jones, A.E.O., see Owen-Jones
Jones, A.G.P., see Parry-Jones
Jones, Arnold H., 440
Jones, Arthur H., 199
Jones, A.L., 513, 532
Jones, A.P., 174
Jones, A.W., 217
Jones, C.O., 524, 532
Jones, C.S., 174
Jones, D.A., 101
Jones, D.F., 526
Jones, Rev. D.G., 532
Jones, Rev. D.M., 527
Jones, D.T., 135
Jones, E.A., see Atherley-Jones
Jones, Sir E.D., Bt., 547
Jones, Sir E.R., 221, 518, 535
Jones, E.W.C., see Cemlyn-Jones
Jones, F.E., 258
Jones, F.L., see Llewellyn-Jones
Jones, G.D., 25
Jones, G.H., 447, 475
Jones, G.H.H., see Howard-Jones
Jones, G.J., 140
Jones, G.M. Edwardes, see Edwardes Jones
Jones, G.M.G., see Garro-Jones
Jones, G.W., 217
Jones, Sir G.W.H., 52
Jones, H., 524
Jones, H.C., see Conway-Jones
Jones, H.E., 375
Jones, H.H., 540
Jones, H.J., 399
Jones, H.L.M., 40

Jones, H.M., 540
Jones, John, 537
Jones, Rev. Joseph, 631
Jones, J.E.E., see Emlyn-Jones
Jones, J.F., 213
Jones, J.G., 539
Jones, J.H., 90
Jones, Sir J.H.M., see Morris-Jones
Jones, J.J., 259
Jones, John Lees, see Lees-Jones
Jones, John Lloyd, 127, 527
Jones, J.R., 521
Jones, J.R.H., see Hayes-Jones
Jones, Prof. J.S., 434
Jones, J.S.G., see Griffith-Jones
Jones, J.T., 529
Jones, J.W., 538
Jones, Sir L., 523
Jones, L.H.D., 347, 369
Jones, Rt. Hon. L.S., 294, 430
Jones, M., 534
Jones, N.C., 336
Jones, P.A., 357
Jones, P.H., 291
Jones, P.P., 522
Jones, R.E., 224, 436
Jones, R.L., 536
Jones, R.O., 161
Jones, R.T., 526
Jones, R.V., 461
Jones, T.A., 289, 500, 522
Jones, Sir T.G., 533, 538, 545
Jones, T.I.M., see Mardy-Jones
Jones, T.M., see Miller-Jones
Jones, T.W., 540
Jones, W.E.E., 513, 526
Jones, W.K., 140
Jones, W.L.M., see Mars-Jones
Jones, W.N., 528
Joseph, F.L., 169
Joseph, M.C., 63
Jowett, Rt. Hon. F.W., 94
Jowitt, Rt. Hon. Sir W.A., 64, 135, 210, 628
Joy, J., 238
Joyce, E.C., 1
Joynson-Hicks, Hon. L.W., 467
Joynson-Hicks, Rt. Hon. Sir W., Bt., 411
Junor, J.D.B., 555, 582

K

Kane, C.J., 320
Kavanagh, E., 424
Kay, A.D., 265
Kay, Sir R.N., 498
Kaylor, J., 100
Keast, J.E.V., 208
Keatinge, E.M., 453
Kedward, Rev. R.M., 4, 147, 363
Keeling, E.H., 46, 245, 411
Keenan, W., 170
Keens, T., 278, 545
Kegie, H., 187, 423
Keighley, T.D., 92
Keighley-Bell, G.H., 271
Keir, D.E., 592, 607, 615
Keith, Sir H.S., 560, 601

Kellaway, Rt. Hon. F.G., 272
Kellett, E.O., 74, 528
Kellett, R.G., 324
Kelley, Sir F.A., 218
Kelley, S., 31
Kelly, C.J., 6, 197
Kelly, J.S., see Sherwood-Kelly
Kelly, S., 574
Kelly, W.T., 213, 442
Kemsley, C.N.T., see Thornton-Kemsley
Kendall, C.W., 103, 344, 450
Kendall, W.D., 398
Kennedy, A., 32
Kennedy, A.P., 436
Kennedy, A.R., 210
Kennedy, J.A., 570
Kennedy, M.S.N., 383
Kennedy, Rt. Hon. T., 575, 577
Kennedy, W.S., 58
Kenney, R., 95
Kenworthy, Hon. J.M., 147, 218
Kenyon, B., 303
Kenyon, C., 375
Kenyon, F., 222
Kenyon, H., 179
Kenyon-Slaney, P.P., 313
Ker, J.C., 617
Kerby, H.B., 410
Kerr, C.I., 147, 419, 523, 577
Kerr, H.W., 202
Kerr, Dr. J., 632
Kerr, Sir J.G., 632
Kerr, S.P., 458, 460
Kerr, T.A., 566
Kerran, F.L., 52, 149, 273
Kerrigan, P., 563, 571
Kerry, Earl of, 309
Kershaw, F.W., 369
Keswick, H., 590
Key, C.W., 39
Key, E.M.C., see Cooper-Key
Keyes, Sir R.J.B., Bt., 208
Keymer, Sir D.T., 18
Kidd, G. le B., 467
Kidd, J., 606
Kiley, J.D., 51
Kilner, E.E.R., 118
Kimball, L., 147, 395
Kincaid-Smith, T.M.H., 438
Kindell, A.A.G., 236
Kindersley, G.M., 357
King, E.M., 296
King, F.V., 387
King, F.W., 319
King, H.D., 38, 416
King, Dr. H.M., 349
King, J., 143, 271
King-Hall, W.S.R., 387
Kingesley-Johnson, R., 279
Kinghorn, E., 130, 424
Kingsmill, W.H., 442
Kinley, J., 91
Kinloch, A.D., 596
Kinloch, J.L., 565, 574, 583
Kinloch-Cooke, Sir C., Bt., 204, 515
Kirby, B.V., 167
Kirby, J.A., 160

Kirby, R.E.W., 34, 317
Kirby, W.H., 394
Kirkpatrick, W.M., 210
Kirkwood, D., 551
Kitson, A., 198
Knatchbull, Hon. M.H.R., 363
Knebworth, Viscount, 45, 357
Kneeshaw, J.W., 81, 489
Knight, A., 184
Knight, A.M., 388
Knight, E.A., 485
Knight, G.W.H., 20, 103, 200, 204, 481
Knight, T.H., 246, 274
Knights, H.N., 8
Knowles, F.J., 361, 401, 402
Knox, Sir A.W.F., 281
Kynaston, J.W., 266

L

Lacey, C.G., 407
Lacey, J., 209
Lakin, C.H.A., 536
Lakin, J., 472
Lamb, E.G., 353
Lamb, Sir J.Q., 449
Lamb, R.A., 447
Lamb, T., 554
Lambert, Rt. Hon. George, 312
Lambert, Hon. George, 312
Lambert, J., 494
Lambert, W.A., 224
Lambton, Viscount, 324
Lamert, S.S., 487
Lampard-Vachell, B.G., 164, 254, 310
Lampson, Rt. Hon. G.L.T.L., see Locker-
  Lampson
Lampson, O.S.L., see Locker-Lampson
Lamsley, A.T., 232
Lancaster, C.G., 379
Lancaster, S.M., 258
Landa, M.J., 152
Landau, F.M., 374
Lane, H., 135
Lane, H.E., 267
Lane-Fox, Rt. Hon. G.R., 494
Lang, C.D.C., 312
Lang, C.H.D., see Durrad-Lang
Lang, Rev. G., 202, 291
Langdon, H.T., 311
Langdon-Davies, J., 458
Langford, E.W., 352, 353
Langford-Holt, J.A., 435
Lansbury, Rt. Hon. G., 39
Lapthorn, F.D., 34
Lapthorn, T.H.F., 208
Larmor, Sir J., 627
Lascelles, E.ff.W., 495
Lassen, E.J., 247
Latham, C., 54, 409
Latham, Sir H.P., Bt., 218, 492
Lathan, G., 229, 359, 406
Laughland, Rev. J.V., 173
Laurie, Dr. A.P., 557
Laverack, F.J., 31
Lavers, S.R.C., 321
Law, Albert, 90

Law, Arthur, 217, 222
Law, Rt. Hon. A.B., 562
Law, Sir A.J., 213, 305
Law, D.B., 452
Law, Rt. Hon. R.K., 30, 150
Lawder, J.C., 56
Lawley, D.B., 241, 435
Lawrence, Rt. Hon. F.W.P., see Pethick-
   Lawrence
Lawrence, G.K., 495
Lawrence, S.C., 628
Lawrence, W.E., 230
Lawrie, H.H., 291
Lawson, C.F.C., 488
Lawson, F., 158
Lawson, Sir Henry M., 209
Lawson, Hugh M., 134, 509
Lawson, Rt. Hon. J.J., 324, 329
Lawther, W., 235, 321
Laycock, H.C., 487
Laycock, R.E., 426
Layton, E.S., 34
Layton, W.T., 104, 516, 629
Lazarus, J., 33
Leach, W., 93
Lean, J., 607
Leaper, W.J., 508
Leather, E.H.C., 101
Leckie, J.A., 250
Leckie, J.V., 553
Ledbury, S., 347
Leddy, C.E., 621
Ledsom, W.H., 169
Lee, Frank, 307
Lee, Frederick, 181
Lee, H.W., 363
Lee, Rev. R., 268
Leeburn, W.J., 619
Leech, Dr. J.W., 195
Leechman, W.G., 566
Lees, J., 302
Lees, L., 71
Lees-Jones, J., 123, 177
Lees-Smith, Rt. Hon. H.B., 497, 500
Leeson, W., 330
Legge-Bourke, E.A.H., 361
Leicester, O.H., 6
Leigh, Sir J., Bt., 55
Leigh, J.C., 390, 485
Leigh, J.C.G., 6
Leighton, A.L., 264
Leighton, B.E.P., 434
Leith-Hay-Clark, N., 58
Le Mesurier, P.R., 156
Lemon, A.B., 480
Lennox-Boyd, A.T., 274, 535
Leonard, A.W., 410
Leonard, W., 570, 574
Le Quesne, C.T., 355
Leslie, J.R., 330, 407
Lesser, H., 10
Lessing, E.A., 275
Letham, J., 601
Letts, W.H., 338
Lever, Sir A.L., Bt., 18
Lever, L.M., 182
Lever, N.H., 179

Lever, Sir T.J.P., Bt., 20
Levick, H.D., 187
Levinson, B.A., 404
Levy, B., 280
Levy, T., 498
Lewer, A.J., 25
Lewin, J., 430
Lewington, W.J., 28
Lewins, W.A., 105
Lewis, A.W.J., 261
Lewis, C.G., 259
Lewis, D., 525
Lewis, E., 51
Lewis, H.M., 122
Lewis, I.L., 462
Lewis, Dr. John, 130
Lewis, John, 90
Lewis, Joseph, 285
Lewis, Rt. Hon. J.H., 631
Lewis, J.S., 631
Lewis, K., 386
Lewis, O., 333
Lewis, R.H., 472
Lewis, R.J., 174
Lewis, S.K., 250
Lewis, Thomas (1), 232
Lewis, Thomas (2), 97
Lewis, T.A., 539, 631
Lewis, T.C., 101
Lewisham, Viscount, 257
Leyland, Rev. A.S., 448
Lidbury, C.A., 395
Liddall, Sir W.S., 164, 497
Liddell Hart, A.J., 89
Liddiard, E.S., 373
Lidiard, Sir H., 38
Lincoln, F.A., 133
Lincoln, H.J., 263
Lindemann, Prof. F.A., 630
Lindgren, G.S., 357, 422
Lindley, Rt. Hon. Sir F., 628
Lindley, F.W., 152, 218
Lindner, A.F.H., 468
Lindsay, A.D.L., 203
Lindsay, G.H.M.B., see Broun-Lindsay
Lindsay, K.M., 203, 270, 408, 585, 628
Lindsay, M.A., 473
Lindsay, N.K., 101
Lindsley, J., 327, 328
Linfield, F.C., 274, 402, 489
Ling, W., 366
Lingen-Barker, E.N., 236
Linklater, E., 592
Linsey, T.T., 456
Linstead, H.N., 56
Lipson, D.L., 108
Lipton, M., 31
Lisburne, Earl of, 527
Lister, Sir R.A., 344
Lister, T.F., 64
Litchfield, J.L., 201
Lithgow, S., 204
Little, Sir E.G.G.G., see Graham-Little
Little, G., 53
Little, Rev. Dr. J., 624
Little, Rev. J.H., 624
Liverman, M.G., 15, 263

Livesey, A.H.H., see Henderson-Livesey
Livingstone, A.M., 367, 596, 598
Llewellin, Rt. Hon. J.J., 47, 412
Llewellyn, D.T., 533
Llewellyn, D.W.A., 113
Llewellyn, W.M., 517
Llewellyn-Jones, F., 532
Llewelyn, Sir L.W., 545
Llewelyn, W.C., 285, 286
Llewelyn-Williams, H., 528
Lloyd, Charles E., 536
Lloyd, Cyril E., 119
Lloyd, E.G.R., 613
Lloyd, F.G., 82, 448, 485
Lloyd, Rt. Hon. Sir G.A., 463
Lloyd, G.B., 435
Lloyd, Rt. Hon. G.W., 48, 81
Lloyd, H.M., 515
Lloyd, I.B., 443, 456
Lloyd, J.S.B., 289, 292
Lloyd, W.D., 53, 263
Lloyd George, Rt. Hon. D., 513
Lloyd George, Rt. Hon. G., 547
Lloyd-Greame, Rt. Hon. Sir P., see
  Cunliffe-Lister, Rt. Hon. Sir P.
Lobnitz, Sir F., 613
Lochrane, F.H.A.J., 117
Locker-Lampson, Rt. Hon. G.L.T., 413
Locker-Lampson, O.S., 79, 360
Lockhart, Sir R.C., 575
Lockwood, A., 228
Lockwood, J.C., 18, 70
Lockwood, J.H., 508
Lockwood, S.S., 493
Loder, Hon. J. de V., 158, 465
Lodge, T., 41
Lodge, T.C.S., see Skeffington-Lodge
Loftus, P.C., 451
Logan, A., 579
Logan, D.G., 171
Loman, G.H., 151
Lomax, J.W., 391
Lomax, S., 90
Long, Hon. R.E.O., 482
Long, Rt. Hon. W.H., 59
Longbottom, A.W., 132
Longbottom, Rev. H.D., 170
Longden, F., 75
Longden, G.J.M., 189
Longhurst, H.C., 404
Longmore, Sir A.M., 398
Looker, H.W., 147, 340
Lord, Sir W.G., see Greaves-Lord
Lorden, J.W., 42
Lorimer, H.D., 308
Lorimer, R., 550
Lort-Williams, J.R., 3
Loseby, C.E., 94, 201
Lough, Rt. Hon. T., 28
Lougher, Sir L., 514, 515
Lovat-Fraser, J.A., 98, 447, 536
Loverseed, J.E., 287
Loverseed, J.F., 454
Loveys, A.W., 437
Low, T.A.R.W., 88
Lowe, Sir F.W., Bt., 77
Lowe, S.R.D., see Drury-Lowe

Lowell, W., 539
Lowndes, R.L., 55
Lowth, T., 176
Lowther, Hon. C.W., 249, 298, 301
Lowther, C.W.H., 107, 383
Lowther, Sir H.C., 299
Lowther, Rt. Hon. J.W., 299
Lowthian, E., 107
Loyd, A.T., 275
Lucas, A.L., 112
Lucas, J., 571
Lucas, Sir J.M., Bt., 209
Lucas, P.B., 16
Lucas-Tooth, Sir H.V.H.D., Bt., 138, 361
Luce, Sir R.H., 117
Lucy, Sir H.W.C-R.F., Bt., see Fairfax-Lucy
Ludlow, F., 203
Lumley, G., 329
Lumley, L.R., 148, 271
Lumsden, W.F., 548
Lunn, Sir G., 194
Lunn, Sir H.S., 97
Lunn, W., 507
Lunnon, J., 439
Lupton, A., 58, 258
Lupton, O., 135
Luxmoore, A.F.C.C., 370
Lyburn, Dr. E.F.St.J., 374
Lygon, Hon. H., 270, 386
Lyle, Sir C.E.L., Bt., 92, 260, 334
Lyle-Samuel, A., 398, 450
Lymington, Viscount, 347
Lynch, A.A., 2, 18
Lynch, J., 90
Lynch, Dr. J.J., 250
Lynch, T., 428
Lyne, A.W., 443
Lyne, J., 252
Lynn, Sir R.J., 621
Lyon, L., 136
Lyon, M.D., 453
Lyons, A.M., 158, 304
Lyons, Dr. R., 409
Lyons, T., 625
Lyster, Dr. R.A., 210, 351
Lyttelton, Rt. Hon. O., 346
Lytton-Bernard, Dr. B., 410

**M**

Mabane, Rt. Hon. W., 141
McAdam, W., 220, 558
McAllister, G., 565, 604, 605
MacAlpine, J.W., 371
MacAndrew, Sir C.G., 568, 584, 585
MacAndrew, J.O., 586
McArthur, D., 613
McArthur, J., 575
McCall, J.B.P., see Pollok-McCall
McCall, T., 153, 384
McCallum, D., 583
McCallum, Sir J.M., 578
MacCallum, Rev. M., 583
MacCalman, H.T., 565
McCartan, M., 625
McCarthy, M.D., 324, 331
McClure, Alexander (1), 564, 604

McClure, Alexander (2), 564
McColl, I., 590
McConnell, Sir J., Bt., 622
McConnell, T.E., 619
McConnell, W., 130
MacCormick, J.M., 560, 565, 578, 596
McCormick, P., 622
McCorquodale, Rt. Hon. M.S., 264, 458, 510
McCourt, B., 599
McCowan, H., 598
McCracken, M.J., 551, 559
McCrae, Sir G., 554, 579
McCrossan, D., 625
McCulloch, J., 264, 565, 578
McCullough, W.D., 415
McCurdy, Rt. Hon. C.A., 196
MacDermot, F., 621
MacDiarmid, J.M., 597, 598, 611
Macdonald, A.J.F., 615
McDonald, Dr. B.F.P., 248
Macdonald, D., 573
Macdonald, D.H., 599
MacDonald, D.J., 552
Macdonald, G., 381
MacDonald, H., 359
Macdonald, J., 597
Macdonald, Rt. Hon. J.A.M., 579
MacDonald, Rt. Hon. J.R., 60, 160, 329, 533, 632
Macdonald, Sir M., 596
MacDonald, Rt. Hon. M.J., 426, 597
Macdonald, Dr. P., 632
Macdonald, Sir P.D., 362
MacDonald, R., 561
McDonald, S., 555
McDonald, T.P., 555
Macdonell, A.G., 164
McDonnell, Hon. A., 366
MacDonnell, J.H., 58, 273
McDougal, A.R., 615
MacDougall, J.D., 573, 605
McDougall, J.P., 288
McDougall, Dr. P., 184
McDougall, R., 305
McElwee, A., 181
McEnteen, V.L.T., 252
MacEwen, Sir A.M., 585, 598
McEwen, J.H.F., 588
MacEwen, M., 591
McFadyean, Sir A., 12
Macfadyen, Rev. D., 106, 211, 357
Macfadyen, E., 479
Macfarlane, C., 135
McFarlane, C.S., 560
MacFarlane, Sir F.N.M., see Mason-MacFarlane
McGhee, F.L., 172
McGhee, H.G., 227, 502
McGilley, J.A., 325
McGleenan, C.E., 623
McGovern, J., 571
McGowan, J., 608
McGree, L.J., 171
MacGregor, A.A., 135, 561, 587
McGuffie, D.J., 484
McGurk, J., 377
Machin, A.G.F., 272
Machin, E.A., 87

McIlroy, W.G., 211
McInnes, J., 562, 569
MacInnes, R.I.A., 589, 617
Macintosh, A.F., 548, 577, 580
McIntosh, G.R., 549
MacIntosh, H.D., 597
McIntyre, H., 591
McIntyre, H.W., 298
MacIntyre, I., 558
McIntyre, Dr. R.D., 603
MacIver, Dr. I.H., 583
Mack, J.D., 191, 248
Mack, R., 348
Mackay, A.B., 561, 569
Mackay, A.M., 585, 599
MacKay, B.S., 23, 357, 461, 609
Mackay, D.N., 596
McKay, J., 249
McKay, J.W., 109
Mackay, R.W.G., 149, 438, 536
McKeag, E.L., 335, 367
McKeag, W., 194, 326
McKean, J.A.D., 578
McKee, Dr. J.T., 623
McKenna, Rt. Hon. R., 545
Mackeson, H.R., 142
Mackie, J.H., 554, 595
Mackie, W., 568
Mackinder, Sir H.J., 560
Mackinder, W., 508
McKinlay, A.S., 568, 591, 612
McKinnon, Rev. C., 611
Mackintosh, A.M., 597
Maclagan, O.F., 472
McLaine, W., 97, 404, 549
MacLaren, A., 238
McLaren, Hon. H.D., 393
McLaren, R., 604, 605
McLaren, S.P., 559, 592
McLaughlin, J.C., 464
Maclay, Hon. J.P., 578
Maclay, Hon. J.S., 577
McLean, A., 418, 534
McLean, C.W.W., 400
Maclean, Rt. Hon. Sir D., 295, 515, 585, 608
Maclean, F.H.R., 382
Maclean, J., 563
Maclean, N., 564
Maclean, N.G., 596
McLean, T., 168, 380
McLean, Dr. W.H., 573
McLean, W.R., 567
McLeavy, F., 94
McLellan, R., 563, 601
Macleod, I.N., 598
MacLeod, J., 597
MacLeod, J.M., 566
Macleod, T., 487
McManus, A., 132
Macmaster, D., 456
McMicking, G., 595
Macmillan, Rt. Hon. M.H., 103, 237
Macmillan, M.K., 598
Macmillan, M.V., 329
McNab, E.R., 604, 607
Macnaghten, E.L., 432, 626
Macnaghten, Hon. Sir M.M., 626

McNair, J., 98
MacNair, T.A., 565, 577
Macnamara, J.R.J., 261, 332
Macnamara, Rt. Hon. T.J., 9, 250
McNamee, T., 379
McNeil, H., 566, 574, 597
McNeill, H., 595
McNeill, Rt. Hon. R.J., 364
McNicol, J., 572
McNicol, J.M., 571
Maconochie, A.W., 254
Macpherson, D., 587
MacPherson, G., 566
Macpherson, Rt. Hon. Sir J.I., Bt., 597
MacPherson, M., 442, 579
Macpherson, N.M.S., 590
Macpherson, T., 216
McPhie, J.R., 334, 346
Macquisten, F.A., 572, 583
MacRobert, Rt. Hon. A.M., 576, 613
MacRobert, J., 593
McShane, H., 563
McShane, J.J., 250
McSkimming, J., 572
Mactaggart, I.A., 563
MacVeagh, J., 241
McVey, C., 71, 72
MacWhinney, C., 626
Maddison, F., 211, 319, 488
Maddock, H.L., 159
Maddocks, Sir H., 471
Maden, H., 383
Maden, Sir J.H., 217
Maggs, H.J., 99
Magnay, T., 128, 323
Magnus, Sir P., Bt., 629
Magnus, S.W., 18
Mahon, J., 42
Mahon, S., 168
Mainwaring, W.H., 520
Mais, A.R., 372
Maitland, Sir A., 368
Maitland, Rt. Hon. Sir A.H.D.R.S., Bt., see
  Steel-Maitland
Maitland, J.F.W., 402
Maitland, L.L., 288
Makins, E., 30, 288
Malbon, F.W., 236
Malcolm, I.Z., 113
Malcolm, P., 585
Malindine, E.T., 28, 162, 413
Malkin, S., 238
Mallaby-Deeley, Sir H.M., Bt., 263
Mallalieu, E.L., 400, 495
Mallalieu, F.W., 495
Mallalieu, J.P.W., 141
Mallet, Sir C.E., 549
Mallison, W.C., 309
Mallon, J.J., 339, 359
Malone, C.J.L., 64, 162, 196
Malone, H.J., 6
Malone, P.B., 244
Mancor, C.J.M., 555
Mander, Sir G. Le M., 267, 353, 444, 486
Mander, J.A.H., 317
Manfield, J., 196
Mann, T., 199

Mann, W., 123
Manning, C.A.G., 8
Manningham-Buller, Sir M.E., Bt., 196, 420
Manningham-Buller, R.E., 419
Mansel, Sir C.C., Bt., 109, 296, 528, 631
Mansfield, J., 421
Mansfield, W.T., 490
Manville, Sir E., 109
March, S., 40
Marcus, M., 552
Marcy, W.N., 102
Mardy-Jones, T.I., 539
Margesson, Rt. Hon. H.D.R., 261, 472
Marjoribanks, E., 463
Markham, Sir C., Bt., 306
Markham, S.F., 33, 200, 214, 460
Marklew, E., 131, 495
Marks, Sir G.C., 295
Marks, H., 49
Marley, J., 42
Marlow, A.E., 158
Marlowe, A.A.H., 97
Marnham, R.J., 456
Marples, A.E., 248
Marquand, H.A., 515
Marriott, Sir J.A.R., 203, 271
Mars-Jones, W.L., 530
Marsden, A., 1, 456
Marshall, A.E., 148
Marshall, Sir A.H., 64, 141, 247
Marshall, A.J., 463
Marshall, A.P., 80, 352
Marshall, D., 293
Marshall, F., 224
Marshall, J.Y., 571
Marshall, S.H., 242
Marshall, T.H., 459
Martel, Sir G. Le Q., 321
Martell, E.D., 3
Martell, E.K., 274
Martin, A.E., 338
Martin, F., 580, 581
Martin, G.W., 157
Martin, J.C., 378
Martin, J.H., 46, 130
Martin, R., 234
Martin, T.B., 8, 323, 327
Martin, W.E., 407
Martin, W.H.P., 549, 562, 591
Martineau, H.M., 544
Marwick, W.H., 590
Marwood, A.T., 307, 430
Mashford, W.E., 148
Mason, A., 285
Mason, D.J., 301
Mason, D.M., 109, 310, 338, 365, 555
Mason, Hon. G.K.M., 112
Mason, J.F., 163
Mason, R., 425
Mason, S., 170
Mason, T.J., 411
Mason-MacFarlane, Sir F.N., 37
Masterman, Rt. Hon. C.F.G., 184, 260, 304
Mather, B., 157
Mathers, G., 558, 606
Mathew, C.J., 51
Mathew, R., 586

Mathew, T., 129
Mathews, A.M., 244, 251, 339, 340
Mathias, Sir R., Bt., 518
Matters, L.W., 32
Matthews, A.S., 496
Matthews, D., 522
Matthews, D.M., 555
Matthews, G.R., 75
Matthews, R.B., 337, 363, 374, 432
Maude, J.C., 127
Maudling, R., 139
Maw, H., 194
Mawdesley, J., 200
Maxton, J., 559
Maxwell, A.T., 73
Maxwell, J., 603
Maxwell, Hon. S.A., 415
May, H.A., 337
May, H.J., 616
May, J.H., 432
May, L.A., 9
May, T.J., 74, 200
Maycock, J.W., 120
Mayer, E.R., 8
Mayer, S., 452
Mayhew, C.P., 417
Mayhew, Sir J., 123, 335
Maynard, Sir H.J., 15, 344, 415
Meakin, W., 80, 239, 395, 448, 449
Meares, C.H., 189
Medland, H.M., 205, 315
Medlicott, F., 404, 414
Meech, T.C., 86
Meek, A.M., 82
Meggitt, J.C., 536
Mell, R., 150
Mellanby, R.A., 451
Meller, Sir R.J., 8, 366, 461
Mellick, J., 561
Melling, L., 471
Mellish, R.J., 3
Mellor, Sir J.S.P., Bt., 301, 474, 475
Mellor, W., 406
Melville, Sir J.B., 128
Mendel, E.I., 179
Mennell, R.O., 457
Menzies, J.H., 593
Mercer, H., 454
Mercer, T.W., 182, 385
Meredith, W.R., 541
Merriman, Sir F.B., 184
Messel, R.P., 74, 113, 312
Messer, F., 244
Messer, W.W., 24
Meston, Hon. D., 233
Mesurier, P.R. Le, see Le Mesurier
Metcalfe, G.H., 491
Metcalfe, H., 161
Metcalfe, J., 374
Meyer, Sir F.C., Bt., 130
Meyler, H.M., 6, 87
Meysey-Thompson, E.C., 79
Michell, T.F.T., 297
Mickle, N., 272
Middlebrook, Sir W., 155
Middleton, C.F., 85
Middleton, E., 25

Middleton, G., 107, 283
Middleton, G.W., 570
Middleton, J.T., 64, 202
Midgley, Rt. Hon. H.C., 620, 621
Mikardo, I., 211
Mildmay, Rt. Hon. F.B., 316
Millar, A.E.R., 355
Millar, I.A.D., 587
Millar, J.D., 592, 603
Miller, E., 459
Miller, F.N., see Norie-Miller
Miller, J.H.C., 275
Miller, J.M.R., 571
Miller, W.J., 53, 362
Miller-Jones, T., 49
Millett, A.E., 441, 442, 464
Millican, R., 301
Milligan, Sir W., 222
Milligan, W.R., 570
Millington, E.R., 332
Mills, Sir F., Bt., 162
Mills, Henry (1), 28
Mills, Henry (2), 200, 483
Mills, J.D., 349
Mills, J.E., 366
Mills, J.F.F.P., see Platts-Mills
Millwood, P.L., 273
Milne, C., 551, 555, 593
Milne, D.L., 531
Milne, J.L., 549
Milne, Sir J.S.W., see Wardlaw-Milne
Milne, W.G., 482
Milner, D., 494
Milner, G., 181
Milner, G.C., 372
Milner, Rt. Hon. J., 156
Milnes, H.H.M., 104
Milton, F., 27
Minns, O.A., 57
Minto, J., 393
Mitchell, A., 69, 132, 492, 502
Mitchell, D.K., 174
Mitchell, E., 94
Mitchell, E.R., 562, 578
Mitchell, F., 112
Mitchell, G.W., 366
Mitchell, H.P., 405, 616
Mitchell, J., 595
Mitchell, M.E., 87, 385
Mitchell, Sir P.C., 632
Mitchell, R.M., 612
Mitchell, S., 602
Mitchell, T., 299
Mitchell, T.W.H., 512
Mitchell, W., 556, 582, 608
Mitchell, W.F., 339
Mitchell, Sir W.L., 57
Mitchell-Thomson, Rt. Hon. Sir W., Bt., 113, 567
Mitcheson, G.G., 44, 96
Mitchison, G.R., 80, 420
Mitford, W.B., 415
Moeran, E.W., 429, 493
Moffat, A.B., 605
Moffat, J., 599
Moffatt-Pender, I.M., 425, 598
Molden, J.W., 2, 28, 53, 437, 479
Moles, Rt. Hon. T., 620

Moller, N.H., 332
Molloy, L.G.S., 87
Molson, A.H.E., 305, 496, 517
Molson, J.E., 401
Molteno, P.A., 611
Mond, Rt. Hon. Sir A.M., Bt., 523, 528
Mond, Hon. H.L., 165, 361
Money, Sir L.G.C., 236, 244
Money, R.I., 224
Monkhouse, O., 321
Monks, A.E., 397, 431
Monro, J.D., 480
Monsell, Rt. Hon. Sir B.M.E., see Eyres-Monsell
Monslow, W., 67, 192
Montagu, Rt. Hon. E.S., 282
Montague, F., 28
Montague-Barlow, Rt. Hon. Sir C.A., 221
Monteith, A., 496
Montgomery, R.M., 286
Moody, A.R., 72
Moody, A.S., 169
Moody, W., 328
Moon, Dr. R.O., 203, 265
Moore, B., 76
Moore, D.E., 510
Moore, F., 601
Moore, F.D., 93
Moore, H.D., 182
Moore, M., 66
Moore, M.W., 398
Moore, Hon. Sir N.J., 26, 212
Moore, S.C., 153
Moore, Sir T.C.R., 550, 600
Moore, W., 367
Moore, W.H., 174, 214
Moore, W.L., 519
Moore-Brabazon, J.T.C., 214, 248
Moores, J., 304, 471
Moran, T.P., 259
Morden, C.R., 14, 21
Morden, W.G., 405
Mordey, T.H., 129
Moreing, A.C., 210
Moreing, A.H., 294, 487
Morel, E.D., 552
Morgan, B., 319
Morgan, C., 440
Morgan, C.J.E., 566
Morgan, D.W., 520
Morgan, Hon. E.F., 49
Morgan, G.H., 146, 222, 296, 541
Morgan, Rev. H., 537
Morgan, H.A., 531
Morgan, Dr. H.B.W., 9, 213
Morgan, I.J., 527
Morgan, J., 160, 371, 393, 464, 472, 496
Morgan, Sir K.P.V., see Vaughan-Morgan
Morgan, M., 261, 543
Morgan, P.T.H., 514
Morgan, R.H., 486
Morgan, R.L.R., 263
Morgan, S.C., 106, 196
Morgan, Rev. S.J.W., 368, 458
Morgan, S.W., 359
Morgan, T.R., 538
Morgan, W.P., 592
Morison, T.B., 596

Morland, J.C., 440
Morley, Ralph, 232
Morley, Robert, 229, 496
Morris, E.H.F., 228, 408
Morris, H., 225
Morris, H.S., 99
Morris, J.P., 220
Morris, J.R., 311
Morris, J.W., 143
Morris, O.T., 515, 534
Morris, P., 523
Morris, R., 1
Morris, R.H., 527, 528
Morris, S., 80
Morris, T., 434
Morris, T.A., 173, 248
Morris, T.C., 211
Morris, T.E., 447
Morris-Jones, Sir J.H., 530
Morrison, Dr. G.A., 632
Morrison, H., 480
Morrison, Rt. Hon. H.S., 20, 35
Morrison, J.G., 480
Morrison, R.C., 243
Morrison, R.J., 212
Morrison, Rt. Hon. W.S., 342, 598
Morrison-Bell, Sir A.C., Bt., 311
Morrow, J., 620
Morse, W.E., 437, 441
Mort, A., 290
Mort, D.L., 125, 266, 522
Mortimer, A., 92
Mortimer, G.V., 62
Morton, D.S., 185, 289
Morton, T.E., 24
Moseley, S.A., 233
Moses, J.J.H., 205
Mosley, Sir O.E., Bt., 81, 230, 240, 408
Moss, A., 179, 283
Moss, E.O., 501
Moss, H.J., 571, 605
Motion, V., 50
Mott-Radclyffe, C.E., 277
Moulton, Hon. H.L.F., 480
Mount, W.A., 276
Mowat, D.M.S., 146
Mowatt, G.F., 464
Moyle, A., 315, 486
Muff, G., 96, 148, 285
Muggeridge, H.T., 113, 338
Muir, J.R.B., 213, 403, 492, 628
Muir, J.W., 567
Muirhead, A.J., 440
Muirhead, R.E., 614
Mulholland, Hon. H.G.H., 104
Mullan, C.H., 624
Mulley, F.W., 474
Mullins, D.E., 310
Mulvey, A., 625
Munro, H., 597
Munro, Rev. J.M., 613, 632
Munro, P., 536
Munro, Rt. Hon. R., 615
Munro, R.M., 632
Munro, W.B., 551
Munthe, M.G., 124
Murchison, Sir C.K., 148, 360

Murfitt, G.P., 21
Murney, M., 624
Murnin, H., 579
Murphy, J.T., 20, 180, 224
Murray, Hon. A.C., 582
Murray, B.A., 41, 583
Murray, C.D., 557
Murray, C. de B., 573, 607
Murray, Hon. C.G., 570
Murray, Dr. D., 598
Murray, Dr. D.S., 212
Murray, G., 371
Murray, Prof. G.G.A., 630
Murray, J., 157, 505, 575
Murray, J.D., 331
Murray, R., 614
Murray, R.G., 225
Murray, Sir T.D.K., 600, 607
Murray, W., 590
Murray, W.G., 213
Murray-Philipson, H.R., 411, 608
Murrell, F.E.J., 441
Muter, W., 569
Myer, R., 37
Myers, P., 504
Myers, T., 389, 511

N

Nabarro, G.D.N., 257
Nall, Sir J., 181
Nall-Cain, A.R.N., 173
Nally, W., 266
Nash, P., 621
Nathan, H.L., 5, 51, 54, 516
Nation, J.J.H., 148
Naylor, G.D., 278
Naylor, H.D., 300
Naylor, J.M., 546
Naylor, T.E., 48
Neal, A., 228, 401, 426
Neal, H., 304
Neal, J., 66, 425
Neathercoat, E.T., 516, 535
Needham, C.T., 181
Neep, E.J.C., 152, 451, 452
Neft, R., 441
Neill, W.F., 619
Nelson, Sir A., 190
Nelson, E.J.B., 51
Nelson, Sir F., 344
Nelson, G., 174
Nelson, R.F.W.R., 603
Nesbitt, R.C., 365
Neven-Spence, B.H.H., 610
Nevill, R.C.R., 365
Neville, Sir R.J.N., 155, 262, 414
Neville, T., 223, 489, 502
Newbold, J.T.W., 334, 603
Newbold, T.C., 117
Newbould, A.E., 163
Newbound, P.S., 150
Newdegate, Hon. J.M.F., see Fitzroy-Newdegate
Newell, Dr. A.G., 244
Newman, J., 580
Newman, J.R.P., 407
Newman, Sir R.H.S.D.L., Bt., 127

Newsom, G.H., 320
Newsome, N.F., 299
Newson, Sir P.W., Bt., 475
Newton, Sir D.G.C., 106
Newton, G.D., 189
Newton, H.K., 335
Nichol, R., 613
Nicholas, Rev. T.E., 517
Nicholl, Sir E., 296
Nicholls, G., 294, 394, 421, 453, 476
Nicholls, H., 190, 210
Nicholls, H.R., 260
Nicholson, F.D., 331
Nicholson, G., 189, 459
Nicholson, J., 569
Nicholson, J.C., 261
Nicholson, J.S., 58
Nicholson, O.W., 58
Nicholson, P.B., 512
Nicholson, R., 496
Nicholson, Rt. Hon. W.G., 350
Nicol, E.M., 213
Nicolson, Hon. H.G., 112, 160, 628
Nield, B.E., 285
Nield, Rt. Hon. Sir H., 120
Nield, H.K., 289, 358
Nightingale, P.R., 226
Nixon, H., 129, 429, 436
Nobbs, H., 380
Noble, A.H.P., 11
Noble, B., 136, 363
Noel-Baker, F.E., 405
Noel-Baker, P.J., 79, 109, 117
Nordon, C.L., 4, 46, 629
Norie-Miller, F., 612
Norman, A.C.W., 203
Norman, C.P., 6
Norman, Rt. Hon. Sir H., Bt., 86
Normand, W.G., 558
Normansell, F.B., 74
Norris, F.B.V., 221
Norris, Sir H.G., 15
North, E.T.T., 471
Norton, H., 31
Norton-Griffiths, Sir J., Bt., 54
Norwood, Rev. F.W., 52
Nunn, W., 195, 235, 300
Nunneley, C.W., 112
Nuttall, E., 72
Nuttall, J., 384
Nutting, H.A., 396

O

Oakes, L., 388
Oakley, A.B.L., 544
Oakley, T., 436
Oates, B.H., 512
O'Brien, M.R., 221
O'Brien, T., 201
O'Brien, W., 236
O'Connell, R.J.E.F., 10
O'Connor, T.J., 198, 273
O'Connor, Rt. Hon. T.P., 171
Oddie, G.S., 628
Odell, H.J., 79, 426
Odey, G.W., 489

O'Donnell, C.A., 298, 565
O'Donovan, Dr. W.J., 50
Ogden, F., 96
Ogden, J.W., 510
Ogden, R., 466
O'Grady, J., 156
O'Hagan, P.F., 624
Oldfield, J.R.A., 340
Oldfield, W.H., 180
Oliver, G., 135, 423
Oliver, G.H., 306
Oliver, G.L.J., 247
Oliver, P.M., 177, 283
Olliver, A.G., 506
O'Malley, B.L.A., 36
Oman, C.G., 589
Oman, Sir C.W.C., 630
O'Neill, J.J., 210, 382
O'Neill, Rt. Hon. Sir R.W.H., Bt., 622
Onions, A., 534
Oram, A.E., 465
Orbach, M., 263, 360
Orchard, A.J., 520
O'Reilly, S., 623
Ormiston, T., 603
Ormond, H.J., 52
Ormsby-Gore, Rt. Hon. W.G.A., 448
Orpen, H.F., 346
Orr, J., 606
Orr, Sir J. Boyd, see Boyd Orr
Orr, Dr. J.F., 606
Orr-Ewing, I.L., 128, 441
Osborn, H., 123
Osborn, W.S., 466
Osborne, C., 403
Osburn, A.C., 250
O'Sullivan, R., 193
Outhwaite, R.L., 239
Over, J.J., 256
Owen, D.P., 457
Owen, E., 161
Owen, Rev. E.T., 528
Owen, Sir G., 308, 526
Owen, H.F., 352
Owen, P.L.W., 546
Owen, T.D., 248
Owen-Jones, A.E., 451

P

Packham, D.G., 464
Paddon, B., 223
Padley, W.E., 404
Paget, J.W.F.G., 1
Paget, R.T., 196
Paget, T.G.F., 393
Pain, P., 459
Paish, Sir G., 179, 558, 562
Pakenham, Hon. F.A., 203
Palfrey, H.E., 486
Palin, J.H., 95, 195
Paling, Rt. Hon. W., 496, 512
Paling, W.T., 118, 443
Palmer, A.M.F., 265
Palmer, A.W., 208
Palmer, C.F., 436
Palmer, E.T., 17, 364

Palmer, F.N., 244, 459
Palmer, F.N.B., see Beaufort-Palmer
Palmer, G.E.H., 351
Palmer, G.L., 482
Palmer, G.M., 328
Palmer, J., 15, 374
Palmer, O.L.P., see Prior-Palmer
Palmer, R.G.F., see Fenwick-Palmer
Pannell, T.C., 157
Pargeter, T., 465
Pargiter, G.A., 410
Parish, J., 337
Parish, L., 247
Parker, A.D.D., see Dodds-Parker
Parker, Charles Sandbach, 310
Parker, Charles Stanley, 543
Parker, Harper, 239
Parker, Herbert, 212
Parker, James, 444
Parker, John, 114, 338, 397
Parker, O., 420
Parker, R.G., 86
Parkes, H.E., 257
Parkin, B.T., 344
Parkinson, A.L., 87
Parkinson, D.H., 275
Parkinson, J.A., 262
Parkman, S.M., 136
Parlour, W., 491
Parnell-Smith, W., 470
Parrott, Sir J.E., 558
Parry, D.M., 235
Parry, T.H., 532
Parry-Jones, A.G., 433
Parsloe, C.G., 57
Partridge, E., 2
Paterson, C.E., 55
Paterson, F.G., 411, 451
Paterson, J.S., 590
Paton, A.H., 576
Paton, H.W., 469
Paton, J., 197, 549, 584
Paton, R.M.R., 536
Patrick, C.M., 313
Pattinson, R., 164, 398
Pattinson, S., 402
Paul, E., 285
Paul, H.M., 422
Paul, W., 184, 381
Pavely, H., 319
Paxton, Rev. W., 93
Pay, E.J., 279, 472
Payne, C., 110
Payne, E.G., 324
Payne, H., 399
Payne, J.W., 282
Peace, J.W.G., 239
Peach, L. du G., 117
Peacock, Sir P., 253
Peacock, T., 287
Peacock, Sir W., 294
Peake, E.C., 323
Peake, Rt. Hon. O., 118, 153
Peake, R., 281
Pearce, Sir W., 49
Pearson, A., 539
Pearson, A.J., 348

Pearson, J., 93
Pearson, W.G., 327, 328
Peart, T.F., 301
Pease, E.H., 115
Pease, Rt. Hon. H.P., 115
Pease, W.E., 115
Peat, C.U., 115
Peck, S., 460
Peel, Hon. A.G.V., 397, 472
Peel, H.W., 96
Peel, R.F., 452
Peel, Hon. S., 412
Pemberton, Dr. W.B.J., 4
Pender, I.M.M., see Moffatt-Pender
Pender, J.C.D.D., see Denison-Pender
Pennefather, Sir J. de F., Bt., 170
Pennington, J., 248
Penny, A.J., 127
Penny, Sir Frederick George, Bt., 151
Penny, Frederick George, 258
Penrose, A.P.D., 415
Penston, A.J., 289
Penton, Sir E., 35, 314
Pepper, J.T., 429
Percy, C., 246
Percy, Rt. Hon. Lord Eustace, 136, 147
Perkins, E.K., 232
Perkins, W.F., 349
Perkins, W.R.D., 344
Perks, T.P., 500
Perowne, J.T.W., 362
Perriman, F., 232
Perring, W.G., 37
Perrins, W., 85
Perry, J., 476
Perry, S.F., 236, 420
Peters, A., 265
Peters, S.J., 360
Petherick, M., 296
Pethick-Lawrence, Rt. Hon. F.W., 27, 160, 555
Peto, B.A.J., 80
Peto, Sir B.E., Bt., 310
Peto, C.H.M., 310
Peto, G.K., 266, 403, 438
Petrie, C.A., 295
Petter, Sir E.W., 59, 100
Phibbs, C., 540
Philby, H.St.J.B., 142
Philipps, Sir I., 232
Philipps, Sir O.C., 285
Philipps, Hon. R.H., 525
Philipson, H., 128, 423, 425
Philipson, H.R.M., see Murray-Philipson
Phillipps, H.V., 213, 558
Phillips, A.S., 61
Phillips, E.A., 496
Phillips, E.H., 218
Phillips, G.I., 10, 370
Phillips, H., 248
Phillips, S., 249
Picciotto, C.M., 41
Pickering, E.H., 160
Pickering, E.W., 118
Pickles, W., 141, 149, 504
Pickstone, C., 380
Pickthorn, K.W.M., 627
Pielou, D.P., 486

Pierrepont, C.E., 127
Pigott, W., 108, 352
Pike, C.F., 223, 495, 506
Pike, M.J., 13, 230
Pilcher, G., 296
Pilcher, T.D., 345
Pilditch, Sir P.E., 410
Pile, A.W., 515
Pile, J., 350
Pilkington, Sir A., Bt., 507
Pilkington, R.A., 392
Pilkington, R.R., 500, 552
Pilley, W.C., 44
Pimblott, W., 289
Pinard, W.J., 14
Pinkham, C., 264
Pinson, C.H., 267
Piratin, P., 50
Pirie, D.V., 548
Pitman, I.J., 68
Pitt, W., 246
Pitt-Rivers, G.H.L.F., 318
Pitts, J.H., 293
Pittwood, E., 401
Plaisted, E.J., 370, 480
Plaistowe, C., 108, 319
Platt, J., 173
Platt, Sir T.W.C., see Comyn-Platt
Platts-Mills, J.F.F., 14
Plugge, L.F., 214
Plumer, Hon. T.H.R., 508
Plummer, S.J., 437
Pole, D.G., 308, 464, 514, 516, 556
Pollard, Prof. A.F., 629
Pollard, P.F., 53, 433
Pollard, R.S.W., 92
Pollitt, A.G., 125
Pollitt, H., 51, 259, 304, 329, 520
Pollock, Rt. Hon. Sir E.M., Bt., 476
Pollock, J., 585
Pollock, R.D., 624
Pollok-McCall, J.B., 586
Polson, Sir T.A., 367
Ponsonby, A.A.W.H., 224, 553
Ponsonby, C.E., 373
Poole, C.C., 108, 435, 447
Poole, Sir F.C., 293
Poole, J.L., 289
Poole, O.B.S., 434
Pope-Hennessy, L.H.R., 374
Popplewell, E., 195
Porritt, R.W., 380
Porter, Edward (1), 86, 210, 253
Porter, Edward (2), 435
Porter, G., 152, 169
Potter, J., 69, 125
Potter, S.B.M., 83
Potts, J., 66
Powell, D.L., 538
Powell, E.C.L.H., see Hulbert-Powell
Powell, E.G.H., 48
Powell, F.J., 151
Powell, G.H., 201
Powell, J.E., 501
Powell, J.F., 520
Powell, T.D.F., 202
Power, Sir J.C., Bt., 265

Power, W., 583
Powis, H., 503
Powlesland, J.J., 523
Pownall, Sir A., 35
Pratt, H.M., 205
Pratt, Sir J.W., 181, 241, 552, 561, 566
Pratt, T.A., 159
Pre, W.B. Du, see Du Pre
Prentice, J., 266
Prescott, Sir W.H., 243
Prescott, W.R.S., 377
Prescott-Decie, C., 56
Press, R.H., 622
Prestige, J.T., 13
Preston, H.W., 11
Preston, W., 250
Preston, Sir W.R., 50, 108
Pretyman, Rt. Hon. E.G., 332
Price, C.W.M., 547
Price, E.G., 45
Price, G., 499
Price, M.P., 129, 300, 343
Price, S.L., 20
Price-Heywood, F.B., 477
Price-White, D.A., 513
Prichard, Rev. A.G., 11
Prichard, W.A., 521
Priestley, J.B., 627
Priestley, L., 429
Priestley, Sir W.E.B., 94
Pringle, J.A., 625
Pringle, W.H., 550, 588
Pringle, W.M.R., 184, 502, 550, 572
Prior, R.M., 74, 260
Prior-Palmer, O.L., 470
Pritt, D.N., 21, 241
Privett, F.J., 207, 209
Proby, R.G., 454
Procter, H.A., 62, 260
Proctor, T., 199, 294
Proctor, W.T., 125
Profumo, J.D., 420
Prosser, C.F.H.W., see Wegg-Prosser
Prothero, Rt. Hon. R.E., 630
Pryce, E.C., 433
Pryde, D.J., 608
Puddicombe, R.W., 162
Pudney, J.S., 373
Pugh, R., 222
Pughe, Rev. D., 150
Pulley, C.T., 352
Purbrick, R., 172
Purcell, A.A., 109, 182, 343
Purchase, H.G., 32, 87, 159, 401, 485
Pursey, H., 148
Putt, S.G., 315
Pybus, P.J., 335, 508
Pym, L.R., 544

Q

Queen, I., 571
Quelch, L.E., 211
Quesne, C.T. Le, see Le Quesne
Quibell, D.J.K., 400
Quick, A.S., 31
Quin, D.J.M., 562

R

Radcliffe, L., 305
Radclyffe, C.E.M., see Mott-Radclyffe
Radford, E.A., 184, 221
Radford, W.G.W., 9
Radice, E.A., 31
Rae, H.G., 566
Rae, Sir H.N., 508
Raeburn, Sir W.H., 591
Raffan, P.W., 161, 550, 556
Raffety, F.W., 36, 68, 102, 108, 317
Raikes, H.V.A.M., 173, 306, 340
Raine, Sir W., 241
Rait, R.L., 370
Ramage, C.B., 195, 234
Ramage, J., 108
Ramage, W., 183, 257
Ramsay, A., 257
Ramsay, A.H.M., 608
Ramsay, Hon. S., 594
Ramsay, T.B.W., 571, 598
Ramsbotham, H., 382
Ramsden, A.M., 69, 155
Ramsden, Sir E.J.S.H., 95, 511
Ramsden, G.T., 498
Ramsden, T., 377
Randall, H.E., 376
Randles, Sir J.S., 179
Ranger, J., 145, 334
Rankin, J., 569, 573
Rankin, J.S., 165
Rankin, R., 170
Ransom, S., 206
Raper, A.B., 25
Raper, J.B., 258
Raphael, J.R., 51
Raphael, R.A., 422
Ratcliffe, Alexander, 579
Ratcliffe, Arthur, 446
Ratcliffe, E.B., see Brotherton-Ratcliffe
Ratcliffe, H.B., 93
Rathbone, H.R., 173
Rathbone, J.R., 293
Ravenshaw, J., 191
Raw, Dr. N., 173
Rawlins, P.L.E., 57
Rawlinson, Rt. Hon. J.F.P., 627
Rawson, Sir A.C., 97
Rawson, B., 227
Ray, Rev. A., 444
Ray, E.P., 83
Ray, H.W., 112
Ray, Sir W., 14, 212
Rayner, R.H., 316
Raynes, W.R., 117
Razzall, L.H., 492
Rea, A.L., 201
Rea, Sir W.R., Bt., 95, 118, 190, 202, 439
Read, J., 401
Reade, A.E.E., 275
Reade, R.St.J., 482
Reakes, G.L., 248
Reckitt, Sir H.J., Bt., 45
Redwood, V.C., 103
Reece, F.B., 533
Reed, A.C., 127

Reed, Sir H.S., 278, 486
Reed, P., 204, 293
Rees, D., 539
Rees, F.J., 529
Rees, Sir J.D., 199
Rees, J.T.T., 310
Rees, Sir W.B., 101, 444
Rees, W.D., 522
Rees-Williams, D.R., 113
Reeves, J., 17, 61
Reeves, S., 390
Reeves, W.O., 34
Regan, W., 605
Reid, A.S.C., see Cunningham-Reid
Reid, D.D., 624
Reid, J., 186
Reid, Rt. Hon. J.S.C., 565, 579
Reid, T., 290, 481
Reid, Sir William, 586
Reid, William (1), 566, 591
Reid, William (2), 560
Reid, W.A., 117
Reiss, R.L., 43, 210, 333
Reith, Rt. Hon. Sir J.C.W., 232
Remer, J.R., 289
Remnant, C.W.E., 57
Remnant, Sir J.F., Bt., 24
Rendall, A., 345
Renton, A.F.G., 157, 196
Renton, D.L-M., 360
Rentoul, Sir G., 451
Renwick, Sir G., Bt., 192
Renwick, G.A., 389
Rew, Sir R.H., 432
Rewcastle, C.S., 227, 420
Reynolds, E.E., 397
Reynolds, Sir J.F.R., Bt., 90
Reynolds, Sir J.P., Bt., 168
Reynolds, J.W., 497
Reynolds, W.G.W., 159
Rhodes, D., 500
Rhodes, H., 64, 388
Rhodes, J.A., 494
Rhodes, J.P., 291
Rhymer, E.T., 126
Rhys, Hon. C.A.U., 26, 338, 460
Rhys, D., 530
Rhys, Hon. D.R., 347
Rhys, H.T., 413
Rhys, T.A., 513
Rhys Williams, Sir R., Bt., 431, 539
Rice, Sir F.G., 335
Richards, Rev. D., 631
Richards, R., 531
Richards, Rt. Hon. T., 543
Richardson, Sir Alexander, 369
Richardson, Arthur, 201, 396
Richardson, A.H.H., 10
Richardson, H.B., 477
Richardson, James, 489
Richardson, John, 551
Richardson, Prof. J.H., 628
Richardson, J.J., 115
Richardson, Sir P.W., 456
Richardson, R., 327
Richardson, T., 393
Richardson, T.A., 241

Rickards, G.W., 500
Rickett, Rt. Hon. Sir J.C., see Compton-Rickett
Riddiough, H., 509
Ridge-Beedle, P.D., 560, 599
Ridgway, W., 412, 456
Ridley, G., 304
Ridsdale, H.A.C., 194
Riley, B., 118
Riley, F.F., 159, 237, 272
Riley, J.A.L., 630
Riley, T., 447
Risdon, W., 319
Ritchie, A.L., 561
Ritson, John, 189
Ritson, Joshua, 326
Rivers, G.H.L.F.P., see Pitt-Rivers
Roach, R.B.K., 431
Robens, A., 425
Roberts, A.O., 165, 170, 531
Roberts, A.R.N., 36
Roberts, C., 612
Roberts, C.D., 243
Roberts, C.H., 117, 164, 198, 417
Roberts, E.H.G., 532
Roberts, E.O., 540
Roberts, Rt. Hon. F.O., 257
Roberts, G.D., 127, 262
Roberts, Rt. Hon. George Henry, 197
Roberts, George Henry, 268
Roberts, G.O., 526
Roberts, G.P.H., see Hardy-Roberts
Roberts, H., 79
Roberts, J.C., 294
Roberts, J.J., 540
Roberts, O.L., 262
Roberts, P.G., 226
Roberts, R.C., 531
Roberts, R.O., 524
Roberts, Rt. Hon. Sir Samuel, Bt., 226
Roberts, Sir Samuel, Bt., 226, 352
Roberts, W.H.W., 298
Roberts, W.R., 478
Robertson, D., 57
Robertson, F.J., 553, 563, 571, 589
Robertson, J., 599
Robertson, J.A.St.G.F.D., see Despencer-Robertson
Robertson, J.J., 588
Robertson, Rt. Hon. J.M., 249, 409
Robertson, Rt. Hon. Sir M.A., 188, 461
Robertson, T.A., 22, 278, 407, 611
Robertson, T.G., 561
Robertson, W., 586
Robins, S.J., 205, 545
Robins, T., 320
Robins, W.R., 342, 478
Robinson, E., 508
Robinson, Dr. J., 185, 389
Robinson, J.C.H., 236
Robinson, J.R., 87, 89, 392
Robinson, K., 42
Robinson, R.D., 401
Robinson, S., 525
Robinson, Sir S.W., 252, 332, 334, 340
Robinson, Sir T., 389
Robinson, W.A., 168, 173, 175, 219, 508
Robinson, W.C., 64, 202, 498

Robinson, W.E., 238
Robson, Hon. H.B., 235, 423
Robson, N., 500
Rocke, W.L., 481
Rodd, Rt. Hon. Sir J.R., 41
Roderick, E.J., 517
Rodger, A.K., 605
Rodocanachi, E.M., 469
Rodwell, C.H., 49
Roebuck, F., 510
Rogers, G.H.R., 29, 212
Rogers, G.V., 115
Rogers, Sir H., 82
Rogers, L.V., 328
Rogers, W.J., 419
Rogerson, J.E., 321
Romeril, H.G., 2, 43
Romilly, E.C., 352
Roome, H.D., 42, 211
Ropner, L., 330, 494
Rosbotham, Sir S.T., 387
Rose, F.H., 548
Rose, T.F.D., 163
Ross, D.A., 41
Ross, J.J.A.N., 497
Ross, Sir R.D., Bt., 329, 626
Ross, William (1), 420
Ross, William (2), 550, 585
Ross, W.C., 185, 382
Ross Taylor, W., 452
Rothschild, J.A.E. de, 361
Rothschild, L.N. de, 278
Rothwell, C., 377, 393
Rothwell, J., 220
Rothwell, T.S., 305
Round, J.H., 347
Roundell, R.F., 509
Routledge, G.A., 333
Rowbotham, W.B., 117
Rowe, F.A.P., 172, 294, 308
Rowe, G.J., 235
Rowland-Entwistle, A., 238
Rowlands, G., 521, 532, 534, 545
Rowlands, J., 366
Rowlandson, T., 262
Rowntree, A.S., 271
Rowntree, H.D., 492
Rowntree, J.W., 492
Rowse, A.L., 296
Rowsell, P.F., 316
Rowson, G., 378
Roxburgh, R., 566
Roxburgh, W., 563
Royce, W.S., 397
Royden, Sir T., Bt., 91
Royds, E., 398
Royds, P.M.R., 151
Royle, Charles (1), 236
Royle, Charles (2), 222, 382
Rubin, H., 254
Rudd, E., 378
Rudkin, C.M.C., 209, 467
Ruggles-Brise, Sir E.A., Bt., 337
Rumsey, F.A., 13
Runciman, Rt. Hon. W., 97, 118, 297, 423, 523, 556
Rush, G.E., 385

Rushton, J., 104, 509
Russell, A., 575
Russell, Sir A.W., 246
Russell, Hon. B.A.W., 11
Russell, F., 35
Russell, H.F., 224, 226
Russell, R., 276
Russell, R.J., 287
Russell, R.S., 571, 600
Russell, S.H.M., 377
Russell, W., 90
Russell-Wells, Sir S., 629
Rust, W., 20
Ruston, J.G.C., 460
Rutherford, Sir J., Bt., 377
Rutherford, Sir J.H., Bt., 166
Rutherford, James R., 548, 585
Rutherford, John R. (formerly Chalmers), 126
Rutherford, Dr. V.H., 241, 322
Rutherford, Sir W.W., 166
Ryan, H.F., 378, 381
Rycroft, F.W.R., 220
Rye, F.G., 395
Ryle, Prof. J.A., 627

S

Sadler, J.R., 420
Sadler, S.A., 187
Sainsbury, A.J., 454
Saklatvala, S., 1, 571
Salmon, Sir I., 408
Salt, Sir E.W., 85
Salter, Dr. A., 4
Salter, F.R., 106
Salter, G., 266
Salter, Rt. Hon. Sir J.A., 630
Samson, G., 483
Samuel, A.L., see Lyle-Samuel
Samuel, Sir A.M., Bt., 459
Samuel, Rt. Hon. Sir H.L., 377, 490
Samuel, Rt. Hon. Sir H.S., 34
Samuel, H.W., 523
Samuel, M.R.A., 47, 56
Samuel, Samuel, 56
Samuel, Sigmund, 264, 447
Samuel, W.I., 517, 537
Samuels, H., 226
Samuels, M.T., see Turner-Samuels
Samuelson, R.E.H., 307
Samways, H., 315
Sandelson, B.M., 152
Sandeman, Sir A.N.S., Bt., see Stewart-Sandeman
Sanders, C.F., 514
Sanders, C.J.O., 50
Sanders, Rt. Hon. Sir R.A., Bt., 437, 440
Sanders, R.M-D., 422
Sanders, W.S., 1
Sanderson, Sir F.B., Bt., 120, 121, 377
Sanderson, J.R., 402
Sandham, E., 170, 375
Sandilands, G.S., 11, 408
Sandison, G.R., 233
Sandon, Viscount, 435
Sandys, Rt. Hon. E.D., 34
Sanger, S., 441
Sara, H.T.W., 244

Sargant, N.T.C., 26
Sargant, T., 208, 350
Sargood, R., 4
Sassoon, Rt. Hon. Sir P.A.G.D., Bt., 142
Savery, S.S., 488
Savill, C.J.F., 331
Saville, G.S., 401
Savory, Prof. D.L., 633
Sawyer, E.E., 38
Sawyer, G.F., 76
Sayer, J.C., 103
Scardifield, F., 315
Scholefield, J., 499, 503
Schultz, J.L., 488
Schuster, Sir G.E., 250
Scobell, W.B., 68
Scollan, T., 614
Scone, Lord, 604, 612
Scott, A.H., 14, 115, 260
Scott, A.M., 559, 568
Scott, D., 246
Scott, E., 194
Scott, E.K., 155
Scott, J., 582, 609, 614
Scott, J.D., 599
Scott, J.H.M., 153
Scott, Sir L.F., 168
Scott, M.S., see Stoddart-Scott
Scott, P.M., 255
Scott, R.D., 425
Scott, Sir S.E., Bt., 41
Scott, T.M., 383
Scott, Lord William, 615
Scott, William (1), 594
Scott, William (2), 328
Scott, W.T., 448
Scott-Cowell, J., 135
Scott-Elliot, W.T., 62
Scott-Stokes, H.F., 441
Scovell, G.J.S., 427
Scriven, C.R., 4
Scrymgeour, E., 552
Scrymgeour-Wedderburn, H.J., 575, 614
Scurr, J., 50, 279
Scutts, L., 356
Seager, Sir W.H., 515
Seamark, W.S., 196
Sears, J.E., 44
Searson, C.W., 46
Seaton, A., 539
Seaverns, J.H., 401
Seddon, J.A., 239
Sedgwick, F.H., 51
Seely, Hon. A.P.W., 199
Seely, Sir C.H., Bt., 427
Seely, Sir H.M., Bt., 30, 414, 423
Seely, Rt. Hon. J.E.B., 306, 362
Seely, V.B.J., 503
Segal, Dr. S., 74, 210, 246
Selby-Bigge, Sir L.A., Bt., 628
Self, H.L., 450
Sellars, B.C., 180
Sellers, F.A., 137, 390
Selley, E., 356
Selley, H.R., 2
Sells, A., 272, 399
Sessions, W.H., 493, 498

Seuffert, S., 464
Sexton, Sir J., 219
Sexton, T.M., 321
Shackleton, E.A.A., 92, 210, 458
Shackleton, R., 86
Shackleton, W.H., 194
Shadforth, W., 5
Shakesby, A.E., 150
Shakespeare, Rt. Hon. Sir G.H., Bt., 197, 422
Shann, G., 85
Sharkey, F.R., 77
Sharman, A.W., 429
Sharman, H.J., 294
Sharp, G.G., 334
Sharp, G.M., 511
Sharp, H., 180
Shattock, B.A., 1
Shaw, Albert, 191
Shaw, Hon. Alexander, 585
Shaw, A.D.M., 559, 572, 578, 614
Shaw, F., 574
Shaw, G.R.D., 510
Shaw, Rev. J.A., 267
Shaw, Dr. J.V., 306
Shaw, O.L., 371
Shaw, P.S., 173
Shaw, R., 14
Shaw, S., 609
Shaw, Rt. Hon. T., 210
Shaw, W.T., 594
Shaw, W.W., 327, 482
Shawcross, C.N., 392
Shawcross, H.W., 219
Shawcross, M.R., 490
Shearer, E.W., 278
Shearman, H.C., 362
Shee, Sir M.A., see Archer-Shee
Sheehan, D.D., 49
Sheffield, Sir B.D.G., Bt., 400
Sheilds, W.F.W., see Wentworth-Sheilds
Shelford, C.W., 444
Shenfield, A.A., 77
Shephard, S., 429
Shepherd, A.L., 115
Shepherd, W.G., 42
Shepherd, W.S., 284
Sheppard, J.T., 28, 61
Sheppard, M., 224
Sheppard, R.P., 479
Shepperson, Sir E.W., 353
Sherman, S., 411
Sherrott, J.C., 44
Sherwood, G.H., 247
Sherwood, W.J., 115, 135
Sherwood-Kelly, J., 304
Shield, G.W., 424, 425
Shields, N.S., 42
Shiels, Dr. T.D., 555
Shillaker, J.F., 404
Shingfield, W.J., 454
Shinwell, E., 329, 606
Shinwell, M., 584
Shipwright, D.E.B.K., 296
Shoesmith, F., 570
Sholl, W.J., 408
Short, A., 254, 496
Shortt, C.S., 189

Shortt, Rt. Hon. E., 195
Shrapnell-Smith, E.S., 60
Shurmer, P.L.E., 83
Shute, Sir J.J., 168
Shuttleworth, J.W.W., 118
Sidebottom, R., 434
Sidebottom, S.R., 428
Sidney, W.P., 11
Sievier, R.S., 45
Silkin, L., 10, 52, 54
Silverman, J., 78, 82
Silverman, S.S., 168, 190
Simcock, W.I., 449
Simcox, A.H.A., 230
Simm, M.T., 249
Simmonds, Sir O.E., 76
Simmons, C.J., 78, 84
Simmons, E.B., 466
Simms, Very Rev. J.M., 624
Simon, Sir E.D., 185, 296, 552, 628
Simon, Rt. Hon. Sir J.A., 251, 511
Simpson, F.B., 64
Simpson, F.R., 323
Simpson, J.H., 439
Simpson, J.W., 33
Simpson, R.L.G., 254
Simpson, Dr. R.W., 194
Simpson-Hinchliffe, W.A., 510
Sims, J.H.L., 364
Sinclair, Rt. Hon. Sir A.H.M., Bt., 589
Sinclair, H.M., 598
Sinclair, T., 633
Sinclair, W.A., 555
Singleton, J.E., 382
Sinkinson, G., 588
Sitch, C.H., 445
Sitwell, F.O.S., 492
Sixsmith, Dr. C.F.G., 536
Skeffington, A.M., 36, 57
Skeffington-Lodge, T.C., 272
Skelsey, F.W., 118
Skelton, A.N., 612, 632
Skelton, J.O.M., 100, 101
Skelton, S., 172
Skinnard, F.W., 133
Skinner, J.A., 55, 409
Skinner, J.E., 373
Slack, G.G., 245
Slack, T., 471
Slaney, P.P.K., see Kenyon-Slaney
Slater, J., 463
Slater, T.I., 421
Sleigh, H., 554
Slesser, Sir H.H., 152, 156
Sloan, A., 584, 586
Small, G.L.R., 127, 250
Small, R., 412
Smallwood, E., 25, 124
Smethurst, S., 202
Smiles, Sir W.D., 86, 624
Smillie, R., 189
Smith, Albert, 190
Smith, Alfred, 163, 241, 317
Smith, Arthur, 500
Smith, Sir A.M., 113, 568
Smith, A.V., 452
Smith, Dr. A.W.L., 80

Smith, Rt. Hon. Sir Benjamin, 3
Smith, Sir Bracewell, 7
Smith, Brian, 416
Smith, Dr. C.A., 7, 349
Smith, C.G.P., 333
Smith, D.C.W., see Walker-Smith
Smith, D.N., 463
Smith, E., 240
Smith, E.E.D., see Dorman-Smith
Smith, E.P., 363
Smith, E.S.S., see Shrapnell-Smith
Smith, F., 53, 84, 471
Smith, Rt. Hon. Sir F.E., Bt., 174
Smith, Sir Harold, 173, 253
Smith, Harold, 299, 374
Smith, Harry, 23
Smith, Rt. Hon. H.B.L., see Lees-Smith
Smith, H.M., 117
Smith, H.N., 200, 368
Smith, James, 192
Smith, John, 267
Smith, Joseph, 152
Smith, Sir J.W., see Walker-Smith
Smith, L., 419, 440, 448
Smith, L.W., 227
Smith, Sir M., 610
Smith, P., 178
Smith, P.G., 502
Smith, P.J.L., 610
Smith, Rennie, 502
Smith, Robert, 584
Smith, R.A.A., see Alec-Smith
Smith, R.D., 172
Smith, R.F., 119
Smith, R.H.D., see Dorman-Smith
Smith, Sir R.W., 580
Smith, S.H., 150
Smith, S.W., 495
Smith, T., 501, 503
Smith, T.M.H.K., see Kincaid-Smith
Smith, Ward, 70
Smith, William, 451
Smith, W.C., 456, 560, 567
Smith, W.P., see Parnell-Smith
Smith, Walter R., 197, 422
Smith, Prof. William R., 632
Smith-Carington, N.W., 399
Smithers, A.W., 365
Smithers, Sir W., 365, 372
Smithson, F., 494
Smuts, J.C., 504
Smyth, J.G., 54
Snadden, W.M., 611
Snelgrove, E., 227
Snelgrove, E.C., 224
Snell, H., 60, 141
Snook, C.E., 397
Snow, J.W., 207
Snowball, N.M., 412
Snowden, J.S., 94
Snowden, Rt. Hon. P., 86, 495
Snowden, T., 62, 225, 508, 509
Soames, A.G., 450
Solley, L.J., 341
Solomon, A.J., 368
Solomon, H.J., 243
Solomon, R.B., 50

Somerset, R.H.E.H., 78
Somerset, T., 619
Somervell, Rt. Hon. Sir D.B., 286
Somervell, W.H., 500
Somerville, A.A., 277, 629
Somerville, D.G., 67, 263
Soper, R.J., 66
Sorensen, Rev. R.W., 163, 232, 451
Sorley, Prof. W.R., 627
Soskice, F., 71
Sotheron-Estcourt, T.E., 503
Southby, Sir A.R.J., Bt., 458
Southern, F.W., 502
Sparkes, H.W.S., 312, 314
Sparks, J.A., 279, 332, 404, 439
Sparrow, A.H., see Hanbury-Sparrow
Sparrow, G.M., 126
Spearing, T.A.E., 136
Spearman, A.C.M., 180, 428, 492
Spears, Sir E.L., 107, 393, 395
Spedding, Rev. R.K., 90
Speir, R.M., 606
Spence, B.H.H.N., see Neven-Spence
Spence, E., 321
Spence, H.R., 580
Spence, J.L.T.C., 607
Spence, R., 588, 613
Spencer, C.G., see Gordon-Spencer
Spencer, G., 350
Spencer, G.A., 427
Spencer, H.H., 96
Spencer, I., 573
Spencer, M., 92, 215
Spencer, R.A., 219
Spender, E.H., 68
Spender-Clay, Rt. Hon. H.H., 374
Spens, W.P., 44, 363
Spero, Dr. G.E., 16, 52, 160
Spero, L., 55, 452
Spicer, L.D., 30, 252
Spires, F., 83
Spofforth, W.A., 187
Spon, J.S., 29
Spoor, B.C., 322
Spranger, F.J.G., 232
Spreull, J.M., 99
Springman, P.E., 427
Sprot, Sir A., Bt., 592, 604
Spurr, J.C., 156
Squire, J.C., 405, 627
Squire, W.J., 48
Stainer, F., 349
Stamford, T.W., 157
Stamp, A.R., 236, 351
Stancomb, Dr. E.H.M., 232
Stanfield, C., 518
Stanford, C.T., see Thomas-Stanford
Stanford, E., 46, 469
Stanier, Sir B., Bt., 433
Stanley, Rt. Hon. Lord, 379
Stanley, Rt. Hon. Sir A.H., 64
Stanley, Hon. Sir A.L., 288
Stanley, Hon. G.F., 210, 263
Stanley, H., 564
Stanley, Rt. Hon. O.F.G., 102, 166, 477
Stanley, S.H., 32
Stanley, Hon. V.A., 87

Cranufluld, J.W., 103
Stanton, A.W., 129, 344, 478
Stanton, C.B., 517
Stanton, W.T., 471
Stark, A., 148
Starkey, J.R., 429
Starmer, Sir C.W., 330, 490
Starr, M., 265
Staub, M.K., 51
Steel, S.S., 363
Steel, W.L., 5, 449
Steel-Maitland, Rt. Hon. Sir A.H.D.R., Bt., 78, 475
Steele, J.F., 90
Steele, T., 602
Steer, W.B., 119, 251
Stein, L.J., 4, 29, 367
Stennett, S., 281
Stephen, Rev. C., 518, 550, 560
Stephen, P.C., 584
Stephens, Sir A., 528
Stephens, A.L.N., 82
Stephens, R., 148
Stephens, S., 205
Stephens, Sir W., 222
Stephenson, H.K., 229
Stephenson, H.M., 176
Stephenson, T., 300
Stevens, G.P., 229
Stevens, M., 125
Stevenson, A.M.S., 337
Stevenson, Sir D.M., Bt., 568
Stevenson, James (1), 471
Stevenson, James (2), 560
Stevenson, John, 405, 415
Stevenson, J.T., 413
Stevenson, Dr. R.S., 593, 632
Stevenson, W.E., 571
Steward, W.A., 46
Stewart, Earl Castle, see Castle Stewart
Stewart, A., 616
Stewart, D., 153
Stewart, G., 292
Stewart, J., 570
Stewart, J.F., 625
Stewart, J.H., see Henderson-Stewart
Stewart, J.M., 452
Stewart, P.D., 56
Stewart, R., 534, 552
Stewart, R.M.M., 15, 36
Stewart, R.S., 237, 301
Stewart, Rev. W.D., 611
Stewart, William John, 620
Stewart, William Joseph, 327
Stewart-Sandeman, Sir A.N., Bt., 384
Stirling, A., 611
Stockdale, J.H., 254
Stocker, E.J., 317
Stocks, Prof. J.L., 630
Stockton, Sir E.F., 179
Stoddart-Scott, M., 504
Stoker, R.B., 184
Stokes, H.F.S., see Scott-Stokes
Stokes, R.R., 146, 562
Stone, G., 152, 193, 308
Stone, J.G., 407
Stones, J., 378

Stonestreet, W., 244
Stooke-Vaughan, J.S., 24
Storey, L.H., 173
Storey, S., 241
Stott, G.G., 558, 580
Stott, J., 380
Stott, T., 182
Stott, W.H., 71, 72
Stourton, Hon. J.J., 221
Strachey, E.J.St.L., 74, 552
Strain, J., 613
Stranger, I.H., 276
Strangman, Sir T.J., 267, 286
Stratton-Hallett, C.S., 438
Strauss, A., 37
Strauss, E.A., 47
Strauss, G.R., 33
Strauss, H.G., 197, 628
Streatfeild, S.R., 326, 595
Strickland, Sir G., 382
Strickland, W.F., 109, 111
Stringer, C.H., 507
Strong, H.V., 363
Strong, Prof. J., 628
Stross, Dr. B., 239
Strutt, G.St.J., 335
Stuart, Lord Colum Crichton, see Crichton-Stuart
Stuart, Rt. Hon. J., 609
Stuart-Bunning, G.H., 325
Stubbs, A.E., 282, 396
Studholme, H.G., 313
Sturrock, J.L., 243, 577
Styles, H.W., 373
Suenson-Taylor, A.J., 308, 346, 370
Sueter, Sir M.F., 356
Sugden, Sir W.H., 26, 135, 163, 183, 217, 388
Suggett, G.B., 276
Suirdale, Viscount, 421
Sullivan, J., 599, 604
Summers, G.S., 196
Summersby, C.H., 45
Summerskill, Dr. W.H., 53
Sunderland, J.W., 210
Sunley, B., 122
Sunley, T., 493
Sunlight, J., 435
Surtees, H.C., 128, 331
Sutcliffe, H., 388
Sutcliffe, J.H., 169
Sutcliffe, T., 131
Sutherland, H., 236
Sutherland, Dr. H.G., 632
Sutherland, Rt. Hon. Sir W., 66, 583
Sutton, A.S.E., see Elwell-Sutton
Sutton, E.F.M., 184
Sutton, J.E., 178
Swaffield, G., 43
Swain, A.B., 356
Swan, H.D., 197
Swan, J.E., 321
Swietochowski, Dr. G. de P., 37
Swift, B.R., 484
Swift, R.P.W., 219
Swingler, S.T., 448
Sykes, Sir A.J., Bt., 288
Sykes, Sir C., Bt., 141
Sykes, F., 132

Sykes, Rt. Hon. Sir F.H., 198, 227
Sykes, Sir M., Bt., 147
Sylvester, G.O., 501
Symonds, A.L., 106
Syrett, P.M., 15

T

Tagg, C.W., 10
Tait, F., 299
Talbot, A., 88
Talbot, B.C., see Chetwynd-Talbot
Talbot, Rt. Hon. Lord Edmund, 467
Talbot, G.A., 355
Tanner, E.W., 337, 454
Tanner, H.D., 233
Tapp, A.W., 215
Tapsell, W.T.L., 49
Tarachand, Dr. N.M., 428
Tasker, Sir R.I., 5, 24, 25
Tatham, C.K., 191
Tattersall, J.L., 291
Tawney, R.H., 213, 244, 481
Tayler, J.A., 357
Taylor, Albert, 226
Taylor, Arthur, 435
Taylor, Austin, 487
Taylor, A.J.S., see Suenson-Taylor
Taylor, A.T., 614
Taylor, A.T.W., see Waters-Taylor
Taylor, C.E.P., 408
Taylor, C.J., 184
Taylor, Dr. C.R.C., see Cooke-Taylor
Taylor, C.S., 463
Taylor, E.A., 14, 38, 60
Taylor, E.G., 445
Taylor, E.M., 28
Taylor, F.K., 369
Taylor, H.A., 496
Taylor, Harry B., 428
Taylor, Herbert B., 224
Taylor, John (1), 551
Taylor, John (2), 568, 578, 605
Taylor, J.J., 98
Taylor, J.P., 90
Taylor, J.W., 324
Taylor, R.A., 164
Taylor, R.J., 189
Taylor, Dr. S.J.L., 354
Taylor, T., 554, 564
Taylor, W., 195, 375
Taylor, W.B., 414, 418
Taylor, W.J., 94
Taylor, Dr. W.O.G., 561
Taylor, W. Ross, see Ross Taylor
Tee, C.E., 427
Teeling, L.W.B., 97, 259
Teff, S., 50
Temple, C.G.W., see Wodehouse-Temple
Temple, F.G., 278
Temple, F.W., 405, 410
Temple, H.J., 218
Temple, W., 193
Templeton, W.P., 571, 587, 600
Tennant, Rt. Hon. H.J., 562, 588
Tennant, J.E., 609
Terrell, E., 33, 47, 359

Terrell, G., 223, 470
Terrell, R., 432
Terrett, J.J., 213, 236
Terry, E., 152
Tetley, G.S., 10
Tett, H.L., 542
Tevenan, P.J., 166
Thickett, J., 250
Thirlestane and Boltoun, Lord, 232
Thom, J.G., 591
Thomas, A.L.U., see Ungoed-Thomas
Thomas, B.P., 519
Thomas, C.E.T., 88
Thomas, D.E., 517
Thomas, D.R., 518
Thomas, D.W., 319
Thomas, G.B., 547
Thomas, G.C., 209
Thomas, I., 500, 511
Thomas, I.O., 436
Thomas, J.A., see Aeron-Thomas
Thomas, Rt. Hon. J.H., 117
Thomas, J.P.L., 352, 529
Thomas, J.R., 367
Thomas, L.B., see Beaumont-Thomas
Thomas, L.M., 446
Thomas, L.P., 615
Thomas, Sir O., 524
Thomas, P.H., 55
Thomas, Sir R.J., Bt., 524, 531
Thomas, T.G., 514
Thomas, W.D., 520
Thomas, Dr. W.S.R., 143, 232, 580, 597
Thomas-Stanford, C., 97
Thompson, E.C.M., see Meysey-Thompson
Thompson, G., 377
Thompson, G.H., 153
Thompson, H., 322
Thompson, J., 193
Thompson, J.W.H., 143, 440
Thompson, K.F., 373
Thompson, L., 241
Thompson, P.G., 315
Thompson, S.J., 266
Thomson, C.B., 98, 358
Thomson, D.C., 264, 557, 576, 632
Thomson, Sir F.C., Bt., 549
Thomson, Rt. Hon. G.R., 555
Thomson, J.A.C., 615
Thomson, Sir J.D.W., Bt., 549
Thomson, J.F.G., 579
Thomson, J.G., 558
Thomson, J.L., 212, 365
Thomson, R.J., 194
Thomson, R.W., 38
Thomson, W., 140
Thomson, Rt. Hon. Sir W.M., Bt., see
  Mitchell-Thomson
Thomson, W.T., 187
Thoresby, F., 211, 443
Thornborough, F.C., 148, 184, 189, 304, 481
Thorne, G.R., 267
Thorne, W.J., 258
Thorneycroft, G.E.P., 448, 544
Thorneycroft, H., 87, 178
Thorneycroft, W., 444
Thornley, E.J., 207

Thornton, M.R., 313
Thornton-Kemsley, C.N., 582
Thorp, L.T., 190, 459
Thorp, R.A.F., 423
Thorpe, F., 495
Thorpe, J.H., 184
Thorpe, T.E., 178
Thruston, E.H., 441
Thurtle, E., 6, 45
Thwaites, N.G., 228
Thyne, R.C., 555
Tibbles, H.M., 42
Tickler, T.G., 131
Tiffany, S., 421
Tillett, B., 220
Tillett, N.R., 414
Tillotson, J.C., 74
Tily, W.J.W., 322
Timmons, J., 599
Tinker, C., 141
Tinker, J.J., 161
Tinne, J.A., 173
Tiptaft, N., 79
Titchfield, Marquess of, 429
Titler, E.J., 10
Titt, G.F., 390
Titterington, M.F., 96
Todd, A.J.K., 423
Todd, A.L.S., 445
Todd, D.F., 324
Todd, J.W., 211, 459
Todd, W.R., 623
Tolley, L., 485
Tomlinson, A., 478
Tomlinson, G., 378
Tomlinson, R.P., 379, 382
Tompson, G.C., 314
Tones, J.H., 398
Tonge, J., 391
Toole, J., 167, 221, 509
Tooth, Sir H.V.H.D.L., Bt., see Lucas-Tooth
Tootill, R., 90
Tossell, G.L., 237
Touche, G.C., 26, 64, 462
Toulmin, Sir G., 105
Toulmin, J.M., 210
Tout, W.J., 202, 379, 510
Town, B.R.W., 95
Townend, A.E., 107, 177, 236
Townend, W., 155
Townley, M.G., 274, 361
Townroe, B.S., 201
Townsend, C.H., 313
Townsend, E., 509
Townsend, G., 449
Townshend, Sir C.V.F., 436
Toynbee, W.F., 332, 337, 374
Train, J., 561, 605
Travess, R.J., 127
Travis, C.H., 178
Tree, A.R.L.F., 394
Treherne, C.G., 539
Treleaven, S.L., 167, 173
Trench, P.E., 93
Trestrail, A.E.Y., 315
Trevelyan, Rt. Hon. Sir C.P., Bt., 192, 498
Tribe, A.A.W., 467

Tritton, G.E., 432
Tronchin-James, R.N., 211
Trotter, T.A., 355
Trout, E.J., 205
Troward, E.R., 211
Troyte, G.J.A., see Acland-Troyte
Truman, F.C., 164
Truman, S., 308
Trumble, J., 112
Tryon, Rt. Hon. G.C., 97
Tubbs, S.W., 344
Tucker, J.M., 374, 393
Tufnell, N.C., 277
Tufnell, R.L., 106
Turnbull, S.P., 492
Turner, A.E.M., 506
Turner, A.H., 389
Turner, Sir B., 69
Turner, H.F.L., 37
Turner, Rev. J.B., 388
Turner-Samuels, M., 129, 152, 321
Turnor, C.H., 403
Turton, E.R., 493
Turton, R.H., 493
Twells, G., 199
Twist, H., 161
Tyers, C.H., 156
Tyler, F.L., 288
Tyler, T.G., 130
Tyrer, R., 215

U

Underdown, T.H.J., 316
Ungoed-Thomas, A.L., 536
Unsworth, E.I.G., 378
Urquhart, H.F., 289
Usborne, H.C., 73
Usher, H.B., 159
Usmani, S., 43, 511

V

Vachell, B.G.L., see Lampard-Vachell
Vaizey, J.T.D.H., 336
Valentine, Rev. L.E., 526
Van Abbé, D.M., 173
Van den Berg, F.J., 397
Vane, E.D.T., 276
Vane, W.M.F., 477
Vant, W.A., 413
Varley, F.B., 428
Varley, H., 429
Vasey, C.J., 148
Vassie, J.D., 609
Vaughan, D.J., 101, 343
Vaughan, J.J., 6, 183
Vaughan, J.S.S., see Stooke-Vaughan
Vaughan, R., 540
Vaughan-Davies, M.L., 527
Vaughan-Morgan, Sir K.P., 15
Veasey, A.C.T., 362
Veness, G.T., 340
Verney, Sir H.C.W., Bt., 279, 347, 431, 487, 509
Vernon, C., 195
Vernon, W.F., 7
Viant, S.P., 264

Vick, G.R., 135, 322
Vickers, D., 227
Vickers, H.H., 487
Vickery, C.E., 323
Villiers, E.A., 55
Vivian, H.H., 126, 196, 316
Voisey-Youldon, W.J., 569
Vos, P., 390

W

Waddington, E., 330
Waddington, R., 217
Wade, F.R., 506
Wade, G.A., 191
Wade, W.E., 431
Wadsworth, G., 487
Wainwright, F.N., 190
Wakefield, W.A., 231
Wakefield, Sir W.W., 41, 481
Waldron, W.J., 15
Walford, J.E.S., 330
Walkden, A.G., 101, 268, 380
Walkden, E., 217, 496
Walker, A.W., 548
Walker, Sir C.L.F., Bt., see Forestier-Walker
Walker, G.E.O., 585
Walker, G.H., 86, 217
Walker, Harry, 481
Walker, Henry, 167
Walker, H.G., 233
Walker, J., 218, 519, 603
Walker, J.C., 21
Walker, P.C. Gordon, see Gordon Walker
Walker, P.J.F.C., see Chapman-Walker
Walker, R.B., 387, 415
Walker, R.F., 118, 154, 388, 495
Walker, S., 238
Walker, W.H., 392
Walker-Smith, D.C., 356
Walker-Smith, Sir J., 67
Wall, A.M., 57
Wallace, D.E., 140, 472
Wallace, F.L., 581
Wallace, F.W., 552
Wallace, G.D., 365
Wallace, H.R., 586
Wallace, H.W., 105, 251
Wallace, Sir J., 553
Wallace, R.E.H., 87
Wallhead, R.C., 109, 518
Wallington, H.J., 103
Walmsley, J.B., 381
Walsh, Rt. Hon. S., 381
Walston, H.D.L.G., 360
Walters, Rt. Hon. Sir J.T., 224, 296, 504
Walters, S.E., 98, 344
Walton, A., 45
Walton, James, 497
Walton, Sir Joseph, Bt., 66
Walton, R.H., 33
Wandless, W.H., 67
Wansbrough, A.G., 61
Want, J.R., 46
Warbey, W.N., 273
Ward, A.E., 280
Ward, Sir A.L., Bt., 149

Ward, George (1), 200, 402
Ward, George (2), 393
Ward, G.L., 494
Ward, Hon. G.R., 270
Ward, H.J., 124
Ward, J., 240
Ward, J.A., 126
Ward, P.H., 291
Ward, Rt. Hon. W.D., 232
Ward, W.E., 319
Ward, W.G., 202, 477
Ward-Jackson, C.L.A., 353, 408
Warde, J.R., 316
Warde-Aldam, J.R.P., 186, 225
Warde-Aldam, W.St.A., 496
Warder, W.E., 434, 484
Wardlaw-Milne, Sir J.S., 485
Wardle, G.J., 236
Waring, W., 249, 323, 588
Waring, W.J., 440
Warlow, R.E., 307
Warne, G.H., 425
Warner, Sir T.C.T., Bt., 447
Warner, W.W., 274
Warren, Sir A.H., 126
Warren, J.H., 248
Warren, V., 559
Warrender, Sir V.A.G.A., Bt., 398
Warwick, T., 45
Wason, J.C., 610
Waterhouse, Rt. Hon. C., 159, 307
Waters, W.A., 360
Waters-Taylor, A.T., 267
Waterson, A.E., 198, 420
Watkins, F.C., 18, 278
Watkins, H.M., 382, 426
Watkins, T.E., 525
Watkins-Evans, I., 417, 514
Watson, A.A., 56
Watson, Sir F., 504
Watson, G., 175
Watson, H., 247
Watson, J.B., 237
Watson, J.L., 128
Watson, Prof. J.R., 549
Watson, Rt. Hon. W., 107, 595
Watson, W.M., 553
Watson-Armstrong, Hon. W.J.M., 423
Watt, F.C., 554
Watt, G.S.H., see Harvie-Watt
Watt, H.A., 564, 567, 583
Watts, J., 240
Watts, J.A.W., 386
Watts, J.W., 325
Watts, Sir T., 185
Waudby, Rev. F., 425
Wayland, Sir W.A., 364
Weaver, H.E., 362, 457
Webb, D.G., 419
Webb, Sir H., Bt., 343, 515
Webb, J.B., see Baldwin-Webb
Webb, M., 93
Webb, Rt. Hon. S.J., 329, 629
Webb, W.H., 445
Webbe, Sir H., 58
Weber, H.E., 39
Webster, E.R., 172

Wedderburn, H.J.S., see Scrymgeour-Wedderburn
Wedgwood, Rt. Hon. J.C., 191
Wedgwood, J.H., 449
Weeple, J.G., 545
Wegg-Prosser, C.F.H., 38
Weigall, W.E.G.A., 402
Weinberg, J., 304
Weir, A.M., 583
Weir, J.D., 390
Weir, J.M., 602
Weir, L.M., 583, 616
Weir, R.S., 632
Weir, W., 424
Weitzman, D., 52
Welch, J., 558
Welch, P., 545
Wellock, W., 486
Wells, H.G., 629
Wells, P.L., 368
Wells, R.S., 226
Wells, Sir Sydney Richard, Bt., 272
Wells, Sir Sydney Russell, see Russell-Wells
Wells, W.T., 250
Welsh, J., 578
Welsh, J.C., 599, 600, 602
Wentworth-Sheilds, W.F., 240
West, A., 24, 143
West, D.G., 545
West, F.R., 21, 29
West, H., 343
West, W.J., 2, 351, 370
Westcott, J.T., 22
Weston, Sir A.G.H., see Hunter-Weston
Weston, H., 110
Weston, J.W., 477
Weston, W.G., 289
Westwood, Rt. Hon. J.C., 579, 592, 608
Westwood, J.W., 343
Westwood, W., 206, 612
Wetton, E.D., 22
Weymouth, Viscount, 438
Whaite, H.H., 427
Wheater, H., 97
Wheatley, Rt. Hon. J., 571
Wheatley, Rt. Hon. J.T., 555, 559, 584
Wheatley, M.J., 317
Wheeler, H.F., 399
Wheler, G.C.H., 368
Whetham, W.C.D., 627
White, B.S., 80
White, Charles Frederick (Senr.), 309
White, Charles Frederick (Junr.), 239, 309
White, D.A.P., see Price-White
White, F.E., 102, 344
White, G.C., 301
White, Sir G.D.D., Bt., see Dalrymple-White
White, G.R.B., 397
White, Henry (1), 180
White, Henry (2), 307
White, H.A.D., see Dalrymple-White
White, Rt. Hon. H.G., 71
White, J.B., 364
White, J.D., 187, 562, 573
White, R., 425
White, R.C., 323
White, R.C.B., see Brooman-White
White, Sir R.D., Bt., 348

White, T., 175
Whitehead, J., 104
Whitehead, J.A., 361
Whitehouse, E.R., 295
Whitehouse, J.H., 52, 232, 239, 345, 352, 601
Whiteley, E., 185
Whiteley, J.P., 74, 279
Whiteley, Wilfrid, 81, 495
Whiteley, Rt. Hon. William, 323
Whiteley, Hon. W.T., 156
Whiteside, B.N.H., 155, 256
Whitfield, Dr. E.A., 41, 281
Whiting, A., 130, 338, 375
Whitla, Sir W., 633
Whitley, Rt. Hon. J.H., 132
Whitlow, C.H., 440
Whittaker, H., 83
Whittaker, J.E., 380
Whittaker, Rt. Hon. Sir T.P., 511
Whittaker, W., 217
Whittingstall, W.A.F., see Fearnley-Whittingstall
Whitwham, J.O., 430
Whitworth, F., 219
Whybrew, J.S.W., 347
Whyte, J.B., 307
Whyte, W., 561
Wickham, E.T.R., 439
Wickhart, F.A., 25
Widdicombe, D.G., 142
Wigan, J.T., 275
Wigg, G.E.C., 119
Wiggins, W.M., 202
Wignall, J., 343
Wigoder, B.T., 92
Wigzell, R.L., 274
Wilcock, C.A.B., 117
Wild, Sir E.E., 261
Wilde, H., 125
Wildman, L.J., 28
Wiles, Rt. Hon. T., 27, 463
Wilkes, L., 192
Wilkie, A., 552
Wilkie, R.B., 560, 614
Wilkins, W.A., 101
Wilkinson, V.G., 460
Wilkinson, W., 309
Willbery, J., 475
Willcock, C.H., 65
Willey, A.W., 152
Willey, F.T., 241
Willey, Hon. F.V., 96
Willey, O.G., 84, 490, 509
Williams, Aneurin, 325
Williams, Arnold, 510
Williams, A.J., 515
Williams, A.L., 234, 351
Williams, A.M., 295
Williams, A.V., 307
Williams, C., 313, 315
Williams, C. a'B., 342, 459, 484
Williams, C.P., 531
Williams, D., 522
Williams, D.C., 166
Williams, D.H., 535
Williams, D.J., 537
Williams, D.R., 174, 267
Williams, D.R.R., see Rees-Williams

Williams, E.J., 538
Williams, E.L.H., see Howard-Williams
Williams, F.J.W., 524
Williams, G.C., 529
Williams, G.W., 374
Williams, H., 465
Williams, Sir H.G., 113, 211, 254, 628
Williams, H.H., see Heathcote-Williams
Williams, H.L., see Llewelyn-Williams
Williams, I.A., 11
Williams, I.A.J., 310
Williams, Jesse, 76
Williams, John (1), 535
Williams, John (2), 289, 290
Williams, J.A., 365
Williams, J.D., 531
Williams, J.E., 539
Williams, Dr. J.H., 529
Williams, J.L., 566
Williams, J.R.L., see Lort-Williams
Williams, L.G., 530
Williams, M.E.B., see Bransby-Williams
Williams, Penry, 186, 423
Williams, Percy, 270
Williams, P.F., 102, 419
Williams, Sir Robert, Bt., 320
Williams, Robert, 109, 533
Williams, Rowland, 528
Williams, R.C., 544
Williams, Sir R. Rhys, Bt., see Rhys Williams
Williams, R.S.A., 373
Williams, R.W., 262
Williams, Rt. Hon. T., 497
Williams, T.E., 14
Williams, T.J., 522
Williams, Rev. T.R., 106
Williams, T.S.B., 32, 437, 463
Williams, Sir W.E.H., Bt., see Hume-Williams
Williams, W.H., 533, 542
Williams, William Llewellyn, 208
Williams, William Llewelyn, 527
Williams, W.R., 139
Williams, W.T., 22
Williamson, Rt. Hon. Sir A., Bt., 609
Williamson, C.A.W., 468
Williamson, J., 379
Williamson, J.W., 366
Williamson, Thomas (1), 392
Williamson, Thomas (2), 400
Williamson, W.H., 212
Willink, Rt. Hon. H.U., 112, 146
Willis, E.G., 556
Willis, R.C., 234, 382
Willison, H., 75, 471
Willmett, P.J., 370
Willoughby, Hon. C.H-D., 399
Willoughby de Eresby, Lord, 399
Wills, G., 437
Wills, Sir G.A.H., Bt., 441
Wills, W.D., 69
Wilmot, J.C., 13, 15, 32, 35
Wilson, A.S., 488
Wilson, Sir A.T., 357
Wilson, B.P., 507
Wilson, C., 173
Wilson, Cecil H., 223
Wilson, Sir Charles H., 152

Wilson, C.T., 33, 175
Wilson, D., 619
Wilson, F.C., 154
Wilson, Hon. G.G., 149
Wilson, G.H.A., 627
Wilson, H.C.B., 507
Wilson, James, 119, 202, 430
Wilson, John, 498
Wilson, Joseph, 194
Wilson, J.E., 489
Wilson, J.G., 565
Wilson, James H., 387
Wilson, John H., 417
Wilson, Joseph Havelock (Senr.), 235
Wilson, Joseph Havelock (Junr.), 130
Wilson, J.M., 128
Wilson, J.R., 534
Wilson, Rt. Hon. J.W., 486
Wilson, Rt. Hon. L.O., 59, 209, 211
Wilson, M.J., 491
Wilson, Sir M.R.H., Bt., 6
Wilson, R.F., 576
Wilson, R.J., 194, 328
Wilson, Dr. R.M., 339
Wilson, R.R., 447
Wilson, S.E.D., 325
Wilson, S.S., 339
Wilson, W.C., 394
Wilson, W.T., 391
Wilson-Fox, H., 475
Wilton, E.W., 35, 113
Wilton, W.M., 621
Wiltshire, A.W., 319
Wiltshire, F.H., 140
Winby, L.P., 394
Windham, W.G., 36
Windle, J.L., 96
Windsor, Viscount, 433
Windsor, W., 5, 147, 199
Windsor-Clive, G., 433
Winfield, A., 2
Winfrey, Sir R., 401, 418
Winfrey, R.P., 397, 422
Wing, T.E., 131, 327, 331, 366
Wingfield, L.A., 431
Winn, H.J., 489
Winning, J., 566
Winstone, J., 518
Winterton, Rt. Hon. Earl, 468, 469
Winterton, G.E., 395
Winterton, P., 364, 461
Wintle, A.D., 34
Wintringham, T., 403
Wintringham, T.H., 346, 607
Wise, A.R., 230, 334
Wise, E.F., 95, 158
Wise, Sir F., 143
Wise, F.J., 394, 415, 451
Witard, H.E., 197
Withers, Sir J.J., 627
Wodehouse-Temple, C.G., 260
Woffenden, T., 509
Wolff, H.M.C.D., see Drummond-Wolff
Wolmer, Rt. Hon. Viscount, 346
Womersley, Rt. Hon. Sir W.J., 131
Wood, Dr. A., 106, 627
Wood, A.E., 388

Wood, A.F., 338
Wood, B.C., 437
Wood, Hon. C.I.C., see Irwin, Lord
Wood, Rt. Hon. E.F.L., 505
Wood, E.W.H., 291
Wood, Rt. Hon. Sir H.K., 61
Wood, Sir J., Bt., 291
Wood, Sir M.M., 550, 580, 587
Wood, R.A.E., 184
Wood, R.M., 394
Wood, Sir S.H.H., Bt., see Hill-Wood
Wood, Rt. Hon. T.M., 18, 570
Wood, W.W., 136
Woodard, A.N.P., 49
Woodard, M.H., 467
Woodburn, A., 557, 576, 616
Woodcock, G.R., 154
Woodcock, H.B.D., 214
Woodcock, H.C., 167, 345
Woodgate, H.P., 465
Woodhead, E., 141, 228, 504
Woodroffe, M.F., 214
Woods, Rev. G.S., 14, 184, 385, 439, 494
Woods, P.J., 620
Woodwark, G.G., 415
Woolcock, W.J.U., 18
Woolf, A.H., 58
Woolf, L.S., 628
Wooll, E., 147, 219
Woolley, W.E., 511
Wootton-Davies, J.H., 380
Wormald, S., 292, 628
Worrall, J.H., 24, 295
Worrall, T.F., 536
Worsfold, Dr. T.C., 461
Worsnop, L.M., 412, 460
Worsthorne, A.L.W.K., 378
Worth, G.A., 398
Worthington, Sir J.V., 343
Worthington-Evans, Rt. Hon. Sir L., Bt., 59, 333
Woulfe-Brenan, F.G.J., 206
Wragg, H., 302
Wreford-Glanvill, H.W., 314
Wrentmore, J.H., 23
Wright, A.W., 470
Wright, H.F., 117
Wright, H.H., 60
Wright, J.A.C., 78
Wright, J.W., 324
Wright, L.H., 171
Wright, O.W., 302
Wright, P.H.G., 5
Wright, R.A., 115
Wright, R.W., 305
Wright, W., 605
Wright, W.D., 313
Wrightson, H., 163
Wrigley, A., 130
Wyatt, H.F., 153
Wyatt, W.L., 74
Wylie, J.M., 615
Wynne, A.W.E., 523

Y

Yate, Sir C.E., Bt., 396
Yates, H., 472

Yates, J.A., 475
Yates, V.F., 81
Yeaman, F.C., 555
Yeo, Sir A.W., 40, 420
Yerburgh, R.D.T., 319
Yexley, L.J.W., 208
Yonge, J.A., 507
York, C., 505
Youldon, W.J.V., see Voisey-Youldon
Young, Allan, 64, 83
Young, Andrew, 568
Young, A.S.L., 568
Young, D.C.C., 575
Young, E., 21
Young, Rt. Hon. Sir E.H., 197, 373
Young, E.J., 186, 217, 328, 599
Young, E.P., 149
Young, Frank W., 288
Young, Sir Frederick W., 481
Young, G., 281, 417

Young, Sir H.W., 134, 166
Young, J.A., 558
Young, J.B., 600
Young, J.D., 233, 409, 606
Young, J.L., 23
Young, P.R.C., 77
Young, Sir R., 386
Young, R.S., 26
Young, S.A.J., 201
Young, W., 612
Young, W.T., 440
Younger, Sir G., Bt., 550
Younger, G.A., 568
Younger, Hon. K.G., 131

Z

Zilliacus, K., 128
Zimmern, Prof. A.E., 513
Zorn, J.C.L., 35

# SECTION TWO — — — WOMEN

## A

Acland, Lady, 127
Adamson, Mrs. J.L., 70, 366
Alderton, Mrs. C.B., 149, 557
Allen, Miss M.S., 59
Annesley, Lady Clare, 102, 272
Anstey, Mrs. A.J., 34
Apsley, Lady, 98
Archibald, Mrs. D.H., 68
Ashby, Mrs. M.I.C., 81, 212, 355, 359, 409, 453
Astor, Viscountess, 206
Atholl, Duchess of, 611

## B

Bacon, Miss A.M., 154
Balfour, Miss H.C.M., 377
Barlow, Hon. Lady, 305, 306
Barton, Mrs. E., 80, 198
Bayfield, Mrs. B.A., 180
Beaumont, Mrs. G., 507
Beavan, Miss M., 167
Beer, Mrs. N., 176
Bell, Mrs. F.N.H., 273
Bentham, Dr. Ethel, 25
Bentwich, Mrs. H.C., 7, 408
Bevan, Mrs. J., see Lee, Miss J.
Billson, Miss M.G., 112
Blackman, Mrs. A.B., 43
Bliss, Miss B.E.M.S., 107, 464
Bondfield, Rt. Hon. Margaret G., 196, 249
Bonham Carter, Lady Violet, 440
Borrett, Mrs. C.E.M., 344, 374, 441
Bowen-Davies, Mrs. C., 534
Braddock, Mrs. E.M., 168
Brodrick, Hon. Mrs. A.G., 530
Brook, Mrs. I., 276
Brown, Mrs. A.S.G., 33
Brown, Mrs. I., 39, 585, 603
Brown, Mrs. N.S., see Stewart-Brown
Browning, Miss H.A., 55
Buckmaster, Miss H.M.A., 332, 337
Bulley, Miss A.L., 285, 292
Burton, Miss E.F., 135, 138
Buxton, Lady Noel, see Noel-Buxton

## C

Cadbury, Mrs. E.M., 80
Campbell, Miss E., 570
Carter, Lady Violet Bonham, see Bonham Carter
Castle, Mrs. B.A., 86
Cazalet, Miss T., see Cazalet-Keir, Mrs. T.
Cazalet-Keir, Mrs. T. (formerly Cazalet), 25
Chamberlayne, Mrs. R.F., 467
Churchill, Dr. Stella, 19, 405
Clarkson, Mrs. J., 82
Coats, Lady Glen, see Glen-Coats
Colman, Miss G.M., 142, 227, 246
Cooper, Lady, 250
Cooper, Miss N.A., 625
Copeland, Mrs. I., 240

Corbet, Mrs. F.K., 9, 35
Corner, Mrs. A.E., 459
Cowan, Miss M.G., 555, 578
Cowley, Mrs. M., 505
Cox, Miss L.A., see Middleton, Mrs. L.A.
Crawfurd, Mrs. H., 548, 599
Crisp, Miss D., 59, 404
Crosfield, Lady, 26
Cullen, Mrs. A., 563
Currie, Lady, 479

## D

Dalton, Mrs. F.R., 322
Dart, Miss V., 374
Davidson, Viscountess, 355
Davies, Mrs. C.B., see Bowen-Davies
Davies, Mrs. F.R., 311
Davies, Mrs. R.D.Q., 440
Despard, Mrs. C., 1
Dimsdale, Mrs. E., 282
Dollan, Mrs. A.J., 590
Dott, Mrs. M., 555
Dower, Mrs. A.L.G., 512
Drake, Mrs. B., 36
Driver, Miss G.M., 133
Duncan, Mrs. K.S., 17

## E

Eden, Mrs. J., 79
Edmondes, Mrs. D.C., 538
Edwardes, Miss E., 43
Edwards, Miss F., see Kerby, Mrs. F.
Elias, Mrs. E.C., 48
Elst, Mrs. V. Van Der, see Van Der Elst
Emmott, Lady, 202
Evans, Miss D., 38

## F

Folland, Mrs. L., 535
Fox, Mrs. N.D., 212
Fraser, Mrs. B., 57
Fraser, Miss H., 564, 601
Fremantle, Hon. Mrs. A., 59

## G

Ganley, Mrs. C.S., 2, 37
Garland, Miss A.V., 209, 253, 366
Gatty, Mrs. L.M.S., see Scott-Gatty
Gault, Mrs. H.E., 612
Gaved, Miss J.A., 206
Gavin, Dr. Catherine I., 559, 586
George, Lady Megan Lloyd, see Lloyd George
Gibbon, Miss M.M., 20
Glen-Coats, Lady, 578
Goddard, Miss I.G., 136
Gordon, Mrs. M.M.O., 136
Gorsky, Mrs. D.M., 19
Gould, Mrs. B.A., 33, 34, 137, 181, 290
Grant, Miss M.P., 156, 222, 503

Grant of Monymusk, Lady, see Tweedsmuir, Lady
Graves, Miss F.M., 20
Gwynne-Vaughan, Dame Helen, 8

**H**

Hamilton, Mrs. M.A., 86, 214
Hardie, Mrs. A., 572
Henderson, Miss J.M., 354
Henney, Miss W.C., 408
Herbison, Miss M.M., 604
Hilyer, Mrs. C.I., 512
Hitchcock, Mrs. M., 454
Hoffman, Mrs. Z.K., 416
Holland, Miss H.L., 142
Hornabrook, Mrs. B., 75
Horsbrugh, Rt. Hon. Florence, 552
Hulse, Mrs. H., 117

**I**

Iveagh, Countess of, 233

**J**

Jackson, Miss E.B.H., 304
Jacobs, Dr. Elizabeth, 41
Jalland, Miss M.W., 385
Jewson, Miss D., 197
Jones, Miss E.L., 532
Jones, Dr. Gwenan, 631
Jones, Miss M.L.K., 176
Josephy, Miss F.L., 347, 351, 479
Judd, Mrs. H.O., 242

**K**

Keeble, Mrs. I.M.N., 452
Kerby, Mrs. F. (formerly Edwards), 377, 532
Keynes, Miss H.M., 233, 458, 469
Kidd, Miss M.H., 606

**L**

Lakeman, Miss E., 358
Lapthorn, Miss E., 357
Lawrence, Miss A.S., 9, 123, 237
Lawrence, Mrs. E.P.P., see Pethick-Lawrence
Lawson, Lady, 272
Lee, Miss J. (Mrs. Bevan), 98, 444, 604
Lewis, Mrs. B.E., 79
Lloyd George, Lady Megan, 524
Lucas, Mrs. A., 32

**M**

Macarthur, Miss M.R., 486
McCall, Miss C.A.W., 453
MacDonald, Mrs. M.I., 611
McEwan, Mrs. J.L., 406
MacInerney, Mrs. M.A., 86
Mackenzie, Mrs. H.M., 631
Mackinnon, Miss A., 488
Macmillan, Miss C., 556
Mann, Mrs. J., 600, 614
Manning, Mrs. E.L., 25, 241, 334
Marcoursé, Miss I., 24

Markham, Miss V., 428
Marshall, Miss M.E., 230
Martyn, Mrs. E.H., 409
Massingham, Mrs. G.S., 350, 371
Masterman, Mrs. L.B., 480
Maxton, Miss A., 560, 613
Melville, Dr. Frances H., 632
Mercer, Mrs. M.A., 71, 169
Middleton, Mrs. L.A. (formerly Cox), 38, 206, 504
Middleton, Mrs. M.K., 425
Mitchell, Miss E.B., 602, 604
Mitchison, Mrs. N., 632
Mobbs, Miss D.W., 355
Monymusk, Lady Grant of, see Tweedsmuir, Lady
Moody, Mrs. A., 239
Moore, Mrs. R., 97
Morgan, Dr. Elizabeth T., 241, 435
Morgan, Mrs. F.E.G., 127
Mosley, Lady Cynthia, 240
Murray, Miss E.G., 559
Muspratt, Miss N., 373

**N**

Nichol, Mrs. M.E., 95
Nicholson, Miss M., 277
Noel-Buxton, Lady, 197, 416

**O**

O'Conor, Miss M., 362
Osborn, Miss D.F., 466

**P**

Pakenham, Hon. Mrs. E., 108
Paling, Mrs. G.N., 443
Pallister, Miss M., 92
Palmer, Mrs. E., 362
Pankhurst, Miss C., 230
Parnell, Miss N.S., 263
Parsons, Miss R.M., 381
Paton, Mrs. F.B. (formerly Widdowson), 108, 430
Pease, Mrs. M., 457
Penny, Mrs. E.M., 154, 423
Pethick-Lawrence, Mrs. E.P., 184
Philipson, Mrs. M., 423
Phillips, Dr. Marion, 241
Phipps, Miss E.F., 11
Pickford, Hon. Mary A., 21, 378
Picton-Turbervill, Miss E., 26, 344, 436
Pilkington, Miss M.E., 219
Porter, Mrs. M.M., 136
Power, Mrs. M.M., 140
Purser, Mrs. J., 474

**R**

Rackham, Mrs. C.D., 332, 339
Rathbone, Mrs. B.F., see Wright, Mrs. B.F.
Rathbone, Miss E.F., 165, 628
Rhys Williams, Lady, 144, 539
Richardson, Mrs. A.N.S., see Stewart-Richardson
Richardson, Miss M.R., 346, 404
Rickards, Dr. Esther, 37
Ridealgh, Mrs. M., 144

Roberton, Miss V.M.C., 570
Roberts, Miss A.G., 534
Roddick, Miss M.D., 258
Runciman, Mrs. H., 297, 313
Runge, Mrs. N.C., 3
Russell, Hon. Mrs. D.W., 11

S

Sandeman, Dr. Laura S., 548
Sayle, Miss A., 355
Scarborough, Miss F.E., 543
Schilizzi, Miss A.H., 196
Scott-Gatty, Mrs. L.M., 360
Sharpe, Dr. Dorothy A., 11
Shaw, Mrs. C.M., 550, 585
Shaw, Mrs. H.B., 599
Short, Mrs. E.V., 477
Shufeldt, Miss M.D., 11
Simpson, Mrs. L., 320
Smith, Miss R., 428
Spearman, Mrs. D.V.C.E., 40, 147
Spurrell, Miss K.F., 294, 316
Stephen, Miss J., 209, 485
Stewart, Lady, 29
Stewart, Miss E., 556
Stewart-Brown, Mrs. N., 390
Stewart-Richardson, Mrs. A.N., 38
Stocks, Mrs. M.D., 628, 629
Stoneham, Mrs. N.J., 534
Strachey, Mrs. R., 405
Strauss, Mrs. P., 30
Summerskill, Dr. Edith, 16, 56, 105
Swan, Miss A.S., 567
Swinburne, Miss I., 457

T

Tate, Mrs. M.C., 264, 438
Tennant, Mrs. E.E.F., 56, 259
Tennant, Mrs. W.M., 343
Terrington, Lady, 281

Thompson, Mrs. B.J.K., 134
Townsend, Mrs. R., 281
Turbervill, Miss E.P., see Picton-Turbervill
Tweedsmuir, Lady (formerly Lady Grant of
    Monymusk), 548, 549
Tylecote, Dr. Mabel P., 379, 384

V

Van Der Elst, Mrs. V., 46, 56, 336
Vaughan, Dame Helen Gwynne, see Gwynne-
    Vaughan
Vickers, Miss J.H., 40

W

Wadham, Mrs. C.M., 36, 215, 349
Ward, Miss I.M.B., 189, 249
Ward, Mrs. S.A., 444
Warner, Miss P.M., 108
Warwick, Countess of, 476
West, Miss D., 3
Weston, Mrs. E.A., 347
Whately, Miss M.M., 55, 358
Wheeler, Dr. Olive A., 631
White, Mrs. A.B., 409
White, Miss F., 210
Whitehead, Miss M.M., 318
Widdowson, Miss F.B., see Paton, Mrs. F.B.
Wilkinson, Rt. Hon. Ellen C., 64, 186, 328
Williams, Miss H.U., 325
Williams, Miss M.L.G., 539
Williams, Lady Rhys, see Rhys Williams
Williamson, Mrs. C.E., 363, 364
Wills, Mrs. E.A., 76
Wintringham, Mrs. K., 607
Wintringham, Mrs. M., 278, 403
Wood, Miss W., 559
Woodburn, Mrs. B., 557
Woodman, Miss D.V.A., 278, 413
Wright, Mrs. B.F. (formerly Rathbone), 293

# INDEX TO CONSTITUENCIES

This index shows the constituency reference number which is given, following the name of the constituency, at the top of each page. It does *not* refer to the folio number which appears in small type at the foot of each page. The index has been extensively cross-indexed for ease of reference.

The names of borough constituencies are followed, within brackets, by the name of the administrative county in which they are situated. The only exceptions are boroughs which bear the same name as the county and London Boroughs which are already grouped together in the pages of constituency results. This information will allow readers to collate election results on a county basis.

For those who may wish to compare the 1918-1949 constituencies with those of pre-1918 or post-1950, it should be noted that the following counties have changed their names during this century: Angus (formerly Forfarshire), East Lothian (formerly Haddingtonshire), Hampshire (formerly Southamptonshire), Midlothian (formerly Edinburghshire), Moray (formerly Elginshire), West Lothian (formerly Linlithgowshire).

The following county abbreviations have been used:

| | | | |
|---|---|---|---|
| Berks. | Berkshire | Lincs. | Lincolnshire |
| Glam. | Glamorganshire | Middx. | Middlesex |
| Glos. | Gloucestershire | Mon. | Monmouthshire |
| Hants. | Hampshire | Staffs. | Staffordshire |
| Lancs. | Lancashire | Worcs. | Worcestershire |

## A

Abbey, see Westminster
Aberavon, see Glamorganshire
Aberdare, see Merthyr Tydfil
ABERDEEN
  North, 548
  South, 549
Aberdeen University, see Combined Scottish
  Universities
ABERDEENSHIRE and KINCARDINESHIRE
  Central, 580
  Eastern, 581
  Kincardine and Western, 582
Abertillery, see Monmouthshire
Abingdon, see Berkshire
ACCRINGTON (Lancs.), 62
Acock's Green, see Birmingham

Acton, see Middlesex
Aldershot, see Hampshire
Altrincham, see Cheshire
ALTRINCHAM and SALE (Cheshire), 63
ANGLESEY, 524
ANTRIM, 622
Arbroath, see Montrose Burghs
Ardrossan, see Ayr Burghs
Ardwick, see Manchester
ARGYLL, 583
ARMAGH, 623
Ashford, see Kent
ASHTON-UNDER-LYNE (Lancs.), 64
Aston, see Birmingham
Attercliffe, see Sheffield
Aylesbury, see Buckinghamshire

AYR DISTRICT of BURGHS, 550
AYRSHIRE and BUTE
  Bute and Northern, 584
  Kilmarnock, 585
  South Ayrshire, 586

**B**

Balham and Tooting, see Wandsworth
Banbury, see Oxfordshire
BANFFSHIRE, 587
Bangor, see Caernarvon Boroughs
BARKING (Essex), 65
Barkston Ash, see Yorkshire
Barnard Castle, see Durham
Barnet, see Hertfordshire
BARNSLEY (Yorkshire), 66
Barnstaple, see Devon
BARROW-IN-FURNESS (Lancs.), 67
Barry, see Glamorganshire
Basingstoke, see Hampshire
Bassetlaw, see Nottinghamshire
BATH (Somerset), 68
BATLEY and MORLEY (Yorkshire), 69
BATTERSEA
  North, 1
  South, 2
Bedford, see Bedfordshire
BEDFORDSHIRE
  Bedford, 272
  Luton, 273
  Mid, 274
Bedwellty, see Monmouthshire
BELFAST (Antrim)
  East, 618
  North, 619
  South, 620
  West, 621
Belfast University, see Queen's University
Belper, see Derbyshire
BERKSHIRE
  Abingdon, 275
  Newbury, 276
  Windsor, 277
BERMONDSEY
  Rotherhithe, 3
  West, 4
Berwick-upon-Tweed, see Northumberland
BERWICKSHIRE and HADDINGTONSHIRE, 588
BETHNAL GREEN
  North-East, 5
  South-West, 6
Bewdley, see Worcestershire
BEXLEY (Kent), 70
Bilston, see Wolverhampton
BIRKENHEAD (Cheshire)
  East, 71
  West, 72
BIRMINGHAM (Warwickshire)
  Acock's Green, 73
  Aston, 74
  Deritend, 75
  Duddeston, 76
  Edgbaston, 77
  Erdington, 78
  Handsworth, 79
  King's Norton, 80

Ladywood, 81
Moseley, 82
Sparkbrook, 83
West, 84
Yardley, 85
Birmingham University, see Combined English
  Universities
Bishop Auckland, see Durham
BLACKBURN (Lancs.), 86
Blackley, see Manchester
BLACKPOOL (Lancs.), 87
  North, 88
  South, 89
Blaydon, see Durham
Bodmin, see Cornwall
BOLTON (Lancs.), 90
BOOTLE (Lancs.), 91
Boston, see Lincolnshire
Bosworth, see Leicestershire
Bothwell, see Lanarkshire
BOURNEMOUTH (Hants.), 92
Bow and Bromley, see Poplar
BRADFORD (Yorkshire)
  Central, 93
  East, 94
  North, 95
  South, 96
Brechin, see Montrose Burghs
BRECONSHIRE and RADNORSHIRE, 525
Brentford and Chiswick, see Middlesex
Bridgeton, see Glasgow
Bridgwater, see Somerset
Brigg, see Lincolnshire
BRIGHTON (Sussex), 97
Brightside, see Sheffield
BRISTOL (Glos.)
  Central, 98
  East, 99
  North, 100
  South, 101
  West, 102
Bristol University, see Combined English
  Universities
Brixton, see Lambeth
BROMLEY (Kent), 103
Bromley, see Poplar
Broxtowe, see Nottinghamshire
Buckhaven, see Kirkcaldy Burghs
Buckingham, see Buckinghamshire
BUCKINGHAMSHIRE
  Aylesbury, 278
  Buckingham, 279
  Eton and Slough, 280
  Wycombe, 281
Bucklow, see Cheshire
Buckrose, see Yorkshire
BURNLEY (Lancs.), 104
Burntisland, see Kirkcaldy Burghs
Burslem, see Stoke-on-Trent
Burton, see Staffordshire
BURY (Lancs.), 105
Bury St. Edmunds, see Suffolk
Bute, see Ayrshire and Bute

**C**

CAERNARVON DISTRICT of BOROUGHS, 513

CAERNARVONSHIRE, 526
Caerphilly, see Glamorganshire
CAITHNESS and SUTHERLAND, 589
CAMBERWELL
  Dulwich, 7
  North, 8
  North-West, 9
  Peckham, 10
Camborne, see Cornwall
CAMBRIDGE, 106
CAMBRIDGE UNIVERSITY, 627
CAMBRIDGESHIRE, 282
Camlachie, see Glasgow
Cannock, see Staffordshire
Canterbury, see Kent
CARDIFF (Glam.)
  Central, 514
  East, 515
  South, 516
CARDIGANSHIRE, 527
CARLISLE (Cumberland), 107
Carmarthen, see Carmarthenshire
CARMARTHENSHIRE
  Carmarthen, 528
  Llanelly, 529
Carnarvon, see Caernarvon
Carshalton, see Surrey
Cathcart, see Glasgow
Chatham, see Rochester
Cheam, see Sutton and Cheam
Chelmsford, see Essex
CHELSEA, 11
CHELTENHAM (Glos.), 108
Chertsey, see Surrey
CHESHIRE
  Altrincham, 283
  Bucklow, 284
  City of Chester, 285
  Crewe, 286
  Eddisbury, 287
  Knutsford, 288
  Macclesfield, 289
  Northwich, 290
  Stalybridge and Hyde, 291
  Wirral, 292
Chester, see Cheshire
Chesterfield, see Derbyshire
Chester-le-Street, see Durham
Chichester, see Sussex
Chippenham, see Wiltshire
Chislehurst, see Kent
Chiswick, see Middlesex
Chorley, see Lancashire
Christchurch, see Hampshire
Cirencester and Tewkesbury, see Gloucestershire
City of Chester, see Cheshire
CITY of LONDON, 12
Clackmannanshire, see Stirlingshire
  and Clackmannanshire
Clapham, see Wandsworth
Clay Cross, see Derbyshire
Clayton, see Manchester
Cleveland, see Yorkshire
Clitheroe, see Lancashire
Clydebank, see Dumbarton Burghs
Coatbridge, see Lanarkshire
Cockermouth, see Cumberland

Colchester, see Essex
Colne, see Nelson and Colne
Colne Valley, see Yorkshire
COMBINED ENGLISH UNIVERSITIES, 628
COMBINED SCOTTISH UNIVERSITIES, 632
Consett, see Durham
Conway, see Caernarvon Burghs
CORNWALL
  Bodmin, 293
  Camborne, 294
  Northern, 295
  Penryn and Falmouth, 296
  St. Ives, 297
COVENTRY (Warwickshire), 109
  East, 110
  West, 111
Cowdenbeath, see Dunfermline Burghs
Crewe, see Cheshire
Cromarty, see Inverness-shire and Ross and
  Cromarty
CROYDON (Surrey)
  North, 112
  South, 113
CUMBERLAND
  Northern, 298
  Penrith and Cockermouth, 299
  Whitehaven, 300
  Workington, 301

**D**

DAGENHAM (Essex), 114
DARLINGTON (Durham), 115
DARTFORD (Kent), 116
Dartford, see Kent
Darwen, see Lancashire
Daventry, see Northamptonshire
Dean, Forest of, see Gloucestershire
Denbigh, see Denbighshire
DENBIGHSHIRE
  Denbigh, 530
  Wrexham, 531
DEPTFORD, 13
DERBY, 117
DERBYSHIRE
  Belper, 302
  Chesterfield, 303
  Clay Cross, 304
  High Peak, 305
  Ilkeston, 306
  North-Eastern, 307
  Southern, 308
  Western, 309
Deritend, see Birmingham
Devizes, see Wiltshire
DEVON
  Barnstaple, 310
  Honiton, 311
  South Molton, 312
  Tavistock, 313
  Tiverton, 314
  Torquay, 315
  Totnes, 316
Devonport, see Plymouth
DEWSBURY (Yorkshire), 118
Doncaster, see Yorkshire
Don Valley, see Yorkshire

DORSET
  Eastern, 317
  Northern, 318
  Southern, 319
  Western, 320
Dover, see Kent
DOWN, 624
Drake, see Plymouth
Duddeston, see Birmingham
DUDLEY (Worcs.), 119
Dulwich, see Camberwell
DUMBARTON DISTRICT of BURGHS, 551
DUMFRIESSHIRE, 590
DUNBARTONSHIRE, 591
DUNDEE (Forfarshire), 552
DUNFERMLINE DISTRICT of BURGHS (Fife), 553
Durham, see Durham (County)
DURHAM (County)
  Barnard Castle, 321
  Bishop Auckland, 322
  Blaydon, 323
  Chester-le-Street, 324
  Consett, 325
  Durham, 326
  Houghton-le-Spring, 327
  Jarrow, 328
  Seaham, 329
  Sedgefield, 330
  Spennymoor, 331
Durham University, see Combined English Universities
Dysart, see Kirkcaldy Burghs

E

EALING (Middx.), 120
  East, 121
  West, 122
Eastbourne, see Sussex
East Grinstead, see Sussex
EAST HAM (Essex)
  North, 123
  South, 124
East Toxteth, see Liverpool
Ebbw Vale, see Monmouthshire
ECCLES (Lancs.), 125
Ecclesall, see Sheffield
Eddisbury, see Cheshire
Edgbaston, see Birmingham
Edge Hill, see Liverpool
EDINBURGH (Midlothian)
  Central, 554
  East, 555
  North, 556
  South, 557
  West, 558
Edinburgh University, see Combined Scottish
  Universities
EDMONTON (Middx.), 126
Elland, see Yorkshire
Ely, Isle of, see Isle of Ely
Enfield, see Middlesex
English Universities, see Combined English
Epping, see Essex
Epsom, see Surrey
Erdington, see Birmingham
ESSEX
  Chelmsford, 332

Colchester, 333
Epping, 334
Harwich, 335
Hornchurch, 336
Maldon, 337
Romford, 338
Saffron Walden, 339
South-Eastern, 340
Thurrock, 341
Eton and Slough, see Buckinghamshire
Everton, see Liverpool
Evesham, see Worcestershire
Exchange, see Liverpool
Exchange, see Manchester
EXETER (Devon), 127
Eye, see Suffolk

F

Fairfield, see Liverpool
Falkirk, see Stirling and Falkirk Burghs
Falmouth, see Cornwall
Fareham, see Hampshire
Farnham, see Surrey
Farnworth, see Lancashire
Faversham, see Kent
FERMANAGH and TYRONE, 625
FIFE
  Eastern, 592
  Western, 593
Finchley, see Middlesex
FINSBURY, 14
FLINTSHIRE, 532
Forest of Dean, see Gloucestershire
Forfar, see Montrose Burghs
FORFARSHIRE, 594
Frome, see Somerset
FULHAM
  East, 15
  West, 16
Fylde, see Lancashire

G

Gainsborough, see Lincolnshire
GALLOWAY (Kirkcudbrightshire and
  Wigtownshire), 595
GATESHEAD (Durham), 128
Gillingham, see Rochester
GLAMORGANSHIRE
  Aberavon, 533
  Caerphilly, 534
  Gower, 535
  Llandaff and Barry, 536
  Neath, 537
  Ogmore, 538
  Pontypridd, 539
GLASGOW (Lanarkshire)
  Bridgeton, 559
  Camlachie, 560
  Cathcart, 561
  Central, 562
  Gorbals, 563
  Govan, 564
  Hillhead, 565
  Kelvingrove, 566
  Maryhill, 567

GLASGOW (Cont.)
  Partick, 568
  Pollok, 569
  St. Rollox, 570
  Shettleston, 571
  Springburn, 572
  Tradeston, 573
Glasgow University, see Combined Scottish
  Universities
GLOUCESTER, 129
GLOUCESTERSHIRE
  Cirencester and Tewkesbury, 342
  Forest of Dean, 343
  Stroud, 344
  Thornbury, 345
Gorbals, see Glasgow
Gorton, see Manchester
Govan, see Glasgow
Gower, see Glamorganshire
Grangemouth, see Stirling and Falkirk Burghs
Grantham, see Lincolnshire
Gravesend, see Kent
GREAT YARMOUTH (Norfolk), 130
GREENOCK (Renfrewshire), 574
GREENWICH, 17
GRIMSBY (Lincs.), 131
Guildford, see Surrey


                         H


HACKNEY
  Central, 18
  North, 19
  South, 20
Haddingtonshire, see Berwickshire and
  Haddingtonshire
HALIFAX (Yorkshire), 132
Hallam, see Sheffield
Hamilton, see Lanarkshire
HAMMERSMITH
  North, 21
  South, 22
HAMPSHIRE
  Aldershot, 346
  Basingstoke, 347
  Fareham, 348
  New Forest and Christchurch, 349
  Petersfield, 350
  Winchester, 351
HAMPSTEAD, 23
Handsworth, see Birmingham
Hanley, see Stoke-on-Trent
Harborough, see Leicestershire
HARROW (Middx.)
  East, 133
  West, 134
Harrow, see Middlesex
HARTLEPOOLS, THE (Durham), 135
Harwich, see Essex
HASTINGS (Sussex), 136
Hemel Hempstead, see Hertfordshire
Hemsworth, see Yorkshire
HENDON (Middx.)
  North, 137
  South, 138
Hendon, see Middlesex
Henley, see Oxfordshire

Hereford, see Herefordshire
HEREFORDSHIRE
  Hereford, 352
  Leominster, 353
Hertford, see Hertfordshire
HERTFORDSHIRE
  Barnet, 354
  Hemel Hempstead, 355
  Hertford, 356
  Hitchin, 357
  St. Albans, 358
  Watford, 359
HESTON and ISLEWORTH (Middx.), 139
Hexham, see Northumberland
Heywood and Radcliffe, see Lancashire
High Peak, see Derbyshire
Hillhead, see Glasgow
Hillsborough, see Sheffield
Hitchin, see Hertfordshire
HOLBORN, 24
Holderness, see Yorkshire
Holland, Parts of, see Lincolnshire
Holland with Boston, see Lincolnshire
Honiton, see Devon
Horncastle, see Lincolnshire
Hornchurch, see Essex
HORNSEY (Middx.), 140
Horsham, see Sussex
Horsham and Worthing, see Sussex
Houghton-le-Spring, see Durham
Howdenshire, see Yorkshire
HUDDERSFIELD (Yorkshire), 141
Hull, see Kingston upon Hull
Hulme, see Manchester
HUNTINGDONSHIRE, 360
Hyde, see Cheshire
HYTHE (Kent), 142


                         I


ILFORD (Essex), 143
  North, 144
  South, 145
Ilkeston, see Derbyshire
Ince, see Lancashire
Innerleven, see Kirkcaldy Burghs
Inverbervie, see Montrose Burghs
Inverkeithing, see Dunfermline Burghs
Inverness, see Inverness-shire and Ross and
  Cromarty
INVERNESS-SHIRE and ROSS and CROMARTY
  Inverness, 596
  Ross and Cromarty, 597
  Western Isles, 598
IPSWICH (Suffolk), 146
Irvine, see Ayr Burghs
ISLE of ELY, 361
Isle of Thanet, see Kent
ISLE of WIGHT, 362
Isleworth, see Heston and Isleworth
ISLINGTON
  East, 25
  North, 26
  South, 27
  West, 28

**J**

Jarrow, see Durham

**K**

Keighley, see Yorkshire
Kelvingrove, see Glasgow
Kennington, see Lambeth
KENSINGTON
  North, 29
  South, 30
KENT
  Ashford, 363
  Canterbury, 364
  Chislehurst, 365
  Dartford, 366
  Dover, 367
  Faversham, 368
  Gravesend, 369
  Isle of Thanet, 370
  Maidstone, 371
  Orpington, 372
  Sevenoaks, 373
  Tonbridge, 374
Kesteven, Parts of, see Lincolnshire
Kettering, see Northamptonshire
Kidderminster, see Worcestershire
Kilmarnock, see Ayrshire and Bute
Kincardineshire, see Aberdeenshire and Kincardine
Kinghorn, see Kirkcaldy Burghs
King's Lynn, see Norfolk
King's Norton, see Birmingham
KINGSTON UPON HULL (Yorkshire)
  Central, 147
  East, 148
  North-West, 149
  South-West, 150
KINGSTON UPON THAMES (Surrey), 151
Kingswinford, see Staffordshire
Kinross-shire, see Perthshire and Kinross-shire
KIRKCALDY DISTRICT of BURGHS (Fife), 575
Kirkcudbrightshire, see Galloway
Kirkdale, see Liverpool
Knutsford, see Cheshire

**L**

Ladywood, see Birmingham
LAMBETH
  Brixton, 31
  Kennington, 32
  North, 33
  Norwood, 34
Lanark, see Lanarkshire
LANARKSHIRE
  Bothwell, 599
  Coatbridge, 600
  Hamilton, 601
  Lanark, 602
  Motherwell, 603
  Northern, 604
  Rutherglen, 605
LANCASHIRE
  Chorley, 375
  Clitheroe, 376
  Darwen, 377

Farnworth, 378
Fylde, 379
Heywood and Radcliffe, 380
Ince, 381
Lancaster, 382
Lonsdale, 383
Middleton and Prestwich, 384
Mossley, 385
Newton, 386
Ormskirk, 387
Royton, 388
Stretford, 389
Waterloo, 390
Westhoughton, 391
Widnes, 392
Lancaster, see Lancashire
Leamington, see Warwickshire
LEEDS (Yorkshire)
  Central, 152
  North, 153
  North-East, 154
  South, 155
  South-East, 156
  West, 157
Leeds University, see Combined English
  Universities
Leek, see Staffordshire
LEICESTER
  East, 158
  South, 159
  West, 160
LEICESTERSHIRE
  Bosworth, 393
  Harborough, 394
  Loughborough, 395
  Melton, 396
LEIGH (Lancs.), 161
LEITH (Midlothian), 576
Leominster, see Herefordshire
Lewes, see Sussex
LEWISHAM
  East, 35
  West, 36
LEYTON (Essex)
  East, 162
  West, 163
Lichfield, see Staffordshire
Limehouse, see Stepney
LINCOLN, 164
LINCOLNSHIRE
  (PARTS of HOLLAND)
  Holland with Boston, 397
  (PARTS of KESTEVEN, and
    RUTLANDSHIRE)
  Grantham, 398
  Rutland and Stamford, 399
  (PARTS of LINDSEY)
  Brigg, 400
  Gainsborough, 401
  Horncastle, 402
  Louth, 403
Lindsey, Parts of, see Lincolnshire
LINLITHGOWSHIRE, 606
LIVERPOOL (Lancs.)
  East Toxteth, 165
  Edge Hill, 166
  Everton, 167

LIVLIII'OOL (Cont.)
Exchange, 168
Fairfield, 169
Kirkdale, 170
Scotland, 171
Walton, 172
Wavertree, 173
West Derby, 174
West Toxteth, 175
Liverpool University, see Combined English
Universities
Llandaff and Barry, see Glamorganshire
Llanelly, see Carmarthenshire
Lochgelly, see Dunfermline Burghs
London, City of, see City of London
LONDON UNIVERSITY, 629
LONDONDERRY, 626
Lonsdale, see Lancashire
Loughborough, see Leicestershire
Louth, see Lincolnshire
Lowestoft, see Suffolk
Ludlow, see Shropshire
Luton, see Bedfordshire

M

Macclesfield, see Cheshire
Maidstone, see Kent
Maldon, see Essex
Malton, see Yorkshire
MANCHESTER (Lancs.)
Ardwick, 176
Blackley, 177
Clayton, 178
Exchange, 179
Gorton, 180
Hulme, 181
Moss Side, 182
Platting, 183
Rusholme, 184
Withington, 185
Manchester University, see Combined English
Universities
Mansfield, see Nottinghamshire
Maryhill, see Glasgow
Marylebone, see St. Marylebone
Melton, see Leicestershire
MERIONETHSHIRE, 540
Merthyr, see Merthyr Tydfil
MERTHYR TYDFIL (Glam.)
Aberdare, 517
Merthyr, 518
Methil and Innerleven, see Kirkcaldy Burghs
MIDDLESBROUGH (Yorkshire)
East, 186
West, 187
MIDDLESEX
Acton, 404
Brentford and Chiswick, 405
Enfield, 406
Finchley, 407
Harrow, 408
Hendon, 409
Spelthorne, 410
Twickenham, 411
Uxbridge, 412
Wood Green, 413

Middleton and Prestwich, see Lancashire
MIDLOTHIAN and PEEBLESSHIRE
Northern, 607
Peebles and Southern, 608
Mile End, see Stepney
MITCHAM (Surrey), 188
Mitcham, see Surrey
Monmouth, see Monmouthshire
MONMOUTHSHIRE
Abertillery, 541
Bedwellty, 542
Ebbw Vale, 543
Monmouth, 544
Pontypool, 545
MONTGOMERYSHIRE, 546
MONTROSE DISTRICT of BURGHS
(Forfarshire and Kincardineshire), 577
MORAY and NAIRNSHIRE, 609
Morley, see Batley and Morley
MORPETH (Northumberland), 189
Moseley, see Birmingham
Mossley, see Lancashire
Moss Side, see Manchester
Motherwell, see Lanarkshire

N

Nairnshire, see Moray and Nairnshire
Neath, see Glamorganshire
NELSON and COLNE (Lancs.), 190
Newark, see Nottinghamshire
Newbury, see Berkshire
NEWCASTLE-UNDER-LYME (Staffs.), 191
NEWCASTLE UPON TYNE (Northumberland)
Central, 192
East, 193
North, 194
West, 195
New Forest and Christchurch, see Hampshire
NEWPORT (Mon.), 519
Newton, see Lancashire
NORFOLK
Eastern, 414
King's Lynn, 415
Northern, 416
Southern, 417
South-Western, 418
Normanton, see Yorkshire
NORTHAMPTON, 196
NORTHAMPTONSHIRE and the SOKE of
PETERBOROUGH
Daventry, 419
Kettering, 420
Peterborough, 421
Wellingborough, 422
NORTHUMBERLAND
Berwick-upon-Tweed, 423
Hexham, 424
Wansbeck, 425
Northwich, see Cheshire
NORWICH (Norfolk), 197
Norwood, see Lambeth
NOTTINGHAM
Central, 198
East, 199
South, 200
West, 201

**NOTTINGHAMSHIRE**
Bassetlaw, 426
Broxtowe, 427
Mansfield, 428
Newark, 429
Rushcliffe, 430
Nuneaton, see Warwickshire

**O**

Ogmore, see Glamorganshire
OLDHAM (Lancs.), 202
ORKNEY and SHETLAND, 610
Ormskirk, see Lancashire
Orpington, see Kent
Oswestry, see Shropshire
Otley, see Yorkshire
OXFORD, 203
OXFORD UNIVERSITY, 630
**OXFORDSHIRE**
Banbury, 431
Henley, 432

**P**

**PADDINGTON**
North, 37
South, 38
PAISLEY (Renfrewshire), 578
Park, see Sheffield
Partick, see Glasgow
Peckham, see Camberwell
Peeblesshire, see Midlothian and Peeblesshire
PEMBROKESHIRE, 547
Penistone, see Yorkshire
Penrith and Cockermouth, see Cumberland
Penryn and Falmouth, see Cornwall
Perth, see Perthshire and Kinross-shire
**PERTHSHIRE and KINROSS-SHIRE**
Kinross and Western, 611
Perth, 612
Peterborough, see Northamptonshire
Petersfield, see Hampshire
Plaistow, see West Ham
Platting, see Manchester
**PLYMOUTH (Devon)**
Devonport, 204
Drake, 205
Sutton, 206
Pollok, see Glasgow
Pontefract, see Yorkshire
Pontypool, see Monmouthshire
Pontypridd, see Glamorganshire
**POPLAR**
Bow and Bromley, 39
South Poplar, 40
**PORTSMOUTH (Hants.)**
Central, 207
North, 208
South, 209
PRESTON (Lancs.), 210
Prestwich, see Lancashire
Prestwick, see Ayr Burghs
Pudsey and Otley, see Yorkshire
Putney, see Wandsworth
Pwllheli, see Caernarvon Burghs

**Q**

QUEEN'S UNIVERSITY of BELFAST, 633

**R**

Radcliffe, see Lancashire
Radnorshire, see Breconshire and Radnorshire
READING (Berks.), 211
Reading University, see Combined English
Universities
Reigate, see Surrey
**RENFREWSHIRE**
Eastern, 613
Western, 614
**RHONDDA (Glam.)**
East, 520
West, 521
RICHMOND (Surrey), 212
Richmond, see Yorkshire
Ripon, see Yorkshire
ROCHDALE (Lancs.), 213
**ROCHESTER (Kent)**
Chatham, 214
Gillingham, 215
ROMFORD (Essex), 216
Romford, see Essex
Ross and Cromarty, see Inverness-shire and Ross
and Cromarty
ROSSENDALE (Lancs.), 217
ROTHERHAM (Yorkshire), 218
Rotherhithe, see Bermondsey
Rother Valley, see Yorkshire
Rothwell, see Yorkshire
ROXBURGHSHIRE and SELKIRKSHIRE, 615
Royton, see Lancashire
Rugby, see Warwickshire
Rushcliffe, see Nottinghamshire
Rusholme, see Manchester
Rutherglen, see Lanarkshire
Rutland and Stamford, see Lincolnshire
Rutlandshire, see Lincolnshire
Rye, see Sussex

**S**

Saffron Walden, see Essex
St. Albans, see Hertfordshire
St. Andrews University, see Combined Scottish
Universities
St. George's, see Stepney
St. George's, see Westminster
ST. HELENS (Lancs.), 219
St. Ives, see Cornwall
ST. MARYLEBONE, 41
**ST. PANCRAS**
North, 42
South-East, 43
South-West, 44
St. Rollox, see Glasgow
Sale, see Altrincham and Sale
**SALFORD (Lancs.)**
North, 220
South, 221
West, 222
Salisbury, see Wiltshire

Saltcoats, see Ayr Burghs
Scarborough and Whitby, see Yorkshire
Scotland, see Liverpool
Scottish Universities, see Combined Scottish
Seaham, see Durham
Sedgefield, see Durham
Selkirkshire, see Roxburghshire and Selkirkshire
Sevenoaks, see Kent
SHEFFIELD (Yorkshire)
 Attercliffe, 223
 Brightside, 224
 Central, 225
 Ecclesall, 226
 Hallam, 227
 Hillsborough, 228
 Park, 229
Sheffield University, see Combined English
 Universities
Shetland, see Orkney and Shetland
Shettleston, see Glasgow
Shipley, see Yorkshire
SHOREDITCH, 45
Shrewsbury, see Shropshire
SHROPSHIRE
 Ludlow, 433
 Oswestry, 434
 Shrewsbury, 435
 The Wrekin, 436
Silvertown, see West Ham
Skipton, see Yorkshire
Slough, see Buckinghamshire
Slough, see Eton and Slough
SMETHWICK (Staffs.), 230
Soke of Peterborough, see Northamptonshire
Solihull, see Warwickshire
SOMERSET
 Bridgwater, 437
 Frome, 438
 Taunton, 439
 Wells, 440
 Weston-super-Mare, 441
 Yeovil, 442
SOUTHALL (Middx.), 231
SOUTHAMPTON (Hants.), 232
SOUTHEND-ON-SEA (Essex), 233
South Molton, see Devon
SOUTHPORT (Lancs.), 234
SOUTH SHIELDS (Durham), 235
SOUTHWARK
 Central, 46
 North, 47
 South-East, 48
Sowerby, see Yorkshire
Sparkbrook, see Birmingham
Spelthorne, see Middlesex
Spennymoor, see Durham
Spen Valley, see Yorkshire
Springburn, see Glasgow
Stafford, see Staffordshire
STAFFORDSHIRE
 Burton, 443
 Cannock, 444
 Kingswinford, 445
 Leek, 446
 Lichfield, 447
 Stafford, 448
 Stone, 449

Stalybridge and Hyde, see Cheshire
Stamford, see Lincolnshire
STEPNEY
 Limehouse, 49
 Mile End, 50
 Whitechapel and St. George's, 51
STIRLING and FALKIRK DISTRICT of
 BURGHS, 579
STIRLINGSHIRE and CLACKMANNANSHIRE
 Clackmannan and Eastern, 616
 Western, 617
STOCKPORT (Cheshire), 236
STOCKTON-ON-TEES (Durham), 237
Stoke, see Stoke-on-Trent
STOKE NEWINGTON, 52
STOKE-ON-TRENT (Staffs.)
 Burslem, 238
 Hanley, 239
 Stoke, 240
Stone, see Staffordshire
Stourbridge, see Worcestershire
Stratford, see West Ham
Streatham, see Wandsworth
Stretford, see Lancashire
Stroud, see Gloucestershire
Sudbury, see Suffolk
SUFFOLK (East)
 Eye, 450
 Lowestoft, 451
 Woodbridge, 452
SUFFOLK (West)
 Bury St. Edmunds, 453
 Sudbury, 454
SUNDERLAND (Durham), 241
SURREY
 Carshalton, 455
 Chertsey, 456
 Eastern, 457
 Epsom, 458
 Farnham, 459
 Guildford, 460
 Mitcham, 461
 Reigate, 462
SUSSEX (East)
 Eastbourne, 463
 East Grinstead, 464
 Lewes, 465
 Rye, 466
SUSSEX (West)
 Chichester, 467
 Horsham, 468
 Horsham and Worthing, 469
 Worthing, 470
Sutherland, see Caithness and Sutherland
Sutton, see Plymouth
SUTTON and CHEAM (Surrey), 242
Sutton Coldfield, see Warwickshire
SWANSEA (Glam.)
 East, 522
 West, 523
Swindon, see Wiltshire

T

Tamworth, see Warwickshire
Taunton, see Somerset
Tavistock, see Devon

Tewkesbury, see Gloucestershire
Thanet, Isle of, see Kent
Thirsk and Malton, see Yorkshire
Thornbury, see Gloucestershire
Thurrock, see Essex
Tiverton, see Devon
Tonbridge, see Kent
Tooting, see Wandsworth
Torquay, see Devon
Totnes, see Devon
TOTTENHAM (Middx.)
  North, 243
  South, 244
Toxteth, see Liverpool
Tradeston, see Glasgow
Troon, see Ayr Burghs
TWICKENHAM (Middx.), 245
Twickenham, see Middlesex
TYNEMOUTH (Northumberland), 246
Tyrone, see Fermanagh and Tyrone


                    U

Universities, see Cambridge, Combined English,
  Combined Scottish, London, Oxford, Queen's
  (Belfast), Wales
Upton, see West Ham
Uxbridge, see Middlesex


                    W

WAKEFIELD (Yorkshire), 247
WALES UNIVERSITY, 631
WALLASEY (Cheshire), 248
WALLSEND (Northumberland), 249
WALSALL (Staffs.), 250
WALTHAMSTOW (Essex)
  East, 251
  West, 252
Walton, see Liverpool
WANDSWORTH
  Balham and Tooting, 53
  Central, 54
  Clapham, 55
  Putney, 56
  Streatham, 57
Wansbeck, see Northumberland
WARRINGTON (Lancs.), 253
Warwick and Leamington, see Warwickshire
WARWICKSHIRE
  Nuneaton, 471
  Rugby, 472
  Solihull, 473
  Sutton Coldfield, 474
  Tamworth, 475
  Warwick and Leamington, 476
Waterloo, see Lancashire
Watford, see Hertfordshire
Wavertree, see Liverpool
WEDNESBURY (Staffs.), 254
Wellingborough, see Northamptonshire
Wells, see Somerset
WEMBLEY (Middx.)
  North, 255
  South, 256
Wentworth, see Yorkshire
WEST BROMWICH (Staffs.), 257

Westbury, see Wiltshire
West Derby, see Liverpool
Western Isles, see Inverness-shire and Ross and
  Cromarty
WEST HAM (Essex)
  Plaistow, 258
  Silvertown, 259
  Stratford, 260
  Upton, 261
Westhoughton, see Lancashire
WESTMINSTER
  Abbey, 58
  St. George's, 59
WESTMORLAND, 477
Weston-super-Mare, see Somerset
West Toxteth, see Liverpool
Whitby, see Yorkshire
Whitechapel and St. George's, see Stepney
Whitehaven, see Cumberland
Widnes, see Lancashire
WIGAN (Lancs.), 262
Wight, Isle of, see Isle of Wight
Wigtownshire, see Galloway
WILLESDEN (Middx.)
  East, 263
  West, 264
WILTSHIRE
  Chippenham, 478
  Devizes, 479
  Salisbury, 480
  Swindon, 481
  Westbury, 482
WIMBLEDON (Surrey), 265
Winchester, see Hampshire
Windsor, see Berkshire
Wirral, see Cheshire
Withington, see Manchester
WOLVERHAMPTON (Staffs.)
  Bilston, 266
  East, 267
  West, 268
Woodbridge, see Suffolk
WOODFORD (Essex), 269
Wood Green, see Middlesex
WOOLWICH
  East, 60
  West, 61
WORCESTER, 270
WORCESTERSHIRE
  Bewdley, 483
  Evesham, 484
  Kidderminster, 485
  Stourbridge, 486
Workington, see Cumberland
Worthing, see Sussex
Wrekin, The, see Shropshire
Wrexham, see Denbighshire
Wycombe, see Buckinghamshire


                    Y

Yardley, see Birmingham
Yarmouth, see Great Yarmouth
Yeovil, see Somerset
YORK, 271
YORKSHIRE (East Riding)
  Buckrose, 487

YORKSHIRE (East Riding) (Cont.)
Holderness, 488
Howdenshire, 489
YORKSHIRE (North Riding)
Cleveland, 490
Richmond, 491
Scarborough and Whitby, 492
Thirsk and Malton, 493
YORKSHIRE (West Riding)
Barkston Ash, 494
Colne Valley, 495
Doncaster, 496
Don Valley, 497
Elland, 498
Hemsworth, 499
Keighley, 500
Normanton, 501

Penistone, 502
Pontefract, 503
Pudsey and Otley, 504
Ripon, 505
Rother Valley, 506
Rothwell, 507
Shipley, 508
Skipton, 509
Sowerby, 510
Spen Valley, 511
Wentworth, 512

Z

Zetland, see Orkney and Shetland

# INDEX TO FOOTNOTES

The number or numbers indicate the constituency reference number which is given after the name of the constituency, at the top of each page. It does *not* refer to the folio number which appears in small type at the foot of each page.

Where a candidate's name appears in a footnote relating to a constituency which he contested the entry will be found in the Index to Candidates commencing on page 721 and the name is not indexed again here.

## A

Acland, Sir R.T.D., Bt., 248, 467
Acton Democratic Labour Party, 404
Agriculture, policy on (see also National Farmers' Union), 488
Anti-Parliamentary Communist Federation, 571
Anti-Waste League, 31, 32, 36, 38, 56, 59, 97, 212, 356, 367, 369, 370
Asquith, Rt. Hon. H.H., 294, 516

## B

Baldwin, Rt. Hon. S., 41, 100
Beaverbrook, Lord, 59
Belfast North Temperance Council, 619
Birmingham City Council, 79
Bottomley, H.W., see Independent Parliamentary Group
Brighton and Hove Conservative Association, 97
British Citizens' League, 61
British Legion, 117, 571
British National Party, see English National Association
British Reform and Women's Party, 210
British Socialist Party, 126, 162
Brown, W.J., 429, 467

## C

Candidates retiring after nomination, 28, 128, 192, 495, 533, 539
Capital punishment, policy on, 46, 56, 336
China, policy on, 47
Churchill, R.F.E.S., 34
Churchill, Rt. Hon. W.L.S., 97, 547, 596, 597
Coalition 'coupon' (the letter sent by Lloyd George and Bonar Law to official Coalition candidates), 43, 149, 161, 162, 181, 186, 187, 189, 191, 197, 228, 230, 236, 244, 301, 302,
303, 329, 385, 427, 510, 540, 546, 563, 574, 594, 601
Common Wealth Movement, 98, 248, 309, 377, 421, 437, 453
Communist Party, 1, 5, 6, 46, 64, 129, 184, 404, 563, 566, 574
Comrades of the Great War, 152, 155, 157
Conservative Party and constituency associations (unofficial Conservative organisations are indexed under their titles), 30, 41, 47, 97, 100, 127, 143, 194, 218, 294, 366, 370, 385, 403, 411, 416, 417, 508, 510, 518, 547, 578, 579, 588, 595, 597, 608, 611, 624
Conservative working men's clubs, 259, 521, 534

## D

*Daily Express,* 59
Diagnostic clinics, policy on, 374
Dorset North Agricultural Defence League, 318

## E

Ecclesall Tenants' Protection Association, 226
Edmonton Pro-Ally and Labour Party, 126
Election petitions, 205, 307
Empire Free Trade Crusade, 25
English National Association (formerly British National Party), 404

## F

Farmers' Rights Association, 433
Federal Union, 632
Fife, Kinross and Clackmannan Miners' Association, 553, 593
Fife, Kinross and Clackmannan Mineworkers' Reform Union, 593
Free trade, policy of, 12, 76, 411

**G**

Germany, policy of aerial reprisals, 23, 80, 119, 140, 436
Greenock and District Dockers' Union, 574

**H**

Harrow Electors' League, 408
Hastings Independent Progressive Movement, 136

**I**

Ilford Conservative Forward Association, 143
India, policy on, 34, 173
Independent Labour Party (ILP) 349, 421, 564, 589, 598, 613, 616
Independent Parliamentary Group (Horatio Bottomley's group), 58, 150, 236, 298, 339, 356, 366, 367, 383, 436
Industrial insurance, policy on, 148
Irish Labour Party, 236
Irish nationalist movement, 171, 621, 626

**K**

Kendall, W.D., 429, 467
Kensington South Conservative Emergency Association, 30

**L**

Labour Independent Group, 14, 21, 128, 184, 341
Labour Party and constituency parties, 1, 5, 6, 46, 47, 58, 64, 129, 135, 151, 162, 171, 184, 203, 232, 248, 260, 309, 334, 349, 398, 404, 420, 437, 456, 472, 509, 552, 564, 565, 566, 569, 574, 578, 589, 598, 613, 621, 622
Law, Rt. Hon. A.B., 230
League Against Imperialism, 412
Liberal Party and constituency associations, 37, 58, 69, 87, 100, 130, 132, 151, 162, 165, 191, 203, 208, 240, 294, 339, 366, 371, 378, 385, 389, 414, 437, 456, 478, 516, 546, 551, 578, 579, 588, 595, 596, 597, 632
Liberty Restoration League, 459
Liverpool City Council, 165
Liverpool Women's Citizenship Association, 165
Lloyd George, Rt. Hon. D., 92, 100, 230, 294, 456, 516, 546
Lower-Deck, Parliamentary Committee, 208, 215
Lucas, F.A. (died after nomination), 32

**M**

Manchester Land Values League, 184
Members of Parliament, expulsion of, 20, 369
Moss Side Tenants' Protection Society, 182

**N**

National Amalgamated Coal Porters' Union, 45
National Amalgamated Union of Labour, 225
National Association of Discharged Sailors and Soldiers, 152, 155, 157, 510
National Democratic and Labour Party, 130, 150, 403, 427, 551

National Farmers' Union, 321, 353, 356, 387, 399, 414, 488, 489, 491, 528
National Federation of Discharged and Demobilized Sailors and Soldiers, 2, 4, 6, 13, 16, 28, 31, 34, 37, 55, 79, 109, 130, 131, 152, 155, 157, 167, 181, 189, 193, 244, 248, 357, 410, 533
National Federation of Women Teachers, 11
National Government, 87, 97, 132, 352, 363, 513, 524, 526, 547, 578, 592, 597, 611, 632
National Liberals (1922-23), 30, 339, 366, 518, 579
National Liberals (1931 onwards), 100, 578, 596, 597, 632
National Party, 356
National Peace Council, 346
National Sailors' and Firemen's Union, 91, 130, 150, 235
National Socialist Party, 104, 109
Newcastle North (1940) Conservative Association, 194
New Party, 595
'1941 Committee', 480
Norfolk South Independent Conservative Association, 417

**O**

Orange (Protestant) movement, 603

**P**

Peace Pledge Union, 80, 616
Plymouth Conservative Imperial Party, 206
Polling, postponed by death of candidate, 32, 147, 309, 472
Popular Front, 58, 203, 437
Portsmouth South Constitutional Association, 209
Preston Progressive Labour Party, 210
Priestley, J.B., 480
Prohibition, see Temperance
Protestant Action Society, 576

**Q**

Quakers, see Society of Friends

**R**

Representation of the People Act, 1918, 610
Russia, policy of aid, 23

**S**

St. George's, Hanover Square, Independent Conservative Association, 59
St. Marylebone Conservative Association, 41
St. Marylebone Conservative and Constitutional Union, 41
Samuel, Viscount, 456
Scottish Anti-War and No Conscription League Council, 616
Scottish nationalism, policy of, 554, 559, 560, 561
Scottish Protestant League, 579
Scottish Socialist Party, 616
Sinn Fein, 621, 623, 624, 626

Social Credit Secretariat, 78, 95
Society of Friends (Quakers), 125
Spain, policy on, 611
Speaker of the House of Commons, 132, 299, 419, 424
Spinsters Pensions' Association, 210
Stewart, W.J., 622
Stockport Irish Election Committee, 236

T

Temperance and prohibition, 206, 210, 619

U

Ulster Independent Unionist Association, 621

Ulster Progressive Unionist Association, 622
United Carters' and Motormen's Association, 181
United Empire Party, 25, 38
United Socialist Movement, 559, 560, 562

W

Ward, W. Dudley, 403
Welsh nationalism, policy of, 531, 536
Whitechapel Street-Sellers' and Costers' Union, 51
Woman MP, first to take seat in House of Commons, 206
Women's Parliamentary League, 409
Woolton-Teviot agreement, 547
Wright, W. (died after nomination), 617